Antique Trader®
POTTERY & PORCELAIN
CERAMICS

4TH
EDITION

Edited by
Kyle Husfloen

Contributing editor
Pat McPherson

Published by
Antique Trader Books, A Division of

 **krause publications**
An F&W Publications Company

700 East State Street • Iola, WI 54990-0001
715-445-2214 • 888-457-2873
www.krause.com

Please, call or write us for our free catalog of antiques and collectibles
publications. Our toll-free number to place an order or obtain a free catalog is 800-258-0929 or please use our regular business telephone,
715-445-2214.

Library of Congress Catalog Number: 99-68141
ISBN: 0-87349-638-8

Printed in the United States of America

TABLE OF CONTENTS

Introduction

It was over 30 years ago that The Antique Trader produced our first general price guides covering all types of antiques and collectibles. Since the founding of our new Antique Trader Books & Price Guides division in 1994, we have greatly expanded our offerings in the category of price guides as well as other specialized references for the collecting field.

The first new product in our expanded price guide line-up was *Antique Trader Books Pottery & Porcelain—Ceramics Price Guide,* released in early 1994. This well-illustrated reference covered all major categories of pottery and porcelain, foreign and domestic, and was well received by the collecting community. The popularity of this guide has led to further editions and we're pleased to present here the all new 4th Edition. Although similar in format to our earlier editions, we greatly expanded the number of ceramics categories included. All of our listings are new or updated with many contributions by leading authorities in specific ceramics fields. Highlighting the listings are even more quality photographs, that add to this guide's usefulness and eye appeal. As in the earlier editions, this guide covers ceramics produced as far back as the eighteenth century in Europe, but also includes expanded sections on popular twentieth century American chinawares and pottery. Whatever segment of the vast ceramics market you find most appealing, we'll have information included here.

We always pride ourselves on providing the most accurate and detailed descriptions possible for each item included. Each category also begin with a brief introductory paragraph and, in most sections, sketches of typical manufacturers' marks found on the pieces.

Ceramics, like most collecting specialties, has a vocabulary all its own. To give you a better understanding of terms used throughout this guide, we begin with a general introduction to the collecting of ceramics followed by several pages of sketches showing a wide variety of pieces and forms you will find listed. The sketches include brief notes on the forms and body parts which will make it easier to study and use our guide. As an additional reference source we are including, at the conclusion of our price listings, a Glossary of Selected Ceramics Terms followed by several special Appendices covering individual collecting groups, museums of interest and references to pottery and porcelain marks. Since English ceramics of the nineteenth and early twentieth century make up quite a large portion of collectible ceramic wares found in this country, we also include an appendix explaining the unique system of English Registry Marks.

My staff and I have put many hours of effort into producing an attractive and useful guide, and it took many hands and hearts to produce the volume you now hold. A special note of thanks goes to our many Special Contributors for preparing a variety of categories covering some of today's most popular and collectible ceramics. Special thanks also to Pat McPherson for her work on a number of popular American ceramic wares. You will find a complete listing of these Special Contributors on another page. Their efforts have assured that we are presenting a well rounded and comprehensive guide.

I sincerely hope that all who add *Antique Trader Books Pottery & Porcelain—Ceramics Price Guide* to their library will find it handy, easy to use and authoritative. Use it as a guide in your collecting pursuits and it should serve you well. If you have special comments or questions, we'll be happy to answer your inquiries. Enjoy this guide and may it bring you new knowledge and appreciation of your ceramic treasures and those waiting your discovery.

Kyle Husfloen, Editor

Photography Credits

Photographers who have contributed to this volume include: Carole A. Berk, Bethesda, Maryland; Susan N. Cox, El Cajon, California; Jane Fehrenbocher, Pasadena, California; Don Hoffmann, Aurora, Illinois; Robert Jason-Ickes, Olympia, Washington.

For other photographs, artwork, data or permission to photograph in their shops, we sincerely express appreciation to the following auctioneers, galleries, museums, individuals and shops:

Brown Auctions, Mullinville, Kansas; Charlton Hall Galleries, Columbia, South Carolina; Cincinnati Art Galleries, Cincinnati, Ohio; A Collector's Passion Shop, Olympia, Washington; Armans, Portsmouth, Rhode Island; DeFina Auctions, Austenburg, Ohio; William Doyle Galleries, New York, New York; Garth's Auctions, Delaware, Ohio; Green Valley Auctions, Mt. Crawford, Virginia; Gene Harris Antique Auction Center, Marshalltown, Iowa; Jackson's Auctions, Cedar Falls, Iowa; Joy Luke Gallery, Bloomington, Illinois; Russ McCall Auctioneers, Onawa, Iowa; Dave Rago, Lambertville, New Jersey; Skinner, Inc., Bolton Massachusetts; Sotheby's, New York, New York; Temples Antiques, Minneapolis, Minnesota; Treadway Gallery, Cincinnati, Ohio; and Wolf's Fine Arts & Auctioneers, Cleveland, Ohio.

ON THE COVER:

"Left to right: Noritake cologne bottle with flower cluster stopper, decorated with a colorful Art Deco lady, $450-550; Hand-painted porcelain 7 3/4" d. plates, $50; Songbird pie bird, marked "USA," $50.

Please note: Though listings have been double-checked and every effort has been made to insure accuracy, neither the compilers, editors nor publisher can assume responsibility for any losses that might be incurred as a result of consulting this guide, or of errors, typographical or otherwise.

Special Contributors

ABC Plates

Joan M. George, Ed.D
67 Stevens Ave.
Old Bridge, NJ 08857
e-mail: drjgeorge@nac.net

Abingdon

Elaine Westover
210 Knox Highway 5
Abingdon, IL 61410-9332

American Painted Porcelain

Dorothy Kamm
P.O. Box 7460
Port St. Lucie, FL 34985-7460
e-mail: dorothykamm@adelphia.net

Amphora-Tepliz

Les and Irene Cohen
P.O. Box 17001
Pittsburgh, PA 15235
(412) 795-3030
fax (412) 793-0222
e-mail: am4ah@yahoo.com

Amphora Collectors International
10159 Nancy Dr.
Meadville, PA 16335
Web site: www.amphoracollectors.org

Belleek (American)

Peggy Sebek, ISA, AAA
3255 Glencairn Rd.
Shaker Heights, OH 44122
e-mail: pegsebek@earthlink.net

Belleek (Irish)

Del E. Domke
16142 N.E. 15th St.
Bellevue, WA 98008-2711
(425) 643-3359 (phone/fax)

e-mail: delyicious@aol.com
Web site: The Beauty and Romance of
Irish Belleek

Blue and White Pottery

Steve Stone
12795 W. Alameda Pkwy.
Lakewood, CO 80225
e-mail: Sylvanlvr@aol.com

Blue Ridge Dinnerwares

Patricia McPherson
Country Town Antiques
738 Main St.
Ramona, CA 92065
(619) 871-6060

Brayton Laguna Pottery

Patricia McPherson
Country Town Antiques
738 Main St.
Ramona, CA 92065
(619) 871-6060

Buffalo Pottery

Phillip Sullivan
P.O. Box 69
South Orleans, MA 02662
(508) 255-8495

Caliente Pottery

Patricia McPherson
Country Town Antiques
738 Main St.
Ramona, CA 92065
(619) 871-6060

Catalina Island Pottery

James Elliot-Bishop
500 S. Farrell Dr., S-114
Palm Springs, CA 92264
e-mail: gmcb@ix.netcom.com

Ceramic Arts Studio of Madison

Tim Holthaus
CAS Collectors Association
P.O. Box 46
Madison, WI 53701-0046
e-mail: CAScollectors@Ameritech.net

Cleminson Clay

Patricia McPherson
Country Town Antiques
738 Main St.
Ramona, CA 92065
(619) 871-6060

Cowan

Tim and Jamie Saloff
e-mail: tgsaloff@erie.net
Web site: http://www.erie.net/~jlsaloff

Czech Pottery

Cheryl Goyda
Box 137
Hopeland, PA 17533
e-mail: Mzczech@aol.com

deLee Art

Patricia McPherson
Country Town Antiques
738 Main St.
Ramona, CA 92065
(619) 871-6060

Doulton & Royal Doulton - Bunnykins

Reg. G. Morris
7360 Martingale
Chesterland, OH 44026
e-mail: min@modex.com

Florence Ceramics

David G. Miller
1971 Blue Fox Dr.
Lansdale, PA 19446-5505
(610) 584-6127

Florence Ceramics Collectors Society
e-mail: FlorenceCeramics@aol.com

Flow Blue

Vivian Kromer
1 1 800 Shankin St.
Bakersfield, CA 93312
(661) 588-7768

Franciscan Pottery

James Elliot-Bishop
500 S. Farrell Dr., S-114
Palm Springs, CA 92264
e-mail: gmcb@ix.netcom.com

Frankoma Pottery

Patricia McPherson
Country Town Antiques
738 Main St.
Ramona, CA 92065
(619) 871-6060

Geisha Girl Porcelain

Elyce Litts
P.O. Box 394
Morris Plains, NJ 07950
(908) 964-5055
e-mail: happy-memories@worldnet.att.net

Gonder

James R. Boshears
354 Whitewater Dr., Apt. 107
Bolingbrook, IL 60440-7911
e-mail: jrbosh@uillinois.edu

Hall China

Marty Kennedy
4711 S.W. Brentwood Rd.
Topeka, KS 66606
(785) 554-5837
(785) 273-4981

e-mail: martykennedy@cox.net
Web site: http://www.inter-
services.com/HallChina

Harker Pottery

Neva Colbert
69565 Crescent Rd.
St. Clairsville, OH 43950
e-mail: colbert@1st.net

Haviland

Nora Travis
13337 E. South St.
Cerritos, CA 90701
(714) 521-9283
e-mail: Travishrs@aol.com

Head Vase Planters

Maddy Gordon
P.O. Box 83H
Scarsdale, NY 10583

Hull

Joan Hull
1376 Nevada SW
Huron, SD 57350

Hull Pottery Association
11023 Tunnel Hill N.E.
New Lexington, OH 43764

Ironstone

Bev Dieringer
P.O. Box 536
Redding Ridge, CT 06876
e-mail: dieringer1@aol.com

Jewel Tea - Autumn Leaf

Jo Cunningham
535 E. Normal
Springfield, MO 65807-1659
(417) 831-1320
e-mail: hiresearcher@aol.com

Kitchen Collectibles

Butter Pats:

Mary Dessoie
265 Eagle Bend Dr.
Bigfork, MT 59911-6235

Cow Creamers:

LuAnn Riggs
1486 Moonridge Ct.
Upland, CA 91784
e-mail: st-ark-bucks@netwebb.com or
st-ark-bucks@worldnet.att.net

Egg Cups:

Joan M. George, Ed.D
67 Stevens Ave.
Old Bridge, NJ 08857
e-mail: drjgeorge@nac.net

Napkin Dolls, Reamers:

Bobbie Zucker Bryson is the co-author,
with Deborah Gillham and Ellen
Bercovici, of the pictorial price guide
Collectibles for the Kitchen, Bath &
Beyond, 2nd Edition, published by
Krause Publications. It covers a broad
range of collectibles including napkin
dolls, stringholders, pie birds, figural egg
timers, razor blade banks, whimsical
whistle milk cups and laundry sprinkler
bottles. Bryson can be contacted via e-
mail at Napkindoll@aol.com.

String Holders, Egg Timers, Pie Birds:

Ellen Bercovici
Dynamite Antiques
5118 Hampden Ln.
Bethesda, MD 20814-2308

Limoges

Debby DeBay, Ret. USAF
Limoges Antiques Shop
20 Post Office Avenue
Andover, MA 01810
(978) 470-8773

e-mail: dquinn1@flash.net
www.limogesantiques.com

LuRay Pastels

Joe Zacharias
P.O. Box 99516
Raleigh, NC 27624-9516
(919) 848-6966
e-mail: IBUYLURAY2@aol.com

Majolica

Michael G. Strawser Auctions
P.O. Box 332
Wolcottville, IN 46795
(260) 854-2859
www.majolicaauctions.com

Mettlach

Gary Kirsner
Glentiques, Ltd.
1940 Augusta Terrace
P.O. Box 8807
Coral Springs, FL 33071
e-mail: gkirsner@myacc.net

Morton Potteries

Burdell Hall
201 W. Sassafras Dr.
Morton, IL 61550
(309) 263-2988
e-mail: bnbhall@mtco.com

Mulberry

Ellen Hill
Mulberry Hill South
655 10th Ave. N.E., Apt. 5
St. Petersburg, FL 33701

Nicodemus

Patricia McPherson
Country Town Antiques
738 Main St.
Ramona, CA 92065
(619) 871-6060

Nippon

Jackson's International Auctioneers &
Appraisers
2229 Lincoln St.
Cedar Falls, IA 50613
(319) 277-2256
(319) 277-1252 (fax)
www.jacksonsauction.com

Noritake

Janet and Tim Trapani
145 Andover Place
West Hempstead, NY 11552
e-mail: ttrapani1946@yahoo.com

Old Ivory

Alma Hillman
362 E. Main St.
Searsport, ME 04974
e-mail: oldivory@acadia.net

Oyster Plates

Michael G. Strawser Auctions
P.O. Box 332
Wolcottville, IN 46795
(260) 854-2859
www.majolicaauctions.com

Pacific Clay Products

Patricia McPherson
Country Town Antiques
738 Main St.
Ramona, CA 92065
(619) 871-6060

Phoenix Bird Porcelain

Joan Collett Oates
685 S. Washington
Constantine, MI 49042
(269) 435-8353
e-mail: koates120@earthlink.net

Pierce (Howard) Porcelains

Patricia McPherson
Country Town Antiques
738 Main St.
Ramona, CA 92065
(619) 871-6060

Quimper

Sandra V. Bondhus
P.O. Box 100
Unionville, CT 06085
nbondhus@pol.net

Red Wing

Charles W. Casad
801 Tyler Ct.
Monticello, IL 61856-2246

Royal Bayreuth

Mary McCaslin
6887 Black Oak Ct. E.
Avon, IN 46123
(317) 272-7776
e-mail: maryjack@indyrrcom

Royal Copley

Tim Holthaus
CAS Collectors Association
P.O. Box 46
Madison, WI 53701-0046
e-mail: CAScollectors@Ameritech.net

R.S. Prussia

Mary McCaslin
6887 Black Oak Ct. E.
Avon, IN 46123
(317) 272-7776
e-mail: maryjack@indyrrcom

Rozart

Patricia McPherson
Country Town Antiques
738 Main St.

Ramona, CA 92065
(619) 871-6060

Russel Wright Designs

Kathryn Wiese
Retrospective Modern Design
P.O. Box 1138
Kamuela, HI 96743
e-mail: retrodesign@earthlink.net

Sascha Brastoff

Patricia McPherson
Country Town Antiques
738 Main St.
Ramona, CA 92065
(619) 871-6060

Schoop (Hedi) Art Creations

Patricia McPherson
Country Town Antiques
738 Main St.
Ramona, CA 92065
(619) 871-6060

Shawnee

Linda Guffey
2004 Fiat Ct.
El Cajon, CA 92019-4234
e-mail: Gufantique@aol.com

Shelley China

Mannie Banner
6412 Silverbrook W.
W. Bloomfield, MI 48322-1034

Steins

Gary Kirsner
Glentiques, Ltd.
1940 Augusta Terrace
P.O. Box 8807
Coral Springs, FL 33071
e-mail: gkirsner@myacc.net

Torquay Pottery

Judy Wucherer
Transitions of Wales, Ltd.
P.O. Box 1441
Brookfield, WI 53045

North American Torquay Society
Marlene Graham, Secretary
214 N. Ronda Rd.
McHenry, IL 60050
(815) 385-2040

Uhl Pottery

Lloyd Martin
1582 Gregory Lane
Jasper, IN 47546
e-mail: lmartin@psci.net

Vernon Kilns

Pam Green
You Must Remember This
P.O. Box 822
Hollis, NH 03049
e-mail: ymrt@aol.com
www.ymrt.com

Warwick

Otto Zwicker
48 Arcadia Ave.
Wheeling, WV 26003
(304) 242-1872

Watt Pottery

Dennis Thompson
6715 Stearns Rd.
N. Olmsted, OH 44070
e-mail: Dennis.M.Thompson@nasa.gov

Zeisel (Eva) Designs

Pat Moore
695 Monterey Blvd., Apt. 203
San Francisco, CA 94124
e-mail: ezcclub@pacbell.net

Zsolnay

Federico Santi / John Gacher
The Drawing Room Antiques
152 Spring St.
Newport, RI 02840
(401) 841-5060
www.drawrm.com

Collecting Guidelines

Whenever I'm asked about what to collect, I always stress that you should collect what you like and want to live with. Collecting is a very personal matter and only you can determine what will give you the most satisfaction. With the wide diversity of ceramics available, everyone should be able to find a topic they will enjoy studying and collecting.

One thing that every collector should keep in mind is that to get the most from their hobby they must study it in depth, read everything they can get their hands on, and purchase the best references available for their library. New research material continues to become available for collectors and learning is an ongoing process.

It is also very helpful to join a collectors' club where others who share your enthusiasm will support and guide your learning. Fellow collectors often become your best friends and sources for special treasures to add to your collection. Dealers who specialize in a ceramics category are always eager to help educate and support collectors and many times they become a mentor for a novice who is just starting out on the road to the 'advanced collector' level.

With the very ancient and complex history of ceramic wares, it's easy to understand why becoming educated about your special interest is of paramount importance. There have been collectors of pottery and porcelain for centuries, and for nearly as long collectors have had to be wary of reproductions or 'reissues.' In Chinese ceramics, for instance, it has always been considered perfectly acceptable to copy as closely as possible the style and finish of earlier ceramics and even mark them with

period markings on the base. The only problem arises when a modern collector wants to determine whether their piece, 'guaranteed' antique, was produced over two hundred years ago or barely a century ago.

With European and, to some extent, American wares, copying of earlier styles has also been going on for many decades. As far back as the mid-nineteenth century, 'copies' and 'adaptions' of desirable early wares were finding their way onto the collector market. By the late nineteenth century, in particular, revivals of eighteenth century porcelains and even some early nineteenth century earthenwares were available, often sold as decorative items and sometimes clearly marked. After a hundred years, however, these early copies can pose a real quagmire for the unwary.

Again, education is the key. As you're building your store of knowledge and experience, buy with care from reliable sources.

Another area that calls for special caution on the part of collectors, especially the tyro, is that of damaged and repaired pieces. A wise collector will always buy the best example they can find and it is a good policy to save up to buy one extra fine piece rather than a handful of lesser examples. You never want to pass up a good buy. But, in the long run, a smaller collection of choice pieces will probably bring you more satisfaction (and financial reward) than a large collection of moderate quality.

Purchasing a damaged or clearly repaired piece is a judgment only the collector can make. In general I wouldn't recommend it unless the piece is so unique that another example is not likely to come your way in the near future. For certain classes of expensive and rare ceramics, especially early pottery that has seen heavy use, a certain amount of damage may be inevitable and more acceptable. The sale price, however, should reflect this fact.

Restoration of pottery and porcelain wares has been a fact of life for many decades. Even in the early nineteenth century before good glues were available, 'make-do' repairs were sometimes done to pieces using small metal staples and today some collectors seek out these quaint examples of early recycling. Since the early twentieth century glue and repainting have been common methods used to mask damages to pottery and porcelain and these repairs can usually be detected today with a strong light and the naked eye.

The problem in recent decades has been the ability of restorers to completely mask any sign of previous damages using more sophisticated repair methods. There is nothing wrong with a quality restoration of a rare piece as long as the eventual purchaser is completely aware such work has been done.

It can take more than the naked eye and a strong light to detect some invisible repairs today and that's where the popular 'black light,' using ultraviolet rays, can be of help. Many spots of repair will fluoresce under the 'black light.' I understand, however, that newer glues and paints are becoming available which won't show up under the black light. The key then, especially for the beginner, is know your ceramic or your seller and be sure you have a money-back guarantee when making a major purchase.

I certainly don't want to sound too downbeat and discourage anyone from pursuing what can be a wonderfully fun and fulfilling hobby, but starting from a position of strength, with confidence and education, will certainly pay-off in the long run for every collector.

Ceramics, in addition to their beauty and charm, also offer the collecting advantage of durability and low-maintenance. It's surprising how much pottery and porcelain from two centuries ago is still available to collect. There were literally train-cars full of it produced and sold by the late nineteenth century, and such wares are abundantly available and often reasonably priced. Beautiful dinnerwares and colorful vases abound in the marketplace and offer exciting collecting possibilities. They look wonderful used on today's dining tables or gracing display shelves.

A periodic dusting and once-a-year washing in mild sudsy, warm water is about all the care they will require. Of course, it's not recommended you put older pottery and porcelains in your dishwasher where rattling and extremely hot water could cause damage. Anyway, it's more satisfying to hold a piece in your hand in warm soapy water in a rubber dishpan (for added protection) and caress it carefully with a dishrag. The tactile enjoyment of a ceramic piece brings a new dimension to collecting and this sort of T.L.C. can be nearly as satisfying as just admiring a piece in a china cabinet or on a shelf.

Whatever sort of pottery or porcelain appeals to you most, whether it be eighteenth century Meissen or mid-twentieth century California-made pottery, you can take pride in the fact that you are carrying on a collecting tradition that goes back centuries when the crowned heads of Europe first began vying for the finest and rarest ceramics with which to accent their regal abodes.

Kyle Husfloen

Typical Ceramic Shapes

The following line drawings illustrate typical shapes found in pottery and porcelain pitchers and vases. These forms are ferred to often in our price listings.

Pitcher - Barrel-shaped

Pitcher - Jug-type

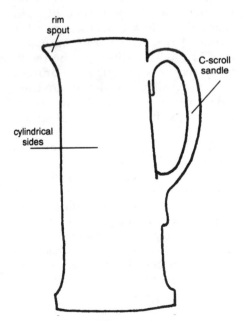

rim
spout

C-scroll
sandle

cylindrical
sides

Pitcher - Tankard-type with cylindrical
sides, C-scroll handle, and
rim spout.

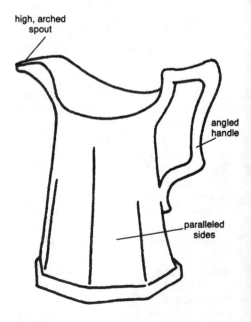

high, arched
spout

angled
handle

paralleled
sides

Pitcher - Tankard-type with panelled
(octagonal) sides, angled handle and high, arched spout.

Vases

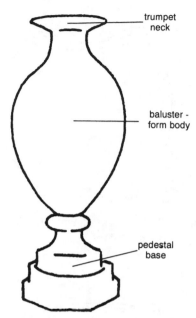

trumpet
neck

baluster -
form body

pedestal
base

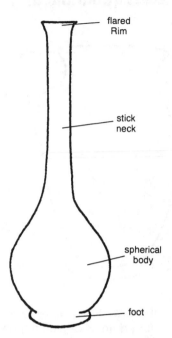

flared
Rim

stick
neck

spherical
body

foot

Vase - Baluster-form body with trumpet neck on a pedestal base.

Vase - Bottle-form — Spherical footed body tapering to a tall stick neck with flared rim.

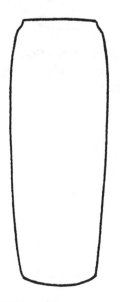

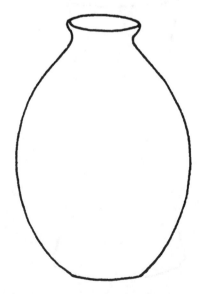

Vase - Cylindrical

Vase - Ovoid body, tapering to a short, flared neck.

Vases (Continued)

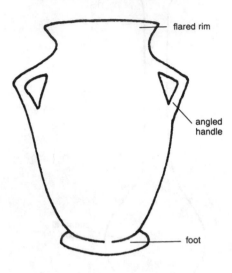

Vase - Ovoid, footed body with flared rim & angled handles.

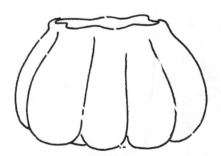

Vase - Pillow-shaped with molded rim; on knob feet.

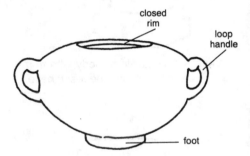

Vase or bowl vase - Spherical, footed body with closed rim and loop handles.

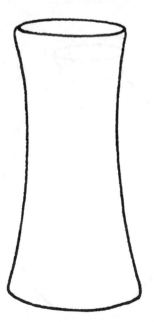

Vase - Waisted cylindrical form.

Vase - Squatty bulbous body with lobed sides.

CERAMICS

ABC Plates

These children's plates were popular in the late 19th and early 20th centuries. An alphabet border was incorporated with nursery rhymes, maxims, scenes or figures in an apparent attempt to "spoon feed" a bit of knowledge at mealtime. An important reference book in this field is A Collector's Guide to ABC Plates, Mugs and Things *by Mildred L. and Joseph P. Chalala (Pridemark Press, Lancaster, Pennsylvania, 1980)*

Girl with Alphabet Book ABC Plate

Letter "A" ABC Plate

"A, Apple, Ape, Air," 6" d., black transfer w/color added to an apple and ape w/large "A" in center & words "Apple, Ape, Air" above picture, red line on rim, probably part of a series (ILLUS.)............... **$225**

ABCs, 4 3/4" d., purple transfer of small girl reading alphabet book to dog in doghouse, letters "N," "S" & "Z" reversed (ILLUS. top of page)....................................... **200**

"Baked Taters All Hot" ABC Plate

"Baked Taters All Hot," 7 1/8" d., blue transfer of man & woman dressed for the cold selling potatoes at a stove on the street (ILLUS.)... **175**

"Band of Hope" ABC Plate

"Band of Hope - The Sabbath Keepers," 6" d., center illustration of congregation filing into church over "Rise early and thankfully put up your prayer - Be at school in good time and be diligent there," color has been added (ILLUS. previous page) **250**

"Base Ball Caught on a Fly" Plate

"Base Ball Caught on a Fly," 6 3/16" d., from the "American Sports" series, black transfer of a baseball game in action showing a fielder catching the ball (ILLUS.) **600**

"Base Ball Running to First Base"

"Base Ball Running to First Base," 6 1/4" d., from "American Sports" series, illustration of field w/several boys playing baseball, crazing, small rim flake (ILLUS.)............ **600**

"Base Ball Striker and Catcher" Plate

"Base Ball Striker and Catcher," 7 1/8" d., from the "American Sports" series, green transfer of a batter ("striker") & catcher (ILLUS.)... **600**

"The Beggar's Petition" ABC Plate

"Beggar's Petition (The)" 7 1/4" d., black transfer w/some color added of young girl giving something to a begging dog (ILLUS.)... **225**

Bird ABC Plate

Bird, 7 1/4" d., brown transfer of titmouse in branches & print alphabet, marked "England" (ILLUS.) **175**

Letter "C" ABC Plate

"C, Cow, Cat, Clown," 5 1/4" d., black & white, large letter "C" surrounded by images of cow, cat & clown, part of alphabet series (ILLUS.)... **275**

"Commander A.H. Foote," 5 1/8" d., black transfer portrait, no mark **350**

"Contemplation" ABC Plate

"Contemplation," 6 5/16" d., from the "Flowers that Never Fade" series, transfer w/color added, "Lord, what is life? - Tis like a flow'r. That blossoms & is gone! We see it flourish for an hour. With all its beauty on" & related illustration of young girls looking at a flower (ILLUS.) **250**

ABC Plate from "Conundrum" Series

Conundrum, 6 1/8" d., from "Conundrum" series, "What fruit does our sketch represent?" under illustration of two figures sitting at table piled high, both waving spoons, one rubbing his stomach (ILLUS.) **250**

Cricket ABC Plate

Cricket game, 7 1/4" d., brown transfer of cricket game in progress (ILLUS.) **175**

"Crusoe Finding the Foot Prints"

"Crusoe Finding the Foot Prints," 8" d., from "Robinson Crusoe" series, Brownhills Pottery Company, sepia transfer w/color added of Robinson Crusoe discovering Friday's footprints, letters printed in sepia around edge of plate (ILLUS.) **175**

"Diamond" Series ABC Plate

Diamond, 7 5/8" d., from "Diamond" series, center diamond shows man & horse, four sepia pictures surrounding center diamond illustrate the rest of the story, also known as a comic book of the 1800s (ILLUS.) **175**

"England's Hope" ABC Plate

"England's Hope. Prince of Wales," 7" d., black transfer of image of young prince astride pony, black lines around edge (ILLUS.) **450**

"Exhibition Prize Rabbits" ABC Plate

"Exhibition Prize Rabbits," black transfer of long-eared rabbits, writing under picture hard to decipher (ILLUS.) **275**

"The Favorite Rabbits" ABC Plate

"Favorite Rabbits (The)," 5" d., one of a series, black & white, "How joyous at each sunshine hour - I haunted ev'ry green retreat - of forest, garden, heath & bower -

Their cell to store with clover sweet" surrounds center illustration of girl in period dress feeding pet rabbits, older plate (ILLUS.) **300**

"Federal Generals" ABC Plate

"Federal Generals," 6" d., black transfer showing four Civil War generals on horseback (ILLUS.) **400**

"The Finding of Moses" ABC Plate

"Finding of Moses (The)" from the "Bible Pictures" series, multicolor scene of two women finding Moses in the bulrushes, letters & floral decorations in space not taken up by center scene (ILLUS.) **250**

"Franklin's Proverbs," 5" d., "Keep thy shop and thy shop will keep thee" over center illustration of merchant (ILLUS. below) **175**

Small "Franklin's Proverbs" Plate

"Franklin's Proverbs" ABC Plate

"Franklin's Proverbs" 7" d., "Keep thy shop
and thy shop will keep thee" around colorful central transfer of merchant in front
of shop, J. & G. Meakin, 1851 (ILLUS.)........ **175**

ABC Plate, "The Lord's Prayer" series

"Give Us This Day Our Daily Bread,"
6 1/4" d., from "The Lord's Prayer" series, blue transfer picture of children giving food to an old man w/a cane (ILLUS.)...... **225**

"Gathering Cotton" ABC Plate

"Gathering Cotton," 6" d., black transfer
w/color added of two slaves picking cot-
ton (ILLUS.) **275**

"The Gleaners" ABC Plate

"Gleaners (The)," 5 5/8" d., illustration of
woman w/bundle on her head walking
across bridge w/two children (ILLUS.)........... **175**

George Washington ABC Plate

George Washington, 7 1/2" d., black portrait
of George Washington, same as picture
used on one-dollar bill (ILLUS.)..................... **500**

"The Graces" ABC Plate

"Graces (The)," 7 1/4" d., black transfer of three girls in period dress embracing, red luster rim (ILLUS.) **300**

"The Guardian" ABC Plate

"Guardian (The)," 7 1/4" d., brown transfer w/color added of sleeping girl guarded by large dog (ILLUS.) **225**

Hens & Rooster ABC Plate

Hens & rooster, 6 1/2" d., colorful transfer of rooster & hens, pale blue embossed alphabet border, probably Germany (ILLUS.) **85**

"Highland Dance" ABC Plate

"Highland Dance," 5 1/2" d., black transfer w/color added of several people dancing (ILLUS.) **175**

"The Irish Jig" ABC Plate

"Irish Jig (The)," 6 1/4" d., pink transfer of a girl dancing, "The Irish Jig" printed at top (ILLUS.) **200**

"John Gilpin" ABC Plate

"John Gilpin Pursued as a Highwayman," 6 1/4" d., black print w/slightly painted details, one of a series showing the humorous anniversary adventures of a 19th-c. draper, illustrations based on Cruikshank's published in 1828 (ILLUS.) **300**

Kite ABC Plate

Kite, 5 1/8" d., black transfer w/colors added
of three boys holding a large yellow kite
(ILLUS.)... **220**

"Leopard and the Fox" ABC Plate

"Leopard and the Fox," 6 1/2" d., part of early "Aesop Fables" series, black & white,
center w/illustration of leopard & fox in
wooded setting, large letters around rim
(ILLUS.)... **275**

"The Lion" ABC Plate

"Lion (The)," 7 5/16" d., from the "Wild Animals" series, Brownhills Pottery Compa-
ny, sepia transfer w/color added (ILLUS.)..... **255**

"The Little Jockey" ABC Plate

"Little Jockey (The)" 7" d., center illustration
of child in dress & plumed hat riding on
the back of a large dog, large black let-
ters on rim (ILLUS.)... **300**

"The Little Play-fellows" ABC Plate

"Little Play-fellows (The)," 5 1/2" d., black
transfer of young boy w/hoop or net & two
girls w/wheelbarrow (ILLUS.) **350**

"Little Red Riding Hood" ABC Plate

"Little Red Riding Hood," 8 3/16" d., from the
"Nursery Tales" series, multicolor transfer in reserve of Little Red Riding Hood &
the wolf, scattered alphabet to the side,
Staffordshire (ILLUS.)...................................... **250**

"Little Strokes Fell Great Oaks"

"Little strokes fell great Oaks," 8 1/4" d., black transfer w/red, yellow & green illustration of man w/ax standing by felled tree, Staffordshire (ILLUS.) **150**

"Marine Railway Station, Manhatton [sic] Beach Hotel," 7" d., illustration of station in center, Staffordshire (ILLUS.) **135**

"The Milk Girl" ABC Plate

"London Dogseller" ABC Plate

"London Dogseller," 7 1/8" d., black transfer w/color added of man in period dress holding two dogs in his arms & one on a leash, w/small dog in back pocket (ILLUS.) **175**

"Milk Girl (The)," 5 1/2" d., black transfer of girl carrying bowl, another woman milking a cow in a field (ILLUS.) **350**

Boys Playing Music ABC Plate

Musicians, 6" d., mulberry transfer of two children playing stringed instruments, made for H.C. Edmeston, England (ILLUS.) **175**

Boys Playing Marbles ABC Plate

Marbles, 6 3/16" d., blue transfer of three boys in period clothes playing marbles, red lines around rim (ILLUS.) **250**

"My Face is My Fortune" ABC Plate

"My Face is My Fortune," 6 3/4" d., blue & white transfer picture of a sitting bulldog (ILLUS.) **175**

"Marine Railway Station" ABC Plate

Riddle ABC Plate

Riddle, 6 1/16" d., blue transfer w/riddle "I ever live man's unrelenting foe - mighty in mischief though I'm small in size - And he at last that seems to lay me low - My food and habitation both supplies" and answer ("Worm") printed around center illustration of two girls playing a game w/hoops & sticks (ILLUS.) **250**

"Rupert and Spot" ABC Plate

"Rupert and Spot," multicolor image of young boy on hands & knees being watched over by a big dog in center, letters in black around image, Roman numerals up to XII & decorative border around letters (ILLUS.) **250**

Sign Language ABC Plate with Owls

Sign language, 6 1/2" d., center w/illustration of schoolmaster owl at desk, little owls in attendance, circled by illustrations of hand signs & letters, red line around rim (ILLUS.) **300**

Sign Language ABC Plate

Sign language, 7" d., illustrations of hands forming letters of sign language in boxes in the middle of the plate, h.p. flowers on rim, extremely rare (ILLUS.) **600**

Children Sledding ABC Plate

Sledding, 7 3/8" d., center illustration of children & toy bears sledding, circled by printed letters of the alphabet in addition to the embossed letters on the rim (ILLUS.).............. **250**

"Soldier Tired" ABC Plate

"Soldier Tired," 7 1/4" d., black transfer of sleeping boy in dress w/a sword & hat nearby guarded by a dog (ILLUS.) **300**

"The Sponge Bath" ABC Plate

"Sponge Bath (The)," 7 7/8" d., black & white, image of young boy bathing in large tub, laughing as he pulls fully clothed child into the water, large printed letters on rim (ILLUS.) **175**

"Thames Tunnel" ABC Plate

"Thames Tunnel," 5 1/4" d., black transfer picture illustrating the opening of the Tunnel in London, 1843, w/people in period dress (ILLUS.) **225**

"Turk" ABC Plate

"Turk," 7 1/4" d., from the "Nations of the World" series, Brownhills Pottery Company, transfer w/polychrome highlights depicts woman in costume, letters to the side rather than in circle on rim of plate (ILLUS.) **225**

Girls Holding Umbrella ABC Plate

Umbrella, 7" d., black transfer w/color added of two girls under an umbrella, an old woman & other children watching from a doorway (ILLUS.) **250**

"Union Troops" ABC Plate

"Union Troops in Virginia," 6 1/8" d., black transfer w/color highlights of a large number of soldiers in formation (ILLUS.) **400**

"Victoria Regina" ABC Plate

"Victoria Regina," 5 1/16" d., black transfer of portrait of Queen Victoria as a young girl over words "Born 25 of May 1918. Proclaimed 20 of June 1837" (ILLUS.)....... **1,000**

"Whom Are You For" ABC Plate

"Whom are you for," 5 1/8" d., center picture of a field sentry w/bayonet stopping two solders, colors added (ILLUS.)...................... **250**

"William Penn" ABC Plate

"William Penn," 7 1/2" d., pink transfer portrait, no mark (ILLUS.)...................................... **350**

Woman Riding Spotted Horse Plate

Woman riding, 5 3/16" d., center illustration of woman balancing large basket on her head & riding on spotted horse (ILLUS.)....... **175**

Abingdon

Abingdon Mark

From about 1934 until 1950, Abingdon Pottery Company, Abingdon, Illinois, manufactured decorative pottery, mainly cookie jars, flowerpots and vases. Decorated with various glazes, these items are becoming popular with collectors who are especially attracted to Abingdon's novelty cookie jars.

Ashtray, Leaf, in the shape of a maple leaf, white interior, black exterior, No. 660, 1948-50, 5 1/2" d. (ILLUS. below) **$20**

Abingdon Leaf Ashtrays

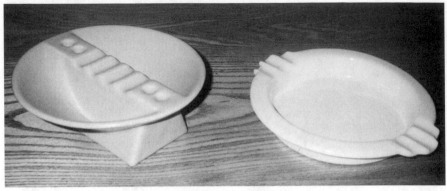

Abingdon Ashtrays

Ashtray, New Mode, round, divided in half by ridge to hold cigarettes, rectangular base, pink, No. 456, 1939-48, 5 3/4" d. (ILLUS. left)... 30

Ashtray, round, black w/black donkey standing on top, No. 510, 1940-41, 5 1/2" d. (ILLUS. left, w/elephant ashtray, below)........ **150**

Abingdon Octagonal Ashtray

Ashtray, octagonal, turquoise, No. 551, 1941-46, 7 x 7" (ILLUS.).................................. **25**

Abingdon Round Ashtray

Ashtray, round, turquoise, No. 555, 1941-46, 8" d. (ILLUS.).. **25**

Abingdon Donkey & Elephant Ashtrays

Abingdon Russian Dancer Book Ends

Ashtray, round, white, No. 334 (ILLUS. right, w/New Mode ashtray) **20**
Ashtray, round, white w/black elephant standing on top w/trunk raised, No. 509, 1940-41, 5 1/2" d. (ILLUS. right, w/donkey ashtray) **150**
Book ends, figures of Russian dancers w/arms crossed at chest, fez-type hats, rectangular bases, white, No. 321, 1934-40, 6 1/2" h. (ILLUS. above) **250-300**
Book ends, model of Scottie dog, No. 650, 7 1/2" h., pr. **200**
Book ends, model of sea gull, spread wings, No. 305, ivory glaze, 1934-1942, 6" h., pr. (ILLUS. left w/model of sea gull) **150-165**

Book ends/planters, model of cactus, No. 374, 1936-8, 7" h., pr. (ILLUS.) **125**
Book ends/planters, model of dolphin, No. 444D, blue glaze, 5 3/4" h., pr. **65**

Abingdon Chinese Bowl

Bowl, 9 x 11" oval, Chinese, gently flaring body on short rectangular feet, white floral decoration on white ground, No. 345, 1935-37 (ILLUS.) **90**
Bowl, 9 x 14" rectangular, turquoise, Han patt., No. 523, 1940 (ILLUS. below) **40**

Cactus Book Ends/Planters

Abingdon Han Bowl

Abingdon Salad Bowl & Candleholders

Bowl, salad, 10" d., 5" h., Rope, scalloped
  rim, ropetwist foot, turquoise, No. 313,
  1934-36 (ILLUS. center w/Quatrain can-
  dleholders)... 75
Candleholder, double, No. 479, Scroll patt.,
  4 1/2" h. 15

Abingdon Shell Candleholder

Candleholder, double, Shell line, green, No.
  505, 1940-49, 4" h., pr. (ILLUS.)...................... 25

Bamboo Candleholders & Console Plate

Candleholders, Bamboo patt., No. 716, pr.
  (ILLUS. w/console plate)................................... 30
Candleholders, Quatrain, quatrefoil shapes
  w/center hole for candle, turquoise, No.
  360, 1935-36, pr. (ILLUS. w/Rope salad
  bowl)... 50
Candleholders, Sunburst, in the form of
  three ribbed connected semicircles, rose,
  No. 447, 1938, 8" l., pr. (ILLUS. right &
  left w/window box, below) 60
Console bowl, No. 532, Scroll patt.,
  14 1/2" l.. 20
Console plate, Bamboo patt., No. 715,
  10 1/2" d. (ILLUS. w/candleholders)............. 125
Cookie jar, Baby, No. 561, 11" h............. 750-1,000

Sunburst Candleholders & Window Box

Abingdon Bo Peep Cookie Jar

Cookie jar, Bo Peep, No. 694D, 1950, 12" h.
(ILLUS.)... **375**

Abingdon Choo Choo Cookie Jar

Cookie jar, Choo Choo, No. 651D, 1948-50,
7 1/2" h. (ILLUS.)... **225**
Cookie jar, Clock, No. 563, 9" h. **100**

Abingdon Daisy Cookie Jar

Cookie jar, Daisy, No. 677, 1949-50, 8" h.
(ILLUS.).. **95**

Fat Boy Cookie Jar

Cookie jar, Fat Boy, No. 495, 1940-46,
8 1/4" h. (ILLUS.).. **500-700**
Cookie jar, Floral/Plaid, No. 697, 8 1/2" h. . **350-550**
Cookie jar, Hippo, No. 549, plain & decorat-
ed, 8" h.. **350-550**
Cookie jar, Humpty Dumpty, No. 663,
10 1/2" h.. **208**
Cookie jar, Little Girl, No. 693, 9 1/2" h. **225**

Little Ol' Lady Cookie Jars

Cookie jar, Little Ol' Lady, No. 471, 9" h.,
various decorations, each (ILLUS.)........ **200-300**
Cookie jar, Miss Muffet, No. 662D, 11" h. **350**
Cookie jar, Money Bag, No. 588D, 7 1/2" h. **40**

Mother Goose Cookie Jar

Cookie jar, Mother Goose, No. 695D, 1950,
12" h. (ILLUS.).. **425**

Pineapple Cookie Jar

Cookie jar, Pineapple, No. 664, 1949-50,
10 1/2" h. (ILLUS.).............................. **200**
Cookie jar, Pumpkin, No. 674D, 8" h................. **550**
Cookie jar, Three Bears, No. 696D, 8 3/4" h.
(light hairline in lid)............................. **40**
Cookie jar, Windmill, No. 678, 10 1/2" h. **500**
Cookie jar, Witch, No. 692, 11 1/2" h. **1,000**

Wigwam Cookie Jar

Cookie jar, Wigwam, No. 665D, 11" h.
(ILLUS.)... **750-1,000**

Abingdon Display Sign

Display sign, marked "Abingdon" (ILLUS.)........ **300**

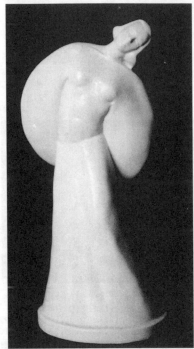

Scarf Dancer Figure

Figure, Scarf Dancer, No. 3902, 13" h.
(ILLUS.).. **800 up**
Flower boat, Fern Leaf, oblong ribbed leaf
shape, pink, No. 426, 1937-38, 13 x 4"
(ILLUS. left w/fruit boat, below)...................... **100**

Abingdon Flower Boat & Fruit Boat

Various Flowerpots

Flowerpots, Nos. 149 to 152, floral decoration, 3 to 6" h., each (ILLUS. of three) **15-30**
Fruit boat, Fern Leaf, oblong ribbed leaf shape, white, No. 432, 1938-39, 6 1/2 x 15" (ILLUS. right w/flower boat) **100**

Lamp base, No. 254, draped shaft, 13" h. (ILLUS.) **200**
Model of heron, No. 574, tan glaze, 5 1/4" h. **68**
Model of peacock, No. 416, turquoise glaze, 7" h. **96**

Abingdon Penguin Figurine

Model of penguin, black, wearing top hat, No. 573, 5" h. (ILLUS.) **50**
Model of penguin, white, 3" h. **25**
Mantel pieces, cov., handled, bird & floral decoration on white ground, No. KR22, rare, each (ILLUS. of two, below) **65**

Abingdon Lamp Base

Two Abingdon Mantel Pieces

Abingdon Gull Figurine & Book Ends

Model of sea gull, w/spread wings, No. 562,
    1942, 5" h. (ILLUS. right w/book ends)...... **50-75**
Model of swan, No. 661, 3 3/4" h. **150**

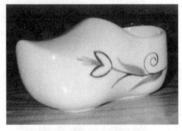

Abingdon Dutch Shoe Planter

Planter, Dutch shoe, stylized tulip decora-
    tion on white ground, No. 655D, 1948,
    5" l. (ILLUS.).. **95**
Planter, model of a puppy, No. 652D,
    6 3/4" l. **50**
Planter, short foot, flared sides rising to
    scroll ends, No. 476, 10" w., 3" h.
    (ILLUS. below) **30**
String holder, Chinese head, No. 702,
    5 1/2" h. **500**

Grecian Pitcher & Vase

Pitcher, 15" h., Grecian patt., No. 613
    (ILLUS. right w/vase)...................................... **150**

Abingdon Planter

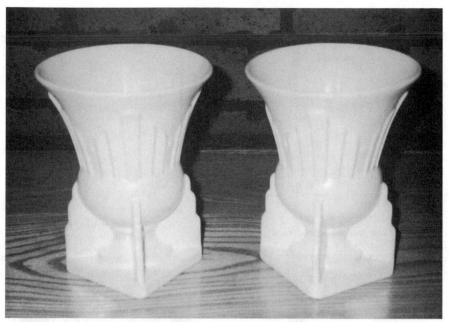

Abingdon Capri Vases

Abingdon Cattail Vase

Vase, 6 1/4" h., vertical ribs, three h.p. cat-
  tails, No. 152 (ILLUS.) **32**
Vase, 3 1/2" h., No. A1, whatnot type................ **100**
Vase, 4 1/2" h., No. C1, whatnot type **100**
Vase, 5" h., No. B1, whatnot type **100**
Vase, 5" h., white floral decoration on blue
  ground, small handles, No. 567D, 1942-
  46 (ILLUS. right w/window box No. 570D)....... **40**
Vase, 5 1/2" h., No. 142, Classic line **40**
Vase, 5 3/4" h., Capri, urn form w/quatrefoil
  bases, white, No. 351, 1935-37, each
  (ILLUS. of two top of page)............................. **125**
Vase, 7" h., No. 171, Classic line **40**
Vase, 7 1/4" h., Fern Leaf, ribbed leaf-style
  sides flaring to bowl-style opening,
  green, No. 423, 1937-38 (ILLUS. right
  w/taller Fern Leaf vase) **85**

Figural Blackamoor Vase

Vase, 7 1/2" h. figure of Blackamoor, No.
  497D (ILLUS.)... **150**

Abingdon Delta Vase

Vase, 8" h., Delta, handles, ribbed base, rose, No. 108, 1938-39 (ILLUS.)..................... **40**

Abingdon Scroll Vase

Vase, 8" h., Scroll, bulbous body, neck w/four handles tapers out at top, green, No. 417, 1937-38 (ILLUS.)................................ **80**

Abingdon Gamma Vase

Vase, 8" h., Gamma, short bulbous base connected to tall slightly flaring lobed neck by applied side handles, turquoise, No. 107, 1938-39 (ILLUS.)............................... **40**

Abingdon Wreath Vase

Vase, 8" h., Wreath, circular on ribbed ogee base, leaf garland, bow & star decoration, pink, No. 467, 1938-39 (ILLUS.) **95**

Abingdon Boot Vase

Vase, 8" h., model of a boot, white, No. 584, 1947 (ILLUS.)....................................... **45**
Vase, 8" h., No. 132, Classic line.......................... **40**

Abingdon Swedish Vase

Vase, 8 1/4" h., Swedish, handled, white, No. 314, 1934-36 (ILLUS.)................................ **85**

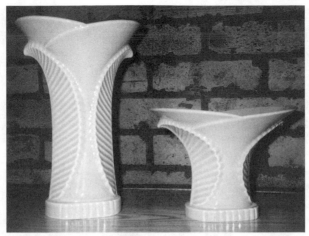

Abingdon Fern Leaf Vases

Vase, 10 1/4" h., Fern Leaf, tall ribbed leaf-shape sides taper out to top opening, blue, No. 422, 1937-39 (ILLUS. left w/smaller Fern Leaf vase)................................ **95**

Lung Pattern Vase

Vase, 11" h., Lung patt., No. 302 (ILLUS.)........ **225**
Vase, 15" h., floor-type, Grecian patt., No. 603 (ILLUS. left w/pitcher)............................... **150**

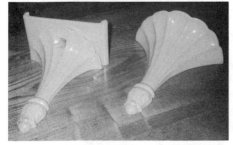

Abingdon Acanthus Wall Bracket & Wall Pocket

Wall bracket, Acanthus, pink, No. 589, 1947, 7" h. (ILLUS. left w/wall pocket)............. **65**
Wall pocket, Acanthus, pink, No. 648, 1948, 8 3/4" h. (ILLUS. right w/wall bracket)............. **65**
Wall pocket, figural butterfly, No. 601, 8 1/2" h... **150**
Wall pocket, figural Dutch boy, No. 489, 10" h. **150**
Wall pocket, figural Dutch girl, No. 490, 10" h. **150**

Abingdon Wall Pockets

Wall pocket, Leaf, overlapping pink veined leaves, No. 724, 1950, scarce, 10 x 5 1/2" (ILLUS. top w/Triad wall pocket)... **75**

Abingdon Window Box & Vase

Double Trumpet Wall Pocket

Wall pocket, Morning Glory, double trumpet
form, No. 375, 1936-40, 6 1/2" h.
(ILLUS.).. **45-55**

Morning Glory Wall Pocket

Wall pocket, Morning Glory, trumpet form,
pink, No. 377, 1936-50, 7 1/2" h.
(ILLUS.).. 35
Wall pocket, Triad, in the form of three pink
connected flowerpots, No. 640, 1940,
5 1/2 x 8" (ILLUS. bottom w/Leaf wall
pocket)... **40-50**
Window box, oblong, scalloped rim, white
floral decoration on blue ground, No.
570D, 1942-46, 10" l. (ILLUS. left w/vase
No. 567D, above).. 35
Window box, Sunburst, in the form of three
connected ribbed semicircles, rose, No.
448, 1938-39, 9" l., (ILLUS. center
w/Sunburst candleholders) 80

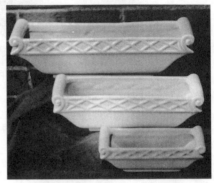

Various Size Window Boxes

Window boxes, No. 477, 13 1/2" l., No. 476,
10 1/2" l., No. 475, 7" l., each (ILLUS.)...... **25-35**

American Painted Porcelain

*During the late Victorian era American artisans pro-
duced thousands of hand-painted porcelain items,
including tableware, dresser sets, desk sets, and bric-a-
brac. These pieces of porcelain were imported and usually bear the marks of foreign factories and countries. To
learn more about identification, evaluation, history and
appraisal, the following books and newsletter by Dorothy Kamm are recommended:* American Painted Porcelain: Collector's Identification & Value Guide,
Comprehensive Guide to American Painted Porcelain,
and Dorothy Kamm's Porcelain Collector's Companion.

Berry spoon holder, pierced handles, decorated w/two clusters of blackberries, light
blue border, burnished gold rim & handles, marked "Bavaria," ca. 1894-1914,
4 5/8 x 10".. **$45**

Bonbon Box with Peacock Decor

Bonbon box, cov., round, low domed cover decorated w/a conventional design of three intertwined peacocks, baby blue base, burnished gold rims & feet, opal luster interior, marked "T&V Limoges - France," 1892-1907 (ILLUS.)............................ **95**

Bonbon dish, round w/gold upright ring handles, decorated w/clusters of currants on a multicolored ground, an inner border band w/gilded outlines of spider webs & currant clusters, burnished gold rim, signed "I.A. Johnson, 1915" & marked "UNO-IT - Favorite - Bavaria," 6 3/8" d. **40**

Bouillon cup & saucer, decorated w/a curvilinear geometric design in burnished gold outlined in dark blue, burnished gold rims & handles, marked "T & V - Limoges - France," ca. 1892-1907 .... **30**

Small Footed Bowl

Bowl, 5 1/2" d., 2 3/4" h., pedestal foot, decorated w/a conventional border in moss, yellow, orange & burnished gold on an ivory ground, dark green base, burnished bold rim & band, marked w/"La Seynie - P and P - Limoges - France," 1903-17 (ILLUS.)... **50**

Bowl, 7 1/2" d., cereal, decorated w/a border design of daisy clusters on an ivory ground, light blue border & burnished gold rim, marked "HR - Hutschenreuther - Selb - Bavaria," ca. 1905-18.......................... **22**

Bowl, 8 3/4" w., square fruit-type, decorated on the interior w/geraniums on a poly-chrome ground, on the exterior w/scrolls on a graduated green ground, burnished gold rim, ca. 1880-1900.................................... **70**

Butter dish, cover & liner, decorated on the domed cover & dished base w/clusters of pink roses & greenery on a pale pink & green ground, burnished gold rim & handle, signed "R.O. BRIGGS, AUSTIN, IL (?)," marked w/crowned double-headed eagle & "MZ - Austria," 1884-1909 .... **75**

Butter tub, round, decorated w/forget-me-nots on an ivory ground, burnished gold rim & handles, signed "Tossy," marked "T & V - Limoges - France," ca. 1892-1917 (no pierced insert) **50**

Cake plate, pierced rim handles, scalloped edge, decorated w/a four-panel design w/conventional-style flowers in each panel, burnished gold border outlines, dotted grounds & rim, signed w/illegible cipher & marked "HR - Charlotte - Bavaria," ca. 1887+, 9 1/8" d. **75**

Individual Cake Plate with Wild Roses

Cake plate or cookie tray, individual size, paneled sides, open handles, decorated w/a cluster of pink wild roses on a multi-colored pastel ground, signed "R.J. '30" (ILLUS.)... **22**

Celery dish, long narrow shallow boat-form w/squared ends, decorated w/a border design of daisies & leaves on a pastel polychrome ground, ivory center, signed "Weiler," 1900-20, 5 3/4 x 12 3/4" (ILLUS., below)... **60**

Celery Dish with Daisy Border

Chocolate cup & saucer, decorated w/yellow primrose on a shaded yellow brown ground, burnished gold rims, cup base & handle, signed "A. Brown," marked "Haviland - Limoges - France," ca. 1894-1931 35

Chocolate pot, cov., decorated w/cluster of pink roses on a pastel polychrome ground, burnished gold knob & handle, signed "M.H. Dorothy," marked "GDA - France," ca. 1900-41 175

Coffeepot, cov., decorated w/a conventional-style dandelion design, burnished gold rims, spout interior, upper lip & handles, signed "M. Lamour," marked "J. & C. Bavaria," ca. 1902, 10" h. 225

Morning Glory-decorated Compote

Compote, 8 7/8" d., 4 1/4" h., open, wide shallow round flaring bowl raised on a flaring pedestal base, the interior decorated w/a cluster of pink & white morning glories, rim & foot decorated w/bands of conventional pink butterflies, burnished gold rim & foot, signed "CL April 13th, 188(1)," marked "CFH" (ILLUS. of interior) 200

Cracker & cheese dish, decorated w/a conventional Chinese-style floral design, an opal lustre ground, burnished gold borders & rims, illegible signature, marked w/a wreath & star & "R.S. Tillowitz - Silesia," ca. 1920-38, 8 1/2" d. 110

Cracker jar, cov., decorated w/white wild roses on a pastel polychrome ground w/burnished gold handles, signed "A.S.S.," marked "Royal" & wreath w/"O. & E.G.," 1898-1918 62

Creamer & cov. sugar bowl, each w/a tapering cylindrical form, the base decorated w/a conventional blue & green floral border on a burnished gold band, ivory ground, burnished gold lips, spout, rims & handles, signed "Helen Hurley," 1900-20, pr. (ILLUS., bottom of page) 55

Creamer & open sugar bowl, decorated w/yellow roses on a light green border band, burnished gold borders, rims, base rims & handles, creamer marked w/a bird & "C.T. - Altwasser - Silesia," marked "KPM," ca. 1909-1930, pr. 35

Cup, after dinner size, decorated w/panels of Japanese-style medallions in antique green & bright gold on a dull red ground, signed "MA 12/92" (no saucer) 12

Breakfast Cup & Saucer with Clover

Cup & saucer, breakfast-size, decorated w/a clover design on a light blue ground, burnished gold rims & handle, signed "A. H. h.," ca. 1880s-90s (ILLUS.) 45

Cup & Saucer with Celtic Border

Cup & saucer, cylindrical cup w/angled handle, decorated w/a conventional Celtic border design in celadon, light blue border, ivory center & interior, burnished gold rims & handle, signed "L.E.S.," marked w/a crown in double circle & "Victoria Austria," 1900-20, the set (ILLUS.) 35

Cup & saucer, decorated w/pink roses on a pastel polychrome ground, opal lustre interior, burnished gold rims & handle, marked "Favorite - Bavaria," ca. 1908-18, the set 25

Decorated Creamer & Covered Sugar

Cup & Saucer with Floral Border

Cup & saucer, tapering cylindrical cup w/angled handle, decorated w/a conventional blue floral garland border design, burnished gold rims & handle, signed "Jane Bent Telin," marked "Favorite Bavaria,"1910-25, the set (ILLUS.) 40

Fern pot, decorated w/pink wild roses on a graduated green ground, signed "B.E. Miehling 99," marked "Elite" in a shield & "Limoges - France," 1899, 7 1/2" d., 4 3/4" h. 200

Gold-decorated Hair Receiver

Hair receiver, cov., squatty round form on three gold curved legs, decorated w/a conventional rose design in burnished gold, burnished gold rim & feet, signed "Ferver," ca. 1900-10, 3 7/8" d., 3 1/4" h. (ILLUS.) 50

Decorated Hairpin Box

Hairpin box, cov., oval, decorated w/a conventional-style rose, leaf & stem border on a burnished gold ground, ivory top, light blue base, marked "Favorite - Bavaria," ca. 1908-1915, 1 1/2 x 4 1/2", 1 3/4" h. (ILLUS.) 30

Handkerchief box, cov., decorated w/peach-tinged yellow roses on a pastel polychrome ground, signed "WSO - 1913,"

marked "D. & Co. - France," 5 1/4" sq., 3" h. 75

Honey dish, on three ball feet, decorated w/pink clover & wheat sheaves, light grey border, white enamel trim, burnished gold rim, marked "Bavaria," ca. 1891-1914, 7 1/8" d. 40

Ice cream bowl, decorated w/a winter scene w/burnished gold border & rim, signed "F.L. Hey," marked "CFH - GDM," ca. 1920-30, 6 3/4 x 10 5/8", 2 3/16" h. 115

Jelly tray, round, individual size, decorated w/a conventional border design in greens, blue, yellow & burnished gold, outlined in black, burnished gold rim & handles, signed "LMC," marked "Made in Japan," ca. 1925, 7 1/8" d. 30

Lobster or shrimp salad bowl, decorated w/border clusters of seashells & seaweed, white enamel trim, pale polychrome ground colors on exterior, burnished gold rim, marked "H and Co. - Limoges - France," ca. 1888-1896, 7 3/4 x 10 1/2" 125

Luncheon set: 7 1/2" d. plate, cup & saucer; decorated in a conventional-style floral border w/white enameled flower centers & burnished gold rims & handle, marked "Germany," ca. 1914-18, the set 35

Mayonnaise bowl & underplate, decorated w/clusters of forget-me-nots on a pale blue border, ivory ground, burnished gold rims & feet, signed "AG," marked "Stouffer," 1906-1914, bowl 4 1/2" d., underplate 5 7/16" d., 2 pcs. 30

Muffin dish, cov., round, decorated w/pink wild roses & greenery on a pastel polychrome ground, burnished gold rim & handles, signed "E. Starer," marked "J & C - 'Louise' - Bavaria," ca. 1902, 9 1/4" d., 4" h. 325

Mug, decorated w/colorful yellow & yellowish red gooseberries on a polychrome ground, marked w/a crown & two shields w/"Vienna - Austria," ca. 1900-15, 4 3/4" h. 65

Mustard jar w/attached underplate & cover, decorated w/conventional-style water lilies on a light blue & burnished gold ground, burnished gold handle & rims,

marked "D. & Co. - France," ca. 1879-
1900, 3" h. **40**
Napkin ring, decorated w/forget-me-nots,
white enamel trim & burnished gold rims,
signed "Luken," ca. 1895-1926, 2" d. **20**
Napkin ring, half moon-shape, decorated
w/a purple columbine on an ivory
ground, ca. 1880-1915, 2 1/2" w. **25**
Nut bowl, decorated in polychrome colors
w/a squirrel, acorns & oak leaves on a
branch, opal lustre interior, burnished
gold feet & fluted rim, signed "Mrs. O.C.
Oakes," 1900-20 .... **100**
Olive dish, ring-handled, decorated w/helio-
trope, w/etched & burnished gold border
& burnished gold handle, marked "T & V
- Limoges - France," ca. 1892-1907,
7 3/8" d. **50**

Decorated Orange Cups

Orange cups, footed, decorated w/designs
of orange blossoms on light blue & yellow
grounds, embellished w/white & yellow
enamel, burnished gold rim, base band,
foot & prongs, signed "CKI," marked "T &
V - France - Deposé," ca. 1900-15,
3 1/4" d., 2 3/4" h., pr. (ILLUS.) **100**

Perfume with Honeysuckle Decor

Perfume bottle w/original gold stopper,
ovoid body w/a short neck & large ball
stopper, decorated w/a conventional design of honeysuckle in matte bronze
greens, outlined in burnished gold, on a
matte pale green ground, burnished gold
lip & stopper, signed "M.L. Cushman" &
"CFH/GDM," 1882-1890, 4 3/4" h.
(ILLUS.) **85**

Perfume Bottle with Daisy Decoration

Perfume bottle w/original gold stopper,
squatty bulbous base tapering to a tall
slender cylindrical neck, decorated
around the lower body w/daisies &
leaves on an ivory ground, burnished
gold rim & stopper, marked w/a wreath &
"O. & E.G. - Royal - Austria," 1898-1918,
4 3/4" h. (ILLUS.) **75**

Pin Tray with Moth Decoration

Pin tray, oval, decorated w/a border design
of four blue & burnished gold moths, connected by a burnished gold & black band,
ivory ground, burnished gold rim, signed
"E. Arrindell - 1-2/18," marked w/a crown
& double-headed eagle & "MZ - Austria,"
1918 (ILLUS.) **50**
Pitcher, 9 3/4" h., claret-type, decorated w/a
conventional Art Nouveau-style floral design outlined in gold, burnished gold handle & edges, signed "V.B. Chase," ca.
1890-1914 .... **50**
Pitcher, 5 3/4" h., lemonade, bulbous body,
decorated w/currants on a polychrome
ground, ca. 1900-1920 .... **225**
Pitcher, 5 3/4" h., lemonade-type, decorat-
ed w/clusters of purple grapes on an ivory ground, antique green beaded handle
& border band at top, ca. 1900-16 .... **225**

Pitcher & underplate, 3 3/8" h. milk-type pitcher, 5 1/4" d. plate, decorated w/conventionalized orange blossoms w/burnished gold borders, rims, spout & handle, signed "J.M. Cliffe, 11/28" & marked "Japan," the set **30**

Coupe Plate with Cornucopias

Plate, 6 3/4" d., coupe-style, decorated w/a border design of pink roses in burnished gold cornucopias, interspersed on a pink band, ivory ground, burnished gold rim & banding, marked w/a crown & scepter & "Silesia," ca. 1900-20 (ILLUS.) **25**

Plate Decorated with Pansies

Plate, 7 3/4" d., round w/lightly scalloped rim, decorated w/multicolored pansies & greenery & burnished gold scrolls, ivory center, lavender rim border, burnished gold rim band, signed "BS" & marked "J&C - Louise - Bavaria," ca. 1902+ (ILLUS.) **50**

Plate with Well-painted Nasturtiums

Plate, 8 3/4" d., decorated w/orange nasturtiums, green leaves & light green scrolls accented w/gilded dots, burnished gold border band & rim, signed "G. Leykauf - 1908," marked "J.P.L. - France" (ILLUS.) **275**

Tulip-decorated Plate

Plate, 8 1/4" d., decorated w/large red tulips & green leaves on a shaded rust to cream ground w/burnished gold rim, marked w/a bird & "Altwasser - Germany," ca. 1909-34 (ILLUS.) **45**

Poppy-decorated Plate

Plate, 8 3/4" d., decorated w/large orange poppies & green leaves on a shaded green ground, burnished gold rim, stamped on bottom "J. Lycett - St. Louis, Mo. - The Odeon," ca. 1900-15 (ILLUS.)......... **50**

Plate, 5 1/4 x 9 1/2", salad-type, crescent-shaped, decorated w/multicolored sweet peas on a pale violet & green ground, burnished gold rim, ca. 1900-24 .... **42**

Hand-painted Pomade Jar

Powder Puff Box & Pin Tray

Pomade jar, cov., small cylindrical form, decorated w/a conventional geometric design in baby blue & burnished gold outlined in brown, marked "W. G. & Co. - Limoges - France," ca. 1901, 2 1/2" d., 1 1/2" h. (ILLUS.) **35**

Powder puff box & pin tray, round box w/domed cover & gold scroll loop finial, oblong lobed tray, each decorated w/a conventional dark bluish violet floral & pale green leaf border design w/burnished gold rims & vines outlined in black, on a pale pecan background, ivory ground, burnished gold finial, pin tray marked "GDA - France," box marked "T&V Limoges - France," 1900-20, tray 4 1/2 x 5 5/8", box 4 7/8" d., the set (ILLUS., above) **100**

Punch cups, decorated w/clusters of forget-me-nots, opal lustre interiors, burnished gold stems & rims, marked w/"Royal," a wreath & "O. & E.G.," 1898-1918, 4" h., set of 5 .... **125**

Pretty Painted Relish Pot

Relish pot, cov., ovoid body w/small inset domed cover w/gold loop handle, gold side handle, decorated w/a conventional design of fruits & flowers in polychrome colors, yellow enamel accents, baby blue ground, burnished gold rim & handles, signed "L Hogue," marked in a circle "K&L - Germany," 1915-30, 3 5/8" h. (ILLUS.) **30**

Salt dips, cauldron-shaped, decorated w/pink roses on a pale blue & yellow

ground, burnished gold rims & ball feet, signed "P. Putzki," marked w/a crown, double-head eagle & "MZ - Austria," ca. 1884-1909, set of 6 .... **120**

Decorated Nippon Porcelain Shakers

Salt & pepper shakers, decorated w/delicate panels of conventional-style hawthorn berries & leaves on an opal lustre ground, burnished gold tops & branch-shaped borders, signed "A.E.F.," marked "Noritake Nippon," 1914-21, 2 1/2" h., pr. (ILLUS.) **35**

Salt & Peppers with Blue Insects

Salt & pepper shakers, tapering square form w/domed gold top, white ground decorated w/a conventional design of blue-winged insects, burnished gold tops, 1905-20, 3" h., pr. (ILLUS.) **35**

Sandwich tray, double pierced handles, decorated w/a polychrome conventional design, burnished gold rim & handles, marked w/a crown & crossed scepters w/"Rosenthal - Bavaria," 1908-25, 10" l. **85**

Sherbet, decorated w/daisies on an ivory ground, mother-of-pearl lustre interior, burnished gold border, rim & foot, signed "M. Paddock," marked "Epiag - Czechoslovakia," ca. 1920-39, 3 1/8" h. **35**

Soup plates, flanged rim decorated w/three clusters of seashells & seaweed on a very pale polychrome ground, burnished gold rims, signed "ALB," marked "H. & Co. - Haviland - Limoges - France," 1876-1879, 9" d., pr... 50

Sugar shaker, decorated w/Art Nouveau-style florals & squiggling border band in burnished gold, burnished gold pierced top, signed "E.C.R.," ca. 1905-15, 2 3/4" d., 4 1/2" h. 50

Syrup jug, cov., decorated w/pink & ruby roses on a polychrome ground, burnished gold handle, knob & rims, opal lustre spout interior, marked "ADK - France," ca. 1891-1910, 4" h. (missing underplate).. 30

Table top centerpiece, decorated w/a cluster of daisies on a pastel polychrome ground, burnished gold rim, signed "E. Miller," marked "T & V - Limoges - France," ca. 1892-1907, 11 5/8" d. 90

Toast set: plate & cup; 9 3/16 w. plate decorated w/conventional-style strawberries on an ivory ground, opal lustre cup interior, burnished gold borders, rims & handle, ca. 1925-30, 2 pcs............................. 60

Toothpick holder, decorated w/double violets on a pastel ivory & green ground, burnished gold rim, signed "Wats" & "Pitkin & Brooks Studio," marked "T & V - Limoges - France," 1903-10, 2 3/4" h................. 30

Tumbler, decorated w/ruby roses on a polychrome ground, burnished gold rim, illegible signature, marked "La Seynie - PP - Limoges - France," ca. 1903-17, 3 3/8" h. 22

Art Deco Design Painted Vase

Vase, 7 7/8" h., bulbous baluster-form w/wide flared neck, decorated w/two Art Deco-style floral panels in lustre & burnished gold, gold center band & base & neck bands, signed "M.D.P. 1920," marked w/a shield & "Thomas" (ILLUS.)......... 85

Vase, 7" h., bulbous base tapering to a tall slender neck, two-handled, decorated w/pink & yellow roses on a pastel polychrome ground, burnished gold rim, accents & handle, ca. 1900-20 45

Jewelry

American painted porcelain jewelry comprises a unique category. While the metallic settings and porcelain medallions were inexpensive, the painted decoration was a work of fine art. The finished piece possessed greater intrinsic value than costume jewelry of the same period because it was a one-of-a-kind creation, but one that was not as expensive as real gold and sterling silver settings and precious and semiprecious jewels. Note that signatures are rare, backstamps lacking.

Dorothy Kamm

Bar pin, decorated w/pink roses & greenery, brass-plated bezel, ca. 1880s, 7/16 x 1 1/2" 30

Bar pin, decorated w/pink roses on a pale green ground, burnished gold tips & brass-plated bezel, ca. 1900-1915, 2 5/8" w. 50

Belt Buckle Brooch with Portrait

Belt buckle brooch, oval, decorated w/a profile of a woman wearing a pink top & white shawl, pink roses in her curly brown hair, black choker at her neck, burnished gold rim, gold-plated bezel, signed "M.e.M.," 1900-17, 1 7/8 x 2 3/8" (ILLUS.).. 175

Belt Buckle Brooch with Pansy

Belt buckle brooch, oval, decorated w/a white pansy, accented w/white enamel, on a burnished gold ground, gold-plated bezel, 1900-17, 1 11/16 x 2 1/4" (ILLUS.)........ 75

Art Nouveau Florals on Belt Brooch

Belt buckle brooch, oval, decorated w/an Art Nouveau-style water lily design outlined w/raised paste, petals filled in w/lavender enamel, burnished green & gold background, gold-plated bezel, 1900-17, 1 7/8 x 2 5/8" (ILLUS.) **110**

Bachelor Buttons on Belt Brooch

Belt buckle brooch, oval, decorated w/blue bachelor buttons & greenery on a polychrome ground, irregular burnished gold border outlined in black, gold-plate bezel, 1900-17, 1 7/8 x 2 5/8" (ILLUS.) **95**

Belt buckle brooch, oval, decorated w/roses & greenery on a polychrome ground, burnished gold scalloped border outlined in black, gold-plated bezel, 1900-17, 1 15/16 x 2 11/16" **115**

Brooch, decorated w/violets on a light yellow brown ground w/raised paste scrolled border covered w/burnished gold & burnished gold rims, gold-plated bezel, ca. 1890-1920, 1 1/2" d. **45**

Brooch, diamond-shaped, decorated w/a water lily & waterscape w/white enamel highlights, sky & clouds in background, burnished gold rim, gold-plated bezel, ca. 1930s-1940s, 7/8" sq. **35**

Heart-shaped Brooch with Roses

Brooch, heart-shaped, decorated w/a pink & a ruby rose w/leaves on a polychrome ground, white enamel accents, burnished gold rim, gold-plated bezel, 7/8 x 7/8" (ILLUS.) **30**

Brooch, horseshoe shape, decorated w/pink & ruby roses on a green & yellow ground, white enamel highlights & burnished gold tips, ca. 1880s-1915, 1 1/4 x 1 1/2" **75**

Forget-me-nots on Long Oval Brooch

Brooch, long oval, decorated w/forget-me-nots & leaves on a pastel polychrome ground, white enamel highlights, burnished gold rim, gold-plated bezel, 1 x 1 3/4" (ILLUS.) **45**

Brooch, lozenge shape, decorated w/forget-me-nots on a pink & pale yellow ground w/white enamel highlights & burnished gold rim, brass-plated bezel, ca. 1890-1920, 7/8 x 1 5/8" **35**

Brooch, oval, decorated w/a conventional-style Colonial dame in light blue & yellow w/opal lustre background & burnished gold rim, brass-plated bezel, ca. 1915-25, 1 5/8 x 2 1/8" **60**

Brooch, oval, decorated w/a conventional-style lavender iris & green leaves outlined in black on a yellow lustre ground w/white enamel highlights on petal edges & yellow enamel highlights on flower centers, burnished gold rim, gold-plated bezel, ca. 1900-20, 1 5/8 x 2 1/8" **75**

Pink Rose on Oval Brooch

Brooch, oval, decorated w/a large pink rose & green leaves on a light blue ground, burnished gold rim, gold-plated bezel, 1 1/8 x 1 3/8" (ILLUS.) 40

Brooch, oval, decorated w/a sunset landscape scene w/house by stream, trees in background, burnished gold rim, gold-plated bezel, 1 1/2 x 1 15/16" 125

Brooch, oval, decorated w/a tropical Florida scene, burnished gold border & brass-plated bezel, ca. 1920s, 1 1/2 x 2"................... 65

Florida River Landscape on Brooch

Brooch, oval, decorated w/a tropical river landscape in polychrome colors, signed on the lower left "OC" (Olive Commons, Coconut Grove, Florida), gold-plated bezel, ca. 1920s, 1 3/8 x 1 1/4" (ILLUS.)........ 75

Brooch, oval, decorated w/an Art Nouveau maiden's portrait surrounded by forget-me-nots on an ivory ground, white enamel highlights, framed by burnished gold raised paste scrolls & dots, gold-plated bezel, 1 1/4 x 1 5/8" (ILLUS.) 80

Brooch, oval, decorated w/forget-me-nots on a pale yellow center w/pale blue border, gold-plated bezel, signed "A. Jibbing," ca. 1900-20, 1 3/8 x 1 1/2" 75

Brooch, oval, decorated w/pink & white & ruby roses & green leaves on a rich blue ground w/white enamel highlights, burnished gold border & rim, gold-plated bezel, ca. 1940s, 1 1/2 x 2" 65

Brooch, rectangular, decorated w/a tropical scene of palm tree in white on a platinum ground, painted by Olive Commons, Miami, Florida, sterling silver bezel, ca. 1920s-1940s, 3/4 x 1" 80

Brooch, round, decorated w/a conventional-style trillium w/raised paste & burnished gold pistols & burnished gold background, brass-plated bezel, ca. 1910-15, 1 9/16" d... 35

Brooch/pendant, heart shape, decorated w/daisies on a light shading to dark blue ground, gold-plated bezel, ca. 1900-20, 1 13/16 x 2".. 55

Brooches, oval, decorated w/forget-me-nots on a pale pink & blue ground w/white enamel highlights on petal edges, burnished gold rims, gold-plated bezels, gold wear, ca. 1900-20, 13/16 x 1", pr............. 70

Brooches with Pink & Ruby Roses

Brooches, round, decorated w/pink & ruby roses & green leaves on a polychrome ground, burnished gold rim, gold-plated bezel, 7 /8" d., pr. (ILLUS.) 70

Cuff pin, rectangular, decorated w/a purple iris outlined & bordered in burnished gold, brass-plated bezel, ca. 1900-15, 1/4 x 1 1/16"... 15

Art Nouveau Maiden on Brooch

Cuff Pins with Forget-me-nots

Cuff pins, rectangular, decorated w/forget-me-nots on a burnished gold ground, gold-plated bezel, ca. 1900-15, 1/4 x 1 1/4", pr. (ILLUS.).. **45**

Flapper pin, oval, decorated w/a stylized, elegant red-haired woman wearing blue dress & fur stole, pink flower & large comb in her hair, white ground w/burnished gold border, gold-plated bezel, ca. 1922-30, 1 11/16 x 2 1/8" **85**

Flapper pin, oval, decorated w/bust of stylized red-haired flapper on a pastel polychrome ground, burnished gold rim & brass-plated bezel, ca. 1924-28, 1 5/8 x 2 1/8" **75**

Handy pin, crescent shape, asymmetrically decorated w/a purple pansy on an ivory ground, burnished gold tip & brass-plated bezel, ca. 1880-1915, 2" w. **35**

Handy pin, crescent shape, decorated w/forget-me-nots '& leaves on a burnished gold ground, gold-plated bezel, ca. 1890-1915, gold wear, 1 13/16" w. **30**

Handy pin, crescent shape, decorated w/pink & ruby roses & green leaves on an ivory ground, w/white enamel highlights & one burnished gold tip, gold-plated bezel, ca. 1890-1915, 2 3/16" w. **45**

Hatpin, circular head, decorated w/a conventional geometric design in raised paste dots & scrolls, covered w/burnished gold, turquoise enamel jewels, cobalt blue flat enamel, gold-plated bezel, ca. 1905-20, 1" d., 6 3/8" shaft **110**

Hatpin, circular head, decorated w/pink roses & greenery on a pale blue & yellow ground, burnished gold border, gold-plated bezel, ca. 1890-1920, some gold wear, 1" d., 7 3/4" shaft **115**

Hatpin Head with Wild Roses

Hatpin, circular head, decorated w/pink wild roses & greenery on a yellow ground, burnished gold rim, gold-plated filigree setting, head 1 1/16" d., shaft 9" l. (ILLUS. of head).. **135**

Hatpin Head with Ruby Roses

Hatpin, circular head, decorated w/ruby roses & green leaves, embellished w/burnished gold scrolls, gold-plated bezel, head 1 3/8" d., shaft 7 3/4" l. (ILLUS. of head).. **125**

Pendant, decorated w/a purple pansy w/white enamel center accents & burnished gold border, gold-plated bezel, ca. 1880s-1914, 1" d. **50**

Pendant, oval, decorated w/forget-me-nots on a pastel polychrome ground w/white enamel highlights & burnished gold rim, gold-plated bezel, ca. 1900-25, 1 1/4 x 1 3/4" **65**

Scarf pin, medallion-shaped, decorated w/violets, brass-plated bezel & shank, ca. 1880-1920, medallion 1 1/4" d., shank 3" l. **50**

Shirtwaist Button with Clover Leaf

Shirtwaist button, oval w/shank, decorated w/a three-leaf clover in green on a yellow & brown ground, burnished gold rim, 7/8 x 1 1/16" (ILLUS.) **20**

Shirtwaist Button with Flower

Shirtwaist button, round w/eye, decorated w/a conventional stylized long blossom flanked by pointed oval leaves in pale yellow, dark blue & black on a burnished gold ground, 1 1/16" d. (ILLUS.) **30**

Unusual Portrait Shirtwaist Button

Shirtwaist Buttons with Pinwheels

Shirtwaist button, round w/shank, decorated w/the bust portrait of a young blonde-haired girl, wearing a pale blue dress, against a shaded yellow to black ground, 1 3/8" d. (ILLUS., previous page)..................... **80**

Shirtwaist buttons, heart-shaped, decorated w/pink roses, raised paste scrolled border covered w/burnished gold, ca. 1890-1910, 1 1/8 x 1 3/16", pr. **75**

Shirtwaist buttons, round, each decorated w/a geometric pinwheel design in light blue, black & gold trimmed w/burnished gold dots & a center turquoise "jewel," on a burnished gold ground, two 1" d., three 7/8" d., the set (ILLUS., above)........... **115**

Shirtwaist set: oval brooch & pr. of oval cuff links; decorated w/blue forget-me-nots on an ivory background w/white enamel highlights, brass-plated mounts, ca. 1900-10, brooch w/burnished gold free-form border & rim, 1 3/8 x 1 3/4", cuff links w/burnished gold rims, 13/16 x 1 1/16", the set **250**

Brooch from Shirtwaist Set

Shirtwaist set: oval brooch & two round buttons w/shank; each decorated w/forget-me-nots & greenery on a pastel polychrome ground, burnished gold rim, gold-plated bezel, brooch 1 1/4 x 1 3/4", buttons 15/16" d., the set (ILLUS. of brooch)....... **90**

Shirtwaist set: oval cuff links & three round buttons w/shanks; decorated w/clusters of violets on pale yellow ground, burnished gold rim, gold-plated bezel on cuff links, ca. 1900-15, cuff links 3/4 x 1 1/4", buttons 1 1/4" d., the set **175**

Watch chatelaine, oval, decorated w/a woman wearing a rose-colored bodice, light shading to dark warm green ground, set in gold-plated rim w/twisted gold edge, ca. 1880s, 1 1/8 x 1 3/8" **125**

Amphora - Teplitz

In the late 19th and early 20th centuries numerous potteries operated in the vicinity of Teplitz in the Bohemian region of what was Austria but is now the Czech Republic. They included Amphora, RStK, Stellmacher, Ernst Wahliss, Paul Dachsel, Imperial and lesser-known potteries such as Johanne Maresh, Julius Dressler, Bernard Bloch and Heliosine.

The number of collectors in this category is growing while availability of better or rarer pieces is shrinking. Consequently, prices for all pieces are appreciating, while those for better and/or rarer pieces, including restored rare pieces, are soaring.

The price ranges presented here are retail. They presume mint or near mint condition or, in the case of very rare damaged pieces, proper restoration. They reflect such variables as rarity, design, quality of glaze, size and the intangible "in-vogue factor." They are the prices that knowledgeable sellers will charge and knowledgeable collectors will pay.

Amphora - Teplitz Marks

Bowl, 10 1/4" w., 5 1/4" h., consisting of two wonderfully detailed high-glazed fish swimming around the perimeter, each executed in the Art Nouveau style w/flowing fins & tails, tentacles drip from their mouths, high-relief w/gold & reddish highlights, rare theme, impressed in ovals "Amphora" & "Austria" w/a crown.. **$3,800-4,200**

Exotic Paul Dachsel Bowl

Bowl, 14 1/2" w., 4 3/8" h., an exotic Paul Dachsel design of calla lilies growing out of stems which originate at the bottom & gracefully extend around the sides to fully developed calla lilies at each end, in the center on each side are several 'jewels' w/abstract leaves of high-glazed green w/gold overtones, mottled texture w/'jeweled' greenish gold embellishments, stamped over glaze w/intertwined "PD - Turn-Teplitz," handwritten over glaze "0/45" (ILLUS.)........................ **5,000-5,500**

crown, 1431 & "A" in blue, 13 1/2" w., 18 1/4" h. (ILLUS.)............................. **3,000-4,000**

Bust of Richard Wagner

Bust of a Sultry Princess

Bust of a woman, perhaps Sarah Bernhardt in the role of a sultry princess, magnificently finished w/plentiful gold & bronze glazes without excessive fussiness, mounted on a base featuring a maiden on a horse in a forest setting, the bust seemingly supported by stag horns protruding from each side, impressed "Amphora" & "Austria" in a lozenge w/a

Bust of Richard Wagner, the somber looking composer mounted on a pedestal emblazoned "Wagner" on the front, the head w/a beautiful soft flesh-toned Amphora glaze, the pedestal w/a shriveled tan & white glaze w/shades of olive green highlights, one of a rare series of composers, impressed "Amphora" & "Austria" in ovals w/a crown, a circle w/"Imperial Amphora" & "250 -1," 19 3/4" h.
(ILLUS.)... **2,000-2,500**

Rare Amphora Candlestick

Candlestick, rare Amphora piece w/many of their special characteristics including jewels, spider webs, butterflies & wonderful soft muted Amphora glazes w/reds, blues & gold, a large handle extends from near the top of the socket, four smaller handles extend up & outward from the base, eleven jewels of various sizes & colors, impressed "Amphora" in an oval & a crown & "28," 14" h. (ILLUS.).. **4,000-4,500**

Centerpiece, an expansive bowl w/a 'jeweled' effect along the rim, supported by two seated male lions w/fine details, a round base w/a 'jeweled' effect, the underside of the bowl suggests a tropical jungle, a better example of a design featuring animals supporting a bowl, multi-colored 'jewels,' lion in a natural brownish glaze, stamped "Amphora - Made in Czecho-slovakia" in an oval, "734 - 261" in black ink, 12" w., 9 5/8" h............. **1,000-1,500**

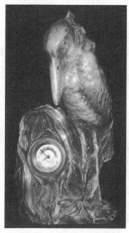

Fantasy Stork Clock

Clock, table model, a fantasy stork, similar to Martin Bros. birds, stands next to a clock dial framed by Art Nouveau-style leaves, fine detailing, soft brownish tan glaze, rare, raised rectangle w/factory logo & "AK-Turn," impressed "319," 13" h. (ILLUS.).................................... **4,000-4,500**

Amphora Teplitz Ewer

Ewer, an Art Nouveau design w/extraordinary detail combining a reticulated handle suggesting Paul Dachsel & varied circles on the body suggesting Gustav Klimt, a reticulated top, many 'jewels' of different colors & sizes randomly located over the body suggesting a spectrum of stars in the milky way, unusual gold bud spout, high-glazed blue garlands randomly draped about the body, heavy gold trim on the upper part of the handle, top & spout, a subdued gold trim extends down the handle to & around the bottom where there is an abstract tree design, very difficult to produce, rare, impressed "Amphora" in a circle & "40 -537," 14" h. (ILLUS.)....... **6, 000-6,500**

Figure group, a small fine scenic figural group w/a rooster & hen perched side by side overlooking a pond, a small gold frog climbing into the pond, gives a barnyard feeling, soft muted shades of tan w/highlights of gold, a realistic theme & valuable because of the small size, impressed "Amphora" in an oval & illegible numbers, 6 1/2" w., 7 3/4" h. **850-1,100**

Unique Figural Humidor

Humidor, cov., figural, a fantasy piece featuring a large globe representing the world being shot from a tiny cannon & caught by a jester lying on his back, the jester reputedly represents a prime minister of the time, a hat at the top of the globe forms the handles, soft muted grey Amphora glaze, rare, impressed "Amphora" in an oval & "4216," 14" w., 9" h. (ILLUS.).. **3, 500-4,500**

Indian Heads Amphora Humidor

Humidor, cov., figural, a massive Native American theme composed of three Indian heads w/high-glazed pink & green feathered headdresses, 'jeweled' & draping beaded necklaces on two, a draping necklace of animal teeth on the third, high-glaze green & cobalt blue finial handle on a decorative mixed glazed top, basic color of Campina brown w/much contrasting high-glaze in green, pink, brown & blue, rare, impressed ovals w/"Amphora" & "Austria," a crown & "Imperial - Amphora - Turn" in a circle & "S-1633-46," 10 1/2" h. (ILLUS.)............................ **2,500-3,500**

Amphora Model of a European Boar

Model of a boar, seated European boar leaning to one side as though attempting to rest from a hunter's pursuit, finished in brownish gold glaze, very lifelike, rare, impressed "Amphora" & "Austria" in oval, a crown, #8236/36 & artist's mark "H" in gold, 10" h. (ILLUS.).......................... **1,500-1,700**

Large Model of a Crowing Rooster

Model of a rooster, larger-than-life crowing rooster designed by Berwiel & glazed in mottled golden brown, this example found in Germany, another reported to be in a Scandinavian art museum, incised "Berwiel 08" on the side, impressed "Amphora" & "Austria" in oval, a crown, "Imperial - Amphora - Turn" in a circle & 8237/37, 26" h. (ILLUS.)........................... **4,500+**

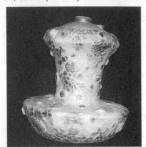

Unusual Amphora Lamp - Vase

Oil lamp-vase, a massive tiered form w/a swelled shoulder & wide flat-topped lower section decorated w/a variety of multicolored 'jewels,' w/a removable lamp font insert, rare, impressed "Amphora" & "Austria" in ovals & 8796/52, 12 1/2" h. (ILLUS.).. **4,500+**

Plaque, a large oval shape centered by an Art Nouveau woman in high relief attired in a luminescent pink dress blowing a double-horned musical instrument and seated on a rocky ledge, the border of the plaque consisting of garlands of flowers & leaves in high relief, especially the buds, basic color of seafoam green, the surrounding florals in greens & tans, impressed "Ernst Wahliss," 17 x 19 1/2".. **1,600-2,000**

Plaque with Art Nouveau Woman

Plaque, terra cotta rectangular form depicting a very stylized beautifully coifed Art Nouveau woman in profile in high relief, her unique elegance suggesting a woman of high social stature, the borders garlanded leaves & buds in high relief, organic mossy shades of green, soft purples, tans & warm browns, impressed marks "Ernst Wahliss - Made in Austria - Turn - Wien - 157," 11 3/4 x 17" (ILLUS.)... **1,400-1,700**

Vase, 5 3/4" h., figural, elegantly executed Paul Dachsel creation w/a greenish cast & numerous vertical ribs extending up from the base, four intertwined gold-bodied dragonflies form a reticulated top, immediately below a series of smaller dragonflies encircle the vase, two multilayered handles within handles complete the design, stamped over glaze w/intertwined "PD - Turn - Teplitz," impressed "104"...................................... **2,000-2,500**

Fine Figural Vase with Maiden

Vase, 7" h., figural, demure, elegant wonderfully detailed young woman seated & reaching down to retrieve a flower, against an upright flowering vine-covered wall, mixed iridescent colors of blue, magenta, silver, purple & gold all w/a bronze-like finish, a top-of-the-line creation of Ernst Wahliss, marked "EW - Turn - Vienna - Made in Austria" & an incised "I" & 4838/8/360/7 (ILLUS.) **1,500-2,500**

Vase, 7 1/2" h., a playful expression of Amphora w/a pink snake draped around the body of the bulbous vase & extending to the top where its delicate tongue protrudes, a subtle leaf design extends around the bottom, the pink color of the snake distinguishes this piece from more drab versions, impressed in ovals "Amphora" & "Austria," & "4114 - 52"...... **1,500-1,800**

Vase, 7 3/4" h., round bulbous shape, decorated w/a profile of a young girl w/long flowing brownish hair full of numerous multicolored high-glazed flowers w/gold touches, all surrounded by a brownish tan forest scene, finely executed, impressed "Amphora - 663," overglaze red mark "RStK - Turn - Teplitz - Made in Austria".. **2,000-2,200**

Vase, 8 3/4" h., four-paneled high-shouldered squared form w/a front-faced Mucha-style Art Nouveau princess portrait, elaborate gold enameling against a landscape decorated w/blue & purple trees w/gold highlights above a base decorated w/Paul Dachsel-style abstract red flowers in a green base, impressed "Amphora" in oval & "579-40," red "RStK

Austria" overglaze mark, artist mark "Fr" in gold overglaze **3,500-4,000**

Paul Dachsel Forest Scene Vase

Vase, 9" h., a bulbous Paul Dachsel forest scene w/reticulated gold top & varied reddish mushrooms in high relief encircling the bottom, a production mold but handpainted to produce a uniquely different forest scene, stamped over the glaze w/intertwined "PD - Turn - Teplitz," impressed "1106 -2," blue overglaze "094" (ILLUS.).. **3,500-4,000**

Rare Amphora Cat Head Vase

Vase, 9" h., wide bulbous tapering form, rare form suggesting an inverted Tiffany lamp shade, four large Persian cat heads molded in full relief & projecting from the sides w/a forest of abstract trees w/160-170 opal-like translucent 'jewels' symbolizing fruits, the jewels in various sizes & shades of opal blue mounted in gold surrounds, heavy gold rim, the tree branches extending to the jewels on a background of Klimt-like subtle gold circles, holes behind the jewels permit candlelight or an electric bulb to illuminate the

jewels, cat heads finished in a soft pinkish gold w/traces of green & gold highlights on the ears, impressed "Amphora -
Austria" in a lozenge, a crown & "8183 -
28" (ILLUS.) **14,000-16,000**

Abstract Paul Dachsel Vase

Vase, 9 7/8" h., a Paul Dachsel abstract design w/a reticulated geometric top & a reticulated handle within a reticulated handle sweeping in an arc from the top to the
bottom w/abstract tendrils extending
around the bottom of the body & back of
the handles, several high-glazed green
pods resembling teardrops of various sizes hang from the abstract handle, vines
& a center funnel, the top rim & top of
handle finished in gold, rare, stamped
over glaze w/intertwined "PD - Turn -
Teplitz" (ILLUS.).................................. **4,000-4,500**
Vase, 10" h., a Paul Dachsel abstract archi-
tectural style w/a geometric design consisting of a rounded bottom from which
four handles begin flush & extend to the
top of the rim where they flare open, each
handle suggests an abstract candelabrum w/charcoal flames rising from each,
finished in iridescent gunmetal grey
w/charcoal black sheen touches, gold
wash on top, modern in all respects even
though produced in the 1904-10 period,
rare form, stamped over glaze w/inter-
twined "PD - Turn - Teplitz," impressed
"1049" **4,500-5,500**
Vase, 10 5/8" h., figural, in the form of a
prancing male lion, snarling open mouth,
standing on a broad base narrowing at
the top, numerous concentric circles form
bands around the top & bottom, lion re-
flects an iridescent gold, green & rose
combination of color, body of base in metallic green w/undertones of blues &
splotches of reds, impressed "Amphora"
& "Austria" in oval, a crown & "500-52,"
handwritten in black ink over glaze "CB -
613417," estimated value without jewels,
$1,500 to 2,000, value w/jewels **2,500-3,500**

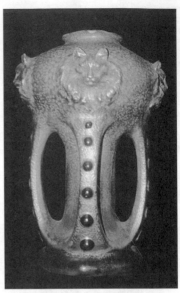

Vase with Persian Cat Heads

Vase, 11" h., four gold Persian cat heads
adorn a center-pillared body w/four surrounding gold 'jeweled' arms extending
from each cat head to the base, metallic
blue w/a gold wash, cobalt blue 'jewels,'
rare design, more common versions
have cabochons instead of animal
heads, marked "Amphora" & "Austria" in
ovals, a crown & impressed "Imperial"
circle mark & "11677 - 51"
(ILLUS.).. **2,500-3,000**

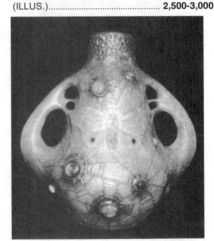

Ornate Jeweled Art Nouveau Vase

Vase, 11 1/4" h., tapering lobed ovoid form
of exceptional Art Nouveau design w/nu-
merous 'jewels,' spider webs & two butterflies w/heavy pierced extended handles suggesting a larger butterfly, 17
'jewels' in varying sizes & colors, red abstract circles drape from the gold-edged

top, soft muted tan, red, blue & green glazes w/gold iridescence, impressed "Amphora" & "Austria" in ovals, a crown & "8551-42," red "RStK Austria" overglaze mark (ILLUS.) **4,500-5,000**

Czech Vase with Figural Dragon

Vase, 12" h., a wonderful & colorful dragon hugs the circumference of the top w/its huge, detailed wings draping along the sides, detailed claw-like feet decorated in two glazes, one predominately blue, the other predominately tan, a Czechoslovakian creation w/no Austrian counterpart, stamped over the glaze "Amphora - Made in Czech-slovakia" in an oval (ILLUS.) **3,500**

Amphora Figural Cockatoo Vase

Vase, 12" h., figural, three standing cockatoos, fully feathered, extend around the body of the vase, their plumes rising over the rim, very detailed w/glossy glaze, subtle color mix of blues, greens & tans w/brown streaks, semi-rare, impressed "Amphora" & "Austria" in ovals, a crown & Imperial circle & "11986 - 56" (ILLUS.) **2,000-2,500**

Elegant Leaf-form Amphora Vase

Vase, 12 3/4" h., elegant form consisting of four beautifully veined tall leaves forming the funnel of the vase w/the stem of each leaf forming a handle extending into the bottom, each stem issues an additional flat leaf extending across the bottom, leaves finished in a mottled orange w/touches of greens & yellows w/gold overtones (although marked by Ernst Wahliss the design indicates the work of Paul Dachsel who worked at various Amphora factories), rare, stamped over glaze "EW" red mark, impressed "9491," "9786a - 10" in ink over the glaze (ILLUS.) **4,000-4,500**

Dachsel "Enchanted Forest" Vase

Vase, 13" h., wide-shouldered tapering cylindrical body, a fantasy design by Paul Dachsel worthy of the description "enchanted forest," the design consists of slender molded abstract trees extending from the narrow base to the bulbous top, lovely heart-shaped leaves extend in clusters from the various branches, trees in muted green, the leaves in pearlized off-white w/gold framing, the symbolic sky in rich red extending between the trees from the bottom to the top, rare, intertwined "PD" mark rubbed off (ILLUS.).. **6,000-6,500**

Vase, 14" h., figural, a fantasy dragon featuring two flaring wings, one extending practically from the top to the bottom of the body, the other well above & beyond the rim, creature w/a convoluted tail, spine & teeth, the head w/open mouth positioned at top of the vase, bluish green gold iridescence, glazes vary from a flat tan to a variety of very iridescent colors, made in 14" & 17" size, impressed "Amphora" in oval, illegible numbers, large size w/better glazes, $6,500, 14" size w/drab glazes **4,500**

Vase, 14 5/8" h., a figural fantasy piece, a different variety of dragon vase but not highly glazed, the dragon is mostly brown but it features a well-defined head, body, clawed feet & tail, a snake tongue drapes from the mouth, hideously beautiful, the body contrasts nicely w/the metallic greenish blue iridescence of the mottled background, found in various glazes, impressed "Amphora" & "Austria" in oval, a crown & "C 4543".............................. **3,500-4,000**

Tall Amphora Vase with Insects

Vase, 14 3/4" h., tall gently tapering ovoid body w/a swelled top, decorated w/eight three-dimensional iridescent indigo blue insects of varying sizes crawling up the side toward a series of leaves adorned w/berries, above the berries is a four-handled 3" h. heavily gilded top, the rest of the body in iridescent light blue w/gold highlights, rare, impressed "Amphora" & "Austria" in ovals, a crown & 3987/58 (ILLUS.).. **4,500**

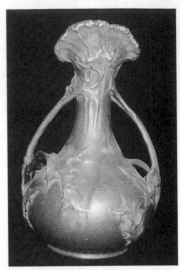

Flower-decorated Art Nouveau Vase

Vase, 15" h., bulbous squatty base tapering to a slender neck w/fanned rim, unique Art Nouveau design w/an open flower blossom tinged in gold at the top, two curved vine handles extend from the neck to the base, the base relief-molded w/detailed leaves, found in numerous color variations & glazes, the most magnificent being a bronze glaze, value depends on the glaze w/bronze being the rarest, impressed "Amphora" & "Austria" in oval, a crown & 3852/42 (ILLUS.)... **2,500-4,000**

Amphora Vase with Golden Grapes

Vase, 15 1/2" h., cascades of golden grapes stream down on all sides between four funnel necks, the central funnel projecting skyward, this funnel design suggests Paul Dachsel, especially desirable because the piece is viewable from any angle, metallic purplish glaze w/metallic gold highlights containing numerous little gold circles, marked "Amphora" & "Austria" in ovals, a crown & "3680" (ILLUS.).. **1,500-2,000**

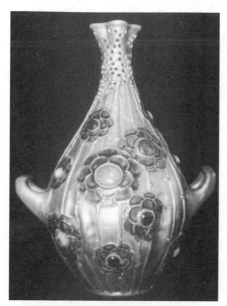

Rare Jeweled Amphora Vase

Vase, 16" h., bulbous ovoid body tapering to
a slender flaring lobed reticulated neck,
outswept loop handles at the lower sides,
shimmering burnished gold ground w/red
touches, adorned randomly w/twenty
large variously colored 'jewels,' one handle in red, the other in gold, overall molded vertical ribbing, rare form, impressed
"Amphora" in an oval, crown, old "RStK"
mark & "3349" (ILLUS.).................... **7,500-8,000**

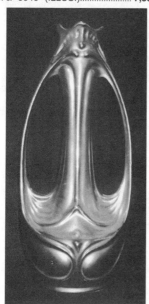

Tall Heliosine Ware Art Nouveau Vase

Vase, 16" h., tall elegant Heliosine Ware
piece w/a striking Art Nouveau design,
two curved slender handles swoop
gracefully from the top rim to the bottom
w/a slender central shaft, a wide array of
iridescent metallic glazes, an increasingly popular line, marked "Heliosine Ware -
Austria" & impressed "21020 -D"
(ILLUS.).. **1,000-1,500**

Rare Amphora Octopus Vase

Vase, 16 1/2" h., a massive fantasy piece
w/a large golden iridescent octopus
around the bottom, its tentacles extending around the sides & up to the top
where they grab a large swimming sea
horse, a particularly rare style of octopus
w/only one known at present, impressed
"Amphora" & "Austria" in ovals, a crown &
"4597 - 50" (ILLUS.).......................... **8,000-8,500**
Vase, 16 1/2" h., fine Paul Dachsel creation
in an undulating freeform design consisting of several abstract trees extending
from the bottom to the top where a
branch wraps around the top & then
down dividing into other branches w/a
series of red-glazed leaves, numerous
white 'jewels' suggesting seeds & seed
pods attached to the branches & trunks,
red leaves w/gold-tinged ends, very rare
form, stamped over the glaze w/inter-
twined "PD - Turn - Teplitz," impressed
"1115".. **4,500-5,500**

Rare Large Vase with Owl Heads

Vase, 16 3/4" h., wide bulbous body w/small shoulder handles, tapering to a short flaring neck, the design suggests an ominous nightfall w/four dark owl heads peering from among tree branches w/150 or so translucent 'jewel-like' leaves, when a candle is placed inside it softly lights these jewels, rare form recently discovered in Europe, impressed "Amphora" & "Austria" in ovals, a crown, incised "D" & 8180 (ILLUS.) .... **18,000+**

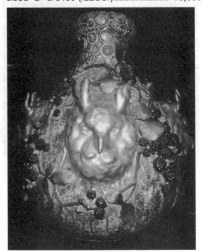

Rare Owl Head Vase

Vase, 17" h., massive bulbous bottle-form w/four finely detailed gold-finished owl heads projecting from the sides surrounded by brambles, leaves & many clusters of berries & numerous 'jewels' of various sizes & colors interspersed among the brambles, unusual & complicated design, some similar pieces w/other animal heads exist but few survive intact, rare, impressed "Amphora" in oval, a crown & "8160" (ILLUS.) **8,500-9,500**

Vase, 17 1/8" h., tall Art Nouveau form gradually tapering to a narrower top, the bottom w/seven delicate female heads w/long flowing hair emerging from a swirling ocean, tan w/highlights of gold & green, a similar example found in a Berlin museum, marks include a raised Art Nouveau girl's head & "Amphora" in a raised rectangle, red "RStK Austria" mark over the glaze, impressed illegible numbers, handwritten "1081 - L - 372" over the glaze **2,000-3,000**

Rare Reticulated Amphora Vase

Vase, 17 1/2" h., an important reticulated piece composed of a basket-like vase within a vase elaborately entwined w/swooping gold handles joined in the middle, numerous varied colored 'jewels' around the sides, viewed through the reticulation a high-glazed blue swirly design w/gold highlights is seen, the exterior w/a metallic bluish green w/gold wash & gold highlights, high-glazed gold rim, only one known so far, impressed "Amphora" & "Austria" in ovals, a crown & "3791 -45" (ILLUS.) **12,000-14,000**

Rare Tall Triangular Amphora Vase

Vase, 17 1/2" h., tall tapering triangular ovoid body w/a flared rim, iridescent &

heavily gilded w/multiple 'jewels' on each panel, rich magenta glaze blends into each gilded panel, rarely seen shape, impressed "Amphora" & "Austria" in oval, 8658/55 (ILLUS.) **7,500**

Amphora Vase with Coiling Beast

Vase, 18 1/4" h., a fantasy piece w/a coiling beast not really a dragon, snake or octopus but w/characteristics of each, finished in a golden color w/gold highlights, the head extends above the top, the body entwines down around the sides, mottled metallic purplish blue background, impressed "Amphora" & "Austria" in ovals, a crown & "4539 -50," values vary w/the glaze (ILLUS.) **4,000-4,500**

Rare Large Figural Amphora Vase

Vase, 18 1/4" h., figural, a massive Art Nouveau form featuring an elegant woman wearing a diaphanous gown & standing in front of the body of the vase, her extended hand holding a 'jewel' like those adorning the sides of the piece, reticulated top finished in rich gold, impressed "Amphora - Austria" in a lozenge, 8171 (ILLUS.) **14,000-15,000**

Amphora Dragon Vase

Vase, 20" h., footed tall wide cylindrical body w/squatty bulbous base & closed-in rim, mottled mauve glaze w/relief-molded dragon figure in yellow, tan & gilt glaze conforming entirely around body & rim, minor restorations to chips, impressed "AMPHORA" in a lozenge, a crown & "4548 50" (ILLUS.) **6,000-6,500**

Tall Vase with Pine Cones

Vase, 20" h., tall slightly tapering cylindrical form w/a widely flared base, boldly molded pine cones hang around the top section from symbolic green trees divided by red indented vertical panels, a Paul Dachsel Secessionist design, rare, stamped over the glaze w/intertwined "PD - Turn - Teplitz" & impressed "2038 - 6" (ILLUS.) **9,000-10,000**

Massive Amphora Mermaid Vase

Vase, 21" h., 18" w., figural, a wide squatty
bulbous base centered by a tall neck, Art
Nouveau style w/a mermaid clinging to
the top rim, her well-defined body extends down along the side, applied berries, vines & leaves complete the decoration, finished in a matte tan w/gold wash
& highlights, bluish berries, red stems,
greenish red leaves & a high-glazed gold
rim, important & very rare, would be rare
even without the applied foliage, impressed "Amphora" in oval & "07 - 7 - 3"
(ILLUS.)... **8,000-10,000**

"Amphora" & "Austria" in a lozenge, a
crown & "02047 - 28" (ILLUS.) **15,000-16,000**

Tall Amphora Vase with Bats

Vase, 21 1/2" h., tall bottle-form w/swarms
of gold bats feeding on golden fruits
around the reticulated top, they are about
to be joined by other bats flying up the
sides, tall graceful form w/the rounded
base encircled by golden lily pad leaves
w/the stems extending up the sides on an
eggshell off-white ground, impressed
"Amphora" in oval, red "Austria RStK"
mark over glaze, impressed "41 - 668" &
"750 - 1029" in ink (ILLUS.) **7,000-9,000**

Tall Amphora Portrait Vase

Vase, 21 1/2" h., portrait-type, a very large
profiled Sarah Bernhardt portrait inspired
by Gustav Klimt featuring a majestic bird
headdress w/eleven 'jewels' of various
sizes & colors, the figure w/long flowing
hair streaming from under the headdress
to her shoulders, below her neck is a jeweled butterfly, on one side a golden sun
rises from the ocean emitting numerous
golden rays, bluish green metallic background w/heavy gold detail, impressed

Somber, Eerie Dragon Vase

Vase, 22" h., figural, a somber swampy-green dragon encircles the tall body several times, its wings spread like a cobra's hood, leering down hungrily at a frog restrained by his tail at the base, this piece can be found finished in other colors including red & tan, this eerie somber look compensates for what the glaze may lack, impressed "Amphora" & "Austria" in ovals, a crown & "4536 - 6" (ILLUS.)... **5,500-6,000**

Unusual Vase with Figural Bear

Vase, 23 1/2" h., figural, a squatty bulbous base w/flattened shoulder mounted w/a huge gilded bear licking his extended paws, decorated w/a variety of subtle colors & circles, rare subject matter, found in South America, impressed "Amphora" & "Austria" in ovals & 4509, also in overglaze red "RSstK - Turn - Teplitz - Made in Austria" (ILLUS.)..................................... **4,500**

Vases, 10 1/2" h., footed bulbous ovoid body tapering to a slender cylindrical neck w/a flattened disk rim, painted in shades of purple, pink, green, blue, black & gilt w/the bust of a young maiden wearing a voluminous hood surmounted by a Byzantine crown surrounded by a gilt aura, a lower border of roses, the crown & roses w/applied bosses, one printed w/mark "Turn - Teplitz - Bohemia - R.St. - Made in Austria," the other impressed "Amphora," each impressed "2014 -28," pr. **6,900**

Amphora Sea Life Vases

Vases, 19 1/2" h., tapering cylindrical form w/cushion foot & spiky rim, applied w/a realistically modeled octopus capturing a crab, covered in a sponged blue, white & yellow glaze, the creatures in beige & burnt orange, printed in blue "AMPHORA - Made in Czecho-Slovakia" & impressed numbers, pr. (ILLUS.)....................... **5,500-6,500**

Arequipa

Dr. Philip King Brown established The Arequipa Sanitorium in Fairfax, California, in the early years of the 20th century. In 1911 he set up a pottery at the facility as therapy for his female tuberculosis patients since he had been impressed with the success of the similar Marblehead pottery in Massachusetts.

The first art director was the noted ceramics designer Frederick H. Rhead who had earlier been art director at the Roseville Pottery.

In 1913 the pottery was separated from the medical facility and incorporated as The Arequipa Potteries. Later that year Rhead and his wife, Agnes, one of the pottery instructors, left Arequipa and Albert L. Solon took over as the pottery director. The corporation was dissolved in 1915 and the pottery closed in 1918 although the sanitorium remained in operation until 1957.

Arequipa Marks

Bowl, 6 1/2" d., 2 1/4" h., wide flat bottomed form w/squatty bulbous incurved sides w/a wide flat mouth, embossed w/eucalyptus branches under a dark matte green & blue glaze, stamped mark, incised "KH - 11".. **$880**

Early Arequipa Vases

Vase, 3 1/4" h., 3" d., miniature, simple wide ovoid form w/closed rim, decorated in squeeze-bag w/stylized leaves in a fine organic matte green w/small red circles, against a matte yellow ground, incised mark "?27 - Arequipa - California - 1912" (ILLUS. center with larger vases)................ **6,325**

Early Arequipa Squatty Vase

Vase, 4 1/4" h., 7" d., footed wide squatty bulbous form w/the wide shoulder tapering to a short flared neck, enamel-decorated w/a plant w/white berries against a semi-matte greyish blue ground, rare early mark, incised "AP - 1911" (ILLUS.)....... **660**

Vase, 4 3/4" h., 3 1/4" d., swelled cylindrical body w/a narrow rounded shoulder to the short, wide neck, smooth matte leathery dark green glaze, incised "3 - Arequipa - Cal." (ILLUS. right with 7" squeeze-bag vase) **358**

Vase, 6" h., 3 1/4" d., simple ovoid body w/wide incurved rim, decorated w/incised abstract leaves in a flowing, glossy dark blue against a turquoise ground, restoration to small inner rim chip, Frederick Rhead period, signed in ink "Arequipa California - 1912 - 463 - 4" (ILLUS. center with 7" squeeze-bag vase).......................... **2,420**

Vase, 6 1/4" h., 5" d., bulbous shouldered ovoid body w/a wide flat rim, decorated in squeezebag w/stylized yellow flowers over large, bright green leaves w/blue veins, from the Frederick Rhead period, blue ink mark "Arequipa - California," ca. 1911-12, minute glaze nick on raised point (ILLUS. left with miniature vase) **9,350**

Rare Miniature Arequipa Vase

Vase, 3 1/2" h., 2 1/2" d., miniature, simple ovoid body w/closed rim, decorated in squeeze-bag w/a rim band of holly leaves & red berries against a matte, mottled greenish blue ground, by Frederick Rhead, white & brown glaze mark (ILLUS.)... **6,325**

Variety of Arequipa Vases

Vase, 7" h., 4" d., simple ovoid body decorated in squeezebag w/stylized leaves in brown on a matte feathered green ground, a dark green drip down from each leaf, fine glaze nicks on rim, Rhead period, ca. 1912, blue enamel mark (ILLUS. left with two other vases) **3,740**

Vase, 7 1/2" h., 4" d., bulbous base below tapering cylindrical sides, decorated in squeezebag w/a wreath of heart-shaped leaves under a fine leathery pea green matte glaze, Frederick Rhead period, marked in ink "Arequipa California 1913 - 2123 - 123" (ILLUS. right with miniature vase) **1,980**

Vase, 11" h., 6 1/4" d., baluster-form w/a short flaring neck, hand-cut w/large upright bell-shaped flowers around the sides & small daisy-like blossom heads around the neck, clear brown glossy glaze, die-stamped mark & "403-22 -WI" **770**

Bauer

The Bauer Pottery was moved to Los Angeles, California, from Paducah, Kentucky, in 1909 in the hope that the climate would prove beneficial to the principal organizer, John Andrew Bauer, who suffered from severe asthma. Flowerpots made of California adobe clay were the first production at the new location, but soon they were able to resume production of stoneware crocks and jugs, the mainstay of the Kentucky operation. In the early 1930s, Bauer's colorfully glazed earthen dinnerwares, especially the popular Ring-Ware pattern, became an immediate success. Sometimes confused with its imitator, Fiesta Ware (first registered by Homer Laughlin in 1937), Bauer pottery is collectible in its own right and is especially popular with West Coast collectors. Bauer Pottery ceased operation in 1962.

Bauer Mark

Baking dish, cov., individual, Ring-Ware patt., green or yellow, 4" d., each **$40**

Batter bowl, Ring-Ware patt., green, 1 qt. **125**

Ring-Ware Beater Pitcher

Beater pitcher, Ring-Ware patt., red, 1 qt. (ILLUS.) **85**

Bowl, batter, Ring-Ware, large **75-100**

A Variety of Bauer Ring-Ware Pieces

Bowl, berry, 5 1/2" d., Ring-Ware patt., delphinium (ILLUS. far left)...................................... 30
Bowl, berry, 5 1/2" d., Ring-Ware patt., yellow... 25
Bowl, soup, cov., 5 1/2" d., lug handles, Ring-Ware patt., orange, green, ivory or cobalt blue, each.. 90
Bowl, 13" d., Cal-Art line, green 35
Bowl, 15" d., wide low sides, white & brown speckled glaze, No. 149 95
Butter dish, cov., round, Ring-Ware patt., red 155
Cake plate, Monterey patt., yellow..................... 185
Candleholders, spool-shaped, Ring-Ware patt., jade green, pr. 130
Casserole, w/holder, Ring-Ware, 5 1/2" h. 60-75
Casserole, cov., individual, Ring-Ware patt., cobalt blue, 5 1/2" d... 300
Casserole, cov., individual, Ring-Ware patt., ivory, 5 1/2" d. 300
Casserole, cov., individual, Ring-Ware patt., orange/red, 5 1/2" d.. 200
Coffee carafe, cov., Ring-Ware patt., copper handle, delph blue 250
Coffee carafe, cov., Ring-Ware patt., copper handle, orange/red 150
Console set: bowl & pr. of three-light candlesticks; Cal-Art line, pink, semi-matte finish, 3 pcs.. 145
Cookie jar, cov., Monterey Moderne patt., chartreuse... 100
Cookie jar, pastel Kitchenware................... 100-150

Monterey Midget Creamer

Creamer, midget, Monterey patt., orange/red (ILLUS.)... 20
Creamer & cov. sugar bowl, Ring-Ware patt., ivory, pr... 150
Creamer & cov. sugar bowl, Ring-Ware patt., orange, pr... 75
Cup & saucer, demitasse, Ring-Ware patt., yellow.. 125
Cup & saucer, Monterey Moderne patt. 20-30
Cup & saucer, Ring-Ware patt., yellow (ILLUS. third from right w/bowl) 45-50
Custard cup, Ring-Ware 15-25

Flowerpot, Ring-Ware patt., cobalt blue 45
Flowerpot, Speckleware, flesh pink, 8 1/4" d., 6 1/2" h.. 40
Gravy boat, Monterey Moderne patt., pink........... 40
Gravy boat, Monterey patt. 30-40
Gravy boat, Ring-Ware patt., burgundy.............. 145
Jug, ball-shape, La Linda patt. 40-50
Mixing bowl, Atlanta line, No. 24, cobalt blue 100
Mixing bowl, nesting-type, Ring-Ware patt., No. 18, chartreuse... 75
Mixing bowl, nesting-type, Ring-Ware patt., No. 36, ivory 55
Mixing Bowl, speckled, 1950s, 6" h. (ILLUS.)... 15-20
Mug, barrel-shaped, Ring-Ware patt., jade green or yellow, each.. 150
Oil Jar, #122, 20" h....................................... 750-100

Bauer Oil Jar

Oil jar, No. 100, orange, 16" h. (ILLUS.)......... **1,000**
Oil jar, No. 100, cobalt blue, 22" h. **1,700**
Oil jars, No. 100, white, 12" h., pr. **3,000**
Pie plate, Ring-Ware patt., green 45
Pitcher, Ring-Ware patt., orange, 1 qt. 85
Pitcher, Ring-Ware patt., delph blue, 2 qt. 200
Pitcher, cov., jug-type, ice water, Monterey patt., turquoise... 325
Pitcher, water, w/ice lip, Monterey patt., green 125
Planter, model of a swan, chartreuse, medium 95
Plate, chop-type, Ring-Ware, 15" d. (ILLUS. center back with pieces)............. **75-100**
Plate, luncheon-type, Ring-Ware **20-25**
Plate, 5" d., bread & butter, Ring-Ware patt., green (ILLUS. center front w/bowl).................. 15
Plate, salad, 7 1/2" d., Ring-Ware patt., yellow (ILLUS. center front w/bowl)....................... 30
Plate, 9" d., Ring-Ware patt., grey 65
Plate, 10 1/2" d., dinner, Ring-Ware patt., cobalt or delph blue, each................................ 95
Plate, 10 1/2" d., dinner, Ring-Ware patt., jade green, orange or yellow, each 85
Plate, chop, 12" d., Ring-Ware patt., burgundy.. 150

Plate, chop, 12" d., Ring-Ware patt.,
white.. 230
Plate, chop, 14" d., Ring-Ware patt.,
yellow.. 125
Plate, chop, Monterey Moderne patt., yellow....... 45
Plate, grill, Monterey Moderne patt., char-
treuse... 35
Plate, luncheon, Ring-Ware patt., yellow
(ILLUS. center back w/bowl)...................... 40
Punch bowl, Ring-Ware patt., three-footed,
cobalt blue, 14" d................................. 850
Punch bowl, Ring-Ware patt., three-footed,
jade green, 14" d................................. 550
Punch cup, Ring-Ware patt., delph, cobalt
blue, green, yellow or burgundy, each........... 35
Refrigerator set, stacking, Ring-Ware, 4
pcs... 250-350
Relish dish, divided, Ring-Ware patt., cobalt
blue... 195
Salt & pepper shakers, beehive-shaped,
Ring-Ware patt., orange/red, pr.................. 60
Salt & pepper shakers, Ring-Ware patt.,
black, pr. (ILLUS. back, second from left
w/bowl).. 85
Shakers, La Linda patt., old style.................. 20-25
Sugar bowl, cov., demitasse, Ring-Ware
patt., burgundy.................................... 60
Sugar bowl, Monterey patt......................... 20-25
Sugar shaker, Ring-Ware patt., jade green....... 350
Syrup pitcher, Ring-Ware patt., cobalt blue..... 285
Teapot, cov., Ring-Ware patt., burgundy, 2-
cup size... 325
Teapot, cov., Ring-Ware patt., yellow, 2-cup
size... 125
Teapot, Ring-Ware, 6 cup capacity........... 100-150
Tumbler, Ring-Ware patt., green, large
(ILLUS. second from right w/bowl).............. 45-65
Tumbler, Ring-Ware patt., delphinium, small
(ILLUS. far right w/bowl)........................ 40
Vase, 8" h., Billy-type.......................... 50-75
Vase, 4 1/4" h., bulbous, Fred Johnson Art-
ware line, jade green............................. 65
Vase, 8" h., Hi-Fire line, deep trumpet-
shaped form w/widely flaring sides fluted
on the exterior, yellow.......................... 90

Matt Carlton Line Vase

Vase, 8" h., ovoid base w/widely flared rim,
twist shoulder handles, orange, Matt Carlton Artware line (ILLUS.)...................... 650
Vase, 10 1/2" h., cylindrical, Ring-Ware
patt., delph blue................................. 95
Vase, 13" h., ovoid base w/widely flared rim,
twist shoulder handles, jade green, Matt
Carlton Artware line............................. 1,200

Large Rebekah Vase

Vase, 24" h., Rebekah, tall slender baluster-
form w/loop handles near the short flaring neck, jade green, Matt Carlton Art-
ware line (ILLUS.).............................. 2,500

Belleek

American Belleek

*Marks:American Art China Works - R & E, 1891-95
AAC   (superim-   posed,   1891-
95 American Belleek Company - Company name
,banner & globe Ceramic Art Company - CAC palette,
1889- 1906 Colombian Art Pottery - CAP, 1893-1902
Cook Pottery - Three feathers w/"CHC," 1894
-1904 Coxon Belleek Pottery - "Coxon Belleek" in a
shield, 1926-1930 Gordon Belleek - "Gordon Belleek,"
1920-28 Knowles, Taylor & Knowles - "Lotusware" in
a circle w/a crown, 1891-96 Lenox China - Palette
mark, 1906-1924 Ott & Brewer - Crown & shield, 1883-
1893 Perlee - "P" in a wreath, 1925-1930 Willets
Manufacturing   Company   -   Serpent
mark, 1880-1909 Cook Pottery - Three feathers
w/"CHC,"*

Baskets and Bowls

Lenox, bowl, 10 1/2" d., 3" h., h.p. Art Deco
cameos of tulips accented w/heavy gold,
artist-signed "Clara May," dated "22,"
palette mark $350
Lenox, fernery, h.p. violets on a bowl-
shaped base on shell gilded feet, artist
palette mark, 7" d., 6" h....................... 500

Ott and Brewer, basket, applied floral & leaf decoration, crown & sword mark, 6 x 8", 3" h. **600**

Ott and Brewer, bowl, h.p. flowers on a cream ground w/gilded thistle handles, crown & sword mark. **500**

Ott and Brewer, tazza, hand-decorated w/twig feet & gilt paste ferns, crown, sword & O.B. mark, 8" d. **900**

Hand-painted Bowl with Gilt Trim

Willets, bowl, ovoid form w/small h.p. sprays of flowers over entire outside, gilding on ruffled rim, foot & handles, serpent mark (ILLUS.). **600**

Willets, bowl, 6 1/4" d., 5" h., handled, h.p. apple blossoms, leaves & twigs accented w/heavy gold, artist-signed "ES James," serpent mark **650**

Willets, bowl, 6 1/2" d., 3" h., handled, h.p. delicate floral sprays, ruffled top trimmed w/gold, gilt shaped handles, serpent mark. **425**

Ruffled Rim Bowl with Gold Accents

Willets, bowl, 7" d., 3" h., ovoid form h.p. w/decoration of roses, heavy gold accents on ruffled rim, foot & two applied handles, serpent mark (ILLUS.) **625**

Willets, bowl, fruit, 10" d., 4" h., deep scalloped rim, h.p. inside & out w/images of grapes & foliage, highlighted w/heavy gold **700**

Candlesticks and Lamps

Lenox, candlestick lamps, hexagonal inverted tulip shaped shades, h.p. roses joined by green swags & gilding, artist-signed "Trezisc," palette mark, shades 6" d., overall 18" h., pr. **560**

Lenox, candlesticks, black w/Art Deco-style enameled flowers accented w/raised gold, palette mark, 8 1/4" h., pr. **225**

Cups and Saucers

Ceramic Art Company, cabinet cup, on square footed base, enameled pink & gold saucer, 3 3/4" h. **175**

Ceramic Art Company Cabinet Cup

Ceramic Art Company, cabinet cup, no saucer, delicately enameled fretwork on footed base, CAC palette mark, 3 3/4" h. (ILLUS.). **75**

Ceramic Art Company, cup & saucer, "Tridacna" body shape, cream-colored exterior, blue lustre interior w/gold handle & trim, CAC palette mark, saucer 5 1/4" d. **350**

Ceramic Art Company, demitasse cup & saucer, decorated w/scenes of elves & pixies inspired by illustrator Palmer Cox, CAC palette mark, saucer 4" d. **750**

Coxon Belleek, demitasse cup & saucer, h.p. "Boulevard" patt. gold around the rim of the cup & saucer, saucer 5" d. **125**

Lenox, bouillon cup & saucer, cream-colored body w/gold banding around top of cup & saucer, palette mark, saucer 6" d. **125**

Cup with Sterling Holder & Saucer

Lenox, demitasse cup & saucer, colored porcelain w/double gold rim & pink border w/enameled flowers, hammered sterling holder & saucer, palette mark, 2 1/2" d. saucer (ILLUS.). **125**

Art Deco Silver Overlay Cup, Saucer

Lenox, demitasse cup & saucer, cov., sterling silver overlay of Art Deco design w/orange & green enameling, silver overlay around rim of cup & octagonal saucer, palette mark, 4 1/2" w. saucer (ILLUS.).. **125**

Demitasse Cup & Saucer with Holder

Lenox, demitasse cup & saucer, cream-colored porcelain w/double gold bands, flared rim, sterling saucer & reticulated holder w/angled handle, palette mark, 2" h. cup, 2 3/4" d. saucer (ILLUS.).............. **125**

Lenox, demitasse cup & saucer, filigree sterling silver overlay on two sides of the cup & around the rim of the cup & saucer, palette mark, saucer 1 1/2" d......................... **125**

Morgan, cup & saucer, h.p. in the "Orient" patt., urn mark, saucer 5 1/4" d..................... **250**

Morgan, demitasse cup & saucer, w/heavy gold embossed rims & handle, footed cup, 2 3/4" d. x 1 7/8" h. cup **125**

Ott and Brewer, cup & saucer, "Tridacna" body shape, cream-colored exterior, blue lustre interior w/gold handle & rim, crown & sword mark, saucer 5 1/4" d. **300**

Willets, bouillon cup & saucer, h.p. flowers w/gold trim, serpent mark, saucer 5 1/2" d. **350**

"Tridacna" Bouillon Cup and Saucer

Willets, bouillon cup & saucer, "Tridacna" body patt., pearlized pale blue exterior & white interior, serpent mark, 6 1/2" d. saucer (ILLUS.)... **225**

Pink Luster Bouillon Cup & Saucer

Willets, bouillon cup & saucer, "Tridacna" body patt., pink luster finish interior, cream color exterior w/gold trim & double handles, serpent mark, 3 1/2" d. cup, 5 1/4" d. saucer (ILLUS.).................................. **250**

Willets, cup & saucer, coffee-size, cream-colored fluted body w/gold handle & trim, serpent mark, saucer 5 1/2" d. **175**

Willets, demitasse cup & saucer, fluted white body w/purple monogram "W," outlined in gold w/gold-flecked purple dragon-shaped handle, serpent mark, saucer 4" d.. **110**

Jars, Boxes and Miscellaneous

Ceramic Art Company, box, cov., lid w/ruffled edge, h.p. w/violets & foliage, accented w/gold, CAC palette mark, 1 3/4" h., 3 7/8" w. **295**

Lidded Dresser Jar

Ceramic Art Company, dresser jar, hand-decorated w/gold paste roses & stripes, CAC palette mark, 3 1/2" d., 5" h. (ILLUS.).. **220**

Knowles, Taylor & Knowles Lotus Ware, rose jar, cov., "Orleans," body & lid w/ornately patterned & pierced overall design.. **3,200**

Lenox, condiment jar & cover, tapering hexagonal form w/domed cover, white ground w/blue jewel beading w/gold

paste swags, sterling finial, palette mark,
4 1/2" w., 5 1/2" h. 325
Lenox, ice bucket, h.p. w/Deco-style basket
of flowers, palette mark, 5 1/2" h.,
6 1/4" w. 225

Covered Mustard

Morgan, mustard, cov., h.p. cobalt band
w/Deco-style enameled basket of fruit on
front, gold-colored finial on lid w/opening
for spoon, 5" h., 4" d. (ILLUS.)....................... 175
Ott and Brewer, cracker jar & cover, hand-
decorated w/gold paste flowers & gold
handles, sword & crown mark, 5" d., 7" h. 475

Geisha Dresser Jar

Ott and Brewer, dresser jar, cov., cylindrical
form, h.p. w/illustration of geisha, gold
accents on lid, sword & crown mark,
5 1/2" h., 3 1/2" d. (ILLUS.) 425
Willets, humidor, cov., h.p. college crest on
one side & painting of cigarettes &
matches on other, serpent mark,
5 1/2" h., 4 1/4" w. 375

Mugs

Ceramic Art Company, Art Deco design
w/heavy gold accents, CAC palette mark,
7" h.. 295

Baluster-form Mug

Ceramic Art Company, baluster-form, h.p.
overall w/flowers & foliage on green
ground, artist signed, CAC palette mark,
6" h. (ILLUS.)... 245
Ceramic Art Company, h.p. chrysanthe-
mums & leaves, artist-signed in gold
"A.B. Wood," CAC palette mark, 5 1/2" h....... 225
Ceramic Art Company, h.p. design of
grapes of various colors & grapevines,
accented w/heavy gold on a pink pastel
body, artist-signed "KR" & dated 1904,
CAC palette mark, 6" h.................................. 350
Ceramic Art Company, h.p. peasant women
in the Delft style of monochromatic blue
on white, CAC palette mark, 5 1/2" h............. 275
Ceramic Art Company, h.p. scene of children flying kites, artist-signed "CHT,"
CAC palette mark, 4 3/4" h., 5 1/4" d. 325

Mug with Blackberries

Ceramic Art Company, ovoid form w/h.p.
blackberries & foliage on pastel pink
ground, CAC palette mark, 5" h. (ILLUS.)...... 325
Ceramic Art Company, portrait-type, h.p.
"Colonial Drinkers," artist-signed by Fred
Little, CAC palette mark, 5" h. 325
Ceramic Art Company, portrait-type, h.p.
portrait of a Native American Chief, CAC
palette mark, 6" h. 1,100
Ceramic Art Company, portrait-type, h.p.
portrait of an old man w/a stein seated at
a table, artist-signed "E.D. Westphal,"
CAC palette mark, 5 3/4" h. 300

Stein-type Mug with Grape Design

Ceramic Art Company, stein-type, h.p. all over w/images of grapes & foliage on blue & purple ground, CAC palette mark, 7 1/2" h. (ILLUS.) **375**

Lenox, h.p. bird decoration, palette mark, 4 1/4" h. **110**

Lenox, h.p. heavy enameled flowers in the Art Deco style, artist-signed "HRM," palette mark, 7" h. **150**

Lenox, h.p. off-white & multicolored poppies on a soft cream matte ground accented w/gold & a gold curved handle, palette mark, 7" h. **200**

Lenox, h.p. w/intense green leaves & berries on a rust & brown ground, palette mark, 5" h. **175**

Plum-decorated Mug

Lenox, ovoid shape, w/h.p. Deco-style blue plums & foliage in cream panel around top, lower mug solid green, palette mark, 4 1/2" h. (ILLUS.) **120**

Rust Mug with Grape Decoration

Willets, cylindrical shape flaring at base, decorated w/h.p. grapes & foliage on a rust ground, serpent mark, 5 1/2" h. (ILLUS.) **175**

Willets, goblet, toasting-type, "Aforetone," h.p., artist-signed "E.S. Wright," dated "1903," serpent mark, 5" d., 11" h. **350**

Willets, h.p. blackberries & foliage on a pastel ground, serpent mark, 4 1/2" h. **125**

Willets Belleek Mug with Monk

Willets, h.p. scene of a monk w/a wine cask, deep maroon base & handle, serpent mark, 6" h. (ILLUS.) **325**

Orange Mug w/Currants

Willets, ovoid form, h.p. orange currants & green leaves on orange ground, serpent mark, 5" h. (ILLUS.) **125**

Art Nouveau-style Mug

Willets, ovoid form w/Art Nouveau-style h.p. hearts & whiplash decoration in pale lilac, serpent mark, 4" h. (ILLUS.) **85**

Mug with Handpainted Cherries

Willets, slightly tapering cylindrical form w/panel at base w/raised design, decorated w/cherries, h.p. & marked "D'Arcy's Hand Painted," serpent mark, 5 1/2" h. (ILLUS.)... **190**

Willets, small h.p. bunches of grapes & foliage all around, heavy gilded handle & rim, serpent mark, 4 1/2" h............................ **275**

Mug with Rose Swags & Gilding

Willets, tall cylindrical form w/slightly flaring base, applied handle, h.p. rose swags on cream ground, heavy gilding on rim, handle & raised leaf design around base, serpent mark, 5 1/2" h. (ILLUS.) **260**

Mug with Design of Ripe Plums

Willets, tall cylindrical form w/slightly flaring base, applied handle, h.p. all over w/images of ripe plums & foliage, artist-signed, additional "Darcy's Hand Painted, #6007," serpent mark, 5 1/2" h. (ILLUS.)... **270**

Willets Mug with Peaches

Willets, tall, slightly ovoid form w/h.p. decoration of peaches & foliage on deep orange ground, serpent mark, 5 3/4" h. (ILLUS.)... **160**

Artist-signed Mug

Willets, tapering cylindrical form w/gilt handle, h.p. w/grape foliage on lilac band on paler ground, artist signed "M. Schaffer '10," serpent mark, 6" h. (ILLUS.) **145**

Pitchers, Creamers and Ewers

Ceramic Art Company, cider pitcher, h.p. all around w/large pink roses & leaves, accented w/gold, beaded gold handle, CAC palette mark, 8" h., 6" d., ... **600**

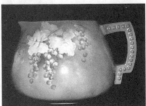

Cider Pitcher with Currants

Ceramic Art Company, cider pitcher, h.p. orange & currants & pale green leaves, 8" h., 6" d., CAC palette mark (ILLUS.)......... **450**

Ceramic Art Company, creamer, footed swan-form, gold highlights, artist-signed "ES," dated "1903," CAC palette mark, 3 1/2" h. **225**

Ceramic Art Company, pitcher, 6 1/2" h., tankard-type, h.p. grapes, leaves & vines on rust ground, heavy gold accents, CAC palette mark **800**

Water Lily Cider Pitcher

Lenox, cider pitcher, h.p. overall w/water lilies & leaves, artist-signed, 6 1/2" h., palette mark (ILLUS.) **750**

Lenox Silver Overlay Creamer

Lenox, creamer, cream-colored body w/swags of silver overlay, 5 1/4" h., palette mark (ILLUS.) **110**

American Belleek Ewer

Lenox, ewer, cream-colored body w/design of flowing colors in yellow, green & mauve, 5 1/2" h., 3 1/2" d., palette mark (ILLUS.)... **295**

Lenox, lemonade pitcher, w/h.p. lemons & foliage over entire body, artist-signed, 10 1/2" h., palette mark................................... **750**

Lenox, pitcher, 9" h., jug-type, handled, h.p. w/an overall floral design, trimmed in gold, palette mark **600**

Lenox, pitcher, 14" h., tankard-type, h.p. grapes, leaves & vines, embossed handle trimmed in gold, palette mark................... **725**

Ott and Brewer, creamer, cream-colored, hand-decorated w/gold paste foliage & an applied gilded thistle handle, crown & sword mark, 3 1/2" h. **450**

Ott and Brewer, ewer, shaped form w/raised gold paste stylized leaf decoration on a matte ground, cactus-shaped handle, crown & sword mark, 8" h., 7 1/2" d. **1,500**

Willets, apple cider pitcher, decorated w/h.p. apples & foliage on purple to pale ground, 6" h. **600**

Willets Creamer

Willets, creamer, thin porcelain w/arched, ruffled spout & forked handle, delicate h.p. pink blossoms & green leaves, 3 1/2" h., 3" d. (ILLUS.)..................... **125**

Willets, pitcher, 7" h., jug-shaped, h.p. large poppies w/soft gold-accented foliage & handle, artist-signed "A.B. Julia," dated "1910," serpent mark **250**

Willets Jug with Cavalier

Willets, pitcher, 8" h., jug-type, handled wide ovoid form w/short neck, h.p. scene of a bearded cavalier seated at a table w/a wine jug & goblet, serpent mark, (ILLUS.).. **600**

Willets, pitcher, 10 1/2" h., tankard-type, h.p. fruit decoration all over, artist-signed, serpent mark **750**

Willets, pitcher, 11 1/4" h., tankard-type, dragon-handled, h.p. w/wisteria, artist-signed **900**

Willets, pitcher, 15" h., tankard-type, h.p. blackberries, leaves & vines on light green matte ground, artist-signed "Fisher," serpent mark **825**

Willets, pitcher, 15" h., tankard-type, h.p. w/berries all around **825**

Plates and Platters

Gordon Belleek, plate, 8" d., decorated w/birds, heavy enameling & gold trim **75**

Lenox, plate, 7 1/2" d., cream-colored w/sterling silver overlay of festoons of ribbons, silver around outer rim, palette mark **40**

Lenox, plate, 7 1/2" d., h.p. medallions surrounded & connected by heavy silver overlay by the Rockwell Silver Company, palette mark **65**

Lenox, plate, 8" d., h.p. w/a few flowers, palette mark **50**

Lenox, platter, 16 1/2" l., Art Deco design w/h.p. border & solid handles w/gold trim, palette mark **130**

Morgan, plate, 10 1/2" d., decorated w/intricate enameled design of fruit, flowers & birds **225**

Morgan, plate, 10 5/8" d., Orient, Deco-style h.p. enamel decoration **150**

Ott and Brewer, plate, 8 1/2" d., scalloped rim w/h.p. ferns in pink, dark green, mauve & light green, crown & sword mark **125**

Salt Dips

Scalloped-rim Salt Dip

Ceramic Art Pottery, h.p. violets & leaves, scalloped gold rim, CAC palette mark, 1 1/2" d. (ILLUS.) **96**

Lenox, h.p. w/a soft pink ground & small purple blossoms & green leaves w/gold trim, palette mark, 1 1/4" d., set of 12 .... **500**

Artist-signed Lenox Salt Dip

Lenox, h.p. w/a stylized band & blossom design, signed by E. Sweeny, palette mark, 1 1/2" d. (ILLUS.) **55**

Footed Lenox Salt Dip

Lenox, three-footed, lustre body, gold-trimmed feet & scalloped rim, palette mark, 1 1/4" d. (ILLUS.) **56**

Willets Salt with Lustre Exterior

Willets, pink lustre exterior, cream-colored interior, serpent mark, 2" d. (ILLUS.) **56**

Footed Willets Salt Dip

Willets, three-footed, lustre exterior w/gold rim & feet, serpent mark, 3" d. (ILLUS.)........... **35**

Sets

Lenox, cider set: pitcher & six cups; h.p. red apples, leaves & stems in an overall design, palette mark, cups 5" h., pitcher 6" h., the set **950**

Lenox, coffee set: pedestal-based cov. coffeepot, cov. sugar & creamer; h.p. flowers in gold shields w/heavy gold accents, artist-signed "Kaufman," palette mark, the set.. **1,450**

Lenox Creamer & Sugar Bowl

Lenox, creamer & cov. sugar bowl, pedestal base, urn-form bodies, cream ground w/hand-decorated Art Deco design of enameled beading & gold paste, palette mark, 7" h., pr. (ILLUS.) **600**

Creamer & Sugar in Sterling Holders

Lenox, creamer & open sugar, cream color porcelain inserts w/flaring rims in sterling silver reticulated footed holders, palette mark, 3 1/2" h. creamer, 2 1/2" h. sugar, pr. (ILLUS.) **275**

Silver Overlay Creamer & Sugar

Lenox, creamer & open sugar, cream color w/silver overlay of flying geese, trees & foliage, palette mark, 3" h., pr. (ILLUS.) **325**

Lenox Rose-decorated Tea Set

Lenox, salt & pepper shakers, h.p. w/small
sprays of flowers, palette mark, 2 1/2" h.,
pr. **120**
Lenox, tea set: cov. teapot, cov. sugar bowl
& creamer; each w/a pedestal base &
square foot, boat-shaped body w/angled
handle, h.p. w/pink roses & blue blossoms w/green leaves, gold handles & finial, palette mark, teapot 11" l., the set
(ILLUS.) **1,050**

Vases

Vase with Chrysanthemums

Ceramic Art Company, 7 1/2" h., ovoid body
w/short neck & flared rim, h.p. chrysanthemums on a light green matte ground
w/gold trim & gold on neck & neck rim,
artist-signed "DeLan," CAC palette mark
(ILLUS.) **625**

Vase with Jonquil Decoration

Ceramic Art Company, 8 1/4" h., cylindrical
body tapering to small 4 1/2" top
opening, h.p. w/large yellow jonquils &
leaves all around on a pale blue ground,
some gold highlights, CAC palette mark
(ILLUS.) **975**
Ceramic Art Company, 10" h., w/h.p. roses
& gold embellishments, CAC palette
mark **700**
Ceramic Art Company, 10 1/2" h., ovoid
body w/narrow waisted neck opening to
flaring rim, h.p. w/large pink roses on a
lavender ground, high glaze, CAC palette
mark **800**

Ceramic Art Company, 10 1/2" h., pear-shaped body w/short neck opening w/slightly flaring rim, h.p. w/large pink roses on a green ground, high glaze, CAC palette mark **800**

Artist-signed Vase with Flowers

Ceramic Art Company, 13" h., ovoid body w/short narrow neck & flaring rim, decorated w/h.p. orange flowers & green leaves on pale green & cream ground, artist-signed, CAC palette mark (ILLUS.) **900**

Ceramic Art Company, 16" h., 7" d., portrait-type, cylindrical, h.p. Art Nouveau-style standing woman w/flowing hair, CAC palette mark **1,600**

Ceramic Art Company, 17" h., w/h.p. wisteria decoration, artist-signed, CAC palette mark **1,400**

Knowles, Taylor and Knowles Lotus Ware, 8" h., 5" d., front h.p. w/a scene of a Victorian woman standing by a beehive looking up at two flying cherubs, the back w/a bouquet of flowers, applied "fishnet" work on body **1,400**

Basket-style Lenox Vase

Lenox, basket-style, w/scalloped rim & foot, h.p. w/Deco-style baskets of flowers & gold highlights on white ground, palette mark (ILLUS.) **175**

Early Lenox Urn-shaped Vase

Lenox, 8" h., urn-shaped on a flaring pedestal & square foot, swan's-neck handles, white ground h.p. w/a central floral medallion on the front & back, early wreath mark (ILLUS.) **300**

Lenox, 8" h., 3" d., h.p. flowers w/fine gilding, signed "Valborg, 1905," fluted top w/attached handle to side of tilted bowl, palette mark.. **650**

Lenox, 8" h., 5" d., bulbous body, h.p. floral decoration in mint condition, palette mark...... **510**

Lenox, 9 1/2" h., 3" d., cylindrical, h.p. bird on branch w/flowers, palette mark.................. **450**

Lenox, 10 1/4" h., ovoid body tapering to short, wide, flared neck, h.p. decoration of open roses, leaves & petals on mauve matte ground, palette mark............................ **550**

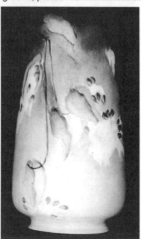

Lenox Vase with Blossom Seeds

Lenox, 10 1/4" h., tapering cylindrical body w/a short wide flared neck, h.p. w/open seed pods w/white & brown seeds & green leaves, shaded brown to cream ground, palette mark (ILLUS.) **700**

Lenox, 10 1/4" h., 3" d., cylindrical, decorated w/a stylized bird highlighted in gold, artist-signed "E.R. Martin," palette mark **300**

Lenox, 11 1/2" h., 5 1/2" d., impressionistic h.p. decoration w/gold trim, palette mark **500**

Lenox, 12 1/2" h., ovoid body tapering to a short flared neck, h.p. w/large chrysanthemums w/soft gold highlights, palette mark **895**

Lenox Vase with Landscape Band

Lenox, 13" h., cylindrical w/slightly incurved rim, a wide rim band h.p. w/a stylized country landscape & gold border, the lower body w/a pale ground h.p. overall w/diamond devices, palette mark (ILLUS.) **675**

Lenox, 15 1/2" h., cylindrical, h.p. Oriental women, trees & foliage, palette mark **350**

Lenox, 18 1/2" h., decorated w/h.p. roses accented w/gold, heavily gilded shaped handles, palette mark **3,200**

Gourd-style Vase

Willets, 7" h., gourd-type, w/h.p. flowers & foliage on white ground, serpent mark (ILLUS.) **325**

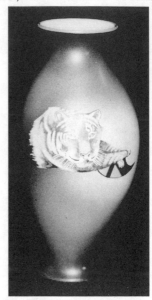

Willets Vase with a Tiger

Willets, 9" h., 4" d., baluster-form w/flared foot & rim, dark green ground decorated w/a h.p. tiger on one side, serpent mark (ILLUS.) **900**

Willets, 10" h., bulbous form w/all over floral decoration, artist-signed, dated 1905, serpent mark **1,200**

Willets, 10" h., 3" d., cylindrical, h.p. design of three Japanese women in kimonos on a pale green ground, serpent mark **450**

Willets, 10" h., 8" d., bulbous body w/a short pinched neck & fluted rim, h.p. overall w/large pastel roses & foliage, serpent mark **500**

Willets Vase with Birds & Wisteria

Willets, 10 1/2" h., 6" d., ovoid form w/h.p. decoration of birds & wisteria, serpent mark (ILLUS.) **900**

Willets, 10 1/2" h., 6" d., h.p. Pickard decoration of a full-length Art Nouveau woman w/flowing hair & gown on a pink lustre ground, serpent mark **1,600**

Willets, 11" h., h.p. chrysanthemums accented w/gold on white ground, serpent mark **665**

Willets, 11" h., 6 1/2" d., bulbous shape w/a short, small neck w/fluted rim, h.p. w/flowers & heavy gold paste accents, serpent mark **900**

Willets, 11 1/2" h., cylindrical, h.p. w/large roses of different shades of pink w/green leaves & gold trim, serpent mark **625**

Willets, 12" h., tapering from a small top to a flared bottom, h.p. clusters of roses, artist-signed "M.A. Minor - 1902," serpent mark **1,400**

Willets, 13" h., 6" d., bulbous form w/a short flared neck, h.p. overall w/pink, red & white roses w/soft gold highlights, serpent mark **1,800**

Willets, 13" h., 9" d., bulbous shape w/a short pinched neck w/fluted rim, h.p. overall w/pink, red & white roses, serpent mark **1,850**

Willets, 13 3/4" h., 8" d., undecorated, urn-shaped w/curved applied handles, serpent mark **125**

Willets, 15 1/2" h., waisted cylindrical form, h.p. overall w/hyacinths w/gold accents, artist-signed "E. Miler," serpent mark **1,050**

Willets, 15 1/2" h., 3" d., h.p. large flowers, artist-signed "J. Brauer," serpent mark **1,200**

Willets, 15 1/2" h., 4" d., cylindrical w/flared bottom & flared scalloped top, h.p. completely w/pink & red roses on a soft pastel pink ground, serpent mark **1,200**

Miscellaneous

Ceramic Art Company, loving cup, h.p. images of grapes & foliage, gilded rim, base & handles, topped w/figural children's heads, serpent mark, 8 1/4" h., 6 1/4" d. ... **2,000**

Knowles, Taylor & Knowles Lotus Ware rose bowl, 5" d., 6" h., "Columbia," raised cameo-style flowers w/gold branching ornamentation **760**

Knowles, Taylor & Knowles Lotus Ware rose bowl, 7" d., 7 1/2" h., cov., h.p. ornately patterned pierced cover & handles, applied gilded roses & "jewels" **2,500**

Lenox Teapot with Roses Decoration

Lenox, teapot, cov., pedestal base on square foot, boat-shaped body w/angled handle, h.p. sprays of pink & white roses w/green leaves, gold band trim, palette mark, 10" l., 8" h. (ILLUS.) **450**

Lenox, toothpick holder, h.p. ravens sitting on pine branches, straight sides, palette mark, 2 1/4" h. **150**

Three-handled Loving Cup

Willets, loving cup, three-handled ovoid form on pedestal base, decorated w/h.p. chrysanthemums & foliage in teal on white ground, serpent mark, 5 1/2" d., 8" h. (ILLUS.) **200**

Willets Sherbet in Holder

Willets, sherbet, porcelain insert in sterling silver reticulated holder w/pedestal base, serpent mark, 3 1/2" d., 3 3/4" h. (ILLUS.) **125**

Irish Belleek

Belleek china has been made in Ireland's County Fermanagh for many years. It is exceedingly thin porcelain. Several marks were used, including a hound and harp (1865-1880), and a hound, harp and castle (1863-1891). A printed hound, harp and castle with the words "Co. Fermanagh Ireland" constitutes the mark from 1891. The earliest marks were printed in black followed by those printed in green. In recent years the marks appear in gold.

The item identification for the following listing follows that used in Richard K. Degenhardt's reference "Belleek - The Complete Collector's Guide and Illustrated Reference," first and second editions. The Degenhardt illustration number (D...) appears at the end of each listing. This number will be followed in most cases by a Roman numeral "I" to indicate a first period black mark while the Roman numeral "II" will indicate a second period black mark. In the "Baskets" section an Arabic number "1" indicates an impressed ribbon mark with "Belleek" while the numeral "2" indicates the impressed ribbon with the words "Belleek - Co. Fermanagh." Both these marks were used in the first period, 1865-1891. Unless otherwise noted, all pieces here will carry the black mark. A thorough discussion of the early Belleek marks is found in this book as well as at the Web site: http://members.aol.com/delyicious/index.html.

Prices for items currently in production may also be located at this site, especially via the 1983 Suggested Retail Price List. Prices given here are for pieces in excellent or mint condition with no chips, cracks, crazing or repairs, although, on flowered items, minimal chips to the flowers is acceptable to the extent of the purchaser's tolerance. Earthenware pieces often exhibit varying degrees of crazing due to the primitive bottle kilns originally used at the pottery.

Basket Ware
Basket, cov., oval, small size
   (D114-I) **$6,000**

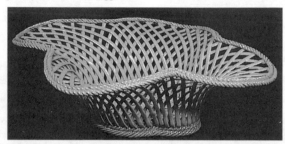

Lobed Belleek Basket

Basket, four-lobed form w/widely flared rims, D1693-1 (ILLUS.) **3,000**

Large Henshall's Twig Basket

Basket, Henshall's Twig Basket, large size,
   D120-1 (ILLUS.) **2,600**

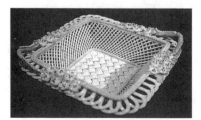

Belleek Melvin Basket

Basket, Melvin Basket, painted blossoms,
   D1690-5 (ILLUS.) **800**

Round Belleek Handled Basket

Basket, round, center arched handle, flattened rim w/applied colored blossoms, flat rod, D1274-1 (ILLUS.) **5,000**

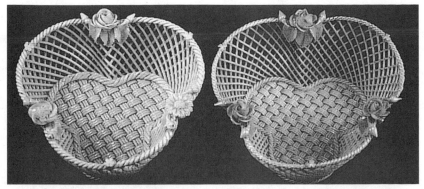

Two Belleek Shamrock Baskets

Basket, Shamrock basket, three different flowers around the rim, small size, D109-1, each (ILLUS. of two) **520**

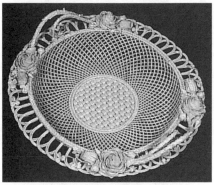

Large Sydenham Twig Basket

Basket, Sydenham Twig Basket, large size, D108-1 (ILLUS.) **4,400**

Box, cov., Forget-Me-Not trinket box, flower blossoms on the cover (D111-III) **600**

Brooch, flowered, (D1525-II) **400**

Belleek Flower Bouquet in Frame

Flower bouquet, hand-formed in green ware, features samples of all flower styles used on Belleek wares, mounted in a shadowbox frame, marked with two ribbons & "Belleek (R) Co. Fermanagh," ca. 1955-79 (ILLUS.) **2,200**

Very Rare Belleek Frame

Frame, photo or mirror, oblong w/two oval picture openings, ornately applied overall   w/flowers, D66-II (ILLUS.) **6,200**

Unique Belleek Woven Mirror Frame

Frame, woven mirror frame, oval, unique,
  Second Period Mark II (ILLUS.) **4,000**

Woven Flowered Jewel Stand

Jewel stand, Woven Flowered Jewel Stand,
  D1575-II (ILLUS.) **1,200**
Menu holder, decorated w/applied flowers,
  various designs, D275-II, each **600**

Comports & Centerpieces

Cherub Candelabra

Candelabra, Cherub Candelabra, w/drip
  cups, D341-II (ILLUS.) **6,000**

Bird Nest Stump Vase-Centerpiece

Centerpiece, Bird Nest Stump Vase, w/eggs
  in nest, D57-II (ILLUS.) **3,200**

Rare Belleek Bittern Comport

Comport, Bittern Comport, figural tall birds
  form pedestal, gilt trim, D6-II (ILLUS.) **10,000**

Boy on Swan Figural Comport

Comport, Boy on Swan Comport, beetlefys
  on base, D33-I (ILLUS.) **8,000**

Earthenware

Earthenware Bowl with Inscription

Bowl, deep sides, Celtic inscription that translates "Friendship is Better than Gold," D857-II (ILLUS.)................................. **400**

Chamber Pot with Gladstone

Chamber pot, printed portrait of William Gladstone on the inside bottom, D2082-I (ILLUS.)... **1,600**

Jelly mold, deep slightly flaring rounded sides, design on the interior (D880-I)............. **460**
Mug, cylindrical, scenic transfer-printed decoration (D858-II).. **360**

Pottery Scene on Earthenware Plate

Plate, 10" d., black transfer-printed pottery scene in the center, a crest on the flanged rim, D887-I (ILLUS.).......................... **400**

Earthenware Serving Dish

Serving dish, open, oval, embossed end handles, pedestal base, D915-II (ILLUS.)...... **400**
Toothbrush tray, cov., found w/various transfer-printed designs (D932-I)................... **440**

Floral-decorated Earthenware Tray

Tray, oval, brown transfer-printed floral de-

sign, D900-I (ILLUS.).. **400**

Figurines

Belgian Hawkers Figurines

Belgian Hawker, female, fully-decorated, D15-II (ILLUS. right) **3,000**
Belgian Hawker, male, fully-decorated, D21-II (ILLUS. left) **3,000**

Belleek Bust of Clytie

Bust of Clytie, low pedestal base, D14-II (ILLUS.) **2,200**

Bust and Figure of Lesbie

Bust of Lesbie, trimmed w/flowers & high-lighted w/colors, D1651-I (ILLUS. right) **3,600**

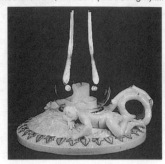

Shepherd & Dog Candleholder

Candleholder, figure of a sleeping shepherd & his dog on the rounded base, ring handle, green tint & gilt trim, D1603-I (ILLUS.) **4,000**

Boy & Girl Figural Candlesticks

Candlestick, boy w/basket on shoulder, fully-decorated & pierced, D1126-I (ILLUS. left) **3,200**
Candlestick, girl w/basket on her shoulder, fully-decorated & pierced, D1137-I (ILLUS. right with Boy candlestick) **3,200**

Figures of Affection & Meditation

Figure of Affection, fully-decorated, D1134-I (ILLUS. left) **3,400**

Rare Belleek Figure of Erin

Figure of Erin, standing figure by well, D1-I
(ILLUS.).. **10,000**
Figure of Lesbie, standing, highlighted
w/colors, D1656-I (ILLUS. left with bust
of Lesbie)... **3,600**
Figure of Meditation, fully-decorated, D20-I
(ILLUS. right with Affection)........................ **3,400**

Belleek Figure of a Cavalier

Figure of Cavalier, standing, D22-II (ILLUS.).. **3,400**

Very Rare Horse & Snake Figurine

Model of Horse & Snake, D1139-III
(ILLUS.).. **12,000**

Museum Display Patterns (Artichoke, Chinese, Finner, Five O'Clock, Lace, Ring Handle Ivory, Set #36 & Victoria)

Rare Belleek Crouching Venus

Figure of Crouching Venus, gilt highlights,
D16-I (ILLUS.)... **10,000**

Bone China Bread Plate & Cup & Saucer

Bone china bread plate, heavy pink ground
& gilt trim, D844-I (ILLUS. left) **680**
Bone china teacup & saucer, heavy pink
ground & gilt trim, D848-I (ILLUS. right) **620**
Chinese creamer w/dragon head spout &
open sugar bowl, decorated (D485-I &
D486-I), pr.. **880**
Chinese tea urn, figural cover, ornate
winged dragon spout, twisted rope-form
overhead handle, large winged dragon
support on round base w/paw feet, deco-
rated (D482-I)... **15,000**

Chinese Pattern Teacup & Saucer

Chinese teacup & saucer, decorated, D483-
I (ILLUS.)... **520**
Chinese teapot, cov., small size, decorated
(D484-I) **2,000**

Lace Medium-sized Teapot

Lace teapot, cov., medium size, D800-II
(ILLUS.).. **1,000**
Lace tray, round, decorated (D803-I)............. **6,000**
Ring Handle bread plate, Limoges decora-
tion (D824-I) **1,400**

Religious Items & Lithophanes
Figure of the Blessed Virgin Mary, large size
(D1106-II)... **1,800**

Cherub Holy Water Font

Holy water font, Cherub head w/spread
wings, D1110-VI (ILLUS.) **100**
Holy water font, Coral & Shell (D1111-V)........... **100**

Sacred Heart Font #4

Holy water font, Sacred Heart font, #4,
D1115-III (ILLUS.) **260**

Holy water font, Sacred Heart font, #8
(D1114-II) **320**
Lithophane, Madonna, Child & Angel
(D1544-III)... **3,200**
Lithophane, Madonna, Child & Angel
(D1544-VII) **600**

Child Looking in Mirror Lithophane

Lithophane, round, child looking in mirror,
D1539-VII (ILLUS.).. **480**

Tea Ware - Common Patterns (Harp Shamrock, Limpet, Hexagon, Neptune, Shamrock & Tridacna)

Harp Shamrock Butter Plate

Harp Shamrock butter plate, D1356-III
(ILLUS.)... **200**

Harp Shamrock Plate for Butter

Harp Shamrock butter plate, D1356-VI
(ILLUS.).. **100**

Harp Shamrock Teakettle

Harp Shamrock teakettle, overhead handle,
large size, gilt trim, D1359-III (ILLUS.)........... **660**

Hexagon Pattern Breakfast Set

Hexagon breakfast set: small teapot, open
sugar & creamer, two plates & two cups
& saucers, h.p. floral decoration, no tray,
D396-II (ILLUS.) **2,600**

Marmalades & Mustard

Hexagon Pattern Teapot

Hexagon teapot, cov., large size, D407-II
(ILLUS.).. **600**
Neptune biscuit jar, cov. (D531-II) **460**
Neptune creamer & open sugar bowl, green
tint, pr. (D416-II & D417-II)............................. **400**
Neptune mustard jar, cov., D298-III (ILLUS.
left with marmalades, top of page)................. **100**

Neptune Pattern Cup & Saucer

Neptune teacup & saucer, green tint, D414-
II (ILLUS.) 240
Neptune teapot, cov., medium size, green
tint (D415-II) **480**
Neptune tray, green tint (D418-II)................... **1,200**
Shamrock bread plate, round w/loop han-
dles (D379-III) 180
Shamrock egg cup, footed (D389-II)................. 120

Shamrock Large & Name Mugs

Shamrock mug, large size, D216-II (ILLUS.
right).. **120**

Shamrock mug, Name Mug, impressed reserve for name, small size, D216-II
(ILLUS. left) 140

Shamrock marmalade jar, cov., barrel-shaped, D1561-IV (ILLUS. right, top of previous page) **100**
Shamrock marmalade jar, cov., cup marmalade, D1323-III (ILLUS. center, top previous page) **100**
Shamrock pitcher, milk, jug-form (D390-II) **320**

Shamrock Low-Shape Cup & Saucer

Shamrock teacup & saucer, low shape, D366-III (ILLUS.) **160**

Tridacna Boat-shaped Creamer

Tridacna creamer, boat-shaped, D247-VI (ILLUS.) **60**

Large Tridacna Gilt-trimmed Sugar

Tridacna sugar bowl, open, gilt-trimmed, large size, D472-I (ILLUS.) **440**

Tea Ware - Desirable Patterns (Echinus, Limpet (footed), Grass, Hexagon, Holly, Mask, New Shell & Shell)

Echinus creamer & open sugar bowl, decorated (D647-I & D648-I), pr. **1,000**
Echinus cup & saucer, egg shell, crested (D358-I) **500**
Echinus egg cup, footed (D666-I) **400**
Echinus teapot, cov., pink tint w/gold trim, small size (D659-I) **900**
Grass coffeepot, cov., large size (D1402-I).... **1,600**

Grass Pattern Tea & Coffee Service

Grass creamer & covered sugar bowl, middle size, D746-I & D748-I, pr. (ILLUS. left & right with set) **800**

Grass Egg Cup with Crest

Grass egg cup, footed, crested decoration, D754-I (ILLUS.) **420**
Grass honey pot, cover & stand, model of a beehive on a low table-form base, the set (D755-I) **1,000**
Grass mustache cup & saucer (D739-I) **620**
Grass teakettle, cov., large size, D751-I (ILLUS. at back with the set) **1,000**
Grass teapot, cov., small size, D750-I (ILLUS. center front with set) **800**
Grass tray, round, D736-I (ILLUS. with set)... **2,000**

Small Mask Pattern Powder Bowl

Mask powder bowl, small size, D1548-III (ILLUS.) **160**

Tea Ware - Rare Patterns (Aberdeen, Blarney, Celtic (low & tall), Cone, Erne, Fan, Institute, Ivy, Lily (high & low), Scroll, Sydney, Thistle & Thorn)

Aberdeen Pattern Breakfast Set

Aberdeen breakfast set: cov. teapot, cream-
er, open sugar & cups & saucers; no tray,
D494-II (ILLUS.).. **2,200**
Celtic teacup & saucer, low shape, painted
(D1456-III & D1457-III) **400**
Cone teacup & saucer, pink tint (D432-II) **440**

Fan teacup & saucer, decorated, D694-II
(ILLUS.).. **600**
Institute plate, 6" d., pink tint (D724-I)................ **160**

Institute Decorated Sugar Bowl

Institute sugar bowl, cov., decorated, D728-
I (ILLUS.).. **600**
Thorn brush tray & scent bottles, turquoise
& gilt decoration, D333-I & D335-I
(ILLUS., below)... **2,200**

Fan Pattern Teacup & Saucer

Thorn Brush Tray & Scent Bottles

Thorn creamer & open sugar bowl, small
size (D760-I & D761-I), pr. **1,000**

Thorn teapot, cov., small size, decorated
(D759-I).. **800**
Thorn tray, oval, decorated (D762-I)............... **2,600**

Tea Ware - Miscellaneous
Items produced, but with NO matching tea set pieces.

Cardium on Shell Dish & Sycamore & Worcester Plates

Cardium on Shell dish, Size 2, pink tint,
  D261-I (ILLUS. center, top of page) **180**
Cleary salt dip, oblong, pink tint & gilt trim
  (D295-II) **100**

Decorated Belleek Flask

Flask, ovoid form, gilt Harp, Hound & Castle
logo at the center in gold, D1523-I
(ILLUS.) **2,000**

Greek Dessert Plate with Scene

Greek dessert plate, tinted & gilt-
trimmed, h.p. center scene titled "Eel
Fishery on the Erne," by E. Sheerin, D29-
I (ILLUS.) **3,200**

Flower-decorated Heart Plate

Heart plate, scalloped edges, Size 2, h.p.
flowers, D635-III (ILLUS.) **120**

Irish Pot Creamer & Open Sugar

Irish Pot creamer & open sugar bowl, Size 2,
D232-II, pr. (ILLUS.) **240**

Armorial Souvenir Loving Cup

Loving cup, three-handled, armorial souvenir, D1503-I (ILLUS.) 400

Shell-shaped Nautilus Creamer

Nautilus creamer, shell-shaped, pink tint, D279-I (ILLUS.) 600

Small Model of an Irish Harp

Ring Handle Decorated Plate

Ring Handle plate, 6" d., Limoges Decoration, D822-I (ILLUS.) 600
Shell creamer, large size (D601-I) 720

Bowl-shaped Shell Plateau

Shell Plateau, bowl-shaped, medium size, D792-I (ILLUS.) 380

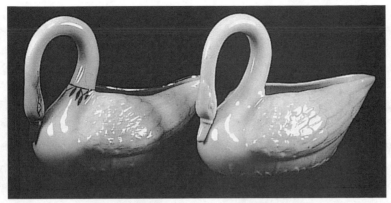

Two Large Swan Creamers

Swan creamer, figural, large size, D254-III
(ILLUS. left).. **320**
Swan creamer, figural, large size, D254-VI
(ILLUS. right)... **120**
Sycamore plate, leaf-shaped, Size 2, pink
tint, D642-II (ILLUS. right with Cardium
on Shell dish).. **120**
Toy creamer & open sugar bowl, Cleary
patt. (D249-III), pr. **160**
Toy creamer & open sugar bowl, Ivy patt.,
small size (D241-I), pr...................................... **240**
Worcester plate, Size 2, D682-II (ILLUS. left
with Cardium on Shell dish) **120**

Vases & Spills
Aberdeen vases, left & right, flowered, me-
dium size (D58-II), pr. **1,600**
Celtic Vase-J, D1199-III, each **460**

Clam Shell & Griffin vase, pink tint, D140-I
(ILLUS.)... **2,200**

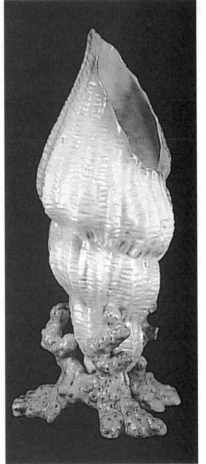

Clam Shell & Griffin Vase

Belleek Coral and Shell Vase
Coral and Shell Vase, D133-II (ILLUS.).............. **880**

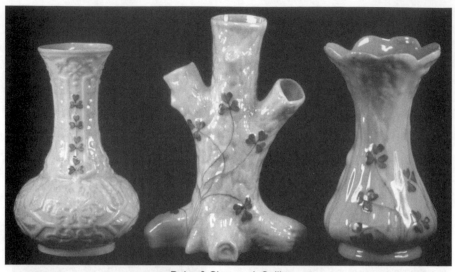

Daisy & Shamrock Spills

Daisy Spill, D178-III (ILLUS. right)...................... **220**

Ivy Stump Spill (D147-I)... **420**

Belleek Flowered Spill

Flowered Spill, raised on twig feet, large size, D45-III (ILLUS.).. **380**

Belleek Marine Jug Vase

Marine Jug Vase, coral designs, ruffled foot, D134-II (ILLUS.) **800**

Prince Arthur Vase, flowered (D1218-II)............. **920**

Belleek Figural Frog Vase

Frog Vase, model of frog w/head up & mouth open, large size, D181-II (ILLUS.).. **1,000**

Belleek Ram's Head Flower Holder

Ram's Head Flower Holder, figural, D1180-I (ILLUS.)... **1,400**

Belleek Rathmore Flowerpot

Rathmore Flowerpot, bulbous w/flaring scalloped rim & applied flowers, D43-II
(ILLUS.).. **2,200**

Belleek Ribbon Vase

Ribbon Vase, flowered, D1220-III (ILLUS.)....... **340**

Seahorse and Shell Flower Holder

Seahorse and Shell Flower Holder, rectan-
gular base, D129-I (ILLUS.)........................ **1,200**
Shamrock Spill, D191-III (ILLUS. left with
Daisy Spill).. **220**
Shamrock Tree Stump Spill, D1224-III
(ILLUS. center with Daisy Spill)...................... **240**
Triple Fish Vase, painted (D1231-I)................. **4,600**

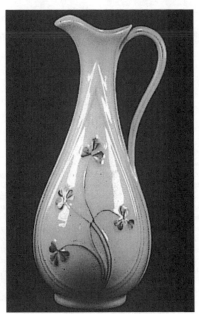

Belleek Typha Jug Spill

Typha Jug Spill, decorated w/shamrocks,
D1790-VI (ILLUS.)... **120**

Bennington

*Bennington wares, which ranged from stoneware to
parian and porcelain, were made in Bennington, Vermont, primarily in two potteries, one in which Captain
John Norton and his descendants were principals, and
the other in which Christopher Webber Fenton (also
once associated with the Nortons) was a principal. Various marks are found on the wares made in the two major
potteries, including J. & E. Norton, E. & L. P. Norton, L.
Norton & Co., Norton & Fenton, Edward Norton,
Lyman Fenton & Co., Fenton's Works, United States
Pottery Co., U.S.P. and others.*

*The popular pottery with the mottled brown on yel-
lowware glaze was also produced in Bennington, but
such wares should be referred to as "Rockingham" or
"Bennington-type" unless they can be specifically attributed to a Bennington, Vermont factory.*

Book flask, binding marked "Departed Spirits," Flint Enamel glaze, 5 5/8" h. (minor
edge wear).. **$468**
Bottle, figural coachman, mottled running
Rockingham glaze, 1848-49 marks,
10" h. (chips, spider crack in base) **385**
Butter churn, stoneware, elongated ovoid
body w/eared handles & molded rim, cobalt blue slip-quilled floral spray decoration, impressed mark of E. & L.P. Norton,
4 gal., brown-glazed cover & wooden
dasher, 1861-81, 17 1/2" h. (chips)................ **575**
Candlestick, ringed columnar form w/heavy
socket ring & flaring round base, overall
mottled brown Flint Enamel glaze, hairline in foot & line around flange of base,
probably manufacturing defect, 7 3/4" h........ **385**

Crock, stoneware, cylindrical w/molded rim
& eared handles, slip-quilled cobalt blue
decoration of a recumbent stag in a landscape w/shrubs, fences & a tree, impressed "J. & E. Norton - Bennington VT
- 2," mid-19th c., 2 gal., 10 3/4" d.,
9 1/4" h. **5,460**
Wash bowl, Flint Enamel glaze, widely flar-
ing ribbed sides molded w/diamonds,
13" d., 4 1/2" h. (wear, hairline) **413**

Berlin (KPM)

*The mark KPM was used at Meissen from 1724 to
1725, and was later adopted by the Royal Factory,
Konigliche Porzellan Manufaktur, in Berlin. At various
periods it was been incorporated with the Brandenburg
scepter, the Prussian eagle or the crowned globe. The
same letters were also adopted by other factories in Germany in the late 19th and early 20th centuries. With the
end of the German monarchy in 1918, the name of the firm
was changed to Staatliche Porzellan Manufaktur and
though production was halted during World War II, the
factory was rebuilt and is still in business. The exquisite
paintings on porcelain were produced at the close of the
19th century and are eagerly sought by collectors today.*

Bowl, handled oblong form, decorated in a
colorful floral design w/a gilt edge, underglaze-blue K.P.M. mark, ca. 1890,
11 1/4" l. **$173**
Cabinet cup, painted w/a military figure
seated before a brick wall, w/a battle
waging in the background, within gilt borders, blue scepter mark, impressed let-
ters & numbers, mid-19th c., 4 3/4" h. **345**
Cabinet plate, octagonal w/reticulated rim,
the center w/a color portrait of Frederick
the Great, 19th c., 9 1/8" w. **230**
Figure group, depicting a peasant couple
w/an infant, late 19th c., 12" h. (minor
losses) **374**
Figure group, depicting two bacchantes & a
goat, decorated in color, 19th c., 8" l. (re-
pairs) **173**
Plaque, rectangular, h.p. landscape scene
w/a farm girl, impressed K.P.M. mark,
late 19th - early 20th c., giltwood frame,
4 x 5 3/4" **1,610**

Berlin Porcelain Plaque

Plaque, "Rose de Mai," signed, titled &
stamped in lower right "Wagner,"
stamped & titled on verso, 5 x 7" (ILLUS.).. **2,576**
Plaque, oval, bust portrait of a young brunette beauty facing right, wearing a grey
shift w/a red sash, a bundle of wheat at
the lower left, late 19th - early 20th c., impressed monogram & scepter mark, art-
ist-signed, 6 5/8 x 8 7/8" **4,600**
Plaque, rectangular, h.p. scene of an Arab
maiden in colorful attire standing next to
a fountain & looking off to the left w/one
hand shielding her eyes, titled "Expecta-
tions," artist-signed, w/raised gilt trim, ca.
1900, unframed, 6 x 9" **3,450**
Plaque, oval, bust portrait of a young girl
w/short wind-blown dark hair, head
turned to one side, wearing a locket &
open-collared blouse, impressed
mark & scepter, late 19th c., 6 3/4 x 9" **1,495**
Plaque, rectangular, "September Morning,"
painted in a soft palette in the Art Nouveau style w/a young nude woman
standing & bathing in a highland lake
w/mountains in the distance, early 20th
c., impressed scepter & monogram mark,
various ciphers, in a black frame,
7 1/2 x 9 7/8" **2,875**
Plaque, rectangular, finely painted w/a
scene of a Renaissance woman standing
before a church door, a rosary & book of
prayers in her right hand, late 19th c., impressed scepter & monogram mark, titled, w/paper label & signed by F. Wag-
ner, in a giltwood frame, 6 7/8 x 10"........... **3,680**
Plaque, rectangular, bust portrait of a young
peasant woman turned to the side w/her
smiling face turned to the viewer, her
blonde hair braided atop her head, wearing a colored scarf & white blouse, impressed "KPM" & scepter, ca. 1900,
7 1/2 x 10"... **2,875**
Plaque, rectangular, painted w/a figural
scene of a woman kneeling by a small girl
holding a water ewer, impressed mark, in
a giltwood frame, 19th c., 7 1/2 x 10"........ **3,680**
Plaque, oval, allegorical bust portrait of
"Beauty," a young woman facing right
wearing a low-cut gown, her long brown
hair flowing over her shoulders, impressed scepter mark & "K.P.M.," 19th c.,
framed, 8 1/2 x 10 1/4" **8,050**
Plaque, oval, a half-length portrait of a seat-
ed gypsy girl, her long dark hair under a
gold coin-trimmed cap, leaning on one elbow & looking left, blue scepter & K.P.M.
mark, late 19th c., 10 3/4" h........................ **3,900**
Plaque, rectangular, "La Fiammetta," half-
length portrait of a young maiden looking
left, a laurel wreath in her long brown
hair, wearing a white, blue & gold-
trimmed gown, impressed marks, artist-
signed, late 19th c., 12 1/2" h...................... **7,200**

"Return from His First Voyage" Plaque

Plaque, rectangular, polychrome enamel interior scene of a sailor & family sitting around a table entitled "Return from His First Voyage," impressed "K.P.M." mark, 19th c., giltwood frame, 10 x 12 1/2" (ILLUS.) 9,200

Plaque, rectangular, three-quarter length portrait of a young maiden standing in the dark & shielding a candle w/one hand, the light reflecting back on her face & body, titled "Gute Nacht," after Hom, artist-signed, late 19th c., impressed mark & scepter, 8 x 13" 2,875

Plaque, rectangular, porcelain, full figure portrait of young dark-haired girl in field of flowers, after Marowsky, titled "Ophelie" ornate scrolled leafy frame, early 20th c., impressed "KPM" scepter mark & dimensions, 8 x 13 1/4" 6,900

Plaque, oval, porcelain three-quarter portrait of young girl w/long dark hair pulled to one side & over her shoulder, floral background, artist-signed, late 19th c., impressed "KPM - 6" & scepter mark, 13 1/2" h. 13,800

Plaque, rectangular, painted w/a scene of a young woman in Mideastern attire standing beside a well & leaning on a jug, palm trees in the background, impressed scepter mark & "K.P.M.," late 19th c., giltwood frame, 11 1/4 x 13 1/2" 7,475

Plaque, rectangular, scene of a Greek maiden w/a water jug, artist-signed, ca. 1900, giltwood frame, 10 x 15 1/2" 6,900

Plaque, rectangular, a half-length portrait of a standing young maiden wearing a white long-sleeved loose robe, her hand held to her throat & her eyes looking heavenward, long curly brown hair hanging loose, tall slender green leafy stems w/large feathery lavender blossoms behind her, artist-signed, impressed marks, late 19th c., 10 3/4 x 16" 7,800

Plaque, rectangular, a scene of a young woman wearing a tightly wrapped classical off-the-shoulder gown standing & holding a mandolin in front of her, a dark tropical landscape behind her, artist-signed, late 19th c., 11 1/4 x 19" 11,400

Plaques, rectangular, one depicting a pair of peasant girls seated among ruins w/a large basket of grapes, one counting change in her hand, the second scene of two young boys & a seated dog w/a basket of fruit & one eating slices, after Murillo, late 19th c., 10 x 12 1/2", pr. **13,800**

Berlin Urn

Urns, cov., square base w/flared foot below wide ovoid body, two ring handles w/lion's head masks, decorated w/h.p. & gilded multicolored foliage, domed cover w/blossom finial, late 19th c., 8 1/2" h., pr. (ILLUS. of one)...................... **1,035**

Vase, 10" h., pâte-sur-pâte, square-form handles w/scrolled ends, stylized gilt foliage designs around the pâte-sur-pâte cartouche of a child w/fruit basket on one side, enameled floral reserve on the other side, KPM mark, late 19th c. **5,175**

K.P.M. Gourd-shaped Vase

Vase, 14" h., double gourd form, one side decorated w/figural reserves, reverse w/foliate spray, turquoise ground (ILLUS.)........................... 633

Vases, cov., 17" h., a round stepped base below the ringed tapering pedestal supporting the tall tapering ovoid body molded around the shoulder w/gadrooning and around the base w/a band of serpents & acanthus leaves, upright looped shoulder handles, the domed cover w/a berry finial, white ground w/heavy gold trim, the sides decorated on the front w/a colored scene of an amorous couple in 18th c. costume & on the back w/a floral bouquet, also trimmed in pink & green, blue scepter & iron-red orb marks, late 19th c., pr. **5,750**

Vegetable tureen, cov., oval, decorated in tones of lavender & green w/flower-filled urns & scrolls, 1850-70, 14" l. **460**

Bisque

Bisque is biscuit china, fired a single time but not glazed. Some bisque is decorated with colors. Most abundant from the Victorian era are figures and groups, but other pieces, from busts to vases, were made by numerous potteries in the United States and abroad. Reproductions have been produced for many years, so care must be taken when seeking antique originals.

Bust of a young boy, holding a letter, 8" h. **$138**

Figure group, a young boy & girl standing on a rockwork base, he holding a fishing pole up in one hand & another projecting out while the girl ties the fishing line to it, fine detailing & delicate coloring, marked by Heubach, 8 1/2" h. **165**

Bisque Dutch Girl Figure

Figure of a Dutch girl, seated pose w/hands on her knees, wearing a white bonnet over light brown hair, tinted face & arms, blue dress w/white bodice & trim on sleeves & at waist, unmarked, 3 1/2 x 5", 6 1/2" h. (ILLUS.) **195**

Figure of young girl, w/cat on a swing, 5 3/4" h. **110**

Figures, a male & female w/gilt & yellow enamel trim, he standing holding a fishing net, she holding a small keg, Germany, late 19th c., 28" h., pr. **920**

French Skating Figures

Figures of a woman & man, each in 18th c. costume, wearing ice skates & depicted in skating pose, each on a shaped platform base, France, late 19th c., facing pair, minor restorations, 28" h., pr. (ILLUS.) **2,070**

Bisque Seated Boy

Figure of a Dutch boy, seated w/one hand on knee, orange jacket, yellow pants, grey hat & shoes, black & white neck scarf, unmarked, 3 1/2 x 5 1/2", 6" h. (ILLUS.) **195**

Blue & White Pottery

The category of blue and white or blue and grey pottery includes a wide variety of pottery, earthenware and stoneware items widely produced in this country in the late 19th century right through the 1930s. Originally marketed as inexpensive wares, most pieces featured a white or grey body molded with a fruit, flower or geometric design and then trimmed with bands or splashes of blue to highlight the molded pattern. Pitchers, butter crocks and salt boxes are among the numerous items produced, but other kitchenwares and chamber sets are also found. Values vary depending on the rarity of the embossed pattern and the depth of color of the blue trim; the darker the blue, the better. Some entries refer to several different books on Blue and White Pottery. These books are: Blue & White Stoneware, Pottery & Crockery by Edith Harbin (1977, Collector Books, Paducah, KY); Stoneware in the Blue and White by M.H. Alexander (1993 reprint, Image Graphics, Inc., Paducah, KY); and Blue & White Stoneware by Kathryn McNerney (1995, Collector Books, Paducah, KY).

Apple cider cooler, cov., w/spigot, 13" d.,
15" h. **$425**

Miniature Blue & White Bank

Bank, miniature, jug-form, stenciled rectangular w/"Money Bank" (ILLUS.) **650**
Basin, embossed Bow Tie patt. w/rose decal, Brush-McCoy Pottery Co., basin 15" d. **150**
Basin, embossed Apple Blossom patt., Burley-Winter Pottery Co., 9" d. **185**
Basin, embossed Apple Blossom patt., Burley-Winter Pottery Co., 14 d. **295**
Batter jar, cov., stenciled Wildflower patt., Brush-McCoy Pottery Co., small, 6" d., 5 3/4" h. (ILLUS. right, bottom of page) **350**
Batter jar, cov., stenciled Wildflower patt., Brush-McCoy Pottery Co., large, 7" d., 8" h. **400**
Batter pail, bail handle, stenciled Wildflower patt., Brush-McCoy Pottery Co., 4 7/8" h. (ILLUS. left with batter jar) **375**

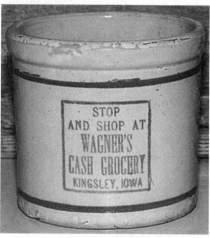

Advertising Beater Jar

Beater jar, advertising-type, "Stop And Shop at Wagner's Cash Grocery, Kingsley, Iowa," 4 3/4" h. (ILLUS.) **325**

Wildflower Batter Jar & Pail

Flying Bird Berry Bowl & Grease Jar

Miniature Birdbath

Bird bath, miniature, embossed birds around base, Western Stoneware Co., 10" h. (ILLUS.)... **2,500**
Bowl, 4" d., 2" h., berry, embossed Flying Bird patt., w/advertising, A.E. Hull Pottery Co.. **450**
Bowl, 4" d., 2" h., berry or cereal, embossed Flying Bird patt., A.E. Hull Pottery Co. (ILLUS. right, top of page).............................. **250**
Bowl, 4 1/2" d., 2 1/2" h., embossed Reverse Pyramids patt., Ruckles Pottery....... **65-75**
Bowl, 6" to 12" d., embossed Greek Key patt., Red Wing Pottery Co., ranges...... **100-170**
Bowl, 7 1/2" d., 2 3/4" h., embossed Apricot with Honeycomb patt., A.E. Hull Pottery Co.. **135**

Reverse Pyramids-Picket Fence Bowl

Bowl, 7 1/2" d., 5" h., embossed Reverse Pyramids w/Reverse Picket Fence patt., Ruckles Pottery (ILLUS.)........................... **90-100**
Bowl, 9 1/2" d., 3 3/4" h., embossed Apricot with Honeycomb patt., A.E. Hull Pottery Co. **150**
Bowl, 9 1/2" d., 5" h., embossed Currants and Diamonds patt.. **230**
Bowl, 10" d., 5" h., embossed Heart Banded patt.. **135**
Bowl, embossed Heart patt................................. **450**

Stenciled Nautilus Pattern Bowl

Bowl, stenciled Nautilus patt., rim handles, A.E. Hull Pottery Co. (ILLUS.)........................ **325**

Embossed Venetian Pattern Bowl

Bowl, 7" d., 2 1/2" h., embossed Venetian patt., same as Reverse Pyramids w/Reverse Picket Fence but w/honeycomb at bottom, Roseville Pottery (ILLUS.).................. **50**
Bowls, nesting-type, embossed Basketweave patt., depending on size............. **220+**
Bowls, nesting-type, embossed Zig-Zag patt., depending on size........................... **100-150**
Bowls, embossed Ringsaround (Wedding Ring) patt., A.E. Hull Pottery Co., six sizes, ranges... **85-225**

Bowls, nesting-type, embossed Cosmos patt., A.E. Hull Pottery Co., depending on size, each.. **65-275**

Stenciled Wildflower Bowl

Bowls, nesting-type, stenciled Wildflower patt., Brush-McCoy Pottery Co., 4" to 14" d., depending on size (ILLUS. of 10" d. size)... **150-450**

Brush vase, embossed Bow Tie (Our Lucile) patt., w/rose decal, Brush-McCoy Pottery Co., 5 1/2" h....................................... **115**

Willow Pattern Brush Vase

Brush vase, embossed Willow (Basketweave & Morning Glory) patt., Brush-McCoy Pottery Co., small, 4 3/4" h. (ILLUS.)... **325**

Butter crock, cov., advertising-type, 6" d., 6" h.. **100**

Butter crock, cov., embossed Butterfly patt., Nelson McCoy Sanitary Stoneware Co., 10 lb. size, 9 1/2" d., 6" h. **275**

Butter crock, cov., embossed Daisy and Basketweave patt., 7" d., 6 3/4" h.................. **350**

Butter crock, cov., embossed Diffused Blues with Inverted Pyramid Bands patt., 6" d., 4" h. **150**

Butter crock, cov., embossed Greek Column (Draped Windows) patt., Red Wing Pottery Co. & Nelson McCoy Sanitary Stoneware Co., found in 2, 3, 4 & 5 lb. sizes, ranges **225-295**

Butter crock, cov., embossed Indian Good Luck Sign (Swastika) patt., produced by Nelson McCoy Sanitary Stoneware Co., Robinson-Ransbottom Pottery Co. & The Crooksville Pottery Co., 6 1/4" d., 5 1/4" h. **175**

Jersey Cow Butter Crock

Butter crock, cov., embossed Jersey Cow patt., 4" h. (ILLUS.) **1,000**

Butter crock, cov., embossed Rose & Waffle patt., 5" d., 4 1/2" h.. **300**

Butter crock, cov., embossed Peacock patt., w/bail handle, Brush-McCoy Pottery Co., 1 lb., 4" h... **1,000**

Peacock Butter Crock & Salt Box

Butter crock, cov., embossed Peacock patt., w/bail handle, Brush-McCoy Pottery Co.,

3 lb., 5" h. (ILLUS. right)................................. **800**

Embossed Willow Canisters

Canister, cov., embossed Willow (Basketweave & Morning Glory) patt., "Barley," Brush-McCoy Pottery Co., average 6 1/2 to 7" h., each. **1,000**

Canister, cov., embossed Willow (Basketweave & Morning Glory) patt., "Cereal," Brush-McCoy Pottery Co., average 5 1/2 to 6 1/2" h. (ILLUS. center row, far left, top of page)... **550**

Canister, cov., embossed Willow (Basketweave & Morning Glory) patt., "Coffee," Brush-McCoy Pottery Co., average 5 1/2 to 6 1/2" h. (ILLUS. middle row, second from left).............................. **275**

Canister, cov., embossed Willow (Basketweave & Morning Glory) patt., "Crackers (short)," Brush-McCoy Pottery Co., average 5 1/2 to 6 1/2" h., each. (ILLUS. top row, third from right) **550**

Canister, cov., embossed Willow (Basketweave & Morning Glory) patt., "Crackers (tall)," Brush-McCoy Pottery Co., average 6 1/2 to 7" h., each. (ILLUS. top row, third from left).. **1,000**

Canister, cov., embossed Willow (Basketweave & Morning Glory) patt., "Raisins," Brush-McCoy Pottery Co., average 5 1/2" to 6 1/2" h. (ILLUS. top row, second from right)................................ **625**

Canister, cov., embossed Willow (Basketweave & Morning Glory) patt., "Rice," Brush-McCoy Pottery Co., average 6 1/2 to 7" h., each. **1,250**

Canister, cov., embossed Willow (Basketweave & Morning Glory) patt., "Salt," "Beans," or blank, Brush-McCoy Pottery Co., average 5 1/2 to 6 1/2" h., each (ILLUS. of Salt, middle row, center; Beans, top row, far right) **375**

Canister, cov., embossed Willow (Basketweave & Morning Glory) patt., "Sugar," Brush-McCoy Pottery Co., average 5 1/2 to 6 1/2" h. (ILLUS. middle row, second from right)... **275**

Canister, cov., embossed Willow (Basketweave & Morning Glory) patt., "Tea," Brush-McCoy Pottery Co., average 5 1/2 to 6 1/2" h. (ILLUS. middle row, far right)...... **275**

Canister, cov., embossed Willow (Basketweave & Morning Glory) patt., "Tobacco," Brush-McCoy Pottery Co., average 6 1/2 to 7" h., each. (ILLUS. top row, far left)... **1,000**

Stenciled Floral Pattern Canister

Canister, cov., stenciled Floral patt., probably A.E. Hull Pottery co., 5 7/8" h. (ILLUS.).. **275**

Canister, cov., stenciled Wildflower patt., "Barley," "Cornstarch" or "Grape Nuts," Brush-McCoy Pottery Co., 5 3/4" h., each (ILLUS. second row from bottom with other canisters & spice jars).................... **550**

Wildflower Canisters & Spice Jars

Canister, cov., stenciled Wildflower patt., "Beans," or "Peas," Brush-McCoy Pottery Co., 5 1/2 to 6 1/2", each (ILLUS. of Beans, second row from bottom) **325**

Canister, cov., stenciled Wildflower patt., blank title, Brush-McCoy Pottery Co. (ILLUS. bottom row with other canisters & spice jars) **475**

Canister, cov., stenciled Wildflower patt., "Butter," tall w/flared rim, Brush-McCoy Pottery Co., 5 3/5" h. (ILLUS. top row with other canisters & spice jars) **350**

Canister, cov., stenciled Wildflower patt., "Cereal (Sago)," Brush-McCoy Pottery Co., 5 1/2 to 6 1/2" h. (ILLUS. bottom row with canisters & spice jars) **400**

Canister, cov., stenciled Wildflower patt., "Choice Sour Pickles," Brush-McCoy Pottery Co., 12" h. **850**

Canister, cov., stenciled Wildflower patt., "Coffee," "Rice" or "Tea," 5 1/2 to 6 1/2", each (ILLUS. second, third & bottom rows with canisters & spice jars) **225**

Canister, cov., stenciled Wildflower patt., "Corn Meal" (tall), Brush-McCoy Pottery Co., 10" h. (ILLUS. top row, right, with canisters & spice jars) **750**

Canister, cov., stenciled Wildflower patt., "Crackers" (tall), Brush-McCoy Pottery Co., 5 1/2 to 6 1/2" h. (ILLUS. top row with canisters & spice jars) **700**

Canister, cov., stenciled Wildflower patt., "Currants," Brush-McCoy Pottery Co., 5 1/2 to 6 1/2" (ILLUS. bottom row with canisters & spice jars) **425**

Canister, cov., stenciled Wildflower patt., "Farina," "Prunes" or "Raisins," Brush-McCoy Pottery Co., 5 1/2 to 6 1/2", each (ILLUS. second row from bottom & bottom row with canisters & spice jars) **375**

Canister, cov., stenciled Wildflower patt., "Flour," Brush-McCoy Pottery Co., 5 1/2 to 6 1/2" h. (ILLUS. top row with canisters & spice jars) **800**

Canister, cov., stenciled Wildflower patt., "Genuine German Dills," Brush-McCoy Pottery Co., 12" h. (ILLUS. top row, far left with canisters & spice jars) **850**

Canister, cov., stenciled Wildflower patt., "Oatmeal," Brush-McCoy Pottery Co., 5 1/2 to 6 1/2", each (ILLUS. second row from bottom with canisters & spice jars) **400**

Canister, cov., stenciled Wildflower patt., "Sugar," Brush-McCoy Pottery Co., 5 1/2 to 6 1/2" (ILLUS. bottom row, far right, with canisters & spice jars) **250**

Canister, cov., stenciled Wildflower patt., "Sugar" (tall), Brush-McCoy Pottery Co., 10" h. (ILLUS. top row, second from left with canisters & spice jars) **500**

Canister, cov., stenciled Wildflower patt., "Tapioca," Brush-McCoy Pottery Co., 5 1/2 to 6 1/2" h. (ILLUS. second row from bottom with canisters & spice jars) **450**

Canister, cov., stenciled Wildflower patt., "Tobacco," Brush-McCoy Pottery Co., 5 1/2 to 6 1/2" h., each **600**

Canister, cov., stenciled Wildflower patt., blank, Brush-McCoy Pottery Co., 2 gal. **425**

Canister, cov., stenciled Wildflower patt., blank, Brush-McCoy Pottery Co., 3 gal. **525**

Canister/cookie jar, cov., embossed Willow (Basketweave & Morning Glory) patt., "Put Your Fist In," Brush-McCoy Pottery Co., average 6 1/2 to 7" h., each. (ILLUS. top row, second from left w/other Willow canisters) **1,000**

Embossed GrapeWare Casserole

Casserole, cov., embossed GrapeWare patt., Brush-McCoy Pottery Co. (ILLUS. with extra cover)... **425**

Apple Blossom Chamber Pot

Chamber pot, cov., embossed Apple Blossom patt., Burley-Winter Pottery Co., 11" d., 6" h. (ILLUS.).. **375**

Chamber pot, cov., embossed Bow Tie patt. w/rose decal, Brush-McCoy Pottery Co., 11" d., 6" h. **225**

Chamber pot, cov., embossed Open Rose and Spearpoint Panels patt., A.E. Hull Pottery Co., 9 1/2" d., 6" h. **300**

Chamber pot, cov., embossed Willow (Basketweave & Morning Glory) patt., Brush-McCoy Pottery Co., 9 1/2" d., 8" h. (ILLUS. right, bottom of page)........................ **325**

Chamber pot, open, embossed Apple Blossom patt., Burley-Winter Pottery Co., 11" d., 6" h. **325**

Willow Chamber Pot & Slop Jar

Rare Peacock Coffeepot & Pitcher

Coffeepot, cov., embossed Peacock patt., Brush-McCoy Pottery Co., 6 1/2" d., overall 10 3/4" h. (ILLUS. right).................. **4,000**

Cold fudge crock, w/tin lid & ladle, marked "Johnson Cold Fudge Crock," various sizes known, 12" d., 13" h. **300**

Cooking or preserving kettle, cov., bail handle, embossed Peacock patt., Brush-McCoy Pottery Co., 5 qt.................................... **1,100**

Cup, embossed Paneled Fir Tree patt., Brush-McCoy Pottery Co., 3" d., 3 1/2" h....... **175**

Cuspidor, embossed Poinsettia and Basketweave patt., 9 3/4" d., 9" h. **180**

Cuspidor, embossed Willow (Basketweave & Morning Glory) patt., Brush-McCoy Pottery Co., 7 1/2" d., 5 1/2" h........................ **185**

Miniature Diffused Blue Cuspidor

Cuspidor, miniature, souvenir-type, Diffused Blue patt., 2" h. (ILLUS.) **325**

Custard cup, embossed Fishscale patt., A.E. Hull Pottery Co., 2 1/2" d., 5" h.............. **125**

Stenciled Dutch Boy Creamer

Creamer, ovoid form, stenciled Dutch Boy patt., 4 1/4" h. **225**

Blue & White Ewer & Pitcher

Ewer, embossed Apple Blossom patt., large, Burley-Winter Pottery Co., 12" h.

(ILLUS. right with embossed Feathers & Plume pitcher).. **450**

Decorated Bow Tie Ewer & Basin Set

Small-mouthed Apple Blossom Ewer

Ewer, embossed Apple Blossom patt., small
    mouth, Burley-Winter Pottery Co., 8" h.
    (ILLUS.).. 395
Ewer, embossed Bow Tie (Our Lucile) patt.,
    w/rose decal, Brush-McCoy Pottery Co.,
    11" h.. 175
Ewer, Floral Decal (Memphis patt.), West-
    ern Stoneware Co., small, 7" h...................... 175
Ewer & basin set, embossed Apple Blossom
    patt., Burley-Winter Pottery Co., pr.............. 700
Ewer & basin set, embossed Bow Tie patt.
    w/Flying Birdbird decal, Brush-McCoy
    Pottery Co., basin 15" d., ewer 11" h., pr.
    (ILLUS., top of page)...................................... 625

Bow Tie Ewer from Set

Ewer & basin set, embossed Bow Tie patt.
    w/stenciled   Wildflower   decoration,
    Brush-McCoy Pottery Co., basin 15" d.,
    ewer 11" h., pr. (ILLUS. of ewer only)............ 625
Ewer & basin set, Floral Decal (Memphis
    patt.), Western Stoneware Co., basin
    15" d., ewer 11 1/4" h., pr. 365
Foot warmer, signed by Logan Pottery Co. 250
Grease jar, cov., embossed Flying Bird
    patt., A. E. Hull Pottery Co., 4" h. (ILLUS.
    left with berry bowl) 1,100
Grease jar, embossed Flying Bird patt., A.E.
    Hull Pottery Co., 4" h. 1,100
Iced tea cooler, cov., plain barrel shape,
    printed "3 - Iced Tea Cooler," 3 gal.,
    11" d., 13" h... 310
Jardiniere & pedestal, embossed Cosmos
    patt., green & cream spongeware, possi-
    bly Weller or Burley-Winter Pottery Co.,
    jardiniere 6" h., pedestal 5 1/2" h. 2,500

Cosmos Jardiniere & Pedestal

Jardiniere & pedestal, embossed Cosmos
    patt., possibly Weller or Burley-Winter
    Pottery Co., jardiniere 6" h., pedestal
    5 1/2" h. (ILLUS.)... 2,000
Match holder, model of a duck, 5 1/2" d.,
    5" h.. 250

Lovebird Pattern Milk Crock

Figural Rooster Match Holder

Match holder, model of a rooster (ILLUS.) **435**
Meat tenderizer, stenciled Wildflower patt.,
  Brush-McCoy Pottery Co., 3 1/2" d. at
  face **370**
Milk crock, embossed Apricot patt., A.E.
  Hull Pottery Co., 10" d., 5" h. **225**
Milk crock, embossed Lovebird patt., w/bail
  handle, A. E. Hull Pottery Co., 9" d.,
  5 1/2" h. (ILLUS., top of page) **500**

Mug, embossed Apple Blossom patt., Burley-Winter Pottery Co., 5" h. (ILLUS.) **700**

Embossed Cattail Advertising Mug

Mug, embossed Cattail patt., w/advertising,
  Western Stoneware Co., 3" d., 4" h.
  (ILLUS.).. **275**
Mug, embossed Cattail patt., Western
  Stoneware Co., 3" d., 4" h. **130**

Rare Apple Blossom Mug

Columns & Arches Mug & Pitcher

Mug, embossed Columns and Arches patt.,
extremely rare, Brush-McCoy Pottery
Co., 4 1/2" h. (ILLUS. left) .... **650+**

Embossed Rose & Fishscale Mug

Mug, embossed Rose & Fishscale patt., A.
E. Hull Pottery Co., 5" h. (ILLUS.) **750**
Mug, stenciled Cattail patt., Western Stone-
ware Co., 3" d., 4" h. **130**
Mustard jar, cov., Diffused Blue, stenciled
"Mustard," 3" d., 4" h. **200**

Bluebird Decal Hallboy Pitcher

Pitcher, 9" h., 7" d., Bluebird decal, hall boy-
style, Brush-McCoy Pottery Co. (ILLUS.) **425**
Pitcher, 7" h., 3 1/2" d., Diffused Blue
w/rose decal, A.E. Hull Pottery Co. **125**
Pitcher, Diffused Blue, plain smooth shape,
found in 1/4, 1/2, 5/8 & 1 gallon size,
smallest is rarest, depending on the
size **150-225**

Embossed Loop Pie Baker

Pie baker, embossed Loop patt., light blue,
unglazed rim & under collar, 8" d.
(ILLUS.) **40**

Avenue of Trees Pitcher

Pitcher, 8" h., embossed Avenue of Trees
patt. (ILLUS.) **325**

Pitcher, embossed Bands and Rivets patt.,
1 gal. **275**

Pitcher, embossed Bands and Rivets patt.,
1 pt. **285**

Pitcher, embossed Bands and Rivets
patt., 1/2 gal. **285**

Pitcher, embossed Bands and Rivets
patt., 1/4 gal. **285**

Pitcher, embossed Bands and Rivets
patt., 5/8 gal. **225**

Beaded Swirl Pattern Pitcher

Pitcher, 6 1/2" h., embossed Beaded Swirl
patt., A. E. Hull Pottery Co. (ILLUS.) **950**

Small Embossed Butterfly Pitcher

Pitcher, 4 3/4" h., embossed Butterfly patt.,
Nelson McCoy Sanitary Stoneware Co.
(ILLUS.) **600**

Embossed Cattails Pitcher

Pitcher, 5 3/4" h., embossed Cattails patt.
(ILLUS.) **400**

Embossed Cherry Band Pitcher

Pitcher, 9 1/2" h., embossed Cherry Band
patt., Red Wing Pottery Co., 8 pt., available in numerous sizes, the smallest being the most valuable, often seen w/print-
ed advertising, which adds $300
minimum to the value, without advertis-
ing (ILLUS.) **225-400**

Cherry Cluster & Grape Pattern Pitchers

Pitcher, 10" h., 8 1/2" d., embossed Cherry Cluster with Basketweave patt., A.E. Hull Pottery Co. (ILLUS. bottom row, left, on previous page) 325

Pitcher, 9" h., embossed Columns and Arches patt., Brush-McCoy Pottery Co. (ILLUS. right with mug) 600

Large Sized Cow Pitcher

Pitcher, embossed Cow patt., A.E. Hull Pottery Co., five sizes, rarest 5 3/4" h. to 9" h. (ILLUS. of 9" size) 250-600

Pitcher, 7 1/2" h., 6 1/4" d., embossed Dainty Fruit patt., A.E. Hull Pottery Co. 550

Embossed Dandy Pitcher

Pitcher, 7" h., embossed Dandy patt., Brush-McCoy Pottery Co. (ILLUS.) 425

Pitcher, 8" h., embossed Feathers & Plume patt. (ILLUS. left with Apple Blossom ewer) 650

Rare Embossed Grape Pitcher

Pitcher, 7 1/2" h., embossed Grape patt., Burley-Winter Pottery Co. (ILLUS.) 1,000

Pitcher, embossed Grape Cluster on Trellis patt., four sizes, 5" to 9 1/2" h., depending on size, each 165-245

Pitcher, 7" h., embossed Grape Cluster on Trellis patt., squat body w/cover, Uhl Pottery Co. 350

Pitcher, 7" h., embossed Grape Cluster on Trellis patt., squat body w/no cover, Uhl Pottery Co. (ILLUS. top center with Cherry Cluster pitcher) 200

Pitcher, embossed Grape with Rickrack patt., three sizes, smallest the most valuable, each (ILLUS. of smallest & largest, front center & right with the Cherry Cluster pitcher) 195-325

Pitcher, embossed Lincoln Head patt., Uhl Pottery Co., several sizes, depending on size 900

Graduated Lincoln Head with Log Cabin Pitchers

Pitcher, embossed Lincoln Head with Log Cabin patt., Uhl Pottery Co., five sizes, one gallon size largest & most valuable, depending on size (ILLUS.) 575-1,500

Old Fashioned Garden Rose Pitcher

Pitcher, 7" h., 7" d., embossed Old Fashioned Garden Rose patt., Burley-Winter Pottery Co. (ILLUS.)...................................... **500**
Pitcher, 8 1/2" h., embossed Peacock patt., Brush-McCoy Pottery Co. (ILLUS. left with coffeepot)... **1,250**

Rare Remember Pitcher

Pitcher, embossed Remember patt., molded figure of Columbia standing beside an American shield, "Remember" on the interior rim (ILLUS.)... **1,500**

Scroll & Leaf Advertising Pitcher

Pitcher, 7" h., embossed Scroll & Leaf patt., printed Iowa advertising (ILLUS.) **750**

Embossed Scroll Pitcher

Pitcher, 8" h., embossed Scroll patt., Logan Pottery Co. (ILLUS.)....................................... **650**

Embossed Strutting Stag Pitcher

Pitcher, 8 1/2" h., 6" d., embossed Strutting Stag patt., possibly Brush-McCoy Pottery Co. (ILLUS.) **525**
Pitcher, 8 1/2" h., 6" d., embossed Swan patt., Burley-Winter Pottery Co. **450**
Pitcher, 9" h., embossed Windmill and Bush patt., J.W. McCoy Pottery Co. & Brush-McCoy Pottery Co. .... **400+**
Pitcher, 7" h., embossed Windmill & Bush patt., J.W. McCoy Pottery Co. & Brush-McCoy Pottery Co. **250**
Pitcher, 8 1/2" h., Flying Bluebird decal, J.W. McCoy Pottery Co. **250**

Three Stenciled Blue & White Pitchers

Pitcher, 8" h., stenciled Acorn patt., Brush-McCoy Pottery Co. (ILLUS. center) **300**

Pitcher, 8 1/2" h., stenciled Dutch Scene (Dutch Landscape) patt. w/two Dutch children **275**

Stenciled Bow Tie Pitcher

Pitcher, 7 3/4" h., stenciled Bow Tie patt., possibly A.E. Hull Pottery Co. (ILLUS.) **175**

Pitcher, 5 3/4" h., stenciled Cattail patt. , Brush-McCoy Pottery Co. (ILLUS. left with Acorn pitcher) **250**

Pitcher, 5" h., stenciled Conifer Tree patt., Brush-McCoy Pottery Co. (ILLUS. right with Acorn pitcher) **250**

Stylized Floral Pattern Pitcher

Pitcher, 8 3/4" h., stenciled Stylized Floral patt., A.E. Hull Pottery Co. (ILLUS.) **225**

Pitcher, 6 3/4" h., stenciled Wildflower patt., hall boy-type w/cylindrical body & one stencil per side, Brush-McCoy Pottery Co. **375**

Two Wildflower Hall Boy Pitchers

Pitcher, 6" h., stenciled Wildflower patt., hall boy-type w/waisted body & five stencils

per side, Brush-McCoy Pottery Co. (ILLUS. right) **750**

Small Wildflower Rolling Pin

Pitcher, 6 3/4" h., stenciled Wildflower patt., hall boy-type w/cylindrical body & five stencils per side, Brush-McCoy Pottery Co. (ILLUS. left) **550**

Pitcher, 7 1/2" h., 4" d., stenciled Wildflower patt., hall boy-type, Brush-McCoy Pottery Co. **275**

Pitcher, 9" h., 4" d., Swirl patt., Diffused Blue swirled bands up around sides **275**

Ramekin or nappy, embossed Peacock patt., Brush-McCoy Pottery Co., 4" d. **300**

Refrigerator jar, cov., Diffused Blue, stenciled "Refrigerator Jar," 3 lb., 7" d., 6 1/2" h. **325**

Stenciled Wildflower Roaster

Roaster, cov., stenciled Wildflower patt., Brush-McCoy Pottery Co., 12" d., 8 1/2" h. (ILLUS.) **450**

Rolling pin, stenciled Wildflower patt., Brush-McCoy Pottery Co., small, 8" l. (ILLUS., top of page) **300**

Rolling pin, stenciled Wildflower patt., w/advertising, large baker's type, Brush-Mc-Coy Pottery Co., stoneware roller 14 1/2" l. **3,000**

Salt box, cov., Blue Band patt., 5" d., 6" h. **130**

Advertising Hanging Salt Box

Salt box, cov., Diffused Blue patt., Western Stoneware advertising-type, "You Need Salt, We Need You - The Hodgin Store, Whittier, Iowa," 4 1/4" h. (ILLUS.) **600**

Salt box, cov., embossed Apple Blossom patt., Burley-Winter Pottery Co., 6" d., 4" h. **400**

Salt box, cov., embossed Basketweave & Grapes, patt., sponged blue decoration, 6" d., 4" h. **375**

Salt box, cov., embossed Daisy patt., 6" d., 6 1/2" h. **250**

Salt box, cov., embossed Good Luck Sign (Swastika) patt., Nelson McCoy Sanitary Stoneware Co., Robinson-Ransbottom Pottery Co. & The Crooksville Pottery Co., 6" d., 4" h. **250**

Salt box, cov., embossed Grape & Waffle patt. **350**

Salt box, cov., embossed Raspberry patt., Brush-McCoy Pottery Co., 5 1/2" d., 5 1/2" h. **250**

Salt box, cov., embossed Waffle patt. **220**

Salt box, cov., hanging-type, embossed Peacock patt., Brush-McCoy Pottery Co., 5" d., 5" h. (ILLUS. left with butter crock) **425**

Salt box, cov., plain **100**

Wildflower Salt with Compass Decor

Salt box, cov., stenciled Wildflower patt., hinged wooden cover, compass design around "Salt" on front, J.W. McCoy Pottery Co., 6" d., 4 1/2" h. (ILLUS. with no cover) **300**

Sand jar, embossed Polar Bear patt., Uhl Pottery Co., 11" d., 13 1/2" h. **750**

Sand jar, embossed Polar Bear patt., Uhl Pottery Co., 12 1/4" d., 14 1/2" h. **1,250**

Shaving mug, scuttle-form, 4" d., 6" h. **1,250**

Cat Head & Lion Head Soap Dishes

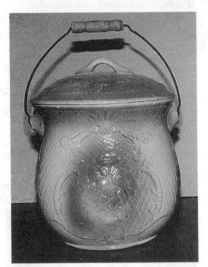

Embossed Apple Blossom Slop Jar

Slop jar, cov., embossed Willow (Basketweave & Morning Glory) patt., Brush-McCoy Pottery Co., 9 1/2" d., 12 1/2" h. (ILLUS. left with chamber pot) 350

Soap dish, embossed Cat Head patt., small round style, 3 3/4" d. (ILLUS. right, top of page) 155

Soap dish, embossed Lion Head patt., small round style, 3 3/4" d. (ILLUS. left) 155

Soap dish, stenciled Wildflower patt., slab-type, Brush-McCoy Pottery Co., 3 5/8 x 5 1/4", 3/4" thick.............................. 275

Wildflower/Arches & Columns Soap

Soap dish, cover & drainer, stenciled Wildflower patt. on embossed Arches & Columns shape, Brush-McCoy Pottery Co., 5 1/4" d., 2" h. (ILLUS.).................................... 600

Slop jar, cov., embossed Apple Blossom patt., Burley-Winter Pottery Co., 10" h. (ILLUS.)... 350

Slop jar, cov., embossed Rose & Fishscale patt., A.E. Hull Pottery Co., 10" h.................. 325

Willow Pattern Spice Jars

Spice jar, cov., embossed Willow (Basketweave & Morning Glory) patt., "Cinnamon," "Nutmeg," "Allspice," "Ginger,"

"Cloves" & "Pepper," each (ILLUS. of group)... 250-300

Near Wildflower "Pepper" Spice Jar

Spice jar, cov., stenciled Near Wildflower patt., uncommon design, found in "Allspice," "Pepper," "Cinnamon," "Nutmeg," "Ginger" & "Cloves," possibly by Brush-McCoy or A.E. Hull Pottery Co., 3 3/4" h., each (ILLUS. of Pepper).................................. 500
Spice jar, cov., stenciled Near Wildflower patt., uncommon design, "Nutmegs" (plural) & "Mustard," possibly by Brush-McCoy or A.E. Hull Pottery Co., 3 3/4" h., each 700

Stenciled Plume "Nutmeg" Jar

Spice jar, cov., stenciled Plume patt., "Nutmeg," A.E. Hull Pottery Co., 4 1/4" h. (ILLUS.)... 150
Spice jar, cov., stenciled Wildflower patt., "Allspice," "Pepper," "Cinnamon," "Nutmeg," "Cloves" & "Ginger," Brush-McCoy Pottery Co., 3 1/4" h., each (ILLUS. third row from bottom with canisters & spice jars)... 250
Spice jar, cov., stenciled Wildflower patt., "Allspice," "Pepper," "Cinnamon," "Nutmeg," "Cloves" & "Ginger," Brush-McCoy Pottery Co., very rare size, 2 3/4" h., each (ILLUS. third row from bottom with canisters & spice jars).................................... 400
Spice jar, cov., stenciled Wildflower patt., "Nutmegs" (plural) & "Mustard," extremely rare, Brush-McCoy Pottery Co.,

3 1/4" h., each (ILLUS. third row from bottom with canisters & spice jars)................ 500
Spice jar, cov., stenciled Wildflower patt., "Nutmegs" (plural) & "Mustard," extremely rare & rare small size, Brush-McCoy Pottery Co., 2 3/4" h., each (ILLUS. third row from bottom with canisters & spice jars).. 800

Windy City Pattern Stein

Stein, embossed Windy City patt., 5 1/2" h. (ILLUS.) 165
Stewer, cov., embossed Willow (Basketweave & Morning Glory) patt., Brush-McCoy Pottery Co., 2 qt. 325
Stewer, cov., embossed Willow (Basketweave & Morning Glory) patt., Brush-McCoy Pottery Co., 4 qt. 275
Stewer, cov., stenciled Wildflower patt., Brush-McCoy Pottery Co., 4 qt. 285
Tumbler, stenciled Wildflower patt., tapering cylindrical form, no printed designs inside, 5" h.. 300

Stenciled Wildflower Tumbler

Tumbler, stenciled Wildflower patt., tapering cylindrical form, printed designs inside, 5" h. (ILLUS.).. 350
Umbrella stand, embossed Two Stags patt., solid blue, Logan Pottery Co., 21" h.......... 1,500

Two Daffodil Vases

Vase, 8" h., embossed Daffodil patt., incised
on the bottom "WPC" (ILLUS. left)................. **200**
Vase, 12" h., embossed Daffodil patt., in-
cised on the bottom "WPC" (ILLUS. right)..... **275**

Diffused Blue Ovoid Vase

Vase, Diffused Blue, wide ovoid body
w/short flared neck & pointed shoulder
handles (ILLUS.)... **300+**

Apple Blossom Water Cooler

Water cooler, cov., embossed Apple Blos-
som patt., w/spigot, 13" h. (ILLUS.)............ **1,000**
Water cooler, cov., embossed Cupid patt.,
w/spigot, Western Stoneware, 5 gal.............. **725**
Water cooler, cov., embossed Polar Bear
patt., w/ spigot, Uhl Pottery Co., 10 gal. **1,250**
Water cooler, cov., embossed Polar Bear
patt., w/ spigot, Uhl Pottery Co., 2 gal. **600**
Water cooler, cov., embossed Polar Bear
patt., w/ spigot, Uhl Pottery Co., 4 gal. **725**

Flying Bird Water Set

Water set: pitcher & six mugs; embossed
Flying Bird patt., A.E. Hull Pottery Co.,   the set (ILLUS.)... **2,400**

Blue Ridge Dinnerwares

The small town of Erwin, Tennessee, was the home of the Southern Potteries, Inc., originally founded by E.J. Owen in 1917 and first called the Clinchfield Pottery.

In the early 1920s Charles W. Foreman purchased the plant and revolutionized the company's output, developing the popular line of handpainted wares sold as "Blue Ridge" dinnerwares. Freehand painted by women from the surrounding hills, these colorful dishes in many patterns continued in production until the plant's closing in 1957.

Blue Ridge Dinnerwares Mark

Ashtray, individual, Tralee Rose patt.................. $18
Bonbon, shell-shaped, flat, Nove Rose patt. 75

Shell-shaped Blue Ridge Bowl

Bowl, 9" d., deep shell shape, in shades of
   blues & pinks (ILLUS.)...................................... 75
Bowl, berry, Bountiful patt., large 20
Butter pat/coaster, Lyonnaise patt., 4" d.............. 48

Pomona Pattern Cake Lifter

Cake lifter, Pomona patt., 9" l. (ILLUS.)............... 32
Cake tray, maple leaf shape, French Peas-
   ant patt. 145
Cake tray, maple leaf shape, Rose of
   Sharon patt., 10 1/4" l 95
Cake tray, maple leaf shape, Verna patt............. 85
Candy box, cov., Rose Marie patt. 195

Fruit Fantasy Pattern Celery

Celery, leaf-shaped, Fruit Fantasy patt.,
   10 1/2" l. (ILLUS.).. 75
Character jug, American Indian........................... 725
Cigarette box, cov., French Peasant patt. 159
Coffeepot, cov., ovoid, various floral pat-
   terns, 10 1/2" h., each...................................... 150

Cock o' the Walk Creamer

Creamer, Candlewick shape, Cock o' the
   Walk patt., 7" l. (ILLUS.).................................... 35
Creamer, Mardi Gras patt. 15

Garden Lane Creamer & Sugar

Creamer & cov. sugar bowl, Colonial shape,
   Garden Lane patt., the set (ILLUS.)................ 55
Creamer & cov. sugar bowl, Ridge Daisy
   patt., pr.. 45
Cup, Crab Apple patt. 9
Cup, Square Dance patt... 79
Cup & saucer, demitasse, china, Rose
   Marie patt.. 85

French Peasant Pattern Gravy Boat

Gravy boat, Colonial shape, French Peasant patt., 7 1/4" l. (ILLUS.) 65
Mug, child's, Chanticleer patt. 165
Pie plate, Cassandra patt., wine-colored border 35
Pie plate & server, Cross Stitch patt., 2 pcs. 75
Pie server, blue & white lattice design 30
Pitcher, 5" h., china, Annett's Wild Rose patt., Antique shape 85
Pitcher, 6 1/4" h., earthenware, Fairmede Fruits patt., Alice shape (small smear on red line trim) 135
Pitcher, 7" h., Sculptured Fruit patt., ... 85
Pitcher, china, decorated w/grapes, Helen shape 95
Pitcher, Milady patt. 195
Plate, 6" d., Bluebell Bouquet patt. 8
Plate, 6" sq., "Milkmaid," Provincial Farm Scene, Candlewick shape 65
Plate, dinner, Chanticleer patt. 38
Relish dish, deep shell-shaped, French Peasant patt. 150
Salt & pepper shakers, Dogtooth Violet patt., pr. 75
Salt & pepper shakers, figural Mallard hen & drake, pr. 450

Blue Ridge Salt & Pepper Shakers

Salt & pepper shakers, tall, footed, various floral decorations, 5 1/2" h. pr. (ILLUS.) 89
Sugar bowl, cov., Nocturne patt. 22

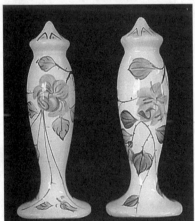

Adoration Pattern Teapot

Teapot, cov., Ball shape, Adoration patt., 6 3/4" h. (ILLUS.) 135
Teapot, cov., Ball shape, Bluebelle Bouquet patt. 225

Cherry Pattern Teapot

Teapot, cov., Colonial shape, Cherry patt., 8 3/4" h. (ILLUS.) 150
Tray, Trellis shape, Daffodil patt. 150

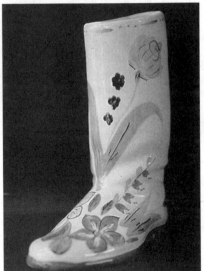

Vase in a Boot Shape

Vase, 8" h., boot shape, various floral decorations (ILLUS.) 89
Vase, 5 1/2" h., china, Hampton patt., Hibiscus shape 100
Vase, 9 1/4" h., ruffle-top style, Delphine patt. 115
Vegetable bowl, cov., Mardi Gras patt. 100
Vegetable bowl, open, round, Ridge Daisy patt. 29

Boch Freres

The Belgian firm, founded in 1841 and still in production, first produced stoneware art pottery of mediocre quality, attempting to upgrade their wares through the years. In 1907, Charles Catteau became the art director of the pottery, and slowly the influence of his work was absorbed by the artisans surrounding him. All through the 1920s wares were decorated in distinctive Art Deco designs and are now eagerly sought along with the hand-thrown gourd-form vessels coated with earthtone glazes that were produced during the same time. Almost all Boch Freres pottery is marked, but the finest wares also carry the signature of Charles Catteau in addition to the pottery mark.

Boch Freres Mark

Box, cov., low rectangular form w/rounded corners, decorated w/crossed bands of stylized flowers in turquoise, sapphire blue, yellow & black on a crackled ivory ground, brass hinge & border, base w/circular stamp "Boch F La Louvière," brass stamped "France," ca. 1920s, 4 x 5 1/2", 1 1/2" h. **$288**

Boch Freres Charger & Vases

Charger, large round form w/flanged rim, decorated in the center w/a large grazing antelope, the border band w/round geometric devices, in sapphire blue, turquoise green & black on a crackled ivory ground, marked "D943 - Ch. Catteau - 22p C K," ca. 1920s, 14 1/2" d. (ILLUS. center) **1,150**

Inkstand, stoneware, white w/h.p. blue floral sprigs & bands, rectangular dished base w/rounded corners & serpentine sides centering a rectangular upright block fitted in the top w/an open inkwell & covered sander, 19th c., 8 3/4" l. **110**

Boch Freres Pottery Lamp Base

Lamp base, bulbous ovoid body tapering to a short flared neck w/lamp fittings, inscribed w/stylized vines & fruits descending from the shoulder in shades of yellow, brown & blue against an oatmeal ground, glossy glaze, marked "Keramis - Made in Belgium," ca. 1928, crazing, 24 1/4" h. (ILLUS.)... **316**

Vase, 7" h., bulbous ovoid body tapering sharply to a small neck, decorated w/a repeating floral design of yellow blossoms, bluish green leaves & burgundy berries on branches, on a sapphire blue ground, separated by bands of blue, green, orange & black, circular stamp mark "Boch F La Louvière," ca. 1920s (crazing) **920**

Vase, 8 1/2" h., ovoid body tapering to a tall slender & slightly tapering neck, decorated w/three stylized flowers & leaves in a basket w/double swag, repeated in three sections, divided by border of multiple ovals, in yellow, orange, sapphire blue & light blue on an ivory crackled ground, circular mark "Boch F La Louvière," Belgium, ca. 1920s... **403**

Two Boch Freres Vases

Vase, 8 3/4" h., footed ovoid body w/the swelled shoulder tapering to a wide, short flared neck, decorated overall w/large stylized yellow blossoms & leafy vines in yellow, turquoise, sapphire blue, orange & pale green w/blue borders on a crackled ivory ground, partial stamp "Keramis - Made in Belgium - 31," ca. 1920s (ILLUS. right)... **690**

Vase, 8 3/4" h., low footring supporting a wide bulbous cylindrical body w/a wide rounded shoulder centering a thick molded rim band, decorated w/a wide center band featuring a continuous row of large upright stylized penguin-like birds in black against a yellow ground, black borders at the base & top, signed & stamped "Ch. Catteau - Keramis - Made in Belgium - Grès Keramis - 1059 C," ca. 1928-29 .... **6,600**

Vase, 9" h., wide ovoid body w/a wide rounded shoulder centering a short cylindrical neck, decorated w/a continuous band of large grazing antelope in sapphire blue, turquoise, bluish green & black on a crackled ivory ground, marked "Boch F La Louvière - D943 - 13 - 1291," ca. 1925 (ILLUS. left with flower-decorated vase)... **1,265**

Vase, 9 1/4" h., very wide bulbous ovoid body tapering to a short cylindrical neck, decorated w/symmetrical stylized floral reserve in sapphire blue, bluish green & orange on a crackled white ground, stamped "Keramis - Made in Belgium - D60 - R V Larouche Belge - 1293," ca. 1920s **805**

Vase, 9 1/2" h., bulbous ovoid body tapering to a tiny cylindrical neck, decorated w/a white central band painted w/large stylized black bears against a white band w/narrower brown upper & lower bands trimmed w/black banding & zigzag lines, signed & stamped "Ch. Catteau - D. 1487 - Keramis - Made in Belgium - Grès Keramis - 996 C" **5,100**

Vase, 10 1/2" h., flat-bottomed wide ovoid body w/a small cupped neck, decorated w/large brown & black flying bats against a greenish grey sky w/dark grey clouds, design 1378, signed & impressed "D. 1378 - Ch. Catteau - Keramis - Made in Belgium - Grès Keramis - 1053 C.," ca. 1929 (drilled)................................. **3,840**

Boch Freres Vase with Sunbursts

Vase, 10 1/2" h., simple ovoid body tapering to a flat molded mouth, decorated w/four large repeating stylized swirled sunburst flowers in sections separated by a wavy line w/alternating oval dots, in turquoise, yellow & sapphire blue on an ivory crackled ground, turquoise border bands, stamped & signed "Boch F La Louvière - D889 - CT - K 899," ca. 1920s (ILLUS.) **575**

Vase, 10 1/2" h., simple ovoid form w/a footring & rim ring, decorated w/wide color vertical bands of stylized tulips & flowers w/leaves in yellow, sapphire blue, green & brown on an ivory crackled ground, sapphire blue bands, marked "Keramis - Made in Belgium - D2779 - 9 - 899," ca. 1920s **690**

Vase, 11" h., simple ovoid form tapering to a small flat mouth, decorated around the sides w/large black flamingos running the full length of the sides against a mottled yellowish green ground, signed & stamped "C. Catteau - D. 979 - Keramis - Made in Belgium - Grès Keramis - 987," ca. 1925 .... **9,000**

Vase, 11 1/8" h., ovoid body tapering slightly to a wide short neck w/molded rim, the upper portion decorated w/a wide band featuring large stylized oblong black & white birdlike creatures against a mottled dark grey ground, a wide lower band w/a lattice design in light brown & black, a narrow crosshatch band around the rim, signed & stamped "Ch. Catteau - D. 1025 - Keramis - Made in Belgium - 967 - Grès Keramis," ca. 1925 .... **10,200**

Vase, 12" h., large wide ovoid body tapering gently to a wide, short cylindrical neck, decorated w/stylized flowers & leaves in pinks, sapphire blue, yellow, brown & grey on a pale yellow ground, bordered w/a ring of small blossoms & leaves & sapphire blue bands, marked "Keramis - Made in Belgium - 2243 - 909," ca. 1920s (crazing) **805**

Vase, 12 1/8" h., wide ovoid body tapering to a short rolled neck, decorated w/a wide central band featuring a continuous design of large stylized black & white owls against a tan ground, white dash & solid thin bands above & below the center band, black bands around the top & base, signed & stamped "Ch. Catteau - D. 1060 - Keramis - Made in Belgium - Grès Keramis - 914 C," ca. 1925 .... **5,760**

Catteau-designed Boch Freres Vase

Vase, 12 1/4" h., ovoid body tapering slightly to a short, flaring molded neck, decorated w/a wide center band w/a continuous row of large white stylized birdlike creatures against a black ground w/thin brown lines, white upper & lower bands w/thin brown scalloped designs, signed & stamped "Ch. Catteau - D 1026 - Boch Frs. - La Louvière - Made in Belgium - Fabrication Belgique - Grès Keramis - 911 C," ca. 1925 (ILLUS.) **6,600**

Vase, 12 1/2" h., stoneware, tall simple ovoid form w/a thick short rolled neck, a wide central band decorated in black & cream w/a row of large stylized birds, the upper & lower bands in black w/cream fishscale designs, designed by Charles Catteau, signed "Ch. Catteau - D. 1026A" & incised "Gres Keramis" w/wolf mark & "Keramis - Made in Belgium," original retailer's sticker, ca. 1925 .... **3,300**

w/overall geometric ring designs in matching colors, designed by Charles Catteau, signed "Ch. Catteau - D. 943," stamped "Keramis - Made in Belgium - 24," inscribed "762" **3,300**

Vase, 19 1/4" h., large ovoid form w/a heavy rolled rim, the body painted w/large stylized exotic birds among large rounded blossoms & leafy branches w/berries in greenish yellow on a dark brown ground w/black base & rim bands, designed by Jules-Ernest Chaput, signed, ca. 1930.... **12,000**

Large Boch Freres Floral Vase

Vase, 19 1/2" h., large, tall ovoid form tapering to a tiny neck w/deeply rolled rim, wide vertical bands of stylized creamy white blossom clusters & green scrolls alternating w/narrow creamy white zigzag stripes, stamped & signed "Ch. Catteau - D. 1003 - Boch Frs. - La Louvière - Made in Belgium - Fabrication Belgique - Grès Keramis - 961 - V.," ca. 1925 (ILLUS.) **6,000**

Vases, 11 1/2" h., ovoid body tapering to a short cylindrical neck w/molded rim, decorated w/two large stylized standing birds w/extended wings among leafy vines, in sapphire blue, blue, bluish green & pale green on an ivory crackled ground, striped border bands, stamped "Keramis - Made in Belgium - D4507," ca. 1920s, pr. (ILLUS. left & right with charger)............... **920**

Boch Freres Antelope Vase

Vase, 13 1/2" h., wide ovoid body tapering to a wide cupped neck, decorated w/a wide central band of stylized antelope in dark blue & black grazing on blue & green grass at the bottom & w/leaves & geometric designs around the top, against a crackle-glazed white ground, signed & stamped "Ch. Catteau - Boch Frs. - La Louvière - Made in Belgium - Fabrication Belgique - 911," ca. 1924 (ILLUS.)... **6,000**

Vase, 16" h., tall baluster form w/a cylindrical short neck, decorated w/a wide band of gazelle in dark blue, purple & black among stylized foliage against a creamy white ground, the neck & lower body

Brayton Laguna Pottery

Durlin Brayton was ahead of other California upstart companies of the 1940s when he began Brayton Laguna Pottery in Laguna Beach, California, in 1927. Collectors need to familiarize themselves with the various lines created by Brayton during its more than forty years in business. Hand-turned pieces were the first to be made, but there were many other lines: Children, the mark usually including the name of the child; White Crackle; White Crackle with a small amount of brown stain; Brown Stain with some White Crackle, which is not as popular among today's collectors as is the overall White Crackle or the White Crackle with some brown stain; Calasia, an Art Deco line, mostly vases and planters; Gay Nineties; Circus; Provincial, which was a brown stain with gloss glazes in an assortment of colors; African-American; Animals; Walt Disney sanctioned items, which are much sought after and treasured; Webton Ware, popular today as it represents a country theme; and others.

Just as Brayton had numerous lines, the company also had various marks, no less than a dozen. Stickers were also used, sometimes in combination with a mark. Designers incised their initials on some regular sized items, and many times their initials were the only mark on a piece that was too small for Brayton's other marks.

Foreign imports were instrumental in the failure of many U.S. companies, and Brayton was no exception. Production ceased in 1968.

Circus Series Clowns Book Ends

Book ends, Circus Series, clowns sitting w/legs outstretched, white clothes w/green & red ruffles at sleeve & leg cuffs & collar, red hats, 1940s walk-a-dog & pots stamp mark "Brayton," 6" h. (ILLUS.).. **$315**

Bowl, 10" d., 2" h., Calasia line, feather design in bottom, scalloped rim w/raised circles on inner rim, pale green **75**

Bust of woman, White Crackle glaze, 12" h. **525**

Candleholder, figural, three choirboys **165**

Candleholders, figural Blackamoor, pr. **250**

Cigarette box, cov., black flecked glossy red, stamp mark "Brayton Calif. U.S.A.," 3 1/4 x 5", 2" h. **45**

Cookie jar, cov., light brown matte body w/overall honeycomb texture, dark brown straight tree branches w/five partridges around body in pale blue, yellow & orange, glossy white interior, pale blue lid, Model No. V-12, Mark 2, 7 1/4" h. (ILLUS., to the right).. **250**

Honeycomb Texture Cookie Jar

Garden Motif Creamer & Sugar

Cookie jar, figural Mammy, burgundy base & turquoise bandanna, rare early version.. **1,425**

Cookie jar, figural Provincial Lady, textured woodtone stain w/high-gloss white apron & scarf tied around head, red, green & yellow flowers & hearts motif on clothing, being reproduced so must be marked, "Brayton Laguna Calif. K-27," 13" h............... **525**

Cookie jar, figure of Swedish Maid (Christina), produced 1941, incised mark, 11" h...... **600**

Creamer, figural cat... **65**

Creamer & sugar, in the form of a sprinkler can & wheelbarrow, w/floral design in pale pinks & blues on white ground, stamp mark "1948," 3" h., pr. (ILLUS., top of page) **75**

Creamer & sugar, individual, eggplant, unglazed bottom, created by Durlin Brayton, incised mark "Brayton Laguna Pottery," pr. **225**

Provincial Line Cup with Tea Bag Holder

Cup w/tea bag holder, Provincial line, brown bisque stain w/white & yellow flowers & green leaves outside, gloss yellow inside, marked "Brayton Laguna Calif. K-31," 1 3/4" h. (ILLUS.) **24**

Figure, African-American baby w/diaper, seated, green eyes, 3 3/4" h. **145**

Figure, baby on all fours **95**

Figure, baby sitting up.. **95**

Figure, Blackamoor, kneeling & holding open cornucopia, heavily jeweled w/gold trim, 10" h.. **250**

Figure, Blackamoor, kneeling, jeweled trim, 15" h.. **315**

Figure, Blackamoor, walking & carrying a bowl in his hands, glossy gold earrings,

white bowl & shoes, burgundy scarf, shirt & pantaloons, 8 1/4" h. **225**

Figure, boy, Alice in Wonderland, not Walt Disney, marked "R," designer Frances Robinson, 3 3/4" h... **300**

Figure, boy wearing swimming trunks, Hillbilly Shotgun Wedding series, marked, produced 1938, designed by Andy Anderson, 4 1/4" h. **200**

Children's Series "Ann" Figure

Figure, Children's Series, "Ann," girl seated w/legs apart, knees bent, 4" h. (ILLUS.)........ **135**

Figure, Children's Series, "Ellen," girl standing w/pigtails & a hat tied at neck, arms bent & palms forward, one leg slightly twisted, 7 1/4" h. **110**

Figure, Children's Series, "John," boy w/horn.. **125**

Figure, Children's Series, "Jon," boy standing & carrying a basket in one hand, rooster in other, 8 1/4" h................................. **115**

Figure, peasant woman w/basket at her side in front & basket at her left in back, blue dress, yellow vest, incised mark "Brayton Laguna Pottery," 7 1/2" h. **115**

Figure, sailor boy holding a gun **325**

Figure, woman w/two wolfhounds, one on each side, woman w/red hair & wearing a long yellow dress, 9 1/2" h. **145**

Figure, woman wearing a blue dress & bonnet & holding a book **135**

African-American Boy & Girl

Figure group, African-American boy & girl, boy holding basket of flowers in each hand, black shoes, yellow socks, barefoot girl, created by L.A. Dowd, early 1940s, paper label, 4 1/4" base, boy 7" h., girl 5 1/2" h. (ILLUS.) **495**

Figure group, Bride & Groom, the bride standing on the left w/white dress & pink flowers w/green leaves & pink hat, bouquet in left hand, her right hand on the groom's shoulder, man seated wearing striped trousers, black jacket, brown shoes & brown hat in left hand, black hair & mustache, stamp mark, 4 3/4" l., 8 1/2" h. **195**

Figure group, "One Year Later," mother seated on left w/green dress holding baby in white dress, man standing w/striped trousers, black hair, mustache, jacket & shoes, stamp mark, 4" l., 8 1/4" h. **160**

Figure of woman, Gay Nineties Series, holding parasol, unglazed bottom, incised mark "Brayton Laguna Pottery," 9 1/2" h. **245**

Figures, African-American boys on hands & knees playing dice, w/original die, 4 3/4" l., 3 1/2" h., 3 pcs................... **265**

Figures, Children's Series, "Eric" & "Inger," Swedish boy & girl, pr. **225**

Figures, Hillbilly Shotgun Wedding series, 8 pcs... **1,850**

Flower holder, figural, "Francis," girl standing & holding small planter in front, White Crackle glossy glaze dress, yellow pot, brown hair w/blue ribbon, brown-stained face & arms, bluebird on right arm, 6 1/2" h. **65**

Brayton Laguna Turquoise Bear

Model of bear, turquoise, sitting w/front legs outstretched, incised underglaze mark "Brayton's Laguna, Cal.," 3" h. (ILLUS.) **65**

Model of carousel horse, rearing position, 16" h. **162**

Model of cat, "Kiki," seated on oval base, tail wraps around to hide back legs and paws, socks on front paws, hat perched on head & tied at front, eyes closed, colorful sweater, assorted colors of pink, blue, black & white, marked on unglazed bottom, "Brayton Laguna" above a line & "Kiki" below the line, 6" l. base, 9 1/4" h. **145**

Brayton-Laguna Cat

Model of cat, lying down, head up, yellow body w/brown accents, green eyes, stamp mark, "Copyright 1941 by Brayton Laguna Pottery," 6 1/2" l., 4 1/4" h. (ILLUS.)... **75**

Model of cat, seated on oval base, socks on front paws w/left paw over right paw, head turned to left looking back, blue eyes open, hat perched on head between ears, bluebird in front of hat, colorful colors of blue, pink, white & black, unglazed, bottom w/no marks, 6 1/4" l. base, 9" h...................................... **125**

Model of dog, sniffing, "Pluto," Walt Disney, 6" l., 3 1/4" h................................. **165**

Model of duck, standing w/head down, Provincial line, brown overall stain w/glossy yellow bill, 6 1/2" h. **50**

Model of fawn, standing, ears up, brown & white spots, unmarked, 6 1/2" h........ **75**

Model of fox, seated, No. H-57 .... **145**

Model of owl, brown & white, 7" h.......... **65**

Model of purple cow, original sticker **115**

Brayton-Laguna Quail

Model of quail standing on base, turquoise, black & grey, underglaze mark "Brayton's Laguna Beach, Calif.," 10 3/4" h. (ILLUS.).. **145**

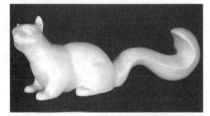

Brayton-Laguna White Squirrel

Model of squirrel, crouched w/tail behind & curving slightly upward on end, head & ears up, nondescript face, White Crackle glaze, incised mark, "Brayton's Laguna Calif. T-15," 12 3/4" l, 6" h. (ILLUS.)............. **125**

Brayton-Laguna Monkeys

Models of monkeys, male & female, White Crackle w/brown stain faces, unmarked, 13" h., pr. (ILLUS.) **450**

Pair of Brayton Laguna Quails

Models of quails, brown w/black speckles on white breasts, black & white feather details on wings, incised mark "Brayton's Laguna Beach," 9" & 11" h., pr. (ILLUS.) **150**

Mug, w/pretzel-shaped handle, raised pretzel shapes on gold, stamp mark "Brayton Calif. U.S.A.," 5" h. **32**

Pencil holder, figural, gingham dog **85**

Pitcher, cream-size, model of a calico kitten, high glaze white body w/pink, light blue & mauve flowers & brown stitching, pale blue ribbon around neck, black nose & eyes, stamp mark "Copyright 1942 by Brayton Laguna Pottery," 6 1/2" h. **85**

Planter, in the form of a peasant man w/flower cart, assorted glazes, unmarked, 6 x 11", 11" h. **165**

Salt & pepper shakers, figural, gingham dog & calico cat, pr. **85**

Salt & pepper shakers, figural mammy & chef, 5 1/2" h., pr. **150**

Salt & pepper shakers, figural peasant couple, Provincial patt., pr. **65**

Teapot & cover on stand, Provincial patt., tulip stand, the set **125**

Tile, chartreuse & yellow bird, turquoise, yellow & white flowers, black background incised mark, "Laguna Pottery," 7 x 7".......... **395**

Brayton Laguna Tile

Tile, square, w/scene of man in sombrero napping under palm tree, man dressed in white serape & cobalt blue pants & sombrero, cacti & palm tree in greens & turquoises, pale green ground, unglazed back, created by Durlin Brayton, incised mark, "Brayton Laguna Pottery," 6 3/4" sq. (ILLUS.)... **495**

Vase, 5 1/2" h., model of grey elephant wearing diaper & open blue hat, 1940s walk-a-dog & pots stamp mark "Brayton" **165**

Vase, 7 1/4" h., 7" w., 7" l., pillow shape w/feather design on each side & raised circles on recessed short base, fern green.. **85**

Sea Horse Vase

Vase, 8 1/2" h., model of a sea horse, white body w/pink, yellow & turquoise accents, stamp mark underglaze "Brayton Calif. U.S.A." (ILLUS.)... **295**

Russian Woman Wall Plaque

Wall plaque, figure of woman, arms above head, Russian dress, Webton Ware mark, hard to find, 13 1/2" h. (ILLUS.) **225**

Wall plaque, model of a large zebra, black & gold **115**

Webton Ware Wall Pocket Bowl

Wall pocket, model of a bowl w/shaped rim, two holes for hanging, Webton Ware mark on unglazed back, 2 3/4" w., 4 1/4" h. (ILLUS.)... **85**

Buffalo Pottery

Incorporated in 1901 as a wholly-owned subsidiary of the Larkin Soap Company, founded by John D. Larkin of Buffalo, New York, in 1875, the Buffalo Pottery was a manufactory built to produce premium wares to be included with purchases of Larkin's chief product, soap.

In October 1903, the first kiln was fired and Buffalo Pottery became the only pottery in the world run entirely by electricity. In 1904 Larkin offered its first premium produced by the pottery. This concept of using premiums caused sales to skyrocket and, in 1905, the first Blue Willow pattern pottery made in the United States was introduced as a premium.

The Buffalo Pottery administrative building, built in 1904 to house 1,800 clerical workers, was the creation of a 32-year-old architect, Frank Lloyd Wright. The building was demolished in 1953, but many critics considered it to be Wright's masterpiece.

By 1910 annual soap production peaked and the number of premiums offered in the catalogs exceeded 600. By 1915 this number had grown to 1,500. The first catalog of premiums was issued in 1893 and continued to appear through the late 1930s.

John D. Larkin died in 1926, and during the Great Depression the firm suffered severe losses, going into bankruptcy in 1940. After World War II the pottery resumed production under new management, but its vitreous wares were generally limited to mass-produced china for the institutional market.

Among the pottery lines produced during Buffalo's heyday were Gaudy Willow, Deldare, Abino Ware, historical and commemorative plates and unique hand-painted jugs and pitchers. In the 1920s and 1930s the firm concentrated on personalized wares for commercial clients including hotels, clubs, railroads and restaurants.

In 1983 Oneida Silversmiths bought the pottery, an ironic twist since, years before, Oneida silver had been featured in Larkin catalogs. The pottery has now ceased all domestic production of ceramics. - Phillip M. Sullivan.

Buffalo Pottery Mark

Abino Ware (1911-1913)

Matchbox holder w/ashtray **$1,600**
Pitcher, 7" h., jug-form, octagonal, Portland
   Head Light.. **2,300+**
Pitcher, 10 1/2" h., tankard-type....................... **1,900**
Vase, 8" h., seascape decoration **2,200**

Blue Willow Pattern (1905-1916)

Note: Pieces dated 1905 and marked "First Old Willow Ware Manufactured in America" are worth double the prices shown here.

Chop plate, scalloped edge, 11" d. **250**
Match safe, 2 3/4 x 6" **200**
Oyster tureen, notched cover **550**

Blue Willow Wash Pitcher

Pitcher, wash, Blue Willow patt. (ILLUS.) **750**
Pitcher, jug-type, "Hall Boy," 6 1/2 oz., 3 pts. **300**
Pitcher, cov., jug-type, 3 1/2 pts. **400**
Pitcher, jug-type, "Chicago," 4 1/2 pts. **400**
Salad bowl, square, 9 1/4" w. **275**

Sauceboat w/attached stand, oval, double-
   handled, 1 pt. **400**
Teapot, cov., square, 2 pts., 5 1/2 oz................. **350**
Teapot, cov., individual size, 12 oz. **300**
Vegetable dish, cov., square, 7 1/2 x
   9 1/2" **300**

Deldare Ware (1908-1909, 1923-1925)

Note: "Fallowfield Hunt" and "Ye Olden Days" scenes are similarly priced for the equivalent pieces in this line.

Calendar plate, 1910, 9 1/2" d...................... **2,500+**

Buffalo Deldare Ware Card Tray

Calling card tray, round w/tab handles, "Ye
   Olden Days" scene, 7 3/4" d. (ILLUS.)........ **450+**

Deldare Shield-back Candleholder

Candleholder, shield-back style, "Ye Olden
   Days" scene, 7" h. (ILLUS.)....................... **1,800+**

Deldare Candlestick & Pitcher

Candlestick, "Ye Olden Days" scene, 9 1/2" h. (ILLUS. right) **750**
Dresser tray, rectangular, "Dancing Ye Minuet" scene, 9 x 12"... **750**
Fruit bowl, 9" d., 3 3/4" h. **600**
Humidor, cov., octagonal, 7" h. **1,200**

Jardiniere & garden seat pedestal base, "Ye Lion Inn" scenes on jardiniere, two "Ye Olden Days" scenes on base, 1908, jardiniere 9" h., base 13 1/2" h., the set (ILLUS.)... **12,000**

Buffalo Deldare 8" Octagonal Pitcher

Pitcher, 8" h., octagonal, "Ye Olden Days" scene (ILLUS.).. **850**
Pitcher, 12 1/2" h. tankard-type, "Ye Olden Days" scene (ILLUS. left with candlestick) .... **1,000+**
Plate, 6 1/4" d., salesman's sample .... **2,200+**

Very Rare Deldare Jardiniere & Base

Deldare "Fallow Field Hunt" Plates

Plates, 9 1/4" d., "The Fallow Field Hunt - The Start," artist-signed, set of 4, each

(ILLUS.) **225**
Punch bowl, footed, 14 3/4" d., 9 1/4" h. ...... **7,000+**

Relish dish, oblong, 6 1/2 x 12" **500**
Salad bowl, 12" d., 5" h. **500**
Vase, 8 1/2" h., 6" d., footed tapering ovoid
　body w/a flaring rim, "Ye Olden Days"
　scene, black ink mark .... **1,200+**

Rare Deldare Vase

Vase, 9" h., tall waisted cylindrical form, "Ye
　Olden Days" scene (ILLUS.) **1,400**
Wall plaque, 12" d. **850**

Emerald Deldare (1911)
Candlestick, Bayberry decoration, 9" h. **1,000**

Emerald Deldare Chocolate Pot

Coffee/chocolate pot, cov., tall tapering hex-
　agonal form w/pinched spout & angled D-
　form handle, inset lid w/blossom finial,
　stylized symmetrical designs highlighted
　w/white flowers on body & lid, band just
　under spout w/stylized moths & large but-
　terfly, decorated by L. Newman, ca.
　1911, artist's name in green slip, ink
　stamp logo & "7," 10 1/2" h. (ILLUS.) **3,000**

Very Rare Emerald Deldare Pitcher

Pitcher, 8 3/4" h., octagonal, angled handle,
　color scene of "Dr. Syntax Setting Out to
　the Lakes," signed by M. Gerhardt, dated
　1911 (ILLUS.) **18,000-19,000**
Plaque, round, "Friday," scene of monks at
　a long table eating fish on Friday, 12" d. . **1,900+**
Plaque, round, "Lost," scene of herd of
　sheep in blizzard, 13 1/2" d. .... **2,000+**

"Dr. Syntax" Emerald Deldare Plate

Plate, 7 1/4" d., h.p. floral border & center
　scene, "Dr. Syntax Soliloquizing," by E.
　Missel, marked w/Emerald Deldare logo,
　"1911" & "4," (ILLUS.) **1,400**
Plate, 8 1/4" d., stylized floral & geometric
　decoration **750**

Emerald Deldare Vase

Large display of Gaudy Willow Pottery

Vase, 8" h., 6 1/2" d., ovoid w/a wide shoulder tapering to a short flaring neck, olive green ground decorated in shades of green & white w/a kingfisher & iris, signed by J. Gerhardt, 1911 (ILLUS., on previous page) 1,800

Gaudy Willow (1905-1916)

Note: Pieces dated 1905 and marked "First Old Willow Ware Manufactured in America" are worth double the prices shown here. This line is generally priced five times higher than the Blue Willow line. (ILLUS. above)

Bone dish, 3 1/4 x 7 1/4"...................................... 225
Boston egg cup, 7 oz. 350
Butter dish, cover & insert, the set,
    7 1/4" d. 750
Cake plate, double-handled, 10 1/4" d. 500
Creamer, round, 1 pt., 2 oz. 500
Gravy/sauceboat, 14 1/2 oz. 400
Pickle dish, square, 4 1/2 x 8 1/4"...................... 350
Plate, dinner, 10 1/2" d. 275
Platter, 18" l., oval.. 1,000
Saucer, 6 1/2" d. 50
Sugar bowl, cov., round, 24 1/4 oz. 500
Teacup, 10 oz... 175

Jugs and Pitchers (1906-1909)

Jug, "George Washington," blue & white,
    1907, 7 1/2" h. 650

Jug, "Mason," brown/beige colors, 1907,
    8 1/2" h.. 1,000+
Pitcher, "Art Nouveau," gold & blue, 1908,
    9 1/2" h.. 1,200+

"Buffalo Hunt" Pitcher

Pitcher, "Buffalo Hunt," jug-form, Indian on horseback hunting buffalo, dark bluish green ground, 6" h. (ILLUS.) 350
Pitcher, "Chrysanthemum," dark green,
    1908, 7 1/2" h.. 500

"Gloriana" & "Holland" Pitchers

Buffalo "Cinderella" Pitcher

Pitcher, "Cinderella," jug-type, ca. 1907, marked w/Buffalo transfer logo & date, "Cinderella" & "1328," 6" h. (ILLUS.) **700**

Pitcher, "Gloriana," blue on white, ca. 1908, 9" h. (ILLUS. right, top of page)...................... **900**

Pitcher, "Holland," decorated w/three colorful h.p. scenes of Dutch children on the body w/band near the rim decorated w/a rural landscape, ca. 1906, marked w/Buffalo transfer logo & date, "Holland" & "9," overall consistent staining, 5 3/4" h. (ILLUS. left with Gloriana Pitcher) **750**

Pitcher, "John Paul Jones," blue & white, 1908, 8 3/4" h.. **1,000+**

Pitcher, "Marine Pitcher, Lighthouse," blue & white, 1907, 9 1/4" h................................ **1,000**

Pitcher, "New Bedford Whaler - The Niger," bluish green, 1907, 6" h................................ **850**

Pitcher, "Pilgrim," brightly colored, 1908, 9" h.. **1,000**

Pitcher, "Robin Hood," multicolored, 1906, 8 1/4" h. **575**

Pitcher, "Roosevelt Bears," beige, 1906, 8 1/4" h. **3,200**

Buffalo "Sailor" Pitcher

Pitcher, "Sailor" patt., waisted-tankard form, decorated in blues w/the heads of two seamen above scenes of sailing ships, opposite side w/a lighthouse & rocky coastline, 1906, 9 1/4" h. (ILLUS.)... **1,000-1,100**

Pitcher, "Whirl of the Town," brightly colored, 1906, 7" h. **675**

Plates - Commemorative (1906-1912)

Great Falls, Montana Plate

B. & M. Smelter, and the largest smokestack in the world. Great Falls, Montana, deep green, ca. 1909, 7 1/2" d. (ILLUS.)............... **125**

Gen. A.P. Stewart Chapter, United Daughters of the Confederacy, No. 81, Richmond, Virginia, blue & white, 1907, 10 1/2" d........................ **300**

George Washington & Martha Washington, deep bluish green, 7 1/2" d., each............... **250**

Improved Order of the Redman, green border w/multicolored design, 7 1/2" d. **175**

Locks (The), Lockport, New York, deep bluish green, 7 1/2" d. **125**

New Bedford, Massachusetts, blue & white, 1908, 10 1/2" d................................ **175**

Buffalo Pottery Niagara Falls Plate

Niagara Falls, dark blue w/Bonrea pattern border, ca. 1907, 7 1/2" d. (ILLUS.)............... **150**

Richest Hill in the World, Butte, Montana, deep bluish green, 7 1/2" d............................ **150**

State Capitol, Helena, Montana, deep bluish green, 7 1/2" d. **150**

Plates - Historical - Blue or Green (1905-1910)

Capitol Building, Washington, D.C., 10" d........... **75**
Faneuil Hall, Boston, 10" d. **75**
Independence Hall, Philadelphia, 10" d............... **75**
Mount Vernon, 10" d... **75**
Niagara Falls, 10" d.. **75**
White House, Washington, 10" d........................... **75**

Miscellaneous Pieces

First Buffalo China Christmas Plate

Christmas Plate, 1950, first of a series of annual plates ending in 1962, 9 1/2" d. (ILLUS.).. **65**

Bluebird Pattern Pieces

Cup & saucer, Bluebird patt, china mark   (ILLUS. right).. **125**

Large & Small Geranium Pitchers

Dolly Dingle Child's Feeding Dish

Feeding dish, child's, alphabet border, color center scene of Dolly Dingle children signed by Grace Drayton (ILLUS.)................. **175**

Dutch Children Feeding Dish

Feeding dish, child's, alphabet border, Dutch children at play in center, ca. 1916, Buffalo China, 7 3/4" d. (ILLUS.)......... **125**

Seneca Pattern Gravy Boat

Gravy boat, Seneca patt., 8 1/2" l. (ILLUS.)......... **45**
Pitcher, 8 3/4" h., bone china, melon-shaped, white, 1909..................................... **1,000**
Pitcher, Geranium patt., blue & white, small size (ILLUS. front row, right with other Geranium pitchers, top of page) **275**
Pitcher, Geranium patt., pale green & brown on white, small size, 1906-1909 (ILLUS. front row, left with other Geranium pitchers)...................................... **175**

Rare York Pattern Pitcher

Pitcher, York patt., white body w/blue & red flowers, 1910, rare, 7 1/2" h. (ILLUS.) **650**
Pitchers, Geranium patt., large sizes, multi-colored design or dark blue & white, 1906-1909, each (ILLUS. in back row) **400**
Plate, 6 1/2" d., Bluebird patt., china mark (ILLUS. left with cup & saucer)......................... **75**

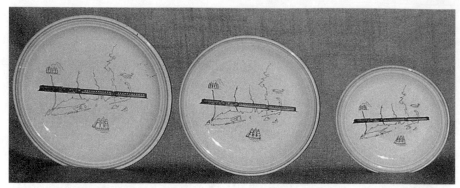

NY, NH & H Railroad Plates

Plate, 6 3/8" d., bread & butter, made for the New York, New Haven & Hartford Railroad, ca. 1935 (ILLUS. right) **75**

Plate, 8 3/8" d., luncheon, made for the New York, New Haven & Hartford, Railroad, ca. 1935 (ILLUS. center with other railroad plates) **125**

Plate, 9" d., dinner, Hotel Robert Fulton service, Buffalo China.. **250**

Plate, 9" d., Multifleure patt., Buffalo China....... **300**

Plate, 9 1/2" d., Bing Crosby portrait, Buffalo China **500**

Plate, 9 1/2" d., dinner, Roycroft Inn service..... **300**

Plate, 9 3/4" d., dinner, made for the New York, New Haven & Hartford Railroad, ca. 1935 (ILLUS. left with other railroad plates) **150**

Plate, 10" d., New York World's Fair, 1939 ...... **500**

Plate, 10 1/4" d., dinner, Bangor patt., eagle backstamp, 1906 .... **600**

Plate, 10 1/4" d., dinner, Japan patt., multicolored, 1906.. **250**

Plate, 10 1/2" d., Stuyvesant Hotel service, green & gold **250**

Plate, 10 3/4" d., Jack Dempsey photograph, Buffalo China **500**

Plate, 10 3/4" d., Pere Marquette Hotel service, Ye Olde Ivory **300**

Plate, 11" d., Breakfast at the Three Pigeons, Fallowfield Hunt line, on Colorido Ware **750**

C.& O. Railroad Washington Plate

Plate, George Washington portrait, gold-embossed border band, made for the Chesapeake & Ohio Railroad, 1932, 11" d. (ILLUS.) **750**

Rare Buffalo China Turkey Platter

Platter, 13 1/4 x 18 1/2", Turkey patt., large colorful turkey in landscape in center, fall landscape border scenes, Colorido Ware, 1937, Buffalo China (ILLUS.)........... **3,000**

Portland vase, reproduced in 1946, 8" h. **1,000**
Teapot, cov., tea ball-type w/built-in tea ball,
Argyle patt., blue & white, 1914 .... **300**
Tom & Jerry set: punch bowl & 12 cups; Col-
orido Ware, the set...................................... **1,000**

Caliente Pottery

Virgil K. Haldeman was a leader in the ceramic field through the heyday of California art pottery. After earning a B.S. degree in Ceramic Engineering in 1923 from the University of Illinois, Virgil worked for a Pennsylvania tile company for several years and concentrated on industrial tile production after moving to Southern California in 1927. He did a brief stint at the Santa Catalina Clay Products on Catalina Island. Dissatisfied with the limitations of the native Catalina clay, he quit his job as ceramics engineer and plant superintendent in 1933 and moved to the mainland. Virgil established the Haldeman Pottery in Burbank, and the Caliente line was born that same year. Haldeman created the Caliente glazes, Andrew Hazelhurst was the chief designer, and Virgil's wife, Anna, handled the administration and marketing areas. In 1951, when the construction of the Interstate 5 Freeway threatened the pottery's location, the Haldemans moved the business to Calabasas, 25 miles to the west. Items produced were shallow flower bowls called "floaters," with overlapped, irregular edges; baskets with hand-coiled handles; ewers; candleholders; and miniature animals. Figures of Art Deco women, most in dancing positions, were also created. Many pieces featured hand-applied floral decorations. These items were extremely fragile and collectors should carefully inspect before purchasing, as condition is key to value.Unfortunately, it was only a short time after the move that foreign imports caused a decline in the demand for the more expensive American-made ceramic products. In 1953, the Haldemans decided to give up production of the Caliente line and Virgil returned to the field of industrial tile, working for firms in Texas, New Mexico and Southern California. Retiring in 1973, Virgil died in 1979.At best, items were randomly marked and some simply bear a deeply impressed "Made in California" mark. In 1987 (and in a 1997 update), however, Wilbur Held wrote a privately printed book titled Collectable Caliente Pottery, which added tremendously to identifying Caliente products by a numbering system that the Haldeman Company used. According to Held, molded pieces are usually numbered in the 100s and are the ear-

liest made; handmade pieces, 200s; most animals and fowl (solid colors and hand-brushed), 300s; dancing girls, 400s; continuation of handmade pieces, 500-549; and molded pieces with applied roses, 550 and above. Caliente Pottery stickers were also used.In the early years, the word "Caliente" was used as a line name to designate flower frogs, figurines and flower bowls. Collectors now use the Caliente name almost exclusively to indicate all products made at the Haldeman pottery.

Basket, round, footed rim w/rope handle,
green, Model No. 222, incised "Hand-
made Calif.," 7" l. **$35**

Caliente Pottery Basket

Basket, w/hand-coiled center handle, pink,
Model No. 221, 5" l. (ILLUS.)............................ **29**
Bowl, 4 3/4" h., bulbous ivy-type, satin
matte white gloss, two pink applied roses
& one rosebud w/two green leaves, Model No. 560 (ILLUS. center, bottom of
page) **70**
Bowl, 8" d., 2 1/2" h., green, rolled edge,
Model No. 14-1, early ware (ILLUS. right
w/handled vases) **145**
Candy dish, figural, swan w/head bent at
neck serving as handle, pink inside,
white outside, Model No. 64, 9" l., 6" h. **65**
Ewer, w/handles, ivory base & lower half of
body darkening to pink w/overall pink inside, applied w/two ivory leaves, one pink
rose & one white rose & white rosebud,
marked "558 Handmade Cal.," 9 1/2" h. **80**
Ewer, w/handles, yellow gloss ground w/ap-
plied two white roses & three yellow
leaves in relief, incised mark "554
U.S.A.," 5 1/2" h. **35**

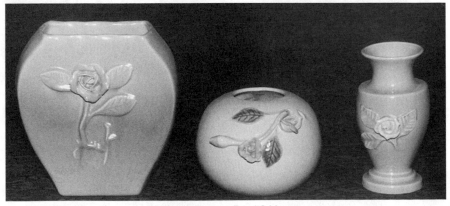

Caliente Pottery Bowl & Vases

Caliente Dancing Girl Figures

Figure of a dancing girl, arms outstretched w/each hand holding up tip of skirt, right foot visible, head bent far to the right touching right shoulder, pale green, impressed mark "Made in California," Model No. 408, 6 1/2" h. (ILLUS. left) **120**

Figure of a dancing girl, head bent w/right hand to shoulder, left hand holding dress up, kicking left leg, pale pink, impressed mark "Made in California," Model No. 407, 7" h. (ILLUS. right) **135**

Figure of dancing girl in bloomers, a scarf in each hand draping to the floor, head bent & slightly tilted, face features indistinct, left hand resting on waist, Model No. 406, very hard to find, 6 1/2" h. **165**

Figure of woman standing, holding lower section of long dress away from body exposing legs, head tilted slightly w/hat on her head, impressed mark "Made in California" in block letters, Model No. 405, 6 1/4" h. (ILLUS. center) **100**

rings in two rose petals & four inward rim bends, script-incised mark, Model No. 509, 16" l. **65**

Floater, pink inside, white outside, Model No. 205 14" l. **35**

Flower frog, model of a sailboat, satin matte white glaze, Model No. 73, 5" h. **65**

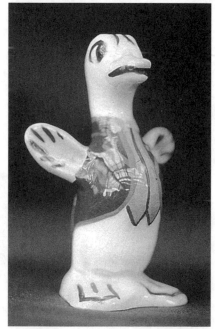

Model of a Duck with Wings Flapping

Model of a duck, wings up, details brush painted, well marked w/sticker, incised Model No. 334 & in-mold mark, 4" h. (ILLUS.). **85**

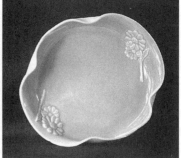

Caliente Pottery Floater

Floater, blue inside, white outside, floral design in relief, 12" l. (ILLUS.) **45**

Floater, flat & shallow dish to float flowers, oval w/two overlapping rim cuts w/candle

Caliente Rooster & Hen

Model of a hen, standing on round base, unusual hand-decorated, brown body
w/darker brown highlights, green & white
base incised "336" & "USA," 3 1/2" h.
(ILLUS. left)... **75**
Model of a pointer dog, on oval base, walk-
ing position, tail & head up, white base &
lower portion of dog's body, upper half
caramel gloss, Model No. 360, 6 3/4" l.,
4" h.. **75**
Model of a rooster, seated on round base,
unusual hand-decorated brown body
w/darker brown highlights, green & white
base, incised "306" & "USA," 3 3/4" h.
(ILLUS. right w/hen) **75**
Model of an egret, white, Model No. 369,
4 1/4" h. (ILLUS., right) **75**
Planter, model of a Dutch shoe w/one rose
& leaves, green glaze w/pink, unmarked,
Model No. 555, 5" l., 2 1/2" h. **30**

Model of an Egret

Sign, Caliente Pottery dealer, unnumbered,
3 1/4" h., 9 1/2" l. **425**
Vase, 3 3/4" h., one handle, yellow, Model
No. 37 (ILLUS. second from left w/han-
dled vases & bowl)... **35**

Caliente Handled Vases & Bowl

Vase, 7" h., footed w/ring at shoulder & two handles at top, orange, Model No. 9 (ILLUS. left w/handled vases & bowl) **175**

Vase, 7" h., urn-shaped w/three rings around base, pale pink body w/applied white rose & pink leaves, script incised mark, Model No. 581 (ILLUS. right w/bowl & vase).. **80**

Vase, 8" h., flat front & back w/curved sides, slightly scalloped rectangular opening, one applied green rose & leaves blending to gold top w/two applied rosebuds, one rose & one leaf, "Model No. 570" & "Calif." etched into glazed bottom, a hard-to-find glaze combination (ILLUS. left w/bowl & vase)... **80**

Vase, 9" h., two small handles at top, green early ware, Model No. 1-1 (ILLUS. second from right w/handled vases & bowl)...... **225**

Wall pocket, heart-shaped w/piecrust edge & applied rose & leaves at center top, Model No. 7, 7" h. **70**

Wall pocket, three plumes w/bow near bottom, satin matte white glaze, incised mark, Model No. 6, 6 1/2" h. **75**

Canton

This ware has been decorated for nearly two centuries in factories near Canton, China. Intended for export sale, much of it was originally inexpensive blue-and-white hand-decorated ware. Late-18th- and early-19th-century pieces are superior to later ones and fetch higher prices.

Basket & undertray, flaring oval basket w/reticulated sides, on a matching oval undertray, 19th c., 10 1/4" l., 3 3/4" h., 2 pcs. (minor edge chips) **$805**

Basket & undertray, oval basket w/deep slightly flared reticulated sides, on a matching undertray, 19th c., 7 1/2 x 8 3/4", 2 pcs. (glaze imperfections) **575**

Bowl, 9" d., round, w/scalloped edge **523**

Bowl, 8 1/4 x 10", lobed shape, orange peel glaze, ... **330**

Container, cov., round w/two wire bale handles, lid w/flat wafer finial, 6 3/4" d., 3 1/4" h.. **990**

Creamer, "bullnose" spout w/flared rim, orange peel glaze, 3 3/4" h.............................. **220**

Creamer, helmet-shaped w/angled branch handle, 4" h.. **495**

Creamer, helmet-shaped, w/Oriental hooked crosses on foot & molded swirls on branch handle, 4 1/8" h. (ILLUS. second from left w/other pieces) **578**

Creamer, squat body w/high handle, 3 1/4" h.. **220**

Fruit basket & undertray, deep oval reticulated basket w/gently flaring sides & flanged rim, in a deep matching undertray w/reticulated flanged rim, 19th c., basket 8 5/8" l., 4 1/2" h., undertray 9 7/8" l., 2 pcs. **1,150**

Fruit basket & undertray, oval gently flaring basket w/reticulated sides, on a matching undertray w/reticulated edges, 19th c., 10 1/4" l., 3 3/4" h., 2 pcs. (minor edge chips).. **805**

Hot water plate, rounded slightly paneled rim, edge spout opening, 19th c., 9 1/2" d... **303**

Pitcher, 6" h., bulbous body w/high, thin handle w/molded fan end & exaggerated slope to spout, orange peel glaze................... **880**

Pitcher, 4 1/2" h., jug-form w/double twisted strap handle, 19th c. **605**

Platter, 11 1/2" l., oblong w/canted corners, 19th c.. **413**

Platter, 11 1/2 x 14 1/2", oblong w/cut corners, well-and-tree-type, cloud borders, 19th c.. **1,210**

Platter, 13 x 16", octagonal w/dark slate blue & white decoration (some firing imperfections in glaze)...................................... **330**

Platter, 13 3/4" w., 16 7/8" l., oblong w/canted corners, 19th c. **748**

Platter, 14 x 17 1/2" rounded octagonal shape, medium blue decoration of a bridge, pagodas & an island, orange peel glaze **495**

Platter, 14 3/4 x 17 7/8" oval, 19th c., (minor imperfections) **1,093**

Platter, 17 x 21 1/8", oblong w/wide cut corners, 19th c. (minor glaze irregularities) **1,840**

Platter & strainer, 13 3/4 x 17 1/8", deep oval form, oblong w/canted corners, 19th c., 2 pcs. (minor glass irregularities, color variations).. **978**

Serving bowl, oblong octagonal form, 11 x 13 1/2" **880**

Serving dish, cov., footed oval form w/snout-shaped handles, 19th c., 8 3/4 x 10", 6" h. (chip) **805**

Serving dish, square w/lobed corners, orange peel glaze, 8 1/2" sq. **440**

Sugar bowl, cov., cup-shaped w/double, intertwined handles w/applied decorative ends, fruit finial, 3 7/8" d., 4 1/2" h., minor flakes on foot (ILLUS. second from right w/other pieces) **523**

Canton Porcelain Pieces

Teapot, cov., canister-shaped body & intertwined, reeded handle w/ornate, applied floral ends, fruit finial, straight spout, 5 1/2" h., some rim flakes (ILLUS. far left w/other pieces).. **908**

Teapot, cov., cylindrical body tapering in at top, intertwined handle w/decorative ends, fruit finial on lid, curved spout, 6 3/4" h. (ILLUS. far right w/other pieces)..... **578**

Tureen, cov., footed oblong body w/animal head end handles, 10 x 12", 8" h. **1,540**

Tureen, cov., rectangular w/rounded corners, flared base, the cover decorated w/a leaf-shaped knop, boar's head end handles, 19th c., 13" l., 8 1/2" h. (minor small firing cracks).. **1,955**

Vegetable bowl, open, oblong w/cut corners, 9 3/4 x 11 1/2" **605**

Vegetable dish, cov., almond-shaped w/flanged rim, low domed cover w/pine cone finial, 10 1/4" l. (chips)........................... **385**

Vegetable dish, cov., rectangular form, 19th c., 7 1/2 x 8 3/4", 4 1/2" h. (small rim nick) **345**

Warming dish, cov., high base w/blue & white design on interior, lid has fruit finial, 9 3/8" d., 5" h... **660**

Water bottle, ovoid, w/long neck, white ground w/hint of blue, darker blue design of buildings w/hills, 7 5/8" h., short hairlines at lip (ILLUS. center w/other pieces)..... **688**

Capo-di-Monte

Production of porcelain and faience began in 1736 at the Capo-di-Monte factory in Naples. In 1743 King Charles of Naples established a factory there that made wares with relief decoration. In 1759 the factory was moved to Buen Retiro near Madrid, operating until 1808. Another Naples pottery was opened in 1771 and operated until 1806 when its molds were acquired by the Doccia factory of Florence, which has since made reproductions of original Capo-di-Monte pieces with the "N" mark beneath a crown. Some very early pieces are valued in the thousands of dollars but the subsequent productions are considerably lower.

Bowl, 8 3/4" d., wide shallow form w/upright sides molded in relief w/a continuous colorful scene of frolicking bacchantes in a landscape, molded lappets around the bottom, the interior & scalloped rim painted w/foliate scrolls & sprays, 19th c. **$431**

Box, cov., rectangular, molded in relief w/polychrome classical figures & a battle scene, brass-framed hinged cover, 19th c., 3" l. **431**

Casket, cov., rectangular w/high domed hinged cover, on leafy scroll tab feet, the cover & sides decorated w/colorful relief-molded panels of putti around the sides & a scene of Psyche w/putti on the cover, 19th c., 9 1/2" l., 7 1/2" h. **518**

Dessert service: twelve 7 3/4" d. dessert plates, eight teacups & seven saucers; each plate painted w/a crested coat-of-arms trimmed in gilt, the border molded in low relief w/mythological figures at leisure pursuits, the bases marked w/blue crowned "N" mark & museum accession

numbers & two w/gilt inscription "A Madame la Comtesse de Spilinbergo," late 19th - early 20th c., the set **1,410**

Pitcher, 9" h., cylindrical w/enameled relief-molded figural w/a gilt background, scrolled handles, underglaze-blue mark, 19th c. **288**

Plaques, oblong octagonal form, each decorated in color w/a Classical battle scene, in molded octagonal frames, 19th c., 5 1/2" x 6 12", pr. **920**

Capo-di-Monte Stein

Stein, cov., cylindrical body decorated in relief w/a classical scene, a figural cherub finial on the domed cover, applied elephant head handle, trimmed overall in color, 14" h. (ILLUS.) **605**

Triptych, the three sections w/a continuous scene of a coach & figurines surmounted by a crest, 9 3/4" l., 9 7/8" h. **316**

Urns, cov., a stepped square base supporting a short pedestal below the tall slightly flaring cylindrical body w/molded lion mask side handles & a high stepped cover w/pineapple finial, decorated w/molded low-relief Bacchic putti riding a goat & a donkey decorated in color, gold trim, 20th c., 12" h., pr. **353**

Capo-di-Monte Wall Plaque

Wall plaque, teardrop shield-form, a large central scroll-framed landscape scene of warriors w/horses, border cartouches w/military trophies & a grotesque head at the top, in a tooled leather frame, wear, late 19th c., 27" h. (ILLUS.)............... **863**

Carlton Ware

The Staffordshire firm of Wiltshaw & Robinson, Stoke-on-Trent, operated the Carlton Works from about 1890 until 1958, producing both earthenwares and porcelain. Specializing in decorative items like vases and teapots, it became well known for its lustre-finished wares, often decorated in the Oriental taste. The trademark Carlton Ware was incorporated into its printed mark. Since 1958, a new company, Carlton Ware Ltd., has operated the Carlton Works at Stoke.

Cracker jar, cov., footed bulbous ovoid form w/short waisted neck fitted w/a silver plate rim, cover & swing bail handle, decorated around the sides w/a transfer-printed colorful peony design, 7" h. **$115**

Carlton Ware Pitcher

Pitcher, 6 3/4" h., 5" d., "Rouge Royale," footed ovoid body w/large rim spout & long squared gold handle & gold ringed foot, the body w/a deep rouge iridescent ground decorated w/a large flying bird in gold, yellow, green, pink, blue & orange against an ornate gilt foliate ground, mother-of-pearl interior (ILLUS.)................... **595**

Potpourri jar, cov., wide ovoid body w/a fitted domed cover, deep yellow ground decorated on each side & the top of the cover w/cartouche-shaped reserves showing Oriental buildings & people in colored enamels against a black satin ground, gold borders, 7 1/2" d., 9 3/4" h. **425**

Toast holder, Art Deco-style, black & orange edged wedges w/loop handles on a yellow-glazed ground, 2 1/2 x 6 1/2", 2 1/4" h. **144**

Vase, 8 1/4" h., 7 3/4" d., flaring foot & tall wide trumpet-form body w/angled loop handles below the rim, a gilt decoration of an Oriental landscape w/a pagoda & gilt borders on a dark green ground.............. **275**

Catalina Island Pottery

The Clay Products Division of the Santa Catalina Island Co. produced a variety of wares during its brief ten-year operation. The brainchild of chewing-gum magnate William Wrigley, Jr., owner of Catalina Island at the time, and business associate D.M. Retton, the plant was established at Pebbly Beach, near Avalon, in 1927. Its twofold goal was to provide year-round work for the island's residents and to produce building material for Wrigley's ongoing development of a major tourist attraction at Avalon. Early production consisted of bricks and roof and patio tiles. Later, art pottery, including vases, flower bowls, lamps and home accessories, were made from a local brown-based clay; in about 1930, tablewares were introduced. These early wares carried vivid glazes but had a tendency to chip easily, and a white-bodied, more chip-resistant clay imported from the mainland was used after 1932. The costs associated with importing clay eventually caused the Catalina pottery to be sold to Gladding, McBean & Co. in 1937. Gladding, McBean items usually have an ink stamped mark and can be distinguished from Island ware by the glaze and clay as well.

Catalina Island Pottery Mark

Ashtray, figural bear, Monterey brown glaze... **$475**
Ashtray, figural fish, decorated, Model No. 551, Toyon red glaze, 6 1/2" **225**
Ashtray, model of a baseball glove..................... **950**
Ashtray, model of a cowboy hat, Descanso green or blue glaze, each **195**
Ashtray, figural goat, 4" w. **495**
Ashtray, figural fish, decorated, Model No. 550, Toyon red glaze, 4 1/2" l. **150**
Book ends, Monterey brown glaze, pr. **600**
Book ends, figural monk, pearly white glaze, 4 x 5", pr... **950**
Bowl, 7 1/2" d., Starlight **145**
Bowl, flower-type, fluted, 10 x 15", 2" h. **125**
Bowl, fruit, 13" d., footed, blue glaze................. **175**
Bowl, 9 1/2 x 14", flared sides, white glaze... **150**
Bowl, 17 1/2" l., oval, flared, pearly white glaze... **200**
Candelabra, No. 382, Descanso green glaze, pr. **350**
Candleholder, footed, 4" h., Model No. 381 .... **85**

Candleholder, low, Model No. 380........................ 90
Candleholders, No. 380, sea foam glaze,
    pr. 200
Carafe, cov., handled, Toyon red glaze 125
Carafe, cov., handled, turquoise glaze................ 95
Casserole, cov., rope edge 125
Charger, Mexican scene, 11 1/2" d. 750

Charger with Marlin

Charger, relief-molded marlin, Monterey
    brown glaze, 14" d. (ILLUS.)...................... 1,200
Charger, relief-molded swordfish, Descanso
    green glaze, 14" d. 1,200
Charger, rolled edge, Toyon red glaze,
    14 1/2" d. 225
Coaster 75
Coffee server, cov. 150
Compote, footed, w/glass liner, Toyon red
    glaze 225
Console bowl, fluted... 225
Creamer, rope edge 75
Creamer, 6" h. 250
Cup, demitasse 45
Cup & saucer, rope edge....................................... 45
Cup & saucer, Rope patt. 5-10
Custard cup 45
Flask, model of a cactus, Descanso green,
    6 1/4" h. 600
Flower frog, model of a pelican 250
Flower frog, model of a stork, 7" h. 295
Flowerpot, 4 1/2" h. 95
Flowerpot, Toyon red, 4 1/2" h. 65
Indian bowl, rare 475
Lamp base, basketweave design, Descan-
    so green glaze... 1,200
Model of clamshell, pearly white glaze.............. 300
Mug, 6" h.. 55
Oil jar, No. 351, Toyon red glaze, 18" h.......... 1,200
Pipe holder/ashtray, figural napping peon,
    No. 555, Descanso green or blue glaze,
    each 450
Pitcher, 7 1/2" h., Toyon red glaze..................... 350
Planter, model of a cat, cactus planter, Cat-
    Lina 475
Plate, Moorish design decoration........................ 425
Plate, 8 1/2" d., salad, rope edge......................... 28
Plate, 10 1/2" d., dinner, rope edge 32
Plate, chop, 11" d., Descanso green
    glaze 65
Plate, 11 1/4" d., painted desert scene 550
Plate, chop, 12 1/2" d., Toyon red glaze............. 70
Plate, chop, 13 1/2" d., rope edge........................ 95

Plate, 14" d., submarine garden
    decoration 1,250

Clover-shaped Relish Tray

Relish tray, handled, clover-shaped, sea
    foam glaze (ILLUS.)....................................... 650
Salt & pepper shakers, figural senorita & pe-
    on, Toyon red & yellow glaze, pr. 150
Salt & pepper shakers, gourd-shaped,
    pr.. 75
Salt & pepper shakers, model of cactus,
    pr... 95
Salt & pepper shakers, model of cactus, tall,
    pr... 65
Salt & pepper shakers, model of tulip, blue
    glaze, pr... 85
Shot tumbler, nude figure, "Bottoms Up,"
    3 1/4" h... 195
Sugar bowl, cov., rope edge................................. 55
Sugar bowl, Rope patt. 30-50
Tea tile, 8" w... 295
Teapot, cov., rope edge 265
Tile, Spanish design, 6 x 6" sq............................ 150

Tile Plaque with Macaw

Tile plaque, depicting green macaw,
    12 x 18" (ILLUS.)... 2,500+

Tortilla Warmer

Tortilla warmer, cov., Monterey brown glaze
(ILLUS.)... 750
Tumbler 50
Tumbler, blue glaze.................................. 35
Vase, trophy-type, Toyon red 395
Vase, 5" h., handled, Model No. 612, Man-
darin yellow glaze.................................. 125
Vase, 5" h., stepped form, blue glaze........ 275
Vase, 5" h., stepped, handled, turquoise
glaze.. 350
Vase, bud, 5" h., Model No. 300, Descanso
green glaze... 145
Vase, 5 1/2" h., Model No. 600, tan glaze 135
Vase, 5 1/2" h., Model No. 603, tan
glaze.. 100
Vase, 6" h., ribbed body, blue glaze..................... 85
Vase, 7" h., Model No. 636, turquoise
glaze.. 145
Vase, 7 1/4" h., sawtooth edge..................... 175
Vase, 7 1/4" h., sawtooth edge on each
side, Model No. 601, turquoise glaze........... 200
Vase, 7 1/2" h., trophy-form, handled, Toy-
on red glaze.. 350
Vase, 7 1/2" h., trophy-form, orange glaze........ 325
Vase, 7 3/4" h., Model No. 627, blue
glaze.. 135
Vase, 9" h., experimental multicolored
glaze.. 800
Vase, 10" h., fluted 225
Vase, 10" h., pearly white glaze........................ 195
Vinegar bottle w/stopper, gourd-shape 165
Wall pocket, basketweave design, 9" l......... 375
Wall pocket or vase, seashell form, white
clay.. 350

Ceramic Arts Studio of Madison

During its 15 years of operation, Ceramic Arts Studio of Madison, Wisconsin, was one of the nation's largest producers of figurines, shakers and other decorative wares. Its originality and high production standards make its wares highly collectible works of art. In 1940, the artistic talent of Lawrence Rabbitt merged with the business acumen of Reuben Sand to start Ceramic Arts Studio. Their partnership was successful. Rabbitt remained artist in residence and the Studio produced hand-thrown bowls, pots and vases exploring the potential of Wisconsin clay. After Rabbitt's departure in 1942, a serendipitous meeting between Sand and Betty Harrington brought her artistic talents to the Studio. Under her artistic direction, the focus was changed to finely sculpted decorative wares, including figurines of people, animals and fantasy figures. Metal Art accessories to complement the ceramic pieces were assembled at the Studio under the direction of Zona Liberace (stepmother to the famous pianist), who also functioned as the Studio's decorating director.

From 1942 to 1948, the Studio's business flourished while imports from Europe and the Far East were suspended as a result of World War II. Annual production of 500,000 pieces and employment of 100 people were typical for these years. Harrington, although not the only designer on staff, is credited with the creation of the vast majority of the 800+ pieces put into production. This level of output and quality helped to solidify the Studio's reputation as one of the most original and enduring ceramic producers in America.

The popularity of the Studio's work drew many poor quality imitations and outright copies. After World War II, lower-priced decorative imports began to flood the market, forcing the Studio's eventual close in 1955. Attempts to continue the enterprise in Japan resulted in products bearing the name Ceramic Arts Studio - Japan and/or Mahana Imports. Some of the original molds were taken there and many of the models were produced with little or no design change, but with wide variations in quality. The ink stamp on these Japanese Studio wares is in red or blue and the clay color is bright white. In contrast, the semicircle mark, Ceramic Arts Studio, Madison, WI is always in black and the clay is ivory and heavier. But since only one out of four Madison Ceramic Arts Studio works were ink-stamped, other clues to authenticity are the decoration and clarity of the glaze.

Ceramic Arts Studio Marks

Accordion Lady, 8 1/2" h. **$500-600**
Adam & Eve (one-piece), 12" h. .... **Too rare-price**
Adonis, 9" h. **250-350**

African Man Mask Vase

Realistic Bear Cub & Mother

African Man vase, stylized mask on ringed
base, dark brown, 8" h. (ILLUS.)............ **125-150**
African Man wall pocket, 7 3/4" h............... **150-175**
African Woman vase, 8" h.......................... **125-150**
African Woman wall pocket, 7 3/4" h......... **150-175**
Ancient Cat, 4 1/2" h. **80-100**
Ancient Kitten, 2 1/2" h. **70-90**
Aphrodite, 7" h.. **250-350**
Autumn Andy, Four Seasons group, 5" h. **160-190**
Baby Mermaid, diving, 2 1/2" h.................... **150-175**
Baby Mermaid, sitting, 3" h. **175-200**
Barbershop Quartet mug, 3 1/2" h. **650-750**
Bedtime Boy, 4 3/4" h. **75-95**

Black Bear Cub Realistic, 2 1/4" h. (ILLUS.
left, top of page).. **140-160**
Blythe, 6 1/2" h... **150-175**
Boy Doll, 12" h. **1,200-1,400**
Boy with Puppy, shelf-sitter, 4 1/4" h. **75-100**
Boy with Towel, 5" h.................................... **300-350**
Butch Boxer, 3" l. **60-80**
Cellist Man, 6 1/2" h. **500-600**
Children in Chairs, boy looking over back of
one armchair, girl looking over matching
chair, 1" to 1 1/2" h., each set (ILLUS.,
top of next page)... **60-80**

Bedtime Girl

Bedtime Girl, 4 3/4" h. (ILLUS.)........................ **75-95**
Billy Boxer, 2" l. **60-80**

Rare Egyptian Woman Figure

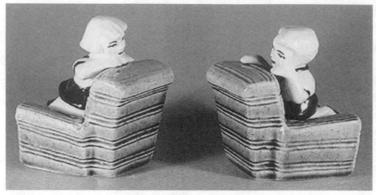

Boy & Girl in Armchairs

Cowboy, shelf-sitter, 4 1/2" h. **125-150**
Cowgirl, shelf-sitter, 4 1/2" h. **125-150**
Cupid, 5" h. **275-500**
Dawn, 6 1/2" h. **175-200**
Drum Girl, 4 1/2" h. **160-180**
Drum Girl bank, 4 1/2" h. **220-250**
Dutch Dance Boy, 7 1/2" h. **200-250**
Dutch Dance Girl, 7 1/2" h. **200-250**
Egyptian Man, 9 1/2" h. **700-750**
Egyptian Woman, 9 1/2" h. (ILLUS., previ-
  ous page) **700-750**
English Setter, Kirby, 2" l. **150-175**
Fire Man, 11 1/4" h. **200-250**
Fire Woman, 11 1/4" h. **200-250**
Flute Girl, 4 1/2" h. **140-160**
Flute Lady, 8 1/2" h. **500-600**
French Horn Man, 6 1/2" h. **500-600**
Girl with Kitten, shelf-sitter, 4 1/4" h. **75-100**
Gleeful Imp, sitting, 3 1/2" h. **500-550**
Gremlin, sitting, 2" h. **250-300**
Gremlin, standing, 4" h. **250-300**
Guitar Man, stylized seated figure, grey
  glaze, 6 1/2" h. (ILLUS., next
  column) **500-600**

Rare Guitar Man Figure

Hamlet & Ophelia Wall Plaques

Hamlet wall plaque, 8" h. (ILLUS. right)..... **180-220**
Happy Imp, lying, 3 1/2" h. **500-550**
Harem Girl, kneeling, 4 1/2" h..................... **100-125**
Harem Girl, reclining, 6" l........................... **100-125**
Harlequin Boy with mask, 8 3/4" h. **900-950**
Harlequin Girl with mask, 8 1/2" h.............. **900-950**

Hear No Evil Candleholder

Hear No Evil candleholder, 5" h. (ILLUS.)... **80-100**
Honey or Sonny Spaniel bank, 5 3/4" h.,
    each **300-350**
Honey Pot with bee, 4" h. **150-175**
Honey Spaniel, 5 3/4" h. **200-225**
Hunter, Al, 7 1/2" h. **125-200**

Jack in Beanstalk Wall Plaque

Jack in Beanstalk wall plaque, 6 1/2" h.
    (ILLUS.)... **360-400**
Joey, baby kangaroo, 2 1/2" h........................ **70-90**
Kangaroo Mother, 4 3/4" h............................... **60-80**
King's Jester Flutist Man, 11 1/2" h. **100-200**
King's Jester Lutist Woman, 12" h............... **100-200**
Lightning Stallion, 5 3/4" h. **150-175**

Jack Be Nimble Wall Plaque

Jack Be Nimble wall plaque, 5" h.
    (ILLUS.)... **400-450**

Madonna with Halo Figure

Lion & Lioness Figures

Lion, 7 1/4" l. (ILLUS. left) **170-190**
Lion King, 4" h. **350-400**
Lioness, 5 1/2" l. (ILLUS. right with
   lion) **170-190**
Lorelei on Shell planter, 6" h...................... **250-300**
Madonna with Bible, 9 1/2" h. **325-350**
Madonna with Halo, 9 1/2" h. (ILLUS., on
   previous page) **300-700**
Mary Contrary wall plaque, 5" h.
   (ILLUS., on next column)......................... **160-180**
Mermaid on Rock, 4" h. **150-175**
Modern Doe, reclining, 3 3/4" h.................. **100-125**
Modern Fawn, 2" h. **75-100**
Mother Black Bear Realistic, 3 1/4" h.
   (ILLUS. right with cub) **180-220**
Mother Seal on rock, 5" h. **500-600**
Mouse, Hickory Dickory Dock, 3" l.............. **90-110**

Mary Contrary Wall Plaque

Mermaid, Neptune & Sprites

Mermaid wall plaque, 6" h. (ILLUS.   top left) **350-400**

Mr. Blankety Blank Bank

Mr. Blankety Blank bank, 4 1/2" h.
(ILLUS.)... **120-140**

Mrs. Blankety Blank Bank

Mrs. Blankety Blank bank, 4 1/2" h.
(ILLUS.)... **120-140**
Neptune wall plaque, 6" h. (ILLUS. bottom
left with Mermaid) **350-400**
Nineteenth (19th) Century Man, 6 3/4" h. .. **250-300**
Nineteenth (19th) Century Woman,
6 1/2" h. **250-300**

Ophelia wall plaque, 8" h. (ILLUS. left with
Hamlet wall plaque) **180-220**

Paisley Pig Figure

Paisley Pig, 5 1/2" l., 3" h. (ILLUS.)........... **325-375**
Panda with hat, 2 3/4" h. **200-225**
Pensive, 6" h. **150-175**

Promenade Man & Woman

Promenade Man, 7 3/4" h. (ILLUS.
right).. **100-150**
Promenade Woman, 7 3/4" h. (ILLUS. left
with Promenade Man) **100-150**
Sad Imp with spear, 5" h. **500-550**
Saucy Squirrel, 2 1/4" h................................. **175-350**
Seal Mother, 6" l. **400-450**
Seal Pup, 3" l... **350-400**
Seal Pup on rock, 5" l. **450-500**
See No Evil candleholder, 5" h. **80-100**
Skunky bank, 4" h... **260-280**
Sonny Spaniel, 5 3/4" h................................. **200-225**
Space bowl, 5 1/4" h. **100-125**
Speak No Evil candleholder, 5" h. **80-100**
Spring Sue, Four Seasons group, 5" h. **140-170**
Sprite wall plaque, fish down, 4 1/4" h.
(ILLUS. bottom right with Mermaid)........ **300-350**
Sprite wall plaque, fish up, 4 1/4" h.
(ILLUS. top right with Mermaid) **300-350**
Square Dance Boy, 6 1/2" h. **100-125**
Square Dance Girl, 6 1/2" h.......................... **100-125**
Squeaky Squirrel, 3 1/4" h. **50-70**
St. Agnes with Lamb, 6" h............................. **260-285**
Sultan on Pillow, 4 1/2" h. **120-145**
Sultan only, 4" h... **130-155**
Summer Sally, Four Seasons group,
3 1/2" h.. **100-130**
Swan Lake Man, 7" h..................................... **900-950**
Swan Lake Woman, 7" h................................ **900-950**

Tembino & Tembo Elephants

Tembino Elephant, realistic, trunk down,
   2 1/2" h. (ILLUS. right) **160-190**
Tembo Elephant, realistic, trunk up,
   6 1/2" h. (ILLUS. left with Tembino)....... **185-225**
Temple Dance Man, 7" h............................. **450-500**
Temple Dance Woman, 6 3/4" h. **450-500**
Thunder Stallion, 5 3/4" h........................... **150-175**
Tony the Barber bank, bust of man,
   4 3/4" h. **75-100**
Tortoise with cane, 2 1/4" h......................... **120-140**
Triad Girl center, 5" h. **90-120**
Triad Girl left, 7" h.. **80-110**
Triad Girl right, 7" h. **80-110**
Violin Lady, 8 1/2" h. **500-600**

Water Woman, chartreuse, 11 1/2" h.
   (ILLUS. left) **175-200**
White Willy, ball down, 4 1/2" h................... **240-270**
White Winnie, sleeping, 5 1/2" l. **240-270**
White Woody, 3 1/4" h. **240-270**
Winter Willie, Four Seasons group, 4" h. **90-120**
Zebra, 5" h. **350-450**

Chinese Export

Large quantities of porcelain have been made in China for export to America from the 1780s, much of it shipped from the ports of Canton and Nanking. A major source of this porcelain was Ching-te-Chen in the Kiangsi province, but the wares were also made else-where. The largest quantities were blue and white. Prices fluctuate considerably depending on age, condition, decoration, etc.

CANTON and ROSE MEDALLION export wares are listed separately.

Water Man & Water Woman

Water Man, chartreuse, 11 1/2" h. (ILLUS.
   right).. **175-200**

Chinese Export Armorial Bowl

Pair of Chinese Export Bowls

Bowl, 9 1/4" d., armorial, octagon-form rim decorated w/alternating panels of birds, flowers & shells, center w/arms of Mercer, ca. 1755 (ILLUS.).......................... **$1,064**
Bowls, 9 3/4" d., "Tobacco Leaf" patt., wide rim, overall vibrant painted overlapping leaf & floral spray design, ca. 1800, pr. (ILLUS., top of page).................................... **2,576**
Coffeepot, cov., blue Nanking patt., footed bulbous ovoid body tapering to a small neck fitted w/a domed flanged cover w/fruit finial, short shaped rim spout & applied entwined strap handle, gilt trim, 9 1/8" h. (small flakes on cover).................. **1,045**
Dish, Famille Rose palette, irregular wide rounded & lobed form, shallow w/flared rim, floral-decorated rim band, interior w/scattered designs of figures, fish, Chinese characters, etc., 19th c., 11 1/4" l. **825**
Mug, cylinder shape w/applied twig handle, blue enamel bands & Batten coat of arms, ca. 1790, 5 1/2" h. **728**
Plate, 9" d., scalloped edge, made for the Continental market w/polychrome & gilt armorial decoration, late 18th c. (minor edge chips) **633**
Plates, 9 1/4" d., honeycomb border interspersed w/pictures of duck & woman, the center w/scene of women w/parasol & group of ducks, in Chinese Imari palette, ca. 1735, pr. **2,912**
Platter, 11 1/2" l., oval, blue Fitzhugh patt., 19th c.. **385**
Platter, 13 7/8" l., rectangular w/deeply angled corners, blue Nanking patt., orange peel glaze, 19th c. **770**
Platter, 14 1/2" l., oval, flanged rim, gilded "A" in circle mark, 19th c. (spot of rim repair).. **633**
Platter, 15 5/8'" l., oval, green Fitzhugh patt., 19th c. **1,725**
Platter, 13 3/8 x 16 1/8", blue Nanking patt., oblong w/cut corners, 18th c. (rim chips) **575**

Platter, 16 1/8" l., 13 3/8" w., blue Nanking patt., oblong w/beveled corners, 18th c. (rim chips).. **575**
Platter, 16 1/2" l., oval, blue Nanking patt., w/pierced oval insert, 19th c., 2 pcs. **440**
Platter, 16 1/2" l., 13 1/2" w., blue Nanking patt., oblong w/canted corners, late 18th c. (glaze bubbles, minor rim chips)................ **690**
Platter, 20" oval, blue Fitzhugh patt., 19th c. **805**
Platter, 20 1/2" l., oval w/cut corners, blue Nanking patt., painted w/a monogram within a shield w/lion crest & Latin motto, early 19th c.. **978**

Chinese Export Punch Bowl

Punch bowl, armorial, footed, rounded flared sides decorated w/arms of Campbell the Duke of Argyll and motto "NE OBLIVISCARIS, VIX EA NOSTRA VOCO" & chinoiserie cartouche, chain design rim, ca. 1770 (ILLUS.)......................... **2,688**
Punch bowl, armorial, footed, rounded flared sides, decorated w/scroll band, spearhead & floral border, coat of arms & floral sprays, ca. 1790, 10 1/4" d., 4 1/4" h. **1,064**
Sauce tureen, cov., blue Fitzhugh patt., footed squatty bulbous oval form w/flared rim & low domed cover w/a large blossom finial, entwined lapped end handles, 19th c., 8 1/4" l., 5 1/2" h. **920**
Teapot, cov., cylindrical w/h.p. polychrome & gilt eagle w/wings down & shield decoration, entwined strap handle, 19th c., 5 3/4" h. (chips, hairline, scratches) **690**

Tray, blue Nanking patt., oval w/wide flared & reticulated border & shallow center w/landscape scene, 19th c., 10 3/4" l............ **495**

Tureen, cov., blue Fitzhugh patt., high-footed large deep bulbous oval body w/an upright rim band supporting a tapered domed cover w/large blossom finial, entwined lapped end handles, 19th c., 14" l., 11 1/4" h.. **2,645**

Tureen, cov., decorated w/spearhead band, coat of arms & floral sprays, pineapple finial & bent twig handles, 13 1/2" l., 11" h.. **532**

Tureen, cov., flared pedestal foot below oval form w/rounded sides, twisted twig handles, domed cover w/blossom finial, decorated in green & gold designs on cream ground, 14" l., 11 1/2" h............................... **3,360**

Covered Tureen with Underplate

Tureen, cover & underplate, oblong, footed, in Claerbout design in rust, blue & green on white ground, ca. 1790, 9 1/2 x 14", 9 1/2 h. (ILLUS.)... **1,904**

Chinese Export Vase

Vase, baluster form, cylindrical neck w/flaring lip, decorated in famille verte w/scenic panels, late 19th c., 21 1/2" h. (ILLUS.).. **448**

Vegetable bowl, cov., Famille Rose palette, footed rectangular form w/notched corners & stepped domed cover w/fruit finial, heavy gilt trim, orange peel glaze, 9 1/2" l.. **1,045**

Vegetable dish, cov., blue Fitzhugh patt., rectangular w/notched corners, stepped domed cover w/large fruit finial, trimmed in gilt, 19th c., 9 1/2" l........................... **825**

Vegetable dish, cov., blue Nanking patt., almond-shaped w/flanged rim, low domed cover w/pine cone finial, 19th c., 10 3/4" l. (edge chips).......................... **330**

Vegetable dish, open, blue Nanking patt., oval w/slightly scalloped flanged rim on flaring sides, orange peel glaze, 19th c., 11 1/2" l.. **275**

Warming plate, blue Nanking patt., octagonal shape w/picture of a man w/an umbrella walking across bridge, flowers on wide edge, 9 1/4" d. **385**

Chintz China

There are over fifty flower patterns and myriad colors from which Chintz collectors can choose. That is not surprising considering companies in England began producing these showy, yet sometimes muted, patterns in the early part of this century. Public reception was so great that this production trend continued until the 1960s.

Sweet Pea Bowl in Crown Shape

Bowl, Sweet Pea patt., Crown shape, Royal Winton (ILLUS.)... **$750**

Royal Winton Sunshine Butter Pat

Butter pat, Sunshine patt., Royal Winton (ILLUS.).. **135**

Summertime Cheese Dish

Cheese dish, cov., Summertime patt., Dane shape, Royal Winton (ILLUS.)...................... **350**

Queen Anne Compote

Compote, open, oblong shallow shaped bowl on a flaring rectangular pedestal base, Queen Anne patt., Royal Winton (ILLUS.).. **225**
Creamer & cov. sugar bowl, Chintz patt., Old Cottage shape, Royal Winton, pr........... **250**

Sunshine Pattern Gravy Boat

Gravy boat & undertray, Sunshine patt., Royal Winton, 2 pcs. (ILLUS.)...................... **295**

Triumph Mustard Jar

Mustard jar, cov., footed barrel shape, Triumph patt., Royal Winton (ILLUS.)... **155**

Royal Winton Chelsea Pitcher

Pitcher, 3" h., jug-form, miniature milk-type, Chelsea patt., Globe shape, Royal Winton (ILLUS.)... **110**
Teapot, cov., Joyce-Lynn patt., Ascot shape, Royal Winton.................................... **1,295**

Royal Winton Silverdale Trivet

Trivet, round, Silverdale patt., Royal Winton (ILLUS.)... **95**

Clarice Cliff Designs

Clarice Cliff was a designer for A. J. Wilkinson, Ltd., Royal Staffordshire Pottery, Burslem, England when it acquired the adjoining Newport Pottery Company whose warehouses were filled with undecorated bowls and vases. About 1925 her flair with the Art Deco style was incorporated into designs appropriately named "Bizarre" and "Fantasque" and the warehouse stockpile was decorated in vivid colors. These hand-painted earthenwares, all bearing the printed signature of designer Clarice Cliff, were produced until World War II and are now finding enormous favor with collectors.

Note: Reproductions of the Clarice Cliff "Bizarre" marking have been appearing on the market recently.

Clarice Cliff Mark

Bowl, 5" d., 3" h., footed flared cylindrical form, Autumn Crocus patt., a yellow band on the inside rim, the exterior w/blue, orange & purple flowers, ca. 1930s (minor glaze scratches)... **$345**

Bowl, 6 1/4" d., octagonal flanged rim on the rounded body, Woodland patt., stylized landscape w/trees in orange, green, black, blue, purple & yellow, marked............. **550**

Bowl, 6 1/2" d., 3" h., "Bizarre" ware, footed deep slightly flaring sides, Crocus patt., the sides divided into two horizontal bands of color w/a band of small crocus blossoms along the upper half, in orange, blue, purple & green, stamped mark... **550**

Bowl, 7 1/2" d., 3 1/8" h., Forest Glen patt., a thin footring below the deep upright round sides curved around the base, a variation w/an orange & brown sky produced in Delicia runnings, mottled orange interior, marked, ca. 1936 (glaze flaking around rim)... **288**

Bowl, 8" d., 3 3/4" h., "Bizarre" ware, deep gently rounded sides tapering to a footring, Original Bizarre patt., a wide band of blocks & triangles around the upper half in blue, orange, ivory & purple, purple band around the bottom section, marked.. **650**

Bowl, 8" d., 4 1/4" h., "Bizarre" ware, octagonal, h.p. w/Original Bizarre patt., large crudely painted bands of maroon, dark orange & dark blue diamonds above an ochre base band, ink mark **1,100**

Bowl, 8 3/8" d., 3 1/2" h., round w/deep upright sides, Keyhole patt., a geometric design in yellow, black & green, stamped marks, ca. 1929 (glaze wear) **374**

Bowl, 9" d., deep rounded sides, the upper half w/a wide band in polychrome featuring large stylized cottages w/pointed orange roofs beneath arching trees, lime green banding, marked................................... **800**

Bowl, 9 1/2" d., 4 1/2" h., orange, green & blue h.p. poppies **600**

Butter dish, cov., "Bizarre" ware, Crocus patt., a wide shallow base w/low, upright sides fitted w/a shallow, flat-sided cover w/a slightly domed top & flat button finial, the top decorated w/purple, blue & orange blossoms on an ivory ground, marked, 4" d., 2 3/4" h..................... **550**

A Variety of Clarice Cliff Patterns

Butter dish, cov., "Bizarre" ware, short wide cylindrical body w/an inset cover w/large button finial, Secrets patt., decorated w/a stylized landscape in shades of green, yellow & brown w/red-roofed houses on a cream ground, marked, 4" d., 2 5/8" h. (ILLUS. left) **550**

Candleholders, figural, modeled as a kneeling woman w/her arms raised high holding the candle socket modeled as a basket of flowers, My Garden patt., orange dress & polychrome trim, marked, 7 1/4" h., facing pr. **575**

Various Clarice Cliff Items

Candleholders, Fantasque line, cylindrical form w/flared base & rim, Melon patt., decorated w/a band of overlapping fruit in predominantly orange glaze w/yellow, bluish green & brown outline, stamped on base "Hand Painted Fantasque by Clarice Cliff Wilkinson Ltd. England," ca. 1930, minor glaze nicks, two small firing cracks to inside rim of one, 3 1/4" h., pr. (ILLUS. front)... **1,380**

Candlestick, loop-handled, Tonquin patt., red **30**

Two Pairs of Clarice Cliff Candlesticks

Candlesticks, slender baluster-form shaft above a disk foot & w/a wide flattened rim, painted w/bold geometric designs in blue, orange & green, Delicia Citrus patt., brightly painted fruits on a cream ground pr. (ILLUS. left & right)................................. **2,500**

Candlesticks, squared pedestal foot supporting a tall square tapering shaft & cylindrical socket w/flared rim, decorated in bold geometric designs in orange, cream, green, blue & yellow, pr. (ILLUS. center) **2,900**

Clarice Cliff Figural Centerpiece

Centerpiece, "Bizarre" ware, model of a stylized Viking longboat, raised on trestle supports & w/a frog insert, glazed in orange, yellow, brown & black on a cream ground, printed factory marks, ca. 1925, restored, 15 3/4" l., 9 5/8" h., 2 pcs. (ILLUS.)... **1,500**

Rare Crest Pattern Charger

Charger, large round dished form, Crest patt., three large Japanese-style crests in gold, blue, rust red, black & green on a mottled green ground (ILLUS.)................. **12,000**

Charger, Taormina patt., round, decorated w/large stylized trees on a cliff top w/the sea in the distance in tones of orange, yellow, green & blue, marked, 17" d. (minor crazing) **1,093**

Coffee service: cov. coffeepot, creamer, open sugar bowl, five cake plates & six cups & saucers; Ravel patt., creamer & sugar w/pointed conical bodies supported by buttress legs, other serving pieces w/flaring cylindrical bodies, marked, coffeepot 6" h., the set...................................... **1,100**

Condiment set: two jars w/silver-plated lids & a small open bowl fitted in a silver-plated frame w/a looped center handle; each piece h.p. w/stylized red & blue flowers on an ivory ground, marked, tray 4 1/2 x 5", the set (small chip on one piece).. **523**

Cracker jar, cov., "Bizarre" ware, Blue Chintz patt., stylized blue, green & pink blossom forms w/blue border band (ILLUS. center w/plate)............................... **1,800**

Cracker jar, cov., "Bizarre" ware, bulbous barrel shape w/large side knobs to support the arched woven wicker bail handle, wide flat mouth w/a slightly domed cover centered by a large ball finial, Gayday patt., decorated w/a wide band of large stylized flowers in orange, rust, amethyst, blue & green above a lower band in orange on a cream ground, the cover w/an orange finial & yellow band, 5 7/8" d., 6 1/4" h. (ILLUS. right w/butter dish).. **975**

Delicia Citrus Cracker Jar & Vases

Cracker jar, cov., "Bizarre" ware, squatty kettle-form w/side knobs supporting the swing bail handle, Delicia Citrus patt. (ILLUS. right)... **1,400**

Cracker jar, cov., Celtic Harvest patt., spherical footed body decorated w/embossed fruit & sheaves of wheat, chromed metal cover, 6 1/2" h. (chrome wear).. **173**

Cup & saucer, "Bizarre" ware, Autumn Crocus patt., Athens shape.................................... **300**

"Bizarre" Demitasse Set

Demitasse set: cov. coffeepot, six demitasse cups & saucers, creamer & open
sugar bowl; "Bizarre" ware, Fantasque
patt., decorated w/a stylized tree on one
side, the other w/stylized hollyhocks,
small chips to one saucer, 15 pcs.
(ILLUS. of part).. **3,200**

Dinner service: four dinner plates, thirteen
luncheon plates, fifteen soup bowls, eight
fruit plates, seven appetizer plates, four
dessert plates, seven cups & saucers,
cov. sugar, creamer & serving bowl; Biar-
ritz patt., the square plates w/deep
rounded wells, the creamer & sugar
w/upright flattened round shapes, each
decorated w/concentric bands in black,
maroon, taupe, gold & yellow on a cream
ground, ca. 1929, marked, the set............. **1,150**

Figures, "Bizarre" ware, flat cutouts, com-
prising two groups of musicians & two
groups of dancing couples, all highly stylized & glazed in reddish orange, yellow,
lime green, cream & black, printed facto-
ry marks, ca. 1925, 5 5/8 to 7" h., 4 pcs.. **29,000**

Jam jar, cov., cylindrical body, Melon patt.,
decorated w/a band of overlapping fruit,
predominantly orange w/yellow, blue &
green w/brown outline, ca. 1930, restoration to rim & side, marked, 4" h. (ILLUS.
top right w/candleholders) **690**

Jam pot, cov., Blue Firs patt., flat-sided
round form on small log feet, domed cover w/flat round knob, stylized landscape
w/trees, marked, 4 1/4" h. **900**

Lemonade set: 8" h. tankard pitcher & four
cylindrical tumblers; each decorated in
an abstract geometric pattern in orange,
blue, purple, green & yellow, marked, the
set.. **1,100**

Pitcher, 5 1/8" h., "Fantasque" line, squared
base w/flattened spherical sides, Autumn
(Balloon Trees) patt. in blue, yellow,
green, orange, black & purple, stamped
on base "Registration Applied For Fantasque Hand Painted Bizarre by Clarice
Cliff Newport Pottery England," ca. 1931,
minor glaze bubbles & nicks (ILLUS. cen-
ter right w/candleholders) **920**

Pitcher, 5 3/4" h., "Fantasque" line, Melon
patt., wide conical body w/solid triangular
handle, orange & thin black bands flanking a wide central band of stylized mel-
ons in yellow, blue, green & orange,
marked, ca. 1930 (tiny glaze nicks at rim
& base, faint scratch in lower orange
band).. **875**

Pitcher, 6 7/8" h., "Bizarre" ware, flaring cylindrical body w/a wide rim & wide arched
spout opposite an angled handle, Secrets patt., decorated w/a stylized landscape in shades of green, yellow &
brown w/a red-roofed house on a cream
ground, stamped mark...................................... **900**

Pitcher, 7" h., 7" d., "Bizarre" ware, tapering
cylindrical body w/flat rim & wide pointed
spout, flattened angled handle from rim
to base, Sliced Fruit patt., wide band of
abstract fruit in yellow, orange & red,
stamped mark **1,800**

Pitcher, 9 1/4" h., My Garden patt., wide rim
tapering to a flared base w/embossed
flowers ornamenting the handle in orange, green & brown on a light tan
ground, post-1936 .... **288**

Pitcher, 9 3/4" h., 7 3/4" d., jug-type, "Bizarre" ware, Isis shape, Summerhouse
patt., decorated w/trees & gazebos in
yellow, green, purple, red & blue against
an ivory ground, marked **3,900**

Lotus Pitcher in Delicia Citrus Pattern

Pitcher, 12" h., "Bizarre" ware, Lotus shape,
ringed ovoid body tapering to a wide cylindrical neck, heavy loop handle, Delicia
Citrus patt., large stylized red, yellow &
orange fruits around the top w/green
leaves & streaky green on a cream
ground (ILLUS.) **2,200**

Pitcher, 12" h., jug-type, "Bizarre" ware,
Trees & House patt., ovoid w/molded
narrow rings, decorated w/wide bands of
orange & black flanking a wide central
band w/green-roofed houses & black &
orange trees, marked, ca. 1930 .... **1,265**

Plate, 7 3/4" d., Broth patt., predominantly
orange w/bubbles & orange, purple &
blue cobwebs (few glaze scratches)............ **230**

Plate, 9" d., "Bizarre" ware, Blue Chintz
patt., decorated w/stylized flowers in
green, blue & pink against an ivory
ground, marked.. **650**

Plate, 9 3/4" d., Forest Glen patt., a stylized
cottage in a woodland scene in orange,

ivory & green, die-stamped "Clarice Cliff - Newport Pottery - England" **950**

Plate, 10" d., "Fantasque" line, Autumn (Balloon Trees) patt. w/blue, yellow, green & purple trees & orange striped border bands, base stamped "Fantasque Hand Painted Bizarre by Clarice Cliff Newport Pottery England" (ILLUS. center left w/candleholders) **1,725**

Sugar shaker, Autumn patt., sharply pointed conical form w/rows of small holes pierced around the top, decorated in pastel autumn colors, marked, 5 1/2" h. **1,200**

Sugar shaker, "Bizarre" ware, Crocus patt., sharply pointed conical form, decorated w/blue, purple & orange crocus flowers, marked, ca. 1930, 5 5/8" h. (chips on base) **460**

Sugar shaker, "Bizarre" ware, flattened egg-shaped body set on two tiny log-form feet, Crocus patt., banded body w/a central row of stylized crocus blossoms, in yellow, blue, orange & purple, stamped mark, 2 1/2" w., 5" h. **750**

Tumbler, Sunray patt., conical form, polychrome decoration of a stylized sun, orange banding, marked, 3" h. **600**

Vase, 5 1/4" h., "Bizarre" ware, Shape No. 341, squatty bulbous chalice-form, Delicia Citrus patt., bright fruits on a creamy ground (ILLUS. left w/cracker jar) **900**

Vase, 8" h., "Bizarre" ware, Nasturtium patt., footed ovoid body w/a flaring rolled rim, decorated w/vivid orange, red & yellow blossoms w/black, red, yellow & green leaves atop a mottled caramel & tan ground against a white background, marked "Nasturtium - Bizarre by Clarice Cliff - Hand painted - England" **900**

Vase, 8" h., "Bizarre" ware, Shape No. 362, ovoid upper body above a heavy ringed & waisted base, Delicia Citrus patt., brightly painted fruits on a cream ground (ILLUS. center w/cracker jar) **1,200**

Vase, 8" h., "Bizarre" ware, Shape No. 386, swelled cylindrical base below the angled shoulder & tall gently flaring neck, Crocus patt., a yellow rim band & brown bottom section below a cluster of colorful crocus blossoms on a cream ground (ILLUS.) **1,500**

Vase, 9" h., 4 3/4" d., "Bizarre" ware, baluster-shaped, Original Bizarre patt., a wide middle band of multicolored triangles flanked by a dark blue rim band & yellow & orange base bands, No. 264, ink mark (minor wear) **2,500**

Vase, 9 1/2" h., 6 1/2" d., "Bizarre" ware, Isis shape, ovoid body tapering to a wide, flat rim, decorated in the Melon patt., bold stylized abstract fruits in dark red, blue, orange, green & yellow around the middle flanked by wide dark orange bands, ink mark **3,200**

Vase, 10 7/8" h., "Bizarre" ware, My Garden patt., cylindrical form tapering to flared foot decorated w/h.p. relief-molded orange & yellow flowers & black leaves on golden mushroom ground, shape No. 664, Wilkinson, Ltd. **650**

Vase, 11 3/4" h., 10" d., "Bizarre" ware, Lotus shape, Geometric patt., urn-form, handled, decorated w/a wide maroon base band & wide green neck band flanking a wide central band of triangular devices in a row in cream, purple, blue, maroon & green, blue & cream rim bands & cream handles, marked **2,900**

Vase, 12 1/4" h., gently flaring conical body on a wide round foot, molded in bold relief w/green & yellow budgie birds on a leafy branch against a light blue shaded to cream ground **410**

Clarice Cliff Crocus Vase

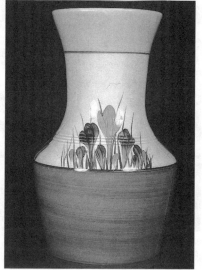

Crocus Pattern Vase

Vases, 8" h., "Bizarre" ware, footed ovoid
body w/flared rim, Crocus patt., orange,
blue & purple crocuses, green, brown &
yellow bands, small glaze chip, marked,
pr. (ILLUS. of one)... **690**

Cleminson Clay

*Betty Cleminson began her home-based business,
Cleminson Clay, in Monterey Park, California, in 1941.
Begun as just a hobby for Betty, most items were decorated by her hand and greeted with great enthusiasm. It
became necessary by 1943 to move to larger facilities
where mass production could begin. A factory was built
in El Monte, California, and Betty enlisted the help of
her schoolteacher husband, George, to handle business
affairs while she continued to create. The company name
was also changed at this time to "The California Cleminsons."One of her first pieces, a crude but delightful pie
bird, was so popular that Betty concentrated her initial
efforts on kitchen-related items. She created butter
dishes, canisters, cookie jars, etc. By the mid-'40s, with
up to 150 employees, she was able to expand her lines
with giftware such as vases, wall plaques, cups and saucers, figurines, and a full line of tableware called Dis-
tlefink.Business remained good in the 1950s as most
Cleminson items were inexpensive and could compete
with the imported Japanese wares. In the 1960s, however, due to the large amount of hand work and costs to
produce quality pieces, it became increasingly difficult
to compete. In 1963, Betty and George Cleminson
decided to close the pottery.Betty Cleminson's incised
"bc" mark is the earliest mark found. More common is a
stamped mark, "The California Cleminsons," which can
be found with or without a boy and girl on either side of
a circular shield.*

Cleminson Cleanser Shaker

Cleanser shaker, figure of a woman standing, yellow hair, pink scarf over head,
pink & white dress w/grey trim, five holes
in top of head, originally included a card
around her neck w/a poem explaining
that she was a cleanser shaker, marked
w/copyright symbol & the plate w/a girl &
boy on each side, 6 1/2" h. (ILLUS.) **48**
Cleanser shaker, figure of woman standing,
yellow hair, brown scarf, white & brown
apron over yellow dress, blue accents,
very common, 6 1/2" h...................................... **38**

Galagray Line Bowl

Bowl, 3" d., 2 3/4" h., straight 1/4" base rising to a lightly flared rim, Galagray line,
grey ground w/red gloss inside & red abstract leaves around the outside center
(ILLUS.)... **$29**
Butter dish, cov., figural, model of a Dis-
tlefink sitting on an oblong base, bird's
head turned toward back, brown glossy
glaze w/dark brown & rust accents,
7 1/2" l., 5 3/4" h. **59**
Butter dish, cov., figural, round model of a
pudgy woman w/her skirt forming the lid
& her upper body forming the handle,
green dish w/cover in white gloss w/dark
& light green, dark brown & black glazes,
7" h.. **145**

Cleminson Clay Creamer

Creamer, figural, model of rooster, white
w/green & pink accents, stamped mark,
5 1/2" h. (ILLUS.)... **49**

"For A Good Egg" Egg Cup

Egg cup, boy's face on front, "For A Good Egg" on reverse, no mark, 3 3/4" h. (ILLUS.) **42**

"Morning After" Mug

Mug, cov., irregular shape w/front showing man's face w/hung-over expression, model of water bag forms lid, "Morning After" on reverse & "Never Again" on inside bottom, stamped mark, 5" h. (ILLUS.) **49**

Mug, girl & boy drinking on front, "Now Is The Hour" on reverse, stamped mark, 3 1/4" h. **24**

Juvenile Mug

Mug, juvenile, round knobs on sides, scene of Native American boy & his dog playing on front, stamped mark, 4 1/4" h. (ILLUS.) **65**

Cleminson Clay Laundry Sprinkler

Laundry sprinkler, figural, Oriental man, hat forms metal top, stamped mark, 9" h. (ILLUS.) **85**

Cleminson Clay Pie Bird

Pie bird, figural, model of a bird, white body decorated in pink, blue & green, early mark, 1941, 4 1/2" h. (ILLUS.) **75**

Pitcher, 10 1/2" h., figural, model of a Distlefink, beak forms spout, tail is handle, white body w/brown & green accents **58**

Plate, 6 1/2" d., pale blue background w/white & black silhouette, woman standing & churning butter **25**

Plate, 7" d., ecru ground w/stylized fruit in center w/green leaves, blue rectangles around verge, two factory-drilled holes for hanging **20**

Plate, 7" d., scalloped rim, decorated w/flowers & butterflies, two holes for hanging, stamped mark **32**

Razor blade bank, model of a man's face, w/hand holding razor, slot in top for used blades, unglazed bottom w/stamped mark, 3 1/4" h. **55**

Recipe holder, small footed oblong base rising to scalloped sides & rim, hearts & flowers motif, "Recipe holder" in brown & black, 4" l., 3" h. **34**

Cleminson Clay Ring Holder

Ring holder, figural, model of a dog w/tail straight up to hold jewelry, white body w/tan & dark brown accents, marked w/copyright symbol & plate w/a boy & girl on either side, 3" l., 2 3/4" h. (ILLUS.) **38**

Salt box w/hinged wooden lid, figural bucket, white ground w/"Salt" in maroon & green & maroon leaves, cherry fruit & leaves at top near drilled hole for hanging, 8" h. **69**

Salt & pepper shakers, figural man & woman on square bases, Galagray line, red & grey colors, 6" h., pr. **35**

Cleminson Sock Darner

Sock darner, white ground w/h.p. woman's face & brown hair, blue & maroon accents, words "darn it" on front near bottom, feet on bottom unseen from standing position, 5" h. (ILLUS.) **70**

Spoon rest, elongated quatrefoil w/gloss grey & orange, dark grey & tan leaves & blossoms, 8 1/2" l. **29**

String holder, heart-shaped **75**

Tea bag holder, model of a teapot w/"Let Me Hold The Bag" in center, stamped mark, 4 1/4" w. **22**

Vase, model of a watering can **30**

Wall Plaque with Applied Flowers

Wall plaque, oval w/scalloped rim trimmed in brown on inside edge, applied flowers & leaves in center w/h.p. background flowers, green gloss leaves, pink flower bud & two pink flowers w/yellow centers, two factory holes for hanging, boy & girl mark, 6 3/4" h. (ILLUS.) **45**

Cleminson Clay Wall Plaque

Wall plaque, oval w/scalloped rim trimmed in brown on inside edge, applied pansy-like flowers & leaves in center, one in pinks, one yellow & blue, h.p. background flowers, green gloss leaves, two factory holes for hanging, 6 3/4" h. (ILLUS.) **45**

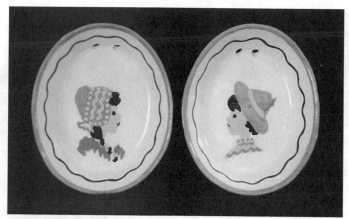

Cleminson Clay Wall Plaques

Wall plaques, oval, white ground, blue rims, scalloped brown line inside rims, centers w/bust profiles of boy in blue Alpine-type hat & girl in blue & pink bonnet, both w/brown hair & eyes, each plaque w/two holes for hanging, bc mark, 4 1/4" h., pr (ILLUS.).. **29**

Wall pocket, model of a frying pan w/design on bottom, "Them that works hard eats hearty," hole in handle for hanging, ink stamp mark, 11 3/8" l. including handle.......... **45**

Wall Pocket in Form of Scoop

Wall pocket, model of a scoop, white body w/blue & red flowers & green leaves, second mark without boy & girl on each side, marked "hand painted" & copyright symbol, 9" l. (ILLUS.)... **45**

Wall pocket, model of a teapot, wire & wood handle painted w/flowers, blue & brown glazes w/heart-shaped motif w/"Kitchen bright & a singing kettle make home the place you want to settle," marked w/boy & girl, 9" d., 6" h. **49**

Wall pocket, slightly flared top & bottom w/top showing "Let's pay off the Mortgage" & bottom showing a house & trees, gloss rose, 7" h. **38**

Wall pocket, white ground w/scalloped blue edge, "Once burned" at top, "Twice shy" at bottom, woman holding spoon facing away from a black wood-burning kitchen stove, ink stamp mark, 5 1/4" sq...................... **42**

Clewell Wares

Although Charles W. Clewell of Canton, Ohio, didn't operate a pottery, he is responsible for a category of fine art pottery through his development of a unique metal coating placed on pottery blanks obtained from Owens, Weller and others. By encasing objects in a thin metal shell, he produced copper- and bronze-finished ceramics. Later experiments led him to chemically treat the metal coating to attain the bluish green patinated effect associated with copper and bronze. Although he produced metal-coated pottery from 1902 until the mid-1950s, Clewell's production was quite limited, for he felt no one else could competently recreate his artwork, therefore operated a small shop with little help.

Clewell Wares Mark

Bowl-vase, a small footring supporting a wide bulbous body w/a short widely flared rim, fine bronzed & verdigris patina, incised "Clewell 417-2-G," 5 1/4" d., 4 1/2" h. **$495**

Vase, 3 3/8" h., bulbous body w/short molded rim, brown patina on upper half w/crusty green patina below, marked "Clewell" (minor scuffs).................................... **252**

Vase, 4 5/8" h., bulbous ovoid shouldered body tapering to cylindrical neck w/flaring rim, green over brown patina, base incised "Clewell 466" (patina polished away in small spots about the shoulder) **224**

A Variety of Copper-clad Clewell Vases

Vase, 5 1/2" h., 7" d., copper-clad, squatty
  bulbous body tapering to a short cylindrical neck w/slightly flaring rim, loop handles from center of body to rim, incised
  "Clewell - 408-2-6," normal wear to fine
  bronze to verdigris patina, tight lines in
  copper on shoulder (ILLUS. lower left) **788**
Vase, 6 1/4" h., 3 1/2" d., simple ovoid body
  w/molded rim, copper-clad w/fine verdigris to bronze patina, some patination
  flakes to rim, incised "Clewell - 321 - 24"
  (ILLUS. lower center) **619**

Clewell Vase with Shiny Patina

Vase, 7" h., simple ovoid form tapering to a
  small flat mouth, overall shiny coppery
  patina, signed, light scratches & wear
  (ILLUS.) **374**

Small Slender Clewell Vase

Vase, 6 1/2" h., a wide round base tapering
  to a slender waisted body, deep red patina w/pale green patina band around the
  base, small glaze chips around base
  (ILLUS.) **287**

Clewell Vase with Original Patina

Vase, 7 1/4" h., round foot below the bulbous lower body tapering to tall trumpet-
  form sides, even dark bronze original pa-
  tina, signed (ILLUS.) **287**

Clewell Vase with Shaded Patina

Vase, 7 1/2" h., 3 1/2" d., ovoid body w/the
rounded shoulder centering a small flaring neck, dark green verdigris shaded to
dark reddish bronze patina, incised
"Clewell - 351 - 215" (ILLUS.)..................... **1,725**

Vase, 7 3/4" h., bulbous base tapering to tall
cylindrical neck w/flared rim, early 20th
c., inscribed "Clewell 293-29" **575**

Clewell Vase No. 463

Vase, 8 1/2" h., broad-shouldered tapering
ovoid body w/a small, short rolled neck,
No. 463, some surface glaze flaws & flak-
ing (ILLUS.) **431**

Clewell Vase with Dark Green Patina

Vase, 7 1/2" h., 3 3/4" d., ovoid body w/the
rounded shoulder centering a small flaring neck, overall shaded dark green to
lighter green verdigris patina, couple of
small patina flakes near base, incised
"Clewell - 351- 6" (ILLUS.) **920**

Ovoid Clewell Vase

Vase, 8 1/2" h., 5" d., simple ovoid form tapering to a flat rim, deep reddish bronze
& verdigris patina, pea-sized colored
spot near base, incised "Clewell - 60-
215" (ILLUS.)..**978**
Vase, 9" h., 4 1/2" d., tall slender tapering
urn-form body w/a flattened shoulder
centering a short rolled neck flanked by
small angled handles, bronze & verdigris
patina, incised "C.W. Clewell - 520-220"
(few patina chips on base).......................... **1,125**

Clifton Pottery Humidor

Humidor, cov., Indian Ware, cylindrical w/in-
set cover w/large knob handle, dark
brown ground w/black stylized geometric
designs, two chips at rim (ILLUS.)............. **$109**
Pitcher, 7" d., wide squatty bulbous body tapering to a wide slightly rolled rim w/low
arched spout, D-form loop handle, cream
ground incised & painted w/stylized geo-
metric black flying birds................................. **176**
Vase, 6" h., wide bulbous tapering ovoid
body w/a small cylindrical neck w/flared
rim, bold Greek key-style Native American designs in deep brick red outlined in
cream against a black ground, incised
mark... **275**
Vase, 6 1/2" h., tall slender tapering cylindri-
cal body w/a tiny cylindrical neck, the
body in green & tan crystalline glaze decorated overall w/a silver overlay design of
stylized blossoms & long tendrils ar-
ranged as oblong reserves up the sides
& around the neck, incised mark **1,430**
Vase, 8" h., 11" d., Native American design,
"Homolobi," large squatty bulbous body
centered by a wide, short cylindrical
neck, decorated w/large repeating S-
scroll design & borders in black on a terra
cotta ground, incised "Clifton 233" & titled
(typical glaze flaking) **495**

Clewell Vase No. 305-6

Vase, 10" h., tall baluster-form body, fine
bronzed patina, No. 305-6, signed
(ILLUS.).. 862
Vase, 11" h., 7 3/4" d., copper-clad wide
slightly flaring cylindrical body w/a narrow angled shoulder to the wide closed
rim, unusual striated gold, green & copper patina, minor ceramic loss inside rim,
incised "Clewell" (ILLUS. far right, with
group) 1,392
Vase, 11 1/4" h., 8 1/2" d., a large gently
flaring cylindrical body w/a wide angled
shoulder centering a low squatty neck,
verdigris finish, signed 2,760
Vase, 14 1/2" h., 6 1/4" d., tall baluster-form
copper-clad body w/flared rim on the
short cylindrical neck, bronze to verdigris
patina, small flakes to verdigris & some
splits to copper on neck, incised "Clewell
- 378 - 26" (ILLUS. top center, with group).. 2,588

Clifton Pottery

*William A. Long, founder of the Lonhuda Pottery,
joined Fred Tschirner, a chemist, to found the Clifton
Art Pottery in Newark, New Jersey, in 1905. Crystal
Patina was their first art pottery line and featured a subdued pale green crystalline glaze later also made in
shades of yellow and tan. In 1906 its Indian Ware line,
based on the pottery made by American Indians, was
introduced. Other lines they produced include Tirrube
and Robin's-egg Blue. Floor and wall tiles became the
focus of the production after 1911, and by 1914 the
firm's name had changed to Clifton Porcelain Tile Company, which better reflected its production.*

Clifton Native American-style Vase

Vase, 9 1/2" h., Native American form vessel w/a wide squatty bulbous base centered by a wide cylindrical neck, incised

& painted w/geometric designs in black, cream, tan & dark brown, incised mark (ILLUS.).. **330**

Vase, 9 1/2" h., 4 1/2" d., ovoid form tapering to a short cylindrical neck, Crystal Patina, mottled creamy white & greenish yellow glaze, incised "Clifton - 158" **385**

Vase, 10" h., 7" w., a gently flaring cylindrical lower body below a wide shoulder centering a tall cylindrical neck, long pointed angled handles from the rim to the shoulder, Crystal Patina glaze, incised mark... **495**

Copeland & Spode

W.T. Copeland & Sons, Ltd., has operated the Spode Works at Stoke, England, from 1847 to the present. The name Spode was used on some of its productions. Its predecessor, Spode, was founded by Josiah Spode about 1784 and became Copeland & Garrett in 1843, continuing under that name until 1847. Listings dated prior to 1843 should be attributed to Spode.

Copeland & Spode Mark

Rare Copeland Majolica Candlestick

Candlestick, majolica, Water Lily patt., baluster-form standard w/a cobalt blue ground molded w/pink blossoms & green leaves below brown molded socket bands, the round base w/brown ribbed band & a band of green leaves on a blue ground, grey rim band, Copeland, late 19th c., minor hairline in top, 6 1/2" h. (ILLUS.)... **$770**

Compote, open, green floral decoration, ca. 1860, 9 3/8" d., 4 3/4" h.................................... **66**

Dessert plates, decorated w/raised floral border against lapis blue & overglazed floral enamel centers against white ground, ca. 1891-1915, No. 2694S, England, set of 12 .... **180**

Dessert plates, each finely decorated in raised paste gilding w/a different exotic bird perched on rockwork or branches detailed in turquoise & white enamel, within a scalloped gilt-edged rim, painted by C.B. Brough, printed Copeland-Spode mark, artist-signed, retailer's mark, ca. 1884, 8 1/4" d., set of 10 (some slight rubbing)... **5,700**

Dessert service: footed oval dish, eleven dessert plates; each piece of festoon-embossed shape, each finely painted w/two panels of oranges alternating w/two panels of different colorful flowers reserved on a pierced border richly decorated w/raised paste gilding, green printed "Spode Copeland's China England" & retailer's mark, ca. 1937, the set................ **7,800**

Dinner service: 14 soup plates, 23 luncheon plates, a large 15" l. cov. tureen & undertray, a small tureen w/mismatched cover, two small trays, four graduated oval platters, largest 21" l., & ten 10 1/4" d. dinner plates; all in an Imari-style colorful transfer-printed decoration of black florals in center & around borders decorated w/underglaze-blue & red enamels, the set (chips, stains) **990**

Dinner service: eleven dinner plates, eight each luncheon plates, salad/dessert plates, bread & butter plates, cream soup bowls, saucers & teacups, sauce dishes, cereal bowls, six coffee cups & saucers, seven square dessert plates, two graduated platters, one each oval open vegetable dish, relish dish, butter cover, cov. teapot, milk pitcher, cov. sugar bowl, creamer & gravy boat w/undertray; Tower patt., pink, early 20th c., 112 pcs. (one dinner plate chipped, gravy boat stained) **1,100**

Dinner service: nine each dinner plates, salad/dessert plates, bread & butter plates, saucers & teacups, demitasse cups & saucers; Maritime Rose patt., R4118, late 19th-early 20th c., 63 pcs. **950**

Dinner service: thirteen 9 3/4" d. dinner plates, three rimmed soup plates, six dessert plates; each round w/a central botanical specimen on a white ground, continuing to a wide rim w/molded scrolling leafage & dolphin decoration ending in a gilt edge, Spode, ca. 1813-15, some w/iron-red factory mark, the set **920**

Dinner service: twelve each dinner plates, luncheon plates, teacups & saucers, fourteen square dessert plates, ten each bread & butter plates, soup/cereal bowls, sauce dishes, cream soup bowls & saucers, six egg cups, two each round meat platters & square open vegetable dishes, one each teapot, cov. sugar bowl, creamer, gravy boat w/undertray, round cov. vegetable bowl, cov. soup tureen w/ladle, scalloped round vegetable bowl, rectangular cov. vegetable dish, triple divided relish server & relish dish; Tower patt., blue, early 20th c., 134 pcs. **1,900**

Figure of St. Filomena, parian, standing w/a lamp & staff, Copeland, late 19th c., 26" h. (losses) **748**

Pitcher, 6 1/2" h., majolica, Lotus patt., rounded four-panel sides w/each panel molded w/a pink blossom & green leaves, squared neck, brown branch handle, Copeland, late 19th c. **1,430**

Pitcher, 8 1/4" h., "Chicago" design, stoneware, decorated w/molded medallions & vignettes depicting the early history of Chicago in white on a matte blue ground, impressed "Copeland England - Copeland Late Spode, England" & "Chicago Pitcher - Designed by Frank E. Burley, Edition Delux, Burley & Co., Chicago," late 19th c. **460**

Pitcher, 8 1/2" h., majolica, Wheat patt., ovoid body w/rim spout & angled handle, cobalt blue ground molded w/pink & yellow wheat & green leaves, Copeland, late 19th c. **1,045**

Pitcher, 9" h., majolica, tall ovoid body w/a wide arched spout & undulating handle, the sides w/lavender panels molded in colors w/a woman & swan in water on one side & a woman w/a dolphin on the other, panels surrounded by bouquets of flowers, pedestal base molded w/shells, green, yellow & brown trim, Copeland, late 19th c. **1,925**

Plate, 8 1/4" d., Caramanian patt., medium blue, Spode, first half 19th c. **220**

Plate, 10" d., Caramanian patt., light to medium blue, Spode, first half 19th c. **176**

One of a Pair of Spode Cabinet Plates

Plates, 9 3/4" d., gilt rim & turquoise border, center cartouche w/painted landscape, marked "Copeland and Garret," ca. 1845, pr. (ILLUS. of one).............................. **252**

Plates, dinner, 10 1/2" d., powder blue banded border w/gilt floral & foliate deco-

rations, impressed & printed marks, 20th c., set of 12.. **374**

Platter, 18 7/8" l., oval, ironstone, bluish black transfer-printed design of delicate leaf swags & blossoms around the wide flanged rim, stylized leafy scrolls & stems of stylized flowers around the inner border, impressed "Copeland," 19th c. **105**

Soup plate, Caramanian patt., medium blue, Spode, first half 19th c., 10" d. **220**

Teapot, cov., pâte-sur-pâte, nearly spherical body w/an inset domed cover, swan's-neck spout & C-scroll handle, dark cobalt blue ground w/bluish white-relief band of classical figures below a leaf sprig shoulder band, the cover w/white radiating pointed leaves around the white knop, marked, ca. 1894-1910, 5" h. **165**

Vegetable set: 13" l. oval cov. vegetable bowl & seven matching bowls; blue & white transfer-printed foliate design, factory marks, ca. 1880, the set (wear) **201**

Cowan

R. Guy Cowan opened his first pottery studio in 1912 in Lakewood, Ohio. The pottery operated almost continuously, with the exception of a break during the First World War, at various locations in the Cleveland area until it was forced to close in 1931 due to financial difficulties.

Many of this century's finest artists began with Cowan and its associate, the Cleveland School of Art. This fine art pottery, particularly the designer pieces, are highly sought after by collectors.

Many people are unaware that it was due to R. Guy Cowan's perseverance and tireless work that art pottery is today considered an art form and found in many art museums.

Cowan Mark

Ashtray, model of a ram, green, designed by Edris Eckhardt, 5 1/4" l., 3 1/2" h. (ILLUS. lower left with chick ashtray/nut dish)... **$200**

Ashtray, center relief-molded unicorn decoration, caramel glaze, designed by Waylande Gregory, w/footed foliate metal stand, Shape No. 925, 3/4 x 5 1/2"..................... **90**

Ashtray, three-section base w/figural leaping gazelle & foliage on edge, Oriental Red glaze, designed by Waylande Gregory, 5 3/4" h. (ILLUS. lower right with horse book end & boy & girl book ends)........ **350**

Ashtray/nut dish, ivory glaze, Shape No. 769, 1" h... **25**

Cowan Clown Ashtrays & Vases

Ashtray/nut dish, figural clown Periot, blue or ivory glaze, designed by Elizabeth Anderson, Shape No. 788, 2 1/2 x 3", each (ILLUS. lower center) **150**

Cowan Ashtrays, Flower Frog & Vase

Ashtray/nut dish, model of a chick, green glaze, Shape No. 768, 3 1/2" h. (ILLUS. bottom center) **75**
Book ends, figural, model of a fish, Oriental Red glaze, Shape No. 863, 4 5/8" h., pr. **750**
Book ends, figural Art Deco-style elephant, push & pull, tan glaze, designed by Thelma F. Winter, one Shape No. 840 & one Shape No. 841, 4 3/4" h., pr. **1,600**

Cowan Book Ends & Model of Horse

Book ends, figural, model of a seated polar bear, front paws near face, ivory glaze, designed by Margaret Postgate, 6" h., pr. (ILLUS. left) **1,600**
Book ends, figural, a nude kneeling boy & nude kneeling girl, each on oblong bases, creamy white glaze, designed by Frank N. Wilcox, Shape No. 519, Marks 8 & 9, ca. 1925, 6 1/2" h., pr. (ILLUS. with Cowan ashtray & kicking horse book end) **550**
Book ends, figural, a little girl standing wearing a large sunbonnet & full ruffled dress, verde green, designed by Kat. Barnes Jenkins, Shape No. 521, 7" h., pr. **700**

Variety of Cowan Animal Pieces

Book ends, figural, model of a unicorn, front legs raised on relief-molded foliage base, orange glaze, designed by Waylande Gregory, Shape No. 961, mark No. 8, 7" h., pr. (ILLUS. left) **1,000**

Book ends, figural, model of a ram, black, thick rectangular base w/slanted top, Shape No. E-3, designed by Waylande Gregory, 7 1/2" h., pr.................................... **2,500**

Elephant Book Ends & Paperweights

Book ends, figural, modeled as a large rounded stylized elephant w/trunk curved under, standing on a stepped rectangular base, overall Oriental Red glaze, designed by Margaret Postgate, Shape No. E-2, 7 1/4" h., pr. (ILLUS. top center & lower left).. **2,000**

Book ends, "Pierette," stylized figure of young woman wearing a short flaring skirt & holding a scarf behind her, russet & salmon glaze, designed by Elizabeth Anderson, Shape No. 792, 8 1/4" h. (ILLUS. center with polar bear book ends) **2,300**

Cowan Book Ends & Ashtray

Book ends, model of a stylized horse, back legs raised in kicking position, black, designed by Waylande Gregory, Shape No. E-1, 9" h., pr. (ILLUS. of one, with ashtray & boy & girl book ends)........................ **2,500**

Book ends, figural, a little girl standing wearing a sunbonnet & full ruffled dress, on a thick rectangular base, ivory semi-matte glaze, Shape No. 521, impressed mark & "Z," ca. 1925, 4" w., 7 1/4" h., pr. **550**

Bowl, miniature, 2" d., footed, flared body, Shape No. 514, mark No. 5, orange lustre **60**

Bowl, 5 1/4" d., individual, green & black, designed by Arthur E. Baggs **3,000**

Bowl, 7 1/2" w., octagonal, the alternating side panels hand-decorated w/floral design, brown & yellow glaze, Shape No. B-5-B **375**

Bowl, 2 1/2 x 9 1/4", Egyptian blue glaze, designed by R.G. Cowan, Shape No. B-12 .... **75**

Bowl, w/drip, 3 x 9 1/2", blue lustre finish, Shape No. 701-A... **80**

Bowl, 10" d., 2 1/2" h., Egyptian blue, Shape No. B-12... **75**

Bowl, 2 1/4 x 10 1/4", blue pearl finish................ **140**

Bowl, 3 x 11 1/4", designed to imitate hand molding, two-tone blue glaze, Shape No. B-827 .... **300**

Bowl, 3 x 10 x 11 1/2", leaf design, ivory & green, designed by Waylande Gregory **125**

Bowl, 3 x 9 1/4 x 12 1/4", copper crystal glaze, Shape No. B-785-A **150**

Bowl, 3 x 6 x 12 1/2" oblong, caramel w/light green glaze, Shape No. 683 .... **50**

Bowl, 2 3/4 x 11 1/2 x 15", Oriental Red glaze, designed by Waylande Gregory, Shape No. B-4 .... **200**

Bowl, 3 x 8 1/2 x 16 1/4", footed shallow form, flaring scalloped sides & rim, down-curved side handles, ivory exterior w/blue interior glaze, Shape No. 743-B **120**

Bowl-vase, green & gold, Shape No. B-4, 11".. **300**

Cowan Bust

Various Cowan Pieces

Bust of a woman, close-cut hair in ringlets, original sculpture by Jose Martin, terra cotta, 13 1/2" h. (ILLUS.)............................ **6,200**

Buttons, decorated w/various zodiac designs, by Paul Bogatay, 50 pcs. **500**

Candelabrum, "Pavlova," porcelain, two-light, Art Deco style, a footed squatty tapering central dish issuing at each side a styllzed hand holding an upturned cornucopia-form candle socket, the center fitted w/a figure of a nude female dancer standing on one leg w/her other leg raised, her torso arched over & holding a long swirled drapery, Special Ivory glaze, stamped mark, 10" l., 7" h. (chip under rim of one bobeche) **400**

Candleholder, flaring base w/flattened rim, black & silver, Shape No. 870, 1 1/2" h. **50**

Candleholder, figural, model of a Viking ship prow, green glaze, Shape No. 777, 5 1/4" h. **35**

Candleholders, Etruscan, Oriental Red glaze, Shape No. S-6, 1 3/4" h., pr. **75**

Candleholders, ivory glaze, Shape No. 692, 2 1/4" h., pr. **30**

Candleholders, footed, designed by R.G. Cowan, ivory, Shape No. 811, 2 3/8" h., pr. **50**

Candleholders, blue lustre finish, Shape No. 528, 3 1/2" h., pr. **35**

Candleholders, semicircular wave design, white glaze, Shape No. 751, 4 3/4" h., pr. **125**

Candlestick, flared base below twisted column, blossom-form cup, green & orange drip glaze, Shape No. 625-A, 7 3/4" h. (ILLUS. far right, top of page).......................... **90**

Candlestick, figural, Byzantine figure flanked by angels, golden yellow glaze, designed by R.G. Cowan, 9 1/4" h. (ILLUS. left, below).. **300**

Byzantine Angel Candlesticks

Candlestick, figural, Byzantine figure flanked by angels, salmon glaze, designed by R.G. Cowan, 9 1/4" h. (ILLUS. right)... **350**

Cowan Figural Nude Candlestick

Candlestick, two-light, large figural nude standing w/head tilted & holding a swirling drapery, flanked by blossom-form candle sockets supported by scrolled leaves at the base, matte ivory glaze, designed by R.G. Cowan, Shape No. 745, 7 1/2" w., 9 3/4" h. (ILLUS.) **1,200**

Cowan Figural Nude Candlestick

Candlestick, figural, seminude female standing before figural branches on round base w/flared foot, one arm across her body & the other raised overhead, shaded tan & green glaze, designed by R.G. Cowan, Shape No. 744-R, 12 1/2" h. (ILLUS.)...................................... **1,000**

Candlestick/bud vase, tapering cylindrical shape w/flared foot & rim, blue lustre, Shape 530-A, 7 1/2" h...................................... **80**

Candlestick/bud vase, tapering cylindrical shape w/flared foot & rim, rainbow blue finish, Shape 530-A, 7 1/2" h........................... **50**

Candlesticks, curled form, royal blue, 1 1/2" h., pr. **125**

Candlesticks, figural grape handles, ivory glaze, 4" h., pr... **80**

Candlesticks, w/loop handle, green, Shape No. 781, 4" h., pr. **75**

Candlesticks, figural sea horse w/flared base, green, Shape No. 716, 4 3/8" h., pr. **60**

Candlesticks, "The Girl Reserve," designed by R.G. Cowan, medium blue, Shape No. 671, 5 1/2" h., pr. **275**

Cowan Candlesticks & Vase

Candlesticks, model of a marlin on wave-form base, verde green, designed by Waylande Gregory, 8" h., pr. (ILLUS. right)... **1,300**

Centerpiece set, 6 1/4" h. trumpet-form vase centered on 8" sq. base w/candle socket in each corner, Princess line, vase Shape No. V-1, Mark No. 8, candelabra Shape No. S-2, Mark No. 8, black matte, 2 pcs., together w/four nut dishes/open compotes, green glaze, Shape No. C-1, Mark No. 8, the set........................... **900**

Charger, "Polo" plate, incised scene w/polo players & flowers under a blazing sun, covered in a rare glossy brown & cafe-au-lait glaze, designed by Victor Schreckengost, mark Nos. 8 & 9, Shape No. X-48, impressed "V.S. - Cowan," 11 1/4" d. (grinding chips to retaining ring)... **900**

Charger, wall plaque, yellow, 11 1/4" d. **150**

Charger, octagonal, hand-decorated by Thelma Frazier Winter, 13 1/4" **1,200**

Cigarette holder, w/wave design, Oriental Red glaze, designed by Waylande Gregory, Shape No. 927-J, 3 1/4" **100**

Cigarette/match holder, sea horse decoration, pink, No. 726, 3 1/2 x 4" **65**

Cigarette/matchholder, flared foot w/relief-molded sea horse decoration, orange glaze, Shape No. 72, 3 1/2" h. **40**

Clip dish, green, 3 1/4" d. (part of desk set, Shape PB-1)... **20**

Comport, footed, square, green & white glaze, Shape No. 951, 4 1/2" sq., 2 1/4" h.. **40**

Console bowl, octagonal, stand-up-type, verde green, Shape No. 689, 3 x 8 x 8 1/2" **95**

Console bowl, footed, low rounded sides w/incurved rim, orange lustre, Shape No. 567-B, 2 3/4 x 9 3/4"... **45**

Console bowl, footed, flaring fluted sides, white glaze exterior, blue glaze interior, Shape No. 713-A, 3 1/2 x 7 1/4 x 10 1/2" **90**

Console bowl, April green, Shape No. B-1, 11 1/2" l., 2 1/4" h. **95**

Console bowl, turquoise & dark matte blue, Shape No. 690, 3 1/2 x 8 x 16" **120**

Console bowl, ivory & pink glaze, Shape No. 763, 3 1/4 x 9 x 16 1/2".................................... **80**

Console bowl, w/wave design, verde green, designed by Waylande Gregory, 2 3/4 x 9 x 17 1/2"... **325**

Console bowls, 3 3/4 x 4 1/2 x 11", two-handled, footed, widely flaring fluted sides, verde green, Shape No. 538, pr. **280**

Console set: 6 1/2 x 10 1/2 x 17" bowl & pr. of candleholders; footed bowl w/figural bird handles, lobed sides, designed by Alexander Blazys, Shape No. 729, mottled blue glaze, the set.................................... **550**

Console set: 9" d. bowl & pair of 4" h. candleholders; ivory & purple glaze, Shape Nos. 733-A & 734 .... **125**

Cowan Decanters & Wine Cups

Decanter w/stopper, figural King of Clubs, a seated robed & bearded man w/a large crown on his head & holding a scepter, black glaze w/gold, designed by Waylande Gregory, Shape E-4, 10" h. (ILLUS. left) **1,100**

Decanter w/stopper, figural Queen of Hearts, seated figure holding scepter & wearing crown, Oriental Red glaze, designed by Waylande Gregory, Shape No. E-5, 10 1/2" h. (ILLUS. with King of Clubs decanter).. **950**

Desk set, w/paper clip dish, Oriental Red glaze, Shape PB-1, 2 1/2 x 5 1/2", the set...... **125**

Cowan Figurines & Flower Frog

Figurine, "Spanish Dancer," female, white, designed by Elizabeth Anderson, Shape No. 793, 8 1/2" h. (ILLUS. right)..................... **900**

Figurine, "Spanish Dancer," male, white, designed by Elizabeth Anderson, Shape No. 793, 8 3/4" h. (ILLUS. left) **900**

Figurine, kneeling female nude, almond
glaze, 9" h. **350**

Russian Tambourine Player Figurine

Figurine, Russian peasant, "Tambourine
Player," white crackle glaze, designed by
Alexander Blazys, Shape No. 757-760,
9" h. (ILLUS.) **1,000**

"Persephone" Figurine

Figurine, "Persephone," standing female
nude holding a long scarf out to one side
and near her shoulder, ivory glaze, designed by Waylande Gregory, Shape No.
D-6, 15" h. (ILLUS.) **3,500**
Figurine, "Nautch Dancer," female w/a flar-
ing pleated skirt on rectangular base,
semi-matte ivory glaze w/silver accents,
incised "Waylande Gregory," impressed
mark, 6 3/4 x 9 1/4", 17 3/4" h. **8,500**
Figurines, "Spanish Dancer," male & female
figures h.p. in polychrome glazes, the

male mark No. 9, Shape No. 794-D,
8 1/4" h. & the female mark No. 8, Shape
No. 793-D, 8 1/2" h., designed by Eliza-
beth Anderson, impressed marks, pr. **2,400**
Finger bowl, Egyptian blue, Shape No. B-
19, 3" **80**
Flower frog, model of an artichoke, light
green, Shape No. 775, 3" h. **90**
Flower frog, figure of a nude female, one leg
kneeling on thick round base, head bent
to one side & looking upward, one arm
resting on knee of bent leg w/the other
hand near her foot, ivory glaze, designed
by Walter Sinz, 6" h. (ILLUS. left with Div-
er flower frog) **450**

Cowan Flower Frogs

Flower frog, figural Art Deco-style nude
dancing woman in a curved pose, standing on one leg & trailing a long scarf, ivory
glaze, designed by Walter Sinz, Shape
No. 698, 6 1/2" h. (ILLUS. left) **275-325**

Various Cowan Flower Frogs

Flower frog, figural, "Repose," Art Deco
style, a seminude sinewy woman standing & slightly curved backward, her arms
away from her sides holding trailing drapery, in a cupped blossom-form base, ivory glaze, designed by R.G. Cowan,
Shape No. 712, 6 1/2" h. (ILLUS. lower
center) **450**
Flower frog, figural, "Scarf Dancer," Art
Deco-style nude dancing woman in a
curved pose standing on one leg & holding the ends of a long scarf in her outstretched hands, ivory glaze, designed
by R.G. Cowan, Shape No. 686, 7" h.
(ILLUS. top with "Repose" flower frog) **350**

Flower frog, figural, Art Deco nude scarf dancer, No. 35, ivory glaze, signed, 7 1/4" h. **400**

Flower frog, figural, an Art Deco dancing nude woman leaning back w/one leg raised & the ends of a long scarf held in her outstretched hands, overall white glaze, impressed mark, 7 1/2" h..................... **300**

Flower frog, figural, Art Deco style, two nude females partially draped in flowing scarves, each bending backward away from the other w/one hand holding the scarf behind each figure & their other hand joined, on an oval base w/flower holes, ivory glaze, designed by R.G. Cowan, Shape No. 685, 7 1/2" h. (ILLUS. lower right with "Repose" flower frog) **850**

Cowan Female Form Flower Frogs

Flower frog, "Diver," wave-form base w/tall wave supporting nude female figure, back arched & arms raised over head, ivory glaze, designed by R.G. Cowan, Shape No. 683, 8" h. (ILLUS. right) **1,200**

Flower frog, "Marching Girl," Art Deco style, a nude female partially draped w/a flowing scarf standing & leaning backward w/one hand on her hip & the other raising the scarf above her head, on an oblong serpentine-molded wave base w/flower holes, ivory glaze, designed by R.G. Cowan, Shape No. 680, 8" h. (ILLUS. lower left with "Repose" flower frog) **450**

Flower frog, model of a deer, designed by Waylande Gregory, ivory glaze, Shape No. F-905, 8 1/4" h. (ILLUS. right with unicorn book ends)... **550**

Flower frog, figural, "Awakening," an Art Deco woman draped in a flowing scarf standing & leaning backward w/her arms bent & her hands touching her shoulders, on a flower-form pedestal base, ivory glaze, designed by R.G. Cowan, Shape

No. F-8, impressed mark, 1930s, 9" h. (ILLUS. right with flower frog No. 698)... **550-650**

Flower frog, figural Pan sitting on large toad-stool, ivory glaze, designed by W. Gregory, Shape No. F-9, 9" h. (ILLUS. with ram & chick ashtrays) **1,000**

Flower frog, a standing seminude Art Deco woman, posed w/one leg kicked to the back, her torso bent back w/one arm raised & curved overhead, the other arm curved around her waist holding a long feather fan, a long drapery hangs down the front from her waist, on a rounded in-curved broad leaf cluster base, overall Original Ivory glaze, designed by R.G. Cowan, Shape No. 806, stamped mark, 4" w., 9 1/2" h. **1,700**

"Swirl Dancer" Flower Frog

Flower frog, figural, "Swirl Dancer," Art Deco nude female dancer standing & leaning to the side, w/one hand on hip & the other holding a scarf which swirls about her, on a round lobed base w/flower holes, ivory glaze, designed by R.G. Cowan, Shape No. 720, 10" h. (ILLUS.).............................. **1,200**

Flower frog, "Wreath Girl," figure of a woman standing on a blossom-form base & holding up the long tails of her flowing skirt, ivory glaze, designed by R.G. Cowan, Shape No. 721, 10" h. (ILLUS. center with Diver flower frog) **1,000**

Flower frog, fluted flower-form base centered by relief-molded stalk & leaves supporting the figure of a female nude standing w/one leg bent, knee raised, leaning backward w/one arm raised overhead & the other resting on a curved leaf, ivory glaze, designed by R.G. Cowan, Shape No. F-812-X, 10 1/2" h. (ILLUS. center with Spanish Dancers).................................. **900**

Flower frog, model of a reindeer, designed by Waylande Gregory, polychrome finish, Shape No. 903, 11" h. (ILLUS. center with unicorn book ends) **1,600**

Flower frog, figural nude w/long flowing scarf, ivory, designed by R.G. Cowan, Shape No. 687, 11 3/4" h.............................. **1,000**

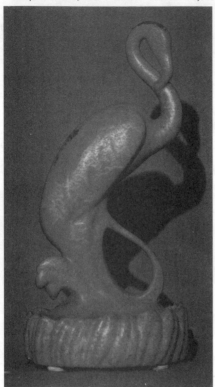

Cowan Flamingo Flower Frog

Flower frog, model of a flamingo, orange glaze, designed by Waylande Gregory, Shape No. D2-F, 11 3/4" h. (ILLUS.).......... **1,000**

Flower frog, figural, "Triumphant," figure of a standing seminude Art Deco woman w/one leg raised, leaning back w/one arm raised above her head & the other on her hip, a clinging drapery around her lower body, standing on a round incurved leaf cluster base, overall Original Ivory glaze, stamped mark, 4 1/2" w., 15" h........ **2,200**

Ginger jar, cov., blue lustre, Shape No. 513, 6 3/4" h. **300**

Ginger jar, cov., orange lustre, Shape No. 583, 10" h.. **500**

Lamp, foliage decoration, 9" h. **375**

Lamp, candlestick-form, a disk foot & spiral-twist standard w/a flaring molded socket fitted w/an electric bulb socket, overall marigold lustre glaze, impressed mark, 11" h... **90**

Lamp, girl w/deer decoration, ivory, 18" h. **450**

Lamp, w/fittings, moth decoration, blue, 13" h., overall 22" h. **350**

Lamp base, Art Deco style, angular, green, designed by Waylande Gregory, Shape No. 821, 8 3/8" h. **200**

Cowan Lamp Base

Lamp base, round domed base below modernist teardrop-shaped body decorated w/nude female figure, ivory & brown glaze, designed by Waylande Gregory, 11" h. (ILLUS.) **1,500**

Bird on Wave Model

Cowan Lakeware Urn & Vases

Model of bird on wave, Egyptian blue, designed by Alexander Blazys, Shape No.
749-A, 12" h. (ILLUS.)................................. **1,500**
Model of elephant, standing on square
plinth, head & trunk down, rich mottled
Oriental Red glaze, designed by Margaret Postgate, ca. 1930, faint impressed
mark on plinth & paper label reading
"X869 Elephant designed by M....et P....,"
10 1/2" h.. **5,500**
Model of horse, standing animal on an ob-
long base, Egyptian blue glaze, designed
by Viktor Schreckengost, 7 3/4" h.
(ILLUS. right with polar bear book ends)... **3,900**
Model of ram, Oriental Red glaze, designed
by Edris Eckhart, 3 1/2" h.............................. **250**
Paperweight, figural, modeled as a large
rounded stylized elephant w/trunk curved
under, standing on a stepped rectangular
base, ivory glaze, designed by Margaret
Postgate, Shape No. D-3, 4 3/4" h.
(ILLUS. lower center with elephant book
ends)... **400**
Paperweight, figural, modeled as a large
rounded stylized elephant w/trunk curved
under, standing on a stepped rectangular
base, blue glaze, designed by Margaret
Postgate, Shape No. D-3, 4 3/4" h.
(ILLUS. lower right with elephant book
ends)... **450**
Paperweight, figural, modeled as a large
rounded stylized elephant w/trunk curved
under, standing on a stepped rectangular
base, overall Oriental Red glaze, de-
signed by Margaret Postgate, Shape No.
D-3, 4 3/4" h. (ILLUS. top right with ele-
phant book ends)... **500**
Pen base, maroon, Shape No. PB-2, 3 3/4"........ **80**
Plaque, seascape decoration, designed by
Thelma Frazier Winter, 11 1/2" d. **900**
Plaque, hand-decorated by Arthur E.
Baggs, Egyptian blue, artist-signed
"AEB," 2 1/2 x 12 1/2" **2,500**
Plaque, terradatol, designed by Alexander
Blazys, Egyptian blue, Shape No. 739,
15 1/2" **1,000**

Strawberry jar w/saucer, light green, designed by R.G. Cowan, Shape No. SJ-6,
6" h., 2 pcs.. **200**
Strawberry jar w/saucer, Oriental Red
glaze, designed by R.G. Cowan, Shape
No. SJ-1, mark No. 8, 7 1/2" h., 2 pcs. **350**
Trivet, round, center portrait of young wom-
an's face encircled by a floral border,
white on blue ground, impressed mark &
"Cowan," 6 5/8" d. (minor staining from
usage) **275**

Urn, Lakeware, blue, Shape V-102, 5 1/2" h.
(ILLUS. left, top of page)................................. **90**
Urn, classical form w/trumpet foot support-
ing a wide bulbous ribbed body w/a wide
short cylindrical neck flanked by loop
handles, overall Peacock blue glaze,
stamped mark, 8" d., 9 1/2" h. **100**

Cowan Urn w/Figural Grape Handles

Urn, cov., black w/gold trim & figural grape cluster handles, Shape No. V-95, 10 1/4" h. (ILLUS.) **450**

Vase, 3 1/4" h., footed, baluster-form, Feu Rouge glaze, Shape No. 533 .... **100**

Vase, 4" h., bulbous ovoid tapering to cylindrical neck, Jet Black glaze, Shape No. V-5 (ILLUS. center w/urn) **300**

Vase, 4" h., waisted cylindrical body w/bulbous top & wide flaring rim, mottled orange glaze, Shape No. 630 (ILLUS. second from left w/No. 625-A candlestick) **80**

Vase, 4 1/4" h., mottled green, Shape No. V-54 .... **75**

Vase, 4 3/4" h., bulbous body w/horizontal ribbing, wide cylindrical neck, mottled turquoise glaze, Shape No. V-30 .... **80**

Vase, 4 3/4" h., bulbous body w/horizontal ribbing, wide cylindrical neck, green glaze, Shape No. V-30 (ILLUS. lower left with clown ashtrays) **90**

Vase, 4 3/4" h., waterfall, designed by Paul Bogatay, maroon, hand-decorated, Shape No. V-77 .... **1,000**

Vase, 4 3/4" h., wide tapering cylindrical body, mottled orange, brown & rust, Shape No. V-34 (ILLUS. second from right w/No. 625-A candlestick) **80**

Vase, 5" h., fan-shaped, designed by R.G. Cowan, golden yellow, Shape No. V-801 ...... **70**

Vase, 5 1/4" h., Lakeware, melon-lobed shape **90**

Vase, 5 1/2" h., footed wide semi-ovoid body w/flaring rim, dark bluish green, Shape 575-A, mark No. 4 .... **50**

Vase, 5 1/2" h., Lakeware, bulbous base w/wide shoulder tapering to wide cylindrical neck, blue glaze, Shape No. V-72 .... **90**

Vase, 5 1/2" h., orange lustre, Shape No. 608 .... **40**

Vase, 6 1/4" h., experimental, polychrome, designed by Arthur E. Baggs, Shape No. 15-A, artist signed "AEB" **1,500**

Vase, 6 1/4" h., six-sided w/stepped neck, blue rainbow glaze, Shape No. 546 .... **75**

Vase, bud, 6 1/4" h., flaring domed foot below ovoid body tapering to cylindrical neck w/flaring rim, plum glaze, Shape No. 916 .... **80**

Vase, 6 1/2" h., blue & green, Shape No. V-55 .... **160**

Cowan Decorated Vases

Vase, 6 1/2" h., bulbous body w/short molded rim, black w/Egyptian blue bands & center decoration, designed by Whitney Atchley, Shape No. V-38 (ILLUS. right) **2,000**

Vase, 6 1/2" h., footed, squatty bulbous base w/trumpet-form neck, flattened sides w/notched corners, green glaze, Shape No. V-649-A (ILLUS. right w/urn) **150**

Vase, 6 1/2" h., mottled dark blue & green, Shape No. V-55 .... **160**

Vase, 6 1/2" h., spherical body w/flaring cylindrical neck flanked by scroll handles, Egyptian blue, designed by Viktor Schreckengost, Shape No. V-99 .... **650**

Vase, 6 1/2" h., wide bulbous body, yellow glaze, Shape V-91 .... **250**

Vase, cov., 6 1/2" h., wide bulbous body, blue glaze, Shape V-91 .... **250**

Vase, 6 5/8" h., bright yellow glaze, Shape No. 797 .... **80**

Vase, 6 3/4" h., footed bulbous ovoid body w/wide tapering cylindrical neck, Jet Black glaze, Shape V-25 .... **500**

Vase, 7" h., fan-shaped w/scalloped foot & domed base decorated w/relief-molded sea horse decoration, pink glaze, Shape No. 715-A **60**

Vase, 7" h., footed bulbous base, the narrow shoulder tapering to tall wide cylindrical neck, Oriental Red glaze, Shape No. V-79 .... **250**

Vase, 7" h., Lakeware, bulbous base w/trumpet-form neck, Oriental Red glaze, Shape No. V-75 .... **90**

Vase, bud, 7" h., blue lustre glaze **75**

Vase, 7 1/4" h., footed slender ovoid body w/flaring rim, Oriental Red glaze, Shape No. V-12 .... **175**

Vase, 7 1/2" h., baluster-form w/trumpet-form neck, blue rainbow lustre, Shape No. 631 .... **90**

Vase, 7 1/2" h., flared foot below paneled ovoid body, orange lustre glaze, Shape No. 691-A, mark No. 6 .... **75**

Vase, 7 1/2" h., footed, tapering cylindrical body, green drip over yellow glaze, Shape No. 591, 8" h. (ILLUS. far right with clown ashtrays) **275**

Vase, 7 1/2" h., tall slender ovoid body w/short cylindrical neck, orange lustre, Shape No. 552 (ILLUS. lower right with chick & ram ashtrays) **90**

Vase, 5 1/4 x 7 3/4", flared tulip-shaped body, squared feet, blue **80**

Vase, 8" h., blue lustre, Shape No. 615 .... **100**

Vase, 8" h., bulbous body tapering to cylindrical neck w/flaring rim, verde green, Shape No. V-932 .... **180**

Vase, 8" h., bulbous body tapering to cylindrical neck w/flaring rim, gold, Shape No. V-932 (ILLUS. far left w/No. 625-A candlestick) **250**

Vase, 8" h., bulbous body tapering to cylindrical neck w/flaring rim, Feu Rouge (red) glaze, Shape No. V-932 .... **550**

Vase, 8" h., bulbous body tapering to cylindrical neck w/flaring rim, black drip over Feu Rouge (red) glaze Shape No. V-932 (ILLUS. top with clown ashtrays) **550**

Vase, 8" h., cylindrical body, black w/overall turquoise blue decoration, triple-signed (ILLUS. left with bulbous vase) **880**

Vase, 10 1/2" h., footed bulbous ovoid body, Star patt., decorated w/relief-molded foliage, orange glaze, designed by Waylande Gregory, Shape V-32, mark No. 8 & 9 .... **600**

Vase, 13 1/2" h., baluster-form body w/flaring rim, light blue glaze, Shape No. 563 (ILLUS. left w/marlin candlesticks)................. **275**

Wall plate, flat, blue, 11 1/4" d. **150**

Wine cups, Oriental Red glaze, Shape No. X-17, 2 1/2" h., each (ILLUS. of two, front left with decanter) **45**

Cybis

Though not antique, fine Cybis porcelain figures are included here because of the great collector interest. They are produced in both limited edition and non-numbered series, so there can be a wide range available to the collector.

Cybis Mark

Burro, "Fitzgerald," No. 632, 1964, 7" h. **$175**

Carousel Pony, "Sugarplum," No. 651, 1981, 12" h. **875**

Little Match Girl, No. 4067, 1983, 5 3/4" h........ **350**

Little Princess, No. 457, 1968-1970, 10" h. **550**

Raccoon, "Raffles," No. 636, 1965, signed, 7 1/2 x 9" **170**

Sea King's Steed (The), "Oceania," 1977, limited edition, 14 1/2" h. **985**

Czechoslovakian

Czechoslovakia did not exist until the end of World War I in 1918. The country was put together with parts of Austria, Bohemia and Hungary as a reward for the help of the Czechs and the Slovaks in winning the war. In 1993 Czechoslovakia split and became two countries: the Czech Republic and the Slovak Republic. Items are highly collectible because the country was in existence only 75 years. For a more thorough study of the subject, refer to the following books: Made in Czechoslovakia Books 1 and 2 by Ruth A. Forsythe; Czechoslovakian Glass & Collectibles Books I and II by Dale & Dian Barta and Helen M. Rose and Czechoslovakian Perfume Bottles and Boudoir Accessories by Jacquelyne Y. Jones North.

Ashtray Topped with Figure of Dog

Ashtray, rectangular yellow tray topped w/figure of white dog w/nose to ground, ears flapping & tail erect, black & red detailing, 5" h. (ILLUS.) **$175**

Various Czechoslovakian Pieces

Basket, orange & green h.p. floral decoration on cream ground, low orange handle, 4 1/2" h. (ILLUS. front row, left w/various Czechoslovakian pieces) **85**

Various J. Mrazek Pieces

Bell, w/original pottery heart clapper, geometric patt. on black ground, J. Mrazek, Peasant Art Industries, 4 1/4" h. (ILLUS. front row, left w/various J. Mrazek pieces) **150**

Hand-painted Beverage Set

Beverage set: cov. pitcher & four tumblers; tapering cylindrical shapes, pitcher w/applied black C-scroll handle & knobbed lid, h.p. floral decoration in red, blue, green & yellow on white ground w/black trim, the set (ILLUS.) **275**

Biscuit jar, w/rattan handle, decorated w/orange flower, 7" h. **125**
Book ends, in the form of a boy & girl, Erphila, 6" h., pr. **125**
Book ends, in the form of Indian heads, pr. **125**
Bowl, 14" l., shallow shape, green & yellow, Eichwald **65**

Various Peasant Art Pieces

Box, cov., round, floral decoration on yellow sponge ground, J. Mzarek, Peasant Art Industries, 6" d., 6" h. (ILLUS. front row, second from left w/various Peasant Art pieces).............. **225**

Cache pot, decorated w/cherries, 4 1/2" h. **65**

Cup & saucer, "Highlander" patt. **25**

Flower frog, round, w/airbrushed hoses around middle **150**

Humidor, cov., ovoid shape, geometric patt. on light green sponge ground, knobbed lid, J. Mrazek, Peasant Art Industries, 7 1/2" h. (ILLUS. back row, right w/various J. Mrazek pieces)...................................... **375**

Slip Decorated Candlestick

Candlesticks, sharply waisted circular form slip decorated overall in orange, blue, yellow & black flower-in-circle designs, 3" h., pr. (ILLUS. of one) **150**

Canister set, green background w/floral decoration, 15-piece set **600**

Cigarette box, white, w/horse finial, 4" h. **150**

Console bowl, footed, lilac, purple & green, Eichwald, 6" h.. **150**

Crab ramekin, cov. **25**

Creamer, decorated w/orange cherries, 4 1/2" h. **55**

Creamer, floral decor on blue sponge ground, J. Mrazek, Peasant Art Industries, 3" h. (ILLUS. front row, second from right, w/various Peasant Art pieces)............... **65**

Creamer, w/handle in the form of a cat, white iridescent, 4" h. **65**

Slip Decorated Covered Jar

Jar, cov., cylindrical shape, slip decorated overall in orange, blue, green & black, w/stylized fan on front, 7" h. (ILLUS.)............. **475**

Model of bulldog, white w/brown & black splotches, 7" h. **135**

Model of Toucan

Model of toucan, bird w/large yellow beak perches on black base, white body w/green, blue, yellow & red detail, 8" h. (ILLUS.).. **750**

Models of horse heads, white high glaze, 9" h., pr.. **175**

Mug with Bird Handle

Mug, cylindrical form w/figure of bird forming handle, cream w/red & black accents, Erphila (ILLUS.).. **175**

Mug, "Monte Carlo" patt., 1/2 liter......................... **40**

Mug, slightly tapering cylindrical form w/floral medallion on orange sponge ground, Peasant Art Industries, 5" h. (ILLUS. front row far right, w/various Peasant Art pieces)... **65**

Mustard w/underplate, cov., floral decor on green sponge ground, J. Mrazek, Peasant Art Industries, 4" d., 4" h. (ILLUS. middle row, second from right, w/various Peasant Art pieces)... **145**

Hand-painted Pitcher

Pitcher, bulbous form w/short circular base, C-scroll handle, h.p. w/decoration of large flower on front & back w/green leaves as accents, "BATNA," Ditmar-Urbach (ILLUS.).. **350**

Pitcher, 1-liter, bulbous body w/flaring cylindrical neck, short base & S-scroll applied handle, h.p. decoration of orange, blue & black ellipses, green leaves & orange trim, LOSTRO (ILLUS. second from right w/other pitcher & vases, below)...................... **150**

Czechoslovakian Pitchers & Vases

Pitcher, 1-liter, cov., ovoid body w/cylindrical neck, short base & C-scroll applied handle, h.p. overall floral decoration (ILLUS. second from left w/other pitcher & vases) **125**

Pitcher, 1-liter, white stencil design on cobalt blue ground, Ditmar-Urbach (ILLUS. back row, left w/various Czechoslovakian pieces) **125**

Airbrushed "Himalaja" Pitcher

Pitcher, 1 1/2-liter, footed bulbous form w/tapering neck & flared rim, black C-scroll handle dividing into two sections at base, "Himalaja" patt., airbrushed purple, white, yellow & green, CORA, Ditmar-Urbach (ILLUS.) **275**

Pitcher, 4" h., spherical form, geometric design on yellow sponge ground, J. Mrazek, Peasant Art Industries (ILLUS. front row, center w/various J. Mrazek pieces) **175**

Pitcher, 4 1/2" h., in the form of a standing cow, w/blue, yellow & orange spots **95**

Pitcher, 6" h., figural, in the form of a girl holding flowers, orange & white, Erphila **85**

Pitcher, 6 1/2" h., w/stencil of man & woman w/heart in red & green **45**

Pitcher, 7" h., simple form w/overall h.p. floral decoration on white ground, angled handle, BERN (ILLUS. front row, right w/various Czechoslovakian pieces) **85**

Cat Pitcher

Pitcher, 8" h., figural, in the form of a seated cat w/head turned to side, tail forms handle, one ear forms spout, cream w/red & black accents, imported by Eberling & Reuss (Erphila) (ILLUS.) **950**

Pitcher, 8" h., straight-sided, in the form of blown-out fruit **150**

Pitcher, 9" h., "Monte Carlo" patt., red, black & white striped **195**

Pitcher, cover & underplate, 9" h., decorated on front w/orange flower w/green leaves, 3 pcs. **150**

Plate, 6 1/2" h., geometric patt. on orange sponge ground, J. Mrazek, Peasant Art Industries (ILLUS. back row, center w/various J. Mrazek pieces) **55**

Plate, 8 1/2" d., white, each decorated in center w/different fruit: one w/pear, one w/grapes, one w/apple, one w/orange, one w/strawberries, one w/plums, each **25**

Plate, 9 1/2" d., white w/border decorated w/images of lobster, crab & shrimp **45**

Plate, 10" d., "Highlander" patt., red, blue & black plaid **25**

Plate, 12" d., cheese & crackers, white w/green airbrushed lines in several places, center w/figural multicolored rooster & holes for toothpicks **125**

Plate, 12" d., floral center on yellow sponge ground, J. Mrazek, Peasant Art Industries (ILLUS. back row, w/various Peasant Art pieces) **85**

Punch bowl w/underplate, "Highlander" patt., 15" d., the set **175**

Salt & pepper shakers, "Monte Carlo" patt., pr. **30**

Airbrushed Salt & Pepper Shakers

Salt & pepper shakers, ovoid form, airbrushed decoration of stagecoach w/horses & attendants in black silhouette against white ground w/blue, gold & green, 4 1/2" h., pr. (ILLUS.) **35**

Toby, Mr. Bumble, Erphila, 3 1/4" h. **45**

Vase, 4 1/2" h., cylindrical form, geometric design on light green sponge ground, J. Mrazek, Peasant Art Industries, 7 1/2" h. (ILLUS. front row, right w/various J. Mrazek pieces) **110**

Vase, 5" h., bulbous form w/two small side handles at shoulder, decorated w/orange flowers & green leaves (ILLUS. front row, center w/various Czechoslovakian pieces) **75**

Czechoslovakian Vases

Vase, 5 1/2" h., squatty shape, h.p. multi-color floral decoration (ILLUS. second from left w/other Czechoslovakian vases)..... **110**

Vase, 6" h., ovoid w/flaring rim & tapering out at base, overall floral design, Peasant Art Industries (ILLUS. front row, far left, w/various Peasant Art pieces)...................... **125**

Vase, 6" h., slightly ovoid cylindrical form w/floral band on black ground, Peasant Art Industries (ILLUS. middle row, second from left w/various Peasant Art pieces) **115**

Vase, 7" h., bulbous form w/flaring neck & short circular base, decorated w/red flowers w/black trim on cream ground, Ditmar-Urbach (ILLUS. second from right w/other Czechoslovakian vases) **175**

Vase, 7" h., fan-shaped, w/multicolored h.p. slip decoration.. **195**

Vase, 7" h., segmented ovoid form w/flaring rim & base, h.p. overall floral decoration (ILLUS. far right w/other vase & pitchers)..... **175**

Vase, 7 1/2" h., waisted cylindrical form, geometric patt. on orange sponge ground, J. Mrazek, Peasant Art Industries (ILLUS. back row, left w/various J. Mrazek pieces)... **275**

Vase, 8" h., bulbous form w/short flared neck, short circular base, two side loop handles, airbrushed in purple & red (ILLUS. far left w/other vase & pitchers)....... **150**

Vase, 8" h., flaring neck & short stepped base, airbrushed w/crosshatching & dots in lavender, red, brown & pink (ILLUS. far right w/other Czechoslovakian vases)........... **125**

Vase, 8" h., flaring rim, short circular base, slip decorated w/orange circles w/green centers outlined in blue w/black spider webbing on white ground, trimmed in yellow & black (ILLUS. far left w/other Czechoslovakian vases)................................ **250**

Vase, 8" h., octagonal form w/flaring rim & base, h.p. floral decoration on white ground (ILLUS. back row, right w/various Czechoslovakian pieces) **125**

Vase, 8" h., two-handled, brown & yellow w/image of cottage on front.............................. **55**

Vase, 8" h., white matte finish w/decoration of woman's head at base **175**

Vase, 9" h., bulbous body w/cylindrical neck flaring slightly at rim, wide floral band on yellow sponge ground, Peasant Art Industries (ILLUS. middle row far right, w/various Peasant Art pieces)........................ **250**

Slip-decorated Czechoslovakian Vase

Vase, 12" h., tall, slightly ovoid cylindrical shape, slip decoration, cream & dark green swirls on ground of large purple & orange circles, cobalt trim (ILLUS.)................ **450**

Vase, 12 1/2" h., short bulbous base w/long cylindrical neck flaring out slightly at rim, blue sponge ground w/floral medallions, Peasant Art Industries (ILLUS. middle row, far left w/various Peasant Art pieces)... **350**

Wall pocket, decorated w/orange flower, 7" h... **65**

Dedham & Chelsea Keramic Art Works

Dedham & Chelsea Keramic Art Works Marks

This pottery was organized in 1866 by Alexander W. Robertson in Chelsea, Massachusetts, and became A.W. & H. Robertson in 1868. In 1872, the name was changed to Chelsea Keramic Art Works and in 1891 to Chelsea Pottery, U.S.A. About 1895, the pottery was moved to Dedham, Massachusetts, and was renamed Dedham Pottery. Production ceased in 1943. High-fired colored wares and crackle ware were specialties. The rabbit is said to have been the most popular decoration on crackle ware in blue.

Since 1977, the Potting Shed, Concord, Massachusetts, has produced quality reproductions of early Dedham wares. These pieces are carefully marked to avoid confusion with original examples.

Large Dedham Rabbit Bowl

Bowl, 8" d., 3" h., footed wide & deep rounded form w/flat rim, Rabbit patt., blue ink stamp (ILLUS.)... **$633**

Bowl, 8" d., 3" h., footed wide rounded form, Rabbit patt., blue ink stamp (ILLUS. top row, far left, bottom of page)........................... **506**

Cup & saucer, extra large coffee-size, Rabbit patt., blue ink stamp, 5" d., 3" h., the set (ILLUS. center, bottom row with bowl)... **338**

Cups & saucers, tea-size, Rabbit patt., blue ink stamp, saucer 6" d., set of 6 (ILLUS. bottom row, far left with bowl).................... **1,238**

Unusual Chelsea Keramic Jar

Jar, cov., oval flattened "pilgrim flask"-form, raised on four wide rounded tab feet, small scroll side handles, the flattened & domed cover w/a fanned finial, a molded oval side scene base on a printed image by L. Knauss showing a little girl feeding geese under a glossy dark teal blue glaze, the border, foot & cover in glossy green, modeled by Hugh Robertson, stamped Chelsea Keramic Art Works mark, 10 1/2" w., 9 1/4" h. (ILLUS.).. **1,840**

Variety of Dedham Crackleware Pieces

Medallion, oval, molded w/a scene of a trumpeting post boy riding a horse & viewed from behind, based on an image by J.E. Kelly, covered in a forest green glaze, by Hugh Robertson, incised "HCR - James Kelley," w/a rare catalog "American Decorative Tiles 1870-1930" which includes the piece, medallion 4 x 4 3/4"....... **844**

Pitcher, 5" h., 5 1/4" d., "Night and Day" design, blue ink stamp (ILLUS. top row, far right with bowl) **619**

Pitcher, 7 3/4" h., tall rectangular tapering form w/a squared stepped rim spout & square loop handle, incised w/a Greek key border & geometric linear border at the rim, handle & base, glossy green glaze later painted w/birds & nest in a flowering tree, impressed Chelsea Keramic Art Works mark, ca. 1885..... **800-1,000**

Plate, breakfast, 8 3/8" d., Iris patt., pre-1932, blue stamp mark & impressed rabbit mark, East Dedham, Massachusetts **144**

Plate, 8 1/2" d., luncheon size, Grape patt., blue ink stamp, bruise to table ring (ILLUS. bottom row, second from right with bowl) **141**

Plate, 8 1/2" d., luncheon size, Turkey patt. (ILLUS. top row, second from right with Rabbit bowl **100-200**

Plate, 10" d., Dolphin patt., early mark.............. **844**

Plates, 6" d., bread & butter size, Rabbit patt., restoration to small chip on rim of one, blue ink mark, set of 6 (ILLUS. bottom row, second from left with bowl)............. **619**

Plates, 8 1/2" d., luncheon size, Horse Chestnut patt., blue ink mark, pr. (ILLUS. bottom row, far right with bowl) **309**

Plates, 8 1/2" d., luncheon size, Rabbit patt., blue ink mark, short, tight line in one, set of 6 (ILLUS. top row, second from left with bowl)................................. **844**

Table service: six Crab patt. plates, one Crab patt. bowl, four Lobster patt. plates, three Lobster patt. serving platters & four Rabbit patt. ashtrays; stamped mark, ca. 1920s, the set... **5,520**

blood, green & blue mottled glaze, by Hugh Robertson, short opposing firing lines in rim, Dedham mark (ILLUS.) **575**

Chelsea Keramic Bottle-form Vase

Vase, 6 1/2" h., 4" d., footed bottle-form, squatty bulbous body tapering to a tall cylindrical neck, unusual oxblood & slate grey glaze, stamped Chelsea Keramic Art Works mark (ILLUS.)............................. **1,725**

Chelsea Keramic Pilgrim Vase

Vase, 6 3/4" h., 4" w., flattened upright rectangular flask form w/rounded flat borders & a small spout neck, embossed on the

Miniature Dedham Robertson Vase

Vase, 2 3/4" h., 2" d., miniature, simple ovoid form w/flat mouth, dripping ox-

side panel w/a scene of an elderly bearded pilgrim walking through a landscape,
panel w/a deep teal blue glossy glaze,
the border w/an olive green glossy glaze,
by H. Robertson, short, tight opposing
lines at the rim, small stilt pull chip on the
back, stamped "CKAW - HCR" (ILLUS.) **731**

Chelsea Keramic Pilgrim Flask Vase

Vase, 7 1/2" h., 6 1/4" w., flattened round
pilgrim flask form on four peg feet, tapering to a short cylindrical neck, the sides
incised w/pine boughs & flowers under a
speckled amber glossy glaze, by George
Ferrety, stamped mark & artist-signed
(ILLUS.) **1,495**
Vase, 8" h., 3" d., slender tall ovoid form, ex-
perimental fine mirrored oxblood glaze,
by Hugh Robertson, incised Dedham
Pottery mark **605**
Vase, 8" h., 6 1/2" d., pilgrim flask form, flat-
tened round form w/a short tapering cylindrical neck, raised on four short peg
feet, the lower half carved in high relief
w/an ivory hunting dog in a field against a
blue ground, by Hugh Robertson, die-
stamped & initialed (small chips on feet).. **4,125**
Vase, 8 1/4" h., 3 1/2" d., slightly flaring cylindrical body w/a wide angled shoulder
tapering to a short cylindrical neck, fine
oxblood "orange peel" semi-matte glaze,
unsigned Chelsea Keramic Art Works
(ILLUS. center with experimental vase)..... **1,760**

Fine Lustre Glazed Dedham Vase

Vase, 7 1/2" h., 4" d., ovoid body tapering to
a tall, wide cylindrical neck, fine experimental lustered oxblood glaze, by Hugh
Robertson, Dedham mark (ILLUS.) **4,313**
Vase, 7 1/2" h., 5" d., wide baluster form
w/short cylindrical neck, experimental example by Hugh Robertson, covered in a
superior mirrored oxblood dripping glaze,
incised "Dedham Pottery - HCR" (ILLUS.
left, bottom of page) **1,980**

Dedham & Chelsea Keramic Vases

Vase, 8 1/2" h., 5 1/4" h., Chinese bronze-shaped, squared, tapering double-lobe form embossed in the side panels w/flowers or geometric designs resembling decorated bronze, overall white crackled glaze, Dedham rabbit ink stamp (ILLUS. right with experimental vase) **550**

Large Chelsea Keramic Pillow Vase

Vase, 11" h., tall flattened ovoid pillow-form body on knob feet, tapering to a flared scalloped mouth, the sides embossed w/scrolls & overall flowers, butterflies & bees, mottled glossy green glaze, artist-signed, Chelsea Keramic Art Works mark (ILLUS.) **633**

deLee Art

The deLee Art company was founded in 1937 in Los Angeles by Jimmie Lee Adair Kohl. The name deLee means "of or by Lee" and is a French derivation. After earning an art degree from UCLA, Jimmie Lee taught art and ceramics at Belmont High School in Los Angeles while starting her ceramics business.More than 350 different pieces, most modeled by Jimmie Lee herself, were offered during the company's 21 years of business. The line included figurines of children, animals and birds as well as cookie jars, banks and wall pockets. Pieces of deLee Art were sold to wholesale buyers only, through catalog sales or in deLee booths at New York and Los Angeles gift shows.Jimmie Lee gave names to all her creations. All deLee pieces left the factory with name and logo stickers. Many items are also incised with the words "deLee Art" and sometimes the year of production. Pieces void of any identification can be authenticated by those familiar with Jimmie Lee's distinct designs and detailed hand painting. The deLee colors

are also easily recognized, as they remained the same for more than 20 years.Like many California pottery companies, deLee Art sales declined in the late 1950s due to Japanese production of less expensive ceramics, especially those that closely copied deLee. In 1958, the pottery closed. On September 9, 1999, Jimmie Lee died. Her wonderful contributions to the California pottery craze are only now becoming recognized.

Bank, figural, model of chicken w/black feathers & green bonnet, no mark, 6" h. **$135**
Bank, "Money Bunny," figural rabbit, ears up, pink w/blue purse w/flower on purse, silver w/black lettering sticker, "deLee" sticker & incised underglaze "deLee," 9" h. **125**
Cookie jar, model of boy chef, head down, eyes closed, arms folded over chest w/spoon in hands, colorful flowers on sleeves, apron forms bulbous bottom, marked "deLee Art 1944," 12 1/2" h. **395**
Figure of African American boy, "8 Ball," incised mark "deLee Art © 40 USA - A Walter Lantz Creation," 4 1/2" h. **165**
Figure of angel, standing, head tilted slightly to right, eyes closed, arms together in front at waist, overall glossy white glaze w/brown & blue tiny flowers & scallops on dress front & at wrist & neck, 6 1/2" h. **55**
Figure of boy, lying on his stomach, head up, arms folded under his chest, 2 3/4" l. **85**
Figures of boy & girl, lying on their backs w/legs crossed, boy w/dark green short pants, white shirt w/green buttons, brown hair, soles & straps of shoes, girl w/brown hair, blue eyes, white dress w/blue polka-dots, barefooted, both pieces marked w/a black & silver paper label "deLee Art, California, Hand decorated," 2 1/2" l., pr. **195**
Figures of Latino dancers, black & white w/gold accents, incised "deLee Art, U.S.A.," 11 1/2" & 12 1/2" h., pr. **295**
Model of bunny, "Bunny Hug" on sticker, ears up, white ground w/tan on ears, colorful small flowers on top of head & chest, marked "deLee," 6" h. **48**
Model of elephant, seated on back legs, trunk up, head bent to right touching shoulder, white ground w/small pink & blue flowers w/green leaves, 4 3/4" h. **65**
Model of skunk, "Phew," standing w/tail up, black gloss glaze w/white, wide stripe from top of head to middle of tail, white & black eyes, pink nose, paper label, 4 1/2" l. **35**
Models of elephants, "Lucky & Happy," trunks up, pastel floral on white, "Lucky" standing w/back leg up, "Happy" sitting on back legs, deLee stickers on both, name sticker on "Happy," no mark, 5" h., pr. (ILLUS., top next page) **130**
Models of lambs, "Tom & Jerry," "Tom" has blue bell, "Jerry" has blue flower, no marks, 4" h., pr. (ILLUS., middle next page) **85**
Models of pigs, "Grunt & Groan," "Groan" sitting & "Grunt" standing, no marks, 4 1/4" h. & 3 1/2" h., pr. (ILLUS., bottom next page) **95**

"Lucky & Happy" Elephants

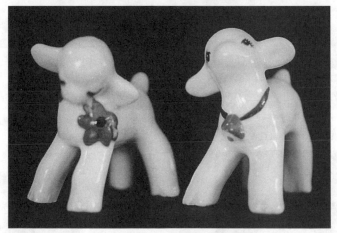

deLee Art "Tom & Jerry" Lambs

"Grunt & Groan" deLee Art Pigs

"Daisy" Figural Planter

Planter, "Daisy," figural, girl dressed in white w/blue & pink flowers, small bonnet w/flowers, planter in front formed by dress folds, incised mark "deLee Art © 1946, L.A., U.S.A.," 8" h. (ILLUS.) **65**

"Hopalong" Planter

Planter, "Hopalong," model of a bunny w/closed eyes, planter w/bow at side, deLee sticker, incised "deLee Art," 6" h. (ILLUS.)... **62**

Figural deLee Girl Planter

Planter, figural, girl dressed in white w/blue polka-dots, brown piping at edge of apron & collar of dress, large blue bow at waist in back, eyes closed w/brown eyelashes, holds up apron to form small planter in front, incised underglaze mark "deLee Art, 1938, Irene," 6" h. (ILLUS.).......... **65**

"Mr. Skunk" Planter

Planter, "Mr. Skunk" on sticker, model of skunk w/black body & white upright tail, pink mouth & nose, white eyes & hair, blue derby hat, tiny planter is formed where tail meets back, marked "deLee Art 1940 ©," 6" h. (ILLUS.)................................ **49**

"Nina" Figural Planter

Planter, "Nina," figural, girl dressed in white w/blue & pink flowers, head scarf, apron is double planter, no mark, 7" h. (ILLUS.) **49**

Planter, "Sahara Sue," model of a camel seated w/front hoofs crossed, head up & slightly tilted to right, pale pink gloss w/caramel glaze highlights on hoofs, mouth & ears, flowers between neck, open hump forms small planter, 5 1/2" h. **95**

Salt & pepper shakers, "Salty & Peppy," baby chicks w/chef hats, sitting in eggshells, no mark, 5" h., pr. **85**

Wall pocket, "Mr. Stinkie," model of a skunk, gloss black w/white, colorful flowers at left shoulder, small opening near stomach for matches, marked "deLee Art," 7 1/4" h. **39**

Delft

In the early 17th century Italian potters settled in Holland and began producing tin-glazed earthenwares, often decorated with pseudo-Oriental designs based on Chinese porcelain wares. The city of Delft became the center of this pottery production and several firms produced the wares throughout the 17th and early 18th century. A majority of the pieces featured blue on white designs, but polychrome wares were also made. The Dutch Delftwares were also shipped to England and eventually the English copied them at potteries in such cities as Bristol, Lambeth and Liverpool. Although still produced today, Delft peaked in popularity by the mid-18th century.

Charger, round, decorated in blue on white w/the "Peacock" patt., edged in yellow, blue "MP" monogram & "5/1" probably for Pieter Paree, director at De Metalen Pot, mid-18th c., 13 1/2" d. **$705**

Dry drug jar, ovoid body, h.p. in blue w/a cherub & shell label inscribed "U:AEGYPTIAC:," ca. 1730, England, 7 1/8" h. (large chip to foot, some crazing) **1,150**

Dry drug jar, ovoid body, h.p. in blue w/an angel's head & ribbon label inscribed "V:POPULNEU" above the initials

"i.G.," ca. 1680, London, 7 7/8" h. (cracks & some cracking & flaking of surface glaze) **2,070**

Plate, 8 3/4" d., polychrome decoration, painted in the center in blue, red & green w/a dolphin spouting a spray of water flanked by two distant ships, within a border of concentric blue lines & a blue & white checkered band at the rim, England, ca. 1730 (typical minor glaze loss at rim) **2,760**

Puzzle jug, bulbous body inscribed in blue "Here Gentlemen Come try your Skill - I'll hold a wager if you will - That you don't drink this liqr all - Without you spill or let some fall," flanked by stylized flowering plants beneath a cylindrical neck pierced w/a pattern of hearts & flowers, ca. 1760, probably Liverpool, 7 1/2" h. (two spouts missing & some restored-over glaze flaking to the rim) **1,150**

Derby & Royal Crown Derby

William Duesbury, in partnership with John and Christopher Heath, established the Derby Porcelain Works in Derby, England about 1750. Duesbury soon bought out his partners and in 1770 purchased the Chelsea factory and six years later, the Bow works. Duesbury was succeeded by his son and grandson. Robert Bloor purchased the business about 1814 and managed successfully until illness in 1828 left him unable to exercise control. The "Bloor" Period, however, extends from 1814 until 1848, when the factory closed. Former Derby workmen then resumed porcelain manufacture in another factory and this nucleus eventually united with a new and distinct venture in 1878 which, after 1890, was known as Royal Crown Derby.

A variety of anchor and crown marks have been used since the 18th century.

Derby & Royal Crown Derby Marks

Candlestick, "Birds in Branches" style, modeled w/two figural birds, one w/orange & purple plumage, the other pale yellow, each perched among branches of white blossoms below a foliate-molded candle socket, ca. 1765, 9 3/8" h. (minor chips & repair) **$3,162**

Creamer, helmet-shaped, flattened rim & naturalistically colored twig handle, painted on the front w/a bouquet of summer flowers & on the back w/honeysuckle, w/floral sprigs on the rim & foot, ca. 1760, 5 1/8" h. (tiny chips) **1,265**

Royal Crown Derby Dessert Service

Dessert dish, lozenge-shaped, the central oval panel painted w/two huntsmen & hounds within a gilt frame & a wide gilt foliate border at the lobed rim, probably painted by William Cotton, ca. 1815, crowned crossed batons & D in iron-red, painted initial I or number 7, 11 1/4" l. (slight rubbing) **1,380**

Dessert service: platter, 12 1/4" l., 5 dessert plates, 7" d., & small sauce boat; in the Imari palette, early 20th c., the set (ILLUS., top of page)..................................... **532**

Crown Derby Dessert Set

Dessert set: 12 plates, small cov. tureen, cov. vegetable dish, open dish, cov. teapot, cov. sugar bowl & three miscella-neous pieces; each in mostly cream ground w/red, green & gilt scrolls in the borders, Crown Derby, early 19th c., the set (ILLUS. of part)................................... **518**

Dish, cov., Imari pattern, w/dome-shaped lid w/gilt handle, early 20th c., 4 1/2" h., 8 3/4" d. **532**

Figure group, "Tithe Pig," modeled w/the farmer's wife offering her baby to the black-clad parson, in lieu of the piglet held by her husband, all standing before a leafy tree on a grassy mound base w/a further piglet, a basket of eggs & a wheat sheaf, ca. 1770, 7 1/4" h. (some minor chips & restoration, fine hairline in base) **862**

Jar, cov., globular form, floral decoration in colored enamels & gilt, ca. 1890, 12" h. **1,150**

Plates, 9" d., Imari patt., early 20th c., set of four.. **553**

Platters, 13 1/2" l., oval, King's patt., painted in an Imari palette w/a central flowering prunus tree, peonies & other flowers within an elaborate foliate scroll border, ca. 1825, crowned crossed batons & D marks in iron-red, number 36 in underglaze-blue & incised 13, pr. (some rubbing to the gilding at the rim edges) **690**

Royal Crown Derby Tea Set

Tea set: cov. teapot, cov. sugar bowl & creamer; oval cylindrical bodies, each decorated in an Imari-style design w/stylized Oriental blossoms in rust red w/green leaves against an oval black-ground center reserve w/gilt trim & rust red-outlined blossoms, a black-ground rim band w/gilt leafy bands & rust blossoms, Royal Crown Derby, ca. 1850, teapot 5 3/4" h., the set (ILLUS.)........................... **523**

Handsome Royal Crown Derby Tray

Teapot, cov., globular form, painted in bright colors w/two Oriental figures seated beside a table, the reverse w/a figure walking between two large vases, the small domed cover painted w/a butterfly & vases within an iron red & gilt chain link border, 5 3/8" h. (cracks between body & handle terminals, handle possibly reaffixed, tiny chips to foot rim) **3,737**

Tray, rectangular w/cut corners & rounded tab end handles, an ornate Imari-style design w/large stylized rust red Oriental blossoms w/scrolls over black & gold leaves on two sides & fan-shaped black-ground reserves at the ends, one w/birds in a tree, the other w/flowers, overall white ground w/outlined blossoms & leaves, black-ground border band w/gold & rust red leaves & blossoms, Royal Crown Derby, ca. 1850, 12 1/2 x 19" (ILLUS., top of page).................................. **1,320**

Vase, 8 1/4" h., bottle form, enamel & gilt-decorated w/fruits, flowers & foliage, ca. 1887 .... **403**

Vase, 10" h., bulbous body, a beige ground decorated w/multicolored rocaille designs w/gilt trim, factory marks, late 19th c. **173**

Ornate Royal Crown Derby Vase

Vase, 12" h., tall baluster-form body on a bell-form flaring foot & w/a tall tapering slender neck w/a flaring blossom-form cupped rim, teal blue ground decorated w/ornate raised gold scrolls, brackets &

long swags of blossoms around the sides w/gilt striping down the neck, gilt scalloped trim on the rim & base, Royal Crown Derby, 1896 (ILLUS.).......................... **288**

Doulton & Royal Doulton

Royal Doulton Mark

John Doulton, the founder, was born in 1793. He became an apprentice at the age of 12 to a potter in south London. Five years later he was employed in another small pottery near Lambeth. His two sons, John and Henry, subsequently joined their father in 1830 in a partnership he had formed with the name of Doulton & Watts. Watts retired in 1864 and the partnership was dissolved. Henry formed a new company that traded as Doulton & Co.

In the early 1870s the proprietor of the Pinder Bourne Co., located in Burslem, Staffordshire, offered Henry a partnership. The Pinder Bourne Co. was purchased by Henry in 1878 and became part of the Doulton & Co. in 1882.

With the passage of time the demand for the Lambeth industrial and decorative stoneware declined whereas demand for the Burslem manufactured and decorated bone china wares increased.

Doulton & Co. was incorporated as a limited liability company in 1899. In 1901 the company was allowed to use the word "Royal" on its trademarks by Royal Charter. The well known "lion on crown" logo came into use in 1902. In 2000 the logo was changed on the company's advertising literature to one showing a more stylized lion's head in profile.

Today Royal Doulton is one of the world's leading manufacturers and distributors of premium grade ceramic tabletop wares and collectibles. The Doulton Group comprises Minton, Royal Albert, Caithness Glass,

Holland Studio Craft and Royal Doulton. Royal Crown Derby was part of the group from 1971 until 2000 when it became an independent company. These companies market collectibles using their own brand names.

Animals & Birds

Bird, Bullfinch, blue & pale blue feathers, red breast, HN 2551, 1941-46, 5 1/2" h. **$325**

Cat, seated animal, red "Flambé" glaze, 1920-96, 4 1/2" h. **100**

Cat, seated animal, red "Flambé" glaze, 1977-96, 11" h. **525**

Siamese Cat

Cat, Siamese, seated, glossy cream & black, DA 129, 4" h. (ILLUS.) **25**

Cat, Siamese Cat, standing, cream & black, HN 2660, 1960-85, 5" h. **115**

Dog, Airedale Terrier, Ch. "Cotsford Topsail," standing, dark brown & black, light brown underbody, HN 1024, 1931-68, 4" h. **250**

Dog, Alsatian, "Benign of Picardy," dark brown, HN 1117, 1937-68, 4 1/2" **225**

Dog, American Great Dane, light brown, HN 2602, 1941-60, 6 1/2" h. **625**

Dog, Boxer, Champion "Warlord of Mazelaine," golden brown coat w/white bib, HN 2643, 1952-85, 6 1/2" h. **125**

Dog, Bulldog, HN 1047, standing, brown & white, 1931-38, 3 1/4" **165**

Dog, Bulldog, HN 1074, standing, white & brown, 1932-85, 3 1/4" **165**

Dog, Bulldog, K 1, seated, tan w/brown patches, 1931-77, 2 1/2" **95**

Dog, Bulldog Puppy, K 2, seated, tan w/brown patches, 1931-77, 2" **85**

Dog, character dog yawning, white w/brown patches over ears & eyes, black patches on back, HN 1099, 1934-85, 4" h. **85**

Dog, Chow (Shibu Ino), K 15, golden, 1940-77, 2 1/2" **110**

Dog, Cocker Spaniel, Ch. "Lucky Star of Ware," black coat w/grey markings, HN 1021, 1931-68, 3 1/2" h. **165**

Dog, Cocker Spaniel, golden w/dark brown patches, HN 1187, 1937-69, 5" **125**

Dog, Cocker Spaniel, "Lucky Star of Ware," black coat w/grey markings, HN 1020, 1981-85, 5" **165**

Dog, Cocker Spaniel, seated, K9A, golden brown w/black highlights, 1931-77, 2 1/2" h. **80**

Dog, Cocker Spaniel w/pheasant, seated, white coat w/dark brown markings, red & brown pheasant, HN 1029, 1931-68, 3 1/2" h. **175**

Dog, Cocker Spaniel w/Pheasant, seated, white coat w/dark brown markings, red, brown & green pheasant, HN 1062, 1931-68, 3 1/2" **175**

Dog, Cocker Spaniel, white w/black markings, HN 1078, 1932-68, 3" h. **165**

Dog, Cocker Spaniel, white w/black markings, HN 1109, 1937-85, 5" **140**

Dog, Cocker Spaniel, white w/light brown patches, HN 1037, 1931-68, 3 1/2" **175**

Dog, Collie, Ch. "Ashstead Applause," dark & light brown coat, white chest, shoulder & feet, HN 1057, 1931-60, 7 1/2" h. **750**

Dog, Collie, dark & light brown coat, white chest, shoulders & feet, HN 1059, 1931-85, 3 1/2" **175**

Dog, Collie, dark & light brown coat, white chest, shoulders & feet, medium, HN 1058, 1931-85, 5" h. **185**

Dog, Dalmatian, "Goworth Victor," white w/black spots, black ears, HN 1113, 1937-85, 5 1/2" **225**

Dog, Dalmatian, "Goworth Victor," white w/black spots, black ears, HN 1114, 1937-68, 4 1/4" **325**

Dog, Doberman Pinscher, Ch. "Rancho Dobe's Storm," black w/brown feet & chin, HN 2645, 1955-85, 6 1/4" **155**

Dog, Dog of Fo, Flambé, RDICC, 1981, 5 1/4" h. **175**

Dog, English Setter, Ch. "Maesydd Mustard," off-white coat w/black highlights, HN 1051, 1931-68, 4" h. **220**

Dog, English Setter, "Maesydd Mustard," off-white coat w/black highlights, HN 1050, 1931-85, 5 1/4" h. **145**

Dog, English Setter w/pheasant, grey w/black markings, reddish brown bird, yellowish brown leaves on base, HN 2529, 1939-85, 8" h. **475**

Dog, Foxhound, K 7, seated, white w/brown & black patches, 1931-77, 2 1/2" **110**

Dog, Great Dane, "Rebeller of Ouborough," light brown, HN 2562, 191-52, 4 1/2" **750**

Dog, Greyhound, standing, golden brown w/dark brown markings, cream chest & feet, HN 1065, 1931-55, 8 1/2" h. **1,150**

Dog, Greyhound, white w/dark brown patches, HN 1077, 1932-55, 4 1/2" **625**

Dog, Irish Setter, Ch. "Pat O'Moy," reddish brown, HN 1054, 1931-60, 7 1/2" h. **725**

Dog, Irish Setter, "Pat O'Moy," reddish brown, HN 1055, 1931-85, 5" **140**

Dog, Labrador, "Bumblikite of Mansergh," black, HN 2667, 1967-85, 5 1/4" **145**

Dog, Labrador, standing, black, DA 145, 1990-present, 5" h. **48**

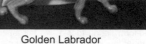

Golden Labrador

Dog, Labrador, standing, golden, DA 145, 1990-present, 5" h. (ILLUS.) **48**

Dog, Pekinese, Ch. "Biddee of Ifield," golden w/black highlights, HN 1012, 1931-85, 3" 100

Dog, Rough-haired Terrier, Ch. "Crackley Startler," white w/black & brown markings, HN 1014, 1931-85, 3 3/4" h. 165

Dog, Scottish Terrier, Ch. "Albourne Arthur," black, HN 1015, 1931-60, 5" 305

Dog, Scottish Terrier, Ch. "Albourne Arthur," black, HN 1016, 1931-85, 3 1/2" 175

Dog, Sealyham, Ch. "Scotia Stylist," white, HN 1031, 1931-55, 4" 405

Dog, Springer Spaniel, "Dry Toast," white coat w/brown markings, HN 2517, 1938-55, 3 3/4" 175

Dog, Springer Spaniel, white w/black markings, HN 1078, 1932-68, 3" 135

Dog, St. Bernard, lying, brown & cream, K 19, 1940-77, 1 1/2 x 2 1/2" 110

Dog, Wire Fox Terrier, K 8, seated, white w/brown & black patches, 1931-77, 2 1/2" 85

Dog, Airedale Terrier, K 5, 1931-55, 1 1/4 x 2 1/4" 225

Dog, Bull Terrier, K 14, lying, white, 1940-59, 1 1/4 x 2 3/4" 325

Dog, Scottish Terrier, seated, black & white, K 18, 1940-77, 2 1/4 x 2 3/4" 150

Dog, Irish Setter, Ch. "Pat O'Moy," HN 1056, 1931-68, 6" l., 4" h. 225

Dog, Cocker Spaniel w/pheasant, seated, white coat w/black markings, HN 1137, 1937-66, 6 1/2 x 7 3/4" 435

Dogs, Cocker Spaniels sleeping, white dog w/brown markings & golden brown dog, HN 2590, 1941-69, 1 3/4" h. 110

Duck, Drake, standing, green, brown & white, HN 807, 1923-77, 2 1/2" h. 95

Duck, Drake, standing, white, HN 806, 1923-68, 2 1/2" h. 95

Elephant, trunk in salute, grey w/black, HN 2644, 1952-85, 4 1/4" 175

Horse, Punch Peon, Chestnut Shire, brown w/black mane & black & white markings on legs, HN 2623, 1950-60, 7 1/2" h. 795

Horses, Chestnut Mare and Foal, chestnut mare w/white stockings, fawn-colored foal w/white stockings, HN 2522, 1938-60, 6 1/2" h. 625

Kitten, licking hind paw, brown & white, HN 2580, 2 1/4" 75

Kitten, looking up, tan & white, HN 2584, 1941-85, 2" 75

Kitten, on hind legs, light brown & black on white, HN 2582, 1941-85, 2 3/4" 75

Kitten, sleeping, brown & white, HN 2581, 1941-85, 1 1/2" 75

Monkey, Langur Monkey, long-haired brown & white coat, HN 2657, 1960-69, 4 1/2" h. 225

Penguin, grey & white w/black tips, K 22, 1940-68, 1 3/4", ... 150

Shetland Pony

Pony, Shetland Pony (woolly Shetland mare), glossy brown, DA 47, 1989 to present, 5 3/4" (ILLUS.) 45

Salmon, curved leaping pose, printed mark, 1940-50, 12" h. 431

Tiger, crouching, brown w/dark brown stripes, HN 225, 1920-36, 2 x 9 1/2" 525

Tiger on a Rock, brown, grey rock, HN 2639, 1952-92, 10 1/4 x 12" 1,250

Bunnykins Figurines

60th Anniversary, DB 137, yellow & white, 1994 70

Ace, DB 42, white & blue, 1986-89 250

Aerobic, DB 40, yellow, blue, 1985-88 225

Airman, DB 199, limited edition of 5000, 1999 75

American Firefighter, DB 268, yellow pants, red hat, 2002, colorway limited edition of 2001 (part of proceeds donated to New York Firefighters 9/11 Disaster Relief Fund) 80

Angel, DB 196, white & yellow, 1999 to present 45

Artist (The), DB 13, burgundy, yellow & blue, 1975-82 375

Astro, DB 20, white, red & blue, 1 983-88 155

Bunnykins Astro Music Box

Astro, Music Box, DB 35, white, red, blue, 1984-89 (ILLUS.) 300

Aussie, DB 58, gold & green, 1988 750

Aussie Surfer, DB 133, gold & green outfit, white & blue base, 1994 115

Bunnykins Australian Digger

Australian Digger, DB 248, brown, yellow
webbing, edition limited to 2001 (ILLUS.)..... **125**
Ballerina, DB 176, pink dress, yellow foot-
stool, 1998 to present **45**
Banjo Player, DB 182, white & red striped
blazer, black trousers, yellow straw hat,
1999, limited edition of 2,500......................... **150**
Basket Ball Bunnykin,   DB 262, yellow
w/blue trim, limited edition of 2,000, 2002..... **150**
Basket Ball Players, DB 208, limited edition
of 2,500, the set (sold only in set of 5) **625**

Bath Night Bunnykins

Bath Night, DB 141,tableau RDICC exclusive, limited edition of 5,000, 2001
(ILLUS.)... **160**
Bathtime, DB 148, white bathrobe w/grey
trim, yellow towel & duck, 1994-97 .... **50**
Batsman, DB 144, white, beige & black,
1994, limited edition of 1,000......................... **265**
Be Prepared, DB 56, dark green & grey,
1987-96 .... **60**

Fourth Variation of Bedtime

Bedtime, DB 103, fourth variation, yellow &
green striped pajamas, brown Teddy
bear, 1991 (ILLUS.) **265**
Bedtime, DB 55, blue & white striped paja-
mas, 1987-98 .... **40**
Bedtime, DB 63, second variation, red &
white striped pajamas, 1987, limited edi-
tion **425**
Bedtime, DB 79, third variation, light blue &
white, 1988 .... **850**
Beefeater, DB 163, red, gold, black & white
livery, black hat w/red, blue & white band,
1996, limited edition of 1,500 .... **525**
Billie and Buntie Bunnykins Sleigh Ride, DB
4, blue, maroon & yellow, 1972-97 .... **45**
Billie and Buntie Bunnykins Sleigh Ride, DB
81, green, yellow & red, 1989......................... **155**
Billie Bunnykins Cooling Off, DB 3, burgun-
dy, yellow & greenish grey, 1972-87 .... **185**
Bogey, DB 32, green, brown & yellow, 1984-
92 .... **150**
Bowler, DB 145, white, beige & black, 1994,
limited edition of 1,000................................... **265**
Boy Skater, DB 152, blue coat, brown pants,
yellow hat, green boots & black skates,
1995-98 .... **45**
Boy Skater, second variation, DB 187, blue
jacket, white trousers, red boots, 1998,
limited edition of 2,500..................................... **55**

Bunnykins Bride

Bride, DB 101, cream dress, grey, blue & white train, 1991 to 2001 (ILLUS.) **45**

Bridesmaid, DB 173, yellow dress, dark yellow flowers, 1997-99 .... **40**

Britannia, DB 219, blue, 2000, limited edition of 2,500 .... **100**

Brownie, DB 61, brown uniform, yellow tie, 1987-93 .... **75**

Buntie Bunnykins Helping Mother, DB 2, rose-pink & yellow, 1972-93 .... **65**

Business Man, DB 203, 1999, limited edition of 5,000 .... **85**

Busy Needles, DB 10, white, green & maroon, 1973-88 .... **75**

Captain Cook, DB 251, dark blue & yellow, 2002, limited edition of 2,500 .... **150**

Carol Singer, DB 104, dark green, red, yellow & white, 1991, UK Backstamp, limited edition of 700 .... **250**

Bunnykins Christmas Surprise

Christmas Surprise, DB 146, cream & red, 1994-2000 (ILLUS.) **50**

Cinderella, DB 231, pink & yellow, RDICC exclusive, 2001 .... **70**

Clarinet Player, DB 184, blue & white striped jacket, grey trousers, yellow straw hat, 1999, limited edition of 2,500 .... **150**

Clown, DB 128, white costume w/black stars & pompons, red square on trousers & red ruff at neck, 1992, limited edition of 750 .... **750**

Clown, DB 129, white costume w/red stars & black pompons, black ruff around neck, 1992, limited edition of 250 .... **1,500**

Collector Bunnykins

Collector, DB 54, brown, blue & grey, 1987, RDICC (ILLUS.) **550**

Cook, DB 85, white & green, 1990-94 .... **85**

Cooling Off, DB 3, maroon coat, 1972-87 .... **185**

Cowboy, DB 201, 1999, limited edition of 2,500 .... **125**

Cymbals, DB 107, dark green, red & yellow, from the Oompah Band series, 1991, limited edition of 250 .... **525**

Cymbals, DB 25, red, blue uniform & yellow cymbals, from the Oompah Band series, 1990, limited edition of 250 .... **525**

Cymbals, DB 25, red, blue & yellow, from the Oompah Band series, 1984-90 .... **115**

Cymbals, DB 88, blue coat, 1990, limited edition of 250 .... **525**

Carol Singer Bunnykins

Carol Singer, DB 104, dark green, red, yellow & white, 1991, USA Backstamp, limited edition of 300 (ILLUS.) **400**

Carol Singer, Music Box, DB 53, red, yellow & green, 1986-89 .... **325**

Cavalier, DB 179, red tunic, white collar, black trousers & hat, yellow cape, light brown boots, 1998, limited edition of 2,500 .... **265**

Cheerleader, DB 142, red, 1994, limited edition of 1,000 .... **300**

Cheerleader, DB 142, second variation, yellow, 1994, limited edition of 1,000 .... **225**

Choir Singer, DB 223, white cassock, red robe, 2001, RDICC exclusive **45**

Father, Mother and Victoria, DB 68, blue,
grey, maroon & yellow, 1988-96 .... **65**
Federation, DB 224, blue, Australian flag,
limited edition of 2,500.................................. **165**
Federation, DB 224, green, Australian flag,
2000, limited edition of 2,500........................ **125**
Fireman, DB 183, red jacket & helmet, black
trousers, yellow boots, 1998, limited edi-
tion of 3,500... **75**

Fireman Bunnykins

Fireman, DB 75, dark blue & yellow, 1989 to
present (ILLUS.)... **45**
Fisherman, DB 170, blue hat & trousers,
light yellow sweater, black wellingtons,
1997-2000... **45**

Bunnykins Fisherman

Fisherman, DB 84, maroon, yellow & grey,
1990-93 (ILLUS.).. **125**
Flamenco Dancer, DB 256, yellow & black,
2002, limited distribution.................................... **50**
Footballer, DB 117, green & white, 1991,
limited edition of 250 .... **650**

Bunnykins Footballer

Footballer, DB 119, red, 1991, limited edi-
tion of 250 (ILLUS.).. **650**
Footballer, DB 121, blue shirt & white
shorts, 1991, limited edition of 250................ **650**
Footballer, DB 123, blue & white, 1991, lim-
ited edition of 250 .... **650**
Fortune Teller, DB 218, red, black & yellow,
white ball, 2000.. **65**
Fortune Teller, DB 218, red, black & yellow,
white ball, produced only in 2001 .... **55**
Freefall, DB 41, grey, yellow & white, 1986-
89 .... **325**

Bunnykins Friar Tuck

Friar Tuck, DB 246, brown w/green, 2001
(ILLUS.).. **60**
Gardener, DB 156, brown jacket, white shirt,
grey trousers, light green wheelbarrow,
1996-98 .... **50**
Girl Skater, DB 153, green coat w/white trim,
pink dress, blue books, yellow skates,
1995-97 .... **45**
Goalkeeper, DB 116, green & black, 1991,
limited edition of 250...................................... **650**

Limited Edition Magician

Magician, DB 159, black suit, yellow shirt, yellow table cloth w/red border, 1998, limited edition of 1,000 (ILLUS.)..................... **695**

Maid Marion, DB 245, pink, yellow & green, 2001... **60**

Mandarin, DB 252, yellow & black, 2001, limited edition of 2,500.................................. **185**

Mary, Mary, Quite Contrary, DB 247, pink, 2002.. **55**

Master Potter, DB 131, blue, white, green & brown, 1992-93, RDICC Special.................. **250**

Mermaid, DB 263, 2003, limited edition of 3,000.. **125**

Merry Christmas, DB 194, tableau, 1999, limited edition 2000 .... **525**

Milkman, DB 125, white, green & grey, 1992, limited edition of 1,000........................ **750**

Minstrel, DB 211, 1999, limited edition of 2,500.. **105**

Morris Dancer, DB 204, multicolored, 1999, limited edition of 2,000.................................... **45**

Mother, DB 189, blue, white & red, 1999, Figure of the Year series **45**

Mother and Baby, DB 167, brown, light pink dress, red shoes, yellow blanket, 1997-2000... **45**

Mother and Baby, DB 226, blue, white apron, 2001, limited edition of 2,000, pr. (sold only w/Father)............................ **150**

Mother's Day, DB 155, brown & blue, 1995-2000... **45**

Mountie, DB 135, red jacket, dark blue trousers, brown hat, 1993, limited edition of 750 .... **800**

Mountie, Sergeant, DB 136, red coat w/yellow stripes on sleeve, blue & brown, 1993, limited edition of 250......................... **1,500**

Mr. Bunnybeat Strumming, DB 16, pink & yellow coat, blue & white striped trousers, white w/blue polka dot neck bow, 1982-88... **200**

Mr. Bunnybeat Strumming, Music Box, DB 38, pink, white, yellow, 1987-89..................... **355**

Mr. Bunnykins at the Easter Parade, DB 18, red, yellow & brown, 1982-93........................... **85**

Mr. Bunnykins at the Easter Parade, DB 51, blue tie & hat band, maroon coat, light grey trousers, pink ribbon on package, 1986... **850**

Mr. Bunnykins Autumn Days, DB 5, maroon, yellow & blue, 1972-82 .... **300**

Mr. Punch, DB 234, blue, red, yellow stripes, 2002, limited edition of 2,500 .... **180**

Mrs. Bunnykins at the Easter Parade, DB 19, pale blue & maroon, 1982-96 .... **75**

Mrs. Bunnykins at the Easter Parade, DB 52, maroon dress, white collar, blue bow on bonnet, multicolored bows on packages, 1986 .... **950**

Mrs. Bunnykins at the Easter Parade, Music Box, DB 39, blue, yellow & maroon, 1987-91.. **295**

Mrs. Bunnykins Clean Sweep, DB 6, blue & white, 1972-91 .... **75**

Bunnykins Mystic

Mystic, DB 197, green, yellow & mauve, 1999 (ILLUS.)...................................... **55**

New Baby, DB 158, blue dress w/white trim, white cradle, pink pillow, yellow blanket, 1995-99... **45**

Nurse, DB 74A, dark & light blue & white, red cross, 1989-94 .... **250**

Bunnykins Nurse with Green Cross

Nurse, DB 74B, dark & light blue & white, green cross, 1994-2000 (ILLUS.)..................... **40**

Old Balloon Seller, DB 217, multicolored, 1999, limited edition of 2,000........................ **195**

Olympic, DB 28A, white & blue, 1984-88........... **195**

Olympic, DB 28B, gold & green, 1984 .... **600**

On Line, DB 238, pink & blue, 2001, limited edition of 2,500.. **135**

Oompah Band, DB 105, 106, 107, 108, 109, green, 1991, limited edition of 250, the set... **2,750**

Oompah Band, DB 23, 24, 25, 26B, 27, red, 1990, the set.. **650**

Oompah Band, DB 86, 87, 88, 89, blue, 1990, limited edition of 250, the set........... **2,750**

Out for a Duck, DB 150, white, beige & green, 1995, limited edition of 1,250 .... **315**

Out for a Duck, DB 160, white, beige & green, 1995, limited edition of 1,250 .... **315**

Paperboy, DB 77, green, yellow, red & white, 1989-93... **105**

Partners in Collecting by Bunnykins

Partners in Collecting, DB 151, red, white & blue, 1995, RDICC (ILLUS.) **125**

Pilgrim, DB 212, tableau, brown & green, 1999, limited edition of 2,500........................ **125**

Piper, DB 191, green, brown & black, 1999, limited edition of 3,000.................................... **150**

Policeman, DB 64, dark blue uniform, 1988-2000 .... **45**

Bunnykins Polly

Polly, DB 71, pink, 1988-93 (ILLUS.) **125**

Bunnykins Postman

Postman, DB 76, dark blue & red, 1989-93 (ILLUS.)... **120**

Prince Frederick, DB 48, green, white & red, Royal Family series, 1986-90......................... **125**

Prince Frederick, DB 94, red, blue & yellow, Royal family series, 1990, limited edition of 250.. **465**

Prince John, DB 266, orange & green cloak, 2002... **60**

Princess Beatrice, DB 47, pale green, Royal Family series, 1986-90..................................... **105**

Princess Beatrice, DB 93, yellow & gold, Royal Family series, 1990, limited edition of 250.. **465**

Queen Sophie, DB 46, blue & red, Royal Family series, 1986-90 .... **145**

Queen Sophie, DB 92, pink & purple, Royal Family series, 1990, limited edition of 250 .... **465**

Rainy Day Bunnykins

Rainy Day, DB 147, yellow coat & hat, blue
trousers, black boots, 1994-97 (ILLUS.)......... **40**
Ringmaster, DB 165, black hat & trousers,
red jacket, white waistcoat & shirt, black
bow tie, 1996, limited edition of 1,500........... **500**
Rise and Shine, DB 11, maroon, yellow &
blue, 1973-88 .... **125**
Robin Hood, DB 244, green, 2001...................... **60**
Robin Hood resin stand, for Robin Hood
Collection, brown & green, 2001...................... **60**
Rock and Roll, DB 124, white, blue & red,
1991, limited edition of 1,000.......................... **395**
Runners, DB 205, 1999, limited edition of
2,500, the set (sold only in set of 5).............. **625**
Sailor, DB 166, white & blue, 1997, Bun-
nykins of the Year series **45**
Sandcastle Money Box, DB 228, 2002, to
mark the 30th anniversary of Bunnykins
figures... **225**

Sands of Time Bunnykins

Sands of Time, DB 229, yellow, 2000, limited order period of three months (ILLUS.)....... **60**

Santa Bunnykins Happy Christmas

Santa, DB 17, red, white & brown, 1981-96
(ILLUS.)... **45**

Santa Christmas Tree Ornament

Santa, DB 62, Christmas tree ornament, red
& white, edition limited to 1987 (ILLUS.)... **1,500**

Santa Music Box

Santa, Music Box, DB 34, red, white, brown,
1988-91 (ILLUS.).. **215**
Santa's Helper, DB 192, red, green & yel-
low, 1999, limited edition of 2,500 .... **65**
Saxophone Player, DB 186, navy & white
striped shirt, blue vest, black trousers,
1999, limited edition of 2,500 .... **180**
School Days, DB 57, dark green, white &
yellow, 1987-94.. **125**
Schoolboy, DB 66, blue, white & grey, 1988-
91 .... **155**
Schoolmaster, DB 60, black, green & white,
1987-96.. **60**
Scotsman (The), DB 180, dark blue jacket &
hat, red & yellow kilt, white shirt, sporran
& socks, black shoes, 1998, limited edi-
tion of 2,500... **185**
Seaside, DB 177, blue bathing costume,
white & blue bathing cap, yellow sandy
base, Bunnykins of the Year, 1998 .... **55**

Sheriff of Nottingham, DB 265, red cross on white apron, blue cloak, 2002 .... **65**

Shopper, DB 233, green, pink, brown, Bunnykins of the Year, 2002 .... **50**

Sightseer, DB 215, pink dress, 2000 .... **50**

Sleepytime, DB 15, brown, white, yellow, blue & red, 1975-93 .... **75**

Sleighride, DB 4, 1972-91 .... **45**

Bunnykins Sleighride

Sleighride, DB 81, green, yellow, red, 1989 (ILLUS.) **155**

Soccer Player, DB 123, dark blue & white, 1991, limited edition of 250 .... **650**

Soccer Players, DB 209, 1999, limited edition of 2,500, the set (sold only in set of 5) **625**

Sousaphone, DB 105, dark green, red & yellow, Oompah Band series, 1991, limited edition of 200 .... **500**

Sousaphone, DB 23, red, blue & yellow, Oompah Band series, 1984-90 .... **115**

Sousaphone, DB 86, blue uniform & yellow sousaphone, Oompha Band series, 1990, limited edition of 250 .... **500**

Statue of Liberty, DB 198, red, white & blue, 1999, limited edition of 3,000 .... **140**

Stopwatch, DB 253, green & yellow, produced only in 2002 .... **55**

Storytime, DB 59, dress w/green polka dots on white, yellow shoes & yellow dress w/green shoes, 1987 .... **345**

Storytime, DB 9, white dress w/blue design & pink dress, 1972-97 .... **45**

Strawberries, DB 278, tableau, issued in a pair w/Tennis, 2003, limited edition of 3,000, pr. **150**

Sundial, DB 213, red, blue & white, produced only in 2000 .... **50**

Susan, DB 70, white, blue & yellow, 1988-93 .... **125**

Susan as Queen of the May

Susan Bunnykins as Queen of the May, DB 83, white polka dot dress w/blue, brown chair, 1990-91 (ILLUS.) **165**

Sweet Dreams Baby Bunnykins, DB 276, 2002 .... **60**

Sweetheart, DB 130, yellow sweater, blue trousers, red heart, 1992-97 .... **50**

Bunnykins Sweetheart

Sweetheart, DB 174, white & blue, pink heart, 1997, limited edition of 2,500 (ILLUS.) **205**

Swimmers, DB 206, 1999, limited edition of 2,500, the set (sold only in set of 5) **625**

Sydney, DB 195, blue, white, black & brown, 1999, limited edition of 2,500 .... **175**

Tally Ho!, DB 12, burgundy, yellow, blue, white & green, 1973-88 .... **105**

Tally Ho Bunnykins

Tally Ho!, DB 78, light blue coat & white rocking horse, yellow sweater, 1988 (ILLUS.) **205**

Tally Ho!, Music Box, DB 33A, maroon coat, yellow jumper, 1984-93 .... **255**

Tally Ho!, Music Box, DB 33B, "William," red coat, maroon tie, 1988-91 .... **300**

Tennis, DB 277, tableau, issued in a pair w/Strawberries, 2003, limited edition of 3,000, pr. **150**

Tom, DB 72, brown, white & blue, 1988-93 .... **90**

Touchdown, DB 100 (University of Indiana), white & red, 1990, limited edition of 200 ...... **625**

Touchdown, DB 29A, blue & white, 1985-88 ..... **165**

Touchdown, DB 29B (Boston College), maroon & gold, 1985, limited edition of 50 ...... **2,000**

Touchdown, DB 96 (Ohio State University), grey & orange, 1990, limited edition of 200 .... **625**

Touchdown, DB 97 (University of Michigan), yellow & blue, 1990, limited edition of 200 ..... **625**

Touchdown, DB 98 (Cincinnati Bengals), orange & black, 1990, limited edition of 200 ..... **625**

Touchdown, DB 99 (Notre Dame), green & yellow, 1990, limited edition of 200 .... **625**

Tourist, DB 190, blue & yellow, ICC on hat, 1999, limited order period of three months **85**

Town Crier, DB 259, black, red & yellow, 2002, limited edition of 2,500 .... **175**

Trick or Treat, DB 162, red dress, black hat, shoes & cloak, white moon & stars, 1995, limited edition of 1,500 .... **850**

Trumpet Player, DB 210, green striped coat, 2000, limited edition of 2,500 .... **175**

Trumpeter, DB 106, dark green, red & yellow, Oompah Band series, 1991, limited edition of 250 .... **500**

Trumpeter, DB 24, red, blue & yellow, Oompah Band series, 1984-90 .... **105**

Trumpeter, DB 87, blue uniform & yellow trumpet, Oompah Band series, 1990, limited edition of 250 .... **500**

Tyrolean Dancer, DB 246, black & white, 2001 .... **60**

Uncle Sam, DB 175, red jacket, yellow shirt, blue & white striped trousers, red, white & blue hat, platinum bow tie, 1997, limited edition of 1,500 .... **205**

Uncle Sam, DB 50, blue, red & white, 1986 to present **45**

Vicar, DB 254, 2002, limited to renewing members of RDICC **45**

Waltzing Matilda, DB 236, yellow, red jacket, brown hat, 2001, limited edition of 2,001 .... **225**

Wee Willie Winkie, DB 270, blue w/yellow tinges to nightgown, 2002 .... **55**

Welsh Lady, DB 172, light pink & yellow dress, black hat, 1997, limited edition of 2,500 .... **225**

Wicket Keeper, DB 150, white, beige & black, 1995, limited edition of 1,000 .... **265**

Will Scarlet, DB 264, green & orange, 2002 .... **60**

William, DB 69, red & white, 1988-93 .... **85**

With Love, DB 269, tinged yellow, w/engraveable nameplate, 2002 .... **65**

Wizard, DB 168, brown rabbit, purple robes & hat, 1997, limited edition of 2,000 .... **400**

Character Jugs

Anne Boleyn

Anne Boleyn, large, D 6644, 7 1/4" h. (ILLUS.) **85**

Anne of Cleves

Anne of Cleves, large, D 6653, 7 1/4" h. (ILLUS.) **85**

Antony & Cleopatra, large, D 6728, 7 1/4" h. **125**

Aramis

Aramis, large, D 6441, 7 1/4" h. (ILLUS.) **115**
Aramis, miniature, D 6508, 2 1/2" h...................... **45**
'Arriet, tiny, D 6256, 1 1/4" h.............................. **175**
'Arry, large, D 6207, 6 1/2" h.............................. **185**
'Arry, tiny, D 6255, 1 1/2" h. **175**
Athos, small, D 6452, 3 3/4" h. **60**
Auld Mac, miniature, D 6253, 2 1/4" h.................. **45**
Auld Mac "A," large, D 5823, 6 1/4" h.................. **85**

Bacchus

Bacchus, large, D 6499, 7" h. (ILLUS.)................ **95**
Bacchus, miniature, D 6521, 2 1/2" h.................. **50**
Baseball Player, small, D 6878, 4 1/4" h............. **120**

Beefeater

Beefeater, large, D 6206, 6 1/2" h.
 (ILLUS.)... **85**
Beefeater, small, D 6233, 3 1/4" h....................... **90**
Ben Franklin, small, D 6695, 4" h. **90**

Blacksmith

Blacksmith, D 6571, large, 7" h.
 (ILLUS.).. **140**
Bootmaker, small, D 6579, 4" h. **70**
Busker (The), large, D 6775, 6 1/2" h. **125**
Buzfuz, small, D 5838, 4" h.................................. **110**
Cap'n Cuttle, mid, D 5842, 5 1/2" h. **175**
Capt. Ahab, large, D 6500, 7" h. **145**
Capt. Ahab, small, D 6506, 4" h........................... **65**

Capt. Henry Morgan

Capt. Henry Morgan, large, 6 3/4" h.
 (ILLUS.)... **95**
Capt. Hook, small, D 660, 4" h. **350**
Cardinal (The), small, D 6033,
 3 1/2" h... **65**
Cardinal (The), tiny, D 6258, 1 1/2" h.................. **210**

Catherine Howard

Catherine Howard, large, D 6645, 7" h.
(ILLUS.).. **165**

Catherine of Aragon

Catherine of Aragon, large, D 6643, 7" h.
(ILLUS.).. **120**

Catherine Parr

Catherine Parr, large, D 6664, 6 3/4" h.
(ILLUS.).. **190**
Cavalier (The), large, D 6114, 7" h. **135**
Cavalier (The), small, D 6173, 3 1/4" h. **60**
City Gent, large, D 6815, 7" h. **150**
Cliff Cornell, large, variation 2, dark blue
suit, red tie w/cream polka dots, 9" h. **300**

Cliff Cornell Toby Jugs

Cliff Cornell, large, variation No. 1, light
brown suit, brown & cream striped tie,
9" h. (ILLUS. left)... **450**
Cliff Cornell, large, variation No. 3, dark
brown suit, green, black & blue designed
tie, 9" h. (ILLUS. right) **300**
Cliff Cornell, small, variation No. 1, light
brown suit, brown & cream striped tie,
5" h. **1,500**
Cliff Cornell, small, variation No. 2, blue suit,
5" h. **3,500**
Cliff Cornell, small, variation No. 3, dark
brown suit, 5" h. **300**
Clown w/red hair (The), large, D 5610,
7 1/2" h. **2,600**

Clown with White Hair

Clown w/white hair (The), large, D 6322,
7 1/2" h. (ILLUS.).. **1,200**
Collector (The), large, D 6796, 7" h. **175**

Davy Crockett & Santa Anna, large, D 6729,
7" h. **150**
Dick Turpin, horse handle, large, D 6528,
7" h. **100**
Dick Turpin, horse handle, miniature, D
6542, 2 1/4" h. **60**
Dick Turpin, miniature, D 6128, 2 1/4" h. **45**
Dick Turpin, pistol handle, small, D 5618,
3 1/2" h. **55**
Dick Turpin "A," pistol handle, D 5485,
6 1/2" h. **130**
Drake, small, D 6174, 3 1/4" h. **65**
Falconer (The), miniature, D 6547,
2 3/4" h. **55**
Falconer (The), small, D 6540, 3 3/4" h. **60**

Falstaff

Falstaff, large, D 6287, 6" h. (ILLUS.) **110**
Farmer John, large, D 5788, 6 1/2" h. **135**
Farmer John, small, D 5789, 3 1/4" h. **65**
Fat Boy, mid, D 5840, 5" h. **175**
Fat Boy, miniature, D 6139, 2 1/2" h. **60**

The Fortune Teller

Fortune Teller (The), large, D 6497,
6 3/4" h. (ILLUS.) **550**
Fortune Teller (The), small, D 6503,
3 3/4" h. **330**

Friar Tuck, large, D 6321, 7" h. **425**
Gaoler, small, D 6577, 3 3/4" h. **70**

The Gardener

Gardener (The), large, D 6630, 7 3/4" h.
(ILLUS) **160**
General Gordon, large, D 6869, 7 1/4" h. **215**
Genie, large, D 6892, 7" h. **225**
George Washington, large, D 6669,
7 1/2" h. **165**

George Washington

George Washington and George III, large, D
6749, 7 1/4" h. (ILLUS. of Washington
side) **175**
Gladiator, small, D 6553, 4 1/4" h. **395**
Gone Away, miniature, D 6545,
2 1/2" h. **60**
Gone Away, small, D 6538, 3 3/4" h. **55**
Granny, large, D 5521, 6 1/4" h. **95**
Granny, miniature, D 6520, 2 1/4" h. **60**

The Guardsman

Guardsman (The), large, D 6568, 6 3/4" h.
(ILLUS.)... **95**

Gulliver

Gulliver, large, D 6560, 7 1/2" h. (ILLUS.) **825**
Gulliver, miniature, D 6566, 2 1/2" h.................... **395**
Gunsmith, small, D 6580, 3 1/2" h. **65**

Hamlet

Hamlet, large, D 6672, 7 1/4" h. (ILLUS.)........... **165**
Happy John "A," large, D 6031, 8 1/2" h.............. **95**

Henry V

Henry V, embossed flag, large, variation No.
1, D 6671, 7 1/4" h. (ILLUS.) **205**
Henry V, flag decal, large, variation No. 3, D
6671, 7 1/4" h.. **140**

Henry VIII

Henry VIII, large, D 6642, 6 1/2" h. (ILLUS.)...... **105**

Izaac Walton

Izaac Walton, large, D 6404, 7" h. (ILLUS.) **95**

Jane Seymour

Jane Seymour, large, D 6646, 7 1/4" h.
(ILLUS.).. **115**
Jarge, small, D 6295, 3 1/2" h. **135**
Jester, seated, medium, D 6910, 5" h. **175**
Jester, small, D 5556, 3 1/8" h. **90**
Jockey, large, D 6625, 7 3/4" h. **275**
John Barleycorn, small, D 5735,
3 1/2" h.. **55**
John Doulton, small, two o'clock, D 6656,
4 1/4" h. **50**

John Peel

John Peel, large, D 5612, 6 1/2" h.
(ILLUS.).. **125**
John Peel, tiny, D 6259, 1 1/4" h.......................... **200**
John Shorter, small, D 6880, 4 1/4" h. **165**

Johnny Appleseed

Johnny Appleseed, large, D 6372, 6" h.
(ILLUS.).. **260**
Juggler (The), large, D 6835,
6 1/2" h.. **155**
King Charles I, large, D 6917,
7" h... **375**

The Lawyer

Lawyer (The), large, D6498, 7" h.
(ILLUS.).. **115**
Lawyer (The), small, D 6504, 4" h. **60**
Leprechaun, large, D 6847, 7 1/2" h. **145**
Little Mester Museum Piece, large, D 6819,
6 3/4" h... **165**
Lobster Man, large, D 6617, 7 1/2" h. **90**
Long John Silver, miniature, D 6512,
2 1/2" h.. **50**

Lord Nelson

Lord Nelson, large, D 6336, 7" h. (ILLUS.)........ **380**

Louis Armstrong

Louis Armstrong, large, D 6707, 7 1/2" h.
(ILLUS.).. **200**

Lumberjack

Lumberjack, large, D 6610, 7 1/4" h.
(ILLUS.)... **90**
Macbeth, large, D 6667, 7 1/4" h. **135**

Mad Hatter

Mad Hatter, large, D 6598, 7 1/4" h.
(ILLUS.).. **175**
Mark Twain, small, D 6694, 4" h. **135**
Mephistopheles, large, w/verse, D 5757,
7" h.. **2,750**
Mephistopheles "A," small, two-faced,
w/verse, D 5758, 3 3/4" h................................. **950**

Merlin

Merlin, large, D 6529, 7 1/4" h.
(ILLUS.) **90**
Merlin, small, D 6536, 3 3/4" h. **50**
Mine Host, miniature, D 6513,
2 1/2" h... **60**
Mr. Micawber, mid, D 5843, 5 1/2" h. **165**

Paddy, tiny, D 6145, 1 1/4" h............................... **75**

Mr. Pickwick

Mr. Pickwick, large, D 6060, 5 1/2" h.
(ILLUS.)... **185**
Mr. Pickwick, tiny, D 6260, 1 1/4" h. **165**
Mr. Quaker, large, D 6738, 7 1/2" h.................... **650**
Neptune, small, D 6552, 3 3/4" h. **55**
North American Indian, small, D 6614,
4 1/4" h. **50**
Old Charley, large, D 5420, 5 1/2" h..................... **95**

Parson Brown

Parson Brown "A," large, D 5486, 6 1/2" h.
(ILLUS.).. **125**
Pearly King, large, D 6760, 6 3/4" h. **125**
Pearly Queen, large, D 6759, 7" h....................... **115**
Pied Piper, large, D 6403, 7" h............................ **125**
Poacher (The), variation 2, large, D 6429,
7" h.. **175**

Old King Cole

Old King Cole, large, D 6036, 5 3/4" h.
(ILLUS.)... **275**
Old Salt, large, D 6551, 7 1/2" h........................... **105**

Paddy

Paddy, large, D 5753, 6" h. (ILLUS.) **110**

Punch & Judy Man

Punch & Judy Man, large, D 6590, 7" h.
(ILLUS.)... **750**
Queen Victoria, small, D 6913,
3 1/2" h... **165**
Red Queen (The), large, D 6777,
7 1/4" h... **135**

The Ringmaster

Ringmaster (The), large, D 6863, 7 1/2" h.
(ILLUS.).. **175**

Rip Van Winkle

Rip Van Winkle, large, D 6438, 6 1/2" h.
(ILLUS.).. **100**

Robin Hood

Robin Hood, 2nd version, large, D 6527,
7 1/2" h. (ILLUS. left)....................................... **105**
Robin Hood, 2nd version, small, D 6234,
3 1/4" h. (ILLUS. right)...................................... **65**

Robinson Crusoe

Robinson Crusoe, large, D 6532, 7 1/2" h.
(ILLUS.).. **120**
Robinson Crusoe, miniature, D 6546,
2 3/4" h.. **55**
Romeo, large, D 6670, 7 1/2" h. **105**
Ronald Reagan, large, D 6718,
7 3/4" h.. **750**
Sairey Gamp, tiny, D 6146,
1 1/4" h.. **80**
Sam Johnson, large, D 6289,
6 1/4" h.. **325**

Sam Weller

Sam Weller, large, D 6064, 6 1/2" h.
(ILLUS.).. **325**
Sam Weller, tiny, D 6147, 1 1/4" h. **75**
Sancho Pança, large, D 6456,
6 1/2" h.. **125**

Santa Claus w/Doll & Drum Handle

Santa Claus, doll & drum handle, large, D
6668, 7 1/2" h. (ILLUS.)................................... **148**

Sir Thomas More

Sir Thomas More, large, D 6792, 6 3/4" h.
(ILLUS.).. **215**

Santa Claus with Plain Handle

Santa Claus, plain handle, large, D 6704,
7 1/2" h. (ILLUS.) **165**
Simon the Cellarer, large, D 5504,
6 1/2" h. **110**
Simon the Cellarer, small, D 5616,
3 1/2" h. **60**

The Sleuth

Sleuth (The), large, D 6631, 7" h. (ILLUS.) **105**

Simple Simon

Simple Simon, large, D 6374, 7" h. (ILLUS.)..... **495**
Sir Francis Drake, large, D 6805, 7" h................ **225**

St. George

St. George, large, D 6618, 7 1/2" h. (ILLUS.)...... **350**

Tam O'Shanter, miniature, D 6640, 2 1/2" h. **85**
Toby Philpots, large, D 5736, 6 1/4" h. **120**

Tony Weller

Tony Weller, large, D 5531, 6 1/2" h.
   (ILLUS.).. **145**
Touchstone, large, D 5613, 7" h........................ **245**
Town Crier, large, D 6530, 7" h......................... **245**

Ugly Duchess

Ugly Duchess, large, D 6599, 6 3/4" h.
   (ILLUS.).. **650**
Uncle Tom Cobbleigh, large, D 6337, 7" h. **550**

Veteran Motorist

Veteran Motorist, large, D 6633, 7 1/2" h.
   (ILLUS.)... **165**

The Walrus & Carpenter

Walrus & Carpenter (The), large, D 6600,
   7 1/4" h. (ILLUS.)... **195**

Shakespeare

William Shakespeare, large, D 6689,
   7 3/4" h. (ILLUS.)... **150**
Winston Churchill, style 1, large, D 6907,
   Union Jack & bulldog handle, 7" h................. **325**

Yachtsman

Yachtsman, large, D 6626, 8" h. (ILLUS.).......... **145**

Figurines

The Auctioneer

Autumn Breezes

Bedtime

Bedtime Story, HN 2059, pink, white, yellow & blue, 1950-98 .... **450**

Belle, HN 2340, green dress, 1968-88 .... **85**

Bernice, HN 2071, pink & red, 1951-53 .... **995**

Biddy, HN 1513, red dress, blue shawl, 1932-51 .... **275**

Bill Sykes, M 54, black & brown, 1932-81 .... **80**

Blacksmith of Williamsburg, HN 2240, white shirt, brown hat, 1960-83 .... **375**

Bo Peep, HN 1811, orange dress, green hat, 1937-95 .... **150**

Bride (The), HN 2166, pale pink dress, 1956-76 .... **250**

Bride (The), HN 2873, white w/gold trim, 1980-89 .... **175**

Bride (The), HN 3284, style 4, white, 1990-97 .... **225**

Bridesmaid, M 30, pink & lavender, 1932-45 .... **300**

Bridesmaid (The Little), M 12, multicolor gown, 1932-45 .... **295**

Broken Lance (The), HN 2041, blue, red & yellow, 1949-75 .... **650**

Bunny, HN 2214, turquoise, 1960-75 .... **225**

Bunny's Bedtime, HN 3370, pale blue, pink ribbon, 1991, RDICC Series, limited edition of 9,500 .... **225**

Buttercup, HN 2309, green dress w/yellow sleeves, 1964-97 .... **210**

Buz Fuz, M 53, black & red, 1932-83 .... **80**

Camellia, HN 2222, pink, 1960-71 .... **350**

Captain Cook, HN 2889, black & cream, 1980-84 .... **500**

Captain Cuttle, M 77, yellow & black, 1939-82 .... **80**

Captain (The), HN 2260, black & white, 1965-82 .... **300**

Carpet Seller (The), HN 1464, (hand open), green & orange, 1929-? **315**

Carpet Seller (The), HN 1464A, (hand closed), green & orange, 1931-69 .... **275**

Carpet Seller (The), HN 2776, Flambé, 1990 to present **225**

Catherine, HN 3044, white, 1985-96 .... **65**

Catherine of Aragon, HN 3233, green, blue & white dress, 1990, limited edition of 9,500 .... **525**

Charlotte

Charlotte, HN 3813, brown figure, ivory dress, 1996-97 (ILLUS.) **285**

Chief (The), HN 2892, gold, 1979-88 .... **265**

Child from Williamsburg, HN 2154, blue dress, 1964-83 .... **265**

China Repairer, HN 2943, blue, white & tan, 1983-88 .... **175**

Chloe, HN 1765, blue, 1936-50 .... **475**

Christmas Parcels

Christmas Parcels, HN 2851, black, 1978-82 (ILLUS.) **235**

Cissie

Cissie, HN 1809, pink dress, 1937-93 (ILLUS.) **175**

Claire, HN 3209, red, 1990-92 .... **215**

Claribel, HN 1951, red dress, 1940-49 .... **425**

Clarinda, HN 2724, blue & white dress, 1975-81 .... **210**

Coachman, HN 2282, purple, grey & blue, 1963-71 .... **625**

Cookie, HN 2218, pink & white, 1958-75 .... **215**

Coralie, HN 2307, yellow dress, 1964-88 .... **175**

Cup O' Tea, HN 2322, dark blue & grey, 1964-83 .... **315**

Curly Locks, HN 2049, pink flowered
dress,1949-53 .... **265**
Daffy Down Dilly, HN 1712, green dress,
1935-75 .... **405**
Dainty May, M 67, pink skirt, blue overdress,
1935-49 .... **625**

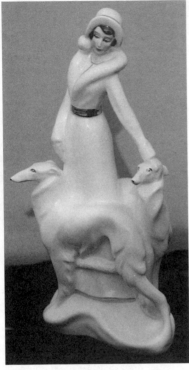

Daisy

Daisy, HN 3805, ivory & gold, Charleston
series, 1996-97 (ILLUS.) **285**
Darling, HN 1319, white w/black base,
1929-59 .... **225**
Darling, HN 1985, white nightshirt, 1946-97 .... **95**
David Copperfield, M 88, black & tan, Dick-
ens Miniatures Series, 1949-83 .... **85**
Deborah, HN 2701, green & white,
1983-84 .... **215**
Delight, HN 1772, red dress, 1936-67 .... **265**
Diana, HN 1986, red, 1946-75 .... **250**
Discovery, HN 3428, matte white, 1992 .... **375**
Duchess of York (The), HN 3086, cream,
1986, limited edition of 1,500 .... **1,450**
Duke of Edinburgh (The), HN 2386, black &
gold, 1981, limited edition of 1,500 .... **500**
Dulcie, HN 2305, blue, 1981-84 .... **220**
Easter Day, HN 1976, white dress, blue
flowers, 1945-51 .... **525**
Easter Day, HN 2039, multicolored, 1949-
69 .... **500**
Eliza, HN 2543, gold, Haute Ensemble Se-
ries, 1974-79 .... **405**
Eliza, HN 3179, red & lilac, 1988-92 .... **200**

Ellen

Ellen, HN 3816, ivory & light blue dress,
1996-97 (ILLUS.) **285**
Elyse, HN 2429, blue dress, 1972-95 .... **225**
Embroidering, HN 2855, grey dress, 1980-
90 .... **275**
Emily, HN 3204, style 2, white & blue, 1989-
93 .... **175**
Enchantment, HN 2178, blue, 1957-82 .... **200**
Fagin, M 49, brown, 1932-83 .... **80**
Fair Lady, HN 2832, red gown, green
sleeves, 1977-96 .... **225**
Fair Maiden, HN 2211, green dress, yellow
sleeves, 1967-94 .... **135**
Fair Maiden, HN 2434, red gown, 1983-94 .... **135**
Falstaff, HN 2054, red jacket, brown belt &
boots, 1950-92 .... **195**
Falstaff, HN 3236, brown, yellow & laven-
der, 1989-90 .... **135**
Farmer's Wife, HN 2069, red, green &
brown, 1951-55 .... **545**
Fat Boy, M 44, blue & white, 1932-83 .... **80**
Favourite (The), HN 2249, blue & white,
1960-90 .... **275**
Fiona, HN 2694, red & white, 1974-81 .... **225**
First Dance, HN 2803, pale blue dress,
1977-92 .... **250**
First Steps, HN 2242, blue & yellow, 1959-
65 .... **615**
First Waltz, HN 2862, red dress, 1979-83 .... **375**
Fleur, HN 2368, green dress, 1968-95 .... **265**
Flirtation, HN 3071, pale blue, 1985-95 .... **185**
Flower Seller's Children, HN 1342, purple,
red & yellow, 1929-93 .... **575**
Foaming Quart (The) HN 2162, brown,
1955-92 .... **235**

Fond Farewell

Fond Farewell, HN 3815, red, 1997-99 (ILLUS.) **375**

Fortune Teller

Fortune Teller, HN 2159, multicolor, 1955-67 (ILLUS.) **825**

Forty Winks, HN 1974, green & tan, 1945-73 .... **350**

Francine, HN 2422, green & white dress, 1972-81 .... **160**

French Peasant, HN 2075, brown & green, 1951-55 .... **625**

Frodo, HN 2912, black & white, Middle Earth Series, 1980-84 .... **150**

Gaffer (The), HN 2053, green & brown, 1950-59 .... **450**

Gamekeeper (The), HN 2879, green, black & tan, 1984-92 .... **295**

Gandalf, HN 2911, green & white, Middle Earth Series, 1980-84 .... **275**

Geisha (The), HN 3229, Flambé, RDICC, 1989 .... **250**

Genie (The), HN 2989, blue, 1983-90 .... **325**

Genie (The), HN 2999, Flambé, 1989-95 .... **350**

George Washington at Prayer, HN 2861, blue & tan, 1977, limited edition of 750 .... **3,500**

Gillian, HN 3042, green, 1984-91 .... **215**

Gimli, HN 2922, brown & blue, Middle Earth Series, 1981-84 .... **235**

Giselle, The Forest Glade, HN 2140, white & blue, 1954-65 .... **500**

Golfer, HN 2992, blue, white & pale brown, 1988-91 .... **215**

Good King Wenceslas, HN 2118, brown & purple, 1953-76 .... **550**

Good Morning, HN 2671, blue, pink & brown matte, 1974-76 .... **200**

Goody Two Shoes, M 80, blue skirt, red overdress, 1939-49 .... **135**

Graduate (The), HN 3017, male, black & grey, 1984-92 .... **235**

Granny's Shawl, HN 1647, red cape, 1934-49 .... **625**

Gypsy Dance, HN 2230, lavender dress, 1959-71 .... **475**

Happy Anniversary, HN 3097, style one, purple & white, 1987-93 .... **275**

Harmony

Harmony, HN 2824, grey dress, 1978-84 (ILLUS.) **300**

Hazel, HN 1797, orange & green dress, 1936-49 .... **475**

He Loves Me, HN 2046, flowered pink dress, 1949-62 .... **425**

Hilary, HN 2335, blue dress, 1967-81 .... **275**

Home Again, HN 2167, red & white, 1956-95 .... **225**

Homecoming (The), HN 3295, blue, pink & green, 1990, limited edition of 9,500, Children of the Blitz series **400**
Honey, HN 1909, pink, 1939-49 .... **525**
Hornpipe (The), HN 2161, blue jacket, blue & white striped trousers, 1955-62 .... **900**

The Huntsman

Huntsman (The), HN 2492, grey coat, cream pants, black hat & boots, 1974-79 (ILLUS.)... **325**
Ibrahim, HN 2095, brown & yellow, 1952-55 ..... **700**
Innocence, HN 2842, red, 1979-83.................... **225**
Irene, HN 1621, pale yellow dress, 1934-51 ..... **550**
Isadora, HN 2938, lavender, 1986-92 .... **350**
Ivy, HN 1768, pink hat, lavender dress, 1936-79 .... **135**
Jack, HN 2060, green, white & black, 1950-71 .... **235**
Jacqueline, HN 2001, pink dress, 1947-51 .... **800**
Jane, HN 2806, yellow dress, 1983-86 .... **225**
Jane, HN 3260, green, blue & yellow, 1990-95 .... **275**
Janet, HN 1537, red dress, 1932-95 .... **150**
Janet, M 69, pale green skirt, green over-dress, 1936-49 .... **495**
Janet, HN 1916, pink & blue, 1939-49 .... **350**
Janice, HN 2022, green dress, 1949-55 .... **715**
Jennifer, HN 2392, blue dress, 1981-92 .... **295**
Jester (A), HN 2016, pink, purple & orange, 1949-97 .... **325**
Jill, HN 2061, pink & white, 1950-71.................. **250**
Joan, HN 2023, blue, 1949-59........................... **225**
Joker (The), HN 2252, white, 1990-92 .... **250**
Judge (The), HN 2443, red & white, 1972-76 ..... **250**
Judge (The), HN 2443A, gloss, red & white, 1976-92 .... **260**
Judith, HN 2278, yellow, 1986-89 .... **275**
Julia, HN 2705, gold, 1975-90 .... **265**
June, HN 2991, lavender & red, 1988-94 .... **235**
Karen, HN 1994, red dress, 1947-55 .... **450**
Karen, HN 2388, style two, red & white, 1982 to present.. **475**
Kate, HN 2789, white dress, 1978-87 .... **200**
Kathleen, HN 3100, purple, cream & pink, 1986.. **300**
Katrina, HN 2327, red, 1967-69 .... **475**

Kelly, HN 2478, white w/blue flowers, 1985-92 .... **220**
Kirsty, HN 3213, red, 1988-97 .... **150**
Ko-Ko, HN 2898, yellow & blue, 1980-85........... **650**
L'Ambitieuse, HN 3359, rose & pale blue, 1991, RDICC, limited edition of 5,000............ **350**
La Sylphide, HN 2138, white dress, 1954-65... **475**
Lady April, HN 1958, red dress, 1940-49.. **360**
Lady Betty, HN 1967, red, 1941-51 .... **450**
Lady of the Georgian Period (A), HN 41, gold & blue, 1914-38.................................. **1,900**

Lambing Time

Lambing Time, HN 1890, light brown, 1938-80 (ILLUS.).. **300**
Last Waltz, HN 2315, apricot dress, 1967-93 .... **220**
Laura, HN 2960, pale blue & white w/yellow flowers, 1984-94 .... **300**
Laura, HN 3136, dark blue & white, 1988 .... **300**
Lavinia, HN 1955, red dress, 1940-79 .... **145**
Lawyer (The), HN 3041, grey & black, 1985-95 .... **225**
Leading Lady, HN 2269, blue & yellow, 1965-76 .... **325**
Legolas, HN 2917, cream & tan, Middle Earth Series, 1981-84..................................... **175**
Lights Out, HN 2662, blue trousers & yellow spotted shirt, 1965-69 .... **325**
Lilac Time, HN 2137, red, 1954-69.................... **400**
Lily, HN 1799, green & blue, 1936-49................. **550**
Lisa, HN 2394, yellow & lilac, 1983-90 .... **200**
Little Boy Blue, HN 2062, blue, 1950-73.. **200**
Lizzie, HN 2749, green, white & red, 1988-91 .... **190**
Lorna, HN 2311, green dress, apricot shawl, 1965-85.. **260**
Love Letter, HN 2149, pink & blue dress, 1958-76.. **500**
Lucy Locket, HN 524, yellow dress, 1921-49.. **700**
Lynne, HN 2329, green dress, 1971-96............. **225**
Madonna of the Square, HN 2034, light green-blue, 1949-51.................................. **1,100**

Make Believe

Make Believe, HN 2225, blue dress, 1962-88 (ILLUS.) 180

Margaret, HN 1989, red & green, 1947-49 500

Marguerite, HN 1928, pink dress, 1940-49 450

Marie, HN 1370, style 2, purple dress, 1930-88 95

Marietta, HN 1341, black & red, 1929-49 .... **1,650**

Marjorie, HN 2788, blue & white dress, 1980-84 375

Mary, HN 3375, blue & white, Figure of the Year Series, 1992 650

Mary Had a Little Lamb, HN 2048, lavender, 1949-88 150

Mary, Mary, HN 2044, pink, Nursery Rhymes Series, 1949-73 225

Masque, HN 2554, hand holds wand of mask, blue, 1973-82 325

Master (The), HN 2325, green & brown, 1967-92 225

Maxine, HN 3199, pink & purple, 1989-90 215

Mayor (The), HN 2280, red & white, 1963-71 450

Maytime, HN 2113, pink dress w/blue scarf, 1953-67 400

Melissa, HN 2467, purple & cream, 1981 to present 225

Melody, HN 2204, blue & peach, 1957-62 350

Mendicant (The), HN 1365, brown, 1929-69 325

Meriel, HN 1931, pink dress, 1940-49 .... **1,650**

Michelle, HN 2234, green, 1967-94 185

Midsummer Noon, HN 2033, pink, 1949-55 750

Minuet, HN 2019, white dress, floral print, 1949-71 400

Miss Demure, HN 1402, lavender & pink dress, 1930-75 250

Miss Fortune, HN 1897, blue & white shawl, pink dress, 1938-49 .... **1,600**

Modesty, HN 2744, white, 1987-91 225

Monica, HN 1467, flowered purple dress, 1931-95 175

Monica, M 66, shaded pink skirt, blue blouse, 1935-49 700

Mr. Micawber, HN 1895, brown, black & tan, 1938-52 450

Mr. Micawber, M 42, yellow & black, 1932-83 80

Mr. Pickwick, HN 1894, blue, tan & cream, Dickens Series, 1938-42 475

Mrs. Bardell, M 86, green, 1949-82 80

My Love, HN 2339, white w/red rose, 1969-97 325

News vendor, HN 2891, gold & grey, 1986, limited edition of 2,500 260

Newsboy, HN 2244, green, brown & blue, 1959-65 625

Nicola, HN 2839, flowered lavender dress, 1978-95 350

Nina, HN 2347, matte blue, 1969-76 200

Ninette, HN 2379, yellow & cream, 1971-97 325

Old Country Roses

Old Country Roses, HN 3692, red, 1995-99 (ILLUS.) 360

Old King Cole, HN 2217, brown, yellow & white, 1963-67 695

Olga, HN 2463, turquoise & gold, 1972-75 315

Oliver Twist, M 89, black & tan, Dickens Miniatures Series, 1949-83 80

Once Upon a Time, HN 2047, pink dotted dress, 1949-55 475

Orange Lady (The), HN 1953, light green dress, green shawl, 1940-75 315

Orange Vendor (An), HN 1966, purple cloak, 1941-49 .... **1,050**

Paisley Shawl, HN 1392, white dress, red shawl, 1930-49 475

Paisley Shawl, M 4, green dress, dark green shawl, black bonnet w/red feather & ribbons, 1932-45 450

Pamela, HN 3223, style 2, white & blue, 1989-89 250

Pantalettes, HN 1362, green & blue, 1929-
38 ...... **600**

Pantalettes, M 16, red skirt, red tie on hat,
1932-45 ...... **400**

Parisian, HN 2445, blue & grey, matte
glaze,1972-75 ...... **250**

Partners, HN 3119, black, blue & grey,
1990-92 ...... **300**

Paula, HN 3234, white & blue, 1990-96 ...... **250**

Pauline, HN 2441, peach, 1984-1989 ...... **250**

Pearly Boy, HN 2035, reddish brown, 1949-
59 ...... **250**

Pearly Boy, HN 20352, hands clasped, red
jacket, 1949-59 ...... **250**

Pearly Girl, HN 1483, red jacket, 1931-49 ...... **350**

Pecksniff, HN 2098, black & brown, 1952-67 ...... **400**

Peggy, HN 2038, red dress, green trim,
1949-79 ...... **135**

Penelope, HN 1901, red dress, 1939-75 ...... **400**

Penny, HN 2338, green & white dress,
1968-95 ...... **130**

Pensive, HN 3109, white w/yellow flowers
on skirt, 1986-88 ...... **250**

Pied Piper (The), HN 2102, brown cloak,
grey hat & boots, 1953-76 ...... **395**

Piper (The), HN 2907, green, 1980-92 ...... **375**

Polka (The), HN 2156, pale pink dress,
1955-69 ...... **465**

Polly, HN 3178, green & lavender,
1988-91 ...... **325**

Polly Peachum, HN 550, red dress,
1922-49 ...... **495**

Polly Peachum, M 21, red gown, 1932-45 ...... **650**

Premiere, HN 2343, hand holds cloak,
green dress, 1969-79 ...... **250**

Pride & Joy

Pride & Joy, HN 2945, brown, gold & green,
RDICC, 1984 (ILLUS.) **325**

Priscilla, M 24, red, 1932-45 ...... **600**

Promenade, HN 2076, blue & orange, 1951-
53 ...... **1,650**

Prue, HN 1996, red, white & black, 1947-55 ...... **550**

Puppetmaker, HN 2253, green, brown &
red, 1962-73 ...... **500**

Queen Anne, HN 3141, green, red & white,
1989, Queens of the Realm Series, limited edition of 500 ...... **425**

Queen Elizabeth I, HN 3099, red & gold,
1987, Queens of the Realm Series, limited edition of 5,000 ...... **550**

Queen of the Ice, HN 2435, cream, Enchantment Series, 1983-86 ...... **225**

Rachel, HN 2919, gold & green, 1981-84 ...... **265**

Rebecca, HN 2805, pale blue & lavender,
1980-96 ...... **425**

Regal Lady, HN 2709, turquoise & cream,
1975-83 ...... **250**

Rosabell, HN 1620, red & green,
1934-38 ...... **1,450**

Rosamund, M 32, yellow dress tinged
w/blue, 1932-45 ...... **750**

Rosemary

Rosemary, HN 3698, mauve & yellow,
1995-97 (ILLUS.) **375**

Rowena, HN 2077, red, 1951-55 ...... **650**

Sabbath Morn, HN 1982, red, 1945-1959 ...... **350**

Sailor's Holiday, HN 2442, apricot jacket,
1972-79 ...... **315**

Sairey Gamp, HN 2100, white dress, green
cape, 1952-67 ...... **550**

Salome, HN 3267, red, blue, lavender &
green, 1990, limited edition of 1,000 ...... **1,100**

Sam Weller, M 48, yellow & brown,
1932-81 ...... **80**

Samwise, HN 2925, black & brown, Middle
Earth Series, 1982-84 ...... **450**

Sandra, HN 2275, gold, 1969-97 ...... **163**

Sara, HN 2265, red & white, 1981-97 ...... **150**

Schoolmarm, HN 2223, 1958-81 ...... **375**

Secret Thoughts, HN 2382, green
1971-88 ...... **275**

Sharon, HN 3047, white, 1984-95 ...... **150**

The Shepherd

Shepherd (The), HN 1975, light brown,
1945-75 (ILLUS.) **350**
Shore Leave, HN 2254, 1965-79 .... **325**
Simone, HN 2378, green dress,
1971-81 .... **195**
Sir Edward, HN 2370, red & grey, 1979, lim-
ited edition of 500 .... **550**
Skater (The), HN 3439, red, 1992-97 .... **325**

Sleeping Beauty

Sleeping Beauty, HN 3079, green, 1987-89
(ILLUS.) **275**
Sleepyhead, HN 2114, 1953-55 .... **1,850**
Soiree, HN 2312, white dress, green over-
skirt, 1967-84 .... **200**
Solitude, HN 2810, cream, blue & orange,
1977-1983 .... **375**
Sophie, HN 3257, blue & red, 1990-92 .... **250**
Southern Belle, HN 2229, red & cream,
1958-97 .... **250**
Spring, HN 2085, 1952-59 .... **465**
Spring Flower, HN 1807, green skirt, grey-
blue overskirt, 1937-59 .... **450**
Spring Morning, HN 1922, green coat,
1940-73 .... **325**
Spring Morning, HN 1922, pink & blue,
1940-73 .... **325**

Spring Walk

Spring Walk, HN 3120, blue, 1990-92
(ILLUS.) **325**
St. George, HN 2051, 1950-85 .... **625**
St. George, HN 2067, purple, red & orange
blanket, 1950-76 .... **2,250**
Stiggins, M 50, black suit, 1932-1982 .... **80**
Summer, HN 2086, red gown, 1952-59 .... **575**
Summer's Day, HN 2181, 1957-62 .... **400**
Summertime, HN 3137, white & blue, 1987,
RDICC Series **250**
Sunday Morning, HN 2184, red & brown,
1963-69 .... **475**
Susan, HN 2952, blue, black & pink, 1982-
93 .... **350**
Sweet Anne, HN 1330, red, pink & yellow
skirt, 1929-49 .... **350**
Sweet Anne, HN 1496, pink & purple dress
& hat, 1932-67 .... **375**
Sweet April, HN 2215, pink dress,
1965-67 .... **550**
Sweet Dreams, HN 2380, multicolored,
1971-90 .... **225**
Sweet Lavender, HN 1373, green, red &
black, 1930-49 .... **1,050**
Sweet Seventeen, HN 2734, white w/gold
trim, 1975-93 .... **250**
Sweet Sixteen, HN 2231, 1958-65 .... **325**
Sweet Suzy, HN 1918, 1939-49 .... **1,250**
Sweet & Twenty, HN 1298, red & pink dress,
1928-69 .... **450**
Sweeting, HN 1935, pink dress,
1940-73 .... **250**
Teatime, HN 2255, 1972-95 .... **275**

Teresa, HN 1682, red and brown,
1935-49 .... **1,250**

Thanks Doc

Thanks Doc, HN 2731, white & brown,
1975-90 (ILLUS.) **275**
This Little Pig, HN 1793, red robe, 1
936-95 .... **150**
Tiny Tim, HN 539, black, brown & blue,
1922-32 .... **80**
Top O' The Hill, HN 1833, green & blue
dress, 1937-71 .... **400**

Top 'O The Hill

Top 'O The Hill, HN 2126, mauve & green,
1988, miniature (ILLUS.) **150**
Treasure Island, HN 2243, 1962-75 .... **225**
Tumbler, HN 3183, pink & yellow, 1989-91 .... **225**
Uriah Heep, HN 554, black jacket & trou-
sers, 1923-39 .... **450**

Valerie, HN 2107, red gown w/white apron,
1953-95 .... **150**
Vanity, HN 2475, red, 1973-1992 .... **175**
Veneta, HN 2722, green & white, 1974-81 .... **200**
Veronica, HN 3205, style 3, white & pink,
1989-92 .... **200**
Victoria, HN 2471, patterned pink dress,
1973 to present **400**
Victorian Lady (A), HN 728, red skirt, purple
shawl, 1925-52 .... **525**
Victorian Lady (A), M 1, red-tinged dress,
light green shawl, 1932-45 .... **550**
Virginia, HN 1693, yellow dress, 1935-49 ...... **1,750**
Wendy, HN 2109, blue dress, 1953-95 .... **100**
Willy-Won't-He, HN 2150, red, green, blue &
white, 1955-59 .... **250**
Windflower, M 79, blue & green, 1939-49 ...... **1,650**
Winter, HN 2088, shaded blue skirt, 1952-
59 .... **425**
Winter's Walk (A), HN 3052, pale blue &
white, 1987-95 .... **250**

Wintertime

Wintertime, HN 3060, 1985, RDICC
(ILLUS.) **350**
Wizard (The), HN 2877, blue w/black &
white hat, 1979 to present **525**
Writing, HN 3049, flowered yellow dress,
1986, limited edition of 750, Gentle Arts
Series **1,650**
Young Dreams, HN 3176, pink, 1988-92 .... **250**
Young Master, HN 2872, purple, grey &
brown, 1980-89 .... **325**
Yvonne, HN 3038, turquoise, 1987-92 .... **225**

Miscellaneous

Pitcher, 5 1/2" h., brightly colored rose design on a salmon pink background, angled handle, mottling on the collar & base
rim, gold trim, Doulton, Burslem, artist-
signed **110**
Pitcher, 5 1/2" h., stoneware, bulbous form,
the tan ground incised w/playful cats, the
shoulder & neck glazed w/cobalt blue

strap work, decorated by Hannah Bar-
low, impressed Doulton Lambeth mark,
late 19th c. **920**

Pitcher, 9" h., stoneware, bulbous ovoid
body tapering to a cylindrical neck
w/pinched spout, C-form handle, the upper half w/a dark brown glaze over a tan
glaze on the lower half, lower half applied
w/white relief designs including a windmill, dogs chasing deer, men drinking,
etc., Model No. 6859, Doulton, Lambeth
mark, late 19th c. **116**

Plates, 10 1/4" d., each w/a central rosette,
the border elaborately gilded & enameled
in the Art Nouveau style w/displaying
peacocks, spade ornaments & trailing
berried branches, the outer paneled blue
border gilded w/beaded flowers, dated
1902, retailed by Tiffany & Co., New
York, set of 4 .... **2,300**

Tyg (three-handled drinking vessel), waisted cylindrical shape decorated w/applied
figures & animals in relief, Sheffield silver
rim band marked "Maypin and Webb,"
Doulton, Lambeth, late 19th - early 20th
c., 4 3/4" d., 6 1/2" h. **193**

Florence Ceramics

Florence Marks

*Some of the finest figurines and artwares were pro-
duced between 1940 and 1962 by the Florence Ceramics
Company of Pasadena, California. Florence Ward
began working with ceramics following the death of her
son, Jack, in 1939.*

*Mrs. Ward had not worked with clay before her
involvement with classes at the Pasadena Hobby School.
After study and firsthand experience, she began production in her garage, using a kiln located outside the
garage to conform with city regulations. The years 1942-
44 were considered her "garage" period.*

*In 1944 Florence Ceramics moved to a small plant in
Pasadena, employing fifty-four employees and receiving
orders of $250,000 per year. In 1948 it was again neces-
sary to move to a larger facility in the area with the most
up-to-date equipment. The number of employees
increased to more than 100. Within five years Florence
Ceramics was considered one of the finest producers of
semi-porcelain figurines and artwares.*

*Florence created a wide range of items including fig-
urines, lamps, picture frames, planters and models of
animals and birds. It was her extensive line of women in
beautiful gowns and gentlemen in fine clothes that gave
her the most pleasure and was the foundation of her
business. Two of her most popular lines of figurines were
inspired by the famous 1860 Godey's Ladies' Book and
by famous artists from the Old Master group. In the mid-
1950s two bird lines were produced for several years.
One of the bird lines was designed by Don Winton and
the other was a line of contemporary sculpted bird and
animal figures designed by the well-known sculptor
Betty Davenport Ford.*

*There were several unsuccessful contemporary art-
ware lines produced for a short time. The Driftware line
consisted of modern freeform bowls and accessories.
The Floraline is a rococo line with overglazed decoration. The Gourmet Pottery, a division of Florence
Ceramics Company, produced accessory serving pieces
under the name of Scandia and Sierra.*

*Florence products were manufactured in the tradi-
tional porcelain process with a second firing at a higher
temperature after the glaze had been applied. Many
pieces had overglaze paint decoration and clay ruffles,
roses and lace dipped in slip prior to the third firing.*

Figures

"Abigail," Godey lady, beige full-skirted
dress, cape & bonnet w/green bow tied
under chin, 8" h. **$100-150**

"Adeline" Figure

"Adeline," brown hair w/applied roses in
both sides of hair, green off-the-shoulder
full pleated dress, holding a pink shawl
wrapped around her lower arms, 9" h.
(ILLUS.)... **275-325**

"Amber," brown hair, pink ruffled long dress
& large bonnet, right arm bent & holding
a pink parasol at right shoulder, left arm
extended w/fingers touching her dress,
articulated fingers, 9 1/4" h. **425-475**

"Amelia," Godey lady, 8 1/4" h. **175-225**

"Amelia," Godey lady, brocade fabric dress,
12" h. **1,500-2,000**

Florence "Angel," Downcast Eyes

"Angel," downcast eyes, yellow hair, arms
bent across upper body, part of angel's
wings showing, white robe w/gold
trimmed rope sash, cuffs & collar, gold &
brown ribbon sticker, 7" h. (ILLUS.)............ **50-75**

Rare Version of Florence "Angel"

"Angel," rare late version w/spread wings,
7 3/4" h. (ILLUS.)..................................... **100-125**
"Anita," standing w/right arm bent, palm ex-
tended near waist, left arm almost
straight down at side, gold brocade long

dress w/short sleeves & fitted waist, artic-
ulated fingers, 15" h. **1,500-2,000**
"Ann," pink dress & white hat, 6" h. **50-75**
"Annabel," Godey lady, standing w/right arm
bent & carrying a basket of flowers, left
arm in outward position, long full jacket
w/gold trim, large hat, articulated fingers,
8 " h. **400-450**
"Annabel," Godey lady, standing w/right arm
bent & holding a card in hand, left arm in
outward position, long full jacket w/gold
trim, large hat, articulated fingers,
8 " h. **375-400**

Early "Annabelle" Florence Piece

"Annabelle," woman standing wearing a
large dished hat & long flaring coat w/ruf-
fled collar over a long striped dress, arms
extended w/articulated hands, bird
perched on her right hand
(ILLUS.)... **450-500**
"Ava," dirndl-type dress w/brown skirt & tan
peasant blouse, left hand on hip & right
arm raised & holding a large green bas-
ket on her head, 10 1/2" h....................... **175-225**
"Ballet," 7" h. **225-250**
"Barbara," Colonial era woman standing in a
full gown w/slipper toe showing under
front, applied decor in her tall hairdo,
8 1/2" h.. **550-600**
"Barbara," girl standing wearing a large pic-
ture hat & long dress w/puffed sleeves,
holding a basket of flowers, 6" h.............. **75-100**
"Bea," teal dress w/white hat, 6" h. **100-125**

Rare Birthday Girl Figure

"Birthday Girl," standing w/her arms bent & hands close together, wearing a long flaring aqua gown, 9 3/4" h. (ILLUS.).......... **750-825**

"Blossom Girl," Chinese girl standing wearing a round cap and long side-button coat flaring at the hem above a floor-length dress, 8 1/4" h. **100-125**

Florence "Blueboy" Figure

"Blueboy," figure of man standing on base, blue pants & coat w/white trim, white stockings, holding plumed hat in right hand, 12" h. (ILLUS.)................................ **350-400**

"Blynkyn," young girl standing in long pink nightgown, holding a doll at her side, 5" h.. **150-200**

"Bride," lace veil, 8 1/2" h. **1,250-1,500**

"Bride," porcelain veil, 8 1/2" h. **1,000-1,250**

Florence "Bryan" Figure

"Bryan," young man in dress suit standing next to pedestal, gray suit, 11" h. (ILLUS.)... **2,000-2,500**

"Butch," boy w/hands in pockets, 5" h........ **100-125**

"Camille," figure of standing woman wearing white dress trimmed in gold, shawl over both arms made entirely of hand-dipped lace, brown hair, white triangular hat w/applied pink rose, ribbon tied to right side of neck, 8 1/2" h. **175-225**

"Camille," figure of standing woman wearing white dress trimmed in gold, shawl over both arms, triangular hat w/applied pink rose, ribbon tied to right side of neck, articulated hands, no lace, 8 1/2" h. **125-150**

"Camille," figure of standing woman wearing white dress trimmed in gold, shawl over both arms made entirely of hand-dipped lace, brown hair, white triangular hat w/applied pink rose, ribbon tied to right side of neck, one hand, 8 1/2" h. **250-275**

"Camille," woman standing & wearing white dress trimmed in gold, shawl over both arms made entirely of hand-dipped lace, brown hair, white triangular hat w/applied pink rose, ribbon tied to right side of neck, two hands, 8 1/2" h. **300-350**

"Carmen," woman dancer w/head slightly turned & tilted to left, right arm bent w/fingers touching black hair, left arm across body at waist, ruffled lace short-sleeved white dress w/red & gold trim, 14" h. **1,200-1,500**

Florence "Cecile" Figure

"Carol," girl standing wearing a high-front bonnet & jacket w/tiered shoulders above a widely flaring dress over tiered pantaloons, 7 3/4" h. **200-250**

"Carol," woman standing wearing a wide gown, one hand holding up the front hem exposing her foot, the other arm away from her body, 10" h. **550-600**

"Caroline," brocade fabric dress, 15" h. **3,500-4,500**

"Catherine," seated on an open-backed settee, holding a hat, 7 3/4" l., 6 3/4" h. **500-600**

"Catherine," seated on an open-backed settee, no hat variation, 7 3/4" l., 6 3/4" h. **650-700**

"Cecile," woman standing wearing a long full gown & a lace shawl, aqua gown, 8 1/2" h. (ILLUS., to the left) **1,200-1,250**

"Charles," man standing & wearing 18th c. attire w/a long cape, 8" h. **150-175**

"Charmaine," woman holding a parasol, ruffled long dress, large hat w/flowers, 8 1/2" h. **175-200**

"Charmaine," woman holding a parasol, wearing ruffled long dress, large hat w/flowers, w/articulated hands, 8 1/2" h. **250-350**

"Chinese boy," standing wearing flaring jacket & long flaring pants, holding a vase under one arm, 7 3/4" h. **100-125**

"Chinese girl," standing wearing a flaring jacket applied w/roses & long flaring pants, 7 3/4" h. **100-125**

"Choir Boys," royal red robes, 6 " h., set of 3 (ILLUS.)... **150-225**

"Choir Boys" Florence Figures

"The Christening" Figure Group

"Christening (The)," woman w/dress trimmed in lace at neck, sleeves & front of dress holding an infant in a long white christening dress, articulated fingers, 10" h. (ILLUS.) **2,000-2,500**

"Cinderella and Prince Charming" Figure Group

"Cinderella & Prince Charming," dancing couple on raised base, both in white Renaissance period costume, white w/gold

trim & gold tiara on her blonde hair, he holds a silver slipper behind her back in his right hand, 11 3/4" h. (ILLUS.).. **1,750-2,000**

"Cindy," young woman standing in long flaring gown, arms bent & away from the body, 8" h.................................. **225-300**

"Clarissa," woman in full-sleeved jacket & long swirled & pleated skirt, bonnet & holding a muff in right hand, left hand on her shoulder, 7 3/4" h. **125-150**

"Clarissa," woman in full-sleeved jacket & long swirled & pleated skirt, bonnet & holding a muff in right hand, left hand on her shoulder, articulated hand, 7 3/4" h... **175-200**

"Claudia," ruffled dress w/lace trim, lace shawl on shoulders, large hat, bouquet in left hand, no hands showing, 8 1/4" h. **175-200**

"Claudia," ruffled dress w/lace trim, lace shawl on shoulders, large hat, articulated hands, 8 1/4" h. **250-275**

"Claudia," ruffled dress w/lace trim, no lace shawl, large hat, articulated hands, 8 1/4" h. **200-225**

Florence "Cleopatra" Figure

"Cleopatra," exotic figure in flowing blended blue robes, standing on square base, 12" h. (ILLUS.) **1,200-1,250**

"Colleen" with Articulated Hands

"Colleen," woman standing w/head slightly
turned to left, both arms at the front w/ar-
ticulated hands, long wind-blown dress
w/white collar, bonnet w/ribbon tied un-
der chin, 8" h. (ILLUS.) **225-250**
"Colleen," woman standing w/head slightly
turned to left, right hand behind back &
left arm to the front w/articulated hand,
long wind-blown dress w/white collar,
bonnet w/ribbon tied under chin, 8" h. .. **150-200**

Florence "Cynthia" Figure

"Cynthia," standing w/left arm extended
slightly backward, head turned slightly to
left, right hand holding large white hat
trimmed w/flowers, aquamarine over-
dress w/white underskirt, lacy jabot at
neck & lace cuffs, articulated fingers,
9 1/4" h. (ILLUS.) **450-500**

Florence Figure of "Darleen"

"Darleen," standing w/head tilted, brown
hair w/curls & roses at neck, long dress
w/white underskirt, white lace trim on
bodice & extending to bottom of dress,
right arm bent & holding an open parasol
at right shoulder, left arm at waist, articulated fingers, 8 1/4" h. (ILLUS.) **600-650**
"Dear Ruth," 9" h.. **800-1,000**
"Dear Ruth," lady on bench,
7 1/2" h. **1,500-1,750**
"Deborah," woman in a long flaring & swirl-
ing gown w/lace at collar & shoulder
cuffs, moss green gown, 10" h.
(ILLUS., top of next page)...................... **650-725**
"Denise," off-the-shoulder white dress
w/gold trim extending down the dress
front, violet overskirt, brown hair w/roses,
both arms bent at waist w/right hand
holding a closed fan, articulated fingers,
10" h. **500-650**
"Diane," woman in Victorian costume wear-
ing a high rounded bonnet w/feather & a
high-collared long coat opening over a
ruffled dress, one arm down at side hold-
ing a muff, 8" h. **200-225**
"Diane," woman in Victorian costume wear-
ing a high rounded bonnet w/feather & a
high-collared long coat opening over a
ruffled dress, one arm down at side holding a muff, articulated hands,
8" h. **225-275**
"Don," man standing in 1950s era tuxedo,
9" h.. **225-275**

Florence "Deborah" Figurine

"Dora Lee," woman wearing a long widely flaring & swirling royal red gown, a small round hat on her head w/a ribbon, arms away from the body, 9 1/2" h. (ILLUS.)... **750 TO 900**

"Douglas," man standing in front of square column wearing Victorian outfit w/top hat, dress coat & vest, one arm behind his back, one hand on lapel, 8 1/4" h. **125-150**

"Edward," man in late Victorian costume sitting in an armchair, holding his bowler hat on one knee, 7" h. **200-250**

Florence "Elaine" Figure

"Elaine," woman wearing a long, flaring Victorian coat w/wide sleeves, a small bonnet tied on w/a large ribbon under her chin, her hands in a muff at the front, 6" h. (ILLUS.).. **50 -75**

Rare "Dora Lee" Figure

Rare Variation of "Elizabeth"

"Elizabeth," woman in 18th c. costume w/a wide flaring aqua gown w/half-sleeves & a lace-trimmed bodice, long curls down her neck, seated on a white settee, rare white settee variation, 7" w., 8 1/4" h. (ILLUS.).. **1,200-1,400**

"Elizabeth," woman in 18th c. costume w/a wide flaring aqua gown w/half-sleeves & a lace-trimmed bodice, long curls down her neck, seated on a grey settee, 7" w., 8 1/4" h. **250-300**

"Eve," woman standing wearing a long slightly flaring gown, one hand holding up the front hem to expose lace-trimmed petticoat, other hand at shoulder, lace-trimmed collar & cuffs on half-sleeves, 8 1/2" h. **200-225**

"Fair Lady," woman in Gay Nineties gown standing on scrolled base decorated w/roses & gold trim, rose dress w/ornate white lace trim panel in front of dress, rose trim at bodice, upswept brown hair w/roses, right hand raised, articulated fingers, 11 1/2" h. **1,750-2,000**

Florence Figure of "Geoff"

"Geoff," boy wearing 18th c. costume standing beside a seated dog, 6" h. (ILLUS.).. **375-400**

Variation of "Fair Lady" Figure

"Fair Lady," woman in Gay Nineties gown standing on scrolled base decorated w/a small basket of strewn flowers across the front, royal red dress w/ornate white lace collar, upswept brown hair w/roses, arms away from body w/articulated fingers, 11 1/2" h. (ILLUS.).............................. **1,750-2,000**

Rare "Georgia" in Brocade Gown

"Georgia," woma standing wearing a long wide real brocade fabric gown, her hands lifting sides of gown at the front, 12" h. (ILLUS.).. **1,500-2,000**

"Grandmother and I" Figure Group

"Grandmother & I," two women sitting at a round table covered w/a white tablecloth w/a teapot on it, the older woman sitting on a white chair holding a teacup in her right hand, wearing a violet dress w/lace trimmed cuffs & collar, the young woman dressed in a pink dress w/lace trim at the neck & a bow tied in the back, holding a teacup in her left hand, 6 3/4" h. (ILLUS.)... **2,000-2,500**

Florence "Her Majesty" Figure

"Her Majesty," woman in 18th c.-style long dress w/long sleeves, fitted bodice w/standup collar, white w/gold trim, 7" h. (ILLUS.).. **175-200**
"Irene," Godey lady in long dress w/gold trim, flower in upswept hair, right hand holding muff near face, 6" h. **50-75**
"Jeannette," Godey lady, rose colored full-skirted dress w/peplum, white collar, flower at neck, left hand holding hat w/bow, right hand holding parasol, 7 3/4" h. **125-150**
"Jeannette," Godey lady, rose colored full-skirted dress w/peplum, white collar, flower at neck, left hand holding hat w/bow, right hand holding parasol, articulated hands, 7 3/4" h. **175-200**
"John Alden," man dressed in dark grey kneebritches, light grey coat, shoes & large brim hat & holding a gun, 9 1/4" h... **175-200**
"Josephine," woman in Gay Nineties costume wearing a large feathered hat & long gown w/leg-o-mutton sleeves, one hand on her hip, the other holding up hem of gown, 9" h. **250-275**
"Joyce," woman wearing full off-the-shoulder gown w/shoulder ruffles, a wide-brimmed picture hat, arms away at the front, 8 1/2" h.. **325-350**
"Joyce," woman wearing full off-the-shoulder gown w/shoulder ruffles, a wide-brimmed picture hat, arms away at the front, 9" h. **400-475**

Florence "Karen" Figure

"Karen," woman in late Victorian costume, wearing a narrow-waisted fur-trimmed half-length coat over a widely flaring gown, small fur-trimmed hat, w/arms away from body, articulated fingers, 8 1/2" h. (ILLUS.) **1,250-1,500**

"Karla," ballerina, standing "en pointe" w/head tilted & one arm stretched out, the other curved close to her face, deeply ruffled tutu, 9 3/4" h. **200-225**

"Lady Diana," woman stepping forward w/her arms away from her body, wearing flowers in her piled hair & a low-cut narrow lilac gown w/a flaring lacy collar, tight waist & overgown pulled into a bustle, the half-length sleeves w/lace cuffs, 10" h. **425-475**

"Lady Diana" with Plain Cuffs

"Lady Diana," woman stepping forward w/her arms away from her body, wearing flowers in her piled hair & a low-cut narrow lilac gown w/a flaring lacy collar, tight waist & overgown pulled into a bustle, the half-length sleeves w/plain cuffs, 10" h. (ILLUS.) **500-575**

"Lantern Boy," 8 1/4" h. **100-125**

"Leading Man," man standing w/right leg in front of left, royal red kneebritches, white stockings w/gold-trimmed shoes, knee-length coat w/lacy jabot at neck, left arm bent at elbow & raised upward, left arm extended outward holding a scroll, black hair, 10 1/4" h. **300-350**

"Lillian Russell," woman in Gay Nineties gown, her hair piled high & her arms away from her body, the off-the-shoulder gown w/floral trim around the collar & bands down around the widely flaring

skirt w/wide overlapping ruffled panel, 13 1/2" h. **1,750-2,000**

Florence "Linda Lou" Figure

"Linda Lou," girl standing wearing a long full green dress w/peplum & long sleeves, holding a bouquet of flowers to her cheek, a high-fronted bonnet on her head, 7 3/4" h. (ILLUS.) **100-125**

Florence "Little Don" Figure

"Little Don," boy standing w/a grey cat at right side w/both arms extended outward, red pants & shirt w/ruffled lace trim, white cummerbund & shoes, from the Old Master group, Francisco Goya's "Don Manuel Osorio," 7 3/4" h. (ILLUS.) **1,000-1,250**

Rare "Little Princess" Figure

"Little Princess," girl standing in a long-sleeved very wide 17th c. farthingale gown, her hair in long curls, arms outstretched to edges of gown, 8 1/2" h. (ILLUS.)... **1,000-1,250**
"Lorry," youth wearing late Victorian outfit w/cap & short jacket, books under one arm, 8" h. **400-450**

Florence "Love Letter" Figurine

"Love Letter," woman standing reading a small letter, her hair piled on her head, wearing an off-the-shoulder long gown w/lace bands, 12" h. (ILLUS.).......... **1,500-1,750**

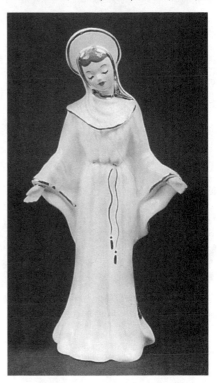

Florence "Madonna" Figure

"Madonna," woman standing wearing white hood and long-sleeved long white gown w/gold trim, halo around head, 10" h. (ILLUS.)... **100-125**
"Marc Antony," Roman warrior wearing helmet, breastplate, white short garment & long flowing cape, one sandaled leg resting on a rectangular block on a square base, 13" h. **750-1,000**
"Marcella," girl ballerina standing w/right foot pointed in front of left leg, arms w/elbows slightly bent & pointed downward, pink tutu, applied roses in brown hair, 7" h. **125-150**
"Marie Antoinette," woman in ornate 18th c. gown, her hair piled high & trimmed w/flowers, high lace collar & wide rounded gown w/center flower-trimmed drapes opening over tiered lace panels, arms in front, one holding a closed fan, smaller skirt style, 10" h. **225-250**
"Marie Antoinette," woman in ornate 18th c. gown, her hair piled high & trimmed w/flowers, high lace collar & wide rounded gown w/center flower-trimmed drapes opening over tiered lace panels, arms in front, one holding a closed fan, large skirt style, 10" h.. **300-350**

Florence "Marilyn" Figure

"Marilyn," woman standing wearing 18th-c. moss green gown w/half-length sleeves w/lace cuffs & large balloon gathers at the waist above the long flaring gown, carrying a basket over one arm, 8 1/2" h. (ILLUS.) **350-400**

"Marlene" Figure in Brocade Gown

"Marlene," woman standing w/her hair up w/curl down the back, arms away in front, wearing a mint green brocade gown, 10" h. (ILLUS.) **1,500-2,000**

"Mary," woman seated in balloon-back arm-chair, wearing a large picture hat, gown w/lace jabot & long sleeves, her hands in lap & on chair arm, 7 1/2" h. **600-625**

"Mary," woman seated in balloon-back arm-chair, wearing a small feathered hat, gown w/lace jabot & long sleeves, her hands in lap & on chair arm, 7 1/2" h. **500-550**

"Melanie," Godey lady, wearing a close-fitting bonnet & long-sleeved long coat over a wide dress, arms at her side, 7 1/2" h. **100-125**

"Memories" Figure

"Memories," elderly woman sitting in a white wing chair w/gold trim, reading a book, white dress w/gold trim, white lace shawl around shoulders, 5 3/4" w., 6 1/2" h. (ILLUS.) **650-700**

"Mikado," very tall Japanese man wearing small round cap, floor-length long-sleeved jacket above draped lower garment on round base, 15" h. **300-350**

"Musette," Godey lady, standing & slightly leaning forward, wearing a picture hat & off-the-shoulder gown w/lace collar & cuffs, front gathers expose slips, 8 3/4" h. **300-325**

"Our Lady of Grace," Madonna figure wearing long cloak w/gathered arms over long gown, on rounded domed base, 10 3/4" h. **175-200**

"Pamela," girl standing but not wearing a bonnet, long swirling short-sleeved dress, a basket of flowers in one hand, 7 1/2" h. **400-450**

"Pamela" Bonnet & Basket

"Pamela," girl standing wearing a flower-trimmed bonnet & long swirling short-sleeved dress, a basket of flowers in one hand, 7 1/2" h. (ILLUS.) **450-475**

"Peter," boy standing w/legs apart & holding a package in his right hand, white jacket, shirt & shoes, pale blue pants & hat, brown hair, 5 1/2" h. **100-125**

"Peter," man standing wearing Victorian frock coat over lacy cravat, one leg to side & leaning on a scroll pedestal w/a hand holding his top hat, 9 1/4" h. **225-250**

Florence "Pinkie" Figure

"Pinkie," figure of woman standing on base, wearing white dress w/rose trim & hat w/loose ribbon, right arm behind back, left arm held in front of body, 12" h. (ILLUS.) **350-400**

"Prima Donna," woman in ornate 18th c. costume, her hair piled high & trimmed w/flowers, wearing a wide gown w/up-right lacy collar, long ruffle-edged sleeves, the front of the gown formed by wide drapes opening over a tiered lacy underskirt, arms away from front, 10" h. **550-625**

"Princess," woman in simple 18th c. cos-tume, the gown w/flower trim at neck, large bow tied to right side of waist w/ruf-fle extending down the dress front, left hand holding fan, roses in hair, articulat-ed fingers, 10 1/4" h. **500-550**

"Reggie," boy standing wearing Victorian outfit, Eton jacket & vest & long pants, scrolls at the side bottom, 7" h. **225-250**

"Rhett," man standing in front of low stone wall, right hand on vest, left hand in pock-et, white ruffled shirt trimmed in color, flaring frock coat, 9" h. **150-175**

"Rhett," man standing in front of low wood fence, right hand on vest, left hand in pocket, white ruffled shirt trimmed in col-or, flaring frock coat, 9" h. **175-200**

"Rosalie" Figure by Florence

"Rosalie," woman wearing long dress w/lace ruffle at the off-the-shoulder neckline, brown hair w/roses, holding skirt out at each side, articulated fingers, 9 1/2" h. (ILLUS.) **550-600**

"Sally," woman wearing Victorian outfit, high rounded bonnet tied w/bow, simple ruf-fled collar & long-sleeved coat over wide swirled & ruffled gown, both hands at sides, 6 3/4" h. **125-150**

"Story Hour" Figure with Boy

Florence "Scarlett" Figure

"Scarlett," Godey lady, wearing royal red dress & bonnet, right hand holding a muff near face, left hand holding handbag, no hands showing, 8 3/4" h. (ILLUS.) **100-125**

"Scarlett," Godey lady, wearing royal red dress & bonnet, right hand holding a muff near face, left hand holding handbag, articulated hands showing, 8 3/4" h. **250-300**

"Spring Reverie," maiden standing in long simple dress, arms away from body at front w/bird on one hand, 12 1/2" h. **1,000-1,250**

"Story Hour," seated mother & girl, woman reading book held in left hand, rose dress w/lace at neck, roses in her hair, girl w/blonde hair w/right arm on bench, ruffled lace short-sleeved white dress w/blue & pink trim, no little boy, 8" l., 6 3/4" h. **800-850**

"Story Hour," seated mother & girl, woman reading book held in left hand, rose dress w/lace at neck, roses in her hair, girl w/blonde hair w/right arm on bench, ruffled lace short-sleeved white dress w/blue & pink trim, small boy dressed in blue shirt & pants & standing near girl 8" l., 6 3/4" h. (ILLUS., top of page).... **900-1,000**

"Susan/Susann," woman standing in simple off-the-shoulder Victorian gown, hair pulled back w/long side curls & cluster of flowers, one hand holding up side of dress, other arm holding basket of flowers to her side, 9" h. **300-350**

"Suzanna," woman in Gay Nineties outfit, standing w/one hand up to rim of large tilted picture hat, the long fur-trimmed jacket w/leg-o-mutton sleeves, other hand holding back coat to expose lace-tiered long gown, 9 1/4" h. **350-400**

"Tess," woman standing wearing long dress w/lace ruffle at neckline, large picture hat, arms away w/one hand holding edge of skirt up over shoe, 7 1/4" h. **250-300**

"Tess," woman standing wearing long dress w/no lace ruffle at neckline, large picture hat, arms away w/one hand holding edge of skirt up over shoe, 7 1/4" h. **200-250**

"Victor," man w/head tilted wearing a Victorian outfit, holding top hat in right hand, frock coat over long pants, swirling long cape, 9 1/4" h. **175-225**

Florence Figure of "Victoria"

"Victoria," woman in Victorian dress seated on serpetine-back tufted Victorian settee, wearing a small bonnet tied w/a bow, rose red gown w/ruffle-trimmed panels at waist, ruffled hem trim, arms away, 8 1/4" l., 7" h. (ILLUS.) **250-300**

"Victoria," woman in Victorian dress seated on serpetine-back tufted Victorian settee, variation w/no bonnet, rose red gown w/ruffle-trimmed panels at waist, ruffled hem trim, arms away, 8 1/4" l., 7" h. **325-350**

"Virginia" Figure with Lace Collar

"Virginia," woman standing wearing a wide picture hat & off-the-shoulder gown w/lace-trimmed collar & short sleeves, long flaring & tiered moss green gown, 9" h. (ILLUS.) **1,500-1,750**

"Virginia" Figure with No Lace

"Virginia," woman standing wearing a wide picture hat & off-the-shoulder gown, variation w/no lace at collar or sleeves, long flaring & tiered rose red gown, 9" h. (ILLUS.) **900-1,000**

"Wood Nymph" Ballerina Figure

"Wood Nymph," girl ballerina standing on domed base w/flower-trimmed tree stump at back, one arm outstretched behind, one bent in front, 7 3/4" h. (ILLUS.) **225-275**

"Wynkin," boy toddler wearing long blue pajamas & holding a Teddy bear,
5 1/2" h. **150-200**

"Yvonne" Florence Figure

"Yvonne," woman standing wearing Victorian outfit, small ribbon-trimmed bonnet, long-sleeved jacket w/peplum over long wide dress, arms at side, one holding a small ribbon-trimmed box, 8 3/4" h. (ILLUS.)... **200-225**

"Yvonne," woman standing wearing Victorian outfit, small ribbon-trimmed bonnet, long-sleeved jacket w/peplum over long wide dress, articulated hands w/one arm out & other one holding a small ribbon-trimmed box, 8 3/4" h............................... **275-300**

Other Items

Ford Dog Advertising Bank

Bank, "Ford," model of dog standing w/left paw across body w/"Ford" advertising under left paw & right paw on top of head, head turned slightly to left, glossy grey w/black highlights, in-mold mark "Florence Ceramics Pasadena, California" & copyright symbol, 6 3/4" h. (ILLUS.).......... **25-30**
Bust, "American Lady," heavy lace trim, 7 3/4" h. **350-400**
Bust, "David," young boy w/crewcut, 9 1/2" h. **100-125**
Bust, "Gigi," 10" h. **175-200**
Bust, "Modern Boy," 9 1/2" h. **100-125**
Bust, "Modern Girl," 9 1/2" h. **100-125**
Bust, "Pamela," girl w/ponytail, 9 1/2" h...... **100-125**
Bust, "Shen," Chinese woman w/wide upright scrolling headdress, scroll-trimmed jacket, 7 1/2" h. **175-200**
Flower holder, "Belle," Gay Nineties woman w/a large hat & long flaring gown, holder at the back, 7 1/2" h. **50-75**
Flower holder, "Beth," woman standing in a dirndl-style dress & holding up one corner of her long apron, holder at the back, 7 1/2" h.. **50-75**
Flower holder, "Blossom Girl," Chinese woman standing wearing a round cap and long side-button coat flaring at the hem above a floor-length dress, w/flower vase, 8 1/4" h. **50-75**
Flower holder, "Chinese Boy," holder at the back, 7 3/4 .... **40-50**
Flower holder, "Chinese Child/Boy," bamboo-form holder at side, 7" h. **100-125**
Flower holder, "Chinese Child/Girl," bamboo-form holder at side, 7" h. **100-125**
Flower holder, "Chinese Girl," holder at the back, 7 3/4 .... **40-50**
Flower holder, "Jerry," young man standing in white suit trimmed in blue, pink tie, holding a white bass fiddle trimmed w/gold, 7 3/4" h. **175-200**
Flower holder, "Lantern Boy," 8 1/4" h. **50-75**
Flower holder, "Molly," standing girl wearing long gown w/short ruffled sleeves at shoulder, standing beside a large cylinder vase embossed w/leafy boughs, 6 1/2" h. **35-40**
Flower holder, "Rene," standing woman in European peasant costume w/lobed upright headpiece on head, dirndl outfit w/long sleeves & a wide apron w/peasant decoration over long dress, a basket in each hand at sides, 8 1/2" h. **150-175**
Flower holder, "June," girl in front of pleated-edge block, 6" h. **35-40**
Head vase, "Fern," girl wearing wide lightly ruffled hat & dress w/small ruffled collar & wide ruffles at the shoulders, 7" h. **125-150**
Powder box, "Ballet," 6" h. **300-325**
TV lamp, "Dear Ruth," 9" h. **800-1,000**

Flow Blue

ABBEY (George Jones & Sons, ca. 1900)
Beeker, 3 1/2" d., 4" h.. **$100**
Bowl, 8" d., 4 1/2" h... **550**
Bowl, 9" d., 4 1/2" h... **600**
Hot water pot, 6" h.. **125**

Abbey Punch Bowl

Punch bowl, 10 1/2" d., 6" h. (ILLUS.)............... **750**
Shredded wheat dish, 6 1/4" l., 5" w................... **150**

ABBEY (Petrus Regout Co., Maastricht, Holland, date unknown)

Abbey Cup & Saucer

Farmer's cup & saucer, oversized, cup 5" d.,
    4" h. & saucer, 8" d. (ILLUS.).......................... **165**

ABERDEEN (Bourne & Leigh), ca. 1900, Floral,
Butter pat, 3 1/2" d... **40**

ACME (Sampson Hancock & Sons, ca. 1900)
Plate, 9" d., five-sided.. **150**

Acme Plate

Plate, 9" d., scalloped (ILLUS.)............................ **125**

ADDERLEY (Doulton & Company, ca. 1886), Floral
Vegetable bowl, open, round, 8 1/2" d.,
    2 3/4" h... **195**

ALASKA (W.H. Grindley & Company, ca. 1891)
Bowl, berry, 5" d. **40**
Creamer, 5 1/4 h... **200**
Plate, 10" d., scalloped.. **115**
Platter, 14" l... **300**
Soup plate w/flanged rim, 9" d. **90**

ALBANY (Johnson Bros., ca. 1900)
Plate, 8" d. **65**
Tea cup & saucer, cup, 2 1/2" h., 3 1/2" d,
    saucer, 6" d. **115**

ALBANY (W.H. Grindley & Company, ca. 1899)
Butter pat, 3 1/2" d. **45**
Plate, 6 1/2 d. **50**

Albany Platter

Platter, 14 1/2" l. (ILLUS.)... **275**

ALTHEA (Podmore, Walker & Company, ca. 1834-1859)

Althea Coffeepot

Coffeepot, cov., 11" d. (ILLUS.)....................... **1,200**
Creamer, 6" h. **300**
Sugar, cov., footed, two-handled, 7" h. **475**
Tea cup & saucer, cup, 4" d., 2 1/2" h., sau-
  cer, 5 3/4" d. **165**

ALTON (W.H. Grindley & Company, ca. 1891)

Alton Platter

Platter, 18" l. (ILLUS.) **550**

AMOUR (Societé Céramique, Dutch, ca. 1865)

Armour Footed Compote

Compote, footed, two-handled, 10" d.
  (ILLUS.).. **575**

ANDORRA (Johnson Bros., ca. 1901)

Andorra Vegetable Bowl

Vegetable bowl, open, round, 9 1/2" d.
  (ILLUS.).. **165**

ANEMONE (Lockhart & Arthur, ca. 1855)

Plate, 10 1/4" d. **135**
Platter, 16" l. **525**

ARGYLE (W.H. Grindley & Company, ca. 1896)

Argyle Platter

Platter, 16" l. (ILLUS.)... **450**
Platter, 18" l. **575**

ASHBURTON (W.H. Grindley & Company, ca. 1891)

Plate, 9" d. **90**
Plate, 8" d. **75**
Platter, 12" l. **175**
Platter, 14" l. **295**

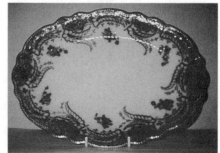

Ashburton Platter

Ashburton Sauce Ladle

Platter, 16" l. (ILLUS., bottom prev. page)......... 425
Platter, 18" l. 550
Sauce ladle, 7" l. (ILLUS., top of page)............. 295
Plate, 10" d. 115

ATALANTA (Wedgwood & Company, ca. 1900)

Atalanta Platter

Platter, 14" l. (ILLUS.) 295

BALTIC (W.H. Grindley & Company, ca. 1891)
Gravy boat, 7" l. 125
Plate, 10" d. 100

BEAUFORT (W.H. Grindley & Company, ca. 1903)

Beaufort Underplate

Underplate, for cov. butter, two-handled, 9" d. (ILLUS.).. 125

BELMONT (J.H. Weatherby & Sons, ca. 1892)
Plate, 9" d. 75
Plate, 10" d. 95

BLUE DANUBE, THE (Johnson Bros., ca. 1900)
Creamer, 4" h.. 200
Plate, 10" d. 95
Soup bowl, open, 9" d... 80
Sugar, cov., 5" h. 275
Tea cup & saucer 100

BLUEBELL (Dillwyn-Swansea, Welch, ca. 1840)

Bluebell Syrup Pitcher

Syrup pitcher w/pewter lid, 8 1/2" h (ILLUS.)...... 800

BOUQUET (Henry Alcock, ca. 1895)

Bouquet Vegetable Dish

Vegetable dish, cov., footed, 12" l. (ILLUS.) **300**

BRAZIL (W.H. Grindley & Company, ca. 1891)

Brazil Sugar Bowl

Sugar bowl, cov., 5" h. (ILLUS.) **250**

BRITISH SCENERY (Davenport & Company, ca. 1856)

Charger, 13" d. **350**

British Scenery Platter

Platter, 19" l. (ILLUS.) **750**
Vegetable bowl, oval, 10" l., 3 1/2" h. **400**

BURMESE (Thomas Rathbone & Company, ca. 1912)

Serving dish, rectangular, pierced, two-handled, 13 1/2 l., 9" w. **375**

CALICO (Warwick China Company, American, ca. 1900, aka Daisy Chain)

Calico Tankard-type Pitcher

Pitcher, 7 1/2" h., 9" w. (ILLUS.) **275**

CAMBRIDGE (Alfred Meakin, ca. 1891)

Platter, 14" l. **325**
Relish dish, oval, 8 1/2" l. **145**

CANNISTER (Unknown, marked "Germany," ca. 1891)

Sugar Canister

Canister, cov., marked "Sugar," 6" d., 8" h. (ILLUS.) **225**
Spice jar, cov., 5" h. **75**

CASHMERE (Francis Morley, ca. 1850)

Cashmere Plate & Underplate

Plate, 10 1/2" d. (ILLUS. left) **250**
Underplate, 8" d. (ILLUS. right) **175**

CECIL (F. Till & Son, ca. 1891)
Bone dish, crescent-shaped **65**
Plate, 6" d. **50**

CHINESE (Dimmock, ca. 1845)

Chinese Pattern Teapot

Tea set: cov. teapot, oversized cov. sugar &
creamer; Primary body shape, teapot
9" h., the set (ILLUS. of teapot).................. **2,800**

CHRYSANTHEMUM (Myott, Son & Co., ca. 1907)

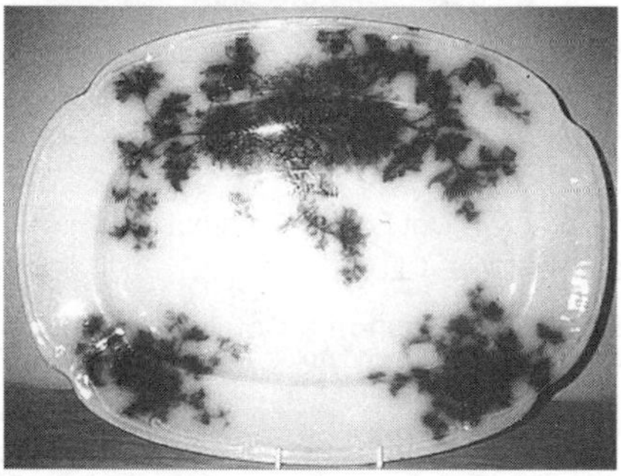

Chrysanthemum Platter

Platter, 14" l. (ILLUS.) **400**

CLARENCE (W.H. Grindley & Co., ca. 1900)

Clarence Platter

Platter, 16" l. (ILLUS.) **450**

CLAYTON (Johnson Bros., ca. 1902)

Part of Clayton Chamber Set

Chamber set: pitcher & bowl, chamber pot,
shaving mug & small water pitcher; the
set (ILLUS. of part)..................................... **2,500**
Chamber set: pitcher & bowl, chamber pot,
toothbrush holder & shaving mug; the set.. **2,000**
Platter, 16" l. **450**

Clayton Soup Plate

Soup plate w/flanged rim, 9" d. (ILLUS.) **95**
Vegetable dish, open, oval, 9" l........................... **165**

CLYTIE (Wedgwood & Co., Ltd., ca. 1908)
Plate, 10" d., w/turkey design **175**
Platter, 19" l., w/turkey design **1,000**

COLONIAL (J. & G. Meakin, ca. 1891)
Butter pat, 3 1/2" d. **45**
Vegetable bowl, open, oval, 9" l.......................... **125**

CONWAY (New Wharf Pottery, ca. 1891)

Conway Vegetable Bowl

Vegetable bowl, open, 9 1/2" d. (ILLUS.) **195**

DAISY (Burgess & Leigh, ca. 1897)

Daisy Soup Plate

Soup plate w/flanged rim, 9" d. (ILLUS.).............. **95**

DELFT (Minton, ca. 1893)

Delft Oyster Plate

Oyster plate, 10" d. (ILLUS.).............................. **300**

Delft Platter

Platter, 14" l. (ILLUS.) **325**

DERBY (W.H. Grindley, ca. 1891)
Plate, 9" d... **85**

Derby Platter

Platter, 14" l. (ILLUS.).. **295**
Soup plate w/flanged rim, 9" d. **85**
Vegetable dish, cov., 12" l., 7" h. **275**

DOT FLOWER (Unknown, ca. 1840)

Dot Flower Creamer

Creamer, 5" h. (ILLUS.)... **275**

EGERTON (Doulton & Co., Ltd., ca. 1905)
Cheese dome w/underplate, half-Stilton, very unusual, dome 8" w., 6" h., under-plate, 10" d. **325**
Plate, 8 1/2" d.. **65**
Plate, 9 1/2" d.. **90**
Plate, 10 1/2" d. **100**
Platter, 12" l... **165**
Platter, 16" l... **400**
Platter, 18" l... **500**
Soup plate w/flanged rim, 10 1/2" d. **100**

Egerton Covered Vegetable

Vegetable dish, cov., 13" w., 6 1/2" h. (ILLUS.).. **375**

ENGLISH ROSE (Unknown, ca. 1891)

English Rose Soup Plate

Soup plate w/flanged rim, 9" d. (ILLUS.).............. **90**

FAIRY VILLAS III (W. Adams & Sons, ca. 1891)
Plate, 8" d... **75**
Plate, 10 1/4" d... **125**
Platter, 16" l. **450**

FLORA (Thomas Walker, ca. 1845)

Flora Plate

Plate, 10 1/2" d. (ILLUS.).................................... **200**

FLORIDA (Ford & Sons, ca. 1891)
Plate, 10 1/4" d.. **100**

Florida Platter

Platter, 17" l. (ILLUS.) **500**
Vegetable dish, cov., 12" w., 7" h. **300**

GAINSBOROUGH (Ridgways, ca. 1905)
Creamer, 4" h... **200**
Sugar, cov., 5" h. **275**

GERANIUM (Doulton & Co., ca. 1890s)
Bowl, heavily gilded, scalloped, footed, 10" l. **400**

GIRONDE (W.H. Grindley, ca. 1891)

Gironde Gravy Boat

Gravy boat, 6 1/2" l. (ILLUS.).............................. **125**
Plate, 10 1/4" d., 14-sided................................... **100**

GLOIRE DE DIJON (Doulton & Co., ca. 1895)

Gloire de Dijon Pitcher

Pitcher, belonging to pitcher/bowl wash set (ILLUS.)... **275**

GRACE (W.H. Grindley, ca. 1897)
Butter pat, 3 1/2" d. **45**
Platter, 16" l.. **375**

GRECIAN SCROLL (T.J. and J. Mayer, ca. 1850)

Grecian Scroll Teapot

Teapot, 10" h. (ILLUS., previous page).............. **695**

HADDON (Libertas, ca. 1891, Prussian)
Butter pat, 3 1/2" d.. **45**
Butter w/insert, cov.................................. **325**
Plate, 9" d.. **90**
Plate, 10" d. **100**
Platter, 12" l. **175**
Vegetable bowl, cov., round, 11" d.,
 6 1/2" h. **300**
Vegetable bowl, open, oval, 9" d........................ **165**

HEATH'S FLOWER (Thomas Heath, ca. 1830)

Heath's Flower Plate

Plate, 9 1/2" d., 12-sided (ILLUS.)..................... **165**

HOLLAND (Johnson Bros., ca. 1891)oll
Gravy boat, 6 1/2" l... **125**
Soup bowl, open, 8" d.. **85**
Vegetable dish, cov., footed, 12" l.,
 6 1/2" h. **275**

HONC (Petrus Regout, ca. 1858)

Honc Bedpan

Bedpan (ILLUS.) **1,000**

IVANHOE (Wedgwood & Co., ca. 1900)
Plate, 9 1/2" d.. **125**

Ivanhoe Plate

Plate, 10 1/2" d. (ILLUS.) **150**

IVY (Davenport Potteries, ca. 1820-60)

Ivy Platter

Platter, 22" l., w/meat well (ILLUS.).................... **875**

JENNY LIND (Arthur Wilkinson Ltd., Royal Staffordshire Pottery, ca. 1895)
Cup & saucer, cup 3 1/2" d., saucer
 5 3/4" d. **100**
Plate, 6" d. **55**

KENWORTH (Johnson Bros., ca. 1900)
Berry bowl, 5" d.. **45**

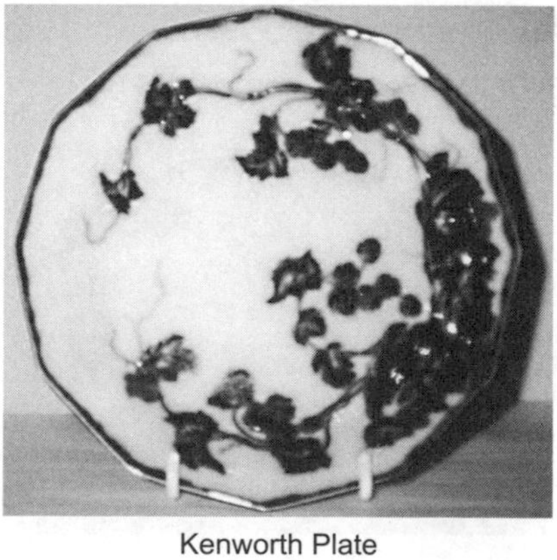

Kenworth Plate

Plate, 10" d. (ILLUS.)... **100**
Soup bowl, open, 9" d... **80**

KNOX (New Wharf Potteries, ca. 1891)
Plate, 7" d.. 48
Tea cup & saucer, cup 4" h., 3 1/2" d., sau-
cer 6" d. 125

KYBER (W. Adams & Co., ca. 1891)
Plate, 9" d... 85

LABELLE (Wheeling Pottery, ca. 1900)
Charger, 13" d...................................... 450

Labelle Portrait Plate
Portrait plate, 13" d., Lovely Ladies (ILLUS.)..... 495

LaBelle Ring-handled Dish
Ring-handled dish, 11" l., 10 1/2" w.
(ILLUS.).. 325

LAKEWOOD (Wood & Sons, ca. 1900)
Butter pat, 3 1/2" d.. 60
Tea cup & saucer, cup 4" h., 3 1/2" d., sau-
cer 6" d. 110

LORNE (W.H. Grindley, ca. 1900)
Bowl, berry, 5" d.. 45
Platter, 12" l. 165

MANHATTAN (Henry Alcock, ca. 1900)
Bowl, berry, 5" d.. 45
Butter dish w/insert, cov. 325
Cake plate, two-handled..................................... 175
Plate, 8" d.. 55
Plate, 9" d.. 95

Platter, 14" l. 275
Platter, 16" l. 400
Soup plate w/flanged rim, 9" d. 90-95
Tea cup & saucer 100

Manhattan Covered Sugar
Tea set: teapot, sugar & creamer; the set
(ILLUS. of sugar) 1,100
Vegetable dish, cov., footed 300

MARIE (W.H. Grindley, ca. 1891)

Marie Pitcher
Pitcher, 7" h. (ILLUS.)... 275
Plate, 10 1/4" d. 100

MARLBOROUGH (W.H. Grindley, ca. 1891)
Butter pat, 3 1/2" d. 45

Marlborough Graduated Pitchers
Pitcher, 6" h. (ILLUS. right)................................... 225
Pitcher, 8" d. (ILLUS. middle).............................. 325
Pitcher, 10" h. (ILLUS. left) 400

Marlborough Open Vegetable Bowl

Vegetable bowl, open, oval, 9" l. (ILLUS.)......... **165**

MARTHA WASHINGTON (Unknown, English, ca. 1900, aka Chain of States)

Martha Washington States Plate

Plate, 9" d. (ILLUS.)... **150**

MEISSEN (F. Mehlem, ca. 1891)

Meissen Vegetable Bowl

Vegetable bowl, open, 10" d. (ILLUS.)............... **165**

MELBOURNE (W.H. Grindley, ca. 1891)
Bowl, berry, 5" d.. 45
Butter pat, 3 1/2" d.. 45
Cake plate, 12" d., two-handled **165**
Plate, 6" d.. 50
Plate, 8" d.. 70
Plate, 9" d.. **90-95**

Melbourne Dinner Plate

Plate, 10" d. (ILLUS.)... **125**
Platter, 14" l. **275**
Platter, 16" l. **200-375**
Platter, 18" l. **495**

Melbourne Soup Tureen

Soup tureen, cov., oval, footed, 14" l.,
   7 1/2" h. (ILLUS.).. **650**
Vegetable bowl, cov., oval **300**
Vegetable bowl, open, round.............................. **200**

MELROSE (Doulton & Co., ca. 1891)
Platter, 20" l. **600**
Plate, 10 1/4" d. 90

MIKADO (A.J. Wilkinson, ca. 1896)

Mikado Dinner Plate

Plate, 10 1/2" d. (ILLUS.) **100**
Platter, 18" l. **600**
Soup plate w/flanged rim, 10 1/2" d. **100**

MILTON (Poutney & Bristol, ca. 1890s)

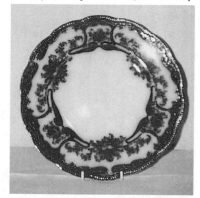

Milton Luncheon Plate

Plate, 9" d. (ILLUS.).. 90
Platter, 18" l. 575
Sauce boat w/ladle & underplate, cov., oval,
    footed.. 425
Plate, 10" d. 115

MONGOLIAN (F. & W., Unidentified Manufacturer, mid-to-late Victorian)
Charger, 14" d. 400

Mongolian Gravy Boat

Gravy boat, footed 195

MONTANA (Johnson Bros., ca. 1900)

Montana Luncheon Plate

Plate, 9" d. (ILLUS.).. 85

MORNING GLORY (Elsmore/Forster, ca. 1853-71)

Morning Glory Cup & Saucer

Cup & saucer, no handle (ILLUS.)...................... 195

MURIEL (Upper Hanley Potteries, ca. 1895)

Muriel Platter

Platter, 14"l. (ILLUS.).. 325

NANKIN (Mellor, Venables & Co. or Thomas Walker, ca. 1845)

Plate from Nankin Tea Set

Tea set: teapot, oversized cov. sugar,
    creamer, 6 cups w/no handles & 6 sau-
    cers, 6 9" d. plates; Primary body style,
    the set (ILLUS.)... 3,200

NON PAREIL (Middleport Potteries, ca. 1891)
Butter pat 50
Platter, 16" l. 475
Soup plate w/flanged rim, 9" d. 95

NORMANDY (Johnson Bros., ca. 1900)
Bowl, berry, 5" d.. 45
Butter pat, 3 1/2" d.. 45
Plate, 9" d.. 95-120

Normandy Soup Plate

Soup plate w/flanged rim, 10" d. (ILLUS.) 115

OLD CURIOSITY SHOP (Ridgways, ca. 1910)

Old Curiosity Shop Platter

Platter, 16" l. (ILLUS.) 450
Vegetable bowl, open, oval, 10" l....................... 195

ORCHID (John Maddock & Sons, Ltd., ca. 1896)
Platter, 16" l. 375
Platter, 18" l. 475

ORIENTAL (Samuel Alcock, ca. 1840)
Plate, 9 1/2" d.. 150
Platter, 16" l. 600

Oriental Underplate

Underplate, two-handled w/reticulated tab
handles, 13" d. (ILLUS.)................................... 450
Plate, 10 1/2" d. 200

ORMONDE (Alfred Meakin, ca. 1891)
Plate, 8" d. 65
Plate, 10 1/4" d. 100

PAISLEY (Mercer, ca. 1890)

Paisley Platters, Bone Dishes, Gravy

Bone dish, crescent-shaped (ILLUS. lower
left) 60
Gravy boat (ILLUS. lower right)........................... 125
Platter, 20" l. (ILLUS. upper right)...................... 650
Relish dish, 9" l. 125
Soup tureen, cov., round 675

PEKIN (Johnson Bros., ca. 1891)

Pekin Dinner Plate

Plate, 10" d. (ILLUS.)... 90

PLYMOUTH (New Wharf Pottery, ca. 1891)

Plymouth Dinner Plate

Plate, 10" d. (ILLUS.)... 100
Tea cup & saucer 100

POPPY (Doulton & Co., ca. 1902)
Jardiniere, 10" h. **650**

PORTMAN (W.H. Grindley, ca. 1891)

Portman Platter

Platter, 14" l. (ILLUS.) **225**

QUEBEC (Paul Utzchneider, ca. 1891)

Quebec Plate

Plate, 10" d. (ILLUS.) **85**

RALEIGH (Burgess & Leigh, ca. 1906)

Raleigh Gravy Boat

Gravy boat, 6 1/2" l. (ILLUS.) **125**

REBECCA (George Jones, ca. 1900)

Rebecca Luncheon Plate

Plate, 9" d. (ILLUS.) **125**

REEDS & FLOWERS (Unknown, ca. 1855)

Reeds & Flowers Soup Plate

Soup plate w/flanged rim, 10 1/2" d.
(ILLUS.) **200**

REGENT (Johnson Bros., ca. 1910)
Plate, 8" d. **65**
Plate, 9" d. **90**
Platter, 18" l. **575**
Tea cup & saucer **100**
Tea set: cov. teapot, sugar & creamer; the
set **1,000**
Plate, 10" d. **100**

ROSEVILLE (John Maddock & Sons, ca. 1891)

Roseville Celery Dish

Celery dish, 11" l. (ILLUS.) **175**

SCINDE (J&G Alcock, 1840)

Scinde Jam Jar

Jam jar w/attached tray, w/lion's head handles, only one of its kind **6,000**

Scinde Platter

Platter, 18" l. (ILLUS.) **750**

Scinde Teapot

Teapot, primary body style, 9" h. (ILLUS.)......... **900**

SEVILLE (New Wharf Pottery, ca. 1891)

Seville Dinner Plate

Plate, 10" d. (ILLUS.) **115**

SHANGHAI (W.E. Corn, ca. 1900)

Shanghai Dinner Plate

Plate, 10" d. (ILLUS.) **100**

SHUSAN (F. & R. Pratt & Co., ca. 1855)

Shusan Dinner Plate

Plate, 10 1/2" d. (ILLUS.) **195**

SLOE BLOSSOM (Wm. Ridgway & Co., ca. 1830)

Sloe Blossom Waste Jar

Waste jar, part of dresser set (ILLUS.)............ **1,500**

Sloe Blossom Water Pitcher

Water pitcher, 7 1/2" h. (ILLUS.) **475**

SPINACH (Brushstroke, maker unknown)

Spinach Waste Bowl

Waste bowl, 5" d. (ILLUS.).................................. **125**

SYRIAN (W.H. Grindley, ca. 1892)

Syrian Chamber Pot

Chamber pot, cov., 11" w., 7" h. (ILLUS.)........... **325**

TOKIO (Johnson Bros., ca. 1900)

Tokio Luncheon Plate

Plate, 9" d. (ILLUS.) **95**

TULIP (Copeland & Garrett, ca. 1845)

Tulip Fruit Compote

Fruit compote, footed, 10" d., 6" h. (ILLUS.)...... **875**

TURKEY (Cauldon, Ltd., ca. 1905)

Turkey Dinner Plate

Plate, 10 1/2" d. (ILLUS.).................................... **200**

TURKEY (Ridgways, ca. 1900)

Turkey Set

Turkey set: platter, 22" l., & 12 dinner plates, 10" d.; the set (ILLUS. of platter)................ **3,200**

VERMONT (Burgess & Leigh, ca. 1895)

Vermont Sauceboat with Underplate

Sauceboat w/underplate, 9" l., 5" h. (ILLUS.).. **275**

VIRGINIA (John Maddock & Sons, ca. 1891)

Virginia Platter

Platter, 16" l. (ILLUS.)... **450**

WATER NYMPH (Josiah Wedgwood, ca. 1872)

Bowl, footed, 8" d., 5" h. **295**

WATTEAU (Doulton & Co., ca. 1900)

Oil lamp, converted to electric, 26" h. **2,200**

Watteau Dinner Plate

Plate, 10 1/2" D. (ILLUS.).................................... **150**

WAVERLY (John Maddock & Son, ca. 1891)

Waverly Platter

Platter, 16" l. (ILLUS.).. **425**

WENTWORTH (J. & G. Meakin, ca. 1907)

Butter pat, 3 1/2" d. **40**

Wentworth Dinner Plate

Plate, 10" d. (ILLUS.) **90**
Vegetable bowl, cov., 12" l., 6 1/2" h. **250**

Franciscan Ware

Franciscan Ware Mark

A product of Gladding, McBean & Company of Lincoln, California, Franciscan Ware was one of a number of lines produced by that firm over its long history. Products made at the Lincoln Plant were Architectural Terra Cotta, Terra Cotta Tiles, and Garden Ware. In 1923, Gladding, McBean purchased the Tropico Pottery in Glendale, California. At this location Gladding, McBean began producing dinnerware. Franciscan Ware was introduced in 1934 beginning with the colorful dinnerware pattern of El Patio. Coronado, a swirled pattern offered in satin and gloss glazes, was introduced in 1935. Gladding, McBean also introduced Art Ware in 1934 as Tropico Art Ware; later, after the acquisition of the Catalina Clay Products company on Catalina Island in 1937, the line was marketed as Catalina Art Ware as well as Franciscan Art Ware. In 1940, Gladding, McBean introduced the handpainted dinnerware line Apple and in 1941 Desert Rose. Desert Rose has the distinction of being one of the most popular patterns ever produced in dinnerware history. In 1942, Gladding, McBean introduced the first of many lines of fine china. Art Ware was discontinued in 1942. In the 1950s, Franciscan introduced three very popular patterns on the Eclipse shape designed by George James: Starburst, Oasis, and Duet. In 1962, Gladding, McBean merged with the International Lock Pipe and Joint Co. to form the company Interpace. Fine china was discontinued in 1977. In 1979, Interpace's Glendale Franciscan Ware Division was purchased by Wedgwood, Ltd. Finally, in October of 1984, the Glendale Franciscan Ware Plant was closed and all dinnerware operations were moved to

England. All Franciscan dinnerware patterns produced prior to 1984, except for Apple, Desert Rose and Fresh Fruit, were discontinued. Fresh Fruit was discontinued in 1989. Wedgwood continues to manufacture Desert Rose and Apple, adding new pieces each year. In 2001, Wedgwood, Ltd. reintroduced Franciscan Ivy.

Ashtray, Apple patt., 4 3/4" sq. **$150**
Ashtray, Apple patt., 4 1/2 x 9" oval **95**
Ashtray, Desert Rose patt., 4 3/4 x 9" oval **85**
Ashtray, Desert Rose patt., square **125**
Ashtray, El Patio tableware, coral satin
    glaze **8**
Ashtray, individual, California Poppy patt. **65**
Ashtray, individual, Wildflower patt., Mari-
    posa Lily shape, 3 1/2" d. **95**
Ashtray, individual, Desert Rose patt.,
    3 1/2" d. **22**
Ashtray, individual, Apple patt., apple-
    shaped, 4" w., 4 1/2" l. **28**
Ashtray, individual, Ivy patt., leaf-shaped,
    4 1/2" l. **32**
Baker, half-apple-shaped, Apple patt.,
    4 3/4" w., 5 1/4" l., 1 3/4" h. **225**
Baking dish, Apple patt., 1 qt. **275**
Baking dish, Cafe Royal patt., 8 3/4 x 9 1/2",
    1 qt. **160**
Baking dish, Desert Rose patt., 1 qt. **208**
Baking dish, October patt., 1 qt. **100**
Baking dish, Apple patt., 1 1/2 qt. **350**
Baking dish, Desert Rose patt., 9 x 14",
    2 1/4" h., 1 1/12 qt. **225**
Baking dish, Meadow Rose patt., 9 x 14",
    1 1/2 qt. **145**
Bank, figural pig, Desert Rose patt. **160**
Batter bowl, pitcher-form, Apple patt., 7" l. **395**
Bell, Desert Rose patt., Danbury Mint,
    4 1/4" h. **75**
Bell, Cafe Royal patt., 3 3/4" d., 6" h. **95**
Bell, dinner, Franciscan **95**
Bowl, bouillon soup, cov., 4 1/2" d., Desert
    Rose patt. **275**
Bowl, fruit, 4 1/2" d., California Poppy patt. **33**
Bowl, fruit, 5 1/4" d., Apple patt., ca. 1940 .... **11**
Bowl, fruit, 5 1/4" d., Desert Rose patt. **12**
Bowl, fruit, 5 1/2" d., Ivy patt. **15**
Bowl, fruit, 5 1/2" d., Wildflower patt. **95**
Bowl, soup, footed, 5 1/2", Apple patt. **32**
Bowl, soup, footed, 5 1/2" d., Desert Rose
    patt. **32**
Bowl, soup, footed, 5 1/2" d., Ivy patt. **36**
Bowl, cereal, 6" d., Desert Rose patt. **18**
Bowl, cereal or soup, 6" d., Apple patt., ca.
    1940 .... **16**
Bowl, cereal or soup, 6" d., Fresh Fruit patt. **18**
Bowl, cereal or soup, 6" d., Ivy patt. **25**
Bowl, cereal or soup, 6" d., Meadow Rose
    patt. **12**
Bowl, cereal or soup, 6" d., Wildflower patt. **125**
Bowl, 7" d., Picnic patt. **8**
Bowl, cereal, 7" d., October patt. **18**
Bowl, salad, 10" d., Apple patt. **95**
Bowl, salad, 10" d., Desert Rose patt. **95**
Bowl, salad, 10" d., Wildflower patt. **450**
Bowl, salad, 11" d., Daisy patt. **45**
Bowl, salad, 11 1/4" d., Ivy patt., green rim
    band **145**
Bowl, fruit, Arden patt. **12**
Box, cov., Desert Rose patt., heart-shaped,
    4 1/2" l., 2 1/2" h. **150**

Desert Rose Covered Butter Dish

Box, cov., Desert Rose patt., egg-shaped,
1 1/2 x 4 3/4" **200**
Box, cov., Apple patt., round, 4 3/4" d.,
1 1/2" h. **245**
Box, cov., Cafe Royal patt., heart-shaped,
5 x 5", 2 1/4" h. **85**
Box, cov., Twilight Rose patt., heart-shaped **225**
Butter dish, cov., Apple patt. **40**
Butter dish, cov., California Poppy patt. **175**
Butter dish, cov., Desert Rose patt. (ILLUS.,
top of page) **45**
Butter dish, cov., Ivy patt. **75**
Butter dish, cov., October patt. **55**
Butter dish, cov., Twilight Rose patt. **125**
Candleholders, Apple patt., pr. **95**
Candleholders, Desert Rose patt., pr. **75**
Candleholders, Starburst patt., pr. **175**
Casserole, cov., Apple patt., 1 1/2 qt. **90**
Casserole, cov., Apple patt., individual size,
handled, 4" d., 3 1/4" h. **60**
Casserole, cov., Apple patt., in metal holder .. **1,500**
Casserole, cov., Desert Rose patt., 1 1/2
qt., 4 3/4" h. **95**
Casserole, cov., Wildflower patt., 1 1/2 qt. **850**
Casserole, cov., Desert Rose patt., 2 1/2 qt. **245**
Celery dish, Apple patt., 7 3/4 x 15 1/2" **28**
Cigarette box, cov., Apple patt.,
3 1/2 x 4 1/2, 2" h. **140**

Cigarette box, cov., Desert Rose patt.,
3 1/2 x 4 1/2", 2" h. **150**
Coaster, Apple patt., 3 3/4" d. **53**
Coffee server, El Patio tableware, red/or-
ange glossy glaze (ILLUS., below) **40**
Coffee server, El Patio tableware, turquoise
glossy glaze **40**

El Patio Coffee Server

Westwood Coffee & Tea Service

Coronado Demitasse Pieces

Coffee & tea service: cov. coffeepot, cov. teapot, round serving plate, creamer & cov. sugar; Westwood patt., the set (ILLUS., previous page).................................. **165**

Coffeepot, cov., Apple patt., ... **100**

Coffeepot, cov., Desert Rose patt., 7 1/2" h. **140**

Coffeepot, cov., Ivy patt., green rim band, 7 1/2" h. **235**

Coffeepot, cov., 10" h., Daisy patt. **65**

Coffeepot, cov., demitasse, Coronado Table Ware, coral satin glaze (ILLUS. rear, w/demitasse pieces, top of page) **95**

Coffeepot, individual, cov., Desert Rose patt. **425**

Compote, open, Apple patt., 8" d., 4" h. **75**

Compote, open, Desert Rose patt., 8" d., 4" h. **65**

Compote, open, Meadow Rose patt., 8" d., 4" h. **85**

Condiment set: oil & vinegar cruets w/original stoppers, cov. mustard jar & three-part tray; Starburst patt., the set.................... **275**

Cookie jar, cov., Apple patt. **245**

Cookie jar, cov., Desert Rose patt. **200**

Creamer, Apple patt. **21**

Creamer, Bountiful patt. **35**

Creamer, individual, Desert Rose patt., 3 1/2" h. **65**

Creamer, Ivy patt., 4" h. **30**

Creamer, Desert Rose patt., 4 1/4" h. **28**

Creamer, October patt. **24**

Creamer & cov. sugar bowl, Apple patt., pr. **55**

Creamer & cov. sugar bowl, Daisy patt., pr. **45**

Creamer & cov. sugar bowl, Desert Rose patt., pr. **55**

Creamer & cov. sugar bowl, El Patio tableware, Mexican blue glossy glaze, pr. **35**

Creamer & cov. sugar bowl, Ivy patt., pr. **90**

Creamer & cov. sugar bowl, Meadow Rose patt., pr. **45**

Creamer & cov. sugar bowl, October patt., pr. **45**

Creamer & cov. sugar bowl, individual, Apple patt., pr. **53**

Creamer & open sugar bowl, Tiempo patt., lime green, pr. **25**

Creamer & open sugar bowl, individual, Desert Rose patt., pr. **140**

Creamer & open sugar bowl, individual, El Patio Nuevo patt., orange, pr. **50**

Apple Pattern Plate, Cup & Saucer

Cup & saucer, Apple patt. (ILLUS. w/bread   & butter plate) **9**

Cup & saucer, Apple patt., jumbo size 78
Cup & saucer, Arden patt. 15
Cup & saucer, California Poppy patt. 35
Cup & saucer, Coronado Table Ware, coral
satin glaze 10
Cup & saucer, demitasse, Coronado, vari-
ous colors, each set (ILLUS. of variety of
colors w/demitasse coffeepot) 22-28
Cup & saucer, Desert Rose patt., jumbo size 60
Cup & saucer, El Patio tableware, glossy
yellow glaze 6
Cup & saucer, Ivy patt. 22
Cup & saucer, October patt. 16
Cup & saucer, Starburst patt. 16
Cup & saucer, tall, Desert Rose patt. 55
Cup & saucer, tea, Desert Rose patt. 5
Cup & saucer, Twilight Rose patt. 26
Cup & saucer, demitasse, Apple patt. 55
Cup & saucer, demitasse, Desert Rose patt. 42
Cup & saucer, demitasse, El Patio table-
ware, golden glow glossy glaze 18
Cup & saucer, demitasse, El Patio table-
ware, Mexican blue glossy glaze 20
Cup & saucer, demitasse, El Patio table-
ware, turquoise glossy glaze 18
Dinner service: 6 each dinner plates, soup
plates, berry bowls, cups & saucers, 3
salad plates, one each open sugar bowl,
creamer, oval platter & vegetable bowl;
Coronado patt., matte coral, the set 135
Dish, Desert Rose patt., heart-shaped,
5 3/4" l. 95
Egg cup, Desert Rose patt., 2 3/4" d.,
3 3/4" h. 36
Egg cup, Meadow Rose patt., 2 3/4 d.,
3 3/4" h. 36
Egg cup, Twilight Rose patt., 2 3/4" d.,
3 3/4" h. 350
Egg cup, Apple patt., double 32
Ginger jar, cov., Apple patt. 395
Ginger jar, cov., Desert Rose patt. 295
Goblet, footed, Desert Rose patt., 6 1/2" h. 225
Goblet, Meadow Rose patt., 6 1/2" h 85
Goblet, Picnic patt., 6 1/2" h. 20
Gravy boat, Arden patt. 65
Gravy boat, California Poppy patt. 95
Gravy boat, Desert Rose patt. 45
Gravy boat, Tiempo patt., lime green 20
Gravy boat w/attached undertray, Apple
patt. 42
Gravy boat w/attached undertray, Desert
Rose patt. 42
Gravy boat w/attached undertray, Ivy patt. 62
Hurricane lamp, Desert Rose patt. 325
Jam jar, cov., Apple patt., redesigned style 275
Jam jar, cov., Desert Rose patt. 95
Microwave dish, oblong, Desert Rose patt.,
1 1/2 qt. 275
Mixing bowl, Apple patt., 6" d. 75
Mixing bowl, Desert Rose patt., 6" d. 75
Mixing bowl, Apple patt., 7 1/2" d. 95
Mixing bowl, Desert Rose patt.,
7 1/2" d. 95
Mixing bowl, Apple patt., 9" d. 125
Mixing bowl, Desert Rose patt., 9" d. 125

Mixing bowl set, Apple patt., 3 pcs. 350
Mixing bowl set, Desert Rose patt.,
3 pcs. 350
Mug, Apple patt., 7 oz. 28
Mug, Cafe Royal patt., 7 oz. 16
Mug, Desert Rose patt., 7 oz. 18
Mug, Apple patt., 10 oz. 120
Mug, Desert Rose patt., 10 oz. 125
Mug, Desert Rose patt., 12 oz. 65
Mug, Apple patt., 17 oz., rare 110
Mug, Meadow Rose patt. 25
Napkin ring, Desert Rose patt. 45
Pepper mill, Duet patt. 75
Pepper mill, Starburst patt. 165
Pickle dish, Desert Rose patt., 4 1/2 x 11" 42
Pickle/relish boat, Desert Rose patt., interior
decoration, 4 1/2 x 11" 350
Pitcher, 4" h., Desert Rose patt. 395
Pitcher, milk, 6 1/4" h., Apple patt., 1 qt. 90
Pitcher, milk, 6 1/2" h., Desert Rose patt.,
1 qt. 85
Pitcher, milk, 8 1/2" h., Daisy patt. 50

Apple Pattern 2 Qt. Pitcher

Pitcher, water, 8 3/4" h., Apple patt., 2 qt.
(ILLUS.) 125
Pitcher, water, 8 3/4" h., Desert Rose patt.,
2 1/2 qt. 95
Pitcher, water, Coronado Table Ware, bur-
gundy glaze 75
Pitcher w/ice lip, El Patio tableware, golden
glow glossy glaze, 2 1/2 qt. 65
Pitcher w/ice lip, El Patio tableware, tur-
quoise glossy glaze, 2 1/2 qt. 85
Plate, bread & butter, Arden patt. 6
Plate, dinner, Arden patt. 15
Plate, luncheon, Arden patt. 12
Plate, salad, Arden patt. 8
Plate, bread & butter, 6 1/4" d., California
Poppy patt. 15
Plate, bread & butter, 6 1/4" d., Ivy patt. 10
Plate, bread & butter, 6 1/2" d., Apple patt.
(ILLUS. w/cup & saucer) 6
Plate, bread & butter, 6 1/2" d., Desert Rose
patt. 6

Various El Patio Plates & Tumblers

Plate, bread & butter, 6 1/2" d., El Patio, apple green (ILLUS. w/various El Patio plates & tumblers).. **6**

Plate, bread & butter, 6 1/2" d., October patt. **8**

Plate, bread & butter, 6 1/2" d., Wildflower patt. **45**

Plate, coupe dessert, 7 1/4" d., Meadow Rose patt.. **29**

Plate, coupe dessert, 7 1/2" d., Apple patt. **65**

Plate, coupe dessert, 7 1/2" d., Desert Rose patt. **65**

Plate, dessert, 7 1/2" d., El Patio, Mexican blue (ILLUS. w/various El Patio plates & tumblers) **12**

Plate, salad, 8" d., California Poppy patt. **45**

Plate, snack, 8" sq., Apple patt............................ **145**

Plate, snack, 8" sq., Desert Rose patt................ **125**

Plate, side salad, 4 1/2 x 8", Apple patt., crescent-shaped **38**

Plate, side salad, 4 1/2 x 8", Desert Rose patt., crescent-shaped **35**

Plate, side salad, 4 1/2 x 8", Ivy patt., crescent-shaped.. **49**

Plate, side salad, 4 1/2 x 8, Meadow Rose patt., crescent-shaped **29**

Plate, salad, 8 1/2" d., Apple patt....................... **16**

Plate, salad, 8 1/2" d., Desert Rose patt............. **13**

Plate, salad, 8 1/2" d., El Patio, bright yellow (ILLUS. w/various El Patio plates & tumblers)... **14**

Plate, salad, 8 1/2" d., Ivy patt............................ **28**

Plate, salad, 8 1/2" d., Meadow Rose patt. **15**

Plate, salad, 8 1/2" d., October patt..................... **16**

Plate, salad, 8 1/2" d., Picnic patt. **8**

Plate, salad, 8 1/2" d., Wildflower patt................. **95**

Plate, child's, 7 x 9" oval, divided, Desert Rose patt., ... **125**

Plate, child's, 7 1/4 x 9", divided, Apple patt. **145**

Plate, luncheon, 9 1/4" d., ivy patt. **28**

Plate, luncheon, 8 1/2" d., El Patio, coral satin (ILLUS. w/various El Patio plates & tumblers) **14**

Plate, luncheon, 9 1/2" d., Apple patt................... **19**

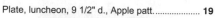

Coronado Table Ware Plate

Plate, luncheon, 9 1/2" d., Coronado Table Ware, coral satin glaze (ILLUS.)...................... **10**

Plate, luncheon, 9 1/2" d., Coronado Table Ware, glossy coral glaze **10**

Plate, luncheon, 9 1/2" d., Desert Rose patt........ **22**

Plate, luncheon, 9 1/2" d., Wildflower patt.......... **125**

Plate, small dinner, 9 1/2" d., El Patio, maroon (ILLUS. w/various El Patio plates & tumblers).. **14**

Plate, coupe, party w/cup well, 10 1/2" d., Desert Rose patt. **160**

Plate, dinner, 10 1/2" d., Apple patt...................... **15**

Dessert Rose Dinner Plate

Toast cover, Desert Rose patt., 5 1/2" d.,
3" h. 145
Trivet, tile, Desert Rose patt. 145
Trivet, Apple patt., 6" d. 245
Tumbler, El Patio tableware, apple green
(ILLUS. w/various El Patio plates & tum-
blers) 28
Tumbler, El Patio tableware, coral glaze 28
Tumbler, El Patio tableware, flame orange
(ILLUS. w/various El Patio plates & tum-
blers) 28
Tumbler, El Patio tableware, glacial blue
glossy glaze (ILLUS. w/various El Patio
plates & tumblers) 28
Tumbler, El Patio tableware, golden glow
(ILLUS. w/various El Patio plates & tum-
blers) 28
Tumbler, El Patio tableware, redwood
glossy glaze 28
Tumbler, Apple patt., juice, 6 oz., 3 1/4" h. 30
Tumbler, Desert Rose patt., juice, 6 oz.,
3 1/4" h. 35
Tumbler, Ivy patt., 10 oz., 5" h. 55
Tumbler, Apple patt., 10 oz., 5 1/4" h. 38
Tumbler, California Poppy patt., water, 10
oz., 5 1/4" h. 125
Tumbler, Desert Rose patt., 10 oz., 5 1/4" h. 38
Tumbler, Wildflower patt., water, 10 oz.,
5 1/2" h. 250
Tumbler, El Patio tableware, Mexican blue
glossy glaze 28
Tureen, cov., flat-bottomed, Desert Rose
patt., 8" d., 5" h. 425
Tureen, cov., footed, Apple patt., 8 3/4" d.,
5 3/4" h. 450
Vase, bud, 6" h., Desert Rose patt. 95
Vase, bud, 6" h., Meadow Rose patt. 65
Vegetable bowl, divided, Apple patt.,
7 x 10 3/4" 42
Vegetable bowl, divided, Desert Rose patt.,
7 x 10 3/4" 55
Vegetable bowl, divided, Ivy patt.,
8 x 12 1/4" 95
Vegetable bowl, open, oval, Arden patt.,
large 45
Vegetable bowl, open, oval, Daisy patt.,
6 3/4 x 13 3/4", 2 1/4" h. 38
Vegetable bowl, open, oval, Desert Rose
patt., 9" l. 35
Vegetable bowl, open, round, Apple patt.,
7 3/4" d. 35
Vegetable bowl, open, round, Apple patt.,
8 1/4" d. 45
Vegetable bowl, open, round, Apple patt.,
9" d. 50
Vegetable bowl, open, round, California
Poppy patt., 9" d. 125
Vegetable bowl, open, round, Desert Rose
patt., 8" d. 24
Vegetable bowl, open, round, Ivy patt.,
7 1/4" d. 45
Vegetable bowl, open, round, Ivy patt.,
8 1/4" d. 47
Vegetable bowl, open, round, Wildflower
patt., 9" d. 225

Frankoma

Frankoma Mark

John Frank began producing and selling pottery on a part-time basis during the summer of 1933 while he was still teaching art and pottery classes at the University of Oklahoma. In 1934, Frankoma Pottery became an incorporated business that was successful enough to allow him to leave his teaching position in 1936 to devote full time to its growth. The pottery was moved to Sapulpa, Oklahoma, in 1938 and a full range of art pottery and dinnerware was eventually offered. In 1953 Frankoma switched from Ada clay to clay found in Sapulpa. Since John Frank's death in 1973, the pottery has been directed by his daughter, Janiece. In early 1991 Richard Bernstein became owner and president of Frankoma Pottery, which was renamed Frankoma Industries. Janiece Frank serves as vice president and general manager. The early wares and limited editions are becoming increasingly popular with collectors today.

John Frank studied at the Chicago Art Institute and was fortunate to train under two noted ceramic artists: Mrs. Myrtle Merritt French and Dr. Charles F. Binns. When a Dr. Jacobsen asked Professor French to find someone to begin a new ceramic art department at the University, she highly recommended John Frank. That position enabled him to study and formulate various glazes. From these experiments he was able to create a beautiful rutile glaze that had been used only sparingly in the past.

When he founded Frankoma Potteries in 1933, Mr. Frank almost always used the rutile technique, which helped to create beautiful glazes for his pottery.

With his family, Mr. Frank moved his operation from Norman, Oklahoma, to Sapulpa, Oklahoma. He felt he had come home. The family and its company have remained in Sapulpa since that time.

Over the years Frankoma products have been marked in a variety of ways. The "pot and leopard" mark was used from 1935 to 1938, when a fire on November 11, 1938 destroyed everything including the mark.

A creamy looking clay known as "Ada" is highly collectible today but it was discontinued in 1953. Frankoma then began using the clay from Sapulpa, which resulted in a red brick color.

In May 1970 John Frank was contacted by a writer, and Mr. Frank personally responded to the writer's questions. There has been much controversy over the actual date when John Frank changed from Ada clay (which is more valuable) to Sapula clay. Below is a paragraph from John Frank's letter to the writer, signed by him, that explains the date. You can find the entire letter printed beginning on page 13 of the Collectors Guide to Frankoma Pottery, Book II, by Susan N. Cox. "...We have always used an Oklahoma clay as the base of all our pottery. The first clay came from Ada, and we used it until 1953 when we switched over to a local brick shale that we dig right here in Sapulpa. Using this as a base we add other earths and come up with what we call our Frankoma Pottery. Peculiar in itself, and it is not available anywhere else, nor is it used by any other pottery, it fires a brick red and we are able to temper it in the cooling so that all of our ware is guaranteed oven proof."

When Richard Bernstein purchased Frankoma in 1991 a new era began, resulting in different products and glazes. True Frankoma collectors search for the products made before 1991 and certainly those made before 1953. Lucky ones can find pot and leopard-marked pieces and those marked "Frank Potteries."

Baker, Westwind patt., Model No. 6vs, Peach Glow glaze, 1 1/2 qt. **$24**
Bell, Joniece Frank wedding commemorative, 1-11-62, White Sand, unmarked, 1 3/4" h. **55**
Book ends, Bucking Bronco, Model No. 423, Prairie Green glaze, 5 1/2" h., pr. **550**

Frankoma Leopard Book End

Book ends, model of leopard, Pompeian Bronze glaze, Model No. 431, 9" l., 5 1/2" h., pr. (ILLUS. of one) **1,100**
Book ends, seated figure, Ivory glaze, Model No. 425, pot & leopard mark, 1934-38, 5 3/4" h., pr. **1,050**

Ocelot Book Ends

Book ends, Walking Ocelot on a two-tiered oblong base, black high glaze, Model No. 424, signed on reverse of tiered base "Taylor" denoting designer Joseph Taylor, pot & leopard mark on bottom, 7" l., 3" h., pr. (ILLUS.) **1,300**
Bottle-vase, V-1, 1969, limited edition, 4,000 created, small black foot w/Prairie Green body, 15" h. **175**
Bottle-vase, V-7, limited edition, 3,500 created, Desert Gold glaze, body w/coffee glazed stopper & base, signed by Joniece Frank, 13" h. **110**

Frankoma Advertising Bowl

Bowl, 5 3/4" d., shallow form, advertising "Oklahoma Gas Company - Golden Anniversary," 1956, Desert Gold, marked "Frankoma" (ILLUS.) **175**
Bowl, 11" l., divided, Lazybones patt., Brown Satin glaze, Model No. 4qd **20**
Brooch, four-leaf clover-shape, Desert Gold glaze, w/original card, 1 1/4" h. **50**
Candleholder, miniature, Aladdin lamp w/finger hold, Prairie Green, marked "Frankoma No. 305," 2 1/4" h. **90**
Catalog, 1953, unnumbered sixteen pages, dated July 1, 1953, two versions for color cover, one w/photograph of Donna Frank or one w/photograph of Grace Lee Frank, each **50**
Christmas card, figural fish tray, Woodland Moss glaze, marked, "1960 the Franks, Frankoma Christmas Frankoma," 4" l. **75**
Christmas card, "Statue of Liberty Torch," White Sand glaze, created by Grace Lee Frank Smith for her & Dr. A. Milton Smith's friends, 1986, 3 1/2" l. **85**

Bronze Green Cigarette Box

Cigarette box, cov., rectangular, cover w/single raised & hard-to-find curved leaf handle, Bronze Green glaze, Ada clay, marked "Frankoma," 4 x 6 3/4", 3 1/2" h. (ILLUS.) **165**
Figure of Fan Dancer, seated, No. 113, Ivory glaze, Ada clay, 14" l., 9" h. **800**
Figure of farmer boy, wearing dark blue overalls, light blue short-sleeved shirt, black scarf tied around neck, yellow hair & ivory wide-brim hat w/only brim showing from front, black shoes, bisque arms, hands, face & neck, marked "Frankoma 702," 6 3/4" h. **145**

Figure of gardener girl, holding pale green apron to form a basket in front of her, light blue dress w/short puffed sleeves & scooped neckline, long yellow hair w/dark blue bow on top, bisque face, neck, arms & hands, marked "Frankoma 701," 5 3/4" h. **145**

Frankoma Indian Chief Figure

Figure of Indian Chief, No. 142, Desert Gold glaze, Ada clay, 7" h. (ILLUS.) **165**

Jar, cov., rose form, black rim base & lid, Ivory body, #32, 1934-38, pot & leopard mark, 4 1/2" h. **225**

Model of fish, miniature, Turquoise, Ada clay, marked "Frankoma," 2 1/2" **350**

Advertising Mortar & Pestle

Mortar & pestle, advertising "Schreibers Drug Store," White Sand, marked "Frankoma," 3 1/4" (ILLUS.).............................. **85**

Mug, 1968, (Republican) elephant, white **90**

Mug, 1970, (Republican) elephant........................ **65**

Mug, 1971, (Republican) elephant **60**

Mug, 1973, (Republican) elephant **40**

Mug, 1974, Nixon/Ford elephant.......................... **575**

Frankoma Ornament

Ornament, "the ABCs of life," gift w/purchase from Tulsa shopping mall, 1987, white background w/sketch of three children, 3 1/2" d. (ILLUS.)..................................... **55**

Pitcher, Wagon Wheel patt., Model No. 94d, Prairie Green glaze, Ada clay, 2 qt.................. **85**

Plate, 8 1/2" d., Bicentennial Series, Limited Edition No. 1, "Provocations," eleven signers of the Declaration of Independence, White Sand glaze, 1972, misspelling of United States as "Staits" **175**

Plate, 7" d., Wildlife Series, Limited Edition No. 1, Bobwhite quail, Prairie Green glaze, 1,000 produced **150**

Plate, 7 1/2" d., Easter 1972, "Jesus Is Not Here...He Is Risen," scene of Jesus' tomb.. **30**

Political chip, John Frank's profile on front surrounded by the words, "Honest, Fair, Capable," & at bottom "Elect John Frank Representative 1962," obverse w/outline of Oklahoma state w/"One Frank" inside it, around it "Oklahomans deserve outstanding leadership" & "For statesmanship vote Republican," unglazed red brick color, 1 3/4" d., 1/8" h.......................... **25**

Postcard, color photograph of Joniece Frank sitting w/various Frankoma products used to show the current Frankoma glazes, 5 1/2 x 6 1/2" **15**

Salt & pepper shakers, model of a Dutch shoe, Desert Gold glaze, Model No. 915h, ca. 1957-60, 4" l., pr. **65**

Salt & pepper shakers, model of an elephant, Desert Gold glaze, No. 160h, produced in 1942 only, Ada clay, 3" h., pr. **160**

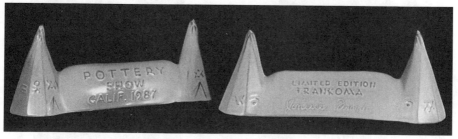

Frankoma Advertising Sign

Sign, advertising "Pottery Show - Calif.   1987," Prairie Green, 9" l. (ILLUS.) **100**

Frankoma Dealer Teepee Sign

Sign, dealer teepee, Prairie Green, 1940s,
marked "Frankoma," 6 1/2" h. (ILLUS.)......... **695**

John Frank Tournament Stein

Stein, footed, advertising-type, for John
Frank Memorial Charity Gold Tourna-
ment, Blue, 150 created, 1973 (ILLUS.)......... **25**
Teapot, cov., Wagon Wheel patt., Model
No. 94j, Desert Gold glaze, Ada clay, 2
cup **40**

Frankoma Eagle Trivet

Trivet, Eagle sitting on branch, large wings
fill up most of the trivet, Peach Glow
glaze, Model No. 2tr, 6" sq. (ILLUS.)............... **65**
Tumbler, juice, Plainsman patt., Model No.
51c, Autumn Yellow glaze, 6 oz. **9**

Vase, 3 1/2" h., round foot rising to bulbous
body w/short neck & rolled lip, unusual
high gloss deep blue, marked "Frank Pot-
teries".. **550**
Vase, 4" h., small foot rising to a flat, narrow
body w/tab handle on each side, Ivory
glaze, marked "Frankoma"................................ **95**
Vase, 4" h., small foot rising to a flat, narrow
body w/tab handle on each side, Ivory
glaze, pot & leopard mark................................ **190**
Vase, 6" h., square-shaped w/relief-molded
flying goose, relief-molded reed decora-
tion on reverse, No. 60B **50**
Vase, 7" h., Art Deco-style w/round foot
w/panel on each side at base, rising to a
plain, flat body w/stepped small elongated handles, Jade Green glaze, Model
No. 41, pot & leopard mark............................... **195**

Frankoma Stovepipe Vase

Vase, 8 3/4" h., stovepipe, Prairie Green
w/silver overlay, 1940s, marked "Franko-
ma" (ILLUS.).. **550**
Vase, 9" h., round stepped ring base rising
to handle on each side, Ivory, #78, pot &
leopard mark **210**
Wall masks, bust of Oriental man, No. 134 &
Oriental woman, No. 133, Jade Green
glaze, pot & leopard mark, Ada clay, man
5 1/2" h., woman 4 3/4" h., pr....................... **595**

Frankoma Billiken Wall Pocket

Wall pocket, figural, billiken, Prairie Green,
Ada clay, marked "Tulsa Court, No. 47,
R.O.J.," 7" h. (ILLUS.) **155**

Fulper Pottery

The Fulper Pottery was founded in Flemington, New Jersey, in 1805 and operated until 1935, although operations were curtailed in 1929 when its main plant was destroyed by fire. The name was changed in 1929 to Stangl Pottery, which continued in operation until July of 1978, when Pfaltzgraff, a division of Susquehanna Broadcasting Company of York, Pennsylvania, purchased the assets of the Stangl Pottery, including the name.

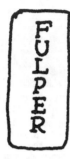

Fulper Marks

Book ends, figural, each molded as a large
spread-winged eagle perched atop a
large thick rectangular platform w/an embossed American shield at the front, Cucumber green matte Crystalline glaze,
rectangular ink stamp, 7 1/2" w., 9" h., pr.
(restoration to beak & neck of one) **$1,069**
Book ends, figural, "Roman Mausoleum"
model, bold classical doorway w/peaked
roof over fan light above the door which
stands ajar, sheer mottled ivory & white
matte glaze w/clay showing through,
rectangular ink mark, 5 1/2" w., 6" h., pr.
(small chip & restoration to corner of one) **605**

Fulper Liberty Bell Book Ends

Book ends, model of the Liberty Bell in
mounting, Verde Antique crystalline
glaze, rectangular ink mark & paper la-
bel, 4" w., 7 1/4" h., pr. (ILLUS.) **690**
Bottle, footed bulbous base tapering to tall
cylindrical neck w/flat rim, embossed
salamander at base of neck, Cat's Eye
flambé glaze, rectangular ink mark, 8" h.,
4" d. **1,800**
Bowl, 10" d., 4" h., wide low cushion form
w/the wide shoulder centered by a wide,
low cylindrical neck, rich Flemington
Green flambé glaze over a mustard yel-
low ground, rectangular ink mark **1,013**
Bowl, 10" d., 6" h., deep rounded sides, the
slightly rounded shoulder tapering to a
wide, flat molded mouth, decorated
w/molded thistles & branches & covered
in an ivory to Chinese blue flambé glaze,
rectangular ink mark (rim chip & hairline)..... **523**
Bowl, 11 1/2" d., a small, low cylindrical foot
supporting a wide rounded & cupped
blossom-form bowl w/wide ribs around
the exterior & a lightly scalloped & pointed rim, exterior w/multi-toned green crystalline glaze, pale yellow interior, incised
vertical mark (minor flakes on foot) **231**
Bowl, 11 1/2" d., 6 1/2" h., footed, deep flaring sides, interior covered in Flemington
green glaze, exterior in Famille Rose
glaze, unmarked **825**

Fulper Vaz-bowl and Small Vases

Bowl w/flower frog, 7 1/4" d., 5" h., "Vaz-bowl," a wide flat-bottomed compressed squatty form on tiny feet, a ringed shoulder w/a flattened rim, the center w/a tall waisted three-legged flower frog, Blue Wisteria & Mirrored Green glaze, rectangular ink mark, Pan-Pacific & original Fulper paper labels (ILLUS. left, bottom previous page) **518**

Bulb bowl, shallow round body w/wide closed rim, glossy streaked brown, blue & green glaze interior, glossy & matte dark blue & rose exterior, early 20th c., faint vertical Fulper stamp, 9 1/4" d., 2 1/4" h. **144**

Center bowl, figural, "Ibis" model, three stylized birds w/wings spread support the wide shallow bowl w/incurved sides, Flemington Green flambé exterior & brown flambé over mustard matte exterior, rectangular ink mark, 11" d., 5 3/4" h. **935**

Center bowl, wide flat bottom w/low incurved sides, embossed fish design covered in a green & Butterscotch flambé glaze, rectangular ink mark, 11" d., 3" h. **1,125**

Console bowl, a very wide shallow form w/rounded incurved sides, raised on three short peg legs, dark green crystalline matte glaze, stamped vertical mark, 10 1/2" d. (minor flakes)................................. **523**

Doorstop, model of a cat, reclining animal facing viewer, tail curled along the body, creamy ground w/streaky brown cat's-eye flambé glaze, ink racetrack mark, 9" l., 6" h.. **1,069**

Flower frog, figural, modeled as an Indian maiden seated in a canoe perched on a rocky outcrop, in green, mahogany, & brown matte glazes, unmarked, 7" l., 4" h. (small flat bottom chip, probably in the making)... **520**

Flower frog, model of a medieval castle on grassy base, brown & green matte glaze, early ink mark, 5 x 5" (a few minor nicks to edges) **440**

Flower frog, figural, a penguin standing atop a large rocky outcrop base w/flower holes, the bird in cream, brown & blue matte glazes w/brown matte glaze on the base, rectangular ink mark, 7" h. **303**

Flower frog, figural, standing full figure Egyptian by John Kunzman, green & turquoise flambé glaze, rectangular ink stamp & "Made by John Kunzman, 1909," 7 1/2" h. (two small chips & bruise to base) **788**

Flower frog, figural, frog on lily pad, mirrored green & caramel flambé glaze, vertical inkstamp rectangle mark, 7" d....................... **220**

Incense burner, cov., wide squatty bulbous body on four tiny feet & w/four tiny squared buttresses around the shoulder, the low neck w/a domed, pierced cover, matte green crystalline glaze, rare, early, unmarked 5" d., 4" h. (bruise to lip interior, restoration to chip)................................. **1,069**

Jug, inverted pear-shaped body w/flared foot, the wide shoulder w/short cylindrical neck & spout w/molded rims, loop handle from shoulder to rim, blue, green & ivory flambé glaze, one of three known, rect-

angular ink mark, 7" d., 9 3/4" h. (chip to base, mostly under foot)............................. **2,588**

Rare Fulper Lamp Base & Shade

Lamp, table model, an 18" d. domical pottery shaded in Chinese blue flambé glaze w/bands of triangular & almond-shaped caramel slag glass segments flanking green slag eyebrow segments around the rim, raised on a matching pottery base w/a knopped standard & widely flaring squatty bulbous base, original porcelain sockets, invisible repair to shade, rectangular ink & Vasecraft marks, 18" h. (ILLUS.).. **10,350**

Pipe holder, figural, modeled at the front w/a fox (?) lying on a snag log w/a large & smaller cylindrical upright log forming holders behind, match striker section to one side of the base, overall Mahogany glossy glaze, unmarked, 6 1/2" w., 3 1/4" h. (repair to fox ears & largest log)...... **900**

Urn, a small foot supporting a wide, deep urn-form body w/an angled shoulder tapering to a short flared neck, upright pierced square handles at the edge of the shoulder, fine frothy blue to Famille Rose flambé glaze, inked racetrack mark, 8" d., 9 1/2" h. **1,575**

Urn, small round pedestal foot supporting a large bulbous ovoid body w/a wide rounded shoulder to a short wide flat mouth flanked by small loop handles, fine ochre, mahogany & pale blue flambé glaze over textured body, raised racetrack mark, 9" d., 9" h. **935**

Urn, tall slender classical form w/wide shoulders & a short neck w/widely rolled rim, upright scroll-tipped handles from the shoulder to the rim, overall Mirror Black glaze on a "hammered" body, rectangular ink mark, 5 1/2" d., 11" h. **495**

Urn, Chinese-form, footed tapering bulbous ovoid body w/a tall cylindrical neck & flared rim, small squared loop shoulder handles, overall Mirror Black glaze over a "hammered" body, raised racetrack mark, 8" d., 11" h. (reglued handle tip) **1,045**

Urn, footed baluster form, shoulder tapering to cylindrical neck w/molded rim, flanked by scrolled handles, covered in a glossy & matte Chinese blue flambé glaze, rectangular ink mark, 11 1/4" h., 5 3/4" d. **715**

Vase, 3" h., squatty bulbous body tapering gently to a closed rim, overall dark purple & matte blue matte glaze, vertical stamped mark.................... **176**

Vase, 3 3/4" h., 6" d., low squatty bulbous lower body centering an upright short wide neck w/incurved mouth, fine green to Chinese Blue flambé glaze, rectangular Prang mark.......................... **366**

Vase, 4" h., 5" d., nearly spherical melon-lobed form, green & Chinese Blue flambé glaze, ink racetrack mark (ILLUS. right with Vaz-bowl) **633**

Vase, 4 1/2" h., swelled cylindrical body w/an angled shoulder to a short, wide cylindrical neck, green over blue to red overall drip glaze, unmarked.......................... **176**

Vase, 4 1/2" h., 4 1/2" d., footed, lobed bell pepper-shaped, w/small closed mouth, blue over Famille Rose flambé glaze, rectangular ink mark **660**

Vase, 5" h., wide half-round lower body w/an angled center shoulder below the wide tapering neck w/flat rim, squared curled C-scroll handles from rim to shoulder, overall purple & blue mottled matte glaze, stamped vertical mark...................... **231**

Vase, 5" h., 7 1/4" d., a wide half-round lower body below a wide angled shoulder centered by a short, wide cylindrical neck, frothy Flemington Green flambé glaze, rectangular ink mark (ILLUS. center with Vaz-bowl) **431**

Vase, 5 1/4" h., 6 3/4" d., footed spherical body w/incurved rim, light blue to elephant's breath flambé glaze, ink racetrack mark **385**

Vase, 5 1/2" h., 4 1/2" d., bulbous ovoid body tapering to a wide short flared rim, dark mirrored green & blue flambé glaze, raised mark........................ **330**

Vase, 6" h., 9" d., squatty bulbous form, the wide shoulder tapering to molded rim, Mirrored Black flambé glaze, ink racetrack mark **619**

Vase, 6" h., 9" d., wide footed squatty bulbous form w/a wide rounded shoulder centered by a small rolled neck, frothy Wisteria Matte glaze, minor grinding chip on base of footring, mark obscured by glaze (ILLUS.)................................ **863**

Vase, 6 1/4" h., 3 1/4" d., footed squatty bulbous base tapering to a tall cylindrical body w/a bulbed neck w/a flat rim, Rose Famille glaze, experimental, squat rectangular ink mark & "121 - McConnell" **1,463**

Vase, 6 1/4" h., 8 1/2" d., footed spherical body w/short wide cylindrical neck, three loop handles, matte Wisteria glaze, incised racetrack mark............................. **385**

Vase, 6 1/2" h., 8" d., wide bulbous body w/angled shoulder handles, purple & blue crystalline glaze, impressed racetrack mark......................... **275**

Vase, 6 3/4" h., ovoid body w/cream flambé over Wisteria glaze, raised vertical mark....... **303**

Vase, 6 3/4" h., 4" d., footed cylindrical body w/rolled rim, incised vertical ribbed bands, covered w/a rich, flowing brown matte finish, impressed mark **3,080**

Vase, 7" h., a flaring pedestal base supporting a large spherical body tapering to a tiny flared neck, the upper body in cream shading to a striped cream, blue & green drip glaze & mottled blue pedestal, impressed mark **286**

Vase, 7" h., wide gently tapering cylindrical body w/a rounded bottom edge & closed flat rim, cat's-eye flambé glaze, impressed vertical mark (minor grinding chips to base)................................ **248**

Fulper Vase with Frothy Blue Glaze

Vase, 7" h., 4 1/2" d., swelled cylindrical body w/a narrow angled shoulder & wide short rolled neck w/short buttress handles from rim to shoulder, lustered frothy turquoise glaze over a matte blue ground, obscured racetrack mark (ILLUS.)................................ **978**

Fulper Vase with Wisteria Matte Glaze

Vase, 10 1/2" h., footed wide bulbous body, the wide shoulder tapering to a short cylindrical neck, Mirror Black flambé glaze, raised racetrack mark **1,870**

Vase, 12" h., large classic baluster-form body w/flaring rim covered in a Rouge flambé glaze, raised racetrack mark **715**

Vase, 12" h., raised & flared neck on a tall ovoid body, ochre rim & sparse cobalt blue crystals on a periwinkle blue ground, vertical black ink stamp mark, ca. 1915 .... **633**

Vase, 12" h., 4 1/2" d., tall slender baluster-form body w/a rounded shoulder to the small flared neck, Butterscotch flambé glaze, inked racetrack mark **619**

Vase, 12" h., 7" d., simple ovoid body tapering to wide cylindrical neck w/flaring rim, frothy Rouge Flambé glaze, raised racetrack mark **731**

Vase, 12" h., 7 1/2" d., tall baluster-form body w/heavy loop handles arching from the neck rim down to the shoulder & along the sides, fine Mirrored Green, Mahogany & Ivory flambé glaze, rectangular ink mark **1,350**

Vase, 12 1/2" h., bulbous ovoid body w/four shoulder handles, collared neck w/flat rim, Chinese blue flambé over Famille Rose glaze, vertical die-stamped racetrack mark (one handle reglued) **715**

Vase, 12 1/2" h., footed bulbous ovoid body w/short cylindrical neck w/molded rim, loop shoulder handle, Leopard Skin crystalline glaze, incised racetrack mark **2,530**

tress projections supporting a narrow flaring shoulder below the tapering cylindrical neck molded w/pointed panels, speckled cafe-au-lait glaze, long hairline from rim, few glaze chips on base, rare & early, rectangular ink mark (ILLUS.) **1,265**

Vase, 12 3/4" h., 7 3/4" d., bullet-shaped body w/two ring handles, covered in textbook Cucumber & Leopard Skin crystalline glaze, ink racetrack mark **3,850**

Tall Fulper Vase with Cattails

Vase, 13" h., 4 3/4" d., tall, slightly waisted cylindrical form, embossed w/tall cattails under a Cucumber Matte crystalline glaze, rectangular mark, shown in Paul Evans pottery book (ILLUS.) **5,750**

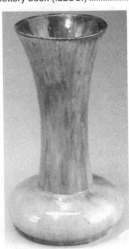

Tall Trumpet-form Fulper Vase

Rare & Early Tall Fulper Vase

Vase, 12 3/4" h., 5 1/4" d., Vasekraft, tall cylindrical lower body below four small but-

Vase, 13" h., 5 1/2" d., low squatty bulbous base w/a wide shoulder to the tall trumpet-form neck, overall Cat's Eye to blue flambé glaze, impressed racetrack mark, early (ILLUS., previous page)` **1,955**

Vase, 13" h., 12" d., Roman Urn form, a large bulbous ovoid body tapering to a short cylindrical neck & molded rim, the shoulder mounted w/four small C-scroll handles, Mirror Black crystalline glaze, incised racetrack mark (restoration to handles, tight lines in rim, several short scratches) **788**

Vase, 15" h., 8" d., tall, classical urn form, the angled shoulder mounted w/two upright inwardly scrolled handles, Mirror Black to Copperdust Crystalline glaze, paper label & "MR" in red (glaze chip on one handle)... **1,575**

Vase, 16" h., 5" d., tapering cylindrical shouldered body w/molded rim, Cat's Eye flambé glaze, incised racetrack mark .. **2,813**

Vase, 16 1/4" h., tall slightly expanding cylindrical body w/short molded rim, covered in a frothy Moss to Rose glaze, ink racetrack mark **1,540**

Vase, 17" h., 8" d., floor type, tall swelled cylindrical form tapering to a short cylindrical neck, Chinese blue & brown mirror flambé glaze, rectangular ink mark (drilled hole in bottom) **1,688**

Vase, 17 1/2'" h., 9" d., floor type, tall baluster form w/a short rolled neck, mirrored Flemington Green flambé glaze, incised racetrack mark (burst bubble near base)...... **495**

Wall pocket, spearpoint-form Pipes of Pan design w/a cluster of tapering tubes forming the upper body, Cucumber green matte glaze, rectangular ink mark, 4 3/4" w., 10 1/2" l... **450**

Vase, footed, wide bulbous base tapering to short wide cylindrical neck, large loop handles from mid section to rim, matte purple & blue glaze, black vertical Fulper in lozenge mark... **460**

Gallé Pottery

Fine pottery was made by Emile Gallé, the multitalented French designer and artisan who is also famous for his glass and furniture. The pottery is relatively scarce.

Gallé Pottery Mark

Gallé Lion Candlestick

Candlesticks, figural, in the form of a seated roaring lion wearing a crown that forms the socket, a large shield at the front decorated w/a thistle & other floral decoration in grey, black & red on a light blue ground w/gilt trim, signed, late 19th c., repairs, 8" h., pr. (ILLUS. of one) **$575**

Dish, foliate-shaped bowl, the interior painted in naturalistic colors w/wildflowers in front of a shore landscape, gilded rim, base w/red stamp mark, late 19th c., 10 1/4" w. (restored) **316**

Gallé Pottery Seated Cat

Model of cat, seated w/head turned facing the viewer, bulging eyes w/smiling expression, glazed in white & decorated w/scattered ringed dots & heart-like devices, signed, ca. 1890, 13" h. (ILLUS.) **3,600**

Gallé Cat with Flowers & Stripes

Model of cat, seated w/head turned facing the viewer, bulging eyes w/smiling expression, glazed in white & decorated w/pale lavender bands & reddish orange & green floral clusters, a painted neck chain w/a locket holding a dog portrait, minor chips to paws & one ear, ca. 1895, 12 3/8" h. (ILLUS.)... **5,700**

Rare Gallé Pottery Dog

Model of dog, seated Boston Terrier-like animal facing the viewer, open front legs, bulging eyes & angry expression, painted in white w/scattered ringed dots & heart-like devices, signed, ca. 1890, 12 5/8" h. (ILLUS.)` **6,000**

Gallé Owl

Model of owl, faience, molded in full relief, perched owl w/glass eyes, glazed in shades of grey & amber on russet base, inscribed (ILLUS.)... **3,737**

Gaudy Dutch

This name is applied to English earthenware with designs copied from Oriental patterns. Production began in the 18th century. These copies flooded into this country in the early 19th century. The incorporation of the word "Dutch" derives from the fact that it was the Dutch who first brought the Oriental wares into Europe. The ware was not, as often erroneously reported, made specifically for the Pennsylvania Dutch.

Creamer, Double Rose patt., 3 3/4" h. **$495**
Cup & saucer, handleless, Butterfly patt. (minor enamel flaking & small table ring chips) **660**
Cup & saucer, handleless, Carnation patt., cup 2 1/2" h., saucer, 5 1/2" d. (imperfections).. **468**
Cup & saucer, handleless, Dahlia patt., cup 2 1/4" h., saucer 5 1/2" d............................. **7,975**
Cup & saucer, handleless, Dove patt., cup 2 1/2" h., saucer 5 1/2" d. (imperfections)...... **495**
Cup & saucer, handleless, Grape patt., cup 2 1/2" h., saucer 5 3/4" d. (minor imperfections).. **495**
Cup & saucer, handleless, Oyster patt., cup 2 1/4" h., saucer 5 1/2" d.......................... **468**
Cup & saucer, handleless, Sunflower patt., cup 2 1/2" h., saucer 5 1/2" d. (imperfections).. **715**
Cup & saucer, handleless, Urn patt., cup 2" h., saucer 5 1/4" d. **550**
Plate, 10" d., Carnation patt............................. **1,265**
Plate, 7 1/2" d., Double Rose patt., framed, a gift from Max Hess...................................... **605**
Plate, 7 1/2" d., Dove patt. **523**
Plate, 7 1/2" d., Oyster patt................................ **578**
Plate, 7 1/2" d., Single Rose patt........................ **495**
Plate, 8" d., Single Rose patt............................. **440**
Plate, 8" d., Urn patt...................................... **715**
Plate, 8 1/4" d., Carnation patt. **935**
Plate, 8 1/4" d., Grape patt., wear, stains, faded enamel (ILLUS. center)........................ **297**

Gaudy Dutch Plates

Plate, 8 1/4" d., Carnation patt., wear & repair (ILLUS. left)... **220**
Plate, 8 3/8" d., Butterfly patt., chip on back rim, wear, repair, retouched colors (ILLUS. right)...................................... **385**
Plate, 9 1/4" d., Grape patt.................... **440**
Plate, 9 3/4" d., Sunflower patt. (imperfections)... **825**
Plate, 10" d., Oyster patt., ... **1,540**
Plate, 10" d., Single Rose patt.,.......................... **935**
Plate, 10" d., Urn patt........................... **935**
Soup plate w/flanged rim, Double Rose patt., 10" d.. **1,760**
Soup plate w/flanged rim, Single Rose patt., 10" d.. **1,495**
Soup plate w/flanged rim, Zinnia patt., impressed "Riley" on underside, 10" d. **4,675**
Sugar bowl, cov., Sunflower patt., shell handles, 5 1/2" h. (damage on lid)....................... **770**
Tea set: child's, cov. teapot, creamer, cov. sugar bowl, two cups & saucers, two waste bowls & two plates; Wagon Wheel patt., 11 pcs. (imperfections) **523**
Teapot, cov., Single Rose patt, 5 1/2" h. (restoration on spout)................................... **1,045**
Teapot, cov., Single Rose patt, 6" h. (chip on spout).. **1,210**
Teapot, cov., Urn patt., 6 1/4" h. **825**
Waste bowl, Sunflower patt., 6 1/2" d. **495**
Waste bowl, transitional design & colors w/flowers in shades of orange & green, 6 1/4" d., 3 1/4" h. (minor wear)...................... **55**
Waste bowl, footed deep flaring sides, Dove patt., 6 3/8" d. (wear, stains, hairline)............ **660**

Gaudy Welsh

This is a name for wares made in England for the American market about 1830 to 1860, with some examples dating much later. Decorated with Imari-style flower patterns, often highlighted with copper lustre, it should not be confused with Gaudy Dutch wares, the colors of which differ somewhat.

Compote, 8 1/4 d., 4"h., open, round bowl w/molded designs & painted interior in a Grape patt., underglaze-blue, red & green w/lustre trim (minor wear & scratches) **$358**
Mug, Grape variant in cobalt, green, orange & lustre, 3 3/4" h. **193**
Pitcher, 6 1/8" h., footed squatty bulbous body w/a wide gently flared neck & wide arched spout, high arched loop handle, decorated in red & green w/pink & copper lustre trim in the Llanberis patt., first half 19th c... **220**
Serving tray, Tulip variant in cobalt, orange, yellow, green & lustre, molded handles, 9 1/4" l. (light stains on back)......................... **138**
Soup plate, Oyster patt. in cobalt, orange, unusual teal green & lustre, 10 1/4" d. (minor enamel wear) **83**

Teapot, cov., bulbous body, short fluted foot, flattened domed lid, molded feet, handle, spout & finial, Columbine patt. in orange, cobalt, pink & green w/lustre in band around body & lid, 8" h. **275**
Teapot, cov., bulbous lobed body tapering to flaring base w/fluted rim, w/molded acanthus leaves & flower finial, C-scroll handle, Vine patt. in orange, cobalt, green & lustre, 7" h. (damaged rim flange, chip on lid) **220**

Geisha Girl Wares

Geisha Girl Porcelain features scenes of Japanese women in colorful kimonos along with the flora and architecture of turn-of-the-century Japan. Although bearing an Oriental motif, the wares were produced for Western use in dinnerware and household accessory forms favored during the late 1800s through the early 1940s. There was minimal production during the Occupied Japan period. Less ornate wares were distributed through gift shops and catalogs during the 1960s-70s; some of these are believed to have been manufactured in Hong Kong. Beware overly ornate items with fake Nippon marks that are in current production today, imported from China. More than a hundred porcelain manufacturers and decorating houses were involved with production of these wares during their heyday.

Prices cited here are for excellent to mint condition items. Enamel wear, flaking, hairlines or missing parts all serve to lower the value of an item. Prices in your area may vary.

Over 275 Geisha Girl Porcelain patterns and pattern variations have been catalogued; others are still coming to light.

The most common patterns include:

Bamboo Tree

Battledore

Child Reaching for Butterfly

Fan series

Garden Bench series

Geisha in Sampan series

Meeting series

Parasol series

Pointing series

The rarest patterns include:

... And They're Off

Bellflower

Bicycle Race

Capricious

Elegance in Motion

Fishing series

Foreign Garden

In Flight

Steamboat

The most popular patterns include:

Boat Festival

Butterfly Dancers

By Land and By Sea

Cloud series

Courtesan Processional

Dragonboat

Small Sounds of Summer

So Big

Temple A

A complete listing of patterns and their descriptions can be found in The Collector's Encyclopedia of Geisha Girl Porcelain. Additional patterns discovered since publication of the book are documented in The Geisha Girl Porcelain Newsletter.

References: Litts. E., Collector's Encyclopedia of Geisha Girl Porcelain, Collector Books, 1988; Geisha Girl Porcelain Newsletter, P. O. Box 3394, Morris Plains, NJ 07950.

Geisha Girl Porcelain features scenes of Japanese women in colorful kimonos along with the flora and architecture of old Japan. Although bearing an Oriental motif, the wares were produced for sale in the West and are primarily found in Occidental dinnerware and decorative forms. Geisha Girl Porcelain was primarily an offshoot of the fine Kutani hand-painted porcelains. Less expensive production methods, e.g. stenciling as a foundation for hand painting, enabled their sale to a larger target market. Geisha ware was sold in five-and-dime stores and used as marketing premiums in addition to being sold through distributors and in high-end department stores. Among the hundreds of patterns and producers, quality can vary greatly. Advanced collectors favor those examples that are well executed, with detailed and careful painting and gilding. Beware, however, of overly ornate and gilded items, which are often indicative of modern day reproductions that combine Kutani and Satsuma styling on ware with fake Nippon marks.Collectors tips: Geisha Girl Porcelain is found in a variety of border colors, the most common being shades of red-orange. Other border colors include shades of blue and green as well as multi-colors and patterns. Geisha ware was sold in sets as well as open stock; actual sets will share the same pattern, border color and border embellishments. Cocoa sets were not sold with sugars and creamers. Teacups and saucers, 7" lunch plates, powder jars and hair receivers are among the most common forms found. Despite being destined for the Western market where an even number of accessory items is considered standard, many Japanese sets were produced with five accessory pieces, e.g. individual nut bowls, cups and saucers. Therefore, sets may be found with either five or six accessory pieces. Due to the proliferation of Geisha ware manufacturers, Geisha ware can bear a wide variety of makers' marks. Many examples, however, are unmarked. With perhaps the exception of Nippon collectors, Geisha collectors do not currently place much focus or value on particular marks. Reference: Litts, E. The Collector's Encyclopedia of Geisha Girl Porcelain, Collector Books, 1988 (out of print).

Bowl, Garden Bench C patt., tri-footed, rose, cobalt blue border w/gold embellishments... **$45**
Bowl, 4 1/2" d., 1 1/4" h., rice, Garden Party patt., multicolor border..................................... **15**
Bowl, 8 1/2" d., Drum D patt., pale cobalt blue border, signed "Kutani" **55**

Geisha Girl Trinket Box

Box, cov., trinket, Temple B patt., butterfly-shaped, red-orange border, marked "Japan," 2 3/4 x 2 x 1 1/4" (ILLUS.) **25**
Box, manicure, Lady in Kaga patt., red border, 2 1/2" d... **15**
Butter pat, Lantern Processional patt., red-orange border w/gold lacing **15**

Geisha Girl Candlesticks

Candlesticks, Temple A patt., multicolor border, Noritake's green M-in-wreath Nippon mark, 5 3/4" h., pr. (ILLUS.).............. **250**
Celery set (child's): master plus six salts; Flower Gathering A patt., pine green border w/white dots.. **45**

Geisha Girl Chocolate Pot

Chocolate pot, cov., Parasol F patt., cobalt blue border w/gold lacing, unusual spout, 8 1/2" h. (ILLUS.)... **125**

Chocolate pot, Parasol C patt., red border
w/gold buds, marked "Japan," 9 1/2" h. **45**
Cup & saucer, child's, bouillon w/lid, Pointing D patt., black border, signed in Japa-
nese "Tashiro" **45**
Cup & saucer, child's demitasse, Torii patt.,
gold border, marked "Made in Japan" **15**
Cup & saucer, cocoa, Bamboo Trellis patt.,
wavy red border w/gold lacing......................... **18**
Cup & saucer, tea, four decorative reserves
including Meeting & Parasol patts., or-
nate all-over design **25**
Cup & saucer, tea, Parasol C patt., red bor-
der, marked "Japan".. **10**
Dish, Fan F patt., footed sherbet, red-or-
ange border **35**
Dish, Garden Bench F patt., figural leaf
shape, ornate multicolor border & highly
gilded decoration **25**

Geisha Girl Dresser Tray

Dresser tray, rectangular, Blind Man's Bluff
patt., designs in floral medallions on co-
balt blue ground, 11 1/2 x 8" (ILLUS.)............. **85**
Egg cup, double, Playing Catch patt., red
border **18**

Geisha Girl Hanging Match Holder

Match holder, Temple B patt., hanging type,
red-orange border, unusual divided style,
3 5/8 x 5" (ILLUS.)... **65**
Mustard jar w/lid & spoon, Lunchtime patt.,
blue-green border, marked "Made in Ja-
pan" **25**

Geisha Girl Perfume Bottle

Perfume bottle, Temple A patt., multicolor
border, R K Nippon mark, 4 1/2" h. (IL-
LUS.) **95**

Small Geisha Girl Pitcher

Pitcher, 4 5/8" h., 7" spout to handle, Gardening patt., ornately molded bottom,
swirl fluted body, gold striations & buds
over red-orange border, signed in Japa-
nese "Made in Japan by Kato" (ILLUS.).......... **55**

Geisha Girl Plate with Enamel Detail

Plate, 7 1/4" d., Parasol patt. variant, dark
green border w/unusual raised white
enamel detailing (ILLUS.) **15**
Plate, 8 1/2" d., Child Reaching for Butterfly
patt., red-orange border **15**

Geisha Girl Music Recital B Plate

Plate, 8 1/2" h., Music Recital B patt., cobalt
blue border w/gold lacing (ILLUS.).................. **35**
Platter, 10" l., Duck Watching A patt., gold
border, marked "Made in Japan" **35**

Geisha Girl Ring Tree

Ring tree, Temple B patt., red-orange border w/interior gold lacing, signed "Kutani," 2 3/4" h., 3 1/2" d. (ILLUS.) 30

Salt & pepper shakers, Lantern Boy patt., pine green border, 2 3/4" h., pr. 15

Geisha Girl Sauce Dishes

Sauce dish, Fan A patt., refined, detailed & unusual underglaze blue, signed in Japanese, 2 5/8" d., 1" h. (ILLUS. of two) 30

Sugar & creamer, Chinese Coin patt., signed "Terazawa".. 45

Geisha Girl Carp Sugar Shaker

Sugar shaker, Carp patt., red-orange border, floriate foot w/gold lacing, gold line around neck, gold star on top (ILLUS.).......... 65

Geisha Girl Tea Caddy

Tea caddy, cov., Parasol B patt., cobalt blue, scalloped border w/gold, missing interior lid, 4" h. (ILLUS.) 28

Teapot, cov., Battledore patt., apple green border 35

Teapot, cov., Bow B patt. in reserve on floral backdrop, cobalt blue border w/gold striping, gold upper edge & spout rim 45

Teapot, cov., Dragonboat patt., red & cobalt blue border w/gold lacing, swirl ribbed body 40

Toothpick holder, Carp A patt., three-sided, red border w/interior gold lacing...................... 25

Geisha Girl Serving Tray

Tray, dual-handled, Parasol G patt., gold embellished red-orange border w/ornate interior framing, signed in Japanese "Nagoya Mukomatsu sei," 10 x 13 1/4" (ILLUS.)... 80

Geisha Girl Vase

Vase, 6 3/4" h., Gardening patt., red border w/interior band of gold lacing (ILLUS.)............. 28

Gonder

Lawton Gonder founded Gonder Ceramic Arts in Zanesville, Ohio, in 1941 and it continued in operation until 1957.

The firm produced a higher priced and better quality of commercial art potteries than many firms of the time and employed Jamie Matchet and Chester Kirk, both of whom were outstanding ceramic designers. Several special glazes were developed during the company's history and Gonder even duplicated some museum pieces of Chinese ceramic. In 1955 the firm converted to the production of tile due to increased foreign competition. By 1957 its years of finest production were over.

Increase price ranges as indicated for the following glaze colors: red flambé - 50 percent, antique gold crackle - 70 percent, turquoise Chinese crackle - 40 percent, white Chinese crackle - 30 per cent.

Ashtray, boomerang shape, Mold No. 223, 6 1/4 x 10 1/2" l... $25-40

Center Rest Cigar Ashtray

Ashtray, Center Rest Cigar, marked "Gonder Original 219" in script, Red Flambe glaze, 2 1/4 x 7 1/2" (ILLUS.)........ 50-75

Ashtray, form of a bird, Mold No. 224, 8 7/8" l. 25-40

Ashtray, form of a fish, Mold No. 113, 4 x 9" l. 75-100

Ashtray, round, piecrust rim, Mold No. 807, 9" d... 20-40

Ashtray, "S" Swirl, Mold No. 626, 6 1/2 x 9 1/8" l. 20-30

Ashtray, Sovereign Fluted Rectangular, Mold No. 807, 1 7/8 x 3 1/4" l. 20-30

Ashtray, Sovereign Fluted Round, Mold No.
808, 2 3/4" d. **20-30**
Ashtray, spiked fish, Mold No. 224,
4 x 7 3/8" l. **40-60**
Ashtray, square, Mold No. 1800A, 10 11/16"
sq. **50-75**
Ashtray, square, w/inside concentric ridges,
Mold No. 815, 10" sq. **25-50**
Ashtray, square w/rounded corners, Mold
No. 814, 8" sq. **20-40**

Ashtray with Trojan Horse Head

Ashtray, oblong w/model of Trojan horse
head on rim, Mold No. 548, gunmetal
glaze, 6 x 6 1/2" (ILLUS.) **25-50**
Ashtray, square, Mold No. 805, 9 1/4" w. **20-40**
Ashtray, "S" swirl design, Mold No. a 408,
2 1/2 x 10" **25-35**
Ashtray, square, Mold No. 586 .... **20-30**
Ashtray set: ashtray, cigarette holder; Mold
No. 406, 3 7/8" sq. **50-75**
Ashtrays, Mold No. 808, set of 3, each **20-30**
Bank, figural Sheriff, 8" h. **200-250**
Base, for Chinese Imperial dragon handle
vase No. 535, footed, 4 5/8 x 5 13/16", 2
1/16" h. **45-65**
Base for bottle vase, Mold #527-B **25-50**
Base for ginger jar, Mold No. 530-B **100-125**
Basket, shell shape w/overhead handle,
Mold No. 674, 7 x 8" **25-50**
Basket, Mold No. L-19, 9 x 13" **20-30**
Bell, figural "Sovereign Bonnet Lady," Mold
No. 800, 3 1/2" h. **50-75**
Beverage set: 8" h. pitcher & six 5" h. mugs;
LaGonda patt., Mold No. 917 & 909, the
set. **50-75**
Book end, model of horse, Mold No. 582,
10" h. **100-125**
Book ends, in the form of horses, Mold No.
211, 10" h. **100-125**

Trojan Horse Head Book Ends

Book ends, model of Trojan horse head,
mottled green glaze, Mold No. 220,
7 1/2" h., pr. (ILLUS.) **100-150**
Bowl, 4 3/8" d., fruit, La Gonda, Mold No.
905 .... **15-20**
Bowl, 5 11/16" d., 1 3/8" h., w/small leaves,
Mold No. B-17 .... **40-60**
Bowl, 6 7/8 x 11 7/8", 2 1/2" h., S-shaped,
Mold No. 592 .... **20-40**
Bowl, 8 1/2" w., 5 1/8" h., hexagonal, w/Chi-
nese figures, Mold No. 742 .... **25-40**
Bowl, 8" d., 2 3/8" h., Mold No. 715 .... **15-25**
Bowl, 8" d., 2 7/8" h., fluted, Mold No. 629 or
H-29 .... **20-30**
Bowl, 13" d., oak leaf design, Mold No. 591 .. **40-60**
Bowl, low, scalloped tulip shape, Mold No.
523 .... **35-50**
Butter warmer, cover & candleholder base,
Mold No. 996, 2 1/2 x 4 1/2", 3 pcs. **25-40**
Candleholder, cubic, Mold No. 726, 3 x 3",
2 1/4" h. **20-30**
Candleholder, fluted, Mold No. 314, 414, E-
14, 4 5/8" w., 1 7/8" h. **10-15**
Candleholder, Mold No. 517, Double Cornu-
copia, 3 3/4" w. x 6 7/8" l., 4" h. **60-80**
Candleholder, Mold No. 518, Triangle,
12 1/2" w. x 10 1/4" l. **100-125**
Candleholder, Mold No. 520/C, Freeform,
4 1/4" w. x 5 1/2" l., 1 13/16" h. **20-35**
Candleholder, single shell, Mold No. 506,
2 3/4" w., 4 5/8" h. **10-20**
Candleholders, La Gonda, Mold No. 915,
2 x 2, 2 1/8" h. **15-20**
Candleholders, Mold No. 521/C, Shell,
6 1/4" l., 3 3/4" h., pr. **25-35**
Candleholders, starfish, Mold No. 501,
7 7/8" w., each **25-35**
Candleholders, model of dolphin, Mold No.
561, 2 1/4 x 5", pr. **40-60**
Casserole, cov., handled lid, La Gonda,
Mold No. 953, 5 1/4 x 8 1/4", 4" h. **20-30**
Casserole, cov., handled lid, La Gonda,
Mold No. 954, 6 1/2 x 10 1/8", 5 1/4" h. **30-40**
Casserole, cov., tab handled lid, La Gonda,
Mold No. 955, 6 3/4 x 11", 5 3/8" h. **75-100**
Chop plate, oblong, Mold No. 912,
8 7/8 x 12 1/4" **100-125**
Cigarette box, cov., Mold. No. 806,
3 1/2 x 4 3/8", 2 5/8" h. **60-80**
Cigarette cup, Sovereign, Mold No. 804,
2 5/8" h. **40-60**
Cigarette holder, Mold No. 804, 2 5/8" h. **40-60**
Console bowl, fluted, w/flowers, Mold No. J-
71, 5 1/8 x 12 3/4", 4 3/4" h. **50-75**
Console bowl, Mold No. 520,
8 7/8 w. x 11 1/4" l, 2 5/8" h. **50-75**

Shell-shaped Console Bowl

Console bowl, oblong shell-molded w/point-
ed ends & starfish molded at the sides,
speckled brown on yellow glaze, Mold
No. 500 (ILLUS.) **100-125**

Console bowl, w/dolphins, Mold No. 556, 11 1/4" d., 4 5/8" h. **55-70**

Console bowl, lobed incurved sides, Mold E-12, 2 1/2 x 7" **5-15**

Console bowl, crescent moon shape, Mold J-55, 5 x 12"...................... **15-30**

Console bowl, seashell shape, Mold No. 521, 7 x 12"...................... **25-40**

Console bowl, rectangular base, body w/relief-molded center fan shape flanked by cornucopia forms, Mold K-14, 7 1/2 x 12 1/2" **150-200**

Console bowl, seashell design, Mold No. 505, 7 1/4 x 17 1/2" **50-65**

Console set: 14" l. bowl & pr. of 5" h. candleholders; shell shape, Mold Nos. 505 & 552, the set **100-125**

Console set: 16" l. bowl & pr. of candleholders; "Banana Boat" bowl, Mold Nos. 565 & 567, the set **75-100**

Cookie jar, cov., bulbous shape w/sleeping dog finial, Mold No. 924, 8 1/2" h. **75-100**

Cookie jar, cov., Pirate, Mold No. 951, 10 1/2" or 12" h. **1,500-1,800**

Cookie jar, cov., "Ye Olde Oaken Bucket," brown w/tan & yellow glaze, marked "Gonder Original 974" in script, only two known to exist, 7" h. RARE......................

Cookie jar, cov., Pirate, 8" h. **200-250**

Cookie jar, cov., Mold No. P-24, 8 1/2" h........ **15-30**

Cookie jar, cov., Sheriff, Mold No. 950, green glaze, 12" h. **1,200-1,400**

Cornucopia-vase, flattened form, square base, Mold 305 E-5, 3 3/8 x 7", 7 3/8" h. **15-30**

Cornucopia-vase, ribbed, Mold No. 360, 7" h. **20-35**

Cornucopia-vase, w/round handles, Mold No. 380, 7" h...................... **20-35**

Cornucopia-vase, leaves at base, Mold No. 691, 7 1/2" h. **50-75**

Cornucopia-vase, held by figural hand, oval base, Mold No. 675, 7 1/2 x 8" **75-100**

Cornucopia-vase, ribbed, curled handles, Mold No. 419, 8" h...................... **30-45**

Cornucopia-vase, shell form, Mold No. H-84, 8" h. **25-40**

Cornucopia-vase, square base, Mold No. H-14, 9" h. **20-35**

Cornucopia-vase, w/leaf design, Mold No. J-61, 9" h...................... **50-65**

Cornucopia-vase, uneven double swirl design, Mold No. H-48, 4 x 9 3/4" **50-60**

Cornucopia-vase, on flat square base, Mold No. J-66, 10" l...................... **20-35**

Cornucopia-vase, double loop handle, Mold J-69, 11" h...................... **50-65**

Cream soup dish, handled, La Gonda, Mold No. 908, 5 1/2 x 5 3/4", 3 3/8" h. **20-25**

Creamer, La Gonda, Mold No. 907, 7" w., 4" h...................... **15-20**

Creamer, La Gonda, Mold No. P-33, 3 1/2" h. **15-25**

Creamer, squashed shape, Mold No. 404, 7" h...................... **25-40**

Creamer, squashed shape, Mold No. 904........ **8-10**

Custard, cov., handled, La Gonda, Mold No. 952, 3 1/4" h. **15-25**

Dish, flat, dog bone shape, Mold No., 2 x 11 1/2"...................... **25-50**

Gonder Slant-top Ewer

Ewer, bulbous base tapering to a tall slanted top w/pointed spout & integral handle, Mold 410, Chinese Turquoise Crackle glaze (ILLUS.)...................... **75-100**

Ewer, fluted, Mold No. E-60, 6" h. **5-15**

Ewer, "Z" handle, Mold No. E-65, 6 1/4" h. **10-20**

Ewer, Mold No. H-73, 8" h. **15-25**

Carafe-shaped Ewer

Ewer, w/stopper, carafe-shaped, gunmetal glaze, Mold No. 994, 8" (ILLUS.).............. **75-100**

Ewer, Mold H-33, 9" h...................... **30-50**

Ewer, scrolled handle, Mold No. H-606 & 606, 9" h...................... **50-75**

Ewer, Mold No. J-25, 8 x 11"...................... **50-75**

Ewer, shell-shaped, Mold No. 508, 14" h. (no starfish) **75-100**

Ewer, shell-shaped w/starfish on base, Mold No. 508, 14" h. **40-60**

Figure group, pair of chair bearers w/chair, Mold No. 765, 12 1/2" h........................... **150-175**

Figure of bearded Oriental man, Mold No. 775, 8 5/8" h...................... **50-60**

Figure of Chinese peasant, kneeling & reaching forward, Mold No. 546, 4 1/2 x 6 1/2"...................... **25-40**

Figure of Chinese peasant, standing figure, Mold No. 545, 8" h... **15-30**
Figure of coolie, kneeling & bending forward, Mold No. 547, 5" h.............................. **15-30**
Figure of Fatima, w/rosary, Mold No. 772, 9 1/2" h.. **75-100**
Figure of madonna, standing, Mold No. 549, 9 1/4" h.. **50-75**
Figure of Oriental male, Mold No. 773, 11" h.. **40-60**
Figure of Oriental man, Mold No. 551, 7" h.... **40-60**
Figure of Oriental mandarin, Mold No. 755, 8 3/4" h... **50-75**
Figure of Oriental woman, holding ginger jar, Mold No. 573, 4 7/8" h. **40-60**
Figure of Oriental woman, w/hands together, Mold No. 570, 6 1/4" h. **40-60**
Figure of Oriental woman, w/right hand to head, Mold No. 776, 9" h............................. **60-80**
Figure of turbaned woman w/baskets, Mold No. 762, 14 1/2" h.. **50-75**
Flower frog, three-tier flower, Mold No. 250, 5 7/8" w., 2 5/8" h. **100-125**
Ginger jar, cov., square, 10" h.................... **100-150**
Ginger jar, cov., decorated w/Oriental dragon on pedestal base, Mold No. 533, 11" h., 3 pcs... **150-200**
Jar, cov., in the form of an Oriental plum, Mold No. 529, 9 3/16" h.......................... **125-150**
Lamp, Aladdin oil style, no number.............. **75-100**
Lamp, bullet-shaped, Mold No. 2228, 11" h.. **75-100**
Lamp, Double Swirl, Mold No. 2020, 30" h. ... **40-60**
Lamp, Driftwood, Mold No. 2017, 30" h. **75-100**
Lamp, ewer form, Mold No. 4046, 11" h. **35-55**
Lamp, figural, elephant, Mold No. 207, 10 3/4" l., 9 1/4" h. **125-150**
Lamp, figural, young woman, Mold No. 587, 4 1/4" sq., 9 3/16" h................................. **125-150**
Lamp, Geometric Planes, Mold No. 4037, 9" w., 10" h.. **40-60**
Lamp, Hollywood Headboard Unit Books, Mold No. 5087, 11 1/2" w., 6 3/8" h. **125-150**
Lamp, Horse Head TV or Console, Mold No. 1901, 14 3/8" h... **75-100**
Lamp, Keystone, Mold No. 4085, 9 1/4" w., 12 3/4" h.. **40-60**
Lamp, Mill TV, Mold No. 1905, 12" w., 8 1/4" h.. **75-100**
Lamp, Mold No. 522, Scarla Sunfish, 10" l., 9" h... **100-125**
Lamp, Mold No. H-77, double handle w/vine leaves, metal base, 7 3/4" w., 8 1/2" h. **50-75**
Lamp, no number, "LG," 8 1/2" h., 6 3/8" w. **75-100**
Lamp, Scroll, Mold No. 2255, 9 1/4" w., 12 3/4" h.. **75-100**
Lamp, Swirl, Mold No. 3060, 7 3/4" w., 5 1/2" h... **40-60**
Lamp, Tall Bottle, Mold No. 5506, 17 1/2" h. **100-125**
Lamp, Vine & Leaves, Mold No. 3031, 9 1/2" h.. **40-60**
Lamp, model of Foo dog, 8" h. **125-150**
Lamp, cookie jar shape, Mold No. P-24, 8 1/2" h... **20-40**
Lamp, model of Trojan horse head, Mold No. 540, 10" h. **75-100**
Lamp, driftwood design, 12" h. **25-50**

Lamp, model of two horse heads, 12" h. **40-50**
Lamp, Oriental dual figures on side, 16" h. **150-200**

Dogwood Globe Lamp Base

Lamp base, Dogwood Globe, Catalog #5507, no mark, Italian Pink Crackle glaze, scarce, 15 1/4" h. (ILLUS.)........... **175-200**

Figure Eight Swirl Lamp Base

Lamp base, Figure Eight Swirl, no mark, Gunmetal Black glaze, 15 5/8" h. (ILLUS.)... **75-100**

Gonder Frappe Lamp Base

Lamp base, Frappe, Catalog #2067, no mark, Rutile Green w/Green Overlay glaze, 15 3/4" h. (ILLUS.).............................. **50-75**

Gonder Lyre-form Lamp Base

Lamp base, Lyre style, no mark, Wine
Brown glaze, 15" h. (ILLUS.) **100-125**

Gonder Wine Brown Lamp Base

Lamp base, Rectangular Flower Center, no
mark, Wine Brown glaze, 4 1/8 x 6 1/8",
11" h. (ILLUS.)... **25-40**

Rose Lady Head Lamp or Figurine

Lamp base, Rose Lady Head, no mark,
Light Blue glaze, Mold #588, can be used
as figurine, 12 1/4" h. (ILLUS.)............... **150-175**
Lamps, Double Link, Mold No. 4039,
24 1/2" h., pr.. **45-65**
Lazy Susan, medium, Mold No. 8,
11 1/2" d... **80-110**
Model of cat, seated "Imperial Cat," Mold
No. 521, 12" h. **200-250**
Model of elephant, Mold No. 207, 11 1/2" l.,
8 7/8" h.. **75-100**
Model of elephant, Mold No. 209, 8" l,
6 1/8" h... **40-50**

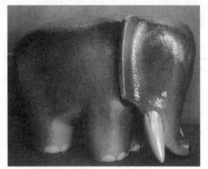

Gonder Model of an Elephant

Model of elephant, stylized standing animal
w/greenish brown glaze & ivory trim,
Mold 108 (ILLUS.) **400-500**
Model of frog, standing, pistachio w/black
trim glaze, experimental, no mold num-
ber or mark, 10 1/2" h. RARE................................
Model of gamecock, w/flowers, Mold No.
525, hard to find, 7 1/8" w., 10 3/4" h..... **150-175**
Model of gamecock, w/plain tail feathers,
Mold No. 525, hard to find, 7 1/8" w.,
10 3/4" h... **150-175**
Model of head of Chinese coolie, Mold No.
541, 11 1/2" w., 11" h............................... **400-500**
Model of head of racing horse, Mold 874,
9 1/4" h... **165-185**
Model of hen w/worms, Mold No. 525, hard
to find, 9" l., 6 3/4" h.................................. **125-150**
Model of horse head, Mold No. 872, 15" l,
7" h.. **150-175**

Large Reclining Panther by Gonder

Model of panther, large, reclining, marked "Gonder Original 210" in script, Royal

Purple glaze, 6 1/2 x 18 1/2" (ILLUS.)... **200-250**

Large Walking Panther by Gonder

Model of Panther, large, walking, no mark, Pistachio glaze, Mold #206, 4 1/8 x 18 1/2" (ILLUS.) **100-150**

Model of panther, recumbent, Mold No. 217, 12" l. **30-50**

Model of panther, standing, Mold No. 205, 12" h. **40-60**

Model of panther, recumbent, Mold No. 217, 15" l. **75-100**

Model of penguin, Mold No. A-9, 3 1/4" w., 4 7/8" h. **25-50**

Model of racing horse head, Mold No. 576, 13 1/2" l., 5 3/4" h. **150-175**

Model of rooster, Mold No. 212, scarce, 4" w., 10 1/2" h. **150-175**

Model of two running deer, Mold No. 690, 9 1/4" l., 6" h. **75-100**

Models of geese, one looking down & one w/neck stretched upward, Mold Nos. B-14 & B-15, 3 1/2 & 5 1/2" h., pr. **25-40**

Mug, swirled wood finish, Mold No. 902, 5" h. **15-30**

Pedestal base, Mold No. 533-B, 6" d. **25-50**

Pitcher, lizard handle, slotted, Mold No. J-54, 8 1/2" l., 10 5/8" h. **100-125**

Pitcher, pistol grip, Mold No. 102, 9 1/8" h. **125-150**

Pitcher, twisted twig handle, Mold No. 301, 7 1/2" l., 7 7/8" h. **100-125**

Pitcher, 6 1/2" h., squatty bulbous base, cylindrical neck w/flared rim, zigzag handle, Mold No. E-73 & E-373................................ **25-35**

Pitcher, 7" h., ruffled lip, Mold No. 1206.......... **25-50**

Pitcher, 5 x 8", ridged woodtone glaze, Mold No. 901 .... **50-75**

Pitcher, 8 1/8" h., LaGonda patt., Mold No. 917 .... **40-50**

Pitcher, 9" h., plain lip, Mold 1205.................... **50-75**

Pitcher, 9 1/4" h., Classical style, "606 Gonder USA" mark in script, Coral Lustre glaze, Mold No. 606 (ILLUS., next column)... **75-100**

Pitcher, 10" h., Mold No. 682 .... **50-75**

Gonder Pitcher in Coral Lustre Glaze

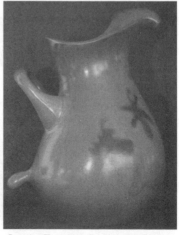

Gonder Two-handled Water Pitcher

Indian Porters Bearing Planter Bowl

Pitcher, 12 1/2" h., water, two-handled, tan glaze decorated w/black figures, Mold No. 104 (ILLUS.)...................................... **350-450**

Planter, African Violet two-piece w/flared top, Mold No. 792, 5 1/4" sq., 5 1/8" h. **20-40**

Planter, cov., rectangular w/ridges & leaves, Mold No. 1004, 5 1/2 x 9 1/2", 4 1/2" h. **35-50**

Planter, double-footed, Mold No. 711, 5 x 8 5/8", 2 7/8" h. **15-25**

Planter, "End of Day," flared square shape, four feet, Mold No. 749/20, 6 1/4" sq., 6" h.. **40-50**

Planter, "End of Day," footed flared rectangle, Mold No. 779/20, 4 3/4 x 10", 3 1/2" h. **40-50**

Planter, figure of Bali woman w/gourds, no bikini top, Mold No. 763, 9 1/8" w., 12 3/8" h. **150-175**

Planter, figure of Gay 90s man w/basket, no mold number, 13 1/4" h. **150-175**

Planter, figure of Gay 90s woman w/basket, no mold number, 13 1/4" h. **150-175**

Planter, figures of Basque dancers, Mold No. 766, 12" h. **125-150**

Planter, four-footed flared square pedestal, Mold No. 753, 7 x 7 1/4", 7 1/4" h............... **25-40**

Planter, four-footed small flared square, Mold No. 748, 5 x 5 1/4", 3 7/8" h. **15-30**

Planter, gondola or lamp, no mold number, 5 3/4" h., 14" l... **60-80**

Planter, Indian Porters Bearing Planter Bowl, marked "© 1950 Gonder Ceramic Arts" in block print, Victorian Wine glaze, Mold No. 764, very hard to find w/bowl, 12 1/4" h., the set (ILLUS., top of page) **100-150**

Large Conch Shell Planter

Planter, Large Conch Shell, no mark, Chinese White Crackle glaze, Mold No. 793,

very hard to find, 5 3/4 x 17 1/4", 8" h. (ILLUS.).. **200-250**

Planter, large rectangle w/round corners, Mold No. 752, 4 1/2 x 9 1/4", 3 1/8" h. **10-20**

Planter, large swan, Mold No. L-14, 8 1/4" h. **50-75**

Planter, Mold No. 510, single hooked square, 3 1/4" w. x 5 3/4" l., 2 3/4" h. **15-25**

Planter, Mold No. 513, single hooked squares, 5 3/4" w. x 5 3/4" l., 2 5/8" h. **20-30**

Planter, reclining panther, Mold No. 237, 5 1/2" h., 14 7/8" l. **125-150**

Planter, rectangular pagoda, Mold No. 727, 5 x 12 1/2", 2 3/4" h. **25-35**

Planter, shell cornucopia, Mold No. 692, 5 1/4 x 9", 4 3/4" h. **50-75**

Planter, square ridges & leaves, Mold No. 1001, 5 1/8" sq., 3 3/4" h. **15-25**

Planter, square w/ridge & leaves, Mold No. 1002, 5 1/4 x 5 1/2", 5 3/16" h. **15-25**

Planter, twist shoe strap, Mold No. 585, 4 5/8 x 10 5/8", 4" h. **40-60**

Planter, Zig Zag, Mold No. 737, 11 3/4 l., 2 1/2" h. **15-30**

Planter, w/hole, Mold No. 738, 2 3/4 x 4 1/4" (top to Mold No. 724) **5-25**

Planter, footed, square w/hole in base, Mold No. 706, 5" h. **10-20**

Planter, bulbous body w/tab handles, decorated w/relief-molded flowers, Mold No. H-83, 5 1/2" h. **50-60**

Planter, model of swan, Mold No. E-44, 5 1/2" h. **5-15**

Planter, figural Madonna, Mold E-303 & R-303, 4 x 6" **10-20**

Planter, square flared form, Mold No. 733, 2 1/2 x 6 1/2" **15-30**

Planter, rectangular, Mold No. 701, 5 3/4 x 7 1/2" **15-30**

Planter, basket shape w/overhead handle, Mold H-39, 7 x 8" **10-20**

Planter, model of swan, Mold No. J-31, 8 1/2" h. **30-45**

Planter, model of wishing well, 6 1/2 x 9 1/4" **100-125**

Planter, model of Chinese sampan (junk), Mold No. 550, 10" l. **10-20**

Planter, figural nude w/deer, Mold No. 593, 9 1/2 x 14" **250-300**

Planter, figural, Oriental water carriers, gold trim, 14" **200-250**

Planter, figural, Bali girl carrying basket on head, 14 1/2" h. **50-75**

Planter, model of large Chinese sampan (junk), Mold No. 520, 15" l. **25-40**

Planter, two-footed w/flared top, Mold No. 716 .... **25-40**

Planter bottom, Mold No. 724, for African Violet planter No. 738, 4 x 5" **5-10**

Planter set, figurine of doe w/turned head, side planters, Mold No. 213, 3 x 4 1/2", 10 5/8" h., the set **75-100**

Planter set: Oriental man & woman water bearers w/baskets; Mold No. 777, man 10 1/2" w., 14 1/8" h., woman 10 1/4" w., 14 1/4" h., each **50-75**

Planter set: top & bottom; Mold No. 738, African Violet, 2 3/4" h., 4 1/4" w., the set **15-25**

Planter top, No. 1000, for African Violet planter No. 738, 4 x 4", 5 1/4" h. **25-40**

Planters, figural, no number, Gay '90s man & woman baskets, man 3 1/4" h., woman, 14" h., each **150-175**

Planters, for doe or rooster figurine, Mold No. 218, 3 3/4 x 3, 2 3/4" h., pr. **25-50**

Planters, figural Bali man & Bali woman w/buckets, 14" h., pr. **60-80**

Plaque, African mask, Mold No. 231, 5 1/8 x 8 1/4" **75-100**

Plaque, African mask, Mold No. 232, 5 x 7 3/4" **75-100**

Plaque, African mask, no number. **75-100**

Plate, square, LaGonda patt. **10-20**

Divided Relish Dish

Relish dish, shallow, divided, six lobe-form sections, mottled yellow glaze, Mold No. 871, 11 x 18" (ILLUS.) **90-120**

Salt & pepper shakers, La Gonda, Mold No. 913, 7 3/4" d., 3" h. **15-20**

Saucer, La Gonda, Mold No. 904, 5 3/8" d. **8-10**

Server, La Gonda, Mold No. 916, 5 7/8 x 9 5/8" **20-30**

Stack set: sugar & creamer; La Gonda, Mold No. 923, 3 7/8 x 4", 2 7/8" h. **30-40**

Sugar bowl, Mold No. P-33, 4 5/8" h. **15-25**

Tankard, shell, Mold No. 400, 9 1/2" h. **150-175**

Tankard, Mold No. M-9, 14" h. **60-80**

Tea cup, La Gonda, Mold No. 903, 2 1/2 x 3 1/4" **8-10**

Teapot, cov., coiled beehive, Mold No. 662, 5 3/4" h. **75-100**

Teapot, cov., rectangular, La Gonda, Mold No. 396, 6 1/4" h. **50-75**

Gonder La Gonda Pattern Teapot

Teapot, cov., upright rectangular form, LaGonda patt., creamy yellow glaze, Mold 914 (ILLUS.). **50-75**

Teapot, cov., vertical ridges, Mold No. P-424, 6 7/16" h. **75-100**

Teapot, cov., Mold No. P-31, 6 1/2" h. **15-25**

Tray, 8-section, Mold No. 100, 10 15/16 x 19 1/4" **150-200**

Tray, shell, Mold No. 865, 12 x 14" **175-225**

Tray, pillow form, flat, Mold No. 544, 7 x 10" **40-60**

Tray, rectangular, flat, Mold No. 700 .... **20-35**
TV lamp, figural "Comedy & Tragedy Mask,"
 Mold No. 519, 6 1/2 x 10" **75-100**
TV lamp, model of Chanticleer rooster,
 9 1/2 x 14" **40-60**
TV lamp, model of masted ship, 14" h. **15-25**
Urn, Sovereign cigarette footed, Mold No.
 801, 3 1/2" h. **40-60**
Vase, applied leaf, Mold No. 370, E-70 .... **20-35**
Vase, large cylindrical, Mold No. 712 .... **25-35**
Vase, modeled pillow, Mold No. 506 .... **50-75**
Vase, Mold No. 511, double hooked square,
 5 1/2" w., x 5 1/2" l. **40-60**
Vase, pigtail handles, Mold No. H-608 .... **100-150**

Gonder Oriental-style Vase

Vase, squared Oriental-style w/angular
 neck handles, pale green glaze, Mold
 537 (ILLUS.) **100-125**
Vase, 2 1/2" h., square mini, Mold No. 407 .... **15-20**
Vase, 3 1/2" h., footed Chinese rectangle,
 Mold No. 707 .... **15-25**
Vase, 3 1/2" h., small round, Mold No. 745 .... **15-20**
Vase, 5" h., cylindrical, Mold No. 710 .... **10-20**
Vase, 5" h., small square footed, Mold No.
 706 .... **10-20**
Vase, 5 x 5" sq., flared, leaf decoration,
 Mold No. 384 .... **25-35**
Vase, 5 5/8" h., olive branch, Mold No. 361 ... **50-75**
Vase, 5 3/4" h., square pillow form, Mold
 No. 705 .... **10-20**
Vase, 6" h., bulbous base w/flared top, leaf
 decoration, Mold E-66 .... **10-20**
Vase, 6" h., fan shape w/relief-molded scroll
 design, Mold No. H-82 .... **25-35**
Vase, 6" h., footed, bulbous lobed base
 w/flaring square top, Mold E-71 .... **20-35**
Vase, 6" h., footed, squatty bulbous base,
 cylindrical neck w/flared rim, applied leaf
 decoration, Mold E-68 .... **15-30**
Vase, 6" h., waisted twisted form, Mold
 E-64 .... **10-20**
Vase, 6 1/16" h., "Z"-handled ewer, Mold
 No. 365, E-65, E-365 .... **15-25**
Vase, 6 1/8" h., small V horn, Mold No.
 E-5 .... **30-50**

Vase, 5 x 6 1/4", rectangular, Mold No.
 709 .... **10-25**
Vase, 6 1/4" h., applied leaf, Mold No.
 E368 .... **20-25**
Vase, 6 1/4" h., square banded, Mold No.
 369, 703, E-69, E-369 .... **20-30**

Gonder Butterfly-shaped Vase

Vase, 6 3/8" h., 8 1/2" w., Ribbed Fan, but-
 terfly-like shape, marked "Gonder H-82
 USA" in script, Antique Gold Crackle
 glaze (ILLUS.) **40-60**
Vase, 6 1/2" h., bulbous base w/scalloped
 trumpet-form neck, Mold E-49 .... **10-25**
Vase, 6 1/2" h., footed bulbous base
 w/trumpet-form neck, leaf-shaped han-
 dles, Mold No. E-67 .... **15-25**
Vase, 6 1/2" h., hourglass shape w/large
 applied leaf, Mold E-70 .... **15-25**
Vase, 6 1/2" h., large flat rectangular, Mold
 No. 708 .... **15-25**
Vase, 6 1/2" h., metallic-look pitcher form,
 Mold No. 382 .... **30-45**
Vase, 6 1/2" h., Mold No. 216, double horn,
 11 1/2" w. **50-75**
Vase, 6 1/2" h., ribbed bulbous base w/cy-
 lindrical neck, angled handles, Mold No.
 E-48 .... **10-25**
Vase, 6 1/2" h., ribbed, swirl design, Mold
 No. 381 .... **20-35**
Vase, 6 1/2" h., ribbon handle ewer, Mold
 No. 373, E-73, E-373 .... **25-35**
Vase, 6 1/2" h., seashell shape, Mold No.
 216 .... **70-90**
Vase, 6 1/2" h., two-handled, draped invert-
 ed bell design, Mold No. 418 .... **40-55**
Vase, 6 1/2" h., urn shape w/leaf design,
 single handle, Mold No. H-80 .... **20-30**
Vase, 6 5/8" h., shell & seaweed, Mold No.
 402, H-401 .... **75-100**
Vase, 6 3/4" h., opposite leaf handle, Mold
 No. H-602 .... **75-100**
Vase, 4 1/2 x 7", ovoid body w/flared top,
 shoulder handles, Mold E-1 .... **5-15**
Vase, 7" h., bottle form, Mold No. 1203 .... **30-50**
Vase, 7" h., pinched leaf design, Mold No.
 E-372 .... **20-35**
Vase, 7" h., ribbed cornucopia, Mold No.
 360 .... **20-35**
Vase, 7" h., small flat horn, Mold No. 305, E-
 5 .... **15-30**
Vase, 7 1/16" h., 6 1/2 x 6 3/8", 4-footed
 large flared square, Mold No. 750 .... **25-35**
Vase, 6 1/2 x 7 1/4", scroll footed, Mold No.
 E-4, 304 .... **30-40**
Vase, 7 3/8" h., Mold No. 303, E-3, flower
 design **10-20**

Vase, 4 1/2 x 7 1/2", footed, model of single flower, Mold No. E-3 .... **10-20**

Vase, 7 1/2" h., basketweave w/knothole design, Mold No. 867 .... **30-50**

Vase, 7 1/2" h., flared foot below inverted pear-shaped body, flaring lobed top, Mold No. E-6.. **10-20**

Vase, 7 x 7 1/2", model of seashell w/two dolphins at base, Mold No. 558................... **50-75**

Vase, 7 x 7 1/2", two-handled, bulbous base w/wide flaring neck, Mold H-42 .... **25-35**

Vase, 7 3/4" h., bottle form, Mold No. 1209 .... **50-70**

Vase, 7 3/4" h., two-handled, Mold No. H-49.. **40-60**

Vase, 7 7/8" h., raised circular bud, Mold No. 1208.. **40-60**

Vase, 6 x 8", model of starfish, Mold No. H-79 .... **15-25**

Vase, 7 1/4 x 8", cuspidor top, Mold No. 559 .... **200-250**

Vase, 8" h., flared bulb to square top, Oriental design, Mold No. 537 or 718 .... **100-125**

Vase, 8" h., flaring form w/relief-molded swans at base, Mold No. H-47 .... **20-30**

Vase, 8" h., flat, Lotus design, Mold No. 402.. **25-40**

Vase, 8" h., medium ewer form, Mold No. 673, H-73 .... **15-25**

Vase, 8" h., raised circular ewer, Mold No. 410 .... **25-40**

Vase, 8" h., rectangular footed maze, Mold No. 401 .... **35-50**

Vase, 8" h., two-handled, relief-molded fern decoration, Mold No. H-77 .... **20-35**

Vase, 8 5/16" h., butterfly w/flowers, Mold No. H-88... **50-75**

Vase, 8 1/16" h., berries & leaves, Mold No. H-55 .... **75-100**

Vase, 8 1/4" h., pine cone, Mold No. 507 .... **65-85**

Vase, 8 3/8" h., medium cylindrical, Mold No. 711 .... **15-75**

Vase, 5 x 8 1/2, rectangular, Mold No. H-74 .... **15-25**

Vase, 6 x 8 1/2", modified rectangle w/raised flowers, Mold No. 687 .... **50-75**

Vase, 7 x 8 1/2", flaring body w/one angled handle at rim, the other at base, Mold No. H-56 .... **15-30**

Vase, 8 1/2" h., bottle form, Mold No. 1204.. **40-60**

Vase, 8 1/2" h., bottle form, Mold No. 1211.. **50-75**

Vase, 8 1/2" h., footed bulbous body w/flaring rim, triple loop handles, Mold No. H-75 .... **15-25**

Vase, 8 1/2" h., model of a stylized swan, Mold No. 511... **35-50**

Vase, 8 1/2" h., rectangular, decorated w/relief-molded crane, Mold No. H-76 ...... **30-40**

Vase, 8 1/2" h., relief-molded double leaf form w/berries, Mold J-70 .... **35-50**

Vase, 8 1/2" h., six-fluted top w/raised leaf design, Mold H-11 .... **20-35**

Vase, 8 1/2" h., tapering pillow form, Mold No. 702... **35-50**

Vase, 8 1/2" h., triple leaf form, Mold No. H-67 .... **15-25**

Vase, 8 1/2" h., two-handled, flared foot below horizontal ribbed base & bulbous lobed top, Mold No. H-52 .... **15-30**

Vase, 8 5/8" h., flat multi-leaf design, Mold No. 478, H-78.. **30-45**

Vase, 4 1/4 x 8 3/4", fluted handle, Mold H-34 .... **15-30**

Vase, 6 1/2 x 9", model of stylized horse w/wings, Mold No. 553 .... **10-25**

Vase, 6 x 9", basketweave design w/flared top, Mold H-36 .... **40-50**

Vase, 6 x 9", flame shape, Mold No. H-69 ..... **25-40**

Vase, 6 x 9", tulip form, Mold No. H-68.......... **15-30**

Vase, 9 1/8" h., 4 x 6 3/16", tapering cylindrical form w/relief-molded pea pod decoration, Mold No. 487 H-87 .... **30-40**

Gonder Sunfish Vase

Vase, 9" h., 10 1/4" w., Scarla Sunfish, marked "Gonder 522," Sea Swirl glaze (ILLUS.).. **100-125**

Vase, 9" h., bottle form, Mold No. 1210.......... **25-50**

Vase, 9" h., double open handles, Mold No. 604.. **75-100**

Vase, 9" h., footed, square double bulb form, Mold No. 607 & H-607................... **125-150**

Vase, 9" h., footed, two-handled, bulbous base, squared top, Mold No. H-7.............. **20-30**

Vase, 9" h., gazelle, Mold No. 215 .... **50-75**

Vase, 9" h., lyre shape, Mold No. J-57 .... **75-100**

Vase, 9" h., shell form, three dolphins at base, Mold No. H-85................................... **50-65**

Vase, 9" h., squatty bulbous base, tapering cylindrical neck, twisted handles, Mold No. H-5... **25-35**

Vase, 9" h., standing Oriental male, Mold No. 519... **15-25**

Vase, 9" h., tieback drape design, Mold No. 605 & H-605... **50-75**

Gonder Mother-of-Pearl Glaze Vase

Vase, 8 1/2" h., 6 3/4" d., Leaf with Berries, Mold #H-86 or H-486, marked "H-86 Gonder U.S.A.," Mother-of-Pearl glaze (ILLUS.).. **20-35**

Vase, 9" h., two-handled fan vase, Mold No.
H-10 .... **15-30**
Vase, 9 1/4" h., fan shape, Mold No. H-601... **35-50**
Vase, 9 1/4" h., footed leaf form w/open cir-
cle in center, Mold No. H-603 .... **35-50**
Vase, 9 1/4" h., large square, footed, Mold
No. 704 .... **25-40**
Vase, 9 3/8" h., swan handle, Mold No.
J-65 .... **100-125**

Gonder Vase on Base

Vase, 9 3/8" h., w/base, bottle form w/bul-
bous bottom in Chinese Turquoise
Crackle glaze, sits on base in White
glaze, marked on base "Gonder 527B,"
very hard to find as set, the set
(ILLUS.) **150-200**
Vase, 9 1/2" h., model of fawn head, Mold
No. 518 .... **75-100**
Vase, 9 1/2" h., two-handled, twisted balus-
ter-form body, Mold No. H-62 .... **15-30**
Vase, 9 9/16" h., large double shell cornuco-
pia, Mold No. 509 .... **150-175**
Vase, 9 5/8" h., Chinese w/uneven handles,
Mold No. 720 .... **75-100**
Vase, 9 3/4" h., Art Deco cactus, Mold No.
686 .... **60-80**
Vase, 9 3/4" h., bottle form w/ridges, Mold
No. 383 .... **50-75**
Vase, 10" h., Art Deco freeform design,
Mold No. 636 .... **80-100**
Vase, 10" h., feather form, Mold No. 539........ **50-75**
Vase, 10" h., hooked squares design, Mold
No. 512 .... **75-100**
Vase, 10" h., model of Trojan horse head,
Mold No. 540 .... **75-100**
Vase, 10" h., square form w/impressed flow-
er design, Mold No. 688 .... **50-75**
Vase, 10" h., two-handled, flared footed,
w/bulbous base & square neck w/flaring
rim, Mold No. H-604 .... **40-55**
Vase, 7 x 10", conical w/relief-molded
leaves at base, Mold J-64 .... **40-50**
Vase, 7 x 10", model of a butterfly, Mold No.
523 .... **100-150**
Vase, 7 x 10", model of leaves on branch,
Mold No. 683 .... **50-75**
Vase, 9 x 10", model of angel fish on waves,
Mold No. 522 .... **75-125**
Vase, 6 x 10", model of swan, Mold No. 802.. **25-50**
Vase, 10 1/4" h., bent tube, Mold No. 595... **75-100**
Vase, 10 1/4" h., flared flower, Mold No.
876 .... **150-175**

Vase, 10 1/4" h., swirled "S" handle, w/four
lips, Mold No. 872...................................... **50-75**
Vase, 10 1/4" h., zigzag & buttons design,
Mold No. 517... **75-100**

Gonder Pegasus Vase

Vase, 10 1/2" h., 9 3/4" w., Pegasus,
marked "Gonder 526," French Lilac
glaze, very hard to find (ILLUS.) **175-225**
Vase, 4 1/2 x 10 1/2, square form w/round
top, Mold No. 534 .... **50-75**

Gonder Freeform Vase

Vase, 10 3/4" h., Nubby Freeform shape,
marked "869 Gonder Original" in script,
Dijon glaze, hard to find (ILLUS.)............ **150-200**
Vase, 10 3/4" h., round leaf-in-leaf, Mold
No. J-59.. **60-80**
Vase, 10 7/8" h., off-center double handle,
Mold No. J-35.. **75-100**
Vase, 11" h., ewer form, J-25 .... **50-75**
Vase, 11" h., flat form, model of swan, Mold
No. 530.. **100-125**
Vase, 11" h., Mold No. 869, J-69, ewer type,
double curved handle **50-65**
Vase, 8 1/2 x 11", flame design, Mold No.
510 .... **60-75**
Vase, 8 x 11", figural leaf design, Mold No.
504 .... **25-35**
Vase, 11 1/8" h., Mold No. 513, 813, footed
double leaf, 5 5/16" w. x 9 1/2" l. **40-60**
Vase, 11 1/2" h., blades of grass design,
Mold No. 861.. **100-125**
Vase, 11 1/2" h., fan shape, relief-molded
shell decoration, Mold No. J-60 .... **40-55**
Vase, 11 1/2" h., orchid design, Mold No.
513 .... **50-75**
Vase, 7 x 11 1/2", triple "S" design, Mold
No. 594 .... **50-75**
Vase, 8 x 11 1/2", leaf swirl design, Mold
No. 596.. **50-75**

Vase, 11 3/4" h., peacock fan, Mold No. K-
15 .... **75-100**
Vase, 11 3/4" h., seahorse, Mold No. 524. **175-225**
Vase, 11 3/4" h., swallow design, Mold
K-25 .... **150-200**
Vase, 12" h., raised flowers & leaves, Mold
No. M-8.. **75-100**
Vase, 12" h., sea gull on piling, Mold No.
514 .... **175-225**
Vase, 12" h., swirl design w/two openings,
Mold No. 862... **75-125**
Vase, 6 x 12", Chinese Imperial dragon
handle, w/base, Mold No. 535, 2 pcs. ... **200-250**

Gonder Vase in Cocoa Glaze

Vase, 12 1/2" h., 5 3/4" d., Rounded Square
Tall Flowers, rectangular w/rounded cor-
ners at base, decorated w/flowers and
stalks, no mark, Cocoa glaze, Mold No.
863 (ILLUS.) **50-75**
Vase, 12 1/2" h., Mold No. M-4 .... **125-150**
Vase, 6 3/4 x 12 1/2", model of cactus, Mold
No. K-26 or 826... **50-75**
Vase, 12 3/4" h., two storks, Mold No. 562 . **75-100**
Vase, 9 3/4" h., uneven double swirl cornu-
copia, Mold No. H-48 .... **50-60**
Vase, 13" h., trellis w/flowers design, Mold
No. 863... **50-75**

Double Cylindrical Form Vase

Vase, 6 1/2 x 13", double, tall slender cylindrical forms joined at triangular-form
base, slanted rim, mottled green glaze,
Mold No. 868 (ILLUS.) **150-200**

Vase, 6 1/2 x 13", double, triangular, Mold
No. 368.. **70-100**

Gonder Seashell Vase

Vase, 13 3/8" h., Seashell Ewer with Star-
fish, marked "508 Gonder U.S.A." in
script, Chinese Turquoise Crackle glaze
(ILLUS.).. **95-120**
Vase, 14 1/2" h., tall tapered, Mold No.
598 .... **75-100**
Vase, 15 3/4" h., leaves & twigs design,
Mold No. 599... **100-150**
Vase, 18 3/8" h., large bottle form, Mold No.
531 .... **175-200**

Gouda

*While tin-enameled earthenware has been made in
Gouda, Holland since the early 1600s, the productions
of modern factories are attracting increasing collector
attention. The art pottery of Gouda is easily recognized
by its brightly colored peasant-style decoration, with
some types having achieved a cloisonné effect. Pottery
workshops located in or near Gouda include Regina,
Zenith, Plazuid, Schoonhoven, Arnhem and others. Their
wide range of production included utilitarian wares as
well as vases, miniatures and large outdoor garden
ornaments.*

Gouda Pottery Marks

Bowl, 8 1/2" l., oval, squatty bulbous form
w/rolled rim & loop end handles, black interior & handles, the sides w/a tannish orange ground decorated w/large lobed
black leaves & burnt orange scrolls, "Regina" crown mark, glossy glaze, ca. 1900 ...... **$83**

Bowl, 10" d., colorful peacock feather design, ca. 1920s **650**

Bowl, 13" d., pierced to hang, shallow w/widely flaring flattened rim, a cream ground decorated w/large multicolored flowers & green leaves in the center w/blossom heads around the rim, orchid banding, house mark & "2610 - 36 - Panow Co 4820 W. Gouda Holland," early 20th c. **66**

Butter pat, polychrome Art Nouveau design, marked "Regina 155 - (crown) - Lydia - WB - Gouda Holland," 3 1/2" d. **50**

Candy dish, squared flaring sides w/a loop end handle, raised on three feet, dark matte green ground decorated w/bands of multicolored leaves & flowers around the exterior & interior, marked "Regina - Gouda - Holland - Luxor - 505H"..................... **61**

Clock garniture, circular clock mount w/painted ceramic face supported by four ceramic arms on a baluster-shaped body & flared base, together w/two candle-holders of similar form, all decorated w/Art Nouveau-style flowers in glossy glaze of pink, purple, blue, green & tan, signed "Zuid Holland" & w/impressed house & "R" on base, early 20th c., clock 20 1/2" h., candleholders 16 3/4" h., 3 pcs. (repairs to candleholder base) **2,875**

Ewer, bulbous ovoid body tapering to a short rim spout & high arched strap handle, interior & handle in black, exterior in tannish orange ground w/overall large lobed black leaves, burnt orange scrolls & cream highlights, marked "Regina - Robur -Gouda - Holland," glossy glaze, early 20th c., 4 1/2" h. **72**

Early Gouda Jug

Jug, bulbous ovoid body tapering to a short cylindrical neck w/a rolled incurved rim w/long spout & integral loop handle extending from rim to shoulder, the top in orchid, the sides decorated w/full-length tapering stripes of white stylized leaves alternating w/green bands w/white dots, scalloped orchid base band, "Zuid Hol-land" mark & "No. 2140," 20th c., 10 1/2" h. (ILLUS.)... **385**

Lamp base, footed wide squatty bulbous tapering base w/a wide shoulder centering a tall cylindrical neck w/small domed cap, decorated around the sides w/floral & leaf designs & linear & dot decorative bands, glazed in shades of blue, rust, green & mustard yellow on a shaded green & brown ground, two-socket metal fixture, mounted on a circular patinated metal base w/impressed Greek key design, ca. 1937, 13 1/4" h. (minor rim nick)... **546**

Toothpick holder, No. 4341, blue, gold, yellow, brown & black **55**

Vase, 7 3/4" h., raised rim on oval body tapering to base, decorated w/central band w/upside down stylized tulip blossoms in blue, green & cream on a green ground, painted marks include "Holland 091/1" **173**

Vase, 4 1/8" h., 3 1/2" d., two-handled, footed bulbous form, decorated w/stylized flowers in blue, gold, rust, tan & black on off-white ground, bands in shades of green on rim, black interior, foot & handles **95**

Small Gouda Handled Vase

Vase, 4 1/4" h., 3 3/4" d., footed bulbous ovoid body w/a ringed neck & small loop handles at the sides, decorated w/stylized designs in dark yellow, brown, white, beige & black, marked "Benda Gouda Holland" (ILLUS.)... **110**

Vase, 7 3/8" h., bulbous, nearly spherical body w/shoulder tapering to short cylindrical neck w/wide flared rim, handles from shoulder to rim, decorated w/colorful Art Nouveau flowers, blue, tan & cream on dark green to black ground, marked "Made in Zuid Holland" on bottom in black slip & incised "18," also marked w/small house & "W" in black slip...... **770**

Vase, 8 1/4" h., 4 1/2" d., a squared foot issuing four curved buttress handles flanking the cylindrical central body w/a cylindrical neck, decorated w/stylized flowers in deep green & purple, marked w/factory symbol & "A to H" & "Zuid, Holland" **345**

Unique Gouda Pottery Vase

Vase, 13" h., a round flared foot supporting a wide squatty bulbous body w/integral handle at each side curving up to form a high rounded continuous handle, the flattened shoulder centered by a bulbed neck, decorated w/Art Nouveau stylized iris blossoms in purple, blue, green & taupe w/a glossy glaze, marked "Made in Zuid, Holland" & house mark, small nick (ILLUS.)... 920

Vases, 11 1/4" h., ovoid body tapering to a flared rim, decorated w/geometric & stylized foliage designs in blue, yellow, orange & green on a mottled greyish green ground, blue painted & impressed marks (minor base chips)... 518

Grueby

Some fine art pottery was produced by the Grueby Faience and Tile Company, established in Boston in 1891. Choice pieces were created with molded designs on a semi-porcelain body. The ware is marked and often bears the initials of the decorators. The pottery closed in 1907.

GRUEBY

Grueby Pottery Mark

Book ends, upright square form, "The Pines," decorated w/a polychrome cuenca designs of two large trees in the foreground & hills in the distance, in shades of green, blue & brown, designed by Addison Le Bouthillier, mounted in fine period hammered-copper frames, 6" sq., pr.. **$8,800**

Bowl, 4" d., low squatty bulbous form w/incurved sides, incised w/short vertical leaves around the sides, dark green matte glaze, artist-initialed, impressed mark & partial paper label 990

Bowl, 5 1/2" d., low wide form w/flaring rounded sides & a wide incurved rim, exterior w/dark blue matte glaze, impressed mark & two paper labels.................................. **935**

Grueby Bowl with Square Rim

Bowl, 7 1/2" w., 3 1/2" h., deep rounded sides curving up to a wide square rim, tooled & applied overlapping pointed leaves around the exterior under a smooth speckled ochre matte glaze, glossy green interior glaze, by Wilhelmina Post, minute nick on edges of some leaves, small glaze miss on side, stamped mark (ILLUS.) **2,300**

Wide & Shallow Grueby Bowl

Bowl, 8" d., 2 1/2" h., wide flat bottom below low incurved sides & wide flat rim, speckled matte green glaze w/mineral deposits, glaze bubbles on side, signed (ILLUS.)... 575

Bowl-vase, spherical form w/flared raised rim, repeating raised leaf design decorating the sides, mustard yellow matte glaze, impressed mark & label on base, 7" h. (small rim chip) **4,600**

Rare Grueby Papyrus Bowl-vase

Bowl-vase, wide squatty bulbous form w/the wide shoulder centered by a short rolled neck, tooled & applied papyrus design under a fine oatmealed matte green glaze, by Wilhelmina Post, minor glaze flakes on base, 10" d., 5" h. (ILLUS.) **10,925**

Grueby Jardiniere by W. Post

Jardiniere, slightly tapering ovoid form w/a wide & low rolled rim, tooled & applied up the sides w/long, wide leaves, frothy matte green glaze, by Wilhelmina Post, few minor glaze nicks, stamped mark, 10 1/2" d., 6" h. (ILLUS.) **5,175**

Large Grueby Jardiniere

Jardiniere, wide bulbous body w/a narrow rounded shoulder & wide, low rolled rim, molded w/continuous wide pointed leaves up the sides alternating w/blossoms on thin stems, green matte glaze, impressed mark, artist-signed, minor rim repair, 9" d. (ILLUS.) **2,310**

Model of scarab, matte green glaze, early 20th c., impressed pottery mark & partial paper label, 2 3/4" w., 4" l. **633**

Paperweight, figural, oblong model of a large scarab beetle, matte bluish grey glaze, Grueby Faience stamped mark, 2 3/4 x 4" **563**

Paperweight, figural, oblong model of a large scarab beetle, matte greenish brown glaze, Grueby Faience stamped mark, 2 3/4 x 3 3/4" (small glaze flake on front) **731**

Tile, square, depicting a row of four stylized white & brown penguins on a white ice-

berg on green water against a pale blue sky, unmarked, 4" sq. (minor chip, fleck to back edge) **935**

Tile, square, from the Dreamworld Mansion, Scituate, Massachusetts, decorated in cuenca w/a frieze of ivory horses on a green path against a pale blue sky, signed "RE" in glaze, 1902, 6" sq. **1,870**

Vase, 3" h., miniature, bulbous ovoid body w/a thin shoulder centered by a flattened flaring neck, thick dark green matte glaze, impressed mark **1,045**

Vase, 3 1/4" h., 5" d., narrow footring below the wide squatty bulbous body tapering to a wide short neck w/rolled rim, leathery matte green glaze, stamped circular mark **990**

Vase, 4" h., 5 1/4" d., squatty bulbous wide body tapering to a short, wide cylindrical neck, leathery matte green glaze, stamped circular Faience mark **990**

Squatty Bulbous Grueby Vase

Vase, 5" h., 5 1/2" d., footed wide squatty bulbous body w/a wide shoulder tapering to a short, wide flaring neck, tooled & applied w/wide arched & pointed leaves around the lower body alternating w/stems below large yellow blossoms around the rim, circular mark (ILLUS.)..... **12,650**

Vase, 5 1/2" h., 3 3/4" d., wide ovoid body w/wide lightly embossed panels, fine leathery matte green glaze, circular stamp mark.. **1,430**

Vase, 6" h., 3 1/4" d., a thin footring below a squatty bulbous base tapering to a tall cylindrical body, flowing matte green glaze, stamped circular mark **935**

Vase, 6 1/4" h., 5" d., bulbous nearly spherical bottom below a wide cylindrical ringed neck, speckled bluish grey matte glaze, Grueby Pottery stamped mark (touchup to rim nick) **900**

Vase, 6 3/4" h., 7 1/4" d., very wide ovoid body w/a closed rim, molded in low-relief w/tall wide leaves alternating w/slender stems w/tiny yellow & orange buds around the rim, leathery matte green glaze, circular mark & incised "RE," by Ruth Erickson.. **28,125**

Vase, 9 1/2" h., 5 3/4" d., bottle form, a wide bulbous base w/a wide flattened shoulder centering a tall cylindrical neck w/slightly flared rim, the base molded & applied w/an overlapping band of wide rounded leaves, fine organic matte green glaze, touchup to edge & rim, stamped mark & "190" **5,175**

Rare Grueby Vase with Jonquils

Vase, 10" h., large bulbous ovoid body w/a wide shoulder & short flaring neck, unusual decoration w/three sets of sculpted & applied jonquils, the flowers in red, green & yellow on green leafy stems against a fine suspended green matte background, by Marie Seaman, impressed mark (ILLUS.)............................. **46,000**

Vase, 10" h., 6" d., tall ovoid form w/molded flat mouth, full-length tooled & applied oblong leaves under a curdled ochre glaze, circular stamp mark & "RE" (glaze miss on side, minor chips under tips of two leaves)... **3,850**

Vase, 10 1/4" h., 8" d., footed wide ovoid body w/short flaring neck, molded w/wide leaves alternating w/buds, curdled matte green glaze, circular Grueby Faience stamp & "AL - 100" (four opposing hairlines, drilled hole at base, few minor glaze nicks to edges, glaze chip to base) **2,588**

Vase, 11" h., 5 1/4" d., tall ovoid body w/slightly flared & pinched rim, decorated w/relief-molded daffodils in profile in yellow, red & blue on long slender green leaves outlined in yellow, leathery matte green glaze, circular Grueby paper label & paper label from Geo. W. Benson Art Shop, Buffalo, incised "RE," by Ruth Erickson (small chip to inner rim, color run to one flower)....................................... **21,375**

Very Rare Grueby "Kendrick" Vase

Vase, 12" h., 8" d., "Kendrick" design, tall gourd-form w/low incurved rim, sides & rim tooled w/long pointed leaves in a fine pulled & leathery matte green glaze, chip to base, few small chips on leaf tips, circular mark (ILLUS.)..................................... **51,750**

Vase, 13 3/4" h., a narrow footring supporting the tall tapering & waisted cylindrical body, molded w/tall overlapping tapering leaves around the sides, some leaf tips showing the clay body, heavy matte green glaze, faint round impressed mark, attributed to Ellen R. Farrington, ca. 1902.. **7,475**

Large Ovoid Grueby Vase

Vase, 13 3/4" h., 9" d., large bulbous ovoid body tapering to a cylindrical neck w/flat rim, tooled & applied around the lower half w/overlapping bands of broad rounded leaves below alternating blossoms & tall buds, fine leathery matte green glaze, circular "Faience" mark, w/letter from Grueby family member, through whose family it descended, restoration to inner rim chip (ILLUS.)... **8,625**

Rare & Unusual Tall Grueby Vase

Vase, 17 1/2" h., 8 1/2" d., large bottle form w/squatty bulbous base & tall slender cylindrical neck w/flaring rim, tooled & applied small quatrefoils around the rim, broad pointed leaves around the lower body, fine leathery green matte glaze, No. 133A, stamped mark & paper label (ILLUS.) **57,500**

Unusual Grueby Wall Pocket

Wall pocket, bulbous ovoid form w/flat arched backplate, the front tooled & applied w/broad, ribbed, rounded, overlapping leaves, leathery matte green glaze, enlarged hanging holes, unmarked, 5 3/4" w., 7" h. (ILLUS.) **1,840**

Grueby Wall Pocket with Leaves

Wall pocket, long ovoid body molded w/long pointed leaves up to the flared rim, w/a molded bulbed bottom tip, thick oatmealy matte green glaze, unmarked, 3 1/2" w., 8 1/2" l. (ILLUS.) **3,738**

Hall China

Hall Marks

Founded in 1903 in East Liverpool, Ohio, this still-operating company at first produced mostly utilitarian wares. It was in 1911 that Robert T. Hall, son of the company founder, developed a special single-fire, lead-free glaze that proved to be strong, hard and nonporous. In the 1920s the firm became well known for its extensive line of teapots (still a major product), and in 1932 it introduced kitchenwares, followed by dinnerwares in 1936 and refrigerator wares in 1938.

The imaginative designs and wide range of glaze colors and decal decorations have led to the growing appeal of Hall wares with collectors, especially people who like Art Deco and Art Moderne design. One of the firm's most famous patterns was the "Autumn Leaf" line, produced as premiums for the Jewel Tea Company. For listings of this ware see "Jewel Tea Autumn Leaf."

Helpful books on Hall include, The Collector's Guide to Hall China by Margaret & Kenn Whitmyer, and Superior Quality Hall China - A Guide for Collectors by Harvey Duke (An ELO Book, 1977).

New England Shape Bean Pots

Ashtray, triangular, deep, No. 683, turquoise $15
Ashtray w/match holder, closed sides, No. 618 1/2, cobalt.................. 20
Baker, French Fluted shape, Blue Bouquet patt. 25
Baker, French Fluted shape, Silhouette patt. 30
Baker, French Fluted shape, Yellow Rose patt. 25

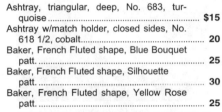

Five Band Batter Bowl

Batter bowl, Five Band shape, Chinese Red (ILLUS.)......................... 95
Batter jug, Sundial shape, Blue Garden patt. 250
Bean pot, cov., New England shape, No. 2 & No. 4, each (ILLUS., top of page) **120-140**
Bean pot, cov., New England shape, No. 4, Blue Blossom patt.......................... 225
Bean pot, cov., New England shape, No. 4, Crocus patt. 325
Bean pot, cov., New England shape, No. 4, Shaggy Tulip patt............................ 275
Bean pot, cov., New England shape, No. 4, Wild Poppy patt........................ 250
Bean pot, cov., New England shape, No. 488 patt. 275
Bean pot, cov., one handle, orange.................... 55

Pert Shape Bean Pot

Bean pot, cov., Pert shape, Chinese Red (ILLUS.)......................... 100
Bean pot, cov., tab-handled, Pert shape, Rose Parade patt. 135
Bowl, 6" d., Medallion shape, Silhouette patt.................. 23
Bowl, 6" d., Radiance shape, No. 4, Crocus patt.................. 25
Bowl, 6" d., Radiance shape, Yellow Rose patt.................. 20
Bowl, 6" d., Thick Rim shape, Blue Blossom patt.................. 40
Bowl, 7" d., Medallion shape, Silhouette patt.................. 25
Bowl, 7" d., Radiance shape, Crocus patt............ 40
Bowl, 7 1/2" d., straight-sided, Rose White patt.................. 18
Bowl, 8 1/2" d.,Thick Rim shape, Tulip patt. 30
Bowl, 8 3/4" d., Five Band shape, Cactus patt.................. 45
Bowl, 9" d., Radiance shape, Crocus patt............ 45
Bowl, 9" d., salad, Rose Parade patt. 44
Bowl, 9" d., salad, Serenade patt. 20

Bowl, 9" d., salad, Silhouette patt. 25

Medallion Shape Bowl

Bowl, 10" d., Medallion shape (ILLUS.) **45**
Butter dish, cov., Crocus patt., Zephyr
shape, 1 lb. **1,200**

Primrose Cake Plate

Cake plate, Primrose patt. (ILLUS.) **20**
Canister, cov., Radiance shape, Chinese
Red.. **200**

Casserole with Chrome Base

Casserole, cov., Art Deco w/chrome reticu-
lated handled base (ILLUS.) **75**
Casserole, cov., Five Band shape, Flamin-
go patt.. **75**
Casserole, cov., Medallion shape, Silhou-
ette patt. **60**
Casserole, cov., Radiance shape, Blue
Bouquet patt. **60**
Casserole, cov., Radiance shape, Crocus
patt. **65**
Casserole, cov., Ribbed line, russet **45**
Casserole, cov., round, No. 76, Wild Poppy
patt., 10 1/2" d. **75**
Casserole, cov., Sundial shape, No. 4, Chi-
nese Red.. **55**

Casserole, cov., tab-handled, Rose Parade
patt... **42**
Casserole, cov., tab-handled, Rose White
patt... **35**

Casserole with Inverted Pie Dish Lid

Casserole w/inverted pie dish lid, Radiance
shape, No. 488, 6 1/2" d., 4" h.
(ILLUS.)... **60**
Coffeelator, cov., cobalt blue **125**
Coffeepot, cov., Drip-O-Later, Duse
shape.. **50**
Coffeepot, cov., Drip-O-Later, Sash shape,
red **70**

Hall Coffeepots

Coffeepot, cov., Drip-O-Lator, Jerry shape
(ILLUS. left) **50**
Coffeepot, cov., Drip-O-Lator, Scoop shape,
Wildflower patt. **40**
Coffeepot, cov., Drip-O-Lator, Waverly
shape... **35**
Coffeepot, cov., drip-type, all-china, Jordan
shape, Morning Glory patt. **275**

Crocus Pattern Coffeepot

Coffeepot, cov., drip-type, all-china, Kadota
shape, Crocus patt. (ILLUS.) **350**

Coffeepot, cov., drip-type, all-china, Medal-
lion line, lettuce green **175**
Coffeepot, cov., electric percolator, Game
Birds (Ducks & Pheasants) patt. **85**
Coffeepot, cov., melt-down w/basket, Cro-
cus patt. **90**

Crocus Pattern Coffeepot

Coffeepot, cov., Terrace shape, Crocus
patt. (ILLUS.) **80**

Ansel Shape Tricolator Coffeepot

Coffeepot, cov., Tricolator, Ansel shape,
yellow art glaze (ILLUS.) **75**
Coffeepot, cov., Tricolator, Coffee Queen,
Chinese Red **55**

Coffee Queen Tricolator Coffeepot

Coffeepot, cov., Tricolator, Coffee Queen,
yellow (ILLUS.) **35**
Coffeepot, cov., Tricolator, Ritz shape, Chi-
nese Red (ILLUS. right w/Jerry Drip-O-
Lator) **135**
Coffeepot, cov., Waverly shape, Minuet
patt. **65**
Cookie jar, cov., Five Band shape, Blue
Blossom patt. **330**

Five Band Cookie Jar

Cookie jar, cov., Five Band shape, Chinese
Red (ILLUS.) **125**

Meadow Flower Cookie Jar

Cookie jar, cov., Five Band shape, Meadow
Flower patt. (ILLUS.) **325**
Cookie jar, cov., Flareware, Gold Lace de-
sign **75**

Flareware Cookie Jar

Cookie jar, cov., Flareware (ILLUS., previous page).. 65
Cookie jar, cov., Grape design, yellow, gold band... 60
Cookie jar, cov., Owl, brown glaze..................... 120
Cookie jar, cov., Red Poppy patt......................... 500
Cookie jar, cov., Sundial shape, Blue Blossom patt. 400

Sundial Cookie Jar

Cookie jar, cov., Sundial shape, Chinese Red (ILLUS.)... 235
Cookie jar, cov., Zeisel, Gold Dot design............. 95
Creamer, Art Deco, Crocus patt. 25
Creamer, Medallion shape, Silhouette patt. 18
Creamer, Modern, Red Poppy patt..................... 35

Creamer in Autumn Leaf Pattern

Creamer, Radiance shape, Autumn Leaf patt. (ILLUS.)... 45
Creamer, individual, Sundial shape, Chinese Red, 2 oz.. 65
Creamer, Sundial shape, Chinese Red, 4 oz... 45
Creamer & cov. sugar bowl, Blue Bouquet patt., pr. 70
Custard, straight-sided, Rose Parade patt. 32
Custard cup, Medallion line, lettuce green 12
Custard cup, Radiance shape, Serenade patt. 20
Custard cup, straight-sided, Rose White patt. 25
Custard cup, Thick Rim shape, Meadow Flower patt. 35

Radiance Shape Drip Jar

Drip jar, cov., Radiance shape, Chinese Red (ILLUS.) 60
Drip jar, cov., Thick Rim shape, Royal Rose patt... 25
Drip jar, open, No. 1188, Mums patt. 35
Gravy boat, Red Poppy patt. 125
Gravy boat, Springtime patt................................. 35

Humidor with Walnut Lid

Humidor, cov., Indian Decal, walnut lid (ILLUS.)... 55
Leftover, cov., loop handle, Blue Blossom patt. 150

Leftover with Loop Handle

Leftover, cov., loop handle, Chinese Red (ILLUS.)... 95
Leftover, cov., rectangular, Blue Bouquet patt. 100
Leftover, cov., square, Crocus patt. 125

Zephyr Shape Leftover

Leftover, cov., Zephyr shape, Chinese Red
(ILLUS.)... **110**

Fantasy Leftover

Leftover, cov., Zephyr shape, Fantasy patt.
(ILLUS.)... **225**
Mixing bowl, Thick Rim shape, Royal Rose
patt., 8 1/2" d. **30**
Mug, beverage, Silhouette patt. **60**
Mug, flagon shape, Monk patt. **45**

Irish Coffee Mug

Mug, Irish coffee, footed, 6" h. (ILLUS.).............. **15**

Hall Commemorative Mug

Mug, Irish coffee, footed, commemorative,
"Hall China Convention 2000" (ILLUS.)........... **40**

Commemorative Irish Coffee Mug

Mug, Irish coffee, footed, commemorative
United States Bicentennial "Era of
Space" Series (ILLUS.) **35**
Mug, Tom & Jerry, Red Dot patt. **15**

Orange Poppy Pie Plate

Pie plate, Orange Poppy patt. (ILLUS.) **45**

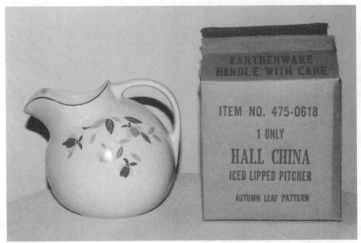

Autumn Leaf Pitcher with Box

Pitcher, ball shape, Autumn Leaf patt., 1978, w/box (ILLUS.) 65

Pitcher, ball shape, No. 3, Chinese Red.............. 55

Pitcher, ball shape, No. 3, Delphinium blue 35

Hall Ball-type Pitcher

Pitcher, ball shape, No. 3, orchid (ILLUS.) 85

Pitcher, ball shape, Royal Rose patt. 95

Pitcher, cov., jug-type, Radiance shape, No. 4, No. 488 patt.. 195

Pitcher, jug-type, Doughnut shape, cobalt blue 75

Doughnut-shape Jug-type Pitcher

Pitcher, jug-type, large, Doughnut shape, Chinese Red (ILLUS.) 135

Pitcher, jug-type, Loop-handle, Blue Blossom patt. 195

Pitcher, jug-type, Loop-handle, emerald green 65

Pitcher, jug-type, Medallion line, No. 3, Silhouette patt. 45

Pitcher, jug-type, No. 628, maroon........................ 50

Pitcher, jug-type, Nora, yellow................................ 25

Pitcher, jug-type, Pert shape, Rose Parade patt. 30-40

Pitcher, jug-type, Radiance shape, No. 5, Wildfire patt. 45

Pitcher, jug-type, Streamline shape, canary yellow... 55

Pitcher, Rose White patt., large 35

Tankard-type Pitcher

Pitcher, tankard-type, black (ILLUS.) 65

Pert Pitchers in Various Sizes

Pitchers, Pert shape, Chinese Red, three
  sizes (ILLUS. of three).................................. **35-55**
Plate, salad, 8 1/4" d., No. 488 patt...................... **15**
Plate, dinner, 9" d., Silhouette patt....................... **15**
Plate, dinner, 10" d., Wildfire patt.......................... **20**
Platter, 11 1/4" l., oval, Springtime patt................ **20**
Platter, 13 1/4" l., oval, Mums patt....................... **50**
Pretzel jar, cov., Crocus patt................................ **225**
Pretzel jar, cov., Pastel Morning Glory patt....... **125**
Punch set: punch bowl & 10 punch cups;
  Old Crow, punch bowl reads "May YOU
  always - have an eagle in your pocket ...a
  turkey on your table - and Old Crow in
  your glass," the set.. **175**

Canister-style Salt & Pepper Shakers

Salt & pepper shakers, canister style, red,
  pr. (ILLUS.)... **90**
Salt & pepper shakers, Five Band shape,
  Blue Blossom patt., pr...................................... **75**
Salt & pepper shakers, handled, range-type,
  Blue Blossom patt., pr...................................... **80**
Salt & pepper shakers, handled, Royal
  Rose patt., pr... **34**
Salt & pepper shakers, Medallion line, let-
  tuce green, pr. **85**
Salt & pepper shakers, Novelty Radiance
  shape, Orange Poppy patt., pr. **95**

Pert Salt & Pepper Shakers

Salt & pepper shakers, Pert shape, Chinese
  Red, pr. (ILLUS.).. **35**
Salt & pepper shakers, Pert shape, Rose
  Parade patt., pr.. **35**
Salt & pepper shakers, Radiance shape,
  canister-style, Chinese Red, pr..................... **120**

Rose White Salt Shaker

Salt & pepper shakers, Rose White patt.,
  holes form letters "S" & "P," pr. (ILLUS. of
  one) **35**
Salt & pepper shakers, Teardrop shape,
  Blue Bouquet patt., pr....................................... **35**
Soup tureen, cov., Clover style, Crocus patt....... **350**
Soup tureen, Thick Rim shape, Blue Bou-
  quet patt. **300**
Stack set, Medallion line, lettuce green **95**
Stack set, Radiance shape, Carrot patt............. **125**
Sugar bowl, cov., Art Deco, Crocus
  patt... **35**

Automobile Shape Teapot

Sugar bowl, cov., Medallion line, Silhouette patt. **35**
Sugar bowl, cov., Modern, Red Poppy patt. **40**
Syrup pitcher, cov., Five Band shape, Blue Blossom patt. **165**
Tea tile, octagonal, art-glaze blue & white **65**
Tea tile, round, Chinese Red **50**

Adele Shape Teapot

Teapot, cov., Adele shape, Art Deco style, olive green (ILLUS.) **200**
Teapot, cov., Airflow shape, Chinese Red **130**
Teapot, cov., Airflow shape, cobalt blue w/gold trim, 6-cup **100**
Teapot, cov., Aladdin shape, cobalt blue w/gold trim, 6-cup **125**
Teapot, cov., Aladdin shape, Crocus patt. **1,950**
Teapot, cov., Aladdin shape, oval opening, w/infuser, cobalt blue w/gold trim **110**
Teapot, cov., Aladdin shape, round opening, Cadet blue w/gold trim **75**

Serenade Teapot

Teapot, cov., Aladdin shape, w/infuser, Serenade patt. (ILLUS.) **350**

Teapot, cov., Aladdin shape, yellow w/gold trim, w/infuser **65**
Teapot, cov., Albany shape, emerald green w/"Gold Special" decoration **60**
Teapot, cov., Albany shape, mahogany w/gold trim, 6-cup **75**
Teapot, cov., Automobile shape, Chinese Red (ILLUS., top of page) **800**
Teapot, cov., Automobile shape, turquoise w/platinum **750**
Teapot, cov., Baltimore shape, Gold Label line, ivory **125**
Teapot, cov., Basket shape, Cadet blue w/platinum decoration **150**

Basket Shape Teapot

Teapot, cov., Basket shape, Chinese Red (ILLUS.) **300**
Teapot, cov., Basket shape, warm yellow **175**
Teapot, cov., Basketball shape, cobalt blue **600**
Teapot, cov., Basketball shape, emerald green w/gold decoration **650**

Orange Poppy Teapot

Teapot, cov., Bellevue shape, Orange Poppy patt. (ILLUS.)................................ **1,800**
Teapot, cov., Birdcage shape, maroon.............. **350**
Teapot, cov., Birdcage shape, maroon w/gold decoration, 6-cup **400**

Birdcage Teapot

Teapot, cov., Birdcage shape, yellow, "Gold Special" decoration (ILLUS.)........................... **500**

Blue Garden Teapot

Teapot, cov., Blue Garden patt., morning set (ILLUS.)...................................... **350**
Teapot, cov., Boston shape, canary yellow, 2-cup **45**
Teapot, cov., Boston shape, Chinese Red........ **150**
Teapot, cov., Boston shape, cobalt blue w/gold Trailing Aster design, 6-cup **150**
Teapot, cov., Boston shape, Crocus patt. **225**

Bowling Ball Teapot

Teapot, cov., Bowling Ball shape, turquoise (ILLUS.).. **500**
Teapot, cov., Cleveland shape, turquoise w/gold decoration **75**
Teapot, cov., Cleveland shape, warm yellow........ **60**
Teapot, cov., Coverlet shape, white w/gold cover, 6-cup... **40**
Teapot, cov., Cube shape, emerald green **100**
Teapot, cov., Cube shape, turquoise, 2-cup **140**
Teapot, cov., Doughnut shape, Chinese Red **500**

Orange Poppy Doughnut Shape Teapot

Teapot, cov., Doughnut shape, Orange Poppy patt. (ILLUS.) **450**
Teapot, cov., Flareware line, Gold Lace design **60**

Football Commemorative Teapot

Teapot, cov., Football shape, commemorative, "Hall 200 Haul, East Liverpool, Ohio" (ILLUS.)... **125**
Teapot, cov., Football shape, maroon **600**
Teapot, cov., French shape, Chinese Red & white, 2-cup **125**
Teapot, cov., French shape, maroon w/gold decoration, 6-cup............................... **45**

French Shape Red & White Teapot

Teapot, cov., French shape, "No Blue," red
body, white lid (ILLUS.) 140
Teapot, cov., French shape, old rose w/gold
French Flower decoration, 6-cup 50
Teapot, cov., Game Birds patt. 250
Teapot, cov., Globe shape, no-drip, Addison
grey w/gold decoration, 6-cup 65
Teapot, cov., Hollywood shape, Indian red 150
Teapot, cov., Hollywood shape, silver lustre
decoration 325
Teapot, cov., Hook Cover shape, Cadet
blue w/gold decoration..................................... 50

Hook Cover Teapot

Teapot, cov., Hook Cover shape, Chinese
Red (ILLUS.)... 250
Teapot, cov., Illinois shape, maroon w/gold
decoration 225
Teapot, cov., Illinois shape, Stock Brown
w/gold decoration.. 140
Teapot, cov., Illinois shape, yellow 200
Teapot, cov., Indiana shape, warm yellow
w/gold decoration, 6-cup 450
Teapot, cov., Kansas shape, ivory w/gold
decoration 400
Teapot, cov., Lipton shape, maroon 45

Warm Yellow Lipton Shape Teapot

Teapot, cov., Lipton shape, warm yellow
(ILLUS.).. 40
Teapot, cov., Lipton shape, yellow 60

Los Angeles Teapot in Cobalt

Teapot, cov., Los Angeles shape, Cobalt
w/Standard Gold trim (ILLUS.)......................... 75
Teapot, cov., Los Angeles shape, emerald
green w/gold decoration, 6-cup........................ 85
Teapot, cov., Manhattan shape, Chinese
Red, 8-cup 500
Teapot, cov., Manhattan shape, side han-
dle, cobalt blue, 2-cup 95
Teapot, cov., McCormick shape,
turquoise 50
Teapot, cov., Medallion shape,
Crocus patt. 85
Teapot, cov., Medallion shape, Silhouette
patt... 70
Teapot, cov., Melody shape, Chinese
Red 305
Teapot, cov., Melody shape, Orange Poppy
patt... 370

Moderne Teapot

Teapot, cov., Moderne shape, Marine blue
(ILLUS.)... 85
Teapot, cov., musical-type, blue, 6-cup.............. 200
Teapot, cov., Nautilus shape, turquoise blue
w/gold decoration 225
Teapot, cov., New York shape, Crocus
patt... 200
Teapot, cov., Ohio shape, brown w/gold
decoration... 200

Ohio Teapot

Teapot, cov., Ohio shape, pink, Gold Dot
decoration (ILLUS.).. 250
Teapot, cov., Parade shape, black........................ 65
Teapot, cov., Parade shape, warm yellow
w/gold decoration 75
Teapot, cov., Pert shape, Chinese Red, 4-
cup 80
Teapot, cov., Pert shape, Chinese Red, 6-
cup 75
Teapot, cov., Pert shape, Chinese Red &
white, 2-cup... 80

Teapot, cov., Philadelphia shape, blue w/hearth scene patt.. **150**

Philadelphia Shape Teapot

Teapot, cov., Philadelphia shape, Chinese Red (ILLUS.)...................................... **250**
Teapot, cov., Plume shape, pink........................... **40**
Teapot, cov., Radiance shape, Acacia patt.. **225**
Teapot, cov., Rhythm shape, Chinese Red **350**
Teapot, cov., Rhythm shape, cobalt blue... **180**
Teapot, cov., Rhythm shape, yellow w/gold decoration, 6-cup............................... **150**

Rutherford Ribbed Teapot

Teapot, cov., Rutherford shape, ribbed, Chinese Red (ILLUS.).. **250**
Teapot, cov., Star shape, cobalt blue................. **145**

Star Shape Teapot

Teapot, cov., Star shape, cobalt blue w/gold decoration (ILLUS.).. **125**

Teapot, cov., Streamline shape, Chinese Red **150**

Fantasy Teapot

Teapot, cov., Streamline shape, Fantasy patt. (ILLUS.).. **400**
Teapot, cov., Streamline shape, Orange Poppy patt... **350**
Teapot, cov., Sundial shape, ivory w/gold decoration.. **95**
Teapot, cov., Surfside shape, cadet blue.. **175**
Teapot, cov., Surfside shape, canary yellow... **185**
Teapot, cov., Surfside shape, emerald green w/gold decoration, 6-cup...................... **200**
Teapot, cov., T-Ball round shape, black w/gold label, 6-cup... **195**
Teapot, cov., Tea-for-Four shape, Stock green **125**

Tea-for-Two Teapot

Teapot, cov., Tea-for-Two shape, pink w/gold decoration (ILLUS.) **150**
Teapot, cov., Tea-for-Two shape, Stock brown w/gold decoration **100**
Teapot, cov., Thorley series, Apple design, black w/gold decoration...................................... **95**
Teapot, cov., Thorley series, Starlight shape, pink w/gold & rhinestone decoration **125**
Teapot, cov., Thorley series, white w/rhinestone decoration **295**
Teapot, cov., Thorley series, Windcrest shape, lemon yellow w/gold decoration........... **95**
Teapot, cov., Tip-Pot, Twinspout, emerald green **95**

Birch Teapot

Teapot, cov., Victorian series, Birch shape,
blue w/gold decoration (ILLUS.)...................... 175
Teapot, cov., Victorian series, Bowknot
shape, pink 50
Teapot, cov., Victorian series, Connie
shape, celadon green, 6-cup 45
Teapot, cov., Windshield shape, Gamebird
patt. 250
Teapot, cov., Windshield shape, Gold Label
line, white w/gold dots..................................... 50
Teapot, cov., Windshield shape, turquoise
w/gold decoration.. 68
Twin-Tea set: cov. teapot, cov. hot water pot
& matching divided tray; art glaze
green... 125
Twin-Tea set: cov. teapot, cov. hot water pot
& matching divided tray; Pansy
patt. 225
Vase, Edgewater, No. 630, cobalt
blue 25
Vase, bud, Trumpet, No. 631, Chinese
Red... 35
Vase, bud, No. 631 1/2, maroon 15
Vase, bud, No. 641, canary yellow 10

Zephyr Shape Water Bottle

Water bottle, cov., refrigerator ware line,
Zephyr shape, Chinese Red (ILLUS.)........... 350
Water server, cov., Montgomery Ward re-
frigerator ware, Delphinium blue..................... 55
Water server, Plaza shape, Chinese Red 135
Water server w/cork stopper, Hotpoint re-
frigerator ware, Dresden blue.......................... 85
Water server w/hinged cover, Westing-
house refrigerator ware, Hercules shape,
cobalt blue 110

Hampshire Pottery

Hampshire Marks

*Hampshire Pottery was made in Keene, New Hamp-
shire, where several potteries operated as far back as the
late 18th century. The pottery now known as Hampshire
Pottery was established by J.S. Taft shortly after 1870.
Various types of wares, including Art Pottery, were produced through the years. Taft's brother-in-law, Cadmon
Robertson, joined the firm in 1904 and was responsible
for developing more than 900 glaze formulas while in*

Blue Garden Water Bottle

Water bottle, cov., refrigerator ware line,
Zephyr shape, Blue Garden patt.
(ILLUS.)... 650

charge of all manufacturing. His death in 1914 created problems for the firm, and Taft sold out to George Morton in 1916. Closed during part of World War I, the pottery was later reopened by Morton for a short time and manufactured white hotel china. From 1919 to 1921, mosaic floor tiles became the main production. All production ceased in 1923.

Low Hampshire Bowl in Mottled Blue

Bowl, 5 1/4" d., 2 1/4" h., wide flattened bottom below the squatty bulbous sides tapering to a wide flat mouth, the sides molded w/wide low arches alternating w/triple grooves, mottled dark blue matte glaze, two opposing rim cracks, signed (ILLUS.) **$288**
Bowl, 5 1/2" d., 2 3/4" h., wide low bulbous incurved sides, matte green glaze, signed "Hampshire Pottery L2/1 - M [within] O," designed by Cadmon Robertson **173**

Hampshire Bowl with Trilliums

Bowl, 9" d., wide flat bottom below low incurved sides & a wide mouth, molded around the sides w/large stylized trillium blossoms, matte green glaze w/cream showing through, marked (ILLUS.) **460**

Hampshire Pottery Low Bowl

Bowl, 10" d., 3" h., a wide flat-bottomed round form w/low incurved sides molded

w/a band of rounded lily pads alternating w/buds on stems, dark green matte glaze, signed, glaze miss on rim, tight line from rim (ILLUS.) **345**

Hampshire Green Bowl-Vase

Bowl-vase, wide squatty bulbous form w/the wide shoulder centered by a low rolled rim, heavy matte green glaze, Model No. 136, inscribed mark, chip on glaze drip (ILLUS.) **258**
Bowl-vase, wide squatty bulbous base below sharply tapering incurved sides w/a wide, flat rim, the sides incised w/a wide band of linear & scrolled repeating design, mottled matte green glaze, ink stamp on base, ca. 1910, 4 1/2" d., 2 3/4" h. **690**
Chamberstick, deep tricorner base w/infolded sides centering a cylindrical socket w/flared rim, high loop handle at the back, dark green glossy glaze, impressed mark, 7" w., 3 1/2" h. **253**

Hampshire Pottery Chamberstick

Chamberstick, round dished base tapering to a cylindrical standard w/a wide rolled socket rim, a round loop handle near the base, mottled blue glaze, impressed mark, two chips, firing lines in base rim (ILLUS.) **115**

Hampshire Matte Green Ewer

Ewer, footed squatty bulbous lower body tapering to cylindrical sides w/a high
arched spout opposite & high arched &
looped handle, matte green glaze, 8" h.
(ILLUS.)... **431**
Ewer, wide squatty bulbous form w/the wide
shoulder centered by a short slender
neck w/a wide inwardly folded tricorner
rim, round loop handle from back of rim to
base of neck, shaded dark brown, green
& gunmetal glossy glaze, impressed
mark, 6" h... **143**

Unusual Hampshire Lamp Base

Lamp base, a thick rounded flaring base
molded w/pointed leaves & tapering to a
slender standard molded w/buds on
stems, matte green glaze, missing sock-
et & wiring, 12" h. (ILLUS.)........................... **1,380**
Lamp base, a wide round cushion foot mold-
ed in relief w/five repeating tulips, a tall
tapering slender shaft molded w/the
stems below a bulbed top w/the electric
socket, matte green glaze, marked on

the base, ca. 1910, 11" h. (wear to lamp
fittings).. **920**
Lamp base, squatty wide bulbous gourd-
form lobed form on small tab feet, the
wide shoulder centered by a short wide
cylindrical neck mounted w/electric fittings complete w/a cap & period silk-lined
wicker shade, impressed mark on base,
base 11" d., 6 1/2" h................................... **1,320**

Hampshire Lamp Base with Tulips

Lamp base, tall gently flaring cylindrical
form w/rounded shoulder to a wide flat
mouth, molded up the sides w/broad
pointed tulip leaves alternating with blossoms around the rim, dark matte green
glaze, signed, several burst bubbles,
small grinding chip on base, w/patinated
rim ring (ILLUS.)................................... **1,150**
Lamp base, wide flared disk foot tapering to
a tall slender trumpet-form body w/a wide
rounded shoulder centered by the electric fittings, embossed w/twining lily pads
around the sides, smooth olive green
glaze, verdigris patina on the fittings,
stamped "Hampshire Pottery - 0018,"
7" d., 16" h.. **1,013**

Hampshire Pottery Large Urn-Vase

Urn-vase, a bulbous base tapering to a tall slightly tapering cylindrical neck flanked by slender angled & pierced handles from high on the neck to the shoulder, embossed Greek key design bands around the upper neck & the lower body, matte green glaze, light abrasion to the base, stamped "Hampshire Pottery - 88," 9" d., 15" h. (ILLUS.) **1,913**

Miniature Hampshire Vase

Vase, 3 1/2" h., miniature, bulbous ovoid body tapering to a small flat mouth, embossed around the sides w/large pointed upright leaves, matte brown glaze, marked (ILLUS.)... **690**

Vase, 3 3/4" h., miniature, bulbous ovoid form tapering to a tiny mouth, the sides molded w/wide pointed & veined leaves up the sides, green & brown matte glaze, impressed mark, experimental glaze............ **715**

Vase, 4 1/4" h., simple ovoid form w/a rounded shoulder centering a short, small rolled neck, lightly molded arched panel-style leaves up the sides, mottled green matte glaze, impressed mark, experimental glaze... **413**

Vase, 4 1/2" h., bulbous tapering ovoid form w/a very wide flat mouth, incised around the rim w/a wavy band of stylized leaves & blossoms, dark green matte glaze............ **605**

Hampshire Moss Green Vase

Vase, 4 1/2" h., wide ovoid body tapering to a wide, flat mouth, overall dark moss green matte glaze, raised mark (ILLUS.)...... **517**

Vase, 4 3/4" h., flat-bottomed ovoid body w/a rounded shoulder centered by a short rolled neck, light vertical panels covered w/an overall dark blue matte glaze, impressed mark **286**

Vase, 4 7/8" h., footed compressed bulbous base w/wide cylindrical neck & flat rim, shaded matte green & mauve glaze, by Cadmon Robertson, Keene, New Hampshire, early 20th c., impressed "Hampshire Pottery 155" & "M" within an O cipher **345**

Vase, 5" h., a flat-based wide bulbous ovoid body w/a rounded shoulder tapering to a wide trumpet neck, overall mottled multi-toned greyish blue matte glaze, impressed mark **605**

Vase, 6" h., an oblong boat-shaped base w/pulled-out tapering end handles looping up & connecting asymmetrically to a slender cylindrical neck which tapers up from the lower body, green matte glaze, impressed mark..................................... **660**

Vase, 6" h., slightly flaring cylindrical form w/a rounded shoulder tapering slightly to a wide flat mouth, good green matte glaze, incised mark **385**

Vase, 6 3/4" h., 3 3/4" d., gently tapering cylindrical form w/a wide rounded shoulder centering a flat mouth, embossed around the shoulder w/broad stylized green leaves on a blue ground, incised mark **825**

Vase, 6 7/8" h., swelled cylindrical body w/narrow shoulder & rolled rim, three impressed columns around body, mottled matte mauve glaze over light green, by Cadmon Robertson, Keene, New Hampshire, early 20th c., incised "Hampshire Pottery 157" & "M" within O cypher **748**

Hampshire Handled Blue Vase

Vase, 7" h., a squatty bulbous bottom tapering sharply to a cylindrical body w/a narrow neck & molded small rim flanked by two small shoulder handles, matte blue glaze, impressed mark, clay bubbles on side of base (ILLUS.)....................................... **460**

Vase, 8 1/2" h., ovoid body tapering to a flaring neck, vine-form open handles on each side connecting to long molded spearpoint leaves down the sides, matte green glaze, signed, light line in one handle 748

Vase, 9" h., wide ovoid form tapering to a wide, flat mouth, overall dark brown matte glaze, raised mark 605

Tall Ovoid Hampshire Green Vase

Vase, 11" h., round dished foot w/a slender stem supporting a tall ovoid body w/a molded flat mouth, green matte glaze, impressed mark, small firing line, light crazing (ILLUS.)..................................... 460

Vase, 12" h., a tall gently swelled cylindrical form w/a narrow rounded shoulder & wide cylindrical neck w/flat rim, fine dark blue matte glaze, impressed mark 1,045

Vase, 12" h., tall slender swelled cylindrical form w/a narrow shoulder to the short rolled neck, overall multi-toned blue matte glaze, impressed mark 990

Vase, 12 1/4" h., 5" d., tall slender ovoid body tapering to a short rolled neck, very thick frothy blue & bluish green matte glaze, green spot on side, stamped mark 1,725

Vase, 15" h., wide squatty bulbous base tapering to a tall & slightly tapering cylindrical neck flanked by long slender angled & pierced handles, a narrow geometrical dash band around the top of the neck & a wider matching band around the lower body, green matte glaze, impressed mark 2,070

Harker Pottery

Harker Marks

Harker Pottery was in business for more than 100 years (1840-1972) in the East Liverpool area of eastern Ohio. One of the oldest potteries in Ohio, it advertised itself as one of the oldest in America. The pottery produced two lines that are favorites of collectors: ovenware under the BakeRite and HotOven brands and Cameoware. However, Harker also produced many other lines as well as Rockingham reproductions, souvenir items and a line designed by Russel Wright that are gaining popularity with collectors. Harker was marketed under dozens of backstamps in its history.

Advertising, Novelty & Souvenir Pieces

Harker Advertising Ashtray

Ashtray, advertising Fontainebleau Hotel, dark blue glaze w/white lettering (ILLUS.).. $20

Ashtrays, w/advertising, each........................... 10-20

Harker 1929 Calendar Plate

Calendar plates, 1907 to 1930, later dates of lower value, each (ILLUS. of 1929 plate)... 30-50

Harker Ivy Pattern Pieces

Souvenir plates, 6" d., each **20-25**
Tea tile, "Townsend Plan" **35-50**

Autumn Leaf

Harker made some Autumn Leaf for Jewel Tea before Hall China received the exclusive contract. The design is larger than that used on later ware and no mark has been found.

Cake plate, Virginia shape **200-250**
Casserole, cov. **75-100**

BakeRite, HotOven

Harker was one of the first American potteries to produce pottery that could go from the oven to the table. Most of this ware, made from the late 1920s to 1970, features brightly colored decals that are popular with collectors today. Prices vary somewhat, depending upon the decal pattern. Among the most popular designs are Amy, Colonial Lady, Countryside, red and blue Deco Dahlia, *Fireplace, Ivy, Lisa, Mallow, Monterey, Oriental Poppy, Petit Point, Red Apple and Tulips. We will list examples of some of these patterns here.*

Ivy Pattern

Grease jar, cov., D'Ware shape (ILLUS. left
with other Ivy pieces, above)............................ **25**
Pie baker (ILLUS. second from right with
other Ivy pattern pieces).................................... **15**
Pitcher, jug-type, round (ILLUS. right with
other Ivy pieces) **40**
Plate, 10" d., dinner, plain round (ILLUS.
second from left other Ivy pieces).................... **12**
Spoon, serving (ILLUS. center with other Ivy
pieces).. **15**

Mallow Pattern

Creamer, cov., Ohio shape (ILLUS. top right
with other Mallow pieces)................................... **15**

Harker Mallow Pattern Pieces

Custard cup (ILLUS. top left with other Mal-
low pieces)... **10**
Mixing bowl, 9" d. (ILLUS. bottom right with
other Mallow pattern pieces)............................. **20**

Mixing bowl, 9" d., lipped (ILLUS. bottom left
other Mallow pattern pieces) **40**
Teapot, cov. (ILLUS. top center other Mal-
low pieces)... **45**

Modern Age/Modern Tulip Pieces

Modern Age/Modern Tulip

Created to resemble and compete with Jewel Tea's Autumn Leaf, Modern Tulip's orange and brown pattern was primarily used on Harker's Modern Age shape, easily identified by its flattened oval, "Life-Saver" finials and the impressed arrow fletchings. Unfortunately, Modern Tulip has yet to be discovered by collectors.

Bowl, utility, 4" d., Zephyr shape (ILLUS. middle row, second from left) **8**
Bowls, utility, 3" to 8" d., Zephyr shape, each **3-10**
Cake plate **15-20**
Cookie jar, cov. (ILLUS. bottom row, above)... **20-30**
Creamer (ILLUS. top row center)..................... **10-15**
Custard cup, individual, Zephyr shape (ILLUS. second row, second from right) **3-5**
Pie baker (ILLUS. top right, left)....................... **10-15**
Pitcher, cov., square, jug-type (ILLUS. top row, right).. **20-25**

Plate, 6" d., cake or bread & butter, plain round (ILLUS. middle row, far right) **2-5**

Modern Tulip Rolling Pin

Rolling pin, 14 1/2" l. (ILLUS.) **85**
Sugar bowl, cov. **10-15**
Teapot, cov. (ILLUS. middle row, far left)....... **20-30**

Petit Point Pattern

Au gratin/casserole, cov. (ILLUS. top row, far left with other Petit Point pieces) **25-35**
Batter jug, cov., paneled Ohio shape **30-40**
Batter set: two batter jugs, lifter & utility plate; the set.. **100-150**

Various Petit Point Pattern Pieces

Bean pot, individual (ILLUS. top row, center front with other Petit Point pieces) **8-10**

Bowls, utility, 3" to 5" d., nesting-type, Zephyr shape, each (ILLUS. of 3" d. size, bottom, second from left with other Petit Point pieces) **8-15**

Bowls, utility, 6" to 8" d., nesting-type, Zephyr shape, each **15-25**

Bowls, utility, 10" to 12" d., nesting-type, Zephyr shape, each **20-40**

Butter dish, cov. **30-50**

Butter dish, cov., 1 lb. **40**

Cheese bowl, cov. **30-40**

Cheese tray, Zephyr shape **15-20**

Coffeepot, cov., w/aluminum brewer basket **65-80**

Condiment jar, cov., individual **20-25**

Condiment set: three jars in a holder; the set **50-75**

Cookie jar, cov., Modern Age shape **25-30**

Cookie jar, cov., Zephyr shape **40-50**

Cup & saucer, plain round **20-25**

Custard cup, individual **8-10**

Custard cup set: six cups in a rack; the set **60-75**

Grease jar, cov., D'Ware shape **20-25**

Grease jar, cov., Hi-Rise shape **15-25**

Petit Point Pattern Mixing Bowl

Mixing bowl, large, 10" d., 5 1/2" h. (ILLUS.) .. **25-50**

Mixing bowl, medium, Zephyr shape, 6" to 8" d., each (ILLUS. of 8" bowl, bottom row center with other Petit Point pieces) ... **15-25**

Mixing bowl, w/pouring lip **40-50**

Pie baker **15-25**

Pitcher, jug-type, Regal shape, gargoyle on handle **25-40**

Plate, 6" d., cake or bread & butter, plain round **6-10**

Plate, 8" d., salad, plain round **10-15**

Plate, 10" d., dinner, plain round (ILLUS. middle row, right with other Petit Point pieces) **15-25**

Salad fork or spoon, each (ILLUS. bottom row, front right with other Petit Point pieces) **15-20**

Petit Point Hi-Rise Shape Shakers

Salt & pepper shakers, Hi-Rise shape, 4 1/2" h., pr. (ILLUS.) **15-25**

Scoop **50-150**

Tea tile, octagonal, (ILLUS. top row, center back, with other Petit Point pieces) **15-25**

Teapot, cov. **65-85**

Utility plate, Virginia shape, 12" w. **10-25**

Red Apple I & Red Apple II Patterns

Various Red Apple Pieces

Au gratin or casserole, cov., Red Apple I patt., Zephyr shape (ILLUS. far right with other Red Apple pieces) **25-35**

Bowl, utility, 4" d., Red Apple I patt., Zephyr shape (ILLUS. front row, second from left with other Red Apple pieces) **10**

Red Apple II Swirl Shape Plate

Plate, 7" d., Red Apple II patt., Swirl shape
(ILLUS.) **25**
Plate, 10" d., dinner, plain round, Red Apple
II patt. (ILLUS. second from left with oth-
er Red Apple pieces) **15-25**
Salt & pepper shakers, Hi-Rise shape, pr. **15-25**
Teapot, cov., Red Apple II patt., Zephyr
shape (ILLUS. far left with other Red Ap-
ple pieces) **50**

Other Patterns
Bean pot, Calico Tulip patt., w/original wire
rack **65**

Harker Monterey Cup & Saucer

Cup & saucer, Monterey patt. (ILLUS.) **15**

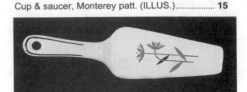

Deco Dahlia Pattern Lifter

Lifter, cake or pie, Deco Dahlia patt., 9" l.
(ILLUS.) **20**
Pitcher, cylindrical, Colonial Lady patt.,
Arches shape **20-30**
Pitcher, jug-type, Deco Dahlia patt., Hi-Rise
shape **50-125**
Syrup pitcher, cov., Colonial Lady pattern,
paneled Ohio shape **25-35**
Utility plate, Calico Tulip patt., Virginia
shape, 12" w **28**

Cameoware

*Created in the early 1930s and based on a Euro-
pean process, the sky blue ware with its white design
that seems to be etched into the surface is Harker's
most widely collected pattern. The process was first
tried by Bennett Pottery, but when Bennett closed, the
Cameoware line was taken over by Harker. After the
blue intaglios met with great success, Harker also
made pink, which was much less popular and rare
today, and yellow, which never went into full production. Because of its rarity and its bright contrast to the
blue engobe, the yellow ware is highly prized and
highly priced today. Prices given are for pink or blue.
Yellow prices are almost double or more, depending
upon the item.*

*In addition, Harker also manufactured a line of blue
and pink intaglio ware for Montgomery Ward with the
name "White Rose." Not so common as the design called
"Dainty Flower," White Rose has its own devoted fans.*

Ashtray, Dainty Flower patt., Swirl or Zephyr
shape, each **5**

Cameoware Pieces

Ashtray, Modern Age shape, Dainty Flower   patt., blue (ILLUS. far left) **15-25**

A Variety of Dainty Flower Pieces

Au gratin/casserole, cov., Zephyr shape **25-45**
Berry/salad set: serving bowl & six individu-
al dishes; the set.. **40-50**
Bowl, cereal, Swirl shape **8-10**
Cake/pie lifter **15-20**
Coffeepot or teapot, cov., each **30-50**
Cookie jar, cov., Dainty Flower patt., Zephyr
shape, blue (ILLUS. far right with ash-
tray)... **50**
Creamer **10-25**
Cup & saucer **10-20**
Custard cup **8-10**
Demitasse cup & saucer **25-30**
Fork or spoon, serving-type, each **15-20**
Fruit dish, Dainty Flower patt., Virginia
shape, blue (ILLUS. top, far right with
other Dainty Flower pieces, above)............... **5-8**
Gravy boat **30-35**
Grease jar, cov., D'Ware shape **15-30**
Grease jar, cov., Hi-Rise shape **10-25**
Mixing bowl **25-45**
Pitcher, jug-type, Hi-Rise shape.................... **75-150**
Pitcher, jug-type, round, blue............................ **30-50**
Pitcher, jug-type, round, Dainty Flower patt.,
yellow (ILLUS. second from left with
Cameoware collection, below) **50**
Pitcher, jug-type, square.................................... **30-50**
Plate, 6" sq., Dainty Flower, Virginia shape,
blue (ILLUS. top row, far left with other
Dainty Flower pieces) **5-8**

Plate, 7" d., luncheon, Dainty Flower patt.,
Swirl shape, blue (ILLUS. back row, left
with ashtray)... **8-12**
Plate, 7" sq., luncheon, Virginia shape **12-15**
Plate, 9" d. **12-15**
Platter, oval, plain... **15-35**
Platter, rectangular, Dainty Flower patt., Vir-
ginia shape, pink (ILLUS. second from
right with Cameoware collection)..................... **25**
Platter, rectangular, Virginia shape, blue........ **20-40**
Rolling pin, blue or pink **90-125**
Salt & pepper shakers, Dainty Flower patt.,
D'Ware shape, teal, pr. (ILLUS. far right
with Cameoware collection).............................. **35**
Salt & pepper shakers, Dainty Flower patt.,
D'Ware shape, yellow, pr. (ILLUS. left
with Cameoware collection).............................. **40**
Salt & pepper shakers, Dainty Flower patt.,
Hi-Rise shape, blue, pr. (ILLUS. top row,
center front with other Dainty Flower
pieces)... **25-30**
Salt & pepper shakers, Modern Age shape,
pr. **10-20**
Soup plate, flat rim, square............................... **10-15**
Sugar bowl, cov. **10-25**
Tea tile **20-30**
Vegetable/salad bowl, Dainty Flower patt.,
Virginia shape, blue, 9" d. (ILLUS. bot-
tom with other Dainty Flower pieces)............. **20**

Harker Cameoware Collection

Children's Ware

Harker's Kiddo sets were made in pink and blue with an occasional rare teal. Their etched classic designs of ducks, elephants, kittens and toy soldiers are loved by many collectors. Harker also made hot water feeders.

Bowl **25-30**
Hot water baby feeder **40-60**

Mug from Kiddo Set

Mug, elephant & toy soldier decorations, pink ground w/white figures, 3" h. (ILLUS. of elephant side).................................. **15**

Child's Mug & Plate

Mug, toy soldier decoration, blue, 3" h. (ILLUS. front with plate).................................... **15**
Plate, Teddy bear w/balloon decoration, blue (ILLUS. w/toy soldier mug)................. **20-30**

Gadroon and Royal Gadroon

With its distinctive scalloped edge, the Gadroon line was extremely popular. It was produced in several glaze colors, but the classic Chesterton grey and Corinthian deep teal are especially elegant and sought after today. These two Gadroon colors are frequently marked "Pate sur Pate."

The Royal Gadroon line was decorated with bright decals and was a perfect foil for colorful designs like Bridal Rose, Currier & Ives, Cynthia, Forget-me-not, Game Birds, Godey, Ivy, Margaret Rose, Morning Glories, Royal Rose, Violets, White Thistle and Wild Rose.

Gadroon

Bowl, cereal/soup, lug handles (ILLUS. middle right with Chesterton collection, below) **8**
Cake set: cake plate, six dessert plates & lifter; 8 pcs. **30-50**
Cake/pie lifter **10-20**
Casserole, cov. **40-50**
Creamer (ILLUS. front right with Chesterton collection)... **8**
Cup & saucer (ILLUS. middle left with Chesterton collection) **10**
Fork or spoon, serving, each **15-25**
Fruit dish **3-5**
Gravy boat (ILLUS. middle row, center with Chesterton collection).. **15**
Nappy **15-20**
Party set: cup & plate; 2 pcs. **10-15**
Pickle dish **8-10**
Plate, 7" w., salad, Virginia shape (ILLUS. rear right with Chesterton collection)................. **8**
Plate, 9" d., dinner (ILLUS. left rear with Chesterton collection)................................... **12-15**
Platter, oval... **20-25**
Rolling pin **85-125**
Salt & pepper shakers, pr. **10-20**
Soup plate, flat... **10-15**
Sugar bowl, cov. (ILLUS. front left with Chesterton collection).. **8**
Teapot, cov... **30-50**

Harker Chesterton Collection

Harker Royal Gadroon Pieces

Royal Gadroon

Bowl, cereal/soup, lug handles, Vintage patt. (ILLUS. bottom row, center with Royal Gadroon pieces, above)............................ 8

Cake plate, Wild Rose patt., 10" d. (ILLUS. bottom row, left with Royal Gadroon pieces) 15

Cake set: cake plate w/six matching serving plates & cake server; Currier & Ives patt., 8 pcs. 35

Casserole, cov. 40-50

Fruit dish, St. John's Wort patt. (ILLUS. middle row, center, with other Royal Gadroon pieces)... 3

Plate, 6" d., luncheon, Bermuda patt. (ILLUS. top row, right with other Royal Gadroon pieces) 8

Plate, 6" d., luncheon, Game Birds patt. (ILLUS. middle row, right with other Royal Gadroon pieces)............................. 8

Plate, 9" d., dinner, Magnolia patt. (ILLUS. top row, center with other Royal Gadroon pieces)... 12-15

Plate, 9" d., dinner, Violets patt. (ILLUS. top row, left with other Royal Gadroon pieces) 12-15

Platter, 15" l., oval, Vintage patt. (ILLUS. middle row, left with other Royal Gadroon pieces)... 20

Teapot, cov., Ivy Vine patt. (ILLUS. bottom row, right with other Royal Gadroon pieces) 50

Later Intaglios

Although highly popular during their time and thus so abundant, the later intaglios produced by Harker are not so in demand today. Therefore the prices are about half of those of Dainty Flower. Often labeled "Cameoware" by dealers, the green, pink-cocoa, yellow and robin's-egg blue ware do not carry the Cameoware
backstamp. Popular designs include Brown-Eyed Susan, Cock O'Morn, Ivy Wreath, Petit Fleur, Springtime, Wild Rice and Wild Rose.

Creamer & sugar bowl, pr. 10-15
Cup & saucer 5-8
Plate, dinner 5-10
Platter 10-20

Rockingham

The dark brown Rockingham glazed pieces were reproduced by Harker in the early 1960s. Because they are often impressed with the date of Harker's founding— "1840"—some confusion among collectors and dealers has arisen. Most items are marked as reproductions, but some are not. Many collectors find the honey-brown and bottle green items more desirable.

Ashtray, model of a tobacco leaf...................... 15-20
Bread tray 20-35
Mug, figural, Daniel Boone head...................... 20-30
Mug, figural hound handle 25-30
Mug, figural Jolly Roger head........................... 15-25

Hound-handled Pitcher

Pitcher, jug-type w/figural hound handle (ILLUS.)... 50-75

Tahiti Ashtray and Shakers

Plate, relief-molded American eagle (Great
    Seal of the U.S.).. **10-20**

Russel Wright

*White Clover intaglio on green, charcoal, coral or
gold.*

Clock, original works **75-100**
Plate **10-20**

Stone China

*Made of genuine Stone China clay, this heavy ware
with its solid pink, blue, white and yellow engobe glazes
over a grey body was manufactured in the 1950s and
1960s. The engobe (colored clay) was mixed with tiny
metallic chips. Later, Harker added hand-decorated
designs like Seafare and used its patented intaglio process to create many other designs.*

Bowl, cereal/soup **5-8**
Bowl, fruit **2-3**
Butter dish, cov. **10-15**
Casserole, cov. **20-30**
Coffeepot, cov., w/aluminum brewer bask
    et... **20-25**
Cookie jar, cov. **20-30**
Creamer & sugar bowl, pr. **10-15**
Cruet set, jug-form, oil & vinegar, pr............... **30-45**
Cup & saucer **5-8**
Nappy **10-15**
Nappy, divided... **8-12**
Pitcher, jug-type **15-20**
Plate, 9" d.. **5-10**
Platter, oval **15-20**
Rolling pin **100-150**
Salt & pepper shakers, D'Ware shape,
    pr.. **10-15**
Teapot, cov. **20-25**
Tidbit tray, three-tier **15-25**

Tahiti

*Originally designed for a restaurant, this labor-inten-
sive hand-decorated line has gained popularity in the
past couple of years.*

Ashtray (ILLUS. right with Tahiti salt & pep-
    per shakers, top of page) **15**
Creamer & sugar, pr.. **20**
Salt & pepper shakers, pr. (ILLUS. left w/Ta-
    hiti ashtray) **10**

Woodsong

*Another latecomer to the Harker line, this unique
ware was impressed with maple leaves and made in
honey brown, bottle green, grey, and dark brown.*

Coffeepot, cov., w/aluminum brewer basket....... **50**

Harker Woodsong Divided Dish

Dish, divided (ILLUS.)... **30**

Harlequin

*The Homer Laughlin China Company, makers of the
popular "Fiesta" pottery line, also introduced in 1938 a
less expensive and thinner ware that was sold under the
"Harlequin" name. It did not carry the maker's trademark and was marketed exclusively through F.W. Woolworth Company. It was produced in a wide range of
dinnerwares in assorted colors until 1964. Out of production for a number of years, in 1979 Woolworth
requested the line be reintroduced using an ironstone
body and with a limited range of pieces and colors
offered. Collectors also seek out a series of miniature
animal figures produced in the Harlequin line in the
1930s and 1940s.*

Ashtray, basketweave, rose................................... **$70**
Ashtray, basketweave, turquoise.......................... **75**
Ashtray, saucer, red... **93**
Ashtray, saucer, spruce green (chip) **50**
Bowl, 5 1/2" d., light green **9**
Bowl, 36s, cereal, 6 1/2" d., rose **20**
Bowl, 36s, oatmeal, 6 1/2" d., chartreuse............. **60**
Bowl, 36s, oatmeal, 6 1/2" d., grey........................ **60**
Bowl, 36s, oatmeal, 6 1/2" d., light green............. **50**
Bowl, 36s, oatmeal, 6 1/2" d., medium
    green **122**
Bowl, 36s, oatmeal, 6 1/2" d., rose........................ **38**
Bowl, 36s, oatmeal, 6 1/2" d., turquoise **30**

Bowl, individual salad, 7" d., chartreuse 31
Bowl, individual salad, 7" d., forest green 41
Bowl, individual salad, 7" d., grey 37
Bowl, individual salad, 7" d., light green.............. 45
Bowl, individual salad, 7" d., mauve blue 45
Bowl, individual salad, 7" d., red 75
Bowl, individual salad, 7" d., turquoise............... 18
Bowl, individual salad, 7" d., yellow 22
Butter dish, cov., turquoise, 1/2 lb. 110
Casserole, cov., chartreuse 240
Casserole, cov., maroon.................................... 205
Casserole, cov., mauve blue.............................. 160
Casserole, cov., spruce green............................ 205
Casserole, cov., turquoise.................................. 165
Casserole, cov., yellow 165
Creamer, forest green.. 25
Creamer, grey 22
Creamer, high-lip, mauve blue 275
Creamer, high-lip, mauve blue 375
Creamer, high-lip, spruce green......................... 225
Creamer, individual size, dark green................... 60
Creamer, individual size, green......................... 110
Creamer, individual size, light green 125
Creamer, individual size, turquoise..................... 25
Creamer, light green.. 25
Creamer, maroon... 25
Creamer, novelty, ball-shaped, grey.................... 75
Creamer, red 25
Creamer, rose 25
Creamer, turquoise... 7
Cup & saucer, demitasse, chartreuse 435
Cup & saucer, demitasse, light green 165
Cup & saucer, demitasse, maroon..................... 173
Cup & saucer, demitasse, mauve blue 100
Cup & saucer, demitasse, red 148
Cup & saucer, demitasse, spruce green........... 195
Cup & saucer, demitasse, turquoise................... 95
Cup & saucer, demitasse, yellow 95
Cup & saucer, turquoise 10
Egg cup, double, grey... 40
Egg cup, double, maroon 24
Egg cup, double, mauve blue 33
Egg cup, double, red.. 40
Egg cup, double, rose 29
Egg cup, double, turquoise................................. 21
Gravy boat, chartreuse 45
Gravy boat, grey 45
Gravy boat, mauve blue...................................... 41
Gravy boat, red 43
Gravy boat, rose 18
Gravy boat, turquoise 21
Gravy boat, yellow 35
Marmalade jar, cov., rose.................................. 685
Marmalade jar, cov., yellow............................... 510
Nappy, medium green, 9" d. 195
Nut dish, individual size, rose 11
Nut dish, individual size, yellow.......................... 13
Nut dish, light green 110
Nut dish, maroon 17
Nut dish, mauve blue 15
Nut dish, red 17
Nut dish, rose 82
Nut dish, spruce green....................................... 32
Nut dish, turquoise... 93
Nut dish, yellow... 11
Pitcher, jug-type, red, 22 oz............................... 95
Pitcher, 9" h., ball-shaped w/ice lip, dark green................. 125

Pitcher, 9" h., ball-shaped w/ice lip, light green 135
Pitcher, 9" h., ball-shaped w/ice lip, maroon...... 120
Pitcher, 9" h., ball-shaped w/ice lip, mauve blue 75
Pitcher, 9" h., ball-shaped w/ice lip, red 93
Pitcher, 9" h., ball-shaped w/ice lip, rose............. 95
Pitcher, 9" h., ball-shaped w/ice lip, spruce green 138
Pitcher, 9" h., ball-shaped w/ice lip, yellow 68
Pitcher, jug-type, grey, 22 oz............................ 110
Pitcher, jug-type, maroon, 22 oz....................... 110
Pitcher, jug-type, rose, 22 oz............................. 95
Pitcher, jug-type, spruce green, 22 oz. 125
Pitcher, jug-type, turquoise, 22 oz. 75
Plate, 6" d., turquoise.. 4
Plate, 7" d., medium green.................................. 55
Plate, 7" d., turquoise.. 6
Plate, 9" d., medium green.................................. 20
Plate, 9" d., turquoise... 11
Plate, 10" d., grey 48
Plate, 10" d., mauve blue 28
Plate, 10 "d., medium green 135
Plate, 10" d., red 30
Plate, 10" d., rose 35
Plate, 10" d., turquoise 22
Platter, 11" l., rose 14
Platter, 11" l., turquoise 22
Relish tray, turquoise w/yellow, red, mauve blue & maroon insert, the set 495
Soup plate, w/flanged rim, maroon, 8" d............. 35
Soup plate, w/flanged rim, medium green, 8" d. 125
Soup plate w/flanged rim, chartreuse.................. 30
Soup plate w/flanged rim, forest green 30
Soup plate w/flanged rim, light green.................. 35
Soup plate w/flanged rim, mauve blue................ 32
Soup plate w/flanged rim, red............................ 40
Soup plate w/flanged rim, rose........................... 35
Soup plate w/flanged rim, turquoise 24
Soup plate w/flanged rim, yellow 30
Spoon rest, yellow 295
Sugar bowl, cov., dark green.............................. 60
Sugar bowl, cov., forest green............................ 60
Sugar bowl, cov., grey 35
Sugar bowl, cov., maroon 45
Sugar bowl, cov., mauve blue 30
Sugar bowl, cov., medium green 220
Sugar bowl, cov., rose 35
Sugar bowl, cov., rose 35
Syrup pitcher, cov., red...................................... 395
Syrup pitcher, cov., yellow................................ 550
Teapot, cov., forest green 258
Teapot, cov., grey.. 205
Teapot, cov., light green................................... 225
Teapot, cov., maroon 210
Teapot, cov., mauve blue.................................. 105
Teapot, cov., red... 175
Teapot, cov., rose 100
Teapot, cov., spruce green 225
Teapot, cov., turquoise 97
Teapot, cov., yellow 145
Tumbler, maroon 80
Tumbler, red... 55
Tumbler, spruce green 50
Tumbler, water, mauve blue 48
Tumbler, yellow.. 43
Tumbler, rose 80

Animals

Haviland

Haviland porcelain was originated by Americans in Limoges, France, shortly before the mid-19th century and continues in production. Some Haviland was made by Theodore Haviland in the United States during the last World War. Numerous other factories also made china in Limoges. Also see LIMOGES.

Haviland Marks

Footed Comport with Reticulated Rim

Comport, pedestal on three feet w/ornate gold shell design, top w/reticulated edge, peach & gold design around base & top, 9" d. (ILLUS.).. **425**

Comport, round, English, shaped like regular pedestal comport without pedestal, Schleiger 56 variation, decorated w/lavender flowers, 9" d.. **125**

Compote, Meadow Visitors patt., smooth blank, 5 1/8" h., 9 7/8" d. **165**

Cracker jar, cov., floral decoration, cobalt, gold & blue bells, 1900 & decorator's marks.. **450**

Cracker jar, cov., Marseille blank...................... **350**

Cream soup w/underplate, Schleiger 31, Ranson blank, decorated w/pink roses, 5" d. bowl, 2 pcs..................................... **55**

Creamer, Schleiger 146, commonly known as Apple Blossom, Theodore Haviland, 4".. **60**

Creamer, Moss Rose patt., gold trim, 5 1/2" h.. **50**

Creamer & open sugar, dessert, Cloverleaf patt., Schleiger 98, pr.................................... **145**

Creamer & open sugar, Ranson blank, Drop Rose patt., w/very ornate gold trim, pr. **695**

Creamer & sugar, Schleiger 223A, Blank 1, decorated w/pink flowers, pr......................... **125**

Creamer & sugar bowl, Mont Mery patt., ca. 1953, pr.. **125**

Cup & saucer, coffee, Schleiger 39D, decorated w/pink roses & gold trim **55**

Cup & saucer, demitasse, Arcadia, bird patt.. **45**

Cup & saucer, tea, Schleiger 19, white w/gold trim... **45**

Cup & saucer, breakfast, Moss Rose patt. w/gold trim... **45**

Cup & saucer, demitasse, Papillon Butterfly patt., floral by Pallandre..................................... **75**

Cup & saucer, Moss Rose patt., "Haviland & Co. - Limoges - France," pr............................. **40**

Cup & saucer, Rosalinde patt.............................. **45**

Meadow Visitors Cup & Saucer

Cups & saucers, Papillon butterfly handles w/Meadow Visitors decoration, six sets (ILLUS. of one set) **900**

Cuspidor, smooth blank, bands of roses decorating rim & body, 6 1/2" h. **193**

Cuspidor, Moss Rose patt, smooth blank, 8" d., 3 1/4" h... **248**

Dessert set: 8 1/2 x 15" tray & four 7 1/4" dishes; Osier Blank No. 637, fruit & floral decoration, the set.. **250**

Dessert set: 9 x 15" oblong tray w/twelve 7" square matching plates; centers decorated w/Meadow Visitors patt. & bordered in rich cobalt blue w/gold trim, commissioned for Mrs. Wm. A. Wilson, 13 pcs...... **2,300**

Haviland Scenic Dish

Dish, shell-shaped, incurved rim opposite pointed rim, h.p. scene of artist's waterside studio, decorated by Theodore Davis, front initialed "D," back w/presidential seal & artist's signature, part of Hayes presidential service, 8 x 9 1/2" (ILLUS.)... **1,925**

Dresser tray, h.p. floral decoration, 1892 mark.. **95**

Egg cup, footed, No. 69 patt. on blank No. 1........ **65**

Egg cups, footed, No. 72 patt., Blank No. 22, pr. **190**

Fish set: 23" l. platter & six 9" d. plates; each w/different fish scene, dark orange & gold borders, Blank No. 1009, 7 pcs.......... **1,250**

Plate from Fish Set

Fish set: 22" l. oval platter & twelve 8 1/2" d. plates; each piece w/a different fish in the center, the border in two shades of green design w/gold trim, h.p. scenes by L. Martin, mark of Theodore Haviland, 13 pcs. (ILLUS. of plate)..................................... **2,750**

Fish set: 23 1/4" l. platter & twelve 7 3/8" plates; Empress Eugenie patt., No. 453, Blank No. 7, 13 pcs...................................... **2,500**

Gravy boat, No. 761 .... **95**

Gravy boat w/attached underplate, No. 98 patt., Blank No. 24.. **145**

Gravy boat w/attached underplate, Schleiger 46, Ranson blank, decorated w/pink & blue flowers... **125**

Haviland Hair Receiver

Hair receiver, cov., squatty round body on three gold feet, h.p. overall w/small flowers in blues & greens w/gold trim, mark of Charles Field Haviland (ILLUS.)..................... **150**

Honey dish, 4" d., bowl-form, Schleiger 33, decorated w/white flowers, pink shading **25**

Ice cream set: tray & 6 individual plates; Old Pansy patt. on Torse blank, 7 pcs. **303**

Jam jar w/underplate, cov., Christmas Rose patt. **795**

Jam jar w/underplate, cov., No. 577 patt., smooth blank **225**

Match box, gold trim, 1882 & decorator's marks **175**

Haviland Mayonnaise

Mayonnaise bowl w/attached underplate, decorated w/pink wild roses touched w/yellow, Schleiger 141D, 5" d. (ILLUS.)...... **145**

Mayonnaise bowl w/underplate, cov., leaf-shaped, Blank No. 271A............................... **166**

Muffin server, No. 31 patt., Blank No. 24........... **225**

Mustache cup & saucer, No. 270A patt., Blank No. 16 .... **220**

Mustard pot, cov., No. 266 patt. on Blank No. 9 .... **220**

Mustard pot w/attached underplate, cov., CFH/GDM, copper color w/gold floral design overall, cov. w/spoon slot, 2 1/2 x 4"..... **225**

Nut dish, footed, No. 1070A patt. **55**

Olive dish, No. 257 patt. **99**

Oyster plate, Ranson blank, Schleiger 42A, decorated w/pink roses................................... **175**

Haviland Oyster Plate

Oyster plate, six clam-shaped sections w/round center section for sauce, white, 8" d. (ILLUS.).. **175**

Oyster plate, The Princess patt., Schleiger 57C, 9 1/2" d. **175**

Oyster plates, four-well, all white w/relief-molded scrolled design, 7 1/2" d., pr............. **250**

Oyster plates, five-well, 72C patt., Blank No. 24??, center indent for sauce, 9" d., pr......... **350**

Oyster scoop, oyster-shaped, CFH/GDM, h.p., 1 3/4 x 2 1/5" **65**

Oyster tureen, Henri II Blank, decorated by Dammouse **1,050**

Pancake server, decorated w/yellow flowers w/pale green stems, smooth blank, 1892 & decorator marks.. **154**

Pickle dish, shell-shaped w/gold trim, leaf mold, 8 3/4" l. **65**

Pin box, cov., oblong, ornate scrolled base & rim, loop finial on h.p. floral decorated lid, marked "H & Co. L. France," 4" l. **175**

Pin tray, rectangular, open handles, decorated w/pink roses, Blank 1, Schleiger 251, 3 x 5".. **125**

Pitcher, syrup-type, Schleiger 144, decorated w/pink roses & green scrolls **145**

Pitcher, 7" h., milk, Schleiger 98, Blank 12, Cloverleaf patt.. **125**

Pitcher with Anchor in Relief

Pitcher, 7" h., milk-type, tankard style w/tapering cylindrical white body w/a large relief-molded anchor under the heavy ropetwist loop handle, bright gold trim, old Haviland & Co. mark (ILLUS.) **125**

Pitcher, 8 3/8" h., Ivy patt. w/gold trim................. **175**

Pitcher, 8 5/8" h., Art Deco stylized figural "Farewell" cat in yellow & white, base inscribed "Theodore Haviland Limoges/France Copyright Depose" & "E.M. Sandoz sc" **895**

Pitcher, 8 5/8" h., Ranson blank No. 1................ **225**

Haviland Lemonade Pitcher

Pitcher, 9" h., lemonade-type, Schleiger
1026B variation, Blank 117, decorated
w/lavender flowers & brushed gold trim,
Theodore Haviland (ILLUS.)......................... **225**

Gold-decorated Lemonade Pitcher

Pitcher, 9" h., tankard-shaped lemonade-
type, Ranson blank, delicate floral band
around the upper body trimmed in gold,
gold handle & trim bands, factory-deco-
rated, Haviland & Co. mark (ILLUS.)............. **225**
Pitcher, 9 1/2" h., No. 279 patt., Blank No.
643 .... **225**
Place setting: dinner, salad, bread & butter
plates, cup & saucer; w/scalloped double
gold edge, Schleiger 91A.............................. **135**
Plate, dinner, No. 72...................................... **40**
Plate, dinner, No. 9 patt., set of 10 .... **300**
Plate, dinner, Rosalinde patt.................................. **35**
Plate, Partridge in a Pear Tree from 12 Days
of Christmas series, 1970 .... **75**

Plate, ice cream, 5" l., leaf-shaped w/han-
dle, cobalt & gold **125**

Paisley Pattern Plate

Plate, bread & butter, 6 1/2" d., Paisley
patt., smooth blanks w/gold edge, brownish red ground w/flowers in yellow, bright
blue, green & white border design w/yel-
low flowers & bright blue leaves, turquoise scroll trim, Haviland & Co. mark
(ILLUS.)... **26**
Plate, bread & butter, 6 1/2" d., Schleiger
340, decorated w/pink roses & blue
scrolls **28**
Plate, coupe salad, 7 1/2" d., Baltimore
Rose patt, Blank No. 207, set of 8 .... **520**
Plate, 8 1/2" d., cobalt & gold Pallandre patt....... **175**

Plate with Draped Pink Roses

Plate, luncheon, 8 1/2" d., smooth edge, de-
sign on border of draped pink roses,
Schleiger 152, Theodore Haviland
(ILLUS.)... **28**

Heart-shaped Baltimore Rose Plate

Double-spouted Sauceboat & Tray

Plate, 7 1/2 x 8 1/2", heart-shaped, Baltimore Rose patt. (ILLUS.) **275**

Plate, 9 1/2" d., scalloped edge, cobalt & gold w/floral center **225**

Plate, dinner, 9 1/2" d., Dammouse antique rose w/gold medallion & flowers.................... **180**

Plate, dinner, 9 1/2" d., Feu de Four, Poppy & Seeds... **125**

Plate, dinner, 9 1/2" d., Schleiger 19, Silver Anniversary.. **35**

Plate, dinner, 9 1/2" d., Schleiger 29-K, decorated w/pink flowers & gold trim **40**

Plate, 9 3/4" d., portrait of woman in forest scene, artist-signed, Blank No. 116............... **125**

Plate, dinner, 10" d., Schleiger 150, known as Harrison Rose, decorated w/small pink & yellow roses... **30**

Plate, 10 1/2" d., service, Blank 20, white w/gold trim.. **45**

Plate, chop, 11 1/4" d., 33A patt., Blank No. 19 .... **125**

Plate, chop, 12" d., Schleiger 233, The Norma, decorated w/small pink & yellow flowers **125**

Plates, luncheon, 8 3/8" d., Club Ware, Meadow Visitors patt. & various fruits, set of 8 .... **242**

Platter, 16" l., rectangular, Marseilles, Schleiger 9.. **125**

Platter, 12 1/4 x 18" oval, Moss Rose patt. w/blue trim, smooth blank **150**

Platter, 14 x 20", Ranson blank No. 1 .... **275**

Pudding set, Schleiger 24, white w/gold trim, complete w/unglazed insert & undertray **475**

Punch bowl, Baltimore Rose patt..................... **2,000**

Punch cup, tapering scalloped pedestal foot supporting wide shallow cup bowl, decorated w/flowers in shades of green w/some pink flowers & green leaves,

variation of Schleiger No. 249B on Blank 17, Haviland & Co. mark, 4" h......................... **75**

Ramekins & underplates, Ranson Blank No. 1, set of 12.. **540**

Relish, oval, Schleiger 570, two-tone green flowers, gold edge, 8" l. **45**

Salad plate, bean-shaped, variation of Schleiger 1190, decorated w/orange flowers & gold trim, 4 1/2 x 9"............................. **95**

Salt, CFH/GDM, h.p. flowers, 1 1/2 x 3/4"............ **45**

Salt, Schleiger 31, decorated w/pink roses & gold trim, 2 x 1".. **65**

Sauce tureen w/attached underplate, cov., No. 146 patt., Blank No. 133, 7" d. underplate, bowl 5 1/4" d.. **145**

Sauce tureen w/attached undertray, cov., oval, Schleiger 619, green design w/gold trim, Theodore Haviland................................ **125**

Sauceboat & undertray, footed double-spouted boat-shaped sauceboat w/looped side handles w/molded rope trim, matching dished undertray, heavy gold trim on white, old Haviland & Co. mark, 2 pcs. (ILLUS., top of page)................ **150**

Serving bowl, Schleiger 235B, 12" d., 2" h........ **195**

Multifloral Serving Dish

Serving dish, quatrefoil form, Multifloral patt., Old H & Co, 9" sq., 2" h. (ILLUS.)......... **125**

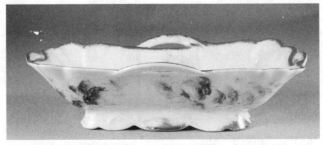

Haviland Serving Dish with Poppies

Serving dish, scalloped rectangular form w/a scalloped footring below the flaring side w/low open side handles, decorated w/pale yellowish green to dark green poppies & pale pink shadows, gold trim, variation of Schleiger No. 665, Haviland & Co. mark, 8 x 10" (ILLUS., bottom previous page) **175**

Serving plate, blue & burgundy Art Deco decoration, black ground, "Haviland & Co. - Limoges - France," 10 1/2" d. **95**

Sipper dishes, Meadow Visitors patt., smooth blank, 4 3/4" d., set of 8 .... **176**

Sorbet, footed, w/gold embossed trim, Schleiger 276 .... **65**

Soup bowls, No. 271A patt., Blank No. 213, set of 8 .... **280**

Soup plate w/flanged rim, No. 761 .... **35**

Soup tureen, cov., pink Drop Rose patt., on Blank No. 22 .... **695**

Soup tureen, round, Ranson blank, Schleiger 29M, decorated w/tiny blue flowers **350**

Haviland Covered Sugar Bowl

Sugar bowl, cov., large cylindrical form w/small loop side handles & inset flat cover w/arched handle, white ground decorated w/sprays of pink daisies touched w/yellow & greyish brown leaves, variation of Schleiger No. 1311, 1 lb. size, Charles Field Haviland, marked "CFH/GDM" (ILLUS.)... **75**

Tea caddy, cov., Ranson blank **275**

Tea set: cov. teapot, creamer & sugar bowl; floral & leaf mold w/gold trim, 3 pcs.............. **400**

Tea set: small cov. teapot, creamer & sugar bowl, six cups & saucers; No. 19 patt., 15 pcs.. **650**

Tea & toast set: scalloped plate & cup; Marseilles blank, decorated w/pink roses, H & Co **175**

Tea & toast tray & cup, No. 482 patt., Blank No. 208, pr. **275**

Tea tray, round, Schleiger 29A, decorated w/pink flowers, unglazed bottom, 16" d. **275**

Butterfly-handled Cup and Saucer

Teacup & saucer, cup w/tapering cylindrical bowl & figural butterfly handle, h.p. grey band design on rim & border, Haviland & Co. (ILLUS.) **125**

Teapot, cov., 4-cup, CFG/GDM, white w/gold, ribbon handle................................... **225**

Teapot, cov., Henri II blank w/gold & silver decoration (inner rim restored)..................... **250**

Toothbrush box, cov., Moss Rose patt. w/gold trim, smooth blank, ca. 1860s-70s, 8" l. **225**

Vases, 15" h., Terra Cotta, brown w/white water lily & large green leaves in relief, Haviland & Co, pr. **4,500**

Vegetable dish, oval, Schleiger 142A, decorated w/pink daisy-like flowers, blue fences & scrolls, gold trim, Theodore Haviland, 8 x 10".. **85**

Vegetable dish, cov., Marseille patt., Blank No. 9, 9 1/2" l. **145**

Vegetable dish, cov., decorated w/small orange roses, Blank No. 24, 10" d. **145**

Wash pitcher, Moss Rose patt. w/gold trim, smooth blank, 12" h. **350**

Waste bowl, Schleiger 233A, The Norma, decorated w/tiny pink & yellow flowers & gold daubs, 5 x 3"... **47**

Head Vase Planters

Head Vase Planters were most popular and most abundant during the 1950s. Whereas some could be found prior to this period, the majority were Japanese imports and a direct product of Japan's postwar industrial boom. Sizes, shapes, styles and quality varied according to importer. American manufacturers did produce some head vase planters during this time, but high quality standards and production costs made it hard to compete with the less expensive imports.

Ardalt, No. 6039, Madonna w/both hands holding roses, pastel coloring in glossy bisque, planter, paper label, 6" h. **$32**

Ardco, No. C1248, high bouffant hair, dark green dress, earrings, necklace, paper label, 5 1/2" h. **62**

"Lita" Head Vase

Betty Lou Nichols, "Lita," redheaded woman in black off-the-shoulder dress w/red-orange flowers, wide-brimmed black hat, eyes closed, rare, 8" h. (ILLUS.).................... **800**

Betty Lou Nichols Head Vase

Betty Lou Nichols, "Mary Lou," woman w/brown hair wearing grey dress w/brown crisscross ribbon at throat, brimmed hat matches ribbon color, closed eyes, 8" h. (ILLUS.) 600

"Mary Lou" Head Vase

Betty Lou Nichols, "Mary Lou," woman w/dark hair wearing blue & white plaid dress w/fancy ruffled high-button shawl collar, w/white-brimmed hat w/hat band in matching blue & white plaid, 8" h. (ILLUS.) 650
Brinn, No. TP2071, molded blonde hair, painted eyes, earrings, right hand near face, 6" h. 100

California Pastels Head Vase

California Pastels, Kaye No. 601, woman in flowered off-the-shoulder grey, pink, black & yellow dress & turban-style blue, yellow, green & pink hat w/big pink rose at front, 10 1/2" h. (ILLUS.) 350
Inarco, King w/full grey beard, red, yellow & black w/gold trim, 4 3/4" h. (small base flake) 75

"Mitzie Gaynor" Head Vase Planter

Inarco, No. 2968, "Mitzie Gaynor," woman wearing white flower in upswept hair, posed w/hand under chin, 6 3/4" h. (ILLUS.) 650

Woman with Heart Necklace

Inarco, No. 5626, blonde w/red bow in hair & red fingernails, wearing heart necklace and pearl earrings, posed w/hand touching lips, 7" h. (ILLUS.) .... **1,500+**
Inarco, No. E1062, head turned to the right, gold clasps on black gown, earrings, necklace, closed eyes w/big lashes, paper label & stamp, 1963, 5 1/4" h. 95
Inarco, No. E1062, ringlet hair, earrings, closed eyes w/big lashes, black gloved right hand holding gilt decorated fan under right cheek, paper label & stamp, 1963, 6" h. 180
Inarco, No. E1611, closed eyes w/big lashes, earrings, gold painted bracelet, left hand under face on right, 1964, 5 1/2" h. 375

Inarco, No. E1756, "Lady Aileen," gold & green tiara & matching painted necklace, paper label, 5 1/2" h. **275**

Inarco Jackie Kennedy

Inarco, No. E1852, Jackie Kennedy wearing black dress & glove w/hand to cheek, paper label, 6" h. (ILLUS.) **500**

Inarco, No. E193/M, applied pink rose in hair, light green dress, earrings, necklace, right hand on cheek, closed eyes w/big lashes, 1961, 5 1/2" h. **100**

Inarco, No. E2254, black dress, pearl finish on hair, earrings, necklace, closed eyes w/big lashes, paper label, 6" h. **70**

Inarco, No. E2322, black dress, black open-edged hat w/white ribbon, gloved hand by right cheek, earrings, necklace, paper label, 7 1/4" h. **215**

Inarco, No. E2523, child w/blue scarf & dress, pigtails, painted eyes, high gloss, stamped, 5 1/2" h. **70**

Inarco Soldier Boy

Inarco, No. E2735, soldier boy w/bayonet, closed eyes, stamped, 5 3/4" h. (ILLUS.) **55**

Inarco, No. E5624, pink hat & blue dress, earrings, painted eyes, paper label & stamp, 5 1/2" h. **125**

Inarco, No. E779, applied blonde hair & peach rose, peach dress, earrings, neck-

lace, right hand by cheek, paper label & stamp, 1962, 6" h. **100**

Inarco, No. E969/S, mint green hat & dress, painted closed eyes w/big lashes, 1963, 4 1/2" h. **65**

Doll-like Head Vase

Japan, doll-like form dressed like Russian peasant w/babushka, red, blue & green, 8 1/4" h. (ILLUS.) **150**

Japan, No. 2261, black dress w/white collar, black bow in blonde hair, painted eyes, earrings, glazed finish, 7" h. **125**

Head Vase Made in Japan

Japan, woman w/platinum blonde hair w/black bow, wearing black ribbon choker w/white flower around neck, eyes closed, rare, 5 1/2" h. (ILLUS.) **550**

Lefton, No. 1086, white iridescent blouse, necklace, paper label, 6" h. **95**

Lefton, No. 1343A, applied flowers on large brimmed hat & collar, painted features, raised right hand, paper label, glossy finish, 6" h. **95**

Lefton, No. 2536, flower in hair, painted earrings & necklace, gloved right hand under chin, 5 1/4" h. **75**

Lefton, No. 2796, blue blouse, blue sash on head, paper label, 6" h. **65**

Lefton, No. 2796, pink blouse, pink sash on head, paper label, 6" h. **65**

Lefton, No. 4596, green hat, scarf & coat, earrings, painted eyes, black gloved hand under cheek, partial Lefton's label, 5 1/2" h.. **95**

Lefton, No. 611B, Lefton paper label & Geo. Z. Lefton stamp, bird on pink floral hat, high collar, closed painted eyes, glossy finish, 6 1/4" h.. **70**

Manchu, Ceramic Arts Studio of Madison, Wisconsin, 7 1/2" h.. **132**

Napco, No. A5120, large pink hat, fur-trimmed pink dress w/blue daisy, closed eyes w/big lashes, paper label, 5" h............... **50**

Napco, No. A5120, orange bonnet w/bow & matching lace-trimmed dress, paper label, 5 1/4" h.. **65**

Napco, No. C1775A, green striped hat w/bow on top right, jeweled green dress, hand by cheek, big lashes, stamped, 1956, 7 1/4" h.. **110**

Napco, No. C2589A, wearing black dress & feather hat, gold painted earring, closed eyes w/big lashes, right hand under right side of chin, bracelet, paper label & stamp, 1956, 5" h.................................... **65**

Napco No. C2632C

Napco, No. C2632C, large lavender hat w/dark trim, matching lavender dress, hand to hat, earring in exposed ear, 7" h. (ILLUS.).. **105**

Napco No. C2633C

Napco, No. C2633C, black hat & dress, gold dots on white hat bow, earrings, necklace, closed eyes w/big lashes, 1956, 5 1/2" h. (ILLUS.).................................... **85**

Napco, No. C2634B, baby w/white bonnet, paper label, 5 1/2" h... **55**

Napco No. C2636B

Napco, No. C2636B, flat white hat w/gold trim, dark green dress, left hand under chin, earrings, necklace, closed eyes w/big lashes, paper label, 1956, 6" h. (ILLUS.)... **95**

Napco, No. C2637C, white round flat hat, black dress, hand under left cheek, painted eyes, earrings, necklace, paper label & stamp, 1956, 7" h. **85**

Napco, No. C2638C, earrings, painted eyes, molded necklace, stamped, 1956, 6" h... **100**

Napco, No. C3205B, wearing crown of gold & white flowers, necklace, paper label, 5 1/2" h.. **70**

Napco, No. C3815, gold & white trim on blue hat, blue high collar jacket, earrings, closed eyes w/big lashes, paper label, 1959, 5 1/2" h... **85**

Napco, No. C3959A, blue hat w/bow & high collar blouse, real lashes, earrings, paper label, 5 1/2" h... **65**

Napco, No. C4556C, child wearing green hat, painted eyes, glossy finish, partial paper label, impressed, 1960, 5 1/4" h. **65**

Napco No. CX2707

Napco, No. CX2707, Christmas girl, green w/red trimmed hat & dress, painted eyes, right hand under cheek, paper label & stamp, 1957, 5 1/2" h. (ILLUS.)......................... **80**

Napco No. CX2708

Napco, No. CX2708, Christmas girl, holly sprigs in hat, painted cross necklace, gloved right hand away from face, closed eyes w/big lashes, paper label & stamp, 1957, 6" h. (ILLUS.).. **250**

Napco, No. CX2709A, Christmas child in fur-trimmed hat & coat, holding song book, painted eyes, paper label & stamp, 1957, 3 1/2" h. (worn paint on back near base)... **75**

Napcoware, No. 8494, gold bow in long hair, gold dress w/white collar, left earring, painted eyes, 7 1/4" h. **225**

Napcoware, No. C6428, three flowers on neck of blue gown, dark gloved hand on left cheek, earrings, closed eyes w/big lashes, stamped mark, 5 1/2" h..................... **125**

Napcoware No. C6429

Napcoware, No. C6429, molded bouffant hair, white floral collar on blue gown, closed eyes w/big lashes, earrings, dark blue glove, hand by cheek, 7" h. (ILLUS.)..... **175**

Napcoware, No. C6985, green dress w/center jewel, closed eyes w/big lashes, earrings, necklace, 8 1/2" h. **225**

Napcoware, No. C7472, dark blue blouse, necklace & earrings, paper label, 6" h. **85**

Napcoware, No. C7473, head turned to right, applied floral decoration on right

shoulder, earrings, necklace, painted eyes, 7 3/4" h. **165**

Napcoware No. C8493

Napcoware, No. C8493, long hair off to right side, gold bow & dress w/white collar, earring in left ear, painted eyes, 6" h. (ILLUS.)... **95**

Relpo, No. 2004, green dress & hair bow, painted eyes, earrings, paper label & stamp, 7" h. **250**

Relpo, No. 2089, Marilyn, grey bow in hair on right, black halter dress, earrings, painted eyes, open lips, paper label & stamp, 7" h. (chip on top of bow, minor paint wear on chin & left cheek)................. **2,700**

Relpo, No. 5634, Christmas girl, hood w/holly, fur-trimmed coat, painted eyes, gloved hand near face, Sampson Import Co., impressed, 1965, 7 1/2" h. **200**

Relpo, No. K1175M, wearing hat & matching dress, w/hands folded under chin, open eyes, earrings, necklace, 5 1/2" h. **95**

Relpo, No. K1633, Japan, black dress w/white decoration, gloved right hand touching chin & cheek, earring, necklace, painted eyes, 7" h.. **200**

Relpo No. K1662

Relpo, No. K1662, floral molded green & lavender hat & green dress, painted eyes, earrings, necklace, paper label & stamp, 6" h. (ILLUS.)...................................... 150

Relpo, No. K1696, wearing green bow in hair & matching top, earrings, necklace, paper label, 5 1/2" h. 55

Woman in Green

Relpo, No. K1835, blonde woman in pale green brimmed hat w/darker green bow, in dark green coat w/beige fur-like collar, 7 1/2" h. (ILLUS.).. 325

Relpo, No. K1836, Japan, white hat w/blue edge & bow, blue dress w/white trim, painted eyes, right earring, 6 1/2" h............... 500

Relpo, No. K1932, black bows in hair & black high collar dress, earrings, painted eyes, paper label & stamp, 5 1/2" h.............. 225

Rare Head Vase Planter

Royal Crown, blonde in white sundress/swimsuit & black floppy-brimmed hat w/white sunglasses sitting on brim, very rare, 7" h. (ILLUS.).............................. 2,000

Ruben, multicolored clown in green & yellow, closed eyes, 5" h. 25

Ruben, No. 4123, white ruffled black dress, earrings, necklace, painted eyes, impression & paper label, 7" h...................................... 75

Ruben, No. 4129, blonde ponytails, painted eyes, earrings, necklace, paper label, 5 1/2" h. 145

Ruben, No. 4185, braided blonde hair w/flower, green dress w/high white collar, impressed mark, 5 1/2" h. 110

Ruben, No. 484, heart-shaped grey hat, necklace, earrings, paper label, 5 3/4" h. 150

Rubens "Lucy"

Rubens, No. 531, Japan, Lucy in top hat w/horse neck piece, shades of grey, stamped & painted lashes, flake in tie end, 7 1/2" h. (ILLUS.).................................... 400

Rubens, No. 531, Japan, Lucy in top hat w/horse neck piece, yellow & green w/glazed finish, stamped & painted lashes, 7 1/2" h. 400

Ucagco Baby

Ucagco, baby dressed in blue bonnet trimmed w/lace & blue bib, paper label, 6" h. (ILLUS.).. 42

"Heads Up" Head Vase Planter

United Design, Abigail 1953 "Heads Up,"
Cameo Girl series, blonde in pink & white
dress & white brimmed hat & gloves,
wearing pearl earrings & necklace, holds
miniature version of similar design in
hand, collector's edition of 500, made for
10th annual Head Vase Convention
(ILLUS.) **250**

Commemorative Head Vase Planter

United Design, Judith "Smart Shopper,"
Cameo Girl series, blonde in leopard
print coat, black gloves & black brimmed
hat trimmed in white, w/six-sided open
box w/miniature head vase inside, limited
edition of 500, commemorative piece for
the 11th annual Head Vase Convention,
5 3/4" h. (ILLUS.) **250**
Velco, No. 3688, Japan, pink hair bow &
dress, w/hand at cheek, paper label,
5 1/2" h. (missing one earring) **75**
Velco, No. 3749, white bow on grey hat,
black dress, rhinestone earrings, closed
eyes w/big lashes, left hand near chin,
paper label & stamp, 5 3/4" h. **125**

Carmen Miranda-style Head Vase

Miscellaneous, stylized black Carmen
Miranda-like woman in pink & yellow
dress w/orange turban w/fruit, unmarked,
7 3/4" h. (ILLUS.) **150**

Woman in Green Dress Head Vase

Miscellaneous, woman in off-the-shoulder
lime green dress, eyes closed, un-
marked, 7 1/2" h. (ILLUS.) **125**

Historical & Commemorative Wares

*Numerous potteries, especially in England and the
United States, made various porcelain and earthenware
pieces to commemorate people, places and events.
Scarce English historical wares with American views
command highest prices. Objects are listed here alpha-
betically by title of the view.*

*Most pieces listed here will date between about 1820
and 1850. The maker's name is noted at the end of the
entry.*

Almshouse, Boston tureen & cover, flowers
within medallions border, dark blue, footed deep ovoid body w/wide angled rim,
domed cover & scroll end handles, Ridgway, 12 3/4" l., 9 1/2" h. (two hairlines in
base, chip on inside edge of cover) **$3,300**
Almshouse, New York platter, vine border,
dark blue, Ridgway, 16 1/2" l. **1,035**

Arms of Delaware Platter

Almshouse, New York platter, flowers within medallions border, Beauties of America series, dark blue, Ridgway, 12 3/4 x 16 1/2" (scratches, scattered minor staining).. **1,265**

Arms of Delaware platter, trumpet flower & vine border, dark blue, Thomas Mayer, ca. 1830, 17 1/8" l. (ILLUS., top of page) **5,600**

Arms of Rhode Island Plate

Arms of Rhode Island plate, flowers & vines border, dark blue, T. Mayer, minor glaze scratches, 8 1/2" d. (ILLUS.)........................... **748**

Baltimore & Ohio Railroad, level (The) plate, shell border, dark blue, E. Wood, 10 1/8" d. (stains, minor roughness on table ring) **990**

Battle of Bunker Hill platter, vine border, dark blue, R. Stevenson, 10 1/4 x 13"........ **8,625**

Boston State House basket & undertray, flowers & leaves border, basket w/reticulated sides & scalloped flaring rim, dark blue, J. Rogers, basket 6 1/2 x 9 1/4", the set **2,760**

Boston State House dish, flowers & leaves on flanged rim, deep sides, dark blue, J. Rogers, 12 3/4" d. (minor glaze scratches) **2,070**

Boston State House pitcher, Rose Border series, fully opened roses w/leaves border, dark blue, Stubbs, 6" h. (small chip on handle) **978**

Boston State House sauce tureen, cover & undertray, flowers & leaves border, pedestal base w/upward looped handles, high domed cover, dark blue, J. Rogers, tureen 7 1/4 x 8 1/4", the set........................ **3,738**

Cadmus (so-called) plate, shell border, irregular center, dark blue, Wood, 10" d. (light scratches) **500-600**

Capitol, Washington (The) serving bowl, vine border, embossed white rim, dark blue, Stevenson, 11" d. (glaze imperfections)... **2,645**

Castle Garden, Battery, New York cup plate, trefoil border, dark blue, Wood, 3 3/4" d. (hairlines).. **138**

Christianburg Danish Settlement on the Gold Coast, Africa platter, shell border, well-and-tree center, dark blue, E. Wood, 18 3/4" l. (minor glaze imperfections)......... **3,220**

City Hall, New York Plate

City Hall, New York plate, flowers within medallions border, medium blue, J. & W. Ridgway, 9 3/4" d. ((ILLUS.) **193**

City Hotel, New York plate, oak leaf border, double portrait reserves at border of Washington & Lafayette, inset view of the Entrance to the Erie Canal, dark blue, R. Stevenson, 8 1/2" d. (minor scratching) **4,600**

Columbia College, New York plate, acorn & oak leaves border, portrait medallion at rim of "President Washington," inset of "View of the Aqueduct Bridge at Rochester," dark blue, R. Stevenson, 7 1/2" d. (minor scratches).. **8,625**

Commodore MacDonnough's Victory plate, shell border, dark blue, E. Wood, 8 3/8" d. (minor wear & knife scratches)....... **358**

Commodore MacDonnough's Victory tea set, shell border, dark blue, cov. teapot, cov. sugar bowl & creamer, E. Wood, teapot 7 1/2 x 11", the set **1,293**

Detroit Platter from Cities Series

Court House, Baltimore plate, fruit & flowers border, dark blue, Henshall, Williamson & Co., 8 1/2" d. (light wear, hairline) **470**

Custom House, Philadelphia cup plate, flowers within medallions border, dark blue, Ridgway, 3 1/2" d. (short hairlines, professional repair).. **275**

Dam & Water Works (The), Philadelphia (Sidewheel Steamboat) plate, fruit & flowers border, dark blue, Henshall, Williamson & Co., 9 7/8" d. **646**

Detroit platter, Cities series, groups of flowers & scrolls border, dark blue, Davenport, minor wear, scratches & small area of professional repair on back rim, 18 3/4" d. (ILLUS., top of page).................. **3,025**

Dix Cove on the Gold Coast, Africa soup tureen, cov., dark blue, shell border, irregular center, pedestal base, loop end handles, E. Wood, 11 x 15" (interior staining).. **4,888**

Doctor Syntax Amused with Pat in the Pond platter, flowers & scrolls border, dark blue, E. Wood, 14 1/4 x 19" (glaze scratches, scattered minor staining) **1,840**

East View of LaGrange, the residence of the Marquis La Fayette plate, dark blue, floral border, E. Wood, 9 1/4" d. (very minor wear)... **303**

Entrance of the Erie Canal into the Hudson at Albany - View of the Aqueduct Bridge at Little Falls pitcher, floral border, dark blue, E. Wood, excellent condition, 6" h. **1,500-1,725**

Esplanade and Castle Garden, New York - Almshouse, Boston pitcher, vine border, dark blue, R. Stevenson, 10" h. **2,300**

Esplanade & Castle Garden Platter

Esplanade and Castle Garden, New York platter, vine border, dark blue, R. Stevenson, minor glaze scratches, 14 1/2 x 18 1/2" ((ILLUS.)
.... **5,750**

Highlands Hudson River Platter

Franklin (Tomb) cup & saucer, handleless, floral border, dark blue, E. & G. Phillips, Longport **385**

Fulton's Steamboat soup plate, floral border, dark blue, unknown maker, 10 1/4" d. (minor scratches & rim chips) **881**

Harper's Ferry, U.S. platter, flowers, shells & scrolls border, scalloped rim, red, Adams, 15 3/8" l. **440**

Highlands, Hudson River platter, shell border, dark blue, E. Wood, minor roughness on interior rim, 10 x 12 3/4" (ILLUS., top of page) **3,335**

Insane Asylum, New York - New York City Hall pitcher, vine border, dark blue, footed bulbous body w/high arched spout & arched handle, Stevenson, 9" h. (minor stains & wear w/some crazing in bottom) **1,100**

Junction of the Sacandaga and Hudson Rivers platter, floral & scroll border, dark blue, Stevenson, 14 1/4" l. **1,955**

Lafayette at Franklin's Tomb coffeepot, floral border, tall footed ovoid body w/flared rim & domed cover, dark blue, Wood, 11 3/4" h. (ILLUS.) **4,888**

Lake George, State of New York platter, shell border, dark blue, E. Wood, 16 1/2" l. (very minor glaze scratches) **2,585**

Landing of Lafayette Plate

Landing of General Lafayette at Castle Garden, New York, 16 August 1824 plate, primrose & dogwood border, dark blue, Clews, minor wear & scratches, 8 7/8" d. ((ILLUS.) **303**

Landing of General Lafayette at Castle Garden, New York, 16 August 1824 pepper pot, floral & vine border, dark blue, 4 5/8" h., Clews (shallow chip & flakes on domed top) **2,750**

Landing of General Lafayette at Castle Garden, New York, 16 August 1824 pitcher, floral & vine border, jug-type, dark blue, Clews, 6 1/4" h. (stained) **1,760**

Lafayette -Franklin's Tomb Coffeepot

Clews Landing of Lafayette Platter

Landing of General Lafayette at Castle Garden, New York, 16 August 1824 platter, floral & vine border, dark blue, Clews, minor glaze scratches, 15 1/4" l. (ILLUS.) **2,070**

Landing of General Lafayette at Castle Garden, New York, 16 August 1824 platter, floral & vine border, dark blue, Clews, 19" l. (slight scratches) **2,970**

Landing of General Lafayette at Castle Garden, New York, 16 August 1824 sauce tureen, cover & underplate, floral & vine border, dark blue, Clews, tureen 8 3/8" l., undertray 9 7/8" l., the set **1,955**

Landing of General Lafayette at Castle Garden, New York, 16 August 1824 sugar bowl & cover, floral & vine border, dark blue, deep boat-shaped form w/flared rim & domed cover, Clews, 6 1/4" h. (chips on rim & cover) **605**

Landing of General Lafayette at Castle Garden, New York, 16 August 1824 tureen, cover & ladle, floral & vine border, dark blue, 11" l., 10" h., Clews (damage) **5,175**

Marine Hospital, Louisville, Kentucky plate, shell border, dark blue, irregular center, E. Wood, 9 1/4" d.(stains, crazing, short internal hairline) **330**

Mendenhall Ferry Platter by Stubbs

Mendenhall Ferry platter, spread eagle border, dark blue, J. Stubbs, minor glaze scratches, 13 3/4 x 16 3/4" (ILLUS.) **2,185**

Mount Vernon, The Seat of the Late Gen'l. Washington tea set: cov. teapot, cov. sugar bowl, creamer, waste bowl & handleless cup & saucer; large flowers border, dark blue, unknown maker, teapot, 10" l., 5" h., the set (minor imperfections) **3,819**

Park Theatre, New York bowl, oak leaf border, dark blue, R. Stevenson, 8 3/4" d. (minute scratches) **2,530**

Pennsylvania Hospital Platter

Park Theatre Plate with Medallions

Park Theatre, New York plate, oak leaf border, four portrait medallions at the border of Jefferson, Washington, Lafayette & Clinton, inset of the Aqueduct Bridge at Little Falls, dark blue, R. Stevenson, 10" d. (ILLUS.)... **3,738**

Pass in the Catskill Mountains undertray, shell border, circular center, dark blue, E. Wood, 8" l. (minor scratches, edge roughness).. **440**

Peace & Plenty Plate by Clews

Peace and Plenty plate, cov., dark blue, wide band of fruit & flowers border, Clews, glaze flakes, 8 7/8" d., (ILLUS.) **330**

Peace and Plenty plate, fruit & flowers border, dark blue, Clews, 10 1/4" d.(minor knife scratches).. **330**

Peace and Plenty vegetable dish, cov., dark blue, wide band of fruit & flowers border, oblong w/flanged rim, Clews, 6 1/2 x 12 1/2" (minute chip under end handle) **1,725**

Pennsylvania Hospital, Philadelphia platter, flowers within medallions border, Beauties of America series, dark blue, Ridgway, few minor scratches, 14 1/8 x 18 3/8" (ILLUS., top of page) **1,880**

Quebec vegetable dish, cov., footed square form w/domed cover & floriform finial, dark blue, E. Wood, 9 1/2" w. .. **2,185**

Sandusky (Ohio) Platter

Sandusky (Ohio) platter, floral border, medium dark blue, harbor scene w/steamship "Henry Clay" & other ships, shoreline in background w/several buildings, unmarked Clews, two small blurred areas in transfer, 16 1/2" l., (ILLUS.)........................ **4,620**

State House, Boston platter, spread-eagle border, dark blue, Stubbs, 14 3/4" l. (minor scratches & crazing) **1,265**

States series pitcher, building, two wings, water in foreground, border w/names of fifteen states in festoons separated by five-point stars border, dark blue, Clews, 6 3/4" h. (minor interior staining) **978**

States series plate, two-story building w/curved drive, border w/names of fifteen states in festoons separated by five-point stars border, dark blue, Clews, 7 3/4" d. (small rim bruise) **330**

Winter View of Pittsfield Platter

States series plate, building, sheep on lawn, border w/names of fifteen states in festoons separated by five-point stars border, dark blue, Clews, 8 3/4" d. (rim w/area of glaze flakes, stain).................................. **289**

States series platter, mansion, foreground a lake w/swans, names of states in festoons separated by five-point stars border, dark blue, Clews, ca. 1830, 16 3/4" l., ... **2,280**

Table Rock, Niagara plate, shell border - circular center, dark blue, E. Wood, 10 1/8" d. (a few scratches) **499**

Tappen Zee from Greensburg, New York vegetable bowl, oblong, shell border, dark blue, E. Wood, 8" l. **935**

Upper Ferry Bridge over the River Schuylkill platter, spread-eagle border, dark blue, Stubbs, 15 1/2 x 18 3/4" (hairline) **705**

Wadsworth Tower tea service: cov. teapot, two large tea cups, one saucer, five regular tea cups, six saucers; shell border, dark blue, E. Wood, 15 pcs. (imperfections).. **2,645**

Washington Standing at Tomb, scroll in hand waste bowl, floral border, dark blue, E. Wood, 6 1/4" d., 3 1/4" h. (minor imperfections).. **748**

West Point Military Academy basket & undertray, reticulated basket & undertray, fruit & flowers border, Celtic China, dark blue, E. Wood, undertray 11 1/2" l., 2 pcs.. **3,738**

West Point Military Academy platter, shell border, dark blue, E. Wood, 9 1/4 x 11 3/4" (minor glaze scratches) **2,760**

Winter View of Pittsfield, Massachusetts platter, vignette views & flowers border, dark blue, Clews, glaze scratches, 14 x 16 1/2" (ILLUS., top of page) **3,450**

Hull

In 1905 Addis E. Hull purchased the Acme Pottery Company in Crooksville, Ohio. In 1917 the A.E. Hull Pottery Company began to make a line of art pottery for florists and gift shops. The company also made novelties, kitchenware and stoneware.

Hull's Little Red Riding Hood kitchenware was manufactured between 1943 and 1957 and is a favoritre of collectors, as are the beautiful matte glaze vases it produced.

In 1950 the factory was destroyed by a flood and fire, but by 1952 it was back in production. Hull added its newer glossy glazed pottery plus pieces sold in flower shops under the names Regal and Floraline. Hull's brown dinnerware lines achieved great popularity and were the main lines being produced prior to the plant's closing in 1986.

References on Hull Pottery include: Hull, The Heavenly Pottery, 7th Edition, 2001 and Hull, The Heavenly Pottery Shirt Pocket Price Guide, 4th Edition, 1999, by Joan Hull. Also The Dinnerwares Lines by Barbara Loveless Click-Burke (Collector Books 1993) and Robert's Ultimate Encyclopedia of Hull Pottery by Brenda Roberts (Walsworth Publishing Co., 1992). -- Joan Hull, Advisor.

Hull Marks

Hull Advertising Piece

Advertising piece, "The A.E. Hull Co. Pottery" in raised lettering within scroll border, very rare, 11 x 5" (ILLUS.)................. **$6,000**

Ashtray, Ebb Tide patt., E8 .... **225**

Ashtray, Butterfly patt., B3, 7" l............................ **55**

Ashtray, Continental patt., No. A1, 8".................. **50**

Ashtray, Serenade patt., No. S23, 10 1/2 x 13".. **95**

Ashtray, Parchment & Pine patt., No. S-14, 14" l.. **175**

Little Red Riding Hood Pieces

Bank, Little Red Riding Hood patt., standing-type (ILLUS. bottom left)........................... **795**

Bank, figural Corky Pig, pink, white & blue, 5".. **225**

Basket, hanging-type, Sun Glow patt., No. 99, 6" h.. **65**

Basket, hanging-type, Woodland Matte patt., cream & blue **575**

Hull Wildflower Basket

Basket, Wildflower patt., fan-shaped, scalloped rim, handle, pink & blue, matte glaze, 12 1/2" h., 16 1/2" w. (ILLUS.)............. **375**

Hull Woodland Basket

Basket, Woodland patt., fan shape, twigform handle, glossy pink, green & beige, 8 3/4" h., 9" w. (ILLUS.).................................... **110**

Basket, Blossom Flite patt., No. T2, 6" h............. **65**

Basket, Parchment & Pine patt., No. S-3, 6" h... **95**

Basket, Sueno Tulip patt., No. 102-33-6", 6" h... **350**

Basket, Open Rose (Camellia) patt., No.142, 6 1/4" h... **350**

Basket, Sun Glow patt., No. 84, 6 1/2" h............. **75**

Tokay Pattern Basket

Basket, Tokay patt., No. 6, overhead branch
handle, white ground, 8" h. (ILLUS.) **95**
Basket, Blossom Flite patt., No. T4, 8 1/2" h. **125**
Basket, Royal Woodland patt., No. W9,
8 3/4" h.. **50**
Basket, Woodland Matte patt., fan-shaped
w/center handle, pink & green, glossy,
W9-8 3/4", 8 3/4" h. **175**
Basket, Woodland Matte patt., fan-shaped
w/center handle, yellow & green, W9-
8 3/4", 8 3/4" h. **245**
Basket, Poppy patt., No. 601, 9" h. **800**
Basket, Ebb Tide patt., E5, 9 1/8" h. **150**
Basket, Wildflower patt., No. 79, 10 1/4" h. **2,000**
Basket, Butterfly patt., three-handled, No.
B17, 10 1/2" h. **350**
Basket, Magnolia Gloss patt., No. H-14,
10 1/2" h. **300**
Basket, Wildflower patt., No. W-16-10 1/2",
10 1/2" h. **375**
Basket, Poppy patt., No. 601, 12" h. **1,300**
Basket, Serenade patt., pink ground, ruffled
sides, No. S14, 12" h. **350**
Basket, Ebb Tide patt., model of a large
shell w/long fish handle, No. E-11,
16 1/2" l. **300**
Bonbon, Butterfly patt., No. B4, 6" d. **45**
Book ends, Orchid patt., No. 316, 7" h., pr..... **1,200**
Bowl, cereal, 6" d., Floral patt., No. 50................. **10**
Bowl, 6 1/2" d., low, Poppy patt., No. 602 .... **295**
Bowl, 7" d., Orchid patt., No. 312........................ **150**

Hull Mixing Bowl

Bowl, 8" d., 4 1/2" h., House 'N Garden line,
pour spout, Mirror Brown glaze w/ivory
foam trim, marked "8 Lip Oven Proof
U.S.A." (ILLUS.)... **18**
Bowl, 8" d., Calla Lily patt., No. 500-32.............. **135**
Bowl, fruit, 9 1/2" d., Tokay patt., No. 7.............. **175**
Bowl, salad, 10" d., No. 49 .... **50**
Bowl, fruit, 10 1/2" d., Butterfly patt., No.
B16... **150**

Little Red Riding Hood Butter Dish

Butter dish, cov., figure of Little Red Riding
Hood (ILLUS.) **475**

Candleholders, Butterfly patt., No. B22,
2 1/2" h., pr. **85**
Candleholders, Ebb Tide patt., No. E-13,
2 3/4" h., pr. **75**
Candleholders, Woodland Matte patt., pink
ground, No. W30, 3 1/2" h., pr. **105**
Candleholders, Bow-Knot patt., No. B17,
4" h., pr. **225**
Candleholders, Dogwood patt., No. 512,
4" h., pr. **160**
Candleholders, Parchment and Pine patt.,
No. S-10, 5" h., pr. **50**
Candleholders, Serenade patt., No. S16,
6 1/2" h., pr. **105**
Candy dish, Butterfly patt., No. B6,
4 3/4 x 5 1/2" **45**
Candy dish, Continental patt., C62,
8 1/4" h. **45**
Candy dish, cov., Serenade patt., No. S3C,
8 1/4" h. **95**
Candy dish, cov., Tokay patt., No. 9C,
8 1/2" h. **100**
Canister, cov., Little Red Riding Hood patt.,
"Cereal" **1,250**
Canister, cov., Little Red Riding Hood patt.,
"Salt" **1,250**
Casserole, cov., French handle-type &
warmer, House 'N Garden line, No. 979,
Mirror Brown, 3 pt., 3 pcs. **125**
Casserole, oval w/figural duck cover, House
'N Garden line, Mirror Brown, 2 pt. **95**
Casserole, cov., Floral patt., No. 42,
7 1/2" d. **60**

Sun Glow Pattern Casserole

Casserole, cov., Sun Glow patt., No. 51-
7 1/2", 7 1/2" d. (ILLUS.) **50**
Casserole, cov., Serenade patt., No.S20,
9" d... **125**
Coaster/spoon rest, Gingerbread Boy patt.,
5" l. **50**
Compote, Tokay patt., No. 9.................................. **65**
Console bowl, Butterfly patt., wide-shoul-
dered disk-form w/closed rim, raised on
long curved tab feet, pebbled white
ground, No. B21, 10" d. **195**
Console bowl, Iris patt., No. 409-12", 12" l........ **250**
Console bowl, Magnolia Gloss patt., No. H-
23, 13" l. **95**
Console bowl, Orchid patt., No. 314,
13" l... **375**
Console bowl, Royal Woodland patt., No.
W29, 13" l. **75**
Consolette, Tokay patt., footed oblong form
w/end branch handles, No. 14,
15 3/4" l. **165**

Cookie jar, cov., Barefoot Boy **450**
Cookie jar, cov., figural Duck **125**
Cookie jar, cov., figural Ginger Bread Man,
  grey Flint Ridge line, 1980s, 12" h. **425**
Cookie jar, cov., Floral patt., No. 48,
  8 1/4" h. **65**
Cookie jar, cov., Gingerbread Man, brown **390**
Cookie jar, cov., Gingerbread Man, sand,
  12" h. **550**

Little Red Riding Hood Cookie Jar

Cookie jar, cov., Little Red Riding Hood,
  closed basket (ILLUS.) **300-1,000**
Cookie jar, cov., Little Red Riding Hood,
  open basket, gold stars on apron................. **395**
Cookie jar, cov., Little Red Riding Hood
  patt., closed-basket style, band of orange
  blossoms around skirt (ILLUS. top with
  bank) **300-1,000**

Parchment & Pine Cornucopia-Vase

Cornucopia-vase, Parchment & Pine patt.,
  No. S-2-5, 7 3/4" h. (ILLUS.) **65**
Cornucopia-vase, Butterfly patt., No. B2,
  6 1/2" h. **40**
Cornucopia-vase, Water Lily patt., pink
  w/gold, L7-6 1/2", 6 1/2" h. **95**
Cornucopia-vase, Ebb Tide patt., No. E3,
  7 1/2" h. **225**
Cornucopia-vase, Wildflower patt., pink, yel-
  low & green, No. W7, 7 1/2" **95**

Hull Bow-Knot Cornucopia-Vase

Cornucopia-vase, Bow-Knot patt., blue &
  pink, No. B-5-7 1/2, 7 1/2" h. (ILLUS.) **250**
Cornucopia-vase, Parchment and Pine
  patt., No. S-2, 7 3/4" h. **65**

Magnolia Gloss Cornucopia-Vase

Cornucopia-vase, Magnolia Gloss patt., No.
  H-10-8 1/2, 8 1/2" h. (ILLUS.) **75**
Cornucopia-vase, Tokay patt., No. 10, white
  ground, 11" l. **65**

Woodland Gloss Cornucopia-Vase

Cornucopia-vase, Woodland Gloss patt.,
  No. W10-11", 11" h. (ILLUS.) **65**
Cornucopia-vase, Woodland Matte patt.,
  pink ground, No. W10-11", 11" h. **198**
Cornucopia-vase, Dogwood patt., No. 511,
  11 1/2" h. **275**
Cornucopia-vase, double, Magnolia Gloss
  patt., No. H-15, 12" h. **125**
Cornucopia-vase, double, Magnolia Matte
  patt., No. 6, 12" h. **175**
Cornucopia-vase, double, Water Lily patt.,
  No. L-27-12", 12" h. **250**
Cornucopia-vase, Parchment & Pine patt.,
  No. S-6, 12" **125**

Bow-Knot Cornucopia-vase

Cornucopia-vase, double, Bow-Knot patt.,
No. B13, 13 1/2" h. (ILLUS.) **295**
Cracker jar, cov., Little Red Riding Hood
patt. **800**
Creamer, Bow-Knot patt., turquoise & blue,
No. B-21-4", 4" h. **175**
Creamer, Water Lily patt., No. L-19-5",
5" h. **75**
Creamer, Rosella patt., No. R-3, 5 1/2" h. **50**
Creamer, Ebb Tide patt., No. E15 .... **60**
Creamer, Royal Woodland patt., No. W28 .... **25**
Creamer & cov. sugar bowl, Little Red
Riding Hood patt., side-pour creamer,
pr. **1,000**
Creamer & open sugar bowl, Open Rose
(Camellia) patt., pink & blue, No. 111-5"
& No. 112-5", 5" l., pr. **200**
Dish, leaf-shaped, Tokay patt., No. 19,
14" l. **95**

Hull Bow-Knot Ewer

Ewer, Bow-Knot patt., No. B-1-51/2,
5 1/2" h. (ILLUS.) **195**

Hull Open Rose Pattern Ewer

Ewer, Open Rose patt., No. 105, 7" h.
(ILLUS.) **225**
Ewer, Open Rose (Camellia) patt., No. 128,
4 3/4" h. **95**
Ewer, Magnolia Gloss patt., No. H-3,
5 1/2" h. **55**

Rosella Pattern Ewer

Ewer, Rosella patt., No. R-9, 6 1/2" h.
(ILLUS.) **75**
Ewer, Royal Woodland patt., No. W6,
6 1/2" h. **45**
Ewer, Woodland Gloss patt., No. W6-6 1/2",
6 1/2" h. **70**
Ewer, Iris patt., No. 401-8", cream & rose,
8" h. **275**
Ewer, Dogwood patt., No. 505-6 1/2",
8 1/2" h. **275**

Hull Wild Flower Ewer

Ewer, Wild Flower patt., pink & blue, No. W-
11-8 1/2", 8 1/2" h. (ILLUS.) **163**
Ewer, Calla Lily patt., No. 506, 10" h. **350**
Ewer, Mardi Gras/Granada patt., No. 31,
10" h. **135**
Ewer, Woodland Gloss patt., No. W24-
13 1/2", 13 1/2" h. **225**
Ewer, Ebb Tide patt., No. E-10, figural fish
handle, 14" h. **275**
Flower dish, Butterfly patt., No. B7,
6 3/4 x 9 3/4" **50**
Flowerpot, Sun Glow patt., No. 98, 7 1/2" h. **45**

Flowerpot & saucer, Calla Lily patt., No. 592, 6" h. **125**

Flowerpot w/attached saucer, Sueno Tulip patt., No. 116-33-4 3/4", 4 3/4" h. **135**

Water Lily Pattern Flowerpot & Saucer

Flowerpot w/attached saucer, Water Lily patt., pink ground, No. L-25-5 1/4", 5 1/4" h. (ILLUS.) **175**

Flowerpot w/attached saucer, Woodland patt., No. W11, 5 1/2" h. **150-175**

Fruit bowl, Serenade patt., No. S15-7", 7" h. **130**

Grease jar, cov., Sun Glow patt., No. 53, 5 1/4" h. **60**

Honey jug, Blossom Flite patt., No. T1, 6" h. **55**

Jardiniere, Dogwood patt., No. 514, 4" h. **110**

Jardiniere, Poppy patt., No. 603, 4 3/4" h. **175**

Jardiniere, Water Lily patt., No. 23-5 1/2", 5 1/2" **125**

Jardiniere, Woodland Matte patt., pink & yellow, No. W7-5 1/2", 5 1/2" h. **145**

Jardiniere, Woodland patt., dark green & blue, No. W7-5 1/2", 5 1/2" h. **125**

Jardiniere, Orchid patt., No. 310, 6" h. **225**

Jardiniere, Calla Lily patt., No. 591, 7" h. **300**

Jardiniere, Sueno Tulip patt., No. 115-33-9", 9" h. **350**

Jardiniere, Bow-Knot patt., wide bulbous body w/short & wide molded neck w/small bows at each side, B-19-9 3/8", 9 3/8" d. **950**

Lamp base, Rosella patt., No. 63-4", 4" h. **300**

Lamp base, Sueno Tulip patt., 6 1/2" h. **600**

Lamp base, Orchid patt., No. 303, 10" h. **600**

Lamp base, Iris patt., No. 414, 16" h. **750**

Lavabo & base, Butterfly patt., Nos. B24 & B25, cream & blue, overall 16" h., 2 pcs. **160**

Mug, Serenade patt., No. S22, 8 oz. **55**

Mustard jar & spoon, Little Red Riding Hood patt., 2 pcs. **500**

Early Art Stoneware Pitcher

Pitcher, 3 3/4" h., Early Art stoneware w/embossed flowers & scrolls, cobalt, maroon & turquoise splotching over cream ground (ILLUS.) **85**

Early Utility Ware Pitcher

Pitcher, 4 1/2" h., Early Utility ware, vertical ribs from base to bottom of handle, white thin horizontal line, wider dark brown line & a second thin white line directly below shoulder, marked "107 - H" in a circle & "36" below it (ILLUS.) **78**

House 'N Garden Pitcher

Pitcher, 7" h., House 'N Garden Rainbow serving ware, Tangerine glaze, two-quart capacity, No. 925 (ILLUS.) **30**

Pitcher, 7 1/2" h., Sun Glow patt., No. 55 .... **85**

Pitcher, 8" h., Sueno Tulip patt., No. 109-33-8" **235**

Pitcher, 8 1/2" h., Blossom Flite patt., No. T3 .... **125**

Dogwood/Wild Rose Ewer

Pitcher, 13 1/2" h., Dogwood/Wild Rose patt., No. 519-13 1/2 (ILLUS.) **800**

Planter, model of a pheasant, No. 61, 6 x 8"........ **50**

Hull Madonna & Child Planter

Planter, bust of the Madonna w/child, pink
semi-glaze, impressed Hull "USA 26,"
No. 26, 7" h. (ILLUS.)... **45**

Planter, baby w/pillow, pink w/gold trim, No.
92, 5 1/2" h. **35**

Planter, model of two Siamese cats, No. 63,
5 3/4" l. **85**

Planter, model of lovebirds, pink & brown,
Novelty line, No. 93, 6" h. **40**

Planter, model of a parrot pulling a flower
blossom-form cart, Novelty line, No. 60,
9 1/2" l., 6" h. **50**

Planter, model of a Dachshund dog, 14" l.,
6" h. **110**

Planter, bust of the Madonna, yellow, No.
24, 7" h. **35**

Planter, Basket Girl, No. 954, 8" h. (ILLUS.,
top of next column) **40**

Basket Girl Planter

Figural Swan Planter

Planter, model of swan, yellow glossy glaze,
Imperial line, No. 69, 8 1/2 x 10 1/2",
8 1/2" h. (ILLUS.).. **50**

Planter, model of Bandanna Duck, Novelty
line, No. 74, 9" h. **50**

Planter, Blossom Flite patt., No. T12,
10 1/2" l. **95**

Little Red Riding Hood Advertising Plaque

Plaque, advertising "Little Red Riding Hood," very rare, only 6 known to exist, 11 3/4" l., 6 1/2" h. (ILLUS.) **20,000**

Rose bowl, Iris patt., No. 412-7", 7" l. **175**

Salt & pepper shakers, Sun Glow patt., No. 54, 2 3/4" h., pr. **20**

Salt & pepper shakers, Floral patt., No. 44, 3 1/2" h., pr. **25**

Sandwich tray, Gingerbread Man patt. **150**

Serving tray, three-part w/butterfly handle, Butterfly patt., gold-trimmed scalloped rim, B23, 11 1/2" l. **200**

String holder, Little Red Riding Hood patt. (ILLUS. bottom right w/bank) **1,600**

Sugar bowl, cov., Blossom Flite patt., No. T16 .... **45**

Sugar bowl, cov., Rosella patt., No. R-4, 5 1/2" h. **60**

Bow-Knot Tea Set

Tea set: cov. teapot, creamer & cov. sugar bowl; Bow-Knot patt., 3 pcs. (ILLUS.) **850**

Tea set: cov. teapot, creamer & cov. sugar bowl; Butterfly patt., Nos. B18, B19 & B20, 3 pcs. **325**

Tea set: cov. teapot No. S-11, cov. sugar bowl No. S-13 & creamer No. S-12; Parchment and Pine patt., 3 pcs. **250**

Tea set: cov. teapot W26, cov. sugar bowl W28 & creamer W27; Woodland Gloss patt., teapot 6 1/2" h., 3 pcs. **275**

Teapot, cov., Serenade patt., No. S17, 5" h., 6-cup **195**

Teapot, cov., Dogwood patt., No. 507, 5 1/2" h. **350**

Teapot, cov., Mardi Gras/Granada patt., No. 33, 5 1/2" h. **200**

Blossom Flite Pattern Teapot

Teapot, cov., Blossom Flite patt., No. T14, 8" h. (ILLUS.) **100**

Teapot, cov., Wildflower patt., No. 72, 8" h. **1,200**

Teapot, cov., Royal Woodland patt., No. W26, 8-cup **95**

Tray, Mirror Brown patt., 10 x 10" **75**

Vase, 4 3/4" h., Magnolia Matte patt., No. 13-4 3/4" **75**

Hull Bow-Knot Pattern Vase

Vase, 5" h., Bow-Knot patt., No. B-2-5, shaded pink to blue matte finish (ILLUS.) **175**

Hull Early Art Ware Vase

Vase, 5 1/2" h., 4 1/2" d., Early Art ware, 1920s, unmarked, cobalt & rose brush-stroke pattern over pale blue w/a hint of green at rim, fake handles from shoulder to rim on each side (ILLUS.) **85**

Vase, 5 1/2" h., Water Lily patt., No. L-2-5 1/2" **75**

Vase, 6" h., Sueno Tulip patt., No. 110-33-6" **150**

Hull Wild Flower Pattern Vase

Vase, 6" h., Wild Flower patt., No. W-3-6", two handles, embossed flower spray, background shading pink at top, cream center, blue at base, matte finish (ILLUS.) **55**

Bow-Knot Pattern Vase

Vase, 6 1/2" h., Bow-Knot patt., blue & cream, No. B-3-6 1/2" (ILLUS.) **250**
Vase, 6 1/2" h., Rosella patt., No. R-6-6 1/2" **40**
Vase, 6 1/2" h., Royal Woodland patt., No. W4 .... **35**

Hull Royal Woodland Vase

Vase, 6 1/2" h., Royal Woodland patt., pale turquoise w/white overall splotching, darker handles & rim, marked "Hull W4-6 1/2 U.S.A." (ILLUS.) **38**

Hull Thistle Pattern Vase

Vase, 6 1/2" h., Thistle patt., blue ground, No. 55 (ILLUS.) **150**

Hull Water Lily Vase

Vase, 6 1/2" h., Water Lily patt., No. L6-6 1/2" (ILLUS.) **95**

Hull Wild Flower Vase

Vase, 6 1/2" h., Wild Flower patt., No. W-5-6 1/2(ILLUS.) **85**
Vase, bud, 6 1/2" h., Serenade patt., No. S1-6 1/2" **55**
Vase, 6 1/2" h., Sueno Tulip patt., blue & pink, 106-33-6 .... **125**
Vase, bud, 6 3/4" h., Orchid patt., No. 306 .... **175**
Vase, 7" h., Butterfly patt., No. B10-7" **55**
Vase, bud, 7" h., Ebb Tide patt., No. E1 .... **75**
Vase, bud, 7" h., Open Rose (Camellia) patt., No. 129 .... **155**
Vase, 7 1/2" h., Royal Woodland patt., No. W8 .... **40**

Hull Bow-Knot Vase

Vase, 8 1/2" h., Bow-Knot patt., No. B-9-8 1/2" (ILLUS.) **325**

Hull Woodland Double Bud Vase

Vase, 8 1/2" h., double-bud, Woodland patt., No. W15-8 1/2", glossy (ILLUS.) **65**

Vase, 8 1/2" h., Magnolia Gloss patt., gold trim, No. H-8 .... **75**

Vase, 8 1/2" h., Magnolia Matte patt., pink & blue, No. 1-8 1/2" **125**

Vase, 8 1/2" h., Magnolia Matte patt., the baluster-form body w/slender scroll handles from the mid-body to the foot, pink & blue, No. 2-8 1/2" **125**

Open Rose Vase

Vase, 8 1/2" h., Open Rose (Camellia) patt., No. 126 (ILLUS.) **325**

Hull Orchid Pattern Vase

Vase, 8 1/2" h., Orchid patt., No. 309-8 1/2, handled, pink & yellow flowers on shaded blue ground (ILLUS.) **195**

Vase, 8 1/2" h., Woodland Matte patt., pink ground, No. W16-8 1/2" **185**

Hull Woodland Pattern Vase

Vase, 8 1/2" h., Woodland patt., Dawn Rose pastel, No. W16-8 1/2 (ILLUS.) **185**

Vase, 9" h., Mardi Gras/Granada patt., No. 48-9" **55**

Vase, 9" h., Mardi Gras/Granada patt., pink & blue, No. 47-9" **55**

Vase, 9" h., Morning Glory patt., No. 215-9" **55**

Vase, 9 1/4" h., Ebb Tide, pink w/gold, No. E-6 .... **175**

Vase, 10" h., Calla Lily patt., No. 520-33 .... **350**

Vase, 10" h., Orchid patt., No. 302 .... **350**

Vase, 10 1/2" h., Butterfly patt., No. B14-10 1/2" **100**

Vase, 10 1/2" h., Magnolia Matte patt., No. 8-10 1/2" **200**

Vase, 10 1/2" h., Poppy patt., No. 605 .... **450**

Hull Poppy Vase

Vase, 10 1/2" h., Poppy patt., No. 607-10 1/2, two-handled, blue bottom, matte finish, original label (ILLUS.) **450**

Large Hull Water Lily Vase

Vase, 10 1/2" h., Water Lily patt., pink & green, No. L-12-10 1/2" (ILLUS.) **300**

Vase, 10 1/2" h., Wildflower patt., yellow & rose, No. 59-10 1/2" **350**

Vase, 12" h., handled, Tokay patt., No. 12-12" **125**

Vase, 12" h., Open Rose (Camellia) patt., No. 124-12" **450**

Vase, 12 1/2" h., Magnolia patt., No. 22-12 1/2" **325**

Vase, 12 1/2" h., Water Lily patt., No. L-16-12 1/2" **395**

Hull Magnolia Vase

Vase, 15" h., Magnolia patt., 16-15", pink & green (ILLUS.) **500**

Wall pocket, model of a flying goose, Novelty line, No. 67, 6" h. **45**

Wall pocket, model of an iron, Sun Glow patt., unmarked, 6" h. **65**

Wall pocket, model of a cup & saucer, Sun Glow patt., No. 80, 6 1/4" h. **75**

Wall pocket, Rosella patt., No. R-10, 6 1/2" h. **85**

Wall pocket, Royal Woodland patt., shell-shaped, No. W13, 7 1/2" l. **50**

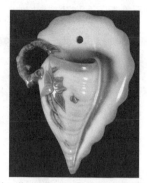

Woodland Gloss Pattern Wall Pocket

Wall pocket, Woodland Gloss patt., conch shell shape, No. W13-7 1/2", 7 1/2" l. (ILLUS.) **95**

Wall pocket, Woodland Matte patt., No. W13-7 12", 7 1/2" l. **190**

Wall pocket, Bow-Knot patt., model of a whisk broom, No. B27-8", 8" h. **285**

Wall pocket, Open Rose (Camellia) patt., fan-shaped, No. 125-8 1/2", 8 1/2" l. **325**

Wall pocket, Bow-Knot patt. **300**

Window box, Dogwood patt., No. 508, 10 1/2" l. **195**

Window box, Parchment & Pine patt., No. S-5, 10 1/2" l. **95**

Window box, Serenade patt., pink, No. S-9, 12 1/2" l. **100**

Hummel Figurines & Collectibles

Hummel Marks

The Goebel Company of Oeslau, Germany, first produced these porcelain figurines in 1934, having obtained the rights to adapt the beautiful pastel sketches of children by Sister Maria Innocentia (Berta) Hummel. Every design by the Goebel artisans was approved by the nun until her death in 1946. Although not antique, these figurines with the "M.I. Hummel" signature, especially those bearing the Goebel Company factory mark used from 1934 and into the early 1940s, are being sought by collectors, although interest may have peaked some years ago. A good reference is Luckey's Hummel Figurines & Plates, Identification and Value Guide by Carl F. Luckey (Krause Publications).Trademarks:TMK 1 - Crown - 1934-1950TMK 2 - Full Bee - 1940-1959TMK 3 - Stylized Bee - 1958-1972TMK 4 - Three Line Mark - 1964-1972TMK 5 - Last Bee - 1970-1980TMK 6 - Missing Bee - 1979-1991TMK 7 - Hummel Mark - 1991-1999TMK 8 - Goebel Bee - 2000-

A   Gentle   Glow   candleholder,   #439, 5 1/4" h., Trademark 6 .... **$200**

A Stitch in Time, #255, 6 3/4" h., Trademark
3.. **550-800**
A Stitch in Time, #255, 6 3/4" h., Trademark
4.. **375-425**

A Stitch in Time

A Stitch in Time, #255, 6 3/4" h., Trademark
6 (ILLUS.)... 300
Accompanist (The), #453, 3" h., Trademark
6.. 100
Accordion boy, #185, 5 1/2" h., Trademark
2.. 425
Adoration, #23/I, 6 1/4" h., Trademark 1........ **1,000-1,300**
Adoration, #23/I, 6 1/4" h., Trademark 2.... **600-800**
Adoration, #23/III, 9" h., Trademark
1... **1,600-2,100**
Angel at Prayer font, #91/A, 4 3/4" h.,
Trademark 2...................................... **200-260**
Angel Cloud font, #206, 2 1/4 x 4 3/4",
Trademark 3...................................... **200-250**
Angel Duet, #261, 5" h., Trademark 5.............. 270
Angel Duet candleholder, #193, 5" h.,
Trademark 2...................................... **600-700**
Angel Serenade, #214D (angel standing),
color decoration, part of Nativity set,
3" h., Trademark 2.............................. **125-145**
Angel Serenade, #214/N (angel standing),
color decoration, part of Nativity set,
5 1/2" h., Trademark 3........................ **250-285**
Angel Serenade with lamb, #83, 5 1/2" h,
Trademark 5...................................... 240
Angel with Accordion, #238B, 2 1/4" h.,
Trademark 5...................................... 55
Angel with Lute candleholder, #III/38/I,
2 1/2" h., Trademark 2........................ **250-300**
Angelic Sleep candleholder, #25, 3 3/4" h.,
Trademark 6...................................... 185
Apple Tree Boy, #142/3/0, 4" h., Trademark
2... **300-350**
Apple Tree Boy, #142/3/0, 4 1/4" h., Trademark 6.. 150
Apple Tree Boy, #142, 6" h., Trademark
2... **600-700**
Apple Tree Girl, #141/3/0, 4" h., Trademark
2... **300-350**
Apple Tree Girl, #141/3/0, 4 1/4" h., Trademark 6.. 150
Apple Tree Girl, #141, 6" h., Trademark
2... **600-700**

Apple Tree Girl table lamp, #229, 7 1/2" h.,
Trademark 2...................................... **900-1,000**
Auf Wiedersehen, #153/0, 5 1/2" h., Trademark 2.. **425-525**
Auf Wiedersehen, #153/0, 5 3/4" h., Trademark 6.. 255
Auf Wiedersehen, #153/I, 7" h., Trademark
3... **475-525**
Ba-Bee Ring plaque, #30/B, boy, 5" d.,
Trademark 2...................................... **350-450**
Ba-Bee Ring plaque, #30/0/B, boy, 5" d.,
Trademark 5...................................... **250-260**
Baker, #128, 4 3/4" h., Trademark 5.................. 245
Baking Day (Die Backerin), #330, 5 1/4" h.,
Trademark 6...................................... 315
Band Leader, #129, 4 1/4", Trademark 2.......... 425
Band Leader, #129, 5 1/4" h., Trademark
5... **245-270**
Barnyard Hero, #195, 4" h., Trademark 5......... 200
Bashful, #377, 4 3/4" h., Trademark
4... **1,000-1,500**
Be Patient, #197/2/0, 4 1/4" h., Trademark
2... **400-500**
Be Patient, #197/I, 6 1/4" h., Trademark
3... **425-475**
Begging His Share, #9, 5 1/2" h., Trademark 1.. **750-900**
Bird Duet, #169, 4" h., Trademark 1........... **425-550**
Bird Watcher, #300, 5" h., Trademark 5......... 255
Birthday Candle candleholder, #440,
5 1/2" h., 1963, Exclusive Special Edition
No. 10 for Members of the Goebel Collectors' Club...................................... 375
Birthday Serenade, #218/2/0, 4" h., Trademark 6.. 185
Birthday Serenade, #218/2/0, 4 1/4" h.,
Trademark 2...................................... **610-650**
Blessed Event, #333, 5 1/2" h., Trademark
6... 365
Book Worm, #8, 4" h., Trademark 1........... **700-850**

Book Worm

Book Worm, #8, 4" h., Trademark 2
(ILLUS.)... 475
Book Worm, #3/III, 9 1/2" h., Trademark
3... **1,600-1,800**
Boots, #143/0, 5" h., Trademark 2.................... 300

Botanist (The), #351, 4 1/4" h., Trademark 6..... **200**
Boy with Bird ashtray, #166, 6 1/4" l., Trademark 3... **195-210**

Boy with Toothache

Boy with Toothache, #217, 5 1/2" h., Trademark 6 (ILLUS.)... **225**
Busy Student, #367, 4 1/4" h., Trademark 6.. **175**
Call to Glory (Fahnentager), #739/I, 5 3/4" h., first issue 1994, three flags included.. **265**
Candlelight candleholder (Engel mit Kerze, Leuchter), #192, 7" h., Trademark 6............ **265**
Carnival, #328, 5 3/4" h., Trademark 6 .... **235**
Celestial Musician, #188/0, 5" h., Trademark 6.. **245**
Celestial Musician, #188, 7" h., Trademark 2.. **850-1,100**
Celestial Musician ornament, #646, 3" h., first issue 1993, original box **105**
Chef, Hello, #124/0, 6" h., Trademark 6............. **240**
Chef, Hello, #124, 6 1/2" h., Trademark 1.. **800-1,000**
Chick Girl, #57/0, 3 1/2" h., Trademark 2... **310-375**

Chick Girl

Chick Girl, #57/I, 4 1/4" h., Trademark 5 (ILLUS.).. **345-355**
Chick Girl candy dish, #III/57, 5 1/4" h., Trademark 2 .... **580-650**

Chicken-Licken (Kukenliesl), #385, 4 3/4" h., Trademark 6...................................... **325**

Chimney Sweep

Chimney Sweep, #12/1, 6 1/2" h., Trademark 2 (ILLUS.)... **475**
Christ Child, #18, 2 x 3 1/4", Trademark 6 .... **150**
Christmas Song, #343, 6 1/2" h., Trademark 6 .... **240**
Cinderella, #337,4 1/2" h., Trademark 6- **320**

Close Harmony

Close Harmony, #336, 5 1/2" h., Trademark 5 (ILLUS.) **365-395**
Close Harmony, #336, 5 1/2" h., Trademark 6 .... **335**
Coffee Break, #409, 4 1/4" h., 1984, exclusive special edition No. 8 for Members of the Goebel Collectors' Club **300**
Confidentially, #314, 5 1/2" h., Trademark 2 .... **4,000-5,000**
Coquettes, #179, 5" h., Trademark 6 .... **325**
Coquettes, #179, 5 1/4" h., Trademark 2.. **500-650**
Crossroads, #331, 6 3/4" h., Trademark 2 .... **4,000-5,000**

Culprits

Culprits, #56A, 6 1/4" h., Trademark 6
(ILLUS.).. **335**
Daddy's Girl, #371, 4 3/4" h.,Trademark
6.. **250**
Daisies Don't Tell, #380, 5" h., 1981, exclu-
sive special edition No. 5 for members of
the Goebel Collectors' Club **275**
Doctor, #127, 4 3/4" h., Trademark
2.. **300-350**
Doctor, #127, 5" h., Trademark 6........................ **165**
Doll Bath, #319, 5 1/4" h., Trademark
3.. **750-1,000**
Doll Bath, #319, 5 1/4" h., Trademark
5.. **350-375**
Easter Greetings, #378, 5" h., Trademark
5.. **245**
Easter Time, #384, 4" h., Trademark
4.. **1,000-1,500**
Evening Prayer (Abengebet), #495, 4" h.,
first issue 1992... **110**
Eventide, #99, 4 3/4", Trademark 2............ **600-750**
Fair Measure, #345, 6" h., Trademark
5.. **365**
Farm Boy, #66, 5 1/4" h., Trademark 6.............. **260**
Favorite Pet, #361, 4 1/2" h., Trademark
6.. **320**
Feathered Friends, #344, 4 1/2" h., Trade-
mark 6... **325**
Feeding Time, #199/0, 4 1/4" h., Trademark
3.. **300-350**
Feeding Time, #199/0, 4 1/4" h., Trademark
6.. **220**
Feeding Time, #199, 5 3/4" h., Trademark
2.. **525-625**
Festival Harmony, #173/4/0, 3" h., first issue
1995.. **100**

Festival Harmony

Festival Harmony, #173/0, 8", Trademark 6
(ILLUS.)... **355**

Festival Harmony, Adventsengel mid Mandolin Figurine

Festival Harmony, Adventsengel mid Mandolin, #172/0, 8", original box, Trademark
6 (ILLUS.) **355**
Flitting   Butterfly   plaque,   #139,
2 1/2 x 2 1/2", Trademark 1 .... **350-550**
Flower Girl, #548, 4 1/2" h., 1989, exclusive
edition M.I. Hummel Club, 5 year mem-
bership, original box... **120**

Flower Madonna, #10/I, white, 9 1/2" h.,
Trademark 1 .... **500-600**
Flower Madonna, #10/I, color, 9 1/2" h.,
Trademark 2 .... **800-950**
Flower Vender, #381, 5 1/4" h., Trademark
6... **275**
Follow the Leader, #369, 7" h., Trademark
3.. **4,000-5,000**
For Father, #87, 5 1/2" h., Trademark
2.. **400-530**
For Father, #87, 5 1/2" h., Trademark 6............. **240**
For Mother, #257, 5 1/4" h., Trademark
6... **225**
Forest Shrine, #183, 9" h., Trademark
1.. **1,500-1,900**

Forest Shrine

Forest Shrine, #183, 9" h., Trademark 6
(ILLUS.)... **625**
Friends, #136/1, 5 3/8" h., Trademark 1
.... **800-950**
Friends, #136/1, 5 3/8" h., Trademark 6 .... **225**
Friends, #136, 10 3/4" h., Trademark
2... **2,000-3,000**
Gift from a Friend (Aus Nachbars Garten),
#485, 5 1/4" h., exclusive edition
1991/92 M.I. Hummel Club, original box....... **275**
Girl with Trumpet, #389, 2 1/2" h., Trade-
mark 4... **175-225**
Globe Trotter, #79, 5" h., Trademark 1 ...... **500-750**
Goebel Hummel Figurines Dealer Display
Plaque #187A, 4 x 5 1/2" h., Trademark
5.. **200**
Going to Grandma's, #52/0, 4 3/4" h.,
Trademark 1 .... **750-1,000**
Going to Grandma's, #52/0, 4 3/4" h.,
Trademark 2 .... **450-600**
Goose Girl, #47/3/0, 4 1/4" h., Trademark 6 ..... **185**
Goose Girl, #47/0, 4 3/4" h., Trademark
2.. **300-400**
Goose Girl, #47/II, 7 1/2" h., Trademark
2.. **700-900**
Happy Birthday, #176/0, 5 1/2" h., Trade-
mark 3.. **325-375**

Happy Traveler, #109/0, 5" h., Trademark
2.. **275-350**
Happy Traveler, #109/II, 8" h., Trademark
1... **1,200-1,500**

Hear Ye, Hear Ye

Hear Ye, Hear Ye, #15/0, 5" h., Trademark
5 (ILLUS.)... **225**
Heavenly Protection, #88/I, 6 3/4" h., Trade-
mark 4 .... **575-660**
Heavenly Protection, #88, 9 1/4" h., Trade-
mark 2 .... **1,300-1,600**
Homeward Bound, #334, 5" h., Trademark
4 .... **475**
I'm Carefree, #633, 4 3/4" h., signature on
back, first issue 1994 .... **875**
It's Cold, #421, 5 1/4" h., 1981, exclusive
special edition No. 6 for members of the
Goebel Collectors' Club................................... **375**
Joyful, #53, 4" h., Trademark 1 .... **350-450**
Joyful, #53, 4" h., Trademark 5 .... **150**
Jubilee, #416, 6 1/4" h., 1980, 50 years, M.I.
Hummel Figurines 1935-1985, "The Love
Lives On" **475**
Just Resting, #112/3/0, 3 3/4" h., Trade-
mark 2 .... **275-350**
Just Resting table lamp, #II/112, 7 1/2" h.,
Trademark 3.. **375-525**
Kindergartner (The) (Schulmachen), #467,
5 1/4" h., Trademark 6................................... **220**
Knit One, Purl One, #432, 3" h., Trademark
5.. **130**
Knitting Lesson, #256, 7 1/2" h., Trademark
3 .... **875-1,150**
Latest News, #184, inscribed "Munchener
Presse," 5 1/4" h., Trademark 3............. **425-500**
Let's Sing, #110/0 , 3 1/4" h., Trademark
5.. **140**
Little Bookkeeper, #306, 4 3/4" h., Trade-
mark 4 .... **425**
Little Cellist, #89/1, 6" h., Trademark 3............... **350**
Little Drummer, #240, 4 1/4" h., Trademark
3 .... **245-260**

Little Drummer

Little Drummer, #240, 4 1/4" h., Trademark
  5 (ILLUS.).. **170**
Little Fiddler, #2/0, 6" h., Trademark 3...... **350-400**
Little Fiddler, #2/II, 11" h., Trademark
  2.. **1,800-2,300**
Little Goat Herder, #200/I, 5 1/2" h, Trade-
  mark 5.. **275**
Little Hiker, #16/I, 5 1/2" h., Trademark 2.. **400-500**
Little Nurse, #376, 4" h., Trademark 6 .... **270**
Little Pair (The), #449, 5 1/4" h., 1990-2000,
  exclusive edition Ten Year Membership,
  M.I. Hummel Club, original box **200**
Little Pharmacist, #322, 6" h., Trademark 6..... **265**
Little Shopper, #96, 4 3/4" h., Trademark
  1.. **430-550**
Little Sleeper, #171/4/0, 3" h., Trademark 6...... **115**
Little Tailor, #308, 5 1/2" h., Trademark 5 .... **275**
Madonna plaque, #48/II, 4 3/4 x 6", Trade-
  mark 2.. **375-525**
Mail Is Here (The), #226, 4 1/4 x 6 1/4",
  Trademark 4 .... **700-800**
Make a Wish (Die Pusteblume), #475,
  4 1/2" h., Trademark 6 .... **225**
March Winds, #43, 5" h., Trademark 5.............. **175**
Max & Moritz, #123, 5 1/4" h., Trademark 5...... **265**

Meditation

Meditation, #13/2/0, 4 1/2" h., Trademark 6
  (ILLUS.).. **165**
Merry Wanderer, #11/2/0, 4 1/4" h., Trade-
  mark 1 .... **450-550**
Merry Wanderer, #7/II, 9 1/2" h., Trademark
  1 .... **3,000-3,500**
Mischief Maker, #342, 5" h., Trademark 5 .... **345**
Mother's Darling, #175, 5 1/2" h., Trade-
  mark 4 .... **300**
Mother's Helper, #133, 5" h., Trademark 4 .... **275**
Not for You, #317, 5 1/2" h., Trademark 4 .... **410**
On Holiday, #350, 4 1/4" h., Trademark 6.......... **165**
On Secret Path, #386, 5 1/2" h., Trademark
  5 .... **310**

Out of Danger

Out of Danger, #56/B, 6 1/2" h., Trademark
  6 (ILLUS.) **335**
Photographer (The), #178, 4 3/4" h., Trade-
  mark 1 .... **750-1,000**
Photographer (The), #178, 4 3/4" h., Trade-
  mark 5 .... **345-370**

The Photographer

Photographer (The), #178, 5" h., Trademark
  6 (ILLUS.) **320**
Pigtails, #2052, 3 1/4" h., M.I. Hummel Club
  Membership Year, 1999/2000, original
  box **75**

Playmates, #58/0, 4" h., Trademark 6................ **185**
Postman, #119, 5" h., Trademark 3................... **300**

Postman

Postman, #119, 5 1/4" h., Trademark 2
   (ILLUS.)... **350-450**

Puppy Love

Puppy Love, #1, 5" h., Trademark 6
   (ILLUS.)... **325**
Retreat to Safety, #201/I, 5 1/2" h., Trade-
   mark 3 .... **475-525**
Ride into Christmas, #396, 5 3/4" h., Trade-
   mark 4 .... **2,000-2,500**

Rare Ring Around the Rosie

Ring Around the Rosie, #348, 6 3/4" h.,   Trademark 2 (ILLUS.).................. **10,000-15,000**

Saint George

Saint George, #55, 6 3/4" h., Trademark 6
(ILLUS.).. **350**
School Boys, #170/I, 7 1/2" h., Trademark
3.. **1,650-1,750**

Serenade

Serenade, #85/II, 7 1/2" h., Trademark 3
(ILLUS.)... **650-700**
She Loves Me, She Loves Me Not!, #174,
4 1/4" h, Trademark 6 .... **225**
Shepherd's Boy, #64, 5 1/2" h., Trademark
6 .... **260**
Shining Light, #358, 2 3/4" h., Trademark 5....... **100**
Silent   Night   candleholder,   #54,
3 1/2 x 4 3/4", Trademark 6 .... **400**
Sing Along (Auf los geht's los), #433,
4 1/2" h., Trademark 6 .... **315**
Singing Lesson, #63, 2 3/4" h., Trademark 5...... **135**

School Girls

School Girls, #177, 9 1/2" h., Trademark 2
(ILLUS.)... **3,000-4,000**
Searching   Angel   plaque,   #310,
4" h.,Trademark 6 .... **115**
Sensitive Hunter, #6, 4 3/4" h., Trademark
1.. **850-1,000**
Serenade, #85/0, 4 3/4" h., Trademark
1 .... **400-500**
Serenade, #85/0, 4 3/4" h., Trademark 3 .... **200**

Sister

Sister, #98/2/0, 4 3/4" h., Trademark 6
(ILLUS.)... **155**
Skier, #59, 5 1/4" h., Trademark 6...................... **220**
Sleep Tight (Schlaf gut), #424, 4 3/4" h.,
Trademark 6.. **240**

Soldier Boy

Soldier Boy, #332, 5 3/4" h., Trademark 5
(ILLUS.).. **255**
Soloist, #135, 4 3/4" h., Trademark 2................. **325**
Song of Praise, #454, 3" h., Trademark 6 .... **110**
Sound of the Trumpet, #457, 3" h., Trade-
mark 6... **110**
Sounds of the Mandolin, #438, 3 1/2" h.,
Trademark 6 .... **135**
Spring Dance, #353/0, 5 1/2" h., Trademark
6... **365**

Star Gazer

Star Gazer, #132, 4 3/4" h., Trademark 3
(ILLUS.).. **350**
Stormy Weather, #71/2/0, 4 3/4" h., Trade-
mark 6... **335**
Storybook Time (Marchenstude), #458,
5" h., First Issue 1992 .... **445**
Street Singer, #131, 5" h., Trademark 1 .... **550-700**
Street Singer, #131, 5 1/2" h., Trademark
3 .... **325**
Strolling Along, #5, 4 3/4" h., Trademark
5... **275**

Supreme Protection, #364, 9 1/4" h., 1984,
"1909-1984, In Celebration of the 75th
Anniversary of the Birth of Sister M.I.
Hummel" **375**
Surprise, #94/3/0, 4 1/4" h., Trademark 6 .... **165**
Sweet Greetings, #352, 4 1/4" h., Trade-
mark 6 .... **200**
Sweet Music, #186, 5 1/4 " h., Trademark
3 .... **300**

Telling Her Secret

Telling Her Secret, #196/0, 5 1/4" h., Trade-
mark 5 (ILLUS.) **365**
Thoughtful, #415, 4 1/2" h., Trademark 6 .... **255**
To Market, #49/3/0, 4" h., Trademark 1 ...... **500-650**
To Market, #49/3/0, 4" h., Trademark 5...... **200-210**
To Market, 6 1/4" h., Trademark 1 .... **1,400-1,700**
Trumpet Boy, #97, 4 3/4" h., Trademark
1 .... **400-425**
Trumpet Boy, #97, 4 3/4" h., Trademark 6 .... **145**
Tuneful Angel, #359, 2 3/4" h., Trademark
5 .... **85**
Two Hands, One Treat (Rechts oder links?),
#493, 4" h., 1991-99, M.I. Hummel Club **125**

Umbrella Boy

Umbrella Boy, #152/0/A, 4 3/4" h., Trade-
mark 6, (ILLUS.) **700**
Umbrella Boy, #152, 8" h., Trademark
2 .... **2,400-2,900**

Umbrella Girl

Umbrella Girl, #152/0/B, 4 3/4" h., Trademark 6 (ILLUS.)... **700**

Umbrella Girl, #152/B, 8" h., Trademark 2.. **2,200-2,700**

Vacation Time plaque, #125, 4 x 4 1/4", Trademark 6 .... **220**

Valentine Gift, #387, 5 3/4" h., 1972, exclusive special edition No. 1 for members of the Goebel Collectors' Club **575**

Valentine Joy, #399, 5 3/4" h., 1979, exclusive special edition for members of the Goebel Collectors' Club................................. **275**

Village Boy, #51/3/0, 4" h., Trademark 1 .. **350-450**

Village Boy, #51/0, 6" h., Trademark 1....... **700-900**

Visiting an Invalid, #382, 5" h., Trademark 4... **1,000-1,500**

Volunteers, #50/2/0, 5" h., Trademark 5... **275-305**

Volunteers, #50/0, 5 1/2" h., Trademark 3... **455-480**

Waiter, #154/0, 6" h., Trademark 6.................... **235**

Waiter, #154/0, 6" h., Trademark 2............. **375-475**

Wash Day, #321/4/0, 3" h., Trademark 6... **115**

Wayside Devotion

Wayside Devotion, #28/2, 7 1/2" h., Trademark 4 (ILLUS.) **575**

Wayside Devotion, #28/III, 8 3/4" h., Trademark 2 .... **1,000-1,200**

Wayside Harmony lamp, #224/II, 9 1/2" h., Trademark 2 .... **650-800**

We Congratulate, #220/2/0, 4" h., Trademark 2 .... **475-575**

Weary Wanderer

Weary Wanderer, #204, 6" h., Trademark 6 (ILLUS.)... **275**

What Now?, #422, 5 3/4" h., 1983, exclusive special edition No. 7 for members of the Goebel Collectors' Club........................... **375**

Which Hand?, #258, 5 1/4" h., Trademark 3 .... **625-825**

Whitsuntide, #163, 6 1/2" h., Trademark 6 .... **325**

Wash Day

Wash Day, #321, 5 3/4" h., Trademark 3 (ILLUS.).. **750-1,000**

Whitsuntide

Whitsuntide, #163, 7 1/4" h., Trademark 1
(ILLUS.) **1,000-1,200**
With Loving Greetings, #309, 3 1/2" h.,
Trademark 6 .... **275**
Worship, #84, 5" h., Trademark 1 .... **475-625**
Worship, #84/0, 5 " h., Trademark 2 .... **350**

Hutschenreuther

The Hutschenreuther family name is associated with fine German porcelains. Carl Magnus Hutschenreuther established a factory at Hohenberg, Bavaria and was succeeded in this business by his widow and sons Christian and Lorenz. Lorenz later established a factory in Selb, Bavaria (1857) that was managed by Christian and his son, Albert. The family later purchased factories near Carlsbad (1909), Altwasser, Silesia (1918) and Arzberg, Bavaria and between 1917 and 1927, acquired at least two additional factories. The firm, noted for the fine quality wares produced, united all these branches in 1969 and continues in production today.

Cup & saucer, deep conical cup, white
ground, the cup transfer-printed w/a
green wreath around a black iron cross,
black & gold inscription dated 1870-
71, ca. 1914, 6 1/2" d., 4 1/4" h. **$138**
Figure group, a slender nude young woman
w/blonde hair kneeling & feeding a small
fawn, on an oval base, signed by C.
Werner, 1930s, 10" h. **253**
Figure group, a young nude woman seated
on her legs, her torso slightly turned &
holding up a handful of blossoms, a
standing fawn looking on from behind
her, small rounded base, all-white except
pink blossoms, ca. 1930s, 9 1/4" h. **127**
Figure group, model of stag w/head raised
standing beside doe w/head down, on
oval base, shades of brown, signed by K.
Tutter, 1930s, 10" h. **288**
Figure group, pair of swallows perched on a
branch, dark blue w/deep red throats &
white bellies, brown branch, signed by G.
Granget, 1950s, 5 1/2" h. **150**
Figure group, "The Red Shoe," ballet cou-
ple, the male dancer standing behind the
ballerina, who wears a long pleated gown
w/a ruffled collar, one leg extended up &
out, all-white, on oval base, signed by C.

Werner, line through mark, 1930s,
12 3/8" h. **265**
Figure group, two cupids dancing, signed
"Tutter," marked "U.S. Zone Germany,"
4" h. **225**
Figure group, two horses side by side, one
posed in a full leap, the other landing on
its front legs w/rear body still raised, both
supported by a tall stand of grass, oval
base, all-white, signed by Fritz, ca.
1930s, 11" h. **230**
Figure group, two mountain goat rams
w/long curved-back horns, both rearing
in opposite directions, shades of brown
on a small round white base, signed by K.
Tutter, 1950s, 6 1/4" h. **138**
Figure group, two small colts, both standing,
one with head up, the other w/head
turned to the back, white w/grey trim,
green-tinted oval base, signed by K.
Tutter, ca. 1930s, 10" h. **161**
Figure group, young nude woman kneeling
down to feed a small fawn, oval base, all-
white, 1930s, 9 7/8" h. **374**
Figure of bather, "After the Bath," kneeling
nude young woman w/her hands up ad-
justing her hair, square base, all-white,
1930s, line through the mark, 7" h. **138**
Figure of dancer, detailed full-action pose of
a young woman wearing a short skirt
down on one knee w/her other leg extended behind her, her torso arched back
& her hair flying, her arms up & away
from her body, pale yellow dress
w/brown edging, a long blue drapery
across thigh, ca. 1930s, 11" h. **575**
Figure of woman, Art Deco-style standing
woman wearing a long pale yellow off-
the-shoulder gown, holding up the sides
w/her hands, round white base, 1930s,
10 1/2" h. **253**
Model of dog, Setter, standing w/head
turned, brown & white, 1950s, 4 1/3" h. **92**
Model of duck, male mallard w/head curved
down w/beak on neck, white oval
base, ca. 1930, 3" h. **104**
Plaque, oval, finely painted w/a bust-length
portrait of a blue-eyed beauty turned to
the right & looking at the viewer, her long
brown hair tied w/a red ribbon, late 19th -
early 20th c., impressed monogram
mark, artist-signed, giltwood frame,
5 1/4 x 6 3/4" **2,070**
Plate, 9 1/2" d., Royal Vienna style, the cen-
ter finely painted w/a bust portrait of Rosalie, Fulie von Bonar after F. Stieler, the
wide border w/elaborate gold banding,
the edge enameled w/blue & red "jewels"
interrupted by gilt diamonds, titled on the
back, impressed shield mark, artist-
signed, late 19th c. **1,380**
Plate, 9 5/8" d., Royal Vienna style, a jew-
eled blue ground wide border heavily
trimmed w/gilt scrolling foliage & applied
w/turquoise & pearl "jewels," the center
finely painted w/a three-quarter length
portrait of a brunette beauty dressed in a
red classical gown & w/long brown hair,
standing & leaning against the landing of
a large temple, artist-signed, late 19th -
early 20th c., blue Beehive mark, im-
pressed & incised numbers **1,725**

Plates, 9 1/2" d., a wide iridescent green ground border decorated w/a gilt Greek key & berried laurel design, the center of each painted in color w/a different Napoleonic scene, each titled on the reverse, late 19th - early 20th c., impressed shield mark, artist-signed, set of 8...................... **10,350**

Imari

This is a multicolor ware that originated in Japan, was copied by the Chinese, and imitated by English and European potteries. It was decorated in overglaze enamel and underglaze-blue. Made in Hizen Province and Arita, much of it was exported through the port of Imari in Japan. Imari often has brocade patterns.

Bowl, 10" d., 4 1/2" h., fluted paneled design, decorated in rust red & cobalt blue, ca. 1875.. **$336**

Imari Shallow Dish

Bowl or charger, round, shallow form w/raised rim, alternating panels of floral motifs & landscapes, all in traditional colors, around central panel in blue & white, late 19th c., 12" d. (ILLUS.) **420**

Charger, round w/scalloped edge, decorated w/center cartouche of floral design surrounded by fan-shaped panels, cobalt blue, rust & green w/gilt decorations, ca. 1860, 14 1/2" d., repair to rim (ILLUS. between vases, below) **308**

Imari Porcelain Charger

Charger, scalloped reeded rim, floral spray & medallion decorations, 1860, 18 1/2" d. (ILLUS.)... **840**

Urn, cov., tall ovoid body w/a high domed cover w/blue foo dog finial, decorated in traditional colors, panels w/dragons, gilt trim, ca. 1900, 20 1/2" h. (two chips on rim)... **960**

Imari Charger Flanked by Imari Vases

Vases, 15 3/4" h., ovoid body decorated w/cartouches painted w/cranes & other birds, molded rim on narrow neck, pedestal base, ca. 1880, pr. (ILLUS. left & right of Charger)... **616**

Vases, 14 7/8" h., tall ovoid body w/flaring trumpet neck, decorated in cobalt blue & rust red w/panels of stylized florals, ca. 1860, pr. **2,900**

Ironstone Cookie Plates

Ironstone

The first successful ironstone was patented in 1813 by C.J. Mason in England. The body contains iron slag incorporated with the clay. Other potters imitated Mason's ware, and today much hard, thick ware is lumped under the term ironstone. Earlier it was called by various names, including graniteware. Both plain white and decorated wares were made throughout the 19th century. Tea Leaf Lustre ironstone was made by several firms.

General

Cabinet plates, each w/a scalloped rim, "Japan" patt., floral border & center, painted in the Imari palette, Hick & Meigh, England, ca. 1830, 10 3/8" d., pr. (one w/hairline).. **$235**

Cabinet plates, each w/a scrolling gilt floral border w/alternating cartouches of birds & flowers, centered by a coat-of-arms, Ashworth, England, ca. 1875, set of 8 (normal surface scratches) **365**

Cookie plate, oval, footed, New York shape, all-white, J. Clementson, ca. 1858, 10" l. (ILLUS., above, two views) **105-125**

Ironstone Handleless Cup & Saucer

Cup & saucer, handleless, Ceres shape, all-white, Elsmore & Forster, ca. 1859 (ILLUS.)... **55-65**

Cups & saucers, handleless, "gaudy" Blackberry patt. in underglaze-blue trimmed w/yellow & orange enamel & lustre, E. Walley mark, ca. 1850, some variation, set of 10 .... **1,375**

Dessert service: 10 5/8" l. shaped dish, 5 3/4" h. open compote, four 10" l. leaf-shaped dishes & fourteen 9 1/4" d. plates; Imari-style designs w/shaped edges & deep green borders, Mason's, mid-19th c., the set....................................... **3,680**

Ironstone Egg Cup

Egg cup, Full Ribbed, all-white, J.W. Pankhurst, ca. 1855, 2 1/4" h. (ILLUS.)... **85-100**

Tulip Ironstone Ewer

Ewer, floral decoration on side, C-scroll
 handle, Tulip, Powell & Bishop, ca. 1870,
 13" h. (ILLUS.)... **250-300**

Wedgwood Ironstone Gravy Boat

Gravy boat, footed, C-scroll handle, Hyacinth patt., all-white, Wedgwood, ca.
 1860s (ILLUS.).. **40-50**
Gravy boat, Long Octagon shape, all-
 white, ca. 1847, T.J. & J. Mayer............. **125-140**

Fig/Union Ironstone Mug

Mug, footed, C-scroll handle, Fig/Union
 shape, all-white, Davenport, ca. 1856,
 3" h. (ILLUS.)... **175-200**
Mug, Gothic patt., all-white, ca. 1840s,
 James Edwards **120-130**

Ironstone Cider Mug

Mug, large mug for cider, w/C-scroll handle,
 floral design on side, Hyacinth patt., all-
 white, Wedgwood, ca. 1860s, 4" h.
 (ILLUS.).. **90-105**
Pitcher, 9 3/4" h., footed wide squatty bul-
 bous body molded w/wide ribs & tapering
 to a wide mouth w/arched spout, high
 arched C-scroll handle, transfer decoration of birds in flowering trees & foliage
 w/polychrome enamel, mark of Ashworth
 Brow., England, ca. 1890 .... **303**
Pitcher, 9 3/4" h., table-type, Grape Octa-
 gon shape, all-white, Pearson &
 Hancock **150-180**
Plate, 8" d., twelve-sided, "gaudy" Bitter-
 sweet patt. w/underglaze flow blue &
 copper luster, impressed "Real Iron-
 stone" (light stains)... **83**
Plate, 8 3/8" w., paneled shape, "gaudy"
 freehand Strawberry patt., underglaze-
 blue w/green & two shades of red enamel
 & copper lustre trim, mid-19th c. **385**
Plate, 8 1/2" d., "gaudy" decoration, vintage
 grape vine design painted in underglaze-
 blue, black, ochre & two shades of green
 (wear, crazing) **110**
Plate, 8 1/2" d., "gaudy" style, center w/urn
 in flow blue w/pink & red flowers & copper
 lustre highlights (stains).................................. **110**
Plate, 8 3/4" w., "gaudy" Strawberry patt.,
 paneled   shape   w/underglaze-blue
 trimmed w/red, pink, green & copper lus-
 tre, impressed mark, mid-19th c. **138**
Plate, 9 1/4" w., paneled shape, "gaudy"
 freehand Morning Glory patt., underglaze-blue trimmed w/two shades of
 green, red & black enamel, mid-19th c. **303**
Plate, 9 1/2" d., Bordered Hyacinth/Lily
 shape, all-white, ca. 1860, W. &
 E. Corn **50-65**

Ironstone Flora Plate

Plate, 9 1/2" d., Flora shape, all-white, Wedgwood & Co., ca. 1860 (ILLUS.) **65-75**

Plate, 9 1/2" w., paneled sides, "gaudy" Floral Urn freehand patt., underglaze-blue & green & trimmed w/two shades of red enamel & copper lustre, mid-19th c. (light stains, tiny enamel flake) **330**

Plate, 9 5/8" d., "gaudy" Blackberry patt., underglaze-blue & black trimmed w/red, yellow & copper lustre, impressed "E. Walley - Niagara Shape," 1850s **193**

Ironstone Trent Plate

Plate, 10" d., Trent shape, all-white, John Alcock, ca. 1855 (ILLUS.) **100-125**

Plate, 10 1/4" d., New York shape, all-white, ca. 1858, J. Clementson **50-65**

Plate, 10 1/4" d., twelve-sided "gaudy" style w/strawberries, pink flowers & underglaze flow blue leaves **248**

Plate, 10 1/2" d., Fig shape, all-white, ca. 1856, Davenport/Wedgwood **60-75**

Plates, 8 1/2" d., decorated w/floral motif in blue & rust, marked "Ashworth Brothers Hanley," England, ca. 1890, set of 9 .... **134**

Plates, 9 5/8" d., paneled edge, central transfer-printed garden landscape w/urn of flowers, flower & scroll border, Florilla patt., purple highlighted w/yellow, green, blue & red enamel, mid-19th c., set of 6 (stains) **138**

Plates, 10 1/2" d., scalloped flanged rim, overall Imari-style transfer decoration in polychrome trimmed w/gold, mid-19th c., pr. **303**

Platter, oval, 10" l., President shape, all-white, John Edwards **30-40**

Strawberry Pattern Platter

Platter, 13 1/2" l., octagonal, "gaudy" Strawberry patt., underglaze-blue w/red, pink & green enamel & luster trim, wear, stains & some enamel flaking (ILLUS.) **770**

Platter, 13 1/2" l., rectangular w/cut corners, "gaudy" freehand Morning Glory patt., underglaze-blue trimmed w/two shades of green, red & black, mid-19th c. (old red flaking, minor stains) **385**

Platter, 11 3/8 x 14 1/8", rectangular, romantic transfer scene of a lakeside cabin w/boaters, marked "Cat, Albion" & "Turnbull, Stepney," light blue, mid-19th c. **121**

Platter, 14 3/4" oval, "gaudy," blue transfer-printed War Bonnet patt. trimmed in red, orange & yellow, marked "Ironstone China," mid-19th c. (wear, scratches) **165**

Platter, 15 3/4" l., rectangular w/cut corners, Florentine patt., light blue, T. Mayer, mid-19th c. (internal hairline) **110**

Wedgwood Ironstone Platter

Platter, 16" l., eight-sided oblong, Fig/Union shape, all-white, Wedgwood, ca. 1856 (ILLUS.) **155-175**

Platter, oval, 16" l., Corn & Oats shape, all-white, Davenport/Wedgwood **65-75**

Platter, rectangular, 16" l., Rolling Star shape, all-white, James Edwards **90-100**

Platter, 16 1/4" l., oval w/lightly scalloped rim, "gaudy" freehand Strawberry patt., underglaze black, mid-19th c. (small chips on one corner) **413**

Platter, 18 1/2" l., Indiana patt., ca. 1880, Wedgwood **196**

Platter, 16 x 21", well-and-tree-type, oval, Rural Scenery patt., broad floral border surrounding a meadow landscape w/figures & animals, Davewell & Goodfellow, England (chips on foot, hairline) **440**

Platter, 21 1/4" l., oval w/flanged rim, the center transfer-printed w/a large landscape scene of a dog holding a stick on the bank of a river w/figures rowing a boat, the river flanked by trees & a country house in the distance, wide floral border, blue & white, back w/printed mark of a ribbon-tied banner inscribed "British Views," mid-19th c. **1,265**

Platter, 22" l., oval, polychrome floral decoration w/gilt trim, Stokes Works mark on base, 19th c. **863**

Platters, 8 1/4 x 10 1/2" & 10 1/2 x 13 1/4", oval, each decorated w/a scrolling gilt floral border w/alternating cartouches of birds & flowers, centered by a coat-of-arms, Ashworth, England, ca. 1875, pr. (normal surface scratches) **300**

Punch bowl, footed deep rounded bowl, floral embellishments around the rim & base, twig urn w/flowers & bird at center & sides, in shades of cobalt blue, yellow, pink, orange & green w/gilt highlights, mid-19th c., 14 1/4" d., 6 1/2" h. **1,035**

Footed Ironstone Punch Bowl

Punch bowl, footed, New York shape, all-white, J. Clementson, ca. 1858, 15" d. (ILLUS.) **375-425**

Relish dish, 1851 Shell shape, all-white, ca. 1851, T. & R. Boote **90-100**

Relish dish, Berlin Swirl, all-white, ca. 1856, Mayer & Elliot **65-75**

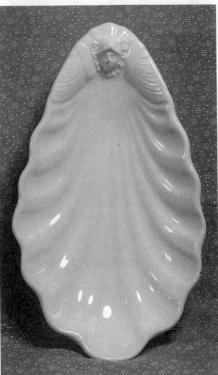

Cameo Gothic Ironstone Relish Dish

Relish dish, elongated shell form, Cameo Gothic, all-white, James Edwards, ca. 1850s, 8" l. (ILLUS.) **100-125**

Relish dish, plain, oval w/two tab handles, all-white, ca. 1870s, Wood, Son & Co. **20-30**

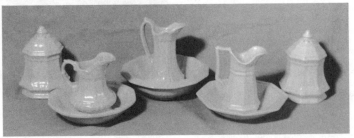

Various Red Cliff Pieces

Salt & pepper shakers, Boote's 1851 shape, all-white, ca. 1960s, Red Cliff, 4" h., pr.

(ILLUS. far right & far left) **50-60**

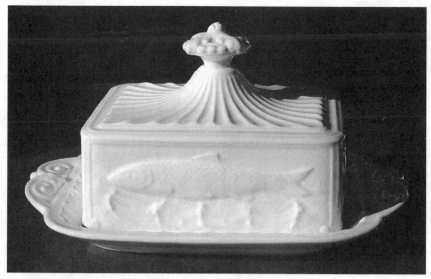

Ironstone Covered Sardine Box

Sardine box, cov., rectangular, all-white, image of sardine on front, lid w/ribbed design curving up to finial-type handle, unmarked, ca. 1870s (ILLUS.) **170-190**

Sauce tureen, cov., oblong form, decorated in color w/the Japanese Garden patt., molded butterfly handles & finial, England, 19th c., 5 3/4" h. **173**

Soup tureen, cover, ladle & underplate, Stafford shape, all-white, ca. 1854, S. Alcock & Co., 4 pcs. **750-800**

Soup tureen, undertray, cover & ladle, Vista England patt., footed deep tureen, grape leaf & vine border, cranberry, tray 14 3/4" l., tureen 10 1/2" h., the set **605**

Ironstone Three-piece Soap Box

Soap box, cover & liner, Pie Crust/Blanket Stitch, all-white, J. & G. Meakin, ca. 1880 (ILLUS.) **30-50**

Soap box, cover & liner, plain oval, all-white, ca. 1872-87, Thomas Elsmore & Son, 3 pcs. **40-45**

Soap box, cover & liner, President shape, all-white, John Edwards, 3 pcs. **120-130**

Soap dish, open, plain hollow rectangular body w/drain holes in well & one on side for cleaning, all-white, various potters **20-30**

Soup plate, flanged paneled rim, Paradise patt., purple floral transfer design w/polychrome trim, mid-19th c., 10 1/2" w. **83**

Soup plate, Sharon Arch shape, all-white, Davenport, 9 1/2" d. **50-60**

Syrup Pitcher with Pewter Lid

Syrup pitcher, w/pewter lid, Lily of the Valley patt., all-white, James Edwards, ca. 1859, 6" h. (ILLUS.) **475-510**

Inverted Diamond Teapot

Teapot, cov., footed, facet effect design, Inverted Diamond, all-white, T.J. & J. Mayer, ca. 1845, 8 1/2" h. (ILLUS.) **225-250**

Teapot, cov., "gaudy" strawberry design, paneled body w/a domed cover w/blossom finial, decorated w/blue flowers, red & green strawberries & gilt trim, ca. 1850, 9 3/4" h. (nick) **2,300**

Teapot, cov., Memnon shape, six panels w/branch handle & bud finial, all-white, ca. 1850s, John Meir & Son, 8 3/4" h. **175-200**

Teapot, cov., tall tapering paneled form w/angled handle & inset high domed cover w/floret finial, "gaudy" Strawberry patt. w/large blossoms highlighted w/flowing blue & copper lustre, mid-19th c., 9" h. (minor flake on spout, reglued finial) **1,375**

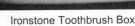

Ironstone Toothbrush Box

Toothbrush box, cov., Sevres shape, all-white, John Edwards, ca. 1860s, 8 1/2" l. (ILLUS.) **90-120**

Vegetable dish, cov., Scotia (Poppy) shape, oval, all-white, ca. 1870, F. Jones & Co., 9" l. **100-120**

Wash bowl & pitcher, miniature, Classic Gothic shape, all-white, Red Cliff, ca. 1960s, overall 4 1/2" h. (ILLUS. second from right w/salt & pepper shakers) **50-75**

Wash bowl & pitcher, miniature, Fig (registered Union shape), all-white, Red Cliff, ca. 1960s, overall 3 1/2" h. (ILLUS. second from left w/salt & pepper shakers) **30-45**

Wash bowl & pitcher, miniature, Sydenham shape, all-white, Red Cliff, ca. 1960s, overall 4 1/2" h. (ILLUS. center w/salt & pepper shakers) **60-90**

Wash bowl & pitcher, "Tudor" patt., transfer-printed overall w/stylized floral medallions, branches & berries in lilac on an ivory ground, William Brownfield & Sons, 1871-91, bowl 15" d., overall 10" h., 2 pcs. **287**

Tea Leaf Ironstone

Apple bowl, fluted sides, Anthony Shaw (some utensil marks) **325**

Baker, rectangular, Victory patt., Edwards, 7 x 9" **50**

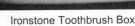

Tea Leaf Scalloped Bone Dish

Bone dish, crescent-shaped w/scalloped rim, Alfred Meakin (ILLUS.) **30**

Boston egg cup, Alfred Meakin (mild crazing) **250**

Brush box, cov., Cable patt., Anthony Shaw **800**

Brush vase, Cable patt., Anthony Shaw **125**

Brush vase, footed, Anthony Shaw **425**

Brush vase, gently waisted cylindrical form w/scalloped rim, Alfred Meakin **205**

Brush vase, Simple Square patt., Wedgwood & Co. **200**

Butter dish, cover & insert, Fish Hook patt., Alfred Meakin **110**

Butter dish, cover & insert, Fleur-de-Lis patt., Wedgwood & Co. **450**

Butter dish, cover & insert, Iona patt., gold motif, Bishop & Stonier, 3 pcs. **70**

Cake plate, Bamboo patt., Alfred Meakin **65**

Cake plate, Basketweave patt., Anthony Shaw (small under rim chip) **500**

Cake plate, Brocade patt., Alfred Meakin **155**

Cake plate, Chelsea patt., Alfred Meakin **190**

Cake plate, Daisy patt., Anthony Shaw **55**

Cake plate, Maidenhair Fern patt., Wilkinson **300**

Cake plate, Polonaise patt., Edge, Malkin **200**

Cake plate, squared shape w/angled handles, Red Cliff, ca. 1960s **40**

Cake plate, Sunburst patt., Wilkinson **130**

Chamber pot, cov., Cable patt., Anthony Shaw **170**

Chamber pot, cov., Daisy 'n Chain patt., Wilkinson **175**

Chamber pot, cov., Lily of the Valley patt., Anthony Shaw **600**

Chamberpot, cov., Maidenhair Fern patt., Wilkinson (mild lustre & glaze wear) **450**

Coffeepot, cov., Square Ridged patt., Red Cliff, ca. 1960s **40**

Compote, open, Hexagon patt., pedestal base, Anthony Shaw **375**

Compote, open, scalloped bowl, pedestal base, Wilkinson (minor pit marks) **325**

Compote, open, square, Red Cliff, ca. 1960s 190

Compote, open, 8 3/4" d., round, Anthony Shaw 275

Creamer, Bordered Fuchsia patt., Anthony Shaw 1,000

Creamer, Cable patt., Anthony Shaw, 5" h. 90

Creamer, gold Tea Leaf, Cartwright Bros., 6 3/4" h. 55

Creamer, LeNoir mark, gold motif, Homer Laughlin, ca. 1930s-40s 130

Creamer, Lily of the Valley patt., Anthony Shaw, 5 1/4" h. 375

Creamer, Lily of the Valley patt., Anthony Shaw, 6 1/2" h. 350

Creamer, Lily of the Valley patt., high-lip variation, Anthony Shaw 375

Creamer, Square Ridged patt., Red Cliff, ca. 1960s 45

Cylindrical Tea Leaf Cup & Saucer

Cup & saucer, handled, cylindrical squatty cup, Wilkinson (ILLUS.) 50

Demitasse cup & saucer, Empress patt., Micratex by Adams, ca. 1960s 35

Doughnut stand, footed, square, Red Cliff, ca. 1960s, 8" w. 135

Egg cup, Empress patt., Micratex by Adams, ca. 1960s 250

Egg cup, unmarked (bottom edge repaired) 275

Gravy boat, Basketweave patt., Anthony Shaw 265

Gravy boat, bathtub-shaped, J. & E. Mayer 180

Gravy boat, Bullet patt., Anthony Shaw 50

Gravy boat, Chinese patt., Anthony Shaw (two pit marks) 210

Gravy boat, Pagoda patt., T. Burgess 110

Gravy boat, Square Ridged patt., Wedgwood & Co. 80

Honey dish, Lily of the Valley patt., Anthony Shaw, 4" d. 170

Ladle, soup-type, Wedgwood & Co. 475

Oyster bowl, footed, unmarked 130

Pitcher, 6" h., Maidenhair Fern patt., Wilkinson 225

Pitcher, 6" h., Sunburst patt., Wilkinson 270

Pitcher, 6 5/8" h., jug-form, Pagoda patt., T. Burgess 170

Pitcher, 7 1/2" h., Chinese patt. Anthony Shaw 325

Pitcher, 7 1/2" h., Square Ridged patt., Mellor, Taylor & Co. 200

Pitcher, 7 3/4" h., Bamboo patt., Alfred Meakin 110

Pitcher, 8" h., Bamboo patt., Alfred Meakin 190

Pitcher, 8" h., Iona patt., gold motif, Powell & Bishop 60

Pitcher, 8" h., Peerless patt., Edwards 400

Pitcher, 8" h., Simple Square patt., Burgess 275

Pitcher, 8 1/2" h., Maidenhair Fern patt., Wilkinson 425

Pitcher, 8 5/8" h., lustre band trim, Grape Octagon shape, Livesley & Powell 85

Pitcher, 8 3/4" h., Rondeau patt., Davenport (flake on base rim) 300

Pitcher, 10" h., water-type, Chelsea patt., Johnson Bros., 3 1/2 qt. 425

Pitcher, milk, Bordered Fuchsia patt., Anthony Shaw 725

Pitcher, hot water-type, Cable patt., Furnival 900

Platter, 10 1/4 x 14 1/4", Chelsea patt., Alfred Meakin 50

Platter, 12 x 17" oval, Brocade patt., Alfred Meakin (minor scratches) 70

Posset cup, Chinese shape, Anthony Shaw 325

Relish dish, Gentle Square patt., T. Furnival 220

Relish dish, mitten-shaped, Chinese patt., Anthony Shaw (some discoloration) 220

Relish dish, mitten-shaped, Grenade patt., Burgess 425

Relish dish, mitten-shaped, Lily of the Valley patt., Anthony Shaw 250

Relish dish, oval, Cable patt., Anthony Shaw 90

Salt & pepper shakers, Empress patt., Micratex by Adams, ca. 1960s, pr. 310

Sauce dish, Lily of the Valley patt., Anthony Shaw 30

Sauce ladle, Anthony Shaw 250

Sauce tureen, cover & ladle, rectangular, Red Cliff, ca. 1960s, the set 225

Sauce tureen, cover, ladle & underplate, Daisy 'n Chain patt., Wilkinson (slight discoloration) 350

Sauce tureen, cover & undertray, Cable patt., Anthony Shaw, 3 pcs. 125

Shaving mug, Cable patt., Anthony Shaw 170

Shaw Chinese Shaving Mug

Shaving mug, Chinese patt., Anthony Shaw (ILLUS.) 120

Shaving mug, Little Cable patt., Thomas Furnival 275

Shaving mug, Niagara Fan patt., Anthony Shaw 750

Shaving mug, Ridged patt., Mellor, Taylor & Co. 600

Slop jar, cov., Cable patt., Anthony Shaw (professional repair on lid) 5,600

Slop jar, Daisy 'n Chain patt., Wilkinson, no cover 800

Slop jar, open, Fish Hook patt., Alfred Meakin (bottom staining) 1,500

Slop jar & silencer, Alfred Meakin (crazing on base & silencer, slight discoloration) **2,000**

Soap dish, slab-type, Grindley (mild wear).. **180**

Soap dish, cover & drainer, Simple Square patt., Wedgwood & Co. (lid w/edge roughness).. **180**

Soap dish, cover & insert, Lion's Head patt., Mellor, Taylor & Co............................... **225**

Soap dish, cover & insert, Ruth Sayers decoration, ca. 1980s...................... **110**

Soup plate, Wedgwood & Co., 9" d. **25**

Soup tureen, cover, ladle & undertray, Simple Square patt., Wedgwood & Co., the set.. **200**

Soup tureen, cover, ladle & undertray, Square Ridged patt., Red Cliff, ca. 1960s, the set... **175**

Sugar bowl, cov., Bordered Fuchsia patt., Anthony Shaw (slight cracks & small chip) **600**

Sugar bowl, cov., Fish Hook patt., Alfred Meakin.. **45**

Sugar bowl, cov., Niagara Fan patt., Anthony Shaw (under rim base chip)..................... **500**

Tea set: cov. teapot, cov. sugar bowl & creamer; Chinese patt., Red Cliff, ca. 1960s, 3 pcs. **500**

Tea set: Daisy 'n Chain patt., Wilkinson **120**

Teapot, cov., Bordered Fuchsia patt., Anthony Shaw (finial repair).............................. **700**

Teapot, cov., child's, East End Pottery (tiny nick on spout lip)...................................... **200**

Vegetable dish, cov., Bamboo patt., square, Alfred Meakin, 6" w. **200**

Vegetable dish, cov., Cable patt., oval, footed, Anthony Shaw, 10" l. **110**

Vegetable dish, cov., Chelsea patt., Alfred Meakin, 12" l.. **120**

Vegetable dish, cov., Daisy 'n Tulip patt., Wedgwood & Co.. **80**

Square Ridged Tea Leaf Vegetable

Vegetable dish, cov., Square Ridged patt., Mellor, Taylor & Co., 12" l. (ILLUS.) **70**

Vegetable dish, cov., Square Ridged patt., Wedgwood & Co.. **110**

Vegetable dish, cov., Sunburst patt., Wilkinson **60**

Wash bowl & pitcher, Bamboo patt., Alfred Meakin, pr.. **225**

Wash bowl & pitcher set, Cable patt., Anthony Shaw, 2 pcs... **325**

Wash bowl & pitcher set, Square Ridged patt., Mellor, Taylor & Co............................. **325**

Wash bowl & pitcher set, Square Ridged patt., Wedgwood & Co., pr. (small hairline in pitcher lip)... **225**

Waste bowl, Chinese patt., Anthony Shaw (one pit mark) **140**

Waste bowl, Lily of the Valley patt., Anthony Shaw.. **230**

Water pitcher, Maidenhair Fern patt., Wilkinson (repaired base chip) **250**

Tea Leaf Variants

Brush box, cov., Morning Glory patt., Portland shape, Elsmore & Forster................... **2,100**

Brush box, cov., Reverse Teaberry patt., Portland shape, Elsmore & Forster (two small chips) **2,500**

Butter dish, cover & insert, Pinwheel patt., Gothic shape, unmarked............................ **1,400**

Cake plate, Berry Cluster & lustre band, Jacob Furnival.. **325**

Cake plate, copper lustre & cobalt blue trim, Lafayette shape, J. Clementson (slight handle roughness) **650**

Cake plate, Teaberry patt., Augusta shape, J. Clementson (one handle flake, some rim roughness)... **400**

Coffeepot, cov., lustre scallop decoration, Wrapped Sydenham shape, E. Walley.......... **500**

Coffeepot, cov., Reverse Teaberry patt., Portland shape, Elsmore & Forster **500**

Creamer, lustre band & cobalt blue trim, Grand Loop shape, unmarked, 5 1/4" h. **425**

Creamer, lustre band decor, Prairie shape, J. Clementson, 6" h.................................... **300**

Creamer, lustre band trim, Gothic shape, Livesley Powell & Co. (minor wear)............... **110**

Creamer, lustre trim, Ceres shape, Elsmore & Forster (light crazing) **210**

Creamer, Pinwheel patt., Gothic shape, attributed to Jacob Furnival (very small nick, glaze damage on foot) **220**

Creamer, Teaberry patt., Elegance shape, Clementson Bros. (slight discoloration, roughness on base) **600**

Cup, handleless, Berry Cluster patt., Jacob Furnival **100**

Cup, handleless, Morning Glory patt., Ceres shape, Elsmore & Forster (tiny rim potting flaw)... **85**

Cup & saucer, handled, child's, Teaberry patt., Clementson Bros. (slight crazing on cup)... **350**

Cup & saucer, handled, Reverse Teaberry patt., Portland shape, Elsmore & Forster (two small chips on saucer) **190**

Cup & saucer, handleless, lustre trim, Ceres shape, Elsmore & Forster **55**

Cup & saucer, handleless, Teaberry patt., Balance Vine shape, J. Clementson **55**

Cup & saucer, handleless, Teaberry patt., New York shape, J. Clementson **160**

Cup & saucer, handleless, Tobacco Leaf patt., Fanfare shape, Elsmore & Forster **95**

Egg cup, Cloverleaf patt. in gold lustre **35**

Gravy boat, copper lustre bands & cobalt blue trim, Tulip shape, Elsmore & Forster (foot flake, medium hairline) **275**

Gravy boat, lustre band trim, Grand Loop shape, J. Clementson **350**

Gravy boat, lustre trim, Ceres shape, Elsmore & Forster **450**

Honey dish, Pomegranate patt., Niagara shape, E. Walley (pinhole in glaze)............... **150**

Mug, lustre Chelsea Grape Sprig patt., paneled sides, unmarked.................................... **225**

Pitcher, 9 1/2" h., Teaberry patt., Chinese shape, J. Clementson 800
Pitcher, milk, Pinwheel patt., attributed to Jacob Furnival (minor wear) 500
Pitcher, milk, Pinwheel patt., Gothic shape, attributed to Jacob Furnival (minor wear) 400
Plate, 9" w., Thistle & Berry patt., ten-sided shape, unmarked 110
Platter, 9 x 11 3/4", lustre band trim, Grape Octagon shape, E. Walley............................. 45
Platter, 19" oval, Morning Glory patt., Portland shape, Elsmore & Forster (mild crazing)... 200
Relish dish, mitten-shape, lustre trim, Ceres shape, Elsmore & Forster (tiny flea bite) 240
Relish dish, mitten-shaped, copper lustre & cobalt blue trim, Tulip shape, Elsmore & Forster (slight edge roughness) 425
Relish dish, mitten-type, Teaberry patt., Elegance shape, Clementson Bros. 625
Soup plate, Teaberry patt., New York shape, Clementson Bros. 60
Sugar bowl, cov., Cinquefoil patt., Wheat shape, unmarked (small discolored spot).. 300
Sugar bowl, cov., copper lustre & cobalt blue trim, Arched Wheat shape, Cochran (lustre wear)... 425
Sugar bowl, cov., copper lustre trim, Ceres shape, Elsmore & Forster 250
Sugar bowl, cov., Reverse Teaberry patt., Portland shape, Elsmore & Forster (mild lid crazing, small hairline in body)................. 450
Sugar bowl, cov., Teaberry patt., Elegance shape, Clementson Bros. (crazing, hairline) 220
Sugar bowl, cov., Teaberry patt., Heavy Square shape, Clementson Bros. (teapot lid, mild crazing & inside rim chips) 450
Sugar bowl, cov., Tobacco Leaf patt., Fanfare shape, Elsmore & Forster (flake on inside lid rim) 325
Teapot, cov., Teaberry patt., Prairie shape, J. Clementson (one hairline in handle, three in base) 400
Vegetable dish, cov., lustre band decor, Ring o' Hearts shape, Livesley Powell & Co. (some discoloration in base, flakes inside cover) 220
Vegetable dish, cov. lustre band, pinstripe & blue leaves, Gothic shape, Elsmore & Forster 450
Vegetable dish, open, oval, Morning Glory patt., Elsmore & Forster, 10" l. (minor crazing)... 190
Vegetable dish, open, oval, Pre-Tea Leaf patt., Niagara shape, E. Walley, 9" l. (minor crazing)...................................... 400
Wash bowl & pitcher set, lustre band trim, Gothic shape, Livesley Powell & Co., 2 pcs.. 350
Wash pitcher, Teaberry patt., Beaded Band shape, Clementson Bros. 475
Waste bowl, lustre band & dot trim, Laurel Wreath patt., Elsmore & Forster................ 375
Waste bowl, Morning Glory patt., Portland shape, Elsmore & Forster 260
Waste bowl, Pepperleaf patt., Crystal shape, Elsmore & Forster 225

Waste bowl, Pinwheel patt., 14-paneled sides, attributed to Jacob Furnival (minor wear)... 140
Water pitcher, lustre band trim, Grape Octagon shape, Livesley Powell & Co., 11" h....... 250

Jasper Ware (Non-Wedgwood)

Jasper ware is fine-grained exceedingly hard stoneware made by including barium sulphate in the clay and was first devised by Josiah Wedgwood, who utilized it for the body of many of his fine cameo blue-and-white and green-and-white pieces. It was subsequently produced by other potters in England and Germany, notably William Adams & Sons, and is in production at the present. Also see WEDGWOOD - JASPER.

Box, cov., miniature, round w/ringed foot, fitted flat cover w/slightly flared rim, the top w/a white relief bust of an Art Nouveau woman w/flowing hair, blue glossy ground, 2 1/2" d. $33
Box, cov., deep round blue jasper base raised on four small tab feet, the sides decorated in white relief w/leafy swags & ribbons, the slightly domed cover w/four small rim tabs decorated w/a blue border band w/white relief blossom & leaf band around a central medallion w/a brown ground & a white relief group of musicians, Germany, ca. 1910, 2 3/4" d., 3 3/4" h. 193
Pitcher, wine, 13" h., King Gambrinus astride a barrel w/incised "Das Jahrist Butbraun Bierist Deralben," also featuring gnomes & leafy vines, blue glazed & white matte finish, late 19th c., Germany... 110
Plaque, oblong, white relief Native American chief w/full headdress, titled "Painted Horse," w/border of owls, green ground, small 125
Plaque, oval, white relief scene of seminude water sprite on a black ground, Limoges, France, early 20th c., unframed, 5 x 7 3/4".. 345
Plaque, rectangular, white relief classical beauty w/a tambourine on a blue ground, Limoges, France, late 19th - early 20th c., framed, plaque 6 x 10" 230

Fisherman Jasper Ware Plaque

Plaque, round, pierced to hang, green ground w/a white relief central scene of a standing fisherman smoking & holding the end of a long coil of rope in his hand, a crate & post behind him, a white relief wide border band of wrapped cattails, Germany, early 20th c., 6 1/4" d. (ILLUS.)... 50-75
Vase, 6" h., white relief scene of women, royal blue ground, Schafer & Vater, Germany 165

Jewel Tea Autumn Leaf

Although not antique, this ware has a devoted follow-ing. The Hall China Company of East Liverpool, Ohio, made the first pieces of Autumn Leaf pattern ware to be given as premiums by the Jewel Tea Company in 1933. The premiums were an immediate success and thousands of new customers, all eager to acquire a piece of the dura-ble Autumn Leaf pattern ware, began purchasing Jewel Tea products. Although the pattern was eventually used to decorate linens, glasswares and tinware, we include only the Hall China Company items in our listing.

Jewel Tea Flat Soup Bowl

Bowl, flat soup, 8 1/2" (ILLUS.) **15**
Bowl, salad, 9" d. (ILLUS., below) **25**

Jewel Tea Butter Dish

Butter dish, cov., square top w/straight finial, 1/4 lb. (ILLUS.) **1,200**

Autumn Leaf Bean Pot

Bean pot, one-handled, 2 1/4 qt. (ILLUS.) **$800**

Butter Dish with Butterfly Handle

Butter dish, cov., w/butterfly-type handle (ILLUS.) **1,500**

Autumn Leaf Cereal Bowl

Bowl, cereal, 6 1/2" d. (ILLUS.) **15**

Drip-type Coffeemaker

Jewel Tea Salad Bowl

Soufflé-style French Baker

Coffeemaker, cov., all china, drip type
(ILLUS., previous page)................................... **350**

Autumn Leaf Electric Percolator

Coffeepot, cov., electric, percolator (ILLUS.)..... **350**
Cup & saucer **10**
French baker, swirled soufflé-style, 2-pt.
(ILLUS., above).. **19**

Gravy Boat with Undertray

Gravy boat (ILLUS.).. **30**

Mixing Bowl

Mixing bowl, 7" d., part of set (ILLUS.) **15**
Pickle dish (gravy undertray)................................... **25**

Jewel Tea Pie Baker

Pie baker, 10" d. (ILLUS.).. **22**

Aladdin Shape Teapot

Jewel Tea Dinner Plate

Plate, 10" d., dinner (ILLUS.)................................ **12**

Jewel Tea Salt & Pepper Shakers

Salt & pepper shakers, small, bell-shaped
(ILLUS.)... **35**
Teapot, cov., Aladdin shape (ILLUS.) **60**
Teapot, cov., Newport shape w/gold trim,
1978 version... **125**

Autumn Leaf Teapot

Teapot, cov., Newport shape w/gold trim
(ILLUS.).. **150**

Oval Vegetable Bowl

Vegetable bowl, 10 1/2" oval (ILLUS.)................. **20**

Jugtown Pottery

This pottery was established by Jacques and Juliana Busbee in Jugtown, North Carolina, in the early 1920s in an attempt to revive the skills of the diminishing North Carolina potter's art as Prohibition ended the need for locally crafted stoneware whiskey jugs. During the early years, Juliana Busbee opened a shop in Greenwich Village in New York City to promote the North Carolina wares that her husband, Jacques, was designing and a local youth, Ben Owen, was producing under his direction. Owen continued to work with Busbee from 1922 until Busbee's death in 1947 at which time Juliana took over management of the pottery for the next decade until her illness (or mental fatigue) caused the pottery to be closed in 1958. At that time, Owen opened his own pottery a few miles away, marking his wares "Ben Owen - Master Potter." The pottery begun by the Busbees was reopened in 1960, under new management, and still operates today using the identical impressed mark of the early Jugtown pottery the Busbees managed from 1922 until 1958.

Jugtown Pottery Mark

Bowl, 4 1/2" d., 1 1/2" h., a small raised foot-ring supporting a wide rounded bowl w/a flat rim, Chinese Blue glaze, impressed mark **$55**

Bowl, 7 1/4" d., 4 1/2" h., a footring supporting a deep rounded bowl w/slightly flared rim, Chinese blue glaze, circular stamp mark (three small glaze misses on interior) **825**

Bowl, 13" d., redware w/a yellow slip-decorated chicken, impressed mark, 20th c. **165**

Pitcher, 10 1/2" h., redware, bulbous ovoid body tapering to a flared rim w/rim spout, small C-form shoulder handle, pumpkin orange glaze, impressed mark **303**

Jugtown Hexagonal Vase

Vase, 3 1/2" h., hexagonal body w/wide shoulder tapering to wide flat rim, semi-matte white glaze, impressed mark (ILLUS.) **248**

Vase, 3 1/2" h., simple ovoid body tapering to a small flat mouth, mottled & streaky glossy brown glaze, impressed mark **121**

Vase, 4" h., 3" d., simple ovoid form tapering to a small flat mouth, Chinese Blue glaze w/mottled dark brown, circular mark **825**

Vase, 4 1/4" h., ovoid body w/closed rim, covered in a frothy semi-matte white glaze, impressed mark.................... **165**

Vase, 5 1/4" h., 4" d., narrow footring below the bulbous ovoid body tapering to a small flat mouth, overall Chinese Blue glaze mottled w/deep red & white, circular stamp mark **770**

Vase, 5 1/4" h., 6 1/4" d., wide bulbous body w/a wide shoulder tapering to a short rolled neck, mottled turquoise, red & purple Chinese Blue glaze, impressed circular mark..................................... **825**

Pear-shaped Jugtown Vase

Vase, 5 1/2" h., 4 1/2" d., pear-shaped body tapering to flat incurved rim, covered in a flowing red & turquoise Chinese Blue glaze, impressed circular mark (ILLUS.)... **660**

Vase, 6" h., ovoid body tapering to a closed mouth, covered in rich Chinese Blue glaze w/red veining, impressed mark............ **495**

Vase, 6 1/4" h., 7" d., bulbous body w/wide shoulder tapering to short neck w/flat rim, Chinese Blue glaze, impressed circular mark.. **1,463**

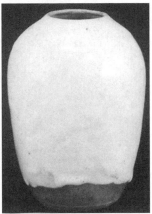

Jugtown Vase with White Drippy Glaze

Vase, 6 1/2" h., 4 1/4" d., ovoid body tapering to a small flat mouth, dripping white semi-matte glaze over a brown clay body, circular stamp mark (ILLUS.)... **495**

Egg-shaped Jugtown Vase

Vase, 7" h., ovoid egg-shaped body tapering to a flat mouth, embossed w/two medallions, mottled light blue glaze w/clay band showing around the base, bruise on rim, short firing line in base of neck, stamped mark (ILLUS.) **288**

Jugtown Chinese Translation Vase

Vase, 8" h., slightly ovoid body tapering to a wide flaring neck, unusual Chinese translation form in dark red & blue mottled glazes (ILLUS.) **698**

Kitchen & Serving Accessories

Butter Pats

Butter pats (sometimes referred to as "butter chips") became an important part of everyday dining beginning in the second half of the 19th century. Victorians placed this little dish by each diner's plate so it could hold a single pat of butter. Thousands of designs were used to decorate ceramic examples, with many sturdy ironstone examples featuring transfer-printed decoration while many finer porcelain ones were hand-painted. Prices here are based on pieces in excellent condition without chips, cracks or crazing.

Noted author and authority Mary Dessoie provided the following broad listing of collectible butter pats. She founded the Butter Pat Patter Association in 1997. It is listed in our Appendix of Collectors Clubs.

Household

Limoges porcelain, decorated w/a garland of green vines w/tiny pink flowers trimmed w/gold, double stamped marks of Charles Field Haviland/GDA Limoges, ca. 1900-1941 .... **$17**

Limoges porcelain, decorated w/apple blossoms on a white ground w/a scalloped rim, Theodore Haviland mark & impressed initials "TH," 1904 - mid-1920s **28**

Tressemann & Vogt Limoges Pat

Limoges porcelain, decorated w/large florals in pinks, pale yellow & blue, scalloped & fluted borders, backstamp for Tressemann & Vogt, Limoges, ca. 1891 (ILLUS.) **50**

Limoges porcelain, five-sided form w/a scalloped gold rim, three h.p. sprays of pink & white dogwood surrounded by pale green leaves, double-stamped Haviland marks, ca. 1880s-1900 .... **30**

Latrille Brothers Floral Butter Pat

Limoges porcelain, gently scalloped side, large pink blossom & green leaf sprigs, backstamp of Latrille Brothers, Limoges, ca. 1900 (ILLUS.) **22**

Limoges porcelain, green floral decoration w/delicately embossed rim, carries the mark of the Alluaud Company of Limoges, France, also a potter's mark of a red rooster standing on one foot, author Mary Gaston notes this mark is rarely found in this country, 1891+ **30**

Limoges porcelain, green & white h.p. decoration w/tiny green flowers on a shiny white ground, a garland of leaves surrounds the rich gold trim, mark of Charles Field Haviland/GDM France, 1891-1900 .... **25**

Limoges porcelain, overall floral design in mint green, amber & traces of pink surrounded by a ruffled rim, double Haviland & Co. marks & the pattern name "The Countess," 1893-1930 .... **30**

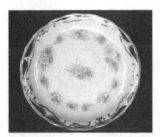

Elite - Limoges Floral Butter Pat

Limoges porcelain, pink & green floral ring & cluster surrounded by a dark blue border band w/ornate gold trim, backstamp for the Elite Works, Limoges, ca. 1900 (ILLUS.).. **42**

Limoges porcelain, round, blue cornflowers, daisies & blue bachelor's buttons on a shiny white ground, mark of Latrille Brothers, Limoges & the pattern name "Old Abbey," ca. 1908-13 .... **22**

Limoges porcelain, round w/a delicate thin sea foam design on the border & gold rim band, double Wm. Guérin stamped mark, 3" d.. **15**

Limoges porcelain, round w/slightly ruffled rim, decorated overall w/autumnal flowers, mark of A. Lanternier, ca. 1891-1914, 3 1/8" d....................................... **22**

Early Theodore Haviland Butter Pat

Limoges porcelain, round w/slightly scalloped rim, pink floral sprigs & green leaves, backstamp for Theodore Haviland, 1903-1925 (ILLUS.).................................. **25**

Early Haviland & Co. Butter Pat

Limoges porcelain, square w/cut corners, blue & yellow bird perched on a flowering branch, scattered blue & pink blossoms, backstamp of Haviland & Co., 1879-1889 (ILLUS.).. **34**

Limoges porcelain, squared form molded to resemble a linen napkin w/folded over corners, one corner w/a h.p. flower, Haviland mark "H & Co" over "L," ca. 1880s.. **35**

Limoges porcelain, squared form w/rounded corners, color scene of a fairy seated on a branch w/pink blossoms, gold trim, Charles Field Haviland mark, 1882-1890 (ILLUS. bottom left with novelty pats).. **55**

Novelty, majolica, molded fan-shaped design trimmed in blue, pink, red, green & gold, unmarked, late 19th c. (ILLUS. bottom right)................................. **110-125**

Novelty, majolica molded fan-shaped design trimmed in blue, pink, yellow, green & gold, unmarked, late 19th c. (ILLUS. top right)................................. **110-125**

Group of Novelty Butter Pats

Novelty, round w/tiny scallops on rim, embossed standing Kate Greenaway-like child wearing a pink bonnet, blue & white cloak & yellow dress, pink blossom & green leaves on green & brown ground, unmarked, late 19th c. (ILLUS. top left) 40

Staffordshire, blue Tower patt., piecrust rim, Copeland - Spode, England............................. 40

Staffordshire, Blue Willow patt., Allerton's, England 30

Staffordshire, Blue Willow patt., Grimwades Ltd., England, ca. 1930+ 25

Staffordshire, Chinese patt., ironstone china decorated w/an Aesthetic Movement design in bluish green featuring an Oriental landscape w/pagodas, a temple, bridge & lush trees & flowers, impressed mark of Wedgwood & Co., England & pattern name, late 19th c. 50

Staffordshire, h.p. bold green ivy design w/large leaves joined by a brown vine surrounded by a green pinstripe, marked by hand on the reverse "Napoleon Ivy as used by Napoleon at St. Helena in 1815 - Wedgwood of Etruria & Barlaston - Made in England - Pattern No. A.L. 4751," 1940+ 45

Staffordshire, ironstone china decorated w/green flowers, Alfred Meakin, England, early 1900s 15

Staffordshire, ironstone china w/a dynamic Art Nouveau design in bold colors of black, orange, blue & gold, mark of J. & G. Meakin, England & registration number for 1902 18

Staffordshire, Jewel Billingsley Rose patt., h.p. rose in full bloom surrounded by green leaves & a smaller rosebud, Copeland - Spode, England pink mark, England registration number & U.S. Patent number dated to June 15, 1926, pattern name & Staffordshire marks also on back 45

Staffordshire, Melbourne patt., flow blue china, W.H. Grindley & Co., England 75

Staffordshire, Roma patt., flow blue china, scrolled gold trim, Wedgwood & Co., England, ca. 1905, 3 1/4" d............................. 80

Copeland-Spode Rosebud Chintz Pat

Staffordshire, Rosebud Chintz patt., bright rosebuds, green vines & a sprinkling of tiny yellow flowers, Copeland - Spode, England mark & pattern name on back, 3" d. (ILLUS.)..................................... 45

Staffordshire, round ironstone decorated overall w/big, bold colorful flowers, bright red pinstripe on the rim, Alfred Meakin, England, ca. 1907.. 16

Round Tea Leaf Pattern Butter Pat

Staffordshire, round ironstone decorated w/the copper lustre Tea Leaf patt., mark of Henry Alcock & Co., England, late 19th c. (ILLUS.) 38

Ironstone China Floral Pat

Staffordshire, square ironstone printed w/an overall black flowering branch design, British registry number 51,058 for 1886 (ILLUS.).. 28

Staffordshire, square ironstone w/a piecrust rim, decorated w/the copper lustre Tea Leaf patt., mark of Wedgwood & C., England, late 19th c. 42

Staffordshire, square ironstone w/copper lustre Tea Leaf patt. & lustre band border, mark of W.H. Grindley, England, late 19th c.. 18

Restaurant Ware

Hospital, decorated w/the hospital's logo in rust & "City Hospital 1871, Worcester, Massachusetts, Science Trimming the Lamp of Life," early, 3" d. 52

Hospital, "Research Hospital" in ornate script framed by a highly stylized border of roses & swags of leaves, heavy duty china, 3 3/4" d.. 50

Hotel, decorated w/a leafy branch w/two berries, from the Mandarin Oriental - Hong Kong, the city's most exclusive hotel, fine porcelain, marked on the back "Mandarin Oriental Hong Kong, Royal Doulton Bone China, England" & the hotel's fan logo, 3" d.................................... 95

Hotel, decorated w/the hotel logo & name "Hotel San Diego," 3" d. 58

Hotel, decorated w/the words "Raffles Hotel, Singapore" & the hotel logo, two green pinstripes on the rim, landmark hotel built in the 19th c., bone china, backstamped w/the Royal Doulton mark & "Specially for Raffles Hotel," 2 7/8" d................................. 95

Restaurant, three green pinstripes surrounding "Barbeque Inn Waikiki," heavy
duty china, mid-20th c. 55

Transportation - Airlines (used in First Class & Business Class)

Aerolineas Argentinas (Argentine Airlines),
airline name on the front, maker's mark
Verbano on the back... 19

Air France First Class Butter Pat

Air France, white ground w/a blue & brown
hippocampus & blue teardrop band
around the rim, "Première Class" (First
Class) presentation-type, made by Ber-
nardaud, Limoges, France, full factory &
airline backmarks, 1970s-1990s, 3" d.
(ILLUS.).. 90

Air New Zealand Butter Pat

Air New Zealand, turquoise ground w/a
Maori tribal design in brown, marked on
the back "Air New Zealand - Crown Lynn
Pottery," 3" d. (ILLUS.)...................................... 30

Alitalia (Italian Airlines), decorated w/a Le-
onardo DaVinci design of a winged flying
machine, marked on the back "Alitalia -
Richard Ginori," 3 1/2" d................................... 15

Alitalia (Italian Airlines), decorated w/a
scene of a vintage airplane, marked on
the back "Alitalia - Richard Ginori,"
3 1/2" d... 15

Alitalia (Italian Airlines), squared form, decorated w/an early hot air balloon in blue,
gold & white (ILLUS. top left, bottom of
page) 15

American Airlines, white w/cobalt blue & silver trim, used in first class for international travel, airline & Jackson China
backmarks, ca. 1980s, 3 7/8" d....................... 18

BOAC (British Overseas Airways), blue
speckled band trimmed in silver, designed exclusively for use in the first
class cabins by Royal Doulton in 1989,
marked on the back w/the airline & Royal
Doulton marks, 3" d. 30

BOAC (British Overseas Airways), Coat-of-
Arms patt. in gold on white, airline & Royal Doulton backstamps, used from 1972-
1989, 3" d. 32

BOAC (British Overseas Airways), Golden
Net patt., Copeland - Spode & airline
marks on the back, 1960s, 2 13/16" d. 32

Canadian Pacific, white ground w/a mustard
yellow airline logo & pinstripe border,
used 1968-1988, backmark reads "Made
exclusively for C.P. Air," 3" d........................... 20

Civil Aviation Administration (China), porcelain w/stylized Oriental floral design in
blue, the organization was formed in
1949 after the establishment of the People's Republic of China (ILLUS. bottom
left).. 85

Delta Airlines, Blue-Gold Rope patt., a cobalt blue band w/the rope & pinstripes in
gold, airline backmark... 15

Delta Airlines, top marked w/airline name in
script... 18

Transportation-related Butter Pats

Finnair, butter ramekin decorated in grey &
silver, presented to First Class passen-
gers in a special box marked "Finnair,"
back-stamped "Arabia" 70

Gulf Air, octagonal, the top w/the airline logo
in gold & a gold rim band, airline & Wedgwood & Co., England back marks 90

Iberia (Spanish Airline), white w/a yellow
pinstripe border & the Iberia logo in red &
yellow w/a crown, manufacturer's & airline name & logo on the back, 3 11/16" d. 50

PanAm, all-white, marked on the back
"Bauscher Weiden, Bavaria, Germany -
PanAm," 3 1/8" d. 30

SwissAir, all-white, back-stamped in green
"SwissAir - Suisse, Langenthal," 2 3/4" d. 25

Thai Airlines, floral design in light & delicate
pink & green tones w/"Thai" in gold, Nori-
take back stamp, 3 3/4" d. 55

Transportation - Ocean Liners

Clipper Line (Sweden), white w/a blue &
gold logo w/line name & gold pinstripe
border, Rorstrand factory mark on re-
verse, 3 3/8" d. 40

Cunard White Star Line, white shell-shaped
form w/a gold fleur-de-lis & gold trim,
used on the Queen Mary & Queen Eliza-
beth, Minton backstamp 45

Greek Line, heavy ceramic in white w/the
company logo in cobalt blue, used on
trans-Atlantic liners between 1939 and
1975, backstamp for A.J. Wilkinson, En-
gland, 2 7/8" d. 32

Transportation - Railroads

Atchison, Topeka & Santa Fe, Adobe patt.,
heavy ceramic w/tan design, distinctive
Econo-Rim form on this stock pattern
used from 1941 to 1969, no railroad logo,
marked on the back "Syracuse China 92-
E USA," 3" d. 15

Baltimore & Ohio, Centenary patt., dark blue
on white, introduced in 1927 to celebrate
the railroad's centennial, full railroad &
Shenango China backstamps, 3 7/16" d.
(ILLUS. top right with animal) 98

British Rail, heavy white body decorated w/a
leaf design surrounded by a gold pinstripe, back marked "BTH" for "British
Transport Hotel," as well as a decorator's
mark & Ridgways Potteries, Ltd. mark,
used in railroad-owned hotels, 4" d. 28

Chicago, Burlington & Quincy, Violets and
Daisies patt., Buffalo China backstamp 78

Chicago, Milwaukee, St. Paul & Pacific Railroad, Traveler patt., dark pink decoration
w/a flying goose in the center, made by
Syracuse China (ILLUS. top right with
animal design pats) 70

Early steam engine, square ironstone china
w/a scene of an early steam engine &
passenger car printed in black within a
black border band, novelty piece not
used on a railroad, England, late 19th c.
(ILLUS. bottom right w/Alitalia) 14

Erie Railroad, Starucca patt. 325

Kansas City Southern Railroad, Roxbury
patt., flower on the top surrounded by the
distinctive Syracuse China Econo-Rim,
Syracuse backstamp, stock pattern, 3" d. 35

Advertising

Don (Edward) & Co., printed on the top
"Compliments of Edward Don & Co., Chicago National Restaurant Exposition,
October, 1940 - Made by Jackson China
Company of Falls Creek, Pa.," backstamped "Ed Don & Co. Chicago - Jack-
son - Made in USA," 3 3/4" d. 50

Royal Copenhagen, white w/the Royal
Copenhagen logo in blue, intricately embossed trim, probably designed as an advertising piece or corporate gift, Royal
Copenhagen backstamps & logo,
2 3/4" d. 90

Syracuse China, printed on the top "Syracuse China - 1871-1971 - A century of
fine services," 100th Anniversary commemorative, Syracuse China backs-
tamp, 3 3/4" d. 38

Warsaw Restaurant, printed on the top
"Warsaw Restaurant 820 N. Ashland
Ave. Chicago," backstamp logo of the
Jackson Vitrified China Company, 1917-
1930s, 3 5/8" d. 55

Fraternal Organizations

Benevolent & Protective Order of Elks,
round ironstone china decorated in green
"BPOE Lodge 374," 3 3/8" d. 30

Fraternal Order of Eagles, round top decorated w/an eagle w/a banner reading
"F.O.E. 1090," Aerie No. 1090 was located in Clifton Forge, Virginia, instituted on
June 1, 1905, charter surrendered Janu-
ary 2, 1920 35

International Order of Odd Fellows, square
ironstone china printed on top "IOOF
1081," backstamp for Greenwood China,
late 19th - early 20th c. 30

Masons, top printed in blue w/a picture of a
Victorian-era Temple & "Harrisburg Association Masonic Temple" in ornate
script lettering, marked on the back "O.P.
Co. Syracuse China" which dates this
piece to 1911 58

Masons, top printed w/the Masonic logo in
green on a pale yellow ground w/a gold
pinstripe border, 3 7/8" d. 32

Military

Grand Army of the Republic (GAR), top
printed in gold "Amasa B. Watson,
W.R.C. 171," gold trim, Major Watson
was a Civil War veteran & The Amasa B.
Watson Post No. 395 of the Department
of Michigan Grand Army of the Republic
was established in his memory in 1888,
back impressed w/"91" in a circle, the
Syracuse China date code for 1911,
3 1/8" d. 75

Hill Military Academy, Portland, Oregon,
printed on the top w/the school logo &
name in green, pre-1948 Shenango Chi-
na Co. backstamp, 3 1/2" d. 65

United States Army Military Academy, West
Point, round heavy duty type, top printed
w/the West Point logo & "Duty - Honor -
Country - West Point - MDCCCII - US-
MA," backstamped "Made by Carr China
Co. for James M. Shaw & Co. expressly
for The Cadet Mess, West Point, New
York," early to mid-20th c., 3" d. 65

Butter Pats with Various Animals

Miscellaneous

Animal design, ironstone china, squared w/napkin-style folded corners, Aesthetic Movement-style transfer-printed design in brown & black showing birds & plants, England, late 19th c. (ILLUS. bottom right).. **22**

Animal design, porcelain w/lightly scalloped rim, decorated w/brown & black crab in blue water, unmarked (ILLUS. bottom left).. **12**

Animal design, porcelain w/lightly scalloped rim, decorated w/brown & black fish in blue water, unmarked (ILLUS. top left, top of page)... **12**

German Porcelain Butter Pat

Oscar & Edward Gutherz, Altrohau, Germany, round porcelain w/a gold band of stamped shamrocks within a green rim band, 1899-1918 (ILLUS.) **50**

Portrait design, asymmetrical porcelain shape decorated w/a bust portrait of a peasant girl wearing a straw hat & white & blue dress, unmarked, late 19th c. (ILLUS. top right, top next page)................ **50-90**

Portrait design, porcelain shell-form w/small tab handle, portrait of a Victorian boy wearing a large straw hat w/feather & lace-collared blue suit on a gold ground, unmarked, late 19th c. (ILLUS. bottom left, top next page) **50-90**

Portrait design, porcelain shell-form w/small tab handle, portrait of a Victorian girl wearing a blue bonnet w/white fur trim & pink ribbon, pink dress w/wide white collar, unmarked, late 19th c. (ILLUS. bottom right, top next page) **50-90**

Buffalo China Singapore Pattern Pat

Buffalo Pottery, Singapore patt., stylized flower sprigs in red, dark gold, dark blue, green & brown w/a red border band, ca. 1930 (ILLUS.)... **25**

Fine Porcelain Portrait Butter Pats

Portrait design, porcelain w/h.p. bust portrait of a Renaissance woman w/large hat & high-collared gown in reddish brown, black & white on a gold ground, unmarked, late 19th c. (ILLUS. top left).......... **50-90**

Bisque porcelain, highly textured bisque body, black spots, pink bow, w/yellow bell at neck, all glazed, "Japan" paper label, 4 1/4 x 5 3/4" (ILLUS.)........................... **20-24**

Cow Creamers

Bennington Pottery Cow Creamer

Bennington pottery, platform-type, Rockingham glaze, rare, missing lid, chip on one horn, tail repair, expect damage as this creamer is a rare find in any condition, 5 x 7" (ILLUS.)... **450-550**

Black Ceramic Cow Creamer

Ceramic, black high-gloss glaze over red clay pottery, highly detailed, cold-painted features, maker unknown, 5 x 5 1/2" (ILLUS.).. **39-44**

Blue Painted Japanese Cow Creamer

Ceramic, blue painted flowers on both sides, molded green bell around neck, flowers in various colors, ink stamped "Japan" on bottom, 5 1/4 x 7 3/4" (ILLUS).. **32-35**

Bisque Cow Creamer

Blue Polka-dotted Cow Creamer

Ceramic, blue polka-dots on white glazed pottery, molded bell at neck, eyes accented w/long lashes, unmarked, maker unknown, 5 1/2 x 5 3/4" (ILLUS.) **49-55**

Brahma Cow Creamer

Ceramic, Brahma, laying down, black at top, graduating to reddish brown over cream pottery, highly glazed, unglazed bottom, very unusual, maker unknown, 3 3/4 x 8 3/4" (ILLUS.) **39-45**

Brown & White Cow Creamer

Ceramic, brown markings on white glazed ceramic, h.p. eyes, tail curls down & connects to back hind leg forming handle, unmarked, 4 x 7" (ILLUS.) **21-24**

Common Cow Creamer

Ceramic, brown markings over highly glazed white ceramic, ink stamped number "B544" underneath, common, 3 1/2 x 5 3/4" (ILLUS.) **22-26**

Ceramic, bull, brown & white, grey hooves & facial shading, tail curls under to form handle, ink stamped "K393," maker unknown, 4 1/2 x 7 3/4" **29-35**

Grouping of Bull Creamers

Ceramic, bull creamers, also found w/matching salt & pepper shakers, stamped "Made in Japan," also "Occupied Japan," 3 x 3", each (ILLUS.) **19-24**

Ceramic, bull creamers, also found w/matching salt & pepper shakers, stamped "Made in Japan," also "Occupied Japan," larger sizes, each **24-35**

Cow Creamer Bust

Ceramic, bust-form, brown markings on white w/pink ears, cheeks & mouth, bulging eyes, yellow horns & bell at neck, commonly found in various other animal shapes, h.p. marked "Japan," 4 x 4" (ILLUS.) **24-28**

Artmark Originals Cow Creamer

Ceramic, bust-form, dark brown w/lighter brown paint-dripping effects, gold highlights on tips of horns, lashes & bell, bottom red & gold foil paper label, h.p., "Artmark Originals, Japan," 3 1/2 x 5 3/4" (ILLUS.) **25-29**

Smiling Cow Creamer

Ceramic, bust-form, golden ringlets & horns at crown, molded blue bell about the neck, black markings, highly detailed smiling features, ink stamped "M6149 Japan," original price 49 cents, 4 x 4 1/4" (ILLUS.) **49-55**

Comical Cow Creamer

Ceramic, comical, pink on white, ink stamped "Japan" on bottom, original ink stamp price of 19 cents on bottom of hoof, 4 x 5" (ILLUS.) 19-24

Ceramic, dark brown over red clay, highly glazed, w/gold accents about the feet & eyes, light brown drippings of paint at opening, missing paper label, Japan, 4 1/2 x 5 1/2" 19-23

Ceramic, dark green shamrocks on white glaze, tail curls underneath to form handle, marked "Cream" on front side, unmarked, 5 x 8" 40-45

Blue Floral Cow Creamer

Ceramic, dark & light blue flowers on white glaze, w/blue nose & ears, tail curled up over back to form handle, "Cream" stamped on one side, bottom ink stamp "E-3801," 4 1/4 x 7" (ILLUS.) 39-46

Flat-Bottomed Cow Creamer

Ceramic, flat bottom, turquoise spots on cream glazed pottery w/brown accents, molded bell at neck, rouge painted jaw area, unmarked, unglazed bottom, 5 1/2 x 7" (ILLUS.) 65-69

Handpainted Cow Creamer

Ceramic, h.p. floral on white, molded bell at neck, many found with "Souvenir" label from places visited, Japan, 3 1/4 x 5 1/4" (ILLUS.) 14-19

Holly Ross Cow Creamer

Ceramic, h.p. flower on one side, bud on reverse, facial features, hooves & ribbon in gold, w/gold under glaze bottom marks, artist signed "Holly Ross, LaAnna, PA. Made in the Poconos," 5 x 7 1/2" (ILLUS.) 39-45

Otagiri Cow Creamer

Ceramic, h.p., w/gold foil label "M O C Japan, Otagiri 1981," embossed underneath, foil label on side, "Handpainted," still being produced, common, by Otagiri, 3 x 5 1/2" (ILLUS.) 12-15

Black Cow Creamer

Ceramic, highly-glazed black over red clay, cold-painted features in pink, blue & gold, pottery bell w/painted flower attached by metal chain, original lid w/tip of tail ornamental to top, unmarked, 5 1/2 x 6" (ILLUS.) 34-39

Sponged Design Cow Creamer

Ceramic, laying down, legs tucked underneath, dark green sponging over brown, yellow & cream glazed pottery, "Made in Japan" bottom ink stamp, rare sponged design, 3 1/2 x 7 1/4" (ILLUS.) 95-100

Brown & White Cow Creamer

Ceramic, light brown over white, sometimes mistaken as the popular "Elsie" creamer, h.p. dark green garland at neck & bow on tail, black hooves, eyes shut w/fine lashes, unmarked, 6 x 6" (ILLUS.) **25-29**

Tan & White Japanese Cow Creamer

Ceramic, light tan over white, high glaze, large black painted eyes & hooves, bottom ink stamp "B588," "Japan," 3 3/4 x 5 3/4" (ILLUS.) **14-19**

Calico Cow Creamer

Ceramic, lying down, dark blue on white, "Milk" stamped on one side, bottom ink stamp "Calico Burleigh Staffordshire England," new, still in production, 3 x 7 1/4" (ILLUS.) **35-39**

Cow Creamer with Eyes Shut

Ceramic, lying down, eyes shut, yellow crown, pink nose, highlighted in brown on white glazed pottery, tail curled up to form handle loop over rear, impressed branding iron marking "R" within a "G" on back side, unglazed pottery bottom, maker unknown, 5 x 6 1/2" (ILLUS.) **42-45**
Ceramic, lying down, feet tucked under, lustreware w/black spots & gold accented horns, red ink stamp "Made in Japan," 4 x 6" **27-32**

Handpainted Japanese Cow Creamer

Ceramic, lying down, red dotted flowers on white w/dark green tail, hooves & crest, pink nose & ribbon, bottom marking "Hand Painted Japan," 1950-60, 4 x 6 1/2" (ILLUS.) **24-29**

Miniature Japanese Cow Creamer

Ceramic, miniature, h.p. flower on each side, stamped "Japan" on front hooves, 2 1/4 x 3 1/2" (ILLUS.) **16-20**

Orange & White Cow Creamer

Ceramic, orange spots on both sides over white, black tail & facial features, unmarked, 1960 (ILLUS.) **19-24**

Petite Cow Creamer

Ceramic, petite, decorated w/flowers on white glaze, molded bell at neck, unmarked, Japan, 4 1/2 x 4 3/4" (ILLUS.) **16-19**
Ceramic, pink mottled high glaze, grey base, horns & tail, black ink stamp "Made in Japan" w/flower in middle, very unusual, 4 1/2 x 6 1/4" **49-55**

Gold Accented Cow Creamer Pitcher

Ceramic, pitcher, black high gloss w/22 kt. gold detailed accents, bottom stamped in gold "Pearl China Co., hand decorated, 22 kt. Gold, U.S.A.," impressed "#635," larger than usual cow creamer, 6 1/2 x 6 1/2" (ILLUS.) **29-35**

Kenmar Purple Cow Creamer

Ceramic, purple glazed, small tin bell attached at neck w/fine wire, gold foil label marked "Kenmar, Japan," various colors, common, mint w/bell, 4 1/2 x 6 1/2" (ILLUS.) **25-29**

Cow Creamer w/Pink Flowers

Ceramic, reddish brown on cream, pink flowers at base, unmarked, w/flat bottom base, 1950-60, 3 3/4 x 5 1/2" (ILLUS.)....... **19-25**

Common Japanese Cow Creamer

Ceramic, reddish brown over cream, Japanese, mass-produced before, during & after the war, found in many sizes, colors & various markings, common, 3 1/2 x 5 1/4" (ILLUS.) **25-28**

Brown Cow Creamer & Sugar Set

Ceramic, set: cow creamer & cov. sugar; brown markings over white, large prominent eyes, molded bells at neck, standing cow creamer, lying down sugar w/lid, tail curls up to form handle on lid of sugar, unmarked, 1950, creamer 5 1/4 x 5 1/2" h., sugar 4 3/4 x 6", the set (ILLUS.)... **42-49**

Purple Cow Creamer & Sugar Set

Ceramic, set: cow creamer & cov. sugar; purple accents on white, sugar has satin ribbon on head, sold by Norcrest China Co., unmarked, "Japan," common, also found w/matching salt & pepper shakers, creamer 6 x 4 3/4" h., sugar 3 x 4 3/4", the complete set (ILLUS.) **29-35**

Cow Creamer & Sugar

Ceramic, set: cow creamer, cov. sugar, salt & pepper; grey & black markings on white, highly glazed, removable salt & pepper heads, warehouse find, "Japan" stamped, mint in box, 5 x 5", the set (ILLUS. of part w/creamer on right) **39-44**

Handpainted Creamer & Sugar Set

Ceramic, set: creamer & cov. sugar; purple over white glaze, large pink flared nostrils, yellow horns, hooves & tails, tails curl up over backs to form handles, ink stamp "52/270" under glaze, foil gold & black paper stickers "Made in Japan," marked "Thames, Handpainted," found w/matching salt & pepper, complete, mint, creamer 5 x 5 1/2", sugar 4 1/2 x 6", the set (ILLUS.).......................... **45-49**

Ceramic, set: creamer & matching cov. sugar; purple over white glaze, yellow horns & molded bell at neck, "Japan" paper label, 1950-60, both 5 x 5", the set **29-32**

Blue Tulip Decorated Cow Creamer

Ceramic, sitting, blue tulips on white glaze, bottom ink stamp "Japan" under glaze, 1950-60, common, 3 3/4 x 4" (ILLUS.) **14-19**

Kent Ceramic Cow Creamer

Ceramic, sitting, brown w/white spots, gold molded bell around neck, tail curled up connecting at back of neck to form handle, bottom impressed stamp "Kent," 5 1/4 x 6" (ILLUS.)....................................... **24-29**

Sitting Bust Cow Creamer

Ceramic, sitting bust, reddish brown, bottom ink stamp "Made in Japan," 3 1/2 x 3 3/4" (ILLUS.)... **29-35**

Sitting Cow Creamer w/Flowers

Ceramic, sitting, flowers on both sides over deep yellow chrome, enhanced gold highlights around features, no bottom markings, 4 3/4 x 6 1/2" (ILLUS.)................ **39-45**

Sitting Cow Creamer

Ceramic, sitting, mottled brown on white pottery, yellow tail forming handle, found w/many other color variations, top of head is both opening & pouring vessel, unmarked (ILLUS.) **14-19**

Japanese Ceramic Cow Creamer

Ceramic, small, blue, w/molded green bell around neck, "Made in Japan" ink stamp underneath, 3 1/2 x 5" (ILLUS.) **30-35**

Nashville Souvenir Cow Creamer

Ceramic, souvenir-type from Nashville, Tennessee, Music City, U.S.A., usually gold in color, found w/all states printed on side, paper label "Made in Japan," common, 3 1/2 x 5" (ILLUS.) **14-19**

Early 1940s Cow Creamer

Ceramic, two large black spots on cream w/black hooves, unmarked, early 1940s, formerly used as a planter, also found in brown on cream, 5 1/2 x 7" (ILLUS.) **39-45**
Ceramic, very simple in form & markings w/five light spots about body, horns & hooves highlighted in brown, paper label missing, 4 1/4 x 5 3/4" **24-29**

Cow Creamer w/Pink & Grey Transfers

Ceramic, w/pink & grey flower transfer on both sides & gold hooves, found in various floral designs, unmarked, 5 1/2 x 7" (ILLUS.) **39-45**
Czechoslovakian pottery, sitting, orange spots on white porcelain, black tail, circle black ink stamp "Made in Czechoslovakia," 4 3/4 x 5 3/4" **75-78**

Czechoslovakian Cow Creamer

Czechoslovakian pottery, sitting, orange w/black ears & tail, dime size circle black ink stamp "Made in Czechoslovakia," minor paint wear, 4 3/4 x 5 3/4" (ILLUS.) **59-65**

Delft Faience Cow Creamer

Delft faience, exceptional blue coloring, windmill scene on front side, unmarked, 4 1/4 x 6 1/2" (ILLUS.) **124-130**

Delft Pottery Cow Creamer

Delft pottery, handpainted, light blue w/darker blue accents, signed by the artist, lidded opening, unusual that tail doesn't form handle, bottom marking under glaze "Made in Holland," mint, 3 3/4 x 6" (ILLUS.) **129-135**
Delft pottery, painted & lightly glazed porcelain, cow dressed in assorted men's clothing, either sitting or standing, rare & very desirable **165-179**

Standing Cow Creamer w/Infant

German china, standing in upright position, reddish brown cow wearing a white & blue dress, holding an infant in a blanket, bottom circular ink stamp "Made in Germany," rare, 3 3/4" w., 5 3/4" h. (ILLUS.) **400-475**

German Porcelain Cow Creamer

German porcelain, brown markings over white, black highlights on tail, hooves & horns, unmarked, 4 1/2 x 5 1/2" (ILLUS.).. **48-52**

Brown & Cream German Cow Creamer

German porcelain, brown on cream porcelain, black accented tail, horns & hooves, red ink stamped "Germany," 3 1/2 x 5" (ILLUS.).. **55-59**
German porcelain, lying, w/tail curled up to form handle, impressed "Germany 1391" on back side, unusual light green color, mint, 3 1/2 x 7 1/2".................................... **114-120**

Miniature German Cow Creamer

German porcelain, miniature, grey/black on fine white porcelain, impressed on back "Germany," 2 5/8 x 3 5/8" (ILLUS.)............. **45-55**
German porcelain, reddish brown graduating to white on softly glazed fine porcelain, extremely detailed features, impressed on reverse side "Germany 8610," 7 1/2" h., 4 3/4" l. **75-82**

Goebel China Cow Creamer

Goebel china, brown markings on cream glazed ceramic, tin gold bell on string, tail curls under to form handle, unmarked, opening 2 1/4", 3 3/4 x 5 3/4" (ILLUS.) **32-36**
Goebel china, brown markings on white, original tin bell on cord, full "Bee" blue ink stamp, "Germany," 5 x 7 1/2" **74-79**

Ironstone China Cow Creamer

Ironstone china, lying, w/legs tucked under, burgundy floral transfer on both sides, backstamp reads "Charlotte Royal Crownford Ironstone England," commonly found mold w/markings of different companies in various colors, marked "Made in England," 3 1/2 x 7" (ILLUS.)...... **39-45**

Black Platform-Style Cow Creamer

Jackfield pottery, high-gloss black glaze over red clay w/gold trim, on platform w/lid, Shropshire, England, 4 1/2 x 6 1/4" (ILLUS.)... **139-145**

Jackfield Cow Creamer

Jackfield pottery, platform base, high-gloss black glaze over red clay, gold details, w/original lid, Shropshire, England, 5 x 7 1/4" (ILLUS.)..................................... **195-225**

Limoges Porcelain Cow Creamer

Limoges porcelain, solid white, highly glazed, stamped in green ink inside top opening "Limoges, France," common mold, used for some souvenir items, 4 1/2 x 6 1/2" (ILLUS.) **25-29**

Rare Occupied Japan Cow Creamer

Occupied Japan china, lying down, legs folded underneath, irregular spots, graduating colors of greens & brown on cream, ink stamped "Made in Occupied Japan," rare, mint, 5 1/4 x 7" (ILLUS.) **69-75**

Occupied Japan Cow Creamer

Occupied Japan china, various dark brown markings, white background, glazed, tail curls up to form handle, found w/many different Japan stamps, common, prices depend on bottom markings, largest size 5 x 8" (ILLUS.)... **35-39**

Japanese Cow Creamer w/Lacy Collar

Porcelain, grey on white w/gold accents, very delicate & lacy collar around neck w/bell attached, eyes shut, red ink stamp "Japan" on hoof, 3 3/4 x 4 1/2" (ILLUS.).. **21-24**

German Porcelain Cow Creamer

Porcelain, white, tail & horns missing black cold-paint due to wear, "Germany" impressed on back underneath, 4 3/4 x 7" (ILLUS.).. **64-69**

Brown Pottery Cow Creamer

Pottery, medium brown sponged markings, blue molded bell at neck, unmarked, 1970-80, 4 1/2 x 6" (ILLUS.) **12-17**

Pottery Cow Creamer

Pottery, pink accents on cream, green dots around neck forming a bow, lock handle tail, unmarked, 3 1/2 x 5" (ILLUS.)............. **14-19**

Staffordshire pottery, cov., platform-type, sponged dark brown & orange over white pottery, milkmaid seated on green base, facing forward, ca. 1810-20, 6 1/2" l. **1,200-1,400**

Staffordshire pottery, cov., sponged purple lustre over cream glazed pottery, orange backstamp "Old Staffordshire Ware, England," 1910-20, small chip on ear, 6 1/2" l. **165-179**

Staffordshire pottery, cov., standing, sponged in manganese & yellow, milk-

maid seated performing her task at oblong platform base, facing left, ca. 1780, repair, 6 3/4" l................................... **1,400-1,800**

Staffordshire Cow Creamer

Staffordshire pottery, pink floral transfer on white, w/yellow bell at neck, unmarked, 5 x 8" (ILLUS.)... **80-95**

Staffordshire pottery, platform-type, reddish brown spots over white, embossed green flower on platform, w/original lid, early, dates from 1870, minor paint loss to be expected, 4 1/2 x 6 1/2" **225-250**

Staffordshire solid agate, cov., body, two legs & suckling calf w/brown & ochre striations, the group modeled standing on a domed rectangular plain creamware base, the cover applied w/a creamware flower-form knop, ca. 1775, 8" l. (restoration to front of base, cover, calf's legs, horns & tail, tiny glaze chips)...................... **2,875**

Sterling silver, cov., ornate flowers around lid w/fly perched on top, marks "RC" w/"M" in a shield, lion w/raised paw facing left, leopard's head, letter "e," English, ca. 1960, still being produced, expect to pay more for earlier versions, 5.2 oz., 4 x 6" **500-700**

White Lusterware Cow Creamer

White lustreware china, w/gold horns & tail, opening highlighted in gold, unmarked, mint, 4 3/4 x 6 1/2" (ILLUS.) **74-79**

Yellowware pottery, cov., standing on a platform, lid w/little or no repair, similar to the Bennington cow creamer, very rare... **1,500-2,000**

Egg Cups

Ceramic egg cups were a common breakfast table accessory beginning about the mid-19th century and were used for serving soft-boiled eggs. Ceramics egg "hoops" or "rings" were used for many years before the cup-form became common. Egg cups continue to be produced today, and modern novelty and souvenir types are especially collectible.

The descriptions and values listed here were provided by collector Dr. Joan M. George, who notes that values for older egg cups are based on their marks, rarity and recent sales results.

Bucket-style, blue monogram "EIIR," for Queen Elizabeth II, England, 1950s **22**

Bucket-style, commemorates death of Princess Diana, England, 1997.................................. **35**

Bucket-style, souvenir of Portsmouth, England w/picture of the HMS Victory, England, 1996 .... **8**

English Gollywog Egg Cup

Bucket-type, colored design of a Gollywog pointing to a stove, Robertsons & Sons, England, ca. 1960s (ILLUS.) **50**

Bjorn Wiinblad Designed Egg Cup

Bucket-type, colorful stylized modernistic design, Bjorn Wiinblad, Rosenthal, Germany, 1985 (ILLUS.) **45**
Double, decorated w/a chick & a green stripe, Roseville Pottery, ca. 1919 .... **250**
Double, Garland patt., dark red flower on a grey ground, Stangl Pottery, ca. 1960s **20**
Double, Luckenbach Line, pennant w/logo, unmarked, American-made **50**
Double, Mexicana patt. by Homer Laughlin, ca. 1930s **30**

Singapore Bird Pattern Egg Cup

Double, Singapore Bird patt., Oriental-style design of birds & flowering branches on a celadon   green   ground,   Adams, England, ca. 1950s (ILLUS.) **20**
Double, souvenir of Caesar's Palace, Las Vegas, Nevada, brown design, 1993 .... **18**

Early Staffordshire Egg Hoop

Hoop-style, green transfer-printed design of people & houses, Staffordshire, England, 19th c. (ILLUS.) **65**

Haviland Porcelain Egg Hoop

Hoop-style, white decorated w/green garland band & gilt scrolls, Haviland, Limoges, France, 1990s (ILLUS.) **85**

W.H. Goss Crest Egg Cup

Single, banner w/crest marked "Ye Ancient Port of Seaford," W.H. Goss, England, 1930s (ILLUS.) **45**

French Bart Simpson Egg Cup

Single, Bart Simpson bust, yellow w/blue base, France, 1997, large (ILLUS.) **35**
Single, Bayeux Tapestry, white ground w/a picture showing a portion of the tapestry, Limoges, France, 1998 .... **15**

French Bellhop Egg Cup

Single, bellhop wearing blue hat & coat, cigarette in his mouth, France, ca. 1920 (ILLUS.) **70**

Rare Betty Boop Egg Cup

Single, Betty Boop head, red dress, grey lustre hair, Germany, ca. 1930s (ILLUS.) **200**

Minton Blue Delft Pattern Egg Cup

Single, blue floral Delft patt., gold band trim, Minton, England, 1990s (ILLUS.)..................... **85**

Single, Booth's "Pompadour" patt., multicolored flowers, Silicon China, England, ca. 1920s **30**

Figural Bugs Bunny Egg Cup

Single, Bugs Bunny head, grey & white, part of a set including Tweety Bird, Tasmanian Devil & Sylvester the Cat, unmarked, large size, 1980s (ILLUS.)....... **35**

Handled Quaker Oats Man Egg Cup

Single, bust of the Quaker Oats Man, handled, tall, England, 1920s (ILLUS.)................. **65**

Single, CAAC insignia of star & wings, small, current, China **12**

Mona Lisa Egg Cup

Single, color copy of the Mona Lisa on a white cup, unmarked, France, 1998................. **10**

New York-Brooklyn Bridge Egg Cup

Single, color scene of bridge w/"New York & Brooklyn Bridge," Germany, early 20th c. (ILLUS.).. **40**

Souvenir Cup with Dutch Children

Single, color scene of Dutch children around the sides, printed in gold at the top "Souvenir Holland," unmarked, 1930s (ILLUS.).. **32**

Early Goebel Boy's Head Egg Cup

Single, comical boy's head, painted features, high collar below chin, Goebel, Germany, ca. 1930s (ILLUS.)........................ **100**

Single, commemorates the wedding of Princess Grace & Prince Rainier of Monaco, France, 1956 .... **95**

Goebel Girl's Head Egg Cup

Single, comical girl's head, painted features, ruffled collar & pink hair band, Goebel, Germany, ca. 1930s (ILLUS.)........................ **100**

Charles & Diana Divorce Egg Cup

Single, commemorating the divorce of Prince Charles & Princess Diana, Coronet Pottery, England, 1996 (ILLUS.)............... **30**

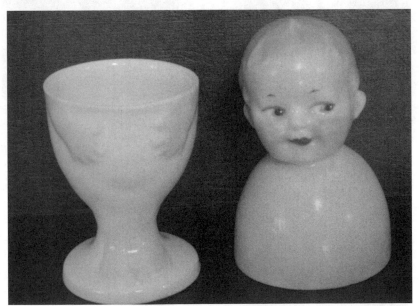

Rare Baby Doll Figural Egg Cup

Single, cov., baby doll head & shoulders painted in natural colors form the top, the footed base shows the hands & feet, unmarked, probably American-made, ca. 1930s, rare (ILLUS.) **150**

Single, cov., full-figure English Beefeater guard, England, 1999 .... **15**

Goebel Daffodil Egg Cup from Series

Single, daffodil blossom, one of an annual series of flowers, birds & animals by Goebel of Germany, 1982 (ILLUS.) **20**

Jasper Ware Egg Cup Souvenir

Single, dark blue jasper ware w/white coat-of-arms of the Dominion of Canada, England, ca. 1950 (ILLUS.) **35**

English Davenport Egg Cup

Single, decorated by hand w/blue scroll arches trimmed w/gold, Davenport, England, 1887 (ILLUS.) **85**

Meissen Blue Orchid Egg Cup

Single, deeply scalloped rim, Blue Orchid patt., Meissen, Germany, 1988 (ILLUS.) **95**

French Faience Egg Cup

Single, faience, h.p. w/colorful blue & yellow florals & scrolls, France, ca. 1920s (ILLUS.) **45**

Swee'pea Figural Egg Cup

Single, figural Swee'pea, from Popeye car-
toons, KFS Vandor Imports, Japan,
1980, large size (ILLUS.) **55**

English Ugly Face Egg Cup

Single, figural ugly man's face in grey clay,
large nose & blue & white eyes, England,
1999 (ILLUS.) **15**

Doulton Watteau Pattern Egg Cup

Single, flow blue Watteau patt., two figures
in landscape having a picnic, Doulton,
Ltd., England, ca. 1900 (ILLUS.) **85**

Figural Staffordshire Egg Cup

Single, "Ham and Eggs," model of a pig
seated at a table which forms the egg

cup,   Staffordshire   bone   china,
England, ca. 1980s (ILLUS.) **35**

Early Mintons Floral Egg Cup

Single, hand-decorated w/a colorful floral &
geometric border band above floral garlands, Mintons, England, ca. 1890s
(ILLUS.) **50**
Single, hand-decorated w/a face, Desimo-
ne, Italy, ca. 1980s **40**

Harrod's Bear Egg Cup

Single, Harrod's bear mascot, standing
wearing trademark green Harrod's
sweater, tall, England, 1999 (ILLUS.) **35**

Unusual Humpty Dumpty Egg Cup

Single, Humpty Dumpty body in blue, sitting on a wall titled "Humpty Dumpty Egg Cup," egg would form the head, unmarked, ca. 1920s (ILLUS.) **60**

Jemima Puddleduck Egg Cup

Single, Jemima Puddleduck standing beside a bush-form cup, one from a set of Beatrix Potter characters, Enesco, 1999, each (ILLUS.) **35**

Single, King Edward VII coronation commemorative, portrait wearing crown, England, 1901 .... **85**

Single, King George V of England coronation commemorative, England, 1911 .... **65**

Royal Albert, England Egg Cup

Single, Lady Carlyle patt., decorated w/large clusters of flowers below a scalloped pink rim band, Royal Albert, England, ca. 1950s (ILLUS.) **35**

Longwy Pottery Egg Cup

Single, large bright pink blossoms & branches on a light blue ground w/dark blue foot & rim, Longwy, France, ca. 1920s (ILLUS.) **65**

Hutschenreuther "March" Egg Cup

Single, lightly scalloped rim, colorful design of exotic bird & flowering branches, one of a series representing the months, marked "MARZ - Hutschenreuther," Germany, 1980s (ILLUS.) **45**

Single, Marilyn Monroe picture transfer-printed on hollow cup, England, 2002 .... **10**

Rare Early Minnie Mouse Egg Cup

Single, Minnie Mouse, pointed nose & large ears, wearing orange skirt & blue blouse on a green base, Japan, ca. 1930s (ILLUS.)... **90**

Modern Cow-form Egg Cup

Single, model of a cow, round, painted black & white over green grass, Knobler, U.S., 1987 (ILLUS.)... **15**

Single, model of a lion supporting the cup on its back, tan lustre glaze, Royal Fenton,

Staffordshire, England, ca. 1930s (ILLUS., below)... **25**

English Lion-form Egg Cup

Single, model of a peacock, colorful bird supporting the cup on its back, Sarreguemines, France, ca. 1930s **50**

Franklin Mint Raccoon Egg Cup

Single, model of a raccoon beside a picnic basket, natural colors, part of the "Forest Friends" set, Franklin Mint, 1986, each one in set (ILLUS., below)................................ **45**

Unusual Train Egg Cup - Whistle

Single, model of a train engine w/whistle at end, marked "Foreign" in a circle on the base, Germany, ca. 1920s (ILLUS.).............. **175**

Figural Noah's Ark Egg Cup

Single, model of Noah's Ark w/cup on the roof, England, ca. 1920s (ILLUS.) **75**

Single, Muppets, either Statler, Waldorf, Sam or Zoot, American-made, 1981, each **50**

Single, Nanking patt., band of stylized colorful flowers & blue ribbons, Royal Doulton, England, ca. 1930s (ILLUS.) **28**

Single, Niagara Falls picture titled "Niagara Falls Prospect Point Canada," Japan, 1930s **28**

Royal Doulton Nanking Egg Cup

Royal Doulton Egg Cup in Orange

Single, orange rim band of stylized floral panels above floral sprigs, gold rim band, Royal Doulton, England, ca. 1930s (ILLUS.) **35**

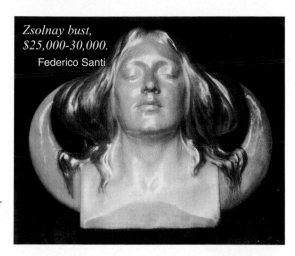

Florence Ceramics "Blueboy," $350-400.
David Miller

Zsolnay bust, $25,000-30,000.
Federico Santi

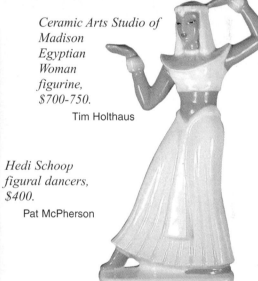

Ceramic Arts Studio of Madison Egyptian Woman figurine, $700-750.
Tim Holthaus

Hedi Schoop figural dancers, $400.
Pat McPherson

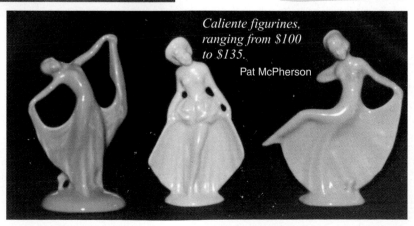

Caliente figurines, ranging from $100 to $135.
Pat McPherson

Czechoslovakian toucan, $750.
Cheryl Goyda

Sascha Brastoff fish-form plate, $75.
Pat McPherson

Nippon lion wall plaque, $575.
Jackson's Auctioneers & Appraisers

Rockingham Ware spaniel, $235.
Skinner, Inc.

Gonder Pegasus vase, $175-225.
James R. Boshears

Nicodemus pig bank, $505.
Pat McPherson

Howard Pierce Porcelains birds, $285 the pair.
Pat McPherson

Napkin doll, $55-65.
Bobbie Zucker Bryson

*Willow Ware
Toby pepper
shaker,
$250-275.*
Jeff Siptak

*Cleminson Clay
sock darner, $70.*
Susan N. Cox

*Reamer
made in
Japan, $75-125.*
Bobbie Zucker Bryson

*Butter pats, round $40, square $55,
fan-shaped $110-125 each.*
Mary Dessoie

*Morton Potteries
waffle set, $150.*
Burdell Hall

Florence Ceramics "Georgia" figurine, $1,500-2,000.

Dave Miller

Noritake dresser jar, $1,075.

Tim Trapani

Inarco head vase planter, $1,500+.

Maddy Gordon

American painted porcelain bonbon box, $95.

Dorothy Kamm

deLee Art planter, $65.

Pat McPherson

Irish Belleek Thorn pattern tray and scent bottles, $2,200 the set.

Del E. Domke

*R.S. Prussia
portrait plate, $3,000-$4,000.*

Mary McCaslin

*Flow Blue LaBelle pattern portrait
plate by Wheeling Pottery, $495.*

Vivian Kromer

*Longwy Art Deco
tile, $400-425.*

Temples Antiques

*Amphora-Teplitz figural vase,
$14,000-15,000.*

Les and Irene Cohen

*Limoges vase,
$3,500.*

Debbie DuBay

Shawnee bank/cookie jars, $450-500 each.
Linda Guffey

Royal Copley clown planter, $100-125.
Tim Holthaus

Cleminson Clay mug, $49.
Pat McPherson

Abingdon train engine cookie jar, $225.
Green Valley Auctions

Royal Doulton Susan Bunnykins figurine, $165.
Reg Morris

Brayton Laguna Pottery book ends, $315.
Pat McPherson

Rozart Pottery Indian portrait mugs, $105 each.

Pat McPherson

Brayton Laguna Pottery tile, $495.

Pat McCaslin

Majolica seal hunter umbrella stand, $22,000.

Michael G. Strawser
Auctions

Warwick Shriner tankard set, $925.

Otto Zwicker

Frankoma teepee sign, $695.

Pat McPherson

American painted porcelain plate, $50.

Dorothy Kamm

"Royal Bayreuth handled vase, $450-500."

Mary McCaslin

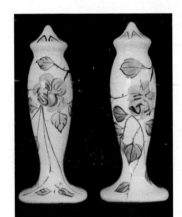

Old Ivory No. 29 spooner, $400.

Alma Hillman

Blue Ridge Dinnerwares salt and pepper shakers, $89.

Pat McPherson

Old Ivory No. 15 demitasse set, $900.

Alma Hillman

Ceramic Art Company mug, $375.

Peggy Sebek

Czechoslovakian beverage set, $275.
Cheryl Goyda

Zsolnay 9 3/4" vase, $12,500-15,000.
Federico Santi

Blue Ridge Dinnerwares Fruit Fantasy celery, $75.
Pat McPherson

Flow Blue Derby pattern platter by W.H. Grindley, $295.
Vivian Kromer

Limoges punch set, $3,500.
Debbie DuBay

*George Jones
majolica jardiniere,
$6,050.*

Michael G. Strawser
Auctions

*Minton
majolica
garden seat,
$2,750.*

Michael G.
Strawser
Auctions

*Buffalo Pottery
Deldare Ware
jardiniere and
garden seat pedestal
base, $12,000.*

Phillip Sullivan

*Blue and White Pottery
Cosmos jardiniere and
pedestal, $2,000.*

Steve Stone

*Uhl Pottery
urn, $175.*

Lloyd Martin

*R.S. Prussia Bird of Paradise
pitcher, $17,000-20,000.*

Mary McCaslin

*Buffalo Pottery
Emerald Deldare
pitcher,
$18,000-19,000.*

Phillip Sulliva

*Royal Bayreuth Butterfly pitcher,
$6000-7,000.*

Mary McCaslin

*Left: Vernon
Kilns Streamline
pitcher, $45-55.*

Pam Green

*Liverpool pitchers, from left:
$2,815, $4,888. $1,150.*

Skinner, Inc.

*Sunderland Pink
Lustre Ware
pitchers, from
left: $3,290,
$646, $1,645.*

Skinner, Inc.

Hall China Pert shape pitchers, $35-55 each.
Marty Kennedy

Russel Wright Designs Casual China creamer ($55), pitcher ($200) and coffeepot ($225).
Ann Kerr

Caliente Pottery small vase ($175), one-handled vase ($35), large vase ($225) and bowl ($145).
Pat McPherson

Red Wing 5-gallon advertising jug, $2,785.
Charles W. Casad

Watt Pottery Tulip pattern mixing bowls, $85-100 each.
Dennis M. Thompson

Frankoma silver overlay vase, $550.

Pat McPherson

Zsolnay owl-form vase, $6,500-8,500.

Federico Santi

Pacific Clay Products vases, $75 the pair.

Pat McPherson

Gonder Conch Shell planter, $200-250.

James R. Boshears

American Belleek Willets vase, $900.

Peggy Sebek

Quimper "Decor Riche" vase, $2,000.

Sandra V. Bondhus

Wedgwood majolica punch bowl, $33,000.

Michael G.
Strawser
Auctions

Mulberry Cyprus pattern gravy boat, Wm. Davenport, $200.

Eve Hill

George Jones majolica cheese dish, $13,750.

Michael G. Strawser
Auctions

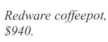

Redware coffeepot, $940.

Skinner, Inc.

HB - Quimper coffee set, $525.

Sandra V. Bondhus

Harker Pottery Cameoware, from left: salt and pepper shakers ($40 pair), pitcher ($50), platter ($25) and salt and pepper shakers ($35).

Neva Colbert

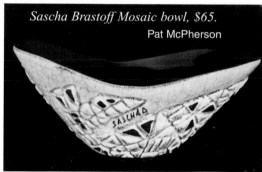

Sascha Brastoff Mosaic bowl, $65.

Pat McPherson

Haviland Multifloral pattern serving dish, $125.

Nora Travis

Harker Pottery Mallow pattern custard cup ($10), teapot ($45), creamer ($15) and mixing bowls ($40 left, $20 right).

Neva Colbert

Cowan kneeling children and bucking horse book ends ($550 and $2,500 respective-ly) and gazelle ashtray ($350).
Tim and Jamie Saloff

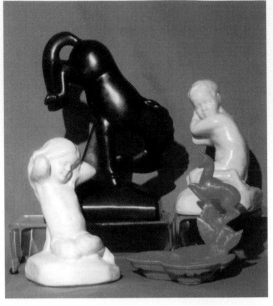

Royal Doulton Bunnykins Santa figurine, $45.

Reg Morris

Royal Bayreuth Santa candle-holder, $8,000-10,000.
Mary McCaslin

Staffordshire Little Red Riding Hood ABC plate, $250.
Mildred L. and Joseph P. Chalala

Hull Little Red Riding Hood plaque, $20,000.
Susan N. Cox

Mintons Egg Cup

Single, overall dark blue branching design on exterior & interior, gold rim stripes, Mintons, England, ca. 1910 (ILLUS.) **50**

Torquay Pottery Egg Cup

Single, painted sea gull & "Torquay" on a dark blue ground, Torquay, England, 1985 (ILLUS.) **45**

Royal Delft Floral-Painted Egg Cup

Single, painted w/small stylized blue flower sprigs, Royal Delft, Germany, 1967 (ILLUS.) **55**
Single, picture of Queen Elizabeth of England as a child, England, 1937 .... **90**

Early Tower of London Egg Cup

Single, pink lustre ground around a white reserve w/a black transfer-printed scene of the Tower of London, Germany, early 20th c. (ILLUS.) **35**
Single, pirate wearing tricorner hat & eye match, unmarked, American-made, modern **12**

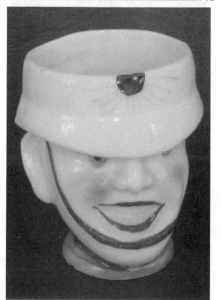

Smiling Policeman Egg Cup

Single, policeman, smiling & wearing a helmet w/a chin strap, unmarked, ca. 1930 (ILLUS.) **40**

Early Figural Popeye Egg Cup

Single, Popeye full-figure, standing wearing a white suit w/blue trim & anchors, Japan, 1930s (ILLUS.) **125**

Blessed Mother Shrine Souvenir

Single, portrait of the Virgin Mary, Blessed Mother Shrine, marked "Present from Carfin" (Scotland), made in Czechoslovakia, 1930s (ILLUS.) **35**

Single, Price William birth commemorative, family portrait, Coronet, England, 1982 .... **30**

Single, Prince Charles, "Spitting Image," Luck & Flaw, England, 1980s **65**

Single, Queen Elizabeth II 70th birthday commemorative, England, 1996 .... **25**

Single, Queen Elizabeth II Golden Jubilee commemorative w/portrait & royal crest, England, 2002 .... **25**

Single, Queen Mary of England coronation commemorative, mate to George V cup, England, 1911 .... **65**

Single, Rhodes, Greece, white w/picture, 2000 .... **6**

Modern Wedgwood Egg Cup

Single, rim band in blue & gold w/tiny red blossoms, Wedgwood, England, 1990s (ILLUS.) **25**

Single, Royal Copenhagen "Flora Danica" patt., hand-painted, Denmark, current **475**

Single, Royal Doulton example decorated w/roses & gold garlands, England, 1927 .... **50**

Chintz "Welbech" Pattern Egg Cup

Single, Royal Winton Chintz "Welbech" patt., England, 1999 (ILLUS.) **35**

Single, "Running Legs," white cup attached to legs w/yellow shoes, Carlton Ware, England, 1970s **40**

Single, scalloped bottom, black transfer-printed scene of "Porta Nigra, Tier," oldest city in Germany, Germany, 1998 .... **15**

Rare Disney Snow White Egg Cup

Single, Snow White, standing beside cup marked w/her name, Walt Disney Enterprises, part of a set, Japan, 1937 (ILLUS.)... **250**

Egg Cup Decorated with Chickens

Single, upper section decorated in color w/scenes of chickens, yellow foot, gold rim bands, unmarked, 1930s (ILLUS.)............. **35**
Single, white ground w/a flag in an oval, titled "Nova Scotia," Canada, 2001.. **7**

The Drunk Figural Egg Cup

Single, The Drunk, silly face of a man w/half-closed eyes & tongue hanging out, unmarked, ca. 1930s (ILLUS.) **75**
Single, Union Pacific Railroad "Winged Streamline" design, Scammell China, 1930s **65**

Winston Churchill-VE Day Egg Cup

Single, Winston Churchill portrait against the Union Jack, commemorates 50th Anniversary of VE Day, Norwich Bone China, England, 1995 (ILLUS.)............................. **55**

Shy Lady Egg Cup by Goebel

Single, woman w/center-parted brown hair
pulled into a bun, shy smile & side-glanc-
ing eyes, yellow bow at neck, Goebel,
Germany, ca. 1930s (ILLUS.) **100**

Egg Timers

*A little glass tube filled with sand and attached to a
figural base measuring between 3" and 5" in height was
once a commonplace kitchen item. Although egg timers
were originally used to time a 3-minute egg, some were
used to limit the length of a telephone call as a cost sav-
ing measure.*

*Many beautiful timers were produced in Germany in
the 1920s and later in Japan, reaching their heyday in
the 1940s. These small egg timers were commonly made
in a variety of shapes in bisque, china, chalkware, cast
iron, tin, brass, wood or plastic.*

*Egg timers had long been considered an essential
kitchen tool until, in the 1920s and 1930s, a German pottery company, W. Goebel, introduced figural egg timers.
Goebel crafted miniature china figurines with attached
glass vials. After the Great Depression, Japanese companies introduced less detailed timers. The Goebel figural egg timers are set apart by their trademark, delicate
painting and distinctive clothes. It is best to purchase
egg timers with their original tube, but the condition of
the figure is most important in setting prices.*

Goebel Baker Egg Timer

Baker, ceramic, Goebel (ILLUS.) **65**

Goebel Bears Egg Timer

Bears, ceramic, brown & tan, white base,
Goebel (ILLUS.) **95**
Bellhop, ceramic, Oriental, wearing red out-
fit, marked "Germany" **50**

Bird, ceramic, sitting on nest, wearing white
bonnet w/green ribbon, Josef Originals
sticker **55**

Bird & Egg Near Stump Egg Timer

Bird, ceramic, standing next to stump w/egg
at base, shades of brown w/green grassy
base & leaves on stump, Japan (ILLUS.)....... **65**

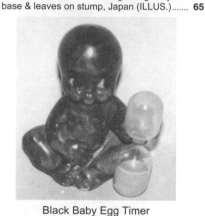

Black Baby Egg Timer

Black baby, ceramic, sitting w/left arm hold-
ing timer (ILLUS.)... **95**
Black chef, ceramic, sitting w/arm up hold-
ing timer, variety of sizes, Germany **85-100**
Black chef, ceramic, standing w/large fish,
timer in fish's mouth, Germany, 4 3/4" h. **100**

Black Chef w/Frying Pan Egg Timer

Black chef with frying pan, composition, Ja-
pan (ILLUS.)... **100**

Bo-Peep Egg Timer

Bo-Peep, ceramic, Japan, "Bo-Peep" on
base (ILLUS.)... **100**
Boy, ceramic, holding rifle, marked "Germa-
ny"... **50**
Boy, ceramic, skiing, marked "Germany,"
3" h.. **50**

Wooden Cat Egg Timer

Cat, wooden, black cat w/yellow eyes & red
collar on domed yellow base, timer lifts
out of back (ILLUS.)... **35**
Cat, ceramic, standing by base of grandfa-
ther clock, Germany, 4 1/2" h............................ **50**
Chef, ceramic, holding blue spoon, marked
"Germany"... **65**
Chef, ceramic, winking, white w/black shoes
& trim, turn on head to activate sand **50**
Chef, composition board, black chef holding
platter of chicken, w/potholder hooks............... **50**
Chef, composition, w/cake, Germany **75**

Egg Timer with Chef Holding Egg

Chef, porcelain, white & blue, holding reddish orange egg, supporting timer, Ger-
many (ILLUS.) **65**
Chef, wood, "Time Your Egg" **25**
Chef, ceramic, winking, white clothes, timer
built in back, turns upside down to tip
sand, 4" h. **40**
Chick, ceramic, white, yellow & purple chick,
marked "Japan" **50**
Chick with cap, ceramic, Josef Originals **55**
Chicken, ceramic, white w/black wings & tail
feathers, marked "Germany" **65**
Chicken, on nest, green plastic, England,
2 1/2" h. **25**

Chimney Sweep Egg Timer

Chimney sweep, ceramic, Goebel, Germa-
ny (ILLUS.) **75**

Chimney sweep, ceramic, wearing black
outfit w/top hat, carrying ladder, Germa-
ny **65**
Chimney sweep, ceramic, carrying ladder,
Germany, 3 1/4" h. **65**

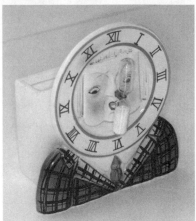

Clockman Planter

Clock, ceramic, clock face, w/man's plaid
suit & tie below, w/planter in back, Japan
(ILLUS.) **40**

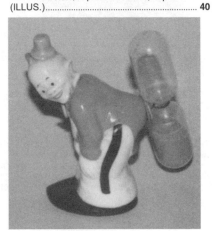

Clown Egg Timer

Clown, ceramic, Germany (ILLUS.) **85**
Clown on phone, ceramic, standing, full-fig-
ured, Japan **60**
Clown on phone, ceramic, standing, yellow
suit, Japan, 3 3/4" h. **60**
Colonial man, ceramic, yellow & white, Ja-
pan **55**
Colonial woman with bonnet, ceramic, vari-
ety of dresses & colors, Germany,
3 3/4" h., each **60**
Dog, ceramic, black poodle, sitting, Germa-
ny **65**
Dog, ceramic, Dachshund, red w/hole in
back for timer, label on back reads
"Shorty Timer" **40**
Dog, ceramic, Pekingese, standing brown &
white dog, marked "Germany" **55**

Dog Egg Timer

Dog, ceramic, sitting, white w/brown tail & ears, timer in head, Germany (ILLUS.) **55**

Lustreware Dog

Dog, white w/brown ears & tail, lustreware, Japan (ILLUS.) **65**

Dogs, ceramic, Scotties, brown, standing facing each other holding timer in paws, marked "Germany" **65**

Duck, wood, hanging-type, duck sitting on green egg, marked "Germany" **35**

Dutch boy, ceramic, wearing blue & white sailor outfit, Germany, small **50**

Dutch boy, ceramic, yellow pants, brown shoes, hat, scarf, Japan **45**

Dutch Boy Egg Timer

Dutch boy, composition, blue pants & hat, red shirt, white tie w/blue polka dots, Germany (ILLUS.) **45**

Dutch boy & girl, ceramic, double-type, unknown modeler, timer marked w/3-, 4- & 5-minute intervals, Goebel, Germany, 1953 .... **95**

Dutch girl, ceramic, talking on telephone, Japan **45**

Dutch girl, ceramic, w/red heart on apron, Germany **45**

Dutch girl & boy, ceramic, Goebel, Germany **95**

Dutch girl w/flowers, chalkware, walking, unmarked, 4 1/2" h **65**

Elephant, ceramic, sitting w/trunk up, white, Germany **65**

Elephant, ceramic, white, sitting w/timer in upraised trunk, marked "Germany" **65**

Elf by well, ceramic, Manorware, England **35**

English Bobby Egg Timer

English Bobby, ceramic, Germany (ILLUS.) **95**

Lustreware Fish Egg Timer

Fish, ceramic, lustreware, burgundy, yellow
& green, Germany (ILLUS.) **85**

Fisherman Egg Timer

Fisherman, ceramic, standing, brown jacket
& hat, tall black boots, carrying a large
white fish on his shoulders, timer at-
tached to mouth of fish, Germany
(ILLUS.) **95**
Friar Tuck, ceramic, single, Goebel, Germa-
ny, 4" h. **65**
Frog, ceramic, multicolored frog sitting on
egg, marked "Japan" **65**
Golliwog, bisque, England **125-150**
Golliwog, ceramic, character-type, marked
"FOREIGN" **125-150**
Happy the dwarf, ceramic, from "Snow
White & the Seven Dwarfs," Maw Co.,
England **100**
Honey bear, ceramic, brown & white, w/tim-
er in mouth made to resemble milk bottle,
Cardinal China Co., No. 1152 .... **65**
House with clock face, ceramic, yellow &
gold, Japan **35**

Huckleberry Finn, ceramic, sitting in front of
post, Japan **95**
Humpty Dumpty, ceramic, wearing hat &
bow tie, turn on head to activate sand,
marked "California Cleminsons" **40**

Indian Egg Timer

Indian, ceramic, kneeling, white, wearing
headdress w/red, blue & green feathers,
holding timer in one hand, marked "Ger-
many," rare (ILLUS.) **125**
Leprechaun, glazed chalkware, sitting on
wishing well, "Porkush" on front base,
marked "Manorware," England **35**
Lighthouse, ceramic, blue, cream & orange
lustreware, Germany, 4 1/2" h. **75**

Little Boy Egg Timer

Little boy, ceramic, standing wearing black
shorts & shoes & large red bow tie, Ger-
many (ILLUS.) **75**
Little girl on phone, ceramic, sitting w/legs
outstretched, pink dress, Germany **65**
Little girl with chick on her toes, ceramic,
Goebel, Germany **100**
Mammy, tin lithographed, mammy cooking
on gas stove, w/potholder hooks **145**

Mammy, tin, w/lithographed picture of her cooking, w/potholder hooks, unmarked, 7 3/4" h. **145**

Minuteman, ceramic, holding rifle & leaning against stone wall, "Kitchen Independence" on front base, marked "Enesco" & "Japan" **25-35**

Mrs. Claus Egg Timer

Mrs. Claus, ceramic, in yellow dress w/green collar, cuffs & hem, w/red bag full of gifts & black bag w/timer (ILLUS.)... **65**

Newspaper boy, ceramic, Japan, 3 1/4" h.. **55**

Oliver Twist, ceramic, wearing red pants & vest, brown jacket, black hat, marked "Germany".. **95**

Mother Rabbit Egg Timer

Mother rabbit, ceramic, holding carrot w/basket, Japan (ILLUS.)................................. **60**

Goebel Owl Egg Timer

Owl, ceramic, Goebel (ILLUS.) **75**

Parlor maid with cat, ceramic, Japan **65**

Penguin, glazed chalkware, standing on green & white base w/"Bagnor Regis" painted on front, marked "Manorware, England".. **50**

Penguin, chalkware, England, 3 3/4" h. **50**

Mouse Chef Egg Timer

Mouse, ceramic, sitting & holding timer, brown w/white apron marked "Chef" in red letters, Josef Originals (ILLUS.).. **35-45**

Rabbit with Carrot Egg Timer

Rabbit, ceramic, sitting, white w/red jacket,
holding carrot which supports the timer,
Germany (ILLUS.) 65
Rabbit with floppy ears, ceramic, standing,
tan, Germany 75
Rabbits, ceramic, double-type, various color
combinations, Goebel, Germany, 4" 75
Rooster, wood, multicolored, standing on
thick base 25

Sailboat Egg Timer

Sailboat, ceramic, lustreware, tan boat
w/white sails, Germany (ILLUS.) 75
Sailboat with sailor, ceramic, lustreware,
Germany 75
Sailor, ceramic, blue, Germany 85
Santa Claus, ceramic, sitting,
unmarked 50-75
Scotsman with bagpipes, plastic, England,
4 1/2" h. 50

Sea Gull Egg Timer

Sea gull, ceramic, timer in beak, Germany
(ILLUS.) 75

Sea Gull Egg Timer with Bottle Opener

Sea gull, iron, white & tan bird w/red beak &
legs, on black & white branch which is
also a bottle opener (ILLUS.) 25
Swiss woman, ceramic, w/multicolored
striped apron, marked "Germany" 65
Telephone, ceramic, black, Japan 35
Vegetable person, ceramic, Japan 95
Veggie man or woman, bisque, Japan,
4 1/2" h., each 75

Waiter Egg Timer

Waiter, ceramic, standing next to ovoid holder for timer, black & white, Germany (ILLUS.).. **65**
Welsh woman, ceramic, Germany, 4 1/2" h. **65**

Windmill w/Pigs Egg Timer

Windmill, ceramic, w/pigs on base, Japan (ILLUS.).. **85**
Windmill, ceramic, w/dog or pigs on base, Japan, 3 3/4" h., each **85**

Napkin dolls

Figure of angel, blonde, wearing blue & white dress w/gold trim, holding maroon flowers w/green leaves, gold halo on head, two slits in shoulders for napkins to form "wings," 5 3/8" h. **100-115**
Figure of bartender/waiter, w/black mustache, red & white checked apron, black bow tie & shoes, holds a tray that serves as candleholder, foil sticker w/"Viking Handmade, Made in Japan," 8 3/4" h. **85-100**
Figure of genie, dressed in white robes trimmed in gold, jewel-decorated turban, holds a gold lantern, label reads "Genie at Your Service," Enesco, 8" h. **100-135**

Byron Molds Napkin Doll

Figure of girl holding flowers, red hair, yellow dress w/matching hair bow, arms clutch flowers to chest, marked "copyright Byron Molds," 8 1/2" h. (ILLUS.).. **65-85**

Atlantic Mold Napkin Doll

Figure of girl holding lily, mouth open as if singing, brown bobbed hair w/yellow headband, bright yellow dress w/green leaf design, holds a blue lily in arms, Atlantic Mold, 11" h. (ILLUS.)......................... **65-75**
Figure of "Miss Versatility," woman in red & white dress w/red scallop trim & matching red picture hat that serves as candleholder, one hand held behind back, California Originals, 13" h. **75-95**
Figure of Santa Claus, in red suit w/black belt & shoes, toothpick holes in hat, marked "Japan," w/a "Sage Store" label, 6 3/4" h... **95-150**

Holt Howard Napkin Doll

Figure of "Sunbonnet Miss," red-haired little girl in yellow dress w/white shoulder ruffle, matching yellow picture hat w/pink rose serves as candleholder, one hand pats hair, other arm is extended, marked "© Holt Howard 1958" (ILLUS.) **125-150**

Napkin Holder/Toothpick Holder

Figure of woman holding tray, blonde, wearing black off-the-shoulder dress, one hand on hip, other holding pink covered tray, the lid w/holes to hold toothpicks, 8 1/2" h. (ILLUS.) **95-110**

Woman in Hat Napkin Holder

Figure of woman in hat, in dress w/yellow drop waist & purple skirt, yellow & purple hat w/upturned brim, marked "Cal. Cer. Mold," 12 1/2" h. (ILLUS.) **65-85**

Holland Mold Napkin Holder

Figure of woman w/daisy, black hair w/bangs, dressed in blue & white dress & long white gloves, one hand fixes daisy behind ear, ca. 1958, marked "Holland Mold," 7 1/4" h. **75-95**

Napkin Doll Holding Fan

Figure of woman w/fan, in 18th-c. white dress w/blue trim on bodice & sleeves & blue bows on front of dress & in her dark hair, one hand holds up white fan w/blue trim, marked "Jam. Calif. ©" (ILLUS.)... **55-65**

Figure of woman w/poodle, blonde, dressed in pink dress trimmed in black, matching hat serves as candleholder, blue jeweled eyes, crystal jeweled necklace & red jewel on finger, holds a white poodle, marked "Kreiss & Co.," 10 3/4" h... **100-125**

Figure of woman w/toothpick tray, bobbed hair, white dress w/yellow scalloped trim, holds oblong toothpick tray attached at waist, 10 3/4" h. **75-85**

Woman with Bird Napkin Doll

Figure of woman w/toothpick tray, brown hair, green lustre dress decorated w/pink roses, one arm holds a toothpick tray w/similar decoration on her head, pink bird perches on other arm, 10 1/2" h. (ILLUS.)... **75-95**

Model of rooster, black w/yellow & white trim, red comb & wattle, yellow beak & feet, paper label w/"Made in Japan," 10 1/4" h.. **35-45**

Oyster Plates

Oyster plates intrigue a growing number of collectors. Oysters were shucked and the meat served in wells of these attractive plates specifically designed to serve oysters. During the late 19th century they were made of fine china and majolica. Some plates were decorated in the realistic "trompe l'oeil" technique while others simply matched the pattern of a dinner service. Also see HAVILAND and LIMOGES.

Majolica, eight-well, shell-form wells in turquoise blue divided by molded green seaweed, a white shell well at the center, George Jones, England, late 19th c. (minor rim nick)..................................... **2,750**

Majolica, six-well, alternating dark pink & white shell-form wells each separated by a band w/a small long shell & a small white shell at the rim, a central ring of small white shells around the dark green center well, 9 1/4" d...................................... **385**

Majolica, six-well, miniature, five pink-trimmed cockle shell wells & one white well centered by a round scalloped green-trimmed well, Wedgwood, late 19th c.,7" d... **1,210**

Majolica, six-well, shell-shaped wells in turquoise blue divided by brown molded seaweed, white shell well at the center, George Jones, England, late 19th c., 10" d.. **1,870**

Very Rare G. Jones Oyster Plate

Majolica, six-well, six cobalt blue shell-form wells separated by brown coral branches & green leaves, white shell-form center well, George Jones, England, late 19th c., 10" d. (ILLUS.)... **4,950**

Fan Pattern Majolica Oyster Plate

Majolica, six-well, six fan-shaped wells in cream & brown decorated w/colorful bugs, cobalt blue round center well, minor glaze rub on rim, S. Fielding & Co., England, late 19th c., 9 1/2" d. (ILLUS.)... **2,310**

Majolica, six-well, six grey shaded to pink cockle shell wells divided by white & centered by a pink central well, Sarreguemines, France, ca. 1920, 9 1/2" d. **110**

Majolica, six-well, six rounded oyster shell-form cobalt blue wells & a long cobalt blue cracker well each separated by a pink fan device & centered by a pink ring around the round cobalt blue center well, Minton, England, late 19th c., 9" d.............. **4,400**

Majolica, six-well, six rounded oyster shell-form turquoise blue wells & a long turquoise blue cracker well each separated by a cobalt blue fan device & centered by a cobalt blue ring around the round turquoise blue center well, Minton, England, late 19th c., 9" d.. **990**

Minton Majolica Oyster Plate

Majolica, six-well, six shell-shaped wells in mottled dark green & brown separated by narrow white shells on brownish green w/small white shells at the rim, inner white shell band around the dark green center well, shape No. 1323, date code for 1870, Minton, England, 9" d. (ILLUS.).. **1,430**

Sunflower Majolica Oyster Plate

Majolica, six-well, six sunflower-shaped wells in yellow & brown separated by green leaves on a white ground, pale blue center well, brown vine border band, Samuel Lear, England, late 19th c., minor hairline, 9 3/4" d. (ILLUS.) **2,090**

Majolica, six-well, turquoise blue ribbed scallop shell wells separated by slender light green shells & dark green seaweed, white round scalloped center shell, George Jones, England, late 19th c., 8 1/2" d. **1,100**

Majolica, six-well, white ribbed scallop shell wells separated by thin yellow shells & green seaweed, round white center well w/pink border, George Jones, England, late 19th c., 8 1/2" d. **1,760**

Majolica, six-well, wide tapering turquoise blue shell wells divided by wide bands w/a slender pink shell on green grass & a small white shell at the rim, a central ring of small white shells around the dark green round center well, Minton, England, late 19th c., 9" d. **770**

Majolica, six-well, yellow ground w/six shell-form wells painted w/dark green & blue stylized scrolls, dots & florals around a pale blue center well, Henriot Quimper, France, ca. 1960, 8 1/2" d. **165**

Majolica, six-well, yellow spiraled arms centered by a brown-banded turquoise blue center well, the arms dividing the dark green fish head-shaped wells w/a large fish-shaped cracker well at one side, 9 3/4" d. (minor rim glaze wear) **660**

Majolica, six-well, six pink shell-form oyster pockets centering a raised & applied shell-form well, George Jones, England, ca. 1872, 10 1/2" d. **2,070**

Pie Birds

A pie bird can be described as a small, hollow device, usually between 3-1/2" to 6" long, glazed inside and vented from the top. Its function is to raise the crust of a pie to allow steam to escape, thus preventing juices from bubbling over onto the oven floor while providing a flaky, dry crust.

Originally, in the 1880s, pie birds were funnel-shaped vents used by the English for their meat pies. Not until the turn of the 20th century did figurals appear, first in the form of birds, followed by elephants, chefs, etc. By the 1930s, many shapes were found in America.

Today the market is flooded with many reproductions and newly created pie birds, usually in many whimsical shapes and subjects. It is best to purchase from knowledgeable dealers and fellow collectors.

Advertising, "Kirkbrights China Stores Stockton on Tees," ceramic, white, England **75**

Advertising, "Lightning Pie Funnel England," ceramic, white, England **75-120**

Paulden's Advertising Pie Bird

Advertising, "Paulden's Crockery Department Stretford Road," ceramic, white, England (ILLUS.) **70**

Advertising, "Roe's Patent Rosebud," ceramic, England, 1910-30 .... **55-65**

Advertising, "Rowland's Hygienic Patent," ceramic, England, 1910-30 .... **55-65**

Advertising, "Sequel...Porcelain," ceramic, white, England **50**

Advertising, "The Gourmet Crust Holder & Vent, Challis' Patent," ceramic, white, England **100**

Advertising, "The Grimmage Purfection Pie Funnel," ceramic, England, 1910-30 .... **55-65**

Jackie Sammond Pie Bird & Owl

Bird, black, ceramic, 3" h., by Jackie Sammond, early 1970s (ILLUS. right) **150**
Bird, ceramic, black, England **20-30**
Bird, ceramic, black on white base, yellow feet & beak, Nutbrown, England **50**

Bird, ceramic, brown & lavender trim, puff-chested, ca. 1940s (ILLUS.) **350**
Bird, ceramic, Camark Pottery, Camden, Ark., ca. 1950s-60s, 6 1/2" h. **95-115**

Hard-to-find Ceramic Pie Bird

Bird, ceramic, LaPere, Zanesville, Ohio, ca. 1930s-60s, hard to find (ILLUS.) **100-150**
Bird, ceramic, "Midwinter," black, England **50-60**

Bird on Log Pie Bird

Bird, ceramic, black, perched on log, England (ILLUS.) **65**

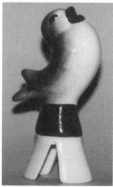

Puff-chested Bird Pie Bird

Sunglow Pie Bird

Bird, ceramic, Sunglow, England (ILLUS.) **95**

Two-headed Pie Bird

Bird, ceramic, two-headed, Barn Pottery, Devon, England (ILLUS.) 85

Rowe Pottery Pie Bird

Bird, ceramic, two-piece w/detachable base, 1992, Rowe Pottery (ILLUS.)................. 25

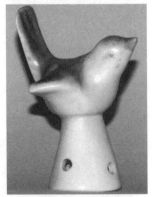

Half-doll Style Pie Bird

Bird, ceramics, half-doll style, blue & yellow on conical base, USA (ILLUS.)....................... 200

Bird, on nest w/babies, Artisian Pottery, USA 450
Bird, pottery, "Scipio Creek Pottery, Hannibal, MO" 25

Bird on Nest Pie Bird

Bird on nest w/babies, ceramic, Artisian Galleries, Fort Dodge, IA (ILLUS.)................. 500
Black chef, ceramic, full-figured, green smock, "Pie-Aire," USA 150

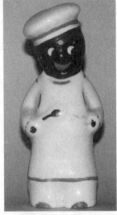

Black Chef w/Gold Spoon Pie Bird

Black chef, ceramic, w/gold spoon, white w/red trim (ILLUS.)... 200

Black Chef with Blue Smock

Black Chef, full-figured, blue smock, "Pie-Aire," USA (ILLUS.).. **125**

Blackbird for Child's Pie

Blackbird, ceramic, for child's pie, 2 3/4" (ILLUS.).. **35-50**
Blackbird, ceramic, Jackie Sammond, USA. ca. 1970s, 3" h............................. **125-150**

Very Large Black Pie Bird

Blackbird, ceramic, very large, 2 1/2" w x 5" h., English (ILLUS.) **125**

Blackbird w/Black Glaze

Blackbird, ceramic, w/black glaze, ca. 1930s-40s, English (ILLUS.)........................... **125**
Blackbird, ceramic, w/yellow trim on brown base... **85**

Wide-Mouth Blackbird

Blackbird, ceramic, wide mouth, yellow beak, fat, English (ILLUS.).............................. **175**
Blackbird, clay w/black & yellow glaze, ca. 1960s-70s.. **65-75**
Blackbird, red clay w/black glaze, ca. 1930s-40s.. **75-85**
Bluebird, ceramic, Japan, post-1960.............. **20-30**
Chef, ceramic, "A Lorrie Design, Japan," Joseph Originals, 1980s.................................. **75-95**

"Benny the Baker" Pie Bird

Chef, ceramic, "Benny the Baker," w/tools & box, Cardinal China Co., USA (ILLUS.).. **150**
Chef, ceramic, half-figure, all-white, England.. **90**

"Pie-Aire" Chefs

Chef, ceramic, "Pie-Aire," solid color, green,
red or yellow, each (ILLUS.) **100**
Chef, ceramic, "Servex Oven China, Bohe-
mia, Guaranteed Heatproof, RD 17494
Aus., RD 4098 N.Z.," Australia,
4 5/8" h. **125**
Chef, ceramic, white, England **80-90**

Holland Servex Chef Pie Bird

Chef, ceramic, white w/black buttons, "The
Servex Chef" in black letters on hat,
marked "Holland" inside (ILLUS.) **125**

Cherry, Apple & Peach Pie Birds

Cherry, apple & peach, ceramic, ca. 1950s,
in original box, set of three
(ILLUS.) **500-600**

Chick w/Dust Cap

Chick, ceramic, w/dust cap, Josef Originals
(ILLUS.) **65**
Chick, ceramic, yellow w/pink lips, Josef
Originals **50**
Donald Duck, ceramic, "Walt Disney"
marked on one side & "Donald Duck" on
the other, rare **1,500**

Dopey Pie Bird

Dopey, ceramic, Disney (ILLUS.) **500**

English Dragon Pie Birds

Dragon, ceramic, Creiciau Pottery, Wales,
United Kingdom **200**
Dragons, ceramic, various shapes & colors,
1980s-1990s, England, each (ILLUS. of
three, top of page) **100**

Duck Head Pie Bird

Duck head, ceramic, pink, England (ILLUS.)...... **125**

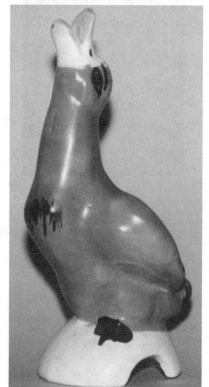

Brown English Duck Pie Bird

Duck, ceramic, brown w/white & yellow
beak, black trim, white base, England
(ILLUS.) **125**
Duck, ceramic, pink, blue or yellow, full-bod-
ied, USA, each **65**

Dutch Girl Multipurpose Pie Bird

Dutch girl, ceramic, doubles as pie vent, measuring spoon holder and/or receptacles for scouring pads & soap, rare (ILLUS.).. **150**

Nutbrown, England Elephant

Elephant, all-grey w/trunk up, ca. 1930s, Nutbrown, England (ILLUS. right)................. **200**
Elephant, all-white w/trunk up, Nutbrown, England (ILLUS. left).. **50**

Elephant Pie Bird

Elephant, ceramic, grey & pink w/swirled pink base, Cardinal China Co., USA (ILLUS.).. **350**

Elephant Pie Bird

Elephant, ceramic, white, ca. 1930s (ILLUS.).. **200**

"Fred the Flour Grader" Pie Bird

"Fred the Flour Grader," ceramic, black & white, from Homepride Flour, ca. 1978 (ILLUS.).. **95**

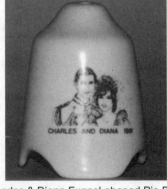

Charles & Diana Funnel-shaped Pie Bird

Funnel-shaped, ceramic, white w/blue transfer-printed image of Prince Charles & Princess Diana above "Charles and Diana 1981" (ILLUS.) **75**

Granny Pie Baker

Granny, ceramic, "Pie Baker," figure of a woman holding a bowl by Josef Originals (ILLUS.) **75**

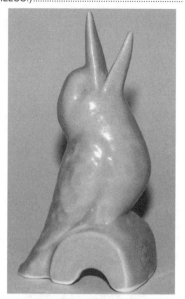

Kookaburra Pie Bird

Kookaburra, ceramic, light blue, Australia (ILLUS.) **250**

Luzianne Mammy Pie Baker

Luzianne Mammy, ceramic, black woman dressed in yellow shirt & green skirt, carrying a red tray w/coffee service, white turban on head (ILLUS.) **95**

Multipurpose Mammy

Mammy, ceramic, doubles as pie vent, measuring spoon holder, and/or receptacles for scouring pads & soap (ILLUS.) **85**

Mammy, ceramic, outstretched arms, USA **85**

Mushroom Pie Bird

Mushroom, ceramic, white w/brown & green trim, designed by Clarice Cliff, ca. 1930s, England (ILLUS.) **125**

Mushroom-shaped Pie Bird

Mushroom-shaped, ceramic, England (ILLUS.) **350**

Josef Originals Owl

Owl, ceramic, "A Lorrie Design, Japan," Josef Originals, 1980s (ILLUS.) **300**

Owl, ceramic, Jackie Sammond, USA. ca. 1970s (ILLUS. left with black bird) **200**

"Patrick" Pie Bird

"Patrick," ceramic, by California Cleminson, many color variations, USA, each (ILLUS.) **60**

Rare Brown "Patrick" Pie Bird

"Patrick," ceramic, tan w/brown trim, California Cleminson, USA, rare (ILLUS.) **250**

Peasant Woman Pie Baker

Peasant woman, ceramic, brown glaze, 1960s-70s (ILLUS.) **95**

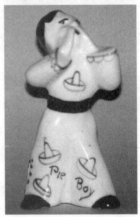

Pie Boy Pie Bird

"Pie Boy," ceramic, white w/black & green trim, Squire Pottery of California, USA (ILLUS.) **500**

"Pie Chef" Pie Bird

"Pie Chef," by Josef Originals, ceramic
(ILLUS.)... **65**
"Pie-Chic," ceramic, given as premium in
Pillsbury Flour, USA... **50**
Rooster, ceramic, Marion Drake...................... **65-85**

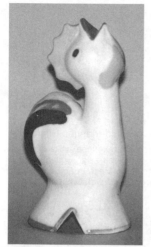

Cleminsons Rooster Pie Bird

Rooster, ceramic, white w/pink & burgundy
trim, thin line around base, California
Cleminsons, rare (ILLUS.).............................. **100**

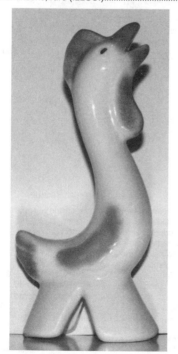

Pearl China Rooster Pie Bird

Rooster, ceramic, white w/tan trim, Pearl
China, USA (ILLUS.)................................ **150-300**

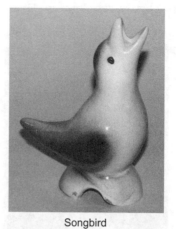

Songbird

Songbird, ceramic, beige, blue & pink varia-
tions, USA, each (ILLUS.)................................... **50**

LaPere Songbird

Songbird, ceramic, black w/gold beak, feet
& trim, LaPere, Ohio, USA (ILLUS.).............. **150**

Sunglow Pie Bird

Sunglow bird, ceramic, orange, ca. 1950s (ILLUS.) **90-110**

Thistle-shaped Pie Bird

Thistle-shaped, ceramic, blue, England (ILLUS.) **250**

"The Bleriot Pie Divider" Pie Bird

Unusual pie vent, ceramic, "The Bleriot Pie Divider," white, 1910-20 (ILLUS.) **395**
Yankee pie bird, ceramic, Millford, New Hampshire, ca. 1960s **40-50**

Reamers

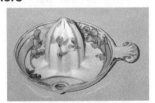

Floral Ceramic Reamer

One-piece, saucer shape w/lipped spout and shell-form handle, white ground w/pink & magenta flowers, green leaves & gold bead trim, marked "Hand Painted Japan" **150-175**

Reamer with Lattice Strainer

One-piece, saucer shape w/spout & side handle, round seed dam w/lattice strainer, white ground w/design of red cherries & green leaves, gold trim, 3" h. (ILLUS.) **85-115**

Gold-trimmed Reamer

One-piece, saucer shape, white w/gold trim, w/figures of tree, swan, butterfly & flowerpot, marked "Made In France - Limoges France," 3 1/2" d. (ILLUS.) **95-125**

Hall Ceramic Reamer

One-piece, simple round shape w/lip & side tab handle, green outside, white inside, marked "Hall," 6" h. (ILLUS.) **550-600**

Souvenir Ceramic Reamer

One-piece, souvenir, saucer shape w/spout & side handle, blue, rust & cream, w/painted image of Victorian woman w/parasol on one side of bowl & mass of flowers on the other, marked "Made in England, A Present From Dobercourt," 3 1/4" d. (ILLUS.) **85-125**
Three-piece, teapot shape, orange & white w/gold trim, cone sits under gold-handled lid, 3 1/2" h. **75-85**
Three-piece w/tray, ceramic w/sterling silver trim, white ground w/orange flowers, green leaves, rust trim, marked "France," 5" h. **225-250**
Two-piece, figure of duck w/white lustre body, blue head, orange beak, yellow top knot, marked "Made In Japan," 2 3/4" h. **35-50**

Oriental Man's Head Reamer

Two-piece, in the shape of an Oriental man's head, w/collar as base, hat as lid/reamer, light blue w/dark grey highlights, incised "9496," 5 3/4" h. (ILLUS.) **95-125**

Two-piece, model of lemon slice, yellow w/green handle, marked "Japan," 6 3/4" h. **40-50**

Reamer with Basketweave Design

Two-piece, pitcher shape w/C-form handle, basketweave design in dark green w/orange & maroon flowers & light green leaves, yellow top & cone, black trim, marked "Maramotoware Hand Painted Japan," 4" h. (ILLUS.) **40-50**

Squat Pitcher-form Reamer

Two-piece, squat pitcher form w/lip & circular handle, white ground w/maroon & yellow flower design, gold trim, marked "Hand Painted Japan," 3 3/4" h. (ILLUS.) **125-150**

Tall Pitcher-form Reamer

Two-piece, tall pitcher form w/lip, C-form handle & short outcurved base, pale pink ground w/painted floral decoration in pinks, blues, yellows & greens, thin green rim decoration, marked "Pantry Bak-In Ware by Crooksville," 8 1/4" h. (ILLUS.) **125-175**

Two-piece, teapot shape on three legs, white ground w/color photograph of Westminster Abbey, marked "Foreign," 3 1/2" h. **100-125**

Figural Painted Ceramic Reamer

Two-piece, teapot shape, with earthtone & purple pansy-type flowers on white ground, green lustre trim on handle & rim of body, lid & spout, ribbed lid w/holes for liquid to pass through, reamer in the form of a head with yellow ribbed cone hat, marked "Made in Japan," 6" h. (ILLUS.) **75-125**

String Holders

String Holders were standard equipment for general stores, bakeries and homes before the use of paper bags, tape and staples became prevalent. Decorative string holders, mostly chalkware, first became popular during the late 1930s and 1940s. They were mass-produced and sold in five-and-dime stores like Woolworth's and Kresge's. Ceramic string holders became available in the late 1940s through the 1950s. It is much more difficult to find a chalkware string holder in excellent condition, while the sturdier ceramics maintain a higher quality over time.

Apple, ceramic, handmade, 1947 .... **35-55**
Apple w/face, ceramic, PY **135**
Apple with berries, chalkware, common **15-35**

Apple with Worm String Holder

Apple with worm, chalkware, "Willie the Worm," ca. 1948, Miller Studio (ILLUS.) **65**

Art Deco Woman String Holder

Art Deco woman, chalkware, green beret & scarf (ILLUS.) **150**

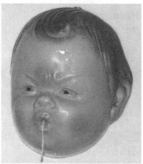

Frowning Baby String Holder

Baby, chalkware, frowning (ILLUS.) **225-275**
Balloon, ceramic, variety of colors, each **45**

Banana String Holder

Bananas, chalkware, ca. 1980s-present (ILLUS.) **25-50**

Bear with Scissors In Collar

Bear, w/scissors in collar, ceramic, Japan (ILLUS.) **50**

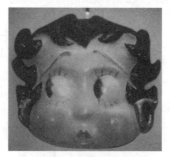

Betty Boop String Holder

Betty Boop, chalkware, original (ILLUS.) **500**
Bird, ceramic, green, "Arthur Wood, England," also found in blue & brown **25**

"String Swallow" Bird String Holder

Bird, ceramic, in birdhouse, "String Swal-
low" (ILLUS.)... 45
Bird, ceramic, yellow bird on green nest,
embossed "String Nest Pull," Cardinal
China, U.S.A. (ILLUS.) 50
Bird, chalkware, in birdcage................................ 100
Bird, chalkware, peeking out of
birdhouse 175
Bird & birdhouse, wood & metal 35
Bird on birdhouse, chalkware, cardboard,
"Early Bird," bobs up & down when string
is pulled, handmade 45-55
Bird on branch, ceramic, Royal Copley................ 60
Bird on nest, ceramic, countertop-type, Jo-
sef Originals... 75-95

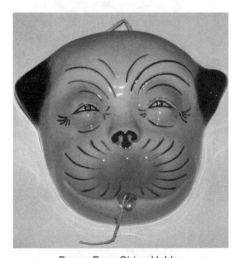

Bonzo Face String Holder

Bonzo face, ceramic, marked "Japan," rare
(ILLUS.)... 350

Boy with Tilted Cap

Boy, w/tilted cap, chalkware (ILLUS.) 100
Boy, w/top hat and pipe, eyes to side, chalk-
ware 50

Man & Woman String Holder

Brother Jacob and Sister Isabel, chalkware,
newer vintage, each (ILLUS.)..................... 55-60
Bunch of balloons, ceramic, green, pink &
blue, ca. 1983, Fitz & Floyd 50
Butler, ceramic, black man w/white lips &
eyebrows, Japan, hard to find .... 350+

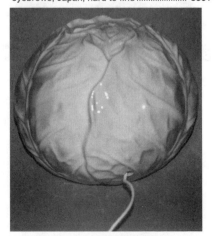

Cabbage String Holder

Cabbage, ceramic, Japan (ILLUS.) 100
Campbell Soup boy, chalkware, face only ...... 500+

Black Cat w/Gold Bow

Cat, ceramic, black w/gold bow, handmade
(ILLUS.)... **50**
Cat, ceramic, climbing a ball of string.................. **65**
Cat, ceramic, full-figured w/flowers & scis-
sors **25-45**

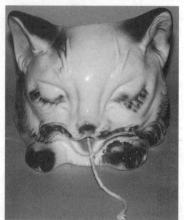

"Knitter's Pal" String Holder

Cat, ceramic, "Knitter's Pal" (ILLUS.) **45**
Cat, ceramic, w/matching wall pocket **95**

Cat with Plaid Collar

Cat, ceramic, w/plaid collar, space for scis-
sors, Japan (ILLUS.)... **50**
Cat, ceramic, w/scissors in collar, "Babba-
combe Pottery, England".................................. **25**
Cat, ceramic, white face w/pink & black pol-
ka dot collar... **50**
Cat, ceramic, white, full-figured on top of ball
of string **55-85**

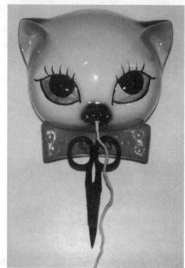

Cat Face String Holder

Cat, ceramic, white, w/large green eyes,
scissors hang on bow (ILLUS.) **35**

Cat on Ball of String String Holder

Cat, chalkware, grinning, on a ball of string,
Miller Studio, 1952 (ILLUS.) **50**
Cat, chalkware, w/bow, holding ball of
string.. **40**
Chef, ceramic, "Gift Ideas Creation, Phila.,
Pa.," w/scissors in head **35**

Chef, chalkware, unusual version of chef w/bushy eyebrows (ILLUS.)........................... **150**

Chef with Rosy Cheeks

Chef, ceramic, w/rosy cheeks, marked "Japan" (ILLUS.)... **50**
Chef, chalkware, baby face w/chef's hat **200**

Chef with Large Hat

Chef, chalkware, w/large hat facing left (ILLUS.)... **150**

Chef with Spoon & Box String Holder

Chef, chalkware, full-figured black chef w/spoon & blue box (ILLUS.)......................... **275**
Chef, chalkware, Rice Crispy.............................. **145**

Chef with Bottle, Glass String Holder

Chef w/bottle & glass, ceramic, full-figured, Japan (ILLUS.).. **175**

Chef with Bushy Eyebrows

Black Chef's Face String Holder

Chef's head, chalkware, black face, white
  hat (ILLUS.) **200**

Rare Chef String Holder

Chef's head, chalkware, "By Bello, 1949,"
  chubby-faced, rare (ILLUS.) **450**

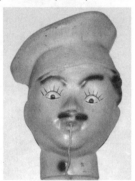

Chalkware Chef's Head String Holder

Chef's head, chalkware, common
  (ILLUS.) **60**
Chef's head, chalkware, "Little Chef," Miller
  Studio **150**
Cherries, chalkware **175**
Chicken, ceramic, "Quimper of France,"
  found in several patterns, still in produc-
  tion **65-85**
Chicken, ceramic, unmarked **40-50**

Chipmunk String Holder

Chipmunk's head, ceramic, white & brown,
  red & white striped hat & bow, bow holds
  scissors, Japan (ILLUS.) **55**
Clown, ceramic, full-figured, "Pierrot," hand
  holds scissors **85**

Jo-Jo the Clown String Holder

Clown, chalkware, "Jo-Jo," ca. 1948, Miller
  Studio (ILLUS.) **200**
Collie, ceramic, "Royal Trico," Japan **135**
Crock, ceramic, "Kitchen String," by Bur-
  leigh Ironstone, Staffordshire, England,
  w/scissors in top **50**

"The Darned String Caddy"

"Darned String Caddy (The)," ceramic,
  marked "Fitz & Floyd, MCMLXXVI"
  (ILLUS.) **35**
Delicious apple, chalkware, w/stem &
  leaves **25-50**
Dog, ceramic, "Bonzo" w/bee on chest **150**
Dog, ceramic, Boxer **95**
Dog, ceramic, German Shepherd, "Royal
  Trico, Japan" **135**

Dog String Holder

Dog, ceramic (ILLUS.) **100**

Scottie String Holder

Dog, ceramic, Scottie, marked "Royal Trico,
Japan" (ILLUS.).. **135**
Dog, ceramic, w/diamond-shaped eyes....... **85-100**
Dog, ceramic, w/puffed cheeks **35-55**
Dog, ceramic, w/scissors as glasses,
marked "Babbacombe Pottery, England" **25**
Dog, chalkware, Bulldog w/studded
collar, ca. 1933... **100**
Dog, chalkware, w/chef's hat, "Conovers
Original"... **275**

Westie with Studded Collar

Dog, chalkware, Westie, white w/studded
color (ILLUS.) **125**
Dog, wood, "Sandy Twine Holder," body is
ball of string **35**

Dog with Black Eye

Dog w/black eye, ceramic, w/scissors hold-
er in collar, right eye only circled in black,
England (ILLUS.)... **45**
Dove, ceramic, Japan **45**
Dutch Boy, chalkware, w/cap **125**

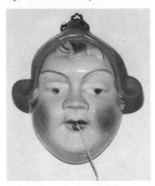

Ceramic Dutch Girl String Holder

Dutch Girl, ceramic, head only, Japan
(ILLUS.).. **50**
Dutch girl, chalkware, w/large hat........................ **60**
Elephant, ceramic, "Hoffritz, England" **40**

Elephant String Holder

Elephant, ceramic, marked "Babbacombe Pottery, England," scissors as glasses (ILLUS.) **25**

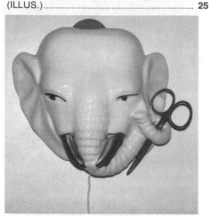

Elephant/Pincushion String Holder

Elephant, ceramic, white w/gold tusks, pincushion on head, Japan (ILLUS.) **50**

Father Christmas String Holder

Father Christmas, ceramic, Japan (ILLUS.) **175**

Flowerpot & Spoon Holder String Holder

Flowerpot, ceramic, yellow w/measuring spoon holder (ILLUS.) **75**

French Chef String Holder

French chef, chalkware, w/scarf around neck (ILLUS.) **185**
Funnel-shaped, w/thistle or cat & ball, ceramic **75**
Gourd, chalkware **150**

Granny String Holder

Granny, ceramic, full-figured, top of nose holds scissors that look like glasses (ILLUS.) **50**

Granny in Rocking Chair String Holder

Granny in rocking chair, ceramic, marked
  "PY," Japan (ILLUS.).. **125**

Humpty Dumpty, ceramic, sitting on wall,
  white & yellow (ILLUS.) **65**
Indian w/headdress, chalkware........................... **300**
Iron w/flowers, ceramic.. **75**
Ladybug, chalkware **225-275**

Cleminson's String Holder

Latchstring house, ceramic, California
  Cleminson's (ILLUS.).. **100**

Grapes String Holder

Grapes, chalkware, bunch (ILLUS.) **150**
Green pepper, ceramic, Lego sticker **65**

Puffed Heart String Holder

Heart, ceramic, puffed, heart reads "You'll
  always have a 'pull' with me!" California
  Cleminsons (ILLUS.)... **50**

Lemon String Holder

Lemon, ceramic, Japan (ILLUS.) **95**

Humpty Dumpty String Holder

Little Bo Peep String Holder

Little Bo Peep, ceramic, white w/red & blue trim, marked "Japan" (ILLUS.) **175**
Little Red Riding Hood, chalkware, head wearing hood **250**

Lovebirds String Holder

Lovebirds, ceramic, Morton Pottery (ILLUS.) **50**
Maid, ceramic, Sarsaparilla, 1984 .... **65**
Mammy, ceramic, full-figured, plaid & polka dot dress, Japan **100**

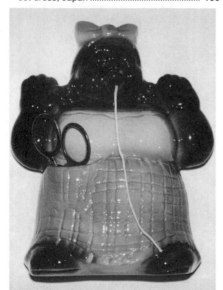

Mammy String Holder

Mammy, ceramic, full-figured, w/arms up & scissors in pocket (ILLUS.) **225**

Mammy Holding Flowers

Mammy, chalkware, full-figured, holding flowers, marked "MAPCO" (ILLUS.) **175**
Mammy, chalkware, head only, marked "Ty-Me" on neck **250**

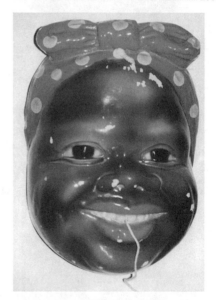

"Genuine Rockalite" Mammy

Mammy, chalkware, head only, w/polka-dot bandana, marked "Genuine Rockalite," made in Canada (ILLUS.) **200**
Mammy, cloth-faced, "Simone," includes card that reads "I'm smiling Jane, so glad I came to tie your things, with nice white strings," rare **150-195**

Coconut Mammy

Mammy, coconut, w/red and blue floral scarf
(ILLUS.) **35**
Mammy, felt, head only, w/plastic rolling
eyes **50-75**
Man, ceramic, head only, drunk, designed
by & marked "Elsa" on back, Pfaltzgraff,
York, Pennsylvania **95**

Pancho Villa String Holder

Pancho Villa, chalkware (ILLUS.) **275**
Parlor maid, ceramic, marked "Sarsasparil-
la," early 1980s **65**
Parrot, chalkware, brightly colored **125-175**
Peach, ceramic **60**
Pear, chalkware **45**

Gigolo Man String Holder

Man, chalkware, head only, marked across
collar, "Just a Gigolo" (ILLUS.) **100**
Mexican man, chalkware, head only, com-
mon **50**
Mexican man, chalkware, w/ornate hat **85-100**
Mexican woman, chalkware, head only,
w/braids & sombrero **150**
Monkey, chalkware, sitting on ball of string,
found in various colors **225-275**
Mouse, ceramic, countertop-type, Josef
Originals sticker **50**
Mouse, ceramic, England **75**
Oriental man, ceramic, w/coolie hat, Abing-
don **400**
Owl, Babbacombe Pottery, England **25**
Owl, ceramic, full-figured, Josef Originals **35**

Peasant Woman Knitting String Holder

Peasant woman, ceramic, full-figured, knitting sock, sticker reads "Wayne of Holly-
wood" (ILLUS.) **175**
Penguin, ceramic, full-figured w/scissors
holder in beak, marked "Arthur Wood,
England" **85**

Floral Decorated Pig String Holder

Pig, ceramic, white w/red & yellow flowers & green leaves decoration, scissors holder on back near tail, Arthur Wood, England (ILLUS.).. **50**

Pineapple, chalkware, "Prince Pineapple," by Miller Studio.................................. **250**

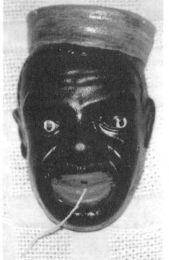

Porter String Holder

Porter, clay, without teeth, marked "Fredericksburg Art Pottery, U.S.A." (ILLUS.).. **145**

Prayer lady, ceramic, by Enesco........................ **175**

Rooster, porcelain, head only, Royal Bayreuth.. **300**

Sailor Boy, chalkware... **150**

Sailor Girl (Rosie the Riveter), chalkware......... **225**

Shaggy dog, ceramic, full-figured, w/scissors as glasses, marked "Babbacombe Pottery, England" **25**

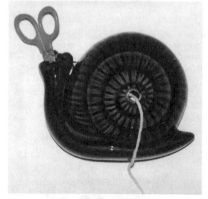

Snail String Holder

Snail, ceramic, dark brown (ILLUS.).................... **35**

Soldier, chalkware, head only, w/hat.................... **50**

Southern Gentleman with ladies, ceramic........... **75**

Strawberry, chalkware, w/white flower, green leaves & no stem.................................... **55**

Sunfish String Holder

Susie Sunfish, chalkware, Miller Studio, 1948 (ILLUS.)... **225-275**

Teapot, ceramic, Japan, w/parakeet..................... **65**

Teddy Bear, ceramic, brown, marked "Babbacombe Pottery, England," hole for scissors in bow at neck **25**

Thatched-roof cottage, ceramic **35**

Tom cat, ceramic, "Takahashi, San Francisco," Japan.. **35**

Tomato String Holder

Tomato, ceramic (ILLUS.)..................................... **55**

Tomato, chalkware.. **50**

Tomato Chef String Holder

Tomato chef, ceramic, "Japan," eyes closed (ILLUS.)... **100**

Westie String Holder

Westie, chalkware (ILLUS.).................................. **200**
Witch in pumpkin, ceramic, winking................... **100**

Woman in Flowered Dress String Holder

Woman, ceramic, full-figured, blue dress w/white & red flowers, Japan (ILLUS.)............ **85**
Woman, ceramic, head only, arched eyebrows **125**

Chalkware, Cardboard & Cloth String Holder

Woman's face, chalkware on cardboard box w/cloth bonnet (ILLUS.).................................. **100**

Young Girl String Holder

Young black girl, ceramic, w/surprised look, Japan (ILLUS.).. **250-295**

Lenox

The Ceramic Art Company was established at Trenton, New Jersey, in 1889 by Jonathan Coxon and Walter Scott Lenox. In addition to true porcelain, it also made a Belleek-type ware. Renamed Lenox Company in 1906, it is still in operation today.

Lenox China Mark

Bouillon cups & holders, deep rounded creamy cup w/flaring gilt-trimmed rim, each in a fitted circular tapering sterling silver geometric openwork frame w/draped garlands & wreaths enclosing a monogram cartouche, w/applied peach C-scroll side handles, raised on a flaring round foot, early 20th c., frame 3 1/2" d., set of 12 .... **$518**
Candlesticks, lyre-shaped, green wreath mark, pr... **40**
Place setting: 10 1/2" d. dinner plate, 9" d. salad plate, 7 1/2" d. bread & butter plate, cup & saucer; Autumn patt., 5 pcs....... **100**
Service plates, the center painted & transfer-printed w/an urn issuing fruit, flowers & foliage within a green rim, the edge w/matching urns & floral panels flanked by scrolled foliage in blue on a cream ground, pattern number 1830/X..77.G, printed mark & mark of retailer Marshall Field & Company, Chicago, early 20th c., 10 1/2" d., set of 12 .... **345**

Limoges

Limoges is the generic name for hard paste porcelain that was produced in one of the Limoges factories in the Limoges Region of France during the 19th and 20th centuries. There are more than 400 different factory identification marks, the Haviland factory marks being some of the most familiar. Dinnerware was commonly decorated by the transfer method and then exported to the United States.

Decorative pieces were hand painted by a factory artist or were imported to the United States as blank pieces of porcelain. At the turn of the 20th century, thousands of undecorated Limoges blanks poured into the United States, where any of the more than 25,000 American porcelain painters decorated them. Today hand-painted decorative pieces are considered fine art. Limoges is not to be confused with American Limoges. (The series on collecting Limoges by Debby DeBay, Living With Limoges, Antique Limoges at Home *and* Collecting Limoges Boxes to Vases *are excellent reference books.)*

Limoges Cache Pot

Cache pot, underglaze factory mark in green "W.G.&Co.," 12" h. (ILLUS.) **$1,500**

Limoges Cake Plate

Cake plate, h.p. in the Picard factory, underglaze factory mark "B&C France," 11 1/2" d. (ILLUS.) 600

Limoges Cake Plate on Pedestal

Cake plate on pedestal, h.p., underglaze factory mark in green "T&V Limoges France Depose" (Tressemann & Vogt), 4 x 12" (ILLUS.) 395

Limoges Candlesticks

Candlesticks, h.p. roses, heavy gold, underglaze factory mark in green "T&V," 16" h., pr. (ILLUS.) 600

Limoges Chalice

Chalice, h.p. violets, underglaze factory mark "J.P.L. France" (Jean Pouyat), 10 1/2" h. (ILLUS.) 700

Limoges Charger with Gold Rim

Charger, dramatic h.p. roses on dark ground, gold scroll on rim, underglaze factory mark in green "AK [over] D France" (A. Klingenberg), 15" d. (ILLUS.) 1,000

Limoges Charger with Roses

Charger, h.p. all over w/light roses, underglaze factory mark in green "AK [over] D France," 15" d. (ILLUS.)............................... **1,000**

Limoges Charger

Charger, h.p. w/dark flowers on light ground, underglaze factory mark in green "AK [over] D France," 15" d. (ILLUS.)......... **1,000**

Limoges Domed Cheese Dish

Cheese dish, cov., rare domed style, h.p., underglaze factory mark in green "J.P.L France," 7" h. (ILLUS.).................................... **400**

Limoges Chocolate Set

Chocolate set: 10 1/2" pot, six cups & saucers; h.p. & signed by factory artist "Magne," underglaze factory mark in green "T&V Limoges France," decorating factory mark "All Over Hand Painted" in red banner, the set (ILLUS.) **3,500**

Limoges 12-piece Chocolate Set

Chocolate set: 12 1/5" pot, 5 cups & saucers, 14" oval tray; h.p., underglaze factory mark in green "J.P.L. France," the set (ILLUS.) **3,000**

Four-piece Limoges Chocolate Set

Chocolate set: 12" pot, two cups, 12" tray; h.p., underglaze factory mark in green "J.P.L. France," the set (ILLUS.)...... **1,500**

Limoges Cracker Jar

Cracker jar, cov., h.p., underglaze mark in green "T&V Limoges France," 7 1/2" h. (ILLUS.)... **325**

Large Limoges Cup & Saucer

Cup & saucer, tea/toast, underglaze factory mark in green "T&V Limoges," 9" d. (ILLUS.).. **200**

Limoges Jardiniere with Cherubs

Limoges Dresser Set

Dresser set: tray, cov. jar & hair receiver; h.p. by amateur artist, underglaze factory mark in green "W.G.&Co., France" (William Guérin), the set (ILLUS.) **500**

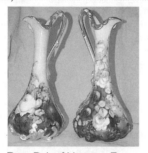

Rare Pair of Limoges Ewers

Ewers, h.p. by unknown amateur artist, underglaze factory mark in green "W.G.&Co.," rare pair, 15 1/4" h., pr. (ILLUS.) **2,500**

Limoges Ice Cream Set

Ice cream set: serving dish & 12 individual dishes in original presentation case; cobalt & gold, two Haviland marks, ca. 1888-1896, the set (ILLUS.) **3,500**

Jardiniere on Fluted Pedestal

Jardiniere, fluted pedestal base, fluted handles, underglaze factory mark in green "J.P.L. France" w/anchor, 12 x 14" (ILLUS.) **2,500**

Limoges Jardiniere, 1897

Jardiniere, footed, h.p. & artist signed "H.E. Page," dated 1897, underglaze factory mark in green "Limoges France" w/anchor (probably A. Lanternier), 10" h. (ILLUS.) **3,000**

Jardiniere, footed, ornate handles, cherub decoration, underglaze factory mark in green "D&Co." (R. Délinieres), 11" h. (ILLUS., top of page) **3,000**

Limoges Planter with Mums

Rare Limoges Jardiniere

Jardiniere, footed, side handles at top, underglaze factory mark in green "T&V France," very rare blank, 11 1/2" h. (ILLUS.).. **2,000**

Jardiniere with Lion Head Handles

Jardiniere, on original base, lion head handles, h.p. roses & detail, underglaze factory mark in green "D&Co.," 12 x 14" (ILLUS.).. **4,500**

Handleless Limoges Jardiniere

Jardiniere, on original base, no handles, underglaze factory mark in green "D&Co.," 11 x 12" (ILLUS.).. **2,500**

Limoges Jardiniere

Jardiniere, original base, elephant head handles, raised gold paste trim, underglaze factory mark in green "J.P.L.," 11 1/5" h. (ILLUS.)... **3,000**

Small Limoges Cider Pitcher

Pitcher, cider, 7" h., h.p. by amateur artist "E. Miler," underglaze factory mark in green "J.P.L. France" (ILLUS.) **600**

Limoges Cider Pitcher

Pitcher, cider, 10 1/2" h., h.p. & signed by factory artist "Roby," underglaze factory mark in green "T&V France," "T&V" decorating mark in purple (ILLUS.) **800**

Limoges Planter or Jardiniere

Planter, h.p. w/vibrant chrysanthemums, gilt handles & four feet, underglaze factory mark in green "D&Co.," 8 x 12 1/2" (ILLUS., top of previous page) **2,000**

Limoges Planter with Roses

Planter, no base, h.p. roses, underglaze factory mark in green "W.G.&Co.," 14" h. (ILLUS.)... **2,500**

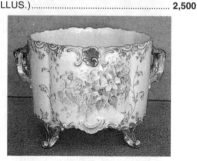

Unusual Limoges Planter

Planter, tall, unusual blank, underglaze factory mark in green "D&Co.," 9 x 9 1/2" (ILLUS.)... **2,000**

Planter or jardiniere, blank attributed to the d'Albis & Romanet Factory, swan handles, overglaze factory decorating mark in red "Elite Works," 8 x 10" (ILLUS., top of page) **1,500**

Limoges Plaque

Plaque, h.p. & trimmed in heavy gold, underglaze factory mark "Limoges" in star (Coiffe), 13 1/4" h. (ILLUS.) **1,200**

Limoges Hanging Plaque

Plaque, underglaze factory mark in green "Limoges France," overglaze decorating mark in red "Limoges France," artist signed "Dubois," pierced factory holes in back for hanging, 14" d. (ILLUS.) **2,500**

Limoges Plate

Plate, 10 1/2" d., heavy gold rim & h.p. roses, underglaze factory mark in green "J.P.L. France," overglaze factory decorating mark w/pink & green wreath (ILLUS.).. **225**

Limoges Plates

Plates, red & gold, underglaze factory mark in green "GDA," overglaze decorating mark in red "GDA" (Gérard Dufraisseix and Abbot), set of 12 (ILLUS. of four) **3,000**

Platter, game, 18" l., h.p. & signed by factory artist "Dubois," "Limoges France" &

star, Flambeau studio decorating mark (ILLUS., bottom of page)............................. **2,000**

Limoges Powder Jar

Powder jar, cov., h.p. roses w/heavy gold, underglaze mark in green "T&V," 5 1/2 x 6 1/2" (ILLUS.)...................................... **550**

Limoges Punch Bowl

Punch bowl, rare mammoth blank w/three gold feet, h.p. w/dramatic roses by unknown artist, underglaze factory mark in green "J.P.L. France," 13 x 26" (ILLUS.)... **5,500**

Limoges Game Platter

Limoges Punch Set

Punch set: bowl, 18" tray, cups; factory-decorated h.p. roses & heavy gilt, all factory artist signed "Aubin," underglaze factory mark in green "T&V Limoges France," factory decorating mark in grey "L.R.L.," the set (ILLUS.) **6,500**

Rare Limoges Punch Set

Punch set: bowl, base, tray, cups; h.p. at White's Art Co., Chicago, underglaze factory mark in green "D&Co.," rare, the set (ILLUS.) **5,500**

Limoges Grape-decorated Punch Set

Punch set: bowl w/original base, tray, cups; h.p. by unknown artist w/dark grapes & heavy gilt, underglaze factory mark in green "T&V Limoges France," the set (ILLUS.) **3,500**

Limoges Seafood Serving Platter

Seafood set: platter, 14 1/2" gravy boat, plates; h.p. w/image of lobster & signed by factory artist "Dubois," "Limoges France" mark w/star, Flambeau studio decorating mark, rare, the set (ILLUS. of platter) **4,000**

Artist-signed Limoges Tea Set

Tea set: cov. teapot, cov. sugar, creamer, tray; unusual pot on pedestal w/roses, artist signed "C. Wynn" & dated 1901, the set (ILLUS.) **1,000**

Large Painting on Porcelain

Tile, h.p. porcelain, artist signed "Ann" & dated 1898, underglaze factory mark in green "T&V Limoges, France," 14 x 17" (ILLUS.) **2,500**

Painting on Porcelain

Tile, h.p. porcelain of woman & cherub, underglaze factory mark in green "T&V France," 11 x 14" (ILLUS.) **3,000**

Limoges Tureen

Tureen, h.p. w/berries, artist signed "Andrew," underglaze factory mark in green "P&P" (Paroutaud Frères), 8 x 9" (ILLUS.)... **1,500**

Limoges Urn with Stopper

Urn, w/original stopper, blank w/split handles, h.p., underglaze factory mark in green "W.G.&Co., Limoges, France," 14" h. (ILLUS.).. **2,000**

Unusual Limoges Vase

Vase, 8" h., 13 1/2" d., underglaze factory mark in green "T&V Limoges France" & artist signed "Vera Gray," unusual shape & size (ILLUS.).. **3,000**

Limoges Vase with Separate Base

Vase, 12 1/2" h., w/separate original base, underglaze factory mark in green "J.P.L.," unusual (ILLUS.) **2,500**

Limoges Vase

Vase, 14" h., factory h.p. & artist signed "Rouncon," underglaze mark in green "PM DE M Limoges, France," overglaze decorating mark in green "Coronet" in crown (ILLUS.)... **3,000**

Limoges Vase with Image of Woman

Vase, 14" h., one of a pair h.p. in a factory in Chicago w/image of woman known to be a factory model in the early 20th c., underglaze mark in green "J.P.L. France," each (ILLUS.) **3,500**

Vase with Lion Head Handles

Vase, 14" h., unique lion head handles, h.p. by "Mrs CW Lamson, Erie, PA," dated March 16, 1901, underglaze factory mark in green "D&Co." (ILLUS.) **2,500**

One of a Pair of Limoges Vases

Vase, 22" h., one of a pair, h.p. w/roses & enameled w/raised gilt, underglaze factory mark in green "W.G.&Co.," each (ILLUS.) **3,000**

Liverpool

Liverpool is most often used as a generic term for fine earthenware products, usually of creamware or pearlware, produced at numerous potteries in this English city during the late 18th and early 19th centuries. Many examples, especially pitchers, were decorated with transfer-printed patriotic designs aimed specifically at the American buying public.

Bowl, 10 1/2" d., creamware, deep rounded sides, the interior transfer-printed in black w/polychrome trim w/a figure of Hope w/a three-masted sailing ship flying two American flags surrounded by six figural reserves around the sides, three transfer-printed country scenes on the exterior, red enamel rim, England, early 19th c. (repaired) **$805**

Mug, tall cylindrical form, creamware w/a black transfer-printed oval portrait medallion of "James Lawrence Esq. late of the United States Navy," scrolled handle w/foliate attachments, early 19th c., 6 1/4" h. (imperfections) **2,990**

Liverpool Masonic Jug

Pitcher, 10 5/8" h., creamware, jug-form, black transfer-printed design on buff ground of "The Mason's Arms" on front, reverse w/the verse "Masonic Secrets" & various Masonic emblems, area under spout decorated w/oval panel of Freemasons in fanciful architectural landscape beneath the script monogram "W.&D.C.," area under handle decorated w/dividers & a square encompassing the letter "G" within a triangle, ca. 1800 (ILLUS.) **3,300**

Pitcher, 11" h., creamware, jug-form, black transfer-printed decorations w/color enamel trim, one side w/an oval reserve centering a portrait medallion of "John Adams President of the United States" surrounded by symbolic figures of Plenty w/a cornucopia of fruit, Justice w/her scale & Cupid, the other side w/a yellow sailing ship flying a red, white & blue American flag & pennant on a green sea above the name "John Adams," an American eagle above a cartouche w/initials under the spout, floral design at the base of the handle, a floral swag border at the neck, w/gold trim, early 19th c. (imperfections) **16,100**

Pitcher, 9 1/2" h., presentation pitcher w/Masonic transfer scenes on all sides in black w/gold foliage & detail, "W.P." & "Success to Delemere" (some wear) **880**

Three Early Liverpool Pitchers

Pitcher, 7 1/4" h., creamware, jug-form, decorated on one side w/a black transfer-printed design of a large round compass & verse, on the other side w/"The Sailors Adieu," early 19th c. (minor imperfections) **748**

Pitcher, 8 1/4" h., creamware, jug-form, transfer-printed in black on one side w/an American eagle & shield & on the other w/a figure of Independence & a poem, early 19th c., imperfections (ILLUS. right with other two pitchers, top of page)............... **1,150**

Pitcher, 8 5/8" h., creamware, jug-form, transfer-printed & enamel-trimmed w/a scene titled "Tom Truelove Going to Sea" on one side & a three-masted sailing ship w/"Success to Trade" on the other, an oval reserve of three figures by a lake w/"Peace to All Nations" under the spout, worn gilt lettering for "John Frank," early 19th c. (imperfections) **1,093**

Pitcher, 8 3/4" h., creamware, jug-form, transfer-printed in black on one side w/"Commodore Prebles Squadron Attacking the City of Tripoli Aug 3, 1804," the other side w/a scene of the Salem Shipyard & a verse, an American eagle & shield below the spout, early 19th c. (imperfections)..................... **2,300**

Pitcher, 9" h., creamware, jug-form, transfer-printed in black w/a large oval reserve showing Washington, Liberty & Franklin examining a large world map, the other side w/a three-masted sailing ship, an American eagle & shield & figure of Hope below the spout, polychrome trim, early 19th c. (imperfections) **978**

Pitcher, 9 1/8" h., creamware, jug-form, black transfer-printed portrait medallion of Commodore Preble on one side, scene of "Commodore Prebles Squadron Attacking the City of Tripoli Aug 3, 1804" on the other, imperfections (ILLUS. left with two other pitchers, top of page)............... **2,815**

Pitcher, 9 1/4" h., creamware, jug-form, one side transfer-printed in black w/poly-chrome trim w/a figure of Hope, a three-masted sailing ship flying the American flag on the other, American eagle below the spout w/a Jefferson quote, dated 1804 (imperfections) **3,738**

Pitcher, 9 1/2" h., creamware, jug-form, one side transfer-printed in black w/poly-chrome trim w/the figure of a Boston Fusilier within an oval reserve, the other side w/"United We Stand - Divided We Fall," American eagle & shield below the spout, early 19th c. (imperfections)......... **17,250**

Pitcher, 10" h., creamware, jug-form, black transfer-printed design of "Peace, Plenty and Independence" w/Classical figures & American eagle on one side, a three-masted sailing ship on the other side, a shield below the spout, England, early 19th c. (imperfections)..................... **920**

Pitcher, 10" h., creamware, jug-form, decorated w/a black transfer-printed design w/color enamel trim, one side w/a Masonic panel, the other w/a sailing ship in brown & black w/yellow masts & flying a red, white & blue American flag & pennant, on a green sea, a cartouche w/initials & the American Eagle under the spout, early 19th c. (imperfections) **1,725**

Pitcher, 10" h., creamware, jug-form, one side transfer-printed in black & trimmed in color w/an oval scenic reserve & "Proscribed Patriots," the other side w/an oval reserve w/a militiaman in uniform & "Success to America whose Militia...," American eagle, shield & Jefferson quote under the spout, dated 1802 (repaired) **3,220**

Pitcher, 10 1/4" h., creamware, jug-form, transfer-printed in black on one side w/a scene titled "Salem Shipyard" & on the other w/a large sailing ship titled "Boston Frigate," polychrome highlights, a cartouche w/monogram above an eagle & shield under the spout, early 19th c., imperfections (ILLUS. center with two other pitchers, top of page)..................... **4,888**

Pitcher, 11 3/4" h., creamware, jug-form, one side transfer-printed in black w/the ship "Massachusetts," the other side w/a map of Newburyport Harbor w/"Success to the Commerce of Newburyport," circular reserve of Columbia under the spout, gilt trim, early 19th c. (minor imperfections)............ **14,950**

Pitcher, 14" h., jug-form, creamware, transfer-printed w/an American eagle & monogram, the ship "America" & a panel depicting George Washington as general, flanked by figures of Justice & Liberty, w/the names of fifteen states, early 19th c........... **6,900**

Pitcher, 14 1/4" h., creamware, jug-form, one side transfer-printed in black trimmed w/color w/vignette showing a seated figure of Hope beside a scene of a sailing ship, a quote "her lefs'ning boat unwilling rows to land," on the other side a three-masted sailing ship flying an American flag below the spout, small transfer scenes scattered around the rim & mast, a reserve w/motto "From Rocks & Sands And every ill May god preserve The Sailor still" below the handle, gilt trim, early 19th c. (imperfections).............. **6,325**

Liverpool Creamware Punch Bowl

Punch bowl, 10" d., creamware, round sides tapering out at top, footrim, black transfer-printed design of bust portrait of Benjamin Franklin or George Washington on front & back, the sides decorated w/pastoral landscapes, the interior w/a three-masted ship in full sail flying the American flag, various trophies around the rim, ca. 1790-1800, chip to footrim, some scratching to interior (ILLUS.)..................... **1,800**

Longwy

This faience factory was established in 1798 in the town of Longwy, France and is noted for its enameled pottery, which resembles cloisonné. Utilitarian wares were the first production here, but by the 1870s an Oriental-style art pottery that imitated cloisonné was created through the use of heavy enamels in relief. By 1912, a modern Art Deco style became part of Longwy's production; these wares, together with the Oriental-style pieces, have made this art pottery popular with collectors today. As interest in Art Deco has soared in recent years, values of Longwy's modern-style wares have risen sharply.

Longwy Floral Cup & Saucer

Cup & saucer, decorated w/overall vibrant colored stylized flowers, ink stamp marks, rim chips on both pieces, cup 2 1/4" h., the set (ILLUS.)............................... **$67**

Art Deco Longwy Tile

Tile, square, decorated in bold colors w/a stylized Art Deco woman in a garden, a deep brick red ground w/the woman in purple, white & black w/a yellow & white landscape w/purple, pink, white & black trees, marked "Longwy France Primavera," 8" w. (ILLUS.).................................. **400-425**

Vase, 11 3/4" h., flared neck on a round flattened body raised on an oval foot, the exterior w/turquoise blue crackle glaze, base w/a green ink stamp mark "Primavera Longwy France," after 1913..................... **230**

Vase, 12 1/2" h., tapering ovoid body w/everted lip, molded w/a mythological ram & bird w/two female nudes amid a stylized landscape, covered in ivory, turquoise blue, cobalt blue, purple & black glaze, green printed mark "Primavera - Longwy - France," ca. 1925......................... **2,587**

Large Longwy Vase

Vase, 22" h., ten sided melon-form body
w/stepped tapering neck & circular foot,
molded w/stylized teal & pink berries on
black vines reserved on a crackled ivory
ground, sawtooth border at neck & cobalt
glazed rim & foot, ca. 1925, printed "So-
ciete Des Faienceries - Longwy - France"
(ILLUS.)... **2,300**

LuRay Pastels

*LuRay Pastels, made by The Taylor, Smith & Taylor
Co. of Chester, West Virginia, from 1938 until 1961, was
a line available in four colors - Windsor Blue, Surf
Green, Persian Cream and Sharon Pink. No one original*

*color seems to be more desirable than the others. A fifth
color, Chatham Gray, ran from 1949 until 1952. Collectors refer to the early-shaped A/D sets as "Chocolate
Sets." Decal-decorated LuRay sets were produced but
are very rare. No known examples of the handleless
sugar, 7" mini platter or gray salad bowl have been
found with the LuRay backstamp. An asterisk (*) indicates an older original mold shape.*

After-dinner chocolate cup, four original colors, each (ILLUS. front, bottom of page). **$20-25**
After-dinner chocolate cup, gray **75-100**
After-dinner chocolate pot, cov., four origi-
   nal colors, each (ILLUS. back)................ **135-175**
After-dinner individual creamer, four original
   colors, each (ILLUS. left)............................ **35-55**
After-dinner individual sugar bowl, cov., four
   original colors, each (ILLUS. right)............. **40-65**
After-dinner saucer, four original colors,
   each (ILLUS. front).. **7-12**
After-dinner saucer, gray................................. **15-25**

Fruit, Grapefruit, Lug Soup Bowls

Bowl, 5" d., fruit, four original colors, each
   (ILLUS. front)...................................... **5-8**

After-Dinner Chocolate Service

Bowl, 5" d., fruit, gray **10-16**

Bowl, 6 1/4" d., grapefruit, rare, four original
   colors, each (ILLUS. left w/fruit bowl) **350-400**

36's & Tab Cereal Bowls

Bowl, 36's bowl (oatmeal), four original colors, each (ILLUS. left) **50-75**
Bowl, 36's bowl (oatmeal), gray **250-300**
Bowl, coupe soup, flat, four original colors, each (ILLUS. right w/fruit bowl) **15-20**
Bowl, coupe soup, flat, gray **30-40**
Bowl, cream soup, four original colors, each .. **65-85**
Bowl, lug soup (tab cereal), four original colors, each **15-20**
Bowl, lug soup (tab cereal), gray **40-50**
Butter dish, cov., four original colors, each **50-75**
Butter dish, cov., gray **150-225**
Cake plate, 11" d., four original colors, each (ILLUS.) **50-75**

"Chocolate set" A/D pot*, cov., four original colors, each (ILLUS. back) **1,000-1,500**
"Chocolate set" A/D saucer*, four original colors, each (ILLUS. front) **25-35**
"Chocolate set" A/D sugar bowl*, cov., four original colors, each (ILLUS. right) **400-500**
Chop plate, four original colors, 15" d., each **30-40**
Chop plate, gray, 15" d. **300-350**
Coaster (nut dish), four original colors, each **65-85**

Compartment (Grill) Plate

Compartment (grill) plate, four original colors, each (ILLUS.) **25-30**
Compartment (grill) plate, gray **100-125**
Cream soup saucer, four original colors, each **20-25**
Creamer, four original colors, each **10-15**
Creamer, gray **30-45**
Egg cup, double, four original colors, each **15-25**
Egg cup, double, gray **75-100**
Epergne (flower vase), four original colors, each (ILLUS.) **125-150**

LuRay 10" Calendar Plate

Calendar plate, 8", 9" or 10" d., each (ILLUS. of 10" d) **35-65**
Casserole, cov., four original colors, each (ILLUS.) **125-175**
"Chocolate set" A/D creamer*, four original colors, each (ILLUS. left) **350-400**

After Dinner Demitasse Service

"Chocolate set" A/D cup*, four original colors, each (ILLUS. front) **75-100**

Flat, Footed & Juice Jugs

Jug, juice, four original colors, each (ILLUS. left) **175-225**
Jug, water, flat, four original colors, each (ILLUS. right) **75-95**

Jug, water, footed*, four original colors,
each (ILLUS. center) **100-125**

LuRay Muffin Cover & Plate

Muffin cover, four original colors, each
(ILLUS. w/an 8" plate) **175-225**
Pepper shaker, four original colors, each **10-15**
Pepper shaker, gray **20-30**
Pickle (celery) dish, four original colors,
each **35-45**
Plate, 6" d., four original colors, each **4-6**
Plate, 6" d., gray **8-12**
Plate, 7" d., four original colors, each
(ILLUS.) **10-15**
Plate, 7" d., gray **20-30**
Plate, 8" d., four original colors, each **20-25**
Plate, 8" d., gray (ILLUS.) **40-50**
Plate, 9" d., four original colors, each **10-15**
Plate, 9" d., gray **20-30**
Plate, 10" d., four original colors, each **15-20**
Plate, 10" d., gray **30-40**

7", 11 1/2" & 13" Platters

Platter, 7" l., mini size, four original colors,
each (ILLUS. top) **200-250**
Platter, 11 1/2" l., four original colors, each
(ILLUS. center) **15-20**
Platter, 11 1/2" l., gray **45-65**
Platter, 13" l., four original colors, each
(ILLUS. bottom) **15-25**
Platter, 13" l., gray **45-65**
Relish dish, four-part, four original colors,
each **125-175**
Salad bowl, four original colors, each **50-75**
Salad bowl, gray **300-400**
Salt shaker, four original colors,
each **10-15**
Salt shaker, gray **20-30**

LuRay Sauceboats

Sauceboat, four original colors, each
(ILLUS. left on celery tray) **30-40**
Sauceboat, w/fixed stand, four original col-
ors, each (ILLUS. right) **35-50**
Sugar bowl, cov., four original colors,
each **15-20**

Regular & Handleless Sugar Bowls

Sugar bowl, cov., gray (ILLUS. left) **45-60**
Sugar bowl, cov., handleless, four original
colors, each (ILLUS. right) **75-125**

Two Different Teapots with Cup & Saucer

Tea cup, four original colors, each (ILLUS.)..... **7-12**
Tea cup, gray **15-25**
Tea saucer, four original colors, each
(ILLUS. w/cup & teapots) **3-5**

Tea saucer, gray **7-10**
Teapot, cov., curved spout, four original col-
ors, each (ILLUS. left w/tea cup) **75-95**
Teapot, cov., curved spout, gray **300-400**

Teapot, cov., flat spout*, four original colors, each (ILLUS. right w/tea cup) **150-200**
Tidbit tray, three-tier, four original colors, each **95-125**
Tidbit tray, two-tier, gray **150-200**

Juice & Water Tumblers

Tumbler, juice, four original colors, 3 1/2" h., each (ILLUS. left) **45-65**
Tumbler, water, four original colors, 4 1/4" h., each (ILLUS. right) **65-85**
Vase, bud, four original colors, each **250-350**
Vase, urn-type, four original colors, each **250-350**
Vegetable bowl (baker), oval, four original colors, each **20-25**
Vegetable bowl (baker), oval, gray **50-65**
Vegetable bowl (nappy), round, four original colors, each **20-25**
Vegetable bowl (nappy), round, gray **50-65**

Lustre Wares

Lustred wares in imitation of copper, gold, silver and other colors were produced in England in the early 19th century and onward. Gold, copper or platinum oxides were painted on glazed objects that were then fired, giving them a lustred effect. Various forms of lustre wares include plain lustre, with the entire object coated to obtain a metallic effect, bands of lustre decoration and painted lustre designs. Particularly appealing is the pink or purple "splash lustre" sometimes referred to as "Sunderland" lustre in the mistaken belief it was confined to the production of Sunderland-area potteries. Objects decorated in silver lustre by the "resist" process, wherein parts of the objects to be left free from lustre decoration were treated with wax, are referred to as "silver resist."

Wares formerly called "Canary Yellow Lustre" are now referred to as "Yellow-Glazed Earthenwares."

Copper

Pepper pot, cov., bulbous body on short foot w/round base, waisted neck tapering to domed lid w/finial, decorated w/light rust band w/pink lustre foliage & blue berries, 4 1/8" h. **$165**
Pitcher, 4 1/2" h., ribbed body, scrolled handle & molded fan spout, white neck w/red, green & pink lustre strawberries, base has a starch blue band **55**
Salt, open, squat bulbous body on flared foot w/round base, ring rim on top, decorated w/blue band of pink lustre foliage & pale yellow berries, 2" h. (minor interior wear) **110**

Silver & Silver Resist

Circus wagon finial, redware, spherical w/molded recumbent lion finial & acanthus leaves, "Bailey & Batkin Sole Patentees" on center band, flat circular base, minor chip to base, lustre wear, 7 7/8" h. **1,265**
Pitcher, 8 3/4" h., jug-form, wide ovoid body w/a short cylindrical neck w/a long pointed spout, C-form handle, silver resist decoration of flowers & vining leaves in silver lustre on a white ground, first half 19th c. (small chips, roughness, crow's foot in side) **248**
Pitcher, 5 3/8" h., jug-form, bulbous ovoid body w/a short concave neck, pointed rim spout & angled loop handle, the body decorated overall in silver resist w/an ornate design of large birds perched among berry clusters, leaves & blossoms, ca. 1815 .... **575**
Pitcher, 5 1/2" h., jug-form, bulbous ovoid body w/a slightly tapering short neck, pointed rim spout & angled loop handle, the sides w/two round purple transfer-printed reserves depicting landscapes w/houses, the remainder of the body decorated in silver resist w/ornately flowering sprigs & a leaf band around the rim, ca. 1810-15 .... **460**
Tea service: cov. teapot, cov. sugar bowl, milk jug & three larger jugs; teapot, sugar bowl, milk jug & larger jug in silver lustre w/floral decoration, another jug w/enamel floral decoration in blues & reds on cream ground beneath silver-lustre neck, spout & handle, & one copper lustre jug w/spout in form of bear's head & dolphin form handle, decorated w/red, yellow, pink & green flowers & leaves on blue ground; Staffordshire, ca. 1820, tallest jug 8 7/8" h., the set (chips, hairline, restuck handle) **1,560**

Sunderland Pink & Others

Pitcher, 4" h., footed wide bulbous squatty body tapering slightly to a short waisted neck w/wide arched spout & scalloped rim, ropetwist arched handle, black transfer-printed village scene w/florals around the neck, overall pink lustre glaze, first half 19th c. **110**
Pitcher, 5 1/4" h., footed wide shell-ribbed lower body below a wide shoulder to the tall waisted neck w/a high, wide arched spout, S-scroll handle, black fruit & floral transfer-printed design around neck, overall pink lustre glaze, early 19th c. (minor surface edge wear) **176**
Pitcher, 6 1/4" h., jug-type, pearlware, the footed bulbous ovoid body tapering to a short cylindrical neck w/rim spout, double-C form handle, the sides molded in relief w/fox hunting scenes highlighted in pink lustre & green enamel against a white ground, first half 19th c. **440**
Pitcher, 7" h., jug-form, black transfer-printed w/two oval reserves, one "Captain Hull of the Constitution" & the other "Pike - be always ready to die for your country," pink lustre trim, early 19th c. (imperfections) **5,750**

Three Early Pink Lustre Pitchers

Pitcher, 7 1/4" h., jug-form, decorated under the spout w/the Mariner's Arms, a ship w/two sailors, lighthouse & cannon in the background, each side w/an inspirational verse within a floral border reserve, ca. 1840 (chips).. **633**

Pitcher, 8" h., Sunderland lustre pitcher w/dark red transfer of ship, verse & two sailors w/"Mariners Arms," h.p. enamel in red, green, yellow & blue (spout has minor wear)... **770**

Pitcher, 8 1/2" h., pearlware, satyr head spout, pink lustre h.p. w/pink queen's roses in blue, green & orange, w/a scene of three sailing ships, verse & "David & Elizabeth Buchannan" (minor flaking, in-the-making hairline on handle).................... **1,320**

Pitcher, 8 3/4" h., jug-form, black transfer-printed design of the farmer's arms flanked by a farmer & wife surrounded by various symbols in a landscape, the other side w/an inspirational verse, oval reserve below the spout signed "Mary Hayward Farmer Sandhurft Kent," polychrome trim, highlighted w/pink lustre trim & florals, early 19th c. (imperfections)... **1,150**

Pitcher, 9" h., jug-form, wide bulbous ovoid body tapering to a short cylindrical neck w/high arched spout, C-form handle, one side w/a black transfer-printed reserve w/Masonic emblems & a verse, the rectangular reserve under the spout w/"Charlotte Todd, Born May 20th, 1825" in brick red enamel, Sunderland pink splash lustre background (wear, stains, chips)............. **770**

Pitcher, 9 3/8" h., jug-form, bulbous cream-colored body decorated w/vignettes on each side, one side w/a polychrome-trimmed black transfer-printed scene of a British sailing ship & a verse in a cartouche reading "May Peace and Plenty On Our Nation Smile and Trade with Commerce Bless the British Isle," the other side w/a verse in a floral wreath, under the spout is "The Sailor's Tear" beneath a printed Mariner's Compass flanked by British ships, red, green & yellow trim, pink lustre squiggles around the sides, early 19th c., imperfections (ILLUS. center w/other pitchers)... **646**

Pitcher, 9 3/8" h., jug-form, the bulbous body decorated on the sides w/large banded reserves, one w/a black transfer-printed figural scene titled "The Sailor's Farewell," the other one w/a sailor's verse, a large panel under the spout inscribed "George Henry Page - Born Sept. 7th 1800 - Charlotte Page - Born Feb. 7th 1802," w/a whimsical puzzle verse, wide Sunderland pink lustre bands around the top & base, polychrome trim in yellow & green, early 19th c., imperfections (ILLUS. left, top of page)............................. **3,290**

Pitcher, 10 1/8" h., jug-form, wide bulbous body decorated w/large black transfer-printed reserves on the sides, one titled "A West View of the Iron Bridge over the Wear under the Patronage of R. Burdon Esq. M.P.," the reverse w/an inspirational verse in a floral wreath, a pouring handle under the spout centering a black transfer-printed sailing ship & an inscription "Arther Rutter 1840," overall spattered pink lustre decoration, minor imperfections (ILLUS. right) **1,645**

Unusual Lustre-trimmed Pitcher

Pitchers, 7 3/8" h., jug-type, bulbous body tapering to a short neck w/large rim spout, angled handle, pink lustre band trim, each transfer-printed in puce w/figural designs, one side w/a standing American Indian & large eagle flanking an American flag above a banner reading "Success to the United States of America," the reverse w/"Peace, Plenty and Independence" & depicting a star & ribbon wreath w/the names of New York & ten other states all surmounted by a large

eagle & American flag & flanked by allegorical figures of Peace & Plenty, a foliate geometric design beneath the spout,
early 19th c., imperfections, pr. (ILLUS.
of one) **2,233**

Watch hutch, figural, a tall central grandfa-
ther clock w/the top open to accept the
watch, case flanked by a small figure of a
boy & a girl, fine underglaze decoration in
yellow, black, blue, green, grey, red,
brown, flesh & pink lustre trim, impressed
on top of the base "Dixon Austin & Co.,"
Sunderland, England, ca. 1820-26, professional restoration to top of clock &
hairline across base, 11 1/4" h. **1,430**

Majolica

*Majolica, a tin-enameled glazed pottery, has been
produced for centuries. It originally took its name from
the island of Majorca, a source of figuline (potter's
clay). Subsequently it was widely produced in England,
Europe and the United States. Etruscan majolica, now
avidly sought, was made by Griffen, Smith & Hill, Phoe-
nixville, Pa., in the last quarter of the 19th century. Most
majolica advertised today is 19th or 20th century. Once
scorned by most collectors, interest in this colorful ware
so popular during the Victorian era has now revived and
prices have risen dramatically in the past few years. Also
see MINTON, ROYAL WORCESTER, SARREGUEM-
INES and WEDGWOOD.*

Etruscan

Majolica Etruscan Mark

Bowl, 8" d., Shell & Seaweed patt., green &
pink exterior, pink interior **$275**
Butter pat, Begonia Leaf on Wicker patt. (mi-
nor rim nick)... **110**
Butter pat, Geranium patt. **55**
Butter pat, Shell & Seaweed patt. w/sea-
weed **193**
Cake plate, Napkin patt., pink & white nap-
kin on yellow ground w/cobalt blue bor-
der (handle repaired) **330**
Cake stand, conventional design w/brown
sunburst w/yellow middle in center surrounded by a band of yellow & an order
band of green leaves, 10" d........................ **385**
Cake stand, Maple Leaves patt., pink
ground **193**
Cake stand, Maple Leaves patt., white
ground **138**
Cake stand, Morning Glory patt., rare bur-
gundy ground, 8" d., 4" h.......................... **358**
Cake stand, Morning Glory patt., rare cobalt
blue morning glories, 8" d., 4" h. **385**

Cake stand, Morning Glory patt., white
ground, 8" d., 4" h..................................... **193**
Cake stand, Morning Glory patt., yellow
morning glories, 8" d., 4" h.............................. **275**

Shell and Seaweed Cake Stand

Cake stand, Shell & Seaweed patt., very mi-
nor rim nicks (ILLUS.).................................. **715**

Rare Etruscan Cheese Dish

Cheese dish, cov., Lily, Fern & Floral patt.,
high domed cover w/large green leaves
& yellow blossoms w/a bud finial on a
white ground, wide base flange w/further
leaves, very minor hairline in cover,
11 1/4" d., 6" h. (ILLUS.) **1,925**

Swan & Water Lily Cheese Dish

Cheese dish, cov., Swan & Water Lily patt.,
tall cylindrical cover w/flat top centered
by a figural swan finial, water lilies,
leaves & butterflies around the sides &
base, fine color (ILLUS.) **1,430**
Cup & saucer, Shell & Seaweed patt................. **220**
Humidor, cov., Shell & Seaweed patt., natu-
ral colors (one shell on cover replaced)..... **1,100**
Mug, Oak Leaf & Acorn patt. **121**
Mug, Pineapple patt.................................. **121**
Mug, Water Lily patt.................................. **121**
Pickle dish, footed oval, Daisy patt., 8 1/2" l.
(rim nick).. **330**
Plate, 8" d., Bamboo patt. **220**

Shell & Seaweed Plates & Platter

Plate, 8" d., Shell & Seaweed patt., great
color (ILLUS. bottom left) 248
Plate, 9" d., Classical Dog patt. 275
Plate, 9" d., Maple Leaf on Basket patt............. 220
Plate, 9" d., Maple Leaves patt., pink
ground, great color 303
Plate, 9" d., Overlapping Begonia Leaves
patt. 165
Plate, 9 1/4" d., Shell & Seaweed patt.,
great color (ILLUS. front right)...................... 330
Plates, 9" d., molded Maple Leaves design,
white background, set of 4 (imperfec-
tions)... 358
Platter, Geranium patt., large leaf w/twig
handles.. 220
Platter, Geranium patt., large leaf w/twig
handles, light pink ground, fine color............ 275
Platter, 14" l., oval w/scalloped rim, Shell &
Seaweed patt. (ILLUS. top with Shell &
Seaweed plates).. 413
Sauce dishes, shell-shaped, natural colors,
pr. 358
Syrup pitcher w/hinged pewter cap, Bam-
boo patt., 7 1/2" h. 495
Syrup pitcher w/hinged pewter cap, Rose
patt., w/butterfly spout................................... 138
Syrup pitcher w/hinged pewter cap, Sun-
flower patt., cobalt blue ground 605
Syrup pitcher w/hinged pewter cap, Sun-
flower patt., white ground 440
Tray, Oak Leaf patt., pink edge, 12" l................ 220

General

Bank, figural, model of a cat w/a ball,
French, 5 1/4" h. 385
Basket, Bird, Fan & Floral patt., oblong
shape pinched in at the center & joined
by an arched handle, pinks & greens
w/cobalt blue trim, 11" l., 8" h. 413
Bowl, 11" l., large shell-shaped bowl w/pink
interior & pale green exterior, on three
brown shell feet, Joseph Holdcroft, En-
gland, late 19th c. 275
Box, cov., round, pale turquoise ground
molded w/flying birds in dark green flanking a central brown twig handle, Joseph
Holdcroft, England, 4 1/2" d. 715
Box w/hinged cover, deep square form
w/flat top, cobalt blue ground molded
w/birds & mice in color & small figural owl
feet at the corners, Joseph Holdcroft, En-
gland, 6" w., 6" h... 3,300
Bread tray, oblong, Napkin patt., woven
napkin design in center in brown & yellow, yellow rope border band, rim embossed "Eat Thy Bread With Thankful-
ness," 15" l.. 413
Bread tray, oblong, Wheat & Basket patt.,
cobalt blue border band embossed

w/"Give Us This Day Our Daily Bread,"
14" l.. 358
Bread tray, oval, Begonia Leaf patt. w/mot-
tled cobalt blue, green, pink & yellow
leaves in center, brown border embossed "Eat Thy Bread With Thankful-
ness," 13" l. 303
Bread tray, oval, Fish patt., low-relief fish in
the center, brown w/green seaweed border trim, border embossed "And Jesus
Broke And Gave Thanks And They Did
Eat," 13 1/2" l. 330
Bread tray, oval, New England Aster patt.,
dark pink blossoms & green leaves on a
cream ground, green border embossed
"Eat To Live Not Live To Eat" 330
Bread tray, oval, Pineapple patt., probably
Wardle & Co., England, 13" l.......................... 275
Bread tray, oval, Wheat patt., brown center,
green leaves & yellow wheat, brown bor-
der band embossed "Eat Thy Bread With
Thankfulness," 13" l. 303
Butter dish, cover & drainer, domed cover,
Shell, Seaweed & Waves patt., in pale
blues, browns & yellow, 19th c....................... 330
Cake stand, on three knob feet, Pond Lily
patt., 9" d.. 165
Cake stand, pedestal base, Pond Lily patt.
in green w/white blossom, pedestal composed of three standing figural storks,
10 1/2" d, 9 1/2" h.. 385
Cake stand, round w/low pedestal, Bird in
Flight patt., large brown bird on a pale
blue pebbled ground, pink blossoms
around rim, Joseph Holdcroft, England,
9 1/2" d.. 220
Candlestick, figural, model of a nude seated
putto beside a tall baluster-form pale blue
candlestick draped w/a pink swag, a shell
at the foot of the figure, on a brown rockwork base, George Jones, England, late
19th c., 10 3/4" h. 660
Center piece, figural, a large wide shallow
bowl w/green interior & wide rolled rim
molded by a band of blue shells, raised
on a leaf-cast pedestal supported by two
winged cupids resting on a shell-molded
round base, Hugo Lonitz & Co., Germany, late 19th c., 16" w., 20" h. (various
professional repairs to high points) 2,475
Chambersticks, footed shell-form triangular
bowl center w/a large ribbed brown socket, a molded classical woman's head at
the base of the C-form upright rim handle, Joseph Holdcroft, England, 6" l.,
1/2" h., pr. 605

Fine George Jones Cheese Dish

Cheese dish, cov., Apple Blossom patt., tall domed cover w/a brown branch handle above a turquoise blue dome decorated w/branches of apple blossoms above a wide band of brown basketweave, basketweave design on flanged base, George Jones, England, late 19th c., 12" h. (ILLUS.)... **2,860**

Large Thos. Forester Cheese Dish

Cheese dish, cov., high domed cover w/branch handle, molded overall w/birds, flowers, leaves & branches in white, yellow, brown & green, flanged rim on base, professional repair on base, Thomas Forester & Sons, England, late 19th c., 11" h. (ILLUS.)................................ **2,200**

Cheese dish, cov., Stilton-type, tall cylindrical cover molded around the side, on the rim of the base & around the cow-form knop w/a band of stiff leaves picked out in shades of green on a pink ground, the interior of the cover & underplate glazed in turquoise, George Jones, England, 1870s, 11 3/8" h. (cows' horns restored, crack in cover)... **5,100**

Very Rare G. Jones Cheese Dish

Cheese dish, cov., Water Lily - King Fisher with Dragonfly patt., tall cylindrical cover w/large water lily leaves in green w/white blossoms & green & brown cattails on a cobalt blue ground, slight domed top w/leaves & a large figural kingfisher finial, brown wicker molded design on base, George Jones, England, minor professional repair to beak, hairline in base, rare, 13 1/2" h. (ILLUS.) **13,750**

Cheese dish, cov., wide cylindrical cover w/flat top, Pansy patt., yellow blossoms on green leafy vines around the sides against a cobalt blue ground, George Jones, England, late 19th c., base 10 1/4" d., overall 7 1/2" h........................... **5,500**

Cheese dish, cov., wide cylindrical cover w/slightly domed top & twig handle, Picket Fence & Floral patt., pink & green blossoms on pale blue ground, George Jones, England, late 19th c., 7 1/2" h. **2,200**

Compote, open, 9" d., low pedestal, Floral & Pinwheel patt., deep red blossoms & brown stems on cream & pale green ground, Samuel Lear, England, late 19th c.. **248**

Victoria Pottery Majolica Compote

Compote, open, 9" d., 5" h., Basketweave & Maple Leaf patt., wide gently fluted shallow bowl w/a turquoise basketweave design & large brown & green leaves, turquoise basketweave pedestal w/green leaves & white blossoms, Victoria Pottery Co. (ILLUS.) **605**

Compote, open, 9 1/2" d., Begonia Leaf patt., unmarked................................. **132**

Compote, open, 10 1/2" d., deep bowl, low pedestal, Tobacco Leaf & Floral Rosette patt.. **209**

Condiment server, four shell-shaped lobes in alternating pink & pale green centered by a shell handle, 9" l..................................... **358**

Creamer & cov. sugar bowl, Bird & Fan patt., blue, brown & pink on a pale yellow ground, S. Fielding & Co., England, late 19th c., pr... **198**

Cup & saucer, Pineapple patt., nice color **275**

Cup & saucer, rounded cup & squared saucer, each molded w/white blossoms & green leaves, bud handle, all on cobalt blue ground, part of the Monkey tea service, George Jones, England **1,550-1,950**

Unique Elephant Majolica Dish

Rare George Jones Game Dish

Dish, cov., figural, a model of a large grey elephant walking & carrying a black trainer & large brown & white howdah on its back, Hugo Lonitz & Co., Germany, late 19th c., 10" l., 9" h. (ILLUS.) 935

Egg server, rounded basket-form frame decorated w/red blossoms & green leaves on a cream ground around the sides, holds six egg cups, S. Fielding & Co., England, late 19th c. (professional repair to base of egg cups) 468

George Jones Game Dish

Game dish, cov., deep oval form, the base molded w/upright green leaves & ferns on a brown ground, yellow rope band around rim centered by a dead game bird in brown & yellow on green ferns on a brown ground, George Jones, England, 11" l. (ILLUS.).. 1,100

Game dish, cov., deep oval form w/brown branch & leaf end handle, the sides molded in relief w/rabbits among green ferns & leaves on a cobalt blue ground, low domed cover molded w/green ferns centered by a large model of a brown quail, George Jones, England, late 19th c., professional repair to bird beak, 11" l. (ILLUS., top of page).................................... 9,350

Humidor, cov., figural, model of a large fat green frog wearing a red smoking jacket, Europe, late 19th c., 6 1/2" h. 468

Humidor, cov., figural, model of a small, long-haired begging dog, 9" h. 440

Ice cream set: one round 16" d. platter & twelve 6 1/2" d. dessert plates; strawberry design on a cream ground w/bow handles, Wedgwood, late 19th c., the set (imperfections).. 633

Jam pot, cov., cylindrical, Strawberry patt., molded green leaves & red berries around the sides, berry finial, Brownfield & Son, England, late 19th c. 143

Jardiniere, a large slightly tapering cylindrical container in cobalt blue w/a molded rim band of green leaves, an oval reserve on the side w/a large pale blue bow at the top & framing a bird perched on a branch, supported around the bottom by three figural caryatids resting on a brown tripartite platform on hoof feet, Joseph Holdcroft, England, late 19th c., 13 1/2" d., 16 1/2" h. (professional repair to one foot & wing tip)................................... 1,925

Jardiniere, figural, modeled w/an eagle w/outstretched wings perched on a branch inclined towards a rabbit crouching in the mouth of its burrow on the opposite side of a large open stump, by Brown-Westhead, Moore & Co., England, signed by painter, ca. 1880, 25" h. (ends of wings & tip of beak restored) 8,400

Rare George Jones Jardiniere

Jardiniere, footed bell-form bowl w/flared yellow rim, the sides in turquoise blue molded w/water lilies, cattails & a bird in shades of green, white, brown & black, George Jones, England, late 19th c., professional hairline repair, 17" d., 15 1/2" h. (ILLUS.).. **6,050**

Jardiniere & underplate, bell-form pot molded w/Neoclassical designs with Gothic arch panels all in pale brown, pale blue, cream w/a cobalt blue rim band, Brownfield & Son, England, late 19th c., 10 1/2" d., 10" h., 2 pcs. **880**

Jardiniere & undertray, the deep rounded body w/gently scalloped rim & small leaf-scrolled side handles molded around the body w/a profusion of ferns, foxgloves & convolvulus on a brown ground, the interior glazed in pink, the undertray molded w/further leaves within a reeded & lobed rim, Mintons, ca. 1869, overall 15 1/2" h., 2 pcs. **9,600**

Unusual Majolica Marmalade Pot

Marmalade pot, cov., Apple Blossom patt., the high domed top w/spoon opening molded w/a brown branch handle & pink blossoms & green leaves on a turquoise ground, the base w/a turquoise ground banded w/brown wicker design & a flanged rim w/further blossoms & leaves, George Jones, England, late 19th c., interior rim chips on rim of cover, 5" h. (ILLUS.)... **2,475**

Model of a cockatoo, naturalistically molded & colored in dark green w/a yellow crest, perched on a green tree stump above rockwork, Minton, Shape No. 1847, ca. 1900, 14 3/8" h. **633**

Mug, Bird in Flight & Water Lily patt., green leaves w/brown & yellow bird on a cobalt blue ground, high relief, great color, 4 1/4" h. **358**

Mug, Picket Fence & Floral patt. **121**

Nut Serving Tray with Squirrel

Nut serving tray, wide, shallow, rounded tray w/large green leaves & brown twigs on a turquoise ground, a figural brown squirrel w/nut seated at the rim, George Jones, England, late 19th c., repair to tail, 10 1/2" w. (ILLUS.).................................... **1,100**

Paperweight, slab-type, rectangular, relief-molded brown owl on branch against a pale green ground, Mayer, late 19th c. **138**

Pitcher, 5 1/2" h., Pineapple patt. **99**

Pitcher, 6" h., Fish on Waves with Shell patt....... **275**

Pitcher, 6 1/2" h., figural, Double Pelican patt., one pelican forms the handle, the other forms the front of the body against green leaves.. **825**

Pitcher, 6 3/4" h., Stork in March patt., brown & white bird on pale blue ground w/cobalt blue rim & base bands, angled branch handle, George Jones, England.... **2,200**

Pitcher, 7" h., Corn patt. **187**

Pitcher, 7" h., Eagle with Rabbit patt., footed w/flat round sides, cobalt blue ground **165**

Pitcher, 7 1/4" h., figural, model of a brown bear w/a drum, great color, Joseph Holdcroft, England, mint...................................... **1,100**

Pitcher, 7 1/4" h., Wheat patt., cylindrical sides molded w/long green leaves & yellow green on a pink ground, ribbon-wrapped brown handle, George Jones, England.. **4,400**

Pitcher, 8" h., Fish patt., flattened round disk sides molded w/pairs of realistic fish on a cobalt blue ground, oval pale blue foot & short neck, angled branch handle, Joseph Holdcroft, England............................. **1,210**

Pitcher, 8 1/2" h., Ram patt., lavender top, great color.. **303**

Pitcher, 8 1/2" h., Sunflower patt., yellow ground.. **143**

Pitcher, 9" h., Bird's Nest patt., branch handle, probably American-made (minor hairline) **440**

Pitcher, 9" h., figural, model of a rooster w/shield on the side reading "Chante Clair Pour La France," Frie Onnaing, France, late 19th c. **660**

Pitcher, 9" h., figural, white swan forms the top of the body w/the neck curving down to form handle, lower ovoid body in cobalt blue w/green leaves, John Bevington, England, late 19th c. **1,100**

Pitcher, 9" h., triangular shape, Owl & Fan patt., yellow ground...................................... **330**

Pitcher, 10" h., figural, model of mother monkey holding her baby, French, late 19th c.. **275**

Pitcher, 10" h., tapering ovoid body, Lily of the Valley, Fern & Rope patt., green & pink on cream ground, lavender rim, Samuel Lear, England, late 19th c. **523**

Pitcher, 10 1/2" h., figural, model of standing pig dressed as waiter, Frie Onnaing, France, late 19th c. **605**

Pitcher, 11" h., figural, model of a seated dog, St. Clement, France, marked "CYPP" on collar, late 19th c. **1,100**

Pitcher, 12" h., Chrysanthemum patt., Avalon Faience mark of the Chesapeake Pottery, Baltimore, Maryland, late 19th c......... **66**

Pitcher, 12 3/4" h., figural, tall model of fish standing on its tail.. 275

Pitcher w/hinged pewter cover, 9 1/2" h., Dogwood patt., mottled brown & green ground 385

Plant stand, model of a tree stump w/four staggered round shelves at the tops of stubby stumps w/three taller in the back & a low one in front, brown tree back decoration w/molded green leaves, late 19th c., 15 1/2" h.. 743

Plate, 7 1/4" d., Strawberry & Vine patt., looped vine border, cobalt blue ground 176

Plate, 7 3/4" d., Strawberry patt., large green leaves w/pink blossoms & berries on a brown ground 154

Plate, 8 1/2" d., Fish & Daisy patt., cobalt blue ground, brown rim band, Joseph Holdcroft, England, late 19th c. 440

Plate, 8 3/4" d., Bellflower patt., pink & white blossoms & green leaves on a cobalt blue ground.. 248

Plate, 8 3/4" d., lightly scalloped rim, Floral & Butterfly patt., leafy vines on a brown ground 154

Plate, 9" d., Pineapple patt., George Jones, England, late 19th c. (very minor rim glaze nick).. 605

Plate, 9" d., Pond Lily patt., overlapping leaves & floral center, George Jones, England, late 19th c. 495

Plate, 9" d., Summer Sun patt., sun face molded in the center surrounded by a bird, butterfly & grapes, in golden yellows & brown 275

Plate, 9" l., model of a wide flattened fish, natural colors.. 176

Plate, 9 1/2" d., Fern & Floral patt., cobalt blue ground & pink Greek key border band 248

Plate, 10" d., large bright pink flowers on green leafy stems against a cobalt blue ground, great color 220

Plates, 8 1/2" d., Overlapping Begonia Leaf patt., dark green w/dark pink borders, set of 4 605

Platter, 11" d., round, molded in the center w/a small cluster of overlapping pink shells on a white ground, orange border band & pink coral edge handles..................... 413

Platter, 11" l., oblong w/scalloped rim, Dog & Doghouse patt., dark brown, green & cream 275

Platter, 12 3/4" l., rectangular w/rounded corners, Tobacco Leaf & Rosette patt., Joseph Holdcroft, England, late 19th c. 275

Platter, 13" l., oval, molded flowers & berries on a pale blue ground around the sides, pink ribbon border & bow handles, mottled dark green center, George Jones, England (hairline).. 1,980

Platter, 13 1/2" l., oval, Bamboo & Fern patt., cobalt blue center, Wardle & Co., England, late 19th c. (scratches in center) 303

Salt dip, figural, large green & pink shell supported atop a green dolphin on an oval foot, 4 3/4" h.. 374

George Jones Sardine Dish

Sardine dish, cov., a rectangular upswept basketweave raft base in mottled green & brown, the rectangular basketweave box w/the cover molded in full relief w/large grey & white fish on green & pink shells & grass, George Jones, England, late 19th c., 9 1/4" l. (ILLUS.) 2,090

Sauce dish, Strawberry patt., round, w/scalloped rim molded w/pink blossoms, green leaves on turquoise ground in sides, George Jones, England, 5" d.............. 440

Strawberry server, Napkin & Strawberry patt., oblong, shallow dish molded w/a creamy napkin & green strawberry leaves, inset at each end, one holding the small pink w/green leaves creamer, the other the matching open sugar, George Jones, England, 15" l., the set 1,430

Strawberry server, round dish w/attached small round cream & sugar wells, embossed strawberry leaves & blossoms, turquoise ground trimmed in yellow, green, brown & pink, England, 19th c., 10" d. 358

Strawberry spoon, green w/pink blossom in bowl & on handle, George Jones, England, 7 1/2" l. 605

Strawberry spoon, green w/pink blossom in pierced bowl, George Jones, England, 4" l. (professional repair to handle)................ 715

Sweet meat dish, figural, modeled as a young girl seated on the side of a rowboat, a fishing net draped along the side, Europe, 19th c., 9" l., 7" h. 385

Syrup pitcher w/hinged pewter cover, Blackberry patt., Edwin Bennett Pottery, Baltimore, Maryland, late 19th c. 165

Syrup pitcher w/hinged pewter cover, Floral & Basket patt., great color, 4 3/4" h................ 385

Syrup pitcher w/hinged pewter cover, Heron patt., Edwin Bennett Pottery, Baltimore, Maryland, late 19th c. 165

Syrup pitcher w/hinged pewter cover, molded floral design, Edwin Bennett Pottery, Baltimore, Maryland, late 19th c. 154

Syrup pitcher w/hinged pewter cover, Sunflower patt., Edwin Bennett Pottery, Baltimore, Maryland, late 19th c. 165

Tea set: cov. teapot, open sugar & creamer, water server, milk pitcher, tray & two cups & saucers; embossed stylized Oriental design of pink blossoms & green leaves among brown angular lines on a cream ground, brown bamboo-form handles, Brownhills Pottery Co., England, late 19th c., the set.. 440

Teapot, cov., Blackberry patt., upright
square shape, blackberries & leaves embossed in side panels on a pale green
ground, figural blackberry finial, 6 1/2" h. **358**
Teapot, cov., spherical body w/large applied
green leaves & white blossoms on a cobalt blue ground, brown branch spout,
figural brown monkey handle, George
Jones, England, 9 1/4" l., 6" h. (repair to
head of monkey, rim of cover & spout) **1,925**

Fine Butterfly & Orchid Tray

Tray, oval, Butterfly & Orchid patt., large
white, pink & green blossoms & green
leaves & large black & brown butterflies
against a dark brown ground, George
Jones, England, late 19th c., 11" l.
(ILLUS.)... **2,420**
Tray, rectangular w/rounded corners, Leaf
patt., molded oak leaf & acorn end handles, mottled dark green, pink & yellow
w/cobalt blue accents, 10" l. **303**
Tureen, cov., figural, long, narrow, oval
brown basket-form base molded on the
top w/a large realistic mackerel on a bed
of green leaves & ferns, George Jones,
England, late 19th c., 19" l. **2,420**

Very Rare Bear Umbrella Stand

Umbrella stand, figural, a model of a large
standing brown bear snarling & holding a
large wooden log bar, molded leafy
branches form the square rockwork
base, Brownfield & Son, England, late

19th c., very rare, professional repair to
oak leaves & feet, 34" h. (ILLUS.) **11,000**

Extremely Rare Umbrella Stand

Umbrella stand, figural, unique design of a
standing dark-skinned bearded man
wearing an Eskimo outfit & holding a
baby seal, on an oblong white & grey ice-
berg base, in shades of black, brown,
grey & white, extremely rare, T.C. Brown,
Westhead, Moore & Co., England, late
19th c., near mint, 39" h. (ILLUS.) **22,000**
Vase, 7" h., baluster-form body w/flaring
rim, angled branch handles, brown
ground molded w/large pink morning glory blossoms & green leafy vines, Brown-
field & Son, England, late 19th c.................... **303**

European Figural Majolica Vases

Vases, 12 1/2" h., figural, Art Nouveau style,
a large cylindrical vase in shaded grey,

blue & pink topped by a ring of pink blossoms w/green vines looping down the sides, one w/a young girl in peasant costume reaching up w/large poppy blossoms beside her, the other w/a young boy in peasant costume holding a basket & standing near a large pink daisy-like blossom, Europe, late 19th c., very minor nick, pr. (ILLUS.)... **440**

Wall pocket, a long cartouche-form backplate in brown molded w/red & green Christmas holly, a long yellow wicker basket holder at the center, T.C. Brown, Westhead, Moore & Co., England, late 19th c., 10 1/2" l. **660**

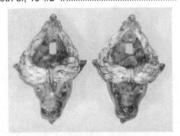

Unusual Bull's Head Wall Pockets

Wall pockets, figural, each modeled as a brown bull's head w/woven green leaf wreath looping up to form the pointed top, browns & greens w/cobalt blue accents, Thomas Sergent, late 19th c., 5 3/4" l., pr. (ILLUS.)..................................... **1,375**

Wall pockets, Palissy Ware, molded as brown branches of green oak leaves & acorns, each w/a model of a lizard on the front, Thomas Sergent, 12" l., pr. (one w/professional repair to rim, other w/repair to lizard's head)..................................... **2,530**

Marblehead

This pottery was organized in 1904 by Dr. Herbert J. Hall as a therapeutic aid to patients in a sanitarium he ran in Marblehead, Massachusetts. It was later separated from the sanitarium and directed by Arthur E. Baggs, a fine artist and designer, who bought out the factory in 1916 and operated it until its closing in 1936. Most wares were hand-thrown and decorated and carry the company mark of a stylized sailing vessel flanked by the letters "M" and "P."

Marblehead Mark

Book ends, square, upright, slant-fronted form, the face incised w/panels enclosing a view of ships under full sail, a different

view on each, midnight blue matte glaze, impressed mark & paper label, ca. 1916, 5 3/8" h., pr. (hairline) **$690**

Book ends, upright, square, wedge-shaped design, the front of each embossed w/a different sailing ship scene in green & orange on a blue ground, stamped mark, 5 1/2" w., 5 1/2" h., pr. (some running glaze & back fleck on one, invisible restoration to corner of other)................................. **880**

Marblehead Two-color Bowl

Bowl, 2 1/2" h., wide squatty flaring form w/a wide tapered shoulder & a wide flat mouth, molded around the shoulder w/a triangular linear design, matte brown on a green ground, impressed mark, by Hannah Tutt, early 20th c. (ILLUS.)............ **1,725**

Bowl, 8" d., 3 3/4" h., a small footring supporting a deep gently flaring bowl w/a widely flaring & flattened rim, lightly molded lotus design on the exterior, dark blue matte glaze on the exterior & a light blue semi-matte interior glaze, stamped mark.. **358**

Marblehead Lotus Leaf Bowl

Bowl, 8 1/4" d., 3 1/4" h., a small footring supporting a deep rounded bowl w/molded overlapping lotus leaves below the widely flaring flattened rim, speckled blue glaze, lighter speckled blue interior, impressed mark, minute rim fleck (ILLUS.)....... **402**

[image of bowl]

Pink-glazed Marblehead Bowl

Bowl, 8 3/4" d., 3" h., small round base below widely flaring slightly rounded sides w/a wide flat rim, speckled dark pink matte glazed exterior & lighter pink interior, unmarked (ILLUS.) **431**

Marblehead Squatty Bowl

Bowl, 8 3/4" d., 4" h., wide rounded incurved sides to a wide flat mouth, speckled matte brown glaze on exterior, celadon green & oxblood glossy interior glaze, stamped mark (ILLUS.)....................... **805**

Bowl-vase, squatty spherical form w/a closed rim, overall dark blue semi-matte glaze, impressed mark, 5" d., 3 1/4" h. **495**

Bowl-Vase with Geometric Band

Bowl-vase, bulbous tapering form w/a wide flat mouth, carved around the top w/a geometric block design in dark brown against a matte green speckled ground, by Arthur Baggs, one-inch bruise, small rim hairline, illustrated in Paul Evans pottery book, marked, 5" d., 3 3/4" h. (ILLUS.)....................... **6,325**

Bowl-vase, a wide bulbous upper body w/wide closed rim, tapering sharply to a cylindrical base, overall lavender matte glaze, impressed mark, 5 1/2" d.................... **770**

Bowl-vase, wide gently flaring rounded cylindrical form w/a wide closed rim, matte green ground, incised w/a wide rim band in darker green of stylized blossoms w/twisted stems forming panels around the sides, marked & artist-initialed, ca. 1916, 6 1/2" d., 4 3/4" h. **6,900**

Bowl-vase, wide squatty spherical form tapering to a closed rim, fine speckled ochre matte glaze, impressed mark, 6 1/2" d., 5" h.. **1,265**

Flaring Marblehead Bowl-Vase

Bowl-vase, cylindrical waisted lower body below widely flaring sides w/a flat rim, yellow matte exterior & teal green matte interior, impressed mark, 8 1/2" d., 5" h. (ILLUS.).. **518**

Chamberstick, dished round base centered by a tall slender shaft w/a flaring cupped socket, a long loop handle from the upper shaft to the base, smooth dark green matte glaze, impressed mark, 5" d., 8 1/2" h.. **550**

Marblehead Squatty Humidor

Humidor, cov., squatty bulbous form w/incurved low sides & inset cover w/large knob handle, the cover painted w/a narrow ochre band of leaves, dark blue matte ground, stamped mark, 6" d., 4" h. (ILLUS.).. **1,750**

Vase, 3" h., 4" d., bulbous nearly spherical lower body w/a rounded shoulder centering a wide, swelled cylindrical neck w/closed rim, incised around the body w/four stylized geometric panels in dark olive brown against a green ground, marked, ca. 1908 (imperfection in the making) **1,265**

Vase, 3" h., 4 1/4" d., low, squatty, wide, bulbous form tapering sharply to a rolled rim, ringed sides, smooth green & charcoal matte glaze, incised "winged M" mark.. **440**

Vase, 3 1/2" h., miniature, small, wide, bulbous, ovoid body tapering to a short flared neck, matte greyish green ground w/a linear band at the rim connecting eight stylized trees around the sides in brown matte glaze w/round blue foliage, by Hannah Tutt, marked, ca. 1912 .... **6,900**

Vase, 3 1/2" h., miniature, small, wide, slightly tapering cylindrical form w/a closed rim, unusual very dark blue matte glaze, impressed mark................................... **385**

Vase, 3 1/2" h., 3 1/2" d., miniature, simple ovoid body tapering slightly to a wide flat mouth, speckled grey ground painted around the rim w/a stylized band of two-tone greyish blue flying geese, stamped ship mark.. **1,688**

Miniature Blue Marblehead Vase

Vase, 3 3/4" h., miniature, swelled cylindrical form tapering slightly to a wide flat mouth, speckled matte blue glaze, impressed mark (ILLUS.)..................................... **460**

Vase, 4" h., 3 1/4" d., cylindrical w/a slightly rounded base, impressed around the rim w/a band of stylized flowers in red w/green leaves on a dark blue ground, impressed mark **1,980**

Vase, 4" h., 4" d., bulbous base tapering to a wide, short cylindrical neck, matte deep blue ground w/incised rim band & stylized geometric border on neck in dark green, by Arthur Baggs, factory mark & artist-initialed **2,415**

Vase, 4 3/8" h., 3 7/8" d., a wide mouth on a cylindrical body, green ground decorated w/a blue linear band at the rim w/eight repeating stylized flowers w/multiple trailing stems in two shades of matte blue, by Hannah Tutt, marks & artist-signed, ca. 1912.. **4,888**

Vase, 5" h., cylindrical w/rounded base & shoulder w/a short rolled rim, medium blue semi-gloss glaze, cipher & paper label.. **259**

Vase, 5" h., small footring supporting a widely flaring trumpet-form body, overall brown matte glaze, impressed mark **550**

Vase, 5" h., wide baluster form w/a wide, short flaring neck, overall dark matte blue glaze, impressed mark (ILLUS., top of next column).. **345**

Vase, 5" h., 3 1/4" d., swelled cylindrical body w/a wide, flat rim, "watermelon rind" glaze, slightly iridescent finish on a textured ground in rich green, stamped mark & paper label, ca. 1908................................. **1,093**

Dark Blue Marblehead Vase

Vase, 5" h., 3 3/4" d., tapering ovoid body w/a wide flat mouth, embossed around the rim w/a repeated band of stylized fruit & leaves in browns & blue, on a speckled grey ground, by Hannah Tutt, impressed mark... **1,430**

Vase, 5 1/8" h., 3 1/4" d., a wide, flat mouth on a swelled tapering cylindrical body, grey ground decorated w/a blue linear rim band w/five repeating stylized flowers w/trailing stems in three shades of matte blue, by Hannah Tutt, marked & artist-signed, ca. 1912 (rim hairlines)................... **1,150**

Vase, 5 1/4" h., 3 3/4" d., tapering ovoid gourd form w/a narrow shoulder to a small flat mouth, incised w/four stylized geometric panels in dark green, by Hannah Tutt, marked & artist-signed............. **19,550**

Vase, 5 1/2" d., a wide, bulbous baluster-form body w/the wide shoulder tapering slightly to a wide flat mouth, dark blue matte glaze, impressed mark (nearly invisible hairline at rim)...................................... **231**

Marblehead Vase with Grapevine

Vase, 5 1/2" h., a wide, flat mouth on a gently tapering ovoid body, decorated w/a band of blue & light green grapevines around the top on a grey ground, chip in base, impressed mark (ILLUS.).................. **1,380**

Marblehead Vase with Brown Glaze

Vase, 5 1/2" h., ovoid body tapering to a widely flaring rim, brown speckled matte glaze, impressed mark, small bruise on rim (ILLUS.) **575**

Vase, 5 1/2" h., ovoid body w/wide, flat mouth, matte blue-grey glaze, early 20th c., impressed mark (crazing) **345**

Vase, 5 1/2" h., 5" d., short cylindrical bottom below widely flaring flat sides, dark blue matte exterior glaze, lighter blue interior, stamped ship mark & paper label **523**

Small Marblehead Bud Vase

Vase, 6" h., bud-type, wide, thick, round, flaring foot tapering to a tall, slender cylindrical body, overall deep rose glaze (ILLUS.) **345**

Vase, 6" h., wide ovoid body tapering to a short flared rim, matte ochre ground decorated w/five tall panels painted w/blueberries & leaves in matte green & matte blue, each panel framed in dark ochre matte glaze, by Hannah Tutt, marked & artist-signed **12,650**

Vase, 6 5/8" h., bulbous octagonal paneled body w/horizontal ribbing, wide mouth, aqua semi-gloss glaze, artist-initialed "A - B - 26," ca. 1926, impressed mark **230**

Unique and Rare Marblehead Vase

Vase, 6 3/4" h., 4" d., simple ovoid form w/a wide, flat mouth, decorated w/triple clusters of tall stylized flowers around the sides w/a lattice-like rim band, in shades of umber, black & cream on a speckled matte green ground, by Hannah Tutt, impressed mark & incised artist mark (ILLUS.) **120,750**

Marblehead Vase with Trees & Berries

Vase, 7" h., gently swelled cylindrical form w/a wide flat rim, painted w/an Arts & Crafts band of tall stylized trees in dark green & brown w/dark red berries against a dark blue ground, impressed mark, original paper label, some minor glaze crawling (ILLUS.) **6,600**

Fine Marblehead Sea Horse Vase

Vase, 7" h., slightly tapering cylindrical form w/a rounded bottom & wide flat rim, decorated around the top w/five delicately painted sea horses & seaweed in shades of blue against a grey ground, by Hanna Tutt, impressed mark (ILLUS.) **11,500**

Simple Ovoid Marblehead Vase

Vase, 8 3/4" h., 5" d., simple ovoid body tapering to a wide, flat mouth, overall smooth matte green glaze, impressed mark (ILLUS.) **1,150**

Vase, 9" h., tall slender simple waisted form, overall lavender matte glaze, impressed mark (faint hairline in rim) **330**

Marblehead Vase with Quatrefoils

Vase, 9" h., 3 3/4" d., tall cylindrical form w/rounded base edge & wide closed rim, incised around the rim w/a band of quatrefoils atop long bands down the sides, dark & lighter green mottled matte glaze, impressed & incised marks (ILLUS.) **9,200**

Vase, 9" h., 5 1/2" d., cylindrical body rounded at the base & at the closed rim, decorated w/stylized upright poppies around the sides w/the arched leaves forming panels around the body, in three shades of matte olive green, two hair-

lines from rim, stamped mark (ILLUS., top of page) **10,350**

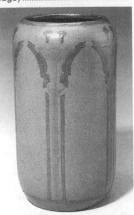

Rare Marblehead Vase with Poppies

Vase, 9 3/4" h., a rounded base edge on the tall gently tapering cylindrical body w/a flat rim, matte green ground incised & surface-painted w/a tapering stalk of stylized flowers in brown matte glaze, marked & artist-initialed, ca. 1912 .... **21,850**

Wall plaque, rectangular, w/profile portrait of an Egyptian in relief, glossy turquoise glaze, early 20th c., impressed mark & paper label, 7 1/2" h., 4 5/8" w. (crazing, minor wear) **546**

Marblehead Ringed Wall Pocket

Wall pocket, tapering conical form w/ringed design, flaring ruffled rim w/hanging hole, dark matte blue glaze, stilt pulls on rim, 4 1/4" w., 8 1/2" h. (ILLUS.) **173**

Wall pocket, widely flaring rounded trumpet form, brown speckled matte exterior glaze, smooth ivory interior glaze, paper label, 7" w., 6" h. (bruise at rim) **450**

Martin Brothers

Martin Brothers Mark

Martinware, the term used for this pottery, dates from 1873 and is the product of the Martin brothers—Robert, Wallace, Edwin, Walter and Charles—often considered the first British studio potters. From first to final stages, their hand-thrown pottery was completely the work of the team. The early wares may be simple and conventional, but the Martin brothers built up their reputation by producing ornately engraved, incised or carved designs as well as rather bizarre figural wares. The amusing face-jugs are considered some of their finest work. After 1910, the work of the pottery declined and can be considered finished by 1915, though some attempts were made to fire pottery as late as the 1920s.

Martin Brothers Gargoyle Dish

Dish, figural, the oblong form w/a crouching, grinning gargoyle at one end, the body forming the open dish composed of two tiered dishes, the neck & body w/fine incised lines to resemble hair, tan unglazed clay, very small edge nicks, signed "Martin Bros. - London & Southall - 4-1894," 5 1/2" l., 2 3/4" h. (ILLUS.) **$1,870**

Martin Brothers Bird Jar on Base

Jar, cov., figural, modeled as a large comical bird w/a rounded oversized head w/droopy beak & sleepy eyes, bulbous body & thick legs w/wide webbed feet, on a round platform base, dark brown, black & tan glazing, firing crack in body secured at factory w/beeswax, incised "R.W. Martin - London & Southall," 5 1/2" w., 11 1/2" h. (ILLUS.) **10,450**

Martin Brothers Bird Jar

Jar, cov., modeled as a grotesque bird w/a bulbous oversized head w/large beak & sleepy expression, feathers in green, light blue & black, marked "Martin Bros - London + Southall - 6-1897," oval base mounted on oval ebonized wooden base, 1897, 10" h. (ILLUS.) **13,500**
Paperweight, figural flying lizard, glazed in black, green & beige, partially obscured mark "Martin Bros - London," 2 1/4 x 4" (restoration to small points) **1,125**
Pitcher, jug-form, 8" h., 7" w., a spherical body molded in relief on each side w/a round smiling face w/curly molded hair, short cylindrical neck w/pinched spout at one side of the top, loop handle from neck rim to shoulder, glazed in dark & warm browns, incised "R.W. Martin Bros. - London - Southall," 1870-80 .... **1,265**

Martin Brothers Decorated Pitcher

Pitcher, 9" h., salt-glazed stoneware, a footed ovoid body tapering to a high widely flaring & pinched neck, D-form strap handle, finely incised & decorated w/birds nestled amid branches, glazed in shades of brown, green & rust against a blue striped ground, marked "6-1-2 - 1-8-50 - Martin Bros London & Southall," 1902 (ILLUS.)... **1,500-2,000**

Pitcher, jug-type, 9 3/4" h., ovoid body w/swelled shoulder under D-form handle, short cylindrical neck w/slightly flared rim & small pinched spout, body incised w/sea reptiles in indigo & amber, mark partially obscured by paper label (fleck to rim) **1,800**

Vase, 10 1/4" h., 6" d., wide ovoid body w/a short cylindrical neck, incised overall w/a design of stylized scrolling leafy vines & blossoms in sand, dark & light brown, marked "27.3.84 - R.W. Martin & Bros. - London & Southall," 1884............................ **1,045**

Massier (Clement)

Massier Mark

Clement Massier was a French artist potter who worked in the late 19th and early 20th centuries creating exquisite earthenware items with lustre decoration.

Charger, round, slightly dished form, overall Mediterranean bay scene w/large pine trees in the right foreground, fine lustred gold on burgundy glazes, impressed "CLEMENT MASSIER - GOLFE JUAN," 13" d. **$1,430**

Massier Vase with Unusual Design

Vase, 3 7/8" h., simple ovoid form w/flat rim, clam & seaweed decoration in brilliant metallic glaze, marked "C.M. Golfe Juan A.M." (ILLUS.) **532**

Vase, 6 3/4" h., 2 1/2" d., bud-type, bottle-shaped, bulbous ovoid body tapering to a very tall slender "stick" neck, decorated w/a design of mistletoe in silky red, gold & green iridescent glaze, unmarked.............. **220**

Vase, 8 3/4" h., baluster-shaped, w/short flaring neck, glossy ruby glaze w/splotch-

es of leaf-like designs, incised "J. Massier, Vallavris, France - 2008/6" (professional repair to rim) **179**

McCoy

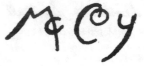

McCoy Mark

Collectors are now seeking the art wares of two McCoy potteries. One was founded in Roseville, Ohio, in the late 19th century as the J.W. McCoy Pottery, subsequently becoming Brush-McCoy Pottery Co., later Brush Pottery. The other was also founded in Roseville in 1910 as Nelson McCoy Sanitary Stoneware Co., later becoming Nelson McCoy Pottery. In 1967 the pottery was sold to D.T. Chase of the Mount Clemens Pottery Co., who sold his interest to the Lancaster Colony Corp. in 1974. The pottery shop closed in 1985. Cookie jars are especially collectible today.

A helpful reference book is The Collector's Encyclopedia of McCoy Pottery, by the Huxfords (Collector Books), and McCoy Cookie Jars From the First to the Latest, by Harold Nichols (Nichols Publishing, 1987).

Book ends, decorated w/swallows, ca. 1956, 5 1/2 x 6"..................................... **$200-250**

Book ends, model of violin, ca. 1959, 10" h., pr... **100-150**

Cache pot, double w/applied bird, ca. 1949, 10 1/2" l. **35-45**

Astronaut Cookie Jar

Cookie jar, Astronaut, 1963, good gold trim (ILLUS.).. **750**

Cookie jar, Bunch of Bananas, ca. 1948.. **125-150**

Chipmunk Cookie Jar

Cookie jar, Chipmunk, ca. 1960 (ILLUS.).. **100-125**
Cookie jar, Christmas Tree, ca. 1959 ..... **800-1,000**
Cookie jar, Corn (ear of corn), ca. 1958..... **150-175**

Freddie the Gleep Cookie Jar

Cookie jar, Freddie the Gleep, 1974
(ILLUS.).. **475**
Cookie jar, Garbage Can, ca. 1978 .... **30-40**
Cookie jar, heart-shaped, Hobnail line, ca.
1940... **400-550**
Cookie jar, Hobby Horse, ca. 1948............. **100-150**

Indian Head Cookie Jar

Cookie jar, Indian Head, ca. 1954
(ILLUS.)... **325-425**

Two Kittens in a Basket Cookie Jar

Cookie jar, Kittens in a Basket, ca. 1950s
(ILLUS.).. **600-700**

Koala Bear Cookie Jar

Cookie jar, Koala Bear, ca. 1983 (ILLUS.) ... **85-100**
Cookie jar, Mr. & Mrs. Owl, ca. 1952 .... **75-95**
Cookie jar, Teepee, 1956-59 .... **350**
Cookie jar, Tomato, ca. 1964 .... **60-70**

Yellow Mouse Cookie Jar

Cookie jar, Yellow Mouse, ca. 1978
(ILLUS.).. **35-45**
Figurine, head of witch, ca. early 1940s,
3" h... **400-600**
Iced tea server, El Rancho Bar-B-Que
line, ca. 1960, 11 1/2" h........................... **250-300**
Jardiniere, swallows decoration, ca. late
1930s, 7" h. **90-125**
Jardiniere, fish decoration, ca. 1958,
7 1/2" h... **350-400**

Leaves & Berries Jardiniere & Pedestal

Jardiniere & pedestal base, Leaves & Berries design, ca. 1930s, overall 21" h., 2 pcs. (ILLUS.)... **250-350**

Sand Butterfly Jardiniere & Pedestal

Jardiniere & pedestal base, sand butterfly decoration, shaded brown & green ground, overall 21" h., 2 pc. (ILLUS.).... **250-350**

Ring Design Jardiniere & Pedestal

Jardiniere & pedestal base, ring design, ca. 1930s, overall 29" h., 2 pcs. (ILLUS.) **450-550**
Lamp w/original shade, model of pair of cowboy boots base, original shade, ca. 1956.. **150-200**

Model of Angelfish

Model of angelfish, aqua, ca. early 1940s, Cope design, 6" h. (ILLUS.).................... **300-400**
Model of cat, ca. 1940s, 3" h. **300-400**

Large Oil Jar

Oil jar, bulbous ovoid body w/slightly flaring rim, angled shoulder handles, shaded blue, ca. 1930s, 15" h. (ILLUS.).............. **250-300**

Large Oil Jar

Oil jar, bulbous ovoid body w/slightly flaring rim, angled shoulder handles, red sponged glaze, 18" h. (ILLUS.)............... **300-400**

Pitcher, embossed w/parading ducks, ca.
   1930s, 4 pt. **90-125**
Pitcher, 7" h., Donkey, marked "NM," early
   1940s **250-300**
Pitcher, 10" h., Butterfly line........................ **150-225**
Pitcher-vase, 7" h., figural parrot, ca.
   1952 .... **150-200**

Rare Madonna Planter

Planter, figural, Madonna, white, ca. 1960s,
   rare, 6" h. (ILLUS.) **200-250**
Planter, model of baby scale, ca. 1954,
   5 x 5 1/2" **60-75**
Planter, model of backward bird, ca. early
   1940s, 4" h.. **60-70**

Figural Bear Planter

Planter, model of bear w/ball, yellow w/black
   trim, red ball, 5 1/2 x 7" (ILLUS.)............ **100-125**
Planter, model of carriage w/umbrella, ca.
   1955, 8 x 9"... **150-200**
Planter, model of Cope monkey head,
   5 1/2" h. **100-200**

Fish Planter

Planter, model of fish, green, ca. 1955,
   7 x 12" (ILLUS.) **1,000-1,200**
Planter, model of lemon, ca. 1953,
   5 x 6 1/2"... **790-110**
Planter, model of Liberty Bell, cold painted
   black bell, base embossed "4th July
   1776," 8 1/4 x 10" **200-350**
Planter, model of pomegranate, ca. 1953,
   5 x 6 1/2"... **200-250**
Planter, model of rooster on wheel of
   wheelbarrow, ca. 1955, 10 1/2" l. **100-125**
Planter, model of snowman, ca. 1940s,
   4 x 6"... **60-75**
Planter, model of stork, ca. 1956, blue &
   pink, 7 x 7 1/2" **60-75**
Planter, model of "stretch" dachshund,
   8 1/4" l. **175-225**
Planter, model of trolley car, ca. 1954,
   3 3/4 x 7"... **50-60**
Planter, model of wagon wheel, ca. 1954,
   8" h... **30-40**
Planter, Plow Boy, ca. 1955, 7 x 8" **100-125**
Planter, rectangular, relief-molded golf
   scene, ca. 1957, 4 x 6" **150-200**
Planting dish, model of swan, ca. 1955,
   10 1/2" l. **350-400**
Planting dish, rectangular, front w/five relief-
   molded Scottie dog heads, white, brown
   & green, ca. 1949, 8" l. **50-60**
Platter, 14" l., Butterfly line, ca.
   1940s... **250-600**

Porch Jar

Porch jar, wide tapering cylindrical body
   w/ribbed base, embossed leaf & berry
   decoration below rim, green, marked
   "NM," ca. 1940s, 9 1/2 x 11" (ILLUS.)... **200-250**
Spoon rest, Butterfly line, ca. 1953,
   4 x 7 1/2"... **90-125**
Sprinkler, model of turtle, green w/yellow
   trim, ca. 1950, 5 1/2 x 10" **80-100**
Tea set: cov. teapot, creamer & open sugar
   bowl; Pine Cone patt., ca. 1946,
   3 pcs. **75-100**
TV lamp, model of fireplace, ca. 1950s,
   6 x 9" **75-100**

Umbrella Stand with Leaf Design

Umbrella stand, cylindrical w/applied handles, ribbed panels alternating w/embossed leaf design panels, glossy brown glaze, ca. 1940s, 19" h. (ILLUS.) **250-350**

Vase, 6" h., footed, heart-shape w/embossed roses, ca. 1940s **60-80**

Vase, 6" h., Hobnail line, Castlegate shape, ca. early 1940s............................. **150-200**

Vase, 6 1/2" h., figural tulip, ca. 1953......... **100-125**

Vase, 8" h., figural chrysanthemum, ca. 1950.. **100-125**

Vase, 8" h., footed bulbous base w/trumpet-form neck & scrolled handles, embossed peacock decoration, ca. 1948..................... **40-60**

Vase, 8 1/4" h., figural magnolia, pink, white, brown & green, ca. 1953............. **150-175**

Vase, 8 1/2" h., figural wide lily-form, white, brown & green, ca. 1956 .... **350-400**

Fawn Vase

Vase, 9" h., boot-shaped w/figural fawn & foliage, chartreuse w/green, ca. 1954 (ILLUS.)... **100-125**

Vase, 9" h. or 10" h., figural lizard handles... **350-500**

Vase, 10" h., 13 1/2" w., Blades of Grass, fan-shaped... **250-350**

Vase, 12" h., strap, double handled, ca. 1947 .... **80-110**

Vase, 14" h., Antique Curio line, ca. 1962 .... **75-100**

Vase, 14" h., figural seated cat, ca. 1960.. **200-250**

Vase, 14 1/2" h., Tall Fan, ca. 1954 .... **150-200**

Wall pocket, Butterfly line, marked "NM," ca. 1940s, 6 x 7" **250-600**

Wall pocket, figural, clown, white w/red & black trim, ca. 1940s, 8" l. **100-150**

Wall pocket, model of apple, ca. early 1950s, 6 x 7" **60-70**

Wall pocket, model of bellows, ca. mid-1950s, 9 1/2" l. **90-110**

Wall pocket, model of bird bath, late 1940s, 5 x 6 1/2".. **90-110**

Wall pocket, model of cuckoo clock, plus chains & weights, ca. mid-1950s, 8" l. .. **125-200**

Wall pocket, model of fan, blue, mid-1950s, 8 x 8 1/2".. **75-90**

Wall pocket, model of lovebirds on trivet, ca. early 1950s, 8 1/2" l. **75-90**

Wall pocket, model of pear, ca. early 1950s, 6 x 7"... **70-85**

Meissen

Meissen Mark

The secret of true hard paste porcelain, known long before to the Chinese, was "discovered" accidentally in Meissen, Germany by J.F. Bottger, an alchemist working with E.W. Tschirnhausen. The first European true porcelain was made in the Meissen Porcelain Works, organized about 1709. Meissen marks have been widely copied by other factories. Some pieces listed here are recent.

Beakers, covers & underplates, the tall slightly tapering cylindrical beaker flanked by gold loop handles, the yellow ground decorated w/reserves of harbor scenes w/merchants in conversation before boats & ships within gilt quatrefoil cartouches, the lower domed cover w/knob finial & similar reserves, decorated gilt rim bands, matching decor on the underplate, late 19th c., blue crossed swords mark & various incised & impressed marks, the underplates 5 5/8" d., two sets **$2,300**

Candlestick, Blue Onion patt., domed stepped foot tapering to the ringed & baluster-form standard below the cylindrical candle socket, blue crossed swords mark, 19th c., 9" h. **413**

Candlesticks, Rococo style, the foliate nozzle & drip pan on a scroll-molded stem encrusted w/flowers & applied w/paired putti each holding an attribute of a different season, the rocaille-molded footed base painted w/scattered flower sprigs, mid to late 19th c., blue crossed swords marks, numbered, after a model by Leuteritz, 13 1/8" h., pr. **2,760**

Centerpiece, Rococo-style, the deep flaring oblong bowl w/a reticulated scroll border above a wide band of encrusted floral garland in pastel colors & gilt, the bottom of the bowl molded as a shell raised on a scrolling palm tree stem similarly decorated & applied w/large figures of an amorous 18th c. couple, on a tall tapering round rocaille-molded base w/gilt trim, ca. 1850, blue crossed swords mark & numbers, modeled by Leuteritz, 19 1/8" h. **4,600**

Compote, three-tier, blue floral decorated, the figure of a female flower seller mounted at the top of the graduated dishes each w/a reticulated basketweave rim, late 19th - early 20th c., 20 3/4" h. **1,380**

Compote, open, 12" h., figural, the figures of two nude youths encircle the stump stem set upon an applied-floral rocky base, supporting a double-handled bowl decorated w/colored applied florals around the exterior & painted decoration on the interior, 19th c. **1,100**

Dishes, figural, each w/a shaped oblong base supporting a reclining male or female figure in 18th c. attire beside a fluted, flaring low oblong dish decorated in the Blue Onion patt., late 19th c., 12 1/2" l., pr. **1,840**

Figure group, a winged Cupid standing & holding a disc-form birdbath sideways w/a group of birds applied to it, on a cylindrical swirled scroll-molded pedestal base, polychrome & gilt trim, marked, late 19th c. (minor chip) **1,495**

Figure group, baby w/a dog, modeled as a child lying on a plaid-covered daybed holding a rattle out to a spaniel standing beside the bed, the child half-naked w/a ribbon-tied cap & shirt over the upper body, on a rectangular molded base w/canted corners & a blue & gilt rim band of egg-and-dart, late 19th - early 20th c., blue crossed swords & line mark, numbered, modeled after M.F. Acier, 7 1/2" h. **2,760**

Figure group, modeled as allegorical female figures set on an oval base, one holding a ribbon at the wings of Cupid, the other feeding doves, blue crossed swords mark, 19th c., 12" h. **5,175**

Figure group, modeled as four children in 18th c. costume at play, alternating boy & girl, playing ring-around-the-rosie about a tall leafy tree, the oval base molded w/gilt rocaille scrolls & applied w/flowers & foliage, late 19th c., blue crossed swords mark & numbers, 11 1/2" h. **3,680**

Figure group, shepherd & shepherdess, seated holding hands, the shepherdess w/a ewe in her lap, another recumbent at her companion's feet, on a rocaille-molded base, late 19th - early 20th c., blue crossed swords mark & incised & impressed numbers, 8 1/2" w. **1,495**

Figure group, two young children dressed in 18th c. attire, on a base, enameled decoration & incised marks, late 19th c., 6 1/2" h. **690**

Figure group, Monkey Band, composed of a conductor, oboe player, flute player, trumpet player, piano player on monkeyback, cello player, French horn player & violin player, late 19th - early 20th c., tallest 7" h., the set (various chips & small damages) **6,038**

Adam & Eve Figure Group

Figure group, Adam & Eve standing among various birds & animals w/the apple tree & serpent behind them, Adam just biting the apple, oblong mound base, polychrome decoration, underglaze-blue crossed swords mark & seconds mark, 19th c., 12" h. (ILLUS.) **4,025**

Figure group, allegorical, "North America," modeled as a Native American wearing a feathered headdress & riding his horse while spearing a charging buffalo, underglaze-blue crossed swords mark, modeled in 1903 by Erich Hoesel, 14" l., 14" h. **3,500-4,500**

Figure of a woman, allegorical, modeled holding a stringed instrument & seated on a scrolled freeform base, polychrome & gilt trim, incised "#369 - 6," late 19th - early 20th c., 16 1/2" h. **3,000-3,200**

Figure of a woman, allegorical, shown seated on a scroll freeform base & holding a staff, the other hand holding the scarf draped across her head, flowing robes w/polychrome florette decoration, gilt-trimmed base, incised "#369 - 5" & printed mark, late 19th - early 20th c., 16 1/2" h. **3,220**

Figure of Apollo, the god clad in a puce & gilt drapery, holding aloft his bow & w/a quiver of arrows slung across his back, seated in a chariot among grey clouds & yellow & white sunbursts, blue crossed-swords mark & incised numbers, 19th c., 8 1/4" h. (some restoration) **1,800**

Figure of Cupid, the young Cupid standing holding a broken heart, on a round socle w/marbleized decoration & gilt bands, late 19th - early 20th c., 8 1/8" h. **1,380**

Figure of female, allegorical, seated on a high scroll-molded base wearing long loose robes & holding a script in one hand, her other arm stretched out, No.

369, late 19th - early 20th c., blue crossed swords mark, 16 1/2" h................. **1,610**

Figure of hunter, standing figure w/boots, breeches & a spotted fur cloak, one hand at belt, the other arm extended, polychrome decoration, blue crossed swords mark, 19th c., No. 1285, 8 3/4" h. **460**

Figures, allegorical, each a putto representing Night & Day, one in the guise of a mythological figure of Athena w/an owl, the other as Perseus w/a torch & sunflower, each on waisted faux marble & gilt-trimmed circular base, late 19th - early 20th c., blue crossed swords mark, incised & impressed numbers, 7" h., pr. **3,220**

Figures of harvesters, one as a peasant woman walking w/a bundle of lettuce under her right arm & beside a milestone incised w/crowned crossed swords, the other a peasant man wearing long pants, a long-sleeved shirt & floral-decorated vest & carrying a scythe & a pail, on oval bases, one w/a commemorative date mark for 1710-1910, blue crossed swords marks & incised & impressed marks, 14 1/2" h., pr..................................... **2,300**

Pair of Meissen Figurines

Figurines, man & woman in 18th-c. floral dress, each carrying flowers in hand, the man w/his coat flaring over a tree stump, each mounted on raised base w/applied flowers, marked w/crossed swords, 17" h., pr. (ILLUS.)... **3,024**

Fruit basket, oval form w/pierced sides, Blue Onion patt., blue crossed swords mark, late 19th c., 19 1/2" l. **633**

Model of a monkey, seated animal holding an apple, 2 3/4" h. **2,000-2,200**

Model of Bolognese hound, seated facing left, brown fur markings, late 19th - early 20th c., blue crossed swords mark, after a model by J.J. Kandler, incised & impressed numbers, 8 3/4" h. **2,070**

Pitcher, cov., 10 1/4" h., ovoid body w/heavy leaf design, scrolling handle, wreath finial, late 19th c................................. **448**

Plaque, rectangular, "Feines Bouquet," a painted scene of a standing Cardinal sampling the bouquet of a white wine from a Venetian glass held in his right hand, a book in his left, in an interior rich w/pre-Renaissance Italian artifacts, late 19th - early 20th c., impressed mono-

gram & sceptre mark, artist-signed, painted wood frame, 7 1/2 x 10"................ **6,900**

Plate, 9" d., flower-encrusted, round form piled high in the center w/a profusion of colorful flowers & fruit within a pierced gilt-edged border, the underside printed & painted w/forget-me-not sprigs & insects, underglaze-blue crossed swords mark, ca. 1830 (some damage & restoration)... **1,955**

Plates, 9 3/4" d., Blue Onion patt., crossed swords mark, late 19th - early 20th c., set of 6 .... **385**

Platter & insert, 21 1/2" l., oval, Blue Onion patt., trimmed w/gold, early 20th c., 2 pcs. **489**

Salt dips, figural, each w/a seated child between two baskets, modeled w/foliate sprays & decorated in polychrome, late 19th c., 5 1/2" l., 5" h., pr...................... **2,070**

Soup tureen, cov., footed squatty bulbous oval form w/upright loop foliate end handle, high stepped & domed cover w/a putto finial, Blue Onion patt., blue crossed swords mark, late 19th - early 20th c., 14 1/4" l... **863**

Fine Meissen tête-à-tête Tea Set

Tea set, tête-à-tête size: cov. teapot, cov. sugar bowl, creamer, two cups & saucers & an oblong tray; each decorated w/colorful encrusted flowers w/painted flowers on the tray, cups w/six feet, underglaze-blue crossed swords mark, 19th c., tray 16" l., the set (ILLUS.) **3,500-4,000**

Teacup & saucer, cobalt blue ground decorated w/a topographical landscape showing the city of Konigstein, late 19th c., 3 7/8" d. **1,380**

Teapot, cov., figural, model of a rooster, enamel decoration, late 19th - early 20th c., 6" l.. **575-600**

Tray, squared form w/ornately molded dished edges w/rocaille shells & blue floral decoration, polychrome floral decoration at center & gilt enamel trim, scrolled loop side handles, late 19th c., 16 1/4" w... **1,093**

Vase, 16" h., double-gourd form, painted & trimmed in gilt in the Kakiemon style w/birds in flight & perched on flowering branches & w/butterflies, blue "AR" monogram & date mark for 1922................... **920**

Vase, cov., 16 1/8" h., pate-sur-pate, tall baluster form w/a ringed pedestal foot supporting the large ovoid body w/a ringed trumpet neck w/rolled rim & high domed cover w/berried finial, tall scrolled lion head handles from the rim to the shoulder, cobalt blue ground w/scrolling gilt trim, the front decorated w/a large oval reserve w/a slip design of a nymph in a diaphanous drapery accompanied by Pan playing a tambourine & two frolicking putti on a celadon ground & within a gilt foliate & platinum border set w/beaded lozenges, ca. 1880, blue crossed swords mark & numbers.. 14,950

Vase, 22 3/4" h., "schneeballen" type, flared baluster form, applied overall w/mayflower blossoms in white & w/brightly plumed birds perched on green leafy branches w/large ball clusters of white blossoms, the short socle foot applied w/a nest of baby birds & eggs attended by a small yellow bird & w/green leafy vines, mid- to late 19th c., blue crossed swords marks, letters & numbers, after a model by J.J. Kandler 9,200

Vases, 19" h., baluster form w/entwined snake handles, cobalt blue ground, the mouth, collar & foot molded & trimmed w/gilt, late 19th - early 20th c., blue crossed swords marks & incised & impressed numbers, mounted as lamps, pr. 2,990

Merrimac Pottery

Merrimac Mark

The Merrimac Ceramic Company of Newburyport, Massachusetts, was initially organized in 1897 by Thomas S. Nickerson for the production of inexpensive garden pottery and decorated tile. Within the year, production was expanded to include decorative art pottery, a change reflected in the new name, Merrimac Pottery Company, adopted in 1902. Early glazes were limited to primarily matte green and yellow, but by 1903 a variety of hues, including iridescent and metallic lustres, was being used. Marked only with a paper label until after 1901, pieces then bore an impressed mark incorporating a fish beneath "Merrimac." Fire destroyed the pottery in 1908. This relatively short span of production makes the ware scarce and expensive.

Bowl-vase, wide flat-bottomed form w/low rounded sides w/a wide shoulder centering a short, wide, cylindrical neck, fine matte green glaze, impressed mark, 9" d., 4" h. (minute fleck on rim) **$1,320**

Jar, cov., tapering cylindrical body w/a wide rounded shoulder centering a slightly domed cover w/knob finial, glossy speckled brown glaze, paper label, 3 1/4" d., 5 1/4" h. (stilt pulls inside rim of cover in the making)... 495

Pitcher, 6 3/4" h., 6 1/2" d., tapering cylindrical body w/a rolled rim, C-form handle, rich matte green mottled glaze, stamped mark (rim chip restoration) 330

Large Merrimac Umbrella Stand

Umbrella stand, tall cylindrical form w/tooled & applied leaves under a leathery matte green glaze, crack to base crawls along the side, a few small chips to decoration & some glaze pooling, paper label, 8 1/2" d., 22 3/4" h. (ILLUS.)........................ **4,125**

Vase, miniature, 4" h., 3 1/2" d., squatty bulbous baluster form w/the wide shoulder centered by a widely flaring trumpet neck, feathered matte green & gunmetal glaze, mark partially obscured by green glaze 495

Vase, 7 1/2" h., 4 1/4" d., slightly swelled cylindrical form w/a small closed mouth, tooled & applied w/dogwood blossoms around the top on tall stems w/leaves around the base, rich leathery matte green glaze, impressed mark (opposing hairlines, one restored)................................. 1,980

Rare Merrimac Vase with Leaves

Vase, 7 3/4" h., 4 1/2" d., gently swelled cylindrical form w/a rounded shoulder to the closed rim, tooled & applied w/swirling leaves, fine feathered matte green glaze, carved "EB," several nicks to edges of leaves (ILLUS.)... 4,219

Vase, 10" h., globular base tapering to tall cylindrical neck w/flat rim, mottled rich green, gunmetal & mauve glaze 825

Large Bottle-form Merrimac Vase

Vase, 10" h., 5" d., bulbous, nearly spherical base tapering to a tall cylindrical neck, fine dark green & mirrored black mottled glaze, unmarked (ILLUS.).............. **1,650**

Tall Green Merrimac Vase

Vase, 10 1/2" h., tall ovoid body tapering to a flat molded mouth, overall matte green glaze, stilt pull & small chips on base (ILLUS.)... **1,035**

Tall Simple Merrimac Vase

Vase, 11 1/2" h., tall, slightly swelled cylindrical body w/a widely flaring rim, overall matte green glaze, impressed chip in rim, small glaze miss at base (ILLUS.).................. **690**

Vase, 11 1/2" h., 6" d., gently swelled cylindrical body w/a widely flared rim, applied stylized plant sprigs around the rim on tall thin stems w/a band of pointed leaves around the base, leathery semi-matte green glaze, stamped mark (restored chip at rim, hairline down body)................. **1,980**

Mettlach

Mettlach Mark

Ceramics with the name Mettlach were produced by Villeroy & Boch and other potteries in the Mettlach area of Germany. Villeroy and Boch's finest years of production are thought to be from about 1890 to 1910. Also see STEINS.

Mettlach Cracker Jar

Cracker jar, cov., silver plate rim, bail handle & flat cover w/knob finial, cylindrical w/molded base & rim bands in dark brown, a wide tan middle band w/a mosaic design of a white-dotted zigzag band forming triangles w/three-petal flowers in brown & white, No. 1306, 4" h. (ILLUS.).. **$230**

Cracker jar, cov., wide, squatty, bulbous body w/a silver plate rim, flat cover w/turned finial & swing handle, mosaic decoration of narrow geometric bands in shades of dark blue, tan, brown & white above a wider base band w/stylized flowering branches, tan ground, No. 1332, 5" d.. **575**

Mettlach Ewer with Figural Handle

Ewer, stoneware, domed-footed ovoid body
w/a tall cylindrical neck & wide mask
spout, green ground applied w/brown

pointed leaves above the foot below a
wide relief-molded band of classical figures in the woods hunting w/dogs against
a dark brown ground, a neck band
w/brown woven design, full-figure Cupid
handle in cream w/brown trim, No. 2356,
4 2/3 liter (ILLUS.) **805**
Flowerpot, a narrow footring below the wide
cylindrical body w/a slightly flared rim,
the sides divided into panels etched
w/color scenes of Cavaliers drinking,
white lappet band around the rim, No.
2170, 6" h. **374**
Jardiniere, Art Nouveau design, a deep
bowl-form container w/gently ruffled rim,
glossy mossy green sides molded w/an
upright cluster of berries & long leaves,
supported on curved & stepped-out short
end legs in dark green w/moss green
bands, pale yellow interior, No. 2735,
13" l., 5 1/4" h. **805**
Jardiniere, Art Nouveau design, low narrow
oblong form w/rounded tapering sides
raised on low brackets, the flat rim
w/stepped ends, decorated w/an etched
design of panels formed by brown lattice
& bars against a tan ground w/clusters of
green buds, No. 2980, 14" l., 5" h **460**
Jardiniere, cameo-style, low long narrow
rectangular form w/low bracket end feet,
flat rim w/stepped ends, the long sides
each w/two oblong dark green panels
w/reclining classical women in white relief, tan border bands w/white stripping,
No. 3041, 11 2/3" l., 4 1/4" h. **311**

Unique Mettlach Garniture Set

Mantel garniture: clock in urn & pair of matching side urns; the large baluster-form central urn w/a mosaic design of stylized floral & leaf panels in alternating cream w/green & tan & rust red w/tan, brown & green, the flared neck w/tan ground & floral swags, raised on a high gilt-metal plinth w/scroll-cast footed base, gilt-metal serpent-form shoulder handles & a scalloped metal rim band & gadrooned domed cover w/leaf bud finial, a clock set into one side within a brass bezel, the matching shorter urns w/similar gilt-metal details, shorter urns 15 1/2", tallest urn 19" h., the set (ILLUS.).............. **3,565**

Girl & Swans Mettlach Plaque

Plaque, pierced for hanging, charming printed-under-glaze color scene of a little Victorian girl wearing a feather hat & purple gown & holding a small basket, standing on the shore of a large lake feeding white swans w/a village in the background, gold trim w/slight wear, No. 1044/1122, 17" d. (ILLUS.).. **920**

Mettlach Woman & Roses Plaque

Plaque, pierced to hang, Art Nouveau design, a large etched bust portrait of an Art Nouveau woman on the left sniffing large

tan roses on dark green leafy stems, tan border band decorated w/dark green & rust red leaf devices, No. 2544, 20" d. (ILLUS.).. **863**

Plaque, pierced to hang, etched w/a surrealistic seascape w/a large black raven flying over stormy dark blue waves between dark brown craggy cliffs, the shaded dark blue sky w/pale blue moon highlighted w/stripes of pink clouds, slight gold wear, No. 2551, 18" d................ **1,668**

Phanolith Plaque with Figures

Plaque, pierced to hang, phanolith, a dark green ground decorated w/white relief w/three seminude classical water nymphs & flying birds, No. 7043, 21" d. (ILLUS.).. **719**

Plaques, pierced to hang, each w/an overall etched scene, one w/a gnome seated on leafy blossoming branches drinking from a mug, various beetles flying & perched, all against a shaded medium to light blue ground, the other w/a gnome seated in a nest on a leafy vine w/butterflies flying about, against a shaded medium to light blue ground, No. 2112 & 2113, 16" d., facing pr... **2,128**

Plaques, pierced to hang, etched designs, each centered by a bust portrait of a Renaissance woman wearing a large feathered hat, in natural tones & dark blue, dark pink & white against a pale blue ground, the wide border band w/overall stylized scrolling leaves in brown, tan & blue on a dark blue ground, No. 1424 & 1425, 15 1/2" d., facing pr............................ **1,035**

Plaques, pierced to hang, rectangular dark green ground, each decorated w/a narrow white relief border around a scene of a classical woman & cupids, No. 7067 & 7068, 4 x 6", facing pair.................................... **806**

Tobacco jar, cov., barrel-shaped, an etched design w/repeating pairs of large herring-bone panels in dark blue & dark red separated by horizontal & vertical white bands w/"Tabac" in black, four alternate white panels etched w/an outlined figure of a man smoking a pipe above another panel w/a dark blue, dark red & dotted black checkerboard design w/another white band w/"Tabac," domed cover w/checkerboard panels & white knob, very rare, No. 4504, 6 1/2" h........................... **719**

Vase, 3 7/8" h., spherical body raised on flaring scroll feet, short, wide cylindrical neck w/molded band, mosaic decoration around body w/a suspended band of tan spearpoints w/stylized blue & brown blossoms alternating w/upright scrolled leaf & bar designs in brown, black & white, No. 1674 .... **399**

Vase, 3 7/8" h., spherical body raised on three scroll feet, mosaic design w/wide vertical brown stripes w/bands of applied blue buttons alternating w/narrow black & tiny red bead stripes, short neck w/molded band w/applied tiny beads, No. 1671....... **400**

Vase, 4 1/4" h., bulbous ovoid body w/short flared neck, on three knob feet, mosaic design w/wide upper & lower grey bands decorated w/brown & blue double circles, narrow brown middle band w/small brown & white roundels, No. 1640 .... **345**

Mettlach Vase with Poppies

Vase, 7" h., bulbous ovoid body tapering to a bulbed neck w/narrow scalloped rim, a dark blue ground etched overall w/an Art Nouveau design w/clusters of large deep pink poppy blossoms & a narrow pale blue ribbon band, tiny pink leaf designs scattered around the sides & neck, No. 2434 (ILLUS.) **460**

Vase, 7" h., footed ovoid body w/short, wide flaring neck, dark blue ground decorated w/an overall mosaic design of almond-form panels composed of brown leaves & stylized four-petal blossoms in rust red & pale blue, small scattered dot blossoms on the shoulder & neck, No. 1573 .... **230**

Vase, 7" h., mosaic decoration on a brick red ground, a funnel foot w/dark blue band & leaf tips below the wide ovoid body decorated w/bands of tiny florets flanking the wide center band w/vertical almond-form devices w/scroll leaves in dark blue & stylized four-petal designs in tan & slate blue, short flaring neck w/band of tiny beads, No. 1573...................... **311**

Vase, 7 3/4" h., wide ovoid body w/a short, flared neck, a mosaic decoration of dark brown horizontal bands decorated w/opposing bands of serrated lappets in dark

blue, green & deep rose, rounded smaller bands of lappets around the base & neck, No. 1596.. **374**

Vase, 9" h., bulbous ovoid form w/a dark blue ground decorated in mosaic w/scattered pink & pale blue three-petal blossoms & tiny blue bead blossoms, a brick red neck band decorated w/a band of applied dark blue beads, No. 2868 .... **288**

Vase, 10 1/2" h., classical-style, a pedestal base in dark brown w/rust red lappet band supporting the bulbous body decorated w/two large heart-shaped reserves w/pink ground & white relief figures of putti under leafy branches, dark brown & rust red border bands continuing up & forming stripes on the tall trumpet neck flanked by long brown S-scroll handles, No. 2432 .... **240**

Vase, 13 1/2" h., tall cylindrical body raised on small scroll legs, Oriental landscape scene, a dark brown matte ground molded in relief w/pairs of geese in white, brown & greyish blue on brown rockwork, tall golden brown bamboo stocks behind them & pale blue water in front of them, No. 1515 (one leg repaired)............................ **719**

Vase, 16 1/2" h., Art Nouveau design, baluster-form body tapering to a tall cylindrical neck w/flared rim, slender serpentine handles from rim to shoulder, decorated w/a glossy moss green glaze w/dark green handles & base bands, the neck & shoulder molded in low relief w/suspended fuchsia blossoms, No. 2731 .... **891**

Very Fine Mettlach Vase with Fairy

Vase, 26" h., tall baluster-form body, beautifully decorated in relief w/a lovely winged fairy dressed in deep rose, blue & white, perched on slender contorted leafy vine w/pink blossoms, all against a subtly shaded dark to medium blue ground, gold highlights, No. 1610 (ILLUS.)............. **5,635**

Vases, 10" h., a low, round foot supporting a tall, squared body w/a short flaring neck, each side w/a large oblong mosaic panel filled w/arabesque entwined scrolls in white, light blue, green & gold w/a maroon almond-form central reserve, dark blue borders, No. 2032, pr. **1,093**

Minton

The Minton factory in England was established by Thomas Minton in 1793. The factory made earthenware, especially the blue-printed variety, and Thomas Minton is sometimes credited with the invention of the blue "Willow" pattern. For a time majolica and tiles were also an important part of production, but bone china soon became the principal ware. Mintons, Ltd., continues in operation today. Also see MAJOLICA.

Minton Marks

Bowl, 4" d., 2 1/2" h., majolica, modeled as a round bird's nest in dark brown supported by molded oak leaves & acorns....... **$330**

Bowl, majolica, deep, rounded, molded & ribbed yellow basketweave exterior w/a band of wide overlapping green leaves around the rim, turquoise interior, shape No. 582, date code for 1865, mint **495**

Cabinet plates, 8 1/8" d., majolica, decorated w/floral motifs, ca. 1873, set of 5 .... **308**

Centerpiece, majolica, figural, a large, wide & shallow deep yellow shell w/pink interior supported atop a figural merman on an oval foot, shape No. 865, date code for 1870, 12" w., 14" h. **1,650**

Unusual Minton Chestnut Server

Chestnut server, majolica, shell-form dish w/scalloped flanged rim molded w/green leaves on brown, large arching green & pink leaves & figural chestnut cover half the turquoise blue bowl, shape No. 494, date code for 1862, 9 1/2" w. (ILLUS.).. **1,540**

Ewer, majolica, monumental piece, large figural handle of a mermaid w/braided hair & fish scale vest & tail reaching down & entwining w/the horns of a bold relief satyr's head, the large wide curved spout above a neck molded in a ruffled pink shell & green leaf design above the bulbous lower portion, which features a full-figure putto at the rim opposite the handle, large green garland bands divide the lower body into panels molded in white relief w/a classical woman & putti against a tan ground, short swirled brown pedestal on the round foot w/a yellow shell-molded edge band, date code for 1871, shape No. 1290, mint, overall 16" w., 21" h. **55,000**

Fancy Minton Game Dish

Game dish, cov., majolica, oval, the tapering brown basketweave base w/green relief oak leaves & acorns, the cover molded in full relief w/dead game & a branch handle, professional handle repair on base, chip on wing of bird, hairline & rim repair on insert, late 19th c., 13" l. (ILLUS.)... **1,210**

Minton Majolica Garden Seat

Garden seat, majolica, large ovoid form w/a flaring, lightly ruffled top, cobalt blue w/a large turquoise blue ribbon & bow around the neck above a large suspended branch of pink & white flowers & green leaves, shape No. 2367, date code for 1881, 17" h. (ILLUS.) **2,750**

Garden seat, majolica, Oriental-style, round turquoise top centered by a circle of molded scrolls, the curved shoulder molded w/oblong panels of pink & green scrolls within yellow borders, S-scroll tapering legs curve down to join at an open center ring, scroll feet, date code for 1863, 19" h. **4,400**

Humidor, cov., majolica, figural, a cylindrical tall coil of yellow rope forming the body, a large seated figure of a sailor drinking from a mug on the flat top, shape No. 716, 9" h. **2,200**

Large Minton Jardiniere

Jardiniere, footed oval urn form w/rolled rim, turquoise blue ground w/white & brown molded snake handles, a green rope band around the foot & shoulder of the body, chain-molded rim band in ochre, green & brown, pink interior, shape No. 532, date code for 1869, professional repair to rim, 24" l., 12" h. (ILLUS.) **3,575**

Jardiniere, majolica, large bulbous urn top w/a flaring cobalt blue neck, the turquoise sides molded w/two large bold-relief lion masks supporting green swags

molded w/colorful fruit, nuts & wheat, floral rosettes w/pink ribbons & bows alternate w/the lion masks, on a pedestal molded w/green leaves above the round turquoise foot w/a golden brown lappet band, date code for 1869, 15" d., 14 1/2" h. **3,300**

Oyster plates, each painted in tones of yellow, pink & green, printed marks, ca. 1900, 9 1/4" d., set of 12 .... **1,035**

Plate, 9 3/4" d., majolica, a dark green center w/the wide border molded w/three large green & yellow sunflower heads separated by deep rose reticulated panels.. **413**

Plates, 10 1/4" d., pate-sur-pate, each wide border set w/three oval blue-ground pate-sur-pate medallions decorated in white slip w/nymphs & putti within gilt surround linked by ribbon-tied gilt garlands on a cream ground, the cavetto & rim w/gilt beads, dated 1921-28, impressed & gilt marks, retailed by Ovington's, New York, Chicago, set of 17 .... **16,100**

Punch bowl, "Japan" patt., deep rounded sides on a thick footring, painted on the exterior in bright colors w/alternating shaped panels of prunus & peony plants below a border of purple & black half flower heads at the gilt rim, the interior similarly decorated about a central orange, yellow & gilt stylized flower head medallion, blue painted pseudo-Sevres mark w/"m" & pattern no. 555, ca. 1810, 10 1/4" d. (piece broken & restored at the rim, fine hairlines in base) **3,105**

Salt dip, master size, majolica, model of a small tapering cylindrical basket in yellow w/a large square tab at one rim, turquoise interior, date code for 1872, 5" h........ **193**

Salt dip, master size, majolica, oblong four-lobed form in a marbleized malachite & gold glaze, 5" l., 2 1/2" h. **165**

Salt dip, master size, majolica, oblong four-lobed form w/pink interior & cobalt blue exterior on a green foot, date code for 1862, 5" l., 2 1/2" h. **330**

Soup tureen, cover & undertray, ironstone china, footed squatty bulbous oval body w/rolled loop end handles, high domed cover w/loop handle, matching dished undertray, decorated w/black transfer-printed Oriental garden landscapes trimmed w/colorful enamels, impressed marks, ca. 1882, handle to handle 14 1/4" l., the set **403**

Spill vases, majolica, figural, a large standing seminude putto beside an upright trumpet-form basketweave basket w/turquoise blue interior & the exterior trimmed w/leafy vines, all on a round leaf-trimmed base, shape No. 405 & 406, date code for 1867, 10 3/4" h., pr. (professional repair to rims of baskets) **3,850**

Toby jugs, majolica, figural Barrister & Lady, stocky figures in colorful 18th c. attire, great detail, 11 1/2" h., pr. (minor professional rim repair) **2,750**

Tray, majolica, round, cobalt blue inner rim band around the mottled green & brown center, wide border band molded in brown, yellow & green w/putti, birds & leafy scrolls, yellow floral rosette border band, 10 3/4" d.. **440**

Minton "Pate-sur-Pate" Moon Flask

Vase, 13" h., moon flask-form, "pate-sure-pate," flattened disk form raised on an oblong foot, w/a short ringed neck & bulbed rim flanked by loop handles to the shoulder, one side decorated w/white slip Chinese figures in a garden setting, the other side w/garden furniture, against a brown background & the body in coral, impressed mark & shape No. 1664, printed factory marks, ca. 1873 (ILLUS.)............ **1,725**

Vase, cov., 22 5/8" h., deep, square plinth w/ovolo corners supporting a short, ringed pedestal below the tall, ovoid, shouldered body w/a short trumpet neck, domed cover w/pointed knob finial, inwardly scrolled gold shoulder handles, the turquoise blue ground decorated overall in the cloisonné style w/geometric grotesque mask, stylized dolphin crests & octagonal mosaic designs, gilt band trim, designed by Christopher Dresser, Model No. 1656, dated 1873, retailer's mark of A.B. Daniell & Son **8,625**

Unusual Minton Wine Cooler

Wine cooler, majolica, oval, deep, slightly flared sides w/a scalloped rim, turquoise ground w/scroll-trimmed side panels molded w/scenes of putti in the forest, large green leaves form end handles, late 19th c., 14 x 23", 11" h. (ILLUS.).. **3,300**

Mocha

Mocha decoration is found on basically utilitarian creamware or yellowware articles and is achieved by a simple chemical reaction. A color pigment of brown, blue, green or black is given an acid nature by infusion of tobacco or hops. When this acid nature colorant is applied in blobs to an alkaline ground color, it reacts by spreading in feathery seaweed designs. This type of decoration is usually accompanied by horizontal bands of light color slip. Produced in numerous Staffordshire potteries from the late 18th until the late 19th centuries, its name is derived from the similar markings found on mocha quartz. In addition to the seaweed decoration, mocha wares are also seen with Earthworm and Cat's Eye patterns or a marbleized effect.

Bowl, 4" d., 2 7/8" h., cylindrical body w/tapering sides on a thin footring, white stripes & brown band w/black seaweed decoration (hairline) **$358**

Group of Mocha Pieces

Bowl, 4 3/4" d., 3 1/2" h., footed bulbous body w/a wide rolled rim, canary yellow ground w/a wide green band decorated in yellow & black w/the Earthworm patt., partial impressed mark "CL & ---Mont---," chips, repairs, appears to have had an eared handle (ILLUS. bottom center)............. **110**

Bowl, 6 1/2" d., yellowware, brown & white stripes (wear & stains w/short rim hairline) 83Bowl, 7" d., footed deep rounded form, marbleized slip in dark blue, medium brown & dark brown on a white ground below a green reeded rim band, early 19th c., base & rim chips, hairline in base, glaze wear, pitting (ILLUS. right with mugs, below)... **881**

Mocha Bowl and Mugs

Bowl, 7" d., 3 1/2" h., white band w/blue seaweed decoration & brown stripes (minor wear)... **385**

Bowl, 8 1/8" d., 3 7/8" h., white band w/green seaweed decoration & brown stripes (wear & small interior flake) **165**

Bowl, 10" d., yellowware w/green seaweed design **250**

Bowl, 10 1/8" d., 4 5/8" h., white band w/green seaweed decoration & brown stripes (wear, stains & shallow interior flakes).. **341**

Bowl, 11" d., 5 1/4" h., footed w/deep, wide bell-form body w/rolled rim, yellowware w/a wide white upper band w/blue seaweed decoration, East Liverpool, Ohio (wear, large foot chip) **220**

Chamber pot, footed squatty bulbous form w/C-form leaf tip handle, a wide two-tone blue band decorated w/a zigzag Earthworm patt. in black & white flanked by narrow double black stripes, 8 3/4" d. (some wear, edge flakes) **121**

Jar, cov., cylindrical w/a flared base & low domed cover w/button finial, the body & cover w/a pale blue band flanked by black stripes & Earthworm or Cat's-eye patt. in white & blue, repairs, hairline in cover, 5" h. (ILLUS. top left w/mocha pieces).. **495**

Master salt, blue stripes & white band w/green seaweed decoration on yellowware, 2 1/4" h. (short hairlines & interior stain).. **770**

Mixing bowl, footed deep round flaring form w/molded rim, yellowware w/a wide white center band w/thin brown line borders & pale blue seaweed decoration, 14 3/4" d., 7" h. (spider crack in base, flaking on interior, rim chip)............................ **330**

Mixing bowl, footed deep round flaring form w/molded rim, yellowware w/a wide white center band w/thin brown line borders & dark green daubs of seaweed decoration, 14 3/4" d., 7" h. (rim hairline w/glaze flakes in bottom)...................................... **385**

Mixing bowl, footed w/deep rounded sides & molded rim, yellowware w/a white band w/brown line borders decorated w/a green seaweed design, 14 3/4" d., 7" h. (spider crack in base, flaking on interior, rim chip)... **303**

Mixing bowl, small footring supporting a deep rounded flaring bowl w/a heavy molded rim, yellowware w/a wide central white band w/blue bands & black seaweed decoration, East Liverpool, Ohio, late 19th - early 20th c., 8 1/2" d., 4 1/4" h.. **385**

Mug, cylindrical, decorated w/thin black & white w/blue stripes & geometric banding, applied ribbed handle w/leaf tips, early 19th c., 2 3/4" h. (stains, minor damage)... **451**

Mug, cylindrical, w/extruded handle w/foliate terminals, banded at the top & base in dark brown & ochre w/dark brown, medium brown & white scroddled dot slip on a rust field, early 19th c., circular crack,

two vertical cracks in body, discoloration, 5 3/4" h. (ILLUS. center with bowl & mug).. **1,175**

Mug with Two Earthworm Bands

Mug, cylindrical, w/extruded handle w/foliate terminals, banded in dark brown & rust w/two rows of blue, dark brown, rust & white Earthworm patt. flanked by upper & lower white rouletted bands, early 19th c., circular & spider cracks in base, three rim chips, 6" h. (ILLUS.) **1,175**

Mocha Mug with Earthworm Bands

Mug, cylindrical, w/molded base & extruded handle, narrow bands of rust at the top & base, wide grey center band decorated in the Earthworm patt. in blue, rust & black, early 19th c., chips, 5 3/4" h. (ILLUS.) **2,350**

Mug, decorated w/brown stripes w/white band & blue seaweed decoration on yellowware, 3 7/8" h... **358**

Mug, miniature, cylindrical, w/arched leaf tip handle, narrow brown & light blue stripes flanking a wide grey band w/brown, white & light blue Earthworm patt., 3 1/8" h. (stains, crack).. **385**

Mug, pearlware, cylindrical, w/extruded handle w/foliate terminals, a pale green rim band over dark brown bands w/Cat's Eye decoration flanking a central grey band w/dark brown, tan, grey & white Earthworm patt., early 19th c., small hairline in base (ILLUS. left with bowl & mug).. **5,288**

Mug, low, wide cylindrical body w/C-scroll leaftip handle, heavy double brown bands flanking a center dark brown band decorated w/the Earthworm patt. in blue, white & tan, hairlines, 3 3/4" h. (ILLUS. bottom left w/mocha pieces)............................ **550**

Mug, cylindrical, blue & brown border bands centering a brown impressed repeating geometric design on a cream ground, 19th c., 5 5/8" h. (very minor chips & cracks, minor staining) **978**

Mustard pot, cov., footed bulbous body w/C-form handle, low domed cover w/knob finial, white w/brown tooled lines, 3 3/4" h. (wear).. **1,210**

Early Mocha Mustard Pot

Mustard pot, cov., low cylindrical body w/D-form handle & inset cover w/knob finial, blue banded cover & blue reeded band above a wide blue band decorated w/the Earthworm patt. in white, black & brown, England, chips to lid, small crack in body, discoloration, early 19th c., 2 1/2" h. (ILLUS.).. **1,293**

Mustard pot, cov., low cylindrical body w/narrow flared rim & foot, inset flat cover w/knob finial, C-form handle, the body w/a wide tan band decorated w/looping Earthworm patt. in white, yellow & black, narrow black stripes at top & bottom, 2 1/2" h. (chips on lid, small lid repair) **605**

Pepper pot, cov., baluster form w/domed top, flared round foot, body decorated w/wide blue band w/black seaweed decoration, tan stripes, 5" h. (slight wear to finial) **770**

Pepper pot, cov., cylindrical body w/short tapered neck w/slightly flared domed top & knob finial, round footed base, wide black band around body w/light blue, orange & white wavy line design, flanked by grey stripes, cobalt feathering on lid, 4 3/4" h. (minor wear, staining, short hairline in top)... **1,155**

Pepper pot, cov., cylindrical, w/domed top & knob finial, blue & tan bands w/brown check tooled bands, 4 1/4" h. (small flakes on base & lid rim, wear on finial) **1,210**

Pepper pot, cov., squat, bulbous yellowware body on short, flared, round, ringed foot, slightly flaring cylindrical neck, body w/white band of pink seaweed decoration, brown & pale blue stripes, 4 1/4" h. (minor flake on base) **1,980**

Pepper pot, cov., footed ovoid body w/domed cap, orangish tan band w/black seaweed decoration, brown stripes, 3 5/8" h. (small flakes) **990**

Pepper pot, cov., footed ovoid body tapering to short cylindrical neck fitted w/a pierced domed top, a wide yellow-ochre band w/Earthworm patt. in white, brown & beige, narrow brown stripes, 3 7/8" h. (small chips on dome)................................. **1,100**

Pitcher, milk, jug-form, 4 5/8" h., C-scroll leaf tip handle, decorated w/a dark bluish grey band flanked by black stripes, the center embossed dark band decorated w/green & black seaweed patt., wear, painted-over flake on spout (ILLUS. top right w/mocha pieces)..................................... **440**

Pitcher, jug-form, 5" h., decorated w/the Earthworm patt., a wide central tan band w/the decoration in white, pale blue & brown, thin upper & lower bands in tan & dark brown, molded leaf tip handle, early 19th c. (professional repair to handle) **660**

Pitcher, jug-form, 5 1/2" h., w/a wide, flat base, narrow blue, white & dark brown bands flanking a wide central tan band w/dark brown Earthworm patt., looped leaf tip handle, early 19th c. (damage) **330**

Small Mocha Pitcher with Seaweed

Pitcher, 6 1/2" h., baluster-form, banded in dark brown & rust w/a green-glazed rouletted upper band, black mocha Seaweed patt. in the wide rust band, extruded handle w/green-glazed foliate terminals, England, early 19th c. (ILLUS.).. **2,585**

Pitcher, 6 3/4" h., barrel-shaped w/leaf tip handle & arched spout, tooled bands w/blue, black & tan stripes & blue band w/Earthworm patt. (short hairlines on bottom & in handle, pinpoint edge flakes)....... **1,155**

Pitcher, 7 1/8" h., footed bulbous body tapering to flat rim, arched spout & molded leaf C-form handle, brown band w/black stripes & light blue & green bands, blue & brown Earthworm patt. (chips, stains & cracks).. **770**

Pitcher, 7 7/8" h., jug-form, pearlware body decorated around the sides w/pumpkin-colored bands at top & bottom w/brown geometric & line decoration on a white ground, embossed leaf decoration on handle & spout, early 19th c. (minor chips, wear, interior glaze flakes) **1,320**

Unusual Banded Mocha Pitcher

Pitcher, 8" h., barrel-shaped, pearlware, banded in rust & black w/rouletted green glazed upper & lower bands, decorated w/blue, dark brown & white Earthworm patt., white & black trailing slip "branches," extruded handle w/green-glazed foliate terminals, England, early 19th c., rim & spout chips, long crack at rim, crack across lower handle terminal, glaze hairlines on base (ILLUS.) **3,525**

Shaker w/domed top, footed short cylindrical body w/tapering neck to domed top, wide tan body band w/seaweed decoration flanked by narrow black stripes & a narrower tan band at neck, 4 1/8" h. (chips) **220**

Tureen, cov., round, decorated w/entwined cables & "cat's eyes" on ochre ground, w/green-glazed foliate handles, cover decorated w/two zigzag cables w/green-glazed floral knop, 19th c., 10 3/8" l. across handles (hairlines, minor chips)...... **5,400**

Waste bowl, footed, deep, gently flaring rounded form, a wide orangish tan band flanked by thin dark brown stripes & an embossed green band, decorated w/the Earthworm patt. in blue, white & dark brown, repairs, 5 5/8" d., 2 7/8" h. (ILLUS. bottom right w/mocha pieces) **550**

Moorcroft

MOORCROFT

Moorcroft Marks

William Moorcroft became a designer for James Macintyre & Co. in 1897 and was put in charge of the art pottery production there. Moorcroft developed a number of popular designs, including Florian Ware, while with Macintyre and continued with that firm until 1913, when it discontinued the production of art pottery.

After leaving Macintyre in 1913, Moorcroft set up his own pottery in Burslem, where he continued producing the art wares he had designed earlier, introducing new patterns as well. After William's death in 1945, the pottery was operated by his son, Walter.

Bowl, 7 1/4" d., 1 1/2" h., Clematis patt., signed **$200-225**

Large Moorcroft Pomegranate Bowl

Bowl, 8 1/4" d., 4" h., footed, wide & deep rounded shape w/flat rim, Pomegranate patt., large red & orange fruits & greenish brown leaves w/purple & red berries in the background, stamped mark (ILLUS.) **805**

Bowl, 9" d., 4" h., footed, wide, rounded form w/flat rim, Waving Corn (wheat) patt., decorated in squeezebag w/large curved heads of wheat in green & maroon on a light celadon green ground, stamped Moorcroft & ink mark **715**

Box, cov., Anemone patt., cylindrical, w/fitted flat cover, decorated around the sides & on the cover w/large anemone blossoms in shades of mauve, blue & green against a shaded green ground, glossy glaze, impressed & painted marks, mid-20th c., 3 1/2" h. **316**

Box, cov., Pansy patt., round, squat form, decorated around the sides & cover w/pansies w/a glossy glaze over shades of mauve, purple & green on a cobalt blue ground, impressed marks, ca. 1930, 6" d., 4" h. **403**

Box, cov., Pomegranate patt., round, squat form, decorated around the sides & cover w/pomegranates under a glossy glaze, in shades of mauve, purple & green on a cobalt blue ground, impressed facsimile signature, "Potter to H.M. The Queen" mark & painted initials, ca. 1930, 6" d., 4" h. (small glaze flake inside bowl) **575**

Compote, open, 11" d., 3 5/8" h., Wisteria patt., circular footed bowl w/flared rim, glossy glaze on a design of wisteria in yellow, green & purple on a cobalt blue ground, impressed & painted mark, ca. 1925 (minor surface scratches) **546**

Tall Moorcroft Floral Lamp Base

Lamp base, a metal round base supporting the slightly waisted cylindrical lamp decorated w/bold stylized flowers in red, green & yellow against a cream & cobalt blue ground, signed, replaced socket , minor crazing, 14" h. (ILLUS.) **546**

Perfume bottle w/stopper, figural, round, flattened sides molded as a large pansy blossom, painted in lavender & yellow on a cobalt blue ground, hallmarked silver cap, unsigned, 1 3/4" w., 2" h. **660**

Pitcher, 5" h., 6" d., footed, bulbous, nearly spherical body w/a wide short cylindrical neck w/pinched spout, C-form strap handle, decorated w/yellow & pink irises on a shaded dark blue to light green ground, impressed "MOORCROFT - MADE IN ENGLAND" & script signature **375-400**

Potpourri jar, cov., footed, bulbous, ovoid, shouldered body w/a fitted flat-topped cover pierced w/small holes, the sides of the body w/incised roundels enclosing a cluster of three small heart-shaped leaves, overall cinnabar red glossy glaze, ink script signature, impressed "W225," 3 1/2" d., 3 1/4" h. (chip to threaded inside rim of cover & base) **440-460**

Tea set: cov. teapot, open sugar & creamer; Pomegranate patt., large red & yellow fruits w/purple seeds & yellowish green leaves, green mark, teapot 7 1/2" d., 8" h., the set (small chip & flat hairline in teapot, repair to spout & crack in handle of creamer) **2,860**

Vase, 1 3/4" h., 2" d., miniature, tiny spherical form w/a small flared neck, painted w/stylized roses & blue flowers on a white ground, stamped "MacIntyre Burslem" & script "WM"....................................... **935**

Vase, 3" h., miniature, Anemone patt., nearly spherical body w/a short flared rim, decorated w/two anemone blossoms in mauve & purple on a cobalt blue ground, impressed mark, mid-20th c. **230**

Vase, 3 1/4" h., miniature, Anemone patt., raised rim on a bulbous body, decorated w/two anemone blossoms in mauve & purple on a cobalt blue ground, impressed facsimile William Moorcroft signature & "Potter to H.M. the Queen" mark, ca. 1947 .... **259**

Vase, 4" h., deep blue ground decorated w/purple plums, grapes & green l eaves **225-250**

Moorcroft Eventide Pattern Vase

Vase, 5" h., footed baluster form, Eventide patt., large stylized trees in shades of brown against a light tan & deep rose ground (ILLUS.) **1,265**

Vase, 5 1/4" h., bulbous ovoid body tapering to a cylindrical neck, bluish red flowers & light green leaves on a green shading to dark blue ground, impressed mark & paper label **230**

Vase, 5 1/4" h., Orchid patt., footed spherical body w/a thick molded rim, decorated w/multicolored orchid blossoms on a cobalt blue ground, impressed mark & facsimile William Moorcroft signature & initials, ca. 1930s **288**

Vase, 5 1/2" h., Hibiscus patt., footed ovoid body tapering to a short flared neck, decorated w/three large hibiscus blossoms in mauve & yellow on a shaded green ground, green stamp & paper label, mid-20th c.. **403**

Vase, 5 3/4" h., Orchid patt., bulbous baluster form w/a wide low molded mouth, decorated w/large orchids in shades of mauve, yellow & blue on a shaded green to blue ground w/a glossy glaze, impressed & painted marks, ca. 1947............... **374**

Vase, 6 1/4" h., Orchid patt., wide ovoid body w/a short flared neck, decorated w/large orchids in shades of mauve, purple, yellow & green on a cobalt blue ground w/a glossy glaze, impressed & painted marks, ca. 1947 .... **518**

Signed Moorcroft Eventide Vase

Vase, 6 1/2" h., 3 1/2" d., baluster form w/short flared neck, Eventide patt., squeezebag design of large stylized trees in shades of reddish orange & green flambé glaze, ca. 1925, signed (ILLUS.).. **220**

Vase, 6 3/4" h., 3" d., Florian Ware, slightly waisted cylindrical form w/a rounded base rim & shoulder tapering to a short cylindrical neck, decorated in squeezebag w/blue stylized jonquils & green leaves on a blue ground, ink mark.............. **1,980**

Moorcroft Clematis Pattern Vase

Vase, 7" h., footed ovoid body w/a wide flat mouth, "Clematis" patt., a large blossom & leaves in dark purplish red & orangish red on a reddish orange ground, initials & impressed mark, paper label, mid-20th c., small glaze scratch (ILLUS.) **489**

Vase, 7 1/4" h., ovoid form w/a flared rim, decorated around the sides w/fish & seaweed under a glossy glaze, in shades of yellow, orange & green against a shaded orange to blue flambé ground, impressed mark & painted initials, ca. 1930 .... **3,680**

Vase, 7 1/2" h., 4 1/2" d., disc foot below the simple ovoid body flaring to a wide, flat mouth, decorated w/purple grapes & yellow leaves on a shaded green to dark blue ground, die-stamped "Moorcroft - MADE IN ENGLAND" & w/ink signature **650-700**

Vase, 7 3/4" h., Orchid patt., footed, nearly spherical body tapering to a short cylindrical neck, decorated w/orchid & flower blossoms in mauve, purple, blue & yellow on a cobalt blue ground, impressed factory mark, painted initials of Walter Moorcroft & printed paper label, mid-20th c. **345**

Moorcroft Vase with Blue Berries

Vase, 9" h., 5 1/4" d., simple ovoid body tapering slightly to a short flaring rim, decorated in squeezebag w/a wide band of large blue berries & pale green leaves around the shoulder against a mottled green & dark blue ground, dark crazing lines around rim, ink signature & stamped mark (ILLUS.) **1,150**

Vase, 9" h., 5 1/2" d., a wide disc foot supporting an ovoid body w/a wide flat mouth, decorated w/large red, garnet & orange fruits & leaves on a dark cobalt blue ground, paper label **2,138**

Vase, 9 3/4" h., Wisteria patt., large baluster-form body w/a short rolled neck, decorated around the sides w/purple, mauve & yellow wisteria blossoms on a cobalt blue ground, impressed factory mark & painted signature, mid-20th c. **431**

Vase, 10 1/4" h., bulbous base tapering to a tall neck w/flared rim, decorated w/trailing rose blossoms in cobalt blue & mauve on a sage green lustre ground, signature mark, second quarter 20th c. **2,185**

Vase, 13" h., decorated w/pomegranates & berries among wild birds, in red, yellow & blue, impressed "Moorcroft - Made in England - WM," ca. 1930-45 .... **977**

Tall Baluster-form Moorcroft Vase

Vase, 13" h., tall baluster-form body, Pomegranate patt., large deep red fruits w/moss green leaves against a dark blue ground, drill hole for lamp in base, signed (ILLUS.) **690**

Tall Moorcroft Claremont Vase

Vase, 14" h., tall baluster form w/a short flared neck, Claremont patt., decorated in red, yellow & purple w/toadstools on a mottled green & blue ground, Moorcroft signature & impressed "Moorcroft - Burslem - England M46," ca. 1916-18 (ILLUS.)... **5,100**

Vase, 14 3/8" h., Palm Tree patt., tall tapered ovoid form w/flared rim, decorated in relief w/palm trees & flowers w/a body of water & rocks in the distance, glossy glaze in shades of green, brown, pink & blue, impressed marks, ca. 1997.................. **690**

Tall Moorcroft Vase

Vase, 16" h., tall slender ovoid body, Wisteria patt. w/flambé glaze, impressed marks, ca. 1930, drilled (ILLUS.).. **975-1,000**

Large Moorcroft Spanish Pattern Vase

Vase, 16" h., 10 1/2" d., a round foot below the tall trumpet-form body, Spanish patt., overall bold scrolling blossoms & leaves in reds, pinks, greens & blues, two chips on base, green slip signature mark & stamped "Made for Liberty & Co.," 1903-13 (ILLUS.) **4,312**

Large Moorcroft Vase with Grapes

Vase, 17" h., "Grape and Leaf" patt., wide baluster form w/a short flaring neck, decorated w/fruit & leaves in shades of orange, red, purple & mauve on a shaded rust & dark blue ground, glossy glaze, impressed mark, ca. 1930 (ILLUS.)............... **4,888**

Morton Potteries

A total of six potteries were in operation at various times in Morton, Illinois, from 1877 to 1976. All traced their origins from the Morton Brick and Tile Company begun in 1877 by six Rapp brothers who came to America in the early 1870s to escape forced military service under Kaiser Wilhelm I. Sons, nephews and cousins of the founding fathers were responsible for the continuation of the pottery industry in Morton as a result of buyouts or the establishment of new and separate operations. The potteries are listed chronologically by beginning dates.

Morton's natural clay deposits were ideal for the Rapps' venture into pottery production. Local clay was used until it was depleted in 1940. That clay fired out to a golden ecru color. After 1940, clay was imported from South Carolina and Indiana. It fired out snow white. The differences in clay allow one to easily date production at the Morton potteries. Only a few items were marked by any of the potteries. Occasionally, paper labels were used, but most of those have long disappeared. Glaze is sometimes a determinant. Early glazes were Rockingham brown, green and cobalt blue, or transparent, to produce yellowware. In the '20s and '30s colorful drip glazes were used. In the later years solid pastel and Deco colors were in vogue.

Most of Morton's potteries were short-lived, operating for twenty years or less. Their products are elusive. However, Morton Pottery Company was in operation for fifty-four years, and its products appear regularly in today's secondary market.

Rapp Brothers Brick & Tile Company & Morton Pottery Works (1877-1915) - Morton Earthenware Company (1915-1917)

Baker, deep, yellowware, 10" d........................ **$125**

Bank, figural acorn, brown Rockingham glaze, no advertising.. **50**

Three Rapp Brothers Mugs

Churn, mottled brown Rockingham glaze, 4
gal. **200**

Rapp Bros. Green-glazed Creamer

Creamer, waisted cylindrical form w/molded
bark & flowers under a dark green glaze,
5" h. (ILLUS.).. **50**

Morton Jardiniere

Jardiniere, tapering cylindrical form, embossed leaf design, green, 7" d. (ILLUS.)....... **50**
Lapel button, model of an elephant w/em-
bossed "GOP" on side, dark brown glaze,
1 1/8 x 1 3/4" **95**

Rapp Bros. Turk's Turban Mold

Mold, food, Turk's turban shape, field tile
clay w/dark brown glaze, 7" d. (ILLUS.).......... **75**

Mug, cylindrical, w/lightly molded lappet rim
band, brown Rockingham glaze,
3 1/4" h., each (ILLUS. left & center, top
of page).. **50**
Mug, cylindrical, yellowware, 2 3/4" h.
(ILLUS. right with other mugs) **75**
Paperweight, model of a bison, advertises
Rock Sand Company, brown Rocking-
ham glaze, 2 7/8" l. (ILLUS.) **70**
Pitcher, jug-type, milk (Dutch jug), brown
Rockingham glaze, 3 1/2 pt. (ILLUS.).............. **80**

Rapp Bros. Sauerkraut Crock

Sauerkraut crock, cover/press, impressed
mark, dark brown glaze, 4 gal., rare,
11" h. (ILLUS.) **150**
Stein, barrel-shaped w/"Trinke was klar ist
und rede was wahr ist" embossed around
rim & base, green, 1 pt. **65**
Teapot, cov., pear-shaped, brown Rocking-
ham glaze, 2 cup **80**

Rapp Bros. Acorn-shaped Teapot

Teapot, cov., acorn-shaped, mottled brown
Rockingham glaze, 3 3/4 cup size
(ILLUS.).. **90**

Cliftwood Art Potteries, Inc. (1920-1940)

Figural Cow Creamer

Creamer, figural cow, standing, tail forms handle, chocolate brown drip glaze, 3 3/4 x 6" (ILLUS.) **90**

Cliftwood Art Deco Lamp Base

Lamp base, Art Deco style, spherical body on four square legs, pinkish orchid drip glaze, base 4" h. (ILLUS.) **40**

Cliftwood Figure of a Billiken

Figure of a Billiken, seated, dark brown Rockingham glaze, 10 1/2" h. (ILLUS.) **100**

Flower frog, figural turtle, holes pierced on back, bluish mulberry drip glaze, 4" l. **30**

Lamp Base with Sailing Ships

Lamp base, waisted cylindrical form w/a stepped shoulder, embossed panels around the sides showing a sailing ship, herbage green glaze, round metal foot, 11" h. (ILLUS.) **50**

Cliftwood Model of a Bison

Model of bison, natural colors of light & dark brown, 9 1/2" l., 6 1/2" h. (ILLUS.) **200**

Cliftwood Model of German Shepherd

Model of dog, German shepherd, reclining,
white, 8 1/2" l., 6" h. (ILLUS.)............................ **70**
Model of elephant, standing, chocolate
brown drip glaze, 7 1/4 x 13 1/2"................... **125**

Clifton Model of a Frog

Model of frog, seated, glass eyes, shaded
green to white glaze, 5" h. (ILLUS.)................. **50**
Model of lioness, standing, chocolate brown
drip glaze, 16" h., 5" h.. **95**

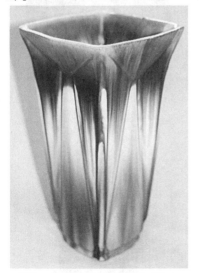

Clifton Deco Vase with Drip Glaze

Vase, 8" h., Art Deco style, square gently
flaring sides w/a widely flared rim, choco-
late brown drip glaze (ILLUS.).......................... **65**

Cliftwood Vase with Chain Design

Vase, 10" h., footed, slightly flaring cylindrical body w/rounded base & shoulder w/a
flat mouth, lightly embossed vertical
chain bands, matte orchid glaze (ILLUS.)........ **65**
Vase, 16" h., footed baluster-form body
w/flat rim, No. 114, bluish grey drip glaze........ **85**
Vase, 18 1/4" h., urn form w/figural snakes
swallowing fish handles, No. 132, choco-
late brown drip glaze... **125**
Wall pocket, bullet-shaped w/handle on
each side, matte turquoise & ivory glaze,
5" w., 7 1/2" h... **70**
Wall pocket, elongated bell shape, No. 123,
matte green glaze, 3 1/3" w., 8 3/4" h.............. **50**

Morton Pottery Company (1922-1976)

Bank, figural, cat, sitting, yellow & white,
8 1/2" h.. **50**
Bank, figural, hen on nest, white w/red cold
painted comb, black feather detail, yellow
beak, 4" h.. **50**
Bank, figural, house, shoe-shaped, yellow
w/green roof, 6 1/2" h. **30**
Bank, figural, Little Brown Church,
2 5/8 x 3 5/8", 3 3/4" h. **25**

Morton Pottery Teddy Bear Bank

Bank, figural, Teddy bear, seated w/legs
outstretched, brown, pink, blue & black
on white, 8" h. (ILLUS.) **40**

Morton Pottery Canister Set

Canister set: marked "Coffee," "Flour," "Sugar" & "Tea;" white cylindrical base w/yellow hat-shaped lid w/high button handle, 9" & 10" h., the set (ILLUS.)............... **45**

Cookie jar, cov., baby bird in blue & yellow spray over white.. **60**

Cookie jar, cov., basket of fruit, green or brown basket w/colored fruit, No. 3720, each **50**

Panda Bear Cookie Jar

Cookie jar, cov., panda bear, black & white, front paws crossed (ILLUS.) **80**

Creamer & sugar bowl, model of chicken & rooster, black & white w/cold-painted red comb, pr. **55**

Morton Pottery Egg Tray

Egg tray, hexagonal cluster of eggs & half-round eggs w/a figural chick in the center, 12" w. (ILLUS.)... **45**

Figure of John F. Kennedy, Jr., standing on square base, right hand to head in salute position, gold paint trim, rare version, 7" h. **125**

Grass grower, bisque, bust of "Jiggs," the comic strip character, 5" h. **35**

Grass grower, bisque, model of a standing pig, 7 1/2" l., 3 3/4" h.. **20**

Head vase, woman w/1920s hairstyle, wide brim hat, white matte glaze.............................. **75**

Head vase, woman w/1940s hairstyle, pill box hat, blue matte glaze................................... **55**

Head vase, woman w/upswept hairstyle, white w/red lips, bow in hair & heart-shaped locket **40**

Morton Pottery Jardiniere

Jardiniere, squared form w/swelled sides, low rectangular mouth, tab side handles, small block feet, pink ground w/embossed floral sprig in blue & green, 4 1/2" h. (ILLUS.)... **24**

Morton Kerosene Lamp

Lamp, kerosene, brass fixture w/glass chimney, cylindrical body w/ribbed base & relief-molded swag design, white glaze (ILLUS.) **55**

Morton Davy Crockett Lamp & Shade

Lamp, table, figural Davy Crockett w/bear beside tree, original shade (ILLUS.) **200**

Dog with Pheasant Lamp Base

Lamp base, model of a black & white dog w/brown pheasant in mouth, relief-molded brown & green grassy base, double opening in planter, 5 x 10", 8 1/4" h. (ILLUS.) **90**

Morton Pottery Bird Planter

Planter, model of a bird w/bright colors of yellow, blue, orange & red on a green grassy base, 5" h. (ILLUS.) **24**

Morton Rooster on Rockers Planter

Planter, model of a rooster on rockers, yellow & pink sprayed glaze w/h.p. black & red trim, 4 1/2" h. (ILLUS.) **24**

Boston Terrier Planter

Planter, model of Boston terrier, sitting, black & white (ILLUS.) **30**

Kitten & Fish Bowl TV Lamp

TV lamp, figural, black kitten seated on chartreuse stump base reaching for glass fish bowl, 9" h. (ILLUS.) **50**
Vase, model of a tree trunk, matte green glaze, No. 260 .... **24**

Morton Heart-shaped Vase

Morton Santa Claus Punch Set

Vase, 12" h., model of a large & small red heart on an oval base, rare (ILLUS.)............... **50**

Christmas Novelties

Figural Santa Claus Head Cigarette Box

Cigarette box, cov., figural Santa Claus head, hat cover becomes ashtray, cold painted red hat (ILLUS.).................................... **50**

Lollipop tree, w/holes to insert lollipops, green bisque, 9 1/4" h............................. **45**

Model of a sleigh, Victorian style, white w/h.p. holly & berries, No. 3015 .... **30**

Model of a sleigh, Victorian-style, red paint, No. 772... **40**

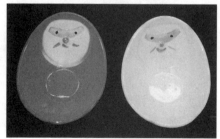

Morton Santa Nut Dishes

Nut dish, oval, stylized Santa face, red background, rare, 2 1/2 x 3" (ILLUS. left)............... **25**

Nut dish, oval, stylized Santa face, white background, rare, 2 1/2 x 3" (ILLUS. right)... **30**

Plate, 8", figural Santa Claus face, h.p. white w/blue eyes, pink cheeks, hat cold painted red.. **50**

Plate, 12", figural Santa Claus face, white w/blue eyes, pink cheeks, hat cold painted red **95**

Punch set: punch bowl & 8 punch cups; figural Santa Claus head, white w/pink trim, green stone eyes, 9 pcs. (ILLUS. of part, top of page) **225**

Midwest Potteries, Inc. (1940-1944)

Midwest Leaping Deer Book Ends

Book ends, Art Deco style, a stylized leaping deer against an upright disc, round foot, blue glaze, 7 3/4" h., pr. (ILLUS.) **40**

Figure of baseball player, batter, grey uniform, 7 1/4" h.. **300**

Figure of baseball player, catcher, white uniform, 6 3/4" h... **275**

Figure of baseball player, umpire, black uniform, 6 1/4" h.. **250**

Model of deer w/antlers, white w/gold trim, 12" h. **50**

Midwest Potteries Ducks

Model of ducks, three attached in graduated
sizes, white w/yellow trim, 6" l. (ILLUS.)......... **36**
Model of flamingo, brownish green spray
glaze, 10 1/2" h. **50**

Midwest Potteries Flying Fish

Model of flying fish, stylized form in leaping
pose, white glaze, 9 1/4" h. (ILLUS.)............... **35**

Midwest Potteries Swan Model

Model of swan, large stylized bird w/tall upright curved & flared wings, long neck

turned to back, dark brown & yellow drip
glaze, 8" h. (ILLUS.)... **24**
Models of golden pheasants, white w/gold
trim, male 4 3/4" h., female 4 1/2" h., pr.
(ILLUS., bottom of page).................................... **45**

Midwest Potteries Hen & Rooster

Models of hen & rooster, white w/cold painted red & yellow trim, hen 7" h., rooster
8" h., pr. (ILLUS.)... **50**
Pitcher, 4 1/2" h., figural, seated cow, brown
& white drip glaze **25**

Midwest Potteries Deco-style Planter

Planter, figural, Art Deco style, standing
draped nude woman flanked by globe-
shaped planters, platinum glaze,
5 3/4" l., 5 1/2" h. (ILLUS.) **40**

Midwest Potteries Golden Pheasants

Calico Cat & Gingham Dog Planters

Planter, figural, Calico Cat, yellow & blue spatter on white, 7 1/2" h. (ILLUS. right)... **24**

Planter, figural, Gingham Dog, blue & yellow spatter on white, 7 1/2" h. (ILLUS. left with Calico Cat)... **24**

Midwest Potteries Owl TV Lamp

TV lamp, model of an owl w/spread wings, sprayed brown on white ground, green eyes, 12" h. (ILLUS.)... **75**

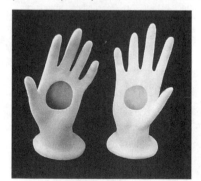

Midwest Potteries Hand Vases

Vase, 4 1/2" h., bud-type, model of an open hand, white matte glaze (ILLUS. right).. **20**

Vase, 4 1/2" h., bud-type, model of open hand, turquoise matte glaze (ILLUS. left) **20**

American Art Potteries (1947-1963)

American Art Candlestick

Candlestick, three-light, open doughnut-shaped ring fitted w/three sockets, wide round foot, dark bluish green glaze, No. 140J, 7 1/2" w., 6 1/2" h. (ILLUS.) **35**

Double Cornucopia Table Lamp

Lamp, table, double cornucopia form, white w/gold trim, 13" h. (ILLUS.)................................ **40**

French Poodle Table Lamp

Lamp, table, figural, model of a seated French poodle, black ground w/sprayed pink on bands of curls, 15" h. (ILLUS.) **50**

Crouching Panther Table Lamp

Lamp, table, figural, stylized crouching panther on a tall tree trunk, rose & black
spray glaze, 11 1/2" h. (ILLUS.) **50**

American Art Bird on Stump Model

Model of bird on stump, white w/gold trim,
7" h. (ILLUS.) **20**
Model of cockatoo on stump, natural colors,
No. 315, 7" h. **30**

Rearing Horse by American Art

Model of horse, rearing position, brown &
green spray glaze (ILLUS.) **18**
Model of pig, black w/white band, No. 89,
5 1/2" h. **40**

Chunky Pony Figural Planter

Planter, figural, model of a chunky standing
pony, dark streaky mauve & pink spray
glaze, sticker on side, No. 49, 5 1/4" l.,
4 3/4" h. (ILLUS.) **15**

Bird on Stump Planter

Planter, figural, model of a long-tailed bird
perched on a stump, green & brown
spray glaze, 7" h. (ILLUS.) **20**

Recumbent Deer Figural Planter

Planter, figural, model of a recumbent deer
w/head turned over shoulder, green &
brown spray glaze, 5" h. (ILLUS.) **20**

Doe and Fawn Figural Planter

Planter, figural, model of a standing doe bending her head down to her reclining fawn, mottled brown glaze, No. 322J, 7 1/4" h. (ILLUS.) 25

Planter, figural, model of a swordfish, blue & mauve spray glaze, No. 307P, 7 1/2 x 11"... 25

Vase, 8" h., ewer-form, blue & mauve glaze w/gold trim, No. 209G 35

Vase, 10 1/2" h., double cornucopia form, white w/gold trim, No. 208B 30

Vase, 12" h., octagonal, pink & mauve spray glaze, No. 214G.. 25

Wall pocket, figural, model of a dustpan, white w/h.p. underglaze decoration, No. 81C.. 24

Wall pocket, figural, model of a red apple on a green leaf, No. 127N................................. 20

Wall pocket, figural, model of a teapot, white w/h.p. underglaze decoration, No. 79C.......... 24

Window sill box, arched diamond design, green & pink spray glaze, No. 32I, 3 1/2 x 4 x 10" 30

Window sill box, white w/h.p. ivy, No. 25D, 2 1/2 x 4 x 13" 30

Mulberry

Mulberry or Flow Mulberry ironstone wares were produced in the Staffordshire district of England in the period between 1840 and 1870 at many of the same factories that produced its close "cousin," Flow Blue china. In fact, some of the early Flow Blue patterns were also decorated with the dark blackish or brownish purple mulberry coloration and feature the same heavy smearing or "flown" effect. Produced on sturdy ironstone bodies, the designs were either transfer-printed or hand-painted (Brushstroke) with an Asian, Scenic, Floral or Marble design. Some patterns were also decorated with additional colors over or under the glaze; these are designated in the following listings as "w/polychrome."

Quite a bit of this ware is still to be found and is becoming increasingly sought-after by collectors, although presently its values lag somewhat behind similar Flow Blue pieces. The standard references to Mulberry wares is Petra Williams' book, Flow Blue China and Mulberry Ware, Similarity and Value Guide and Mulberry Ironstone - Flow Blue's Best Kept Little Secret, by Ellen R. Hill.

ACADIA (maker unknown, ca. 1850)
Creamer, 6" h., Classic Gothic shape $300

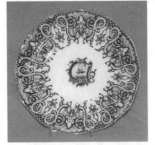

Acadia Plate

Plate, 8" d. (ILLUS.).. 200

AMERILLIA (Podmore, Walker & Co., ca. 1850)
Egg cup 200
Plate, 9 1/2" 95

Amerillia Covered Vegetable Dish

Vegetable dish, cov. (ILLUS.).............................. 350

ATHENS (Charles Meigh, ca. 1845)
Creamer, 6", vertical-paneled Gothic shape 150
Cup plate 100

Athens Pitcher

Pitcher, 6-paneled, 10" h. (ILLUS.)...................... 350
Punch cup 125
Sugar, cov., vertical-paneled Gothic shape 200

ATHENS (Wm. Adams & Son, ca. 1849)
Cup plate 95
Plate, 8 1/2" d... 55
Soup Plate, w/flanged rim, 9" d............................ 90
Sugar, cov., full-paneled Gothic shape.............. 225
Teapot, cov., full-paneled Gothic shape 310

AVA (T.J. & J. Mayer, ca. 1850)
Cup & saucer, handleless, w/polychrome 95
Plate, 9 1/2" d., w/polychrome............................. 85
Plate, 10 1/2" d., w/polychrome 95
Platter, 16" l., w/polychrome 250

Ava Sauce Tureen & Undertray

Sauce tureen, cover & undertray, w/poly-
chrome, 3 pcs. (ILLUS.)................................. 500

BEAUTIES OF CHINA (Mellor Venables & Co., ca. 1845)
Cup plate 95
Plate, 7 1/2" d., w/polychrome.............................. 65
Platter, 14" l., w/polychrome 225
Sauce tureen, cover, ladle & undertray, long
octagon, 4 pcs.. 750

BOCHARA (James Edwards, ca. 1850)
Creamer, full-paneled Gothic shape, 6" h. 150
Pitcher, 7 1/2" h., full-paneled Gothic
shape.. 170
Plate, 10 1/2" d.. 75

Bochara Teapot

Teapot, cov., pedestaled Gothic style
(ILLUS.).. 350

BRUNSWICK (Mellor Venables & Co., ca. 1845)
Plate, 7 1/2" d., w/polychrome.............................. 65
Platter, 16" l., w/polychrome 275
Relish dish, stubby mitten-shaped, w/poly-
chrome... 150
Sugar, cov., Classic Gothic shape, w/poly-
chrome... 225

BRYONIA (Paul Utzchneider & Co., ca. 1880)
Cup & saucer, handled 60
Gravy boat 150
Plate, 7 1/2" d... 50

Bryonia Plate

Plate, 9 1/2" d. (ILLUS.)... 65

CEYLON (Charles Meigh, ca. 1840)
Plate, 9 1/2" d... 75
Plate, 10 1/2" d., w/polychrome............................ 85
Platter, 14" l., w/polychrome 175
Vegetable bowl, open, small................................. 125

CHUSAN (P. Holdcroft, ca. 1850)
Plate, 9 1/2" d.. 80

Chusan Potato Bowl

Potato bowl, 11" d. (ILLUS.) 250

CLEOPATRA (F. Morley & Co., ca. 1850)
Basin & ewer, w/polychrome 750
Plate, 9 1/2" d.. 70
Soap box, cover & drainer, 3 pcs........................ 350
Soup plate, w/flanged rim, 9" d. 90

COREA (Joseph Clementson, ca. 1850)
Cup & saucer, handleless 75
Sugar, cov., long hexagon 250
Teapot, cov., long hexagon 350

COREAN (Podmore, Walker & Co., ca. 1850)
Cup plate 100
Cup & saucer, handled, large.............................. 125
Relish, mitten-shaped... 135

Corean Sauce Tureen

Sauce tureen, cover & undertray, 3 pcs.
(ILLUS.)... 500

Corean Covered Sugar

Sugar, cov., oval bulbous style (ILLUS.) 350

COTTON PLANT (J. Furnival, ca. 1850)
Creamer, paneled grape shape, w/poly-
chrome, 6 5/8" h. 200

Cotton Plant Teapot

Teapot, cov., cockscomb handle, w/poly-
chrome (ILLUS.).............................. **750**

CYPRUS (Wm. Davenport, ca. 1845)
Cup plate **95**

Cyprus Gravy

Gravy boat, unusual handle (ILLUS.)................. **200**
Pitcher, 11" h., 6-sided......................... **250**

DORA (E. Challinor, ca. 1850)
Plate, 9 1/2" d.................................. **85**

Dora Baltic Shape Teapot

Teapot, cov., Baltic shape (ILLUS.).................... **650**

FERN & VINE (maker unknown, ca. 1850)

Fern & Vine Creamer

Creamer, Classic Gothic style, 6" h.
(ILLUS.)...................................... **350**
Plate, 7 1/2" d................................. **95**

FLORA (Hulme & Booth, ca. 1850)
Creamer, w/polychrome, grand loop shape,
6" h... **150**

FLORA (T. Walker, ca. 1847)
Cup & saucer, handleless **65**
Plate, 7 1/2" d................................. **75**
Plate, 9 1/2" d................................. **85**
Sugar, cov., Classic Gothic shape..................... **250**

FLOWER VASE (T.J. & J. Mayer, ca. 1850)
Teapot, cov., w/polychrome, Prize Bloom
shape................................... **560**

FOLIAGE (J. Edwards, ca. 1850)
Gravy boat **150**

Foliage Plate

Plate, 8" d. (ILLUS.) **85**

GERANIUM (Podmore, Walker & Co., ca. 1850)

Geranium Plate

Plate, 8" d. (ILLUS.) **65**
Waste bowl **135**

JARDINIERE (Villeroy & Boch, ca. 1880)
Gravy boat **125**
Plate, 7 1/2" d................................. **55**
Plate, 9 1/2" d................................. **75**
Vegetable bowl, open, round............................... **150**

JEDDO (Wm. Adams, ca. 1849)
Cup plate **95**
Cup & saucer, handleless **85**
Relish dish, octagonal........................... **125**

Jeddo Sugar Bowl

Sugar, cov., full-paneled Gothic shape
(ILLUS.).. 195
Teapot, cov., full-paneled Gothic shape 300

KAN-SU (Thomas Walker, ca. 1847)
Cup & saucer, handleless 75
Plate, 7 1/2" d.. 60
Platter, 14" l. 250

Kan-su Covered Vegetable Dish

Vegetable dish, cov., octagonal (ILLUS.) 375

MARBLE (A. Shaw, ca. 1850)

Marble Creamer

Creamer, 10 panel Gothic shape, 6" h.
(ILLUS.).. 250
Invalid feeder, large.. 500
Waste bowl 150

MARBLE (Mellor Venables, ca. 1845)
Plate, 9 1/2" d... 75
Teapot, cov., child's, vertical paneled
Gothic 350

Marble Teapot

Teapot, cov., vertical paneled Gothic shape
(ILLUS.)... 600

MEDINA (J. Furnival, ca. 1850)
Cup & saucer, handleless 65
Gravy boat 155
Sugar, cov., cockscomb handle 400

NANKIN (Davenport, ca. 1845)

Nankin Pitcher

Pitcher, 8" h., mask spout jug w/polychrome
(ILLUS.)... 350
Plate, 8 1/2" d., w/polychrome............................... 75

NING PO (R. Hall, ca. 1840)
Cup & saucer, handleless 85
Plate, 10 1/2" d. 95
Soup plate, w/flanged rim, 10" d. 95

PARISIAN GROUPS (J. Clementson, ca. 1850)
Plate, 7 1/2" d., w/polychrome............................... 60
Plate, 8 1/2" d., w/polychrome............................... 70
Sauce dish, w/polychrome 65

Parisian Sauce Tureen & Undertray

Sauce tureen, cover & undertray, w/poly-
chrome, 3 pcs. (ILLUS.)............................ 450

PELEW (Edward Challinor, ca. 1850)
Cup & saucer, handleless, pedestaled................ 95
Plate, 7 1/2" d... 60
Plate, 10 1/2" d... 90
Punch cup, ring handle..................................... 100

Pelew Teapot

Teapot, cov., pumpkin shape (ILLUS.).............. 450

PERUVIAN (John Wedge Wood, ca. 1850)

Peruvian Cup & Saucer

Cup & saucer, handleless, "double bulge"
(ILLUS.).. 95
Gravy boat 145
Teapot, cov., 16 paneled.................................. 400
Waste bowl, "double bulge"............................... 150

PHANTASIA (J. Furnival, ca. 1850)

Phantasia Creamer

Creamer, w/polychrome, cockscomb han-
dle, 6" h. (ILLUS.)..................................... 450
Cup plate, w/polychrome.................................. 95
Plate, 9 1/2" d., w/polychrome........................... 85
Sugar, cov., w/polychrome, cockscomb
handle.. 500
Teapot, cov., w/polychrome, cockscomb
handle.. 700

RHONE SCENERY (T.J. & J. Mayer, ca. 1850)
Gravy boat 150
Plate, 7 1/2" d... 45
Plate, 10 1/2" d... 65
Sauce tureen, cover & undertray, 3 pcs. 500
Sugar, cov., full-paneled Gothic shape............. 200

SCINDE (T. Walker, ca. 1847)
Creamer, Classic Gothic shape, 6" h. 150
Plate, 9 1/2" d... 80
Soup plate, w/flanged rim, 9" d. 90
Teapot, cov., Classic Gothic shape.................... 350

SHAPOO (T. & R. Boote, ca. 1850)
Plate, 8 1/2" d... 75
Sugar, cov., Primary shape 300
Teapot, cov., Primary shape.............................. 450
Vegetable dish, cov., flame finial 350

TEMPLE (Podmore, Walker & Co., ca. 1850)
Cup plate 75

Temple Cup & Saucer

Cup & saucer, handled (ILLUS.).......................... 95
Plate, 8 1/2" d... 55
Sugar, cov., Classic Gothic shape...................... 200
Teapot, cov., Classic Gothic shape.................... 350

VINCENNES (J. Alcock, ca. 1840)
Cup & saucer, handleless, thumbprint................ 95
Plate, 7 1/2" d... 60
Plate, 10 1/2" d... 80

Vincennes Punch Cup

Punch cup (ILLUS.)... 125
Soup tureen, cover & undertray, 10-sided, 3
pcs. 2,000

VINCENNES (J. & G. Alcock, ca. 1845)

Vincennes Compote

Compote, Gothic Cameo shape (ILLUS.).......... **650**

WASHINGTON VASE (Podmore, Walker & Co., ca. 1850)
Creamer, Classic Gothic shape, 6" h. **225**
Cup & saucer, handleless **95**
Plate, 10 1/2" d.. **85**
Soup plate, w/flanged rim, 9" d........................... **85**
Teapot, cov., bulbous shape............................... **600**

WHAMPOA (Mellor Venables & Co., ca. 1845)
Gravy boat **165**
Plate, 10 1/2" d.. **95**
Sauce tureen, cov., long octagon shape, 2 pcs... **300**

WREATH (Thomas Furnival, ca. 1850)

Wreath Ewer

Ewer (ILLUS.)... **350**
Plate, 9 1/2" d. **95**

Newcomb College Pottery

This pottery was established in the art department of Newcomb College, New Orleans, Louisiana, in 1897. Each piece was hand-thrown and bore the potter's mark & decorator's monogram on the base. It was always a studio business and never operated as a factory. Its pieces are, therefore, scarce, with the early wares being eagerly sought. The pottery closed in 1940.

Newcomb College Pottery Mark

Bowl, 4 1/2" d., 2 1/2" h., footed half-round form w/flat rim, carved around the rim w/a narrow band of pink buds on a green & blue ground, by Sadie Irvine, 1927, marked "NC - IS - PV71" **$1,238**
Bowl-vase, wide spherical form tapering to a wide flat rim, carved w/a continuous landscape of live oaks draped in Spanish moss w/a full moon behind, 1939, marked "NC - Y38 - FHF," 7" d., 5 1/2" h. (very tight short hairline at rim)................... **3,375**

Newcomb Glossy-glazed Charger

Charger, decorated overall w/large fig branches w/leaves & fruit in dark blue & bluish yellow on a pale blue ground, glossy glaze, by Irene Borden Keep, 1902, few tiny clay pimples, marked, 10 3/4" d. (ILLUS.).................................... **10,350**

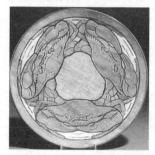

Large Newcomb Charger with Crabs

Charger, incised around the center w/three large blue crabs on a blue ground, by Sabrina Wells, 1904, marked "NC - M - S.E. Wells - YY64," short, tight line on back, 13" d. (ILLUS.) **28,125**

Very Rare Newcomb College Jar

Jar, cov., large bulbous ovoid body w/a fitted domed cover, the upper half of the body carved w/a band of stylized sweet peas, the cover carved w/a central blossom surrounded w/a band reading "Here are sweet peas on tiptoe for a flight," by Mazie T. Ryan, 1903, signed "M.C. - M.T.R. - W - MR - SS - 64," 6" d., 8" h. (ILLUS.)... **42,188**

Newcomb Jardiniere, Teapot & Vase

Jardiniere, large bulbous ovoid form w/a wide flat closed rim, decorated w/large white lilies w/yellow centers raised on green stems against a cobalt blue ground, by Harriet Joor, 1903, marked "NC - JM - X97 - HJ," two rim repairs, 10 1/2" d., 8 3/4" h. (ILLUS. right with teapot & vase).. **13,500**

Teapot, cov., footed conical body w/angled spout & handle, fitted low domed cover w/button finial, carved around the lower body w/a band of wild roses in light pink & yellow on a dark bluish green ground w/dark blue trim, by Alma Mason, 1911, marked "NC - EG44 - A.M. - B.," 5 1/2" d., 4 1/4" h. (ILLUS. front left with jardiniere & vase)... **3,375**

Newcomb College Tyg with Flowers

Tyg (three-handled mug), wide slightly tapering cylindrical body w/three squared tubular handles from the rim to the base, decorated around the rim w/a band of white flowers against bands of dark blue & white, pale blue lower body & white handles, old tight hairline in one handle, by Marie De Hoa LeBlanc, 1905, 5" d., 3 3/4" h. (ILLUS.)... **4,600**

Vase, 3" h., 3 3/4" d., miniature, bulbous ovoid form tapering to a short flat neck, decorated w/a vertical band of light blue bell-shaped flowers & green leaves around the sides on a cobalt blue ground, by Henrietta Bailey, 1929, marked "NC - HB3359 - JM".. **1,463**

Vase, 3 3/4" h., 3 1/4" d., miniature, simple ovoid body w/a flat mouth, painted w/a continuous upright band of strawberries & leaf clusters in dark blue on a pale blue ground, by Ester Elliott, 1902, marked "NC - JM - EHE - R19" (ILLUS. upper left with teapot & jardiniere)................................ **9,000**

Vase, 3 7/8" h., bulbous ovoid body w/narrow molded rim, deeply carved & painted blue & green trees on matte glaze, by Anna Frances Simpson, ca. 1926, impressed w/Newcomb logo, the date, "PO60," shape number "5" & initials of potter, Joseph Meyer, incised artist's initials (two small flat chips off bottom edge) **1,670**

Newcomb Vase with Tall Pines

Vase, 5 1/4" h., 3 1/4" d., ovoid body w/a narrow shoulder tapering to a short, wide cylindrical neck, crisply carved w/a landscape of tall pines in bluish green on a washed blue ground, small stilt-pull chips, by Sadie Irvine, 1917, signed (ILLUS.)... **3,450**

Three Early Newcomb College Vases

Rare Newcomb Vase with Pod Design

Early Newcomb Vase with Egrets

Vase, 7 1/4" h., 5 1/4" d., slightly tapering ovoid body w/a wide closed rim, incised around the shoulder w/large stylized seed pods on long stems in shades of blue & greenish blue, interior firing line at rim, by Marie Benson, 1905 (ILLUS.)....... **10,925**

Vase, 8" h., 6" d., tapering ovoid form w/the shoulder centering a wide low rolled neck flanked by upright angled loop handles, painted w/four different views of large white egrets among sea grass in blue, white & green on a cobalt blue ground, pre-1902, by Marie M. Ross, restoration to one handle, impressed mark (ILLUS., next column) **25,875**

Vase, 8 3/4" h., 4 3/4" d., gently tapering cylindrical form w/a rounded shoulder & short cylindrical rim, decorated w/light periwinkle blue wisteria blossoms on a cobalt blue & celadon ground, by Maude Robinson, 1904, restored rim hairline, marked "NC - JM - Maude Robinson - XX41" (ILLUS. left, top of page)................ **13,500**

Rare Newcomb Vase with Flowers

Vase, 9 1/2" h., 4" d., footed cylindrical form w/rounded base & shoulder tapering to a short, flat neck, decorated w/stylized yellow flowers & dark blue leaves on a pale denim ground, glossy glaze, four hairlines from rim, unknown artist, dated 1902 (ILLUS.).. **27,600**

Fine Newcomb Landscape Vase

Vase, 10 1/4" h., 6 1/2" d., wide ovoid body tapering to a flat mouth, decorated w/a landscape of live oak trees & Spanish moss w/a full moon in the background, shades of dark & light blue & yellow, by Anna Frances Simpson, marked (ILLUS.).. **17,250**

Vase, 10 1/2" h., tall, sharply tapering cylindrical form w/small flared mouth, carved & painted eucalyptus leaves & seed pods suspended from the rim, in light pink & green matte on a blue ground, by Sadie Irvine, impressed mark **4,485**

Vase, 11" h., 5" d., tall ovoid form, crisply carved & decorated w/a tall oak tree w/Spanish moss w/a full moon beyond, shades of dark & light blue w/a yellow moon, by A.F. Simpson, 1927, marked "NC - M - AFS - QC35" (ILLUS. center with wisteria vase) **16,313**

Exceptional Newcomb Landscape

Vase, 11" h., 6" d., slender ovoid form tapering to a short cylindrical neck, decorated w/a continuous landscape of live oak trees draped w/Spanish moss w/a full moon beyond, in shades of dark & light blue, greenish blue & white, exceptional,

by Anna Frances Simpson, 1929 (ILLUS.)... **17,250**

Tall Newcomb Vase with Trees

Vase, 11 1/4" h., 4 1/2" d., tall, slender cylindrical form w/a widely flaring rim, finely carved w/a continuous band of tall cypress & pine trees in medium bluish green on a pale bluish green ground, by Leona Nicholson, 1907, restoration to a hairline, marked "NC - BP46 - M - LN" (ILLUS.)... **8,625**

Very Rare Newcomb College Vase

Vase, 12" h., tall, gently tapering cylindrical form w/a rounded shoulder centering a short rolled neck, carved & painted bamboo stalks in several tones of green against a blue ground, all covered in a glossy glaze, by Henrietta Bailey, ca. 1909 (ILLUS.)... **46,750**

Vase, 12 1/4" h., 7 1/2" d., large tapering ovoid form w/a closed rim, decorated w/tall pine trees in dark blue & green against a background of dark blue & pale & dark yellow, by Harriet Joor, 1902, restoration to line at shoulder, marked "NC - JM - HJ - U87 - Q" (ILLUS. right with wisteria vase).. **21,375**

Rare Newcomb Roadrunner Vase

Vase, 12 1/2" h., 7 3/4" d., wide ovoid body tapering to a short cylindrical neck, decorated around the shoulder w/a wide band of racing roadrunner birds, the birds in bluish white on dark blue, the background in streaky cream & dark blue, glossy glaze, Marie De Hoa LeBlanc, 1902 (ILLUS.)... **43,125**

Very Rare Newcomb Vase with Irises

Vase, 14 1/2" h., 9" d., simple tall ovoid form tapering to a flat mouth, carved overall w/tall blue & yellow irises on tall green leafy stems, glossy glaze, Henrietta Bailey, 1909 (ILLUS.)................................. **46,000**

Rare Newcomb College Wall Pocket

Wall pocket, long slender conical form, carved around the upper body w/a band of stylized trees in cobalt blue & green, dark blue lower body, glossy glaze, by Leona Nicholson, ca. 1904, 4" d., 11" l. (ILLUS.).. **9,350**

Nicodemus

The promise of a job distributing newspapers brought Chester Nicodemus to Cleveland, Ohio, in 1921 to attend the Cleveland School of Art. Studying sculpture, Chester graduated in 1925 and began teaching at the Dayton Art Institute. That same year he married his longtime sweetheart, Florine Massett, a costume designer. In 1930, while attending Ohio State University, where he studied under ceramist Arthur Baggs, Chester accepted a position at the Columbus Art School as head of the Sculpture Department. He later became the dean of the Columbus Art School and president of the Art League. During these early years, Chester was creating mostly portrait heads and fountain figures.During the Depression Chester learned how to do clay casting and began to create smaller pieces that were more affordable to the masses. On a trip through New England in 1939, he carried with him a sampling of his work. He felt encouraged to start his own business after selling all the pieces he carried and receiving orders for many more.

In 1943, due to the war and a subsequent drop in class attendance, Chester left the field of teaching to pursue pottery making full time. His own business, "Ferro-Stone Ceramics," used local clay. Containing a large amount of iron (ferro is the Latin word for "iron"), the Ohio clay had a red color, which imbued a russet brown undertone to the pottery that gave a second dimension to the glaze. It was fired at a very high temperature and rendered stone hard. Known for its durability, it was leak-proof and not easily chipped. Nicodemus Pottery could be purchased at fine showrooms throughout the United States or by knocking on Chester's door and viewing the ceramic pieces in his modest garage salesroom. Keeping stores stocked kept him busy, and in 1973 he decided to retire from the retail business. His home business continued to flourish with new designs.

All created in his studio in Columbus, Ohio, Nicodemus pieces included animals, birds, Christmas cards, medallions, fountains and dinnerware. Colors used were pussy willow, turquoise, dark yellow, mottled green, antique ivory and deep blue. Pieces referred to as "museum quality" are heavily mottled with broken color lines showing more of the red clay body. Most pieces are incised "NICODEMUS" on an unglazed base. Some may also have initials of Nicodemus' students Ellen Jennings or James Thornton. Paper labels bearing the Ferro-Stone name are also found.

Chester Nicodemus was a very talented artist who is just beginning to receive proper recognition for his ceramic excellence. His studio was closed in 1990 after a fall that broke his hip. Chester died later that year at the age of 89. As requested by Chester, shortly after his death all Nicodemus molds and glazes were destroyed by his son Darell.

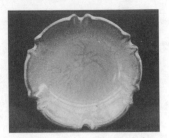

Mottled Green Nicodemus Ashtray

Ashtray, mottled green, incised "Nicodemus," 3 1/2" d. (ILLUS.)................................ **$75**

Nicodemus Promotional Ashtray

Ashtray, round, w/four cigarette rests, advertises "Goucher College Founded 1885," incised "Nicodemus," 4 1/2" d. (ILLUS.).. **110**

Nicodemus Piggy Bank

Bank, in the form of a pig, mottled green, incised "Nicodemus," 3 1/4" h. (ILLUS.)........... **505**

Nicodemus Figure of Joseph

Figure of Joseph, No. 4 in a nine-piece nativity set, turquoise, incised "Nicodemus," 7 1/2" h. (ILLUS.)... **375**

Flower holder, figure of girl, dark yellow, "Nicodemus," 6" h... **325**

Nicodemus Robin

Model of robin, black & red unglazed w/yellow beak, incised "Nicodemus," 3 1/2" h. (ILLUS.).. **225**

Pitcher, 3 1/2" h., dark yellow, incised "Nicodemus" **145**

Nicodemus Mottled Green Pitcher

Pitcher, 3 1/2" h., mottled green, museum-quality glaze, incised "Nicodemus" (ILLUS.).. **325**

Planter, cornucopia, blue, incised "Nicodemus," 10" l.. **275**

Wall pocket, twisted horns, antique ivory, incised "Nicodemus," 9" h. **825**

Niloak Pottery

This pottery was made in Benton, Arkansas, and featured hand-thrown varicolored swirled clay decoration in objects of classic forms. Designated Mission Ware, this line is the most desirable of Niloak's production, which began early in this century. Less expensive to produce, the cast Hywood Line, finished with either high gloss or semi-matte glazes, was introduced during the Depression of the 1930s. The pottery ceased operation about 1946.

ℕILOAK

Niloak Pottery Mark

Bowl, 5" d., Mission Ware, squatty rounded base tapering slightly to the wide, flat rim, swirled red, brown, cream & blue clays, marked **$176**

Niloak Bowl and Vases

Bowl, 6 3/4" d., 3" h., Mission Ware, wide, deep rounded form w/a flat mouth, swirled dark blue, light blue, dark brown, cream & reddish brown clays, impressed mark, paper label (ILLUS. left) **173**

Box, cov., Mission Ware, squatty bulbous body & high squatty mushroom-shaped cover, swirled dark brown, reddish brown, tan & blue clays, impressed mark, 4" h. **1,035**

Jug, spherical body w/flat bottom, a pointed loop handle on the shoulder opposite a short, round spout, overall mottled golden tan & green matte glaze, ink mark, 6" h. **231**

Lamp base, Mission Ware, tapered ovoid form w/flared round base, swirled marbleized clays in red, blue, cream & taupe, two-socket fixture, early 20th c., 10 1/4" h. **374**

Puff box, cov., Mission Ware, footed wide, squatty, bulbous body w/a low rim & flat inset cover w/pointed finial, swirled dark brown, tan & dark blue clays, 4" h. (ILLUS., top next column) **575**

Vase, 3 1/2" h., miniature, Mission Ware, ovoid form tapering gently to a wide flat mouth, swirled light & dark blue, tan & light brown clays, minute flakes (ILLUS. left, bottom of page) **242**

Niloak Mission Ware Puff Box

Vase, 3 1/2" h., miniature, Mission Ware, wide ovoid form tapering to a heavy molded rim, swirled dark & light brown, dark blue, cream & reddish brown clays, impressed mark (ILLUS. right with bowl) **150**

Vase, 5" h., 6" d., Mission Ware, flat-bottomed wide bulbous form curving to a wide flat rim, swirled dark & light brown, cream, reddish brown & blue clays, impressed mark (ILLUS. right with miniature vase) **265**

Large & Small Mission Ware Vases

Niloak Mission Ware Vase

Vase, 6" h., Mission Ware, simple baluster form w/a wide closed rim, swirled red, cream & grey clays, impressed mark (ILLUS.) 209

Vase, 6" h., Mission Ware, wide cylindrical form rounded at the base & top rim, bold swirled bands of dark blue, reddish brown & dark & light brown clays, impressed mark (ILLUS. center with bowl) 403

Two Cylindrical Niloak Vases

Vase, 7 1/4" h., Mission Ware, simple cylindrical form, fine swirls of dark blue, cream & dark brown clays, early impressed mark w/patent pending wording (ILLUS. left) 633

Unusual Mission Ware Incised Vase

Vase, 8 1/4" h., Mission Ware, tall ovoid form tapering gently to flat rim, unusual decoration of overall incised squiggles in a tan matte glaze over a dark brown base, paper label (ILLUS.) 1,150

Vase, 8 3/4" h., Mission Ware, large bulbous ovoid body tapering to a short slightly rolled neck, swirled dark & light brown clays, rare ink stamp mark 1,093

Vase, 10" h., Mission Ware, tall simple cylindrical form, bold swirls of medium blue, dark & light brown, cream & reddish brown clays, impressed mark (ILLUS. right with other cylindrical vase) 288

Vase, 11" h., Mission Ware, tall baluste form w/widely flaring flattened neck, bold squiggly swirls of blue, cream, reddish brown, dark & light brown clays, impressed mark (ILLUS. center with miniature vase) 500

Vase, 12 1/4" h., footed bulbous body tapering to a tall flaring trumpet neck, overall dark matte blue glaze, impressed mark 748

Nippon

"Nippon" is a term used to describe a wide range of porcelain wares produced in Japan from the late 19th century until about 1921. It was in 1891 that the United States implemented the McKinley Tariff Act, which required that all wares exported to the United States carry a marking indicating the country of origin. The Japanese chose to use "Nippon," their name for Japan. In 1921 the import laws were revised and the words "Made in" had to be added to the markings. Japan was also required to replace the "Nippon" with the English name "Japan" on all wares sent to the United States.

Many Japanese factories produced Nippon porcelain, much of it hand-painted with ornate floral or landscape decoration and heavy gold decoration, applied beading and slip-trailed designs referred to as "moriage." We indicate the specific marking used on a piece, when known, at the end of each listing. Be aware that a number of Nippon markings have been reproduced and used on new porcelain wares.

Important reference books on Nippon include: The Collector's Encyclopedia of Nippon Porcelain, Series One through Three, *by Joan F. Van Patten (Collector Books, Paducah, Kentucky) and* The Wonderful World of Nippon Porcelain, 1891-1921 *by Kathy Wojciechowski (Schiffer Publishing, Ltd., Atglen, Pennsylvania).*

Basket, on three feet, finely painted in stylized flowers & gilt w/"coralene" trim, "US Patent" mark, 4 3/4" h $202

Nippon Floral-decorated Bowl

Bowl, 7 1/2" d., 3 3/4" h., wide shallow bowl w/lightly scalloped rim, raised on three

gilt-trimmed scroll feet, gold & cobalt blue rim band, pink & white apple blossoms & green leaves on the interior & exterior, green "M" in wreath mark (ILLUS.) **135**
Bowl, 8 1/2" d., three-handled, decorated w/a scene of a sailing ship w/palm trees & ruins on the shore, green "M" in wreath mark **144**
Bowl, 10" d., low sides, three-footed, decorated w/large open roses, blue "Maple Leaf" mark **56**

Nippon Scenic Chamberstick

Chamberstick, saucer-form base decorated w/scene of house by lake w/trees & mountains, natural colors, green "M" in wreath mark, 4 1/4" d., 2" h. (ILLUS.) .. **100-125**
Chocolate set: cov. pot & six cups & saucers; an Art Deco-style mold copied from R.S. Prussia wares, painted w/open roses, green "I&E" wreath mark, pot 8" h., the set **280**
Cigar receiver, heart-shaped, h.p. in raised enamel w/a playing card motif, 4 3/4" l. **448**
Condensed milk container, cylindrical, decorated w/gilt scrolls & florals, green "M" in wreath mark, 5 1/2" h. **67**
Condensed milk container, cover & underplate, cylindrical handled container, h.p. w/a floral band outlined in gold, magenta "M" in wreath mark, overall 6" h., 3 pcs. **101**
Dresser tray & tumbler, h.p. Egyptian scene w/enameled rim, 2 pcs. **112**
Humidor, cov., decorated w/a tree-lined shore scene, green "M" in wreath mark, 5 1/2" h. **224**
Humidor, cov., squared form, decorated w/four scenic panels of sailboats, green "M" in wreath mark, 4 1/2" h. **308**
Mug, decorated w/a h.p. scene of an Oriental landscape w/a pagoda & garden in raised enamel, green "M" in wreath mark, 5" h. **67**
Mug, h.p. landscape scene w/embossed rim & handle w/raised enameling, green "M" in wreath mark, 5 1/2" h. **112**
Nut tray, molded in relief w/beechnuts painted in natural colors, green "M" in wreath mark, 8" l. **78**

Blossom-decorated Relish Dish

Relish dish, oval w/pierced end handles, cobalt blue & gold rim band, the interior h.p. w/pink & white apple blossoms & green leaves on a creamy pale green ground, green "M" in wreath mark, 5 x 8 1/2" (ILLUS.) **65**
Tankard, cylindrical, finely painted gold-decorated rim & base, applied scroll handle, blue "Maple Leaf" mark, 13" h. (minor gold loss) **345**
Tazza, miniature, footed, decorated w/roses on a stippled gold ground, "Kinran" crown mark, 5" l. **34**
Vase, 9" h., Art Deco form w/"coralene" decoration of lotus leaves & flowers, marked in magenta "KinRan - U.S. Patent Feb. 9, 1909" (minor loss to beading) **661**
Vase, 9" h., molded basketweave body painted w/red & white roses, blue "M" in wreath mark **748**

Vase with Ornate Gilt Decoration

Vase, 10 1/4" h., 5" d., baluster-form body raised on a scalloped flaring foot & tapering to a flaring pointed lobed rim, long slender S-scroll handles up the sides, decorated overall w/heavy gold stylized leaves & berries on vines, blue "Maple Leaf" mark (ILLUS.) **175**
Vase, 11" h., two-handled, rare "sharkskin" glaze, h.p. flowers & grapes, marked "Patent No. 1705 Feb. 26, 1910 - Royal Kinjo Japan" **489**
Vase, 13" h., 7" d., finely painted landscape w/heavy etched gold decoration of flowers & striped band, probably studio decorated, green "M" in wreath mark **489**
Wall plaque, pierced for hanging, h.p. scene of palm trees & sailboats **101**
Wall plaque, pierced to hang, relief-molded w/a squirrel eating peanuts, green "M" in wreath mark, ca. 1915, 10 3/4" d. **575**

Wall Plaque with Lions

Wall plaque, pierced to hang, round, molded
in relief w/a lion & lioness in a rocky landscape, natural coloration, green "M" in
wreath mark, 10 3/4" d. (ILLUS.).................... **575**

Noritake

Noritake china, still in production in Japan, has been
exported in large quantities to this country since early in
this century. Although the Noritake Company first regis-
tered in 1904, it did not use "Noritake" as part of its
backstamp until 1918. Interest in Noritake has escalated
as collectors now seek out pieces made between the
"Nippon" era and World War II (1921-41). The Azalea
pattern is also popular with collectors.

Noritake Mark

Ashtray, center Queen of Clubs decoration,
4" w. **$40**
Ashtray, figural polar bear, blue ground,
4 1/4" d., 2 1/2" h. **230**
Ashtray, center Indian head decoration,
5 1/2" w. **275**
Ashtray, figural nude woman seated at edge
of lustered flower form tray,
7" w. **950**

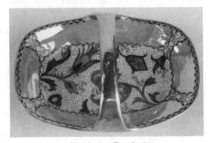

Noritake Basket

Basket, oblong w/center handle, gold lustre
ground, interior w/center stylized floral
decoration & geometric design in each
corner & around rim, 7 3/4" l., 3" h.
(ILLUS.) **90**
Basket, Roseara patt............................... **70**
Basket-bowl, footed, petal-shaped rim,
6 1/2" w. **105**
Basket-vase, 7 1/2" h. **125**
Berry set: master bowl & 6 sauce dishes;
decal & h.p. purple orchids, green leaves
& pods decoration on green ground, 7
pcs. **120**
Bonbon, raised gold decoration,
6 1/4" w. **25**
Bonbon dish, Azalea patt. **40**

Noritake Scenic Bowl

Bowl, 6" sq., flanged rim w/pierced handles,
orange lustre ground decorated w/h.p.
scene w/large tree in foreground
(ILLUS.).. **85**

Art Deco Bowl

Bowl, 6 1/2" d., 2" h., fluted sides of alternating light & dark grey panels w/pointed
rims, center w/Art Deco floral decoration
(ILLUS.).. **190**
Bowl, 7" w., square w/incurved sides, three-
footed, interior w/relief-molded filbert
nuts in brown trimmed w/h.p. autumn
leaves **75**
Bowl, 8 3/4" d., 2" h., Art Deco-style orange
& white checkerboard ground decorated
w/stylized dark brown rose buds & leaves
outlined in grey & grey stems **260**
Bowl, 9" d., footed, scenic interior decora-
tion, lustre finish exterior **50**
Bowl, shell-shaped, three-footed, Tree in
Meadow patt.. **200**
Bowl, soup, Azalea patt............................... **30**
Butter dish, cover & drain insert, Azalea
patt., 3 pcs... **80**
Cake plate, Sheridan patt., 9 3/4" d. **25**

Noritake Cake Plate

Cake plate, rectangular, open-handled, turquoise border w/oval center Oriental scene on black ground, 10" l. (ILLUS.) **120**

Cake plate, open-handled, Tree in Meadow patt. **30**

Cake set: 10" d. handled master cake plate & 6 serving plates; fruit bowl medallions centers, blue lustre rims, 7 pcs. **80**

Cake set: 14 x 6 1/4" oblong tray w/pierced handles & six 6 1/2" d. serving plates; white w/pale green & gold floral border, 7 pcs. **70**

Candlesticks, Indian motif decoration, 3 1/4" h., pr. **150**

Candy dish, octagonal, Tree in Meadow patt. **70**

Candy dish, cov., figural bird finial, scalloped rim, blue lustre finish, 6 1/2 x 7 1/4" **100**

Celery set: celery tray & 6 individual salt dips, decal & h.p. florals & butterflies decoration, 7 pcs. **95**

Celery tray, Azalea patt. **50**

Figural Swan Cigarette Holder

Cigarette holder, footed, figural swan, orange lustre w/black neck & head, black outlining on wing feathers & tail, 3" w., 4 1/2" h. (ILLUS.) **325**

Cigarette holder, bell-shaped w/bird finial, 5" h. **275**

Cigarette holder/playing card holder, pedestal foot, gold lustre ground decorated w/scene of golfer, 4" h. **295**

Cigarette Jar in Art Deco Style

Cigarette jar, cov., bell-shaped cover w/bird finial, Art Deco-style silhouetted scenic decoration of woman in chair & man standing, both holding cigarettes, 4 3/4" h., 3 1/2" d. (ILLUS.) **550**

Coffee set: cov. coffeepot, creamer, cov. sugar bowl & four cups & saucers; greyish blue butterfly, pink florals & grey leaves decoration, 11 pcs. **240**

Cologne bottle w/flower cluster stopper, Art Deco man wearing checkered cape, lustered sides, 6 3/4" h. **450**

Cologne bottle w/stopper, two-handled, Art Deco woman decoration **675**

Noritake Condiment Set

Condiment set: cov. mustard jar & pr. salt & pepper shakers on handled tray; blue lustre w/tops decorated w/flowers, 7" w. tray, the set (ILLUS.) **120**

Figural Condiment Set

Condiment set: cov. mustard jar & pr. salt & pepper shakers on handled tray; bulbous blue lustre mustard jar w/red rosebud finial, green leaves, ovoid shakers w/clown head tops, red, blue, orange & white lustre, blue lustre tray, 7" l., the set (ILLUS.)...... **660**

Condiment set: cov. mustard jar & pr. salt & pepper shakers on handled tray; lustre borders & tops, 5 1/2" w. tray, the set.............. **70**

Noritake Cracker Jar

Cracker jar, cov., footed spherical body decorated w/a black band w/white swords &
shields design & center oval yellow medallion w/scene of white sailboat on lake,
white clouds in distance & blue stylized
tree in foreground, black & white geometric design bands around rim & cover
edge, orange lustre ground, 7" h.
(ILLUS.)... **260**
Creamer, Azalea patt. **25**
Creamer, Tree in Meadow patt............................... **20**
Creamer & cov. sugar bowl, Azalea patt., pr. **80**
Creamer & cov. sugar bowl, blue scenic
decoration, brown borders, pr. **70**

Creamer & Sugar in Art Deco Style

Creamer & open sugar bowl, Art Deco-style
checked decoration in black, blue, brown
& white, orange lustre interior basket-
shaped sugar bowl w/overhead handle,
creamer 3" h., sugar bowl 4 1/2" h., pr.
(ILLUS.).. **115**

Scenic Berry Creamer & Sugar Shaker

Creamer & sugar shaker, berry set-type,
decorated w/a scene of a gondola, or-
ange lustre ground, 6 1/2" h., pr. (ILLUS.)....... **80**
Creamer & sugar shaker, berry set-type, orange lustre interior, scenic decoration
w/cottage, bridge & trees above floral
cluster, blue lustre ground, 6 1/2" h., pr. **95**
Creamer & sugar shaker, berry set-type,
raised gold decoration, 5 3/4" h. creamer
& 6 1/4" h. sugar shaker, pr. **85**

Noritake Cruet Set

Cruet set w/original stoppers, the two conjoined globular bottles set at angles &
joined w/a handle at the shoulder, shaded orange lustre ground decorated
w/green & yellow clover leaves & stems,
6" l., 3 1/2" h. (ILLUS.)..................................... **115**
Cup & saucer, demitasse, Tree in Meadow
patt. **20**
Cup & saucer, Tree in Meadow patt..................... **20**
Desk set: heart-shaped tray w/pen rack at
front & two cov. jars w/floral finials; decal
& h.p. florals, 6 1/2" w................................... **400**
Dinner bell, figural Chinaman, 3 1/2" h. **275**
Dish, blue lustre trim, 5" sq. **25**
Dresser box, cov., figural woman on lid, lus-
tre finish, 5" h. **780**
Figurine, maiden carrying a bundle of sticks
on her head **75**
Fish plates, h.p. & decal w/h.p. center fish
decoration, gold borders, 8 1/2" d., pr........... **125**
Flower holder, model of bird on stump, base
pierced w/four flower holes, 4 1/2" h. **155**

Hair Receiver in Art Deco Style

Hair receiver, cov., Art Deco style, geometric design on gold lustre ground, 3 1/2" d.
(ILLUS.).. **195**
Humidor, cov., model of an owl w/head as
cover, lustre finish, 7" h. **900**
Humidor, cov., relief-molded & h.p. horse
head, 7" h. **600**
Humidor, cov., four panels of decal & h.p.
yellow roses & black leaves on orange
ground within h.p. black oval borders,
7 1/2" h. **350**
Inkwell, model of an owl, Art Deco style,
3 1/2" h. **255**
Jam jar, cover & underplate, melon-shaped,
pink ground w/grey leaves, handle & leaf-
shaped underplate, 5 3/4" l., 4 1/4" h.,
the set **120**
Lemon plate, Azalea patt. **35**
Lobster set: sauce bowl, underplate & ladle;
molded lotus form, petals w/highlights &
lobster decoration on 10 3/4" d. under-
plate **215**
Marmalade jar, cover, underplate & ladle,
flower bud finial, 5 1/4" h. **75**
Mayonnaise set, Azalea patt., 3 pcs. **70**
Night light, figural woman, 9 1/4" h.,
2 pc. **4,200**

Nut bowl, tri-lobed bowl w/figural squirrel
seated at side eating nut, 7 1/2" w **120**
Nut bowl, molded nut shell form w/three re-
lief-molded nuts & side h.p. w/walnuts &
green ferns decoration **90**
Nut set: 6" d. bowl shaped like open chest-
nut & six 2" d. nut dishes; earthtone
ground w/h.p. nuts & leaves, the set **140**
Plate, 6 1/2" d., Azalea patt **15**
Plate, 6 1/2" d., Tree in Meadow patt. **15**
Plate, 7 1/2" d., Azalea patt **15**
Plate, dinner, Azalea patt. **40**
Platter, 10" l., Tree in Meadow patt. **75**
Platter, 14" l., Tree in Meadow patt. **75**
Powder box, cov., figural, an Art Deco-style
female figure on a chair in colors of or-
ange, black, green, white & brown w/a
lustre finish, 1930s, 4 1/4 x 5", 7" h. **7,500**
Powder box, cov., figural bird finial,
3 1/2" d **120**
Powder box, cov., Art Deco decoration,
4" d **450**
Powder puff box, cov., disc-form, stylized
floral decoration in red, blue, white &
black on a white iridized ground w/blue
lustre border, 4" d. **190**
Relish dish, Azalea patt., 8" l. **25**
Ring holder, model of a hand **35**
Salt & pepper shakers, Tree in Meadow
patt., pr **20**
Sauce dish, Azalea patt. **25**
Shaving mug, landscape scene w/tree,
birds & moon decoration **60**
Smoke set: handled tray, cigar & cigarette
jars & match holder; cigars, cigarettes &
matchsticks decoration, the set **350**

Noritake Double Spoon Holder

Spoon holder, double tray-form, oblong
shape w/gold angular center handle, orange lustre interior, exterior decorated
w/flowers & butterfly on black ground,
6 1/2" l., 2 1/2" h. (ILLUS.) **65**
Sugar bowl, cov., Azalea patt. **60**
Sugar shaker, lavender & gold decoration,
blue lustre trim **40**
Syrup jug, Azalea patt **75**
Tea strainer w/footed rest, cov., Azalea patt.
decal & h.p. red roses & gold trim on
green ground, 2 pcs. **95**
Toast rack, two-slice, blue & yellow decora-
tion **55**
Tray, pierced handles, decal & h.p. fruit bor-
der, lustre center, 11" w **80**
Tray, rectangular, pierced end handles, flo-
ral decoration on white ground, green
edge trim w/brown trim on handles,
17 1/2" l. **90**

Scenic Noritake Vase

Vase, 4 1/4" h., 5 1/4" d., footed bulbous
body w/figural leaf & grape cluster handles, gold & blue lustre ground decorated
w/scene of trees & children (ILLUS.) **355**
Vase, 5 1/2" h., orange & gold rim &
handles, h.p. tree & cottage lakeside
scene **75**

Noritake Fan-shaped Vase

Vase, 6 1/2" h., footed, fan-shaped, colorful
Art Deco floral design on orange ground
(ILLUS.) **210**
Vase, 7" h., fan-shaped w/ruffled rim, fruit &
vines decoration, green & blue base **90**
Vase, 8" h., footed ovoid body w/squared
rim handles, butterfly decoration on
shaded & streaked blue & orange ground **240**

Stylized Noritake Vase

Vase, 8 1/4" h., 5 1/4" d., footed ovoid body
w/scalloped rim & scrolled rim handles,
blue interior, exterior base w/blue, brown
& black vertical lines on white, black
band on upper body decorated w/stylized
flowers in yellow, purple, brown & blue
w/green & brown leaves (ILLUS.) 650
Vase, 8 1/4" h., Indian motif & lustre decora-
tion 135
Vase, 8 1/2" h., bulbous body, Tree in
Meadow patt. 100
Vegetable bowl, open, round, Tree in Mead-
ow patt. 35
Vegetable dish, cov., round, Azalea patt. 85

Scenic Noritake Wall Plaque

Wall plaque, pierced to hang, silhouetted Art
Deco-style scene of woman in gown
w/full ruffled skirt, sitting on couch & holding mirror, white lustre ground, 8 3/4" d.
(ILLUS.) 895
Wall plaque, pierced to hang, relief-molded
& h.p. double Indian portraits, 10 1/2" d. 690
Wall pocket, double, conical two-part form
w/arched backplate, decorated w/an exotic blue & yellow bird among branches
of red & blue stylized blossoms against a
cream ground, purple lustre rim band,
8" l. 175
Wall pocket, trumpet-form, wide upper band
decorated w/an autumn sunset scene,
lavender lustre rim band & base, 8 1/4" l. 90
Wall pocket, double, relief-molded floral
cresting backplate, stylized florals & bird
of paradise decoration, lustre border, 8" l. 210
Wall pocket, single, h.p. tree & cottage lakeside scene on blue lustered ground, 8" h. 95
Waste bowl, Azalea patt. 60

North Dakota School of Mines

North Dakota School of Mines Mark

*All pottery produced at the University of North
Dakota School of Mines was made from North Dakota
clay. In 1910, the University hired Margaret Kelly Cable
to teach pottery making, and she remained at the school
until her retirement. Julia Mattson and Margaret Pachl
also served as instructors between 1923 and 1970.
Designs and glazes varied through the years ranging
from the Art Nouveau to modern styles. Pieces were
marked "University of North Dakota - Grand Forks,
N.D. - Made at School of Mines, N.D." within a circle
and also signed by the students until 1963. Since that
time, the pieces bear only the students' signatures. Items
signed "Huck" are by the artist Flora Huckfield and
were made between 1923 and 1949.*

Small North Dakota Bowl

Bowl, 4 1/2" d., 2" h., low, flat-bottomed cylindrical form, incised continuous scrolling band, green matte glaze, signed
(ILLUS.) **$201**
Bowl, 9" d., 4 1/4" h., narrow footring below
the deep rounded upright sides, carved
w/heart-shaped green leaves below a
green rim band on a matte white ground,
mottled glossy light blue interior, circular
mark & name "Schnell" 495

North Dakota Bowl-vases & Vase

Bowl-vase, squatty bulbous body w/a narrow shoulder to a molded rim, carved band decoration of buffalo standing head to head & separated by three wide vertical bands, glossy medium blue carved to rich creamy white, stamped circular mark & incised "JM - 466," 4 1/2" d., 3 3/4" h. (ILLUS. front right, bottom prev. page) **1,913**

Bowl-vase, squatty bulbous body w/short incurved neck & flat mouth, Bentonite clay w/a dark reddish color decorated in the Native American style w/a pattern of birds, stamped circular mark & incised "Armstrong - 1948," 4 3/4" d., 4 1/4" h. (ILLUS. back left w/bowl-vases) **1,013**

Bowl-vase, round, straight tapering sides w/a narrow shoulder & molded rim, decorated w/band of carved birds under a matte chartreuse glaze, ink stamp mark & incised "M. Cable - Meadowlark - 155," 5 1/2" d., 3 1/4" h. (ILLUS. front left w/bowl-vases) **675**

Bowl-vase, wide bulbous body, the shoulder tapering to a short cylindrical neck w/flat mouth, embossed w/a band of oxen & covered wagons under a matte brown glaze, stamped circular mark & incised "MC - 186," 7 1/4" d., 6 1/2" h. (ILLUS. far right w/bowl-vases).................................... **1,463**

North Dakota Wheat Bowl-vase

Bowl-vase, squatty bulbous form w/the shoulder tapering up to a flat mouth, carved around the middle w/a wide band showing shocks of wheat, in shades of dark & light brown, by Flora Huckfield, ink stamped "Hoffman - Huck - 1655 - No. Dakota Wheat," 7" d., 4 3/4" h. (ILLUS.).... **1,350**

North Dakota Round Box

Box, cov., low cylindrical form w/low domed fitted cover, the cover embossed w/the head of a Native American chief wearing a headdress, umber ground w/a mocha matte glaze on the cover, by Margaret Cable, stamped mark, incised "M. Cable - 156," 5" d., 2" h. (ILLUS.)............................ **690**

Charger, decorated w/a large stylized five-petal blossom in yellow, white, deep red, blue & black cuerda seca, by Margaret Cable, 1949, ink stamped "M. Cable - 1949 - June Marks," 9 1/2" d. **534**

Vase, miniature, 3 1/2" h., 3 3/4" d., small spherical form tapering at the base, glossy dark blue ground cut around the center w/a wide band of silhouetted coyotes against an ivory ground, circular mark & "M-298" (flat stilt pull nicks)............ **1,320**

Vase, 3 1/2" h., 5" d., wide conical form tapering to a small molded mouth, incised w/an overall pointed geometric design, matte green glaze, by M.J. Arnegard, 1932, ink stamped "M.J. Arnegard - 42132"... **788**

Vase, miniature, 3 3/4" h., 3 1/4" d., simple ovoid form tapering to a closed rim, incised around the sides w/large upright stylized tulip-like flowers on leafy stems, celadon green semi-matte glaze, ink stamped "53H"... **563**

Vase, 3 3/4" h., 4 3/4" d., wide squatty bulbous form tapering to a wide rolled rim, incised around the upper half w/a band of stylized blossoms & leaves, matte green mirocrystalline glaze, by Flora Huckfield, Ink stamped "E. Ericson - Huck - 106".......... **506**

Vase, 4" h., 5 1/2" d., wide flat-bottomed ovoid form w/a wide rounded shoulder centered by a short tapering wide mouth, the shoulder decorated w/a wide band of pink prairie roses & green leaves on a cream ground, pink background, by Flora Huckfield, ink stamped "Bridgeman - Huck - 4248".. **788**

Vase, 4 3/4" h., 6 1/2" d., wide squatty form w/the flaring lower body below a wide tapering shoulder centered by a short flat mouth, the shoulder carved w/a wide band of stylized flowers, matte caramel glaze, by C.A. Sorbo, ink stamped "C.A. Sorbo - 196".. **506**

Vase, 5" h., 4 3/4" d., wide conical body tapering to molded rim, band around & below rim and at base in shades of blue, the center cream ground decorated w/a blue & green scene of a Viking ship sailing on waves & flying birds, stamped circular mark & incised "J. Mattson - 149A - Viking Ship" (ILLUS. back right w/bowl-vases).. **1,688**

Vase, 5 1/2" h., simple, gently swelled cylindrical form w/a shoulder tapering slightly to a short flaring neck, overall shaded brown & green matte glaze, stamp mark....... **253**

Vase, 5 1/2" h., 6" d., bulbous, nearly spherical form w/a small closed rim, "Prairie Rose" patt., dark sand-colored ground decorated around the mouth w/a wide band of coral stylized roses & green leaves between thin bands, Margaret Cable, circular ink mark & "M. Cable - 131 - A - Prairie Rose".................................... **990**

Vase, 5 3/4" h., 2 3/4" d., gently swelled cylindrical form tapering to a ringed short neck, incised w/his design of a stylized cowboy w/his lariat spelling out "Why not Minot" around the shoulder, light periwinkle blue glaze, by Julia Mattson, ink stamped "JM - 175"... **422**

Vase, 9" h., tapering cylindrical body w/a rounded shoulder centering a short slightly flared neck, overall brownish green matte glaze, stamp mark & signed & numbered by J. Mattson (minor flake on bottom rim) 385

Ohr (George) Pottery

GEO. E. OHR
BILOXI, MISS.

Ohr Pottery Marks

George Ohr, the eccentric potter of Biloxi, Mississippi, worked from about 1883 to 1906. Some think him to be one of the most expert throwers the craft will ever see. The majority of his works were hand-thrown, exceedingly thin-walled items, some of which have a crushed or folded appearance. He considered himself the foremost potter in the world and declined to sell much of his production, instead accumulating a great horde to leave as a legacy to his children. In 1972 this collection was purchased for resale by an antiques dealer.

Bowl, 2 7/8" h., flat base w/tall twisted & crumpled flared floral form, mottled green interior glaze, mottled burgundy exterior glaze, impressed "Geo. E. Ohr Biloxi Miss." **$5,520**

Ohr Matte Glazed Small Bowl

Bowl, 4 3/4" d., 2 1/2" h., footed squatty bulbous form w/a wide rolled & inwardly folded labial rim w/two pulled-out spouts on the rim, rare green, brown & gunmetal dead-matte glaze, stamped "G.E. Ohr - Biloxi, Miss." (ILLUS.) **3,335**

Ohr Bisque Clay Bowl-vase

Bowl-vase, round foot below the compressed four-sided deeply indented & crumpled form w/an incurved pinched & twisted rim, oxidized beige bisque clay, minor kiln kiss, script signature, 5 3/4" w., 3 3/4" h. (ILLUS.) **3,738**

Cup, footed, gently flaring rounded form w/dimpled sides & a crenelated rim, hand-built rounded loop handle, exterior w/a mottled mahogany glaze, interior in gunmetal, signed "Geo. E. Ohr - Biloxi - Miss.," **1,463**

Unusual George Ohr Cup

Cup, small footring below a large nearly spherical body w/wide flat mouth, looped C-scroll handle, fine dripping gunmetal over mottled & speckled glossy green glaze, stamped mark, 6 3/4" d., 4 1/2" h. (ILLUS.) **4,313**

Inkstand, a rectangular base w/serpentine front mounted w/a large mule head w/long pointed ears beside a low squatty bowl w/incurved sides, a small tree stump on the other side of the bowl, overall mottled green, brown & gunmetal glaze, stamped "G.E. Ohr - Biloxi," 4 3/4 x 7 1/4", 4" h. (touchup to both ear tips) **4,500**

Inkwell, figural, a rectangular plaque back w/a high-relief molded face of a mountain lion w/a filling hole at the top of the head, shimmering dark green glaze, stamped "G.E. Ohr - Biloxi - Biloxi Welcome poem," 3 1/2 x 4 1/2" **1,320**

Inkwell, figural, model of a cabin w/a long sloping roof & stick-style chimney on one side, mottled glossy green glaze, stamped "Geo. Ohr - Biloxi, Miss.," 3 x 4 1/2" **2,310**

George Ohr Pottery Hat

Model of a hat, tall tapering crown ripped at the top, crumpled sides & upturned brim, red, green & blue glossy glaze, restoration to small rim chip, marked "G.E. Ohr - Biloxi," 4 1/2" l., 4" h. (ILLUS.) **4,313**

Mug, Joe Jefferson-type, double-gourd form w/long pointed strap handle down the side, incised w/"Here's your good health...," overall speckled & mottled dark bluish green glaze, script signature & dated 1896, 5 3/4" d., 6 1/2" h. **2,363**

Ohr Pinch-sided Pitcher

Pitcher, 2 1/2" h., 5" w., four pinched-in sides forming a diamond-shaped top opening, round foot, pointed angled loop handle, light mauve glaze on exterior, chartreuse green interior glaze, signed "Geo. E. Ohr - Biloxi, Miss.," minute rim nick (ILLUS.) **2,250**

Pitcher, 3" h., 5 1/2" d., footed squatty bulbous body w/a closed rim & small pinched upright rim spout, applied D-form handle, amber, green & gunmetal speckled glaze, signed "G.E. Ohr - Biloxi - Miss." **731**

Ohr Boat-shaped Pitcher

Pitcher, 3" h., 6" l., footed oblong boat-shape w/widely rolled rim w/pinched spout, ear-shaped loop handle, umber glaze speckled w/gunmetal, stamped "G.E. Ohr - Biloxi, Miss." (ILLUS.) **2,185**

Pitcher, 4 1/2" h., pinched & pulled flattened rounded form w/angled integral handle, deeply scalloped & flared rim, mottled charcoal-glazed interior, dark pink glazed exterior, inscribed "G.E. Ohr" **6,900**

Teapot, cov., footed baluster form w/flared rim, simple strap handle & swan's-neck spout, flat inset cover w/knob finial, overall sponged design in dark brown, green

& black on a khaki ground, stamped "Geo. Ohr - Biloxi, Miss.," 4" h. **6,050**

Rare George Ohr Teapot

Teapot, cov., footed, w/a widely flaring flat-sided lower body below the angled shoulder band & domed top compressed down in the center w/a small cover, snake spout, C-scroll handle, cobalt blue glossy glaze, stamped "G.E. Ohr - Biloxi, Miss.," normal abrasion around rim, small nick on tip of spout, 8 3/4" l., 4" h. (ILLUS.) **11,250**

Vase, miniature, 3 3/4" h., 2 1/2" h., a low pedestal foot supporting a slightly tapering cylindrical body w/a deeply crumpled & twisted upper border, green & amber speckled semi-matte glaze, marked "G.E. Ohr - Biloxi, Miss." (minor rim nick) **1,870**

Ohr Vase with Volcanic Glaze

Vase, 4" h., 3 3/4" d., wide baluster-form w/flattened wide rim, fine cadmium yellow, lavender, green & pink volcanic glaze, stamped "G.E. Ohr - Biloxi, Miss." (ILLUS.) **3,038**

Vase, 4 1/2" h., 2 1/2" d., footed bulbous spherical lower body tapering to a tall, upright, twisted, folded & pinched neck, dark speckled olive green glaze, neck in gunmetal glaze, marked "G.E. Ohr - Biloxi, Miss." **2,588**

Four George Ohr Vases

Vase, 4 1/2" h., 4 1/2" w., a footed wide swelled form w/a deeply folded rim & a collapsed side, overall speckled amber & gunmetal glaze, signed "G.E. OHR - Biloxi, Miss." (ILLUS. second from right)... **6,188**

Rare George Ohr Vase

Vase, 4 1/2" h., 4 1/2" w., round foot below the squatty bulbous four-sided body w/a deep in-body twist below the pinched, twisted & crumpled ragged rim, glossy indigo glaze w/red, amber & gunmetal, signed "G.E. Ohr - Biloxi, Miss." (ILLUS.)... **16,100**

Vase, 4 1/2" h., 5 1/4" d., footed squatty bulbous body w/large dimples around the middle, tapering to a short, wide cylindrical neck, fine mottled brown & gunmetal glossy glaze, stamped "G.E. Ohr - Biloxi".. **3,150**

Vase, 4 3/4" h., 4 1/4" d., footed cylindrical two-tiered body w/the wide upper tier impressed w/large swirled dimples below the wide short cylindrical neck, overall

speckled amber glaze, signed "G.E. Ohr - Biloxi"... **3,656**

George Ohr Spotted Vase

Vase, 5" h., 5 1/4" d., bulbous ovoid form w/wide, short cylindrical neck, one side pinched-in, the other side dimpled, large sponged maroon dots, spattered green & red glazes under a sheer semi-matte glaze, clay body showing through, restoration to rim hairline, signed (ILLUS.).. **8,050**

Vase, 6 1/4" h., 5" d., footed ovoid pillow-style body w/an upright crimped rim folded down across the center, rare pink glaze w/a sponged-on green & gunmetal band, stamped "G.E. OHR - Biloxi, Miss.," small kiln kiss on body, minor glaze nick & a few flakes inside rim (ILLUS. far left with other vases) **19,125**

Vase, 7" h., 4" d., baluster-form body w/a medial raised band & a deep in-body twist at the neck below the closed rim, unusual green glaze around the lower body w/a drippy red & teal leathery matte glaze on the upper half, script signature (ILLUS. far right with other vases)... **8,438**

George Ohr Vase with Applied Snake

Vase, 7 1/4" h., 3 3/4" d., flaring foot supporting a tall tapering ovoid body below a cupped neck w/a dimpled band below a plain slightly flared rim band, an applied snake looping around the lower neck & down the body, cobalt blue, amber & raspberry sponged glaze, stamped mark, restoration to base chip, some firing lines on snake, few minute rim nicks (ILLUS.)...................... **10,688**

Vase, 8 1/4" h., flaring foot below the squatty bulbous lower body tapering to a narrow waist below the tall flaring trumpet neck w/wide incurved mouth, red, purple, green, black mottled & volcanic glazes, inscribed "G.E. Ohr" **21,850**

Vase, 9 1/2" h., 5" d., footed bulbous spherical lower body below a tall neck w/a band of dimples at the bottom below tall flutes to the crimped rim, mirrored cobalt blue & gunmetal glaze, restored rim chip, typical abrasion line in body, script signature & "M" (ILLUS. second from left with other vases).. **9,563**

Rare George Ohr Whiskey Jug

Whiskey jug, flat-bottomed wide flaring cylindrical lower body below an angled twisted & pinched shoulder centered by a domed upper body w/a short molded spout, an S-scroll snake-like handle from side of neck to shoulder, mottled green & gunmetal lustered glaze, signed, restoration to handle, two minute flecks inside rim, 6" d., 6 1/2" h. (ILLUS.)........................ **4,888**

Old Ivory

Old Ivory china was produced in Silesia, Germany, in the late 1800s and takes its name from the soft white background coloring. A wide range of table pieces was made with the various patterns, usually identified by a number rather than a name.

The following prices are averages for Old Ivory at this time. Rare patterns will command higher prices, and there is some variance in prices geographically. These prices are also based on the item being perfect. Cups are measured across the top opening.

Basket, handled, No. U2 Deco blank **$400**
Berry set: 10 1/2" master bowl & six small
   berries; No. 7 Clairon blank, the set.............. **300**
Berry set: 9 1/2" master bowl & six small
   berries; No. 12 Clairon blank, the set............ **350**
Berry set: 10 1/2" d. master bowl & six small
   berries; No. 15 Clairon blank, the set............ **285**
Berry set: 9 1/2" master bowl & six small
   berries; No. 84 Empire blank, the set............ **250**
Bonbon, inside handle, No. 62 Florette
   blank, rare, 6" l...................................... **450**
Bone dish, No. 16, Worcester blank, rare **400**
Bouillon cup & saucer, No. 16 Clairon blank,
   3 1/2" d.. **250**
Bowl, 5 1/2" d., No. 7 Clairon blank...................... **45**
Bowl, 5 1/2" d., waste, No. 11 Clairon blank...... **285**

No. 84 Worchester Bowl

Bowl, 5 1/2" d., waste, No. 84 Worchester
   blank (ILLUS.).. **300**
Bowl, 6" d., cereal, No. 76 Louis XVI blank......... **95**
Bowl, 6 1/2" d., No. 22 Clairon blank.................. **100**

No. 28 Alice Bowl

Bowl, 7" d., whipped cream, No. 28 Alice
   blank (ILLUS.).. **300**
Bowl, 9" d., No. 34 Empire blank **150**
Bowl, 9" d., No. 69 Florette blank **200**
Bowl, 9" d., No. 200 Deco blank **100**
Bowl, 10" d., No. 5 Elysee blank.......................... **350**
Bowl, 10" d., No. 10 Clairon blank **200**
Bowl, 10" d., No. 11 Clairon blank **125**
Bowl, 10" d., No. 16 Clairon blank **125**

Bowl, 10" d., No. 73 Empire blank **250**

Old Ivory Bun Tray

Bun tray, oval w/open handles, No. 122 Al-
ice blank, 10" l. (ILLUS.) **300**
Butter pat, No. 15 Mignon blank, 3 1/4" d. **150**
Cake plate, tab-handled, No. U15 Florette
blank, 9 1/2" d. **185**
Cake plate, open-handled, No. 200 Deco
blank, 9 1/2" h. **125**
Cake plate, open-handled, No. 10 Clairon
blank, 10 1/2" d. **150**
Cake plate, open-handled, No. 17 Clairon
blank, 10 1/2" d. **400**
Cake plate, tab-handled, No. 57 Florette
blank, 10 1/2" d. **195**
Cake plate, tab-handled, No. 137 Rivoli
blank, 10 1/2" d. **185**

No. 204 Deco Cake Plate

Cake plate, w/open handles, No. 204 Deco
blank, 10" d. (ILLUS.) **300**
Cake plate, tab-handled, No. 75 Florette
blank (ILLUS., top next column) **250-300**
Cake set: 11" d. serving plate & 5 individual
plates; No. 12 Clairon blank, the set **450**

Florette Cake Plate

Cake set: 10 1/2" d. cake plate & six small
serving plates; No. 69 Florette blank, the
set **450**

Celery dish, No. 12 Clairon blank,
11 1/2" l. **200**
Celery dish, No. 22 Clairon blank,
11 1/4" l. **300**
Celery dish, No. 28 Clairon blank,
11 1/4" l. **150**
Center bowl, No. 84 Deco Variant blank,
12 1/2" d. **500**
Charger, No. 8 Clairon blank, 13 1/2" d. **385**

No. 90 Clairon Charger

Charger, No. 90 Clairon blank, 13 1/2" d.
(ILLUS.) **500**
Charger, No. 16 Clairon blank, 13" d. **300**
Charger, No. 44 Florette blank (ILLUS. back
row, w/Florette pieces, below) **500-650**

No. 44 Florette Blank Pieces

Chocolate pot, cov., No. 44 Florette blank, rare, 9 1/2" h. (ILLUS. far right w/Florette pieces) **600-700**

Chocolate pot, No. 118 Empire blank, rare, 9 1/2" h. **600**

Chocolate set, No. 22 Clairon blank, rare, 7-pc. set **2,500**

Chocolate set: 9 1/2" h. cov. pot & six cups & saucers; No. 53 Empire blank, rare, the set **1,500**

Chocolate set: 9 1/2" h. cov. pot & six cups & saucers; No. 75 Empire blank, the set **900**

Chocolate set, No. 200 Deco blank, 7-pc. set **600**

Chowder cup & saucer, No. U29 Eglantine blank, 4" d. **300**

Cider cup & saucer, No. 16 Clairon blank, 3" d. **150**

Coffeepot, cov., No. 84 Deco variant blank, 9" h. **1,200**

Empire Blank Demitasse Coffeepot

Coffeepot, cov., demitasse, No. 123 Empire blank (ILLUS.) **500-650**

Compote, 9" d., open, No. U11 Alice blank, rare **600**

Cracker jar, No. 11 Clairon blank, 8 1/2" h. **500**

Cracker jar, No. 120 Clairon blank, rare, 8 1/2" h. **650**

Cracker jar, cov., No. 33 Empire blank, 5 1/2" h. **500**

Cracker jar, cov., No. 39 Empire blank, very rare, 5 1/2" h. **900**

Cracker jar, cov., No. 15 Clairon blank, 8 1/2" h. **500**

Cracker jar, No. 44 Florette blank (ILLUS. far left w/Florette pieces) **850-1,000**

No. 75 Deco Variant Creamer

Creamer, No. 75 Deco blank variant, service, 5 1/2" h. (ILLUS.) **195**

Creamer & cov. sugar bowl, No. 4 Elysee blank, 4" h., pr. **300**

Creamer & cov. sugar bowl, No. 10 Clairon blank, 4" h., pr. **175**

Creamer & cov. sugar bowl, No. U15 Florette blank, 4" h., pr. (ILLUS., bottom of page) **250**

Creamer & cov. sugar bowl, No. 16 Deco blank variant, 6" h., pr. **400**

No. 53 Empire Sugar & Creamer

Creamer & cov. sugar bowl, No. 53 Empire blank, 4" h., pr. (ILLUS.) **450**

Creamer & cov. sugar bowl, No. 122 Alice blank, pr. **250**

Creamer & cov. sugar bowl, No. 11 Clairon blank, 5 1/2" h., pr. **175**

Creamer & cov. sugar bowl, No. 202 Deco blank, pr. **185**

No. U15 Florette Sugar & Creamer

Creamer & cov. sugar bowl, service size, No. 84 Deco variant blank, pr. **400**

Creamer & cov. sugar bowl, service size, No. U17 Eglantine blank, pr. **500**

Creamer & cov. sugar bowl, No. 39 Empire blank, rare, 3 1/2" & 5 1/2" h., pr. **400**

Creamer & cov. sugar bowl, No. 99 Empire blank, rare, 5 1/2" h., pr. **450**

Louis XVI Blank Creamer & Sugar

Creamer & cov. sugar bowl, No. 76 Louis XVI blank, rare, pr. (ILLUS.) **300-400**

No. 4 Elysee Chocolate Cup & Saucer

Cup & saucer, chocolate, No. 4 Elysee blank, 2 1/2" d. (ILLUS.) **250**

Cup & saucer, demi, No. 10 Clairon blank, 2 1/2" d. **135**

Cup & saucer, No. 15 Clairon blank, 3 1/2" d. **65**

Cup & saucer, No. 22 Clairon blank, very rare, 3 3/4" d. **500**

Cup & saucer, bouillon, No. 27 Alice blank, rare, 3 1/2" d. **450**

Cup & saucer, cov., bouillon-type, No. 73 Alice blank, rare, 3 1/2" d. **350**

Cup & saucer, No. 99 Empire blank, rare, 3 1/2" d. **450**

Cup & saucer, No. 114 Clairon blank, very rare, 3 1/2" d. **400**

Cup & saucer, No. 204 Deco blank, scarce, 3 3/4" d. **175**

Cup & saucer, No. U30 Alice variant blank w/Y border. **65-75**

Cup & saucer, No. 16 Clairon blank, 3 1/4" d. **75**

No. 90 Clairon Blank Cup & Saucer

Cup & saucer, No. 90 Clairon blank (ILLUS.) **75-95**

Cup & saucer, No. 203 Deco blank, 3 1/4" d. **95**

Cup & saucer, No. 82 Empire blank **75-95**

Cup & saucer, No. 84 Empire blank, 3 1/4" d. **75**

Cup & saucer, 5 o'clock-type, No. 28 Empire blank, 3" d. **85**

Florette Blank Cup & Saucer

Cup & saucer, No. 62 Florette blank (ILLUS.). **150-250**

Demitasse cup & saucer, No. 16 Clairon blank, 2 1/2" d. **125**

Demitasse cup & saucer, No. 22 Clairon blank, 2 1/2" d. **200**

Deco Variant Cup & Saucer & Teapot

Demitasse cup & saucer, No. 75 Deco variant blank (ILLUS. left) **125-140**

Demitasse cup & saucer, No. 5 Elysee blank, rare, 2 1/2" d. **175**

Demitasse pot, No. 16 Clairon blank, 7 1/2" h. **500**

Demitasse pot, No. 97 Clairon blank, very rare, 7 1/2" h. **2,000**

Demitasse pot, cov., No. 73 Clairon blank, 7 1/2" h. **525**

Demitasse pot, cov., No. 33 Empire blank, 7 1/2" h. **500**

Demitasse pot, No. 44 Florette blank (ILLUS. front, second from right w/Florette pieces) **800-900**

Demitasse pot, cov., No. 62 Florette blank, very rare, 7 1/2" h. **1,200**

No. 15 Clairon Demitasse Set

Demitasse set: 7 1/2" pot & 4 cups & saucers; No. 15 Clairon blank (ILLUS.).............. **900**

Demitasse set: 7 1/2" pot & 4 cups & saucers; No. U22 Eglantine blank.................... **1,800**

Dish, tri-lobed, No. 202 Deco blank, 6" w. **95**

Dish, tri-lobed, No. 204 Rivoli blank, 6" w. **175**

Dresser tray, No. 122 Clairon blank, 11 1/2" l. **285**

Dresser tray, No. 90 Clairon blank, 11 1/2" l. **250**

Dresser tray, No. 34 Empire blank..................... **250**

Egg cup, No. 84 Eglantine blank, very rare, 2 1/2" h. **500**

Eglantine Blank Ice Cream Bowl

Ice cream bowl, No. 6 Eglantine blank (ILLUS.)... **300-400**

Jam dish, individual, No. 28 Alice blank............. **150**

Jam jar, cov., No. 137 Deco blank, 3 1/2" h. **250**

No. 200 Deco Jam Jar

Jam jar, cov., No. 200 Deco blank, 3 1/2" h. (ILLUS.).. **400**

Mayonnaise set: dish & underplate; No. 10 Empire blank, 6 1/2" l., the set **275**

Mayonnaise set: dish & underplate; No. 84 Empire blank, 6 1/2", the set **265**

Muffineer, No. 73 Louis XVI blank, 4" h. **485**

Louis XVI Muffineer & Salt & Peppers

Muffineer, No. 84 Louis XVI blank (ILLUS. left).. **350-450**

Mustache cup & saucer, No. 4 Elysee blank, 3 1/2" d. **450**

Mustache cup & saucer, No. 16 Clairon blank, 3 1/2" d. **300**

Mustard pot, cov., No. 12 Clairon blank, 3 3/4" h. **425**

Mustard pot, cov., No. 84 Carmen blank, 3 3/4" h. **325**

Mustard pot, cov., No. 200 Deco blank, 3 3/4" h. **450**

Nappy, No. 65 Clairon blank, rare, 6" l. **550**

Olive dish, No. 17 Clairon blank, 6 1/2" l. **400**

Olive dish, No. 20 Florette blank, rare, 6 1/2" l. **195**

Olive dish, No. 75 Empire blank, 6 1/2" l. **75**

Pickle dish, No. 32 Empire blank, 8 1/2" l. **75**

Pickle dish, No. 84 Empire blank, 8 1/2" l. **85**

Pin tray, No. U22 Eglantine blank....................... **350**

Acanthus Blank Water Pitcher

Pitcher, water, No. 84 Acanthus blank
(ILLUS.)... **1,000-1,200**
Pitcher, 8" h., water, No. 11 Acanthus
blank **1,200**
Plate, 6 1/2" d., No. 121 Alice blank **50**
Plate, luncheon, 8 1/2" d., No. U30 Alice
blank **22**
Plate, 8 1/2" d., No. 60 Alice blank **85**
Plate, 9 1/2" d., No. U30 Alice blank................. **100**
Plate, 6 1/2" d., No. 10 Clairon blank **45**
Plate, 7 1/2" d., No. 12 Clairon blank **85**
Plate, 7 1/2" d., No. 119 Clairon blank, rare...... **300**
Plate, 8 1/2" d., No. 8 Clairon blank.................... **85**
Plate, 8 1/2" d., luncheon, No. 73 Clairon
blank **100**
Plate, 9 1/2" d., dinner, No. 21 Clairon
blank, rare **300**
Plate, 9 3/4" d., dinner, No. 16 Clairon blank..... **200**
Plate, 10" d., No. 16 Clairon blank, open-
handled.. **100**
Plate, 6 1/2" d., No. U4 Deco blank **40**
Plate, 8 1/2" d., No. 200 Deco blank.................... **75**
Plate, 7 1/2" d., No. 4 Elysee blank **65**

Rare No. 99 Empire Plate

Plate, 7 1/2" d., No. 99 Empire blank, rare
(ILLUS.)... **400**
Plate, 7 1/2" d., No. 107 Empire blank, rare...... **250**
Plate, 7 3/4" d., No. 84 Empire blank **65**
Plate, 8 1/2" d., No. 15 Empire blank **75**
Plate, 8 1/2"d., No. 53 Empire blank.................. **125**
Plate, 9 1/2" d., dinner, No. 40 Empire
blank, rare **300**
Plate, 9 3/4" d., dinner, No. 34 Empire blank..... **300**
Plate, 9 1/2" d., tab handle, No. U16 Florette
blank **350**
Plate, 8 1/2" d., luncheon, No. 76 Louis XVI
blank **150**

No. U26 Mignon Dinner Plate

Plate, 9 3/4" d., dinner, No. U26 Mignon
blank (ILLUS.) **385**
Plates, 6 1/4" d., No. 40, set of 5........................ **127**
Platter, 13 1/2" l., No. 75 Alice blank **400**

No. 34 Alice Platter

Platter, 21" l., No. 34 Alice blank (ILLUS.) **800**
Platter, 11 1/2" l., No. 22 Clairon blank.............. **325**
Porringer, No. 39 Empire blank, very rare,
6 1/4" h. **900**
Porringer, No. 82 Empire blank, 6 1/4" d........... **175**
Powder jar, cov., No. U22 Eglantine blank,
rare **450**
Powder jar, No. 84 Deco blank variant,
scarce... **400**
Ramekin & underplate, No. 11 Quadrille
blank, rare, 4 1/2" d., 2 pcs....................... **500**
Salt & pepper shakers, No. 44 Florette blank
(ILLUS. second from left w/Florette piec-
es) **150-250**
Salt & pepper shakers, No. 15 Louis XVI
blank, 2 3/4" h., pr. (ILLUS. right w/muff-
ineer) **125**
Salt & pepper shakers, No. 76 Louis XVI
blank, 2 3/4" h., pr. **200**
Shaving mug, No. 22 Clairon blank, rare,
3 1/4" h.. **1,000**
Soup tureen, cov., No. 84 Deco variant
blank, rare, 13" l.................................... **2,500**
Spoon rest, No. 200 Deco blank, 8 3/4" l. **250**
Spoon rest, lay-down type, No. 204 Deco
blank, 8 1/4" l. **250**

No. 29 Carmen Spooner

Spooner, No. 29 Carmen blank, 4" h.
(ILLUS.).. **400**
Spooner, No. 40 Carmen blank, 4" h. **400**
Tazza, No. U2 Rivoli blank, rare, 9" d. **600**
Tea cup & saucer, No. 4 Elysee blank,
3 1/4" d. **95**
Tea tile, No. 11 Alice blank, 6" d........................ **250**
Tea tile, No. 15 Alice blank, 6" sq...................... **225**
Teapot, cov., No. 204 Deco blank, 5 1/2" h. **700**
Teapot, cov., No. 200 Deco blank, 8 1/2" l........ **500**
Teapot, cov., No. 75 Deco variant blank
(ILLUS. right w/demitasse cup &
saucer) **500-600**
Toothpick holder, No. 15 Clairon blank,
2 1/4" h. **295**
Toothpick holder, No. 73 Clairon blank,
2 1/4" h. **340**
Toothpick holder, No. 121 Quadrille blank,
2 1/4" h.. **325**

Vase, 9" h., No. U12 blank 1,700
Vase, 5" h., No. 134 Deco variant blank 385
Vegetable dish, cov., No. 15 Clairon blank,
   10 1/2" l. 1,000
Vegetable dish, cov., No. 16 Clairon blank,
   10 1/2" l. 1,500

Old Ivory Covered Vegetable Dish

Vegetable dish, No. 28 blank, 10 1/2" l.
   (ILLUS.) 1,500
Vegetable dish, cov., No. 75 Rivoli blank,
   10 1/2" l. 1,500
Vegetable dish, cov., No. 84 Carmen blank,
   10 1/2" l. 1,300
Waste bowl, No. 28 Worcester blank, 5" d. 295

Overbeck

*The four Overbeck sisters, Margaret, Hannah B.,
Elizabeth G. and Mary F., established their pottery in
their old family home in Cambridge City, Indiana, in
1911. Different areas of the house and yard were used
for the varied production needs.*

*Their early production consisted mainly of artware
before 1937, with most pieces being hand-thrown or
hand-built in such forms as vases, bowls, candlesticks,
flower frogs, tea sets and tiles. Pieces during this era
were decorated generally either with glaze inlay or carv-
ing, and several colors of subtle matte glazes were used
first, with brighter glazes added later.*

*After the death of Elizabeth G. in 1937 Mary F.
became the driving force behind the pottery. The output
became less varied, until mainly small molded figures of
various sorts - of humans, some humorous or grotesque,
and animals and birds - were the main products. Work
was carried on alone by Mary F. until her death in 1955.*

*Marked pieces of Overbeck usually carry the "OBK"
cipher, and early wares may carry the initial or initials
of the sister(s) who produced it.*

Bowl, 5 7/8" d., 2 3/4" h., deep half-round
   form w/flat rim, red clay w/a glossy
   glazed interior in rust & maize, matte
   green drip glazed exterior w/whitish drips
   from rim, signed "Overbeck - 5 - 3," early
   20th c. $230
Chalice, round stepped foot & short stem
   supporting a wide & deep thick rounded
   bowl, decorated w/a wide band of incised
   stylized camels & mountains in yellow &
   gunmetal on a raspberry ground, incised
   "OBK - E - F.," 5 1/4" d., 6" h. (tight rim
   crack) 1,688
Figurines, various comical members of a
   band, each w/a different musical instrument, decorated in yellow, pink, green &
   white glazes, incised "OBK," 4 1/2" h.,
   set of 7 (few small chips) 2,363
Tea set: cov. teapot, cov. sugar bowl,
   creamer, round trivet & four cups & saucers; all w/simple rounded forms, each
   decorated w/a panel of stylized white lily-
   of-the-valley in cuerda seca on a celadon

matte ground, marked "OBK - E - H.,"
   teapot 9 1/2" l., 5" h., the set (minor rim
   nick on creamer, small stilt pull chips on
   cups) 2,475
Tumblers, cylindrical, w/rounded bottom
   rim, embossed around the upper body
   w/a band of stylized green crickets on a
   beige ground, stamped "OBK - E - F.,"
   3" d., 3 3/4" h., set of 4 1,463
Vase, 5 3/8" h., tapering cylindrical body,
   green ground w/three panels decorated
   w/deeply carved & painted butterflies in
   green against a chocolate brown ground,
   by Elizabeth & Hannah Overbeck,
   marked w/Overbeck logo & initials "E" &
   "H," together w/copy of "The Chronicle of
   the Overbeck Pottery" (dark line at rim,
   not visible on outside) 1,210

Very Fine Carved Overbeck Vase

Vase, 7 3/8" h., a short cylindrical foot supporting a wide cylindrical body w/a
   stepped shoulder & short rounded neck,
   deeply carved & painted w/five sets of
   stylized lovebirds in rose red & bluish
   green against an elaborately carved
   background in red, blue & green, turquoise blue ground, semigloss glaze,
   Overbeck logo & initials of Elizabeth &
   Mary Frances (ILLUS.) 8,800

Owens

*Owens pottery was the product of the J.B. Owens
Pottery Company, which operated in Ohio from 1890 to
1929. In 1891 it located in Zanesville and produced art
pottery from 1896, introducing "Utopian" wares as its
first art pottery. The company switched to tile after 1907.
Efforts to rebuild after the factory burned in 1928 failed,
and the company closed in 1929.*

Owens Pottery Mark

Bowl, 3 3/4" h., Lotus line, footed spherical body, the wide shoulder tapering to narrow molded rim, decorated w/a dragonfly & a few grass stalks on shaded grey ground, impressed "Owens 202" & "L" **$495**

Bowl, 6 1/8" d., 1 5/8" h., Matt Green line, low round form w/incurved shoulder w/raised lines & flat rim, impressed "Owens 330" **165**

Cruet, matte glaze in cream & grey, shape No. 1216, impressed "Owens 1216," 4 3/4" h. (fine overall crazing) **165**

Cruet, Lightweight line, footed bulbous ovoid body w/tri-point rim & C-form handle, wild rose decoration on shaded green to dark brown ground, by Cecil Excel, incised "CE" & "868," 3 1/4" h. **193**

Cruet, Lightweight line, footed bell-shaped body w/upright petal-shaped spout & loop handle, yellow nasturtium w/green leaves decoration on dark brown ground, decorated by Harry Robinson, incised "HR" & "877" w/impressed "JBO" circular logo, 5 3/8" h. (slight roughness on spout tip) **220**

Ewer, Metal Deposit line, three-footed bulbous body w/arched spout & large loop handle, electroplated copper, slip-decorated w/wild roses by Cecil Excel, marked "2 Owens 921," artist-initialed, 5 3/8" h. **385**

Jardiniere, footed cylindrical body w/scalloped rim, majolica finish w/embossed flowers & birds in blue, white & green, marked w/raised J.B. Owens shield mark, 6 3/4" h. (small glaze flake off rim) **165**

Jardiniere, footed cylindrical body w/scalloped rim, majolica finish w/embossed scrolled designs in blue, green & white, marked w/raised J.B. Owens shield mark, 8 5/8" h. (minor abrasions) **220**

Jug, Utopian line, ovoid body decorated w/orange carnation by Edith Bell, marked "Utopian Owens 967 AE" w/artist's initials in slip below handle, 5 1/2" h. **248**

Mug, Matt Green line, tapering cylindrical body w/C-form handle, decorated w/impressed combed designs & impressed "Owens 46," 3 7/8" h. **220**

Paperweight, rectangular, majolica finish, green glossy ground w/embossed stag head & marked "Edmiston Horney Co. - Zanesville - Ohio" w/embossed scrolled border, "Made by the J.B. Owens Pottery Co." on reverse, 2 3/8 x 3 7/8" **83**

Pitcher, 3 1/4" h., Embossed Lotus line, tapering cylindrical form w/incurved rim, pinched spout & C-form handle, grey ground decorated w/green & purple grape motif, impressed "Owens Lotus X 236" **248**

Owens Lotus Line Pitcher

Pitcher, 8 5/8" h., Lotus line, footed ovoid body tapering to a rolled rim & arched spout, D-form handle, dark green shaded to creamy white ground decorated on one side w/a wading white & blue bird & on the other side w/a lotus blossom, unmarked, some usage staining (ILLUS.) **350-375**

Tall Owens Decorated Pitcher

Pitcher, 12 1/4" h., tankard-form, flaring base below the tall slightly tapering cylindrical body w/a rim spout, arched long handle down the side, underglaze slip decoration of three tulips in yellow, rust & green on a shaded gold to brown ground, impressed mark, minor scratches, early 20th c. (ILLUS.)... **345**

Owens Nursery Rhyme Tile

Tile, square, color scene of Little Bo Peep w/rhyme in black & white in upper corner, in wide flat oak frame, minor edge roughness, 12" sq. (ILLUS.)................................... **2,645**

Vase, 2 1/2" h., Utopian line, squatty four-sided vase w/wild roses on dark brown glossy ground, by Sara Timberlake, marked "1 Owens Utopian 103," artist-initialed in slip on side.. **165**

Vase, 2 7/8" h., Lotus line, short, wide, tapering cylindrical form decorated w/a lotus blossom in white, yellow & green on dark brown ground, impressed "Owens 26".. **303**

Vase, 3" h., Utopian line, footed bulbous base & loop handles from shoulder to rim, pansy decoration on dark brown glossy ground, marked "3 J.B Owens 866" & artist mark in slip on one handle **165**

Vase, 3 1/2" h., Utopian line, two-handled bulbous form w/wild rose decoration on shaded brown ground, most likely by Claude Leffler, marked "Utopian Owens 936" & artist-initialed **248**

Vase, 3 7/8" h., Utopian line, square tapering body w/short cylindrical neck, red clover decoration on shaded brown ground, possibly the work of Virginia Adams, marked "Owens Utopian 2 8 111" w/artist's initials, which appear to be a conjoined "V" and "A".. **138**

Vase, 4" h., Soudaneze line, footed spherical body w/molded rim, decorated w/white pansies on glossy black ground, impressed "Owens 202" (minor glaze scratches & small bruise on rim)................... **330**

Vase, 4 1/4" h., two-handled, squatty bulbous body w/narrow cylindrical neck, shaded brown ground w/wild rose decoration, most likely by Martha Gray, artist-initialed & marked "J.B. Owens Utopian 980" (small nick on rim & 1/2 x 1/2" kiln kiss on back side)... **220**

Owens Utopian Line Vase

Vase, 4 1/4" h., Utopian line, crescent-shaped bowl raised on four tab feet, decorated w/dark red clover & green & brown stems on a dark brown shaded to moss green ground, glossy glaze, artist monogram on back, base w/impressed mark "Utopian J.B. Owens," shape No. 872 (ILLUS.).. **220**

Vase, 4 3/8" h., Utopian line, twisted body w/floral decoration, marked "1 Owens Utopian 117" & obscure artist mark on side **165**

Vase, 4 5/8" h., cylindrical w/bulbous base, raised repeating floral & leaf design, matte aqua glaze, impressed Owensart mark, ca. 1906 .... **173**

Vase, 4 5/8" h., Metal Deposit line, cylindrical body, flaring slightly at base w/flat flared rim, loop handles, electroplated copper w/embossed repeating geometric patterns, impressed "Owens 2" **440**

Vase, 4 3/4" h., Matt Utopian line, twisted body w/small cylindrical neck, pastel slip pansy decoration by Hattie Eberlein, impressed "Owens 102" & artist-initialed (some glaze discoloration & pinhead size glaze nick off base) **165**

Vase, 5" h., Utopian line, footed bulbous body w/wide shoulder tapering to short cylindrical neck w/wide flaring rim, decorated w/orange & green leaves on dark brown glossy ground, by Virginia Adams, marked "Utopian J.B. Owens 975" w/artist's initials on side in slip **193**

Vase, 5 3/8" h., Aborigine line, bulbous shouldered body tapering to wide cylin-

drical neck w/flat rim, light tan earthenware w/rust band & geometric decoration, chocolate brown rim & interior glaze, incised "JBO" & impressed "Owens 29" **165**

Vase, 5 1/2" h., Utopian line, bulbous ovoid body tapering to short cylindrical neck w/molded rim, decorated w/colorful autumn leaves on dark brown glossy ground, marked "Owens Utopian 1048" (minor scratches & small glaze nick off high spot near base) **165**

Vase, 5 5/8" h., majolica finish, bulbous base tapering to cylindrical neck w/flat rim, shape No. 27, impressed "Owens 27".. **83**

Vase, 5 3/4" h., Utopian line, twisted base tapering to square neck w/molded rim, wild rose decoration on shaded brown ground, impressed "2 Owens Utopian 115".. **138**

Vase, 5 7/8" h., Matt Green line, four buttressed feet support the spherical shouldered body tapering to short cylindrical neck w/molded rim, impressed "Owens 1155" (minor glaze nick off one foot) **275**

Vase, 6" h., Art Vellum line, footed, bulbous shouldered body tapering to flaring rim, h.p. horse head in tan shades on shaded brown matte ground, marked "Owens," shape No. 1114 .... **2,500**

Vase, 6" h., bulbous body w/molded rim, green Arts & Crafts-style rectangular designs encircling body, impressed "Owens 218"... **358**

Owens Lotus Line Grey Vase

Vase, 6" h., Lotus line, simple wide ovoid shape tapering slightly to a wide molded rim, a wide shoulder band embossed w/small purple berries & grey leaves on a dark grey ground, a shaded grey to white background, impressed mark, some crazing (ILLUS.).. **287**

Vase, 6" h., Lotus line, waisted cylindrical body w/wide shoulder & flat mouth, decorated w/mushrooms painted by Frank Ferrell, shaded grey to cream ground, artist-initialed, impressed w/"Owensart" torch logo & shape No. 1236 (minor glaze nicks on bottom edge)........................... **468**

Vase, 6 3/8" h., Utopian line, flared rim on a tapered ovoid body, decorated w/rose blossoms & leaves in cream & brown on a shaded brown ground w/a glossy glaze, ornate silver overlay decoration, overlay impressed "Utopian J.B. Owens 923 - Phee F.N. Silver Co." (crazing, scratches, nicks) **288**

Vase, 6 1/2" h., footed spherical form w/incurved flat rim, shaded grey decorated near the rim w/three swimming fish, impressed "L" (minor glaze inconsistencies & discoloration) **280**

Vase, 6 7/8" h., Lightweight line, footed baluster-form body w/slightly flared rim, jonquil decoration by former Rookwood artist Charles J. Dibowski, dark brown glossy glaze ground, incised artist's initials & "846," impressed "JBO" circular logo **358**

Vase, 8 1/2" h., Utopian line, bulbous ovoid base tapering slightly to wide cylindrical neck, nicely detailed ear of corn in yellow w/green husk done in heavy slip, impressed "Owens Utopian 223" (glaze scratches) **330**

Vase, 9 7/8" h., Malachite Opalesce Inlaid line, footed bulbous ovoid body tapering to narrow cylindrical neck w/flared rim, Art Nouveau-style metallic floral decoration (possibly a few missing beads at rim).. **1,650**

Vase, 10 1/4" h., Utopian line, bottle-shaped, coated w/gold & overlaid w/small coral-like beads, underglaze decoration of a rose branch in shades of green, rust & brown, impressed mark & No. 1010, ca. 1905 .... **345**

Vase, 10 3/4" h., 5 3/4" d., tall ovoid form w/three rings molded around the base, decorated overall in sgraffito w/upright stylized iris-like flowers in orange & blue on a dark brown ground, by Henri Deux, pea-sized burst bubble on shoulder, unmarked.. **731**

Vase, 11" h., tall ovoid form tapering to a flat mouth, a black ground w/incised tall iris blossoms on leafy stems in shades of dark brown & blue outlined in cream, unsigned **1,380**

Vase, 13 1/2" h., Lotus line, ovoid body w/short wide cylindrical neck, decorated w/blue & white iris & green leaves on greyish green ground, by Walter Denny, impressed "Owens 1245" & "Denny" in light brown slip (minor color spots in flowers)... **935**

Vase, Art Vellum line, footed bulbous body tapering to wide cylindrical neck, decorated w/scene of harbor w/boats, houses & trees, most likely by C. Minnie Terry, impressed w/Owens torch mark & shape No. 1039, artist-initialed in brown slip (base chip repaired) **1,045**

Pacific Clay Products

In the early 1920s William Lacy merged several southern California potteries to form the Pacific Clay Products Company in Los Angeles. Table and artware pieces of the 1930s have caught the attention of today's collector. In 1932 Hostess Ware, a brightly colored line of dinnerware, was introduced as one of the first competitors to Bauer's Ring Ware. Very distinct in style, Hostess Ware was available in both solid glazes and decorated pieces, in a range of colors including Apache Red, Pacific Blue, Lemon Yellow, Jade Green, Sierra White, Royal Blue and Delphinium Blue. From 1932 to 1942 other lighter-weight dinnerware lines followed, along with an extensive artware line including vases, planters, figurines, candlesticks, etc. Ceramic engineer Frank McCann and art department head Matthew Lattie were largely responsible for Pacific's success. In 1942 the company went into war-related work and pottery manufacture ceased.Collectors may have stoneware pieces such as milk bowls, poultry feeders, crocks, etc. with a Pacific mark. These pieces were produced in the early 1920s by the Pacific Clay Products Company. These stoneware items are not represented here.

Bowl, 6" d., shallow shape, ivory, circular mark "Pacific, Made in U.S.A. 3053"............. **$45**

Jade Green Hostess Ware Bowl

Bowl, 11" d., shallow salad-type shape on short feet, ribbed bands near top & bottom, Hostess Ware, Jade Green, circular mark "Pacific, Made in U.S.A. 311" (ILLUS.)... **195**

Console bowl, shell design, jade & ivory, circular mark "Pacific, Made in U.S.A.," 5 1/4" h... **89**

Figure of ballerina, ivory, circular mark "Pacific, Made in U.S.A.," 7" h. **115**

Pitcher, Pacific Hostessware line, 2-quart **100-125**

Plate, 6" d., Pacific Arcadia ware **4-8**

Plate, 6" d., Pacific Coralitos patt. **5-10**

Platter, 14" d., round, Pacific Arcadia ware.. **20-25**

Salt & pepper shakers, Pacific Hostessware line, pr.. **15-20**

Vase, miniature, 3 1/4" h., ringed cornucopia on base, rust glossy glaze, marked "Pacific U.S.A. 3010" **22**

Blue Vase with Floral Decoration

Vase, 6 1/4" h., molded floral relief, blue high gloss, marked "Pacific Made in U.S.A. 3052" (ILLUS.) 64

Vase, 6 3/4" h., double, aqua & ivory, circular mark "Pacific Made in U.S.A." 75

Light Pink Cornucopia Vase

Vase, 8" h., tall cornucopia form, light pink, marked "Made in U.S.A. 3109" (ILLUS.) 59

Vases, 5 3/4" h., profiles of Martha & George Washington, beading around the profile, Claire Lerner design, green & ivory glazes, circular "Pacific Made in U.S.A. 3060," pr. 75

Parian

Parian is unglazed porcelain in the biscuit stage, and takes its name from its resemblance to Parian marble used for statuary. Parian wares were made in this country and abroad through much of the last century and continue to be made.

Bust of Charles Dickens, mounted on a waisted circular socle, England, 19th c., 15 1/2" h. **$575**

Charles Sumner Parian Bust

Bust of Charles Sumner, mounted on a raised socle base, impressed title, verse & manufacturer's mark of Robinson & Leadbeater, England, ca. 1880, 12 7/8" h. (ILLUS.) 345

Bust of Clytie, mounted on a round waisted socle, England, 19th c., 10 3/4" h. **201**

Bust of General Robert E. Lee, mounted on a raised circular plinth, sculpted by Roland Morris, manufactured by James & Thomas Berington, impressed marks & title, England, ca. 1870, 12 3/4" h. **690**

Bust of Shakespeare, bearded man wearing cord-tied collared shirt & cloak, on a socle base, name impressed on the back, 19th c., 8" h. **110**

Busts of Mozart & Beethoven, each mounted on a raised circular plinth, each titled, attributed to Robinson & Leadbeater, England, ca. 1880, 11 1/4" h., pr. **748**

Figure of fisherman, modeled as a scantily clad male holding a net, England, 19th c., 22 2/12" h. **1,150**

Figure of "The Greek Slave," a standing nude woman leaning on a low draped column, on a ribbed socle base, modeled by Richard Cook after original statue by Hiram Powers, impressed mark "RC 17," mid-19th c., 13" h. **805**

Figure of woman, the kneeling maiden wearing a simple costume, her hands clasped in her lap, raised on a separate molded circular base, impressed marks of the Gustafsberg factory, Sweden, late 19th c., overall 16 1/2" h., 2 pcs. **575**

Figure of woman gathering wheat, full-length figure of woman in long skirt holding small pot & sickle, on round base, 21 3/4" h. (narrow piece of sickle is missing) **660**

Figures, each molded as a child in a different pose, each seated on a trunk, England, 19th c., 13 1/4" h., pr. **1,265**

Figural Owl Match Holder

Match holder, figural, two owls snuggled together on a tree branch w/a small stump in front for the matches, inscribed across the front of the platform base "Match Making," English registry mark for 1871, 5 3/8" w., 7 3/4" h. (ILLUS.) 195

Paris & Old Paris

China known by the generic name of "Paris" and "Old Paris" was made by several Parisian factories from the 18th through the 19th century; some of it is marked and some is not. Much of it was handsomely decorated.

Figurines, a couple in 18th c. costume, he standing playing a flute, she standing & reading a book, each w/colorful costumes, raised on tall waisted pedestal bases w/colorful floral panels & heavy gilt trim & gilt scroll feet, 19th c., 11" h., pr. **$660**

Ice bucket, cylindrical, a blue ground banded w/raised gilt flowers & beadwork & enameled floral panels, festoons & border, retailed by Davis Collamore & Co., Ltd., New York, mid-19th c., 7 3/8" d., 7 1/2" h. (gilt wear on footrim) **575**

Pair of Old Paris Urns/Lamps

Urns, classical form, decorated w/painted floral band on pale blue ground, masked handles, high square base w/green marbelized design w/gilt bands, converted into lamps, ca. 1830, 12" h., pr. (ILLUS.)... **1,344**
Vase, 12" h., portrait decoration on a gilt ground, square enamel-decorated panels on each side, one depicting a female taverner, the other w/an exterior topographical landscape w/building, 19th c. **345**
Vase, 14 3/8" h., tall slender baluster-form body on a slender pedestal base & w/a tall slender trumpet neck, the body w/overall gold trellis & dot design above a band of tulips & stiff leaf-tips at the body, the shoulders w/upright winged Minerva bust-length handles suspending white bisque floral swags down the sides, ca. 1820... **3,680**
Vases, 7 7/8" h., a short round pedestal foot supporting a tall ovoid body tapering slightly to the wide short flaring mouth, a platinum silvery ground w/the mouth rim & foot chased w/gilt diaper bands, one painted in color w/a country maid before an arbor w/a blindfolded Cupid led by a small dog, the reverse w/beehives, the other w/a similar maiden beside a gate accompanied by Cupid offering a bouquet, the reverse w/an open barrel, ca. 1880, the pair **2,300**

Paris Porcelain Vases

Vases, 14 1/2" h., baluster form w/wide ovoid body raised on a short pedestal & square foot, the slender trumpet neck w/a tightly ruffled rim, ornate goat head & fruiting grapevine handles, the blue ground decorated w/a large oval medal-

lion framing a scene of 18th c. women in peasant costume in a landscape, gilt trim, restorations, 19th c., pr. (ILLUS.).......... **575**

Pate-Sur-Pate

Taking its name from the French phrase meaning "paste on paste," this type of ware features designs in relief, obtained by applying successive layers of thin pottery paste, painted one on top of the other. Much of this work was done in France and England, and perhaps the best-known wares of this type from England are those made by Minton.

Box, cov., triangular, the cover molded w/a white nude woman sitting at water's edge silhouetted against blue, trimmed w/gold, marked "Limoges France," late 19th - early 20th c., 5 1/2" w., 2" h. **$220**
Medallion, portrait-type, round, blue ground w/a white slip self-portrait bust profile of Louis Solon, artist-signed & dated 1892, England, 3 7/8" d.. **1,265**
Plaque, rectangular, brown ground decorated w/white slip depicting a classical female figure holding a candlestick surrounded by three putti in flight, gilt-accented, Solon-type, France, unsigned, 19th c., 3 x 5 3/4"................................... **1,840**
Plaque, oval, blue ground w/white slip decoration of a Cupid figure holding a hammer to an anvil to break a chain, artist-signed by Louis Solon, late 19th c., England, in a giltwood frame, 4 3/4 x 6" **1,840**
Plaque, oval, a dark blue ground decorated in white slip w/an angelic winged figure among stars w/a tall lily below, artist-signed by Louis Solon, dated 1908, mounted in an ebonized & giltwood rectangular frame, plaque 5 1/2 x 9 1/2" **3,738**
Plaque, rectangular, blue ground decorated w/a white slip scene of a draped maiden offering drinks to numerous cherubs by her feet, artist-signed by Louis Solon, dated 1908, England, mounted in a flat, wide wood frame, 5 x 10 1/2" **4,313**

Pate-sur-Pate Plate & Vase

Plate, 9 1/8" d., round w/dished rim, deep brown ground w/gilt trim & white slip decoration of a nude child behind a net supported by two small trees, monogram of artist Henry Saunders, printed & impressed marks of Moore Brothers, England, ca. 1885 (ILLUS. left)...................... **748**
Vase, 8 1/2" h., footed, wide, squatty, bulbous body tapering to a narrow neck band supporting a wide squatty cupped neck w/flared & scalloped reticulated rim, dark green ground decorated on one side w/white relief of a triton & crossed staves & on the other side w/a bust of a young

maiden surrounded by blossoms & enclosed in a ribbon band reserve framed w/a leafy wreath, France, late 19th c. **805**

Vases, 6 7/8" h., ovoid body tapering to a short neck w/a flaring cupped rim, curved handles from under rim to shoulders, blue ground w/an oval mauve reserve decorated w/a white slip classical female, printed marks, Germany, 20th c., pr. (ILLUS. of one, right)..................................... **748**

Vases, 7 1/2" h., slender ovoid form, decorated in white pate-sur-pate on an olive green ground w/different scenes of Diana assisting Cupid in the firing of an arrow, beneath a gilt foliate band at the shoulder, the reverse w/either a group of trophies or a heart pierced by two arrows, decorated by A. Birks, Minton marks & numbers, ca. 1900, pr.................................. **8,400**

Paul Revere Pottery

This pottery was established in Boston, Massachusetts, in 1906, by a group of philanthropists seeking to establish better conditions for underprivileged young girls of the area. Edith Brown served as supervisor of the small "Saturday Evening Girls Club" pottery operation, which was moved, in 1912, to a house close to the Old North Church where Paul Revere's signal lanterns had been placed. The wares were mostly hand decorated in mineral colors, and both sgraffito and molded decorations were employed. Although it became popular, it was never a profitable operation and always depended on financial contributions to operate. After the death of Edith Brown in 1932, the pottery foundered and finally closed in 1942.

Paul Revere Marks

Bowl, 5 1/4" d., 2" h., wide flat bottom w/low rounded incurved sides, decorated w/a continuous landscape band w/clusters of trees done in cuerda seca, green, grey & blue, 1915, ink mark "4-15 - S.E.G. - A.G.".. **$935**

Bowl, 5 3/8" d., 2 1/4" h., round, a border of repeating incised rim decoration depicting three running rabbits in cream white against a blue ground, early 20th c. (hairline, glaze imperfections)................................ **805**

Bowl, 6 3/4" d., 3 1/4" h., deep rounded sides decorated around the rim w/a cuerda seca band w/clusters of green trees against a blue sky & brown earth, the background in moss green matte glaze,

marked "S.E.G. - 4-15 - S.G." (crazing lines to rim)... **2,970**

Paul Revere/S.E.G. Large Bowl

Bowl, 7 1/4" d., 3 1/4" h., footed, deep, rounded & gently flaring sides w/rolled rim, decorated in cuerda seca w/an upper wide band w/white trefoil blossoms on a buff & light blue band against the dark blue background, S.E.G. mark (ILLUS.).. **1,610**

Bowl, 8 1/4" d., wide flat bottom & low rounded incurved sides, decorated w/a stylized landscape w/clumps of trees in cuerda seca, in green, blue & grey, dark blue interior, ink mark "SEG - 7-20 - bvc".. **1,650**

Bowl, 8 1/2" d., 2 3/4" h., a wide shallow round form w/upright sides, decorated around the interior rim w/a cuerda seca broad band w/intricate white orchids & green leaves on a two-tone blue & beige ground, the center bottom & exterior in dark blue, signed "S.E.G. - 8 " & illegible initials (short tight hairline)........................ **2,200**

Bowl, 8 1/2" d., 2 3/4" h., round w/tapering sides, matte brown exterior, tan interior, signed "S.E.G.," early 20th c. **173**

Bowl, 10 3/4" d., 4 1/4" h., a small footring supporting a deep flaring round bowl w/a wide flattened flared rim, solid white ground decorated around the inner rim w/a band of white orchids & green leaves on a dark blue band, marked "PR - 11-26"...... **880**

Bowl-vase, wide bulbous form w/a wide closed rim, decorated around the rim w/a cuerda seca band of stylized white flowers & green leaves on beige & celadon green, the lower body w/a bluish grey glaze, signed "S.E.G. 339-12-11 - S.G.," 6" d., 4" h. **4,125**

Breakfast set: child's, cereal bowl, small plate, cup & milk pitcher; each w/a bright yellow ground decorated w/a round central reserve w/a polychrome decoration of chicks or rabbits, a cream-colored rim band on each inscribed "Ellen-Louisa," black outlining, marked "PRP" in ink, 1941, plate 6 1/4" d., the set...................... **1,540**

Cereal bowl, dark blue ground w/a white interior center & an interior cuerda seca rim band inscribed "Robert Bernard Hagan - His Bowl," ink mark "SEG - 251-12-11 - F.L.," 10 1/2" d., 4 1/2" h. (restoration to lines & chips).. **165**

Creamer, short, wide, gently flaring cylindrical form w/a pointed rim spout & D-form handle, plain light blue rim band above alternating dark & light blue stripes, impressed mark, 2 1/4" h. **121**

Paul Revere Plate and Vases

Inkwell, cov., square block-form, the cover decorated w/green trees in a dark blue landscape, base w/dark blue band over lighter blue bottom, inked S.E.G. mark & Bowl Shop paper label, 2 1/2 x 2 3/4", 2" h. **935**

Paperweight, low flat octagonal shape, decorated on the top in cuerda seca w/a green & brown tree on green grass w/a blue sky, marked in ink "S.E.G. - R.B.," 2 1/2" w. **440**

Pitcher, 4 1/4" h., milk-type, gently flaring cylindrical form w/a pinched rim spout & loop handle, a bluish grey ground decorated around the rim w/a cuerda seca band showing a tortoise & a hare in white, black & green w/the motto "Slow but Sure," ink mark **1,650**

Pitcher, 4 1/2" h., slightly flaring cylindrical body w/a small pinched rim spout & loop handle, decorated on the front under the spout w/an oval reserve showing a reclining white rabbit in green grass w/blue sky beyond, black banding on a light blue background, marked "Jane," impressed mark **468**

Plate, 9 3/4" d., dinner, dark blue ground w/a wide white border band decorated in cuerda seca w/black wording "Give Us This Day Our Daily Bread," 1921, ink stamp "S.E.G. 11-21 FL.," bruise to rim (ILLUS. far right, top of page) **619**

Plates, 7 1/2" d., round w/wide flanged rim, overall light blue glaze, impressed mark, set of 3 .... **110**

Tea set: cov. teapot, cov. sugar & creamer; each of simple squatty, rounded form, overall greyish blue glaze, one ink-signed, two pieces stamped, 1927, minute glaze burst on rim of creamer, the set (ILLUS., bottom of page) **288**

Vase, 6" h., bulbous body tapering to small flared rim, matte drip glaze in shades of blue & green, early 20th c., SEG (minor flakes edge of base) **259**

Vase, 4 1/4" h., 3 3/4" d., ovoid body w/a closed rim, dark bluish grey ground, decorated around the upper half w/a landscape in shades of blue outlined in black, stamped circular Paul Revere mark & "5-25 - E.M.," 1925 .... **935**

Vase, 4 1/2"h., 2 1/4" d., swelled & gently tapering cylindrical form w/flared rim, decorated in cuerda seca around the rim w/a band of Greek key design in brown & blue on a pale green ground, ink mark "S.E.G. - E.G. - 4-1-?" **825**

Vase, 4 1/2" h., 3 3/4" d., simple ovoid form w/a closed rim, dark bluish grey ground decorated around the top w/a wide cuerda seca band w/stylized white & blue lotus blossoms, 1914, ink mark "SEG - am - 11-14" (ILLUS. second from right with plate) **1,238**

Vase, 5 1/4" h., 4 1/2" d., wide ovoid body w/a closed rim, a continuous abstract landscape of green trees against a frothy white sky & dark blue & grey ground, glossy glaze, 1922, signed "3-22 - S.E.G. - E.G." **1,540**

Paul Revere Pottery Tea Set

Vase, 5 3/4" h., 4 1/2" d., simple ovoid body w/a closed rim, matte light green ground decorated around the shoulder w/a wide band of stylized yellow tulips & greenish leaves on white w/black border bands, Paul Revere stamp, illegible date (ILLUS. second from left with plate) **1,238**

Vase, 6 1/2" h., 5" d., ovoid body tapering to a thick, rolled rim, dark blue ground decorated around the shoulder w/a wide cuerda seca band w/yellow stylized tulips & dark blue leaves on a light blue ground, stamped mark (ILLUS. far left with plate) .. **1,463**

Vase, 7" h., wide tapering ovoid body w/a closed rim, mottled multi-toned turquoise blue glaze, ink mark, 1927 .... **231**

Pennsbury Pottery

Pennsbury

Pottery

morrisville, Pa.

Pennsbury
Pottery

Pennsbury Pottery Marks

Henry Below and his wife, Lee, founded the Pennsbury Pottery in Morrisville, Pennsylvania, in 1950. The Belows chose the name because William Penn's home was nearby. Lee, a talented artist who designed the well-known Rooster pattern, almost the entire folk art designs and the Pennsylvania German blue and white hand-painted dinnerware, had been affiliated with Stangl Pottery of Trenton, New Jersey. Mr. Below had learned pottery making in Germany and became an expert in mold making and ceramic engineering. He, too, had been associated with Stangl Pottery, and when he and Lee opened Pennsbury Pottery, several workers from Stangl joined the Belows. Mr. Below's death in 1959 was unexpected, and Mrs. Below passed away in 1968 after a long illness. Pennsbury filed for bankruptcy in October 1970. In 1971 the pottery was destroyed by fire.

During Pennsbury's production years, an earthenware with a high temperature firing was used. Most of the designs are a sgraffito-type similar to Stangl's products. The most popular coloring, a characteristic of Pennsbury, is the smear-type glaze of light brown after the sgraffito technique has been used. Birds are usually marked by hand and most often include the name of the bird. Dinnerware followed and then art pieces, ashtrays and teapots. The first dinnerware line was Black Rooster, followed by Red Rooster. There was also a line known as Blue Dowry, which had the same decorations as the brown folk art pattern but done in cobalt.

Canister, cov., Black Rooster patt., w/black rooster finial, front reads "Flour," 9" h. **$175-200**

Cookie jar, cov., Rooster patt. **175-200**

Desk basket, Two Women Under Tree patt., 5" h. **75-95**

Model of a rooster, the large bird realistically molded & decorated in black & white, marked, 11 5/8" h. **275-300**

Model of bird, Crested Chickadee, blue, No. 101, 4" h. **125-150**

Model of chickadee, head down, on irregular base, model No. 111, signed "R.B.," 3 1/2" h. **140-150**

Mug, beer-type, Barber Shop Quartet patt. **35-45**

Mug, beer, Amish patt., dark brown rim & bottom w/dark brown applied handle, 5" h. **38-48**

Oil & vinegar cruets w/stoppers, figural Amish man & woman heads, pr. **75-100**

Commemorative Pie Plate

Pie plate, Dutch Haven commemorative, birds & heart in center, inscribed around the rim "When it comes to Shoo-Fly Pie - Grandma sure knew how - t'is the Kind of Dish she used - Dutch Haven does it now," 9" d. (ILLUS.)................................... **125-150**

Pitcher, 5" h., Delft Toleware patt., fruit & leaves, white body w/fruit & leaves outlined in blue, blue inside **90-110**

Amish Pattern Pitcher

Pitcher, 7 1/4" h., Amish patt. w/interlocked pretzels on reverse (ILLUS.)................... **100-125**

Small Black Rooster Plate

Plate, 6" d., Black Rooster patt. (ILLUS.)........ **25-30**
Plate, 8" d., Courting Buggy patt.................. **75-100**
Plate, 10" d., Red Rooster patt. **45-55**
Relish tray, Black Rooster patt., five-sec-
  tion, each w/different scene, Christmas-
  tree shape, 14 1/2" l., 11" w.................... **225-245**
Salt & pepper shakers, figural head of
  Amish man & Amish woman, pr................. **35-45**

Commemorative Plaque

Wall plaque, commemorative, "What Giffs,
  what ouches you?," reverse marked
  "NFBPWC Philadelphia, PA 1960,"
  drilled for hanging, 4" d. (ILLUS.)............... **30-40**

Plaque with Rooster

Wall plaque, Rooster patt., "When the cock
  crows the night is all," drilled for hanging,
  4" d. (ILLUS.).. **40-50**

"It is Whole Empty" Plaque

Wall plaque, shows woman holding Pennsbury cookie jar, marked "It is Whole Emp-
  ty," drilled for hanging, 4" d. (ILLUS.)........ **35-45**
Wall plaque, Amish man & woman kissing
  over cow, drilled for hanging, 8" d. **90-100**

Donkey & Clown Wall Pocket

Wall pocket, donkey & clown w/dark green
  border, ivory center, 6 1/2" sq. (ILLUS.) **100-125**

Peters & Reed

Peters & Reed Mark

In 1897 John D. Peters and Adam Reed formed a partnership to produce flowerpots in Zanesville, Ohio. Formally incorporated as Peters and Reed in 1901, this type of production was the mainstay until after 1907, when they gradually expanded into the art pottery field. Frank Ferrell, a former designer at the Weller Pottery, developed the "Moss Aztec" line while associated with Peters and Reed, and other art lines followed. Although unmarked, attribution is not difficult once familiar with the various lines. In 1921, Peters and Reed became Zane Pottery which continued in production until 1941.

Moss Aztec Jardiniere

Jardiniere, Moss Aztec line, wide tapering ovoid form w/a wide flat mouth above a molded band of poppy blossoms & four wide buttress panels down the sides, minor chips & nicks, signed, 13" d., 9 3/4" h. (ILLUS.) **$460**

Peters & Reed Cylindrical Jardiniere

Jardiniere, slightly tapering cylindrical form, molded around the sides w/high-relief rounded blossoms above a beaded base band, matte green glaze w/clay showing through, 5 1/2" d., 4" h. (ILLUS.) **115**
Vase, 12" h., Landsun line, tall slender cylindrical body w/a flared base, streaky pale green, brown & blue banded glaze, ca. 1922, light crazing **115**
Vase, 12" h., Shadow Ware, ovoid body tapering to small molded rim, green & black flambé glossy glaze, stamped "PRP" (few shallow scratches to surface) **303**

Large Peters & Reed Floor Vase

Vase, 18" h., floor-type, tall slightly waisted cylindrical form w/a flaring rim, molded around the top w/large stylized blossoms on slender stems slightly spiraling down the sides, dark green matte glaze w/clay showing through, unsigned (ILLUS.) **546**

Pewabic

Mary Chase Perry (Stratton) and Horace J. Caulkins were partners in this Detroit, Michigan, pottery. Established in 1903, Pewabic Pottery evolved from their Revelation Pottery, "Pewabic" meaning "clay with copper color" in the language of Michigan's Chippewa Indians. Caulkins attended to the clay formulas and Mary Perry Stratton was artistic creator of forms & glaze formulas, eventually developing a wide range of colors for her finely textured glazes. The pottery's reputation for fine wares and architectural tiles enabled it to survive the Depression years of the 1930s. After Caulkins died in 1923, Mrs. Stratton continued to be active in the pottery until her death, at age 94, in 1961. Her contributions to the art pottery field are numerous.

Pewabic Pottery Mark

Bowl, 6 3/4" d., 3 3/4" h., hemispherical form w/a slightly flared rim, unusual gunmetal & turquoise dripping lustered glaze, circular stamp mark **$2,025**

Pewabic Footed Bowl

Bowl, 7 1/4" d., 4" h., a small footring below the squatty, wide, bulbous body tapering to a widely flaring rim, flowing matte brown exterior glaze, lavender & turquoise lustered interior glaze, stamped mark & paper label, small glaze nicks on foot (ILLUS.) **805**
Bowl, 3 3/4" d., 1 3/4" h., spherical w/incurved flat rim, iridescent dove grey lustre w/turquoise interior that flows out onto rim, outlined in brick red, the shoulder decorated w/an impressed pattern of rings, impressed mark **252**

Miniature Pewabic Bowl-vase

Bowl-vase, miniature, a small footring supporting a wide squatty bulbous body w/a wide short cylindrical neck, mottled teal blue, green & gunmetal glossy glaze, circular mark, 3 3/4" d., 2 3/4" h. (ILLUS.) **460**

Pewabic Volcanic Glazed Bowl-Vase

Bowl-vase, footed wide half-round form w/a wide slightly rounded shoulder to a wide flat mouth, overall lustered volcanic cobalt blue & celadon greyish green glaze, mark covered by glaze, 9 1/4" d., 4 3/4" h. (ILLUS.) **5,344**

Jar, cov., model of a large eggplant, the top & stem forming the cover, overall dark matte purple flowing glaze, unmarked, 4 1/4" d., 6 3/4" h. (ILLUS., top next column) **2,070**

Jardiniere, footed, large, deep bulbous ovoid body w/a wide flat rim band, lustered cobalt blue glaze, stamped "Pewabic - Detroit," 9" d., 8" h. **2,475**

Pewabic Eggplant-shaped Jar

Plate, 10 3/4" d., flattened form w/wide flanged rim, painted w/a radiating design of dragonflies in blue slip on a white crackled ground, stamped mark, several glaze flakes & chips to footring, stamped mark (ILLUS. center, bottom of page) **1,100**

Miniature Vase with Test Glaze

Vase, miniature, 2" h., 2 1/2" d., test glaze, squatty bulbous body tapering to a short, wide flaring neck, dark Persian blue crackled glaze over a black-glazed lower body, circular stamp & "40B" (ILLUS.) **248**

Pewabic Plate and Vases

Pewabic Miniature Vase

Vase, miniature, 2 1/4" h., 2 1/4" d., flat-bottomed ovoid form w/a closed rim, fine celadon green & lavender lustered glaze, no visible mark (ILLUS.) **385**

Vase, miniature, 2 1/2" h., 2" d., cylindrical form slightly tapered at the base, fine turquoise, green & blue lustered dripping glaze, circular stamp mark (ILLUS. third from right with plate).. **468**

Two Small Pewabic Vases

Vase, miniature, 2 1/2" h., 2" d., flat-bottomed ovoid form, the rounded shoulder centered by a short cylindrical neck w/slightly flared rim, fine celadon & ox-blood lustre glaze, stamped mark (ILLUS. left)... **385**

Vase, miniature, 2 1/2" h., 2 1/4" d., ovoid body tapering to a small flat mouth, dripping pink crackled glaze on a blue lustered ground, stamped "PEWABIC - DETROIT" (some deep crazing lines, minute fleck at rim).. **281**

Vase, miniature, 2 1/2" h., 2 3/4" d., simple wide ovoid form w/a closed rim, fine & thick pink, gold & blue lustered dripping glaze, circular stamp mark (ILLUS. second from left with plate)................................ **1,320**

Vase, miniature, 2 1/2" h., 3 1/4" d., sharply tapering cylindrical sides below a wide shoulder tapering to a wide, flat mouth, fine gold, green & ivory lustered glaze, circular stamp mark & paper label (ILLUS. second from right with plate)............ **605**

Vase, miniature, 3 1/2" h., 2 1/4" d., footed bottle form, fine dripping turquoise & gold lustred glaze, hand-incised "PEWABIC" (stilt pull chip on base).................................... **197**

Bulbous Miniature Pewabic Vase

Vase, miniature, 3 1/2" h., 3 3/4" d., footed bulbous body w/an angled shoulder to a low rolled rim, unusual white semi-matte glaze w/a lustered umber rim, stamped mark & paper label (ILLUS.)........................... **575**

Vase, 3 3/4" h., 3 3/4" d., bulbous, nearly spherical body w/a short cylindrical neck centered on the shoulder, fine thick & leathery cobalt blue & green lustered glaze, circular stamp mark (ILLUS. second from left, below) **731**

Large & Small Pewabic Vases

Vase, miniature, 3 3/4" h., 3 3/4" d., simple ovoid form w/a wide shoulder tapering to a wide, flat mouth, fine dripping turquoise & purple lustered glaze, stamped circular mark 660

Vase, 3 3/4" h., 5" d., wide, squatty, bulbous form w/a wide rounded shoulder centering a short tapering cylindrical neck, overall unusual blue, green & mauve drippy semi-matte glaze, stamped mark, paper label 660

Vase, 4 3/4" h., 3 1/2" d., simple ovoid form w/a flat mouth, fine gold & mauve lustered glaze, circular stamp mark (ILLUS. far right with plate) 715

Vase, 4 3/4" h., 4" d., bulbous ovoid body w/a short cylindrical neck, fine mirrored gold glaze dripping over a glossy dark blue ground, circular stamp mark, small firing chip at base (ILLUS. far left with plate) 1,210

Vase, 4 3/4" h., 4" d., bulbous, wide body w/an angled shoulder tapering to a short, flaring neck, lustered celadon green & purple glaze, stamped cylindrical mark, remnant of paper label (ILLUS. right with miniature vase) 550

Vase, 5" h., 5" d., footed, spherical, ringed body tapering to a narrow mouth rim, overall orange matte glaze, circular stamp mark (restoration to small base chip) 450

Pewabic Vase with Lustered Glaze

Vase, 7 1/2" h., 4" d., simple ovoid body w/a short, flared neck, lustered copper & gold mottled glaze, stamped mark (ILLUS.) **2,530**

Vase, 7 3/4" h., 5 1/2" d., footed, wide, bulbous ovoid body tapering to a short, flared neck w/flattened rim, fine lustered blue & turquoise mottled glaze, stamped "PEWABIC - DETROIT" 1,350

Vase, 8" h., 7" d., the wide, squatty base w/a knobby, sharply angled shoulder tapering to a wide cylindrical neck molded w/light ribbing & knobby prunts around the wide flattened rim, smooth flowing matte green glaze, unmarked (firing lines around base prunts) 2,530

Pewabic Baluster-form Vase

Vase, 6" h., wide baluster-form body w/flaring neck, dark greenish blue glaze, impressed mark, some crazing, small firing line in base, small glaze bubbles (ILLUS.) 345

Vase, 6" h., 4 1/4" d., footed, wide pear-shaped body tapering to a short flared neck, lustered dripping celadon green & purple glaze, circular stamp & paper label 844

Vase, 7" h., 5 1/4" d., flaring cylindrical body w/a wide angled shoulder centering a narrow neck w/molded rim, unusual brown, green & blue dripping matte glaze, stamped mark (reglued chip on base) 660

Pewabic Vase with Unusual Glaze

Vase, 8 1/4" h., 6" d., flaring & swelled cylindrical sides below a wide angled shoulder centered by a small neck w/molded rim, unusual gunmetal brown, celadon & dripping turquoise mottled glaze, circular paster mark (ILLUS.) 1,610

Vase, 9 3/4" h., 6 1/2" d., wide baluster-form body w/a short flared neck, brilliant pulled cobalt blue & turquoise lustered glaze, stamped "Pewabic - Detroit" (ILLUS. second from right with other vases) **5,625**

Pewabic Vase with Modeled Leaves

Vase, 10" h., 5 3/4" d., ovoid form w/hand-modeled impressed arched leaves alternating w/raised wedged ribs continuing to curved shoulder, smooth matte green glaze, Pewabic stamp w/leaves, small glaze chips around base, T-lines in body (ILLUS.)... **4,600**

Vase, 10 1/2" h., 5" d., squatty, bulbous base tapering to a tall ringed body w/a flared mouth, frothy, dripping celadon green & gold lustered glaze, drilled hole in bottom, stamped "PEWABIC - DETROIT" (ILLUS. far right with other vases) **2,363**

Vase, 10 1/2" h., 7" d., wide flaring cylindrical form w/horizontal band, ivory crackle glaze, incised "Pewabic - WBS - 1935"...... **1,125**

Vase, 11" h., 5 3/4" d., bulbous lobed body tapering to a tall slender cylindrical neck & flat rim, covered in a leathery cobalt matte glaze, stamped "Pewabic"................ **2,813**

Vase, 11" h., 8 1/2" d., large, wide, tapering cylindrical form w/a narrow, angled shoulder to a wide, flat mouth, embossed w/nubs around the shoulder, rare dripping matte mustard yellow glaze on a caramel ground, stamped "Pewabic" w/leaves (ILLUS. far left with other vases) **11,250**

Phoenix Bird & Flying Turkey Porcelain

The phoenix bird, a symbol of immortality and spiritual rebirth, has been handed down through Egyptian mythology as a bird that consumed itself by fire after 500 years and then rose again, renewed, from its ashes. This bird has been used to decorate Japanese porcelain designed for export for more than 100 years. The pattern incorporates a blue design of the bird, variously known as the "Flying Phoenix," the "Flying Turkey" or the "Ho-o," stamped on a white ground. It became popular with collectors because of the abundant supply resulting from the long period of time the ware was produced. Pieces can be found marked with Japanese characters, with a "Nippon" mark, a "Made in Japan" mark or an "Occupied Japan" mark. Although there are several variations to the pattern and border, we have grouped them together since values seem to be quite comparable. A word of caution to collectors: Phoenix Bird pattern is still being produced. The standard reference for this category is Phoenix Bird Chinaware by Joan Collett Oates.

Berry server, style "B," w/seven drain holes, 6" d.. **$238**
Bouillon cup & saucer, cov. **61**
Butter pat **14**
Cann, w/handle, straight sides **26**
Casserole, style #1, oval **305**
Celery, style #1, 13 1/2" l. **180**
Cheese & cracker plate, tiered **280**

Style #1 Chocolate Pot

Chocolate pot, style #1, 8 3/4" h., 5 1/4" d. (ILLUS.)... **144**
Chocolate pot, style #2, scalloped body & base **341**
Chocolate set: style #1 pot w/five demi cups & saucers; the set.. **149**
Coffeepot, style #1 .... **72**
Coffeepot, style #6 .... **95**
Condensed milk jar, cov., style #1 .... **110**
Cracker jar, style #3 .... **145**

Phoenix Bird Cup & Saucer

Cup & saucer (ILLUS.)... **15**
Espresso cup & saucer **21**
Gravy boat, style #6 .... **36**
Gravy boat, style #6, w/underplate **75**
Hot water pot **45**
Ice cream dish, w/inverted scallops, 7" l............. **129**
Lemonade glass, w/flared top **56**
Lemonade pitcher **130**
Mustard jar, style #9, w/attached plate **52**
Pancake, cov., w/two steam holes **184**

Phoenix Bird Plate

Pickard

Pickard Mark

Pickard, Inc., making fine decorated china today in Antioch, Illinois, was founded in Chicago in 1894 by Wilder A. Pickard. The company now makes its own blanks but once only decorated those bought from other potteries, primarily from the Havilands and others in Limoges, France.

Pitcher, lemonade, 6 1/4" h., bulbous ovoid body tapering to a flat rim, gilt interior band & gold angled handled, h.p. Classic Ruins by Moonlight patt., artist-signed, 1912-18 mark (ILLUS. left)............................. **$550**
Pitcher, lemonade, 6 1/4" h., bulbous ovoid body tapering to a flat ring, gold angled handle, large pink carnations on golden stems around the sides on a white ground w/gold bands at the rim & bottom, artist-signed, 1905-10 mark (ILLUS. center).. 450
Pitcher, lemonade, 6 1/2" h., squatty, bulbous, ovoid body tapering to a scalloped rim w/wide arched spout, C-form gold handle, wide gold scrolls & red gooseberries w/green leaves on a white ground, Gooseberries Conventional patt., artist-signed, 1903-05 mark (ILLUS. right) 700
Plate, 8 3/4" d., pink floral decoration, artist-signed 88
Sugar bowl, cov., Art Deco design w/gold panels & silver lines w/stylized silver flowers on an off-white ground, artist-signed 150

Tea set: cov. teapot, creamer & cov. sugar bowl; overall etched gold decoration, the set 260
Tray, decorated w/scene of hunting dogs, artist-signed, 16" d. **2,895**

Pierce (Howard) Porcelains

Howard Pierce opened a small studio in 1941 in Claremont, California. Having worked with William Manker, also of Claremont, it is sometimes possible to see Manker's influence in some of Pierce's early work. Always being a studio potter with a tremendous talent (creating his own designs, making molds, firing and painting the items), Howard Pierce's death in February 1994 was felt by collectors. Prices for his pieces have escalated far above what anyone would have imagined.

Wildlife and animals played a large part in Howard and Ellen Pierce's life, with squirrels coming up to their window to be fed from their hands. They lived surrounded by these and other charming creatures. Many of Howard's creations came from watching them. He made roadrunners, monkeys, raccoons, an assortment of eagles, panthers, seals, geese, and many others.

However, his talent did not stop with wildlife and animals. Over time he created nativity scenes, vases, bowls, St. Frances figures, three-piece angel sets, tiles, advertising items and more. A set of three individual angels had one of the shortest runs of any creation Howard produced. They were difficult to make and time consuming. Naturally, they are valued more highly than most pieces because of their scarcity. The angels with black faces are even more difficult to find; fewer of them were made.

Howard used various materials to create his pieces: polyurethane (which caused him an allergic reaction), cement, Wedgwood-type Jasperware, Mount St. Helens ash (use caution not to confuse this treatment with the rough textured pieces), gold leaf, pewter, copper and, of course, porcelain.

Due to Howard's health, Howard and Ellen Pierce destroyed all the molds they had created over fifty years. This occurred in 1992, but it was less than a year before Howard began to make pieces again. In 1993, he purchased a small kiln and began to work on a limited schedule. He created smaller versions of his larger pieces, and collectors practically stood in line to buy them. These pieces are stamped simply "Pierce."

Howard Pierce Marks

Bowl, 7 1/4" d., 4 1/4" h., fluted body flaring to a fluted rim, Manker influence, pale & deep blue w/black accents, incised mark, "Pierce 1983" in script.................................... **$150**

Three Pickard Lemonade Pitchers

Howard Pierce Bowl

Bowl, 13" l., 2" h., freeform, black outside,
speckled black & white inside, 1950s
(ILLUS.)... **85**
Candleholders, comma-shaped, high gloss
grey glaze, 2 3/4" h., pr.................................. **135**
Figure group, boy standing w/head bent &
left arm extended to feed dog seated at
his left side, nondescript mottled brown
glaze, marked "Howard Pierce," 5" h. **100**
Figure group, three monkeys stacked on top
of one another, black, one-piece, Model
No. 300P, 15" h... **360**

Pierce Owls in a Tree

Figure group, two owls in a tree, seated on
branches, three open branches for small
flowers, dull dark brown tree, light & dark
brown owls, larger, unusual size for
Pierce owls in tree, stamp mark "Howard
Pierce," tree, 6" w., 13" h., large owl,
6" h., small owl, 3 1/2" h. (ILLUS.)................. **240**

Howard Pierce Figure of Girl

Figure of girl holding bird, purple high glaze,
"Howard Pierce" stamp, 7" h. (ILLUS.) **100**

Howard Pierce Figure of Man

Figure of man, holds bird in one hand, other
hand is extended, textured brown glaze,
"Howard Pierce" stamp, 11" h. (ILLUS.)........ **195**
Figure of native woman, w/long body, short
legs, arms behind her back, dark brown
glaze w/mottled brown skirt, hard to find,
3 1/2" w., 16 1/2" h... **245**
Figures of Hawaiian boy & girl, overall black
bodies w/green mottled pants on boy,
green mottled grass skirt on girl, both
w/hands in Hula dance position, 1950s,
boy, 7" h., girl, 6 3/4" h., pr. **225**
Jug, bulbous body w/small pouring spout &
small finger hold, brown mottled rough-
textured glaze, stamp mark "Howard
Pierce," 5 3/4" h... **95**
Magnet, model of a dinosaur, gloss grey
glaze, 3" l., 1 1/2" h. **110**
Model of bear, brown, 7" l. **85**
Model of bird on branch, brown & white poly-
urethane, signed "Pierce" on base,
4 1/4" h... **975**
Model of circus horse, head down, tail
straight, leaping position w/middle of
body supported by small, round center
base, light blue w/cobalt accents, experi-
mental glaze, 7 1/2" l., 6 1/2" h. **245**

Howard Pierce Hippopotamus

Model of hippo, standing, short tail, bulbous body, large nose & mouth, small ears & eyes, very distinct features, dark grey bottom, mottled grey top, 1950s, stamp marked "Howard Pierce Porcelain," 9 3/4" l., 3" h. (ILLUS.) **235**

Howard Pierce Mouse

Model of mouse, pink & ivory high glaze, "Howard Pierce Porcelain" stamp, 2" h., 3 1/4" l. (ILLUS.) **380**

Model of panther, pacing position, brown glaze, 11 1/2" l., 2 3/4" h. **400**

Model of rabbit, pale green w/white, cement, no mark, 5 1/2" h., 10 1/2" l............................ **380**

Howard Pierce Skunk

Model of skunk, black w/blue & white stripes on back, "Howard Pierce Porcelain" stamp, 4 3/4" h. (ILLUS.) **160**

Model of skunk, rough textured matte glaze, 6" h. **195**

Model of turkey, miniature, brown high glaze, "Pierce" stamp, 2" h. **235**

Set of Birds on Stumps

Models of birds, blue on black tree stumps, "Howard Pierce Porcelain" stamp & one signed "Pierce" on base, 5" & 4 1/2" h., the set (ILLUS.) **285**

Models of birds, seated, heads up, nondescript bodies except for eyes & beaks, black satin-matte glaze w/orangish red breasts, stamp mark "Howard Pierce," large, 4 1/2" h., medium, 3" h., small, 1 3/4" h., the set **175**

Howard Pierce Dogs w/Drooping Ears

Models of dogs w/drooping ears, dark & light brown, 8" h., & 6" h., pr. (ILLUS.) **205**

Models of fish, each on a half-circle base, dark brown bodies w/speckled bases & fins, large fish, 6" h., medium fish, 4 3/4" h., small fish, 3" h., the set **340**

Models of giraffes, brown & white, 1950s, 9" h., 10" h., pr. **230**

Models of monkeys, grey, pr. **165**

Pencil holder, nude women in relief around outside, tan & brown glaze, one year limited production, 1980, 3 1/2" d., 4 1/4" h. **170**

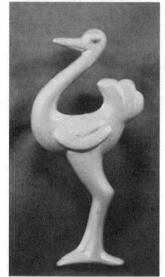

Howard Pierce Ostrich Pin

Pin, figure of ostrich, pewter, incised "Howard Pierce," 2 3/4" h. (ILLUS.)................ **245**

Planter, half-circle alcove in gold leaf w/white bisque angel holding songbook & standing in alcove, hard to find, 7" h. **205**

Howard Pierce Sugar Bowl

Sugar bowl, open, Wedgwood-type white bisque lamb motif, pale blue matte handle & outer edges, produced in 1950s, 2 3/4" h. (ILLUS.) **75**

Howard Pierce Face Vase

Vase, 6 1/2" h., white w/brown faces in relief, very few produced, "Howard Pierce" stamp (ILLUS.) **210**

Vase, 7 3/4" h., lime green w/white fish & coral silhouette, incised underglaze "Howard Pierce, Claremont, Calif., P-400" (number does not denote experimental piece) **125**

Vase, 9" h., tapering body w/a flaring neck & stretched rim, brown bottom half of body & neck, yellow midsection of body & interior, stamp mark, "Howard Pierce," & copyright symbol, hard-to-find color combination **90**

Wall plaque, rectangular, modernistic birds in relief, pale green background w/darker green birds, cement, 19" l., 1/2" deep, 6 1/4" h. **445**

Whistle, bird-shaped w/hole at tail, grey w/white textured glaze, 3 1/2" h. **100**

Whistle, snake crawling, w/body forming an "M" shape, brown w/white glaze, 3 1/4" l., 2 3/4" h. **155**

Pisgah Forest Pottery

Walter Stephen experimented with making pottery with his parents in Tennessee shortly after 1900 . After their deaths in 1910, he eventually moved to the foot of Mt. Pisgah in North Carolina, where he became a partner of C.P. Ryman. Together they built a kiln and a shop, but this partnership was dissolved in 1916. During 1920 Stephen again began to experiment with pottery, and by 1926 he had his own pottery and equipment. Pieces are usually marked and may also be signed "W. Stephen" and dated. Walter Stephen died in 1961, but work at the pottery continues, although on a part-time basis.

Pisgah Forest Marks

Bowl-vase, wide, spherical body w/the wide, round shoulder centered by a short cylindrical neck, amber glaze w/white & blue crystals, raised Stephen mark, dated 1947, 5 3/4" d., 5" h. **$385**

Bowl-vase, wide, spherical form, the rounded shoulder centered by a short, wide neck, amber flambé glaze w/celadon crystals, raised Stephen mark & illegible date, 4 1/2" d., 3 3/4" h. **303**

Teapot, cov., spherical form w/inset cover w/button finial, short, cylindrical spout & D-form shoulder handle, fine Chinese blue glaze w/red, green & blue highlights, raised mark, 8" w. **231**

Vase, 4" h., 5 1/2" d., wide, squatty, bulbous body w/the shoulder sloping to a low, molded, wide mouth, overall streaky white & blue crystalline exterior glaze, raised potter's mark, 1948 .... **605**

Vase, 4 1/2" h., 6" d., wide, bulbous form w/a wide, short, flat neck, overall white crystalline exterior glaze, raised potter's mark, 1942 .... **330**

Vase, 5" h., broad, ovoid form tapering to a wide, flat mouth flanked by strap shoulder handles, glossy soft green & blue glaze, raised mark, 1932 .... **115**

Vase, 5" h., 4 3/4" d., wide, squatty, bulbous lower body tapering to a cylindrical neck w/rolled rim, white & amber glaze w/blue crystals, raised potter mark, dated 1940 .... **358**

Pisgah Forest Vases

Vase, 6 1/2" h., 4" d., simple baluster form w/a short, wide, flaring neck, fine amber glaze w/tightly packed white & dark blue crystals, raised potter mark, dated 1940 (ILLUS. left).. **660**

Vase, 6 1/2" h., 4 1/2" d., tall, deeply corseted form w/a wide, flaring mouth, amber glaze w/grey crystals, raised potter mark & illegible date.. **413**

Pisgah Forest Vase with Blue Crystals

Vase, 7" h., 4" d., ovoid body tapering to a cylindrical neck, brown & amber flambé glaze w/clusters of large blue crystals, grinding chip at base, embossed mark (ILLUS.).. **605**

Vase, 7 1/2" h., 4 3/4" d., baluster form tapering to a short, wide, rolled neck, amber flambé glaze w/a few blue crystals, raised Pisgah Forest mark & illegible date **523**

Vase, 7 3/4" h., 4 1/4" d., baluster form w/flared neck, overall streaky blue, green & white crystalline glaze, raised potter's mark, 1949.. **495**

Vase, 7 3/4" h., 4 3/4" d., wide baluster-form body tapering to a short, wide, flaring neck, amber glaze w/white & blue large crystals around the lower half, raised Stephen mark, dated 1949 (ILLUS. right with two other vases)............... **770**

Vase, 8" h., 5 1/4" d., wide bottle form w/bulbous, tapering body below a tall, waisted, cylindrical neck, overall white glaze w/white crystals, raised potter mark & dated 1941 (ILLUS. center with two other vases).. **715**

Vase, 12 1/4" h., 8" d., wide, bulbous, ovoid base centered by a tall, cylindrical neck, shaded ivory glaze w/blue & pearl scattered crystals, raised potter's mark & "Stephen - 1946" (firing lines around neck base).. **788**

Purinton

The Purinton Pottery Company was founded in Shippenville, Pennsylvania, in 1941 by Bernard S. Purinton. Earlier, beginning in 1936, Mr. Purinton started a smaller pottery operation in Wellsville, Ohio, but by 1941, wanting to expand, he chose the site near Shippenville, where a large, new plant was constructed.

Most of Purinton's products were cast and then hand-painted with a variety of colorful patterns by local people trained at the factory. One of its best known and most popular designs was Peasant Ware, originally introduced at the Wellsville plant in the 1930s. Until the plant was finally closed in 1959, the company continued to produce a colorful, hand-decorated range of tablewares, kitchenwares, vases and novelty items.

Basket planter, Palm Tree, no cutout, 6 1/4" h.. **$299**

Beer mug, Palm Tree, purple intaglio, 16 oz., 4 3/4" h. **380**

Butter dish, tab handle, 6 1/2" l. **80**

Candy dish, w/loop handle..................... **65**

Carafe, Cactus Flower, two-handled, 7 1/2" h.. **264**

Children's cereal bowl, w/puppy, 5 1/4" d. **179**

Chop plate, Crescent, footed, 12" d. **249**

Chop plate, Fruits Blessing, signed by Dorothy Purinton, footed, some for meat, 12" d. (one chip) **501**

Coffee carafe, Autumn Leaves............................. **39**

Coffee mug, 12 oz. **80**

Coffee server, TST shaped, w/lid, 10 1/2"......... **555**

Coffeepot, cov., eight-cup **75**

Cookie jar, rooster **335**

Diamond grill platter, oblong, 12" l........................ **46**

Dinner plate, signed by Dorothy Purinton, w/cabin & trees, 9 3/4" d. **1,031**

Dutch jug, w/ice lip, Cactus, 2 pint..................... **362**

Dutch jug, w/ice lip, Red Ribbon Flower, 2 pint.. **1,226**

Honey jug, Holly, loop handle, 6 1/4" h. **480**
Honey jug, Palm Tree, loop handle,
   6 1/4" h. **130**
Honey jug, Pear, loop handle, 6 1/4" h. **155**
Jam/jelly, tab handle **54**
Oil & vinegar cruet set, tall, 9 1/2" h. **125**
Pig bank, blue **19**
Planter, Napco, Yellow Intaglio, rectangular,
   6" l. **23**
Rebecca jug, Starflower, 7 1/2" h. **255**
Roll tray, oblong **50**
Rum jug planter, 6 1/2" h. **61**
Salt & pepper set, Old Salt & wife **85**
Salt & pepper set, shake-n-pour type, bul-
   bous, 4 1/2" h. **71**
Spaghetti bowl, 14 1/5" d. **205**
Sprinkler, w/red tulips, 5 1/2" h. **114**
Sugar/creamer set, Cactus Flower (sugar
   some damage) **238**
Tumblers, 12 oz. **20**
Winged grease jar **96**

Brown Intaglio
Beanpot, individual **46**
Beverage pitcher, 42 oz., 6 1/4" h. **59**
Candleholder, round, 5" d., 2 1/2" h. **90**
Candy dish, w/loop handle **37**
Canister set, apartment size **128**
Coffeepot, cov., 8 cup **26**
Cookie jar, cov., wide oval, 9 1/2" **50**
Decanter **30**
Dutch jug, w/ice lip, 5 pint **60**
Range grease jar, cov., oval **47**
Range grease & salt & pepper set **60**
Spaghetti bowl, 14 1/2" d. **72**
Tumbler, 12 oz. **38**

Chartreuse
Cup & saucer **14**
Range salt & pepper shakers, 4" h. **128**
Rum jug, loop handle, cutouts **136**

Fruit
Cookie jar, cov., wide oval, 9 1/2" **51**
Flour canister, cov., round, wood lid, 8" h. **89**
Oil & vinegar set, conical shaped **77**
Sugar canister, cov., round, wood lid, 8" h. **50**
Tea 'n' toast plate, Wellsville Pear, 8 1/2" d. **18**

Heather
Kent jug, bulbous body, 4 1/2" h. **45**
Pickle dish, 6" l. **20**

Maywood
Casserole, cov., 9" l. **30**
Cereal bowl, 5 1/2" d. **13**
Jam/jelly, tab handle **53**
Wallpocket, 3 1/2" h. (small hairline) **105**

Ming Tree
Cereal bowl, 5 1/4" d. **43**
Chop plate, footed, 12" d. **250**
Fruit bowl, footed, 12" d. **230**

Mountain Rose
Kent jug **32**
Meat platter, oblong, 12" **179**
Sugar/creamer set, 4-petal **74**

Normandy
Candy dish, w/loop handle **52**
Casserole, cov., 9" l. **36**
Fruit bowl, footed, 12" d. **41**

Mini jug salt & pepper set, 2 1/5" h. **18**
Winged vase, bulbous, 6" h. **25**

Other Intaglios
Chop plate, turquoise, footed, 12" d. **125**
Dinner plate, turquoise, 9 3/4" d. **24**
Salt & pepper set, turquoise, stacking-type,
   2 1/4" h. **43**

Peasant Garden
Grill platter, oblong, 12" l. **257**
Roll tray, oblong **61**
Teapot, cov., 6 cup, domed lid **339**

Pennsylvania Dutch
Chop plate, footed, 12" d. **130**
Dutch jug, 5 pint, ice lip **511**
Meat platter, oblong, 12" **46**
Mini jug salt & pepper set **108**
Sandwich tray, w/metal handle, 12" d. **180**

Petals
Juice mug, 6 oz. **53**
Kent jug, bulbous, 4 1/2" h. **164**

Provincial Fruit
Dessert bowl, 4" d. **24**
Meat platter, oblong, 12" **150**

Red Ivy
Mini sugar, 2" h. **31**
Range grease, cov., oval **26**
Range salt & pepper, 4" h. **27**

Saraband
Beanpot, cov., individual, 3 1/4" h. **44**
Dinner plate, 9 1/2" d. **13**
Jam/jelly, tab handle **82**
Kent jug, bulbous body, 4 1/2" h. **108**
Meat platter, oblong, 12" d. **35**
Tea 'n' toast, w/cup **19**

Seaform
Sugar/creamer set, w/tray, 5" h. **123**

Quimper

Quimper Marks

This French earthenware pottery has been made in France since the end of the 17th century and is still in production today. Because the colorful decoration on this ware, predominantly of Breton peasant figures, is all hand-painted and each piece is unique, it has become increasingly popular with collectors in recent years. Most pieces offered today date from about the mid-19th century to the present. Modern potteries continue to operate today, with contemporary examples available in gift shops.

The standard reference in this field is Quimper Pottery A French Folk Art Faience by Sandra V. Bondhus (privately printed, 1981).

Coffee Set with Music Theme

Baby's feeding pitcher, 4 1/2" h., tiny spout, decorated w/only a flower garland band, unsigned, 19th c., excellent **150**

Basket, exterior w/raised basketweave design, interior w/image of peasant woman w/flower sprays, "HB Quimper - x364," 8 1/4 x 7", 6" h., mint...................................... **350**

Bell, bagpipe shape w/original unglazed clapper, "Ivoire Corbeille" patt., bust portrait of man on front, half sunburst w/sponged circlets design on reverse, "HenRiot Quimper 73," 3 1/4" h., mint............. **75**

Book ends, Modern Movement-style girl toddlers hold onto brown sponged wall as they attempt their first steps, w/white caps & navy dresses, one w/yellow checked apron, one w/pink checked apron, "HenRiot Quimper 136" & artist "J.E. Sevellec," 5 1/2" h., excellent, pr. **450**

Cigarette holder/ashtray, figural, yellow-glazed Modern Movement form of woman wears turquoise polka dotted blouse & red striped apron & holds double baskets w/holes on top for cigarettes, molded indentation on base forms ashtray, "HB Quimper 605," 8 1/2" h., mint **325**

Coffee set: 9 1/4" h. cov. coffeepot, creamer & cov. sugar; each decorated w/different Breton musician & very richly ornamented "Rouenesque" border, "HB Quimper 15," excellent, the set (ILLUS., top of page) **525**

Cup & saucer, "croisille" style, the 4" lip-to-handle cup decorated w/image of seated woman in trefoil cartouche w/"tennis ball" latticework trim, 5" d. saucer, "HR Quimper," mint, pr. **50**

Divided Dish

Dish, divided, double bagpipe shape, "decor riche" patt., bow & twisted knot handles, each division features peasant couple standing beneath sprigs of Breton wildflowers, 13 1/2" l., 11" w., excellent (ILLUS.)... **600**

Dish, fish shape, center w/design of woman wearing the costume of La Rochelle & surrounded by flower branches, "La Rochelle HenRiot Quimper 137," pierced for hanging, 10" l., 4 1/2" w., mint.................... **85**

Doll chamber pot, decorated w/floral band on outside & eye painted on bottom of interior, "HenRiot Quimper 115," 2 1/2" l. from lip to handle tip, mint................................. **35**

Quimper Card Tray

Card tray, rococo amorphous form, "decor riche" patt., center decorated w/pair of Breton musicians surrounded by flower sprays of wild gorse & broom, "HenRiot Quimper 148," 13 x 10 1/2", mint (ILLUS.).. **350**

Charger, w/image of woman in profile holding flower, framed by flower garland band, "HR" mark only, early, 11" d. (slight wear on outer edge).. **100**

Cigarette box, cov., image of woman w/flower branches on lid, geometric patt. on base, "HenRiot Quimper 116," 4 1/2" l., 3 1/4" w., mint.. **95**

Doll's Dish Set

Doll dish set: 4" d. cov. tureen, 4" d. charger, 3" l. gravy boat, two 2 3/4" d. plates & two 1 3/4" d. plates; each w/decoration of sailboat on waves, creamy buff glaze & rose pink sponged border, unsigned, attributable to HenRiot, excellent, set of eight (ILLUS.) **100**

Doll plate, red & blue striped pinwheel geometric patt., "HenRiot Quimper France 115," 1 3/4" d., mint (glaze skips) **45**

Doll plate, Modern Movement colors w/geometric stylized flower patt. in brown, yellow, blue & rose red, "HenRiot Quimper 106," 2 3/4" d., mint **30**

Egg cup, figural, in the form of a yellow-sponged chick w/blue feathers, w/attached 3 1/2" d. underdish, "HB Quimper," mint **75**

Figure group, Modern Movement bride & groom by artist Fanch, from "Noce Blgoudenne" group, the bride wears white dress & loaf coif painted w/yellow "embroidery" work, the groom a dark navy suit & red tie, "HB Quimper," mint **150**

Figure group, Modern Movement-style dancing couple posed so woman's flaring skirt shows off decorative trim on hem, "HenRiot Quimper 78" & artist "R. Micheau-Vernez," 12 1/2" h., mint **450**

Figure of "Fanch," wearing pantaloons & playing flute, Modern Movement colors, "HenRiot Quimper France 597," 3 1/2" h., mint **75**

Figure of St. Anne w/child Mary, "HenRiot Quimper France 127," 5 1/2" h., mint **55**

Figure of St. Yves, the patron saint of lawyers wears legal garb of the period, "HenRiot Quimper," 4 3/4" h., mint **100**

Figure of woman w/cane, Modern Movement-style figure of elderly woman in polka dotted blue shawl & green & orange striped apron leaning on cane, artist "L.H. Nicot" embossed on base, "Henriot Quimper 136," 8" h., mint **325**

Holy water font, base w/figure of the Christ Child holding a cross in relief, the top adorned w/image of eye of God enclosed within radiant sun & two stars, Modern Movement colors, "HB Quimper 119," 5 1/2" l., mint **110**

Inkwell, cov., in the form of a Breton hat, w/original inset & lid w/acorn finial, scene on lid of seated woman w/basket of eggs at her side, "HenRiot Quimper France 72," 5 1/2" w., mint (ILLUS. left, w/plate) **175**

Inkwell, cov., square w/cut corners, design of peasant man w/flowers & red S-link chain border, w/original inset & lid, "HB Quimper 497," 3 1/2" sq., excellent **180**

Quimper Inkwell & Plate

Quimper Inkwell & Pen Tray

Inkwell w/pen tray, cov., oblong, w/four feet & center apron, "demi-fantasie" patt., scene on front of Bretonne woman balancing milk pail on her head surrounded by flowering branches & lattice work, original inset & knobbed lid, "HenRiot Quimper France 99," excellent (ILLUS.)........ **275**

Cradle-shaped Jardiniere

Jardiniere, cradle shape on four tiny feet, double knobs at four upper corners, w/scene of peasant couple executed in the "demi-fantasie" style, back panel displays full-blown red & yellow rose set in flower branch, "HR Quimper," 7 1/4" l., mint (ILLUS.)... **800**

Quimper Crown-shaped Jardiniere

Jardiniere, crown shape, "decor riche" patt. w/seated couple facing each other on front, back w/Crest of Brittany held by lions, "HenRiot Quimper 23," 11 1/2" l., one handle professionally restored (ILLUS.).. **650**

Jardiniere with Ropetwist Handles

Jardiniere, octagonal shape w/country French geometric patt., blue sponged ropetwist handles, unsigned, 19th c., excellent, 12" l. (ILLUS.)..................................... **200**

Handled "Decor Riche" Jardiniere

Jardiniere, oval shape w/cutout rim, short oval outcurved base, dainty scroll handles, "decor riche" patt., main cartouche shows seated woman holding a jug, reverse features crowned Crest of Brittany, "HB Quimper," 12 1/2 l., 7" h., mint (ILLUS.)... **500**

Scalloped-rim Jardiniere

Jardiniere, oval w/scalloped rim, footed, flat ring handles, "decor riche" patt., image of seated musician on front, "HB Quimper 128," 9" l., mint (ILLUS.) **325**

Knife rest, figural, Modern Movement-style form of reclining woman w/her head on her hands & her elbows extended, "HenRiot Quimper" and mark of artist C. Maillard, 4" l., mint **100**

Knife rests, tricorner shape, each decorated w/images of peasant figure & flower branches, HB Quimper "xo" mark, excellent overall, 3" l., six-piece set **100**

"Ivoire Corbeille" Liqueur Set

Liqueur set: barrel keg w/original wooden spigot, wooden stand & six original small handled cups; "Ivoire Corbeille" patt. w/bust portrait of woman in profile on side of keg, "HenRiot Quimper," mint, the set (ILLUS., previous page) **150**

Quimper Liquor Set

Liquor set: 7" d. tray, 6" h. cov. decanter & four 1" h. handleless cups; figure of traditional peasant woman adorns decanter, a bold daisy patt. covers the tray, each cup has flower spray on front, "HenRiot Quimper France 75," mint, the set (ILLUS.) **150**

Match holder, wall-mounted type, pocket features image of peasant woman w/flowers, back panel has lattice & dot geometric design, "HR Quimper," 3 x 2 1/2", mint **175**

Model of swan, figure of seated peasant lad holding pipe is depicted on swan's breast, "HenRiot Quimper France 89," 4" h., 4 3/4" l., mint **120**

Artist-signed Flower Holder

Pique fleurs (flower holder), figural, Modern Movement-style image of a kneeling Bigoudenne lifting a basket of flowers, the basket w/holes for flower stems, "HenRiot Quimper" and signature of artist C.H. Maillard on base, 8" h., 9" l., mint (ILLUS.) **750**

Pitcher, 2 1/2" h., child-size, decorated w/image of Breton man & flowers, "Made in France 12" beneath handle, "HenRiot," mint **65**

Odetta Gresware Pitchers

Pitcher, 3" h., Odetta gresware w/concentric double diamond patt. in white & rich brown on navy blue/cobalt ground, "HB Quimper Odetta 494," mint (ILLUS. top right, w/other Odetta pitchers) **150**

Pitcher, 3 3/4" h., Odetta gresware w/concentric double diamond patt. in white & rich brown on navy blue/cobalt ground, "HB Quimper Odetta 424," mint (ILLUS. bottom right, w/other Odetta pitchers) **150**

Pitcher, 6" h., decorated w/scene of Breton man & flowers, concentric bands of yellow & blue on border, "HenRiot Quimper France 115," mint **35**

Pitcher, 9 1/2" h., Odetta gresware w/a rich deep chocolate brown glaze over a light tan matte glaze "biscuit," bold geometric patt., "HB Quimper Odetta 423-1081+," mint (ILLUS. left, w/other Odetta pitchers) **300**

Plate, 6" d., w/pie crust rim, center shows woman standing in profile w/one hand tucked into apron pocket, flower garland border w/blue sponged edges, "HenRiot Quimper France 72," mint (ILLUS. right, w/inkwell) **100**

"Decor Riche" Pattern Plates

Plate, 8 3/4" d., "decor riche" patt. w/unusual scene of a Breton knight, Bertrand Duguesclin, "HR Quimper," mint (ILLUS. right, w/peasant plate) **525**

Plate, 9" d., yellow glaze w/row of French houses w/a fountain in front & trees on either side of homes & clouds in sky, "HB Quimper France 176," mint **75**

Plate, 9 1/2" d., "decor riche" patt. w/scalloped border & pair of nicely detailed peasant folk, "HR Quimper," mint (ILLUS. left, w/Breton knight plate)............................. **350**

Plate in "Botanique" Pattern

Plate, 9 1/2" d., First Period Porquier Beau, "Botanique" patt., w/display of spray of yellow narcissus & snail, signed w/intersecting "PB" mark in blue, mint (ILLUS.) ... **1,150**

First Period Porquier Beau Plate

Plate, 9 1/2" d., First Period Porquier Beau, entitled "Ramasseur de goemon-Guisseny," scene of fisherman on shoreline holding a pike, w/Crest of Brittany above him in acanthus border, signed w/intersecting "PB" and name of scene, mint (ILLUS.).. **1,250**

Plate, 9 3/4" d., "Broderie Bretonne" geometric patt., ten-pointed star on metallic gold background glaze, intricate raised-to-the-touch heart-shaped patterns in border, "HB Quimper P.F. 163 D 708," mint.. **100**

Pair of Matched Plates

Plates, 7 1/2" d., pale blue sponged ruffled rims, center display shows seated peasant man on one, seated peasant woman on other, "HB" mark only, 19th c., mint, pr. (ILLUS.)... **300**

Set of Five Peasant Plates

Plates, 8 1/2" d., "demi-fantasie" patt., w/different Breton peasant on each, marked w/"HenRiot Quimper France" and various two-digit numbers, mint, set of 5, each (ILLUS.)... **50**

Platter with Courting Scene

Platter, 12" l., 8 1/2" w., oval, "decor riche" patt., center shows courting scene of young Breton couple seated beneath canopy of trees, "HB Quimper," excellent (ILLUS.).. 550

Platter, 13" l., 10" w., rectangular w/cut corners, decorated w/image of open basket w/bouquet of flowers, corners w/black ermine tails, "HenRiot Quimper France," excellent.. 150

"Croisille" Pattern Platter

Platter, 15" l., 10" w., ovoid, in the "croisille" style w/alternating panels of stylized dogwood blossom, finely detailed couple posed in conversation in the center, "HenRiot Quimper France 162," mint (ILLUS.).. 450

Platter, 19" l., 8 1/2" w., oblong shape in Modern Movement Celtic style, center depicts wedding procession walking on path from building in distance, "HenRiot Quimper 72," pierced for hanging, mint (ILLUS. bottom of page)................................ 425

Oval Platter with Peasant Couple

Platter, 14 1/2" l., 11" w., oval, scene of peasant couple & "a la touche" flower garland band, "HB" mark only, 19th c., mint (ILLUS.) 175

Wedding Procession Platter

"Ivoire Corbeille" Fish Platter

Platter, 20 3/4" l., 10" w., oval fish platter, "Ivoire Corbeille" patt. w/portrait busts of young Breton couple framed w/Celtic motifs, "HenRiot Quimper," pierced for hanging, mint (ILLUS.) 275

Porringer, traditional decoration of peasant woman & flowers, blue sponged tab handles, "HenRiot Quimper France," 5 1/2" handle to handle, mint 25

Salt, open oval w/yellow glaze & flower sprig patt. on sides, "HenRiot Quimper," 2" l., mint 25

Salt, pepper & mustard set, "Ivoire Corbeille" patt. "menagere," acorn-shaped mustard pot has figural twig handle & tiny acorn on lid & bust portrait of young peasant girl on the side, salt & pepper are attached open compartments w/twig feet, "HenRiot Quimper," 5 1/2" l., 5" h., mint 125

Tea set: 7" h. cov. teapot, creamer, five cups & six saucers; traditional peasant patt., decorative scalloped borders, "HR Quimper," excellent (ILLUS.) 750

Tobacco jar, cov., figural, Modern Movement style, In the form of a Bretonne woman w/Quimper coif & "embroidery" detailing on blouse & sleeves, the top lifts off at elbow level, by Andre Galland, "HenRiot Quimper A.G. 161," 7" h., mint 300

Tray, pyrographic wooden tray by Paul Fouillen, w/scene depicting interior of cottage where woman serves meal from Quimper cov. tureen, "Fouillen" signature on front & his trademark logo on back, excellent painting w/vibrant colors, 14 3/4 x 7 1/4". 325

Tray with Ropetwist Handles

Tray, yellow glaze w/multi-color ropetwist handles, center features a pitcher-toting woman wearing the headdress of Cherbourg flanked by floral designs (HenRiot made-on-commission example, signed only "Cherbourg"), 12 x 8", mint (ILLUS.) 175

Tumbler/beaker, w/traditional design of Breton woman & flowers, "HenRiot Quimper France 124," 4 1/2" h., mint 65

Scalloped Tea Set

Tureen w/attached underplate, cov., oval shape, the lid decorated w/image of peasant woman w/flower sprays & sea- shell finial, sides adorned w/garlands of flowers, "HenRiot Quimper France 101," 6" l., 4" h., excellent 200

Vase, 3 1/2" h., 5 1/2" w., fan shape, front decorated w/image of peasant man flanked by flower branches, back w/flower sprig & four blue dots, feet are molded butterflies sponged in blue, "HenRiot Quimper," mint 150

Vase, 7 1/2" h., 9" w., Modern Movement style, bust portrait of Breton man is framed in triangular cartouche on front, the reverse displays stone church w/trees & grassy slope, "Quimper" in blue on base, artist "P. Fouillen" signature beside figure of the man, mint............................ 300

"Broderie Bretonne" Vase

Vase, 8 1/2" h., cylindrical form tapering in at top & in to short base, "Broderie Bretonne" patt., w/scene of standing peasants, a woman knitting, a man smoking a pipe, raised-to-the-touch Breton embroidery work on the sides, "HB Quimper," mint (ILLUS.) 450

"Decor Riche" Double Vase

Vase, 9" h., donut shape divided at top center, w/separate openings on each side of division, four short outcurved feet, "decor riche" patt., cartouches featuring woman holding basket & man playing flute flank one w/view of the city of Quimper reflected in the Odet River, reverse side decorated w/multicolor flower garland, dragon-like side handles, mint (ILLUS.).. 2,000

Quimper "Demi-fantasie" Vase

Vase, 15" h., slightly ovoid cylindrical body, flaring to narrow neck w/outcurved rim, side loop handles, "demi-fantasie" patt., portly man smokes pipe on front panel, reverse shows bold double daisy w/wheat flower spray, "HenRiot Quimper France 73," mint (ILLUS.) 350

Vases, 6" h., matched pair, bagpipe shape, "Demi-fantasie" patt. w/man playing horn & woman holding distaff of flax, "HR Quimper," excellent, pr. 375

Wall pocket, bagpipe shape w/double blue bows, decorated w/image of peasant man holding walking stick & posed in an open field, "HB Quimper" beneath figure, 5 1/2" l., mint 100

Redware

Red earthenware pottery was made in the American colonies from the late 1600s. Bowls, crocks and all types of utilitarian wares were turned out in great abundance to supplement the pewter and handmade treenware. The ready availability of the clay, the same used in making bricks and roof tiles, accounted for the vast production. The lead-glazed redware retained its reddish color, although a variety of colors could be obtained by adding various metals to the glaze. Interesting effects occurred accidentally through unsuspected impurities in the clay or uneven temperatures in the firing kiln, which sometimes resulted in streaks or mottled splotches.

Redware pottery was seldom marked by the maker.

Bowl, 10 3/4" d., 4 3/4" h., upright, slightly flared sides w/molded rim, brown sponge decoration around the rim & in lines down the sides, 19th c. (hairlines in base, rim flakes)... $303

Bowl, 7 3/4" d., thin, deep bowl w/brown, green & orange glaze, interior w/orange splotches over green, incised signature "Solomon Miller, 18?5" on bottom, 4" h. (glaze wear, hairlines) 3,300

Bowl, 7" d., 3 1/4" h., flat bottom, flat, flaring, deep sides & molded rim, dark brown sponging on a deep orange ground 440

Canning jar, cylindrical body shape, short shoulder tapers in to outward tapering neck, incised lines on shoulder, glaze w/dark brown splotches on neck & shoulder, 5 3/4" d., 8 3/4" h. (rim chips)................. 330

Chamber pot, footed, deep, rounded form
w/a flat, wide rim & applied strap handle,
incised line decoration, New Hampshire,
19th c., 5 1/2" h. (glaze chips) **690**

Early Redware Coffeepot

Coffeepot, cov., footed baluster-form body
w/a swan's-neck spout, C-form handle &
ribbed domed cover w/fluted acorn finial,
clear lead glaze, England or America,
late 18th c., chips & minor scratches,
11 1/4" h. (ILLUS.) **940**
Cookie mold, Colonial-style man w/decorat-
ed coat mounted on horse & blowing
trumpet, attributed to Ephrata, Pennsyl-
vania, 6 1/8" h. (minor edge wear) **990**
Cookie mold, rectangle divided into six pan-
els w/designs of harp, birds, urn & deer,
5 1/2 x 8 1/4" (minor damage) **440**
Creamer, ovoid body, flared neck, applied
handle, brown shiny glaze w/stylized floral & fern designs on body and band of
design around neck, New Geneva, Penn-
sylvania, 4 3/4" h. (rim flakes) **605**
Creamer, ovoid body w/flared neck, applied
handle, dark brown daubed glaze in zig-
zag design, 4 1/2" h. (rim flakes) **358**
Creamer, paneled, w/high curving handle,
applied rose & two doves under spout, a
rosette on handle, attributed to Anthony
Baecher, Strasburg, Virginia, 4 3/4" h.
(pinpoint glaze flakes) **715**
Crock, tapered ovoid body w/incised lines
around the shoulder, transparent glaze
w/touches of green, New Hampshire,
19th c., 15 1/2" h. (chips, cracks) **920**
Dish, round, shallow form, brown sponging
on an orange ground, 4 3/8" d. (minor
chips) **330**
Dish, shallow, round form, sgraffito decora-
tion of an incised peacock holding a tulip,
yellow & green slip glaze, Pennsylvania,
early 19th c., 9" d. (glaze chips) **1,610**
Flowerpot, slightly tapering cylindrical
shape w/piecrust rim, two incised lines
below, glaze w/brown running splotches,
no saucer, 5 1/4" d., 4 3/4" h. (minor
edge damage) **138**
Food mold, deep, rounded exterior w/cen-
tral shaft on interior surrounded by spiraled flutes below the scalloped rim,
brown sponging on a pinkish amber
ground, 8" d. (wear, slight hairline) **138**

Food mold, Turk's turban form, mottled
brown glaze on the exterior, impressed
"John Bell," Pennsylvania, 6 3/8" d.,
3 3/4" h. (hairlines, small chip on base) **275**
Grease lamp, w/saucer base, ovoid front
w/wick holder & applied strap handle,
brownish red glaze w/some roughness,
5 1/4" h. **303**
Jar, cov., conical form w/sloping shoulder &
tapering base, two handles applied at
shoulder, deep green glaze sprinkled
w/brown, incised decoration on the cover, Massachusetts or Rhode Island, late
18th - early 19th c., 9 1/2" h. (chips to
cover edge, glaze loss at rim) **25,300**
Jar, cov., large, bulbous, ovoid form taper-
ing to a short rolled neck w/an inset flat
cover, overall mottled & spotted green &
tan-spotted slip glaze, a miniature jar
forming the finial on the cover & glazed in
dark brown splashes on tan slip, decorated on the shoulder w/a comical figure
waving a banner w/the initials "S.A.B.,"
the base inscribed "Made in the year
1829 in June the 16th day on Sunday
morning," part of the inscription nearly
obliterated, Massachusetts or Rhode Is-
land, 16" h. (edge chips) **63,000**
Jar, cylindrical body tapering to molded rim,
tooled lines at shoulder rim, glazed base,
green & red mottled glaze w/orange
spots, Galena, Illinois-type, 5" d., 6" h.
(rim flakes) **330**
Jar, ovoid, decorated w/rows of incised lines
at the shoulder & base, a yellow & green
sponged slip decoration, New England,
early 19th c., 6 1/2" h. (edge roughness) .. **1,840**
Jar, ovoid, w/incised lines under raised lip,
two-tone glaze w/wide, brown vertical
bands, 5 1/4"d., 6 1/4" h. (worn glaze on
rim) **275**
Jar, ovoid, w/raised rim, brown daubed
glaze, attributed to Pennsylvania, 4" d.,
4 3/4" h. (small glaze flakes) **193**
Jar, raised bands on the sides w/impressed
geometric & four-pointed star decoration,
running brown glaze w/flakes, Pennsyl-
vania, 8" h. **440**
Jar, slightly concave sides w/reddish glaze
w/yellow splotches, 6" d., 7 1/8" h. (rim
flakes & in-the-making imperfection) **330**
Jar, wide ovoid form w/molded flared rim &
small applied strap handle at rim, mottled
brown glaze, 4 5/8" d., 5 1/8" h. (wear at
rim) **330**
Jar, wide ovoid form w/wide cylindrical neck
& eared shoulder handles, tooled lines,
dark brown glaze w/brown flecks,
12 1/2" h. **176**
Jug, globular, w/strap handle rising from
midsection to rim, dark ivory glaze over
red glaze, sgraffito designs include
chains around shoulder & applied handle, man w/top hat, coat & breeches &
carrying a shovel beside a dog & farm
w/"Samuel Mellvill" above "Always this
full of good Whiskey" & a heart w/banner
reading "SM, JM, 1816," 7 1/8" h. (flaking
glaze & handle crack) **3,850**

Vinegar jar, footed, squatty, bulbous body tapering sharply to a small neck, light green, tan & dark brown mottled glaze, tooled lip & ribbed handle w/thumbprint application, New England, probably Massachusetts, late 18th - early 19th c., 5" h. (minor glaze chips) **9,775**

Whistle, figural bird, a large bird on a perch flanked by two smaller birds & two below on a conical-shaped base, decorated w/a brown drip glaze on a yellow ground, England, late 18th - early 19th c., 9 3/8" h. (chips) **403**

Whistle, figural, model of a bird w/a bulbous, ovoid body w/a flat bottom, a short neck w/head & straight angle cylindrical tail forming whistle opening, mottled black & speckled glaze, 3 1/4" d., 2 1/2" h. **385**

Red Wing

Various potteries operated in Red Wing, Minnesota, from 1868, the most successful being the Red Wing Stoneware Co., organized in 1878. Merged with other local potteries through the years, it became known as Red Wing Union Stoneware Co. in 1894, and was one of the largest producers of utilitarian stoneware items in the United States. After a decline in the popularity of stoneware products, an art pottery line was introduced to compensate for the loss. This was reflected in a new name for the company, Red Wing Potteries, Inc., in 1930. Stoneware production ceased entirely in 1947, but vases, planters, cookie jars and dinnerwares of art pottery quality continued in production until 1967, when the pottery ceased operation altogether.

Red Wing Marks

Art Pottery

Ash receiver, figural, model of a pelican, turquoise, embossed "Red Wing, USA," No. 880 .... **$115**

Basket with 75th Anniversary Seal

Basket, yellow & grey, embossed "Red Wing USA," No. 348, w/75th anniversary seal (ILLUS.) **65**

Cookie jar, cov., Carousel shape, white, blue, red & brown, h.p., very rare, 8 1/2 x 8" **575**

Cookie jar, cov., grape design, royal blue, 10" h. **105**

Cookie Jar with Peasants Design

Cookie jar, cov., Labriego design decorated w/incised dancing peasants, h.p., green, red & yellow, no markings, 9 1/2" h. (ILLUS.) **75**

Figures of cowboy & cowgirl, fully decorated, 11" h., pr. **500**

Planter, hanging-type, No. M-1487 .... **45**

Planter in the Form of a Stove

Planter, in the form of a stove, green & cream, No. 765, 8" h. (ILLUS.) **55**

Planter in the Form of a Log

Planter, in the form of a white birch log, no markings, 11" l. (ILLUS.) **75**

Vase, deer decoration, No. 1120 .... **60**

Vase, figural elephant handle, ivory ground, matte finish, Rum Rill mark **125**

Vase, No. 1079, blue glaze **65**

Vase, No. 839, blue glaze **100**

Vase, 7" h., expanding cylinder w/squared handles rising from narrow shoulder to mouth, No. 163-7, grey & tan glaze **100**

Vase, 7" h., No. 1509-7, black satin matte glaze 35
Vase, 9" h., ribbed, No. 637 145
Vase, 9 1/2" h., No. M1442-9 1/2, Colonial buff & salmon 65
Vase, 10" h., No. 902-10, lustre Dubonnet 100
Vase, 11" h., No. 1377/11, green & yellow glaze 75
Wall pocket, No. M 1630, brown glaze, 10" h................ 80

Brushed & Glazed Wares

Vase, leaf decoration, buff & green, No. 1166................ 35
Vase, 7" h., bulbous body tapering to a short cylindrical neck, angled handles, decorated w/acorn & oak leaf design, dark & light green, No. 149-7 165
Vase, 8" h., flower design decoration, green & mauve, No. 1107 (minor base flake) 75
Vase, 10" h., cemetery vase, green & white, no markings 55
Vase, 15" h., swelling cylindrical body tapering to a flat rim, angled shoulder handles, green & yellow, No. 186-15............. 125

Convention Commemoratives

Bowl, 1980 Red Wing Collectors Society commemorative 925
Cookie jar, 1996 Red Wing Collectors Society commemorative, grey line......... 120
Crock, 1977 Red Wing Collectors Society commemorative, salt glaze 2,250

Commemorative Ball Lock Jar

Jar, cov., ball lock, 2002 Red Wing Collectors Society 25th anniversary commemorative, white glaze (ILLUS.)............. 115
Mug, 1982 Red Wing Collectors Society commemorative, cherry band 750
Planter, 1995 Red Wing Collectors Society commemorative, in the form of a giraffe 105
Poultry waterer, 1993 Red Wing Collectors Society commemorative, bell-shaped w/saucer................ 110

Dinnerwares & Novelties

Ash receiver, figural, model of a seated donkey w/mouth wide open, green glaze............ 55
Beverage server w/stopper, Bob White patt. 75
Beverage server w/stopper, Smart Set patt. 180
Bowl, berry, Bob White patt. 8
Bowl, berry, Capistrano patt................. 9
Bowl, berry, Tampico patt.................. 10
Bowl, cereal, Bob White patt................ 25

Bowl, cereal, Tampico patt. 15
Bowl, salad, Random Harvest patt., large.......... 40
Bowl, soup, Bob White patt................ 20
Bowl, salad, 12" d., Capistrano patt. 45
Bowl, salad, 12" d., Tampico patt. 85
Bread tray, Round Up patt. 150
Bread tray, rectangular, Bob White patt., 24" l................ 100
Butter dish, cov., Bob White patt., 1/4 lb. 75
Butter warmer, Bob White patt................ 95
Candlesticks, Magnolia patt., pr............. 50
Carafe, cov., Bob White patt................ 185
Casserole, Bob White patt., 2 qt................ 40
Casserole, cov., French-style w/stick handle, Town & Country patt., peach glaze.......... 95
Casserole, cov., Smart Set patt., 2 qt. 68

Red Wing Bob White Casserole

Casserole, cov., Bob White patt., 4 qt. (ILLUS.)................ 50
Celery dish, Flight patt................ 175
Cocktail tray, Bob White patt. 40
Coffeepot, cov., Village Green line 35
Cookie jar, cov., Bob White patt............ 60
Cookie jar, cov., figural Katrina (Dutch girl), yellow glaze................ 100
Cookie jar, cov., figural monk, blue glaze.......... 75
Cookie jar, cov., side handle & side top, red glaze................ 225
Creamer, Bob White patt................ 25
Cruets w/stoppers, Bob White patt., pr............. 175
Cruets w/stoppers in metal rack, Bob White patt., the set................ 325
Cup & saucer, Bob White patt. 9
Cup & saucer, Capistrano patt............. 13
French bread tray, Bob White patt., 24" l. 90
Gravy boat, cov., Bob White patt. 55
Gravy boat w/stand, Tampico patt., 2 pcs. 60
Hor d'oeuvres holder, Bob White patt., model of a bird pierced for picks............. 50
Mug, Bob White patt. 80
Pitcher, jug-type, Tampico patt., 2 qt. 65
Pitcher, 12" h., Round Up patt................ 185
Pitcher, water, Bob White patt., 60 oz................ 50
Plate, salad, Flight patt. 60
Plate, 6 1/2" d., Capistrano patt. 5
Plate, 6 1/2" d., Tampico patt. 7
Plate, bread & butter, 6 1/2" d., Bob White patt................ 6
Plate, 8" d., Bob White patt................ 8
Plate, 8 1/2" d., Tampico patt. 12
Plate, 10 1/2" d., Capistrano patt. 10
Plate, 10 1/2" d., Tampico patt. 14
Plate, dinner, 10 1/2" d., Bob White patt. 13
Platter, 13" oval, Bob White patt. 85
Platter, 20" l., Bob White patt. 100
Platter w/metal rack, Bob White patt., large, 2 pcs. 160
Relish, Bob White patt., three-part 70
Relish, Bob White patt., two-part 45
Relish, Tampico patt., 13" l................ 35

Salt & pepper shakers, figural bird, Bob White patt., pr. 35

Salt & pepper shakers, figural pitcher, jug-type w/ice lip, red, Rum Rill mark, pr. 20

Salt & pepper shakers, figural Schmoo, bronze glaze, pr. 95

Salt & pepper shakers, figural Schmoo, cin-namon glaze, Rum Rill mark, pr. 65

Syrup pitcher, Town & Country patt., blue glaze 75

Teapot, cov., Village Green line 22

Teapot & stand, cov., Bob White patt., the set. 140

Tidbit tray, Random Harvest patt., original paper label 27

Tray on warmer, Smart Set patt., large, 2 pcs. 145

Vegetable dish, open, divided, Capistrano patt. 24

Vegetable dish, open, divided, Smart Set patt. 65

Vegetable dish, open, divided, Tampico patt. 45

Specialty Items

Book, "The Clay Giants," 1st edition, history, stoneware of Red Wing, rare, mint, 1977 175

Book, "The Clay Giants," 3rd edition, history w/price guide, stoneware of Red Wing, mint, 1987 160

Bottle, w/iron bailed stopper, amber, em-bossed "Red Wing Brewing Co., Red Wing, Minn.," rare, 14" h. 105

Gunny sack, 100 pounds flour, "Red Wing, Minn." 85

Yard stick, advertising Hi-Park Guernsey Milk, Red Wing, Minn. 45

Stoneware & Utility Wares

Advertising Bean Pot

Bean pot, cov., white & brown glaze, adver-tising, "Christmas Greetings from Chris-tle's Cash Store, Brillion, Wis.," rare (ILLUS.) 125

Bean pot, cov., white & brown glaze, adver-tising "Geo. C. Radloff, Farmersburg, Io-wa" 115

Bean pot, cov., white & brown glaze, adver-tising "Peter Bootzin, Medford, Wis." 105

Bean pot, cov., white & brown glazes, wire handles, marked "Red Wing Union Stoneware" 115

Beater jar, cylindrical, Sponge Band line 280

Beater jar, cylindrical w/a molded rim, white glaze w/blue bands & advertising in a rectangle on front 160

Beater jar, white glaze w/blue band, adver-tising "Klatt & Stueber, Clyman, Wis." 150

Beater jar, white glaze w/blue band, adver-tising "Schulenburg & Thom, Wells, Minn." 140

Bowl, 8" d., spongeware paneled, advertis-ing "Swanson & Nelson, Chisago City" [sic], very rare 275

Bowl, Sponge Band line, South Dakota ad-vertising in bottom, No. 7 285

Bowl, 4" d., spongeware paneled, deep, rounded form 375

Bowl, 6" d., spongeware paneled, advertis-ing "Muscodo Spring Green, Boscobel, Wis.," rare 160

Bowl, 7" d., Dunlap, brown & white glaze, advertising "Columbia Metal Products Co., Chicago, Ill." 75

Bowl, 7" d., "Milk Pan Bowl," white glaze, embossed "RWS Co." on bottom 95

Butter crock, blue sponge glaze, no mark-ings 325

Butter crock, cylindrical, large wing mark, 20 lbs. 800

Butter crock, white glaze, 4" wing mark, "20 lbs" stamped above wing, very rare 925

Churn, white glaze, 4" wing mark, blue oval pottery stamp below wing, 2 gal. 350

Churn, white glaze, 4" wing mark, blue oval pottery stamp below wing, 4 gal. 325

Churn, white glaze, 4" wing mark, blue oval pottery stamp below wing, 5 gal. 375

Churn, white glaze, 4" wing mark, blue oval pottery stamp above wing, 6 gal. 425

Churn w/wooden lid & dasher, swelled cylin-drical body, Union Stoneware Co., large wing mark, 3 gal. 250

Churn w/wooden lid & dasher, swelled cylin-drical body w/eared handles & a molded rim, white-glazed, large wing mark w/oval wing stamp below, 2 gal. 320

Churn w/wooden lid & dasher, swelled cylin-drical body w/eared handles & a molded rim, white-glazed, blue birch leaves over oval & slip-quilled "4," Union Stoneware Co., Red Wing, Minnesota, 4 gal., 20" h. 325

Iced Tea Cooler

Cooler, cov., iced tea, white glaze, wire han-dles, no wing, 5 gal. (ILLUS.) 425

Cooler, iced tea, white-glazed, bail handles, no wing mark, 5 gal., 11 3/4" d. 415

Crock, cylindrical, white-glazed, big wing mark, 1 gal. 435

Crock, white glaze, embossed on base "Minnesota Stoneware, Red Wing, Minn.," no wing, 1 gal. 65

Red Wing Union Stoneware Crock

Crock, cylindrical, w/molded rim, white-glazed, large "2" over double bird leaves & oval marks, Red Wing Union Stoneware, 2 gal., 9 3/4" d. (ILLUS.) 85

"Elephant Ear" Crock

Crock, white glaze, two "elephant ears," oval Union Stoneware Co. stamp in blue, 2 gal. (ILLUS.) 125

Crock, cylindrical, w/eared handles & molded rim, cobalt blue hand-decorated leaf below a "5," grey salt glaze, sidewall stamp, 5 gal. 395

Crock, cylindrical, w/eared handles, white glaze, stamped 4" wing mark, Red Wing oval stamp, 13" d., 6 gal. 85

Crock, salt glaze, cobalt blue design, rare, 8 gal. 1,450

Crock, cov., white glaze, small wing, blue oval stamp below wing, bailed handles, 15 gal. 185

Crock, cov., white glaze, bail handles, 4" wing mark, blue oval stamp below wing, 25 gal. 225

Crock, cov., white glaze, bail handles, 4" wing mark, blue oval stamp below wing, 30 gal. 325

Crock, cylindrical, white-glazed, 6" l. wing mark, 40 gal. 800

Crock, cov., white glaze, bail handles, 4" wing mark, blue oval stamp below wing, rare, 50 gal. 2,400

Crock, cylindrical, white-glazed, large wing mark, 50 gal. 2,300

Crock, white glaze, advertising "Ev-Re-Day Oleomargarine, Wisconsin Butterine Co.," no wing, 2 qt. 60

Fruit jar, cov., white glaze, blue or black stamp, "Stone - Mason Fruit Jar - Union Stoneware Co. - Red Wing, Minn.," very rare, 1 gal. 900

Fruit Jar with Screw-on Lid

Fruit jar, screw-on metal lid, cylindrical w/tapering shoulder, white-glazed, black stamp reads "Stone - Mason Fruit Jar - Union Stoneware Co. - Red Wing, Minn.," 2 qt. (ILLUS.) 255

Jar, cov., applesauce, white glaze, bail handles, ball lock, oval Union Stoneware stamp 185

Jar, refrigerator, white glaze, bail handle, no wing, stamped "5 lbs." 325

Jar, steam table jar, white glaze, cobalt blue #5 stamp, no wing 35

Jar, cov., white-glazed, ball lock, 4" wing over Red Wing oval stamp mark, 5 gal. 195

Jug, brown glaze, embossed "Minnesota Stoneware, Red Wing" on base, 1 gal. 75

Jug, syrup, white glaze, cone-shaped top, embossed "Minnesota Stoneware Co." on base, 1 gal. 90

Advertising Jug

Jug, white glaze, advertising "Creamery Package Mfg. Co. - Manufacturers - Creamery & Dairy Supplies - Minneapolis, Minn. - Poison - Acid," 1 gal. (ILLUS.) 125

Jug, beehive shape, white glaze, two birch leaves, Union Stoneware Co. oval stamp, 3 gal. 395

Jug, brown- & white-glazed shoulder, 4" wing mark, blue oval stamp, 3 gal. 95

Rare Red Wing Jug

Jug, beehive-shaped, small cylindrical neck, dark blue printed diamond w/Iowa advertising above the blue double birch leaf mark, 5 gal. (ILLUS.) **2,785**

Jug, beehive-shaped, white-glazed, w/Portland, Oregon advertising, 5 gal. **950**

Jug, brown- & white-glazed shoulder, 4" wing mark, blue oval stamp, 5 gal. **115**

Jug, cylindrical, w/white-glazed shoulder, 4" wing above Red Wing oval mark, 5 gal. **105**

Jug, beehive shape, Albany slip, North Star Stoneware, large embossed star on base, very rare, 1 qt. **275**

Jug, cylindrical, w/a salt-glazed body & tapering rounded brown-glazed shoulder & neck, oval printed panel w/liquor advertising, 2 qt. **300**

Jug, white glaze, advertising "Ladner Brothers Wines & Liquors, Red Wing, Minn.," 2 qt. **75**

Stoneware "Koverwate"

"Koverwate" (crock cover-weight designed to keep the contents submerged under preserving liquid; bottom & side holes allowed brine to come to the top), white glaze, stamped "Koverwate - Red Wing, Minn.," 15 gal., 13 3/4" d. (ILLUS.) **245**

Poultry feeder, KoRec chicken feeder, white glaze, w/dome top, 1 gal., 2 pcs. **105**

Poultry waterer, cylindrical, w/end opening, "Eureka"-style, marked around opening "Patd. April 7, 1885," Red Wing marking on bottom **245**

Refrigerator jar, stacking-type, short cylindrical form w/a molded rim, white-glazed w/narrow blue bands & "Red Wing Refrigerator Jar" on the side, 5 1/2" d. **165**

Salt box, cov., hanging-type, grey line **1,800**

Trivet, advertising Minnesota Centennial 1858-1958 .... **95**

Water cooler, cov., w/spigot, bail handles, white glaze, 4" wing mark, blue oval Red Wing stamp below wing, 3 gal. **675**

Water cooler, cov., w/spigot, bail handles, white glaze, two birch leaves, no oval stamp, 4 gal. **650**

Water cooler, cov., cylindrical, white-glazed, side handles, large wing mark, 5 gal. **350**

Water cooler, cov., w/spigot, bail handles, white glaze, 4" wing mark, blue oval Red Wing stamp below wing, 6 gal. **625**

Water cooler, cov., w/spigot, bail handles, white glaze, 4" wing mark, blue oval Red Wing stamp below wing, 10 gal. **1,165**

Ridgways

There were numerous Ridgways among English potters. The firm J. & W. Ridgway operated in Shelton from 1814 to 1930 and produced many pieces with scenes of historical interest. William Ridgway operated in Shelton from 1830 to 1865. Most wares marked Ridgway that have been offered in this country were made by one of these two firms or by Ridgway Potteries, Ltd., still in operation.

Also see HISTORICAL & COMMEMORATIVE WARES.

Ridgways Mark

Dinner set: eight 10" d. dinner plates, rectangular cov. vegetable bowl, 19" l. platter, sauceboat w/underplate; Corinthian Flute patt., blue decorated ironstone, 12 pcs. (small unfinished repairs) **$495**

Pitcher, cov.,10 1/2" h., blue-glazed earthenware w/molded & enameled foliate designs, hinged pewter cover, marked by William Ridgway & Co., Hanley & dated "October 1,1835" (minor chip on handle, minor enamel wear) **115**

Pitcher, 12" h., tankard-type, Coaching Days line, "In a Snowdrift" scene **295**

Platter, 15" l., oval, Oriental patt., center landscape scene w/castle & figures, floral border w/temple cartouche, blue **220**

Platter, 15" l., oval, Oriental patt., central landscape scene w/castle & figures, border w/alternating cartouches of flowers & temples, blue **440**

Tea set, child's: cov. teapot & creamer; "Dickensware," scene of Humphrey's Clock, black & white, ca. 1900, 2 pcs. **165**

Vegetable dish, cov., oblong, Oriental patt., decorated w/scenes of temples, trees & flowers, blue, 10 1/2" l. (minor hairline) **825**

Robineau (Adelaide)

Adelaide Alsop Robineau began her career as a china painter and teacher. After her marriage to Samuel Robineau in 1899 they founded the magazine Keramic Studio, which was a practical guide to china painting.

After a few years, frustrated with just decorating wares produced by others, she and her husband began production of earthenware and, later, porcelain.

Between 1904 and 1916 Adelaide Robineau produced a limited number of exquisite, detailed works that garnered her several awards at major international expositions.

After World War I their pottery ceased to operate independently, and Mrs. Robineau joined the staff of Syracuse University in 1920, where she worked until her retirement in 1928. She died in 1929.

The Robineau Pottery was never a major commercial operation and reportedly sold only about 600 pieces over a 25-year period. Many examples were eventually purchased by museums, so few examples of her work are offered for sale today.

Robineau Pottery Marks

Jar, cov., footed spherical form covered in mossy green flambé, the cover completely excised w/a geometric floral design under a bronze glaze, carved "AR - 44 - 1920," 4 1/2 x 4 1/2" (underglaze lines around rim from firing, grinding bruise to edge of base, also in manufacture)....................................... **$14,625**

Robineau Rabbit Tile

Tile, square, deeply carved w/the figure of a stylized crouching rabbit w/a matte celadon glaze, carved "AR" mark, several minute edge nicks, very slight surface abrasion, 4 3/4" w. (ILLUS.)........................ **1,238**

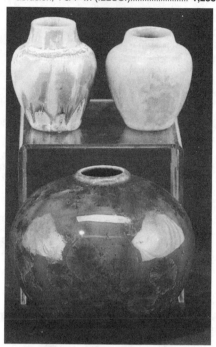

Three Robineau Vases

Vase, miniature, 2 x 2 1/2", ovoid body w/shoulder tapering to wide cylindrical neck w/closed rim, butterscotch flambé glaze, marked "AR - C - 4 - 11-111.," 1904, minor bruise to rim (ILLUS. left w/other vases) **2,363**

Vase, miniature, 2 x 2 1/4", ovoid body tapering to short cylindrical neck w/flat rim, green & blue matte crystalline glaze, marked "AR - C - '04 - 11-111.," 1904 (ILLUS. right w/other vases) **1,913**

Vase, 3 3/4" h., 4 1/4" d., spherical form w/molded rim, cobalt blue crystalline glaze, incised "AR" (ILLUS. bottom w/other vases).. **6,750**

Rockingham Wares

The Marquis of Rockingham first established an earthenware pottery in the Yorkshire district of England around 1745, and it was occupied afterwards by various potters. The well-known mottled brown Rockingham glaze was introduced about 1788 by the Brameld Brothers and became immediately popular. It was during the 1820s that the production of true porcelain began at the factory, and it continued to be made until the firm closed in 1842. Since that time the so-called Rockingham glaze has been used by various potters in England and the United States, including some famous wares produced in Bennington, Vermont. Very similar glazes were also used by potteries in other areas of the United States including Ohio and Indiana, but only wares specifically attributed to Bennington should use that name. The following listings will include mainly wares featuring the dark brown mottled glaze produced at various sites here and abroad.

Cuspidor, footed, round, squatty, bulbous, paneled shape w/rolled & scalloped rim, dark brown running glaze w/bluish green spots on top, 9" d. $110

Flask, model of potato w/small molded mouth, mottled dark brown glaze, 5 1/4" h. 275

Food mold, Turk's turban form, interior w/molded swirled ribs & scalloped rim, mottled brown glaze, 9 5/8" d., 3 1/2" h. (minor roughness) 72

Harvest flask, donut shape decorated w/molded fruit vines on either side w/a man holding a tankard on the neck, dark brown glaze, 8 1/2" d. (minor roughness on lip) 506

Hot plate, round w/ridged edge, three small feet, center w/molded eagle surrounded by four urns, mottled dark brown glaze, 7 3/8" d. 550

Inkwell, figure of girl w/hat reclining on tree stump, 5" l. 193

Loving cup, two-handled, cylindrical, w/applied scenes of men w/a lantern, dogs & a man seated at a table holding a pitcher, raised leaves around the rim, mottled dark brown glaze, 12" d. at handles, 7" h. (glaze bubbles burst on interior & table ring) 358

Model of a dog, in sitting position, w/head turned to side, on scalloped base, 11" h. (repaired edge chips on base & nose) 358

Model of a dog, in sitting position w/head turned to side, open front legs, molded detail, on oblong base, running brown glaze over yellow, 11 1/2" h. (edge chips on bottom of base) 495

Rockingham Cocker Spaniel Puppy

Model of a dog, seated Cocker Spaniel puppy w/long curly hair, attached to an oval base, nicely detailed, England, late 19th c., crack, 13" l., 8 3/4" h. (ILLUS.) 235

Model of a dog, seated Spaniel on a thick rectangular base, freestanding front legs, mottled dark brown glaze, 10 3/4" h. (chips on base) 330

Model of a lion, reclining, amber-colored running glaze, 4 x 9 1/2", 5 3/4" h. 440

Mug, cylinder form w/a relief-molded Toby figure on the front, angled loop handle, mottled dark brown glaze, impressed label of E. & W. Bennett, Baltimore, Maryland, mid-19th c., 4 1/4" h. (chips, slight hairline) 358

Pitcher, 9 1/2" h., footed squatty bulbous base below waisted sides & a wide arched spout, C-scroll handle, molded relief design of soldiers fighting w/stacked rifles, an eagle & snake on the reverse, mottled dark brown glaze, mid-19th c. (chips, hairline) 330

Pitcher, 8 5/8" h., footed, squatty bulbous base tapering slightly to wide cylindrical neck w/slightly flared rim, pinched spout & C-form applied strap handle, mottled brown glaze (flake on end of handle) 303

Platter, octagonal, 9 3/8 x 12 1/2", large splotched glaze design, impressed mark on back (minor firing flaw) 715

Storage jar, cov., cylindrical w/stepped base, relief-molded Gothic arched panels & domed lid, 8" d., 9" h. (minor repair to finial) 660

Toby jug, man in tricorner hat, high, concave base, 5 3/4" h. (glazed-over rim flake) 83

Toby jug, tall bust portrait of a military man w/a tricorner hat & wearing a uniform, wide band around the base embossed "Duke of Wellington - born 1st May 1769 - Died 14th Sept. 1859," base impressed "Thompson," 8" h. (glaze chip on hat rim partially ground) 193

Rookwood

Rookwood Mark

Considered America's foremost art pottery, the Rookwood Pottery Company was established in Cincinnati, Ohio, in 1880 by Mrs. Maria Nichols Longworth Storer. To accurately record its development, each piece carried the Rookwood insignia or mark, was dated, and, if individually decorated, was usually signed by the artist. The pottery remained in Cincinnati until 1959, when it was sold to Herschede Hall Clock Company and moved to Starkville, Mississippi, where it continued in operation until 1967.

A private company is now producing a limited variety of pieces using original Rookwood molds.

Bowl, 4" d., slightly tapering upright flattened sides molded w/an Arts & Crafts design, brown & maroon Matte glaze, No. 1674, 1912 .... $275

Bowl, 5" d., 4 1/2" h., "50th Anniversary" type, deep flaring rounded sides, the interior decorated w/a wide border band of polychrome blossoms & leaves on a mottled ivory ground, Wax Matte glaze, No. 2253D, 1930, Elizabeth N. Lincoln **422**

Bowl, 6 1/2" d., wide low form w/incurved sides molded w/stylized florals below the closed wide rim, dark blue Matte glaze, No. 1709, 1912.. **209**

Bowl-vase, wide spherical body w/a wide flat rim, decorated around the rim w/a narrow band of red cherry blossoms on black branches on an ivory ground, the lower body in bluish grey shaded to rose, Vellum glaze, No. 1375, 1920, E.T. Hurley, 9" d., 6 1/4" h. **1,913**

Bowl-vase, molded production piece in a wide, low, squatty rounded form, the wide top reticulated & molded w/a design of pine cones & needles in light green & pink, No. 1214, Matte glaze, 1909, 7" d., 3" h. **900**

Standard Glaze Cup & Saucer

Cup & saucer, demitasse, the gold ground round saucer w/flared rim, the dark brown cylindrical cup w/D-form handle & gold interior, etched cherry blossom motif w/two blossoms in lighter glaze, the others in silhouette, Standard glaze, No. 208, 1886, Anna Bookprinter, remnants of salesroom label, 3" h., pr. (ILLUS.) **476**

Standard Glaze Dresser Tray

Dresser tray, rectangular, w/ruffled rim, decorated w/h.p. coral carnations on a shaded dark brown ground, Standard glaze, No. 591, 1894, Elizabeth Lincoln, few nicks & rough areas to edge, 7 x 10 3/4" (ILLUS.)... **392**

Ewer, squatty, round, ribbed melon-form base on small tab feet, the top centered

by a tall slender neck w/a wide curled tricorner rim, a slender S-scroll handle from the rim to the shoulder, decorated around the neck w/black-eyed Susans against a dark brown shaded to pale yellow ground, Standard glaze, No. 571C, 1894, H. Wilcox, 5 1/2" d., 8" h. **731**

Ewer, tall slender ovoid body tapering to a rolled rim w/pinched spout, applied shoulder strap handle, decorated w/pale orange chrysanthemum blossoms & green leaves on a warm brown ground, Standard glaze, No. 433, 1888, Harriet Elizabeth Wilcox, 7" h. **748**

Rare Rookwood Jar

Jar, cov., bulbous ovoid body w/reticulated neck & domed cover, white ground decorated around the center w/brightly colored continuous scene depicting seven Chinese figures on horseback riding through rocky terrain w/one rider falling to the ground, by William Hentschel, interior of jar & lid in rich medium blue, artist-initialed, No. 2541, ca. 1921, 9 3/4" h. (ILLUS.)... **4,032**

Jug, floor-type, tall ovoid form w/the rounded shoulder centered by a flared molded neck, applied shoulder strap handle, small molded spout at the bottom front, overall glossy brown glaze, stamped "Rookwood - 1884," 16" d., 28" h. **1,069**

Silver-overlaid Rookwood Jug

Jug w/stopper, double-gourd bulbous form w/a short neck & shoulder handle, the handle, neck & round stopper w/silver overlay, the lower body lobe w/a silver overlay grapevine decoration, the upper lobe decorated w/a large ear of corn in yellow & green on a shaded brown ground, Standard glaze, No. S976, ca. 1890, illegible artist, 4 3/4" d., 8 1/2" h. (ILLUS., previous page).............................. **2,300**

Unusual Rookwood Loving Cup

Loving cup, gently flaring cylindrical sides w/a wide flat rim flanked by two D-form angled handles, decorated w/a color bust portrait of a ragged African-American boy against a shaded light green & tan to brown ground, Standard glaze, No. 259, 1895, Bruce Horsfall, 9 1/2" w., 7" h. (ILLUS.).. **4,600**

Rookwood Mug with Indian Portrait

Mug, swelled bottom & tapering cylindrical sides w/a molded rim band, D-form handle, color bust portrait of Native American chief against a shaded deep gold & brown ground, Standard glaze, No. 656, 1896, Matt Daly, 5" w., 5" h. (ILLUS.)......... **1,380**

Mug, tall tapering cylindrical form w/a large D-form handle, Carved Matt design of stylized oak leaves & acorns in brown & butterfat green, No. 1014D, 1905, 4 1/4" d., 7" h.. **478**

Pitcher, 12" h., 5 3/4" d., tall slender ovoid form tapering to a gently flared rim w/pinched spout, applied C-form strap

handle on the neck, decorated w/large cluster of gooseberry leaves in yellow, green & brown on a shaded light amber to green ground, Standard glaze, No. 567W, 1891, A.R. Valentien **1,800**

Plaque, rectangular, decorated w/an unusual pastoral landscape w/a path & large trees in the foreground & a misty valley in the distance, in soft tones of blue, green, mauve & pink, Vellum glaze, in original wide molded giltwood frame, date obscured, Frederick Rothenbusch, tile 8 1/2 x 11"... **6,600**

Plaque, rectangular, wooded riverside scene w/tall trees on the left river bank, shades of blue, green & peach, Vellum glaze, 1917, Elizabeth McDermott, in original wide flat wood frame w/scroll-molded border band, 6 1/4 x 8 1/4" **3,680**

Rare Sea Green Glazed Plaque

Plaque, unusual design of a songbird in flight near leafy stems on a shaded blue ground, unusual Sea Green glaze, A.R. Valentien, framed, 8 x 10" (ILLUS.).. **19,550**

Rookwood Plaque with Ocean View

Plaque, rectangular, a landscape vista w/a tall lone pine tree in the foreground w/hills & the ocean in the distance, in shades of blue, green, tan & brown, titled "On the Bluffs," mounted in original gilt shadowbox frame, Vellum glaze, 1916, Sara Sax, 8 1/2 x 10 3/4" (ILLUS.).. **8,050**

Rookwood Plaque and Vases

Plaque, rectangular, landscape scene of birch trees on river bank, blue, green & white, Vellum glaze, 1912, E.T. Hurley, wooden frame, plaque 9 x 11" (ILLUS. right, center) 7,088

Plaque with Lake, Trees & Hills

Plaque, a landscape of a meadow leading down to tall slender leafy trees flanking a lake w/mountains in the distance below a pale blue cloudy sky, in shades of purple, blue, dark & light green, tan & brown, Vellum glaze, 1920, Lenore Asbury, framed, 10 x 11 3/4" (ILLUS.) 4,313

Plaque, foreign landscape w/two distant pointed mountains w/a stream & scrubland in the foreground & tall trees in the front left, titled "Mt. Ararat in Armenia," Vellum glaze, 1914, Sara Sax, framed, framed, 9 x 14 1/4" (ILLUS., below) 5,750

Plaque, rectangular, a landscape of trees by a path at dusk, Vellum glaze, 1927, Fred Rothenbusch, framed, 14 x 16"................. 19,550

Plaque, rectangular, a tall unusual mountain & lake vista in shades of blue, green & mauve, mounted in original wide dark coved frame, Vellum glaze, 1912, Ed Diers, 11 1/4 x 16 1/2" (ILLUS., next page) 6,900

Mt. Ararat Vellum Plaque

Large Rookwood Vellum Plaque

Scarce Rookwood Tankard with Imp

Tankard, cov., baluster form w/low domed hinged cover & D-form handle, decorated w/a smiling imp-like character in shaded bright yellow swinging on bare brown branches against a shaded dark to light brown ground, copper overlay on cover, Standard glaze, 1899, Harriet Wilcox, 9" h. (ILLUS.)... **9,200**

Vase, 4" h., 4" d., Jewel Porcelain, bulbous ovoid body tapering to a wide, short, flat mouth, a pale blue band of stylized cherry blossoms around the shoulder against an oxblood glazed ground, dark blue glazed interior, No. 8903, 1920, Sara Sax... **1,800**

Vase, 4 1/2" h., simple ovoid form w/slightly flared wide mouth, a border of raised berry decoration, blue Matte drip glaze w/a slight crystalline effect, No. 212, 1928 .... **288**

Blossoms on Yellow Vellum Vase

Vase, 5" h., 3" h., gently tapering ovoid body w/a flat rim, a pale yellow ground decorated around the bottom w/a band of large & small pink blossoms & green leafy branches, Vellum glaze, 1924, Lenore Asbury (ILLUS.)...................................... **977**

Vase, 5" h., 3 3/4" d., wide simple ovoid form tapering slightly to a wide, flat mouth, decorated w/a continuous landscape scene w/groups of tall trees in a meadow w/hills in the distance, in shades of dark blue, light blue & cream, Vellum glaze, No. 942E, 1919, Ed Diers **1,463**

Vase, 5" h., 7" d., low, wide, squatty, round form w/the wide top tapering up to a short trumpet neck, decorated w/a large cluster of orange & yellow poppies on a dark brown ground, Standard glaze, No. 671B, 1899, E. Lincoln **450**

Vase, 5 1/2" h., 4" d., wide baluster-form body tapering to a flaring trumpet neck, decorated w/stylized apple blossoms on a pink & ivory butterfat ground, Wax Matte glaze, No. 6148, 1937, Kataro Shirayamadani... **1,125**

Rookwood Cherry Blossom Vase

Vase, 5 1/2" h., 5 1/2" d., bulbous footed ovoid body w/a wide, short rolled neck, light pink ground decorated around the shoulder w/a dark grey branch w/pink cherry blossoms, Vellum glaze, 1925, E.T. Hurley (ILLUS.).. **862**

Vase, 5 1/2" h., 6" d., widely flaring trumpet-form body, decorated w/white dogwood blossoms & dark blue leaves against a sheer olive ground, purple interior, Black Opal glaze, No. 2264E, 1925, Kataro Shirayamadani **2,925**

Vase, 5 3/4" h., 4 1/2" d., bulbous ovoid body tapering to a short wide neck, decorated around the shoulder w/a wide band of large yellow roses & green leaves on a pale butter yellow ground, Vellum glaze, No. 1914, 1927, Lenore Asbury **880**

Vase, 5 7/8" h., simple ovoid form w/the flat mouth flanked by small angled shoulder handles, decorated w/honeysuckle blossoms on a shaded gold & brown ground, Standard glaze, 1900, Adeliza Drake Sehon (crazing, minor scratches)...................... **489**

Vase, 6" h., a gently tapering cylindrical form topped by a short cylindrical neck, the sides lightly molded w/tapering pointed panels resembling overlapping tall leaves, good green & rose Matte glaze, No. 1824, 1912... **495**

Rookwood Iris Glaze Vases

Vase, 6" h., 3" d., slightly swelled cylindrical body tapering slightly to a flat mouth, decorated w/large pink & white clover blossoms on green arched leafy stems on a shaded creamy yellow to greyish green ground, Iris glaze, No. 951, 1905, Fred Rothenbusch (ILLUS. right) **1,380**

Vase, 6 1/2" h., footed squatty bulbous base w/the rounded shoulder tapering to a wide cylindrical neck w/flared rim, decorated w/a large yellow iris blossom & green leaves on a golden, green & brown ground, Standard glaze, 1889, Amelia Browne Sprague **575**

Pretty Rookwood Vase with Bayberries

Vase, 6 1/2" h., gently tapering cylindrical form w/a flat rim, decorated w/an elaborate overall design of pink bayberries w/green leaves & brown stems on a pale tan ground, Vellum glaze, No. 2102, 1923, Lorinda Epply (ILLUS.)...................... **4,313**

Vase, 6 1/2" h., tapering cylindrical form w/a flattened closed rim, molded around the shoulder w/repeating design of dragonflies, Matte turquoise glaze, 1927.................. **403**

Vase, 6 1/2" h., 4 1/2" d., tapering bulbous lower body w/a rounded wide shoulder centered by a tall trumpet neck, decorated w/a cluster of white clover blossoms & green leaves on a shaded dark blue to dark grey ground, Iris glaze, No. 754, 1901, Fred Rothenbusch.............................. **1,350**

Vase, 6 1/2" h., 5 1/2" d., bulbous ovoid form tapering to a low rolled mouth, decorated in squeezebag w/an abstract triangle & bar geometric design in dark brown on a coffee-colored ground, No. 6201d, 1931, Jens Jensen.......................... **1,069**

Vase, 6 3/4" h., swelled cylindrical form, decorated w/a waterside landscape in greens, blues & browns against a summer sky of peach, pale green & lavender, Vellum glaze, No. 551, 1921, Fred Rothenbush **1,495**

Vase, 6 3/4" h., 5 1/2" d., Jewel Porcelain, swelled & flaring cylindrical form w/a wide, flat mouth, decorated w/large stylized ivory magnolia blossoms w/ochre trim on a teal blue ground, No. 2189, 1944, Jens Jensen....................................... **1,463**

Rookwood Scenic Vellum Vase

Vase, 7" h., wide cylindrical body w/rounded shoulder & short cylindrical neck, landscape scene of tall leafy trees by a lake w/forest in the background, in shades of light & dark green, blue & cream, Vellum glaze, No. 1873, 1922, Fred Rothenbusch (ILLUS.)... **1,610**

Vase, 7 1/4" h., 3" d., swelled cylindrical body w/a narrow shoulder tapering to a short rolled neck, decorated w/a continuous marsh landscape in umber & brown surrounded by cobalt blue water, Green Vellum glaze, No. 904E, 1911, Sara Sax.. **5,063**

Vase, 7 1/4" h., 3 1/2" d., gently waisted cylindrical form w/a flat rim, decorated in the Japanese style w/a band of swimming fish around the lower third, shaded from creamy white to medium blue w/dark blue, green & cream fish, Vellum glaze, No. 1358, 1908, E.T. Hurley **2,363**

Vase, 7 1/2" h., urn form, swelled cylindrical lower body below the wide flattened shoulder centered by a wide cylindrical neck w/a wide, flattened rim, molded around the lower body w/a band of large pointed leaves alternating w/stylized blossoms on stems, light brown Matte glaze, No. 2413, 1928.................................... **468**

Vase, 7 1/2" h., 3 1/2" d., gently flaring trumpet-form body on a cushion base, continuous landscape of birch trees & hills in pale blues, green, violet & cream, Vellum glaze, No. 1357E, 1920, Fred Rothenbusch **1,913**

Vase, 7 3/4" h., 4 1/2" d., ovoid body tapering to rolled rim, decorated w/purple columbine on shaded blue to pink ground, No. 913D, 1931, Ed Diers (ILLUS. right w/plaque).. **2,025**

Standard Glaze Vase with Blossoms

Vase, 8" h., footed ovoid body tapering to a short neck w/a widely flaring flattened rim, decorated w/large poppy-like blossoms on slender stems against a dark brown ground, Standard glaze, 1899, light crazing, signed (ILLUS.) **805**

Orchids on Matte Rookwood Vase

Vase, 8" h., gently swelled cylindrical form w/a tapering shoulder to a low, flattened rolled rim, decorated w/large purple orchids & dark green leaves & stems against a shaded lavender to pink ground, Matte glaze, No. 904D, 1942, Kataro Shirayamadani (ILLUS.)................. **4,025**

Wisteria Blooms on Rookwood Vase

Vase, 8" h., tall ovoid form w/a rounded shoulder to a short rolled neck, decorated w/large shaded blue wisteria blossoms & green leaves against a dark blue shaded to creamy white ground, Vellum glaze, No. 164E, 1928, E.T. Hurley (ILLUS.)... **2,070**

Vase, 8" h., 3 1/2" d., cylindrical form w/a narrow tapering rim band to the wide flat mouth, decorated w/a continuous landscape w/large leafy trees in the foreground & a lake beyond, in shades of light & dark blue & green w/cream & pale yellow, Vellum glaze, No. 952E, 1918, Ed Diers **1,800**

Vase, 8" h., 3 1/2" d., tall slender ovoid body tapering slightly to a short neck & flat rim, decorated w/a cluster of tall Shasta daisies on green stems against a shaded dark to light blue ground, Vellum glaze, No. 901, 1913, M.H. McDonald.................. **1,350**

Vase, 8" h., 4" d., tapering cylindrical form w/flaring short neck, charcoal ground decorated around the shoulder w/a wide band of stylized pink blossoms & green leaves, Matte glaze, No. 1655E, 1911, O.G. Reed **1,463**

Shirayamadani Vellum Blossom Vase

Vase, 8 1/4" h., 4" d., low flaring foot below
a bulbous flattened lower body below a
tall gently flaring trumpet neck, the upper
body decorated w/large pink cherry blossoms & green leaves on a pink ground
w/violet blue around the lower body & in
the interior, Vellum glaze, 1933, K.
Shirayamadani (ILLUS.) **1,437**

Vase, 8 1/4" h., 4 1/4" d., baluster form,
decorated in squeezebag w/an overall
design of bands of alternating large dark
greenish brown triangles & blue circles
on a pale blue ground, No. 285, 1928,
William Hentschel **1,913**

Vase, 8 1/4" h., 5 1/2" d., six-paneled ovoid
body tapering to a cylindrical neck
w/flared rim, decorated w/large orange
maple leaves against a dark green shaded to mahogany brown ground, Standard
glaze, No. 850, 1903, Sallie Coyne **675**

Iris Glaze Vase with Flying Rook

Vase, 8 1/2" h., gently swelled cylindrical
form w/a narrow shoulder tapering to a
low, flared neck, decorated w/a large
black flying rook w/pine boughs & a full
moon against a dark blue shaded to
creamy white ground, Iris glaze, No. 904,
1908, Clara C. Lindeman (ILLUS.) **8,625**

Vase, 8 1/2" h., 3" d., swelled cylindrical
form tapering to a short cylindrical neck,
decorated w/white arrowhead blossoms
& dark teal blue leaves & grasses on a
shaded pink ground, Vellum glaze, No.
932E, 1921, Kataro Shirayamadani **3,375**

Vase, 8 1/2" h., 4" d., gently swelled cylindrical body w/a short tapering neck w/a
rolled rim, decorated w/large white Shasta daisies w/yellow centers on tall dark
green leafy stems against a shaded pale
blue to cream to pink ground, Vellum
glaze, No. 614E, 1912, Elizabeth
Lincoln **1,350**

Vase, 8 1/2" h., 4 1/2" d., ovoid body tapering to a short cylindrical neck, decorated
w/long stems of yellow & orange roses
against a very dark blue shaded to grey
ground, Iris glaze, No. 926C, 1903, Ed
Diers **2,138**

Rookwood Vase with Landscape Band

Vase, 9" h., footed tapering cylindrical form
w/a short angled shoulder & flat mouth,
decorated around the upper body w/a
wide winter landscape scene in white,
grey, pink & dark blackish brown, on a
dark moss green ground, Vellum glaze,
1912, Shirayamadani (ILLUS.) **2,415**

Flower Band on Jewel Porcelain Vase

Vase, 9" h., Jewel Porcelain, bulbous lower
body below tall tapering sides w/a rolled
rim, painted around the upper body w/a
wide band of stylized flowers in rose,
blue & green on a yellow ground, lower
body in dark greyish blue, turquoise interior, No. 975BT, 1918, Sara Sax
(ILLUS.).. **4,313**

Vase, 9" h., 4 1/2" d., baluster form w/a
swelled shoulder below the short cylindrical neck, decorated w/large white hy-
drangea & green leafy stems against a
dark green to light grey shaded ground,
Iris glaze, No. 909C, 1902, Fred Rothenbusch (ILLUS. left with clover-decorated
vase) **2,185**

Vase, 9" h., 5" d., tapering cylindrical body
w/a narrow angled shoulder centering a
short, wide cylindrical neck, decorated
around the shoulder w/a band of stylized

white cherry blossoms against a midnight blue ground, Vellum glaze, No. 918V, 1915, C.J. McLaughlin **1,688**

Vase, 9 1/8" h., wide ovoid body tapering to a wide flat rim flanked by small angled handles, decorated in low relief w/dark orange poppies & green leaves on a shaded olive green & brown ground, Standard glaze, No. 604C, Kataro Shirayamadani **1,840**

Vase, 9 1/2" h., 5" d., gently flaring cylindrical form w/rounded shoulder tapering to a short molded neck, decorated w/large pink & yellow roses & green leafy stems on a shaded pink to green ground, Iris glaze, No. 943C, 1904, Ed Diers (slight crazing).. **2,200**

Iris Glaze Vase with Poppies

Vase, 9 1/2" h., 5 1/4" d., large ovoid body tapering to a short cylindrical neck w/flared rim, decorated w/large white poppies on green stems against a shaded dark to light grey ground, Iris glaze, No. 849, 1903, Fred Rothenbusch (ILLUS.).. **2,415**

Vase, 9 5/8" h., bulbous nearly spherical body tapering to a tall slender trumpet neck w/wide ruffled rim, decorated w/holly & berries in autumn colors on a shaded yellow, dark green & brown ground, overlaid around the upper neck & bottom w/ornate meandering foliate silver overlay marked "Gorham Mfg. Co. R 727," Standard glaze, No. 614, 1892, indistinct artist's mark **1,840**

Vase, 10 1/4" h., 7 1/4" d., simple ovoid form w/flat rim, decorated w/a continuous meadow landscape w/oak trees, green, blue & grey against cream ground, Vellum glaze, No. 604C, Ed Diers (ILLUS. left, with plaque)... **4,219**

Vase, 10 1/2" h., 4" d., Jewel Porcelain, slightly swelled cylindrical form, a Japanese-style scene of cherry blossoms & flying birds in shades of blue & pink under a glossy pink glaze, No. 951, 1922, Lorinda Epply (ILLUS., top next column)............ **2,070**

Jewel Porcelain Vase with Blossoms

Vase, 10 1/2" h., 5 1/2" d., gently swelled cylindrical form w/a short rolled rim, decorated w/a continuous landscape w/birch trees around a lake, in shades of pale blue, dark blue, greens, purples & cream, Vellum glaze, unglazed, No. 892B, 1931, Ed Diers **5,063**

Vase, 11" h., 5 1/2" d., Jewel Porcelain, swelled cylindrical form w/short rolled neck, decorated w/a continuous wooded landscape w/blue & green trees on a shaded dark blue, white & light blue ground, No.892B, 1940, M.H. McDonald .. **3,190**

Vase, 11 " h., 5 1/2" d., tall ovoid form tapering to a short rolled neck, decorated w/large shaded blue & purple irises & bluish green leaves on a mottled blue ground, Wax Matte glaze, No. 614, 1929, Jens Jensen **2,420**

Fine Rookwood Jewel Porcelain Vase

Vase, 12" h., 5" d., Jewel Porcelain, footed baluster form w/a wide short cylindrical neck w/rolled rim, decorated in the Chinese style w/four panels of stylized flying bluebirds above tall stems of hollyhocks in blues & greens on an ivory butterfat ground, No. 2933, 1929, Lorinda Epply (ILLUS.)... **4,025**

Vase, 12 1/2" h., 4 1/2" d., tall swelled cylindrical form w/a narrow tapering shoulder & rolled neck, decorated w/large pink & white magnolia blossoms on a shaded blue to white ground, Vellum glaze, No. 904C, 1930, Lenore Asbury **7,150**

Vase, 12 1/2" h., 5 1/2" d., slender swelled cylindrical form, decorated w/a continuous sunset landscape w/large tall dark trees in the foreground, in shades of dark blue, black & pale peach pink, Vellum glaze, No. 2032C, 1920, Sara Sax **13,500**

Rookwood Harbor Scene by Schmidt

Vase, 13" h., gently swelling cylindrical form w/an angled shoulder to a short, slightly flared neck, decorated w/a Venetian harbor scene, Glossy glaze, Carl Schmidt (ILLUS.) **13,200**

Tall Scenic Vellum Vase with Trees

Vase, 14" h., baluster form w/angled shoulder to a short rolled neck, painted w/a landscape w/a large leafy tree across a stream w/hills & mountains in the distance on one side & the stream leading to meadows w/trees on the other, Vellum glaze, No. 2251, 1926, Fred Rothenbusch (ILLUS.) **10,350**

Fine Iris Glaze Vase with Irises

Vase, 14 1/2" h., tall slender ovoid form tapering to a flat rim w/a chased silver overlay narrow band, decorated w/large shaded blue irises on green leafy stems against a shaded blue to dark green ground, Iris glaze, No. 879C, 1904, Albert Valentien (ILLUS.) **12,650**

Vase, 16" h., 6 1/2" d., tall slightly tapering cylindrical form w/a thin flared rim, continuous misty landscape of birch trees around a lake at dusk in shades of pale cream, grey, blue & green, Vellum glaze, No. 1660A, 1912, E.T. Hurley **7,313**

Rose Medallion & Rose Canton

The lovely Chinese ware known as Rose Medallion was made through the past century and into the present one. It features alternating panels of people and flowers or insects, with most pieces having four medallions with a central rose or peony medallion. The ware is called Rose Canton if florals and birds or insects fill all the panels. Unless otherwise noted, our listing is for Rose Medallion ware.

Bottle w/cover & basin, Rose Mandarin variant, 19th c., bottle 16" h., basin 15 7/8" d., 4 7/8" h. (chips, minor wear) .. **$1,840**

Bowl, shaped low oval form, 19th c. **288**

Bowl, cov., 5 7/8" d., Rose Mandarin variant, footed deep rounded sides w/C-scroll side handles, mismatched low domed cover w/fruit finial w/underglaze-blue foliage & gilded fruit, the sides of the bowl decorated w/bands of Chinese figures **358**

Bowl, 8 3/8" d., Rose Mandarin variant, shallow round form w/tightly scalloped rim, the interior decorated w/four alternating reserves of figures or florals, the exterior decorated w/15 figures, orange peel glaze, 19th c. **523**

Bowl, 10" d., 4 7/8" h., Rose Mandarin variant, four-lobed, rounded sides w/notched & down-curved rims, orange peel glaze, 19th c. **1,540**

Bowl, 10 5/8" d., 4" h., shallow, w/scalloped sides, 19th c. (minor gilt & enamel wear, minute rim chips) **575**

Brush box, cov., rectangular, w/interior divider, late 19th c., 3 3/4 x 7 1/2" **633**

Cake stand, a wide cylindrical foot supporting a wide shallow dished top decorated on the interior w/alternating floral & figural reserves, 19th c., 8 5/8" d., 3 3/4" h. (minor edge flakes).. **468**

Candlesticks, cylindrical shaft above a flaring round foot, 19th c., 7" h., pr. (minor glaze wear)... **1,495**

Candlesticks, tall slender cylindrical shaft flared at the base & w/a flared, flattened socket rim, 19th c., 9 1/4" h., pr. (minor chips) **1,035**

Charger, round, 12" d., 19th c. (minor glaze wear)... **374**

Charger, ca. 1860, 14 1/2" d............................... **728**

Cider jug, cov., Rose Mandarin patt., w/woven double strap applied handle, lid w/foo dog finial, 19th c., 9 1/2" (glaze wear, finial imperfections) **2,990**

Rose Medallion Coffeepot

Coffeepot, cov., flared base on gently tapering body, domed lid w/finial, C-scroll handle, late 19th c., 10" h. (ILLUS.) **157**

Compote, 9 1/2" d., 3 1/2" h., 19th c.................. **288**

Compote, 11 x 14", 3" h., rounded diamond-shaped shallow bowl on a low flaring matching foot, 19th c. (imperfections).......... **748**

Creamer & cov. sugar, early 20th c., creamer 4 1/2" h., cov. sugar 5" h., pr..................... **134**

Dish, round, w/scalloped edges, 19th c., 8" d. (minor gilt wear)....................................... **316**

Dish, Rose Mandarin variant, rectangular, w/notched rounded corners & incurved shallow sides, central panel w/figures, orange peel glaze, 19th c., 9" l. **660**

Dish, Rose Mandarin variant, oblong, gently lobed form, figural scene in the center, butterflies around the rim, orange peel glaze, 19th c., 10 3/4" l. (chip on table ring).. **605**

Dishes, almond-shaped, each shallow oblong piece decorated w/alternating figural & floral reserves, orange peel glaze, heavy gilt trim, 19th c., 10 3/4" l., pr. **660**

Fruit basket, oval, w/deep, gently flaring reticulated sides w/gilt leaf-form handles, 19th c., 8 1/2 x 10", 4" h. (minor gilt wear)... **403**

Fruit basket, reticulated basket with undertray, 19th c. (glaze wear)................................ **748**

Fruit basket & undertray, oval reticulated basket on matching oval undertray, China, 19th c., 8 3/4 x 10", overall 14 1/4" h... **1,610**

Garden seat, barrel form, paneled decoration of alternating court scenes & floral designs, 19th c., 18" h. (minor glaze wear)... **1,380**

Garden seat, barrel form, three rows of colorfully painted panels separated by bands of gilt bosses, 19th c., 18 1/2" h. (minor gilt wear)... **2,300**

Garden seat, paneled barrel form w/alternating designs of court scenes & floral designs, China, 19th c., 18" h. (minor glaze wear)... **1,725**

Garden seat, Rose Mandarin variant, barrel-form body, decorated w/a court scene surrounding the central body w/upper & lower bands of butterflies & floral designs, China, 19th c., 18 1/2" h. (chips at interior bottom edge, minor glaze wear).... **2,645**

Mug, Rose Mandarin variant, tall cylindrical form w/decorated rim band above a band of three standing figures, entwined arched strap handle, 19th c., 4 7/8" h. **550**

Plates, 9 3/4" d., early 20th c., set of 10 .... **336**

Plates: four 9 5/8" d. dinner plates, eight 8 1/2" d. luncheon plates, eight 6" d. bread & butter plates; 19th c., the set (minor chips, glaze wear) **920**

Plates, 8" d., luncheon, 19th c., set of 6 (minor glaze wear)... **230**

Plates, 8 1/8" d., typical color palette, 19th c., set of 12 (minor rim chips, gilt & enamel wear)... **431**

Plates, 10" d., dinner, 19th c., one marked "Made in China," set of 6 (edge chips).......... **345**

Platter, 11" l., oval form, late 19th c. **308**

Platter, 11 5/8" l., oval, Rose Mandarin variant, wide dished & flanged rim around the figural center scene, 19th c...................... **660**

Platter, 12" l., Rose Mandarin variant, unusual wide rim border decoration w/dragons, goat, horse & Chinese symbols, 19th c. (gilt wear)... **460**

Platter, 13 1/4" l., oval form, late 19th c............. **364**

Rose Medallion Platter

Platter, 13 3/4" l., oval form w/raised rim, late 19th c. (ILLUS.)... **616**

Platter, 15 1/3" l., oval form, late 19th c............. **616**

Platter, 15 3/4" l., oval, Rose Mandarin variant, 19th c. (gilt & enamel wear, minor chips)... **1,093**

Platter, 16 3/4" l., oval, Rose Mandarin variant **880**

Platter, 18" l., oval, 19th c. (minor glaze wear).. **489**

Large Rose Medallion Platter

Platter, 18 1/2" l., oval, gilt rim on raised border, ca. 1840 (ILLUS.)............................ **1,120**

Rose Mandarin Punch Bowl

Punch bowl, Rose Mandarin variant, deep rounded sides, interior & exterior decorated w/colorful panels of figures, florals & birds, 19th c., minor base chips, scratches, glaze loss, 13 1/2" d. (ILLUS.).. **1,495**

Punch bowl, Rose Mandarin variant, 19th c., 14 3/4" d. (glaze wear)................................ **2,645**

Salt dips, low, oval waisted cylindrical base supporting an oval dished top, 19th c., 3 1/4 x 4 1/2", 1 1/2" h., pr. (minor imperfections).. **1,725**

Serving bowl, shaped edges, 19th c., 9 1/2" d., 4 7/8" h. (very minor chips to base)... **1,093**

Serving dish, shallow lobed oval form, 19th c., 8 1/2 x 10 1/8", 1 3/4" h. (wear) **173**

Shrimp dish, irregular shallow rounded form w/a slightly scalloped long floral-decorated flange handle along one side, four panels on the interior, 19th c., 9 1/2 x 10" (glaze wear)... **460**

Shrimp dishes, Rose Mandarin variant, shield form, one w/orange & gilt border, the other w/a floral border, 19th c., 9 3/4" d., 10" d., both (minor glaze wear) **978**

Soup bowls, late 19th c., 4" h., 10" w., 8" d., set of 7.. **420**

Tazza, shallow diamond-shaped bowl w/rounded corners raised on a deep conforming base w/decorative border band, 19th c., 14 1/8" l., 3 1/2" h. (minor gilt & enamel wear)... **805**

Tea set: cov. 4 1/2" h. teapot, sugar, creamer, four cups w/saucers; late 19th c. (restoration to teapot spout, glaze wear)............. **805**

Teapot, cov., Rose Mandarin variant, gilt decorated spout & handle, 19th c., 8 1/4" h. (minor chips, glaze losses) **1,265**

Trembleuses, 19th c., 8 1/4" d., set of 8 (minor glaze wear)... **316**

Urn, cov., Rose Mandarin variant, baluster form w/a rounded domed cover w/a gilt seated foo dog finial, gilt Foo dog mask shoulder handles, 19th c., 16" h. (minor glaze wear)... **1,380**

Vase, 17" h., Rose Mandarin variant, baluster form w/flattened ruffled rim, the neck mounted w/facing pairs of recumbent gilt foo dogs & kylins in gilt, 19th c. (minor glaze wear)... **1,495**

Vases, 9 1/4" h., baluster form w/applied kylins & foo dogs, 19th c., pr. (minor gilt & enamel wear) **633**

Rose Mandarin Ku-form Vase

Vases, 12 3/8" h., 7 3/4" d., Ku-form w/raised acanthus leaf ribbing & gilt archaic dragon design on blue ground, first half 19th c., pr.(ILLUS. of one)................... **3,335**

Vases, 15" h., baluster form, the wide cylindrical neck w/a flaring rim & flanked by a pair of molded foo dog handles, decorated w/panels of Oriental figures, birds & insects, ca. 1850, pr.................................... **2,912**

Rose Medallion Covered Vases

Vases, cov., 18 1/2" h., footed wide ovoid body tapering slightly to cylindrical neck flanked by figural handles, domed cover w/bud finial, on hardwood stands, gilt & enamel wear, minor chips to one lid, 19th c., pr. (ILLUS.) **2,860**

Rose Medallion Vases

Vases, 24" h., ovoid body tapering to tall cylindrical neck w/flaring rim, decorated around the neck w/applied kylins & foo dogs, 19th c., minor gilt & enamel wear, on hardwood stands, pr. (ILLUS.) **2,300**
Vegetable dish, cov., oval shaped form w/strap handles, 19th c., 6 1/4 x 10", 4" h. (minor glaze wear).................................. **460**
Vegetable dish, cov., rectangular, w/shaped corner & flanged rim, interior decoration, 19th c., 7 x 8", 4 3/4" h. (minor glaze wear)... **316**

Rose Medallion Wash Bowl & Pitcher

Wash bowl & pitcher, 14 3/4" h. pitcher w/bulbous ovoid body w/long slender angled handle, paneled decoration, 16" d. bowl w/deep rounded sides & flared rim, interior & rim w/matching decoration, 19th c., the set (ILLUS.)................................. **633**
Water bottle, cov., 19th c., 14 1/2" h. (hairline, minute lid chip, minor gilt & enamel wear).. **431**

Rose Medallion Water Bottle

Water bottle, cov., bulbous base w/tall slender cylindrical neck, small domed cover w/blossom finial, on hardwood stand, 19th c., minor chips to lid, minor gilt & enamel wear, 15" h. (ILLUS.) **805**

Rosenthal

The Rosenthal porcelain manufactory has been in operation since 1880, when it was established by P. Rosenthal in Selb, Bavaria. Tablewares and figure groups are among its specialties.

Cake plate, low pierced & pointed rim handles in gold w/gold rim band, h.p. along one side w/a large bouquet of red & pink roses & green leaves, 11" d. **$58**
Figure group, "Expectation," a woman in late 18th c. costume w/a tall grey hairdo trimmed w/blue & pink blossoms, seated on a bench wearing a deep mustard yellow gown w/pale green & white underskirt, one arm resting on the thick bench arm, looking up at the figure of a kneeling cupid atop a short column in white trimmed w/floral swags & a blue bow, oblong white base, No. K476, signed by A. Opel, ca. 1920, 6 3/4" h................................. **633**
Figure group, "Storming Bacchus," a figure of Bacchus in white, nude except for brown drapery across his thighs, leaning forwarding & striding w/each arm outstretched behind a young Bacchante in white w/brown hair, each seminude w/long dark blue drapery billowing around her legs, oblong white base, No. K190, signed by A. Caasmann, ca. 1922, 8" h.. **748**
Figure group, "Venus & Parrot," a nude woman w/a high blonde pompadour hairdo seated on a bench w/a dark blue drapery & turned toward a white bird perched on the rim of a dark blue urn-bowl w/gold scroll handles resting on short columns w/a molded satyr mask, white oblong base, No. K288, signed by A. Opel, ca. 1920, 6 7/8" h... **546**

Figure group, young girl & fawn, a blonde toddler wearing a blue playsuit & dark red blouse holding up a head of lettuce above the head of a light brown fawn, oval white base, No. 1665, by Friedrich Gronau, ca. 1937, 6 2/3" h. 230

Figure group, modeled as a nude female riding the back of an ostrich, rectangular base, glazed all-white, 18" h. 920

Figure of dancer, young woman in 18th c. peasant costume, wearing a long-sleeved white blouse w/dirndl & full ankle-length rust red dress & large white apron decorated w/scattered rust red blossoms, small cap on her head, posed w/one foot pointed to the side & holding up the corners of her apron, small rounded white base, by Opel, No. 1518/1, 1950s, 8 1/8" h. 288

Figure of Harlequin, standing w/legs together & head raised, playing an accordion, white w/blue trim & gold highlights, white mound base, signed by A. Caasmann, No. K436, ca. 1918, 7 1/2" h. (slight gold wear) 374

Model of dog, Borzoi, long slender reclining animal w/head erect, white & dark charcoal, no base, No. K200/0, signed by M. Valentin, ca. 1929, 9 1/4" l., 4" h. 345

Model of dog, Dachshund puppy, seated, shades of dark brown, signed by Kuspert, No. 1909, 1950s, 3 1/2" h. 150

Model of dog, German Shepherd, seated animal w/open legs, black w/tan face & chest, No. K260/2, by Diller, ca. 1923, 11 3/8" h. 322

Model of dog, Whippet, seated w/one paw raised, white w/black spots, oval base, signed by K. Himmelstoss, No. 511, 2 1/8" h. 196

Model of fish, Angelfish, large graceful fish w/dark & light brown stripes, supported on slender tendrils of sea grass above an oval base, signed by F. Heidenreich, No. 1637, 1950s, 7 3/4" h. 242

Model of horse, large brown animal in prancing pose, black mane & tail & white chest, on narrow oblong white base, by Zugel, No. N958, ca. 1935, 7 3/4" h. 299

Plaque, rectangular, color transfer-printed copy of the Mona Lisa, framed, 1930s, without frame 10 x 12 1/2". 265

Plaque, rectangular, painted w/a scene of the snow-covered Matterhorn w/a lake in the foreground & dark blue sky & white clouds behind, original giltwood shadowbox frame, 10 x 12" 770

Plates, 8 1/2" d., "Rosenthal Ivory" patt., six different colorful fruit designs w/h.p. accents & gilt trim, late 19th - early 20th c., set of 16. 440

Roseville

Roseville Pottery Company operated in Zanesville, Ohio, from 1898 to 1954, having been in business for six years prior to that in Muskingum County, Ohio. Art wares similar to those of Owens and Weller Potteries were produced. Items listed here are by patterns or lines.

Roseville Mark

Apple Blossom (1948)

White apple blossoms in relief on blue, green or pink ground; brown tree branch handles.

Basket, hanging-type, blue ground, 8" **$190**

Console set, 8" l. bowl & pair of 2" h. candle-holders, pink ground, No. 328-8" & No. 351-2", 3 pcs. **500**

Cornucopia-vase, pink ground, No. 321-6", 6" h. **120**

Cornucopia-vases, blue ground, No. 321-6", 6" h., pr. **165**

Cornucopia-vases, green ground, No. 321-6", 6" h., pr. **280**

Jardiniere & pedestal base, blue ground, jardiniere, No. 302-8", 8" h., pedestal, No. 305-8", 2 pcs. **880**

Tea set: cov. teapot, creamer & sugar bowl; blue ground, No. 371-P, the set **440**

Tea set: cov. teapot, creamer & sugar bowl; pink ground, No. 371-P, the set **303**

Vase, 6" h., two-handled, squatty base, long cylindrical neck, pink ground, No. 381-6" **155**

Vase, bud, 7" h., base handles, flaring rim, pink ground, No. 379-7" **99**

Vase, bud, 7" h., base handles, flaring rim, green ground, No. 379-7". **88**

Vase, 8 1/4" h., flaring foot w/ovoid body & wide flaring rim, pointed handles from shoulder to middle of neck, green ground, No. 385-8". **185**

Vase, 10" h., swelled cylindrical body w/shaped rim, base handles, blue ground, No. 389-10". **350**

Vase, 15" h., floor-type, double base handles, short globular base, long cylindrical neck, green ground, No. 392-15". **445**

Apple Blossom Floor Vase

Vase, 15" h., floor-type, double base handles, short globular base, long cylindrical neck, blue ground, No. 392-15" (ILLUS.)...... **776**

Vase, 18" h., floor-type, slender ovoid body w/wide cylindrical neck, blue ground, No. 393-18" (two chips & one bruise to base, hairline to rim)... **358**

Window box, end handles, pink ground, No. 368-8", 2 1/2 x 10 1/2" **50**

Aztec (1915)

Muted earthy tones of beige, grey, brown, teal, olive, azure blue or soft white with slip-trailed geometric decoration in contrasting colors.

Vase, 6 3/8" h., tapering cylindrical body w/bulbous top, slip decoration of stylized mushrooms in white & orange w/blue ribbon bands above & below, on a bluish grey ground, artist-initialed "E" & old oval paper label (base & rim chips) **138**

Vase, 8" h., tapering cylinder swelling slightly at top, squeezebag decoration of white trillium on orange stems against a blue/grey ground, unmarked (lentil-size chip to base & 1" hairline to rim) **523**

Aztec Vase

Vase, 10" h., flared foot w/expanding cylindrical body & flared rim, white & tan decoration against a blue ground, artist-signed (ILLUS.) **248**

Baneda (1933)

Band of embossed pods, blossoms and leaves on green or raspberry pink ground.

Bowl, 6" d., raspberry pink ground, No. 232-6" **385**

Vase, 5" h., footed, pear-shaped w/small loop handles near rim, raspberry pink ground, No. 601-5" **400**

Vase, 6" h., green ground, No. 605-6", original label **518**

Vase, 7" h., footed wide cylindrical body w/wide collared rim, small loop handles from shoulder to rim, raspberry pink ground, No. 610-7" **500**

Wall pocket, flaring sides, green ground, No. 1269-8", gold foil label, 8" h. (small chip to hole in back) **2,645**

Bittersweet (1940)

Orange bittersweet pods and green leaves on a grey blending to rose, yellow with terra cotta, rose with green or solid green bark-textured ground; brown branch handles.

Basket, low overhead handle, shaped rim, green ground, No. 810-10", 10" h. **193**

Bittersweet Planter

Planter w/undertray, grey ground, No. 856-5", slight interior discoloration from usage & small bruise to one of rim points, 5 1/2" h. (ILLUS.)... **67**

Planter w/undertray, green ground, No. 856-5", 5 1/2" h. (minor crazing) **143**

Vase, 7" h., base handles, squared form w/flaring rim, yellow ground, No. 874-7"........ **138**

Vase, 7" h., green ground, No. 879-7"................. **83**

Bittersweet Vases

Vase, 7" h., yellow ground, No. 879-7", embossed "Roseville U.S.A. 879-7"" (ILLUS. right).. **138**

Vase, 10" h., handles at midsection, scalloped rim, grey ground, No. 885-10" (ILLUS. left) **193**

Wall pocket, curving conical form w/overhead handle continuing to one side, grey ground, No. 866-7", 7 1/2" h. **316**

Blackberry (1933)

Band of relief clusters of blackberries with vines and ivory leaves accented in green and terra cotta on a green textured ground.

Basket, hanging-type, 6 1/2" (two flakes to berries) **633**
Bowl, 6" d., No. 226-6" **300**
Jardiniere, two-handled, No. 623-6", 6" h. **495**
Jardiniere, two-handled, 8" h. **1,045**
Planter, hanging-type, No. 348-5", 5" h. (one rim hanging hole only partially pierced) **800**
Planter, six-sided, gold foil label, 3 3/4 x 10" **460**
Vase, 10" h., bulbous base w/wide cylindrical neck, handles at midsection, No. 577-10 .... **1,648**
Vase, 12 1/2" h., ovoid w/loop handles from shoulder to rim, No. 578-12" (minor chip to bottom) **1,320**

Bleeding Heart (1938)

Pink blossoms and green leaves on shaded blue, green or pink ground.

Basket, hanging-type, two-handled, blue ground, No. 362-5", 8" d. **288**
Basket, hanging-type, two-handled, green ground, No. 362-5", 8" d. **242**
Basket, hanging-type, two-handled, pink ground, No. 362-5", 8" w. **225**
Basket w/circular handle, brown ground, No. 360-10", 10" h. **403**

Bleeding Heart Basket

Basket w/circular handle, pink ground, 360-10", 10" h., w/gold foil label (ILLUS.) **331**
Basket w/overhead handle, pink ground, No. 359-8", 7 1/2" h. **200**
Basket w/pointed overhead handle, w/flower frog, pink ground, No. 361-12", 12" h., 2 pcs. **300**
Wall pocket, conical w/pointed overhead handle, blue ground, No. 1287-8", 8 1/2" h. (minor crazing) **619**

Burmese (1950s)

Oriental faces featured on pieces such as wall plaques, book ends, candleholders and console bowls. Some plain pieces also included. Comes in green, black and white.

Candleholders-book end combination, woman & man, white glaze, Nos. 80-B & 70-B, pr. **138**

Bushberry (1948)

Berries and leaves on blue, green or russet bark-textured ground; brown or green branch handles.

Basket, hanging-type w/original chains, russet ground, No. 465-5", 7" **425**

Basket w/asymmetrical overhead handle, green ground, No. 369-6 1/2", 6 1/2" h. **250**
Basket w/asymmetrical overhead handle, ivory ground, No. 369-6 1/2", 6 1/2" h. **112**
Basket w/asymmetrical overhead handle, green ground, No. 370-8", 8" h. **275**
Basket w/asymmetrical overhead handle, blue ground, No. 371-10", 10" h. **353**

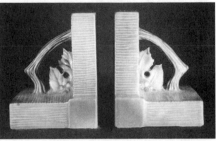

Bushberry Book Ends

Book ends, green ground, No. 9, pr. (ILLUS.) **300**
Bowl, 3" h., small side handles, globular, green ground, No. 657-3" **120**
Flower frog, blue ground, No. 45 .... **160**
Jardiniere, two-handled, blue ground, No. 657-4", 4" h. **165**
Jardiniere, russet ground, No. 657-5", 5" h. **170**
Pitcher, 8 3/4" h., russet w/green branch handle, No. 1325 .... **300**
Urn, two-handled, green ground, No. 411-6", 6" h. (couple of very minor nicks to horizontal ridges) **112**
Vase, 3" h., conical w/tiny rim handles, russet ground, No. 283" **30**

Bushberry Double Bud Vase

Vase, double bud, 4 1/2" h., gate-form, russet ground, No. 158-4 1/2" (ILLUS.) **185**
Vase, 6" h., two-handled, russet ground, No. 30-6" **70**
Vase, 6" h., angular side handles, low foot, globular w/wide neck, green ground, No. 156-6" **138**
Vase, bud, 7 1/2" h., asymmetrical base handles, cylindrical body, russet ground, No. 152-7" **145**
Vase, 10" h., two-handled, russet ground, No. 37-10" **265**
Vase, 12 1/2" h., large asymmetrical side handles, bulging cylinder w/flaring foot, green ground, No. 38-12" **225**

Wall pocket, high-low handles, russet ground, No. 1291-8", 8" h. (glazed over bruise to back).. **259**

Carnelian I (1910-15)

Matte glaze with a combination of two colors or two shades of the same color with the darker dripping over the lighter tone or heavy and textured glaze with intermingled colors and some running.

Bowl, 6 1/2" d., 3" h., two-handled, canted sides, pink & grey **231**

Vase, 5" h., flat pierced handles, rectangular w/slightly bulging sides, rose w/deep purple drip, unmarked, No. 65-2-5 .... **275**

Vase, 5" h., two-handled, squatty bulbous form, shades of green, No. 357-5" **110**

Vase, 5" h., blue & grey ground, No. 642-5" **175**

Vase, 7" h., footed bulbous ovoid w/shoulder tapering to wide molded rim, handles from shoulder to rim, green ground, No. 331-7" **235**

Vase, 7" h., footed bulbous ovoid w/shoulder tapering to wide molded rim, handles from shoulder to rim, rose & grey ground, No. 331-7" **358**

Wall pocket, conical w/ornate side handles, flaring rim, blue & grey, No. 1251-8" (very minor chips around hanging hole) **242**

Carnelian II (1915)

Intermingled colors, some with a drip effect.

Bowl, 12 1/2" d. footed wide shallow round form, deeply mottled dark rose & tan glaze, foil label **1,150**

Console bowl, stepped base, flaring octagonal shape, mottled mauve, grey, cream & black glaze, 9 5/8" l., 3 5/8" h. **220**

Urn, globular body tapering to flaring rim, scrolled shoulder handles, light & dark blue ground, No. 333-6", 6" h. **413**

Vase, 5" h., footed, fan-shaped body w/shaped rim, small base handles, mottled grey, green & pink glaze, No. 351-5 ...... **110**

Vase, bud, 6" h., footed trumpet form w/ornate handles from base to midsection, turquoise ground, No. 341-6" **99**

Vase, 7" h., footed, wide cylindrical body tapering slightly to rolled rim, gloopy pink, mauve, green, black & cream matte glaze (small base chip professionally repaired) **165**

Vase, 8 1/4" h., squatty bulbous body tapering to flared rim, angled scrolled handles, mottled matte mauve drip glaze, partial paper label **423**

Vase, 9" h., ovoid, w/short collared mouth, intermingled shades of pink, purple, green & tan, unmarked **399**

Vase, 10" h., footed tapering cylindrical body w/wide, slightly flaring neck, mottled green glaze **259**

Wall pocket, slender fanned body flanked by double-scroll handles, intermingled shades of pink & blue, 8" h. **345**

Wall pocket, slender fanned body flanked by double-scroll handles, shaded brown ground, 8" h. **460**

Cherry Blossom (1933)

Sprigs of cherry blossoms, green leaves and twigs with pink fence against a combed blue-green ground or creamy ivory fence against a terra cotta ground shading to dark brown.

Basket, hanging-type, brown ground, 8".......... **546**

Jardiniere, squatty bulbous body, two-handled, blue-green ground, No. 627-4", 4" h. (overall crazing w/discoloration at base).. **325**

Jardiniere, shoulder handles, terra cotta ground, No. 627-7", 7" h............................... **550**

Urn, two-handled, terra cotta ground, No. 350-5", 5" h... **420**

Vase, 5" h., two-handled, globular w/wide mouth, terra cotta ground, No. 627-5" **275**

Vase, 10" h., slender ovoid body w/wide cylindrical neck, loop handles from shoulder to middle of neck, blue-green ground, No. 626-10" **1,430**

Vase, 12" h., tall swelled cylindrical form tapering to a short flaring neck flanked by small loop handles, pink ground, No. 627-12".. **546**

Wall pocket, brown ground, No. 1270-8", gold foil label, 8" h. (short tight line to rim)...... **863**

Clematis (1944)

Clematis blossoms and heart-shaped green leaves against a vertically textured ground, white blossoms on blue, rose-pink blossoms on green and ivory blossoms on golden brown.

Console bowl, two-handled, green ground, No. 460-12", 12" l... **140**

Console bowl, green ground, No. 461-14", 14" l. (fleck to one petal).................................. **110**

Vase, 15" h., brown ground, No. 114-15".......... **275**

Vase, 15" h., green ground, No. 114-15"........... **765**

Columbine (1940s)

Columbine blossoms and foliage on shaded ground, yellow blossoms on blue, pink blossoms on pink shaded to green, and blue blossoms on tan shaded to green.

Bowl, 6" d., two-handled, squatty bulbous body w/small angled shoulder handles, tan ground, No. 400-6".................................. **168**

Candleholders, tan ground, No. 1145-2 1/2", 2 1/2" h., pr....................................... **60**

Candlesticks, flat disc base w/handles rising to nozzle, tan ground, No. 1146-4 1/2", 5" h., pr... **224**

Urn-vase, tan ground, No. 150-6", 6" h.............. **165**

Urn-vase, pink ground, No. 151-8", 8" h............ **140**

Vase, 6" h., pink shaded to green ground, No. 13-6" **125**

Vase, 6" h., tan ground, No. 13-6" **135**

Vase, 8" h., handles rising from base, tan ground, No. 19-8"... **195**

Wall pocket, squared flaring mouth, conical body w/curled tip, brown ground, No. 1290-8".. **518**

Corinthian (1923)

Deeply fluted ivory and green body below a continuous band of molded grapevine, fruit, foliage and florals in naturalistic colors, narrow ivory and green molded border at the rim.

Bowl, 5" h., No. 121-5"... **60**

Candlestick, No. 1048-10", 10" h........................ **110**

Vase, 6" h., semi-ovoid....................................... **193**

Vase, 12" h., cylindrical w/flared rim, No. 235-12" (1/8" glaze flake off one vertical rib)... **110**

Wall pocket, No. 1229-12", 12" h. 250

Cosmos (1940)
Embossed blossoms against a wavy horizontal ridged band on a textured ground, ivory band with yellow and orchid blossoms on blue, blue band with white, and orchid blossoms on green or tan.

Basket, hanging-type, handles rising from
midsection to rim, brown ground, No.
361-5", 7" h. 230
Basket w/overhead handle, green ground,
No. 357-10", 10" h. 250
Bowl, 6" d., two-handled, shaped rim, tan
ground, No. 369-6" 60
Bowl, 6" d., No. 376-6" 225
Candlesticks, loop handles rising from disc
base, slightly tapering candle nozzle,
green ground, No. 1137-4 1/2", 4 1/2" h.,
pr. 303
Console bowl, blue ground, No. 371-10",
10" l. 160
Console bowl, footed oblong boat shape
w/an undulating & double-notched rim,
blue ground, No. 374-14", 15 1/2" l. 193
Jardiniere, two-handled, green ground, No.
649-3" 145
Jardiniere & pedestal base, blue ground,
No. 649-10", overall 30" h., 2 pcs. 2,600
Vase, 4" h., double bud, gate-form, tan
ground, No. 133-4" 110
Vase, 4" h., two-handled, globular base &
wide neck, green ground, No. 944-4".......... 135
Vase, 4" h., two-handled, globular base &
wide neck, tan ground, No. 944-4" 99
Vase, 6" h., green ground, No. 947-6" 175
Vase, 7" h., handles at base, trumpet-form
body, green ground, No. 949-7" (small
chip off bottom of rim) 83
Vase, bud, 7" h., slender, slightly tapering
cylinder w/large loop handles at base,
green ground, No. 959-7" 248
Vase, 9" h., handles rising from midsection
of ovoid body to neck, green ground, No.
952-9" 500

Cosmos Vase

Vase, 12 1/2" h., ovoid w/large loop handles, tan ground, No. 956-12"
(ILLUS.)... 300
Wall pocket, fanned conical shape w/high
arched handle across the top, tan
ground, No. 1285-6", 6 1/2" h. 259

Cremona (1927)
Relief-molded floral motifs including a tall stem with small blossoms and arrowhead leaves, wreathed with leaves similar to Velmoss or a web of delicate vines against a background of light green mottled with pale blue or pink with creamy ivory.

Vase, 4" h., squatty, w/narrow flared mouth,
pink ground, No. 351-4" 230
Vase, 10" h., footed square tapering body,
No. 358-10" 220
Vase, 10" h., baluster-form body w/flaring
foot & rim, green ground, No. 350-10"
(fleck to tip of one leaf) 193
Vase, 12" h., footed, slender baluster-form
body w/narrow shoulder to the cylindrical
neck w/flaring rim, green ground, No.
361-12" 385

Della Robbia, Rozane (1906)
Naturalistic or stylized designs executed by hand using the sgraffito method.

Della Robbia Vase with Flower Band

Vase, 9 1/2" h., footed wide ovoid body tapering to a short cylindrical neck, incised
decoration of stylized flowers in large
teardrops w/bands of spade-shaped
leaves around the top & base, in six colors including white, blue, yellow & dark
green, signed, minor chip repairs
(ILLUS.).. 6,325

Unusual Della Robbia Vase

Vase, 10 1/2" h., flaring foot below compressed round base, tall cylindrical body w/flaring rim, deeply carved & cut-back fish decoration under a multi-tone green glaze, partial wafer mark, restored, minor chip to top (ILLUS., previous page) **2,400**

Vase, 10 1/2" h., large spherical body w/short cylindrical neck, flaring rim, cut-back & incised floral design in shades of blue, aqua & olive green, brown & yellow, restoration to top & bottom **8,800**

Large Della Robbia Vase with Poppies

Vase, 17 1/2" h., 9 1/2" d., tall ovoid body w/the rim reticulated in a Greek key design above five tall rectangular panels decorated in seven colors w/excised poppies in ivory & taupe on a mint green ground, unmarked, discreet restoration around rim & to short hairline (ILLUS.) **18,400**

Rare Della Robbia Floor Vase

Vase, 21" h., 10 1/2" d., floor-type, large ovoid form tapering to a small flattened & flared neck, excised, incised & enameled in seven colors w/yellow daffodils & shiny leaves in shades of green on a mint green & indigo blue ground, probably an exhibition piece, wafer mark & original paper price tag marked $50, signed by H. Smith, professional restoration to rim, several underglaze chips on base, invisi-

ble touchups to glaze nicks (ILLUS.) **37,375**

Donatello (1915)
Deeply fluted ivory and green body with wide tan band embossed with cherubs at various pursuits in pastoral settings.

Ashtray, No. 17-3", 3" h. **100**
Basket, hanging-type, No. 327-6", 7" d., 5" h. **201**
Basket w/tall pointed overhead handle, cylindrical body, No. 304-12", 12" h. **358**

Donatello Candlesticks

Candlesticks, flaring base & rim w/tall slender cylindrical stem, No. 1022-10", 10" h., pr. (ILLUS.) **303**
Flower frog, No. 14-2 1/2", 2 1/2" d. **70**
Jardiniere, No. 575-4", 4" h. **95**
Jardiniere, No. 575-6", 7" d., 6" h. **150**
Jardiniere, No. 579-8", 8" h. **250**
Jardiniere, No. 579-10", 10" h. **395**
Jardiniere & pedestal base, 12" h. jardiniere, No. 579-12", overall 34" h., 2 pcs. **1,300**
Planter, No. 238-7" (pinhead nicks on inside rim) **56**
Powder jar, cov., lid decorated w/scene of cherubs playing musical instruments, 5" d., 2" h. **330**
Umbrella stand, cylindrical, No. 753-10", 10" h. (three glaze nicks to rim, a couple of tight lines to relief band, not through) **413**

Vase, double bud, gate-form, No. 8 .... **70**
Vase, bud, 10" h., bottle-form, No. 1 15-10" **255**
Wall pocket, ovoid, No. 1212-9", 9" h. **275-300**
Wall pocket, No. 1202-10", 10" h. **190**
Wall pocket, No. 1219-10", 10" h. **226**
Window box, rectangular, No. 60-12", 6 x 12" l. **295**

Early Embossed Pitchers (pre-1916)
High-gloss utility line of pitchers with various embossed scenes.

Goldenrod Pitcher

Goldenrod, 9 1/2" h., minor bruise to rim &
 touchups around base (ILLUS.) **303**

Landscape Pitcher

Landscape, 7 1/2" h. (ILLUS.) **95-100**

The Cow Pitcher

The Cow, 7 1/2" h. (ILLUS.) **413**

Wild Rose Pitcher

Wild Rose, 9 1/2" h., small spout chip
 (ILLUS.) **125**

Falline (1933)

*Curving panels topped by a semi-scallop separated
by vertical pea pod decorations; blended backgrounds of
tan shading to green and blue or tan shading to darker
brown.*

Console bowl, shallow, w/end loop handles,
 tan ground, No. 244-8", 8" l. **394**

Falline Vase

Vase, 6" h., footed, cylindrical, w/large loop
 handles from midsection to rim, tan shad-
 ing to brown, No. 642-6" (ILLUS.)................. **280**
Vase, 6" h., two-handled, ovoid, tan shading
 to brown, No. 643-6" **392**
Vase, 8 1/4" h., 6" d., footed trumpet form
 w/a widely flaring rim, low arched handles from under the rim to mid-body, tan
 shading to green & blue, 7" l. (Y-shaped
 line from rim) **495**

Florentine (1924-28)

*Bark-textured panels alternating with embossed gar-
lands of cascading fruit and florals; ivory with tan and
green, beige with brown and green or brown with beige
and green glaze.*

Ashtray, brown ground, No. 17-3", 3"................. **165**
Bowl, 7" d., No. 125-7"... **40**
Candlesticks, flaring base, expanding cylin-
drical stem, brown, No. 1050-10", 10" h.,
pr. **358**
Compote, 4" d., brown ground, No. 6-4"........... **195**
Jardiniere, brown, No. 130-4", 7" d., 4" h. **165**
Jardiniere, brown, No. 602-8", 8" h..................... **495**
Sand jar, green ground, 15 x 17"....................... **440**
Wall pocket, conical, No. 1231-12", 12" h. **251**

Foxglove (1940s)

*Sprays of pink and white blossoms embossed against
a shaded matte-finish ground.*

Basket, hanging-type, blue ground, No.
466-5", 10".. **201**
Basket w/circular overhead handle, footed
fan shape w/shaped rim, green ground,
No. 375-12", 12" h. **275**
Candleholders, pink ground, No. 1150-
4 1/2", 4 1/2" h., pr...................................... **250**
Console bowl, oval, w/cut-out rim & pointed
end handles, blue ground, No. 423-12",
12" l.. **154**
Cornucopia-vase, snail shell-type, blue
ground, No. 166-6" **115**
Cornucopia-vase, green ground, No. 164-6"..... **195**
Jardiniere, two-handled, pink ground, No.
659-3", 3" h.. **83**

Foxglove Conch Shell

Model of a conch shell, blue ground, No.
426-6", 6" h. (ILLUS.)...................................... **220**
Vase, 6" h., bulbous base tapering to cylin-
drical neck w/flared rim, angled handles
below rim, blue ground, No. 43-6" **90**
Vase, 8 1/2" h., fan-shaped, handles rising
from disc base to midsection, pink
ground, No. 47-8" **203**

Foxglove Vase

Vase, 8 1/2" h., fan-shaped, handles rising
from disc base to midsection, blue
ground, No. 47-8" (ILLUS.) **134**
Vase, 14" h., conical, w/flaring mouth, four
short handles rising from disc base,
green ground, No. 53-14"................................ **425**
Vase, 16" h., pear-shaped body w/closed
rim, angled handles from lower body to
shoulder, blue ground, No. 55-16".................. **633**
Wall pocket, conical, w/flaring rim, loop handles, blue ground, No. 1292-8", 8" h. **335**

Freesia (1945)

*Trumpet-shaped blossoms and long slender green
leaves against wavy impressed lines, white and lavender
blossoms on blended green, white and yellow blossoms
on shaded blue, or terra cotta and brown.*

Bowl, 6" d., terra cotta ground, No. 464-6"........ **155**
Candleholders, tiny pointed handles, domed
base, blue ground, No. 1160-2", 2" h., pr........ **88**
Console bowl, terra cotta ground, No. 466-
10", 10" l.. **143**
Console set: 12" l., 4 1/2" h. console bowl &
pr. of candlesticks; blue ground, No. 468-
12", 3 pcs.. **88**
Cookie jar, cov., bulbous ovoid body w/an-
gled shoulder handles, slightly domed lid
w/knob finial, green ground, No. 4-8",
8" h... **350**
Cornucopia-vase, terra cotta ground, No.
198-8", 8" h.. **165**
Cornucopia-vases, terra cotta ground, No.
197-6", 6" h., pr.. **121**

Freesia Ewer

Ewer, green ground, No. 19-6", 6" h.
(ILLUS.).. **112**
Lamp, blue ground, No. 145................................ **468**
Urn-vase, two-handled, green ground, No.
463-5", 5" h... **220**
Urn-vase, two-handled, bulbous body taper-
ing to wide cylindrical neck, terra cotta
ground, No. 196-8", 8" h.................................. **225**
Vase, 6" h., terra cotta ground, No. 117-6" **165**
Vase, 7" h., two-handled, fan-shaped, terra
cotta, No. 200-7"... **165**
Vase, 8" h., footed ovoid body flanked by D-
form handles, blue ground, No. 121-8"......... **149**
Vase, 10 1/2" h., two-handled, trumpet-form
body, blue ground, No. 125-10" **165**
Vase, 15" h., tall slender ovoid body taper-
ing to narrow cylindrical neck w/wide flaring rim, pointed shoulder handles, terra
cotta ground, No. 128-15"................................ **275**

Fuchsia (1939)

Coral pink fuchsia blossoms and green leaves against a background of blue shading to yellow, green shading to terra cotta, or terra cotta shading to gold.

Basket, hanging-type, terra cotta ground,
No. 359-5", 7" h... **201**
Bowl, 5" d., two-handled, squatty bulbous
body w/incurved rim, green ground, No.
348-5" **101**
Cornucopia-vase, blue ground, No. 129-6",
6" h. **150**
Jardiniere, two-handled, terra cotta ground,
No. 645-4", 4" h... **190**
Jardiniere, two-handled, blue ground, No.
645-5", 5" h.. **225**

Fuchsia Pitcher

Pitcher w/ice lip, 8" h., blue ground, No.
1322-8" (ILLUS.)... **420**
Vase, 6" h., ovoid, w/handles rising from
shoulder to rim, terra cotta ground, No.
892-6" **130**
Vase, 9" h., footed ovoid body w/flared rim &
large C-form handles, terra cotta ground,
No. 899-9".. **179**
Wall pocket, two-handled, blue ground, No.
1282-8", 8 1/2" h. (minute nick to hanging hole & minor glaze scaling to corner
of rim).. **575**

Futura (1928)

Varied line with shapes ranging from Art Deco geo-metrics to futuristic. Matte glaze is typical although an occasional piece may be high gloss.

Basket, hanging-type, wide sloping shoulders, sharply canted sides, terra cotta &
brown w/embossed stylized pastel foli-
age, No. 344-5", 7 1/2" h. (bruise to rim)...... **288**
Basket, hanging-type, wide sloping shoul-
ders, sharply canted sides, brown w/em-
bossed stylized pastel foliage, 9" h. **230**
Jardiniere, angular handles rising from wide
sloping shoulders to rim, sharply canted
sides, grey ground, No. 616-8", 8" h. **495**
Jardiniere, flaring flat sides below the narrow angled shoulder molded w/stylized
leaves & a short cylindrical neck, small
squared shoulder handles, pink & laven-
der leaves on the grey ground, 9" d., 6" h. **408**
Vase, 6" h., stepped shoulders, square
body w/canted sides, grey w/green &
blue elongated triangles, No. 380-6" **429**

Vase, 6" h., 3 1/2" d., cylindrical body swelling to wider bands at the top & base, long
pierced angled handles down the sides,
apricot w/green bands & handles, one
w/paper label, No. 381-6"............................... **409**
Vase, 6" h., octagonal cone-shaped body
on a conforming low base, bluish green
semi-crystalline glaze, No. 397-6" **376**
Vase, bud, 6" h., widely flaring conical foot
tapering to a slender, tall, slightly flaring
cylindrical body flanked by slender
straight handles from near the rim to the
foot, stylized floral design in blue & green
on a tan shaded to cream ground, No.
422-6".. **413**
Vase, 8" h., 3 3/4" d., star-shaped slender
tapering body on stepped circular base,
pink & grey ground, No. 385-8", un-
marked **392**
Vase, 8" h., 5 3/4" d., a high pyramidal foot
w/four straight pierced legs supporting
the spherical body w/a small conical
mouth, decorated w/white, light blue,
green & yellow circles on blue ground,
No. 404-8"... **1,400-1,500**

Futura "Globe on Legs" Vase

Vase, 8" h., 5 3/4" d., a high pyramidal foot
w/four straight pierced legs supporting
the spherical body w/a small conical
mouth, green ground decorated w/pur-
ple, yellow & orange circles, No. 404-8"
(ILLUS.)... **1,054**
Vase, 8 1/4" h., 4 1/4" w., tall triangular
body tapering slightly to a stepped triangular foot, the body w/wide light blue triangles flanked by slender dark blue triangles, dark & light blue base, unmarked,
No. 383-8"... **935**
Vase, 9 1/2" h., stepped sloping rectangular
foot supporting a body w/flat multifaceted
flat sides on lower half & contrasting panels on upper half tapering to small rectangular neck, shaded yellow & green, No.
412-9"... **5,060**
Vase, 10" h., squatty bulbous base w/mold-
ed ring midsection, wide cylindrical neck
w/flaring rim, No. 435-10" (professional
repair of minor rim chips) **715**
Vase, 10" h., 8 1/2" d., narrow base flaring
to wide shoulder, graduated ringed neck,
orange & green, No. 395-10" **660**

Vase, 10 1/4" h., 5 1/4" d., small buttressed handles at disc base, slightly swollen cylindrical lower portion flaring to a wide mouth, decorated w/blue flowers on green stems against a shaded orange body, No. 431-10", unmarked **1,073**

Vase, 12" h., wide ovoid body on a footring, the neck composed of tapering bands, smooth sides, multi-toned deep green overall glaze, No. 394-12" **920**

Gardenia (1940s)
Large white gardenia blossoms and green leaves over a textured impressed band on a shaded green, grey or tan ground.

Basket w/circular handle, grey ground, No. 609-10", 10" h. **193**

Basket w/circular handle, green ground, No. 609-10", 10" h. **180**

Console set: 11" l. footed oblong boat-shaped bowl & a pair of 2" h. candleholders; green ground, No. 374-11 & 651-2, the set **165**

Cornucopia-vase, tan ground, No. 621-6", 6" h. **80**

Cornucopia-vase, double, green ground, No. 622-8", 8" h. **70**

Cornucopia-vase, double, grey ground, No. 622-8", 8" **60**

Ewer, tan ground, No. 618-15", 15" h. (professional repair to base) **225**

Spooner, green ground, No. 656-3", 3" h. **125**

Vase, 8" h., green ground, No. 684-8" **195**

Vase, 10" h., green ground, No. 658-10 .... **160**

Vase, 10 1/2" h., large handles rising from base to shoulder, ornate rim, tan ground, No. 686-10" **198**

Vase, 12" h., handles rising from low base to midsection, tan ground, No. 687-12" (glaze flakes to bottom) **138**

Wall pocket, large handles, tan ground, No. 666-8", 9 1/2" h. **225**

Good Night Candleholder

Good Night Candleholder

Candleholder, closed back, chamberstick-type, unmarked, 7" h. (ILLUS.) **715**

Imperial II (1924)
Varied line with no common characteristics. Many of the pieces are heavily glazed with colors that run and blend.

Vase, 5 1/2" h., two-handled, bulbous body tapering slightly to short cylindrical neck, blue ground w/glossy mottled ivory glaze on interior that spills over the rim in one area, laced w/tawny yellow, No. 517 .... **150**

Vase, 8 1/4" h., wide ovoid form slightly tapering to a wide, short cylindrical neck, mottled orange & green w/tan glaze w/green, dark brown & blue around the neck **2,415**

Wall pocket, mottled pink & green glaze, No. 1263 .... **403**

Wall pocket, rounded form, relief-molded wavy horizontal lines, red over grey glaze, No. 1262, 6 1/2" h **575**

Iris (1938)
White or yellow blossoms and green leaves on rose blending with green, light blue deepening to a darker blue or tan shading to green or brown.

Basket, hanging-type, brown ground, 305-5", 8 1/2" h. (glaze flake to all three flowers) **259**

Iris Basket

Basket w/pointed overhead handle, compressed ball form, rose ground, No. 354-8", 8" h. (ILLUS.) **112**

Book ends, rose ground, No. 5, pr **425**

Bowl, 5" d., two-handled, footed, tan ground, No. 359-5" **165**

Console bowl, pink ground, No. 362-10", 10" l. **80**

Cornucopia-vase, blue ground, No. 132-8", 8" h. **90**

Ewer, bulbous body, cut-out rim, blue ground, No. 926-10", gold foil label, 10" h. **304**

Jardiniere, two-handled, tan ground, No. 647-4", 4" h **67**

Pedestal base, rose blending w/green ground, unmarked, 16" h **715**

Vase, 4" h., base handles, rose ground, No. 914-4" **99**

Vase, floor-type, 15" h., two large handles rising from shoulder to rim, pink ground, No. 929-15" **475**

Ixia (1930s)

Embossed spray of tiny bell-shaped flowers and slender leaves, white blossoms on pink ground, lavender blossoms on green or yellow ground.

Console bowl, pink ground, No. 331-9", unmarked, 9" l.. **80**
Jardiniere, green ground, No. 640-4", 4" h.......... **60**
Jardiniere, green ground, No. 640-6", 6" h.......... **80**

Jonquil (1931)

White jonquil blossoms and green leaves in relief against textured tan ground, green lining.

Basket, hanging-type, 7 1/4"............................. **345**
Console bowl, oval, No. 220-10", unmarked, black sticker, 10" l.. **225**

Jonquil Crocus Pot

Crocus pot, No. 93-4 1/2", 4 1/2" h. (ILLUS.)..... **413**

Jonquil Jardiniere

Jardiniere, No. 621-5", 5" h. (ILLUS.)................. **112**
Vase, 5 1/2" h., No. 542-5 1/2"............................ **150**
Vase, 6 1/2" h., wide bulbous body tapering to flat rim, C-form handles, No. 543-6 1/2" (ILLUS., top next column).................... **341**
Vase, 8" h., ovoid body tapering to short cylindrical neck, turned-down shoulder handles, No. 529-8".. **325**

Jonquil Vase

Vase, 10" h., compressed bulbous base tapering to wide tapering cylindrical neck w/flat rim, loop handles from midsection to rim, No. 530-10" **303**

Juvenile (1916 on)

Transfer-printed and painted on creamware with nursery rhyme characters, cute animals and other motifs appealing to children.

Juvenile Feeding Dishes

Feeding dish w/rolled edge, "Baby's Plate" around rim, four rabbits around interior, 7" d. (ILLUS. far left with feeding dishes)...... **195**
Feeding dish w/rolled edge, "Baby's Plate," nursery rhyme "Higgledy Piggledy..." stamped in red on rolled rim, "From G.A. Stower's Furniture Co.," unmarked, 7 1/2" d. (ILLUS. second from right with feeding dishes) **190**
Feeding dish w/rolled edge, nursery rhyme "Hickory, Dickory Dock," 8" d. **120**
Feeding dish w/rolled edge, nursery rhyme "Tom, The Piper's Son," 8" d. (slight wear to design).. **100**
Feeding dish w/rolled edge, three ducks, 8" d. (ILLUS. far right with feeding dishes) **238**

Juvenile Mugs & Pitchers

Mug, sitting puppy, 2 3/4" h. (ILLUS. far left)..... **213**
Mug, chicks, 3 1/2" h. (ILLUS. second from left) **149**

Pitcher, 3" h., rabbits (ILLUS. far right).............. **214**
Pitcher, 3 1/2" h., chicks (ILLUS. second from right) **233**

Plate, divided, 9 1/2" d., well worn dressed-up pig, duckling wearing high-top boots & hat & very worn kitten under an umbrella, chick & running rabbit wearing a jacket, stamped "Rv-9," color worn on border (ILLUS. second from left with feeding dishes) **168**

Magnolia (1943)

Large white blossoms with rose centers and black stems in relief against a blue, green or tan textured ground.

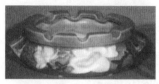

Magnolia Ashtray

Ashtray, two-handled, low bowl form, green ground, No. 28, 7" d., 2" h. (ILLUS.) **83**
Basket, hanging-type, green ground, No. 469-5" **144**
Basket w/ornate overhead handle, footed ovoid body w/long angled overhead handle, green ground, No. 384-8", 8" h. **173**
Bowl, 14" l., tan ground, No. 452-14" **70**
Jardiniere, two-handled, tan ground, No. 665-5", 5" h. **132**
Planter, shell-shaped, w/angular base handles, tan ground, No. 183-6", 6" l. **60**
Vase, 6" h., angular pointed handles from base to midsection, tan ground, No. 88-6" **75-150**
Vase, 9" h., green ground, No. 94-9" **110**

Magnolia Vase

Vase, 14" h., green ground, No. 97-14", repaired base chip (ILLUS.) **431**
Wall pocket, overhead handle w/pointed ends, green ground, No. 1294-8 1/2", 8 1/2" h. **225**

Ming Tree (1949)

High gloss glaze in mint green, turquoise, or white is decorated with Ming branch; handles are formed from gnarled branches.

Basket w/overhead branch handle, ruffled rim, blue ground, No. 509-12", 13" h. **150**

Candleholders, squat melon-ribbed body w/angular branch handles at shoulder, white, No. 551, pr. **50**
Console set: 10" l. bowl, No. 528-10" & pair of candleholders, No. 551; green ground, 3 pcs. **225**

Ming Tree Conch Shell

Model of a conch shell, white ground, No. 563-7, minor crazing, 8 1/2" w. (ILLUS.) **138**
Vase, 8" h., asymmetrical branch handles, blue ground, No. 582-8" **299**

Moderne (1930s)

Art Deco-style rounded and angular shapes trimmed with an embossed panel of vertical lines and modified swirls and circles, white trimmed with terra cotta, medium blue with white, and turquoise with a burnished antique gold.

Bowl, 7 x 11", 4" h., pleated body, white, No. 301-10" **259**
Bowl-vase, low foot, compressed ball form, blue ground, No. 299-6", 6 1/2" **173**
Candleholder, triple, turquoise ground, No. 1112-5 1/2", 5 1/2" h. (small nick in base under foot, not visible from side) **202**
Candleholder, triple, white, No. 1112-5 1/2", 6" h. **170**
Compote, 6" h., blue ground, No. 297-6" **440**
Vase, 6" h., a round foot tapering to a narrow short stem supporting a tall conical body, two small curved handles from foot to lower body, blue ground, No. 788-6" **345**
Vase, triple bud, 7" h., medium blue, No. 792-7" (ILLUS., below) **392**

Moderne Triple Bud Vase

Vase, bud, 8" h., cone-shaped on low foot, asymmetrical handles rising from base, turquoise, No. 791-8" **388**

Vase, 9 1/2" h., white ground, No. 799-9" (1/0 x 1" repair on inside edge of rim) **225**

Montacello (1931)
White stylized trumpet flowers with black accents on a terra cotta band, light terra cotta mottled in blue, or light green mottled and blended with blue backgrounds.

Basket, bulbous base w/wide neck & flaring rim, a long curved upright handle from shoulder to shoulder coming to a point above the neck, green ground, No. 333-6", 6" h. (handle repaired) **358**

Vase, 5 1/4" h., raised rim on an ovoid body w/two handles, decorated w/stylized fleur-de-lis design in cream within a brown band, dark blue ovals on a streaked light green & tan ground.................. **431**

Morning Glory (1935)
Delicately colored blossoms and twining vines in white or green with blue.

Basket, w/high pointed overhead handle, globular body, green ground, No. 340-10", restored handle, 10 1/2" h. **385**

Basket, w/high pointed overhead handle, globular body, white ground, No. 340-10", 10 1/2" h. **638**

Bowl, 4" d., squatty bulbous body w/tiny angled shoulder handles, green ground, No. 268-4" (restoration to nick at rim) **468**

Console bowl, small pointed end handles, white, 4 1/2 x 11 1/2".................................... **330**

Urn-vase, two-handled, green ground, No. 269-6, 6" h. (glaze nick to rim, light bubbling to glaze on one side)............................ **440**

Urn-vase, two-handled, white ground, No. 269-6, 6" h. **550**

Vase, 5" h., footed, flaring sides w/small angled handles at midsection, white ground, No. 723-5" **303**

Vase, 7" d., squatty bulbous body w/small angular handles at the shoulder, white ground **358**

Vase, 7" h., tapering sides, base handles, white ground.. **525**

Vase, 8" h., bulbous ovoid body w/flat mouth, angled shoulder handles, white ground, No. 727-8" (small chip & in-the-making bruise to base) **424**

Vase, 9" h., squatty bulbous ovoid body w/angled handles from midsection to rim, green ground, No. 729-9" (small chip to handle, three glaze nicks to rim).................... **523**

Vase, 12" h., footed flaring cylindrical body w/a wide closed rim flanked by small pointed loop handles, white ground, No. 731-12", ... **880**

Wall pocket, No. 1275-8", 8" h. (tight line to interior) **1,150**

Wall pocket, white ground, No. 1275-8", 8" h. (crack to handle & one corner, one small chip).. **460**

Moss (1930s)
Green moss hanging over brown branch with green leaves; backgrounds are pink, ivory or tan shading to blue.

Basket, hanging-type, blue ground, No. 353-5", unmarked (small abrasion to tip & next to handle) **230**

Bowl, 8" d., pink & green, No. 292-8"................. **170**

Vase, 8 1/2" h., flared foot, bulbous body w/wide flaring rim, tan & green, No. 779-8".. **358**

Moss Wall Pocket

Wall pocket, elongated side handles, flaring rim, blue ground, No. 1278-8", 8 1/2" h. (ILLUS.).. **660**

Wall pocket, bucket-shaped, pink ground, No. 1279-10", 10" h... **431**

Mostique (1915)
Indian designs of stylized flowers and arrowhead leaves, slip decorated on bisque, glazed interiors. Occasional bowl glazed on outside as well.

Basket, hanging-type, heart-shaped leaves & geometric designs, grey ground, No. 334-6", 6" h... **450**

Basket, hanging-type, heart-shaped leaves & geometric designs, tan ground, 8 1/4" h. (small burst bubbles & nicks to rim).. **403**

Bowl, 7 1/2" d., floral design, sandy beige ground, No. 73 .... **60**

Jardiniere, floral design, tan ground, 8" h........... **303**

Mostique Jardiniere

Jardiniere, bulbous form w/molded rim, tan ground w/stylized floral design, small chips to rim & enamel, 9" h. (ILLUS.)............. **397**

Jardiniere, grey ground, unmarked, 10" h. (minor chips to rim, chips to base).................. **330**

Mostique Vase

Vase, 10" h., slightly waisted cylinder w/flaring mouth, arrowhead designs, grey ground, No. 164-10" (ILLUS.)......................... **193**

Wall pocket, conical, pointed end, floral decoration on grey ground, No. 1224-12", 12" h. (chip to hole) **259**

Panel (Rosecraft Panel 1920)
Background colors are dark green or dark brown; decorations embossed within the recessed panels are of natural or stylized floral arrangements or female nudes.

Jar, cov., dark brown ground w/embossed dandelion decoration, No. 295-9, 9" h............ **523**

Vase, 6" h., fan-shaped body w/wide disc foot, brown ground w/nude decoration in orange on either side, unmarked (very minor glaze inconsistencies)........................... **551**

Pauleo (1914)
Prestige line of 222 color combinations and two glaze types, lustre or marbleized.

Lamp, tall ovoid body tapering to a short, wide cylindrical neck w/flared rim, semi-matte blue glaze, original electric lamp fittings, 19" h... **440**

Vase, 16" h., footed tall tapering cylindrical body w/wide cylindrical neck, brown, gold & orange glaze, ink mark **1,610**

Pauleo Vases

Vase, 16 1/2" h., pearl grey to orange lustre glaze w/yellow & red fruit w/pale green leaves decoration bordered by green bands around shoulder, impressed mark (ILLUS. left) **690**

Vase, 18 1/2" h., footed, bulbous base tapering to tall cylindrical neck w/flat rim, shaded red glaze, drilled (ILLUS. right)........ **403**

Vase, floor type, 19" h., footed baluster form w/narrow shoulder tapering to cylindrical neck w/slightly flaring rim, dark brown glaze (chip repair to base, drilled) **322**

Peony (1942)
Floral arrangement with green leaves on textured, shaded backgrounds in yellow with brown, pink with blue, and green.

Basket, fan-shaped w/high overhead handle, pink ground, No. 377-8", 8" h.................. **115**

Peony Book End & Jardiniere

Book ends, pink ground, No. 11, 5 1/2" h., pr. (ILLUS. of one)... **260**

Flower frog, gold ground, No. 47-4", 4" h. **40**

Jardiniere, green ground, No. 661-4", 4" h. (ILLUS. top w/book end) **58**

Jardiniere & pedestal base, gold ground, No. 661-8", 8" h., overall, 24 1/2" h., 2 pcs. (two hairlines & small firing fleck to rim, small chip to one leaf of jardiniere & couple of minute flecks to pedestal)............... **440**

Jardiniere & pedestal base, pink ground, No. 661-8", 8" h., 2 pcs. (shallow glaze scaling 1/2" to shoulder, probably from firing)... **715**

Vase, 7" h., pink ground, No 61-7".................... **145**

Wall pocket, two-handled, brown ground, No. 1293-8", 8" **259**

Wall pocket, two-handled, green ground, No. 1293-8", 8" **225**

Pine Cone (1931)
Realistic embossed brown pine cones and green pine needles on shaded blue, brown or green ground. (Pink is extremely rare.)

Ashtray, brown ground, No. 499, 4 1/2" l. . **200-225**

Book ends, blue ground, No. 1, pr. **288**

Bowl, 4" d., brown ground, bulbous w/incurved irregular rim, No. 441-4" **325**

Bowl, 6 1/2" d., 3 1/4" h., spherical footed form w/small twig handle, blue ground, No. 426-6".. **256**

Candleholders, flat disc base supporting candle nozzle in the form of a pine cone flanked by needles on one side & branch handle on the other, brown ground, No. 112-3", 3" h., pr. **240**

Candlestick, triple, brown ground, No. 1106-5 1/2", 5 1/2" h. **413**

Flowerpot & saucer, blue ground, No. 633-5", 5" h. **288**

Match holder, brown ground, No. 498, 3" h....... **112**

Pitcher w/ice lip, 8" h., footed wide spherical body w/curved rim & squared spout, brown ground, No. 1321.............................. **581**

Planter, boat-shaped, blue ground, No. 455-6", 6" l. **234**

Urn-vase, pedestal foot below a tall, slightly flaring cylindrical body w/two small twig handles, brown ground, No. 907-7", 7" h...... **114**

Urn-vase, pedestal foot below a tall slightly flaring cylindrical body w/two small twig handles, blue ground, No. 907-7", 7" h......... **230**

Vase, 8" h., wide bulbous body w/asymmetrical branch handles, blue ground, gold foil label, No. 114-8" (one handle repaired) **715**

Vase, 14" h., footed, two-handled baluster form w/wide cylindrical neck & slightly flared rim, blue ground, unmarked, No. 713-14" (professional repair to base chips).. **1,210**

Vase, 14" h., floor-type, footed tall ovoid form w/small angled twig handles at shoulder, brown ground, No. 850-14" **805**

Russco (1930s)

Octagonal rim openings, stacked handles, narrow perpendicular panel front and back. One type glaze is solid matte color; another is matte color with lustrous crystalline over glaze, some of which shows actual grown crystals.

Urn-vase, angular handles, orange, No. 108-6, 7" h. **225**

Vase, 8" h., green w/crystalline overglaze......... **193**

Vase, double bud, 8" h., No. 107-8" **200**

Vase, 8" h., rust ground, No. 696-8".................. **220**

Silhouette (1952)

Recessed area silhouettes nature study or female nudes. Colors are rose, turquoise, tan and white with turquoise.

Bowl, 6" d., white, No. 726-6" **70**

Bowl, 8" d., florals, tan ground, No. 727-8"......... **70**

Candleholders, florals, tan ground, No. 751-3", 3" h., pr. **50**

Cornucopia-vase, rose ground, No. 722-6", 6" h. **178**

Ewer, bulging base, florals, rose, No. 716-6", 6" h. **80**

Ewer, bulging base, florals, white, No. 716-6", 6" h. **105**

Jardiniere, footed, wide, nearly spherical body w/an incurved wide irregular rim, small pointed angular shoulder handles, female nudes, blue ground, No. 742-6",

6" h. (tight line to rim, small chip to base, spider lines to base).. **303**

Planter, rose ground, No. 768-8", 8" l. **200**

Rose bowl, female nudes, turquoise blue ground, No. 742-6", 6" h. (repair to base)...... **264**

Urn, four wing-shaped feet on disc base, reclining female nudes, white ground, No. 763-8", 8" h.. **358**

Vase, 5" h., florals, turquoise blue ground, No. 779-5".. **135**

Vase, 7" h., florals, double wing-shaped handles above low footed base, cylindrical w/asymmetrical rim, rose, No. 782-7"........ **78**

Vase, 7" h., fan-shaped, nude woman, rose ground, No. 783-7" (small rim chip professionally repaired)...................................... **383**

Vase, 8" h., urn-form tapering ovoid body raised on four angled feet on a round disc base, wide, slightly flaring mouth, female nude, rose ground, No. 763-8"...................... **374**

Vase, 8" h., rose ground, No. 784-8".................. **245**

Vase, 8" h., white ground, No. 784-8"................. **60**

Vase, 9" h., double, base w/canted sides supporting two square vases w/sloping rims, joined by a stylized branch-form center post, florals, rose ground, No. 757-9".. **245**

Vase, 10" h., small open handles between square base & waisted cylindrical body, shaped rim, female nudes, white ground, No. 787-10" **248**

Vase, 10" h., small open handles between square base & waisted cylindrical body, shaped rim, female nudes, rose ground, No. 787-10" (one corner of base professionally repaired).. **330**

Wall pocket, bullet-shaped w/angular pierced handles, florals, rose ground, No. 766-8", 8" h.. **431**

Snowberry (1946)

Brown branch with small white berries and green leaves embossed over spider-web design in various background colors (blue, green and rose).

Ashtray, round dished form, shaded green ground, 5 1/4" d. **80**

Basket, footed fan-shaped body w/wide looped & pointed handle, shaded green ground, No. 1BK-7", 7" h............................. **193**

Basket, w/asymmetrical overhead handle, shaded blue ground, No. 1BK-8", 8" h.......... **130**

Basket w/curved overhead handle, disc base, shaded green ground, No. 1BK-12", 12" h... **209**

Snowberry Low Bowl

Bowl, 6" d., two-handled, rose ground, small chip at corner of handle, light crazing, No. 1BL1-6" (ILLUS.)...................................... **144**

Sunflower Vases & Wall Pocket

Bowl, 10" d., footed, shaded green ground, No. 1FB-10" **182**

Console bowl, pointed end handles, shaded green ground, No. 1BL1-10", 10" l. **99**

Console bowl, shaded green ground, No. 1BL-8", 11" l. **88**

Cornucopia-vase, shaded green ground, No. 1CC-8", 8" h. **132**

Jardiniere & pedestal, shaded blue ground, No. 1J-8", 2 pcs. **1,350**

Jardiniere & pedestal base, shaded green ground, No. IJ-8", overall 25" h., 2 pcs. **750**

Pedestal base, rose ground, 16" h. **168**

Rose bowl, two-handled, shaded green, No. 1RB-5", 5" h. **165**

Tray, long leaf-shaped, shaded green ground, No. 1BL1-12", 14" l. **200**

Vase, 10" h., shaded green ground, No. 1V2-10" **231**

Vase, 15" h., floor-type, shaded rose ground, 1V1-15" **750**

Snowberry Wall Pocket

Wall pocket, wide half-round form tapering to a pointed base, low angled handles along the lower sides, shaded green ground, No. 1WP-8", 8" w., 5 1/2" h. (ILLUS.) **144**

Window box, shaded green ground, No. 1WX-8", 8" l. **289**

Sunflower (1930)
Tall stems support yellow sunflowers whose blooms form a repetitive band. Textured background shades from tan to dark green at base.

Basket, hanging-type, 6 3/4" (exterior spider lines & horizontal line to rim) **460**

Jardiniere, No. 619-4", 4" h. **616**

Jardiniere, No. 619-6", 6 1/4" h. **1,955**

Planter, wide tapering cylindrical body w/incurved rim, 5 x 6 1/4" **1,265**

Vase, 5" h., No. 486-5", unmarked (ILLUS. second from right, top of page) **560**

Vase, 6" h., swelled cylindrical body w/short cylindrical neck flanked by small loop handles, No. 485-6" (ILLUS. far right, top of page) **669**

Vase, 8" h., two-handled, ovoid, w/flaring rim, No. 491-8" **1,460**

Vase, 9" h., bulbous base w/wide cylindrical neck, small loop handles, No. 493-9" (ILLUS. second from left, top of page) **1,161**

Wall pocket, No. 1265-7", minute glaze nick to front of pierced back brace, glazed over chip to back corner, 7" h. (ILLUS. far left, top of page) **1,427**

Teasel (1936)
Embossed decorations of long stems gracefully curving with delicate spider-like pods. Colors and glaze treatments vary from monochrome matte to crystalline. Colors are beige to tan, medium blue highlighted with gold, pale blue, and deep rose (possibly others).

Jardiniere, footed squatty bulbous body w/a wide cylindrical neck, small angled shoulder handles, rust ground w/green flowers, No. 644-4", 4" h. (small glaze flake off one handle) **83**

Vase, 9" h., closed handles at base, flaring mouth, deep rose, No. 886-9" **110**

Thorn Apple (1930s)
White trumpet flower with leaves reverses to thorny pod with leaves. Colors are shaded blue, brown and pink.

Basket, hanging-type, shaded blue ground, No. 355-5", 7" d., 5" h. **288**

Book ends, shaded blue ground, No. 3, pr........ **140**

Thorn Apple Centerpiece

Centerpiece, shaded blue ground, No. 313-11", 11" l. (ILLUS.) **134**

Jardiniere, shaded brown ground, No. 638-
4", 4" h. **100**
Urn, stepped handles, disc foot, shaded
brown ground, No. 304-4" **80**
Urn, stepped handles, disc foot, shaded
blue ground, No. 305-6", 6" h. **160**
Vase, 4" h., jug form, shaded pink ground,
No. 808-4" **138**
Vase, bud, 7" h., shaded pink ground, No.
813-7" **145**
Vase, 10 1/2" h., angular handles rising
from shoulder to middle of wide neck,
footed, shaded brown ground, No. 822-
10" **138**
Vase, 10 1/2" h., angular handles rising
from shoulder to middle of wide neck,
footed, shaded pink ground, No. 822-10" **225**
Wall pocket, brown ground, No. 356-4",
4" h. (minute nick to back of hole) **978**
Wall pocket, triple, shaded brown ground,
No. 1280-8", 8" h. (small stilt pull chips) **500**

Topeo (1934)
*Simple forms decorated with four vertical evenly
spaced cascades of leaves in high relief at their origin,
tapering downward to a point. A light green crystalline
glaze shades to a mottled medium blue, with cascades in
alternating green and pink. A second type is done completely in a high-gloss dark red.*

Vase, 6 1/2" h., ovoid, w/flaring mouth,
shaded blue glaze, No. 656-6" **201**
Vase, 7" h., compressed globular base &
flaring mouth, green crystalline glaze
shading to blue, No. 658-7 1/4" **403**
Vase, 8" h., blue ground, No. 659-8" **633**
Vase, 8 1/4" h., footed ovoid body w/short
flaring rim, shaded blue ground, No. 660-
8 1/4" **500**
Vase, 12 1/4" h., ovoid tapering sides,
green crystalline glaze shading to blue,
No. 664-12 1/4" **863**

Tuscany (1927)
*Marble-like finish most often found in a shiny pink,
sometimes in matte grey, more rarely in a dull turquoise.
Suggestion of leaves and berries, usually at the base of
handles, are the only decorations.*

Console bowl, rectangular w/rounded ends,
mottled pink, unmarked, 11" l. **225**
Console bowl, rectangular w/rounded ends,
No. 174-12", 12" l. **250**
Flower frog, mottled pink, small **65**
Urn-vase, mottled pink, 4" h. **200**
Vase, 5" h., 7" d., mottled turquoise, No. 70-
5" **88**
Vase, 5" h., 7" d., mottled pink, No. 70-5" **130**
Vase, 5 1/2" h., fan-shaped, mottled pink
ground **95**

Tuscany Vase

Vase, 7" h., tri-shaped, two-handled, grey,
w/original sticker, No. 343-7" (ILLUS.) **202**
Vase, 8" h., mottled pink ground, No. 344-8" **275**
Vase, 10" h., shoulder handles, bulbous
body, mottled pink ground, No. 347-10" **395**
Wall pocket, long open handles, rounded
rim, grey glaze, No. 1255-8", 8" h. **288**

Velmoss (1935)
*Characterized by three horizontal wavy lines around
the top from which long, blade-like leaves extend downward. Colors are green, blue, tan and pink.*

Jardiniere, footed spherical body w/short
wide neck & pointed shoulder handles,
mottled blue glaze, No. 264-5", 5" h. **207**
Urn-vase, angular pointed side handles,
mottled pink, No. 265-6", 6" h. **132**

Velmoss Vase

Vase, 6" h., swelled cylindrical body
w/pointed shoulder handles, mottled
raspberry red glaze, No. 714-6", gold foil
label (ILLUS.) **255**
Vase, 6" h., swelled cylindrical body
w/pointed shoulder handles, mottled tan
& green crystalline glaze, No. 714-6",
gold foil label **358**
Vase, 14 1/2" h., tall trumpet-form body
w/low foot, angular pointed handles, mot-
tled rose glaze, No. 722-14" **616**
Wall pocket, double, mottled green crystal-
line glaze, No. 1274-8", 8 1/2" h. **3,190**

Water Lily (1940s)
*Water lily and pad in various color combinations: tan
to brown with yellow lily, blue with white lily, pink to
green with pink lily.*

Basket, hanging-type, shaded blue ground,
No. 468-5", 9" h. **110**
Basket, w/asymmetrical overhead handle,
curved & sharply scalloped rim, shaded
blue ground, No. 382-12", 12" h. **160**
Basket w/pointed asymmetrical overhead
handle & pleated rim, pink shading to
green ground, No. 381-10", 10" h. **100**
Basket w/pointed overhead handle, cylindri-
cal, w/flaring rim, shaded blue ground,
No. 380-8", 8" h. **140**

Ewer, flared bottom, blended blue ground,
No. 10-6", 6" h... **70**
Flower holder, two-handled, fan-shaped
body, gold shading to brown ground, No.
48, 4 1/2" h. **90**

Water Lily Flowerpot

Flowerpot w/saucer, gold shading to brown
ground, No. 664-5, clay fold on inner rim
of pot, 5" h. (ILLUS.)...................................... **101**
Jardiniere & pedestal base, blended blue
ground, overall 24" h., 2 pcs. **448**
Vase, 9" h., footed bulbous ovoid body w/a
large trumpet neck flanked by angled
handles, gold shading to brown ground,
No. 79-9"... **160**
Vase, 9" h., footed bulbous ovoid body w/a
large trumpet neck flanked by angled
handles, pink shaded to green ground,
No. 79-9".. **207**
Vase, 18" h., floor-type, tall baluster-form
w/pointed shoulder handles, gold shad-
ing to brown ground, No. 85-18" **425**

White Rose (1940s)
*White roses and green leaves against a vertically
combed ground of blended blue, brown shading to
green, or pink shading to green.*

Basket, hanging-type, pink shading to green
ground, No. 463-5", 5" h................................ **325**
Basket w/pointed circular handle, pink shad-
ing to green ground, No. 363-10", 10" h. **303**
Cornucopia-vase, brown shading to green
ground, No. 144-8", 8" h. **190**
Jardiniere & pedestal base, blended blue
ground, No. 653-8", 8" h., 2 pcs.................... **770**
Tea set: cov. teapot, sugar bowl & creamer;
brown shading to green ground, Nos. 1T,
1S, 1C, 3 pcs... **385**
Urn-vase, handles rising from base to rim,
footed, pink shading to green ground,
No. 146-6", 6" h... **150**
Vase, double bud, 4 1/2" h., two cylinders
joined by an arched bridge, brown shad-
ing to green ground, No. 148......................... **160**
Vase, 5" h., footed trumpet-form body
w/notched rim & asymmetrical base loop
handles, brown shading to green ground,
No. 980-6"... **120**
Vase, 7" h., pink shading to green ground,
No. 983-7".. **165**
Vase, 8" h., flattened ovoid body on a rect-
angular foot, small pointed shoulder handles, blended blue ground, No. 984-8"......... **265**

Vase, 9" h., footed, wide tapering cylindrical
body w/large handles from foot to shoulder, notched rim, pink shading to green
ground, No. 986-9".. **300**
Wall pocket, swirled handle, flaring rim, pink
shading to blue ground, No. 1288-6",
6 1/2" h... **345**
Wall pocket, conical w/flaring rim w/over-
head handle continuing to one side, pink
shading to green ground, No. 1289-8",
8 1/2" h... **345**

Wincraft (1948)
*Revived shapes from older lines such as Pine Cone,
Bushberry, Cremona, Primrose and others. Vases with
animal motifs, contemporary shapes in high gloss of
blue, tan, lime and green.*

Ashtray, glossy turquoise blue ground, No.
240-T **60**
Bowl, 8" d., glossy blue ground, No.
226-8".. **132**
Cigarette box, cov., rectangular, glossy
chartreuse, No. 240, 4 1/2" l........................... **165**
Coffeepot, cov., glossy tan, No. 250-P,
9 1/2" h... **140**
Console bowl, brown ground, No. 233-14",
14" l. (small glaze chip to interior, col-
ored-in chip to both rim & base)..................... **173**
Planter, blue, No. 256-5", 5" h........................ **80**
Vase, 6" h., blue ground, No. 241-6"................. **154**
Vase, 8" h., flowing lily form w/asymmetrical
side handles, tulip & foliage in relief on
shaded blue ground, No. 282-8" **121**

Wincraft Vase

Vase, 10" h., cylindrical, tab handles, black
panther & green palm trees in relief on
glossy shaded tan ground, 1/4" dark line
at rim, No. 290-10" (ILLUS.)........................... **550**

Wisteria (1933)
*Lavender wisteria blossoms and green vines against
a roughly textured brown shading to deep blue ground,
rarely found in only brown.*

Basket, hanging-type, brown ground,
7 1/2" h.. **633**
Urn, blue ground, No. 632-5", 5" h. **683**

Wisteria Urn

Urn, bulbous body w/wide flat mouth, small
  loop shoulder handles, brown ground,
  6" h. (ILLUS.)... **518**
Vase, 6" h., ovoid body tapering to short cy-
  lindrical neck flanked by small loop han-
  dles, brown ground, No. 631-6"...................... **480**
Vase, 6 1/2" h., globular, w/angular rim han-
  dles, blue ground, No. 637-6 1/2" **650**
Vase, 6 1/2" h., globular, w/angular rim han-
  dles, brown ground, No. 637-6 1/2".............. **768**

Zephyr Lily (1946)

*Tall lilies and slender leaves adorn swirl-textured
backgrounds of Bermuda Blue, Evergreen and Sienna
Tan.*

Basket, hanging-type, green ground, No.
  472-5", 7 1/2" w.. **188**

Zephyr Lily Candlesticks

Candlesticks, blue ground, No. 1163-4 1/2",
  pr. (ILLUS.) **225**
Console bowl, low oblong form w/curved
  end tab handles, blue ground, No. 474-
  8", 8" l... **110**
Cornucopia-vase, terra cotta ground, No.
  203-6", 6" h. **135**
Ewer, blue ground, No. 22-6", 6" h. **120**
Ewer, footed flaring lower body w/angled
  shoulder tapering to a tall forked neck
  w/upright tall spout, long low arched handle, green ground, No. 23-10", 10" h............. **135**
Rose bowl, terra cotta ground, No. 471-6",
  6" h.. **180**
Vase, 6" h., two-handled, terra cotta, No.
  130-6" **165**

Royal Bayreuth

*Good china in numerous patterns and designs has
been made at the Royal Bayreuth factory in Tettau, Germany since 1794. Listings below are by the company's
lines, plus miscellaneous pieces. Interest in this china*
*remains at a peak and prices continue to rise. Pieces
listed carry the company's blue mark except where noted
otherwise.*

  *Among the important reference books in this field are
Royal Bayreuth - A Collectors' Guide and Royal
Bayreuth - A Collectors' Guide - Book II by Mary
McCaslin (see Special Contributors list).*

Royal Bayreuth Mark

Corinthian

Cake plate, classical figures on black
  ground, 10" d... **$150**
Cake plate, classical figures on black
  ground, 10" d... **150**
Creamer, classical figures on green ground **50**
Creamer & cov. sugar bowl, classical fig-
  ures on black ground, pr. **120**
Pitcher, milk, classical figures on green
  ground **125**

Corinthian Pitcher

Pitcher, tankard, 6 7/8" h., 3 3/4" d., orange
  inside top, classical figures on black satin
  ground, gold bands w/black & white geometric design around neck & base
  (ILLUS.).. **150**
Planter, classical figures on red ground............. **120**
Toothpick holder, classical figures on black
  ground, 2 1/4" h. **175-200**

Devil & Cards

Ashtray **125-150**
Ashtray, two cards... **275-300**
Ashtray w/match holder **250-275**
Candleholder **550**

Creamer, figural red devil, 3 1/2" h. **300-350**
Creamer, 3 3/4" h. **250-325**
Creamer, figural red devil, 4 1/2" h. **375-475**
Match holder, hanging-type, 4" w., 5" h. **500-600**
Mug, 4 3/4" h. **400-500**
Mug, w/blue rim. **395**
Pitcher, milk, 5" h. **450-600**

Devil & Cards Pitcher

Pitcher, water, 7 1/4" h. (ILLUS.). **600-700**
Plate, 6" d. **400-500**
Salt dip, master size **275-325**
Salt shaker **150-175**
Stamp box, cov., 3 1/2" l. **550-600**
Sugar bowl, cov. **350-400**
Sugar bowl, open, short. **300-350**

Mother-of-Pearl
Ashtray, Murex Shell patt. **75-100**
Basket, reticulated rim, ornate handle, rose
  decoration, 3 3/4 x 4" oval, 4 1/4" h. **150**
Bowl, 3 1/2" octagonal, white w/green high-
  lights, pearlized finish. **65**
Bowl, 5 1/2" d., grape cluster mold, pearl-
  ized white finish. **150**
Bowl, 6 1/2 x 9", oak leaf-shaped, footed,
  pearlized finish w/gold trim. **850**
Bowl, 10" oval, handled, figural poppy mold,
  apricot satin finish. **600**
Cake plate, decorated w/roses, 10 1/2" d. **125**
Compote, open, 4 1/2" d., 4 1/2" h., reticu-
  lated bowl & base, decorated w/delicate
  roses, pearlized finish **140**
Compote, open, decorated w/roses, pearl-
  ized finish, small. **50**
Creamer, grape cluster mold, pearlized
  white, 3 3/4" h. **150-175**
Creamer, Murex Shell patt., white pearlized
  finish, 4 1/2" h. **150-200**
Creamer, boot-shaped, figural Spiky Shell
  patt., 4 3/4" h. **250-275**
Creamer, Murex Shell patt., spiky form........ **75-100**
Creamer & cov. sugar bowl, grape cluster
  mold, pearlized yellow, colorful foliage,
  pr. **300-375**
Cup & saucer, demitasse, footed, figural
  Spiky Shell patt., pearlized finish **125-150**
Cup & saucer, demitasse, Oyster & Pearl
  mold **300-350**
Dish, cov., Murex Shell patt., large **175**
Hatpin holder, figural poppy mold, pearlized
  white finish. **550-600**
Hatpin holder, white pearlized finish........... **150-175**
Humidor, cov., Murex Shell patt. **850**

Mustard jar, cov., Murex Shell patt., white
  pearlized finish, 3 1/2" h. **200-250**
Nappy, grape cluster mold, pearlized white
  finish, 6" x 7". **175**
Nappy, handled, figural poppy mold, pearl-
  ized satin finish **150-250**
Pitcher, milk, boot-shaped, figural Spiky
  Shell patt., pearlized finish, 5 1/2" h. **325-375**
Sugar bowl, cov., footed, figural Spiky Shell
  patt., pearlized finish, 3 1/2" h. **250-300**
Toothpick holder, Murex Shell patt. **110-125**
Toothpick holder, Murex Shell patt., pearl-
  ized finish. **150-175**
Wall pocket, figural grape cluster, pearlized
  finish, 9" h. **400-600**

Old Ivory
Basket, 3" h., 7 3/4" l. **200-250**
Bowl, 4 x 6". **200-250**
Pitcher, water, 9" h. **800-1,000**
Toothpick holder **375-425**

Rose Tapestry

Rose Tapestry Basket

Basket, rope handle, base & outer rim, three
  color roses, 4 1/4" w., 4" h. (ILLUS.) **250-350**
Basket, two-color roses, 3" h. **300-350**
Basket, two-color roses, 4 1/4" w., 3 3/4" h. **450**
Basket, miniature, rope handle, tiny pink
  roses frame the rim, small bouquet of yellow roses on each side & yellow roses on
  the interior, shadow green leaves,
  2 1/2 x 4 1/4 x 4 1/2". **325**
Basket, three-color roses, 4 3/4 x 5 1/4". **425**
Basket, miniature, two color roses on yellow
  ground, braided decoration around rim. **375**
Bell, pink American Beauty roses, 3" h. **450-550**
Bell, gold loop handle, three-color roses,
  3 1/4" h. **400**

Rose Tapestry Bowl

Bowl, 10 1/2" d., gently scalloped rim w/four shell-molded gilt-trimmed handles, three-color roses (ILLUS.) **900-1,100**

Bowl, 10 1/2" d., shell- & scroll-molded rim, three-color roses.................................... **950-1,050**

Box, cov., pink & white roses, 2 1/2" sq. **175**

Box, cov., two-color roses, 1 1/2 x 2 1/2"............ **165**

Box, cov., three-color roses, 2 1/2 x 4 1/2", 1 3/4" h. **295**

Box, w/domed cover, three-color roses, 4 1/2" d., 2 3/4" h. **400**

Box, cov., shell-shaped, 3 x 5 1/2"...................... **375**

Cake plate, three-color roses, freeform fancy rim w/gold beading, 9 1/2" w. **425**

Cake plate, pierced gold handles, three-color roses, 10 1/2" d. **500-600**

Candy dish, three-color roses, 8" oval **350**

Chamberstick, a shaped & flattened base centered by a waisted cylindrical short standard supporting the dished socket w/three rim points, an ornate C-scroll handle down the side, three-color roses, 4 1/4" h. **850-950**

Rose Tapestry Chocolate Pot

Chocolate pot, cov., apricot, white, pink & yellow roses, leaf finial, gold trim, 8 1/2" h. (ILLUS.) **1,800-2,000**

Chocolate set: cov. chocolate pot w/four matching cups & saucers, three-color roses. **2,200-2,600**

Clock, table-model, three-color roses, upright rectangular case w/a flaring base & domed top... **1,000**

Creamer, wide cylindrical body slightly flaring at the base & w/a long buttress spout & gilt angled handle, two-color roses on a rose ground, 3" h. **385**

Creamer, ovoid body w/flared base & long pinched spout, three-color roses, 3 1/2" h. **175-200**

Creamer, corset-shaped, three-color roses, 3 3/4" h. **250-300**

Creamer, two-color roses, 3 1/2" d., 4" h.......... **375**

Creamer, pinched spout, two-color roses **355**

Creamer & cov. sugar bowl, pink & white roses, pr. **550-650**

Creamer & cov. sugar bowl, two-color roses, pr. **500-550**

Cups & saucers, demitasse, three-color roses, 2 sets, each set.................................... **150**

Dessert set: large cake plate & six matching small serving plates; three-color roses, 7 pcs... **1,000-1,200**

Dish, three-color roses, 2" w., 4 1/2" l, 1 1/2" h. **195**

Dish, handled, clover-shaped, decorated w/yellow roses, 5" w... **225**

Dish, leaf-shaped, three-color roses, 5" l. .. **225-250**

Dresser box, cov., kidney-shaped, double pink roses, 2 x 5 1/4" **375-400**

Flowerpot & underplate, three-color roses, 3 x 4", 2 pcs.. **295**

Rose Tapestry Hair Receiver

Hair receiver, cov., footed, two-color roses, 4" d., 2 1/2" h. (ILLUS.)................................... **375**

Rose Tapestry Hatpin Holder

Hatpin holder, small red roses at top & base, large yellow roses on body, reticulated base, gold trim, 4 1/2" h. (ILLUS.).. **450-500**

Hatpin holder, two-color roses, scroll-molded reticulated gilt-trimmed foot below the baluster-form body w/a flaring gilt-trimmed rim, 4 1/2" h. **550-650**

Rose Tapestry Humidor

Humidor, cov., three-color roses, 7" h.
(ILLUS.)... **600-650**

Match holder, hanging-type, three-color
roses **460**

Match holder, wall hanging-type, a bulbous
rounded pouch w/a wide arched back-
plate w/hanging hole, white & pink roses **375**

Model of a high-top woman's shoe, pink
roses w/a band of green leaves around
top, 3 1/2" h. **500-700**

Model of a shoe, decorated w/pink roses &
original shoe lace..................................... **450-475**

Model of a Victorian woman's high-heeled
shoe, three-color roses **400-450**

Nappy, tri-lobed leaf shape, decorated w/or-
ange roses, 4 1/2" l. **150-200**

Nappy, open-handled, three-color roses,
5" d... **225**

Nut set: master footed bowl & six small footed bowls; decorated w/pink roses, 7 pcs.. **1,250-
1,275**

Pitcher, 5" h., wide cylindrical body tapering
slightly toward rim, three-color roses, 24
oz.. **350-400**

Rose Tapestry Pitcher

Pitcher, 5 3/4" h., waisted shape, C-scroll
handle angled at bottom, three-color
roses (ILLUS.)... **350-500**

Rose Tapestry Planter

Planter, squatty bulbous base below wide,
gently flaring sides w/a ruffled rim, small
loop handles near the base, three-color
roses, 2 3/4" h. (ILLUS.)................................. **280**

Plate, 6" d. **200-250**

Plate, 7" d., three-color roses **275**

Plate, 7 1/2" d., round, w/slightly scalloped
rim & four sections of fanned ruffles
spaced around the edge, three-color
roses **300-400**

Plate, 10 1/2" d., overall colorful roses
w/four gilded scrolls around the rims **175-200**

Powder box, cov., footed, three-color roses,
4" d., 2 1/2" h.. **350-450**

Powder jar, cov., footed squatty rounded
base w/a squatty domed cover, three-
color roses, 3" d., 2 1/2" h...................... **425-525**

Relish dish, open-handled, three-color
roses, 4 x 8"... **300-350**

Relish dish, oblong, w/gilt-trimmed scalloped rim, decorated w/large pink roses,
4 3/4" w., 8" l. **325-375**

Salt dip, ruffled rim, 3" d. **280**

Salt & pepper shakers, three-color roses, pr....... **495**

Salt shaker, pink roses **250**

Sugar bowl, cov., two-handled, one-color
rose, 3 1/2" d., 3 1/4" h.................................. **350**

Rose Tapestry Tray

Tray, rectangular, with short rim, three-color
roses, 11 1/2 x 8" (ILLUS.)..................... **500-600**

Vase, 4 1/4" h., footed swelled base taper-
ing to cylindrical sides, two-color roses **345**

Vase, 4 1/2" h., decorated w/American
Beauty roses **375**

Rose Tapestry Vase

Vase, 4 1/2" h., ovoid body decorated
w/clusters of small red roses at top &
base, large yellow roses in center, short
neck flaring slightly at rim (ILLUS.)......... **200-300**

Vase, 4 3/4" h., slightly swelled slender cylindrical body w/a short rolled neck,
three-color roses in pink, yellow & white **288**

Vase, 6 1/2" h., decorated w/roses & shad-
ow ferns.. **350-425**

Vase, 7" h., bulbous ovoid body tapering to
a short tiny flared neck **300-375**

Wall plaque, pierced to hang, large pink
roses.. **575**

Wall pocket, three-color roses, 5 x 9" **1,300**

Sand Babies

Trivet **125-150**

Snow Babies

Creamer	**150-175**
Pitcher, 3 1/2" h.	**125**
Salt shaker	**120**
Tea tile	**145**
Trivet	**150**

Sunbonnet Babies

Ashtray, babies cleaning	**250-275**
Bell, babies sewing, unmarked	**400-450**
Candlestick, babies washing, 5" d., 1 3/4" h.	**275-300**
Creamer, babies ironing, 3" h.	**250-300**
Creamer & open sugar bowl, babies sewing, pr.	**475**
Creamer & open sugar bowl, boat-shaped, babies fishing on sugar, babies cleaning on creamer, pr.	**500**
Cup & saucer, babies washing	**250-350**
Dish, diamond-shaped	**200**
Dish, heart-shaped	**200**
Mug, babies washing	**350**
Pitcher, milk, 4 1/4" h., babies washing	**325**

Sunbonnet Babies Plate

Plate, 6" d., babies washing (ILLUS.)	**250-325**
Saucer, babies fishing	**75**
Tea set, child's	**750-900**
Toothpick holder, babies mending	**450-550**
Vase, 3" h., babies fishing	**235**

Tomato Items

Tomato bowl, berry	**50**
Tomato bowls, 5 3/4" d., set of 4	**145**
Tomato box, cov., w/green & brown finial, 3" d.	**45**
Tomato creamer, cov., large	**150-200**
Tomato creamer, cov., small	**45-50**

Tomato Creamer & Sugar Bowl

Tomato creamer & cov. sugar bowl, creamer 3" d., 3" h., sugar bowl 3 1/2" d., 4" h., pr. (ILLUS.)	**125**
Tomato cup & saucer, demitasse	**125**
Tomato mustard jar, cover & figural leaf spoon, 3 pcs.	**125**
Tomato pitcher, milk, 4 1/2" h.	**250-350**

Tomato plate, 4 1/4" d., ring-handled, figural lettuce leaf	**19**
Tomato plate, 5 1/2" d., ring-handled, figural lettuce leaf w/molded yellow flowers	**30-35**
Tomato plate, 7" d., ring-handled, figural lettuce leaf w/molded yellow flowers	**40**
Tomato salt & pepper shakers, pr.	**125-150**
Tomato tea set: cov. teapot, creamer & cov. sugar bowl; 3 pcs.	**325**
Tomato teapot, cov., small	**350**

Miscellaneous

Ashtray, figural elk	**250-275**
Ashtray, figural lobster	**125-150**
Ashtray, figural, oyster & pearl design, 4" l.	**275-325**
Ashtray, figural shell, 4 1/2 x 4 1/2"	**50-75**
Ashtray, mountain goat decoration, 5 1/2" l.	**350-450**
Ashtray, scenic decoration of Dutch woman w/basket, 5 1/2" d.	**50-75**
Ashtray, stork decoration, artist-signed, 4 1/2" l.	**75-100**
Ashtray, stork decoration on yellow ground, 3 1/4 x 5", 1 1/4" h.	**125**
Basket, miniature, scene w/cows, unmarked	**70**
Basket, "tapestry," footed, bulbous body w/a ruffled rim & ornate gold-trimmed overhead handle, portrait of woman w/horse, 5" h.	**550-600**
Basket, handled, boy & donkey decoration, artist-signed, 5 3/4" h.	**150-175**
Basket, w/reticulated handles, decorated w/white roses, 7 3/4" l., 3 1/2" h.	**125**
Bell, nursery rhyme decoration w/Jack & the Beanstalk	**400-450**
Bell, nursery rhyme decoration w/Little Bo Peep	**350-400**
Bell, scene of musicians, men playing a cello & mandolin	**300-350**
Bell, w/original wooden clapper, decorated w/scene of ocean liner being brought into harbor by tugboats	**275**
Bell, peacock decoration, 2 1/2" d., 3" h.	**300**
Berry set: 9 3/4" d. bowl & four 5" d. sauce dishes; decorated w/musicians scene, 5 pcs.	**350-450**
Berry set: 9 1/2" d. bowl & six 5" d. sauce dishes; portrait decoration, 7 pcs.	**650-750**

Royal Bayreuth Bowl

Bowl, 9 1/2" l., 3 3/4" h., raised enameled white roses & foliage on creamy ivory ground, flared, gently ruffled rim, four gold-trimmed reticulated reserves, four short gold feet (ILLUS.)	**225-350**
Bowl, 5 3/4" d., nursery rhyme scene w/Jack & Jill	**125-175**
Bowl, 6" d., figural conch shell	**75**
Bowl, 6 7/8" d., 2 1/2" h., footed, shallow slightly scalloped sides, Cavalier Musicians decoration, gold trim on feet	**100-125**

Bowl, 8" l., 4" h., figural lobster........................... **250**
Bowl, 6 1/4 x 8 1/2", shell-shaped.............. **400-450**
Bowl, 9 1/2" d., figural poppy **135**
Bowl, 10" d., decorated w/gold roses........ **150-200**
Bowl, 10" d., decorated w/pink roses........ **125-150**
Bowl, 5 x 10", footed, handled, figural pop-
   py, apricot satin finish **700**
Bowl, 10 1/2" d., floral decoration, blown-
   out mold.. **250-300**
Bowl, 10 1/2" d., "tapestry," decorated
   w/Colonial scene............................... **1,100-1,300**
Box, cov., four-footed ring base, scenic dec-
   oration of Dutch children **125**
Box, cov., shell-shaped, nursery rhyme
   scene, Little Boy Blue decoration.................. **225**
Box, cov., square, desert scene decoration
   on cover, Arabs w/camels on background colors of pink & brown, un-
   marked, 2 x 2 1/2", 1 3/4" h.............................. **65**

Royal Bayreuth Heart-shaped Box

Box, cov., heart-shaped, decorated w/scene
   of two brown & white cows & trees in pasture, green & yellow background, unmarked, 2 x 3 1/4", 1 1/2" h. (ILLUS.)...... **75-100**
Box, cov., scene of woman on horse, wom-
   an & man w/rake watching, 4 1/4" d.,
   2 1/4" h. **200-225**
Box, cov., figural turtle, 2 3/4 x 5" **1,500**
Box, cov., shell-shaped, Little Jack Horner
   decoration, 5 1/2" d. **250**
Cake plate, decorated w/scene of men fish-
   ing.. **175-225**
Candleholder, figural rose **550-650**
Candleholder, figural, Santa, very rare
   (ILLUS., top next column) **8,000-10,000**
Candleholder, penguin decoration..................... **335**
Candlestick, figural bassett hound, brown,
   4" h.. **500-550**
Candlestick, decorated w/scene of cows,
   4" h.. **75-100**
Candlestick, elks scene, 4" h............................. **145**
Candlestick, decorated w/frog & bee,
   6 1/2" h. **475-525**
Candlestick, figural clown, red,
   4 1/2 x 6 1/2" **575**

Royal Bayreuth Santa Candleholder

Candlestick, w/match holder, figural clown,
   7" h.. **1,300**
Candlestick, oblong dished base w/a stan-
   dard at one edge flanked by downswept
   open handles, tulip-form socket w/flat-
   tened rim, interior of dished base decorated w/scene of hunter & dogs **275-325**
Candy dish, figural lobster **125**
Candy dish w/turned over edge, nursery
   rhyme scene w/Little Miss Muffet................... **125**
Celery dish, figural lobster **150**
Chamberstick, wide, deeply dished, round
   pinched sides, central cylindrical socket
   w/flattened rim, S-scroll handle from side
   of dish to socket, dark brick red ground,
   decorated w/"Dancing Frogs" & flying in-
   sects, rare **1,200-1,500**
Cheese dish, miniature, scenic
   decoration.. **400-500**

Royal Bayreuth Cheese Dishes

Cheese dishes, miniature, decorated
   w/scenes of cattle, each (ILLUS. of
   two)... **450-500**

Royal Bayreuth Child's Tea Set

Child's tea set: cov. teapot, cov. sugar, creamer, two plates, & two cups & saucers; decorated w/scene of children playing, the set (ILLUS., bottom of previous page).. **700-800**

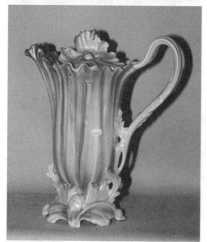

Poppy Pattern Chocolate Pot

Chocolate pot, cov., figural poppy, tall pink blossom w/ruffled rim, figural poppy on cover, light green & white leafy footed base & large leaf & stem handle, 8 1/2" h. (ILLUS.)... **1,400-2,000**
Cracker jar, cov., figural lobster............................ **600**
Cracker jar, cov., figural poppy, 6" h. **800-1,000**
Creamer, Arab scene decoration **95**
Creamer, Brittany Girl decoration......................... **75**
Creamer, cobalt blue, Babes in Woods decoration (unmarked).. **250**
Creamer, decorated w/a colorful Highland cattle scene, gold handle, 4 1/2" h................. **248**
Creamer, decorated w/man in fishing boat scene **145**
Creamer, figural alligator, 4 1/2 " h. **350-400**
Creamer, figural apple **150-225**
Creamer, figural apple, all-green................. **200-250**
Creamer, figural bear, 4 1/4" h. **800-900**
Creamer, figural Bird of Paradise, 3 3/4" h. **450-500**
Creamer, figural black cat **200-300**
Creamer, figural bull, brown........................ **275-325**
Creamer, figural bull, grey........................... **250-325**
Creamer, figural bull head, 4" h................... **175-225**
Creamer, figural butterfly, open wings **350-450**
Creamer, figural cat handle, 4" h. **400-450**
Creamer, figural chimpanzee, 4" h............. **400-450**
Creamer, figural clown, orange outfit, 3 5/8" h. (minor enamel flakes) **375-425**
Creamer, figural clown, red suit.................. **400-450**
Creamer, figural coachman, 4 1/4" h......... **275-300**
Creamer, figural cockatoo, 4" h.................. **400-500**
Creamer, figural crow, black, 4 1/2" h. **150-200**
Creamer, figural crow, black & white.......... **150-200**
Creamer, figural crow, brown beak **150-200**
Creamer, figural crow, brown bill & eyes (rare).. **250**
Creamer, figural dachshund **300-400**
Creamer, figural duck.................................. **250-300**

Eagle Creamer

Creamer, figural eagle, grey (ILLUS.)......... **300-400**
Creamer, figural fish head, grey.......................... **250**
Creamer, figural flounder, 4 1/4" h. **600-800**
Creamer, figural frog.................................... **160-175**
Creamer, figural geranium, 4" h. **450-550**
Creamer, figural girl w/basket, 4 1/4" h....... **550-650**
Creamer, figural girl w/pitcher, red **800-900**
Creamer, figural grape cluster, light green.. **125**
Creamer, figural grape cluster, lilac.................... **100**
Creamer, figural grape cluster, white **100-150**
Creamer, figural grape cluster, yellow (unmarked).. **175**
Creamer, figural hawk, 4 3/4" h................... **450-500**
Creamer, figural ibex head w/trumpet-form bowl, stirrup-type, 4 1/4" h. **700-800**
Creamer, figural lady bug, 4" h. **900-1,100**
Creamer, figural lamplighter **250-300**
Creamer, figural lemon **200-225**
Creamer, figural leopard......................... **6,000-6,500**

Figural Lobster Creamer

Creamer, figural lobster (ILLUS.)................ **125-175**
Creamer, figural Man of the Mountain, 3 1/2" h... **110-125**
Creamer, figural maple leaf, 4" h. **250-325**
Creamer, figural milk maid, red dress, 4 3/4" h... **700-800**
Creamer, figural monk, brown, 4 1/2" h. **600-800**
Creamer, figural monkey, brown................. **425-450**
Creamer, figural monkey, green **500-550**
Creamer, figural mountain goat **275-375**
Creamer, figural Murex shell, colored glaze, 3 3/4" h... **200-300**
Creamer, figural oak leaf............................ **200-250**
Creamer, figural oak leaf, white w/orchid highlights... **250-300**
Creamer, figural orange **200-250**

Creamer, figural pansy, purple, 4" h. 250-300
Creamer, figural parakeet............................ 350-500
Creamer, figural parakeet, green 275-325
Creamer, figural pear 535-550
Creamer, figural pig, blue 775
Creamer, figural pig, grey 500-600
Creamer, figural pig, red, 4 1/4" h. 600-800
Creamer, figural platypus, 4" h. 1,000-1,200
Creamer, figural poodle, black.................... 250-300
Creamer, figural poodle, black &
  white.. 250
Creamer, figural poodle, red,
  4 1/2" h. 500-600
Creamer, figural poppy, peach
  iridescent.. 425
Creamer, figural robin, 4" h. 175-225
Creamer, figural rooster 400-450
Creamer, figural rose, pink, 3" h................. 350-400
Creamer, figural Santa Claus, attached han-
  dle, red, 4 1/4" h.................................. 3,000-3,200
Creamer, figural seal 325-400
Creamer, figural shell w/coral handle 185
Creamer, figural shell w/lobster handle, un-
  marked, 2 1/2" h.................................... 75
Creamer, figural snake............................. 750-1,000
Creamer, figural Spiky Shell, white satin fin-
  ish, 4 1/4" h... 75-125
Creamer, figural St. Bernard, brown.................. 250
Creamer, figural strawberry,
  3 3/4" h. 250-300

Standing Trout Creamer

Creamer, figural trout, standing on tail,
  shaded brown to white w/reddish dots
  (ILLUS.).. 4,500

Water Buffalo Creamer

Creamer, figural water buffalo, black & white
  (ILLUS.).. 175
Creamer, figural water buffalo, souvenir of
  Portland, Oregon 300
Creamer, figural watermelon 300-350
Creamer, flow blue, Babes in Woods deco-
  ration.. 250-300

"Huntsman" Creamer

Creamer, "Huntsman," scene of hunter &
  dogs, small flying bird on flared rim, 4" h.
  (ILLUS.)... 100-125
Creamer, miniature, "tapestry" scene of girl
  & horse... 275
Creamer, scene of girl w/basket, salmon
  color... 600-800
Creamer, stirrup-type, figural ibex head 625
Creamer, "tapestry," Scottish highland
  goats scene 350

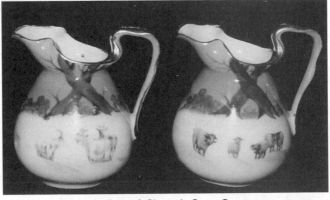

Goats in Snow & Sheep in Snow Creamers

Creamer, w/scene of goats in snow (ILLUS.
  left w/sheep in snow creamer)................ 150-200

Creamer, w/scene of sheep in snow (ILLUS.
  right w/goats in snow creamer).............. 150-200

Creamer, pasture scene w/cows & trees, 3 1/4" h. **75-100**

Creamer, figural clown, green, 3 1/2" h. **400**

Creamer, left-handled, scene of two girls under umbrella, 3 1/2" h. **380**

Creamer, blue cylindrical body w/flared base & figural brown & grey cat handle, 3 3/4" h. **395**

Creamer, figural seashell, boot-shaped, 3 3/4" h. **150-195**

Creamer, "tapestry," footed ovoid body tapering to a wide rounded & flaring neck w/a pinched spout & small C-scroll handle, sheep in the meadow decoration, 3 3/4" h. **300-350**

Creamer, pinched spout, "tapestry," goats decoration, 4" h. **350**

Creamer, crowing rooster & hen decoration, 4 1/4" h. **125-175**

Creamer, figural elk head, shades of brown & cream, 3 1/2" d., 4 1/4" h. **225**

Creamer, figural lamplighter, green, 4 1/2" h. **275**

Creamer, figural crow, black, 4 3/4" h. **225**

Creamer, "tapestry," wide ovoid body w/a flaring foot & a long pinched spout, ornate gilt D-form handle, "The Bathers" landscape scene, 3 1/2" h. **375-425**

Creamer & cov. sugar bowl, figural apple, pr. **350-400**

Creamer & cov. sugar bowl, figural grape cluster, purple, pr. **225**

Creamer & cov. sugar bowl, figural pansy, lavender, pr. **375**

Creamer & cov. sugar bowl, figural poppy, pr. **300-350**

Creamer & cov. sugar bowl, figural rooster, pr. **300-350**

Creamer & cov. sugar bowl, figural strawberry, unmarked, pr. **450-500**

Creamer & open sugar bowl, each decorated w/a mountain landscape w/a boy & donkey, 3" h., pr. **250-350**

Creamer & open sugar bowl, figural poppy, pr. **400-500**

Creamer & open sugar bowl, figural poppy, white satin finish, pr. **500-550**

Creamer & open sugar bowl, figural rooster, creamer w/multicolored feathers & sugar bowl in black, pr. **1,200**

Creamer & open sugar bowl, figural strawberry, unmarked, pr. **500-600**

Creamer & open sugar bowl, "tapestry," barrel-shaped, the creamer w/a long pinched spout, creamer w/goose girl scene, sugar w/Alpine village scene, sugar bowl 3 7/8" h., creamer 4 1/4" h., pr. **675**

Cup & saucer, decorated w/hunting scene of man & dog **100-125**

Cup & saucer, figural rose **150-200**

Cup & saucer, floral decoration on the inside & outside, gold handle on cup, scalloped standard saucer, ca. 1916 .... **35-75**

Cup & saucer, scene of man w/turkeys **125**

Cup & saucer, "tapestry," floral decoration **200-250**

Cup & saucer, demitasse, Castle scene decoration, artist-signed **140**

Cup & saucer, demitasse, figural apple **100-150**

Cup & saucer, demitasse, figural grape cluster **200-250**

Cup & saucer, demitasse, figural orange **150**

Dish, leaf-shaped, nursery rhyme decoration w/Little Miss Muffet **155**

Dish, leaf-shaped, "tapestry," scenic Lady & Prince decoration **125**

Royal Bayreuth Dresser Tray

Dresser tray, rectangular, w/gently ruffled rim, decorated w/depiction of Little Boy Blue sleeping in haystack (ILLUS.)... **450-550**

Dresser tray, rectangular, "tapestry," Lady & Prince scenic decoration, 7 x 9 1/4" **450-550**

Boy & Donkeys Dresser Tray

Dresser tray, rectangular w/rounded corners, scene of boy & three donkeys in landscape, 8 x 11" (ILLUS.).................... **175-250**

Dresser tray, rectangular w/rounded corners, "tapestry" decoration of a young courting couple wearing early 19th c. attire, 11 1/2" l. **500-600**

Dresser tray, decorated w/hunting scene **200-275**

Ewer, scene of hunter w/dog, 4 1/2" h. **225**

Ewer, cobalt blue, Babes in Woods decoration, 6" h. **600-650**

Flower holder w/frog-style cover, hunt scene decoration, 3 3/4" h. **200-225**

Gravy boat w/attached liner, decorated w/multicolored floral sprays, gadrooned border, gold trim, cream ground **60**

Gravy boat & underplate, figural poppy, satin finish, 2 pcs. **250**

Hair receiver, cov., decorated w/scene of boy & donkey **125-150**

Hair receiver, cov., "tapestry," scene of farmer w/turkeys **250-300**

Hair receiver, cov., three-footed, scene of dog beside hunter shooting ducks **250-300**

Hair receiver, cov., decorated w/a scene of a Dutch boy & girl, 3 1/4" h. **150**

Hatpin holder, figural owl................................... **850**

Penguin Hatpin Holder

Hatpin holder, model of a penguin, in red, white & grey, signed (ILLUS.)................. **800-900**

Hatpin holder, footed baluster-form body w/a scalloped rim & top pierced w/holes, "tapestry" design of a youth & maiden in early 19th c. costume, 4 1/2" h. **450-575**

Hatpin holder, hexagonal shape, decorated w/pink & white roses, green leaves & gold trim on rim, satin finish **350**

Humidor, cov., figural elk **950**

Humidor, cov., figural gorilla, black.................. **1,750**

Humidor, cov., tapering cylindrical body w/elk head handles, figural antlers on lid, brown, 6 1/4" h.. **600-800**

Humidor, cov., Arab scene decoration, grey... **500-600**

Humidor, cov., purple & lavender floral decoration.. **325**

Lamp base, "tapestry," slender ovoid body decorated w/"The Chase" scene, hounds after stag in water, raised on a metal ring support w/four short legs w/paw feet, set on an octagonal metal base w/molded swirled leafy stems, fitted for electricity, overall 21" h. (ILLUS.) **900-1,100**

Match holder, hanging-type, figural elk.............. **575**

Match holder, hanging-type, figural shell **275-325**

Match holder, hanging-type, figural spiky shell **275**

Match holder, hanging-type, scene of Arab on horseback... **300**

Match holder, hanging-type, scene of fishermen in boat.. **325-350**

Match holder, hanging-type, stork decoration on yellow ground.............................. **325-350**

Match holder, hanging-type, "tapestry," sheep in landscape scene, 4 1/2" l............... **485**

Match holder w/striker, decorated water scene w/brown "Shadow Trees" & boats on orange & gold ground, unmarked, 3 1/4" d., 2 1/2" h.................................... **75-100**

Mint dish, ruffled, w/Dutch girl decoration, 4 1/2" d... **125**

Model of a man's high top slipper **250-300**

Model of a man's shoe, black oxford.......... **250-300**

Model of Dutch shoe, miniature size, in shape resembling Dutch wooden shoe, w/scenic tapestry decoration of buildings w/trees & clouds in background (ILLUS. right w/man's shoe)................................... **450-500**

Royal Bayreuth Lamp Base

Royal Bayreuth Shoes

Model of man's shoe, two-tone in brown & tan for spat-like effect, 5" l., 2 1/2" h. (ILLUS. left w/miniature Dutch shoe)... **300-350**

Model of woman's shoe, old fashioned high-button shoe in silver tapestry design, 5" l., 3 1/2" h. (ILLUS. center w/vase & sprinkling can, below) **2,000-2,500**

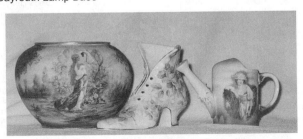

Royal Bayreuth Vase, Shoe & Sprinkling Can

Mug, beer, figural elk **400-450**
Mug, figural clown... **550**
Mug, decorated w/Cavalier scene,
    4 1/2" h. **125-150**
Mug, candle lady decoration,
    5" h... **300-375**

Figural Elk Beer Mug

Mug, beer, figural elk, 5 3/4" h. (ILLUS.)............ **650**
Mustard jar, cov., figural grape cluster, yel-
    low.. **175**
Mustard jar, cov., figural lobster **225**
Mustard jar, cov., figural rose **550**
Mustard jar, cov., figural shell...................... **100-160**
Mustard jar, cov., figural pansy,
    3 1/4" h.. **400-600**
Mustard jar, cover & spoon, figural poppy,
    red, green spoon, 3 pcs.................................. **300**
Nappy, handled, figural poppy........................... **150**
Nut set: large pedestal-based open com-
    pote & six matching servers; each deco-
    rated w/a colorful pastoral scene w/ani-
    mals, 7 pcs.. **450**
Pin dish, decorated w/Arab scene **75-100**
Pin tray, triangular, "tapestry" portrait deco-
    ration of woman wearing large purple
    plumed hat, 5 x 5 x 5" **250**
Pincushion, figural elk head **350**
Pipe holder, figural bassett hound,
    black **450-550**

Royal Bayreuth Water Pitcher

Pitcher, water, bulbous body w/scene of
    fisherman standing in boat against wood-
    ed backdrop, flaring neck & spout, ap-
    plied handle (ILLUS.) **450-500**

Royal Bayreuth Water Pitcher

Pitcher, water, jug-type body w/applied han-
    dle, set-in spout, scenic "tapestry" deco-
    ration (ILLUS.).. **950**

Royal Bayreuth Miniature Pitchers

Pitcher, 2" h., miniature advertising piece
    w/scene of "sanatorium grounds" on
    front, angled handle (ILLUS. left w/minia-
    ture Hupo bird pitcher)............................. **200-250**
Pitcher, 2" h., miniature, w/picture of Hupo
    bird on front, angled handle (ILLUS. right
    w/miniature advertising pitcher) **300-350**
Pitcher, 2 1/2" h., scene w/cows **170**

Royal Bayreuth Pitcher & Vase

Pitcher, 3 1/8" h., 2 3/8" w., squared waist-
    ed body w/short, wide spout & angled gilt
    handle, scene of Arab on horse (ILLUS.
    right).. **125**

Cavalier Pitcher

Pitcher, 3 1/4" h., 2" d., decorated w/Cavalier scene, two Cavaliers drinking at a table, grey & cream ground, unmarked (ILLUS.)... **65**

Pitcher, 3 1/2" h., nursery rhyme scene w/Little Boy Blue **210**

Pitcher, 3 1/2" h., scenic decoration of Arab on horse **75-100**

Pitcher with Musicians Scene

Pitcher, 3 1/2" h., 2 1/4" d., scene of musicians, one playing bass & one w/mandolin, unmarked (ILLUS.)..................................... **65**

Pitcher, 3 3/4" h., corset-shaped, Colonial Curtsey scene w/a couple **165**

Pitcher, miniature, 4 1/2" h., scene of a skiff w/sail.. **100-125**

Pitcher, 5" h., Arab w/horse decoration............. **140**

Pitcher, 5" h., double handles, scene of fisherman in boat w/sails **150-200**

Pitcher, 5" h., figural crow..................................... **175**

Pitcher, 5" h., scene of an Arab on white horse w/brown horse nearby **150**

Pitcher, squatty, 5" h., 5" d., decorated w/hunting scene **100-125**

Royal Bayreuth Santa Pitcher

Pitcher, 5 1/4" h., figural, Santa Claus, pack on back serves as handle (ILLUS.)... **3,500-4,000**

Pitcher, 5 1/4" h., jug-type, narrow handle, decorated w/picture of jester on cream ground shading to light green (ILLUS. right w/hunting stein)................................. **450-550**

Pitcher, 5 1/4" h., pinched spout, "tapestry," scene of train on bridge over raging river...... **550**

Pitcher, 6" h., decorated w/hunting scene **125-150**

Royal Bayreuth Butterfly Pitcher

Pitcher, water, 6 1/2" h., in the form of a perched butterfly, in shades of green, deep pink & light blue, handle in the form of a stem w/leaves (ILLUS.) **6,000-7,000**

Pitcher, 6 3/4" h., wide ovoid body w/a flaring, lightly scalloped base & a long pinched spout, "tapestry" finish w/a color landscape "Don Quixote" scene **525-575**

Royal Bayreuth Pitcher

Pitcher, 7 1/2" h., w/orange, cream & green bands, applied handle (ILLUS.) **150-200**

Pitcher, lemonade, 6 3/4" h., wide ovoid body w/flat foot & long pinched spout, ornate D-shape handle, dark brick red ground w/green "Dancing Frog" & flying insects decoration **1,200-1,500**

Pitcher, lemonade, 7 1/2" h., figural apple... **1,000-1,200**

Pitcher, lemonade, 7 1/2" h., figural lemon.. **1,000-1,200**

Pitcher, milk, babies mending **375-400**

Pitcher, milk, figural coachman **750**

Lobster Milk Pitcher

Pitcher, milk, figural lobster (ILLUS.).................. **250**

Pitcher, milk, figural oak leaf......................... **500-600**

Pitcher, milk, figural red & white parrot handle.. **550-600**
Pitcher, milk, Goose Girl decoration **150-175**
Pitcher, milk, musicians decoration **150-175**
Pitcher, milk, 3" h., figural shell w/lobster handle **150**
Pitcher, milk, 4" h., figural St. Bernard **450-600**
Pitcher, milk, 4 1/4" h., figural rose **600-800**
Pitcher, milk, 4 1/2" h., figural poppy **350-400**
Pitcher, milk, 4 1/2" h., nursery rhyme scene w/Jack & the Beanstalk **325**
Pitcher, milk, 4 3/4" h., figural clown, yellow **900-1,100**
Pitcher, milk, 4 3/4" h., figural coachman . **350-425**
Pitcher, milk, 4 3/4" h., figural cockatoo **695**
Pitcher, milk, 4 3/4" h., figural eagle **550-600**
Pitcher, milk, 4 3/4" h., figural shell w/sea horse handle... **315-350**
Pitcher, milk, 5" h., figural dachshund **600-700**
Pitcher, milk, 5" h., figural fish head **450-500**
Pitcher, milk, 5" h., figural owl, brown........ **400-600**
Pitcher, milk, 5 1/4" h., figural elk............... **275-325**
Pitcher, milk, 5 1/2" h., figural fish head..... **300-400**
Pitcher, milk, 5 1/2" h., figural lamplighter, green... **400-500**
Pitcher, water, tankard, 9 1/2" h., h.p. pastoral cow scene **250-300**
Pitcher, water, 6" h., figural apple **600-700**
Pitcher, water, 6" h., figural pelican **700-900**
Pitcher, water, 6" h., figural Santa Claus, red **6,000-9,000**
Pitcher, water, 6 1/4" h., figural oak leaf **1,700-2,000**
Pitcher, water, 6 1/2" h., figural strawberry **900-1,100**

Figural Sunflower Pitcher

Pitcher, water, 6 1/2" h., figural sunflower (ILLUS.)... **4,000-4,500**
Pitcher, water, 6 3/4" h., figural lobster **395**
Pitcher, water, 6 3/4" h., figural robin **800-900**
Pitcher, water, 7" h., figural coachman.............. **800**
Pitcher, water, 7" h., figural duck............. **800-1,000**
Pitcher, water, 7" h., figural elk.................. **500-700**
Pitcher, water, 7" h., figural orange............ **800-900**
Pitcher, water, 7" h., figural rooster, multicolored.. **3,200-3,600**
Pitcher, water, 7" h., figural seal........... **3,600-4,000**
Pitcher, water, 7 1/4" h., decorated w/frog & bee **900-1,000**
Pitcher, water, 7 1/4" h., pinched spout, scenic decoration of cows in pasture.......... **250-300**
Pitcher, water, 7 1/2" h., figural conch shell, brownish amethyst & yellow mottled body, orange angled coral handle **500-700**
Pitcher, water, 7 3/4" h., 6" d., figural lobster, red shaded to orange w/green handle.. **450-550**
Pitcher, decorated w/scene of hunter & dog **125-175**
Pitcher, sheep scene.. **150**
Plaque, decorated w/scene of Arab on horse, 9 1/2" d... **125-150**

Royal Bayreuth "Tapestry" Plaque

Plaque, pierced to hang, "tapestry," round w/a scroll-molded gilt-trimmed border, center portrait of woman leaning on horse, 9 1/2" d. (ILLUS.)......................... **775-825**
Plate, 5 1/4" d., leaf-shaped, decorated w/small yellow flowers on green ground, green curved handle **40**
Plate, 6" d., decorated w/soccer scene....... **175-200**
Plate, 6" d., handled, figural leaf & flower............. **85**
Plate, 7" d., decorated w/scene of girl walking dog **100**
Plate, 7 1/2" d., nursery rhyme scene w/Little Bo Peep... **125**
Plate, 8" d., decorated w/pink & yellow flowers, gold rim, pink ground, blue mark......... **50-75**
Plate, 8" d., scene of man hunting...................... **125**
Plate, 8 1/2" d., scene of man fishing.................. **135**
Plate, 8 1/2" d., scene of man hunting **135**
Plate, 9" d., candle girl decoration **150-175**
Plate, 9" d., Cavalier Musicians scene **225-275**
Plate, 9" d., figural ear of corn **495**
Plate, 9" d., scene of man smoking pipe **150-175**
Plate, 9 1/2" d., nursery rhyme scene w/Jack & the Beanstalk **250-300**
Plate, 9 1/2" d., scroll-molded rim, "tapestry," toasting Cavalier scene **825**
Plate, 9 1/2" d., "tapestry," landscape scene w/deer by a river **250-300**
Plate, 9 1/2" d., "tapestry," woman w/horse scene... **700-800**
Playing card box, cov., decorated w/a sailing ship scene **195-250**
Powder box, cov., Cavalier Musicians scene...... **175**
Powder box, cov., round, "tapestry," scenic Lady & Prince decoration **150-175**
Powder jar, figural pansy, 4 1/4" h.............. **500-600**
Relish dish, open-handled, footed, ruffled edge, cow scene decoration, 8" l................... **175**
Relish dish, figural cucumber, 5 1/4 x 12 1/2"...................................... **150-250**
Relish dish, figural Murex Shell................... **200-300**
Salt & pepper shakers, figural conch shell, unmarked, pr... **100**
Salt & pepper shakers, figural ear of corn, pr.. **600-800**
Salt & pepper shakers, figural grape cluster, purple, pr.. **150-175**
Salt & pepper shakers, figural poppy, red, pr.. **300-400**

Royal Bayreuth Stein & Pitcher

Salt & pepper shakers, figural shell, pr. **125-150**
Salt shaker, figural elk.. **135**
Shaving mug, figural elk head **500-600**
Sprinkling can, miniature size, "tapestry,"
   decoration of woman & pony, 2 3/4" h.
   (ILLUS. left w/vase & shoe) **500-550**
Stamp box, cov., colorful scene of Dutch
   children.. **125**
Stamp box, cov., "tapestry," Cottage by Wa-
   ter Fall scene.. **225**
Stein, w/pewter hinged top, decorated
   w/scene of stag swimming away from
   hunting dogs, 6" h. (ILLUS. left w/jester
   pitcher, top of page) **450-500**

Hanging Rooster Head String Holder

String holder, hanging-type, figural rooster
   head (ILLUS.).. **400-550**
Sugar bowl, cov., Brittany Girl decoration **100**
Sugar bowl, cov., figural lemon (small finial
   flake) **175**
Sugar bowl, cov., figural pansy, purple (tiny
   rim flake) **225-250**
Sugar bowl, cov., figural poppy, red **225-250**
Sugar bowl, cov., figural rose **300-400**
Sugar bowl, cov., figural shell w/lobster han-
   dle... **200**
Sugar bowl, cov., figural lobster, 3 3/4" h. . **110-150**
Tea strainer, figural pansy, 5 3/4" l. **350-400**
Tea strainer, figural red poppy, 5 3/4" l...... **350-400**
Teapot, cov., child's, decorated w/a scene
   of hunters, 3 3/4" h. **125**
Teapot, cov., child's, boy & donkey decora-
   tion, green, unmarked, 4" h............................. **225**

Teapot, cov., demitasse, decorated
   w/scene of rooster & hen **250-300**
Teapot, cov., figural orange, 6 1/2" h. **425-500**
Teapot, cov., figural poppy, red........................... **350**
Toothpick holder, ball-shaped, w/overhead
   handle, "tapestry," woman w/horse
   scene.. **475**
Toothpick holder, Bird of Paradise decora-
   tion **225-250**
Toothpick holder, decorated w/scene of girl
   w/two chickens.. **150-200**
Toothpick holder, figural bellringer,
   3 1/2" h.. **200-250**
Toothpick holder, figural elk head, 3" h. **225-250**
Toothpick holder, figural Murex Shell................. **175**
Toothpick holder, figural poppy, red **300**
Toothpick holder, man hunting turkeys
   scene.. **200**
Toothpick holder, rooster & hen decoration,
   2 1/2" h.. **200-250**
Toothpick holder, round, one side handle,
   decorated w/scene of man tending tur-
   keys **250-275**
Toothpick holder, "tapestry," scene of wom-
   an w/pony & trees, 2 2/5" h. **450-550**
Toothpick holder, three-handled, floral dec-
   oration, 2 1/4" h. **175-200**
Toothpick holder, three-handled, harvest
   scene decoration **150-200**

Toothpick Holder with Hunt Scene

Toothpick holder, three-handled, hunt
   scene decoration, 3" h. (ILLUS.).................... **265**

Toothpick holder, three-handled, scene of horse & wagon **150-175**

Toothpick holder, three-handled, three feet, nursery rhyme decoration w/Little Boy Blue **225-250**

Toothpick holder, two-handled, four-footed, scene of horsemen, unmarked **75-125**

Tray, club-shaped, scene of hunter w/dog **150**

Tray with Girl & Geese Scene

Tray, decorated w/scene of girl w/geese, molded rim w/gold trim, 9 x 12 1/4" (ILLUS.) **400-450**

Tray, "tapestry," scene of train on bridge over raging river, 7 3/4 x 11" **700-800**

Royal Bayreuth Tureen

Tureen, figural, in the form of a rose on short petal feet, 6" w., 2 3/4" h. (ILLUS.) **450-550**

Royal Bayreuth Vase with Parrots

Vase, baluster-form body w/decoration of red & blue parrots & pink flowers, trumpet neck, short pedestal on disc foot, side handles w/images of human faces where they attach to body (ILLUS.) **450-500**

Vase, miniature, 2 3/4" h., conical body on three tab feet, tapering to a short flaring neck, small knob handles at shoulders, decorated w/a scene of cows **125**

Vase, 3" h., basket-shaped w/overhead handle, square rim, Babes in Woods decoration **325-350**

Vase, 3" h., scene of children w/St. Bernard dog **75-125**

Vase, 3 1/4" d., footed, baluster-form body w/angled shoulder handles, short cylindrical silver rim, Cavalier Musicians scene on grey ground **75-125**

Vase, 3 1/4" h., 1 7/8" d., footed, conical body tapering to a silver rim, small tab handles, decorated w/scene of white & brown cows w/green & brown ground (ILLUS. left, with Arab scene pitcher) **75-125**

Vase, 3 1/2" h., spherical shape w/small gold rim opening, w/scenic "tapestry" decoration of woman in garden (ILLUS. left w/shoe & sprinkling can) **600-650**

Vase, 3 5/8" h., footed conical body tapering to a swelled neck flanked by four loop handles, decorated w/hunting scene, man & woman on horses, unmarked **50-75**

Vase, 3 3/4" h., handled, flow blue, Babes in Woods decoration, scene of girl curtseying **370**

Vase, 4" h., Babes in Woods scene **250-300**

Vase, 4" h., ovoid body w/a tiny, short flaring neck, "tapestry," scene of two cows, one black & one tan **425-475**

Vase, 4" h., two-handled, decorated w/long-tailed Bird of Paradise **300-350**

Vase, 4 1/2" h., sailing scene decoration ... **135-150**

Vase, 4 1/2" h., "tapestry," courting couple decoration **525**

Vase, bud, 4 1/2" h., two handles, Babes in Wood scene, cobalt blue & white **225-325**

Vase, 4 3/4" h., handled, Babes in Woods decoration, girl holding doll **500-550**

Vase, bud, 4 3/4" h., "tapestry," rounded body w/a thin tall neck, Lady & Prince scenic decoration **150-200**

Vase, 5" h., "tapestry," bulbous ovoid body tapering to a short slender flaring neck, "Castle by the Lake" landscape scene .. **300-350**

Vase, 5" h., "tapestry," bulbous ovoid body tapering to a short slender flaring neck, cottage by a waterfall landscape **295-350**

Royal Bayreuth Tapestry Vase

Vase, 5" h., "tapestry," decoration of cock-
fight again scenic ground (ILLUS.) **135-175**
Vase, 5 1/4" h., ovoid body w/short cylindrical neck, medallion portrait framed
w/gold band in incised leaf design
w/enamel trim **200-250**
Vase, 5 1/2" h., decorated w/brown & white
bust portrait of woman on dark green
ground, artist-signed **475**
Vase, 5 1/2" h., portrait decoration **250-300**
Vase, 5 1/2" h., teardrop-shaped, colorful
floral decoration **125**
Vase, 6" h., "tapestry," decorated w/a scene
of an elk & three hounds in a river **425-475**
Vase, 7" h., decorated w/Arab scene **125-150**
Vase, 7" h., decorated w/portrait of a wom-
an **275-350**
Vase, 7" h., "tapestry," a bulbous ovoid body
w/the rounded shoulder centering a tiny
flared neck, a shaded pastel ground centered on one side w/a three-quarters
length portrait of a woman in 18th c. attire
w/a large feathered hat & large muff, the
reverse w/a landscape scene **550-650**
Vase, 7 3/4" h., mercury & floral finish, ca.
1919, artist-signed & signed "Kgl. Priv.
Tettau" **250**

Royal Bayreuth Waterfall Vase

Vase, 8" h., bulbous body on short quatrefoil
foot, side C-scroll handles w/decorative
ends, short reticulated neck w/flaring rim,
decorated w/waterfall scene
(ILLUS.) **200-250**

Royal Bayreuth Girl & Pony Vase

Vase, 8" h., colorful "tapestry" portrait of girl
& pony on blue ground (ILLUS.)............. **375-425**
Vase, 8" h., decorated w/scene of hunter &
dogs **200-250**
Vase, 8 1/4" h., footed, squatty, bulbous
bottom tapering to a tall waisted base w/a
gently scalloped flaring rim, polychrome
boy & two donkeys decoration **250-300**

Vase, 8 1/4" h., "tapestry," slender ovoid
body w/a short cylindrical flaring neck,
"The Bathers" landscape scene **435-550**
Vase, 9" h., tall, slender, waisted, cylindrical
body w/a gently scalloped flaring rim,
three long green scroll & bead loop handles down the sides, the top body w/a
band decorated w/a toasting Cavaliers
scene in color on one side & "Ye Old Bell"
scene on the other, the lower body all in
dark green, ca. 1902 .... **250-300**

Vase with Peacock

Vase, 9 1/2" h., peacock decoration, openwork on neck & at base, ornate scroll
handles, lavish gold trim (ILLUS.)........... **700-750**
Vase, 11 1/2" h., polar bear scene **900-1,100**
Vase, double-bud, ovoid body w/two angled
short flaring necks joined by a small han-
dle, scene of Dutch children **100-150**
Vase, miniature, ball-shaped, footed, silver
rim, Arab scene decoration............................. **150**
Vases, 2 1/2" h., decorated w/sunset scene
of a ship, pr.. **100-150**

Small Royal Bayreuth Vases

Vases, 3 1/8" h., 2 5/8" d., squatty bulbous
lower body below the tall tapering sides
ending in a ringed neck & flanked by loop
handles, one w/scene of Dutch boy & girl
playing w/brown dog & the other w/scene
of Dutch boy & girl playing w/white &
brown dog, green mark, pr. (ILLUS.)........ **75-125**
Wall pocket, figural grape cluster, purple **350**
Wall pocket, figural grape cluster, yellow **350**

Wall pocket, depicts a jester & "Many Kiss
the Child for the Nurses SAKE," green
ground, signed "NOKE," 9" h. **750**
Wall pocket, figural red poppy, 9 1/2" l. **650-700**

Royal Bonn & Bonn

Royal Bonn & Bonn Mark

*Bonn and subsequently Royal Bonn china were pro-
duced in Bonn, Germany, in a manufactory established
in 1755. Later wares made there are often marked
"Mehlem" or bear the initials "FM" or a castle mark.
Most wares were of the hand-painted type. Clock cases
were also made in Bonn.*

Centerpiece, bowl form, h.p w/flowers outlined in raised gold against a matte
cream ground, brushed gold rims, late
19th c., 13 1/2" l., 6" h. **$400**

Ornate Royal Bonn Clock

Clock, mantel-type, upright ornately scroll-
molded case w/a scroll cartouche crest
above the round enameled dial w/Arabic
numerals & a gilt-metal bezel, waisted
scroll-molded sides & floral & scrolling
leaf-decorated lower front, on mold hoof
feet, late 19th - early 20th c., 15 1/2" h.
(ILLUS.) **1,035**
Ewer, slender ovoid shouldered body taper-
ing to a short slender neck w/a tall upright
petal-form spout & a high arched gilt handle, the cream ground decorated w/poly-
chrome flowers & gilt trim, late 19th c.,
12 1/2" h. **110**
Vase, 8 1/4" h., spherical body w/a short cy-
lindrical neck, decorated w/a painted
central vignette of a female surrounded
by a floral landscape, printed mark, ca.
1900 .... **575**
Vase, 8 1/2" h., tapering cylindrical body
w/a short flaring neck, overall sand tapestry decoration, four tall arch-topped

narrow panels w/a cream ground decorated w/multicolored scrolls & blossoms,
dividing bands in dark maroon w/gold
trim & patterned gold around the shoulder & neck, a narrow & white chain band
around the base, one in gold on maroon,
the other w/maroon on green,
marked, ca. 1890 .... **330**

Royal Copenhagen

Royal Copenhagen Mark

*Although the Royal Copenhagen factory in Denmark
has been in business for over 200 years, very little has
been written about it. That is not to say the very beautiful
porcelain it produces is not easily recognizable. Besides
producing gorgeous dinnerware, such as "Blue Fluted"
and "Flora Danica," it produced - and still does - wonderful figurines depicting animals and people. The company employs talented artists as both modelers and
painters. Once you become familiar with the colors,
glazes and beauty of these figurines, you will have no
trouble recognizing them at a glance.*

*Collecting these magnificent figurines seems as pop-
ular now as in the past. As with most objects, and certainly true of these figurines, value will depend on the
complexity, size, age and rarity of the piece. There is
other Danish porcelain on the market today, but the
Royal Copenhagen figurines can readily be recognized
by the mark on the bottom with the three dark blue wavy
lines. Accept no imitations!*

Boy with Teddy Bear Figure Group

Figure group, boy & Teddy bear, toddler
standing wearing blue romper, holding
tan bear behind him, No. 3468, 3 1/2" w.,
7" h. (ILLUS.) **$225**

Girl Feeding Calf Figure Group

Figure group, girl feeding calf, a farm girl bending over to feed a calf from a pail, green oblong base, No. 779, 6 1/2" l., 6 1/2" h. (ILLUS.) **300**

Hans Clodhopper Figure Group

Figure group, Hans Clodhopper, boy seated astride a billy goat, No. 1228, 5 1/2" l., 6 3/4" h. (ILLUS.) **300**

Royal Copenhagen Harvest Group

Figure group, Harvest Group, young farmer & farm girl standing close together, each leaning on a hoe, No. 1300, small, 4" w., 7 1/2" h. (ILLUS.) **400**

Shepherd Boy and Dog

Figure group, shepherd boy w/dog, standing boy wearing cap & long blanket cloak, No. 782, 3 1/2" w., 7 1/2" h. (ILLUS.) **250**

Faun on Tortoise Figure Group

Figure group, young faun seated astride a large tortoise, No. 858, 3 1/2" l., 4" h. (ILLUS.) **175**

Young Children & Puppy Figure Group

Figure group, young girl & boy hugging brown puppy, No. 707, 5 1/2" l., 5 3/4" h. (ILLUS., previous page).................................. **325**

Figure of Young Man Eating Lunch

Figure of young man eating lunch, reclining position, eating from a lunch box, No. 865, 7" l., 4" h. (ILLUS.).................................... **225**

Model of bird, Budgie on Gourd, white bird w/blue trim on dark blue gourd, No. 4682, 4 x 5 1/2" **165**

Model of a Fat Robin

Model of bird, Fat Robin, rounded baby robin in blue, white & rust red, No. 2266, 3" h. (ILLUS.)... **65**

Royal Copenhagen Model of a Grebe

Model of bird, Grebe, handsome swimming bird w/blue crest & grey & white body, No. 3263, 7" l., 4" h. (ILLUS.) **135**

February Boy Juggler Figure

Figure of a boy, February Boy Juggler, standing wearing a top hat & holding a baton to juggle, No. 4524, 6 1/2" h. (ILLUS.)... **175**

Figure of boy, Sandman (Wee-Willie-Winkie), standing on white square stepped base & leaning on an umbrella, holding another, dressed in grey, No. 1145, 6" h. **100**

Royal Copenhagen Sandman Figure

Figure of boy, Sandman (Wee-Willie-Winkie,) standing wearing a long white nightgown & pointed blue cap, a closed umbrella under one arm, opening a brown vial in his hands, No. 1145, 6 3/4" h. (ILLUS.)... **125**

Figure of boy on gourd, young barefoot boy wearing white shirt & blue overalls seated astride a large green gourd, No. 4539, 4 1/4 x 4 1/2" **100**

Royal Copenhagen Icelandic Falcon

Model of bird, Icelandic Falcon, large bird w/speckled bluish grey & white feathers, No. 263, 8 1/2" l., 11" h. (ILLUS.).................. **375**

Model of Finches

Model of birds, pair of blue, white & grey finches perched close together, No. 1189, 5" l., 2" h. (ILLUS.).................................... **80**

Model of cow & calf, Mother cow licking calf nestled against her, white w/shaded grey & black spots, No. 800, 5 x 11" **35**

Royal Copenhagen Great Dane

Model of dog, Great Dane, large recumbent dog in tan w/black striping, No. 1679, 9" l., 4" h. (ILLUS.).. **275**

Model of dog, Male Boxer, standing, white & shaded tan & grey w/black face, No. 3634, 5 1/2 x 7" **150**

Royal Copenhagen Elephant

Model of elephant, walking w/head & trunk raised & mouth open, No. 2998, small size, 6" l., 5" h. (ILLUS.) **120**

Model of elk (moose), reclining position, shaded grey & white w/white antlers, No. 2813, 9 x 10" **450**

Royal Copenhagen Lioness

Model of lioness, recumbent animal, No. 804, 12" l., 6 1/2" h. (ILLUS.)........................... **375**

Model of mink, white w/black eyes & brown nose, No. 4654, 3 3/4 x 7" **180**

Royal Copenhagen Monkey Figure

Model of monkey, seated animal w/head tilted to side, No. 1444, 3" w., 5" h. (ILLUS.).. **125**

Mouse on Ear of Corn Figure

Model of mouse, white & pink mouse perched on an ear of brown corn, No. 512, 5" l., 2" h. (ILLUS.)...................................... **65**

Royal Copenhagen Panda Figure

Model of panda, seated eating bamboo, No.
662, 5 1/2" w., 7" h. (ILLUS.) **350**

Royal Copenhagen Penguins

Model of penguins, two birds seated side by
side, No. 1190, 4" h. (ILLUS.) **100**
Model of piglets, pair of piglets fused togeth-
er, white w/grey spots, pink snout, No.
683, 2 1/2 x 4 1/2" **100**

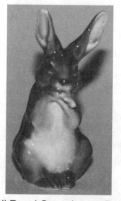

Small Royal Copenhagen Rabbit

Model of rabbit, seated upright eating leaf,
No. 1019, small size, 3 1/2" h. (ILLUS.) **65**

Model of sea lion, head raised, shades of
tan & grey, No. 265, 7 x 12" **350**

Royal Copenhagen Rose Bowl

Rose bowl, squatty spherical form w/wide
flat mouth, dark blue ground painted
w/large white blossoms & green leaves,
No. 424, 8" d., 6" h. (ILLUS.) **200**

Royal Copley

*Royal Copley was a trade name used by the Spauld-
ing China Company of Sebring, Ohio, during the 1940s
and 1950s for a variety of ceramic figurines, planters
and other decorative pieces. Similar pieces were also
produced under the trade name "Royal Windsor" as
well as the Spaulding China mark.*

*The Spaulding China Company stopped producing in
1957, but for the next two years other potteries finished
production of its outstanding orders. Today these originally inexpensive wares are developing a dedicated collector following.*

Figurines

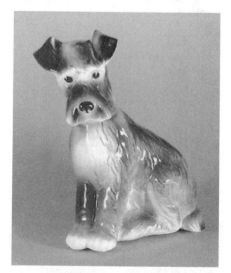

Airedale Figurine

Airedale, seated, brown & white, 6 1/2" h.
(ILLUS.) **$35-40**

Blackamoor Man & Woman Figures

Blackamoor Man & Blackamoor Woman,
   kneeling, 8 1/2" h., pr. (ILLUS.)............... **80-100**
Cockatoos, 7 1/4" h. **40-50**
Cocker Spaniel, 6 1/4" h.................................. **30-35**
Deer & Fawn, 8 1/2" h...................................... **50-60**
Dog, 6 1/2" h... **25-30**
Dog, 8" h. **35-40**
Hen & Rooster, large, Royal Copley mark,
   7" & 8" h., pr. **80-110**
Hen & Rooster, Royal Windsor mark, 6 1/2"
   & 7" h., pr. **100-120**
Hen & Rooster, small, Royal Copley mark,
   6" & 6 1/2" h., pr.. **80-90**
Kingfishers, 5" h. **35-45**
Mallard Duck, 7" h. **35-40**

Spaniel Pup with Collar Figurine

Thrushes, 6 1/2" h. **15-20**
Titmouse, 8" h. **20-30**
Wrens, 6 1/4" h. **15-20**

Planters

Oriental Boy & Girl Figurines

Oriental Boy & Oriental Girl, standing,
   7 1/2" h., pr. (ILLUS.) **30-50**
Parrots, 8" h... **30-40**
Sea Gulls, 8" h. **30-50**
Spaniel Pup with Collar, 6" h. (ILLUS., next
   column).. **35-40**
Swallow with extended wings, 7" h. **90-110**
Swallows on Double Stump, 7 1/2" h.,
   pr. **100-120**

Large Kneeling Angel Planter

Angel, large, kneeling, blue robe, 8" h.
(ILLUS.).. **60-75**

Angel on Star Planter

Angel on Star, white relief figure on creamy
yellow ground, 6 3/4" h. (ILLUS.)................ **25-35**
Apple and Finch, 6 1/2" h. **40-50**
Balinese Girl, 8 1/2" h. **40-50**
Bare Shoulder Lady head vase, 6" h.............. **60-70**
Big Hat Chinese Boy & Girl, 7 1/2" h., pr. **40-50**
Blackamoor Prince head vase, 8" h................. **30-40**
Cinderella's Coach, 6" h., 3 1/4" h. **20-25**

Royal Copley Clown Planter

Clown, 8 1/4" h. (ILLUS.).............................. **100-125**
Cocker Spaniel, 8" h... **25-30**
Deer & Doe, 7 1/2" h. **15-20**

Doe & Fawn Head Planter

Doe & Fawn Head, rectangular log-form
planter, 5 1/4" h. (ILLUS.)............................. **40-50**

Dog with Raised Paw Planter

Dog with Raised Paw, 7 1/2" h. (ILLUS.)........ **60-70**
Dog with Suitcase (Skip), 7" h......................... **40-45**
Dogwood, oval, 3 1/2" h. **25-30**
Dogwood, small, 4 1/2" h. **20-25**
Duck with Mailbox, 6 3/4" h............................... **60-70**
Duck with Wheelbarrow, 3 3/4" h...................... **15-20**
Dutch Boy & Girl with Buckets, 6 1/4" h., pr... **50-75**
Elephant, large, 7 1/2" h.................................... **30-35**

Elf and Shoe Planter

Elf and Shoe, 6" h. (ILLUS.).............................. **50-60**
Elf and Stump, 6" h. **40-50**

Fancy Finch on Tree Stump Planter

Fancy Finch on Tree Stump, red, white & black bird perched on brown leafy branch beside white planter, 7 1/2" h. (ILLUS.) **80-90**
Fighting Cock, 6 1/2" h. **50-60**
Girl Leaning on Barrel & Boy Leaning on Barrel, 6 1/4" h., pr. **40-50**

Girl on Wheelbarrow Planter

Girl on Wheelbarrow, 7" h. (ILLUS.) **40-45**
Goldfinch on Stump, 6 1/2" h. **40 t0 50**
High Tail Rooster, 7 3/4" h. **50-60**

Horse Head with Mane Planter

Horse Head with Flying Mane, 8" h. (ILLUS.) **30-50**

Kitten and Book Planter

Kitten and Book, 6 1/2" h. (ILLUS.) **40-50**
Kitten in Picnic Basket, 8" h. **60-70**

Kitten on Cowboy Boot Planter

Kitten on Cowboy Boot, 7 1/2" h. (ILLUS.) **55-60**
Mallard Drake, sitting, 5 1/4" h. **40-45**
Mallard Duck, standing, 8" h. **15-20**
Mallard Duck on Stump, 8" h. **30-40**
Mature Wood Duck, 7 1/4" h. **30-40**
Nuthatch, 5 1/2" h. **25-30**
Oriental Boy with Basket on Back & Oriental Girl with Basket on Back, 8" h., pr. **120-130**

Palomino Horse Head Planter

Palomino Horse Head, 6 1/4" h. (ILLUS.) **40-50**
Peter Rabbit, 6 1/2" h. **80-90**

Reclining Poodle Planter

Poodle, reclining, white w/black nose & eyes, 8" l. (ILLUS.) **70-80**

Poodle with Bow, posing, 5 1/4" h. **70-80**

Ribbed Star Royal Windsor Planter

Ribbed Star, all-white, "Royal Windsor"
sticker, 4 3/4" h. (ILLUS.) **30-35**

Stuffed Animal Dog Planter

Stuffed Animal Dog, white & brown,
5 1/2" h. (ILLUS.) **60-70**

Stuffed Animal Elephant Planter

Stuffed Animal Elephant, pale green &
white, 6 1/2" h. (ILLUS.) **80-90**

Stuffed Animal Rooster Planter

Stuffed Animal Rooster, pale green & white,
6" h. (ILLUS.) **70-80**
Tanagers, 6 1/4" h. **25-35**
Teddy Bear, 6 1/4" h. **30-40**
Teddy Bear, white, 8" h. **75-90**
Teddy Bear in Picnic Basket, 8" h. **70-90**

Rare Teddy Bear with Concertina

Teddy Bear with Concertina, rare, 7 1/4" h.
(ILLUS.) **100-125**
Teddy Bear with Mandolin, 6 3/4" h. **50-75**

Tony Head Planter

Tony Head, man wearing large blue hat,
8 1/4" h. (ILLUS.) **50-75**
Wide Brim Hat Boy & Wide Brim Hat Girl,
7 1/4" h., pr. **90-100**
Woodpeckers, 6 1/4" h. **25-35**
Wren on Tree Stump, 6 1/4" h. **40-50**

Miscellaneous

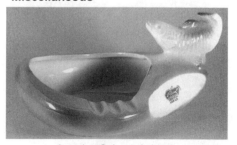

Leaping Salmon Ashtray

Ashtray, Leaping Salmon, oblong boat-
shaped bowl w/figural salmon on rim,
5 x 6 1/4" (ILLUS.)...................................... **30-40**

Bow Tie Pig Bank

Bank, Bow Tie Pig, standing, wearing green
bow tie & blue outfit, 6 1/4" h. (ILLUS.)...... **75-85**
Bank, Teddy Bear, 7 1/2" h. **100-120**

Barber Pole Blade Bank

Blade bank, model of a barber pole in red &
white w/"Blades" on the side, 6 1/4" h.
(ILLUS.).. **70-80**
Pitcher, Floral Beauty, 8" h. **70-85**
Smoking set, models of ducks, 3" & 4" h., 3
pcs. **60-75**
Vase, 5 3/4" h., Fish, open center.................. **45-60**

Happy Anniversary Vase

Vase, 6" h., upright rectangular form w/flar-
ing serpentine rim, dark blue centered by
a large white panel decorated w/wedding
bells & bluebirds & "Happy Anniversary"
in gold (ILLUS.)... **50-60**
Vase, 6 1/4" h., footed pillow-shape, ivy
decoration... **20-25**
Vase, 7" h., Carol's Corsage **25-35**
Vase, 7 1/4" h., Deer, open center **35-40**
Vase, 7 1/4" h., Flying Bird, open center **45-50**
Vase, 8 1/4" h., Dogwood.............................. **30-40**
Vases, 8 1/4" h., cornucopia-shaped w/de-
cal decoration, pr.. **50-60**
Wall plaque-planters, Hen & Rooster,
6 3/4" h., pr. **120-150**

Island Man Wall Pocket

Wall pocket, Island Man, black head wear-
ing white turban, 8" h. (ILLUS.)............... **130-150**
Wall pocket, Salt Box, 5 1/2" h. **60-70**
Wall pocket, Spice Box, 5 1/2" h..................... **80-90**
Wall pocket, Straw Hat, large, 7" h................. **75-85**

Royal Dux

Royal Dux Marks

*This factory in Bohemia was noted for the figural
porcelain wares in the Art Nouveau style it exported
around the turn of the 20th century. Other notable figural pieces were produced through the 1930s. The factory was nationalized after World War II.*

Royal Dux Figural Bowl & Compote

Bowl, 18 1/2" l., figural, oval shell-form bowl w/sloping rim molded w/water plants & a fishing net w/the figure of an Art Nouveau maiden tending the net seated at the upper rim, naturalistic coloring, impressed mark, early 20th c. (ILLUS. left) **$489**

Bust of water nymph, shown emerging from foaming blue waves amid pink orchids & green leaves, her skin & face w/naturalistic coloring, molded rectangular pad mark w/"507," applied pink triangle mark w/"Royal Dux Bohemia," early 20th c., part of one orchid petal missing, small chips to leaves & other petals, 21 1/4" h. (ILLUS. right with bust of woman).............. **4,800**

Two Royal Dux Female Busts

Bust of woman, ornately dressed in late Victorian costume, a large pierced lacy hat w/ribbons & a high & widely flaring ruffled lacy collar w/ribbons, decorated in pale pink, green & yellow w/the hat in pink, molded rectangular pad mark impressed "452 - A," applied pink triangle impressed "Royal Dux Bohemia," early 20th c., some restoration, 21 3/4" h. (ILLUS. left) **1,800**

Ornate Royal Dux Figural Centerpiece

Centerpiece, figural, a large shaped ornately scalloped & pierced bowl atop a pierced curved flowering vine pedestal w/a full-length Art Nouveau maiden in a swirled gown also supporting the bowl, on a scalloped & swirled rounded base, natural colors, ca. 1900, 16" h. (ILLUS.)....... **900**

Centerpiece, figural, a rectangular round-edged platform base molded at the corners w/olive brown branches & molded on the top to represent a pond w/the figures of two young girls, one kneeling & the other sitting & pulling a large jug out of the water, jug & girls' costumes in golden brown w/pastel floral trim on a cream ground, pink triangle mark, 12 1/2" l., 10" h. (minor floral flakes) **770**

Compote, 14 1/2" h., figural, the top molded as a conch-type shell w/an Art Nouveau maiden seated at one end, raised on a wave-molded pedestal base w/another figure below the bowl, naturalistic coloring, impressed mark, early 20th c. (ILLUS. right w/bowl) **748**

Tall Figural Royal Dux Compote

Compote, 20 1/4" h., figural, the wide, shallow, rounded bowl molded w/flowers & leaves & pierced branch handles raised on a tall spiral-twisted tree trunk-form central pedestal surrounded by three dancing Art Nouveau maidens, delicate coloring, impressed & printed marks, early 20th c. (ILLUS.)... **633**

Figure of a woman w/a harp, incised scroll banding on the raised base, impressed mark, early 20th c., 14 1/4" h. **173**

Royal Dux "Tragedy" Figure

Figure of "Tragedy," a standing classical woman wearing a flowing salmon robe trimmed w/gilding & falling from her right shoulder, a laurel wreath in her hair, beside a column on an architectural plinth, holding an actor's mask in one hand & a dagger in the other, some minute chips, early 20th c., 16 5/8" h. (ILLUS.)................ **1,035**

Royal Dux Shepherd & Shepherdess

Figures of a shepherd & shepherdess, each standing beside a goat, raised on a rectangular plinth w/notched corners, colored in moss green & tan, pr. (ILLUS.) **1,250**

Figures of a youth & maiden, each standing on a round base, he wearing a straw hat, kneebreeches, a cloak over one shoulder & a cluster of grain under the other arm, she w/a long peasant dress & carrying a basket over one arm, each trimmed in cobalt blue & white w/gold trim, 20 1/2" h., pr. **1,155**

Vase, 19 1/4" h., bisque, figural, an Art Nouveau-style female figure on one side of the leaf- and floral-molded body, impressed mark, early 20th c. **288**

Large Figural Royal Dux Vase

Vases, 37 1/4" h., figural, a tall flaring cluster of banana tree leaves & fruit behind the standing figure of an Arab girl leaning on a tall jug, other one w/man beneath the tree playing a lute, heavy gold trim on white w/pink trim, marked "Royal Dux - Made in Czechoslovakia," ca. 1920s, pr. (ILLUS. of one) **1,210**

Royal Rudolstadt

This factory began as a faience pottery established in 1720. E. Bohne made hard paste porcelain wares from 1852 to 1920, when the factory became a branch of Heubach Brothers. The factory is still producing in the former East Germany.

Royal Rudolstadt Mark

Bust of an old woman, wearing a polk bonnet & shawl around her shoulders, a small jar in one hand, raised on a square waisted plinth w/scroll feet, shaded beige glaze, 19th c., 7" h. **$138**

Ewer, ivory ground decorated w/multicolored floral sprays strewn around the sides, gold scroll handle, marked **138**

Ewer, a narrow footring below the wide, squatty, bulbous lobed base below a deeply waisted band below a lobed conical shoulder to the tall slightly tapering ribbed & ringed columnar neck w/an upright pointed split spout, long angled bamboo handle from top of neck to shoulder, creamy ground w/all ribbing outlined in gold & delicate painted florals around the lower waisted band, signed, 15" h. **220**

Ewer, bulbous body w/cylindrical neck & ribbed angular handle, the body decorated w/fall-colored branch flowers w/gold trim on an ivory ground, autumn green swirl neck band w/lilac rings, peach-colored handle, marked, 15" h. **121**

Vase, 12 1/4" h., bulbous ovoid shoulder body w/overall swirled ribbing, a small domed section at the base of the cylindrical molded swirl & ring neck topped by a scalloped & reticulated cupped rim, ornate flattened pierced scroll gold handles flanking the neck, creamy beige ground, the body decorated w/a large bouquet of purple flowers w/golden leaves & stems, late 19th c. **193**

Royal Vienna

The second factory in Europe to make hard paste porcelain was established in Vienna in 1719 by Claud Innocentius de Paquier. The factory underwent various changes of administration through the years and finally closed in 1865. Since then, however, the porcelain has been reproduced by various factories in Austria and Germany, many of which have also reproduced the early beehive mark. Early pieces, naturally, bring far higher prices than the later ones or the reproductions.

Royal Vienna Mark

Baskets & underplates, a deep rounded flaring bowl-form basket w/reticulated rim band & reticulated latticework sides raised on a reticulated flaring round pedestal, trimmed overall w/heavy gilt, set in a matching round dished & reticulated underplate w/gold trim, blue shield marks & dated 1812, 10 1/2" d., two sets **$1,955**

Charger, round, colorful scene depicting the Death of Siegfried, paneled gilt foliate border band, ca. 1890, 13 1/2" d. **1,380**

Charger, round, pink & claret ground finely painted w/a central square reserve of a mythological scene emblematic of the Arts & Sciences, named on the reverse, within an elaborately paneled round w/gilt scroll trim & small diamond-shaped reserves w/gilt florals or birds all on a claret, pale pink or lavender ground, mid-19th c., blue beehive mark, artist-signed, 16 7/8" d. **6,325**

Coffeepot, cover & underplate, the footed coffeepot w/a tall tapering cylindrical body w/a scroll-molded long rim spout in gold & a pointed loop handle in gold, fitted w/a stepped domed cover w/urn-form gold finial, the body & cover w/paneled designs on a pale blue ground w/pink reserves on the neck & cover & maroon & white banding, the body painted w/a gold-bordered reserve of putti in gardens, the panels ornately trimmed w/gilt arabesques, leaf-tips & beaded chain, the wide round dished underplate w/matching decoration, late 19th c., blue beehive mark & other marks, 8 1/2" h., the set **2,530**

Plate, 9 5/8" d., painted in the center in color w/a scene of a nymph seated w/flowers in her long blonde hair & being kissed by a winged Eros, a fountain & field in the distance, within an elaborate paneled border band of stylized leaf-tips & gilt flowers, early 20th c., crowned beehive & D mark, artist-signed **1,265**

Portrait plates, 10 3/4" d., each depicting Napoleon or ladies or gentlemen of his court, gilt-beaded borders w/gilt & cobalt band, ca. late 19th c., artist-signed & titled in red enamel, underglaze-blue beehive mark, set of 12 .... **7,475**

Stein, cov., cylindrical w/hinged gilt-metal low domed cover, the front finely painted in color w/a scene of a scantily clad Venus teasing Cupid in a forest glen within a gilt rectangular surround, the burgundy ground trimmed w/gilt scrolling foliage, 19th c., blue beehive mark & iron-red number, 6 1/4" h. **2,990**

Vase, cov., 11" h., slightly tapering cylindrical form w/large molded lion masks w/ring handles near the top & molded gilt scrolls & paw feet supporting the base, the low domed cover w/a gilt blossom finial, a cobalt blue ground, the body decorated on one side w/a large ornate gilt oval reserve w/a right-facing bust portrait of a lightly clad maiden w/a large flower in her long dark hair, printed & incised marks, late 19th c. **1,265**

Vases, cov., 26" h., tapering pedestal round base supporting a tall slender ovoid body w/a short rolled neck & high domed cover

w/double-knop finial, arched gilt leafy scroll shoulder handles down the sides, chestnut brown ground finely painted on the front & back w/putti representing the seasons within molded & gilt ribbon-tied branches, above a band of molded gilt-trimmed flutes & conforming gilt-trimmed base, the neck w/molded stiff-leaf tips, blue beehive mark, late 19th c., pr. **6,325**

Royal Worcester

This porcelain has been made by the Royal Worcester Porcelain Co. at Worcester, England, from 1862 to the present. Royal Worcester is distinguished from wares made at Worcester between 1751 and 1862, which are referred to only as Worcester by collectors.

Royal Worcester Marks

Compote, 7 3/4" d., flower petal shape on poppy pod-form base, decorated in floral design w/gilt decoration, ca. 1888 (ILLUS. lower right w/pitcher & other pieces, bottom next page)........................... **$616**

Ewer, copper-colored glaze w/raised gold decoration including flying birds & molded floral decoration on the handle, ending w/a dragon head finial at the top, green crown mark, also "Patented Metallic" w/an additional impressed crown mark, 11 3/4" h. **220**

Ewer, flared extended rim & gilt handle, ovoid body raised on pedestal base, decorated w/floral design & gilt decoration, 7 3/4" h., ca. 1893 (ILLUS. second from left w/pitcher & other pieces) **224**

Ewer, footed, wide bulbous body w/a wide rounded shoulder centering a short ringed neck & high arched spout w/shaped rim, high arched & scrolled beaded gold handle from rim to shoulder, creamy ground decorated w/large sprays of ferns, late 19th c., Shape No. 1227, 10 1/4" h.. **748**

Ewer, "Patent Metallic" type, raised gold-trimmed foot supporting a bulbous ovoid body tapering sharply to a slender neck w/a large pierced bulbed ring w/gold swirled ribs below the high arched spout, long angled gilt handle from the rim to the lower body, creamy ground decorated w/delicate floral sprigs, 19th c., 13 1/8" h....... **633**

Game plates, each naturalistically painted w/a curing game bird against a yellow ground & within a faux textile-patterned brown border, brown printed crowned globe mark, date code for 1883, 9 1/8" d., set of 11 .... **353**

Pitcher, 5 1/2" h., bulbous body w/floral decoration, gilt twig handle, ca. 1890 (ILLUS. upper right w/other pieces) **224**

Royal Worcester Pitcher & Vase

Pitcher, 6" h., flared scalloped rim, leaf spout & twig handle on bulbous body, decorated in floral design w/gilt decoration, ca. 1889 (ILLUS. left w/vase)..... **476**

Pitcher, 7 1/8" h., lobed melon-form body w/vine handle, bronzed & gilt-decorated, Shape 1111, ca. 1888..................................... **345**

Royal Worcester Beverage Pitcher

Pitcher, 7 3/4" h., gilt rim w/lion head spout & lion paw handle, cylindrical body, decorated in floral design w/gilt decoration, ca. 1889 (ILLUS.)........................ **896**

Pitcher, 8 7/8" h., gilt rim w/lion head spout, cylindrical body w/lion paw handle, decorated in floral design w/gilt decoration, ca. 1889 (ILLUS. far left w/other pieces)... **952**

Plates, 8 3/4" sq., quatrefoil shape, each h.p. w/a different fish, gilt rims w/shells at corners, marked "Manufactured by the Worcester Royal Porcelain

Co. for Richard Briggs Boston" w/the circle mark (no crown), minor wear, the set of 4 (ILLUS. of one, below).............................. **413**

One Plate of Royal Worcester Set

Plates, 9 1/4" d., all decorated w/different polychrome flowers, gilt rims, "Designed by A.H. Williamson," mid-20th-c., set of 12 .... **330**

Service plates, decorated w/a band of Neoclassical gilt enamel, border w/raised gilt enamel w/scrolls & urns, on a lapis blue ground, ca. 1920, 10 3/8" d., set of 18 .... **2,185**

Service plates, round, painted in the center w/colorful summer flowers, surrounded by the blue cavetto gilded w/runs & scrolling foliage continuing around the wide flanged rim, printed factory marks, artist-signed, 10 1/2" d., set of 12 .... **2,300**

Taperstick, lotus form w/a frog mounted on the leaf-form base, Shape No. 687, ca. 1879, 7 3/8" h.. **403**

Tea set: 6 1/2" h. cov. teapot, 3" h. creamer & 3 1/2" h. open sugar; melon ribbed bodies w/applied water lily pad decoration in gilt w/red veins, teapot w/lily pad lid, marked for 1888 & 1889, the set (repaired, minor wear) **220**

Vase, 10 3/4" h., narrow flared rim over bulbous body raised on scalloped pedestal base, decorated w/floral design & gilt decoration, ca. 1891 (ILLUS. right w/pitcher) **1,568**

Vase, 6 1/2" h., majolica, figural, a trumpet-form green vase w/large green leaves behind the figure of a large brown & grey bird (professional repair to vase rim & tail & wing of bird) **413**

Royal Worcester Pieces

Royal Worcester Majolica Vases

Vases, 8 1/2" h., majolica, modeled as large white & tan nautilus shells raised on red coral stems & green seaweed on an oval shell-molded foot, late 19th c., pr. (ILLUS.).. **4,400**

Wall pockets, majolica, molded as a long, pointed bird's nest in greens & brown, a tall pointed leaf-form top w/a large spread-winged bird swooping down, professional repair to points, late 19th c., 12" l., pr. **825**

Rozart Pottery

George and Rose Rydings were aspiring Kansas City (Missouri) potters who, in the late 1960s, began to produce a line of fine underglaze pottery. An inheritance of vintage American-made artware gave the Rydings inspiration to recreate old ceramic masters' techniques. Some design influence also came from Fred Radford, grandson of well-known Ohio artist Albert Radford (ca. 1890s-1904). Experimenting with Radford's formula for Jasperware and sharing ideas with Fred about glazing techniques and ceramic chemistry led the Rydings to a look reminiscent of the ware made by turn-of-the-century American art pottery masters such as Weller and Rookwood. The result of their work became Rozart, the name of the Rydings' pottery.

Many lines have been created since Rozart's beginning. Twainware, Sylvan, Cameoware, Rozart Royal, Rusticware, Deko, Krakatoa, Koma and Sateen are a few. It is rare to find a piece of Rozart that is not marked in some way. The earliest mark is "Rozart" at the top of a circle with "Handmade" in the center and "K.C.M.O." (Kansas City, Missouri) at the bottom. Other marks followed over the years, including a seal that was used extensively. Along with artist initials, collectors will find a date code (either two digits representing the year or a month separated by a slash followed by a two-digit year). George signs his pieces "GMR," "GR," or "RG" (with a backwards "R"). Working on Twainware, Jasperware and Cameoware in the early years, George has many wheel-thrown pieces to his credit. Rose, who is very knowledgeable about Native Americans, does scenics and portraits. Her mark is either "RR" or "RRydings." Four of the seven Rydings children have worked in the pottery as well. Anne Rydings White (mark is "Anne" or "AR" or "ARW") designed and executed many original pieces in addition to her work on the original Twainware line. Susan Rydings Ubert (mark is "S" over "R") has specialized in Sylvan pieces and is an accomplished sculptor and mold maker. Susan's daughter Maureen does female figures in the Art Deco style. Becky (mark is "B" over "R"), now a commercial artist, designed lines such as Fleamarket, Nature's Jewels, and Animals. Cindy Rydings Cushing (mark is "C" over "R" or "CRC") developed the very popular Kittypots line. Mark Rydings is the Rozart mold

maker. The Rozart Pottery is still active today. Pottery enthusiasts are taking notice of the family history, high quality and reminiscent beauty of Rozart. Its affordability may soon cease as Rozart's popularity and recognition are on the rise.

Rozart Box with Lid

Box w/lid, Arts & Crafts style, quatrefoil shape w/image of tree painted on lid and various decorations about sides of box, George Rydings, 6" w. (ILLUS.).................. **$235**

Rozart Ewer with Mouse Design

Ewer, sgraffito mouse design, Rose Rydings, 10" h. (ILLUS.) **200**

Rozart Letter Holders (2 columns)

Letter holders, rectangular, w/various designs painted on front, limited edition, 4 1/2" h., 6 1/2" l., each (ILLUS. of three)........ **45**

Rozart Duck

Rozart Native American Design Mugs

Model of duck, on base (ILLUS.)........................... **65**

Rozart Advertising Mug

Mug, advertising Gatsby Days Excelsior Springs, Missouri, May 1998, w/picture of woman in old-fashioned picture hat on front, 3 1/2" h. (ILLUS.)..................................... **45**

Mugs, w/various incised Native American designs, signed "RR," 5" h., each (ILLUS. of seven, top of page) **105**

Sign, for Rozart Pottery dealer, "Rozart" in script, no base, first issue, 5 1/2" l. **250**

Rozart Pottery Dealer Sign

Sign, for Rozart Pottery dealer, "Rozart Pottery" in script, w/base, Copperverde glaze, 5 1/2" l. (ILLUS.)..................................... **65**

Rare Rusticware Tankard

Tankard, Rusticware, decorated in various motifs, George Rydings, 50 made (ILLUS.)... **395**

Rozart Teapot

Teapot, cov., two-cup size, hi-glaze floral design (ILLUS.)... **155**

Rozart Frog Tile

Tile, frog & leaf design, in wood frame, Copperverde glaze, Susan Ubert, 8" sq. (ILLUS.)... **175**

Rozart Kittypot Vase

Vase, 4 1/2" h., Kittypot, black & white cat on front, Cindy Cushing (ILLUS.)...................... **65**

Rozart Pillow Shape Vase with Bird

Vase, 7 1/2" h., pillow shape w/bird on branch on front, Cindy Cushing (ILLUS.) **135**

Rozart Indian Portrait Vase

Vase, 14 1/2" h., w/Indian portrait on front, Becky White (ILLUS.) **250**

Rozart Royal Vase with Eagle

Vase, 15" h., Rozart Royal, w/eagle in landing position on front, Rose Rydings (ILLUS.) **300**

R.S. Prussia & Related Wares

Ornately decorated china marked "R.S. Prussia" and "R.S. Germany" continues to grow in popularity. According to the Third Series of Mary Frank Gaston's

Encyclopedia of R.S. Prussia (Collector Books, Paducah, Kentucky), these marks were used by the Reinhold Schlegelmilch porcelain factories located in Suhl in the Germanic regions known as "Prussia" prior to World War I, and in Tillowitz, Silesia, which became part of Poland after World War II. Other marks sought by collectors include "R.S. Suhl," "R.S." steeple or church marks, and "R.S. Poland."

The Suhl factory was founded by Reinhold Schlegelmilch in 1869 and closed in 1917. The Tillowitz factory was established in 1895 by Erhard Schlegelmilch, Reinhold's son. This china customarily bears the phrase "R.S. Germany" and "R.S. Tillowitz." The Tillowitz factory closed in 1945, but it was re-opened for a few years under Polish administration.

Prices are high and collectors should beware of the forgeries that sometimes find their way onto the market. Mold names and numbers are taken from Mary Frank Gaston's books on R.S. Prussia.

The "Prussia" and "R.S. Suhl" marks have been reproduced, so buy with care. Later copies of these marks are well done, but quality of porcelain is inferior to the production in the 1890-1920 era.

Collectors are also interested in the porcelain products made by the Erdmann Schlegelmilch factory. This factory was founded by three brothers in Suhl in 1861. They named the factory in honor of their father, Erdmann Schlegelmilch. A variety of marks incorporating the "E.S." initials were used. The factory closed circa 1935. The Erdmann Schlegelmilch factory was an earlier and entirely separate business from the Reinhold Schlegelmilch factory. The two were not related to each other.

R.S. Prussia & Related Marks

R.S. Germany

Berry set: 9" master bowl & six matching 5 1/2" sauce dishes, Iris mold, decorated w/large red roses, 7 pcs. **$500-550**

Bowl, 8" h., handled, decorated w/scene of two colorful parrots, green highlights **275-325**

Bowl, 10" d., decorated w/wild roses, raspberries & blueberries, glossy glaze **125-175**

Bowl, 10 1/2", handled, Lebrun portrait, Tiffany finish, artist's palette, paintbrush **1,800-2,000**

Bowl, large, Lettuce mold, floral decoration.
lustre finish... **300-350**

R.S. Germany Cake Plate

Cake plate, double-pierced small gold side
handles, decorated w/a scene of a maid-
en near a cottage at the edge of a dark
forest, 10" d. (ILLUS.) **275-325**
Coffeepot, cov., demitasse, Ribbon & Jewel
mold, rose garland decoration............... **400-450**
Creamer, Mold 640, decorated w/roses,
gold trim on ruffled rim & ornate
handle... **35-50**

R.S. Germany Cup & Saucer

Cup & saucer, decorated w/blue, black &
white bands on beige lustre ground, cup
w/center silhouette of Art Deco woman in
blue dancing w/blue scarf, cup 3 1/2" d.,
2 1/4" h., saucer 5 3/4" d. (ILLUS.)......... **100-150**
Cup & saucer, demitasse, ornate handle,
eight-footed **75-100**
Gravy boat w/underplate, poppy
decoration.. **75-100**
Mustard jar, cov., calla lily decoration........... **65-100**
Pitcher, 9" h., Mold 343, floral decoration
w/overall gilt tracery on cobalt blue (red
castle mark)... **700-800**
Plate, 7 1/4" d., poppy decoration.................... **30-50**
Plate, 8" d., decorated w/scene of colorful
parrots, gold rim **250-300**
Salad set, 10 1/2" d. lettuce bowl & six 8" d.
matching plates, Mold 12, Iris decoration
on pearl lustre finish, 7 pcs...................... **300-350**
Toothpick holder, two-handled, decorated
w/roses & gold trim, artist-signed............. **75-125**
Tray, handled, decorated w/large white &
green poppies, 15 1/4" l. **275-300**

R.S. Prussia

Bell, tall trumpet-form ruffled body w/twig
handle, decorated w/small purple flowers
& green leaves on white ground, un-
marked, 3 1/2" l... **300-350**

Sheepherder Prussia Berry Set

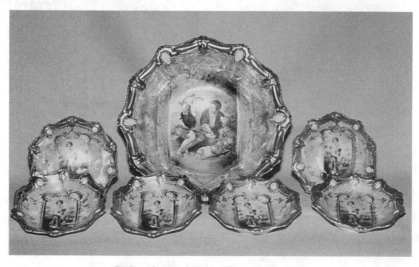

Ribbon & Jewel Melon Eaters Berry Set

Berry set: 11" d. master bowl & five 4" d. sauce dishes; Mold 155, each decorated w/a Sheepherder landscape scene w/cottage & flowering trees & shrubs, the set (ILLUS., previous page) **1,250-1,650**

Berry set: master bowl & six sauce dishes; five-lobed, floral relief rim w/forget-me-nots & water lilies decoration, artist-signed, 7 pcs. **400-450**

Berry set: master bowl & six sauce dishes; Ribbon & Jewel mold (Mold 18) w/Melon Eaters decoration, 7 pcs. (ILLUS, bottom, previous page) **3,500-3,800**

Bowl, 7" d., decorated w/roses, satin finish **150-200**

Bowl, 9 3/4" d., Iris variant mold, rosette center & pale green floral decoration **250-300**

Bowl, 10" d., floral decoration in black & gold **150-175**

Bowl, 10" d., Iris mold, Spring Season portrait decoration **2,400-2,600**

Bowl, 10" d., Mold 202, gold beaded rim, double swans center scene in shades of beige & white, unmarked **200-225**

Summer Season Portrait Bowl

Bowl, 10" d., Mold 85, Summer Season portrait w/mill scene in background (ILLUS.) **2,200-2,600**

Bowl, 10 1/4" d., center decoration of pink roses w/pearlized finish, border in shades of lavender & blue w/satin finish, lavish gold trim (unlisted mold) **400-450**

Bowl, 10 1/4" d., Mold 251, apple blossom decoration, satin finish **250-300**

Bowl, 10 1/2" d., Countess Potocka portrait decoration, heavy gold trim **4,000-4,300**

Bowl, 10 1/2" d., decorated w/pink roses & carnations on white shaded to peach ground, iridescent Tiffany finish **595**

Bowl, 10 1/2" d., decorated w/scene of Dice Throwers, red trim **900-1,200**

Bowl, 10 1/2" d., handled, four-lobed, decorated w/Art Nouveau relief-molded scrolls & colorful sprays on shaded green ground **200-250**

Bowl, 10 1/2" d., Iris mold, poppy decoration **350-400**

Bowl, 10 1/2" d., Mold 101, Tiffany finish around rim, orchid & cream trim on molded border blossoms, central bouquet of pink, yellow & white roses w/green leaves **250-300**

Ornate Mold 211 Bowl with Roses

Bowl, 10 1/2" d., Mold 211, deeply fluted scalloped border, decorated w/large roses in pink, white & yellow, shadow flowers & blue trim around border (ILLUS.) **250-300**

Bowl, 10 1/2" d., Point & Clover mold (Mold 82), decorated w/forget-me-nots & roses, satin finish, artist-signed **300-350**

Bowl, 10 1/2" d., Point & Clover mold (Mold 82), decorated w/pink roses & green leaves w/shadow flowers & a Tiffany finish **250-300**

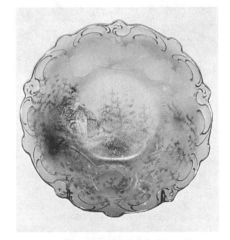

Rare "Tapestry" Bowl

Bowl, 10 3/4" d., Mold 217, "tapestry" center mill scene, gilt scroll border (ILLUS.) **1,100-1,400**

Bowl, 11" d., 3" h., Sunflower mold, satin finish........ **450-500**
Bowl, 11" d., Mold 155, Sheepherder scene decoration in shades of green w/gold & pink........ **350-400**
Bowl, 11" d., Mold 22, four large jewels, satin finish **250-300**

Man in the Mountain Prussia Bowl

Bowl, 11" d., Mold 304, gilt scroll border, overall color scene of the Man in the Mountain (ILLUS.) **550-600**
Bowl, 11" d., 3" h., Fishscale mold, decorated w/white lilies on purple & orange lustre ground, artist-signed........ **325-375**

Rare Icicle Bowl & Chocolate Pot

Bowl, 15" d., Icicle mold (Mold 7), Snow Bird decoration, scenic reserves around the rim, very rare (ILLUS. right with chocolate pot, top of page) **12,000-14,000**
Bread tray, Mold 428, wide oval form w/low flared sides w/a narrow flanged rim, pierced end rim handles, decorated w/a large cluster of roses in peach, pink & green, traces of gold edging, 9 x 12 1/2" **175-225**
Butter dish, cover & insert, Mold 51, floral decoration, unmarked **200-250**
Cake plate, Ribbon & Jewel mold (Mold 18), open-handled, heavy gold border around florals framing the keyhole scene of Dice Players, 9" d. (ILLUS., top next column)........ **1,000-1,200**

Cake Plate with Dice Players

Floral Decorated Cake Plate

Cake plate, open handled, decorated w/pink & white flowers, green leaves, pink & yellow ground, gold trim, 9 3/4" d. (ILLUS.) **225**
Cake plate, open-handled, Fleur-de-Lis mold, Spring Season portrait, 9 3/4" d........ **1,300-1,600**
Cake plate, open-handled, Mold 155, hanging basket decoration, 10" d........ **325-350**
Cake plate, open-handled, Mold 259, decorated w/pink & yellow roses, pearl button finish, 10" d........ **350-400**
Cake plate, open-handled, Fleur-de-Lis mold, decorated w/a castle scene in rust, gold, lavender & yellow, 10 1/4" d........ **1,000-1,300**
Cake plate, open-handled, Medallion mold, center Flora portrait, Tiffany finish w/four cupid medallions, unmarked, 10 1/2" d........ **900-1,000**
Cake plate, Iris mold, yellow poppy decoration, 11" d........ **250-300**
Cake plate, open-handled, Carnation mold (Mold 28), dark pink roses against teal & green w/gold trim, 11" d........ **250-300**
Cake plate, open-handled, modified Fleur-de-Lis mold, floral decoration, beaded, satin finish, artist-signed, 11" d........ **175-225**
Cake plate, Hidden Image mold, light blue highlights, 11 1/2" d........ **450-500**
Cake plate, open handles, Mold 256, satin ground decorated w/flowers in blue, pink & white w/gold trim, 11 1/2" d........ **120-150**
Cake plate, open-handled, Mold 330, decorated w/snapdragons on pastel ground, artist-signed, 11 1/2" d........ **350-375**

Cake plate, open-handled, Mold 343, Winter figural portrait in keyhole medallion, cobalt blue inner border, gold outer border, 12 1/2" d.. **400-450**

Cake plate, Bow-tie mold, pink & gold **500-600**

Cake plate, open-handled, Carnation mold, decorated w/multicolored roses **300-350**

Celery dish, Carnation mold, carnations & pink roses decoration on white shaded to peach ground, iridescent Tiffany finish, 9".. **375**

Celery dish, Hidden Image mold, colored hair, 5 x 12"... **400-450**

Celery dish, Mold 25, oblong, pearlized finish w/Surreal Dogwood blossoms w/gold trim, 6 x 12 1/4" **75-125**

Celery tray, Mold 254, decorated w/green & pink roses, lavish gold tracery, artist-signed, 12" l.. **275-325**

Celery tray, Ribbon & Jewel mold (Mold 18), pink roses & white snowball blossoms within a wide cobalt blue border w/gilt trim, 12" l... **250-300**

Celery tray, Mold 255, decorated w/Surreal Dogwood decoration, pearlized lustre finish, artist-signed, 12 1/4" l..................... **200-225**

Celery tray, open-handled, decorated w/soft pink & white flower center w/lily-of-the-valley, embossed edge of ferns & pastel colors w/gold highlights, 12 1/2" l.......... **200-250**

Celery tray, Carnation mold, decorated w/pink & yellow flowers on lavender satin finish, 6 1/2 x 13 1/4"............................... **300-350**

Centerpiece bowl, Carnation mold, decorated w/pink & yellow roses, 15 1/2" d... **2,300-2,600**

Chocolate cup & saucer, decorated w/castle scene **125-150**

Chocolate pot, cov., Carnation mold (Mold 526), pink background & pink roses w/gold-trimmed leaves & blossoms & ornate gold handle, 12" h. (ILLUS., top of page, next column).................................. **400-500**

Chocolate pot, cov., Icicle mold (Mold 641), rosebush decoration, 10" h. (ILLUS. left with 15" bowl) **300-400**

Carnation Mold Chocolate Pot

Rare Ribbon & Jewel Chocolate Pot

Chocolate pot, cov., Ribbon & Jewel mold (Mold 645), Dice Players scene, jeweled trim, 11" h. (ILLUS.) **2,000-2,300**

Chocolate pot, cov., Hidden Image mold image on both sides, light green, 9 3/4" h.. **1,000-1,100**

Chocolate pot, cov., peacock & pine trees decoration.. **650-750**

Lebrun-decorated Chocolate Set

Melon Eaters Creamer & Sugar

Chocolate pot, cov., Swag & Tassel mold, decorated w/scene of sheepherder & swallows... **900-1,000**

Chocolate set: cov. pot & four cups & saucers; sunflower decoration, the set........ **700-750**

Chocolate set: 10" h. cov. chocolate pot & four cups & saucers; Mold 729, pansy decoration w/gold trim, the set **900-975**

Chocolate set: 10" h. cov. chocolate pot & four cups & saucers; Ribbon and Jewel mold, scene of Dice Throwers decoration on pot & single Melon Eater scene on cups, the set **4,500-5,000**

Chocolate set: tankard-style cov. pot & six cups & saucers; Mold 510, laurel chain decoration, the set **1,000-1,300**

Chocolate set: 10" h. cov. chocolate pot & six cups & saucers; Mold 517, Madame Lebrun portrait decoration, the set (ILLUS., bottom previous page) **7,500-8,200**

Coffeepot, cov., Mold 517, raised floral designs as part of border, unmarked **250-300**

Cracker jar, cov., Mold 540a, beige satin ground w/floral decoration in orchid, yellow & gold, 9 1/2" w. handle to handle, overall 5 1/2" h. **300-350**

Cracker jar, cov., Mold 634, molded feet, surreal dogwood blossoms decoration on pearlized lustre finish, 8" d., 6 1/2" h. **250-300**

Cracker jar, cov., Mold 704, grape leaf decoration, 7" h. **450-500**

Cracker jar, cov., decorated w/hanging basket of flowers, satin finish, 6 x 9 1/2" **325-375**

Cracker jar, cov., Hidden Image mold, image on both sides, green mum decoration **900-1,000**

Cracker jar, cov., Lebrun portrait decoration, no hat, satin finish............................. **1,500-2,000**

Creamer & cov. sugar bowl, floral decoration, green highlights, pr. **125-150**

Creamer & cov. sugar bowl, Mold 505, pink & yellow roses, pr. **125-175**

Creamer & cov. sugar bowl, Ribbon & Jewel mold, single Melon Eaters decoration, pr. (ILLUS., top of page)........................ **1,500-1,800**

Creamer & cov. sugar bowl, satin finish, Tiffany trim, pr.. **175-200**

Cup & saucer, decorated w/pink roses, peg feet & scalloped rim, cup 1 3/4" h., saucer 4 1/4" d., pr.. **125-175**

Dessert set: 9 1/2" d. cake plate & six 7" d. individual plates; Carnation mold, decorated w/carnations, pink & white roses, iridescent Tiffany finish on pale green, the set.. **995**

Dessert set: pedestal cup & saucer, oversized creamer & sugar bowl, two 9 3/4" d., handled plates, eleven 7 1/4" d. plates, nine cups & saucers; plain mold,

decoration w/pink poppies w/tints of aqua, yellow & purple, all pieces are matching, the set **2,200-2,500**

Dresser tray, decorated w/mill scene, shaded green ground, 7 x 11"......................... **350-450**

Dresser tray, Icicle mold, scenic decoration, Man in the Mountain, 7 x 11 1/2"........... **600-700**

Ferner, six vertical ribs, scalloped, decorated w/lilies-of-the-valley on shaded pastel ground, artist-signed, 3 7/8 x 8 1/4" **200-250**

Hair receiver, cov., Mold 814, Surreal Dogwood decoration **150-175**

Match holder w/striker, floral decoration..... **100-125**

Model of a lady's slipper, embossed scrolling on instep & heel & embossed feather on one side of slipper, a dotted medallion w/roses & lily-of-the-valley on the other, shaded turquoise blue w/fancy rim trimmed w/gold, 8" l. **250-300**

Mug, Lily mold, Lebrun portrait decoration (no hat)... **200-250**

Mug, rose decoration on pink satin finish ... **125-175**

Mustache cup, Mold 502 .... **250-300**

Mustard pot, cov., Mold 509a, decorated w/white flowers, glossy light green ground **150-175**

Mustard pot, cov., Mold 521, pink rose decoration, satin finish **150-200**

Nut bowl, footed, Point & Clover mold, decorated w/ten roses in shades of salmon, yellow & rose against a pink, green & gold lustre-finished ground, 6 1/2" d.. **150-200**

Nut dish, Carnation mold (Mold 28), floral decoration w/pearlized finish **200-250**

Pin dish, cov., Hidden Image mold, floral decoration, 2 3/4 x 4 3/4" **350-450**

Unique Bird of Paradise Pitcher

Pitcher, tankard, 12 1/4" h., Mold 569, very rare Bird of Paradise decoration w/shaded gold & light green in the lower half,

white above, gold trim, only one known
(ILLUS.).. **17,000-20,000**

Carnation - Summer Season Pitcher

Pitcher, tankard, 12 1/2" h., Carnation mold
(Mold 526), Summer Season decoration,
pink border trim (ILLUS.).................. **7,000-8,000**

Carnation Mold Pitcher with Roses

Pitcher, tankard, 13" h., Carnation mold
(Mold 526), decorated w/clusters of dark
pink & creamy white roses w/a shaded
dark green ground & pale green molded
blossoms (ILLUS.)............................. **1,000-1,200**
Pitcher, cider, 7" h., iris decoration w/green
& gold background **250-300**
Pitcher, lemonade, 6" h., Mold 501, relief-
molded turquoise blue on white w/pink
Surreal blossoms & fans around scal-
loped top & base, unmarked.................. **250-300**
Pitcher, tankard, 10" h., Mold 584, decorated w/hanging basket of pink & white
roses.. **700-750**
Pitcher, tankard, 11" h., Carnation Mold,
overall decoration of pink poppies & carnations, white ground, iridescent Tiffany
finish **1,100**
Pitcher, tankard, 12" h., Mold 538, decorat-
ed w/Melon Eaters scene (ILLUS.
left, bottom of page).......................... **3,500-4,000**
Pitcher, tankard, 13" h., decorated w/pop-
pies **600-650**
Pitcher, tankard, 13" h., decorated w/scene
of Old Man in Mountain & swans on lake
(ILLUS. right w/other tankard
pitcher, bottom of page) **4,000-4,500**
Pitcher, tankard, 13 1/4" h., Stippled Floral
mold (Mold 525), roses decoration, un-
marked **625-675**
Pitcher, tankard, 13 1/2" h., Carnation Mold,
pink poppy decoration, green
ground **750-850**
Pitcher, water, 8 3/4" h., Carnation mold........... **660**
Plaque, decorated w/scene of woman
w/dog, 9 1/4 x 13"............................... **2,000-2,500**
Plate, 7" d., Fleur-de-Lis mold, Summer
Season portrait decoration...................... **450-500**
Plate, 7 1/2" d., Carnation mold, decorated
w/pink roses, lavender ground, satin fin-
ish... **200-250**
Plate, 7 1/2" d., Carnation mold, decorated
w/pink roses, pink ground, unmarked **175**

R.S. Prussia Tankard Pitchers

Two Rare Bird-decorated Plates

Plate, 7 3/4" d., Medallion mold (Mold 14), Snowbird decoration, landscape scenes in medallions, black rim band (ILLUS. right)... **1,800-2,200**

Plate, 8 1/2" d., Gibson Girl portrait decoration, maroon bonnet **500-550**

Plate, 8 1/2" d., Medallion mold (Mold 14), Reflecting Lilies patt. **125-150**

Plate, 8 1/2" d., Mold 261, Ostrich decoration (ILLUS. left with Snowbird plate)... **2,000-2,500**

Plate, 8 1/2" d., Mold 263, pink & white roses decoration **175-200**

Plate, 8 1/2" d., Mold 300, beaded gold band around the lobed rim, Old Mill Scene decoration in center against a shaded dark green to yellow & blue ground **150-200**

Plate, 8 3/4" d., Mold 278, center decoration of pink poppies on white ground, green border **150-175**

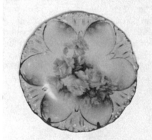

Mold 91 Rose-decorated Plate

Plate, 8 3/4" d., Mold 91, yellow roses decoration on pink ground, shiny yellow border (ILLUS.)... **150-200**

Plate, 9" d., Mold 343, spring figural scenic decoration in keyhole medallion, iridescent Tiffany purple finish at base of figure, gold finish around portrait decoration w/small pink roses **1,800-2,100**

Plate, 9 3/4" d., Icicle mold, swan decoration **800-900**

Plate, 11" d., decorated w/carnations & roses w/gold trim, white shading to peach ground, iridescent Tiffany finish (slight gold wear) **250**

Plate, 11" d., Point & Clover mold, Melon Eater decoration..................................... **900-1,100**

Rare Madame Recamier Plate

Plate, 12" d., Lily mold (Mold 29), Madame Recamier portrait, dark blue Tiffany bronze finish in border panels (ILLUS.).. **3,000-4,000**

Plate, dessert, Mold 506, branches of pink roses & green leaves against a shaded bluish green to white ground w/shadow flowers & satin finish **100-125**

Relish Dish with Spring Season

Relish dish, Iris mold (Mold 25), oval w/scalloped sides & end loop handles, Spring Season portrait surrounded by dark border w/iris, 4 1/2 x 9 1/2" (ILLUS.)... **1,200-1,400**

R.S. Prussia Vases with Animals

Relish dish, Fleur-de-Lis mold, basket of flowers decoration w/shadow flowers, 8" l. **100-125**

Relish dish, scene of masted ship, 4 1/2 x 9 1/2" **250-300**

Relish dish, Icicle mold, scene of swans on lake **450-500**

Relish dish, Mold 82, decorated w/forget-me-nots & multicolored carnations, six jeweled domes **125-175**

Shaving mug, Hidden Image mold, floral decoration **175-225**

Spooner/vase, Mold 502, three-handled, decorated w/delicate roses & gold trim, unsigned, 4 1/4" h. **75-100**

Syrup pitcher, Mold 512, dogwood & pine decoration **175**

Syrup pitcher & underplate, Mold 507, white & pink roses on a shaded brown to pale yellow ground, 2 pcs. **200-250**

Tea set: child's, cov. teapot & four cups & saucers; decorated w/roses, the set **650-700**

Tea set: cov. teapot, creamer & cov. sugar bowl; floral decoration, the set **300-350**

Tea set: cov. teapot, creamer & cov. sugar bowl; mill & castle scene, shaded brown ground, 3 pcs. **900-1,000**

Tea set: cov. teapot, creamer & cov. sugar bowl; pedestal base, scene of Colonial children, 3 pcs. **600-700**

Tea strainer, floral decoration **200-250**

Toothpick holder, ribbed hexagonal shape w/two handles, decorated w/colorful roses **265-300**

Toothpick holder, Stippled Floral mold (Mold 23), white floral decoration **150-175**

Toothpick holder, three-handled, decorated w/white daisies on blue ground, gold handles & trim on top **150-175**

Toothpick holder, urn-shaped, floral decoration, molded star mark **150-175**

Tray, pierced handles, Mold 82, decorated w/full blossom red & pink roses, gold Royal Vienna mark, 8 x 11 1/8" **250-300**

Tray, rectangular, pierced handles, Mold 404, decorated w/pink & white roses, Tiffany border w/gold clover leaves **250-300**

Vase, 4" h., salesman's sample, handled, Mold 914, decorated w/large lilies & green foliage, raised beading around shoulder, gold handles, shaded green ground, artist-signed **150-175**

Vase, 4 1/2" h., Mold 910, decorated w/pink roses, satin finish w/iridescent Tiffany finish around base **250-275**

Vase, 5 1/2" h., cottage & mill scene decoration, cobalt trim **550-650**

Vase, 6 1/4" h., castle scene decoration, brown tones w/jewels **450-500**

Vase, 6 1/4" h., decorated w/brown & cream shadow flowers **75-100**

Vase, 6 1/4" h., decorated w/mill scene, brown w/jewels **450-500**

Vase, 8" h., cylindrical body w/incurved angled shoulder handles, decorated w/parrots on white satin ground, unmarked **2,200-2,600**

Vase, 8" h., ovoid body w/wide shoulder tapering to cylindrical neck w/flared rim, decorated w/scene of black swans (ILLUS. left, top of page) **1,200-1,500**

Vase, 10" h., ovoid body decorated w/scene of two tigers, pastel satin finish (ILLUS. right, top of page) **5,500-7,000**

R.S. Prussia Ovoid Vase w/Parrots

Vase, two-handled, tall, slender, ovoid body w/colorful scene of two parrots, shaded brown foliage, unmarked (ILLUS.)... **1,800-2,000**

Vases, 11 3/4" h., Mold 901, footed, slightly tapering cylindrical body w/a high, flaring, cupped, deeply fluted neck w/jewels, beading & jewels around the shoulder & foot, ornate scrolled gilt handles, Melon

Eaters decoration against a shaded dark green ground, pr., each (ILLUS., below) **1,600-2,000**

Rare Melon Eaters Vases

Other Marks

Bowl, 10" d., Cabbage mold w/center rose decoration (R.S. Tillowitz) **250-300**

Bowl, 10" d., shallow w/very ornate, large Flora portrait, front pose past waist, floral garland, veiling, four different cameo portraits of Flora, wide Tiffany border, lavish gold (E.S. Prov. Saxe) **1,100-1,300**

Chocolate pot, cov., Art Nouveau decoration, glossy finish (R.S. Tillowitz - Silesia)....... **55**

Chocolate pot, cov., lemon yellow ground w/Art Deco decoration & gold trim (R.S. Tillowitz - Silesia) **150**

Coffee set: 6 5/8" l., 3 1/4" d., cov. ovoid coffeepot & two cups & saucers; each piece decorated w/a color oval reserve w/a different romantic scene within a thin gilt border & a deep burgundy panel against a creamy white ground trimmed w/gilt scrolls, a wide red & narrow dark green border band on each, saucers 2 3/4" d., cups 2 1/4" h., blue beehive & R.S. Suhl marks, the set............................... **650**

Fernery, pedestal base, decorated w/pink & white roses, mother-of-pearl finish (R.S. Poland)... **450**

Match holder, hanging-type on attached backplate decorated w/a scene of a man w/mug of beer & pipe (E.S. Prov. Saxe) **175-200**

Plate, 7" d., scene of girl w/rose, trimmed w/gold flowers, beading & a burgundy border **100-125**

Plate, 7 3/4" d., Sunflower mold, rose pink & yellow roses w/Tiffany finish (Wheelock Prussia) **125-150**

Plate, 8" d., peafowl decoration (R.S. Tillowitz - Silesia) **150-200**

Plate, 10 1/2" d., lovely center portrait of Madame DuBarry, four cameos in different poses on a deep burgundy lustre border band (E.W. Prov. Saxe)................... **500-600**

Relish dish, woman's portrait w/shadow flowers & vine border on green ground, 8" l. (E.S. Germany Royal Saxe) **100-125**

E. Schlegelmilch Handled Server

Server, center-handled, decorated w/orange, white & pink poppies on a shaded bluish grey ground, w/a narrow gilt border band, 8 1/2" d., 3 3/4" h., E. Schlegelmilch - Thuringia (ILLUS.)......... **100-150**

Serving dish, center-handled, decorated w/lavender & pink roses, gold trim, 11" d. (R.S. Poland)... **500-550**

Tray, rectangular, open-handled, bright colored bird decoration, 5 x 14" (R.S. Tillowitz) **75-100**

Vase, miniature, 3 1/2" h., cylindrical body w/a rounded shoulder tapering to a tiny rolled neck, decorated w/a colored scene of crowned cranes (R.S. Poland)............ **375-425**

Melon Eaters Vase

Vase, 6 3/8" h., 3" d., wide, ovoid, shouldered body tapering to slender, flaring cylindrical neck, Melon Eaters decoration surrounded by gold border w/reverse decorated w/heart-shaped area w/dainty pink roses on pastel ground, two-thirds of vase covered in purplish lustre w/fine gold leaves & flowers overall, neck in off white w/fine gold floral decoration, artist-signed in gold, Red Crown "Viersa" mark, Suhl or Tillowitz (ILLUS.) **350-400**

R.S. Poland Vase with Geese

Vase, 7" h., footed urn form w/scrolled handles, decorated w/scene of two geese, R.S. Poland (ILLUS.)......................... **1,500-1,800**

Vase, 7 1/2" h., wide, squatty, bulbous base tapering sharply to a tall, slender, cylindrical neck w/an upturned four-lobed rim, long slender gold handles from rim to shoulder, decorated w/a center reserve of a standing Art Nouveau maiden w/her hands behind her head & a peacock behind her framed by delicate gold scrolls & beading & floral bouquets, all on a pearl lustre ground (Prov. Saxe - E.W. Germany) **375-425**

Vase, 9" h., 3" d., tall, slender, ovoid body tapering to a tall, slender trumpet neck, a wide band around the body decorated w/a colored scene of The Melon Eaters between narrow gold & white bands, the neck & lower body in deep rose decorated w/gilt leaf sprigs (R.S. Suhl) **800-1,000**

Vase, 9 1/4" h., gently tapering cylindrical body w/a wide, cupped, scalloped gilt rim, pierced gold serpentine handles from rim to center of sides, decorated around the body w/large blossoms in purple, pink, yellow & green on a shaded brownish green ground (Prove. Saxe) **125-150**

Vase, 9 1/2" h., portrait of "Lady with Swallows," gold beading, turquoise on white ground (Prov. Saxe - E.S. Germany) ... **500-550**

Vase, 10" h., gold Rococo handles, scene of sleeping maiden w/cherub decoration (E.S. Royal Saxe).................................. **350-400**

Vase, 13 1/2" h., portrait of "Lady with Swallows," gold beaded frame, green pearl lustre finish w/gold trim (Prov. Saxe - E.S. Germany) **600-650**

Vase, 13 1/2" h., twisted gold handles, portrait of "Goddess of Fire," iridescent burgundy & opalescent colors w/lavish gold trim (Prov. Saxe, E.S. Germany) **650-700**

Vases, 10" h., gently swelled body tapering to narrow rounded shoulders & a short, flaring, scalloped neck, ornate C-scroll gilt shoulder handles, gold neck band, the body decorated w/a colored scene of a sheepherder leading his flock toward a mill in the background, trees overhead,

the second identical except w/a cottage scene, R.S. Poland, pr. (ILLUS. of one, below)... **1,350-1,400**

R.S. Poland Landscape Vase

Russel Wright Designs

The innovative dinnerwares designed by Russel Wright and produced by various companies beginning in the late 1930s were an immediate success with a society that was turning to a more casual and informal lifestyle. His designs, with their flowing lines and unconventional shapes, were produced in many different colors, which allowed a hostess to arrange creative tables.

Although not antique, these designs, which we list below by line and manufacturer, are highly collectible. In addition to dinnerwares, Wright was also known as a trendsetter in the design of furniture, glassware, lamps, fabric and a multitude of other household goods.

Russel Wright Marks

American Modern (Steubenville Pottery Co.)

Baker, glacier blue, small $55
Baker, granite grey, small 25
Bowl, child's, black chutney 100
Bowl, child's, chartreuse...................................... 100
Bowl, fruit, lug handle, cedar green..................... 30

Group of American Modern Pieces

Black Chutney Celery Tray

Bowl, fruit, lug handle, chartreuse (ILLUS.
　left) 20
Bowl, fruit, lug handle, glacier blue 40
Bowl, salad, cedar green 100
Bowl, salad, white 165
Bowl, soup, lug handle, bean brown 35
Butter dish, cov., granite grey 255
Butter dish, cov., white 365
Carafe, granite grey (no stopper) 200
Carafe w/stopper, bean brown 500
Casserole, cov., stick handle, black chutney 40
Celery tray, black chutney, 13" l. (ILLUS.,
　top of page) 30
Coaster, granite grey 20
Coaster, white 30
Coffee cup cover, black chutney 175
Coffee cup cover, coral 175
Coffeepot, cov., black chutney 250
Coffeepot, cov., cedar green 275
Coffeepot, seafoam blue 275
Coffeepot, cov., demitasse, chartreuse 120
Coffeepot, cov., demitasse, coral 120
Coffeepot, cov., demitasse, granite grey 120
Creamer, cedar green 20
Creamer, white 35
Cup & saucer, coffee, cantaloupe 40
Cup & saucer, coffee, seafoam blue 27
Cup & saucer, demitasse, cantaloupe 60
Cup & saucer, demitasse, chartreuse 30
Gravy boat, chartreuse 20
Hostess plate, chartreuse 75
Hostess plate & cup, cedar green, pr. 100

American Modern Hostess Set

Hostess plate & cup, white, pr. (ILLUS.) 175
Ice box jar, cov., black chutney 225
Ice box jar, cov., coral 225
Mug (tumbler), black chutney 90
Mug (tumbler), cedar green 100
Pickle dish, seafoam blue 25
Pickle dish, white 45
Pitcher, cov., water, cedar green .... 400+
Pitcher, cov., water, white .... 500+
Pitcher, water, 12" h., bean brown 150
Pitcher, water, 12" h., granite grey 100
Pitcher, water, 12" h., seafoam blue 125
Plate, bread & butter, 6 1/4" d., coral 6

Plate, salad, 8" d., seafoam blue 18
Plate, salad, 8" d., white 25
Plate, dinner, 10" d., cantaloupe 40
Plate, dinner, 10" d., granite grey 20
Plate, chop, 13" sq., chartreuse 30
Plate, chop, 13" sq., seafoam blue 50
Plate, child's, coral 60
Plate, child's, seafoam blue 75
Platter, 13 3/4" l., oblong, granite grey 35
Platter, 13 3/4" l., oblong, white 65
Ramekin, cov., individual, bean brown 250
Ramekin, cov., individual, granite grey 188
Relish dish, divided, raffia handle, coral 175
Relish dish, divided, raffia handle, white 300
Relish rosette, granite grey 200
Relish rosette, seafoam blue 250
Salad fork & spoon, coral, pr. 150
Salad fork & spoon, white, pr. 300
Sauceboat, bean brown 75
Sauceboat, coral 40
Shaker, single, chartreuse 8
Shaker, single, glacier blue 20
Stack server, cov., cedar green (ILLUS.
　back, with fruit bowl) 270
Stack server, cov., chartreuse 250
Stack server, cov., granite grey 250
Sugar bowl, cov., chartreuse 15
Sugar bowl, cov., granite grey 15
Teapot, cov., cedar green 150
Teapot, cov., seafoam blue 135
Tumbler, child's, cedar green 140
Tumbler, child's, granite grey 125
Vegetable bowl, cov., cedar green, 12" l. 75
Vegetable bowl, cov., coral, 12" l. 45
Vegetable dish, open, divided, black chut-
　ney 110
Vegetable dish, open, divided, cedar green
　(ILLUS. right front, with fruit bowl) 130
Vegetable dish, open, oval, cantaloupe,
　10" l. 75
Vegetable dish, open, oval, granite grey,
　10" l. 25

Casual China (Iroquois China Co.)

Bowl, 5" d., cereal, ripe apricot 15
Bowl, 5 1/2" d., fruit, ice blue, 9 1/2 oz. 15
Bowl, 5 3/4" d., fruit, oyster grey 20
Bowl, 10" d., salad, pink sherbet, 52 oz. 40
Butter dish, cov., brick red, 1/4 lb. .... 1,000+
Butter dish, cov., white, 1/2 lb. 150
Butter dish, cov., pink sherbet 95
Carafe, cov., charcoal 350
Carafe, cov., oyster grey .... 500+
Casserole, cov., lettuce green, 8" d., 2 qt. 75
Casserole, deep tureen, lemon yellow 250
Casserole, deep tureen, white 260
Coffeepot, cov., nutmeg brown 140

Casual Creamer, Pitcher & Coffeepot

Coffeepot, cov., oyster grey (ILLUS. right)................................... **225**
Coffeepot, cov., sugar white **200**
Coffeepot, cov., demitasse, avocado yellow... **135**
Coffeepot, cov., demitasse, lemon yellow **125**
Cover for casserole, oyster grey, 4 qt. **45**
Cover for cereal/soup bowl **30**
Cover for vegetable bowl, open/divided.............. **35**
Cover for water pitcher **60**
Creamer, family-style, oyster grey (ILLUS. left w/coffeepot & pitcher)................................. **55**
Creamer, family-style, pink sherbet..................... **40**
Creamer, stacking-type, ice blue.......................... **20**
Cup & saucer, avocado yellow **20**
Cup & saucer, coffee, oyster grey (ILLUS. front center w/other cups & saucers).............. **30**
Cup & saucer, tea, charcoal.................................. **25**
Cup & saucer, tea, lemon yellow (ILLUS. front left w/other cups & saucers) **25**

Casual Cups & Saucers & Shakers

Cup & saucer, demitasse, avocado yellow (ILLUS. front right w/other cups & saucers).. **150-175**
Cup & saucer, demitasse, pink sherbet **175**
Cup & saucer, demitasse, sugar white............... **225**
Gravy, redesigned w/cover which becomes stand, ripe apricot...................................... **185**
Gravy, redesigned w/cover which becomes stand, sugar white....................................... **250**
Gravy bowl, 5 1/4", 12 oz. **40**
Gravy stand, ice blue **40**
Gravy stand, oyster grey **70**
Gravy w/attached stand, avocado yellow **100**
Gravy w/attached stand, nutmeg brown **125**
Gumbo soup bowl, cantaloupe, 21 oz.................. **60**
Gumbo soup bowl, charcoal, 21 oz. **50**
Gumbo soup bowl, ice blue, 21 oz. **40**
Hostess set: plate w/well & matching cup; sugar white, 2 pcs. **90**
Mug, pink sherbet, 13 oz. **100**
Mug, restyled, aqua.. **225**
Mug, restyled, ice blue... **100**
Mug, sugar white, 13 oz. **175-200**
Pepper mill, lemon yellow.................................. **300+**
Pitcher, cov., charcoal, 1 1/2 qt......................... **200**
Pitcher, cov., ice blue, 1 1/2 qt. **150**
Pitcher, nutmeg brown.. **200**
Pitcher, redesigned, ripe apricot (ILLUS. center with creamer & coffeepot).................. **200**
Plate, bread & butter, 6 1/2" d., lettuce green.. **10**
Plate, salad, 7 1/2" d. **15**
Plate, luncheon, 9 1/2" d., pink sherbet **17**
Plate, dinner, 10" d., oyster grey **25**
Plate, chop, 13 7/8" d., ice blue............................ **50**
Plate, chop, 13 7/8" d., parsley green **65**

Platter, 10 1/4" oval, individual, lettuce green **50**
Platter, 12 3/4" oval, brick red **90**
Platter, 12 3/4" oval, parsley green **40**
Platter, 14 1/2" oval, sugar white **45**
Salt & pepper shakers, stacking-type, ice blue, pr.. **25**
Salt & pepper shakers, stacking-type, oyster grey, pr. (ILLUS. left rear, with cups & saucers) **60**
Salt & pepper shakers, stacking-type, parsley green, pr. **60**
Salt shaker, single, redesigned......................... **200+**
Salt shaker & pepper mill, redesigned, lemon yellow, pr. (ILLUS. right rear, with cups & saucers)... **500+**
Soup, 11 1/2 oz. **30**
Soup, cov., redesigned, 18 oz.............................. **30**
Sugar, redesigned, aqua...................................... **150**
Sugar, redesigned, brick red .... **275+**
Sugar, stacking-type, pink sherbet **15**
Sugar, stacking-type, sugar white, family size... **40**
Teapot, cov., restyled, aqua .... **3,000+**
Tumbler, iced tea, Pinch patt., seafoam blue, Imperial Glass Co., 14 oz. **50**
Tumbler, water, Pinch patt., ruby red, Imperial Glass Co., 11 oz. .... **125+**
Vegetable dish, open, cantaloupe, 10" d. **85**
Vegetable dish, open, cantaloupe, 8 1/8", 36 oz... **60**
Vegetable dish, open, nutmeg brown, 8 1/8", 36 oz. **35**
Vegetable dish, open or divided (casserole), 10", sugar white.. **60**

Iroquois Casual Cookware

Casserole, 3 qt... **225+**
Dutch oven .... **500+**
Fry pan, cov.. **500+**
Sauce pan, cov... **500+**
Serving tray, electric, 12 3/4 x 17 1/2" .... **2,000+**

Sarreguemines

This factory was established in Lorraine, France, about 1770. Subsequently Wedgwood-type pieces were produced as was Mocha ware. In the 19th century, the factory turned to pottery and stoneware.

Sarreguemines Ducks Centerpiece

Centerpiece, majolica, figural, two large facing ducks in shades of brown & green swimming on an oval turquoise & dark green base, professional repair to wings, late 19th c., 22" l., 8 1/2" h. (ILLUS.)... **$1,760**

Large Sarreguemines Centerpiece

Centerpiece, majolica, large oval bowl w/wide rolled rim over short cylindrical sides molded w/a brown ring band above floral swags in pink, white & green, the pedestal composed of two large mermaids w/their arms entwined w/S-form cornucopias, domed oval base in cobalt blue molded w/green leaf band & palmette feet, minor professional repairs, late 19th c., 22" l., 18" h. (ILLUS.)............... **3,520**

Compote, 10 1/2" l., 9" h., majolica, figural, a large yellow & brown shell-form bowl raised on a mottled dark green & brown dolphin on an oval foot, shape No. 1376 ...... **605**

Ewer, tall, slender, ovoid Art Deco form w/flared foot & shoulder tapering to slender cylindrical neck, flat rim w/tiny spout, D-form handle, crystalline glaze w/striated wine ground & round crystals of various sizes, ink-stamped "Sarreguemines France," 11 7/8" h.............................. **330**

Pitcher, 6 1/2" h., majolica, figural, head of John Bull, naturalistic coloring....................... **138**

Pitcher, 7 1/2" h., majolica, figural, head of Puck, fleshtones on face, wearing green hat, 19th c. **143**

Sarreguemines Figural Planter

Planter, majolica, figural, a large seated monkey wearing a turquoise blue coat, pale green pants & pink slippers at a brown upright piano, which forms the planter, brown base, professional repair to base & tail, late 19th c., 9 1/2" h. (ILLUS.)... **770**

Plaque, majolica, oval, relief-molded color scene of bird dog in the field chasing ducks, fine detail, cobalt blue rim band,

15 x 22" (minor professional rim repair).. **990**

Rare Sarreguemines Game Plaque

Plaque, majolica, oval, w/molded green oak leaf handles, the cobalt blue ground molded in full relief w/three brown quail in a field of gold & green wheat w/a turquoise blue pond at the center, shape No. 571, late 19th c., 16 x 23 1/2" (ILLUS.)... **4,180**

Vase, 17" h., tall, slender cylindrical body w/a flaring ringed foot, incised up the sides w/tall lilies w/an intricate design of leaves & stems in yellow against a dark brown ground, impressed marks (minor flakes to top).. **275**

Sarreguemines Dolphin Vases

Vases, 14 1/2" h., majolica, turquoise blue shell-molded trumpet-form vase supported by an entwined brown & cream dolphin on a round green base, cobalt blue trim, shape No. 400, professional repair to rim, late 19th c., pr. (ILLUS.).................. **1,650**

Sascha Brastoff

Brastoff Marks

Sascha Brastoff dedicated his life to creating works with a flair all his own. He was a costume designer for major movie studios, a dancer, a window dresser and a talented painter. The creator in Sascha put him on the path to ceramics early in life, when he was awarded a scholarship to the Cleveland Art School; however, he also worked with watercolors, charcoals, pastels, resin, fabrics, ceramics, metal sculptures, and enamels. Nelson Rockefeller, Brastoff's friend, understood the uniqueness of his talents and, in 1953, he built a complex in Los Angeles, California, to house the many creations Sascha was able to produce.

A full line of handpainted china with names such as Allegro, La Jolla, Roman Coin and Night Song was created. Surf Ballet was a popular dinnerware line with a look achieved by dipping pieces of blue, pink or yellow into real gold or platinum. Also highly popular was Sascha's line of enamels on copper. Many collectors do not know that Sascha dabbled in textiles. A yard of cloth in good condition might command several hundred dollars on today's market. His artware items included patterns such as Star Steed, a leaping-fantasy horse, and Rooftops, a series of houses where the roofs were the prominent feature. These pieces were - and continue to be - two of the most highly collectible Sascha artware patterns.

Sascha Brastoff also created a line of Alaskan-motif items. Many collectors confuse Matthew Adams pieces with those of Sascha. Even though Adams worked for Brastoff for a period of time, his pieces are not nearly as sought after as those that Sascha created.

Brastoff's crystal ball served him well during his lifetime. In the late 1940s and early 1950s he created a series of Western-motif cache pots that excite any collector when found today. Almost a decade before the poodle craze in the 1950s, Sascha created a line of poodle products. In the 1950s, cigarette smoking was at an all-time high and Sascha was there with smoking accessories.

From 1947 to 1952 pieces were signed "Sascha B." or with the full signature, "Sascha Brastoff." After 1953 and before 1962, during the years of his factory-studio, pieces done by his employees showed "Sascha B." and, more often than not, also included the Chanticleer back stamp. Caution should be taken to understand that the Chanticleer with the full name "Sascha Brastoff" below it is not the "full signature" mark that elevates pieces to substantial prices. The Chanticleer mark is usually in gold and will incorporate Sascha's work name in the same color. Sascha's personal full signature is the one commanding the high prices.

Health problems forced Sascha to leave his company in 1963. After 1962 pieces were marked "Sascha B." and also included the "R" in a circle trademark. Ten years later the business closed.

Sascha Brastoff died on February 4, 1993. The passing of this flamboyant artist, whose special character was well reflected in his work, means that similar creations will probably never be achieved again.

Sascha Brastoff Enamel Ashtray

Ashtray, enamel, floral design on white, 5 1/2" d. (ILLUS.) **$25**
Ashtray, round, leaf decoration, full signature, large **350**
Ashtray, Western scene w/covered wagon, rare promotional piece, 14" w **210**

Sascha Brastoff Mosaic Bowl

Bowl, banana shape, Mosaic design outside, solid color inside (ILLUS.) **65**
Bowl, 8" d., footed, abstract design **45**
Box, cov., Jewel Bird decoration, No. 020 .... **85**
Candleholder, resin, green or blue, 6" h., each **65**
Cigarette box, cov., Rooftops patt., No. 021, 8" l. **100**
Cigarette box, cov., "Star Steed" decoration **100**
Compote, polar bear decoration, No. 085 .... **75**
Dish, horse decoration on green ground, 6 1/2" sq. **45**
Dish, three-footed, fish-shaped (flounder), house decoration, 8 1/4 x 8 1/2" **125**
Gravy boat, w/attached undertray, scalloped rim, pink w/silver accents (ILLUS.) **65**

Sascha Brastoff Gravy Boat

Lamp base, mosaic tile, 27" h............................ **350**
Model of polar bear, blue resin, 10" h. **550**
Model of rooster, mosaic design, 15" h............. **575**
Model of Victorian shoe, Surf Ballet glaze,
   10" h.. **255**
Obelisk, cov., full signature, 21" h....................... **950**

Sascha Brastoff Pipe

Pipe, sinuous shape, abstract design w/gold
   accents, 4" l. (ILLUS.)....................................... **75**
Plate, square, vegetable decoration, full sig-
   nature... **300**

Sascha Brastoff Fish Plate

Plate, 6 1/2" d., fish shape & design
   (ILLUS.)... **75**

Sascha Brastoff Plate

Plate, 8" d., w/house & tree design (ILLUS.)....... **20**
Plate, 9" d., Merbaby patt..................................... **145**

Brown & White S. Brastoff Plate

Plate, 9 1/2" d., wide brown rim w/abstract
   design, white center, full signature
   (ILLUS.).. **750**

Sascha Brastoff Enamel Plate

Plate, 11 1/2" d., enamel, orange & gold abstract design, factory hanger on back
   (ILLUS.).. **85**

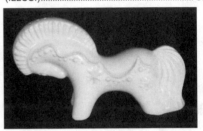

Sascha Brastoff Horse Salt Shaker

Salt shaker, model of a horse, white, pro-
   duced in 1947-1948, 5 1/4" l., 3 1/4" h.
   (ILLUS.).. **150**
Vase, 5" h., Provincial Rooster patt., No.
   F20.. **515**
Wall pocket, Rooftops patt., No. 031, 20" h. **550**

Satsuma

These decorated wares have been produced in Japan since the end of the 18th century. The early pieces are scarce and high-priced. Later Satsuma wares are plentiful and, with prices rising, are also becoming highly collectible.

Satsuma Bowl Decorated in Relief

Bowl, 9 5/8" d., round, decorated w/figures
of man & woman w/haloes in relief sitting
among other painted figures, in gold on

white ground, signed "Hododa, Shimazu Mon," ca. 1868-1912 (ILLUS.).................. **$2,240**

Satsuma Covered Jar

Jar, cov., ovoid body, lid w/foo-lion finial, all decorated w/interior scenes of people, in iron reds, blues & black w/heavy gilding, Meiji period, 10" h. (ILLUS.)........................... **560**

One of Set of Satsuma Cabinet Plates

Plates, 8 1/2" d., set of 12 cabinet plates signed "Kinkozan zo," each decorated w/gilt border, painted flowers w/gilt scroll-work on dark blue ground, centering car-touches of various birds in wooded land-scapes, each different, each marked w/impressed & painted mark on under-side, extremely rare, the set (ILLUS. of one).. **25,760**

Satsuma Signed Vase

Vase, cov., baluster form w/flaring rim, lid w/finial, ringed base, decorated w/haloed Arhats on gold ground, signed "Hododa, Shimazu Mon," ca. 1868-1912, drilled for lamp (ILLUS.).. **504**

Satsuma Miniature Vase

Vase, miniature, 2 1/2" h., classical form w/flaring rim & decorated w/wisteria on cream ground, signed "Kinkozan," ca. 1868-1912 (ILLUS.) **560**

Tall Satsuma Vase

Vase, 22" h., deep rounded lower body be-low a wide flat shoulder centered by a tall cylindrical neck flanked by square bam-boo-form handles w/a bird perched on each, the rim formed into a pierced domed cage, decorated in low relief w/chrysanthemums & leaves, Meiji Peri-od, minor restoration to top cage (ILLUS.)... **330**

Vase, 43" h., elaborately decorated & as-cribed to depict "Kaguyahima" (featuring Shogun w/Courtiers & Samurai), late 19th c., Japan (two minor chips on one handle) **850**

Vases, 10 1/4" h., baluster-shaped, cobalt blue ground decorated w/gilt trim, the front w/a rectangular polychrome land-scape scene, late 19th - early 20th c., pr. (gilt worn) **578**

One of a Pair of Satsuma Vases

Vases, 19 1/4" h., bulbous form w/ring rim, each decorated in fanciful manner w/fig-ures in a garden scene, ca. 1880, pr. (ILLUS. of one) **672**

Schafer & Vater

Founded in Rudolstadt, Thuringia, Germany in 1890, the Schafer and Vater Porcelain Factory specialized in decorative pieces of porcelain usually in white or colored bisque. It produced many novelty figural items such as creamers, toothpick holders, boxes and hatpin holders, and also a line of jasper ware with white relief decoration in imitation of the famous Wedgwood jasper wares. The firm also decorated whiteware blanks.

The company ceased production in 1962, and collectors now seek out its charming pieces, which may be marked with a crown over a starburst containing the script letter "R."

Schafer & Vater Mark

Bottle, figural, a figure of a male golfer in color & wearing a white outfit w/knickers & a cap leaning over a large brown flat-sided round flask w/a short neck projecting at an angle, the flask inscribed "Golf and Good Spirits Make a Good Highball," 4 1/2" h. (missing stopper) **$322**

Bottle, figural, a skeleton standing enveloped in a sheet marked on the front "Gift!" (Poison), white w/brown trim, No. 6109, 9 1/2" h. 334

Bottle, figural, large rounded head of a young man w/wild hair wearing an inverted funnel for a hat, the funnel inscribed "Nurnberger Trichter," overall glossy washed blue glaze, No. 6218, 8" h. 403

Bottle, tall cylindrical form w/rounded shoulder to small cylindrical neck & small shoulder handle, brown, the front molded w/a naughty maiden in color seated in the bowl of a large white champagne glass & holding a single red rose, inscribed below "Prosit Blume," 7" h. (stopper missing) 138

Bottle set: figural bottle, one shot glass & oblong tray; the bottle in the form of a standing stocky man in clown outfit holding up a small pig & w/grapevines below, a small cylindrical short glass molded as a comical face, overall glossy washed dark blue glaze, bottle 7 3/4" h., the set (small chip on bottom of man's foot, stopper missing) 184

Bottle set: figural bottle, six cups & tray; bottle in the form of a comical short, fat doctor w/curled wig standing beside a large upright syringe, six small cylindrical cups w/names of medicines around the base resting on a round tray, pointed tip of syringe forms bottle stopper, overall glossy washed blue glaze, bottle 9 3/4" h., the set.. 575

Figural Chinese Man Creamer

Creamer, figural, in the form of a Chinese man wearing a long orange robe, holding a large white goose by the feet while it tries to fly away, thus forming the spout w/the open beak for pouring, the man's long black pigtail forming the handle, unmarked, 2 1/4" w., 4" h. (ILLUS.) **125**

Figurines, Sun Ladies & Moon Men, two w/a smiling cream-colored sun head on the body of a seated late-Victorian woman, one w/her arms away from her body, wearing a black jacket, white dress & red slippers w/a red handbag in her lap, the other w/a matching outfit but playing a banjo; the three men w/a cream crescent moon head, one head smoking a pipe & attached to the body of a reclining late-Victorian man wearing a short white coat w/black collar & white kneebreeches, a second man wearing a similar outfit but kneeling & holding out a bouquet w/one hand & a pink hat in the other, the third man reclining on his stomach w/his lower legs in the air, No. 3150 through 3155, 3 1/2 to 4 1/2" l., the set of 5 (two women w/minor chip repairs) **1,380**

Schafer & Vater Sugar Shaker

Sugar shaker w/original metal top, bisque, a slender waisted cylindrical white form w/a band of embossed scrolls around the wide bottom & a molded lappet band at the top, the body molded in relief w/figures of Grecian women tinted grey w/an altar in pink & foliage in green, 3 1/4" d., 6 1/8" h. (ILLUS.)... **135**

Tea set: cov. teapot, cov. sugar bowl, creamer & two cups & saucers; figural, all in pink bisque w/grey-green trim, the tea-pot body formed by the wide deep skirt of a woman, a slender ribbed spout at the front, the cover formed by the torso of the woman wearing a ruffled collar & balloon sleeves, a tall ribbon on her head, the handle formed by a slender, elongated figure of a bent-over gentleman wearing a tall top hat, the figural sugar bowl in the form of a similar lady but w/small scroll handles at the sides, the open creamer in the form of a wide skirt w/the handle in the form of the bent-over gentleman, each cup w/a gentleman handle & on a ruffled saucer, all pieces w/molded or-nate scrolls & swags, No. 3861, 3862 & 3863, 4" to 7" h., the set (few small chips, repaired lines)... **834**

Schoop (Hedi) Art Creations

Hedi Schoop left Germany in 1930, then immigrated to Hollywood, California, in 1933. She began producing ceramics of her own designs in 1940. Schoop turned out as many as 30,000 pieces per year once her production was running smoothly. A fire destroyed the pottery in 1958, and Hedi did free-lance work for several California companies. She retired from working full-time in the early 1960s, but her talents would not let her quit completely. She died in 1996 and had painted, although sparingly, until then.

There were a variety of marks ranging from the stamped or incised Schoop signature to the hard-to-find Hedi Schoop sticker. The words "Hollywood, Cal." or "California" can also be found in conjunction with the Hedi Schoop name. You can find items with a production number, artists' names or initials.

Schoop was imitated by many artists, especially some decorators who opened businesses of their own after working with Schoop. Mac and Yona Lippen owned Yona Ceramics, and Katherine Schueftan owned Kim Ward Studio. They used many of Schoop's designs and today have their own following among collectors. There were others, but Schueftan lost a lawsuit Hedi had brought against her in 1942 for design infringements. It is important to buy pieces marked "Hedi Schoop" or buy from a reputable dealer if you want to be sure you have the real thing.

Considering the number of products created, it would be easy to assume that Schoop pieces are plentiful. This would be an erroneous assumption. Collectors will indeed be fortunate to find any Schoop figurines for less than $100, and to amass many of her products takes dedication and determination.

Hedi Schoop Butterfly Ashtray

Ashtray, in the shape of a butterfly w/spread wings, yellow w/gold trim & "eyes" on wings, inkstamp overglaze, 5 1/2" w. (ILLUS.).. **$55**

Candleholder, figural, a mermaid holding a single candle socket in each hand above her head, rare, ca. 1950, 13 1/2" h................ **675**

Hedi Schoop Dancers

Figural group, cowboy & woman dancing, bisque faces & hands, cowboy wears hat & kerchief, woman wears black top & ruf-fled yellow full-length skirt, cowboy has one hand around woman's waist, woman holds skirt out w/one hand, incised un-glazed mark "Hedi Schoop, California," 11" h. (ILLUS.)... **400**

Figure of ballerina, on a thin round base, long skirt flared upward revealing right foot, right arm extended & holding up skirt, left arm extended forward w/head turned to front, bluish grey w/silver over-tones, impressed mark "Hedi Schoop," 9 1/4" h... **145**

Hedi Schoop Chinese Woman Figure

Figure of Chinese woman, standing on a round black base, white floor-length skirt, black, white & green blouse w/long sleeves flaring at wrists, a white flower in black hair above each ear, right fingers bent to hold a pot w/black cloth handle & in same colors as blouse, right leg bent at knee, woman 9" h., pot 2 1/2" h., 2 pcs. (ILLUS.)... **165**

Figure of clown, standing w/one leg crossed over the other, one hand to head, other hand to mouth, bucket & mop at his side, 10 1/2" h. **250**

Figure of girl, "Debutante," standing & holding handmade flowers in both arms, rough textured finish, ca. 1943, 12 1/2" h. **245**

Figure of girl, standing on cobalt blue-glazed round base, legs slightly apart, arms stretched out to sides, hands folded to hold jump rope, rough textured black hair w/pigtails out to sides & held in place w/cobalt blue glossy ties, light blue long sleeved shirt, cobalt blue overblouse w/straps, rough textured cobalt blue short skirt & socks, inkstamp on unglazed bottom, "Hedi Schoop Hollywood, Cal.," 8 1/2" h. **210**

Figure of Woman by Hedi Schoop

Figure of woman, in 19th-c. mint-green off-the-shoulder dress decorated w/h.p. pink flowers on bodice & skirt, light hair w/gold hair bow & curls cascading down one side, holds parasol in one hand, other hand holds skirt, inkstamp underglaze "Hedi Schoop, Hollywood, Cal.," 13" h. (ILLUS.) **235**

Schoop Figure of Woman with Basket

Figure of woman, standing on one foot & holding large basket above her head w/both hands, dressed in yellow top & full yellow skirt w/blue & green stripes, on yellow oval base, incised overglaze "Hedi Schoop Design, California U.S.A.," 14" h. (ILLUS.) **325**

Kneeling Woman Flower Holder

Flower holder, figure of kneeling woman, short light textured hair, white dirndl-type dress w/blue trim & h.p. flowers on skirt, one hand holds apron out for holding flowers, on light blue oval base, inkstamp underglaze "Hedi Schoop, Hollywood, Cal.," 8 1/2" h. (ILLUS.) **85**

Hedi Schoop Flower Holder

Flower holder, figure of woman w/brown hair dressed in pale blue dress w/white textured hem & short puff sleeves, pink rose applied at waist, one hand holds basket on head, other hand holds skirt out to side, creating opening for flowers, inkstamp underglaze "Hedi Schoop, Hollywood, Cal.," 12 3/4" h. (ILLUS.) **195**

Flower holder, figure of woman w/dark brown hair dressed in white dress w/brown & mauve h.p. scalloping & flowers, mauve hat, holds basket in each hand, incised underglaze "Hedi Schoop," 11 1/2" h. **185**

Hedi Schoop Figural Flower Holder

Flower holder, figure of woman w/long light hair, dressed in ruffled teal off-the-shoulder long-sleeved full-length dress & teal picture hat w/scalloped rim, hands clasped in front holding matching basket, all w/applied pink flowers, inkstamp underglaze "Hedi Schoop, Hollywood, Cal.," 11" h. (ILLUS.) **215**

Schoop Jardiniere with Chinese Scene

Jardiniere, cylindrical, incised stylized design of a kneeling Chinese woman w/Ming trees & animals, base & design in gold glaze on a light green body, 7" h. (ILLUS.) **135**

Lamp, figural, TV-type, Comedy & Tragedy masks on a base w/full Comedy, part Tragedy conjoined, dark green w/gold trim, ca. 1954, 10 3/4" l., 12" h. **525**

Model of cat lying down, head up, tail wrapped around side, paws tucked under body, brown collar around neck w/two yellow bells & two small brown pots at-

tached, white rough textured body, inkstamp under glaze, "Hedi Schoop Hollywood, Cal.," 6 3/4" l., 6 1/2" h. **135**

Planter, model of a horse, rough textured mane & tail, white glossy glazed body w/mint green face accents, saddle, bows in assorted areas & scalloped edging at the base, inkstamp mark "Hedi Schoop," 7 1/2" h. **110**

Figural Hedi Schoop Tray

Tray, figural, divided w/irregular leaf-shaped raised edges, the rim mounted w/the figure of a cherub on her knees, arms outstretched beside her, head tilted, beige & gold tray interior, beige w/pink-tinged cherub, gold wings, rose on left wrist, belt of roses around her waist w/rose-glazed bowl exterior & rose hair, bottom of tray also in a glossy rose, incised "Hedi Schoop," 11 1/2" l., overall 6" h. (ILLUS.) **275**

Vase, 9" h. at highest point, 4 1/2" h., at lowest point, 9" l., seashell-form, footed oval base, fluted edge rising from the low end to the higher end, dark green base w/dark green & gold fading to light green, rim trimmed in gold, transparent textured glossy glaze, marked w/a silver label w/red block letters, "Hedi Schoop Hollywood, Calif." on two lines **98**

Sèvres & Sèvres-Style

Sevres marks

Some of the most desirable porcelain ever produced was made at the Sèvres factory, originally established at

Vincennes, France, and transferred, through permission of Madame de Pompadour, to Sèvres as the Royal Manufactory about the middle of the 18th century. King Louis XV took sole responsibility for the works in 1759, when production of hard paste wares began. Between 1850 and 1900, many biscuit and soft-paste pieces were made again. Fine early pieces are scarce and high-priced. Many of those available today are late productions. The various Sèvres marks have been copied, and pieces listed as "Sèvres-Style" are similar to actual Sèvres wares but not necessarily from that factory. Three of the many Sèvres marks are illustrated here.

Busts of the Duc & Duchesse D'Angouleme, bisque, modeled after Baron Francois Joseph Bosio, she wearing an Empire-style gown, her hair in tight curls, he wearing a Napoleonic military uniform, each on a cobalt blue & gold-banded socle, dated January 10, 1821 & October 3, 1823 respectively, blue printed interlaced L's marks, artist & other marks, 10 1/4" h., pr. **$2,760**

Sevres Bisque Figure of Boy & Goat

Figure group, bisque, a bust portrait of a youth holding a kid goat draped around his shoulders, incised factory mark, early 20th c., 15" h. (ILLUS.) **805**

Figure group, bisque, "Le Triomphe de Bacchus," modeled w/the figure of a nude Bacchus seated in an ermine drapery flanked by two nymphs, wrestling putti at his feet, another putto & lioness at the back, the rockwork base w/applied trophies, vases & fruits, after the model by Taraval, impressed marks, dated 1913, 15" h. **2,990**

Jewelry box, cov., cartouche-shaped, w/concave sides & a low domed cover, the hinged cover painted w/a large reserve of 18th c. women in an interior reading a letter surrounded by a cobalt blue ground decorated w/a wide leafy scroll gilt band, the sides each w/a paneled reserve of a landscape within scrolling gilt borders on a cobalt blue ground, the interior painted w/flowers, late 19th - early 20th c., blue crowned wreath & "S" mark, artist-signed, overall 17" l. **8,050**

Pedestals, slightly tapering columnar form w/a gilt-bronze foot & capital, fitted on a square white onyx base & w/a thin square white onyx top, the porcelain column w/dark blue scalloped bands around the top & bottom edged in gold, a central gilt-bronze band dividing the column into two white panels decorated w/light blue figural scenes, late 19th c., top 11 1/2" sq., 44 1/2" h., pr. **20,300**

Pitcher, 7 7/8" h., jug-form, tapering ovoid body w/a short wide neck w/dished spout & notched back edge issuing a high arched gilt loop shoulder handle, the shoulder painted w/a garland of flowers on a yellow band, the lower body w/gilt arches & a band of grapevine on dark blue, mid-19th c. **173**

Plate, 9 1/4" d., the center painted w/flowers, the sky blue rim reserved w/three gilt cartouches centering a pair of exotic birds, painted interlaced L's mark w/crown, number 2,000 & "Trianon," late 18th c. **632**

Urns, cov., tall gilt-bronze mounted baluster form, a stepped squared bronze foot below a short porcelain waisted pedestal w/a bronze connector to the tall ovoid body tapering to a waisted neck & domed cover, fitted w/angular bronze shoulder handles & a figural putto finial, the body w/a central reserve w/a figural color scene of 18th c. country figures w/horses, ornate gilt border on a white ground, the reverse w/a landscape reserve, late 19th c., 45" h., pr. **55,375**

Vase, cov., 34 1/4" h., the tall ovoid body w/a cobalt blue ground, the trumpet-form neck supporting a domed cover w/pod finial, the body raised on an ormolu & porcelain ringed pedestal on a squared ormolu plinth base, the shoulders mounted w/upright ormolu acanthus & bracket ring handles suspending berried laurel, the front painted w/an oval reserve w/a color scene of an amorous couple & an interloper, all within a gilt oval band w/scrolling gilt trim, further gilt trim on the cover, neck & base, ca. 1880, artist-signed **9,775**

Vases, 4 7/8" h., inverted pear-shaped body raised on a small slender pedestal on a square plinth, the short waisted neck w/scalloped rim & gilt fluted panels, the body in dark blue applied w/gilt oak garlands from the shoulder down across the body, gilt base trim, 19th c., pr. **575**

Vases, cov., 22" h., the drum-shaped body w/a rounded bottom raised on a slender pedestal base, the shoulder tapering to a tall waisted neck fitted w/a domed cover w/pine cone finial, the pink ground decorated on the neck & around the mid-body w/oblong reserves w/color scenes of 18th c. figures in landscapes within gold border w/scrolling gilt trim, gilt banding on the cover, body & base, late 19th c., spurious blue interlaced L's marks, the pair **3,680**

Shawnee

Shawnee
U.S.A.

Shawnee Mark

The Shawnee Pottery Company of Zanesville, Ohio, opened its doors for operation in 1936 and, sadly, closed in 1961. The pottery was inexpensive for its quality and was readily purchased at dime stores as well as department stores. Sears, Roebuck and Co., Butler Bros., Woolworth's and S. Kresge were just a few of the companies that were longtime retailers of this fine pottery.

Shawnee Pottery Company had a wide array of merchandise to offer, from knickknacks to dinnerware, although Shawnee is quite often associated with colorful pig cookie jars and the dazzling "Corn King" line of dinnerware. Planters, miniatures, cookie jars and Corn King pieces are much in demand by today's avid collectors. Factory seconds were purchased by outside decorators and trimmed with gold, decals and unusual hand painting, which makes those pieces extremely desirable in today's market and enhances the value considerably.

Shawnee Pottery has become the most sought-after pottery in today's collectible market.

Reference books available are Mark E. Supnick's book Collecting Shawnee Pottery, The Collector's Guide to Shawnee Pottery *by Duane and Janice Vanderbilt or* Shawnee Pottery - An Identification & Value Guide *by Jim and Bev Mangus.*

Shawnee Figural Ashtrays

Ashtray, figural kingfisher, parrot, bird, fish, terrier or owl, marked "U.S.A.," dusty rose, turquoise, old ivory, white or burgundy, 3" h., each (ILLUS. of fish, kingfisher & bird).. **$45-50**

Shawnee Figural Banks

Bank, figural bulldog, 4 1/2" h., unmarked (ILLUS. left) **175-200**

Figural Howdy Doody Bank

Bank, figural Howdy Doody riding a pig, marked "Bob Smith U.S.A.," 6 3/4" h. (ILLUS.)... **500-550**
Bank, figural tumbling bear, unmarked, 4 3/4" h. (ILLUS. right, with bulldog)....... **175-200**
Bank-cookie jar, figural Smiley Pig, chocolate or butterscotch base, marked "Patented: Smiley Shawnee 60 U.S.A.," 10 1/2" h. (ILLUS. right w/Winnie Pig bank-cookie jar) **450-500**

Winnie Pig & Smiley Pig Banks/Cookie Jars

Bank-cookie jar, figural Winnie Pig, chocolate or butterscotch base, marked "Patented: Winnie Shawnee 61 U.S.A." 10 1/2" h. (ILLUS. left w/Smiley Pig bankcookie jar) **450-500**

Rare Shawnee Batter Pitcher

Batter pitcher, Pennsylvania Dutch patt., marked "U.S.A.," rare, 34" h. (ILLUS.) .. **750-900**

Shawnee Figural Book Ends

Book ends, figural, full figure of a man at potter's wheel, brown, marked "Crafted by Shawnee Potteries Zanesville, Ohio 1960," 9" h., pr. (ILLUS.) **400-500**

Indian Motif Cigarette Box

Cigarette box, cov., embossed Indian arrowhead on lid, brown, marked "Shawnee," 3 1/4 x 4 1/2" (ILLUS.) **400-500**
Coffeepot, cov., Pennsylvania Dutch patt., marked "U.S.A. 52," 42 oz. **165-175**
Coffeepot, cov., Sunflower patt, marked "U.S.A.," 42 oz. **165-175**

Valencia Line Coffeepot

Coffeepot, cov., Valencia line, tangerine glaze, 7 1/2" h. (ILLUS.) **95-125**
Cookie jar, cov., figural cottage, marked "U.S.A. 6," 7" h. **800-1,000**
Cookie jar, cov., figural drum major, marked "U.S.A. 10," 10" h. **250-275**
Cookie jar, cov., figural ear of corn, Corn King line, No. 66, 10 1/2" h. **265-275**
Cookie jar, cov., figural fruit basket, marked "Shawnee U.S.A. 84," 8 1/2" h. **95-125**
Cookie jar, cov., figural Jo-Jo the clown, marked "Shawnee U.S.A. 12," 9" h. **225-250**

Jumbo (Lucky) Elephant Cookie Jar

Cookie jar, cov., figural Jumbo (Lucky) elephant, decal decoration & gold trim, marked "U.S.A.," 11 3/4" h. (ILLUS.)...... **550-600**

Muggsy Cookie Jar

Cookie jar, cov., figural Muggsy dog, blue bow, gold trim & decals, marked "Patented Muggsy U.S.A.," 11 3/4" h. (ILLUS.)... **600-650**

Cookie jar, cov., figural Puss 'n Boots, long tail, burgundy bow, marked "Patented Puss N Boots U.S.A.," 10 1/2" h. **150-175**

Cookie jar, cov., figural sailor boy, decorated w/decals & gold trim, marked "U.S.A.," 11 1/2" h.. **650-700**

Cookie jar, cov., figural Smiley Pig, shamrock decoration, marked "U.S.A.," 11 1/4" h.. **195-225**

Winnie Pig Cookie Jar

Cookie jar, cov., figural Winnie Pig, w/peach collar, marked "Patented Winnie U.S.A.," 11 3/4" h. (ILLUS.).................................... **275-300**

Pink Elephant Cookie Jar/Ice Bucket

Cookie jar-ice bucket, cov., figural elephant, pink, marked "Shawnee U.S.A. 60" or "Kenwood U.S.A. 60" (ILLUS.................... **95-100**

Dutch-style Red Feather Creamer

Creamer, ball-type, Dutch style, decorated w/red feather, marked "U.S.A. 12," 4 1/2" h. (ILLUS.)..................................... **125-150**

Dutch-style Creamer & Pitcher

Creamer, ball-type, Dutch style, decorated w/tulip & blue around neck, marked "U.S.A.," 4 1/4" h. (ILLUS. left w/pitcher) **250-275**

Pennsylvania Dutch Creamer & Sugar Bowl

Creamer, ball-type, Pennsylvania Dutch style, marked "U.S.A. 12," 4 1/2" h. (ILLUS. right)... **75-95**

Figural Elephant Creamer

Creamer, figural elephant, w/gold decoration & decals, marked "Patented U.S.A.," 4 3/4" h. (ILLUS.)..................................... **265-285**

Creamer, figural Smiley Pig, decorated w/embossed peach flower, marked "Patented Smiley U.S.A.," 4 1/2" h. **95-125**

Creamer, Lobster Ware, charcoal grey, figural lobster handle, marked "U.S.A. 909," 4 1/2" h... **65-85**

White Corn Line Pieces

Various Shawnee Figurines

Creamer, White Corn line, airbrushed & gold trim, marked "U.S.A.," 4 3/4" h. (ILLUS. third from left, front row, with White Corn Line pieces) **95-125**

Valencia Line Dealer's Display Sign

Dealer's display sign, figural Spanish dancers, "Valencia" embossed across base, tangerine glaze, 11 1/4" h. (ILLUS.) **400-450**

Figurine, model of deer, no mark, 3" h. (ILLUS. far right w/various figurines, top of page) **175-200**

Figurine, model of Pekingese, no mark, 2 1/2" h. (ILLUS. center w/various figurines) **50-55**

Figurine, model of puppy, no mark, 3" h. (ILLUS. second from left w/various figurines) **45-50**

Figurine, model of rabbit, sitting, no mark, 3" h. (ILLUS. second from right w/various figurines) **55-65**

Figurine, model of squirrel, no mark, 2 1/2" h. (ILLUS. third from right w/various figurines) **45-50**

Figurine, model of Teddy bear, no mark, 3" h. (ILLUS. third from left w/various figurines) **45-50**

Figurine, model of tumbling bear, no mark, 3" h. (ILLUS. far left w/various figurines) **65-75**

Shawnee Fern Matchbox Holder

Matchbox holder, embossed Fern patt., marked "U.S.A.," 5 1/2" h. (ILLUS.) **75-100**

Figural Lobster Pin

Pin, figural red lobster, promotion by Shawnee, ink-stamped on back "Kenwood Ceramics Shawnee Potteries Zanesville, Ohio," 3 1/2" l. (ILLUS.) **75-95**

Pitcher, ball-type, Dutch style, w/painted tulips & embossed blue rope decoration around neck, marked "U.S.A.," 64 oz. (ILLUS. right w/Dutch-style creamer).. **375-400**

Pitcher, 7" h., ball-type, Valencia line, burgundy, green, cobalt, orange or yellow, marked "U.S.A." **45-65**

Pitcher, 7 1/2" h., figural Boy Blue, gold trim, marked "Shawnee U.S.A. 46"................. **225-250**

Pitcher, 7 1/2" h., figural Chanticleer rooster, marked "Patented Chanticleer U.S.A." **75-95**

Tandem Bicycle Planter

Pitcher, 7 1/2" h., figural Little Bo Peep, gold
   trim, marked "Shawnee U.S.A. 47"
   (ILLUS.).. **250-275**
Pitcher, 7 3/4" h., figural Smiley Pig, peach
   or burgundy flower decoration, marked
   "Patented Smiley U.S.A." **165-185**
Pitcher, 8" h., White Corn line, airbrushed &
   gold trim, marked "U.S.A." (ILLUS. back
   row, left w/White Corn pieces)............... **195-250**

Clown Planter

Planter, figural clown w/blocks, marked
   "Shawnee U.S.A.," 4 1/2" h.
   (ILLUS.)... **85-100**
Planter, model of a bicycle built for two
   w/man & woman riders dressed in Gay
   Nineties style, gold trim, marked "Shaw-
   nee U.S.A. 735," 6" h. (ILLUS., top of
   page) **75-100**

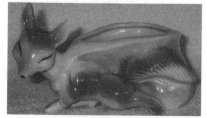

Fox & Bag Planter

Planter, model of a fox & bag, marked
   "U.S.A.," 4 1/2" h. (ILLUS.).......................... **50-75**
Planters, models of train engine, coal car,
   boxcar & caboose, blue, yellow, green &
   butterscotch, decorated, Nos. 550, 551,
   552, 553, 4 pcs. **85-100**

Valencia Relish Tray

Relish tray, Valencia dinnerware line, round
   base w/four wedge-shaped inserts and
   center round insert, Valencia orange, yellow, green & cobalt, no mark, 10 1/4" d.
   (ILLUS.).. **200-250**

Flower & Fern Salt Box

Salt box, cov., Flower & Fern patt., yellow,
   green or blue, marked "U.S.A.," 4 3/4" h.
   (ILLUS.).. **95-125**
Salt & pepper shakers, figural cottage,
   pr. **200-250**

Figural Smiley & Winnie Shakers

Salt & pepper shakers, figural Smiley Pig & Winnie Pig, clover blossom decoration, 3", pr. (ILLUS.) **75-95**

Salt & pepper shakers, figural Smiley Pig & Winnie Pig, clover blossom decoration, 5" h., pr. **175-200**

Salt & pepper shakers, figural Smiley Pig & Winnie Pig, heart decoration, 5", pr. **125-150**

Salt & pepper shakers, White Corn line, airbrushed & gold trim, no mark, 3" h., pr. (ILLUS. front row, far right, in front of larger shakers, w/White Corn pieces) **40-50**

Salt & pepper shakers, White Corn line, airbrushed & gold trim, no mark, 5 1/4" h., pr. (ILLUS. front row, far right, behind smaller shakers, w/White Corn pieces) **85-100**

Lobster Ware Snack Jar/Bean Pot

Snack jar-bean pot, cov., Lobster Ware, tab-handled, figural lobster finial on lid, marked "Kenwood U.S.A. 925," 8" h. (ILLUS.) **275-300**

Sugar bowl-grease jar, Clover Blossom line, w/embossed clover blossoms, marked "U.S.A.," 4 3/4" h. **95-125**

Sugar bowl-grease jar, cov., figural cottage, marked "U.S.A. 8," 4 1/2" h. **325-350**

Sugar bowl-grease jar, cov., White Corn line, airbrushed & gold trim, marked "U.S.A." (ILLUS. front row, far left, w/White Corn pieces) **85-100**

Sugar bowl-grease jar, open, Pennsylvania Dutch patt., w/h.p. heart & tulip design, marked "U.S.A.," 2 3/4" h. (ILLUS. left w/creamer) **95-125**

Sugar shaker, White Corn line, airbrushed & gold trim, marked "U.S.A.," 5 1/4" h. (ILLUS. front row, second from left, w/White Corn pieces) **350-375**

Clover Bud Teapot

Teapot, cov., Clover Bud embossed decoration, marked "U.S.A.," 6 1/2" h. (ILLUS.) **175-225**

Teapot, cov., figural Cottage, marked "U.S.A. 7," 5 1/2" h. **375-450**

Figural Elephant Teapot

Teapot, cov., figural elephant w/burgundy, green & brown h.p. on white ground, marked "U.S.A.," 6 1/2" h. (ILLUS.) **275-300**

Granny Ann Teapot

Teapot, cov., figural Granny Ann, green apron, burgundy & yellow, w/gold decal shawl & trim, marked "Patented Granny Ann U.S.A." (ILLUS.) **400-450**

Tom the Piper's Son Teapot

Teapot, cov., figural Tom the Piper's Son, boy's head finial, pig head spout & tail handle, marked "Tom the Piper's Son Patented U.S.A. 44" (ILLUS.) **85-100**

Teapot, White Corn line, airbrushed & gold trim, marked "U.S.A.," 30 oz. (ILLUS. back row, right w/White Corn pieces) **375-400**

Scotty Dog Wall Pocket

Wall pocket, Scotty dog head, green, burgundy, cobalt, yellow or white, unmarked, 9 1/2" h. (ILLUS.)............................ **65-95**
Wall pocket, Sunflower patt., marked "U.S.A.," 6 3/4" h.. **45-55**

Tropical Fruit Wall Pocket

Wall pocket, Tropical Fruit, pink, marked "U.S.A.," 6 1/2" h. (ILLUS.)........................... **45-55**

Shelley China

Shelley
CHINA
ENGLAND

Shelley Mark

Members of the Shelley family were in the pottery business in England as early as the 18th century. In 1872 Joseph Shelley formed a partnership with James Wileman of Wileman & Co. who operated the Foley China Works. The Wileman & Co. name was used for the firm

for the next fifty years, and between 1890 and 1910 the words "The Foley" appeared above conjoined "WC" initials.

Beginning in 1910 the Shelley family name in a shield appeared on wares, although the firm's official name was still Wileman & Co. The company's name was finally changed to Shelley in 1925 and then Shelley China Ltd. after 1965. The firm changed hands in the 1960s and became part of the Doulton Group in 1971.

At first only average quality earthenwares were produced, but in the late 1890s new shapes and better quality decorations were used.

Bone china was introduced at Shelley before World War I, and these fine dinnerwares became very popular in the United States and are increasingly popular today with collectors. Thin "eggshell china" teawares, miniatures and souvenir items were widely marketed during the 1920s and 1930s and are sought-after today.

Ashtray, advertising-type, "Greer's O.V.H.".... **$100**
Backbar water pitcher, "White Horse" **500**
Bowl, berry, Blue Rock patt. **40**
Breakfast set: two-cup cov. coffeepot, creamer, open sugar bowl, two 8" d. plates, two 6" d. plates, two 5 1/2" d. bowls & one cov. pancake dish; Stocks patt., Dainty shape, the set......................... **1,000**
Butter dish, cov., Dainty White patt. **100**
Butter pat, Primrose patt. **95**
Cake set: 10" handled cake plate & six 6" d. plates; Wild Flower patt., the set.................... **250**
Candlestick, Art Deco-style, orange glaze, 2 1/2" h... **150**
Candlestick, flaring round base below the tapering shaft & bulbed candle socket, down-curved handle from socket to base, Cloisonné patt., 6 1/2" h. **250**
Candy dish, Dainty Pink patt., 4 1/2" l................. **65**
Coffeepot, cov., Bluebells patt., Vincent shape... **350**
Coffeepot, cov., Campanula patt., tall tapering ovoid body w/domed cover, 7" h. **300**
Coffeepot, cov., Dainty Blue patt., Dainty shape **600**
Coffeepot, cov., Violets patt., Mayfair shape... **400**

Dainty Floral Creamer & Sugar Bowl

Creamer & open sugar bowl, Floral patt., Dainty shape w/floral-molded handle, pr. (ILLUS.) **300**
Creamer, open sugar bowl & tray, Blue Rock patt., 3 pcs. **165**
Creamer & sugar bowl, Harebell patt., pr. **90**
Cup & saucer, Begonia patt., six-flute shape... **78**
Cup & saucer, Black Dainty patt., Dainty shape, rare **1,200**

Chinoiserie Pattern Cup & Saucer

Cup & saucer, Chinoiserie patt., Ripon
shape (ILLUS.)............................. 200
Cup & saucer, Countryside (Chintz style)
patt., gold foot & scroll handle 204

Dainty Cup & Saucer w/Floral Handle

Cup & saucer, Dainty shape, lavender &
cream w/floral-molded handle (ILLUS.) 200
Cup & saucer, Dainty shape, solid color 50
Cup & saucer, demitasse, Acacia patt., Re-
gent shape 100

Floral-Handled Cup & Saucer

Cup & saucer, Floral patt., Queen Anne
shape w/floral-molded handle (ILLUS.)......... 400
Cup & saucer, Floral patt., Vogue (Art Deco
style) shape 300
Cup & saucer, Japan patt., Alexandra
shape, Wileman & Co. 100
Cup & saucer, miniature, Lily of the Valley
patt., Westminster shape............................. 325
Cup & saucer, Polka Dot patt. 100
Cup & saucer, Regency patt., Dainty shape 60
Cup & saucer, Rock Garden patt., footed
Oleander shape 170
Cup & saucer, Stocks patt., Stratford shape 60
Cup & saucer, demitasse, Forget-Me-Not
patt. 48
Cups & saucers, demitasse, footed, pink
w/aqua dots, gold lined, 6 each,
12 pcs. 350
Demitasse pot, cov., Wildflowers patt.,
Dainty shape................................... 300

Dessert set: cup & saucer & dessert plate;
Campanula patt., 3 pcs. 130
Dessert set: cup & saucer & dessert plate;
Rosebud patt., 3 pcs..................... 110
Dessert set: cup & saucer & dessert plate;
Rock Garden patt., 3 pcs. 125
Egg cup, Dainty Shamrock patt. 55
Hot water pot, cov., Dainty Blue patt., Dainty
shape (ILLUS. center w/coffeepot & tea-
pot).. 600
Hot water pot, cov., Dainty patt........... 500

Shelley Floral Pattern Invalid Feeder

Invalid feeder, Floral patt. (ILLUS.)...................... 250
Jam pot w/metal cover & holder, Bridal Rose
patt., the set.................................. 175
Jelly mold, model of a large white chicken........ 200
Loving cup, Bermuda commemorative,
"1609-1959," 4 1/2 x 7"...................... 100
Luncheon set: 8" plate, cup & saucer; Hare-
bell patt., 3 pcs.............................. 100
Luncheon set: 8" plate, cup & saucer;
Stocks patt., 3 pcs............................ 90

Blue Iris Luncheon Set

Luncheon set (trio): cup, saucer & plate;
Blue Iris patt., Queen Anne shape, the
set (ILLUS.)...................................... 200

Gladiolus Luncheon Set

Luncheon set (trio): cup, saucer & plate; Gladiolus patt., Eve (Art Deco style) shape, the set (ILLUS.).................................. **250**

Japan Pattern Luncheon Set

Luncheon set (trio): cup, saucer & plate; Japan patt., Fairy shape, Wileman & Co., the set (ILLUS.)................................... **200**

Thistle Pattern Luncheon Set

Luncheon set (trio): cup, saucer & plate; Thistle patt., Alexandra shape, Wileman & Co., the set (ILLUS.) **125**
Mint dish, Dainty Blue patt. **72**

Shelley Model of a Drake

Model of a drake duck, brown head, grey & black body, Bird Series #12, 4 1/2" h. (ILLUS.).. **500**
Mug, decorated w/the coat-of-arms of Wales, 3" h. **100**
Napkin ring, Harmony patt. **100**
Nut dish, Old England patt., signed by Eric Slater **75**
Pitcher, water, jug-form, Blue Dragon patt. **500**
Plate, dinner, Harebell patt...................................... **75**

Festoons & Fruit Pattern Plate

Plate, Festoons & Fruit patt., Roseberry shape (ILLUS.)... **50-100**
Plate, 6" d., Rock Garden patt............................... **40**
Plate, 8" d., luncheon, Blue Rock patt. **56**

Jacobean Pattern Plate

Plate, 8 3/4" d., Jacobean patt. (ILLUS.)........ **50-60**
Platter, 10 x 13", meat, Blue Rock patt.............. **140**

Harmony Pattern Two-piece Reamer

Reamer & base, Harmony patt., streaky mottled pink & green glaze, 2 pc. (ILLUS.).. **350**
Shaving mug, Harmony patt. **175**

Blue Gladiolus Art Deco Tea Set

Tea set, Blue Gladiolus patt., Eve (Art Deco
style) shape, 21 pcs. (ILLUS. of part)......... **3,000**
Tea set, Green Lines & Bands patt., Eve (Art
Deco style) shape, 21 pcs. **2,500**

Red Blocks Art Deco Tea Set

Tea set, Red Blocks patt., Mode (Art Deco
style) shape, teapot & 22 pcs. (ILLUS. of
part).. **3,500**

Sun-Ray Art Deco Tea Set

Tea set, Sun-Ray patt., Vogue (Art Deco
style) shape, 21 pcs. (ILLUS. of
part).. **3,000**
Tea set, Yellow Phlox patt., Regent shape,
teapot & 37 pcs. **2,000**
Teapot, cov., Begonia patt. **400**
Teapot, cov., Dainty Blue patt., Dainty
shape (ILLUS. left w/coffeepot & hot wa-
ter pot) **650**
Teapot, cov., Dainty Blue patt., large **650**
Teapot, cov., Harebell patt. **400**

Harmony Drip-Ware Teapot

Teapot, cov., Harmony Drip-Ware, Cam-
bridge shape (ILLUS.)..................................... **600**
Teapot, cov., Hollyhocks patt., Regent
shape **400**

Rare Laburnum Pattern Teapot

Teapot, cov., Laburnum patt., Eve (Art Deco
style) shape (ILLUS.)....................................... **800**
Toast rack, Harmony Ware patt. **150**

Rare Shelley Umbrella Stand

Umbrella stand, advertising-type, columnar
form w/molded pilasters flanking arched
niches around the side, dark blue ground
printed in white w/"Shelley China - Pot-
ters to The World," 27" h. (ILLUS.)............. **3,500**
Vase, 5" h., Balloons & Flashes patt.................. **125**
Vase, 5" h., Cloisonné patt. **200**

Harmony Ware Moresque Vase

Vase, 6" h., tall waisted shape, Harmony
Ware, Moresque patt., stylized blossoms
in orange, pale & dark blue & brown
(ILLUS.)... **150**

Vegetable bowl, open, oval, Harebell patt.,
9 1/2" l. **160**

Nursery Ware by Mabel Lucie Attwell

Baby feeding plate, color scene inscribed
"Fairy Folk with Tiny Wings..." **350**

Boo-Boo Cruet Set

Cruet set: three mushroom-shaped covered
pots & figural shaker on four-lobed tray;
Boo-Boo set (ILLUS.).................................... **1,000**
Figurine, Boo-Boo with knapsack.................... **1,000**
Figurine, Boo-Boo with mushroom................... **1,000**
Figurine, Golfer **2,200**

Child's Mug and Saucer Set

Mug & saucer, color scene of Mother Rabbit
& baby Rabbity, inscribed "When Rabbity
fell...," the set (ILLUS.)..................................... **375**

Child's Platter with Duck Scene

Platter, 8" l., squared shape w/molded handles, color scene of mother duck & children, inscribed "Will Somebody Kindly
Tell..." (ILLUS.)... **300**

Boo-Boo Figural Tea Set

Tea set: cov. teapot, creamer & open sugar;
Boo-Boo set w/mushroom-shaped open
sugar & mushroom house-shaped teapot
w/figural Boo-Boo creamer, the set
(ILLUS.).. **2,500**

Intarsio Art Pottery (1997-99)

Intarsio Art Pottery Clock

Clock, table model, Art Nouveau-style upright case w/a brown border around a
colored central panel w/a dial above a
scene of a Medieval couple by a sundial
above the inscription "The Days May
Come - The Days May Go..."(ILLUS.)........ **1,800**

Intarsio Art Pottery Cracker Jar

Cracker jar, cov., footed bulbous body w/sil-
ver plate rim, cover & bail handle, wide
color band decorated w/scenes from
Shakespeare plays, 6" h.
(ILLUS.).. **1,000**

Caricature Teapot of Lord Salisbury

Teapot, cov., caricature of Lord Salisbury, dark green, black, tan & brown (ILLUS.).... **1,100**

Toby mug, "The Irishman," 7 1/2" h. **900**

Vase, 8 1/2" h., bulbous body centered by a wide cylindrical neck w/four curved handles from neck to shoulder, decorated w/a central band of brown & white chickens on a blue & green ground, bands of brown scrolls on a green ground above & below & a dark blue neck w/white & yellow flowers & green leaves, green handles.. **2,000**

Intarsio Art Nouveau-style Wash Set

Wash bowl & pitcher set, Art Nouveau design w/large stylized flowers in yellow & shaded blue to white on green swirled leafy stems on a dark green & black ground, bowl 18" d., the set (ILLUS.) **2,500**

Slipware

This term refers to ceramics, primarily redware, decorated by the application of slip (semi-liquid paste made of clay). Such wares were made for decades in England and Germany and elsewhere on the Continent, and in the Pennsylvania Dutch country and elsewhere in the United States. Today, contemporary copies of early Slipware items are featured in numerous decorator magazines and offered for sale in gift catalogs.

Bowl, 8" d., flat bottom w/upright sides, the inside center decorated w/a thin yellow slip wavy cross w/a dot between each arm (wear, edge chip).................................. **$303**

Bowl, 9" d., 1 7/8" h., wide shallow form, redware w/yellow slip squiggled cross design in the center, 19th c............................ **495**

Bowl, 11 1/2" d., wide, round, shallow form w/the wide flanged sides decorated w/three squiggled rows of yellow slip on the redware ground, 19th c. (hairline, glaze flakes) **2,634**

Bowl, 12 1/4 x 15 1/2, oblong redware w/coggled edges, decorated w/three

bands of triple wavy yellow slip bands, 19th c. (imperfections) **605**

Dish, coggle rim, brown slip stylized wide diamond-form veined leaf design across the interior on an amber ground, 5 1/2" d. (old chips) **413**

Dish, shallow round form, a two-line yellow slip band across the center flanked by short two-line bands above & below, 7 1/2" d. (minor wear, crazing) **468**

Loaf dish, oblong, coggled edge, redware yellow slip tree design, wavy lines at top & sides, 10 1/4 x 14", 2 1/2" h. (wear, glaze flake & some old restoration to rim).. **6,600**

Loaf dish, redware, oblong w/coggled edge, three-line yellow slip band around the borders & across the center, 11 1/2 x 15 1/2", 3 1/4" h. (chips, hairlines, flaking)... **220**

Milk bowl, flaring rounded sides, interior glaze w/floral decoration in yellow, green & brown slip, 8 1/2" d., 2 3/4" h. (wear, chips, hairline)... **193**

Pie plate, coggled rim, wide three-line yellow slip band across the middle, 7" d. (minor chips) **220**

Pie plate, round, redware w/three yellow slip double wavy bands across the center, 7 1/2" d., 1 1/2" h. (shallow rim flakes) **468**

Pie plate, round, redware w/coggled edges, decorated w/four squiggled lines in yellow & green slip, 8" d. (imperfections) **330**

Pie plate, coggled rim, a bold yellow slip sweeping monogram w/a "W" across the center, 9" d. (chips, minor flaking w/hairline).. **935**

Pie plate, round slightly dished form, redware w/overall yellow slip S-scrolls & looped squiggles, 9" d., 1 7/8" h. (edge wear, flakes)... **330**

Pie plate, round, redware w/coggled edges, decorated w/large "ABC" above a wavy line & flourish, all in yellow slip, 10 1/8" d. (flaking & hairline) **825**

Pie plate, round, redware w/coggled rim, decorated w/yellow slip wavy lines in center & triple yellow slip squiggled bands at top & bottom, 10 3/4" d. (minor flaking)... **715**

Pie plate, coggled rim, bold wavy three-line band of yellow slip across the center w/slightly wavy bands of slip above & below, 11" d. (glaze & edge chips) **715**

Pie plate, round w/tooled rim, redware w/bold "ABC" in yellow slip, old black on back, 11 1/4" d. (chips).............................. **1,073**

Pie plate, coggled rim, scattered dashes of three-line yellow slip around the top, 11 3/8" d. (edge chips, interior wear, rim hairline) **413**

Pie plate, coggled rim, unusual band of three-line green slip decoration, 11 3/4" d. (shallow rim chips, interior glaze wear)... **880**

Plate, 8 1/4" d., coggled rim, a yellow slip three-line band across the center w/three three-line dashes above & below (shallow rim chips, hairline)..................................... **495**

Plate, 9" d., round w/textured rim, yellow twist slip decoration on redware, 19th c. (hairline, rim chips) **805**

Platter, 11 1/4 x 13 1/2", oval, shallow form w/notched rim, redware w/zigzag & yel-

low slip serpentine designs, 19th c.
(wear, glaze loss).. **518**
Tray, rectangular w/rounded corners, red-
ware w/coggled edges, decorated w/four
bands of triple yellow slip wavy lines,
19th c. (surface wear, chips)...................... **715**

Spatterware

*This ceramic ware takes its name from the "spat-
tered" decoration, in various colors, generally used to
trim pieces handpainted with rustic center designs of
flowers, birds, houses, etc. Popular in the early 19th
century, most was imported from England.*

*Related wares, called "stick spatter," had freehand
designs applied with pieces of cut sponge attached to
sticks, hence the name. Examples date from the 19th and
early 20th century and were produced in England,
Europe and America.*

*Some early spatter-decorated wares were marked by
the manufacturers, but not many. Twentieth century
reproductions are also sometimes marked, including
those produced by Boleslaw Cybis.*

Bowl, 4 3/4" d., 2 1/2" h., footed, flared
sides, yellow spatter w/Tulip patt. in red &
green (hairlines & light stain).................... **$2,310**
Creamer, blue spatter, Fort patt. in grey &
brown w/green spatter trees, 4" h.
(stains)... **248**
Creamer, tapering octagonal form w/wide
spout & angled handle, Fort patt., red,
black, green & yellow building, blue spatter background, 5 5/8" h. (hairline in han-
dle, small chips) **990**
Creamer, yellow spatter, w/peafowl in red,
yellow & slate blue on a green spatter
branch, molded leaf handle, chip & dark-
ened crazing, 3 1/2" h. (ILLUS. third from
right w/assorted spatterware) **4,125**
Cup, handleless, freehand Rooster patt. in
yellow, blue & red w/a blue spatter border .. **1,100**
Cup, miniature, handleless, Rainbow spat-
ter, bands of blue, red & green (small rim
flakes).. **440**
Cup, miniature, handleless, Rooster patt.,
yellow, blue, black & red rooster, blue
spatter rim (rim flakes).................................. **605**
Cup & saucer, green spatter, handleless,
w/schoolhouse design in red & dark
brown, staining, colors differ slightly
(ILLUS. center, front & back row, w/as-
sorted spatterware) **1,870**
Cup & saucer, handleless, blue spatter,
Dahlia patt. in red, blue & green (short
hairlines, some areas where enamel
didn't adhere) **220**
Cup & saucer, handleless, green w/brown
spatter, picture of red schoolhouse in
center, minor stains (ILLUS. front row,
second & third from right, w/group of
spatterware)... **2,750**

Cup & saucer, handleless, Rainbow spatter
border alternating blue & purple stripes......... **385**
Cup & saucer, handleless, Rainbow spatter,
slightly oversized w/red, green & blue
decoration w/blue on inside cup rim (tiny
pinpoint flake on rim of saucer).................. **1,100**
Cup & saucer, handleless, red spatter, light
sponging w/an open-bodied peafowl design in green, light blue & yellow wavy
lines (ILLUS. far right, front & back row,
w/assorted spatterware).............................. **413**
Cup & saucer, handleless, Star patt. in red,
green & dark yellow, blue spatter border,
impressed "R" **1,210**
Cup & saucer, handleless, yellow spatter,
blue, black & green morning glory design, deep yellow (minor wear, blue has
flakes & stains, saucer has hairline).............. **990**
Cup & saucer, handleless, yellow spatter,
design of red tulip w/green leaves, strong
yellow... **3,190**
Cup & saucer, handleless, yellow spatter-
ware, red & green cockscomb center design, cup has minor stain (ILLUS. far left,
front & back row, w/assorted spatter-
ware)... **2,640**
Cup & saucer, Peafowl patt., red spatter
border, cup 2 1/2" h., saucer 5 1/2" d. **523**
Cup & saucer, handleless, Cock's Comb
patt., red, green & black stylized flower,
dark blue spatter border **1,155**
Cup & saucer, handleless, miniature, Rose
patt., red, green & black flower w/blue
spatter background, colors vary slightly
(pinpoint flakes) **330**
Cup & saucer, handleless, Peafowl on
Branch patt., blue, red, yellow & black
bird on a blue spatter ground, impressed
mark "B. and T. Stoneware" (pinpoint
flakes on cup).. **715**
Cup & saucer, handleless, Peafowl patt.,
blue, yellow, black & green bird on a red
spatter ground.. **825-875**
Cup & saucer, handleless, Rainbow spatter,
each piece banded w/alternating stripes
of purple & black spatter **578**
Cup & saucer, handleless, Rose patt., red,
green & black flower, blue spatter border,
impressed Adams mark (minor rough-
ness on cup rim) **605**
Cup & saucer, handleless, Thistle patt., red,
green & black thistle, yellow spatter bor-
ders (pinpoint rim flake on cup)................... **3,410**
Cups & saucers, two cups, two saucers,
handleless, blue spatter rims w/red &
green roses, pr. **385**
Dish, rectangular w/cut corners, Peafowl
patt., yellow, red, black & green bird
against a blue spatter center ground & a
blue spatter border band, 6 x 8 1/4" (minor glaze flakes on rim, yellow glaze
flakes on bird) **2,035**

Assorted Spatterware

Spatterware Group

Mug, Rainbow spatter, purple & blue vertical stripes w/leaf molded handle ends, 2 3/4" h. (ILLUS. third from left w/assorted spatterware, bottom previous page) **935**

Pitcher, 6 1/4" h., squatty bulbous hexagonal body tapering toward the base & to the neck w/a high arched spout, angled scroll handle, Peafowl patt. in red, yellow, green & black, blue spatter background (hairlines in base, wear, stains)..................... **743**

Pitcher, 6 3/8" h., yellow spatter, red & green tulip on both sides, paneled w/a molded fan under spout (some flakes, interior stains & restored spout) **4,675**

Pitcher, 6 5/8" h., slightly bulbous form, blue spatter, red & green parrot design on side, crow's feet, stains (ILLUS. back row, right w/group of spatterware) **3,410**

Pitcher, 7 3/8" h., Rainbow spatter in blue, red, yellow, green & black swirled stripes w/red on inside rim & handle, molded shoulder, scroll handle & spout, rim flake, short hairline (ILLUS. far left w/spatterware group, top of page) **7,150**

Plate, 7 1/4" d., underglaze blue w/red, green & yellow Tulip patt., blue spatter paneled border **825**

Plate, 8 1/4" d., Peafowl patt., blue spatter border **413**

Plate, 8 1/4" d., Rainbow spatter, red & blue rainbow border w/bull's-eye center, hairline, minor surface flake (ILLUS. front row, left, w/group of spatterware)................... **935**

Plate, 8 1/4" d., Thistle patt., red & green center design, red spatter border (three small flakes on feather-molded rim) **1,155**

Plate, 8 3/8" d., deep yellow w/red & green thistle center (chip & light staining)............. **1,540**

Plate, 8 1/2" d., blue spatter, molded feather edge w/red, yellow & blue peafowl center, old paper labels on back w/some history **688**

Plate, 8 1/2" d., Cockscomb patt., red & green center design w/a wide blue spatter border (wear, stains, small flakes) **908**

Plate, 8 1/2" d., Rainbow spatter, light red, blue & yellow stripes on paneled border, minor knife scratches (ILLUS. far right w/spatterware group) **2,640**

Plate, 8 1/2" d., Rainbow spatter w/paneled border of red, yellow & blue stripes **2,860**

Plate, 8 3/4" d., Peafowl patt. freehand bird in red, blue & green, blue spatter overall background (stains)... **770**

Plate, 8 3/4" d., Rainbow spatter, red, blue & yellow border (rim chip) **1,320**

Plate, 9 1/4" d., blue spatter, paneled border, red & green Adam's rose in center (minor stains)... **303**

Plate, 9 1/4" d., Peafowl patt., light blue, yellow, green & black bird against a red spatter ground (minor pinpoint flakes on rim, shallow chip on table ring)...................... **715**

Plate, 9 3/8" d., plain white center w/a wide Rainbow spatter border w/alternating bands of red, blue & green spatter, impressed Adams mark, first half 19th c. (minor wear)... **605**

Plate, 9 3/8" d., white star reserve in center w/Star patt. in dark blue, green & red, blue spatter paneled border............................ **935**

Plate, 9 1/2" d., Peafowl patt., freehand bird in blue, red, green & black, red spatter background.. **1,265**

Plate, 9 1/2" d., Rainbow spatter, plain center w/alternating border bands in red, blue & green spatter, scalloped rim............ **495**

Plate, 9 1/2" d., Star patt. in red, green & blue, blue spatter border **1,073**

Plate, 9 3/4" d., strong yellow spatter paneled rim w/red & green thistle center, light crazing & staining (ILLUS. second from left w/spatterware group)............................. **3,960**

Plate, 10" d., round w/Tulip patt. in red & green, red spatter paneled border (edge wear & stains)... **743**

Platter, 12 1/2" l., Rainbow spatter, octagonal shape w/red & green border, center w/a large red & blue tulip w/green leaves, hairline, stains, flaking (ILLUS. back row, left, w/group of spatterware, top next page) **4,620**

Platter, 15 3/4" l., octagonal oblong shape, decorated w/cluster of buds pattern in burgundy & green on white central ground, blue spatter outer rim has been reglazed (in-the-making hairline at one end of the well) **1,045**

Platter, 15 3/4" l., rectangular w/wide cut corners, overall dark blue spatter (wear, stains)... **330**

Platter, 13 3/4 x 17 1/2", rectangular w/angled corners, Castle patt., freehand red & yellow castle w/green trees & grassy field in the center, wide blue spatter border, ca. 1840 (minor discoloration, crazing) **5,462**

Soup bowl, blue spatter paneled rim, Peafowl patt. freehand bird in red, green & yellow, 10 1/2" d. (rim flakes) **880**

Sugar bowl, cov., footed squatty bulbous form w/rolled rim & inset cover, Fort patt. in black, grey, red & green, blue spatter background, 4 1/4" h. (one small chip & pinpoint flake on base, glazed-over flake on inside flange) **770**

Group of Spatterware

Sugar bowl, cov., Rainbow spatter, ovoid shape w/yellow & blue stripes & red & green thistle design, 5 1/4" h. (hairline & repair) **3,740**

Sugar bowl, cov., Schoolhouse patt., green spatter border, 4 1/2" h. (hairline on rim)... **2,475**

Teapot, cov., baluster shape, paneled w/molded arches on shoulder, Peafowl patt. in green, ochre & pink, blue spatter background, 8 5/8" h. (some flakes & restored finial) **990**

Teapot, cov., miniature, four-footed, bulbous body w/molded C-form handle, swan's neck spout, Peafowl patt., freehand bird in blue, red & yellow on one side, tree on the other, green spatter background, 6" l., 4 1/4" h. (minor roughness on lid edge) **605**

Teapot, cov., octagonal baluster form w/domed cover, C-scroll handle & swan's-neck spout, Peafowl patt., red, blue, black & green bird on a red spatter ground, 9" h. (very minor flakes) **2,420**

Teapot, cov., Peafowl patt., green thumbprint spatter design of leaves w/red, yellow & blue peafowl on a branch, 6 1/2" h. (slightly ground spout, fading to green on lid) **1,870**

Teapot, cov., Rainbow spatter, paneled baluster form w/molded arch designs on shoulder & spout, red & blue spatter, 9 1/4" h. (flakes, hairline & glued finial) **550**

Teapot, cov., tapering octagonal body w/flared rim, swan's-neck spout & high angled handle, fitted high domed cover w/knop finial, over blue spatter decoration, 9" h. (minor hairline, flakes on spout & finial wear) **330**

Vegetable bowl, cov., Rainbow spatter, octagonal shape w/footed base & shell-shaped finial, blue & purple w/brighter colors inside base, impressed "Porcelaine Opaque - & G. Alcock," stains, 7 3/4" h, 10 1/4" l. (ILLUS. far right w/group of spatterware) **2,200**

Vegetable bowl, open, octagonal, w/red & green stripes, red & blue tulip center, 2 x 6", 8 1/2" l., hairlines (ILLUS. second from right w/spatterware group) **2,530**

Washbowl, blue spatter, round paneled bowl, interior w/design of blue & yellow tulip & red blossoms, 14" d., 14 1/2" h. (stains, hairline & spider) **1,210**

Washbowl & pitcher set, Adam's Rose patt. in red, green & black, dark blue spatter background on pitcher & band around the bowl, tall paneled tapering pitcher w/high arched spout & long angled handle, footed flaring bowl w/three roses in panels around the interior, bowl 13 1/2" d., 4 1/2" h., pitcher, 12" h., pr. (hairlines in pitcher, professional restoration on bowl) **2,090**

Waste bowl, flared sides on footed ring base, Peafowl patt., one peafowl in black, ochre & blue, green spatter trim, repair, 5 1/2" d. (ILLUS. center w/spatterware group) **220**

Stick or Cut-Sponge Spatter

Charger, decorated w/large cut-sponge blue foliage w/red & green sprig & flower designs, 12 1/4" d. (minor edge wear & light crazing) **165**

Charger, ironstone w/"gaudy" polychrome cut-sponge decoration in red & green in center, border w/transfer rabbit decoration alternating w/frogs, 13" d. (overall light crazing) **1,100**

Cup & saucer, pale blue spatter decorated w/stick spatter cranberry flowers & green leaves (minor flakes) **330**

Plate, 9 1/8" d., center decorated w/stick spatter red fruit w/green leaves, blue rim w/red stripes (bruise & rim flake) **193**

Plate, 9 1/4" d., ironstone, center round brown transfer-printed scene of three rabbits & a frog, a wide border of small cut-sponge blue blossoms w/freehand green leaves & large trumpet-form red blossoms, brown & yellow trim **413**

Plate, 9 3/8" d., ironstone w/a "gaudy" design, the center w/stick spatter red, blue & green flowers, black transfer border w/rabbits, frogs & trees, yellow & green enamel **468**

Plate, 9 3/4" d., a wide border band of cut-sponge green blossom heads between thin red stripes around the central freehand design of columbine w/a rosebud & thistle in green, blue, red, black & purple (minor wear & stains) **275**

Plate, 10" d., red stick spatter border & leaves w/flow blue stripes & flowers **275**

Plates, 10" d., ironstone china w/a "gaudy" design, the center w/a central bull's-eye w/cut-sponge ring of blossoms surrounded by a wide band of brightly colored stylized leaves & flowers, the rim band w/further cut-sponge flower heads, cobalt blue, green & red, set of 8 (minor edge flakes, one w/hairline, one badly damaged)... **1,650**

Platter, 10 1/4 x 14 1/2", oval, ironstone china w/a "gaudy" design, center w/brown transfer of rabbits & frog in fenced field, yellow enamel field & green frog, border w/red, green & blue stick spatter flowers (minor enamel wear on edge)..................... **1,100**

Sugar bowl, cov., bulbous ovoid body w/a wide low rolled neck, flared footring, inset cover w/button finial, decorated w/spaced vertical stripes alternating w/looped & cut-sponge flower head designs in blue, green & red trimmed w/blue stripes, 5" d., 5" h. (minor roughness inside flange) **275**

Spongeware

Spongeware's designs were spattered, sponged or daubed on in colors, sometimes with a piece of cloth. Blue on white was the most common type, but mottled tans, browns and greens on yellowware were also popular. Spongeware generally has an overall pattern with a coarser look than Spatterwares, to which it is loosely related. These wares were extensively produced in England and America well into the 20th century.

![Spongeware Bank]

Spongeware Bank

Bank, bulbous bottle-shaped form w/blue polka dot sponging & "J.W.B." stenciled in blue, lip chips, 6" h. (ILLUS.)................... **$743**

Bowl, 7 5/8" d., 3 1/4" h., deep rounded sides tapering to a small footring, a central dark blue band flanked by white bands w/outer bands of blue sponging on white (minor wear)... **110**

Bowl, 9 1/4" d., 4" h., tapering round sides w/molded scalloped panels & a molded rim band, blue sponging on white (glaze wear on bottom, rim hairline)........................ **165**

Bowl, 11 1/2" d., wide shallow form w/flanged rim, large dots of green & brown sponging on a white-glazed ground (glaze flakes) **330**

Bowl, 12" d., 5 1/2" h., deep, gently flaring rounded sides w/molded arched panels & a molded rim band, wide upper & lower bands of scalloped blue sponging on white... **275**

Bowl, 12 1/4" d., 5 7/8" h., deep, slightly rounded flaring sides w/a molded rim, wide bands of blue sponging on white w/scalloped edges around the top & base..... **385**

Butter crock, deep cylindrical sides, blue sponging on white w/"Butter" flanked w/small stenciled design & reverse labeled "Village Farm Dairy," chips, hairlines & crazing, 4 5/8" d., 3" h. **330**

Butter crock, cov., cylindrical, blue on white w/"Butter," 7 1/4" d., 5 1/8" h. (minor crazing, lid w/small chips, wire bail missing)... **385**

Crock, cov., cylindrical w/molded rim, inset flat cover, front marked "Butter," overall blue sponging on white, wood & wire bail handle, 5 3/4" d., 3 3/4" h. plus handle.......... **193**

Crock, cov., cylindrical w/molded rim, inset flat cover, overall blue sponging on white, 6 1/2" d., 6 3/4" h. (chips on cover).............. **220**

Crock, deep cylindrical sides w/narrow molded rim w/rim spout, wire bail handle w/turned wooden grip, overall dark blue sponging on white, 6 3/4" d. (rim chips) **330**

Dish, cov., miniature, flat bottom w/low flaring sides & heavy molded flat rim, fitted domed cover w/button finial, overall heavy blue sponging on white, 3 1/4" d. **935**

Inkwell, conical, w/removable insert & pen rest on top, blue on white, 2 5/8" h. (wear & glaze flakes) **165**

Jar, bulbous ovoid body tapering slightly to flared rim, blue on white, pinpoint rim flakes, 4 1/4" h. ((ILLUS. left w/other spongeware items).. **798**

Jardiniere, bulbous ovoid body w/flaring scalloped rim, blue sponging on white w/relief-molded foliage scrolls & gilt trim, 10 1/2" d., 8 3/4" h. (worn gilt, minor crow's foot in bottom & glaze defect on lip) **193**

Jug, cylindrical, w/domed top, small cylindrical neck & strap shoulder handle, yellowware w/overall dark blue sponging, 10 1/2" h... **523**

Pitcher, 7 1/2" h., slightly tapering cylindrical body w/wide pointed rim spout & squared loop handle, relief-molded floral designs covered overall w/heavy blue sponging on white (crazing, hairline in handle) **303**

Pitcher, 7 1/2" h., wide cylindrical form w/small rim spout & squared loop handle, overall design of large circles of blue sponging on white **495**

Pitcher, 8 1/4" h., wide cylindrical body tapering at the shoulder to a wide flat mouth w/rim spout, small loop handle at shoulder, overall banded blue sponging on white (rim flakes) **468**

Spongeware Pitcher

Pitcher, 8 3/4" h., cylindrical body tapering to a flat rim w/a pinched spout, C-form handle, chip on table ring, blue on white (ILLUS.)... **468**

Pitcher, tankard, 8 7/8" h., tall, slightly tapering cylindrical form, C-form handle, overall wide bands of stylized blossom-like sponging in blue on white (small flakes) **550**

Pitcher, 9" h., blue & white, molded rings top & bottom w/bright blue sponging **385**

Pitcher, 9" h., tall cylindrical form w/rim spout & low strap handle, overall light blue sponging on white **495**

Pitcher, 9" h., tall, slender cylindrical body w/pointed rim spout & small C-form handle, heavy overall blue sponging on white **330**

Pitcher, 9 1/2" h., cylindrical w/bulbous base, overall blue sponging on white **715**

Pitcher, 10 3/4" h., bulbous body tapering to a tall flaring neck w/a high arched spout, C-scroll handle, decorated down the sides w/banded blue sponging on white, a painted wide blue band flanked by thin blue bands near the bottom **303**

Pitcher, 11 1/2" h., wide bulbous ovoid body tapering to a waisted neck w/wide arched spout, arched loop handle, the body molded w/ribbons & bows & decorated overall w/wide bands of ovals in blue sponging on white (rim chips) **990**

Platter, 11 3/4" l., oval, w/blue sponge decoration, flow blue edges................................. **303**

Platter, 13 1/2" l., oblong shape w/scalloped sides, blue sponging on white **385**

Soap dish, stoneware, blue sponging on white, 3 1/4 x 4 5/8".. **110**

Teapot, cov., miniature, squatty bulbous body w/C-form handle, swan's-neck spout & inset cover w/blossom finial, blue sponging on white, minor chips, 4 1/8" h. (ILLUS. right w/other spongeware items) **853**

Spongeware Teapot

Teapot, cov., bulbous body w/C-form handle, swan's-neck spout, blue sponging on white, lid chipped & glued, 5 1/2" h. (ILLUS.).. **633**

Tray, scalloped edge, blue sponging on buff-colored ground, 9 1/4" l. **55**

Umbrella stand, slender cylindrical form, wide blue & white bands around the top & base w/overall banded blue sponging on white, 15 1/2" h. **770**

Umbrella stand, tall cylindrical form, the front center w/an oval reserve w/a blue transfer-printed scene of a Dutch girl & boy, wide blue bands near the top & base w/overall banded blue sponging on white, 22 1/4" h. (hairlines) **825**

Staffordshire Figures

Small figures and groups made of pottery were produced by the majority of the Staffordshire, England potters in the 19th century and were used as mantel decorations or "chimney ornaments," as they were sometimes called. Pairs of dogs were favorites and were turned out by the carload, and 19th-century pieces are still available. Well-painted reproductions also abound,

and collectors are urged to exercise caution before investing.

Bear & dog, pearlware, bear-baiting group, modeled w/a chained bear standing four-square on a high rectangular base, a snarling dog at his side, all covered in a thin beige slip, the bear's fur, the dog's spots & the base colored in a watery green glaze, the base edged w/narrow underglaze-blue borders, ca. 1820, 8 1/2" l. (bear's head & edge of base repaired, chain a restoration) **$1,380**

Benjamin Franklin, standing figure of Franklin holds a document in one hand & his tricorner hat in the other, cobalt coat w/purple, green & red vest & striped pants, gold trim, 14 1/2" h. **853**

Benjamin Franklin, standing figure wears dark blue coat & vest w/burgundy & green-on-white pattern, gold lettering on square base spells "Franklin," 14 1/2" h. (crazing, w/areas of blue "pooling" in the glaze).. **990**

Benjamin Franklin, standing on oblong base w/incorrect inscription "Washington," first half 19th c., 15 1/2" h. (cracks, very minor chips) **900-950**

Cats, seated on cobalt blue pillows, looking right & left, w/yellow & black mottled decoration, 4" h., pr. **468**

Cats, seated on cobalt blue pillows, looking right & left, yellow & black mottled decoration, 7 1/2" h., pr... **523**

Dog, Spaniel, seated position, white w/tan head, ears & portion of back, lock & chain collar, glass eyes, worn gold trim, 13 1/2" h. **250-275**

Dogs, black & white dogs seated on yellow, blue & green pillows, 4 1/2" h., pr. **1,540**

Dogs, Dalmatians w/gold chains, on green base, 5" h., pr... **495**

Dogs, full-bodied w/four separate feet, white, tan & black w/glass eyes, gold collars, 14" l., pr. (one foot chipped) **468**

Dogs, poodles looking right & left, standing on footed pedestals w/pink & green accents, 4" h., pr... **605**

Dogs, poodles seated & looking right & left, white w/sanded coats & black muzzles, yellow eyes & gilt collars w/locks, 4 5/8" h., pr.. **413**

Dogs, seated dogs looking right & left, brown decoration & yellow collars, 4 1/2" h., pr... **468**

Dogs, seated dogs looking right & left, hollow body molding w/black & grey decoration, early, 11 1/4" h., pr. (hairlines) **550**

Dogs, seated dogs looking right & left, rust colored decoration, 9" h., pr. **660**

Dogs, Spaniels in seated position, white w/copper lustre spots, ears, neck chain & lock, yellow eyes, black nose, green highlights, open front legs, second half 19th c., 9 1/2" h., pr. (small hairlines)............ **413**

Dogs, Whippets lying on a bed of grass, looking right & left, on raised platform, 4" l., pr. (loss to one tail)................................. **385**

Eggs on nest, a large pile of white eggs in green grass molded to form the cover, oval yellow basket base, impressed "S. & S.," 19th c., 10" l. **440**

Equestrian group, a man on horseback w/a basket of fruit, polychrome trim, 19th c., 9 1/2" h. **303**

Figure group, figure of a Scotsman in kilt w/a dog, ca. 1865, 14 1/2" h. **420**

Figure group, "Heenan-Savers," two dark-haired male figures boxing, one wearing yellow pants w/blue belt, the other w/pink pants & orange belt, oval base w/rectangular panel in background, 9 1/4" h. (minor flakes on hair)... **440**

Figure group, standing figures of man & woman in colorful clothing w/sheep on either side at their feet, raised lettering on base spells "Welsh Shepherds," 14" h. (restoration) **385**

Figure group, standing man & woman in Scottish dress, polychrome decoration, ca. 1850, 14 1/4" h. **448**

Figure group, "Uncle Tom," a tall seated black man w/a little white girl standing on one knee, polychrome decoration, ca. 1860, 10 3/4" h. (crazing).............................. **440**

Figure group, "Uncle Tom," Uncle Tom seated w/Little Eva on his knee, polychrome decoration, 19th c., 10 1/4" h. **770**

Figure group, seated mother poodle & two puppies, all in white w/sanded fur trim, painted facial details, deep blue oblong base, 19th c., 4" h. **375-400**

Figure group, Dick Turpin on horseback, ca. 1840, England, 12 1/4" h. **350-400**

Figure group, man & woman sitting under a woven vine, ca. 1860, 13 1/2" h. **168**

Figure of Scotsman w/rifle, standing wearing kilt & leaning against a low wall, polychrome decoration, oblong base, 7 3/8" h. (minor wear)...................................... **275**

Staffordshire Hen on Nest

Hen on nest, white hen trimmed w/black & brown w/red wattle on light brown basketweave base, bisque finish, 5 3/8 x 7", 7" h. (ILLUS.).. **650-700**

Horse, yellowware, the standing animal wearing reins, head lowered, on a molded oval base, body heavily splashed w/dark brown, attributed to The Don Pottery, England, ca. 1800-22, 6 1/4" h. (tail & both ears restored) **1,000-1,200**

Rabbits, each recumbent animal w/long ears decorated in polychrome & shown nibbling on lettuce leaves, 19th c., 10 1/4" l., pr. **4,000-4,200**

Vase, spill-type, 5 3/4" h., figural model of elephant standing on oval base in front of slender coleslaw tree w/molded leaves, shaded grey w/pink & green blanket, 5 3/4" h. (minor enamel wear & one leg w/in-the-making hairline) **550**

Watch hutch, figural, a man & a woman in Victorian peasant dress standing on each side of a central round watch opening below a smaller top opening flanked by figural peacocks, the holes framed by painted ivy vines, bright polychrome decoration, mid-19th c., 10 3/4" h. (hairlines, chip at back)... **330**

Zebra, a prancing horse-like animal w/painted stripes on body & tail, black mane, wearing reins, on an oval base w/molded shrub under the animal, polychrome trim, 19th c., 8 3/4" h. (wear, crazing).................... **495**

Zebra, black & white zebra stands pawing grassy ground that makes up green & yellow base, 19th c., 5" h. **224**

Zebras, a prancing horse-like animal w/painted stripes on body & tail, looking right & left, on grassy base w/stump, 4 1/2" h., pr.. **468**

Staffordshire Transfer Wares

The process of transfer-printing designs on earthenwares developed in England in the late 18th century, and by the mid-19th century most common ceramic wares were decorated in this manner, most often with romantic European or Oriental landscape scenes, animals or flowers. The earliest such wares were printed in dark blue, but a little later light blue, pink, purple, red, black, green and brown were used. A majority of these wares were produced at various English potteries right up until the turn of the 20th century, but French and other European firms also made similar pieces and all are quite collectible. The best reference on this area is Petra Williams' book Staffordshire Romantic Transfer Patterns - Cup Plates and Early Victorian China (Fountain House East, 1978).

Bowl, 9" d., 4 1/8" h., reticulated, footed bowl w/scalloped edge & molded handles, light blue romantic transfer scene of boatmen on a lake, "Interlachen," marked "Late Spode, Copeland and Garrett" (minor edge wear) **$495**

Bowl, 10" d., blue w/pastoral landscape............ **220**

Rural Scenery Footed Bowl

Bowl, 11" d., 4 1/2" h., footed, deep sides w/lightly scalloped rim, Rural Scenery patt. w/sheep, cow & horse, light blue, Adams, unseen foot rim chip, chip on extreme rim edge (ILLUS.) **300-350**

Brush box, cov., long oblong form, Wild Rose patt., lakeside landscape on cover, medium blue, 7 1/4" l. (very small unseen base flake) **275-300**

Coffeepot, cov., a central reserve depicting a harbor scene w/castle buildings on the heights, surrounded by floral & grapevine transfers, the cover w/a beehive finial, blue, early 19th c., 11 1/2" h. (cover flange broken) **1,035**

Coffeepot, cov., tall baluster-form body w/bulbous tapering neck w/rolled rim & high domed cover w/acorn finial, swan's-neck spout & angled & pointed handle, dark blue scene of two men talking beside a horse near a stable, ca. 1830, 11 1/2" h. (chip on edge of spout) **1,000-1,200**

Cup & saucer, handleless, blue transfer of sparrows near an urn of flowers (minor wear) **248**

Cup & saucer, handleless, central scene of a young couple in a forest setting, floral & scallop border, dark blue, marked "Clews," ca. 1830 (minor wear) **204**

Cup & saucer, handleless, Horse patt., dark blue, Stubbs & Kent (small unseen table ring flake on saucer, cup w/mellowing) **375-400**

Cup & saucer, handleless, white ground w/dark blue floral pattern, Enoch Wood & Sons, Burslem, cup 2 1/2" h., saucer 5 3/4" d. **165**

Ladle, scene of a woman & child by a cottage inside the bowl, dark blue, ca. 1830, 7 1/2" l. **605**

Pitcher, 5 1/2" h., ovoid body, short, slightly tapered neck, applied handle, blue transfer of girl picking flowers & boy robbing a bird's nest, floral border (flake on base, spout has roughness) **495**

Pitcher, 8 1/2" h., Abbey Ruins patt., bulbous body w/short tapered foot & flared neck, molded floral C-scroll handle, light blue romantic transfer scene w/deer & ruins, transfer label "T. Mayer, Longport" (firing separations in handle, minor wear w/crow's feet) **275**

Pitcher, jug-type, 8 1/2" h., wide ovoid body tapering to a short, rolled neck w/long rim spout & C-scroll handle, scene of a large manor house w/covered walkway, a stream w/sailboat in foreground, large leaves around rim, ochre line around mouth rim, dark blue, ca. 1830s, unknown maker (small spout tip chip, traces of two small spiders in base) **375-400**

Pitcher, 10 1/4" h., ornate baroque style w/tapering bulbous footed body, wide arched spout & ornate S-scroll handle, Rural Scenery patt. w/sheep, cow & horse, light blue, Adams, ca. 1840 .... **385**

Plate, toddy, 5 1/8" d., Running Setter patt., Quadrupeds series, dark blue, Hall, ca. 1830s **275-300**

Plate, toddy, 5 1/2" d., scalloped rim, brown printed central rectangular cartouche & floral wreath enclosing wording "A Trifle For Charles," embossed rim scale & rope trimmed in dark blue, impressed Enoch Wood mark, early 19th c. **413**

Plate, 7 1/4" d., Mastiff (Guard Dog) patt., Quadrupeds series, dark blue, Hall, ca. 1830s (stacking wear) **165-185**

Plate, 8 1/2" d., Hunter & Fox patt., Zoological series, dark blue, Wood, ca. 1830s **330**

Plate, 8 3/4" d., Christmas Eve patt., central scene of family in interior, floral border, Wilkie Series by Clews, ca. 1830s **300-350**

Plate, 9" d., center scene of two hunters & hounds w/game, wide floral border, dark blue, ca. 1830 (minor wear)............................ **220**

Plate, 9" d., Cupid & Psyche patt., scalloped edge w/floral border, impressed Adams mark, dark blue, ca. 1830 (slight scratches)... **275**

Plate, 9 3/4" d., Lion patt., Quadrupeds series, dark blue, Hall, ca. 1830s **330**

Plate, 10 1/4" d., Lion patt., blue transfer from the Quadruped series of a lion surrounded by deer, goats, zebras & horses...... **385**

Plate, 10 3/8" d., Fox Hunters patt., scalloped rim, floral border, medium blue, ca. 1840.. **165**

Plate, 10 1/2" d., Canova patt., brown **75**

Platter, pearlware blue decorated, chinoiserie motif, England, mid 19th c., 20 1/2" l. (rim ships, knife marks) **600-625**

Platter, 12 1/4" l., oval, Fountain Scenery patt., medium blue, Adams **175-200**

Platter, 12 1/4" l., oval w/lightly scalloped rim, Caledonia patt., purple, Adams, ca. 1840 (overall mellowing) **308**

Platter, 13 1/4" l., oval, lightly scalloped rim, Palestine patt., light blue, Adams, ca. 1840 .... **250-275**

Platter, 13 3/8" l., oval, Duck Hunting patt., dark blue, ca. 1830s **770**

Platter, 15" l., oval, Caledonia patt., purple, Adams (tiny pit on back rim) **468**

Platter, 15 1/4" l., oval, Moose patt., Quadrupeds series, dark blue, Hall, ca. 1830s (crack off rim, some inner rim wear, light scratches) **550**

Platter, 15 1/2" l., Canova patt., scalloped edge, red transfer scene of canal & gondola, by T. Mayer, Stoke Upon Trent **330**

Platter, 15 1/2" l., oval, Oriental patt., purple, ca. 1840 (slight edge wear) **330-350**

Platter, 13 1/2 x 15 1/2", oval, w/gently scalloped rim, central scene of a group of deer standing in a wooded clearing, vintage border design, marked by Adams, early 19th c. (minor wear) **1,100**

Fine Palestine Pattern Platter

Platter, 17" l., oval, lightly scalloped rim, Palestine patt., light blue, Adams (ILLUS.)... **325-250**

Platter, 17 1/2" l., oval, medium blue transfer-printed center scene of fleet of ships, wide border decorated w/shells & seaweed, John Rogers & Sons (wear & scratches, small rim chips)........................... **1,650**

Platter, 15 1/8 x 17 1/2", wide oval shape w/a gently scalloped rim, the center w/a scene of a man herding cattle, a wide flower & foliage border, dark blue, ca. 1830 (wear)... **990**

Platter, 18 1/2" l., oblong, decorated w/figures, animals, etc., by a country house, blue, Adams, ca. 1830 .... **575**

Platter, 14 3/4 x 18 7/8", wide oval form, a central oval reserve filled w/large fruits including melon, peaches, pears & leaves, the wide flanged rim w/flowers & leaves, dark blue, ca. 1830 (wear)................ **770**

Platter, 19" l., oval, lightly scalloped rim, Tyrolean patt., light blue, Wm. Ridgway, ca. 1840 .... **350-375**

Platter, 14 1/2 x 19", Sheltered Peasants patt., blue transfer w/depiction of man, woman & child w/sheep beneath trees, cathedral in background, fruit & flower border (glaze flaking on rim)........................... **770**

Platter, 15 1/4 x 19 1/4", oval, Palestine patt., central harbor scene w/willow trees & pagodas, geometric foliate border design on the wide scalloped rim, dark blue, R. Stevenson, ca. 1830 (knife scratches)..... **523**

Platter, 14 3/4 x 19 1/2", oval, a central Oriental landscape design w/two people on a hill w/a house, palm trees & a palm border, scalloped rim, blue (stains, glaze wear on underside)... **275**

Platter, 19 5/8" l., oval, lightly scalloped rim, Delhi patt., brown, ca. 1840 .... **475-500**

Lakeside Meeting Platter

Platter, 20" l., oval, Lakeside Meeting patt., medium dark blue, unknown maker, ca. 1830, some scratches & stains on face, few tiny outer rim flakes (ILLUS.).................. **605**

Early Staffordshire Platter

Platter, 20 3/4" l., oval well-and-tree style, Ruins with Horseman in Foreground patt., dark blue, ca. 1830s, unseen foot chip (ILLUS.) **1,200-1,300**

Platter, 21" l., blue transfer, The Italian Pattern, attributed to Spode, early 19th c. (glaze wear, scratches) **575**

Platter, 24" l., oval, Dagger Border patt., blue bands at inner & outer borders w/quatrefoil & dagger designs, by Minton & Boyle, 19th c... **413**

Sauce tureen, cover & undertray, Hare & Pointer patt. on base, Rooster & Fox patt. on undertray, tureen w/footed bulbous body w/rolled rim & domed cover w/berry finial, loop shoulder handles, Quadrupeds series, dark blue, Hall, the set **1,425-1,475**

Sauce tureen, cover & undertray, bulbous oblong deep body w/indented wide corners & a flaring rim, raised on tall heavy scroll legs, inset high domed cover w/flower finial & ladle rim notch, English landscape scenes in dark blue w/a grapevine border, E. Wood, ca. 1835, undertray 7 1/8" l., 6 1/4" h., the set (hairline in cover, unseen rim chips & short hairline, tray w/large spider crack) **1,210**

Sauce tureen undertray, oval, Hyena patt., Zoological series, dark blue, Wood, ca. 1830s, 8" l. (slight scratching) **330**

Soup plate, Common Wolf Trap patt., Oriental Sports series, dark blue, Edward Challinor, ca. 1830s, 8 3/8" d. **300-325**

Soup plate, Shells patt., dark blue, Stubbs & Kent, ca. 1830s, 9 3/4" d. (small unseen table ring flake) **375-475**

Soup plate, Llama patt., Quadrupeds series, dark blue, Hall, 10" d. **325-350**

Rare Caledonia Soup Tureen

Soup tureen, cov., bulbous oval tapering deep ribbed body on four peg feet, upturned loop end handles, high domed cover w/squared ropetwist handle, Caledonia patt., purple, Adams, ca. 1840, in-the-making separations in base & ladle hole, 14" l., 9 3/4" h. (ILLUS.)................. **650-700**

Teapot, cov., bulbous body w/scalloped rim, flared neck & base, applied handle, dark blue transfer of flowers & an urn w/American eagle w/shield, unmarked Clews, 6 1/2" h. (lid has chips).................................... **660**

Teapot, cov., dark blue central transfer of a man fishing w/a manor house in background, surrounded by floral rosette design, molded flower finial, 7 1/2" h................. **468**

Teapot, cov., scene of an early train, the reverse w/rail splitters, floral border & cover, blue, early 19th c., 7 1/2" h. (cracks).... **1,093**

Toddy plate, a central scene of a young woman playing a harp in a landscape, a large manor house in the background, flower & leaf border, medium blue, ca. 1830, 4 3/4" d. **105**

Toddy plate, center scene of a house in the woods, floral border, dark blue, marked "Wood," ca. 1830, 5 3/4" d. **138**

Tray, handled, oblong, Japan Flowers patt., blue, Ridgway, Morley, Wear & Co., England, 1836-42, 10 x 14 1/2"......................... **275**

Undertray, wide rounded form w/gently shaped flanged rim w/molded open oak branch handles, Seashell patt., cluster of shells in the center w/a wide fruit & leaf design border, dark blue, impressed Stubbs mark, ca. 1830, 11 x 15" (roughness on handles) **1,320**

Vegetable dish, cov., Caledonia patt., rectangular, w/wide notched corners, angled loop end handles, domed cover w/blossom finial, purple, Adams, ca. 1840 (small area of mellowing, slight rim wear) **605**

Vegetable dish, open, oblong, Arctic Scenery patt., black transfer of scene of explorer w/Eskimos building igloo, border w/flowers & animals including leopards & buffalo, first half 19th c., 11" l. **935**

Vegetable dish, open, oval, Shell patt., dark blue, Stubbs & Kent, early 19th c., 12 1/4" l., 2 1/2" h. (scratches, wear) **1,150**

Vegetable dish & underplate, open, oblong, open looped rims w/ropetwist handles, medium blue transfer of scene of shepherds near waterfall, impressed & transfer label "Riley's Semi-China," 11" l., 2 pcs... **468**

Wall plaque, pearlware, oval, a black border trim around oval transfer scene of woman on hillside w/tambourine, above inscription "Come and trip it as you go - On the light fantastic toe," England, early 19th c., 6 1/2 x 8 1/2" **431**

Washbowl & pitcher, Aladdin patt., tall ovoid jug-form pitcher w/tall flared neck w/scalloped rim & wide spout, arched loop handle, wide bowl w/scalloped rim, light blue, mid-19th c., bowl 13" d., pitcher 11" h., 2 pcs... **220**

Waste bowl, footed, w/deep, flat & flared sides, large florals & urns w/eagles & shields, interior w/an Oriental building, dark blue, ca. 1830, 5 1/2" d., 3 1/16" h. (minor roughness) **385**

Waste bowl, wide flat flaring sides, scene of a woman w/child talking to a man w/a bundle on his stick, dark blue, ca. 1830s, 5 3/4" d., 3" h. **125-150**

Stangl Pottery

Stangl Mark

Johann Martin Stangl, who first came to work for the Fulper Pottery in 1910 as a ceramic chemist and plant superintendent, acquired a financial interest and became president of the company in 1926. The name of the firm was changed to Stangl Pottery in 1929 and at that time much of the production was devoted to a high grade dinnerware to enable the company to survive the Depression years. One of the earliest solid-color dinnerware patterns was its Colonial line, introduced in 1926. In the 1930s it was joined by the Americana pattern. After 1942 these early patterns were followed by a wide range of hand-decorated patterns featuring flowers and fruits, with a few decorated with animals or human figures.

Around 1940 a very limited edition of porcelain birds, patterned after the illustrations in John James Audubon's "Birds of America," was issued. Stangl subsequently began production of less expensive ceramic birds, which proved to be popular during the war years 1940-46. Each bird was handpainted and well marked with impressed, painted or stamped numerals indicating the species and the size.

All operations ceased at the Trenton, New Jersey, plant in 1978.

Two reference books collectors will find helpful are The Collectors Handbook of Stangl Pottery by Norma Rehl (The Democrat Press, 1979), and Stangl Pottery by Harvey Duke (Wallace-Homestead, 1994).

Birds

Audubon Warbler, pair, No. 3756-D, 7 3/4" h. **$425**

Bluebird, No. 3276-S, 5" h. **125**

Bluebirds (double), No. 3276-D, 8 1/2" h. **250**

Bobolink, No. 3595, 4 3/4" h. **300**

Canary, Blue Flower, No. 3747, 6 1/4" h. **210**

Cardinal (female), pine cones, No. 3444, 6" h. **125**

Chat (Carolina Wren), No. 3590, 4 1/4" h. **260**

Cliff Swallow, No. 3852, 3 1/4" h. **150**

Cockatoo, large, No. 3584, 11 3/8" h. **395**

Duck, flying, No. 3443, 9".................................... **331**

Parakeets, No. 3582D, blue/green, 7" h., pr....... **325**

Red-Headed Woodpeckers, No. 3752-D, 7 3/4" h., pr. **495**

Redstarts, No. 3490-D, 9" h., pr.......................... **325**

Rooster, No. 3445, 9" h. **250**

Scissor-Tailed Flycatcher, No. 3757, 11" h. **895**

Wrens, No. 3401-D, 8", pr.................................... **75**

Steins

Devil Head Character Stein

Character, porcelain, Devil head, grotesque leering expression, by E. Bohne Sohne, 1/4 liter (ILLUS.) **$633**

Dutch Girl Character Stein

Character, porcelain, Dutch Girl, full-figure of a young Dutch girl wearing white cap, orange blouse & tan skirt, shoulders & head form cover, designed by Schierholtz, Musterschutz mark, 1/2 liter (ILLUS.) **2,645**

Indian Chief Head Character Stein

Character, porcelain, Indian Chief head, smiling face in color w/black & white headdress, by E. Bohne Sohne, 1/2 liter (ILLUS.) **460**

Character, porcelain, Skull & Devil, double-sided, one face on each half, unmarked E. Bohne Sohne, 1/4 liter **776**

Faience, cylindrical body decorated in color w/a continuous scene of a milkmaid & two cows w/ruins in the background, pewter base band & low domed cover w/ball thumb lift, Nurnberg mark, mid-18th c., 9" h., 1 1/4 liter (two small chips on upper interior rim, a few minor hairlines) **4,830**

Handpainted Faience Stein

Faience, cylindrical ceramic body in white h.p. in magenta w/a long-billed exotic bird & flowers on rockwork design, stepped flaring pewter band foot & flattened domed pewter lid w/large ball thumb lift, vertical handle strap, probably Thuringia, mid-19th c., 1 1/4 liters (ILLUS.) **1,208**

Mettlach, No. 777 (2140), PUG (printed-under-glaze), color scene of dragoons on horseback, domed pewter lid, 1/2 liter **834**

Mettlach, No. 967 (2184), PUG (printed-under-glaze), color scene of gnomes drinking, signed by Schlitt, inlaid pewter lid, 1/3 liter **304**

Mettlach, No. 1526, handpainted w/wide color scene of a lady & gentleman in 18th c. costume dancing w/a rectangular vertical panel w/inscription & bottom row of red hearts behind them, design by F. Ringer, low domed pewter lid, 1/2 liter **403**

Mettlach, No. 1526, PUG (printed-underglaze), black on cream scene of fox & bird, figural horn on pewter lid, 1/2 liter **546**

Mettlach, No. 1566, etched scene of a man on a high-wheeled bicycle, signed by Gorig, inlaid lid, 1/2 liter **834**

Mettlach, No. 1570, mosaic, a wide center band of horizontal blue leaves & brown vine against white, bands of sawtooth design in dark blue & brown above & below, inlaid pewter lid, 1/2 liter **489**

Mettlach, No. 1724, etched scene of a standing fireman within front panel, figural fireman's hat on inlaid lid, figural fireman thumb lift, 1/2 liter **1,323**

Mettlach, No. 1733, etched scene of a jockey riding a leaping horse in arched front panel, figural jockey cap on inlaid lid, 1/2 liter **1,150**

Mettlach Stein with Gottingen

Mettlach, No. 1742, etched reserve w/scene of the city of Gottingen, inlaid lid, 1/2 liter (ILLUS.)... **633**
Mettlach, No. 2001 B, Book stein, etched & h.p., shows bindings of books on medicine, inlaid lid, 1/2 liter.................................... **446**
Mettlach, No. 2028, etched scene of men drinking in tavern, inlaid lid, 1/2 liter **546**
Mettlach, No. 2050, Slipper stein, etched wide band w/stylized color figures of a Victorian man facing a Victorian woman, a wide inscribed band around the bottom, inlaid lid w/figural slipper, 1/2 liter **1,323**
Mettlach, No. 2089, etched wide scene of an angel serving dinner & beer to a seated gentleman, inlaid lid, 1/2 liter **863**

Mettlach Card Stein

Mettlach, No. 2093, Card stein, bulbous body, etched w/four panels each w/a playing card in color, pewter base band & inlaid lid, 1/2 liter (ILLUS.)............................... **633**

Cavaliers in Tavern Mettlach Stein

Mettlach, No. 2231, etched scene in wide band showing Cavaliers drinking in a tavern, inlaid lid, 1/2 liter (ILLUS.)....................... **575**
Mettlach, No. 2277, etched scene of the city of Nurnberg, inlaid lid, 1/2 liter **575**
Mettlach, No. 2394, etched arched panels w/scenes from Siegfried's youth, inlaid lid, 1/2 liter **690**
Mettlach, No. 2401, etched wide color scene of Tannhauser in the Venusberg, 1/2 liter... **719**
Mettlach, No. 2479, cameo, Hildebrand stein, three arched panels w/white relief scenes against pale blue, brown ground, lid inset w/castle turret, 1/4 liter...................... **334**
Mettlach, No. 2524, Die Kannenburg stein, etched scene of a knight in armor in a castle holding up a stein, pewter turret-form lid, 4 1/4 liters (fine repair line around base)... **1,495**
Mettlach, No. 2808, etched scene of a barmaid bowling w/men looking on, inlaid lid, 1/2 liter **633**
Mettlach, No. 2829, relief decorated, continuous molded design of the Town of Rodenstein, bands of buildings in white & brown between bands of greenery w/inscriptions, inlaid lid w/figural buildings, 1/2 liter **1,955**

Etched Art Nouveau Leaf Stein

Mettlach, No. 2935, etched Art Nouveau design, large white panels w/green three-leaf sprigs, cobalt blue bands & tan stylized wheat stripes, inlaid lid, 1/2 liter (ILLUS.)... **518**
Mettlach, No. 2951, cameo, Prussian eagle emblem in white against a dark green ground, low domed pewter lid, 1/2 liter.......... **575**

Tapestry Postman Mettlach Stein

Mettlach, No. 3085, tapestry-type, large col-
or scene of an elderly postman seated &
drinking from stein, low domed pewter
lid, 1 liter (ILLUS.)............................. **805**

Mettlach, No. 3093, etched scene of a large
hairy brown troll w/long horns holding a
large bottle & seated cross-legged on a
barrel, signed by Schlitt, inlaid lid, 1/2 li-
ter **1,438**

Porcelain, occupational, baker, wide center
band transfer-printed in color w/the crest
of the baker's guild centered by a pretzel,
relief-molded pewter lid w/pretzel, litho-
phane in the bottom, 1/2 liter **460**

Porcelain, occupational, beer wagon driver,
wide center band w/a transfer-printed
color scene of a large horse-drawn beer
wagon, inscriptions around the rim &
base bands, stepped, domed pewter lid,
lithophane in bottom, 1/2 liter **460**

Porcelain, political Socialist design, wide
transfer-printed color center band featuring an allegorical figure of a classical
woman w/banners & flags, inscriptions
around the rim & base bands, includes
owner's name & roster of members,
domed pewter lid, 1/2 liter................................ **719**

Capo-di-Monte-Type Stein

Porcelain, Capo-di-Monte-type, narrow flaring base band w/pink lappet band, tall cylindrical body molded in relief w/a colorful
scene of classical figures bathing & ca-
vorting in water, inset low domed porcelain lid w/full-figure putto finial, crown &
"N" mark, late 19th c., 3/4 liter (ILLUS.) **690**

Porcelain, Capo-di-Monte-type, wide rounded base band below the cylindrical body
molded in relief w/a Roman cavalry battle
scene in color, low domed inset porcelain
lid w/figural helmet finial, crown & "N"
mark, late 19th c., 1/2 liter............................ **546**

Porcelain, color photograph of middle class
gentleman within a gold border against a
deep red ground, inlaid lid, lithophane in
bottom, 1/2 liter **431**

HR No. 425 Pottery Stein

Pottery, cylindrical, w/flaring foot, etched
scene of barmaid & drinkers framed by
scrolling leaves, high domed pewter lid &
thumb rest, Hauber & Reuther No.
425, 1/2 liter (ILLUS.)...................................... **374**

Pottery, tall, slender & slightly tapering cylindrical form decorated in Delft blue
w/large bust portrait of a knight in armor
surrounded by delicate flowering vines &
a crest, hinged domed pewter lid, Royal
Bonn mark, No. 6324, 2 liter............................ **299**

Porcelain Stein with Rugby Scene

Porcelain, cylindrical, w/molded base
band, h.p. dark blue landscape scene of
rugby players, inlaid pewter lid marked
"Yale University," base marked "Delft by
Swaine & Co.," lithophane in bottom, 1/2
liter (ILLUS.) **776**

Delft-style Pottery Stein

Pottery, tall, slender & slightly tapering cylindrical form decorated in Delft blue w/large bust portrait of a knight in armor facing right & surrounded by delicate flowering vines & a crest, hinged domed pewter lid, Royal Bonn mark, No. 4570/4, minor tear in lid, 4 liter (ILLUS.) **460**

Rare Pottery Golfer Stein

Pottery, tall, slightly tapering cylindrical form w/flared base band, etched w/a large scene of a male golfer in brown swinging his club, green grass & grey sky, stepped & domed pewter lid, marked "M.W.G.," very rare, 1/2 liter (ILLUS.) **2,645**

Regimental, porcelain, a wide color band w/a standing figure of a soldier & a large white & blue flag & red shield below a stag head coat-of-arms, inscriptions around top & base bands, two color side scenes, roster list, name of owner, domed pewter lid w/seated soldier finial, Marburg, 1903-05, 12 1/4" h., 1/2 liter **2,070**

Regimental, porcelain, wide center band in color showing soldiers on horseback above a small oval portrait, four side scenes, roster & name of owner, Straubing, 1908-1911, domed pewter lid w/screw-off finial of horse & rider, lithophane in bottom, 12 1/2" h., 1/2 liter (faint lines in lithophane) **518**

Regimental Stein for New Ulm

Regimental, porcelain, wide color band centered by a large red "1" in a white rectangle above a crest, two color side scenes, inscribed bands w/roster & name of owner, pewter lid w/pointed top & figural lion thumb lift, Neu Ulm, 1900-06, 9 1/4" h., 1/2 liter (ILLUS.) **719**

Regimental Stein for Beeskow

Regimental, porcelain, wide color band w/a cluster of oval emblems below vignettes of soldiers in action, four side scenes, printed bands w/roster & name of owner, tall rounded pewter screw-fuse lid, Beeskow, 1907-09, rare unit, 10" h., 1/2 liter (ILLUS.) **863**

Regimental, porcelain, wide color band w/a large round center vignette of a hunter & stag flanked on one side by a waving soldier, a badge above, two side scenes, roster list & name of owner, domed pewter lid w/figural helmet finial & eagle thumb lift, Potsdam, 1904-06, repaired tear in rear of lid, 9 1/2" h., 1/2 liter **1,898**

Regimental, porcelain, wide color center band decorated w/figures of soldiers around a central oval portrait reserve, roster list, inscription for Stuttgart regiment, 1905-07 & name of owner, high domed pewter lid w/figural of seated classical female warrior, 12" h., 1/2 liter **546**

Regimental, porcelain, wide color center band w/a vignette of a city above two bust portraits in ovals flanked by figure of a soldier & the unit number, four side scenes, roster & name of owner, Regensburg, 1911-1913, lithophane in bottom, domed pewter lid w/figural finial of standing soldier, 12 1/3" h., 1/2 liter (faint line in lithophane) **345**

Regimental, porcelain, wide color center band w/scene of soldier on horseback above other figures, four side scenes, inscription & name of owner, Nurnberg, 1909-1912, domed pewter lid w/figural soldier on horseback finial & lion thumb lift, 12 1/4" h., 1/2 liter **834**

Regimental, porcelain, wide color transfer-printed band centered by a crowned shield w/a red cross flanked by standing soldiers, medical side scenes, high domed cover w/wreath thumb lift, Dillingen, 1909-1911, name of owner in bottom band, 9 7/8" h., 1/2 liter **2,415**

Rare Regimental Stein

Regimental, porcelain, wide flared base band below cylindrical sides, wide color center band w/a crown over a blue shield w/"170" in red, flanked by standing figures of soldiers, two side scenes, roster list & name of owner, small color vignettes around base band, domed pewter lid w/large figural griffin thumb lift, Offenburg, 1904-1906, very rare body form, 12 1/4" h., 1/2 liter (ILLUS.)........................... **1,783**

Regimental, pottery, a wide slightly flaring base band molded w/leafy vines & scrolls trimmed in dark green centered by a shield w/monogram, two narrow body bands flank the wide color scene of the Kaiser mounted on horseback in front of large building, inscription around top rim, domed pewter lid w/figural Kaiser on horseback finial, two side scenes, 12-man roster & name of owner, figural eagle thumb lift, Potsdam, 1910-13, very rare units, 14" h., 1/2 liter **5,750**

Art Nouveau-style Stoneware Stein

Stoneware, Art Nouveau style, spherical form w/flattened bottom, bands of incised small diamond & fan designs over a scalloped base band, all highlighted in cobalt blue, flattened hinged pewter lid, by R. Merkelbach, design by R. Riemerschmid, No. 1728, 1/2 liter (ILLUS.)............................. **633**

Stoneware, cylindrical body, grey incised & trimmed in cobalt blue w/a round reserve w/the Munich Child above "XVI Bundestag - Munchen - 1899," pewter lid w/bronze inlay reading "Deutsches Rad Fahrer Bund," 1 liter...................... **403**

Stoneware, cylindrical, decorated on the front w/a colorful coat-of-arms under plumes, all against a speckled brown ground, slightly domed hinged pewter lid, by R. Merkelbach, designed by L. Hohlwein, No. 2176, ca. 1910, 1/2 liter.............. **1,783**

Stoneware, cylindrical, transfer-printed color scene on front of young German maiden holding flowers & reaching out to a facing young man holding his hat out, signed by F. Ringer, flat-topped relief-molded hinged pewter lid, HB, 1903, 1 liter.. **489**

Stoneware, cylindrical, transfer-printed & enameled in color w/the tall figure of an Art Nouveau maiden in a green robe standing in front of a large standing lion, banner with "Gruss aus Munchen" near top, relief-molded pewter lid w/Munich Child, 1 liter **242**

Early Westerwald Stoneware Stein

Stoneware, footed spherical body tapering to a cylindrical neck w/flat rim, incised w/starburst design w/large round rays alternating w/smaller petals, all trimmed in cobalt blue, applied central medallion w/cobalt blue relief initials "GR," purple band trim, Westerwald, mid-18th c., small upper rim chip, 2 liters (ILLUS.)... **776**

Stoneware, plain spherical body molded on the side w/a stylized floret & vine in cobalt blue, raised on three cobalt blue peg feet, hinged pewter lid, by R. Merkelbach, design by R. Riemerschmid, No. 1757, 1/2 liter **863**

Large Stoneware Stein with Crest

Stoneware, tall wide cylindrical tan body, the wide center band molded in relief in the middle w/a family crest surrounded by small white relief shell-like devices, many w/cobalt blue trim, all between thin cobalt blue bands, pewter footring & low domed pewter cover w/large knob thumb lift, repaired tear in rear of lid, Altenburg, 1 1/2 liter (ILLUS.) **2,415**

Stoneware, Third Reich era, engraved color scene of city titled "Regensburg," hinged pewter lid w/impressed eagle & swastika, engraved inscription around base, 1/2 liter **546**

Stoneware

Stoneware is essentially a vitreous pottery, impervious to water even in its unglazed state, that has been produced by potteries all over the world for centuries. Utilitarian wares such as crocks, jugs, churns and the like were the most common productions in the numerous potteries that sprang into existence in the United States during the 19th century. These items were often enhanced by the application of a cobalt blue oxide decoration. In addition to the coarse, primarily salt-glazed stonewares, there are other categories of stoneware known by such special names as basalt, jasper and others.

Batter jug, cov., ovoid shape w/bale handle & old tin lid, angled straight spout w/tin collar, 11" h. **$468**

Batter jug, ovoid body tapering to a molded rim, angled cylindrical spout at the front, small shoulder loops anchoring the wire bail handle w/wooden grip, large brushed cobalt blue crescent-form blossom on the lower front, impressed label of Evan B.

Jones, Pittston, Pennsylvania, 19th c., 10" h. (tin lid missing) **468**

Butter churn, tall, slender, slightly tapering cylindrical form w/short flared neck & eared handles, large cobalt blue slip-quilled sunflower-style blossom on stem w/four leaves below an "8," impressed label "J. Burger, Rochester, N.Y.," late 19th c., 8 gal., 22 3/4" h. (minor lime deposits) **900-1,100**

Churn, tall, slightly waisted cylindrical form w/molded rim & eared handles, brushed cobalt blue crude three-leaf sprig w/two blossoms below a "4," 2nd half 19th c., 4 gal., 16 1/4" h. **358**

Crock, cylindrical, w/cobalt decoration of long-beaked bird on a cherry branch, impressed "6," 10" h. **495**

Crock, two-handled, slip-quilled cobalt blue bird on branch, impressed "F.A. Plaisted, Gardiner, Maine," 11 1/2" h. **400-450**

Crock, cylindrical, w/molded rim & eared handles, large brushed cobalt blue leafy vine up the front w/an impressed "3," 3 gal., 19th c., 11 1/2" h. (small chips) **440**

Stoneware Crock with Codfish Decoration

Crock, ovoid w/flared mouth & eared handles, incised w/horizontal lines & two codfish on front, "Boston" & "JF" on reverse, Jonathan Fenton, Boston, ca. 1794-97, minor chips, 13" h. (ILLUS.) **6,000-6,500**

Jar, cov., eared handles, brushed double flower design, "W.A. MacQuoid & Co., NY, Little West 12th St.," ca. 1870, 1 1/2 gal., 10" h. (minor staining, lid has some damage) **440**

Jar, ovoid body w/thick molded rim, brushed cobalt blue wide band of leafy scrolls & blossoms around the sides, 12 1/4" h. (hairlines) **325-350**

Jar, ovoid body w/a wide, flat mouth, eared handles, brushed cobalt blue band of vining florals around the middle, impressed "4," mid-19th c., 4 gal., 12 3/4" h. (small chips, minor hairlines)...................................... **303**

Jar, slightly ovoid w/molded rim & eared handles, light blue & freehand label w/tulips & leafy vine above "Excelsior Works, Isaac Hewitt, Jr. Rices Landing, Pa. 3," impressed "3," 19th c., 3 gal., 14" h. (minor chips)... **660**

Jar, tall, swelled, cylindrical body w/short cylindrical neck & eared handles, large upright cobalt blue stenciled flower & leaf wreath flanking a central scroll band above a large "4," late 19th c., 4 gal., 15 1/4" h. **440-460**

Jar, tall, wide, cylindrical body tapering slightly to the deep ringed molded mouth flanked by eared handles, upper half w/brushed cobalt blue wide undulating leafy vine w/large blossoms above a central brushed narrow band of scrolled leaves, the bottom w/the blue stenciled label "Hamilton & Jones, Greensboro, PA - 15," 19th c., 15 gal., 24 1/2" h. (hairlines) **1,980**

Jug, ovoid, decorated w/cobalt blue swags, impressed "C. Croleus Stonemaker New York" **1,750-1,850**

Jug, sharply ovoid form w/molded lip & strap shoulder handle, impressed label "S. Purdy" splashed in blue, Tuscarawas County, Ohio, 19th c., 11 1/2" h. **633**

Jug, ovoid, w/ochre decorated flower, impressed "Lyman and Clark, Gardiner," 12 1/2" h. **1,900-2,100**

Jug, ovoid w/small molded neck & strap handle, large brushed cobalt blue tulip blossom on a slender leafy stem, impressed label "T. Reed 2," Tuscarawas County, Ohio, 19th c., 2 gal., 14 1/4" h. **1,870**

Jug, semi-ovoid w/flat base, molded mouth & strap handle, slender brushed cobalt blue bird on a flowering branch, impressed label "Charlestown 2" brushed w/blue, 2 gal., 14 1/2" h. **545**

Jug, ovoid, w/handles, impressed "Lyman and Clark, Gardiner, #3," w/a freehand "3" in ochre in center, 3 gal., 15" h **450-500**

Jug, ovoid body w/molded lip & strap handle, brushed cobalt blue leafy floral sprig decoration & "2" on shoulder, impressed label of J. Maxfield, Milwaukee, mid-19th c., 2 gal., 15" h. (rim chips, stains) **495**

Milk bowl, flat bottom w/deep flared sides & molded top w/rim spout, brushed cobalt blue sprigs of leaves around the sides, impressed "1" in a circle, 11 1/2" d., 4 1/2" h. (small flakes) **440**

Pitcher, 6" h., bulbous ovoid body tapering to a wide cylindrical neck w/a pinched spout & applied ribbed strap handle, wide brushed cobalt blue floral & leaf band around the body & the neck (rim & spout chips) **495**

Stoneware Pitcher

Pitcher, 10" h., bulbous body w/slightly flared base & slightly tapered neck, applied strap handle, freehand cobalt foliage decoration starts at bottom below spout & extends back almost to handle, small fan or leaf designs near the top, wavy lines below the neck rim, incised line detail around the body, firing separations in side & bottom (ILLUS.).................... **3,410**

Pitcher, 10 1/2" h., wide ovoid body tapering to a wide cylindrical neck w/pinched spout & molded rim, strap handle, brushed cobalt blue leaf band around the neck & body (spout chip, stains, some discoloration)... **605**

Pitcher, 10 5/8" h., ovoid body w/raised ring base w/slightly flared rim, short cylindrical neck, applied handle, cobalt floral decoration & line detail around spout & handle (some pot stones) **880**

Preserving jar, semi-ovoid, molded mouth, brushed cobalt blue leafy vine w/two blossoms above three graduated bands, impressed mark of Offord & Federer, West Brownsville, Pennsylvania, 19th c., 10 1/2" h. (chips on lip)..................................... **605**

Iowa Stoneware Preserving Jar

Preserving jar, cylindrical, w/applied eared handles & rolled rim, brushed cobalt blue floral motif & "2," impressed "Tolman, Eldora, IA," 2 gal. (ILLUS.) **3,250-3,500**

Preserving jar, cylindrical, w/heavy molded flat rim, vertical stripes of cobalt blue stenciled stars, 19th c., 9" h. **650-700**

Preserving jar, slightly ovoid w/molded rim, cobalt blue stenciled & freehand decoration, printed "Excelsior Works, Isaac Hewitt, Jr. Rices Landing, PA," 9 1/2" h. **325-350**

Water cooler, tall domed beehive form w/short neck, applied shoulder handles, w/cobalt decoration of chicken pecking at an ear of corn, unusual orange peel glaze, impressed "6" & "New York Stoneware Co. Fort Edward...," 19 1/2" h. (two daubs of translucent glaze & short hairlines at base, made into a lamp but not drilled) **2,750**

Water cooler, tall domed beehive form w/small neck flanked by loop shoulder handles, bung hole w/wooden spigot at the bottom, brushed cobalt blue "6" & a flourish on the shoulder, 18 1/2" h.................. **220**

Teco Pottery

Teco Mark

Teco Pottery was actually the line of art pottery introduced by the American Terra Cotta and Ceramic Company of Terra Cotta (Crystal Lake), Illinois, in 1902. Founded by William D. Gates in 1881, American Terra Cotta originally produced only bricks and drain tile. Because of superior facilities for experimentation, including a chemical laboratory, the company was able to develop an art pottery line, favoring a matte green glaze in the earlier years but eventually achieving a wide range of colors including a metallic lustre glaze and a crystalline glaze. Although some hand-thrown pottery was made, Gates favored a molded ware because it was less expensive to produce. By 1923, Teco Pottery was no longer being made, and in 1930 American Terra Cotta and Ceramic Company was sold. A book on the topic is Teco: Art Pottery of the Prairie School, by Sharon S. Darling (Erie Art Museum, 1990).

Bowl, 4 1/2" d., wide flat bottom w/low incurved sides, green matte glaze, impressed marks, No. 350 .... **$286**

Fine Teco Bowl-vase

Bowl-vase, wide sharply tapering round bowl supported by four heavy squared pierced buttress legs around the rim, design by Holmes Smith, fine green matte glaze w/charcoal highlights, impressed marks, minor crazing on interior, 12" d. (ILLUS.) **5,500**

Box, cov., squatty rounded rectangular form sharply incurved to the rectangular base, w/a flat fitted rectangular cover, smooth matte green glaze w/charcoaling, stamped mark, 2 1/2 x 3 1/2", 2 1/4" h. (bruise on base) **788**

Chamberstick, a wide round dished base w/a tapering short center shaft w/a thick molded socket rim & an open squared handle from the rim to the base rim, good ivory matte glaze, impressed marks, paper label, 5" d. (flaw in glaze on handle in making) **523**

Chamberstick, a wide round dished base w/a tapering short center shaft w/a thick molded socket rim & an open squared handle from the rim to the base rim, good green matte glaze, impressed marks, paper label, 5" d. **605**

Chamberstick, wide cushion foot centered by a tall slender waisted cylindrical shaft molded w/stylized leaves & flowers, a long loop handle from the upper side to the base of the shaft, smooth matte green glaze, paper label, 5" d., 10 3/4" h. **900**

Jardiniere, round bulbous body w/heavily molded wide shoulder band around the wide flat mouth supported on four buttressed legs, smooth matte green glaze, stamped "TECO," 11" d., 7" h. **6,750**

Pitcher, 8 1/2" h., 5" d., tall, slender, waisted body w/a wide rim w/pinched spout & integral pinched & forked loop handle reaching down nearly to the bottom, mottled matte green & charcoal glaze, stamped mark **044**

Pitcher, 9" h., 3 1/2" d., corseted form w/an organic wishbone handle & an undulating rim, smooth matte green glaze, stamped "TECO" (small firing flaw to handle) **1,125**

Vase, miniature, 3" h., 1 1/4" d., simple ovoid form w/two tiny buttress handles at the rim, smooth matte green glaze, original paper label **956**

Vase, 3 3/4" h., 3 1/4" d., footed ovoid body w/dimpled sides, wide molded rim, dark speckled matte green & charcoal glaze, incised "Teco/519" (ILLUS. front row, second from right with group of Teco vases) **619**

Vase, 4" h., bulbous nearly spherical form tapering slightly to a wide, short, flared neck, dark matte green glaze, impressed mark & incised number **440**

Vase, 4" h., slightly tapering cylindrical form w/four deep oval indentations up the sides below the short flared neck, green matte glaze, No. 356 .... **605**

Vase, 4 1/2" h., bulbous rounded base w/a deep indentation on each side & tapering to a wide squared neck, good matte green glaze, impressed mark **660**

Vase, 4 1/2" h., gently flaring wide cylindrical body w/an angled shoulder tapering to a flat mouth, green matte glaze, impressed marks, paper label **770**

Vase, 4 3/4" h., gently tapering cylindrical body w/slightly flared flat rim, molded w/thin rings up the sides, green matte glaze, impressed mark **495**

Vase, 5" h., footed squatty bulbous lower body tapering to a waisted neck w/a four-ruffle flared rim, good green matte glaze, impressed marks **715**

Vase, 6" h., 9 1/2" d., squatty bulbous body, the wide shoulder tapering to a slightly flared rim w/four curled leaves, smooth matte green glaze, restoration to two rim chips, stamped "Teco/272" (ILLUS. bottom row, left with group of Teco vases) **2,700**

Vase, 6 1/4" h., 6 1/2" d., wide, cylindrical, finely ringed body w/three long squared handles from the rim to the base, each handle w/ribbing down the front, smooth matte green glaze, fine charcoaling, stamped mark (bruise to rim) **1,238**

Unusual Pierced Teco Vase

Three Teco Buttress-handled Vases

Vase, 6 1/2" h., bulbous ovoid four-sided form tapering to four short pierced buttress shoulder handles attaching to the flattened pierced rim & mouth, molded leaf design at the bottom center of each side, green matte glaze w/light charcoaling, designed by Fritz Albert, impressed marks (ILLUS.)... **3,850**

Vase, 6 1/2" h., large mug form, the wide cylindrical body w/thin narrow rings & molded looped scrolls at the front, a long low angled open handle down the side, dark matte green glaze, impressed mark.............. **550**

Vase, 6 1/2" h., 5 1/2" d., bulbous ovoid gourd form w/four slight lobes defined by upright scroll bands, four short buttress handles issue from the top & attach to an upper band w/a pierced Oriental design around the closed rim, handles form open loops at the shoulder, also w/pierced openings, matte green glaze, stamped "Teco -113"..................................... **2,420**

Vase, 6 3/4" h., simple ovoid body tapering to a short flared neck, green matte glaze, impressed marks **523**

Double-gourd Teco Handled Vase

Vase, 7" h., 6" d., bulbous double-gourd body w/four heavy curved buttress handles from the rim to the base, fine leath- ery matte green glaze, small long bruise at rim, stamped mark (ILLUS.)................... **2,990**

Vase, 7 1/4" h., 4 1/4" d., conical body tapering to a flared neck w/a thick rim band issuing four heavy squared buttress handles from the rim to the base, smooth medium green matte glaze, short abrasion to rim, stamped mark (ILLUS. left with buttress-handled vases, top of page)......... **4,025**

Vase, 7 1/4" h., 4 1/4" d., ovoid body tapering to a flaring cylindrical neck flanked by heavy square buttress handles going down the sides, mottled matte green glaze, some glaze curdling to base, No. 435, stamped mark (ILLUS. center w/buttress-handled vases, top of page).............. **3,220**

Vase, 7 1/2" h., bulbous spherical base tapering to a tall slender tapering neck topped by a squatty cupped & closed rim, green matte glaze, impressed mark.. **715**

Vase, 7 1/2" h., 4 1/4" d., conical body tapering to a flared neck w/a thick rim band issuing four heavy squared buttress handles from the rim to the base, smooth matte brown glaze, mark obscured by glaze (ILLUS. right with buttress-handled vases, top of page)....................... **3,450**

Vase, 8" h., 5 1/2" d., low footring below the wide ovoid body tapering to a cylindrical neck w/flared rim, long squared handles from the rim down the sides, smooth matte green glaze, stamped mark.............. **2,640**

Vase, 8 3/4" h., 4" d., a tall bullet-shaped body w/a rounded shoulder & small molded mouth, supported by four tall V-form buttresses around the base, smooth medium matte green glaze, stamped mark (ILLUS. back row, left with group of vases, top next page) **4,219**

Vase, 9" h., 4" d., "rocket ship" style, long tapering ovoid body w/a small molded mouth, wide molded V-shaped fins at the base, unusual mauve matte glaze, stamped "Teco" **7,875**

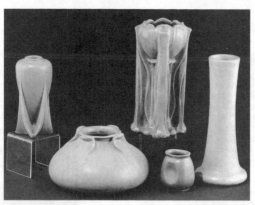

Group of Teco Vases

Tall Teco Vase with Buttresses

Vase, 10 1/4" h., 5 3/4" d., tapering cylindrical body w/a wide flattened rim, four low square buttress handles down the sides, green & charcoal mottled glaze w/a splotch of yellow under the rim, marked, invisible restoration to a few chips, base & mark (ILLUS.) **2,185**

Tall Buttress-handled Teco Vase

Vase, 11 1/4" h., 3 3/4" d., tall, slender, swelled cylindrical body tapering to a slightly flaring neck flanked by squared short buttress handles continuing down the sides to the base, smooth matte green glaze, stamped mark (ILLUS.) **5,175**

Teco Vase with Entwined Handles

Vase, 11 1/2" h., 9" d., large ovoid body w/a narrow shoulder tapering to a wide short cylindrical neck w/a thick flattened rim, pairs of entwined loop handles on each side from rim to shoulder, smooth matte green glaze, stamped mark & remnant of paper label (ILLUS.) **5,175**

Vase, 12 1/4" h., 5" d., a large cupped tulip blossom framed by four heavy buttress leaf-molded supports forming the squared body, matte green glaze, stamped "Teco" (ILLUS. back row, right with group of Teco vases) **5,063**

Unusual Tall Teco Bud Vase

Vase, 12 1/2" h., 5 1/2" d., bud-type, an unusual organic form w/two upturned & two downturned handles projecting from the rim above the slender two-lobed stem above forked short leaves above the multi-petaled foot, heavily charcoaled matte green glaze, No. 153, stamped mark, three tiny chips to base (ILLUS.)...... **2,415**

Vase, 12 1/2" h., 10 1/2" d., large spherical body tapering to a short wide neck w/molded rim, the body raised on four squared short buttress feet, matte green glaze, stamped "Teco - 339" (restoration to two small chips, hairline at rim, two small chips on one foot).............................. **7,700**

Vase, 13 1/4" h., 5 1/4" d., tall slender tapering cylindrical body w/cushion foot, smooth matte grey glaze, stamped "Teco" (ILLUS. far right with group of Teco vases)... **1,688**

Tall Organic-form Teco Vase

Vase, 13 3/4" h., 8 1/4" d., tall cylindrical organic form w/pinched four-petaled scalloped & gently flared rim, long bulbed buttresses down the sides forming feet, smooth green matte glaze, stamped mark, flat chip to one rim petal, bruise to another (ILLUS.) **2,300**

Rare Tall Paneled Teco Vase

Vase, 14 3/4" h., tall tapering four-sided form w/long panels to small open buttresses around the small flat mouth, fine green matte charcoaled glaze, designed by Fritz Albert, No. 181A, marked (ILLUS.)... **33,350**

Vase, 16 1/2" h., 8" d., footed wide squatty bulbous lower body w/a wide shoulder tapering to a very tall slender lobed neck w/flared rim, smooth matte green glaze, stamped mark (restored rim section) **1,688**

Rare Teco Vase

Vase, 17 1/2" h., 6 1/2" d., tall lobed body w/tapering cylindrical neck & molded rim, embossed calla lily between each lobe & extending to rim, light green matte glaze, restoration to small drill hole on side at base, small nick on leaf point (one of two known), stamped "TECO" (ILLUS.) **28,125**

Large Plain Teco Floor Vase

Vase, 20 1/4" h., 10 3/4" d., floor-type, tapering cylindrical body below a wide shoulder tapering to a wide cylindrical neck w/rolled rim, leathery matte green glaze, stamped mark, several small base chips (ILLUS.)... **4,313**

Large Teco Floor Vase

Vase, 22" h., 8 1/2" w., floor-type, a flared stepped foot on the swelled squared body w/molded buttress corners at the closed mouth, molded on each side w/tall slender leaves, microcrystalline matte green glaze, stamped "Teco 343," restoration to base chip, four hairlines at rim (ILLUS.)... **6,188**

Tiffany Pottery

Tiffany Pottery Mark

In 1902 Louis C. Tiffany expanded Tiffany Studios to include ceramics, enamels, gold, silver and gemstones. Tiffany pottery was usually molded rather than wheel-thrown, but it was carefully finished by hand. A limited amount was produced until about 1914. It is scarce.

Tiffany Pottery Square Bottle

Bottle, square upright form w/a small round neck centered on the flat top, incised ab-

stract design around the sides, textured cobalt blue & turquoise matte glaze, incised "LCT," 4" w., 6 1/2" h. (ILLUS.)....... **$1,380**

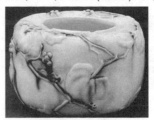

Tiffany Pottery Vase with Vines

Bowl-vase, wide, short, cylindrical form w/flattened rounded base & top rim w/closed mouth, molded w/a bold design of vines, leaves & berries under an Old Ivory glaze, incised "LCT" & etched "Favrile Pottery - P22Y Tiffany," three chips, tight line at rim, nick on branch on top, 7 1/2" d., 5" h. (ILLUS.)........................ **4,500**

Rare Tiffany Pottery Box and Ewer

Box, cov., flat-bottomed w/deep gently rounded flaring sides molded w/a berry & twig design, the domed cover w/a matching design, deep yellow & orange berries on a dark green ground, marked "LCT - 7," 5 1/2" d., 4" h. (ILLUS. right)................. **9,600**

Ewer, flat-bottomed conical form w/a deep cupped neck w/long pinched spout, long tapering handle from edge of neck to base, lightly molded overall w/a design of a stylized parrot, mottled light green & black glaze, marked "L.C.T. - P 159," 8 3/4" h. (ILLUS. left with box)................... **5,100**

Tiffany Vase with Reticulated Shoulder

Vase, 5 1/2" h., wide baluster-form body w/the shoulder reticulated w/a wide band of cherry blossoms on stems, tan bisque finish (ILLUS.)... **1,725**

Vase, 6 5/8" h., wide gently waisted cylindrical form, molded up the sides w/long pointed leaves w/three leaf stems forming arched loop handles down the sides, streaky light & dark blue glaze, signed "LCT - Tiffany Favrile Pottery - P 412" (chip to rim).. **4,800**

Tiffany Pottery Bud Vase

Vase, 7" h., bud-type, slender cylindrical form w/ribbed stems up the sides to swelled molded blossoms at the top just below the flaring rim, rare mottled bluish green glaze w/brown showing through, incised "LCT - 65D - EL," repaired chip on base (ILLUS.) **2,300**

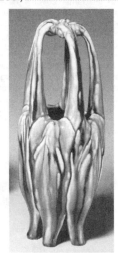

Very Rare Tiffany Pottery Fern Vase

Vase, 11 1/8" h., molded stylized fern design, the body formed by a cluster of molded fern fronds extending down to form short legs, a cluster of tall slender

fronds extending up from the rim & arching together to form open handles, streaky green & dark gold glaze on a creamy body, signed "Tiffany - Pottery - H 9 A - Coll - 49B," firing crack around base (ILLUS.)... **21,450**

Tiles

Tiles have been made by potteries in the United States and abroad for many years. Apart from small tea tiles used on tables, there are also decorative tiles for fireplaces, floors and walls. This is where present collector interest lies, especially in the late 19th century American-made art pottery tiles.

American Encaustic Tiles

American Encaustic Tiling Company, Zanesville, Ohio, rectangular, molded figure of a Colonial gentleman holding a cane & gloves under a glossy brown glaze, impressed "American Encaustic Tiling Co. Limited New York Works Zanesville, O.," minor flaws, 5 7/8 x 18" (ILLUS. right)... **$330**

American Encaustic Tiling Company, Zanesville, Ohio, rectangular, molded figure of a young Colonial woman holding a fan under a glossy brown glaze, impressed "American Encaustic Tiling Co. Limited New York Works Zanesville, O.," minor flaws, 5 7/8 x 18" (ILLUS. left)............. **330**

American Encaustic Stove Tile

American Encaustic Tiling Company, Zanesville, Ohio, rectangular stove tile depicting a seated Roman soldier w/one arm resting across the shoulder of a bear standing beside him, blue high glaze, unmarked, small glaze nicks to edges, 4 1/4 x 7 3/8" (ILLUS.) **280**

Franklin Pottery Faience Tile

Franklin Pottery, Lansdale, Pennsylvania, rectangular, faience tile w/colorful parrot perched on a branch, gloss & matte glazes of blues, green, pink, black & yellow, back die-impressed "Franklin Pottery Faience," ca. 1936, accompanied by photocopy of Franklin Tile catalog, very minor chips to back edges, tile 8 7/8 x 8 3/4" (ILLUS.) **605**

Grueby Faience & Tile Company, Boston, Massachusetts, square, decorated in cuenca w/a stylized yellow stag w/brown antlers under a green leafy tree w/green grass & pale blue sky, in a new wide flat oak Arts & Crafts frame, unmarked, tile 4" w. **1,069**

Grueby Faience & Tile Company, Boston, Massachusetts, decorated in cuenca w/a large pale yellow seated rabbit in a cabbage patch w/light bluish green foliage against a dark green ground, artist-initialed, in a new wide flat oak Arts & Crafts frame, tile 6" w. (some surface abrasion) **3,375**

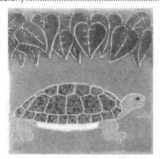

Rare Grueby Turtle Tile

Grueby Faience & Tile Company, Boston, Massachusetts, square, decorated in cuenca w/a turtle in shades of brown & ivory below a bough of green leaves, all on an ochre matte ground, stamped mark & paper label, 6" w. (ILLUS.) **7,450**

Grueby Faience & Tile Company, Boston, Massachusetts, rectangular, decorated in cuenca w/a yellow chamberstick & candle against a green ground below molded wording "Grueby Tile," artist-initialed, in a new wide flat Arts & Crafts oak frame, tile 4 1/2 x 6" **4,500**

Grueby Tile with Horses

Grueby Faience & Tile Company, Boston, Massachusetts, square, decorated w/a row of prancing white horses in cuenca on a blue & green ground, unmarked, restoration to edge chip, 6 1/4" w. (ILLUS.) **3,450**

Grueby Tile in Tiffany Brass Frame

Grueby Faience & Tile Company, Boston, Massachusetts, square, decorated in cuenca w/a yellow tulip blossom flanked by pairs of large arched leaves on a green ground, mounted in a brass Tiffany Studios frame w/squared floral-form feet, 7" w. (ILLUS.) **5,750**

Grueby Tile with Sailing Galleon

Grueby Faience & Tile Company, Boston, Massachusetts, square, a galleon under full sail, in cream & brown on a dark green ground, unsigned, 8" w. (ILLUS.) **2,013**

Exceptional Grueby Seven-tile Frieze

Grueby Faience & Tile Company, Boston, Massachusetts, seven-tile frieze designed by Addison Le Boutillier, titled "The Pines," decorated in cuenca w/pine trees in a valley, green, blue, brown & cobalt matte oatmealy glazes, ca. 1902, small chip to corner of one tile, 6 x 42" (ILLUS.)...................... **42,188**

Grueby Pottery, Boston, Massachusetts, square, decorated in cuenca depicting a cherub w/a cornucopia in matte oatmeal glaze on a grey-blue ground, design by Addison Le Boutillier, Boston, early 20th c., illegible impressed number on side, 6" d. (glaze bursts, minor edge chips).......... **173**

Grueby Pottery, Boston, Massachusetts, square, decorated w/grapevine cluster & leaves in relief in green, brown & dark blue against a tan ground, impressed mark & number 4085A, 6" sq. **748**

Hamilton Tile Works Company, Hamilton, Ohio, rectangular, a woodland scene of deer, brown & tan, back embossed "The Hamilton Tile Works Co Hamilton Ohio," last quarter 19th c., 6 x 12 1/8" (glaze scratches & minor edge chips)....................... **275**

Kensington Art Tile Company, Newport, Kentucky, square, embossed image of a greyhound, shaded tan & brown high glaze, marked w/Kensington logo, minor edge & surface chips, 6" sq. **275**

Low Art Pottery, Chelsea, Massachusetts, square, depicting a profile of a child's head in relief, dark bluish green glossy glaze, impressed marks, early 20th c., 6" sq. (small glaze abrasion) **115**

Marblehead Pottery, Marblehead, Massachusetts, square, a matte-painted stylized landscape silhouetted against an evening sky, in shades of blues & yellows, ship mark, 5 3/4" sq. (several small edge nicks) **1,913**

ral design of blue delphiniums & green leaves on a white ground, in a wide flat oak frame, paper label, 6" w. (ILLUS.)....... **1,100**

Marblehead Pottery, Marblehead, Massachusetts, square, decorated w/a scene of a house in a landscape, the house in colors of transparent rust & blue bordered by green grass, flanked by trees in matte blue & brown, the whole on a matte grey ground, marked, ca. 1908, 6 1/4" w. (few minor edge chips)... **1,150**

Marblehead Pottery, Marblehead, Massachusetts, square, embossed w/a large stylized spreading oak tree in a forest, fine dark green crystalline matte glaze, mounted in a fine flat wide oak frame w/rounded corners in the style of Greene & Greene, tile w/stamped ship mark & paper label, 6 1/4" sq.................................... **3,656**

Minton & Wedgwood Tiles

Minton, Staffordshire, England, molded w/a center ring enclosing a white snowflake-like design flanked by half-designs of diamonds, ochre banding & green leaf edge bands, all on a cobalt blue ground, ca. 1880, 7 3/4" l. (ILLUS. left) **110**

Fine Marblehead Framed Tile

Marblehead Pottery, Marblehead, Massachusetts, square, painted w/a stylized flo-

Unusual Muresque Pottery Tile

Muresque Pottery, Oakland, California, square, a molded Southwestern landscape w/palm tree & adobe home, in cream, tan, green & blue, impressed "Muresque - Oakland," early 20th c., framed, 6" sq. (ILLUS.)..................................... **460**

Newcomb College Tile with Galleon

Newcomb College Pottery, New Orleans, Louisiana, square, molded design depicting a galleon under full sail w/dolphins alongside, Persian blue crackled glaze, by Leona Nicholson, marked, 5 1/4" sq. (ILLUS.)... **805**

Norweta Tile with Minstrels

Norweta (Northwestern Terra Cotta Company), Chicago, Illinois, rectangular, colorful scene of six performing minstrels dancing & playing musical instruments against a cream matte glaze, surface embossed "Norweta," two cast holes in top edge for hanging, professional repair of vertical crack across center, 4 1/2 x 14 1/2" (ILLUS.) **935**

Large Owens Framed Tile

Owens Floor & Wall Tile Company (Empire), Zanesville, Ohio, rectangular, decorated in cuenca w/a landscape of large trees in green, brown & blue, mounted in a narrow wood frame, no visible mark, small chips in two corners, firing bubbles, 8 1/2 x 11 1/2" (ILLUS.)................................ **1,320**

Pardee Tile with Sailing Ship

Pardee (C.) Works, Perth Amboy, New Jersey, square, depicts a large brown & white sailing ship at sea, shaded blue sky & shaded green sea, rich matte glaze, embossed on back "The C. Pardee Works" & "- O," two small nicks on edges, 4 1/4" sq. (ILLUS.)... **330**

Pardee (C.) Works, Perth Amboy, New Jersey, square, yellow & green tulip on pale blue matte glaze ground, artist-initialed in blue slip "PS," the back embossed "The C. Pardee Work," 4 1/4" sq............................. **220**

Rookwood Pottery, Cincinnati, Ohio, square, raised decoration of a Dutch mother holding a baby & little girl at her side by the shore w/a windmill, matte glaze, shades of blue, green, pink & tan, 1924, 5 3/4" w. **316**

Rookwood Pottery, Cincinnati, Ohio, four-tile frieze, decorated in cuenca & forming a continuous landscape w/large green & brown trees & green grass & bushes in the foreground, a long blue lake in the center ground & a series of mountains in green in the background, impressed mark, previously mounted, w/remnants of mounting mortar, one reglued corner, minor corner chips, 12 x 48" (ILLUS., below) **23,000**

Rare Rookwood Tile Frieze

Van Briggle Pottery, Colorado Springs, Colorado, square, a kingfisher perched on a branch, in polychrome glazes including brown, white, green & blue, unmarked, in wide flat oak period frame, minute glaze flecks, 6" w. **4,600**

Wedgwood (Josiah), England, majolica, square, green square center molded w/a portrait of a wigged man in a center ring framed by leafy scrolls, long rectangular brown border panels & pink floret corner blocks, late 19th c., 8" w. (ILLUS. right w/Minton tile) **110**

Torquay Pottery

Torquay Pottery Marks

In the second half of the 19th century several art potteries were established in the South Devon region of England to take advantage of a belt of fine red clay there. The coastal town of Torquay gives its name to this range of wares, which often featured incised sgraffito decoration or colorful country-style decoration with mottos.

The most notable potteries operating in the Torquay area were the Watcombe Pottery, The Torquay Terracotta Company and the Aller Vale Art Pottery, which merged with Watcombe Pottery in 1901 and continued production until 1962. Other firms whose wares are collectible include Longpark Pottery and The Devonmoor Art Pottery.

Early wares feature unglazed terra cotta items in the Victorian taste including classical busts, statuary and vases and some painted and glazed wares including examples with a celeste blue interior or highlights. In addition to sgraffito designs, other decorations included flowers, Barbotine glazes, Devon pixies framed in leafy scrolls and grotesque figures of cats, dogs and other fanciful animals, produced in the 1890s.

The dozen or so potteries flourishing in the region at the turn of the 20th century introduced their most popular product, Motto Wares, which became the bread and

butter line of the local industry. The most popular patterns in this line included Cottage, Black and Colored Cockerels and Scandy, based on Scandinavian rosemaling designs. Most of the mottoes were written in English, with a few in Welsh. On early examples the sayings were often in Devonian dialect. These Motto Wares were sold for years at area seaside resorts and other tourist areas, with some pieces exported to Australia, Canada and, to a lesser extent, the United States. In addition to standard size teawares and novelties, some miniatures and even oversized pieces were offered.

Production at the potteries stopped during World War II, and some of the plants were destroyed in enemy raids. The Watcombe Pottery became Royal Watcombe after the war, and Longpark also started up again but produced simpler patterns. The Dartmouth Pottery, started in 1947, produced cottages similar to those made at Watcombe and also developed a line of figural animals, banks and novelty jugs. The Babbacombe Pottery (1950-59) and St. Marychurch Pottery (ca. 1962-69) were the last two firms to turn out Motto Wares, but these later designs were painted on and the pieces were lighter in color, with less detailing.

Many books on the various potteries are available, and information can be obtained from the products manager of the North American Torquay Society.

Cockerel Pattern

Cup & saucer, Black Cockerel patt., Motto Ware, "Du 'ee 'ave a cup a Tay," Watcombe Torquay Impressed mark, ca. 1910-27, saucer 4 1/2" d., cup 2 1/2" h. **50**

Curling iron tile, Black Cockerel patt., Motto Ware, "O list to me ye ladies fair - and when ye wish to curl your hair - For the safety of your domicile - Pray place your lamp upon this tile," Longpark Torquay mark, scarce, ca. 1903-09, 5 x 7 1/4" **198**

Dairy jug, Black Cockerel patt., Motto Ware, "Good Morning - Straight from the Dairy," no mark, Watcombe, ca. 1910-20, 3 1/2" h. **50**

Hot water pot, cov., Black Cockerel patt., Motto Ware, "Good Morning - Life is a struggle Not a race - A wise man keeps an even pace," Aller Vale mark, ca. 1902-24, overall 7 1/4" h. **176**

Inkwell, Colored Cockeral patt., round, Motto Ware, "Us be always glad tu yer frum 'ee," Aller Vale impressed mark, ca. 1891-1910, 2 1/2" h. **80**

Mug, miniature, Colored Cockerel patt., Motto Ware, "If you can't fly - climb," Longpark Torquay impressed mark, scarce, ca. 1910, 1 5/8" h. **95**

Pitcher, 6" h., Colored Cockerel patt., Motto Ware, "Good Morning - A man may travel thro' the world and sow it thick with friendships," Aller Vale, Devon, England mark, early, ca. 1891-1902 .... **165**

Vase, 5 3/4" h., Black Cockerel patt., four spouts, Motto Ware, "May you never find a mouse in your cupboard with tears in its eyes," desirable motto, Longpark Torquay early mark, ca. 1904-18 .... **279**

Wall pocket, Colored Cockerel patt., Motto Ware, "See a pin pick it up - And all day have good Luck," no mark, H.M. Exeter Pottery, rare, ca. 1920, 6 5/8" l. **225**

Molded Cottageware Pieces

Cottage Pattern

Bowl, 4" d., 3 1/2" h., four-handled, Motto Ware, in Devon dialect, "Come an' zee us in the zummer," Crown Dorset Pottery, ca. 1915.. **134**

Cheese dish, cov., round, Motto Ware, "Masters two will never do," Dartmouth Pottery, ca. 1960, 6 1/2" d., 3 3/4" h............... **99**

Coffeepot, cov., long spout, Motto Ware, "Gude things be scarce take care of me," Watcombe Torquay mark, ca. 1925-35, 7" h.. **151**

Coffeepot, cov., ribbed "beak" spout, Motto Ware, "Say not always what you know - but Always know what you say," Watcombe Torquay mark, ca. 1930, 6 5/8" h. **165**

Creamer, miniature, Motto Ware, "Isle of Wight - Fresh from the cow," Royal Watcombe circle mark, ca. 1950, 1 3/4" h............ **41**

Creamer, Motto Ware, "Tak a little Craim," early Aller Vale mark, ca. 1902-24, 2 3/4" h.. **41**

Cup & saucer, Molded Cottageware, details in relief w/sponged details in rose, green & yellow, Torquay Pottery Co., ca. 1918-24, scarce, saucer 5 1/4" d., cup 3" h., the set (ILLUS. left & right, top of page) **63**

Cup & saucer, Motto Ware, "Where friends there riches," "Made in England" black stamp, Watcombe Torquay mark, ca. 1930s.. **52**

Dog bowl, Motto Ware, "Love Me - Love My Dog," lovely calligraphy & "Tintern," Longpark Torquay, England mark, ca. 1930s, 5 5/8" w. **175**

Honey pot, cov., Watcombe Torquay, ca. 1920s, overall 4 3/8" h. **80**

Humidor, cov., Motto Ware, "When work is done the pipe don't shun," painted Watcombe mark, ca. 1901-20, overall 5 1/4" h. **165**

Inkwell, cov., round, Motto Ware, "Us be always glad tu hear from 'ee," Watcombe Torquay, England mark, ca. 1925-35, scarce w/cover, overall 2 1/2" h. **125**

Pin dish, round, Motto Ware, "I'll take care ov the pins," Longpark Torquay, ca. 1918-30, 3 1/8" d. **45**

Pitcher, 5 1/2" h., Motto Ware, "Be like the Sun Dial - Count only Sunny hours," Watcombe Torquay, "Made in England" mark, ca. 1930s.. **86**

Plate, 6 3/4" d., Molded Cottageware, cottage scene w/thatched roof, sponged design of flowers & trees w/windows & door slip-lined, Torquay Pottery Co. impressed mark, scarce, ca. 1908-15 (ILLUS. center with cups & saucers) **82**

Plate, 8" d., Motto Ware, "Talk little, Hear much, Learn more," Made in DMW England, Watcombe mark, ca. 1918-27 .... **80**

Shaving mug, Motto Ware, "A hair on the head is worth two on the chin," Watcombe Torquay, England mark, ca. 1925-35 (tiny sealed hairline) **151**

Tea set: cov. teapot, cov. sugar & creamer; Motto Ware, "Du' ee zit down an' 'ave a cup a Tay," each also says "Isles of Scilly," Watcombe Torquay incised mark, ca. 1901-20, teapot 3 1/2" h., the set **125**

Teapot, cov., Molded Cottageware, colorful sponged-decorated design, large & heavy, Torquay Pottery Co. mark, ca. 1905-20, overall 9 1/4" l., 6 3/4" h. **152**

Teapot, cov., Motto Ware, "Yu'll 'ave a Cup a Tay now, wa'ant 'ee - Princetown," Watcombe Torquay mark, ca. 1925-35, overall 6 1/2" l., 3 5/8" h. **80**

Toast rack, four large tines, Motto Ware, "Crisp Toast" on front, "Truro" on short side, Watcombe Torquay, England impressed mark, ca. 1930, 5 1/4" l. **178**

Scandy Pattern

Chamberstick, Motto Ware, "I slept and dreamt that life was beauty; I woke and found that life was duty," Aller Vale mark, ca. 1902-24, 5 3/8" h. **99**

Dresser tray, oval, Motto Ware, "A place for everything and everything in its place," Watcombe Torquay mark, ca. 1920s, 7 3/8 x 12".. **176**

Hatpin holder, Motto Ware, "I'll take care of the Hat Pins," Watcombe, ca. 1930, 4 1/2" h. 106

Hot water-coffeepot, cov., Motto Ware, "May we be kind but not in words alone," many details, Aller Vale, ca. 1891-1910, overall 5" h. 108

Hot water-coffeepot, cov., Motto Ware, "Success comes not by wishing - But hard Work bravely done," Aller Vale mark, ca. 1891-1910, overall 6 3/4" h. 140

Inkwell, Motto Ware, "Don't forget the dear ones far away," Watcombe mark, ca. 1920s, 2" h. 61

Jardiniere, ruffled rim, Motto Ware, "It's a long lane that has no turnin'," Watcombe, 5" h. 152

Match holder, Motto Ware, Devon dialect, "No place on earth so plaizes me - as this wan Babbacombe By-the-zay," Longpark Torquay mark, ca. 1903-09, 3 1/4" h. 100

Mug, child's, Motto Ware, "He soars not high who fears to fall," Aller Vale, ca. 1910, 2 1/2" h. 50

Pitcher, 4 1/2" h., Motto Ware, "Another little drink won't do us any harm," Lemon & Crute Pottery, ca. 1920 (rim roughness, spout rub) 53

Pitcher, 6 1/2" h., pierced rim, Motto Ware, "Be always as merry as ever you can - For few will Delight in a sorrowful man," H.M. Exeter Pottery, ca. 1910-10 146

Plate, 5" d., Motto Ware, "Carry a vision in your heart," Watcombe Torquay impressed mark, ca. 1930 59

Plate, 7 3/4" d., Motto Ware, "Work on, Hope on - Self help is noble schooling. You do your best and leave the rest to God Almighty's ruling," early Aller Vale mark, ca. 1891-1901 149

Puzzle jug, Motto Ware, "Within this jug there is good liquor - Fit for Parson or for Vicar. But how to drink and not to spill - will try the utmost of your skill," Longpark, ca. 1920, 4 1/4" h. 125

Large Scandy Pattern Tankard

Tankard, large, slightly tapering cylindrical form, Motto Ware, long motto in Devon dialect, impressed Aller Vale mark, ca.

1891-1910, small sealed hairline, 8 1/4" h. (ILLUS.) 220

Teapot, cov., Motto Ware, "Ye may get better cheer but no' wi' Better heart," Aller Vale mark, ca. 1891-1910, 6 3/4" l., 3 3/4" h. 120

Vase, miniature, 1 3/4" h., two handles at back, Motto Ware, "Niver zay die - Up man an' try," unmarked 70

Other Patterns

Basket, Art Nouveau swags, braided black handle, Barton Pottery, ca. 1922-38, overall 5" h. 135

Large Daisy-decorated Basket

Basket, Daisy patt., large h.p. colorful daisy flowers, Royal Torquay, ca. 1930, overall 8 5/8" h. (ILLUS.) 198

Large Cockington Forge Plate

Bowl, 12" d., Cockington Forge patt., round shallow form w/h.p. scene of the forge, inscribed at rim "Cockington Forge - Torquay," Devon Tors Pottery, ca. 1925-30 (ILLUS.) 335

Aller Vale Jardiniere & Pitcher

Candlesticks, Cherries patt., Motto Ware, one w/"Good - Night," the other "Pleasant Dreams," no mark, Torquay Pottery Co., ca. 1930s, 8" h., pr. **142**

Candlesticks, Primrose patt., Motto Ware, "Many are called but few get up" on one, the other w/"Be the day weary or be the day long - At last it ringeth to Evensong," H.M. Exeter Pottery mark, ca. 1920, 7" h., pr. **125**

Chocolates bowl, cov., commemorative, "Rotary International" on white raised slip wheel against a blue ground, "Service not Self - 1924 Torquay Conference," Hele Cross Pottery, overall 6" h. **125**

Curling iron tile, Forget-me-not patt., Motto Ware, "O list to me ye ladies fair - And when Ye wish to curl your hair - For the safety of this domicile - Pray place your lamps upon this tile," Watcombe Torquay impressed mark, ca. 1920s, 5 1/2 x 7 3/4" **140**

Dog bowl, B1 Scroll patt., Motto Ware, "Love Me - Love My Dog," fancy calligraphy, white clay, early Aller Vale impressed mark, ca. 1891-1902, 4 7/8" d., 2" h. **170**

Humidor, cov., C3 Pattern, Motto Ware, "Help yersel tae a pipe o' bacca," early Scandy-type pattern, Watcombe mark, ca. 1910-20, overall 5" h. **88**

Inkwell, Purple Thistle patt., Motto Ware in Devon dialect, "Gie's a scrae o' yer pen," Longpark, 1 7/8" h. **58**

Jardiniere, Kerswell Daisy patt., commemorative, two handles, "Horton Bucks - 1837 - VR - 1897," made for Queen Victoria's Diamond Jubilee, rare, Aller Vale, 4 1/8" h. (ILLUS. right, top of page)............. **257**

Mug, commemorative, "Coronation of Queen Elizabeth - June 2, 1953," no mark, Sandygate Pottery, 2 3/4" h. **50**

Mug, Sailboat patt., commemorative, "Barbara - Peace Celebrations - Bath - 1919," black sailboat w/rosy sunset background, Torquay Pottery Co. mark, 3 3/4" h. (ILLUS., next column) **122**

Sailboat Commemorative Mug

Mug, two handles, Floral patt., Art Nouveau flower on blue ground, Crown Dorset, ca. 1910, 2 7/8" h. **74**

Pitcher, 2 7/8" h., jug form, Passion Flower patt., Motto Ware, green ground w/motto in a band between the flowers, "May all the hours be winged with joy," H.M. Exeter Pottery, ca. 1930 .... **71**

Pitcher, 4 1/8" h., Q1 Pattern, Motto Ware, two mottoes, "All is not gold that Glitters" & "Adventures are to the Adventurous," no mark, Aller Vale, ca. 1890s **106**

Pitcher, 4 3/4" h., Pixie patt., three pixies in relief amid a colorful leafy scroll design, "Pixy fine - Pixy gay," scarce, impressed Aller Vale mark, ca. 1891-1910...................... **350**

Pitcher, 5 3/4" h., Q1 Pattern, Motto Ware, "Have courage boys to do the right - Be bold, be brave, be strong. By doing right you earn the might - To overcome the wrong," early Aller Vale, repaired base chip, ca. 1890s (ILLUS. left with jardiniere) **76**

Scent bottle, Gardenia patt., black curled handle, Motto Ware, "A thing of beauty is a joy Forever - Gardenia Eau de Cologne - Toogoods - London - England," pink gardenia on blue ground, brass crown-

Small Tintern Abbey Vase

Rare Cavalier Pattern Vase

Fine Fish Pattern Art Vase

Uhl Pottery

Original production of utilitarian wares began at Evansville, Indiana, in the 1850s and consisted mostly of jugs, jars, crocks and pieces for food preparation and preservation. In 1909, production was moved to Huntingburg, Indiana, where a more extensive variety of items was eventually produced including many novelty and advertising items that have become highly collectible. Following labor difficulties, the Uhl Pottery closed in 1944.

Unless it is marked or stamped, Uhl is difficult to identify except by someone with considerable experience. Marked pieces can have several styles of ink stamps and/or an incised number under glaze on the bottom. These numbers are die-cut and impressed in the glazed bottom. Some original molds were acquired by other potteries. Some production exists and should not be considered as Uhl. These may have numbers inscribed by hand with a stylus and are usually not glazed on the bottom.

Many examples have no mark or stamp and may not be bottom-glazed. This is especially true of many of the miniature pieces. If a piece has a "Meier's Wine" paper label, it was probably made by Uhl.

While many color variations exist, there are about nine basic colors: blue, white, black, rose or pink, yellow, teal, purple, pumpkin and browns/tans. Blue, pink, teal and purple are currently the most sought after colors. Animal planters, vases, liquor/wine containers, pitchers, mugs, banks, kitchenware, bakeware, gardenware and custom-made advertising pieces exist.

Similar pieces by other manufacturers do exist. When placed side by side, a seasoned collector can recognize an authentic example of Uhl Pottery.

Ashtray, #199, in the form of a dog lifting its leg at a hydrant, marked (ILLUS. top row, left w/Uhl Pottery pieces)............................... **$525**
Ashtray, brown, American Legion emblem........ **105**
Ashtray, green, hand-turned mark, 3" d............. **145**
Ashtray, round, black, unmarked **25**
Bank, figural, large grinning pig, yellow, unmarked.. **375**
Bank, figural, medium-size grinning pig, white, painted circus theme, unmarked **400**
Bean pot, brown/blue, marked "Boston Bean Pot".. **175**
Bean pot, brown/tan, side handles, marked...... **120**
Bowl, basketweave, blue, unmarked.................. **88**
Bowl, 5" d., picket fence **40**
Bowl, 5" d., shouldered mixing bowl, unmarked.. **140**
Bowl, 8" d., blue, marked "Boonville Implement Company" **90**
Bowl, 8" d., luncheon, blue, marked **70**
Bowl, 8" d., luncheon, green, unmarked............. **50**
Canteen, commemorative of Uhl Collectors Society, 1988.. **260**
Canteen, miniature, blue, Meier Wine paper label **30**
Casserole, cov., blue, #528 & marked **50**
Churn, 3-gal., white, acorn mark.......................... **90**
Churn, 4-gal., cov., white, acorn mark, solid lid.. **185**
Cookie jar, miniature, blue, unmarked **178**

Creamer, light tan, hand-turned square mark, 5 1/2" h.. **150**
Creamer & sugar, cov., robin's-egg blue, both w/hand-turned mark **475**
Flowerpot, ribbed, yellow, no attached saucer, unmarked, 6" **33**
Funnel, brown, unmarked **22**
Jar, 1-gal., white, acorn mark **45**
Jar, 2-gal., white, acorn mark **40**
Jar, 3-gal., tan, Evansville, Ind., mark............... **360**
Jar, 3-gal., white, acorn mark **50**
Jar, 6-gal., white, acorn mark ILLUS. **38**

Miscellaneous Uhl Containers

Jar, blue & white (ILLUS. middle row left w/Uhl containers)... **55**
Jar, cov., cottage cheese, white, metal lid embossed "UHL" **500**
Jar, cov. (ILLUS. top row right w/miscellaneous Uhl containers).. **75**
Jug, 3-gal., light tan, Evansville, Ind., mark........ **200**
Jug, 3-oz., miniature Egyptian, rose, marked #6.. **25**
Jug, 5-gal., blue/white, marked "Dillsboro Sanitarium, Dillsboro, Ind." **575**
Jug, 5-gal., brown/white, acorn mark **60**
Jug, 6-gal., light tan, Evansville, Ind., oval mark.. **90**
Jug, blue Egyptian, marked #133 .... **35**

Various Uhl Pottery Items

Jug, blue & white, "Colonial Mineral Springs, Martinsville, Indiana" (ILLUS. top left w/various Uhl Pottery items)...................... **1,200**
Jug, brown/white, "1939 Merry Christmas," marked **200**

Jug, brown/white, miniature shoulder, front acorn mark.. **550**

Uhl Pottery Pieces

Jug, form of football, large, 5" l., rarer than smaller version (ILLUS. middle row, left w/Uhl Pottery pieces)...................................... **250**

Jug, form of softball, Meier's label, 3 3/8" d. (ILLUS. middle row, right w/Uhl Pottery pieces).. **250**

Jug, in the form of a football, large size, brown, unmarked... **240**

Jug, in the form of a football, small size, brown, unmarked.. **35**

Jug, miniature acorn, marked "Acorn Wares".. **60**

Various Uhl Mugs & Jugs

Jug, miniature, "Canadian Apple Blossom," 3 3/8" h. (ILLUS. bottom left w/various Uhl mugs & jugs) **90**

Jug, miniature, marked, 1" h. **110**

Jug, miniature prunella, black, unmarked............ **25**

Jug, miniature, "Pure Corn, Souvenir Lincoln Birthplace, Kentucky," 3" h. (ILLUS. bottom right w/various Uhl mugs & jugs)...... **225**

Jug, red/green, "1940 Merry Christmas," marked "Uhl Pottery Company," 2 3/8" h. **255**

Jug, "Season's Greetings, 1940-1941, Henderson, Kentucky," 6 5/8" h. (ILLUS. top row w/various Uhl mugs & jugs) **175**

Lamp, Liberty Bell.. **128**

Match holder, marked Uhl, 2 1/4" h. (ILLUS. bottom row right w/miscellaneous Uhl containers).. **120**

Model of cat, potter's name engraved, unmarked **1,000**

Model of cowboy boot, marked (ILLUS. bottom row, right w/Uhl Pottery pieces) **150**

Model of dog & hydrant, similar to ashtray #199, two separate pieces, no marks (ILLUS. top row, center & right w/Uhl Pottery pieces).. **350**

Model of military boot, marked (ILLUS. bottom row, center w/Uhl Pottery pieces)............. **95**

Model of shoe, miniature woman's slipper, blue, marked **75**

Model of shoe, miniature woman's slipper, marked (ILLUS. of two bottom row, left w/Uhl Pottery pieces)....................................... **120**

Model of shoe, miniature woman's slipper, purple, marked... **100**

Model of shoes, tied baby shoes, pink, both marked, pr. **180**

Model of shoes, white, marked #2, pr. **110**

Mug, barrel-shaped, blue & white, marked "Dillsboro Sanitarium".. **300**

Mug, "Chicco Beverage Co." (ILLUS. middle row left w/various Uhl mugs & jugs)................ **90**

Mug, "Chicco Beverage, Norristown" (ILLUS. middle row right w/various Uhl mugs & jugs) **90**

Mug, coffee, blue, marked **55**

Mug, coffee, pink, marked..................................... **55**

Mug, "Homestead Hotel, No. 7 Water" (ILLUS. bottom right w/various Uhl Pottery items) price unknown **125**

Mug, "West Baden Springs Hotel" (ILLUS. bottom left w/various Uhl Pottery items) **110**

Orange blossom jar, #118 (ILLUS. top row left w/miscellaneous Uhl containers)................ **85**

Orange jar (ILLUS. middle row right w/miscellaneous Uhl containers) **85**

Pepper shaker, dark blue, unmarked................... **25**

Pepper shaker, light blue, unmarked **30**

Pitcher, barrel-shaped, blue, marked................... **55**

Pitcher, barrel-shaped, brown, marked................ **40**

Pitcher, barrel-shaped, brown, unmarked **35**

Pitcher, bulbous grape, blue, #183...................... **60**

Pitcher, bulbous grape, pumpkin, #183 .... **55**

Pitcher, globe-shaped, light blue, unmarked........ **28**

Pitcher, Hall Boy, blue & white, unmarked **150**

Pitcher, ice water, yellow, unmarked.................... **50**

Pitcher, miniature, blue, marked "Norristown, Tenn." **180**

Pitcher, miniature, teal green, marked #28 .... **95**

Pitcher, squat grape, blue, unmarked................. **175**

Plaque, Lincoln **550**

Rare Uhl Plate

Plate, 6 3/4" d., stamped "Santa Claus, Indiana," very rare, only three known to exist,
$500+ (ILLUS.).. **500+**
Salt & pepper shakers, pink,
unmarked **77**

Uhl Sand Jar

Sand jar, basketweave design, brushed
green or ivory, used to snuff cigarettes,
Item #530, 20" h., 10 1/2" d.
(ILLUS.)... **200-300**
Stein, 3-oz., miniature, brown, marked **70**
Stein, 3-oz., miniature, teal green, marked **140**
Stein, miniature, w/box, commemorative of
Uhl Collectors Society, 1987......................... **500**
Syrup pitcher, cov., blue, marked...................... **180**
Teapot, 2-cup, blue, marked #131.................... **200**
Thieves jar, miniature, black, #138 .... **83**
Tulip bowl, yellow, marked #119 .... **80**

Uhl Garden Urn

Urn, garden, Roman style, Old Ivory, two
pieces, 19 x 12" (ILLUS.)................................. **175**
Vase, blue, hand-turned mark **600**
Vase, blue, marked #158...................................... **74**
Vase, dark blue, marked #154............................. **90**
Vase, plum, marked #156 .... **75**
Vase, waisted form, "Merrill Park Florist,
Battle Creek, Mich.," extremely rare
(ILLUS. top right w/various Uhl Pottery
items) price unknown ....
Vase, 3 5/8" h., marked "American Legion
Huntingburg Post 221" on bottom
(ILLUS. bottom row left w/miscellaneous
Uhl containers)... **225**
Vase, 4 3/4" h., bud vase, #107, hard to
find, price depends on color, w/blue & es-
pecially purple being most popular
(ILLUS. center w/various Uhl vases).......... **45-75**

Various Uhl Vases

Vase, 5" h., handled, #152, very hard to
find, marked, price depends on color,
w/blue & especially purple being most
popular (ILLUS. bottom left w/various Uhl
vases).. **45-75**
Vase, 5 1/4" h., fan-shaped w/scalloped
rim, #157, hard to find, price depends on
color, w/blue & especially purple being
most popular (ILLUS. bottom right w/var-
ious Uhl vases) **45-75**
Vase, 5 1/4" h., flaring ribbed neck, #158,
incised, hard to find, price depends on
color, w/blue & especially purple being
most popular (ILLUS. top left w/various
Uhl vases)... **45-75**
Vase, 5 1/4" h., side handles, #156, incised,
hard to find, price depends on color,
w/blue & especially purple being most
popular (ILLUS. top right w/various Uhl
vases).. **45-75**
Water cooler, 3-gal., cov., white, acorn mark...... **160**
Water cooler, 5-gal., cov., white, acorn mark...... **200**
Water cooler, 6-gal., blue & white, w/em-
bossed polar bears.. **1,500**

Van Briggle

Early Van Briggle Pottery Mark

*The Van Briggle Pottery was established by Artus
Van Briggle, who formerly worked for Rookwood Pottery, in Colorado Springs, Colorado, at the turn of the
century. He died in 1904, but the pottery was carried on
by his widow and others. From 1900 until 1920, the
pieces were dated. It remains in production today, specializing in Art Pottery.*

Bowl, 6" d., 3" h., wide, flat-bottomed,
squatty, bulbous form w/the sharply tapering top centered w/a wide, flat, molded mouth, light turquoise matte glaze,
Shape No. 50B, 1905 .... **$900**

Van Briggle Bowl-Vase with Leaves

Bowl-vase, large, squatty, bulbous, ovoid form tapering to a wide, flat mouth, molded around the shoulder w/a band of pointed leaves atop long curved stems, matte brown glaze, 1916, 7" d., 4 3/4" h. (ILLUS.).. **920**

Bowl-vase, spherical, w/a low molded mouth, matte brown glaze, Shape No. 200, 1906, 6" h. (staining)............................. **489**

Bowl-vase, squatty, bulbous, deep vessel w/a wide shoulder & molded flat mouth, good matte green glaze, ca. 1905, 5 1/2" h.. **880**

Bowl-vase, wide, bulbous body tapering slightly at the top to a wide, flat mouth, embossed around the rim w/a band of large stylized morning glory blossoms & leaves atop tall slender stems down the sides, feathered blue & green glaze, Shape No. 284, 1905, 7 1/2" d., 6 1/2" h. **1,540**

Fine Early Van Briggle Bowl-Vase

Bowl-vase, wide, squatty, bulbous form tapering to a wide, flat mouth, molded around the sides w/stylized undulating & looping floral designs, dark brown clay shows through the fine suspended blue matte glaze, dated 1907, 5" d. (ILLUS.)..... **4,675**

Candlesticks, wide, seven-sided tapering foot below the tall, tapering paneled shaft w/a paneled bulbous socket, matte green over brown glaze, ca. 1920, 10" h., pr. **633**

Van Briggle Mermaid Chalice

Chalice, round foot & slender stem supporting a squatty bulbous cup tapering to a flat rim, molded around the cup w/the figure of a mermaid, swirled light green & dark blue matte glaze, signed, small glaze miss, paint flecks, 10 1/2" h. (ILLUS.).. **6,325**

Lamp, table model, figural, the base w/a Lady of the Lake design of a maiden kneeling at one end of a shallow oblong pool-form bowl w/incurved sides, the electric lamp fitting behind her supporting the original tapering cylindrical laminated butterfly & dry grass paper shade, base in deep rose glaze w/dark highlights, ca. 1920s, 21" h. **385**

Paperweight, figural horned toad in matte green on an oval mustard base, marked "AA - 1913," ca. 1913, 1 1/2 x 4 3/4" (firing line to base) **1,463**

Vase, miniature, 3" h., 3" d., wide cylindrical base w/shoulder tapering to closed rim, embossed w/trefoils & covered in fine curdled brown glaze, marked "AA - Van Briggle - Colo. Spgs.," ca. 1907-11 .... **563**

Vase, 3 3/4" h., 4" d., flat-bottomed, squatty, bulbous form w/a small, flat mouth, molded around the sides w/crocus blossoms & leaves, leathery matte brown glaze, 1903.. **1,430**

Large Group of Van Briggle Vases

Vase, 3 3/4" h., 4 1/2" h., flat-bottomed spherical form w/a flat molded mouth, pale turquoise matte glaze, dated 1903 (ILLUS. front row, center, with group, bottom previous page).. **900**

Vase, 3 3/4" h., 5" d., flat-bottomed, squatty, bulbous, tapering body w/the wide shoulder centered by a short, wide, cylindrical neck, embossed around the sides w/butterflies, green & pale red matte glaze, Shape No. 626, 1908-11 (overfired, restoration to rim chip)........................... **506**

Vase, 4" h., small footring supporting a bulbous, nearly spherical body tapering slightly to a wide, flat, molded rim, molded down the sides w/swirled florals, unusual purple, grey & green matte glaze, ca. 1907-12............................. **715**

Vase, 4 x 4 3/4", copper-clad, bulbous, ovoid body w/shoulder tapering to wide, flat neck, embossed w/stylized leaves, original dark patina, ca. 1908-11, incised "AA - Van Briggle - Colo. Spgs. - 151".. **3,938**

Vase, 4 3/4" h., 3 3/4" d., squatty, bulbous lower body tapering to a tall, cylindrical neck w/a molded rim, the lower body molded w/swirled pointed leaves, bluish green matte glaze, Shape No. 730, 1908-11 .... **534**

Vase, 5 1/4" h., 3" d., swelled cylindrical form w/a narrow, angled shoulder centering a short neck, molded around the shoulder w/tulip blossoms on slender stems down the sides, thick, frothy & sheer rose & beige matte glaze w/clay showing through, Shape No. 187, 1903 .... **2,200**

Vase, 5 1/4" h., 3 1/2" d., simple ovoid form w/small, molded mouth, embossed w/large stylized crocus blossoms around the shoulder w/stems down the sides, green & pink matte glaze, Shape No. 823, ca. 1910 (ILLUS. front row, second from left w/group of vases)............................. **506**

Vase, 5 3/4" h., 3 3/4" d., wide, low, rounded base below a sharply tapering cylindrical body w/flat rim, matte mustard yellow glaze, Shape No. 825, 1908-11 (ILLUS. front row, second from right w/group of vases)... **534**

Vase, 6" h., slightly tapering swelled cylindrical body w/a tiny flat neck, molded w/small stylized upright buds on stems spaced around the sides, dark brown matte glaze, incised mark, ca. 1915... **440**

Vase, 6" h., 4" d., wide, low, rounded base below a sharply tapering cylindrical body w/flat rim, embossed around the lower body & up the sides w/medallions of wheat sheaves, fine leathery matte green glaze, Shape No. 347, 1905 (ILLUS. front row, far left, with group of vases).............. **2,138**

Small Van Briggle Vase with Flowers

Vase, 6" h., 4 1/4" d., wide, squatty, bulbous base tapering sharply to a cylindrical neck, molded around the lower body w/five-petal blossoms & leaves w/stems & leaves up the sides, chartreuse matte mottled glaze, Shape No. 188, 1903 (ILLUS.).. **2,415**

Bottle-form Van Briggle Vase

Vase, 6 1/2" h., 3 3/4" d., footed, bulbous, bottle-form body tapering to a thick closed rim, embossed down the sides w/stylized flowers & long tiered rows of leaves, feathered dark matte green glaze, 1908-11 (ILLUS.)............................. **1,035**

Vase, 6 1/2" h., 4 1/2" d., footed baluster form w/reticulated shoulder & flat rim, embossed from base to rim w/papyrus plants & covered in green & rose matte glaze, marked "AA - 1916," ca. 1916 (small glaze chip to base)........................... **2,138**

Vase, 7" h., slender cylindrical lower body w/a swelled shoulder tapering slightly to a flat mouth, molded around the shoulder w/dragonflies extending down the sides, dark blue to deep red matte glaze, post-1920s... **319**

Vase, 7" h., 6 1/2" d., wide, bulbous, ovoid body w/a wide, short, rolled rim, embossed around the sides w/large butterflies, cobalt & turquoise matte glaze, 1916... **513**

Van Briggle Vase with Pointed Leaves

Vase, 7 1/4" h., 3 1/4" d., slightly swelled cylindrical form w/a wide, flat mouth, molded around the body w/long downward-pointing spearpoint leaves, frothy & oatmealy green matte glaze w/brown clay showing through, 1905 (ILLUS.) **2,875**

Vase, 7 1/4" h., 3 1/2" d., swelled cylindrical form w/a narrow shoulder centered by a short cylindrical neck, embossed around the neck w/poppy pods w/the slender vines curving down the sides, purple matte glaze, Shape No. 830, 1915 (ILLUS. back row, left, with group of vases) .. **1,125**

Vase, 7 1/4" h., 4" d., gently swelled ovoid body tapering to a short neck w/thick molded rim, embossed around the neck w/stylized flower blossoms on slender stems down the sides, fine leathery dark blue glaze, Shape No. 287, 1905 (ILLUS. back row, right, with group of vases).......... **3,150**

Vase, 7 1/2" h., slender, swelled, cylindrical body tapering to a small, flat, molded mouth, molded around the shoulder w/large tulip blossoms atop long leafy stems, multi-toned blue matte glaze, ca. 1915-20 .... **523**

Van Briggle Vase with Trilliums

Vase, 7 1/2" h., 3 1/2" d., slightly waisted cylindrical form, molded w/crisp trillium leaves & blossoms swirling up around the sides & rim, leathery light blue matte glaze, 1905, Shape No. 296 (ILLUS.)........ **2,090**

Rare Van Briggle "Dos Cebezos" Vase

Vase, 7 3/4" h., 4 3/4" d., "Dos Cebezos," ovoid body tapering to a cylindrical neck, closed shoulder handles molded as two women in flowing garments, unusual mottled charcoal & greyish blue matte flambé glaze, 1902 (ILLUS.)...................... **20,750**

Vase, 7 3/4" h., 5" d., slightly lobed gourd-form body w/a flat mouth, embossed w/stylized flowers around the top, fine teal blue glaze, Shape No. 864, 1912 (tight hairline in rim) **731**

Vase, 8" h., 5 1/2" d., wide, simple, ovoid body tapering to a short, cylindrical neck, overall turquoise matte glaze, Shape No. 269, 1906 (ILLUS. front row, far right, with group of vases).................................... **1,069**

Baluster-form Van Briggle Blue Vase

Vase, 8 1/4" h., 4 1/2" d., baluster form w/a rounded shoulder to a short cylindrical neck, embossed around the shoulder w/stylized blossoms, the stems down the sides, sheer robin's-egg blue glaze w/clay showing through, 1906 (ILLUS.).. **1,840**

Vase, 8 1/2" h., 3 1/2" d., slender baluster form w/a short neck, lavender matte glaze, Shape No. 343C, 1905 .... **1,013**

Vase, 9" h., 4" d., tall, waisted form w/the swelled top below a wide, molded rim, embossed around the shoulder w/large daffodil blossoms on tall leafy stems swirled down the sides, bluish green matte glaze, Shape No. 120, 1920s, two small flat base chips, small bruise on rim, bottom dirty (ILLUS. back row, center, with group of vases) **619**

Vase, 9" h., 4 1/2" d., footed baluster form w/a small, molded mouth, embossed around the neck & shoulder w/large arrowroot leaves w/slender stems down the sides, fine frothy matte green glaze, Shape No. 357, 1905 .... **2,970**

Vase, 9 1/4" h., 4 1/4" d., trumpet form embossed w/jonquils under a fine leathery pink matte glaze, marked "AA - Van Briggle - 1906 - 367," ca. 1906 (drill hole under base) **2,363**

Vase, 10" h., tall, slender, ovoid form w/a flared foot & closed rim, molded around the shoulder w/a repeating design of tulip blossoms on tall leafy stems, dark maroon matte glaze, second quarter 20th c. **259**

Vase, 10 1/2" h., "Lorelei," figural mermaid wrapped around the tall swelled body, black matte glaze, post-1930s **825**

Van Briggle Vase with Leaves & Stems

Vase, 10 1/2" h., 4" d., tall, cylindrical form w/swelled shoulder & tapering neck, embossed around the neck w/large curled leaves on long stems swirled down the sides, matte green & tobacco brown feathered glaze, 1906, Shape No. 289 (ILLUS.) **4,888**

Vase, 10 1/2" h., 4 1/4" d., tapering cylindrical form w/small loop handles, molded rim, covered in unusual veined green & burgundy matte glaze w/melt fissures, marked "AA - Van Briggle - 224 - 1904 - V," ca. 1904 .... **2,475**

Vase, 10 3/4" h., 4" d., tall, slightly tapering cylindrical form molded in relief around

the base w/large spread-winged bats, smooth speckled brown matte glaze, Shape No. 191 (4), ca. 1914 .... **4,400**

Vase, 11" h., 9 1/2" w., "Lady of the Lily" figural design, a large nude Art Nouveau maiden w/arched back & leaning against the side of a large, widely flaring lily-form vase, brown & green mottled matte glaze, 1930s (dirty bottom, few deep crazing lines in base) **2,138**

Lady of the Lily Van Briggle Vase

Vase, 11 1/2" h., 9 1/2" w., "Lady of the Lily," figural w/nude maiden rising from waves & curving back to lean against a large lily-form vase, Persian Rose matte glaze, 1920s, dirt on base (ILLUS.) **1,955**

Vase, 11 3/4" h., 4 1/2" d., tall, ovoid bottle form w/short, cylindrical neck, embossed w/morning glory vines under a frothy chartreuse matte glaze, marked "AA - Van Briggle - 1904 - 108," ca. 1904 .... **2,250**

Vase, 12 3/4" h., 4 14" d., tall, cylindrical form w/swelled, closed rim, embossed near top & on rim w/peacock feathers under an olive green & purple glaze, incised "AA - Van Briggle - 1905 - VV - 12," **3,375**

Vase, 13" h., 6 1/4" d., tall, ovoid form w/four small pierced loop handles around the shoulder & below the short tapering neck, a stylized peacock feather molded between each handle, Persian Rose glaze, Shape No. 119, ca. 1917 .... **990**

Van Briggle Peacock Feather Vase

Vase, 16 1/2" h., 8 1/2" d., tapering cylindrical form w/a bulbed shoulder & flat rim,
embossed up & around the sides w/large
peacock feathers under a frothy turquoise matte glaze on a red clay
body, ca. 1910, Shape No. 07, remnant
of paper price tag (ILLUS.)............................ **7,475**

Vernon Kilns

Vernon Kilns Mark

*The story of Vernon Kilns Pottery begins with the
purchase by Mr. Faye Bennison of the Poxon China
Company (Vernon Potteries) in July 1931. The Poxon
family had run the pottery for a number of years in Vernon, California, but with the founding of Vernon Kilns,
the product lines were greatly expanded.*

*Many innovative dinnerware lines and patterns were
introduced during the 1930s, including designs by such
noted American artists as Rockwell Kent and Don Blan-
ding. In the early 1940s items were designed to tie in
with Walt Disney's animated features "Fantasia" and
"Dumbo." Various commemorative plates, including the
popular "Bits" series, were also produced over a long
period of time. Vernon Kilns was taken over by Metlox
Potteries in 1958 and completely ceased production in
1960.*

"Bits" Series
Plate, 8 1/2" d., Bits of Old New England
Series, The Cove.. **$30**
Plate, 8 1/2" d., Bits of the California Mis-
sions Series, San Rafael Archangel................ **40**
Plate, 8 1/2" d., Bits of the Old South Series,
Cotton Patch.. **40**
Plate, 8 1/2" d., Bits of the Old West Series,
The Fleecing.. **40**
Plate, chop, 14" d., Bits of the Old South-
west Series, Pueblo.. **75**

Cities Series - 10 1/2" d.
Plate, "Atlanta, Georgia," maroon **20**
Plate, "Augusta, Maine," blue **20**

Dinnerwares
Bowl, chowder, tab handle, Gingham patt...... **15-18**
Bowl, fruit, Native California patt....................... **8-10**
Bowl, soup, Coronado patt................................ **15-20**
Bowl, 8 1/2" d., soup, Bel Air patt..................... **15-20**
Bowl, 13" d., salad, Homespun patt..................... **85**
Bowl, Homespun patt. 1 pt.............................. **30-35**
Butter dish, Casual California patt. **25-30**
Butter dish, cov., Tam O'Shanter patt. **35-40**
Butter dish, cov., Tickled Pink patt.................. **30-40**
Butter pat, individual, Organdie patt.,
2 1/2" d. **40-45**

Candleholders, teacup form w/metal fittings,
Tam O'Shanter patt., pr.......................... **100-125**
Casserole, cov., chicken pot pie, Gingham
patt... **35-40**
Casserole, cov., Heavenly Days patt. **35-45**
Casserole, cov., individual, Organdie patt.,
4" d.. **30-35**
Casserole, cov., Tam O'Shanter patt............. **45-55**
Casserole, cov., Vernon's 1860s patt. **75**
Coaster, Gingham patt. **25-30**
Coffee server w/stopper, carafe form, Tam
O'Shanter patt.. **45-55**
Coffeepot, cov., Heavenly Days patt., 8-cup........ **65**
Coffeepot, Ultra California patt..................... **80-100**
Creamer, Modern California patt. **10-15**
Creamer, Ultra patt... **15**

Early California Egg Cup & After Dinner Cups & Saucers

Cup & saucer, after-dinner size, Early Cali-
fornia patt., red or cobalt blue, each (IL-
LUS. front) **25-30**
Cup & saucer, after-dinner size, Monterey
patt... **40-45**
Egg cup, Early California patt., turquoise
(ILLUS. with Early California cups & sau-
cers)... **20**

Organdie Flowerpot & Saucer

Flowerpot & saucer, Organdie patt., 4" d.
(ILLUS.)... **45-50**
Gravy boat, Gingham patt............................... **20-25**
Gravy boat, Native California patt........................ **35**
Mixing bowls, nesting set, Gingham patt., 5"
to 9" d., five pcs. **150-175**
Muffin cover, Early California patt., red, cov-
er only.. **125-150**
Mug, Barkwood patt., 9 oz. **25**
Mug, Homespun patt., 9 oz............................. **35-40**
Pepper mill, Homespun patt. **175**
Pitcher, jug-form, bulb bottom, Tam
O'Shanter patt., 1 pt.................................... **25-30**

Hawaiian Coral Streamline Pitcher

Pitcher, Streamline shape, Hawaiian Coral
patt., 1 qt. (ILLUS.) **45-55**
Pitcher, Streamline shape, Gingham patt., 2
qt. **50-75**
Pitcher, 5" h., Streamline shape, Barkwood
patt., 1/2 pt. 30
Plate, 6 1/2" d., bread & butter, Gingham
patt. 5
Plate, 7 1/2" d., Frontier Days patt. **35-45**
Plate, 7 1/2" d., salad, Tweed patt. **8-10**

Coastline Series Florida Plate

Plate, 9 1/2" d., Coastline series, Florida
patt., Turnbull design (ILLUS.) **100-125**
Plate, 9 1/2" d., luncheon, Organdie
patt. **10-12**
Plate, 9 1/2" d., Native American series, Go-
ing to Town patt., Turnbull design.............. **35-45**
Plate, 9 1/2" d., Trader Vic patt. **100-125**
Plate, 10 1/2" d., Casa California Hermosa
patt., Turnbull design **25-30**
Plate, 10 1/2" d., dinner, Calico patt. 25
Plate, 10 1/2" d., Iris patt., Harry Bird design 50
Plate, chop, 12" d., Frontier Days patt. **150-175**
Plate, chop, 12" d., Organdie patt. **25-30**
Plate, chop, 14" d., Gingham patt. **35-40**
Plate, 17" d., chop-type, Early California
patt. **30-50**
Platter, 12" d., round, Organdie patt. **20-25**
Platter, 14" l., oval, Native California patt. **30-35**
Relish dish, leaf-shaped, four-part, Native
California patt. **40-60**
Relish dish, single leaf shape, Monterey
patt., 12" l. **35-45**
Salt & pepper shakers, large size, Tam
O'Shanter patt., pr. **45-65**
Salt & pepper shakers, Native California
patt., pr. 20
Salt & pepper shakers, regular size, Ging-
ham patt., pr. 20

Trumpet Flower Saucer

Saucer, Trumpet Flower patt., Harry Bird
design (ILLUS.) **8-10**
Spoon rest, Organdie patt. **75-85**

Tweed Pattern Sugar Bowl

Sugar bowl, cov., Tweed patt. (ILLUS.) **30-35**
Teacup & saucer, colossal size, Homespun
patt., 15" d. saucer, 4 qt. **250-275**
Teacup & saucer, jumbo size, Homespun
patt. **45-55**
Teacup & saucer, Ultra patt. 10
Teacup & saucer, Winchester '73 patt. **30-35**

Santa Barbara Pattern Teapot

Teapot, cov., Santa Barbara patt. (ILLUS.) **65-80**
Teapot, cov., Tam O'Shanter patt. **45-55**
Tidbit, two-tier w/wooden handle, Home-
spun patt. **30-35**
Tumbler, Bel Air patt. 20
Tumbler, Homespun patt. 35
Tumbler, Tickled Pink patt. 20

Disney "Fantasia" & Other Items

Bowl, 6" d., chowder, Nutcracker patt. 50
Bowl, 8" d., soup, Flower Ballet patt. 50

Bowl, 8" l., No. 134, decorated figural bird **75-85**
Figure of Baby Weems, No. 37, 6" h. **150-175**
Plate, 17" d., chop, Fantasia patt. .... **600+**
Tray, hors d'oeuvre, May & Vieve Hamilton
design, 16" d. **400-600**
Vase, 4 1/2" h., Pine Cone patt., No. 5, ivory **85-105**
Vase, 12" h., carved handles, May & Vieve
Hamilton design .... **1,500+**

Don Blanding Dinnerwares
Creamer, demitasse size, Hawaiian Flowers
patt., blue **50**
Cup & saucer, Coral Reef patt., blue **50**
Platter, 16 1/2", Lei Lani patt. **200-250**
Sugar bowl, cov., Coral Reef patt., blue **85-95**
Sugar bowl, cov., Hawaiian Flowers patt.,
blue **75-85**
Tumbler, Hilo patt., #4, 5 1/2" h. **125-150**

Rockwell Kent Designs
Bowl, chowder, "Our America" series, coco-
nut tree, blue **45-50**
Creamer, regular, "Our America" series,
houseboaters, brown **50-75**
Cup & saucer, Moby Dick patt., maroon **30-45**
Cup & saucer, Salamina patt. **45-55**
Plate, 6 1/2" d., "Our America" series,
steamship, blue **45-50**
Plate, 6 1/2" d., Salamina patt. **40**
Plate, 9 1/2" d., Moby Dick patt., blue **110-145**
Plate, 17" d., chop, Salamina patt. **400-500**
Sugar bowl, cov., Moby Dick patt., blue **85-105**

States Map Series - 10 1/2" d.
Plate, Connecticut. **20**
Plate, Texas. **40-45**

States Picture Series - 10 1/2" d.
Plate, Alaska, blue **25**
Plate, North Dakota, multicolored **25**
Plate, Vermont, blue. **18-20**
Plate, Virginia, maroon. **18-20**

Miscellaneous Commemoratives
Ashtray, Vermont **20-25**
Cup & saucer, after-dinner size, Niagara
Falls **25**
Plate, 8 1/2" d., Memento Plate of factory **75**

Christmas Tree Pattern Pieces

Plate, 10 1/2" d., Christmas Tree patt. (IL-
LUS. w/Christmas Tree teacup & saucer).. **65-75**
Plate, 10 1/2" d., General MacArthur, brown **20**
Plate, 10 1/2" d., Hollywood Stars, blue.......... **70-80**
Plate, 10 1/2" d., Knott's Berry Farm, Cali-
fornia **35**

Plate, 10 1/2" d., Notre Dame University,
brown **25**
Plate, 10 1/2" d., Old Man of the Mountain,
New Hampshire **25**

1952 Postmasters Convention Plate

Plate, Postmasters Convention, shows
buildings in Boston, border reads "Souvenir of the 48th National Convention of
the National Association of Postmasters
of the United States - Boston, Massachusetts, October 12-16, 1952," multicolor
(ILLUS.). **30-35**
Plate, Statue of Liberty, multicolor. **50-75**
Plates, 8 1/2" d., Cocktail Hour series,
brown transfer, complete set of 8 .... **400-600**
Teacup & saucer, Christmas Tree (ILLUS.
with Christmas Tree plate). **30-35**

Warwick

Warwick Mark

Numerous collectors have turned their attention to the productions of the Warwick China Manufacturing Company that operated in Wheeling, West Virginia, from 1887 until 1951. Prime interest seems to lie in items produced before 1914 that were decorated with decal portraits of beautiful women, monks and Native Americans. Fraternal Order items, as well as floral and fruit decorated items, are also popular with collectors.

Salesman's Sample Ashtray

"June Bride" Sugar & Creamer

Ashtray, salesman's sample, white trimmed in gold w/"Warwick China" in script & knight's helmet in black, no mark on back, ca. 1940s, 4 3/4" l., 3 1/2" w. (ILLUS.).. **$75**

Creamer & cov. sugar, white w/pink roses in "June Bride" decor patt., gold trim, marked w/Warwick knight's helmet, decor code A2003, ca. 1940s, creamer 4" h., sugar 3 1/2" d., pr. (ILLUS., top of page).. **55**

Creamer & cov. sugar, white w/red "Tudor Rose" decor patt. (rare), marked w/Warwick knight's helmet in green, ca. 1940s, creamer 4 1/2" h., sugar 5" d., pr. (ILLUS., bottom of page)................................... **95**

Warwick Ewer

Ewer, matte brown & tan w/hazelnuts, gold trim, marked w/IOGA knight's helmet in green, decor code M2, ca. 1908, 11" h. (ILLUS.).. **175**

Warwick Flow Blue Fern Dish

Fern dish, Pansy decor patt. in Flow Blue, gold trim & highlights, marked "Warwick China" in black, ca. 1896, 4 3/4" h., 7 1/2" d. (ILLUS.)... **475**

Ewer with Poppies

Ewer, brown, tan & cream w/gold rim, pink poppies, embossing around bottom, marked w/IOGA knight's helmet in green, decor code A-6, ca. 1905, 10" h. (ILLUS.).. **70**

"Tudor Rose" Sugar & Creamer

Pheasant Platter

Humidor with B.P.O.E. Elk Logo

Humidor, cov., brown & tan w/elk's head & clock, "Cigars" on back, marked w/IOGA knight's helmet in grey & "Warwick China" in black, decor code A-13 in red, scarce, ca. 1903, 6 1/2" h., 4 1/2" d. (ILLUS.)... **295**

Mug, cylindrical, decorated w/the head of an elk & the "BPOE" emblem **45**

Pitcher, 6 1/2" h., lemonade shape, brown shaded to brown ground, color floral decoration, No. A-27 .... **100**

Pitcher, 6 1/2" h., Tokio #3, brown shaded to brown ground, decorated w/color portrait of Native American, A-12 .... **300**

Pitcher, 7" h., Tokio #2, overall white ground, color bird decoration, D-1 .... **185**

Pitcher, 7 3/4" h., Tokio #1 shape, overall red ground w/color portrait of fisherman in yellow slicker, No. E-3 .... **185**

Pitcher, 9 3/4" h., lemonade shape, overall pink ground w/color "Gibson Girl" type bust portrait of a young woman w/dark hair in a bouffant style & holding purple flowers, No. H-1 (ILLUS.) **265**

Pitcher, 10 1/4" h., monk decoration **165**

Platter, 15" l., h.p. scene of pheasant rooster & hen in field, gold rim, marked w/Warwick knight's helmet in green, signed "Real," ca. 1930s, rare (ILLUS., top of page) **185**

Platter in "June Bride" Pattern

Platter, 22" l., white w/small pink flowers & gold rim in "June Bride" decor patt., marked w/Warwick knight's helmet in maroon, decor code #B2062, ca. 1940s (ILLUS.).................................. **25**

Shaving Mug with Cardinal

Lemonade Pitcher with Woman

Shriner Tankard Set

Shaving mug, brown w/portrait of Cardinal, marked w/IOGA knight's helmet in green & "Warwick China" in black, decor code A-36 in red, ca. 1903, 3 1/2" d., 3 1/2" h. (ILLUS.).. **75**

Portrait Spirits Jug

Spirits jug, matte tan & brown w/woman in low-cut gown & flowing hair, marked w/IOGA knight's helmet in green, decor code M-1 in red, scarce, ca. 1908, 6 1/4" h. (ILLUS) **225**

Stein with Native American Chief

Stein, brown & cream w/portrait of Native American chief in full bonnet, marked w/IOGA knight's helmet in green, ca. 1905, 5" h. (ILLUS.).. **100**

VP Style Stein with Bulldog

Stein, VP style, brown & cream w/photographic transfer of bulldog, "Ch. l'Almassadeur," marked w/IOGA knight's helmet, decor code A-32, ca. 1906, 2 2/4" d., 4 1/2" h. (ILLUS.).................................. **70**
Tankard set: 9 3/4" h. tankard & six 4" h. steins; turquoise & salmon w/Shriner symbol near top & desert scene at bottom, marked w/IOGA knight's helmet in green, no decor code, ca. 1909, scarce, the set (ILLUS., top of page) **925**

Warwick Portrait Teapot

Teapot, cov., h.p. portrait, "Gibson Girl" decor, turquoise & pink, matte finish, signed "H. Richard Boehm," marked w/IOGA knight's helmet in green, decor code M5, rare in this color, ca. 1910, 7 1/2" h. (ILLUS.) **425**
Vase, 4" h., Pansy shape, yellow shading to green ground, color portrait of Anna Potaka, K-1.. **200**

Vase, 4" h., Parisian shape, overall charcoal ground, color nude portrait signed "Carreno," No. C-1... **400**

Violet Vase with Beechnut

Vase, 4" h., Violet shape, brown shading to tan ground, color beechnut decoration, matte finish, M-2 (ILLUS.) **110**

Vase, 4" h., Violet shape, overall charcoal ground, color floral decoration, C-6 .... **130**

Warwick Violet Style Vase

Vase, 4" h., Violet style, brown & tan w/poppies, marked w/IOGA knight's helmet, decor code A-6 in red, scarce, ca. 1904 (ILLUS.).. **110**

Vase, 4 1/2" h., Dainty shape, brown shaded to brown ground, colored floral decoration, No. A-27 .... **145**

Vase, 6" h., Narcis #3 shape, brown shaded to brown ground, decorated w/a fisherman wearing a yellow slicker, No. A-35........ **165**

Vase, 6 1/2" h., Clytie shape, overall red ground w/poinsettia decoration, No. E-2....... **210**

Vase, 6 1/2" h., Clytie shape, tan shaded to brown ground w/beechnut decoration, matte finish, No. M-2....................................... **250**

Clytie Portrait Vase in Red Glaze

Vase, 6 1/2" h., Clytie style portrait vase, portrait of Madame Lebrun, red glaze, marked w/IOGA knight's helmet in grey, decor code I14 in red, rare, ca. 1908 (ILLUS.)... **325**

Vase, 6 1/2" h., Den shape, brown shaded to brown ground, pine cone decoration, No. A-64... **290**

Vase, 6 3/4" h., Narcis #2 shape, overall red ground, color portrait of Princess Potaka, No. E-1 .... **220**

Vase, 7" h., Albany shape, tan shading to tan ground, color nut decoration, matte finish, M-64 .... **200**

Vase, 7 1/4" h., Cuba shape, brown shading to brown ground, color pine cone decoration, A-64 .... **260**

Vase, 7 1/2" h., Verbenia #2 shape, brown shaded to brown ground, adult portrait of Madame Lebrun, No. A-17 .... **220**

Vase, 8" h., Carol shape, green shaded to green ground, red rose decoration, No. F-2.. **255**

Vase, 8" h., Carol shape, overall pink ground decorated w/a "Gibson Girl" type decoration w/portrait of a woman wearing a boa, No. H-1.. **300**

Vase, 8" h., Chicago shape, brown shaded to brown ground w/red & green floral decoration, No. A-40 .... **250**

Vase, 8" h., Duchess shape, brown shading to brown ground, color floral decoration, A-27 .... **155**

Vase, 8" h., Duchess shape, overall white ground w/color bird decoration, D-1 .... **185**

Vase, 8" h., Grecian shape, brown shading to brown ground, color floral decoration, A-6 .... **190**

Vase, 8" h., Rose shape, overall red ground w/color portrait of Madame Recamier, No. E-1 .... **230**

Vase, 8 1/4" h., Narcis #1 shape, overall white ground w/color bird decoration, No. D-1 .... **190**

Vase, 8 1/4" h., Victoria shape, overall red ground w/red poinsettia decoration, No. E-2 .... **190**

Victoria Style Vase with Herons

Vase, 8 1/4" h., Victoria style, white w/gold rim, two herons, marked w/IOGA knight's helmet in grey, decor code D-1 in red, ca. 1909 (ILLUS.)... **190**

Vase, 9" h., Flower shape, green shaded to green ground, portrait of a young woman w/flowing red hair, No. M-1 .... **200**

Warwick Verbena Style Vase

Vase, 9" h., Verbena #1 style, grey w/pink poppies & pink & white daisies, rim trimmed in gold, marked w/IOGA knight's helmet, decor code C-6 in red, ca. 1906 (ILLUS.) **160**

Vase, 9 1/4'" h., brown shaded to brown ground, floral decoration, No. A-23 .... **160**

Vase, 9 1/4" h., Windsor shape, brown shaded to brown ground, acorn decoration, No. A-67 .... **290**

Penn Vase with Acorn Decoration

Vase, 9 1/2" h., Penn shape, brown shaded to brown ground, acorn decoration, No. A-64 (ILLUS.) **195**

Vase, 9 1/2" h., Penn shape, overall green color w/no decoration, matte finish, No. M-6 .... **270**

Warwick Thelma Style Vase

Vase, 9 1/2" h., Thelma style, pink w/h.p. "Gibson Girl" decal, signed "H. Richard Boehm," marked w/IOGA knight's helmet, decor code H-1, scarce, ca. 1909 (ILLUS.) **245**

Vase, 9 1/2" h., Verbenia #1 shape, brown shaded to brown ground, color floral decoration, No. A-6 .... **165**

Vase, 9 3/4" h., Iris shape, brown shaded to brown ground, nut decoration, No. A-64 .... **150**

Warwick Vase with Pink Roses

Vase, 10" h., baluster form w/scroll handles, brown w/pink roses, marked w/IOGA knight's helmet, decor code A-12 in red, scarce, ca. 1904 (ILLUS.) **205**

Vase, 10" h., Flower shape, brown shaded to brown ground, color floral decoration, No. A-6 .... **135**

Vase, 10" h., Henrietta shape, brown shaded to brown ground, color portrait of a seminude young woman, No. A-30 .... **275**

Warwick Portrait Vase

Vase, 10" h., Magnolia style, grey w/picture of partially nude woman, signed "Carreno," marked w/IOGA knight's helmet, decor code #C-2 in red, ca. 1905 (ILLUS.) **850**

Vase, 10" h., Roberta shape, brown shaded to brown ground, portrait of a monk, No. A-36 .... **260**

Vase, 10" h., Royal #2 shape, brown shaded to brown ground, floral decoration, No. A-27 .... **295**

Vase, 10" h., Virginia shape, overall pink ground, "Gibson Girl" type decoration w/portrait of a young woman w/a flower in her hair, No. H-1 .... **300**

woman w/hibiscus flower in hair, marked w/ IOGA knight's helmet in green, decor code A-17 in red, scarce, ca. 1907 (ILLUS.).. **295**

Portrait Vase with Gypsy Girl

Vase, 10 1/4" h., Bouquet #2 portrait style in tan & brown, bust portrait of Gypsy girl in red dress & headscarf, marked w/IOGA knight's helmet in green, decor code M-1 in red, ca. 1908 (ILLUS.) **240**

Warwick Bouquet #2 Style Vase

Vase, 10 1/4" h., Bouquet #2 style in pink w/red, pink & white roses, marked w/IOGA knight's helmet in green, decor code H-4, ca. 1908 (ILLUS.) **190**

Vase with Woman with Red Rose

Vase, 10 1/4'" h., Bouquet #2 style, brown & cream w/decal portrait of young Victorian woman w/red rose in hair, marked w/IOGA knight's helmet in green, decor code A-17 in red, scarce, ca. 1907 (ILLUS.) **295**

Vase with "Gibson Girl" Decor

Vase, 10 1/4" h., Bouquet #2 style, tan & brown matte w/"Gibson Girl" decor of hatted woman holding rose, marked w/IOGA knight's helmet in green, decor code M1 in red, scarce, ca. 1909 (ILLUS.).................... **305**

Vase with Woman with Hibiscus

Vase, 10 1/4" h., Bouquet #2 style, brown & tan w/decal portrait of young Victorian

Bouquet #2 Style Vase with Herons

Vase, 10 1/4" h., Bouquet #2 style, white w/gold rim & two herons, marked w/IOGA knight's helmet in green, decor code D-1 in red, ca. 1909 (ILLUS.) **190**

Vase with Gypsy Girl

Vase, 10 1/4" h., Bouquet #2 style, white w/gold trim & portrait of Gypsy girl, marked w/IOGA knight's helmet in green, ca. 1908 (ILLUS.) **190**

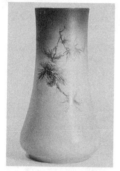

Monroe Style Vase with Pine Cones

Vase, 10 1/4" h., Monroe style, brown & tan matte w/pine cones on branch, marked w/IOGA knight's helmet in green, decor code M-2, ca. 1909 (ILLUS.) **150**

Vase, 10 1/4" h., Orchid shape, overall red ground, poinsettia decoration, No. E-2 .... **210**

Warwick Bouquet #2 Portrait Vase

Vase, 10 1/2" h., Bouquet #2 shape, brown shaded to brown ground, portrait of a young woman w/dark hair holding a branch w/white flowers, No. A-17 (ILLUS.) **225**

Vase, 10 1/2" h., Clematis shape, tan shaded to tan ground w/nut decoration, matte finish, No. M-64 .... **290**

Vase, 10 1/2" h., Magnolia shape, green shaded to green ground, color floral decoration, No. B-30 .... **225**

Vase, 10 1/2" h., Monroe shape, overall pink ground, "Gibson Girl" type decoration w/portrait of a young woman wearing a large hat, No. H-1 .... **275**

Geran Shape Warwick Vase

Vase, 11" h., Geran shape, overall charcoal ground w/red floral cluster, No. C-6 (ILLUS.) **250**

Vase, 11" h., Oriental shape, brown shading to brown ground, color floral decoration, A-21 .... **240**

Vase, 11" h., Royal #1 shape, brown shaded to brown ground w/colored floral decoration, No. A-40 .... **225**

Vase, 11 1/2" h., Bouquet #1 shape, brown shaded to brown ground, portrait of young woman wearing a pearl necklace, No. A-17 .... **215**

Vase, 11 1/2" h., Chrysanthemum #3 shape, brown shaded to brown ground, color floral decoration, No. A-6 .... **160**

Warwick Vase with Hibiscus Flower

Vase, 11 1/2" h., footed ovoid base angling to long narrow neck & flaring rim, slender graceful handles from base to top of neck, brown w/hibiscus flower, marked w/IOGA knight's helmet, decor code A27 in red, scarce, ca. 1904 (ILLUS.) **200**

Hibiscus Vase with Dogs

Vase, 11 1/2" h., Hibiscus shape, brown shaded to brown ground, large color scene of red & black & white setter dogs hunting, No. A-50 (ILLUS.) **375**

Vase, 11 1/2" h., President shape, tan shaded to tan ground, acorn decoration, matte finish, No. M-4 .... **220**

Vase, 11 1/2" h., Regency shape, brown shading to brown ground, color floral decoration, A-40 .... **240**

Vase, 11 1/2" h., Roman shape, overall white ground, color bird decoration, D-1 ...... **220**

Vase, 11 1/2" h., Senator #3 shape, brown shading to brown ground, color floral decoration, A-6 .... **165**

Bouquet Style Vase with Orchid

Vase, 11 3/4" h., Bouquet #1 style, brown & cream w/orchid in shades of pink, marked w/IOGA knight's helmet in green, decor code A-14, ca. 1904 (ILLUS.) **150**

Egyptian Shape Vase with Flowers

Vase, 11 3/4" h., Egyptian shape, brown shaded to brown ground, red floral decoration, No. A-27 (ILLUS.) **245**

Verona Shape Vase with Bird

Vase, 11 3/4" h., Verona shape, overall white ground, color bird decoration, D-1 (ILLUS.) **185**

Vase, 11 7/8" h., Nasturtium shape, brown shading to brown ground, color floral decoration, A-40 .... **240**

Vase, 12" h., Bouquet #1 style, tall cylindrical form w/twig handles, colored transfer of a woman holding long-stemmed yellow roses, shaded ground **225**

Vase, 12" h., Gem shape, brown shading to brown ground, color floral decoration, A-16 .... **190**

Vase, 12" h., Helene shape, color portrait of woman w/large hat, matte finish, M-1 .... **255**

Vase, 12" h., Queen shape, overall charcoal ground, color floral decoration, No. C-6 .... **290**

Vase, 12 1/2" h., Alexandria shape, brown shaded to brown ground w/color floral decoration, No. A-40 .... **275**

Warwick Vase with Poppies

Vase, 12 1/2" h., baluster form, brown w/pink poppies, marked w/IOGA knight's helmet in green, decor code A40, scarce, ca. 1904 (ILLUS.) **200**

Vase with Hazelnuts

Vase, 13" h., Senator #2 style, brown & tan matte w/hazelnuts on branch, marked w/IOGA knight's helmet in green, decor code M-2 in red, ca. 1909 (ILLUS.) **175**

Vase, 13 1/2" h., Chrysanthemum #2 shape, overall charcoal ground decorated w/colored florals, No. C-6 .... **145**

Vase, 13 1/2" h., Senator #2 shape, tan shading to brown ground, color portrait of a gypsy wearing scarf, matte finish, M-1 ...... **190**

Vase, 15" h., A Beauty shape, brown shaded to brown ground w/red rose (American Beauty) decoration, No. A-20 .... **300**

Vase, 15" h., A Beauty shape, white ground w/red rose (American Beauty) decoration, No. D-2 .... **325**

Vase, 15" h., Princess shape, brown shading to brown ground, color floral decoration, A-27 .... **350**

Vase, 15" h., Senator #1 shape, green shading to green ground, color acorn decoration, matte finish, M-4 .... **200**

Vase, 15 1/2" h., Chrysanthemum #1 shape, overall red ground w/a Madame Lebrun child portrait, No. E-1 .... **180**

Commercial China

Bowl, 4 1/4 x 10 1/4" oval, white ironstone w/green band, "Osiris" emblem **20**

Warwick Restaurant Soup Bowls

Bowl, 3 3/4" d., soup, double-handled, white w/black & orange decorative band below rim & on handles, marked w/Warwick knight's helmet in green, ca. 1940s, each (ILLUS. of six) **6**

Bowl, 5" d., white w/bands, star emblem w/"Bethleham Chapter No. 14 O.E.S." **15**

Butter pat, white w/"The Brass Rail" logo, 3" **20**

Warwick Commercial Creamer

Creamer, white w/green tree & bands & "Camp Lone Tree," marked w/Warwick knight's helmet, ca. 1937, 4 1/4" h. (ILLUS.) **21**

Warwick "Sumter Hospital" Creamer

Creamer, white w/two green bands & "Sumter Hospital" logo, 2 1/2" h. (ILLUS.) **22**

Cup, white w/"Johnny's" logo **25**

Cup & saucer, brown wave decoration, Santone finish **25**

Cup & saucer, white w/"Duckwall's" logo **40**

Various Warwick Restaurant Mugs

Cup & saucer, white w/"Liggett's" logo **20**
Cup & saucer, white w/"St. Gregory's" logo **22**
Cup & saucer, white w/Crestwood pattern **25**
Cup & saucer, white w/Dakota pattern **20**
Mug, various decorations, marked w/Warwick knight's helmet in green, ca. 1940s, 3" d., 3 1/4" h., each (ILLUS. of five, top of page) **9**
Mug, white w/green drape & emblem, "The Security Benefit Assoc.," 3 1/2" h. **15**

Warwick "Duckwall's" Mustard Jar

Mustard jar, cov., white w/"Duckwall's" logo (ILLUS.) **28**
Plate, 6 1/4" d., white w/one green band, double headed eagle emblem w/"AASR 32" & "Valley of Wheeling" **24**

Plate, 7 1/4" d., white w/4H camp w/stream & trees in green, two green bands inside rim, marked w/Warwick knight's helmet in green, scarce, ca. 1944 (ILLUS.) **20**
Plate, 9" d., white w/"Hotel Anthony" logo **18**
Plate, 9" d., white w/black & red bands, "Masonic Temple of Austin" emblem **18**
Plate, 10" d., white w/"compliments of Dine Furniture Company" **40**
Plate, 10" d., white w/gold band, "Souvenir of Pleasanton" decal **25**
Plate, 10 1/4" d., white w/"The Washington Duke" logo **35**

Commercial China

Warwick B&O Railroad Platter

Platter, 8 1/4" l., white w/22k gold decorative band on rim & B&O Railroad symbol, marked w/Warwick knight's helmet in green, ca. 1938 (ILLUS.) **125**

Wentworth Military Academy Platter

Platter, 15" l., white w/Wentworth Military Academy crest, maroon band inside rim, marked "Warwick China" in green, ca. 1930s (ILLUS.) **26**

4H Plate by Warwick

Warwick "Sumter Hospital" Sugar Bowl

Sugar bowl, cov., white w/two green bands,
"Sumter Hospital" logo, 3 3/4" h. (ILLUS.)....... **25**
Syrup pitcher, cov., white w/"Johnny's" logo....... **40**
Tray, oval, white w/"The Washington" logo,
3 1/2 x 9 3/4" **30**

"Oakley's" Oval Vegetable Dish

Vegetable dish, individual, oval, white
w/"Oakley's" logo (ILLUS.) **25**

Dinnerwares
Bowl, oval, Pattern No. 2000 .... **25**
Cup & saucer, Pattern No. 9572, Silver Pop-
py decoration.. **10**
Cup & saucer, Pattern No. 9903, Grey Blos-
som decoration... **18**
Cup & saucer, Pattern No. B-9551 .... **20**

Warwick Demitasse Cup & Saucer

Demitasse cup & saucer, Gray Blossom decor patt. w/platinum rim, saucer only
marked w/Warwick knight's helmet in
gold w/patt. name "Gray Blossom - Pat.
#9903," ca. 1940, 2 1/4" h. cup, 5" d.
saucer, cup & saucer (ILLUS.) **26**

Gravy boat w/underplate, Pattern No. B-
9289... **30**
Pitcher, 8" h., buttermilk-type, white ground
w/floral decoration of small pink flowers......... **45**
Pitcher, 8" h., milk-type, white ground w/flo-
ral decoration of blue forget-me-nots.............. **35**
Plate, 6 1/2" d., bread & butter, Pattern No.
9437-M, Windsor Maroon decoration................ **5**
Plate, 6 1/2" d., bread & butter, Pattern No.
D-9351, platinum bands **20**
Plate, 6 1/2" d., bread & butter, Pattern No.
E-9450.. **15**
Plate, 9" d., Pattern AB-9231 .... **8**
Plate, 9" d., Pattern No. B-9059......................... **15**
Plate, 9" d., Pattern No. C-9295, Bird of Par-
adise decoration w/two birds.......................... **12**
Plate, 10" d., dinner, Pattern No. 9584, Bird
of Paradise decoration w/single bird............... **10**
Plate, 10" d., Pattern No. 2098, Venetian
Rose decoration **10**
Platter, 13" l., Pattern No. B-9272, coin gold
trim... **40**
Vegetable bowl, cov., Pattern No. 2001 .... **40**
Vegetable bowl, handled, Pattern No. 2062 .... **30**

Watt Pottery

*In July 1922 the Watt Pottery was incorporated on
the site of the old Burley Pottery in Crooksville, Ohio,
where it was owned and operated by the Watt family of
Perry County, Ohio. It remained in business until a fire
halted production in 1965.*

*Through the 1920s and early 1930s the Watt Pottery
manufactured stoneware crocks, churns and jars. These
are marked with an eagle or acorn in blue, with gallon-
age marked in a circle.*

*In 1935, the pottery dropped its stoneware line in
favor of more modern ovenwares. The lightweight clay
body gave the necessary resilience to go from
icebox to oven. In 1949, the Watt Pottery began hand-
decorating its wares. The pieces were decorated by
teams of three decorators and the patterns were simple
in nature, with as few brush strokes as possible to allow
low production costs. The bright colors against the deep
cream clay give Watt Pottery its unique country appeal.*

*The first hand-decorated patterns are called the
"Classic Patterns" and were produced from 1949 until
about 1953. They are: Rio Rose, Moonflower, Dogwood,
and Daisy and Crosshatch.*

*The patterns most sought after by today's collectors
and their introduction dates are as follows: Starflower
—1951; Apple—1952; Cherry—1952; Silhouette—1953;
Rooster—1955; Dutch Tulip—1956; American Red Bud
(Tear Drop)—1957; Morning Glory—1958; Autumn
Foliage—1959; Double Apple—1959; and Tulip—1961.*

*Most pieces of Watt ware are well marked. The marks
are large, often covering the entire bottom of the piece.
They usually consist of one or more concentric rings
deeply impressed into the bottom. The words "Watt" and
"Oven Ware U.S.A." are impressed as well, although
some pieces have only one phrase, not both. Earlier
marks featured a script "Watt" without circles. Most
pieces also have the mold number impressed in the center, making identification easy. The most significant
pieces that were not marked are the ice bucket (all patterns) and Apple dinner plates.*

—Dennis M. Thompson

Baker, cov., Tear Drop patt., No. 84, square.... **500-600**

Baker, cov., Apple patt., No. 601, 8" d. **100-135**

Baker, cov., Open Apple patt., No. 110, 8 1/2" d. **300-350**

Bean cup, Apple patt., No. 76 .... **225-275**

Bean cup, Starflower patt., five-petal, No. 76, each **25-35**

Bean pot, cov., Tear Drop patt. (American Red Bud), No. 76, decorated lid **200-250**

Bean pot, cov., Tear Drop patt., No. 76, plain lid **75-90**

Bean pot, Double Apple patt., No. 76 .... **400-450**

Bean pot, Starflower patt., five-petal, No. 76.... **150-175**

Apple Pattern Bean Pot

Bean pot, cov., Apple patt., No. 76, 6 1/2" h. (ILLUS.) **175-200**

Bowl, Apple patt., spaghetti, No. 39 .... **125-150**

Two-leaf Apple Spaghetti Bowl

Bowl, Apple patt., two-leaf, spaghetti, No. 39 (ILLUS.) **156-187**

Bowl, chili, Sleeping Mexican **5-7**

Bowl, Cross Hatch Pansy patt., spaghetti, No. 39 .... **250-300**

Bowl, Rio Rose patt., spaghetti, No. 39 .... **50-70**

Bowl, Tear Drop patt., No. 63-65, deep shape, each **60-90**

Bowl, Tear Drop patt., spaghetti, No. 39 .... **200-300**

Dutch Tulip Spaghetti Bowl

Bowl, 13" d., spaghetti, Dutch Tulip patt., No. 39 (ILLUS.) **375-425**

Bowl, spaghetti, 13" d., 3 1/2" h., Autumn Foliage patt., No. 39 .... **125-150**

Canister, cov., "Coffee," Apple patt. **300-375**

Canister, cov., "Coffee," Dutch Tulip patt. **350-400**

Canister, cov., "Flour," Apple patt. **300-375**

Canister, cov., "Flour," Dutch Tulip patt. **350-400**

Canister, cov., "Sugar," Apple patt. **300-375**

Canister, cov., "Sugar," Dutch Tulip patt. ... **350-400**

Canister, cov., "Tea," Apple patt. **300-375**

Canister, cov., "Tea," Dutch Tulip patt. **350-400**

Casserole, Kitch-N-Queen patt., No. 66 & 67, each **85-100**

Casserole, Rooster patt., No. 66 & 67 .... **150-175**

Casserole, cov., Apple patt., No. 18, 5" d. **175-200**

Casserole, cov., French handled, Apple patt., No. 18, 5" d. **200-250**

Cheese crock, Apple patt., No. 80 .... **1,200-1,500**

Cheese crock, Starflower patt., four-petal, No. 80 .... **450-550**

Chip 'n' dip set, Double Apple patt. **300-350**

Churn, stoneware, Eagle or Acorn mark **100-125**

Coffee server, cov., Apple patt., No. 115, rare **2,000-2,300**

Coffee server, cov., Brown Banded, No. 115 .... **150-200**

Cookie jar, cov., Moonflower patt., No. 21 . **150-175**

Cookie jar, cov., Starflower patt., five-petal, No. 21 .... **175-200**

Cookie jar, cov., Rio Rose patt., No. 21, 7 1/2" h. **175-200**

Creamer, Brown Banded, No. 62 .... **400-500**

Creamer, Double Apple patt., No. 62 .... **300-400**

Creamer, No. 62, in various two-tone drip patterns **300-400**

Creamer, Open Apple patt., No. 62 .... **700-850**

Creamer, Tear Drop patt., No. 62 .... **200-250**

Autumn Foliage Creamer & Pitchers

Assorted Watt Pottery, Starflower Pattern (Five-petal)

Creamer, Autumn Foliage patt., No. 62, 4 1/4" h. (ILLUS. right w/Autumn Foliage pitchers).................................. **150-200**
Creamer, Dutch Tulip patt., No. 62, 4 1/4" h. **225-250**
Creamer, Morning Glory patt., cream, No. 97, 4 1/4" h. **300-400**

Crocks, stoneware, Eagle or Acorn patt., various sizes (ILLUS. of two)...................... **35-50**
Cup & saucer, Moonflower patt., pr............... **65-80**
Dog dish **50-75**
"Goodies" jar **200-300**
Ice bucket, Kitch-N-Queen patt., No. 59 .... **125-150**
Ice bucket, Rooster patt., No. 59 .... **250-300**

Rooster Pattern Creamer & Pitchers

Creamer, Rooster patt., No. 62, 4 1/4" h. (ILLUS. left w/pitchers) **175-225**
Creamer, Starflower patt., five-petal, No. 62, 4 1/4" h. (ILLUS. far right w/Starflower pitchers, top of page) **225-275**

Starflower No. 59 Ice Bucket

Ice bucket, Starflower patt., five-petal, No. 59 (ILLUS.) **175-225**
Ice bucket, cov., Dutch Tulip patt., No. 59, 7" h.. **200-225**
Jug, stoneware, Eagle or Acorn mark............ **35-50**
Keg, iced tea, aqua **175-200**
Keg, iced tea, plain.. **45-60**
Keg, iced tea, w/company names............... **100-125**
Mixing bowl **75-100**
Mixing bowl, 16" d., Kitch-N-Queen patt., No. 616... **200-250**
Mixing bowl, 5 or 14" d., Kitch-N-Queen patt., each... **35-74**
Mixing bowl, Apple patt. **40-75**
Mixing bowl, Basket Weave............................. **15-20**
Mixing bowl, Rooster patt................................. **85-100**
Mixing bowl, Wood Grain................................. **15-20**
Mixing bowls, Cross Hatch Pansy patt... **125-150**

Starflower Four-petal Creamer & Pitcher

Creamer, Starflower patt., four-petal, No. 62, 4 1/4" h. (ILLUS. right w/Starflower four-petal pitcher).................................... **350-400**
Creamer, Tulip patt., No. 62, 4 1/4" h......... **190-225**

Watt Pottery Crocks

Watt Pottery Tulip Pattern Mixing Bowls

Mixing bowls, nesting-type, Tulip patt., deep, Nos. 63, 64, & 65, 6 1/2" d., 7 1/2" d. & 8 1/2" d., each (ILLUS.) **85-100**
Mixing bowls, Starflower patt., five-petal, each.. **70-85**
Mug, Autumn Foliage patt., No. 501, 4 1/2" h.. **135-150**

Watt Moonflower Plate & Platter

Pie plate, Autumn Foliage patt., No. 33 ..... **140-160**
Pie plate, Apple patt., No. 33, 9" d............. **125-150**
Pitcher, Apple patt., No 17, plain lip **250-275**
Pitcher, Cherry patt., No. 15 .... **200-250**
Pitcher, Cherry patt., No. 17 .... **200-250**
Pitcher, Cross Hatch Pansy patt., No.
16 .... **200-275**
Pitcher, Dutch Tulip patt., No. 16 .... **175-200**
Pitcher, Dutch Tulip patt., refrigerator, No.
69 .... **400-450**
Pitcher, Kitch-N-Queen patt., No. 17 .... **125-150**
Pitcher, Rio Rose patt., No. 15 .... **175-200**
Pitcher, Rooster patt., No. 16 (ILLUS. right
w/Rooster creamer & pitcher).............. **135-160**
Pitcher, Rooster patt., No. 17, rare **1,200-1,300**
Pitcher, Tear Drop patt., No. 16 .... **175-225**
Pitcher, Tulip patt., No. 16.......................... **125-150**
Pitcher, Tulip patt., No. 17.......................... **200-250**
Pitcher, 5 1/2" h., Apple patt., No. 15 .... **100-125**
Pitcher, 5 1/2" h., Autumn Foliage patt., No.
15 (ILLUS. second from right w/Autumn
Foliage creamer & pitchers)......................... **75-90**
Pitcher, 5 1/2" h., Cross Hatch patt.,
No. 15.. **400-500**
Pitcher, 5 1/2" h., Dutch Tulip patt., No. 15 **175-200**
Pitcher, 5 1/2" h., Rooster patt., No. 15
(ILLUS. center w/Rooster creamer &
pitcher)... **150-175**
Pitcher, 5 1/2" h., Starflower patt., five-pet-
al, No. 15 (ILLUS. second from right
w/Starflower creamer & pitchers) **75-100**
Pitcher, 5 1/2" h., Tear Drop patt., No. 15 ...... **50-60**
Pitcher, 5 1/2" h., Tulip patt., No. 15........... **400-500**
Pitcher, 6 1/2" h., Apple patt., No. 16 .... **90-110**
Pitcher, 6 1/2" h., Autumn Foliage patt., No.
16 (ILLUS. second from left w/Autumn
Foliage creamer & pitchers)................... **100-125**
Pitcher, 6 1/2" h., Cherry patt., No. 16 .... **225-260**
Pitcher, 6 1/2" h., Double Apple patt.,
No. 16 .... **400-500**
Pitcher, 6 1/2" h., Rio Rose patt., No.
16 .... **150-175**
Pitcher, 6 1/2" h., Starflower patt., five-pet-
al, No. 16 (ILLUS. second from left
w/Starflower creamer & pitchers)............... **75-90**
Pitcher, 8" h., Apple patt., w/ice lip, No. 17 **190-225**
Pitcher, 8" h., Autumn Foliage patt., No. 17
(ILLUS. left w/Autumn Foliage creamer &
pitchers).. **135-150**
Pitcher, 8" h., Morning Glory patt.,
No. 96 .... **300-350**
Pitcher, 8" h., Rio Rose patt., No. 17.......... **175-200**

Pitcher, 8" h., Starflower patt., five-petal,
No. 17 (ILLUS. left w/Starflower creamer
& pitchers) **150-170**
Pitcher, 8" h., Starflower patt., four-petal, re-
frigerator, No. 69 (ILLUS. left w/Starflow-
er four-petal creamer)........................... **400-450**
Plate, dinner, Apple patt., w/advertising **325-375**
Plate, 6 1/2" d., Rio Rose patt. **20-30**
Plate, 10" d., Moonflower patt. (ILLUS. right
w/Moonflower platter, top of page)............ **15-25**
Platter, Brown Banded, No. 31...................... **50-75**
Platter, Rio Rose patt., No. 31...................... **80-100**
Platter, 15" d., Autumn Foliage patt., No.
31.. **100-125**
Platter, 15" d, Moonflower patt., No. 31
(ILLUS. left w/Moonflower dinner plate) .. **90-125**
Platter, 15" d., Pansy patt., cut-leaf,
No. 31.. **250-300**
Salt & pepper shakers, Apple patt., hour-
glass shape, pr. **250-275**
Salt & pepper shakers, Autumn Foliage
patt., hourglass shape, each **75-90**
Salt & pepper shakers, Brown Banded,
hourglass shape, pr. **100-150**
Salt & pepper shakers, hourglass shape,
Starflower patt., four-petal, pr................. **225-250**
Salt & pepper shakers, Tear Drop patt.,
hourglass shape, each **125-150**
Salt shaker, Cherry patt.............................. **80-100**
Sugar bowl, cov., Apple patt., No. 98.......... **350-425**
Sugar bowl, cov., Starflower patt., five-petal,
No. 98.. **200-250**
Sugar & creamer, Moonflower patt., cup-
style, each **125-150**
Sugar & creamer, Rio Rose patt., cup-style,
each... **100-150**
Teapot, cov., Apple patt., No. 505, 5" h.
(ILLUS.)... **2,800**

Watt Pottery Apple Teapot

Teapot, cov., Apple (three-leaf) patt., No.
112, rare, 6" h. (ILLUS.) **1,200-1,500**

Wedgwood

WEDGWOOD

Early Wedgwood Mark

Reference here is to the famous pottery established by Josiah Wedgwood in 1759 in England. Numerous types of wares have been produced through the years to the present.

Basalt

Bust of Locke

Bust of Locke, raised on a round socle base, impressed title & mark, ca. 1865, 7 3/4" h. (ILLUS.) **$518**

Figure group, Cupid & Psyche, the seated figures mounted to a freeform oval base, 19th c., impressed title & mark, 8" h. **1,265**

Vase, 8 3/4" h., Krater form, encaustic decoration of iron red & black enamel classical figures on each side, early 19th c., impressed mark, England **2,070**

Basalt Vase

Vase, 9" h., ovoid body tapering to wide flaring rim, C-form handles from rim to shoulder, encaustic decoration of white & black classical figure w/borders in iron red, blue, white & black, early 19th c., impressed mark (ILLUS.) **2,990**

Vase, 12 1/2" h., classical urn form, upswept loop handles, encaustic decoration of iron red, black & white designs w/classical figures to one side, a stylized palmette design to the reverse, borders of gadroon & dot, palmette, laurel & dot & spearhead & dot, ca. 1800, impressed mark **4,313**

Creamware

Condiment set: cov. jug raised on a stand w/two fixed cov. barrel-form pots & filled w/a cov. pepper pot, all supported on a larger circular footed tray; each piece finely painted in brown monochrome w/various gardening implements beneath or within a border of pink thistles edged w/narrow blue enamel bands, ca. 1800, impressed Wedgwood upper & lower case marks, 8 3/4" h. (one cover restored, one cover w/minor crack) **8,050**

Jelly mold, conical, painted w/two groups of colorful flowers above a band of flower swags tied w/blue ribbon & a wreath of flowers on the flat circular base pierced w/four apertures, the rims & tip of the mold edged in brown, impressed mark & "D," 9" h. (minor chips to rim of base) **2,587**

Jelly mold, wedge-shaped, finely painted on each side w/two swags of flowers pendant from a red ribbon, each end painted w/colorful blue & red flower vines, raised on a canted rectangular base pierced w/four apertures, the rims picked out in brown enamel, ca. 1800, impressed "WEDGWOOD L L," 8 1/2" l. (small chips to edge of base) **2,875**

Plate, 9 1/8" d., "Buns! Buns! Buns!," h.p. center scene of man selling buns to woman & child, gold border, artist-signed "E. Lessore," date mark of 1863 .... **325**

Punch pot, cov., bulbous ovoid body, printed in grey & black w/two oval panels of Aurora & Apollo racing across the sky in their respective chariots, within either a border of intertwined husk & laurel garlands enclosing signs of the Zodiac or a border of triangular panels alternating w/groups of instruments & trophies, leaf-molded spout & handle, the slightly domed cover printed w/a garland of flowers about the ovoid knop, ca. 1770-80, impressed mark, 9 5/8" h. (minor restoration to inner flange of cover) **2,185**

Teapot, cov., wide ovoid body w/painted landscape scene & building on each side, entwined loop handle & foliate molded spout, the cover w/flower knop, ca. 1768, 5 3/4" h. (crack, flaked enamels on body & cover restored) **345**

Jasper Ware

Biscuit jar, cov., cylindrical, on circular base, blue jasper dip w/white relief Greek key band interspersed w/profiles of Apollo & the Muses, Sheffield silver plate lid w/scene of Bacchus & a nymph, base by "Mappin & Webb" w/cast foliage & three paw feet, 5 1/2" d., 6 1/4" h. (wear to plating on lid) **358**

Cache pot & underplate, deep bell-shaped cache pot set into a shallow round underplate, light blue dipped decorated w/white relief classical figures, ca. 1900, 8 1/2" d., 8 1/4" h. (small rim chip on underplate) **315**

Cheese dome, cov., the high cylindrical domed top w/an upright white acorn finial, white relief classical figures separated by upright flared bands on lavender, dished base w/heavy rolled rim in lavender w/white relief blossom & leaf bands, late 19th c. **275**

Group of Three-color Jasper Pieces

Medallion, oval, pale blue ground w/dark blue dip sprigged in white w/bust portrait of Benjamin Franklin, after William Hackwood, to dexter, above the impressed title "Dr. FRANKLIN," ca. 1775, impressed "Wedgwood & Bentley," 2 1/4" h. (tiny chips to back edge **1,265**

Medallion, oval, white ground decorated in black relief w/a kneeling chained slave & molded w/the inscription "AM I NOT A MAN AND A BROTHER," mounted in gilt metal as a stickpin, impressed "WEDGWOOD" & "O," late 18th - early 19th c., medallion 1 1/8" h. **1,667**

Pitcher, cov., 7 1/4" h., tankard water-type, slightly tapering cylindrical form w/rim spout, fitted cover w/knob finial & ropetwist handle, solid white ground applied w/relief acanthus & bellflowers alternating in green & lilac, impressed mark, late 19th - early 20th c., cover stained (ILLUS. far right w/vase)................ **1,150**

Tea set: cov. teapot, cov. sugar bowl & creamer; spherical forms w/white relief classical figures & trees on dark blue, the teapot w/a pyramidal cover, marked "Made in England," 3 pcs. **358**

Tea set: cov. teapot, cov. sugar & creamer; solid white ground on wide waisted cylindrical bodies, applied w/foliate relief designs alternating in green & lilac, stained, late 19th - early 20th c., impressed mark, teapot 3 1/2" h., the set (ILLUS. center w/vase).. **1,380**

Teapot, cov., bulbous spherical body w/domed cover & button finial, white relief Grecian women, children & cupids, raised white leaves around lid, spout & handle, on light blue, marked "Wedgwood" only, 5 1/2" d., 5 1/2" h. **210**

Urn, cov., crimson ground w/white relief decoration, a wide cylindrical pedestal base decorated w/swags of grapevines & oval medallions above the acanthus leaf lower border, supporting a short ringed pedestal below the bulbous ovoid body w/matching swag & medallion decoration & short flared neck, low domed cover w/knob finial, Wedgwood only mark, late 19th c., 16" h. **2,970**

Vase, 4 1/4" h., wide ovoid form w/a short wide neck, flaring round foot, solid white ground applied w/acanthus leaf & bellflowers alternating in green & lilac, impressed mark, late 19th - early 20th c. (ILLUS. far left, top of page) **920**

Vase, 8" h., flaring foot tapering to a tall slightly ovoid body w/a wide flared mouth, black ground decorated w/white relief classical figures, 20th c. **180**

Queensware

Dinner service: eleven dinner plates, eight bread-and-butter plates, seven teacups, six bouillon cups, fifteen saucers, creamer, sugar, oval platter, oval vegetable dish, pair of compotes, trumpet-form vase & pair of columnar candlesticks; each applied w/grapevine border, impressed & printed factory marks, ca. 1900, candlesticks 11 1/4" h. (chips & repairs), the set **862**

Miscellaneous

Bowl, 8 1/2" d., "Fairyland Lustre," Kang Hsi-style, the interior decorated w/"Woodland Elves I - Striped Pants" design, the exterior w/"Woodland Elves V - Woodland Bridge Variation II" design on a black background, gold printed mark, Pattern No. Z4968, ca. 1920s **4,500**

Bust of Stephenson

Bust of Stephenson, carrara, designed by E.W. Wyon, on raised circular base, impressed title, factory mark & "E.W. Wyons.F. - 1853," England, 14 3/4" h. (ILLUS.)... **518**

Butter pat, majolica, Oriental Floral patt., turquoise ground.. **193**

Butter pat, majolica, Shell & Coral patt., yellow, green & pink (minor hairline).................. **165**

Cake stand, majolica, Overlapping Leaf patt., green & yellow leaves on round top, raised on a brown trunk base, 8 3/4" d., 5 1/4" h. **165**

Cake stands, "Argenta Ware," Fan patt., impressed marks & date code for 1879, pr. **460**

Center bowl, majolica, oval, upright yellow reticulated basketweave sides above green leafy garland w/pink trim raised on a low cobalt blue base, 15" l. **1,150**

Figural Monkey Centerpiece

Centerpiece, Argenta Ware, figural, a wide rounded bowl patterned w/clambering monkeys supported by a figure of a monkey squatting on a round base molded w/branches, impressed marks, date letter for 1879, 10" h. (ILLUS.). **1,840**

Compote, open, 11" d., majolica, Cauliflower patt., brown, pink & green leaves on a turquoise ground. **248**

Cup, "Fairyland Lustre," small footed cup, decorated w/woodland elves dancing & at various pursuits on a mottled dark purple & green ground, the interior w/birds, butterflies & a bat flying from a leafy border on a mottled mother-of-pearl ground, gilt printed factory mark, ca. 1920, 3" h. **920**

Ewer, majolica, footed spherical body w/tall flaring cylindrical neck, Cattail patt., horizontal green bands of cattails around the middle w/alternating dark brown & yellow bands above & below, 6 1/4" h. **275**

Wedgwood Majolica Fish Set

Fish set: oval platter & four plates; majolica, the platter molded w/a large salmon on a leafy ground, each plate w/other naturalistically colored fish on leafage, date letter for 1879, platter 25" l., the set (ILLUS. of part) **2,875**

Fish set: 6 plates & large oval serving platter; "Argenta Ware," each piece decorated w/a salmon on a bed of leaves, impressed marks & date code for 1875, platter 25" l., the set **977**

Jar, cov., ovoid body w/a domed cover, Lahore patt., decorated around the sides w/figures & animals behind a balustrade beneath brightly enameled swags of fabric around the shoulder, the cover decorated w/multicolored swirling designs,

designed by Daisy Makeig-Jones, Pattern No. Z5266, ca. 1920s, 9 1/2" h. **5,100**

Jar, cov., Fairyland Lustre, a squatty bulbous body fitted w/a domed cover, decorated w/a continuous scene of an enchanted forest full of nymphs & mythical creatures in a variety of oranges, blues & greens w/gold outlines, the cover w/a solitary spider in web bordered w/multicolored foliage, 3 1/2" h. **5,775**

Lily tray, "Fairyland Lustre," round shallow bowl form w/a wide flanged rim, decorated inside with the "Fairy Gondola" design, the exterior printed in gilding w/birds on a mottled greenish black ground, gold printed mark, ca. 1920s, 13" d. (some wear & scratching in the center) **4,500**

Pitcher, 7" h., "Argenta Ware," Ocean patt., molded seashells & coral on a cream ground, shell finial on handle, great color **550**

Pitcher, 7 1/2" h., "Argenta Ware," Bird & Fan patt., pinks & mottled browns & greens on a cream ground **440**

Pitcher, 7 3/4" h., majolica, Overlapping Grapes & Leaves patt., dark greens & browns **550**

Pitcher, 9" h., "Argenta Ware," Bird & Fan patt., pinks & mottled browns & greens on a cream ground **990**

Plaque, "Fairyland Lustre," rectangular, decorated w/a version of "Picnic by a River," orange sky, green river, crimson & purple grass & black & green trees, within a checkered border, together w/its original ebonized wood frame, gold printed mark, Pattern No. Z5279, ca. 1920s, 10 7/8" l., 2 pcs. **6,000**

Plate, 7 3/4" d., "Argenta Ware," Strawberry patt., pink berries & green & brown leaves on a pale yellow ground **220**

Plate, 8 3/4" d., "Argenta Ware," Triple Fish patt., three lifelike fish on a cream ground **385**

Plate, 8 3/4" d., majolica, Strawberry patt., yellow ground **303**

Plate, 9" d., commemorative-type, "Saratoga Monument," cabbage rose border, blue & white, 20th c. **40**

Plate, 9" d., majolica, Angel & Putti patt., four slender standing angels in blue divide the rim into four panels, each molded w/putti & swags on a cream ground, deep rose border band **495**

Plate, 9" d., majolica, green center w/classical putti & drapery, reticulated brown border band **330**

Plate, 9" d., majolica, Ocean patt., pink & brown coral spring on yellow shell in center, mottled brown & green shell border **248**

Plate, 9" d., majolica, Shell & Coral patt., turquoise basketweave ground **660**

Plate, 9" d., majolica, Stork in Marsh patt., reticulated border **880**

Plate, 9" d., majolica, Strawberry & Leaf patt., yellow ground **440**

Plate, 9 1/4" d., majolica, Botanical Bird & Floral patt., reticulated border **275**

Plate, 10" d., Ivanhoe series, "Rebecca Repelling the Templar," blue & white, early 20th c. **95**

Very Rare Wedgwood Punch Bowl

Plate, 10 1/2" d., Ivanhoe series, dark blue & white, scene of "Wamba & Cuzch the Swine Herd" **69**

Plates, 7 7/8" d., majolica, green w/leaves centered on basketweave ground, set of 8.......... **523**

Punch bowl, "Butterfly Lustre," printed on the exterior & foot w/butterflies in gilding on a ruby red & blue ground, the interior similarly decorated on a mottled pale blue & green ground beneath a gold printed Chinoiserie border at the rim, designed by Daisy Makeig-Jones, ca. 1920s, gold printed Portland Vase mark, England & painted pattern number Z4827, 11" d. **690**

Punch bowl, majolica, "Punch & Judy" model, deep sides molded w/a wide rim band of yellow "coins" on a turquoise blue band, four large full-relief heads of Punch around the sides, cobalt blue lower body raised on four seated brown dog legs, each dog wearing a clown hat & ruffled collar, professional repair to dogs' feet & bowl rim, ca. 1878, extremely rare (ILLUS., top of page).................................. **33,000**

Relish tray, majolica, oblong, Onion & Pickle patt., the center w/a large group of molded white onions, green pickles, beans & red cabbage on a cobalt blue ground, yellow wheat head end handles, 9" l. **385**

yellow & deep rose scallop shells & green coral on a cobalt blue ground, silver rim band, silver plate utensils w/matching majolica handles, late 19th c., bowl 9 1/2" d., the set (ILLUS.).............. **1,540**

Sardine box, cov., majolica, Oriental Floral patt., domed cover divided into four panels, two w/small pink blossoms **385**

Strawberry service: 6 plates & 16 1/2" l. serving tray; "Argenta Ware," each decorated w/strawberry plants & ribbons on a reed-molded ground, impressed marks & date code for 1876, the set **977**

Extremely Rare Majolica Tea Set

Tea set: cov. teapot, cov. sugar bowl & creamer; majolica, Punch & Judy patt., squatty bulbous turquoise blue bodies w/flared rims, figural Punch head handles w/cobalt blue & pink hats curving up to rims, low domed covers w/reclining brown dog finials, professional repair to collar of one dog, extremely rare, late 19th c., teapot 7 3/4" l. (ILLUS.)................ **37,400**

Teapot, cov., majolica, Chrysanthemum patt., colored blossoms on a turquoise ground, 6 1/2" h. (very slight hairline) **770**

Tile, "February," Kate Greenaway, green & blue, 6" sq. **138**

Wedgwood Majolica Salad Set

Salad bowl, fork & spoon, majolica, deep round sides molded w/large alternating

Umbrella stand, "Argenta Ware," cylindrical, molded in the Japanese taste w/open vertical fans entwined w/blossoming prunus branches, insects in flight & birds, above a key-pattern band, edged in yellow, date code for 1881, 21 3/4" h. **2,820**

Vase, 8 1/4" h., majolica, Narcissus patt., tapering ovoid body w/flaring rim, raised on three knob feet, yellow blossoms & long green leaves on a dark brown ground **660**

Weller

This pottery was made from 1872 to 1945 at a pottery established originally by Samuel A. Weller at Fulton-ham, Ohio, and moved in 1882 to Zanesville. Numerous lines were produced, and listings below are by pattern or line.

Reference books on Weller include The Collectors Encyclopedia of Weller Pottery *by Sharon & Bob Hux-ford (Collector Books, 1979) and* All About Weller *by Ann Gilbert McDonald (Antique Publications, 1989).*

Weller Marks

Ardsley (1928)
Various shapes molded as cattails among rushes with water lilies at the bottom. Matte glaze.

Bulb bowl, lobed blossom form base w/leaf-form openwork top, half kiln ink stamp logo, 4 7/8" h. **$100-125**

Candleholders, lily pad & blossom disc base centered by a flaring blossom-form socket, half kiln ink stamp logo & old sales tag, one w/original "Weller Ardsley Ware" paper label, 2 3/4" h., pr. (minor glaze inconsistencies)... **125-150**

Vase, 19" h., floor-type, compressed domed base w/lotus blossom & tall trumpet-form body embossed w/cattails & leaves, marked w/full circle kiln ink stamp logo **1,200-1,300**

Aurelian (1898-1910)
Similar to Louwelsa line but with brighter colors and a glossy glaze. Features bright yellow/orange brush-applied background along with brown and yellow transparent glaze.

Lamp, oil, bell-shaped body on small knob feet, decorated w/two medallions of ivory roses, by C. Mitchell, complete w/oil font, artist-signed & stamped "K116," 10 1/2 x 11"... **600-650**

Mug, tapering cylindrical body w/C-form handle, cherry decoration by Charles Chilcote, ca. 1900, impressed w/circular "Aurelian Weller" logo & incised shape

number "435" w/"Chil" painted on side near bottom of handle, 6 1/8" h.............. **275-300**

Aurelian Umbrella Stand

Umbrella stand, decorated w/bright yellow irises, late 19th c., unmarked, removable galvanized sheet metal insert, 23 7/8" h. (ILLUS.)... **1,650-1,750**

Baldin (about 1915-20)
Rustic designs with relief-molded apples and leaves on branches wrapped around each piece.

Baldin Vase

Vase, 5 1/2" h., spherical body tapering to slightly flared rim, impressed "Weller" in large block letters (ILLUS.)..................... **275-325**

Unmarked Baldin Vase

Vase, 10 5/8" h., bulbous base w/slightly tapering wide cylindrical neck & flat rim, un-
marked (ILLUS.)................................. **300 t0 350**

Blue & Decorated Hudson (1919)
*Handpainted lifelike sprays of fruit blossoms and
flowers in shades of pink and blue on a rich dark blue
ground.*

Vase, 9 1/8" h., ovoid body w/rolled rim,
decorated near top w/bright orange &
yellow flowers painted by Hester Pillsbury, unmarked, artist-initialed among
flowers (4" crack descending from rim). **175-200**

Vase, 10" h., slender cylindrical body flaring
at base & tapering to small flat rim, center
of body decorated w/a band of brightly
colored flowers & impressed "Weller" in
large block letters...................................... **250-275**

Six-sided Blue & Decorated Vase

Vase, 11 7/8" h., hexagonal, decorated
w/yellow & pink nasturtiums, unmarked
(ILLUS.)... **504**

Blue Louwelsa (ca. 1905)
*A high-gloss line shading from medium blue to cobalt
blue with underglaze slip decorations of fruits & florals
and sometimes portraits. Decorated in shades of white,
cobalt and light blue slip. Since few pieces were made,
they are rare and sought after today.*

Vase, 5 3/8" h., pillow form w/nasturtium
decoration, unmarked (1/4" chip off left
edge of rim)... **525-550**

Tall Blue Louwelsa Vase with Berries

Vase, 10 7/8" h., tall, slender ovoid body tapering to a very slender neck w/flared
rim, decorated w/dark & light blue blackberries & vines under a shaded light to
dark blue overall glaze, incised "X 431" &
"A 59," very minor glaze scratch
(ILLUS.)... **1,760**

Chase (late 1920s)
*White relief fox hunt scenes, usually on a deep blue
ground.*

Vase, 7 5/8" h., footed baluster form
w/rolled rim, dark blue ground w/white
hunt scene, incised "Weller Pottery" on
bottom **250-275**

Chase Vase with Silver Overlay

Vase, 8 7/8" h., ovoid form w/flat rim, mottled blue matte ground decorated w/ap-
plied silver overlay hunt scene, marked
"Sterling" & impressed "Weller Pottery" in
script (ILLUS.)..................................... **350 to 400**

Claywood (ca. 1910)
*Etched designs against a light tan ground divided by
dark brown bands. Matte glaze.*

Claywood Jardiniere

Jardiniere, bulbous ovoid body divided into
panels by dark brown bands, the creamy
panels w/floral decoration outlined in
brown, unmarked, 3 1/2" h.
(ILLUS.)... **30-50**

A Variety of Coppertone Items

Claywood Vase

Vase, 8" h., tapering cylindrical body w/compressed base, the sides divided into tall panels by dark brown bands, each panel etched w/a grape cluster on leafy vines in creamy white outlined in brown (ILLUS.) **50-75**

Coppertone (late 1920s)

Various shapes with an overall mottled bright green glaze on a "copper" glaze base. Some pieces with figural frog or fish handles. Models of frogs also included.

Bowl w/original flower holder, 11" d., low form w/flaring sides & down-curved rim, incised "Weller Hand Made" (ILLUS. bottom row, second from right, top of page)...... **173**

Coppertone Center Bowl & Frog

Center bowl & flower frog, shallow form w/flaring sides, embossed w/lily pads & buds, flower frog in the form of a cluster of leaves centered by an upright water lily blossom, bowl 12" d., 3" h., 2 pcs. (ILLUS.).. **650-850**

Console bowl, shallow oblong form w/frog seated near water lily on one end, 11" l. (ILLUS. bottom row, left w/bowl & flower holder) **805**
Flower frog, model of lily pad bloom w/seated frog, 3 7/8" h. (small chip inside edge of one petal) **175-200**
Model of frog, green, tan, brown & black matte glaze, 2 1/2" h. (ILLUS. bottom row, third from left w/bowl & flower holder).. **322**

Rare Weller Coppertone Fish Pitcher

Pitcher, 7 5/8" h., bulbous ovoid body w/arched spout, figural fish handle, marked w/half kiln ink stamp logo, couple of burst bubbles inside mouth (ILLUS.) **1,750-1,800**
Vase, 5 3/4" h., wide tapering cylindrical body w/rolled rim, marked in script "Weller Hand Made" **350-375**
Vase, 6" h., tapering ovoid body w/a wide closed flat rim, overall vivid mottled green over dark brown glaze, unmarked (ILLUS. bottom row, far right, with bowl & flower holder) **633**
Vase, 6" h., wide tapering cylindrical form (ILLUS. top row, far right, with bowl and flower holder) **334**
Vase, 6" h., wide tapering cylindrical form w/molded rim (ILLUS. top row, far left, with bowl and flower holder) **161**
Vase, 6 1/2" h., footed, slender, gently flaring cylindrical body, mottled heavy green over a blackish brown ground, incised

mark (ILLUS. top row, fourth from right,
with bowl & flower holder) 297
Vase, 6 1/2" h., footed tapering cylindrical
form, incised "Weller Hand Made"
(ILLUS. top row, third from right, with
bowl and flower holder) 115

Weller Coppertone Spherical Vase

Vase, 7" h., large spherical form tapering to
a wide flaring neck flanked by heavy D-
form handles, signed (ILLUS.)........................ 374
Vase, 8" h., bulbous ovoid body w/molded
rim, figural frog shoulder handles, ink kiln
mark (short tight line to rim) .... 1,525 -1,550
Vase, 8" h., footed, two-handled spherical
base w/wide flaring rim (ILLUS. top row,
third from left, with bowl and flower hold-
er) 265
Vase, 8 3/8" h., bulbous base w/trumpet-
form neck, scrolled handles from base to
below rim, incised "Weller Hand Made"
on bottom (three small burst bubbles on
back side of vase)................................... 225-250
Vase, 8 1/2" h., footed wide trumpet form
(ILLUS. bottom row, third from right, with
bowl & flower holder)..................................... 403
Vase, 9 1/8" h., round foot & trumpet-
shaped body molded around the scalloped rim w/lily pads & buds, matte olive
green shading to tan, black round stamp 374
Vase, 11" h., footed bulbous base w/wide
cylindrical neck w/slightly flared rim,
large loop handles from shoulder to rim
(ILLUS. top row, second from left, with
bowl & flower holder)..................................... 431
Vase, 11" h., footed bulbous base w/wide
trumpet-form neck, heavy strap handles,
incised "Weller Hand Made" (ILLUS. top
row, second from right, with bowl & flow-
er holder) 575
Vase, 15 1/4" h., footed trumpet-form body
(ILLUS. bottom row, second from left,
with bowl & flower holder) 1,144

Dickensware 2nd Line (early 1900s)
*Various incised "sgraffito" designs, usually with a
matte glaze. Quality of the artwork greatly affects price.*

Ewer, tall, slender, cylindrical body w/flaring
ringed foot, C-form handle, decorated
w/a bust profile portrait of "Chief Hol-
lowhorn Bear," shaded tan to dark green
ground, 16" 750-1,250
Mug, depicts detailed image of deer.......... 175-250
Mug, decorated w/scene of monk drinking
from mug, green ground, 5 1/2" h. 385
Mug, bust portrait of American Indian "Tame
Wolf," artist-signed, 6 1/4" h.................... 625-750

Pitcher, 10 1/2" h., portrait of monk, blue &
white, marked "X" 625-750
Vase, 5 1/4" h., 5 1/4" w., pocket-form, flat-
tened bulbous ovoid sides tapering to a
short flaring rim pinched together at the
center, sgraffito marsh scene w/a duck &
reeds by a lake in shades of brown &
green, die-stamped "Dickensware -
Weller - X352"... 220-250
Vase, 8 7/8" h., ovoid body w/short wide
flaring neck, shows scene of a young
woman wearing blue gown, sitting in a
crescent moon playing a long-necked
mandolin, green & yellow, decorated by
Anthony Dunlavy, impressed "Dickensware - Weller" & "X31" w/"M" incised on
base, artist-initialed (glaze nicks on rim) 385
Vase, 9 1/4" h., slightly expanding cylindrical body w/wide flaring rim, golfing scene
featuring a golfer & caddy, trees & a
fence, brown, gold & blue, marked "Dickensware - Weller" & impressed "X 169,"
"12" & "KVV"... 2,200
Vase, 11 7/8" h., tall, waisted, cylindrical
body w/narrow shoulder & short, flaring
neck, depicts an intricately carved & colorfully painted scene of Colonial life
w/seven people, three horses & two stat-
ues in a densely wooded area, all in 18th
c. costume, brown, green, grey & black
glossy glaze, impressed marks "Dickensware - Weller" & "X 48," "8" & "W" (rim
chip has been professionally repaired)...... 1,540
Vase, 12 3/8" h., slender, waisted cylindrical form w/short cylindrical neck & flaring
rim, decorated w/scene of a nude woman
& an angel w/flowers & flowering trees,
impressed "Dickens Ware Weller" (pro-
fession repair of rim chip) 896
Vase, 12 1/2" h., tall cylindrical body w/a
narrow shoulder to the short rolled rim,
continuous landscape scene of white
mounted knights in deep woods, blue sky
above, glossy glaze 3,100-3,750
Vase, 14" h., tall, slender, ovoid body
w/short, narrow, flared neck, decorated
w/an outdoor scene showing a young
mother walking through a wooded area
w/her two daughters, all dressed in white,
shaded brown ground w/green trees in
background, artist-initialed, small chip on
rim, die-stamped "Dickensware - Weller
X 290 0" 990
Vase, 16" h., etched scene w/hunting
dogs.. 1,400-2,500

Two Scenic Dickensware Vases

Vase, 17" h., slender cylindrical form w/incised Venetian scene by C.A. Dusenbery, impressed mark (ILLUS. right) **1,150**

Vase, 17 7/8" h., very tall, slender cylindrical body w/a narrow rounded shoulder to the short rolled neck, decorated w/a standing monk tasting wine, in browns & yellow against a shaded brown to gold ground, glossy glaze, decorated by Mary Gellier, ca. 1900, marked & artist-signed **1,650**

Vase, 20" h., baluster form w/wide cylindrical neck w/flared rim, decorated w/incised & painted scene of marching soldiers, impressed mark, restoration (ILLUS. left) **575**

Eocean and Eocean Rose (1898-1925)

Early art line with various handpainted flowers on shaded grounds, usually with a clear glossy glaze. Quality of artwork varies greatly.

Eocean Mug

Mug, tapering cylindrical body w/C-form handle, wild rose decoration on shaded green ground, 4 7/8" h. (ILLUS.) **125-150**

Vase, 4 7/8" h., pillow form, wild rose decoration on shaded green ground, unmarked (glaze on four stubby feet a bit gritty in the making) **200-225**

Vase, 5 1/8" h., squared shape, pink, white & blue flowers on slate blue ground, ca. 1910 .... **165**

Vase, 5 1/8" h., squatty bulbous body on a narrow footring, tapering to a cylindrical neck w/rolled rim, decorated around the shoulder w/large maroon & grey Virginia creeper leaves & berries, against a grey/green to pale green ground, decorated by Claude Leffler, incised "Eocean Rose Weller" & stamped "9056," artist-initialed (professionally repaired small glaze nicks on rim & foot) **303**

Vase, bud, 5 1/2" h., slip-painted florals on shaded pale blue to grey ground **75**

Vase, 5 3/4" h., corseted form w/pink nasturtium on shaded grey ground, decorated by Mary Pierce, incised "Eocean-Weller 890 6" & artist-signed "MP" **300-325**

Vase, 6" h., 5" d., swelled cylindrical body w/a wide flat shoulder to the short cylindrical neck, decorated w/wild roses in ivory & red on shaded grey ground, incised "Eocean-Rose Weller 9061" **350-400**

Vase, 6" h., 5" d., swelled cylindrical body w/a wide flat shoulder to the short cylindrical neck, decorated w/dogwood branches in white & purple against a shaded dark blue to ivory ground, glossy glaze, marked, Eocean Rose **330**

Vase, 6 1/2" h., 3" d., simple cylindrical body, decorated w/a large polychrome stork standing on one leg against a shaded dark grey to white ground, incised "Eocean - Weller" (crazed).................. **900-1,100**

Vase, bud, 6 5/8" h., decorated w/daisies, impressed "Weller" in large block letters **200-225**

Vase, 8" h., 2 1/2" d., slender cylindrical body w/a narrow round shoulder & short rolled neck, decorated w/purple & green lily-of-the-valley against a shaded black to light green ground, die-stamped circle mark **400-425**

Vase, 8 1/2" h., slender ovoid body decorated w/Virginia creeper against a shaded dark green to cream ground, by William Stemm, incised "Eocean Weller," artist-initialed "F." on side below leaves **650-700**

Vase, 10 3/8" h., gently tapering cylindrical body w/a swelled shoulder tapering to a short cylindrical rim, decorated w/pink wild roses on shaded green glossy ground, decorated by Levi J. Burgess, artist-signed, stamped "Weller" & incised "Eocean," "X" & "50" **935**

Vase, 10 1/2" h., squared shape w/pink thistle decoration on dark green shaded to cream ground, incised "Eocean Rose Weller" & "S" on bottom & impressed "447" & "4" (pinhead glaze nick on top of rim)... **425-450**

Vase, 10 5/8" h., wide slightly tapering cylindrical body w/a wide shoulder to the compressed incurved short neck, decorated w/a band of swimming green fish against a shaded dark green to cream ground, signed, ca. 1905, Eocean Rose **2,500-2,800**

Eocean Vase with Iris Decoration

Vase, 11" h., bulbous ovoid form, painted iris decoration on shaded tan & brown ground, impressed mark, artist-signed (ILLUS.).. **3,163**

Vase, 12 3/4" h., tall ovoid form w/wide rolled rim, decorated w/red & white tulips & green leaves on glossy white ground, incised "Eocean - Weller," "F" & impressed "X 467," artist-signed **1,320**

Vase, 12 3/4" h., 4 3/4" d., slender tapering body w/six open handles rising from narrow shoulder to flared rim, decorated w/large green & violet leaves against a shaded pale pink & dark green ground **900-1,400**

Vase, 12 7/8" h., slender ovoid body w/wide flat mouth, wisteria decoration on shaded brown to yellow ground, glossy glaze, marked & incised "X," artist-initialed (tight 2" hairline from rim) **468**

Vase, 14 1/8" h., tall cylindrical body w/the narrow flat shoulder tapering to a short rolled neck, decorated w/two finely detailed fish swimming among lily pads & flowers, dark greyish green to pale green ground, decorated by Eugene Roberts, incised "Eocean Rose Weller" & impressed with shape number 579, artist-signed **3,850**

Rare Large Weller Eocean Vase

Vase, 24" h., 12" d., large ovoid body tapering to a short widely flaring neck, decorated w/large white tea roses & pale green leafy stems on a dark blue shaded to creamy white ground, by Mae Timberlake, incised mark & artist-signed, couple of minor flakes on base (ILLUS.) **7,313**

Vase, bulbous ovoid tapering to rolled rim, decorated a/portrait of a spaniel w/brown eyes, shaded grey ground, incised "Eocean Weller S" & impressed "2" **1,550-1,575**

Ethel (about 1915)

Circle with profile of Ethel Weller sniffing a rose. Cream color. Matte finish.

Vase, 6 1/4" h., footed fan shape w/reticulated rim & applied ring handles, floral decoration **110**

Vase, 11 1/4" h., disc foot w/tapering cylindrical body, applied ring handles & reticulated rim w/profile of young woman on each side, incised "Weller" **330**

Etna (1906)

Colors similar to Early Eocean line, but designs are molded in low relief and colored.

Lemonade set: 14" h. tankard pitcher & two cylindrical mugs; each w/an angled handle decorated w/a large cluster of deep reddish purple grapes & green leaves at the top against a shaded grey to pink ground, signed, 3 pcs. (hairline in one mug)... **400-450**

Etna Vase

Vase, 5" h., footed squatty bulbous body tapering to wide cylindrical neck w/molded rim, decorated w/purple & mauve nasturtiums, impressed "Etna" on bottom & "Weller" on side & bottom (ILLUS.) **168**

Vase, 6 1/2" h., footed angular bulbous body tapering to a wide cylindrical neck w/slightly flaring rim, slip-painted floral design.. **125**

Vase, 7" h., cylindrical, decorated w/yellow dandelions on grey ground **165**

Vase, 8 3/8" h., gently flaring cylindrical body tapering to a short wide neck, decorated w/embossed flowers in pink & yellow on a shaded grey to pink ground **220**

Vase, 8 1/2" h., cylindrical body tapering to short slightly flared rim, decorated w/embossed pink thistles & green leaves on grey shaded to cream ground, marked "Weller" on side & on bottom in small block letters **248**

Vase, 10 1/2" h., tapering cylindrical body w/flat rim, dark charcoal shaded to grey, decorated at the neck & base w/lavender nasturtium blooms, base impressed "Weller" & "Etna," body incised "Weller" in body near lower blooms (moderate crazing) **190**

Vase, 10 7/8" h., tall, gently flaring cylindrical body w/flat shoulder tapering to a short rolled rim, embossed pink carnation decoration on dark blue shaded to pink ground **220**

Vase, 11" h., tall ovoid body w/bulbous short neck w/closed rim flanked by short twisted strap handles, low-relief floral bouquet in rosy red & pale green leafy stems against a shaded grey ground........................ **300**

Vase, 13 3/8" h., gently swelled cylindrical body tapering to a short cylindrical neck, decorated w/embossed pink roses, grey to ivory ground **550**

Vase, 15" h., baluster-form body w/shoulder tapering to closed mouth, decorated w/embossed grape vines in blues & reds on a shaded green to grey ground, stamped "Weller" **605**

Flemish (mid-teens to 1928)

Clusters of pink roses and green leaves, often against a molded light brown basketweave ground. Some pieces molded with fruit or small figural birds. Matte glaze.

Basket, hanging-type w/chains, 7" h. **125**
Jardiniere, birds on wire scene, 7 1/2" h. **250**
Jardiniere, wide, slightly swelled cylindrical body, pink floral decoration on cream ground, 8 1/2" h. **175**
Jardiniere, decorated w/four lion heads & garlands, 13" d., 10" h. **250**
Pedestal base, decorated w/bright blue cockatoo, 21 5/8" h. (5 1/2" portion of upper rim chipped off & reglued) **336**
Planter, figural log, 4 1/2" h. **35**
Tub, basket-shaped w/rim handles, rose swag on front, 8 1/2" d., 5 1/2" h. **165**

Flemish Cylindrical Vase

Vase, 8 1/2" h., footed cylindrical body w/embossed rose tied w/yellow bow, impressed "Weller" in large block letters (ILLUS.) **193**

Flemish Ovoid Vase

Vase, 12 1/4" h., ovoid form w/flaring cylindrical neck, decorated w/red flowers on green vines, brown matte glaze, minor chip, impressed mark (ILLUS.) **748**

Glendale (early to late 1920s)

Various relief-molded birds in their natural habitats, lifelike coloring. ....

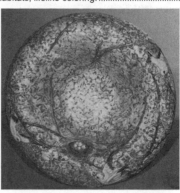

Glendale Bowl

Console bowl w/flower frog, round w/wide flared rim, decorated w/nesting birds w/eggs, 15 1/2" d. bowl marked "Weller" in black slip, frog w/impressed "Weller" in large block letters (ILLUS. of bowl) **770**
Vase, 6" h., cylindrical, large standing marsh bird **400**
Vase, 6 1/2" h., ovoid body w/slightly tapering neck & a flat rim, decorated w/outdoor scene of a bird in flight **365**
Vase, 7" h., baluster-form body w/gently flaring rim, decorated w/a brown bird standing beside its ground nest w/eggs, green grass & white & yellow daisies under a blue sky in background **450**
Vase, double-bud, 7" h., gate-form, tree trunk-form vases flank a panel embossed w/a bird & nest w/four eggs, original label **326**

Glendale Vase

Vase, 11 3/8" h., bulbous base tapering to cylindrical neck & flat rim, decorated w/long-legged plover guarding a nest of speckled eggs surrounded by cattails & a patch of wild berries in red & deep blue, ink stamped "Weller Ware" (ILLUS.) **1,568**

Vase, 11 7/8" h., baluster form tapering to flaring rim, decorated scene of a goldfinch on a nest, yellow & orange butterflies, thistles & daisies, ink stamped "Weller Ware," no artist signature **1,904**

Hudson (1917-34)

Underglaze slip-painted decoration, "parchment-vellum" transparent glaze.

Vase, 6 7/8" h., ovoid body w/wide flat rim, blue pansy decoration by Edith Hood, pink shaded to green ground, marked w/full kiln "Weller Pottery" ink stamp logo (tight line at rim) **225-250**

Vase, 7" h., swelled cylindrical body w/a flaring base & widely flaring rim, decorated around the top w/a pink, yellow & blue blossom against a group of pale green leaves, all against a shaded white to pale green ground, decorated by Sara Timberlake, ca. 1920, marked **250-275**

Vase, 7" h., 3 1/2" d., ovoid, decorated w/white & pink dogwood blossoms against a blue shading to cream to pink ground, artist-signed **300-350**

Vase, 7 1/2" h., octagonal ovoid body w/flat rim, pastel orange & yellow wild rose decoration around top, grey shading to light green ground, faintly impressed "Weller" in small block letters (some dirty crazing especially on interior) **300-325**

Vase, 7 7/8" h., ovoid body w/flat rim, decorated w/white & yellow wild roses, artist-signed, silver foil half kiln label over a half kiln ink stamp logo **448**

Vase, 8 1/4" h., baluster form w/flaring rim, decorated w/blue flowers & green leaves on green shaded to pink ground, by Naomi Walch, marked w/half kiln ink stamp logo & artist-signed **725-750**

Vase, 8 1/4" h., 3" d., cylindrical, decorated w/large blue & yellow iris on a pale yellow to pale sage green ground, matte glaze, artist-signed **500-525**

Vase, 8 1/4" h., 3 1/2" d., baluster form, decorated w/slip-painted trefoil blossoms in dark & light blue w/green leaves on a blue to cream ground, die-stamped "WELLER".. **350-400**

Vase, 8 5/8" h., decorated w/a Spanish caravel under full sail moving over blue sea w/white-capped waves, two other crafts behind, flying sea gulls accompany the boats, shaded blue to pink ground w/red & yellow designs on sails, decorated by Hester Pillsbury, artist-signed on side, the base marked w/"A" in black slip **4,510**

Vase, 8 5/8" h., ovoid body, top decorated w/wild roses & green leaves on green shaded to pink ground, by Sarah Timberlake, impressed "Weller" in large block letters, artist-initialed **425-450**

Vase, 8 7/8" h., swelled cylindrical body w/a short molded mouth, decorated w/large white jonquils on pale green leafy stems against a green to pale cream ground, stamped "Weller" in block letters............ **450-500**

Hudson Vase with Iris Decoration

Vase, 9 3/8" h., footed cylindrical body w/flat rim, decorated w/blue & yellow irises in very heavy slip by Mae Timberlake, shaded green to yellow ground, professional repair of two cracks at rim, artist-signed (ILLUS.).. **600-650**

Vase, 9 3/8" h., swelled cylindrical shouldered body w/a short rounded neck w/flat rim, decorated around the top half w/large creamy white nasturtium blossoms & green leaves & vines against a shaded blue to pale green ground, decorated by Sarah McLaughlin, ca. 1920, artist-signed & marked............................. **500-550**

Vase, 9 1/2" h., 5" d., swelling cylindrical body w/a wide shoulder tapering to a short wide mouth, decorated around the upper half w/large white & blue morning glories & green leaves against a shaded blue to green ground, decorated by Hester Pillsbury, artist's initials on side, black kiln mark on base **600-650**

Vase, 10 1/4" h., footed bulbous base tapering to cylindrical neck w/flat rim, white dogwood decoration by Hester Pillsbury, grey shading to pink ground, impressed "Weller" in script & artist-initialed **775-800**

Unusual Hudson Bud Vase

Vase, bud, 10 1/4" h., slender waisted cylinder w/flaring base, decorated w/pink & white poppies on trailing stems in stylish

Art Nouveau manner, glossy tan ground w/dark band at rim, impressed "Weller" in large block letters (ILLUS.) **775-800**
Vase, 10 5/8" h., cylindrical body w/short, slightly flared rim, blackberry decoration in pastel colors on light grey shading to yellow ground, impressed "Weller" in small block letters **425-450**

Floral Decorated Hudson Vase

Vase, 12" h., ovoid body tapering to flaring rim, pink & blue floral decoration on a shaded green & blue ground, decorated by Sarah McLaughlin, impressed mark (ILLUS.) **2,530**

Large Hudson Vase with Roses

Vase, 12" h., ovoid body w/cylindrical neck & slightly flaring rim, front decorated w/large rose blossoms w/a bee & roses on the obverse, by Hester Pillsbury, incised mark, minor flake to base (ILLUS.) **2,530**
Vase, 12 1/4" h., bulbous ovoid body tapering to a cylindrical neck w/flaring rim, decorated w/a scene depicting a distant city across a bay, tall bamboo shoots & leaves tower over sea gulls flying toward wood pilings in the bay, impressed "Weller" (a 1/2" drill hole in bottom professionally repaired) **2,200**
Vase, 13 1/2" h., urn form, the wide ovoid body tapering to a short cylindrical neck w/rolled rim, wide strap handles from

neck to shoulder, decorated w/a scenic design of a large peacock resting near a large wrought-iron gate & stone fence in shades of blue, white, yellow, green & black against a mottled blue-green to tan ground, attributed to Mae Timberlake, the base marked w/"A" in black slip **4,500-6,000**

Jap Birdimal (1904)

Stylized Japanese-inspired figural bird or animal designs on various solid colored grounds.

Jap Birdimal Umbrella Stand

Umbrella stand, wide cylindrical form w/narrow shoulder & slightly flaring rim, landscape decoration w/large blue trees, impressed mark, minor chips, 20" h. (ILLUS.) **1,035**
Vase, 4 1/2" h., spherical body on three outswept knob feet, tricorner rounded rim, bluish grey ground decorated w/two white geese in flight **265**

Rare Jap Birdimal Weller Vase

Vase, 12 7/8" h., very tall, slender & slightly waisted cylindrical form w/an angled shoulder tapering to a short wide trumpet neck, decorated w/a full-length geisha girl & stylized trees in slip-trail outline, glossy glaze in shades of olive green, yellow, rust, brown & blue on a black ground, incised "Weller Faience - Rhead," ca. 1904 (ILLUS.) **1,955**

L'Art Nouveau (1903-04)

Various figural and floral-embossed Art Nouveau designs.

L'Art Nouveau Four-sided Vase

Vase, 10 1/4" h., slender four-sided body w/embossed panels of flowers & Art Nouveau woman, impressed "Weller" in small block letters (ILLUS.)................................. **350-375**

Large L'Art Nouveau Vase

Vase, 11 1/4" h., waisted cylindrical body w/four-lobed base & molded florals at top, very minor glaze rubs on one side at bottom, impressed "Weller" in small block letters (ILLUS.).. **450-500**

Louwelsa (1896-1924)

Handpainted underglaze slip decoration on dark brown shading to yellow ground; glossy yellow glaze.

Clock, curvilinear stylized five-point star-shaped case decorated w/chrysanthemum blossoms in orange & yellow on standard glaze brown ground, artist-initialed "ER" on side, round white enamel clock face w/black Roman numerals, impressed "Louwelsa Weller," early 20th c., 10" h. (minor foot chip)............................ **850-900**

Clock, mantel-type, scalloped case w/orange nasturtiums, Gilbert clock works, stamped "Louwelsa Weller 706," 4 x 10 1/2 x 12 1/2" (colored-in chip to side & a few glaze flakes & chip to base)... **525-550**

Cruet, bulbous body decorated w/palm fronds, by Mary Gillie, impressed "Louwelsa Weller," artist-initialed, 4 3/8" h...... **75-100**

Ewer, squatty bulbous body decorated w/cherry blossoms, impressed "Louwelsa Weller," 6 1/2" h. **175-200**

Jardiniere, wide flaring waisted cylindrical body w/a wide molded rim, decorated w/a large yellow iris among green leaves on a shaded brown & ochre ground, glossy glaze, impressed mark, 9" h. (glaze scratches).................................... **275-300**

Pitcher, 4 1/8" h., tapering cylindrical body w/pinched spout & C-form handle, decorated w/palm fronds, by William F. Hall, impressed "Louwelsa Weller" & "X 215 11" (small rim chips) **83**

Planter, cylindrical tree trunk form w/three small foxes peeking out at side, 4 1/2" h.. **325-350**

Vase, 5" h., pillow form, decorated w/wild roses, impressed "Louwelsa Weller" on bottom (minor scratches) **83**

Unusual Louwelsa Pillow Vase

Vase, 7" h., pillow form, decorated w/scene of a small house at end of a dirt path w/scruffy plants in foreground & cloudy sky in background, impressed "Louwelsa Weller 41 0" (ILLUS.)........................ **1,000-1,200**

Vase, 9" h., tapering cylindrical form w/wild rose decoration, unmarked (very minor scratches & glaze inconsistencies) **200-225**

Vase, 9 1/4" h., bottle-shaped body w/flaring ruffled neck, decorated w/yellow nasturtiums, stamped mark (small bruise & nick to rim)... **303**

Vase, 10 1/2" h., ovoid form w/flaring rim, decorated w/wild roses, incised artist's initials on side (professional repair to rim, area of loose glaze on shoulder) **193**

Vase, 10 1/2" h., wide cylindrical body decorated w/bright red wild roses, possibly by Albert Haubich, impressed on bottom "Louwelsa Weller 602 5" & artist initialed "A.H." on side (glaze scratches) **350-400**

Vase, 18 1/2" h., slightly tapering cylindrical shouldered body w/small flaring neck, decorated w/lifelike red & purple grapes hanging from finely detailed vine, by Frank Ferrell, impressed "Louwelsa Weller" logo & "200" & "55" (professional repair of small base chip) **1,550-1,575**

Marbleized (Bo Marblo, 1915)

Simple shapes with swirled "marbleized" clays, usually in browns and blues.

Two Marbleized Vases

Vase, 11 1/4" h., square, slightly flared base tapering to flat rim, swirled colors of brown, rust, cream & black, very minor glaze nicks on underside of base, impressed "Weller" in small block letters & incised "Weller" directly over impressed mark (ILLUS. right) **110**
Vase, 12 1/2" h., waisted cylindrical body w/swirled colors of tan, brown, maroon, black & grey, 1/4" chip edge of base, impressed "Weller" in small block letters (ILLUS. left) **110**

Muskota (1915 - late 1920s)

Figural pieces with human figures, birds, animals or frogs. Matte glaze.

Centerpiece, disc base w/two figural baby chicks on grassy mound, unmarked, 5" h. (repair to beaks of both birds)............... **150-175**
Flower frog, Fishing Boy, boy seated on rockwork w/original "Weller Muskota Ware" paper label, 6 7/8" h. **325-350**

Muskota Figural Garden Ornament

Garden ornament, Fishing Boy, boy standing on round base, brown pants w/one leg rolled up to knee, light blue shirt & black hat, marked w/half-kiln ink stamp

logo, two unobtrusive glazed over chips on base, 20 5/8" h. ((ILLUS.)............ **6,225-6,500**

Perfecto (early 1900s)

Predominantly sea green, blending into a delicate pink matte finish, unglazed painted decoration.

Vase, 7 5/8" h., slender ovoid body w/flat rim, embossed scene of nude sitting on a rock, sea gulls overhead, impressed "Weller" in large block letters & signed "Timberlake" on side near base (tight short line at rim) **2,750**

Bird-decorated Perfecto Vase

Vase, 9 1/2" h., footed cylindrical body tapering to short, wide rim, rare carved scene depicting small brown bird perched in a tree of ripe cherries, the background cut back to resemble weathered wood, by Sarah Reid McLaughlin, impressed "Weller" in large block letters & signed "SMcL" on side in black slip (ILLUS.).. **3,300**

Roma (1912-late '20s)

Cream-colored ground decorated with embossed floral swags, bands or fruit clusters...
Vase, 6 7/8" h., footed tapering cylinder w/molded ring rim, floral decoration, impressed "Weller" in large block letters........ **50-75**

Roma Vase

Vase, 12 3/8" h., tapering cylindrical body w/four panels of stylized roses, unmarked (ILLUS.)...................................... **250-275**

Wall pocket, conical, incised vertical lines & decorated w/roses & grape cluster near top, green leaves w/yellow center at base, cream ground, marked "28" in blue slip on back, 8 1/4" h. (very minor staining from use & small bruise on one horizontal band at mid body)........................ **150-175**

Sicardo (1902-07)

Various shapes with iridescent glaze of metallic shadings in greens, blues, crimson, purple or coppertone decorated with vines, flowers, stars or freeform geometric lines.

Jardiniere, very wide, bulbous body raised on short arcaded feet, the sides boldly embossed w/large Moorish arabesques, tapering to a wide, short, flaring, scalloped neck, iridescent purple, gold & green glaze, painted "Weller SICARD" on the side, 14 1/2" d., 12 1/2" h. **1,500-2,000**

Vase, 3 1/4" h., 5 3/4" d., footed wide & low cushion-form body centered by a short, widely flaring trefoil neck, bright satiny decoration of gold arabesques against a lustred green & burgundy ground, signed on the side **700-800**

Vase, 5" h., baluster form, a multicolored iridescent glaze decorated w/mistletoe branches, signed **400-450**

Vase, 5 1/2" h., waisted cylindrical body w/swelled shoulder tapering to small, flat rim, cloud-like decoration, iridescent blue, green & burgundy glaze, unmarked.. **600-650**

Vase, 6 1/2" h., 4 1/4" d., tapering ovoid body w/a bulbous compressed & closed neck flanked by small loop handles, iridescent gold flowers on a deep purple ground, unmarked **850-1,100**

Vase, 7" h., tall, tri-lobed, upright, undulating body, floral designs on sides, covered in iridescent glaze in shades of green & gold **1,150-1,300**

Vase, 8 1/2" h., 5 3/4" d., ovoid gourd form w/wide shoulder & bulbed tapering neck, decorated w/swirling poppies & leaves w/a lustrous gold, blue, green & purple glaze, signed **2,925**

Vase, 8 5/8" h., wide, bulbous, ovoid body tapering sharply to a molded, flat mouth, incurved loop handles on the sides, decorated w/several snails amid leafy vegetation, base cut "36," signed "Weller Sicard," ca. 1905 (glaze flaw from bottom up side 1/2").. **950-1,100**

Vase, 9" h., wide, ovoid, shouldered body tapering to a short, rounded neck w/flat rim, decorated w/flowing chrysanthemums & buds against a background of scattered dots, ca. 1904 .... **2,200-2,600**

Vase, 9 1/4" h., expanding cylinder w/rounded shoulders & rolled rim, decorated w/wild violets, iridescent gold, burgundy & green glaze, signed "Weller Sicard" & impressed "6" **925-950**

Tall Sicardo Vase

Vase, 13" h., 5 3/4" d., bulbous top w/closed small mouth above tapering cylindrical sides, embossed w/large, tall irises, rich burgundy & gold lustre glaze, unmarked (ILLUS.)... **7,700-8,500**

Vase, 14 1/2" h., 7" d., tall ovoid form w/a rounded shoulder centering a short rolled neck, decorated overall w/poppies & vining leaves in celadon & gold on a purple iridescent ground, marked (restored drill hole in base).. **2,925**

Vase, 19 1/2" h., 13" d., Art Nouveau style, ovoid body on scroll-molded feet, the sides tapering to a bulbous, pierced rim molded w/whiplash swirls above large pendent blossoms above the relief-molded figures of two swirling Art Nouveau maidens flanked by long scrolls, the body flanked by large, long, pierced scrolling handles continuing down to the scrolled feet, gold, green, blue & purple iridescent glaze, signed "Weller - Sicard" **7,700-9,500**

Vase, floor-type, 21 3/4" h., wide ovoid body w/a molded mouth, decorated w/large Art Nouveau stylized poppies against a streaked ground, ca. 1905, signed **12,100**

Silvertone (1928)

Various flowers, fruits or butterflies molded on a pale purple-blue matte pebbled ground.

Silvertone Vase

Vase, 6" h., footed squatty, bulbous body w/wide flaring rim, decorated w/embossed pink roses & green leaves against a purple ground, ink mark (ILLUS.).. **325-350**

Woodcraft (1917)

Rustic designs simulating the appearance of stumps, logs and tree trunks. Some pieces are adorned with owls, squirrels, dogs and other animals. Matte finish.

Bowl, 4 1/2" h., shallow bulbous form w/oak leaves & acorns around the rim & figural squirrel seated on rim eating a nut, unmarked (repair to oak leaves on rim opposite squirrel).. **175-200**

Bowl, 5 7/8" d., 2 7/8" h., footed round body w/flared sides & scalloped rim, decorated w/embossed squirrels & trees, unmarked... **200-225**

Bowl, 6 1/4" d., 3" h., footed, deep, gently flaring form w/scalloped rim, relief-molded squirrel decoration, marked in black slip "29".. **101**

Candlestick, double, modeled as an owl perched at the top of an apple tree between candle nozzles, 8" w., 13 1/2" h. **325-350**

Flower frog, figural lobster........................... **120-170**

Woodcraft Jardiniere

Jardiniere, log form w/woodpecker on side, impressed "Weller" in large block letters on bottom, short tight line at rim, 6" h. (ILLUS.)... **350-400**

Lawn ornament, figural, model of a large squirrel seated & holding an acorn, mottled brown & green, stamped "WELLER POTTERY," 11 1/2" w., 11 3/4" h. (restoration to ears, tight hairline in tail).... **2,000-2,500**

Planter, log form w/three embossed foxes on front, crossed branch handles across top, impressed "Weller" in large block letters, 5 3/4" h. **225-250**

Planter, log form w/molded leaf & narrow strap handle at top center, 11" l., 4 1/4" h... **75-100**

Vase, 12" h., smooth tree trunk form w/molded leafy branch around rim & down sides w/hanging purple plums **175-225**

Vase, bud, 10 1/4" h., cylindrical tree trunk form, hollow branch opening in front, flared base & molded apples, branches & leaves, impressed "Weller" in large block letters.. **125-150**

Vase, 13" h., waisted cylindrical tree trunk form w/relief-molded branch, apple & leaves down the front.............................. **250-300**

Wall hanging, model of a large climbing squirrel, matte brown & green glaze, black ink kiln mark, 4 3/4" w., 13 1/2" h... **1,200-1,500**

Woodcraft Squirrel Wall Pocket

Wall pocket, conical w/applied figural squirrel, 9 1/2" h. (ILLUS.) **316**

Wall pocket, relief-molded log w/flowers & berries, marked "Weller" in large block letters on back, 9" h. (minor glaze flakes).. **200-225**

Zona (about 1920)

Red apples and green leaves on brown branches, all on a cream-colored ground; some pieces with molded florals or birds with various glazes. A line of children's dishes was also produced featuring hand-painted or molded animals. This is referred to as the "Zona Baby Line."

Plate, 8 7/8" d., Apple patt., pairs of red apples & green leaves around the border on brown branches against the ivory ground.. **40-50**

Umbrella stand, tapering cylindrical body w/embossed figures of women holding flower garlands, unmarked, 10 " d., 20" h. (three small chips to base & some glaze misses & glazed over chips)............. **1,540**

Wheatley Pottery

Wheatley Marks

Thomas J. Wheatley was one of the original founders of the art pottery movement in Cincinnati, Ohio, in the early 1880s. In 1879 the Cincinnati Art Pottery was formed, and after some legal problems it operated under the name T.J. Wheatley & Company. Its production featured Limoges-style handpainted decorations, and most pieces were carefully marked and often dated.

In 1882 Wheatley disassociated himself from the Cincinnati Art Pottery and opened another pottery, which was destroyed by fire in 1884. Around 1900 Wheatley finally resumed making art pottery in Cincinnati, and in

1903 he founded the Wheatley Pottery Company with a new partner, Isaac Kahn.

The new pottery from this company featured colored matte glazes over relief work designs; green, yellow and blue were the most often used colors. There were imitations of the well-known Grueby Pottery wares as well as artware, garden pottery and architectural pieces. Artwork was apparently not made much after 1907. This plant was destroyed by fire in 1910 but was rebuilt and run by Wheatley until his death in 1917. Wheatley artware was generally unmarked except for a paper label.

Bowl, 6" d., 2 1/2" h., low, upright, corseted sides w/a wide incurved rim, embossed around the sides w/a band of short, upright, pointed, wide leaves, thick matte green glaze, illegible mark **$165**

Teco-style Wheatley Jardiniere

Jardiniere, wide, thick, ovoid body w/a thick squared rim band joining four heavy squared buttresses down the sides, feathered matte green glaze, in the style of Teco, small chip on edge of foot, 9" d., 7" h. (ILLUS.)..................................... **920**

Lamp base, thick, slightly tapering cylindrical body w/a wide squared rim band issuing four thick squared buttresses down the side, a copper tube running through the lower buttresses, fine feathered matte green glaze, unmarked, 8 1/2" d., 11" h. (ILLUS., top next column)................... **575**

Wheatley Lamp with Buttresses

Lamp base, wide, tapering double gourd-form body w/four heavy squared buttress handles from the top rim to the base, leathery matte green glaze, w/original oil font insert, several burst bubbles, incised "WP - 672," 10 1/2" d., 11 1/2" h. (ILLUS. back left, bottom of page) **2,813**

Lamp base, wide, round flaring base tapering to a slender baluster-form standard, embossed oblong leaves around the foot w/the stems continuing up the standard, fine leathery matte green glaze, unmarked, 10" d., 16 1/4" h. **1,575**

Vase, 5 1/2" h., 7" d., wide, bulbous form w/a wide rounded shoulder centered by a wide, flat molded mouth, deeply embossed w/a band of wide ribbed upright leaves alternating w/small buds, thick & frothy matte green glaze, incised "W-685"................... **1,320**

Vase, 6" h., 5" d., wide ovoid body tapering slightly to a wide, flat mouth, embossed w/large upright arrowhead leaves around the sides, matte green glaze, incised "WP," several burst bubbles (ILLUS. front left with lamp base)... **788**

Wheatley Lamp Base and Vases

Large & Small Wheatley Vases

Vase, 6 3/4" h., 5" d., ovoid shouldered form w/a short, wide neck & flat rim, molded w/a continuous vertical band of wide tapering ribbed leaves, mottled matte green glaze, several clay pimples, mark partially obscured (ILLUS. center) **956**

Vase, 7 1/4" h., 7 1/4" d., squatty bulbous body molded around the lower half w/a band of overlapping rounded, pointed leaves, the sides tapering to a cylindrical neck w/narrow molded rings, frothy light green & amber glaze, signed "WP" (several burst glaze bubbles) **900**

Vase, 7 1/4" h., 9" d., a deep, thick rounded form w/a thick squared flat rim band issuing four heavy squared buttresses down the sides, flower dead-matte green glaze, marked "61" (ILLUS. front right with lamp base) **1,800**

Wheatley Vase with Upright Leaves

Vase, 8 1/2" h., slightly ovoid body tapering to a wide flat mouth, the sides molded w/alternating upright pointed & rounded leaves, matte green glaze, several small chips on leaf edges (ILLUS.) **978**

Wheatley Vase with Tendril Handles

Vase, 10 1/4" h., 5" d., footed baluster-form body w/the shoulder issuing four long scrolled tendril-like handles to the rim, matte green glaze, marked (ILLUS.) **1,035**

Wheatley Vase with Buttress Feet

Vase, 10 1/2" h., four heavy square buttress feet tapering up the wide, slightly tapering cylindrical sides, wide molded mouth, overall matte green glaze, illegible mark, several small glaze chips on feet (ILLUS.) **1,438**

Wheatley Vase with Incised Design

Vase, 11 1/2" h., slightly swelled cylindrical form w/a wide bulbed ring around the middle, wide flat rim, mottled matte green glaze w/incised geometric design, unmarked (ILLUS.).. **978**

Vase, 11 1/2" h., 9 1/4" d., small rectangular feet supporting the wide, tapering cylindrical body w/a wide, thick molded rim w/four projecting blocks above buttresses, pulled matte green glaze, base pierced w/five drainage holes in the making, signed, some minor glaze flecks, chips to feet **2,070**

Vase, 12" h., 7 1/2" d., large, slightly tapering cylindrical form w/a thick rolled rim above a recessed neck band w/four small buttress handles, embossed around the sides w/large, rounded veined leaves alternating w/buds on the rim, curdled medium matte green glaze, marked "WP - C13," couple of burst bubbles (ILLUS. back right with lamp base) **2,700**

Vase, 12 1/2" h., 6" d., simple ovoid body tapering to a short cylindrical neck, the sides molded w/tall arrowroot leaves, medium matte green glaze, mark obscured (several clay pimples & burst bubbles) **1,800**

Wheatley Grueby-style Vase

Vase, 12 1/2" h., 9" d., wide baluster form w/wide cushion neck, in the style of Grueby's Kendrick vase, molded around the sides & neck w/wide leaves, fine frothy matte light brown glaze, small chip to edge of neck, remnants of paint (ILLUS.)... **3,450**

"Kendrick" Vase

Vase, 13" h., 9" d., large ovoid body w/a wide, squatty bulbed neck w/incurved rim, molded around the sides w/wide, tapering ribbed leaves w/matching shorter leaves around the neck, leathery green matte glaze, two small chips on side decoration, marked, after a model by G.P. Kendrick (ILLUS.)... **3,938**

Teco-form Wheatley Vase

Vase, 14 1/4" h., 8" d., based on a Teco form, a bulbous bottom tapering slightly to wide cylindrical body w/a four-scallop ring issuing four vine-like handles down the sides, frothy matte green glaze, incised "WP - 615" (ILLUS.)........................... **2,875**

Vase, 14 1/4" h., 8" d., footed bulbous base narrowing slightly to a tall, wide cylindrical neck flanked by four arched & webbed handles from the rim to the shoulder, leathery matte green glaze, incised "WP" (several burst bubbles, few glaze chips at rim, grinding chips to base)... **3,150**

Large Wheatley Vase with Cubes

Vase, 14 1/2" h., 9 1/4" h., footed, tapering, slightly ovoid body molded w/tall ribbed & pointed leaves up the sides alternating w/shorter leaves topped by projecting blocks embossed on the front w/small swastikas, frothy matte green glaze, no visible mark, several burst bubbles, touchups to two corners of cubes & tip of one leaf (ILLUS.) **1,610**

Vase, 18 1/2" h., 10 1/2" d., tall paneled
ovoid form w/a short rolled neck, each
panel molded w/a tall serrated & veined
leaf alternating w/a stem topped by a
three-petal blossom, leathery matte
green glaze, two glaze chips on ribs, incised "WP" (ILLUS. right with small vase).. **3,938**
Vase, 20" h., 10" d., the tall, swelled cylindrical body tapering to a slightly bulbed cylindrical neck flanked by pointed tall buttress handles down the side, each w/a
half-round cut-out, the body molded
w/tall ribbed & pointed leaves alternating
w/stylized blossom buds around the
neck, dark leathery matte green glaze,
mark obscured, long grinding chip on
base (ILLUS. left with small vase) **4,500**
Wall pocket, half-round body composed of
three wide, tapering leaf-form panels
curled in at the top & alternating w/buds,
a low arched backplate w/hanging hole,
curdled medium matte green glaze, un-
marked, 9 1/4" w., 8" h...................................... **675**

Willow Wares

*This pseudo-Chinese pattern has been used by
numerous firms throughout the years. The original
design is attributed to Thomas Minton about 1780, and
Thomas Turner is believed to have first produced the
ware during his tenure at the Caughley works. The blue
underglaze transfer print pattern has never been out of
production since that time. An Oriental landscape incorporating a bridge, pagoda, trees, figures and birds sup-
posedly tells the story of lovers fleeing a cruel father
who wished to prevent their marriage. The gods, having
pity on them, changed them into birds, enabling them to
fly away and seek their happiness together.*

Blue

Ashtray, figural whale, ca. 1960, Japan **$50-55**
Ashtray, unmarked, American **15**
Bank, figural, stacked pigs, ca. 1960, Ja-
pan, 7" h... **50-55**
Batter jug, frosted, Hazel Atlas Glass, 9" h. **100-125**
Batter jug, Moriyama, Japan, 9 1/2" h. **125-150**
Bell, modern, Enesco, Japan.............................. **15**
Bone dish, ca. 1890, unmarked, England........ **40-50**

Blue Willow Bone Dish

Bone dish, Buffalo Pottery, 6 1/2" l. (ILLUS.).. **75-80**
Bowl, 12 1/4" d., serving-type w/beaded rim
(small flake on table ring)................................... **50**
Bowl, berry, Allertons, England **12-15**
Bowl, berry, Japan **8**
Bowl, berry, milk glass, Hazel Atlas..................... **15**
Bowl, cereal, Royal China Co.............................. **11**
Bowl, individual, 5 1/4" oval, J. Maddock............ **20**
Bowl, soup, 8" d., Japan..................................... **18-20**

Bowl, soup w/flanged rim, 8 1/4" d., Royal
China Co.. **10**
Bowl, 6 1/2 x 8 1/4", Ridgways, England........ **50-55**
Bowl, salad, 10" d., Japan.................................. **75**
Bowls, 8", 9 1/4" & 10 1/2" l., rectangular,
stacking-type, Ridgways, set of 3 .... **325**
Butter dish, cov., Ridgways, England.......... **175-185**
Butter dish, in wood holder, 6" d. **50-75**
Butter dish, cov., for stick, Japan, rectangu-
lar, 7" l.. **60-70**
Butter dish, cov., 8" d., England......................... **100**
Butter dish, drain & cover, Ridgways,
3 pcs.. **225**
Butter pat, Buffalo Pottery **25**
Butter pat, Wood & Sons..................................... **25**
Cake plate, Green & Co., 8" sq........................ **40-45**
Canister, cov., round, tin, 5 3/4" h. **20-25**

Blue Willow Coffee Canister

Canister, labeled "Coffee," marked "Willow,"
Australia, ca. 1920s, 5 3/4" h. (ILLUS.) **45-50**
Canister set: cov., "Coffee," "Flour," "Sugar,"
"Tea," barrel-shaped, ca. 1960s, Japan,
the set.. **350-400**
Chamber pot, Wedgwood, 9" d. **175-200**
Charger, 11 3/4" d., Moriyama, Made in Ja-
pan.. **75-95**
Charger, 12" d., Buffalo Pottery **75-95**
Cheese dish, cov., rectangular, unmarked,
England **175**

Blue Willow Cheese Stand

Cheese stand, J. Meir & Sons, England,
8 1/2" d. (ILLUS.)...................................... **195-225**
Condiment cruet set: cov. oil & vinegar &
mustard cruet, salt & pepper; carousel-
type base w/wooden handle, Japan,
7 1/2" h., the set.. **175-200**

Blue Willow Cracker Jar

Cracker jar, cov., silver lid & handle, Minton,
   England, 5" h. (ILLUS.).................................... **175**
Creamer, Allerton, England.................................. **60**

Blue Willow Cow-shaped Creamer

Creamer, cow-shaped, W. Kent, England,
   1920s-50s (ILLUS.) **300-400**
Creamer, individual, Shenango China
   Co.. **25-30**
Creamer, John Steventon **40**

Blue Willow Figural Cow Creamer

Creamer w/original stopper, figural cow
   standing on oval base, mouth forms
   spout & tail forms handle, ca. 1850, unmarked, England, 7" l., 5" h.
   (ILLUS.)... **700-800**

Cruets w/original stoppers, oil & vinegar, Ja-
   pan, 6" h., the set **65**
Cup & saucer, Booth... **40-45**
Cup & saucer, Buffalo Pottery **40-45**
Cup & saucer, child's, ca. 1900, unmarked,
   England.. **50**
Cup & saucer, demitasse, Copeland, En-
   gland... **40**
Cup & saucer, "For Auld Lang Syne," W. Ad-
   ams, England, oversized........................ **100-125**
Cup & saucer, Japan **10-15**
Drainer, butter, ca. 1890, England, 6" sq. **75**
Egg cup, Booths, England, 4" h. **45-50**
Egg cup, Japan, 4" h.. **20-25**
Egg cup, Allerton, England, 4 1/2" h. **40-45**
Ginger jar, cov., Japan, 5" h. **30**
Ginger jar, cov., Mason's, 9" h. **60-75**
Gravy boat, Buffalo Pottery............................. **75-85**

Blue Willow Gravy Boat

Gravy boat, ca. 1890, unmarked, England,
   7" l. (ILLUS.)... **60-65**
Gravy boat w/attached underplate, double-
   spouted, Ridgways, England.................... **75-85**
Hot pot, electric, Japan, 6" h................................. **75**
Invalid feeder, ca. 1860, unmarked, En-
   gland.. **175-200**
Knife rest, ca. 1860, unmarked, England **85-95**
Ladle, pattern in bowl, unmarked, England,
   6" l... **125-135**
Ladle, pattern in bowl, floral handle, un-
   marked, England, 12" l. **185-200**
Lamp, w/ceramic shade, Japan, 8" h.................. **75**
Lamp, w/reflector plate, Japan, 8" h.............. **85-95**
Lamp, Wedgwood, England, 10" h. **200-225**
Lighter, teacup-shaped, Japan....................... **45-50**
Mug, "Farmer's," Japan, 4" h........................... **18-20**

Blue Willow Mug

Mug, barrel-shaped mold, Granger &
   Worcester, England, ca. 1850, 4 1/4" h.
   (ILLUS.).. **250-275**

Willow Ware Mug

Mug, Maling, England, 4 1/2" h. (ILLUS.) **85-95**
Mustache cup & saucer, Hammersley &
Co. **150-175**
Mustard pot, cov., ca. 1870, unmarked, En-
gland, 3" h. **100-125**
Napkin holder, Japan **50-65**

Blue Willow Nut Dish

Nut dish, scalloped shape, ca. 1900, 7" l.
(ILLUS.) **75-85**
Pastry stand, three-tiered plates, Royal Chi-
na Co., Sebring, Ohio, 13" h. **40-50**
Pepper pot, ca. 1870, England, 4" h. **100-125**

Willow Ware Pepper Shaker

Pepper shaker, "Prestopan," unmarked,
Scotland, 5 1/4" h. (ILLUS.) **250-275**

Blue Willow Pitcher

Pitcher, 5 1/2" h., Ridgway, England
(ILLUS.) **85-95**

Buffalo Pottery Blue Willow Pitcher

Pitcher, cov., 5 1/2" h., Buffalo Pottery
(ILLUS.) **200-225**
Pitcher, 6" h., scalloped rim, Allerton, En-
gland **125-150**

Blue Willow "Chicago Jug"

Pitcher, 7" h., "Chicago Jug," ca. 1907, Buf-
falo Pottery, 3 pt. (ILLUS.) **200-225**
Pitcher, 8" h., glass, Johnson Bros., En-
gland **35-40**
Pitcher w/ice lip, 10" h., Japan **100**

Blue Willow Place card Holder

Place card holder, unmarked, England, ca.
   1870s, 2 1/2" d. (ILLUS.) **85-100**
Place mat, cloth, 16 x 12" **18-20**
Plate, bread & butter, Allerton, England **12-15**
Plate, bread & butter, Japan **5-7**
Plate, child's, 4 1/2" d., Japan **10-15**
Plate, "Child's Day 1971," sandman w/wil-
   low umbrella, Wedgwood **65-75**
Plate, dinner, Booth's, England **40-45**

Buffalo Blue Willow Dinner Plate

Plate, dinner, Buffalo Pottery, 1911
   (ILLUS.) **30-35**
Plate, dinner, ca. 1870, unmarked,
   England **40-50**
Plate, dinner, Cambridge, blue patt. on clear
   glass **40-50**
Plate, dinner, flow blue, Royal Doulton **75-85**
Plate, dinner, Holland **18-20**
Plate, dinner, Japan **10-15**
Plate, dinner, Mandarin patt., Copeland, En-
   gland **40-50**
Plate, dinner, modern, Royal Wessex **6-8**
Plate, dinner, Paden City Pottery **30-35**
Plate, dinner, restaurant ware,
   Jackson **15-20**
Plate, dinner, Royal China Co. **10-15**
Plate, dinner, scalloped rim, Allerton, En-
   gland **30-35**
Plate, grill, Allerton, England **45-50**
Plate, luncheon, Wedgwood,
   England **20-25**
Plate, luncheon, Worcester patt. **35-40**

Plate, 7 1/2" d., Arklow, Ireland **20**
Plate, 10" d., tin, ca. 1988, Robert Steffy **10-12**
Plate, grill, 10" d., Japan **18-20**
Plate, 10 1/4" d., paper, Fonda **1-2**
Plate, grill, 10 1/2" d., Holland **18-20**

Blue Willow Wedgwood Platter

Platter, 9 x 11" l., rectangular, Wedgwood &
   Co., England (ILLUS.) **100-125**
Platter, 8 1/2 x 11 1/2" l., oval, scalloped
   rim, Buffalo Pottery **100-125**
Platter, 9 x 12" l., oval, American **15-18**
Platter, 9 x 12" l., oval, Japan **20-25**
Platter, 9 x 12" l., rectangular, Allerton, En-
   gland **150-175**
Platter, 11 x 14" l., oval, Johnson Bros., En-
   gland **65-75**
Platter, 11 x 14" l., rectangular, Buffalo Pot-
   tery **150-175**
Platter, 11 x 14" l., rectangular, ca. 1880s,
   unmarked, England **150-175**
Platter, 15 x 19" l., rectangular, well &
   tree, ca. 1890, unmarked,
   England **350-375**
Platter, 20 1/2" l., oval, English arrow & cir-
   cle mark, late 19th - early 20th c **468**
Pudding mold, England, 4 1/2" h. **40-45**

Willow Ware Punch Cup

Punch cup, pedestal foot, unmarked,
   England, ca. 1900, 3 1/2" h.
   (ILLUS.) **50-75**
Relish dish, leaf-shaped, ca. 1870,
   England **100-125**

Blue Willow Salt Box

Salt box, cov., ca. 1960, wooden lid, Japan,
5 x 5" (ILLUS.).. **195-225**
Salt dip, master, pedestal base, unmarked,
England, 2" h... **100-125**
Salt & pepper shakers, Japan, pr.................... **35-40**

Blue Willow Sauce Tureen

Sauce tureen, cov., England, ca. 1880s,
5" h. (ILLUS.)... **125-150**
Soup tureen, cov., ca. 1880, unmarked, En-
gland **400-450**
Spoon rest, Japan... **35-40**

Blue Willow Sugar Barrel

Sugar Barrel, cov., silver lid & handle, un-
marked, England, ca. 1880s, 5" h.
(ILLUS.)... **175-200**
Sugar bowl, cov., Japan **20-25**

Sugar bowl, cov., Ridgway, England.............. **50-60**
Tea set, child's, Japan, service for six in
box **250-300**
Tea set, child's, tin, Ohio Art Co., Bryan,
Ohio, service for four **125-150**
Tea tile, ca. 1900, unmarked, England, 6"
sq. **75**
Tea tile, Minton, England, 6" sq. **75**
Teapot, child's, Made in Occupied Japan **40-45**
Teapot, cov., ca. 1890, Royal Doulton........ **300-350**
Teapot, cov., child's, Japan **35-40**
Teapot, cov., Homer Laughlin **75-85**
Teapot, cov., round, Allerton, England........ **250-275**

Miniature Teapot

Teapot, cov., miniature, modern, Windsor,
3 3/4" h. (ILLUS.).. **15-20**
Teapot, individual, Moriyama, Japan,
4 1/2" h... **75-100**
Teapot, cov., Sadler, 4 3/4" h. **40-45**

Blue Willow Enamel Teapot

Teapot, cov., enamel, unmarked, 7" h.
(ILLUS.)... **75-85**

Teapot & Trivet

Teapot w/trivet, cov., Grimwades, 6" h., 2 pcs. (ILLUS.)... **250-275**

"Yorkshire Relish" Tip Tray

Tip tray, "Yorkshire Relish," England, 4" d. (ILLUS.)... **50-60**

Blue Willow Tip Tray

Tip tray, "Schweppes Lemon Squash," England, 4 1/2" d. (ILLUS.)............................... **85-95**

Blue Willow Toby Jug

Toby jug, w/Blue Willow jacket, unmarked, England, 6" h. (ILLUS.)......................... **500-600**
Toby jug, w/Blue Willow jacket, W. Kent, England, 6" h... **500-600**
Toothbrush holder, Wedgwood, England, 5 1/4" h. **95**

Tray, round, brass, 6" d.. **50**
Trivet, scalloped foot, Moriyama, 6" (very rare)... **225**
Vegetable bowl, open, Japan, 10 1/2" oval.......... **35**
Warmer, round, holds candle, Japan **58**
Wash pitcher & bowl, ca. 1890, unmarked, England, the set.. **500-600**

Blue Willow Wash Bowl & Pitcher

Wash pitcher & bowl, Royal Doulton, the set **700-900**

Other Colors
Butter dish, rectangular, for stick, red, Japan, 7".. **65-75**
Butter pat, red, Japan **20**
Charger, brown, Buffalo China, 11" d. **60-70**
Coffeepot, cov., ca. 1890, brown, unmarked, England, 8 3/4" h. **200-225**

Purple Willow Ware Cup

Cup, purple, handleless, unmarked, England (ILLUS.).. **75-85**
Cup & saucer, red, ca. 1930, Buffalo China... **30-35**
Egg cup, red, England, 4 1/2" h. **35-40**

Red Willow Ware Pitcher

Pitcher, 5" h., red, "Old Gustavsberg," Sweden (ILLUS.) **65-75**
Plate, 2 3/4" d., green, miniature, modern, Coalport, England **20-25**

Brown Willow Ware Child's Plate

Plate, 4 3/4" d., brown, child's, E.M. & Co. (ILLUS.) **50-60**
Plate, 6" d., restaurant ware, brown, Buffalo China **15**
Plate, 9" d., ca. 1890, brown, John Meir & Son **20-25**
Plate, 9" d., Mandarin patt., red, Copeland **35-40**
Plate, 9" d., purple, Britannia Pottery **35-40**
Plate, bread & butter, 6" d., green, Japan **18-20**
Plate, dinner, pink **10**
Plate, dinner, red, Japan **15-20**
Plate, grill, 11 1/4" d., green, Royal Willow China **30-35**
Platter, 9", brown, early, unmarked, England **90-100**
Platter, cov., 9", red, Petrus Regout, Holland .. **35-45**
Platter, 9 1/4 x 11 1/4", rectangular, red, Allerton, England **175-200**
Platter, 11 x 19" l., rectangular, green, John Steventon & Sons **125-150**
Sugar bowl, red, Japan **25-35**
Teapot, cov., purple, Britannia Pottery **200-225**
Teapot, cov., red, child's, E.M. & Co., England **140-150**
Teapot, cov., red, restaurant ware, Sterling China **75-85**
Vegetable bowl, cov., round, green, Victoria Porcelain **100-125**
Vegetable bowl, red, Allertons, 7" d. **50-60**
Vegetable bowl, red, cov., Japan, 10" d. **30**

Worcester

Flight Barr & Barr

BFB

Worcester Marks

The famed English factory was established in 1751 and produced porcelains. Earthenwares were made in the 19th century. Its first period is known as the "Dr. Wall" period; that from 1783 to 1792 as the "Flight" period; that from 1792 to 1807 as the "Barr and Flight & Barr" period. The firm became Barr, Flight & Barr from 1807 to 1813; Flight, Barr & Barr from 1813 to 1840; Chamberlain & Co. from 1840 to 1852, and Kerr and Binns from 1852 to 1862. After 1862, the company became the Worcester Royal Porcelain Company, Ltd., known familiarly as Royal Worcester, which see. Also included in the following listing are examples of wares from the early Chamberlains and early Grainger factories in Worcester.

Bowl, 6 3/8" d., footed, deep, gently flaring rounded sides, underglaze-blue fruits & flowers exterior decoration, shaded crescent mark, 18th c. (glaze wear) **$173**
Cabinet plates, chain link border & floral bird design, painted in an Imari palette, Barr, ca. 1805, 8 1/2" d., pr. (each cracked & repaired w/staples) **134**
Dessert dish, oval, "Japan" patt., brightly painted w/an Oriental river garden w/exotic birds flying above a bridge, fencing, rockwork & a pagoda, impressed crowned Barr, Flight & Barr marks & redprinted Royal Arms round address mark, ca. 1810, 11 1/8" l. **2,300**
Dessert dish, square scalloped form, painted in the center w/the arms of Somerville, Part. quartering those of Warburton & Meredyth encircled by a garter w/a motto, within a gilt-edged "Barr's orange" border decorated w/a gilt stylized leafy floral vine, Flight & Barr marks, 1801-04, 9 1/4" w. (slight stacking wear) **2,300**
Dessert dishes, shaped oval form, painted w/a central arrangement of flowers amid scattered flower sprays & sprigs within a gilt gadrooned rim, impressed crowned Flight, Barr & Barr mark, ca. 1820, 11 7/8" l., pr. (tiny rim chips) **920**
Dishes, leaf & vine-shaped, molded w/two overlapping leaves edged in green & pale yellow w/puce veining, set w/a brown twig handle, each dish painted in the center w/colorful flower sprays & sprigs, ca. 1765, 7 3/4" l., pr. (slight enamel rubbing) **4,312**
Dishes, lozenge-shaped, painted in the center w/a colorful exotic bird in parkland within border of gilt flower swags suspended from a narrow blue gilt-edged border at the rim, ca. 1780, script W marks in underglaze-blue, 11 5/8" l., pr. (slight rubbing to gilt rim) **1,437**
Egg drainer, the shallow pierced circular bowl in gilt w/a flower sprig within a foliate garland entwined about a narrow blue band, the rim w/a narrow blue & gilt border & set w/a gilt foliate lug handle, underglaze-blue open crescent mark, ca. 1780, 3 1/2" d. **460**
Finger bowl underplate, round w/lightly scalloped rim, painted w/a spray of yellow, pink & orange flowers within four flower & leaf sprigs at the rim, 1758-60, 5 3/4" d. **862**
Pitcher, 5 1/2" h., milk, jug-form, "Japan" patt., bulbous body raised on a circular foot, brightly painted w/an Oriental river

garden w/exotic birds flying above a bridge, fencing, rockwork & a pagoda, below a gilt gadrooned rim, Barr, Flight & Barr, ca. 1810... **2,587**

Pitcher, 9 3/8" h., jug-type, cabbage-leaf style w/mask spout, typically molded w/overlapping leaves & painted below the naturalistically colored mask spout w/the arms of Miss Barbara Band of Hurworth Manor, Darlington within an elaborate puce & gilt foliate & colorful floral cartouche, flanked by turquoise-ground puce scale panels pendent from an underglaze-blue & gilt border below the neck, the gilt dentil-edged rim w/a similar border suspended w/puce leaf swags, underglaze-blue open crescent mark, ca. 1770-75 .... **10,062**

Plate, 7" d., scalloped rim, blue-scale-decorated, gilt-edged mirror & vase-shaped panels enclosing brightly colored flower sprays & sprigs, painted in the workshop of James Giles, ca. 1770, pseudo-seal underglaze-blue mark (slight wear) **1,035**

Plate, 7" d., scalloped rim, painted w/a loose bouquet & sprigs of summer flowers within a gilt-edged rim, decorated in the workshop of James Giles, ca. 1770 (slight gilt rubbing) **575**

Plate, 9" d., shaped rim, a central spray of blackberries surrounded by three exotic birds perched in branches at the gilt-edged rim, painted in the workshop of James Giles, 1768-70 (two minor shallow rim chips)... **2,875**

Plates, 8 1/2" d., dessert, a wide border decorated w/scrolling vines, leaves & floral designs, Chamberlain's, ca. 1815, set of 7 .... **525**

Part of Set of Worcester Dessert Plates

Plates, 8 1/2" d., dessert plates, w/wide border of scrolling vine, leaf & floral motifs, Chamberlains Worcester, ca. 1815, set of 7 (ILLUS. of four)....................................... **308**

Platter, 10 1/8" l., oval, painted in the center in grey, iron-red, black & gold w/the Cookes crest of an armored arm holding a dagger & rising from a gilt battlemented coronet within a grey garter inscribed in black w/a motto, the cavetto & rim w/a wide gilt vermiculé border edged w/salmon-ground gilt-fretwork bands, impressed crowned Barr, Flight & Barr mark, ca. 1810 .... **1,380**

Platter, 12 1/8" l., oval, "Royal Lily" patt., typically painted in underglaze-blue w/radiating foliate panels about a central blue & gilt oval medallion, the brown-edged rim w/a narrow blue & gilt chevron-patterned border, Flight & Barr marks, ca. 1795... **460**

Platters, 10" l., oval, "Japan" patt., painted w/a border of flowering plants, fencing & rockwork in a colorful Imari palette within a gilt-edged rim, impressed crowned Flight, Barr & Barr mark, ca. 1815, pr........ **1,265**

Salad bowls or junket dishes, blue & white, the interior printed in underglaze-blue w/the "Pine Cone" patt. within a border of molded scallop shells printed w/further sprays of flowers & fruit beneath the shaped rim, the exterior printed w/three clusters of root vegetables, scattered insects & flower sprigs, ca. 1775, hatched crescent marks in underglaze-blue, 10 1/2" d., pr. **1,380**

Sauceboat, footed, deep, oblong molded body w/ornate C-scroll handle, underglaze-blue floral panels & a cell border, open crescent mark, 18th c., 7 3/4" l. (firing line under spout) **230**

Soup tureen, cover & stand, each piece printed in underglaze-blue w/the "Pine Cone" patt. within a gadrooned border, the stand & quatrelobed tureen set w/shell-form handles, the cover w/a double bud knop, ca. 1775, hatched crescent mark in underglaze-blue, 12 1/2" w. across handles (very small chip to handle of stand)... **1,840**

Spill vase, the cylindrical body painted w/two assemblages of naturalistically colored feathers on a ground of gilt dots & stars within two gilt patterned orange-red ground borders at the rim & foot, ca. 1800-04, incised B Flight & Barr mark, 4 5/8" h. (star crack to base & chip to foot)... **1,840**

Sweetmeat dish, "Bengal Tiger" patt., "Blind Earl" design, scalloped oval form, molded at each end w/a rose branch handle, painted in the center w/alternating panels of fabulous beasts & vases on tables within a cell-diaper border & gilt-edged rim, ca. 1770, 6 5/8" l. **1,610**

Sweetmeat dish, "Blind Earl" patt., molded w/a twig handle issuing two sprays of rose leaves & two buds picked out in underglaze-blue, the ground also painted in blue w/scattered insects, all within a scalloped rim, ca. 1765, underglaze-blue open crescent mark, 6" d. (small chip to underside edge of rim)............................... **2,587**

Sweetmeat dish, "Blind Earl" patt., round w/a stalk handle & lightly molded rose leaves & buds, finely painted in puce camaieu w/two Oriental figures standing beside a large urn before a house, the scalloped rim painted w/a foliate scroll garland, ca. 1758, 6 1/4" d. (minor chip & hairline) **920**

Sweetmeat dishes, shell-shaped, painted in the center in iron-red, yellow, rose, green

& black w/an Oriental flowering plant growing amid grasses, the fluted scroll handle & ruffled rim edged in puce feathering & molded on the underside w/two rows of uncolored ruffles, 1758-60, 4 7/8" l., pr. (one w/hairline in footrim, interiors w/some speckling) 920

Sweetmeat stand, shell form, the triangular base encrusted w/colorful, naturalistically molded shell, coral & seaweed supporting three tiers of three puce-edged shells w/gilt rims graduating in size & a circular shell above, each painted inside w/polychrome floral sprays, ca. 1770, 8 1/2" h. (some cracks & restorations) 5,175

Tea & coffee service: open sugar bowl, 6" d. waste bowl, 10 coffee cups, 10 tea cups, 10 saucers & a circular plate; each swirl-molded w/a white ground continuing to a cobalt blue border w/gilt leafage highlights, underglaze-blue factory mark, late 18th c., the set 287

Teacups & saucers, richly painted & gilt in underglaze-blue, iron-red, turquoise, green & pink w/a variation of the "Japan" patt., gilt line rims, impressed crown mark of Barr, Flight & Barr, ca. 1807, set of 6 705

Teapot, cov., ovoid body, decorated w/scattered sprays of flowers beneath a gilt dentil-edged rim, the entwined handle & fluted spout decorated w/gilt dots & the domed cover w/an open flower knop, crossed swords & number 9 in underglaze-blue, 1770-75, 6 5/8" h. (knop repaired, minor chips on spout) 805

Teapot, cov., ovoid body w/fluted hexagonal spout, boldly painted w/sprays & sprigs of pink, orange, blue & yellow flowers & butterflies beneath a purple camaieu peony-head & scroll border at the rim, the loop handle w/a purple camaieu foliate sprig & the flattened cover w/a puce striped tulip knop set amid almost botanical flower sprays, ca. 1760, 5 1/8" h. (cover probably assembled & w/a small rim chip) 920

Early Worcester Sauce Tureen

Tureens, cov., sauce-type, swelled oval body w/shell end handles & serpentine rim, domed cover w/artichoke finial, decorated in underglaze-blue w/panels of flowers & cells, pseudo-Chinese marks, 18th c., slight chips to one handle, 6 1/2" l., pr. (ILLUS. of one) 1,955

Yellow-Glazed Earthenware

In the past this early English ware was often referred to as "Canary Lustre," but recently a more accurate title has come into use.

Produced in the late 18th and early 19th centuries, pieces featured an overall yellow glaze, often decorated with silver or copper lustre designs or black, brown or red transfer-printed scenes. Most pieces are not marked.

Today the scarcity of examples in good condition keeps market prices high.

Creamer, urn shape w/molded ring handle, decorated w/black stripes & transfer of fishermen in front of gate house, 5 1/2" h. (colored-in rim flake) **$385**

Creamer, footed, tapering, bulbous body below the wide cylindrical neck w/pointed rim spout & C-scroll handle, yellow ground w/large round brick red h.p. blossoms & green leaves around the body & vining flowers & leaves around the neck, 3 1/2" h. (small chips) 605

Cup plate, decorated w/a polychrome bird perched on a branch w/green spatter foliage, early 19th c., 4 1/4" d. 316

Cup & saucer, handleless, each transfer-printed in brick red w/a fishing scene & castle & windmill in background, all on the yellow ground 495

Cup & saucer, handleless, footed cup w/flaring sides & scalloped rim, matching deep saucer, each h.p. w/large rounded brick red blossoms alternating w/smaller blossom buds among green leaves, green rim bands 1,073

Cup & saucer, handleless, yellow ground transfer-printed in orange & brown w/a scene of a mother & children, early 19th c. 328

Early Yellow-Glazed Flowerpot

Flowerpot & saucer, tapering cylindrical pot w/rounded thick rim band, conforming deep saucer, each w/h.p. large stylized flowers, vines & leaves in red, green & brick red, brick red rims, light spots of wear, early 19th c., saucer 4 1/2" d., 1 1/4" h., pot 4 1/2" d., 4" h. (ILLUS.) 1,045

Garniture set: a pair of vases & a slightly taller vase; each of trumpet-form w/a flaring foot & widely flaring, flattened rim, decorated at the rim & base w/two thin brown stripes, the body decorated w/h.p. flower clusters on leafy vines around the sides, in red, brown & green, two vases 4 1/4" h., third one 4 7/8" h., the set (wear, repair, decoration slightly varies) ... **1,430**

Mug, child's, cylindrical, russet transfer-printed design titled "A Rabbit For William," early 19th c., 2 1/2" h. (minor chips)` **633**

Mug, cylindrical, black transfer-printed inscription "Super Fine Porter Peace and Roast Beef to the Friends of Liberty," silver lustre trim, early 19th c., 3 1/2" d., 3 1/2" h. (repairs to rim & footring)................ **431**

Mug, child's, cylindrical, transfer-printed scene of a coach within an oval wreath w/inscription "A New Carriage For Ann," 2" h. **484**

Mug, child's, cylindrical, brick red transfer-printed scene of a woman & two children in the wood, printed across the top w/"A Present For My Dear Girl," 2 1/4" h. (worn lettering, professional restoration to foot chip)... **220**

Mug, child's, cylindrical w/applied handle, decorated w/stylized multicolored flowers & leaves w/lustre trim, 2 1/4" h. **825**

Mug, child's, cylindrical w/C-scroll leaf tip handle, the front w/a rectangular scroll-trimmed reddish brown transfer-printed cartouche enclosing the motto "My Son, if sinners entice thee, consent thou not lest disgrace come upon thee," 2 3/8" h. (small lip flakes) **413**

Mug, child's, cylindrical w/a brick red transfer-printed wreath enclosing a box reading "Esteem Truth Above All Things," pink lustre band around the base, rim & handle, 2 1/2" h. (pinpoint nick on rim, light lustre wear)...................................... **440**

Mug, child's, cylindrical, yellow ground h.p. w/a pink lustre cottage scene, applied handle, 2 1/2" h.................................... **330**

Mug, child's, cylindrical w/applied handle, the yellow ground decorated w/delicate sprigs of small brick red blossoms on leaf stems, green rim band, 3" h.......................... **743**

Mustard pot, cov., painted w/alternating zig-zag bands of brown & red, ca. 1820-30, 2 7/8" h. **2,520**

Pitcher, 4 3/4" h., mask form, the front molded in relief w/the face of a man w/flesh-toned skin, black hair & beard, the sides molded overall w/large rounded knobs painted brick red w/a green sprigged ground on the yellow ground, angled handle & gently flaring rim & spout w/green band.. **935**

Floral-decorated Yellow-Glazed Pitcher

Pitcher, 7 1/4" h., ovoid, wide-lobed body tapering to a flat rim w/pointed spout & molded feather edging, C-form handle, sides h.p. w/large delicate stylized scrolling brown flowers & leaves w/brown band at rim, fine restoration along side of handle, few spots on spout rim, early 19th c. (ILLUS.)................................. **550**

Pitcher, 7 1/2" h., transfer-printed on each side w/octagonal panel of fruit & birds, inscribed & dated beneath spout in blue enamel "S.Gray:Hodnet, 1810" (rim chip).. **1,080**

Plate, 6 1/2" d., h.p. central design of stylized reddish orange blossoms & green leafy branches on a white ground, yellow-glazed border band.................................. **248**

Plate, 6 1/2" d., scalloped flanged rim w/embossed bird & butterfly design trimmed in brick red, the center w/a large stylized flower & leaf design in brick red & green, all on a yellow ground (repaired) **440**

Plate, 8 1/4" d., yellow ground w/the flanged rim embossed w/fruits & flowers painted in brick red & green, the center w/a large h.p. brick red blossom framed by smaller pointed blossoms & green leaves..... **413**

Yellow-Glazed Earthenware Plate

Plate, 8 3/8" d., modeled as a leafy bunch of grapes resting in a basket, bright yellow, gold & green, ca. 1820-30 (ILLUS.)............ **1,920**

Platter, 9 1/2 x 11", oval, w/gently scalloped rim, h.p. King's Rose center design in reddish orange, yellow & green, reticulated border w/yellow (hairline) **825**

Soup plate w/flanged rim, the rim h.p. w/clusters of small brick red blossoms & green leaves, the center h.p. w/large brick red pinwheel-form blossoms framed by smaller blossoms & green leaves, 8 1/4" d. **2,750**

Tea cup, handleless, raised footring, the flaring rounded sides decorated w/a continuous undulating band of orange blossoms & green leaf bands on the yellow ground, 4 3/8" d., 2 3/4" h. (repair on base rim) **413**

Teapot, cov., ovoid body w/flared rim, black transfer of a woman playing piano or harpsichord accompanied by two children playing triangle & tambourine, black stripes, 5 1/8" h. (short rim hairline & lid repairs) **495**

Teapot, cov., child's, bulbous body w/a short cylindrical neck & inset flat cover, C-form handle & straight angled spout, the body h.p. w/a band of large brick red blossoms & green leaves on the yellow ground, 3 1/2" h. (spout repaired, hairline) **633**

Whistle, model of a bird perched on a round base, the angled tail forming the blowhole, early 19th c., 3" h. (small flake near wing) **385**

Yellowware

Yellowware is a form of utilitarian pottery produced in the United States and England from the early 19th century onward. Its body texture is less dense and vitreous (impervious to water) than stoneware. Most, but not all, yellowware is unmarked and its color varies from deep yellow to pale buff. In the late 19th and early 20th centuries bowls in graduated sizes were widely advertised. Still in production, yellowware is plentiful and still reasonably priced.

Bottle, Toby-type, the upper half molded as a figure of a smiling man wearing a top hat & playing a fiddle, hat forms bottle cap, 19th c., crazing, chip on hat brim, 8 1/2" h. (ILLUS. right) **$715**

Crock, cov., short cylindrical sides w/heavy molded rim & inset cover, the center decorated w/a wide band composed of thin & wider blue bands, 7" d., 3 1/2" h. (crazing, stains) **220**

Yellowware Flask & Toby Bottle

Flask, flattened ovoid sides w/impressed edge bands, one side molded in relief w/an American eagle above flags draped on horizontal poles, the other side molded w/morning glories, 19th c., chips, 7 3/8" h. (ILLUS. left) **1,210**

Model of a dog, seated dog w/brown running glaze, freestanding front feet & nicely detailed coat w/curls, molded base has shells, 10" h. **1,485**

Model of a dog, seated Spaniel w/well-molded fur & facial details, on a thick rectangular base w/cut corners & overall cross-hatched design, overall running brown glaze, signed on the base "Geo. Diehl, Jul. 9th 1870," near Bucks County, Penn-

sylvania, 7 5/8" h. (minor glaze flakes on base) **4,400**

Pitcher, 5" h., jug-form, bulbous baluster form w/rim spout w/strainer & C-form handle, four thin blue stripes around the body, first half 19th c. (flakes) **578**

Pitcher, 5 1/2" h., footed baluster form w/rim spout & C-form handle, decorated w/two wide white bands, each edged by thin brown stripes, 19th c. **550**

Pitcher, 6 1/8" h., jug-form, baluster-form body w/rim spout & C-form handle, two white bands, each divided by four thin black stripes, 19th c. **688**

Pitcher, 7 3/4" h., jug-form, ovoid body w/a rim spout & C-form handle, decorated w/white bands w/dark blue pinstripe borders (minor base flakes) **743**

Pitcher, 7 3/4" h., jug-form, yellow ground w/thin stripes of dark blue & white around the middle & dark blue stripes near the rim & base, 19th c. (minor flakes on bottom) **743**

Soap dish, shallow round form w/a large pierced hole in the center bottom surrounded by six small holes, 5 5/8" d. (some wear) **550**

Zeisel (Eva) Designs

One of the most influential ceramic artists and designers of the 20th century, Eva Zeisel began her career in Europe as a young woman, eventually immigrating to the United States, where her unique, streamlined designs met with great success. Since the 1940s her work has been at the forefront of commercial ceramic design, and in recent decades she has designed in other media. Now in her ninth decade, she continues to be active and involved in the world of art and design.

Castleton - Museum Ware
Bowl, 11" d., salad, White **$160**
Bowl, 13" d., salad, French Garden **375**

Castleton - Museum Ware Coffee Set

Coffeepot, cov., tall, slender form w/C-scroll handle (ILLUS. second from left w/coffee set) **500**
Coffeepot, cov., White **400-500**
Creamer, handleless (ILLUS. second from right w/coffee set) **300**
Creamer, handleless, White **150-175**
Cup & saucer, flat, Mandalay **20**
Cup & saucer, flat, White **40**

Wee Modern Child's Plate

Cup & saucer (ILLUS. far left w/coffee
set) 150-200
Plate, 8 1/4" d., salad, White............................... 30
Plate, 8 1/4" sq., salad, White.......................... 135
Plate, 8 1/4" sq., salad, Wisteria 18
Plate, 10 1/2" d., dinner, White........................ 50
Sugar, cov., handleless (ILLUS. far right
w/coffee set) 250

Goss American - Wee Modern
Child's plate (ILLUS., top of page)..................... 265

Hall China Company - Kitchenware

Golden Clover Cookie Jar

Cookie jar, cov., Golden Clover (ILLUS.).............. 65
Creamer, Tri-tone 45
Marmite, Casual Living 30

Tri-tone Nested Mixing Bowls

Mixing bowls, nested, Tri-tone, set of 5
(ILLUS.)... 250
Refrigerator jug, cov., Casual Living.................. 100
Refrigerator jug, cov., Tri-tone........................... 150

Casual Living Shakers

Shakers, Casual Living, set (ILLUS.) 40
Sugar, Tri-tone 45

Tri-tone Teapot

Teapot, cov., 6-cup, Tri-tone (ILLUS.) 85

Hallcraft - Century Dinnerware
Creamer, Fern.. 30
Cup & saucer, Garden of Eden 15
Gravy boat & ladle, Fern 95

Fern Jug

Jug, Fern, 1 1/4 qt. (ILLUS.) 60
Plate, 10" d., dinner, Sunglow 22
Platter, 15" l., White.. 25
Relish, divided, White 90
Sugar, cov., Fern 30

Century White Vegetable Bowl

Vegetable bowl, 10 1/2" d., White (ILLUS.)......... **18**

Hallcraft - Tomorrow's Classic Dinnerware

Bouquet Cup & Saucer

AD cup & saucer, Bouquet (ILLUS.)..................... **25**
Bowl, 5 3/4" d., fruit, Caprice **9**
Bowl, 9" d., coupe soup, Spring **15**
Creamer & sugar, Harlequin, the set.................. **45**

Hallcraft Creamer & Sugar in White

Creamer & sugar, White, the set (ILLUS.)...... **50-75**

Dawn Cup & Saucer

Cup & saucer, Dawn (ILLUS.) **20**
Cup & saucer, Golden Glo **19**
Cup & saucer, White **25**
Egg cup, double, Arizona **45**
Gravy boat & ladle, Lyric **80**

Jug, Bouquet, 3-qt.. **80**

Bouquet Dinner Plate

Plate, 11" d., dinner, Bouquet (ILLUS.)................ **15**
Plate, 11" d., dinner, Fantasy **18**
Plate, 11" d., dinner, White **18**
Platter, 15" l., Buckingham..................................... **30**

Bouquet Shakers

Shakers, Bouquet, 4" h. (ILLUS.)........................... **15**

White Hallcraft Teapot

Teapot, cov., 6-cup, White (ILLUS.) **160**

Hollydale

Hollydale Chop Plate

Chop plate, 14" l., brown (ILLUS.) **60**
Creamer **62**
Gravy bowl, bird-shape... **85**
Plate, 10 1/4" d., desert yellow **30**
Sauce dish, bird shape, yellow/turquoise **200**
Sugar, cov.. **62**
Tureen & ladle, bird design, the set.................... **300**

Hyalyn "Z Ware"

Bowl, cereal, oxblood, commercial
    grade/restaurant ware.. **40**
Carafe, autumn gold... **90**

Satin Black "Z Ware" Coffee Server

Coffee server, cov., satin black w/white lid
    (ILLUS.).. **125**

"Z Ware" Autumn Gold Compote

Compote, footed, autumn gold, 5" (ILLUS.) **350**
Creamer, handleless, autumn gold,
    4 3/4" h. **85**
Mug & saucer, olive green..................................... **145**

Johann Haviland

Bowl, fruit, Wedding Ring patt. (ILLUS. front
    center, on bread & butter plate, w/Wed-
    ding Ring pieces).. **12**
Coffeepot, cov., Eva White..................................... **75**

Creamer & cov. sugar, Wedding Ring patt.
    (ILLUS. second from left & second from
    right w/Wedding Ring pieces)........................... **60**
Creamer & sugar, Eva White, the set................... **65**
Cup & saucer, Wedding Ring **20**

Wedding Ring Pieces

Dinnerware set, Wedding Ring, 20-pc. ser-
    vice for 4 (ILLUS. of dinner plate, far
    right, & cup & saucer, center, w/Wedding
    Ring pieces) **200-250**
Plate, bread & butter, Wedding Ring patt.
    (ILLUS. front center, under fruit bowl,
    w/Wedding Ring pieces) **10**
Plate, 10 1/4" d., dinner, Wedding Ring............... **18**
Platter, oval, Wedding Ring patt. (ILLUS.
    rear, w/Wedding Ring pieces) **60**
Sauce dish & underplate, Wheat **50**
Serving bowl, round, Wedding Ring patt.
    (ILLUS. far left w/Wedding Ring pieces)......... **40**

Blue Roses Teapot

Teapot, cov., Blue Roses (ILLUS.)........................ **65**
Tureen/vegetable bowl, cov., White **80**

Monmouth Dinnerware

Butter pat, Pals, 4" **16**
Creamer, Blueberry... **18**
Creamer, Lacy Wings **50**
Cup & saucer, Lacey Wings/Rosette **5**

Goose-shaped Gravy Boat

Gravy boat, goose shape, Lacey Wings
    (ILLUS.).. **175**
Sauce dish, Pals.. **140**

Lacey Wings Shakers

Shaker set, Lacey Wings, pr. (ILLUS.)................ **65**
Sugar, cov., bird lid, Blueberry **25**

Monmouth Bird-shaped Sugar

Sugar, cov., bird lid, Lacey Wings
(ILLUS.).. **50**

Pals Teapot

Teapot, cov., Pals, in the form of a stylized
bird w/"dancing turnips" decoration, ce-
ramic ribbon handle (ILLUS.)......................... **375**

Lacey Wings Teapot with Rooster

Teapot, cov., wire handle w/ceramic grip,
Prairie Hen, w/rooster decoration
(ILLUS.)... **150**
Vase, 7 1/2" h., perforated, Lacey Wings **85**
Vegetable bowl, 9 1/2" d.. **65**

Norleans Dinnerware by Meito
(pieces marked "Made in Occupied Japan" are worth 25% more)

Fairfield Cup & Saucer

Cup & saucer, Fairfield (ILLUS.)............................ **8**
Cup & saucer, Livonia... **12**

Livonia Gravy Boat with Underliner

Gravy boat w/underliner, Livonia (ILLUS.) **65**

Livonia Dinner Plate

Plate, dinner, Livonia (ILLUS.) **12**
Plate, salad, Livonia... **10**
Service for six, Livonia, 36-piece set.................. **200**

Norleans Vegetable Bowl

Vegetable bowl, 12" oval, Livonia
(ILLUS.).. **55**

Riverside

Riverside Bowl

Bowl, 8 1/2" d., celadon & moss yellow
(ILLUS.)... **600**
Creamer **175**
Plate, dinner, yellow & olive green........................ **60**

Riverside Vase in Rust

Vase, 4 1/2" h., rust (ILLUS.).................................. **35**

Schmid Dinnerware

Casserole, cov., bird lid, 9 1/2 x 8" **80**

Schmid Dinnerware Coffeepot

Coffeepot, cov., Lacey Wings/Rosette
(ILLUS.)... **35**
Gravy or sauce server, Lacey Wings, 7" d. **175**

Sunburst Mug

Mug, Sunburst (ILLUS.).. **16**

Schmid Dinnerware Pitcher

Pitcher, 10" h., Lacey Wings & Sunburst
(ILLUS.)... **28**
Plate, 10 1/2" d., dinner, Lacey Wings/Sun-
burst... **10**

Schmid Bird-shaped Teapot

Teapot, cov., bird shape, rattan handle,
Lacey Wings (ILLUS.)... **50**

Schramberg

Schramberg Triangular Ashtray

Ashtray, triangular, Gobelin 13 (ILLUS.)............. **160**
Creamer, cov., Mondrian....................................... **170**
Cup & saucer, Gobelin 13 .... **75**

Gobelin 13 Covered Jar

Jar, cov., Gobelin 13, 5" (ILLUS.) **375**

Mondrian Covered Jar

Jar, cov., terraced, Mondrian, 5" (ILLUS.) **1,000**
Jug, cover & undertray, hot water, Mondrian **90**
Pitcher, 4 1/2" h., Mondrian **225**
Plate, salad, matte grun (green) **20**
Plate, 7 1/2" d., dessert, Gobelin 13 .... **60**

Mondrian Covered Sugar

Sugar, cov., Mondrian (ILLUS.) **125**

Gobelin 13 Teapot

Teapot, cov., Gobelin 13 (ILLUS.) **900**
Tray, Mondrian, 12" **450**

Gobelin 8 Vase

Vase, 6" h., offset oval, Gobelin 8 (ILLUS.) **200**

Stratoware

Stratoware Candlestick

Candlestick, brown trim (ILLUS.) **120**
Casserole, cov., beige & brown **100**

Stratoware Cup & Saucer

Cup & saucer, gold interior (ILLUS.) **50**
Plate, 11 1/2" d., yellow & green **60**

Stratoware Refrigerator Jar

Refrigerator jar, cov., blue & beige (ILLUS.) **200**

Stratoware Shakers

Shakers, green trim, pr. (ILLUS.) **80**

Stratoware Covered Sugar

Sugar, cov., gold & beige (ILLUS.) **70**

Town and Country Dinnerware - for Red Wing Potteries

Bowl, 5 3/4" d., chili or cereal................................ **60**
Bowl, 13" d., salad **275**

Town and Country "Yawn" Creamer

Creamer, "yawn," bronze (ILLUS.)........................ **70**

Town and Country Cruets

Cruets, dusk blue & peach, set (ILLUS.) **130**

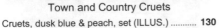

Lazy Susan Relish Set

Lazy Susan relish set w/mustard jar
  (ILLUS.)... **500**

Town and Country Mixing Bowl

Mixing bowl (ILLUS.)... **175**

Town and Country Mustard Jar

Mustard jar, cover & ladle, dusk blue, the set
  (ILLUS.)... **250**

Town and Country Syrup Pitcher

Pitcher, syrup, chartreuse (ILLUS.) **95**
Plate, 6 1/4" d., bread & butter **15**
Plate, 8" d., salad, peach **13**
Plate, 10 1/2" d., dinner, bronze............................ **50**
Plate, 10 1/2" d., dinner, other colors.................... **40**

Comma-shaped Platter

Platter, 15" l., comma shape (ILLUS.)........... **85-100**

Large & Small "Schmoo" Shakers

Shaker, large "schmoo," Ming green
 (ILLUS. right w/small "schmoo" shaker).......... **75**
Shaker, small "schmoo," rust (ILLUS. left
 w/large "schmoo" shaker)................................. **35**
Soup ladle **475**

Salad Serving Spoons

Spoons, salad servers, white, the set
 (ILLUS.)... **1,600**

Bronze Town and Country Teapot

Teapot, cov., bronze (ILLUS.)............................. **250**

Covered Soup Tureen

Tureen, cov., soup, sand (ILLUS.)...................... **650**

Watt Pottery

Watt Pottery Drip Glaze Bowl

Bowl, 8 1/4" d., blue drip glaze
 (ILLUS.).. **25**

Watt Pottery Carafe

Carafe, ribbon handle, Nassau
 (ILLUS.).. **55**
Chop tray, Mountain Road, 14 1/2" **210**
Shaker set, hourglass shape, bisque................... **30**
Teapot, cov., rattan handle, Animal
 Farm **600**

Zsolnay

This pottery was made in Pecs, Hungary, in a factory founded in 1862 by Vilmos Zsolnay. Utilitarian earthenware was originally produced, but by the turn of the 20th century ornamental Art Nouveau-style wares with bright colors and lustre decoration were produced; these wares are especially sought today. Currently Zsolnay pieces are being made in a new factory.

Zsolnay Marks

Zsolnay Domed Box

Box, cov., rectangular, w/domed lid, Ivory
 Ware medieval design w/later metallic
 eosin glaze, incised Zsolnay Factory
 mark, unknown form number, ca. 1900,
 3 1/4" h. (ILLUS.).................................... **$400-600**

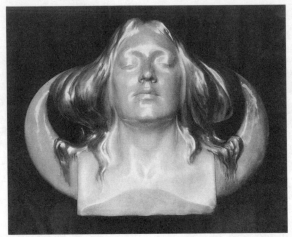

"Luna" Portrait Bust by Zsolnay

Bust, "Luna" by Sandor Apati Abt, realistic portrait of woman w/long hair & closed eyes, various metallic eosin glazes, incised Zsolnay Factory mark, incised form number 5494, exhibited at the Paris Exposition in 1900, ca. 1899, 11" h. (ILLUS.)... **25,000-30,000**

Zsolnay Center Bowl with Polar Bear

Center bowl, oblong boat-shaped form, the top of one end w/a standing figural polar bear peering into water that forms the walls of the piece, waves & fish in relief, iridescent purple, blue & amber glaze w/matte lustre, convex round trademark stamp, early 20th c., chips on base, minor wear, 6 1/2 x 19", 9" h. (ILLUS.).. **690**

Centerpiece, figural, boat-shaped, a reticulated floral border on a boat-shaped vessel decorated w/stylized Oriental flowers in pink, teal & gold tones w/gilt highlights, mounted in an ormolu base w/patinated metal cherubs riding atop wavelike formations & driving a bridled swan at the front, w/seashell feet, impressed "Zsolnay 1211" & blue stamp marks, late 19th c., 13 1/2" l. (hairline) **1,150**

Chalice, organic form w/applied handles curving out connecting base to bowl, multi eosin glazes, printed Zsolnay Factory mark, incised form number 5668, ca. 1900, 6" h. (ILLUS., top next column)... **1,500-2,000**

Zsolnay Chalice

Zsolnay Polychrome Charger

Charger, cream ground w/enameled polychrome flowers & leaves in the Iznik style copying designs from the 18th c., printed factory mark & incised form number 470, ca. 1875, 14 1/5" d. (ILLUS.).......... **750-900**

Zsolnay Armin Klein Charger

Charger, painted w/scene of peasants in folkloric costumes pressing grapes in a vineyard, design by Armin Klein, printed Zsolnay Factory mark, incised form number 470, ca. 1880, 15" d. (ILLUS.) ... **1,500-2,000**

Zsolnay Ewer

Ewer, spherical body and elongated neck fitted w/spout & handle, raised on pedestal base, all-over applied decoration, underside marked "Zsolnay 7," ca. 1830, 12" h. (ILLUS.)... **420**

Figure of woman, seated cloaked woman beside a large low tapering vessel, iridescent gold glaze, gilt stamp mark, early 20th c., 5 1/4" h. (minor glaze wear).............. **374**

Figure of woman, partially clad reclining woman w/green, gold & pink lustre glaze, clothing & rectangular base a blue & green iridescent glaze, stamped company mark, 10" l. **990**

Zsolnay Jardiniere

Jardiniere, realistic polychrome decoration of thistles & leaves, majolica glaze, incised Zsolnay Factory mark & form number 5454, ca. 1899, 18" h. (ILLUS.) **5,000-7,000**

Zsolnay Tadé Sikorsky Jug

Jug, form designed by Tadé Sikorsky, shriveled glaze w/applied pierced decorations, incised Zsolnay Factory mark & form number 1379, ca. 1885, 8" h. (ILLUS.).. **350-550**

Zsolnay Hungarian-style Jug

Jug, on circular base, C-scroll handle, typical Hungarian folkloric form w/cream ground & enameled polychrome flower & leaf decoration, incised Zsolnay Factory mark, incised form number 1157, ca. 1883, 11 1/2" h. (ILLUS.) **550-650**

Zsolnay Lamp by Lajos Mack

Lamp, figural, Art Nouveau model of a woman in the style of Lolie Fuller, w/arms upraised & flowing hair, designed by Lajos Mack, mostly gold/green eosin glazes, round raised Zsolnay Factory mark, incised form number 6324, ca. 1900, 22 1/2" h. (ILLUS.)........................ **20,000-25,000**

Zsolnay Miniature Pitcher

Pitcher, 4 1/2" h., miniature form, squatty footed base tapering to long cylindrical body, flared rim, handle formed by woman peering into the pitcher, exceptional eosin glazes, round raised Zsolnay Factory mark, incised form number 5956, ca. 1900 (ILLUS.)...................................... **2,250-2,750**

Zsolnay Pitcher with Metallic Glaze

Pitcher, 9 1/2" h., slightly bulbous tankard shape w/angular handle, metallic eosin glazed decoration in the style of Loetz Bohemian glass, round raised Zsolnay Factory mark, incised form number 8925, ca. 1918 (ILLUS.) **2,500-3,500**

Pitcher, 12 3/4" h., crackled glaze, red color, modern design by Gabriella Törzsök, printed Zsolnay Factory mark, ca. 1959... **300-500**

Zsolnay Dragon Motif Pitcher

Pitcher, 13" h., cov., decorative Ivory Ware lid, dragon form handle & spout, cream ground w/gilt trim, incised & applied decoration of dragon & gargoyle copying 18th-c. designs, printed Zsolnay Factory mark, incised form number 2994, ca. 1889 (ILLUS.) **600-800**

High-relief Zsolnay Pitcher

Pitcher, 15 1/2" h., tapering tankard style w/C-scroll handle, overall high-relief decoration of oak leaves, acorns & large beetles, pale green eosin glaze, incised Zsolnay Factory mark & form number 4115, ca. 1893 (ILLUS.).................... **4,500-5,500**

Zsolnay Cock-form Pitcher

Zsolnay Plaque-like Tile

Pitcher, 18" h., in the form of a crowing cock w/stylized feathers on oval base, open beak forms spout, pale green eosin glaze, incised Zsolnay Factory mark, incised form number 1132, ca. 1903 (ILLUS.).. **4,000-5,000**

Tile, square, decorated w/flowers & leaves, green & gold eosin glazes, unmarked, unusual & rare, ca. 1900, 5" sq. (ILLUS.).. **1,250-1,500**

Rare Zsolnay Umbrella Stand

Zsolnay Puzzle Jug

Puzzle jug, shriveled yellow glaze w/applied stylized flowers & bird figure attached to C-scroll handle, based on 17th-c. designs, pierced neck & flowers, stepped circular base, incised factory mark & form number 547, ca. 1875, 9 1/2" h. (ILLUS.)... **550-750**

Tile, rectangular plaque form w/oval cartouche w/relief decoration of idyllic setting w/Art Nouveau-style female dancer & Pan-like figures playing musical instruments, multicolored eosin glazes, designed by Lajos Mack, incised Zsolnay Factory mark, incised form number 7892, ca. 1906, 8 1/4 x 10 3/4" (ILLUS., top of page)........................ **7,500-9,500**

Umbrella stand, tall, slightly waisted cylindrical form w/rolled rim, the sides decorated w/dark golden iridescent fish swimming in iridescent swirls of dark blue, purple & gold, impressed "Zsolnay - Pecs - 4036 - 21," ca. 1900, 26 3/4" h. (ILLUS.)............. **14,400**

Miniature Zsolnay Vase

Zsolnay Tile

Vase, miniature, 4" h., wide base tapering to ring foot & long neck, richly decorated w/Hungarian folkloric designs in gold & blue/green eosin glazes, incised Zsolnay Factory mark, ca. 1912 (ILLUS.)...... **1,000-1,250**

Miniature Footed Zsolnay Vase

Vase, miniature, 4 3/4" h., footed form w/ovoid body tapering to narrower neck, decorated w/Hungarian folkloric designs in metallic blue eosin glaze, incised Zsolnay Factory mark, ca. 1906 (ILLUS.)... **750-1,000**

Egyptian Decor Zsolnay Vase

Vase, 5" h., cylindrical, tapering out toward top, then in toward short neck w/small opening, Art Deco Egyptian decor, designed by Teréz Mattyasovszky-Zsolnay, printed Zsolnay Factory mark, ca. 1915 (ILLUS.)... **1,250-1,500**

Scenic Zsolnay Vase

Vase, earthenware, wide ovoid base w/broad flattened shoulder centered by a short cylindrical rim, decorated w/a cara-

van of men on camels carrying guns & spears, in an oasis w/palm trees, below a wavy edged border of scattered flower heads, iridescent red, brown & blue glaze, ca. 1900-10, molded factory seal, impressed "8868" & "19," imperfection at edge of foot, 8" w. (ILLUS.) **2,300**

Zsolnay Vase with Sun & Trees

Vase, 8 1/2" h., slightly ovoid cylindrical shape, decorated w/idyllic view of trees, sun & road, metallic eosin glazes, round raised Zsolnay Factory mark, incised form number 6011, ca. 1906 (ILLUS.)... **12,500-15,000**

Vase, 9" h., baluster form w/figure of draped woman molded in full relief at shoulder, tall cylindrical neck w/flaring scalloped rim, metallic green & blue glaze, stamped company mark **660**

Zsolnay Vase with Landscape Scene

Vase, 9 3/4" h., cylindrical body tapering to short, flared neck, painted w/landscape scene of trees, sunset, clouds & flowers, brilliant eosin glazes, round raised Zsolnay Factory mark, incised form number 8196, ca. 1909 (ILLUS.) **12,500-15,000**

Vase, 10" h., 5" d., tall slender ovoid body tapering to a flat rim, decorated w/ruby red pomegranate design against a nacreous eocin ground, die-stamped & wax-resist mark... **1,760**

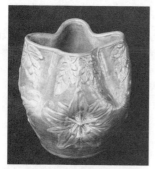

Zsolnay Vase with Metallic Glaze

Vase, 10 1/2" h., freeform body w/quatrefoil opening, decorated w/relief & applied leaves & lilies, highly metallic silver/blue eosin glaze, printed Zsolnay Factory mark, incised form number 5424, ca. 1900 (ILLUS.)............................... **10,000-12,500**

Zsolnay Vase by Sándor Pillo-Hidasy

Vase, 10 3/4" h., ovoid body tapering in at neck, which tapers further to short molded rim, decorated w/three spotted leopards around body, silver metallic leaves w/red early Deco decorations, signed by Sándor Pillo-Hidasy, round raised Zsolnay Factory mark, incised form number 8589, ca. 1912 (ILLUS.) **20,000-25,000**

Zsolnay Owl Vase

Vase, 11" h., figural, consists of three realistic owls in high relief, green/gold metallic eosin glaze, round raised Zsolnay Facto-

ry mark, incised form number 5236, ca. 1898 (ILLUS.).................................... **6,500-8,500**

Zsolnay Iridescent Vase

Vase, 11" h., slightly swelled cylindrical lower body below a bulbed upper body & angled shoulder to the short flared neck, iridescent gold glaze w/purple & blue marbleized striations, impressed "Zsolnay - 7595" & gilt stamp mark, early 20th c. (ILLUS.)` 460

Hungarian Millennium Vase

Vase, 11 3/4" h., bulbous waisted form w/short bulbous applied feet, Hungarian Millennium decoration of painted stylized birds & flowers, round printed Zsolnay Factory mark, incised form number 933, ca. 1882 (ILLUS.) **2,500-3,500**

Zsolnay Vase with Swirled Banding

Vase, 12" h., cylindrical footed body tapering to narrow neck w/highly stylized fluted lip, raised banding in swirl pattern
around body & neck, soft green/blue
eosin glaze, incised Zsolnay Factory
mark, incised form number 4626, ca.
1897 (ILLUS.)..................................... **2,500-3,500**

Zsolnay Vase with Swirl Base

Vase, 12 1/4" h., swirl pattern ovoid base,
long, slightly tapering cylindrical neck,
scalloped rim, cream ground w/enam-
eled painted flowers & leaves, gilt decoration, printed Zsolnay Factory mark, incised form number 3088, ca. 1885
(ILLUS.).. **400-600**

Lajos Mack Vase with Relief Design

Vase, 28" h., tapering cylindrical form
w/squat ovoid neck, decorated w/relief
design of figures in forest setting including Pan-like form, various eosin metallic
glazes, designed by Lajos Mack, incised
Zsolnay Factory mark, incised form num-
ber 5902, ca. 1900 (ILLUS.)........ **25,000-30,000**

GLOSSARY OF SELECTED CERAMICS TERMS

Abino Ware—A line produced by the Buffalo Pottery of Buffalo, New York. Introduced in 1911, this limited line featured mainly sailing ship scenes with a windmill on shore.

Agate Ware—An earthenware pottery featuring a mixture of natural colored clays giving a marbled effect. Popular in England in the 18th century.

Albany slip—A dark brown slip glaze used to line the interiors of most salt-glazed stoneware pottery. Named for a fine clay found near Albany, New York.

Albino line—A version of Griffen, Smith and Hill's Shell & Seaweed majolica pattern with an off-white overall color sometimes trimmed with gold or with pink or blue feathering.

Albion Ware—A line of majolica developed by Edwin Bennett in the 1890s. It featured colored liquid clays over a green clay body decorated with various scenes. Popular for jardinieres and pedestals.

Bas relief—Literally "low relief," referring to lightly molded decorations on ceramic pieces.

Bisquit—Unglazed porcelain left undecorated or sometimes trimmed with pastel colors. Also known as bisque.

Bocage—A background of flowering trees or vines often used as a backdrop for figural groups which were meant to be viewed from the front only.

Bone china—A porcelain body developed in England using the white ashes of bone. It has been the standard English porcelain ware since the early 19th century.

Coleslaw—A type of decoration used on ceramic figurines to imitate hair or fur. It is finely crumbled clay applied to the unfired piece and resembling coleslaw cabbage.

Crackled glaze—A glaze with an intentional network of fine lines produced by uneven contracting of the glaze after firing. First popular on Chinese wares.

Crazing—The fine network of cracks in a glaze produced by uneven contracting of the glaze after firing or later reheating of a piece during usage. An unintentional defect usually found on eathernwares.

Creamware—A light-colored fine earthenware developed in England in the late 18th century and used by numerous potters into the 19th century. Josiah Wedgwood marketed his version as Queensware.

Crystalline glaze—A glaze containing fine crystals resulting from the presence of mineral salts in the mixture. It was a popular glaze on American art pottery of the late 19th century and early 20th century.

Eared handles—Handles applied to ceramic pieces such as crocks. They are crescent or 'ear' shaped, hence the name.

Earthenware—A class of fine-grained porous pottery fired at relatively low temperature and then glazed. It produces a

light and easily molded ware that was widely used by the potteries of Staffordshire, England in the late 18th and early 19th century.

Faience—A form of fine earthenware featuring a tin glaze and originally inspired by Chinese porcelain. It includes early Dutch Delft ware and similar wares made in France, Germany and other areas of Europe.

Fairyland Lustre—A special line of decorated wares developed by Susannah 'Daisy' Makeig-Jones for the Josiah Wedgwood firm early in the 20th century. It featured fantastic or dreamlike scenes with fairies and elves in various colors and with a mother-of-pearl lustre glaze. Closely related to Dragon Lustre featuring designs with dragons.

Flambé glaze—A special type of glaze featuring splashed or streaked deep reds and purple, often dripping over another base color. Popular with some American art pottery makers but also used on porcelain wares.

Flint Enamel glaze—A version of the well known brown mottled Rockingham pottery glaze. It was developed by Lyman Fenton & Co. of Bennington, Vermont and patented in 1849. It featured streaks and flecks of green, orange, yellow and blue mixed with the mottled brown glaze.

Glaze—The general term for vitreous (glass-like) coating fired onto pottery and porcelain to produce an impervious surface and protect underglaze decoration.

Hard-paste—Refers to 'true' porcelain, a fine, white clay body developed by the Chinese and containing kaolin and petuntse or china stone. It is fired at a high temperature and glazed with powdered feldspar to produce a smooth, shiny glaze.

Lead glaze—A shiny glaze most often used on cheap redware pottery and produced using a dry powdered or liquid lead formula. Since it would be toxic, it was generally used on the exterior of utilitarian wares only

Lithophane—A panel of thin porcelain delicately molded with low-relief pattern or scenes which show up clearly when held to light. It was developed in Europe in the 19th century and was used for decorative panels or lamp shades and was later used in the bottom of some German and Japanese steins, mugs or cups.

Majolica—A type of tin-glazed earthenware pottery developed in Italy and named for the island of Majorca. It was revived in Europe and America in the late 19th century and usually featured brightly colored shiny glazes

Married—A close match or a duplicate of the original missing section or piece, such as a lid.

Mission Ware—A decorative line of pottery developed by the Niloak Pottery of Benton, Arkansas. It featured variously colored clays swirled together and was used to produce such decorative pieces as vases and candlesticks.

Moriage—Japanese term for the slip-trailed relief decorations used on various forms of porcelain and pottery. Flowers, beading and dragon decoration are typical examples.

Pâte-sur-pâte—French for 'paste on paste,' this refers to a decorative technique where layers of porcelain slip in white are layered on a darker background. Used on artware produced by firms like Minton, Ltd. of England.

Pearlware—A version of white colored creamware developed in England and widely used for inexpensive eathenwares in the late 18th and early 19th century. It has a pearly glaze, hence the name.

Pillow vase—a form of vase designed to resemble a flattened round or oblong pillow. Generally an upright form with flattened sides. A similar form is the Moon vase or flask, meant to resemble a full moon.

Porcelain—The general category of translucent, vitrified ceramics first developed by the Chinese and later widely produced in Europe and America. Hard-paste is 'true' porcelain, while soft-paste is an 'artificial' version developed to imitate hard-paste using other ingredients.

Pottery—The very general category of ceramics produced from various types of clay. It includes redware, yellowware, stoneware and various earthenwares. It is generally fired at a much lower temperature than porcelain.

PUG—An abbreviation for "printed under glaze," referring to colored decorations on pottery. Most often it is used in reference to decorations found on Mettlach pottery steins.

Relief-molding—A decorative technique, sometimes erroneously referred to as "blown-out," whereby designs are raised in bold relief against a background. The reverse side of such decoration is hollowed-out, giving the impression the design was produced by 'blowing' from the inside. Often used in reference to certain Nippon porcelain wares.

Rocaille—A French term meaning 'rockwork.' It generally refers to a decoration used for the bases of ceramic figurines.

Salt-glazed stoneware—A version of stoneware pottery where common rock salt is thrown in the kiln during firing and produces hard, shiny glaze like a thin coating of glass. A lightly pitted "orange peel" surface is sometimes the result of this technique.

Sanded—A type of finish usually on pottery wares. Unfired pieces are sprinkled or rolled in fine sand, which, when fired, gives the piece a sandy, rough surface texture.

Sang-de-boeuf—Literally French for "ox blood," it refers to a deep red glaze produced with copper oxide. It was first produced by the Chinese and imitated by European and American potters in the late 19th and early 20th century.

Sgrafitto—An Italian-inspired term for decorative designs scratched or cut through a layer of slip before firing. Generally used on earthenware forms and especially with the Pennsylvania-German potters of America.

Slip—The liquid form of clay, often used to decorate earthenware pieces in a process known as slip-trailing or slip-quilling.

Soft-paste—A term used to describe a certain type of porcelain body developed in Europe and England from the 16th to late 18th centuries. It was used to imitate true hard-paste porcelain developed by the Chinese but was produced using a white clay mixed with a grit or flux of bone ash or talc and fired at fairly low temperatures. The pieces are translucent, like hard-paste porcelain, but are not as durable. It should not be used when referring to earthenwares such as creamware or pearlware.

Sprigging—A term used to describe the ornamenting of ceramic pieces with applied relief decoration, such as blossoms, leaves or even figures.

Standard glaze—The most common form of glazing used on Rookwood Pottery pieces. It is a clear, shiny glaze usually on pieces decorated with florals or portraits against a dark shaded backhground.

Stoneware—A class of hard, high-fired pottery usually made from dense grey clay and most often decorated with a salt glaze. American 19th century stoneware was often decorated with slip-quilled or hand-brushed cobalt blue decorations.

Tapestry ware—A form of late 19th century porcelain where the piece is impressed with an overall linen cloth texture before firing. The Royal Bayreuth firm is especially known for their fine "Rose Tapestry" line wherein the finely textured ground is decorated with colored roses.

Tin glaze—A form of pottery glaze made opaque by the addition of tin oxide. It was used most notably on early Dutch Delft as well as other early faience and majolica wares.

Underglaze-blue—A cobalt blue produced with metallic oxides applied to an unfired clay body. Blue was one of the few colors which does not run or smear when fired at a high temperature. It was used by the Chinese on porcelain and later copied by firms such as Meissen.

APPENDIX I
CERAMICS CLUBS & ASSOCIATIONS

ABC Plates
ABC Collectors' Circle
  67 Stevens Ave.
  Old Bridge, NJ 08857-2244

Abingdon Pottery Club
  210 Knox Hwy. 5
  Abingdon, IL 61410-9332

American Art Pottery Association
  P.O. Box 834
  Westport, MA 02790-0697
  www.amartpot.org/

American Ceramic Circle
  520 - 16th St.
  New York, NY 11215

Amphora Collectors Club
  129 Bathurst St.
  Toronto, Ontario
  CANADA M5V 2R2

Arkansas Pottery
National Society of Arkansas Pottery
  Collectors
  2006 Beckenham Cove
  Little Rock, AR 72212
  www.flash.net/~gemoore/nsapc.htm

Pottery Lovers Reunion
  4969 Hudson Dr.
  Stow, OH 44224

Bauer Pottery
  www.bauerpottery.com/

Belleek Collectors International
  Society
  P.O. Box 1498
  Great Falls, VA 22066
  www.belleek.com

Blue & White Pottery Club
  224 12th St. NW
  Cedar Rapids, IA 52405

Blue Ridge Collectors Club
  Rte. 3, Box 161
  Erwin, TN 37650

Carlton Ware Collectors International
  Carlton Works
  Copeland Street
  Stoke-upon-Trent ST4 1PU
  UNITED KINGDOM
  www.lattimore.co.uk/deco/carlton.htm

Ceramic Arts Studio Collectors
  P.O. Box 46
  Madison, WI 53701-0046
  www.ceramicartsstudio.com/

Chintz Connection
  P.O. Box 222
  Riverdale, MD 20738-0222

Clarice Cliff Collectors Club
  Fantasque House
  Tennis Drive, The Park
  Nottingham NG7 1AE
  UNITED KINGDOM
  www.claricecliff.com/

Currier & Ives Dinnerware
  Collectors Club
  29470 Saxon Rd.
  Toulon, IL 61438
  www.royalchinaclub.com

Czechoslovakian Collectors Guild
  International
  P.O. Box 901395
  Kansas City, MO 64190-1395

The Dedham Pottery Collectors
  Society
  248 Highland St.
  Dedham, MA 02026-5833
  www.dedhampottery.com/

Delftware Collectors Association
  P.O. Box 670673
  Marietta, GA 30066
  www.delftware.org/

Doulton & Royal Doulton
Northern California Doulton
  Collectors Club
  P.O. Box 214
  Moraga, CA 94556
  www.royaldoultonwest.com/

Royal Doulton International
  Collectors Club
  701 Cottontail Lane
  Somerset, NJ 08873
  www.royal-doulton.com/

Fiesta Club of America
  P.O. Box 15383
  Loves Park, IL 61115

Fiesta Collector's Club
  P.O. Box 471
  Valley City, OH 44280-0471
  www.chinaspecialties.com/fiesta.html

Flow Blue International Collector's
  Club
  P.O. Box 6664
  Leawood, KS 66206
  www.flowblue.org

Franciscan Pottery Collectors Society
  500 S. Farrell Dr., #S-114
  Palm Springs, CA 92264
  www.gmcb.com/franciscan/

Frankoma Family Collectors
  Association
  1300 Luker Lane
  Sapulpa, OK 74066-6024
  www.frankoma.org/

Gonder Collectors Club
  917 Hurl Dr.
  Pittsburgh, PA 15236-3636
  www.happysemporium.com/gonder_
  collector_club.htm

Goss & Crested China Club
  62 Murray Road
  Horndean
  Waterlooville, Hants. PO8 9JL
  UNITED KINGDOM
  www.gosschina.com/

Gouda Pottery
  See Delftware Collectors Association

Haeger Pottery Collectors of America
  5021 Toyon Way
  Antioch, CA 94509-8426

Hall China Collector's Club
  P.O. Box 360488
  Cleveland, OH 44136-0488
  www.chinaspecialties.com/hallnews.html

Haviland Collectors International
  Foundation
  P.O. Box 271383
  Fort Collins, CO 80527
  www.havilandcollectors.com/

Head Vase Society
  P.O. Box 83H
  Scarsdale, NY 10583-8583

Hull Pottery Association
  13199 Rambo Road
  Crooksville, OH 43731

Hull Pottery Newsletter
  7768 Meadow Dr.
  Hillsboro, MO 63050

Homer Laughlin China Collectors
  P.O. Box 1093
  Corbin, KY 40702-1093
  www.hlcca.org/

Illinois Pottery
Collectors of Illinois Pottery
  & Stoneware
  308 N. Jackson St.
  Clinton, IL 61727-1320

Ironstone China
White Ironstone China Association
  P.O. Box 855
  Fairport, NY 14450-0855
  www.whiteironstonechina.com/

Jewel Tea Autumn Leaf
National Autumn Leaf Collectors Club
  P.O. Box 7929
  Moreno Valley, CA 92552-7929
  www.nalcc.org/

Majolica International Society
  1275 First Ave., Suite 103
  New York, NY 10021-5601
  www.majolicasociety.com/

McCoy Pottery Collectors Connection
2210 Sherwin Dr.
Twinsburg, OH 44087
www.ohiopottery.com/mccoy/

Moorcroft Collectors Club
Sandbach Road
Burslem, Stoke-on-Trent ST6 2DG
UNITED KINGDOM
www.moorcroft.com/

Nemadji Pottery Collectors
P.O. Box 95
Moose Lake, MN 55767

Nippon Porcelain
International Nippon Collectors Club
1521 Independence Ave. SE.
Washington, DC 20003
www.nipponcollectorsclub.com

Lakes & Plains Nippon Collectors'
Club
P.O. Box 230
Peotone, IL 60468-0230

New England Nippon Collectors Club
64 Burt Rd.
Springfield, MA 01118-1848

Sunshine State Nippon Collectors'
Club
P.O. Box 425
Frostproof, FL 33843-0425

Noritake Collectors' Society
145 Andover Place
West Hempstead, NY 11552-1603

North Dakota Pottery Collectors
Society
P.O. Box 14
Beach, ND 58621-0014

Old Ivory China
Society for Old Ivory & Ohme
Porcelains
5946 W. Morraine Ave.
Littleton, CO 80128

The Elegance of Old Ivory Newsletter
28101 S.W. Petes Mountain Road
West Linn, OR 97068-9537

Pewabic Pottery
10125 E. Jefferson Ave.
Detroit, MI 48214
www.pewabic.com/

Phoenix Bird Collectors of America
685 S. Washington
Constantine, MI 49042-1407

Pickard Collectors Club
300 E. Grove St.
Bloomington, IL 61701-5232

Porcelier Collectors Club
21 Tamarac Swamp Road
Wallingford, CT 06492-5529

Purinton Pottery
Purinton News & Views Newsletter
P.O. Box 153
Connellsville, PA 15425

Quimper Club International
5316 Seascape Lane
Plano, TX 75093
www.quimperclub.org/

Red Wing Collectors Society, Inc.
P.O. Box 50
Red Wing, MN 55066-0050
www.redwingcollectors.org

Royal Bayreuth International
Collectors' Society
P.O. Box 325
Orrville, OH 44667-0325

R.S. Prussia
International Association of
R.S. Prussia Collectors Inc.
P.O. Box 446
Mount Joy, PA 17552
www.rsprussia.com/

Shelley China
National Shelley China Club
591 W. 67th Ave.
Anchorage, AK 99518-1555
www.sweetpea.net/shelleyclub/

Southern Folk Pottery Collectors
Society
220 Washington St.
Bennett, NC 27208

Staffordshire
The Transfer Ware Collectors Club
PMB 541
Mt. Vernon, WA 98273
www.transcollectorsclub.org/

Stangl/Fulper Collectors Association
P.O. Box 538
Flemington, NJ 08822
www.stanglfulper.com/

Stoneware
American Stoneware Collectors
Society
P.O. Box 281
Point Pleasant Beach, NJ 08742-
0281

Susie Cooper Collectors Group
P.O. Box 7436
London N12 7QF
UNITED KINGDOM

Tea Leaf Club International
Maxine Johnson, Membership
P.O. Box 377
Belton, MO 64012
www.TeaLeafClub.com

Torquay Pottery
North American Torquay Society
214 N. Ronda Road.
McHenry, IL 60050

Uhl Collectors Society, Inc.
3704 W. Old Road 64
Huntingburg, IN 47542
www.uhlcollectors.org/

Van Briggle Collectors Society
600 S. 21st St.
Colorado Springs, CO 80904
www.vanbriggle.com/

Wade Watch, Ltd.
8199 Pierson Court
Arvada, CO 80005
www.wadewatch.com/

Watt Collectors Association
1431 4th St. SW
P.M.B. 221
Mason City, IA 50401
server34.hypermart.net/wattcollectors/
watt.htm

Wedgwood International Seminar
c/o Mr. R. Mitchell
P.O. Box 890633
Temecula, CA 92589
www.w-i-s.org/

Wedgwood Society of Boston, Inc.
P.O. Box 215
Dedham, MA 02027-0215
htlp://www.angelfire.com/ma/wsb/
index.html

The Wedgwood Society of New York
5 Dogwood Ct.
Glen Head, NY 11545-2740
www.wsny.org/

Wedgwood Society of Washington,
DC
3505 Stringfellow Court
Fairfax, VA 22033

Willow Wares
International Willow Collectors
503 Chestnut St.
Perkasie, PA 18944
www.willowcollectors.org/

Wisconsin Pottery Association
P.O. Box 8213
Madison, WI 53708-8213
www.wisconsinpottery.org/

Eva Zeisel Collectors Club
695 Monterey Blvd. #203
San Francisco, CA 94127
www.evazeisel.org/

APPENDIX II
Museums & Libraries with Ceramic Collections

CERAMICS (AMERICAN)

Everson Museum of Art of Syracuse
& Onondaga County
401 Harrison St.
Syracuse, NY 13202-3019
www.everson.org/

Museum of Ceramics at East
Liverpool
400 E. 5th St.
East Liverpool, OH 43920-3134
www.ohiohistory.org/places/ceramics/

CERAMICS (AMERICAN ART POTTERY)

Cincinnati Art Museum
953 Eden Park
Cincinnati, OH 45202
www.cincinnatiartmuseum.com/

Newcomb College Art Gallery
Woldenberg Art Center
Newcomb College/Tulane
University
1229 Broadway
New Orleans, LA 70118
www.newcomb.tulane.edu/

Zanesville Art Center
620 Military Rd.
Zanesville, OH 43701
www.zanesville.com

OTHER CERAMICS:

BENNINGTON

The Bennington Museum
West Main St.
Bennington, VT 05201
www.benningtonmuseum.com

CATALINA ISLAND POTTERY

Catalina Island Museum
www.ecatalina.com/museum/pottery

CHINESE EXPORT PORCELAIN

Peabody Essex Museum
East India Square
Salem, MA 01970
www.pem.org

CLEWELL POTTERY

Jesse Besser Museum
491 Johnson St.
Alpena, MI 49707
www.ogdennews.com/upnorth/
museum/home.htm

COWAN POTTERY

Cowan Pottery Museum at the Rocky
River Public Library
1600 Hampton Rd.
Rocky River, OH 44116-2699
www.rrpl.org/rrpl_cowan.stm

DEDHAM

Dedham Historical Society
612 High St.
Dedham, MA 02027-0125
www.dedhamhistorical.org

GEORGE OHR

Ohr/O'Keefe Museum of Art
136 G.E. Ohr St.
Biloxi, MS 39530
www.georgeohr.org/

PENNSYLVANIA GERMAN

Hershey Museum
170 W. Hersheypark Dr.
Hershey, PA 17033

ROSEVILLE POTTERY

Roseville Historical Society
91 Main St.
Roseville, OH 43777
www.netpluscom.com/~pchs/
rosevill.htm

WEDGWOOD

Birmingham Museum of Art
2000 Eighth Ave. No.
Birmingham, AL 35203
www.artsbma.org/

GENERAL COLLECTIONS:

The Bayou Bend Collection
#1 Westcott
Houston, TX 77007
www.bayoubend.uh.edu

Greenfield Village and Henry Ford
Museum
20900 Oakwood Blvd.
Dearborn, MI 48124-4088

Museum of Early Southern
Decorative Arts
924 Main St.
Winston Salem, NC 27101

Abby Aldrich Rockefeller Folk
Art Collection
England St.
Williamsburg, VA 23185

The Margaret Woodbury Strong
Museum
700 Allen Creek Rd.
Rochester, NY 14618

Henry Francis DuPont Winterthur
Museum
Winterthur, DE 19735
www.winterthur.org/

APPENDIX III
References to Pottery and Porcelain Marks

*DeBolt's Dictionary of American
Pottery Marks—Whiteware &
Porcelain*
Gerald DeBolt
Collector Books,
Paducah, Kentucky, 1994

*Encyclopaedia of British Pottery and
Porcelain Marks*
Geoffrey A. Godden
Bonanza Books,
New York, New York, 1964

*Kovel's New Dictionary of Marks,
Pottery & Porcelain, 1850 to the
Present*
Ralph & Terry Kovel

Crown Publishers,
New York, New York, 1986

*Lehner's Encyclopedia of U.S. Marks
on Pottery, Porcelain & Clay*
Lois Lehner
Collector Books,
Paducah, Kentucky, 1988

*Marks on German, Bohemian and
Austrian Porcelain, 1710 to
the Present*
Robert E. Röntgen
Schiffer Publishing, Ltd.,
Atglen, Pennsylvania

APPENDIX IV
English Registry Marks

Since the early nineteenth century, the English have used a number of markings on most ceramics wares which can be very helpful in determining the approximate date a piece was produced.

The 'registry' mark can be considered an equivalant of the American patent number. This English numbering system continues in use today.

Beginning in 1842 and continuing until 1883, most pottery and porcelain pieces were printed or stamped with a diamond-shaped registry mark which was coded with numbers and letters indicating the type of material, parcel number of the piece and, most helpful, the day, month and year that the design or pattern was registered at the Public Record Office. Please note that a piece may have been produced a few years after the registration date itself.

Our Chart A here shows the format of the diamond registry mark used between 1842 and 1867. Accompanying it are listings of the corresponding month and year letters used during that period. In a second chart, Chart B, we show the version of the diamond mark used between 1868 and 1883 which depicts a slightly different arrangement. Keep in mind that this diamond registry mark was also used on metal, wood and glasswares. It is important to note that the top bubble with the Roman numeral indicates the material involved; pottery and porcelain will always be Numeral IV.

After 1884, the diamond mark was discontinued and instead just a registration number was printed on pieces. The abbreviation "Rd" for "Registration" appears before the number. We list here these design registry numbers by year with the number indicating the first number that was used in that year. For instance, design number 494010 would have been registered sometime in 1909.

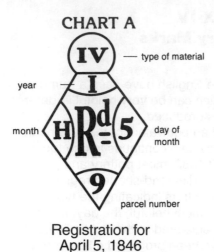

CHART A

— type of material

year

month

day of month

parcel number

Registration for
April 5, 1846

CHART B

— type of material

day of month

parcel number

year

month

Registration for
August 6, 1871

LIST
Month of the Year of Registration

C—January	I—July
G—February	R—August
W—March	D—December
H—April	B—October
E—May	K—November
M—June	A—December

LIST
Year of Registration—1842-1867

1842—X	1851—P	1860—Z
1843—H	1852—D	1861—R
1844—C	1853—Y	1862—O
1845—A	1854—J	1863—G
1846—I	1855—E	1864—N
1847—F	1856—L	1865—W
1848—U	1857—K	1866—Q
1849—S	1858—B	1867—T
1850—V	1859—M	

LIST 3

Year of Registration — 1868-1883

1868—X	1874—U	1879—Y
1869—H	1875—S	1880—J
1870—C	1876—V	1881—E
1871—A	1877—P	1882—L
1872—I	1878—D	1883—K
1873—F		

LIST 4

DESIGN REGISTRY NUMBERS — 1884-1951

Jan. 1884—1	1907—493900	1929—742725
1885—20000	1908—518640	1930—751160
1886—40800	1909—535170	1931—760583
1887—64700	Sep. 1909—548919	1932—769670
1888—91800	Oct. 1909—548920	1933—779292
1889—117800	Jan. 1911—575817	1934—789019
1890—142300	1912—594195	1935—799097
1891—164000	1913—612431	1936—808794
1892—186400	1914—630190	1937—817293
1893—206100	1915—644935	1938—825231
1894—225000	1916—635521	1939—832610
1895—248200	1917—658988	1940—837520
1896—268800	1918—662872	1941—838590
1897—291400	1919—666128	1942—839230
Jan. 1898—311677	1920—673750	1943—839980
1899—332200	1921—680147	1944—841040
1900—351600	1922—687144	1945—842670
1901—368186	1923—694999	Jan. 1946—845550
1902—385180	1924—702671	1947—849730
1903—403200	1925—710165	1948—853260
1904—424400	1926—718057	1949—856999
1905—447800	1927—726330	1950—860854
1906—471860	1928—734370	1951—863970

INDEX

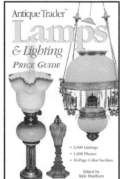